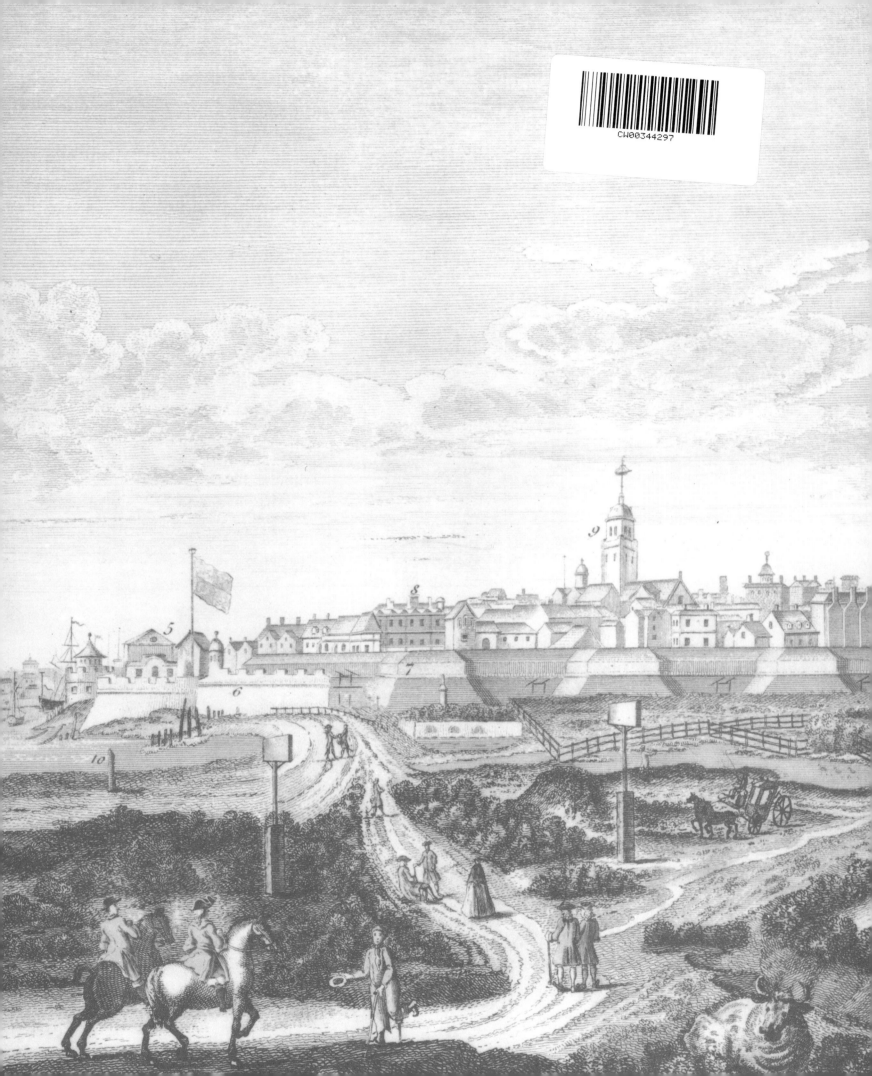

A History of
Napoleonic and American
PRISONERS *of* WAR
1756-1816

Hulk, Depot and Parole

The Prison Hulks at Portsmouth.

A History of
Napoleonic and American
PRISONERS *of* WAR
1756-1816

Hulk, Depot and Parole

Clive L. Lloyd

ANTIQUE COLLECTORS' CLUB

ISBN 978-1-85149-528-3

British Library Cataloguing-in-Publication Data
A catalogue record for this book is available from the British Library

Printed in China
for the Antique Collectors' Club Ltd., Woodbridge, Suffolk

The Antique Collectors' Club

Formed in 1966, the Antique Collectors' Club is now a world-renowned publisher of top quality books for the collector. It also publishes the only independently-run monthly antiques magazine, *Antique Collecting*, which rose quickly from humble beginnings to a network of worldwide subscribers.

The magazine, whose motto is For Collectors–By Collectors–About Collecting, is aimed at collectors interested in widening their knowledge of antiques both by increasing their awareness of quality and by discussion of the factors influencing prices.

Subscription to Antique Collecting is open to anyone interested in antiques and subscribers receive ten issues a year. Well-illustrated articles deal with practical aspects of collecting and provide numerous tips on prices, features of value, investment potential, fakes and forgeries. Offers of related books at special reduced prices are also available only to subscribers.

In response to the enormous demand for information on 'what to pay', ACC introduced in 1968 the famous price guide series. The first title, *The Price Guide to Antique Furniture* (since renamed *British Antique Furniture: Price Guide and Reasons for Values*), is still in constant demand. Since those pioneering days, ACC has gone from strength to strength, publishing many of today's standard works of reference on all things antique and collectable, from *Tiaras* to *20th Century Ceramic Designers in Britain*.

Not only has ACC continued to cater strongly for its original audience, it has also branched out to produce excellent titles on many subjects including art reference, architecture, garden design, gardens, and textiles. All ACC's publications are available through bookshops worldwide and a catalogue is available free of charge from the addresses below.

For further information please contact:

ANTIQUE COLLECTORS' CLUB

www.antiquecollectorsclub.com

Sandy Lane, Old Martlesham
Woodbridge, Suffolk IP12 4SD, UK
Tel: 01394 389950 Fax: 01394 389999
Email: info@antique-acc.com
or
Eastworks, 116 Pleasant Street - Suite 18,
Easthampton, MA 01027, USA
Tel: 413 529 0861 Fax: 413 529 0862
Email: info@antiquecc.com

This book is dedicated
to the memory of
Clive L. Lloyd

1920 – 2004

CONTENTS

Many hundreds of fine books have been published which have dealt with the wars which took place between 1756 and 1815 from a multitude of viewpoints; but in general the subject of the prisoner of war has been neglected or given scant notice within their pages. These introductory notes make no pretence to present potted histories of those wars, except as reminders of dates and to highlight, as appropriate, my own subject – the Prisoner of War.

Clive L. Lloyd

Overleaf: 'The Landings at Savannah', December 1778 by Dominic Serres. NATIONAL TRUST PHOTOGRAPHIC LIBRARY/JOHN HAMMOND.

PART 1

HISTORICAL BACKGROUND

Chapter One

The Seven Years' War 1756–1763

THE SEVEN YEARS' WAR might, with greater truth, have been called the *Nine* Years' War, or, as it is better known in America, the French and Indian War, 1754–1763.

The two uncounted years, '54 and '55, saw the waging of a bloody war between French-Canadians and English-American colonists, made bloodier by the fact that the opposing armies were strongly backed by Indian tribes, pro-British and pro-French. The issue was to decide finally who, Great Britain or France, was to be master of the Upper Ohio Valley and, in effect, add North America to its empire.

For a number of years before the first shot was fired, an uneasy truce had been maintained, with the two governments indulging in a crossfire of claims and counter-claims to territory on the banks of the Forks of the Ohio: both intent on avoiding a mutually injurious war in Europe. When the first shot *was* fired, it came from a small group of Virginian militiamen and Indians, led by a young lieutenant-colonel in his early twenties, whose name would one day transcend all others in American history – George Washington.

That shot was to herald a war which would grow to global dimensions – it is, with veracity, often referred to as the First World War – and marked an inglorious beginning to the story of great Washington's long career. The account of prisoners of war taken in the resulting conflict between French and British colonists is indeed an inglorious and unpleasant one.

News that the French-Canadians were busily building forts on the disputed territory, particularly one fort at the junction of the rivers Allegheny and Ohio, inspired the sending out of a small colonial force which, irresponsibly but unintentionally, was to bring about the outbreak of the Seven (or Nine) Years' War.

In October 1753, Robert Dinwiddie, Lieutenant-Governor of Virginia, sent George Washington, with a scout, an interpreter and four other negotiators, on a diplomatic mission to the French force based at Fort le Boeuf, five hundred miles away and some twenty miles south of Lake Erie. George's task was to warn them convincingly that their fort-building and encroachments on lands claimed by Britain as Crown property, could not be tolerated. In this he failed.

He arrived back in Williamsburg in January of the following year, after a perilous journey which he was lucky to survive – being stalked and fired upon by Indians, and later suffering an icy soaking when he slipped from a raft into the freezing waters of the Allegheny River – but he could only report that, whilst the French commandant had received him with courtesy, he had been firmly informed that 'it was their absolute Design to take possession of the Ohio, and by God they would do it!'.

The building of the fort at the forks of the Ohio river, on the spot where Pittsburg Pa. now stands, had been started by the 'Ohio Company', an enterprise established by Virginian entrepreneurs – among them George Washington's half-brother, Lawrence – to develop lands and trade on the upper Potomac and Ohio rivers; but

the French had now taken possession and named it Fort Duquesne, after Admiral Duquesne the French Governor of Canada. This was too much for the Virginians, and in April, only a couple of months after the first abortive mission, Dinwiddie dispatched Washington on another hazardous trip, this time presumably to repossess the fort, although how he was supposed to achieve this without bloodshed is a good question.

Setting off with 160 militiamen and a band of Indians, the twenty-two year old lieutenant-colonel must have appreciated the dangers involved in the probable foray, but could never have envisaged the possible world-wide repercussions which it might bring about. Although London was understandably worried by the menacing French fort-building which was going on between the Great Lakes and the Mississippi, there could have been no intention to open hostilities at that time, otherwise a very much superior force would have been dispatched to retake Fort Duquesne.

On the 28th May 1754, Washington's small band met up with an even smaller French force – no more than thirty-one men – at Great Meadows, about forty miles from the disputed fort. The detail of the next few minutes is not clear, and it is not recorded who gave the order to fire, but the fact is that the young French-Canadian leader, Ensign Coulon de Jumonville, and nine others in the French vanguard were killed, and twenty-one prisoners of war were taken by the Indians. As only one Frenchman survived to tell the French version of the skirmish at Great Meadows, it is probable that the prisoners were later cruelly murdered by Colonel Washington's Mingo Indians who, with much whooping and dancing, had joyously scalped the ten dead Frenchmen. The fate of the prisoners was probably as barbaric as that inflicted by pro-French Indians on British soldiers captured when reinforcements were sent out from England early in the following year.

Washington had every reason to be worried by the possible outcome of his bungled mission, having little hope that reinforcements could reach him before a larger, and vengeful, French force descended upon him. He withdrew his force southward to a wood-built stockade which was dignified with the name Fort Necessity, there to wait and hope for the best – and it was there, perhaps to his double surprise, that he not only received Virginian and North Carolina troops as reinforcements, which brought his fighting force up to 350 men, but news that he had been promoted to the rank of full colonel.

He was, however, given little time to celebrate as barely a month later his worst fears were realized. On the 3rd July, a 700-strong party of French troops under Captain Louis Coulon de Villiers came to Fort Necessity and the following morning Washington, outnumbered and short of provisions, suffered the ignominy of surrendering and giving up his arms. Captain Coulon de Villiers must have been under very strict instructions from France not to escalate hostilities, but even so he showed great restraint in his dealings with Washington and his Virginians. Ensign Coulon de Jumonville, who had been shot and scalped at Great Meadows a few weeks before, was his brother.

Demanding and receiving a kind of *parole d'honneur* relating to future intrusion on the Ohio, and taking a few hostages – who were later granted their parole at Fort Duquesne – the French captain then allowed the remaining colonists to retreat to the American side of the demarcation line and return to Virginia; but only after Washington had signed an admission of responsibility for *'l'assassinat'* of Ensign de Jumonville.

That it would be hard to imagine what could possibly humble or humiliate a man like Washington, is shown in a famous quote from a letter which he wrote to his brother on his return to Virginia: 'I have heard the bullets whistle; and believe me, there is something charming in the sound'.

Over the weeks which followed, nationally-slanted accounts of the Great Meadows and Fort Necessity affair reached Paris and London. France and England began preparing in secrecy, hoping to send troops to back up or lead their colonial garrisons. They must have realized that once troops were landed, their presence would provoke an undeclared war in North America, a war which both sides hoped would be confined to that side of the Atlantic. The Duke of Newcastle[1] was disturbed by the way things were moving, fearing that the country was 'on the edge of a precipice'. Writing to Lord Albemarle, the British ambassador in Paris, in October 1754, he expressed his concern that the War Office had let the cat out of the bag regarding the undercover dispatch of troops; and urged the ambassador to do his utmost to preserve the peace, by convincing the French that the sole intent was defensive and devoid of any belligerent aims:

> 'A most ill-judged advertisement from the War Office has set all the ministers on fire, and made them believe we are going to war, which is, I hope, the furthest from our thoughts…'

Britain was well aware that trained troops from home would be needed to fight alongside her colonists in the event of full-scale conflict. Although greatly superior in population to the French-Canadians by almost twenty to one, the thirteen American colonies were disunited and uncooperative one with the others; plagued by jealousies, financial quibbles and each Governor's pride in his own state. The problem of a united front did not end there, as it was unlikely that their officers would expect to play second fiddle to the commanders of the troops sent to their aid – or that the latter would take kindly to advice offered by what they would have considered to be backwoods militiamen.

The British plan was to send a small squadron to America under Admiral Keppel, to transport General Edward Braddock and two small regiments of regular soldiers, the '44th' and the '48th', each of about four hundred men. Once there, it was hoped, they were to be backed up by colonial volunteer and militia officers and men. General Braddock was a veteran Guards officer, efficient and courageous, but without experience of the type of fighting he would encounter on the other side of the Atlantic.

On arrival in America he was to take overall command of a four-pronged attack on the French forts, ousting the defenders and establishing the forts as British strongholds. Braddock himself was to lead the attack on Fort Duquesne where the trouble had started; a party led by the Governor of Massachusetts, William Shirley, was to be pitted against Fort Niagara, sited where Lake Erie meets Lake Ontario. Sir William Johnson, an authority on Indian fighting, was

to take Fort Crown Point on Lake Champlain; Colonel Robert Monckton, of the Royal American Regiment, was to march on Fort Beauséjour, at the head of the Bay of Fundy. A well designed strategy on paper, but one which in practice produced a mixed bag of success and disaster.

General Braddock arrived in Virginia in February 1755. There he met Colonel George Washington, and made him his personal aide-de-camp. Each of the four leaders of attacks on the forts faced great trials and difficulties in their efforts to achieve their aims; long arduous marches through wild country, waterways and mountain tracks, opportunist Indians who may or may not prove friendly, according to which side was winning.

The logistics involved and natural hazards to be considered by Braddock when planning his three hundred mile slog, through uncharted country, 'numerous creeks and rivers, swamps, trackless forests, and fifty miles of mountains, some twenty-five hundred feet high', were daunting.

The General's original force of 800 had been increased to about 3,200 by an infusion of colonial volunteers and a few Indians. He calculated that he needed two thousand five hundred saddle-horses and five hundred wagons to carry supplies and ammunition; and seven draft-horses to tow each of the large cannon needed to retake Fort Duquesne.[2]

By the 26th April, 1755, the day the expedition was due to get under way, only one hundred and fifty horses had been obtained, but they set forth nevertheless. 'Three hundred American axe-men marched ahead of the convoy, blazing a trail through the wilderness twelve feet wide'. After six weeks of back breaking and foot-blistering toil through forest and swamp, they reached Fort Necessity, where Washington had suffered the humiliation of capitulation – and where on this occasion he was to offer unwise advice which would cost the British General his objective and his life.

General Braddock, having lost a few men to unseen scalp-hunters on the way, was by now only too conscious of the fact that this was a type of warfare far removed from the 'civilized', and almost formal set-piece battles he was so familiar with in Europe, and sought Washington's opinion as to how they should proceed from thence onward. The young colonel, without considering that had he had sufficient troops to oppose the French a year before he may have made the present expedition unnecessary, advised Braddock to leave half his force behind, and advance on Fort Duquesne with fifteen hundred men. French soldiers and eight hundred Indians, had been kept informed of the British advance for many days by his Indian scouts, and had set up an ambush on a thickly wooded hill on the other side of the River Monongahela.

Early in the morning, with no sign of an enemy presence, Braddock, with his wagon-train, cannon and troops, got safely across the river and then, with no cover, began the steep climb towards the woods.

As they neared the top of the slope they came under fire from Indians waiting in ambush behind every tree and boulder, pouring 'devastating fire upon the conspicuous red-coated soldiers on the open slopes'. The sharp-shooting Indians could hardly miss and, with no visible target ahead of them and Captain Duma's French troops closing in on either flank, the redcoats panicked and fled the massacre.

Braddock and his invading force did not stand a chance. The General himself put up a valiant fight, during which four horses were shot from under him; but with an almost invisible enemy picking off his men at will, and the rear guard which he tried to drive forward colliding with the panic-stricken advance guard fleeing down the hill, the odds were too great for any hope of recovery, and he ordered the retreat. After three hours of hell, more than a thousand men and sixty-three of their eighty-six officers had been killed or wounded, among them General Braddock, Commander in Chief of all British Forces in America.

Edward Braddock was mounting his fifth horse when a bullet pierced his lungs; Washington helped him into a wagon, but he died the next day.

Of course there were prisoners, and these poor fellows could not expect honourable treatment at the hands of their savage captors. In this particular war taking scalps was a bit like winning medals. To quote Furneaux:

> '...behind came the yelling exultant Indians, tomahawking the living, scalping the dead. They did not pursue beyond the river.
> They returned to the fort whooping and shouting and waving their scalps and bringing their prisoners who that night were tied to stakes with fires kindled at their feet. The tormentors poked them with blazing torches and red hot irons. Captain Strobo [one of the hostages taken from Washington at Fort Necessity], safe in his cell [at Fort Duquesne] listened to their blood-curdling shrieks.'

The devastating defeat at Duquesne and the death of the British Commander-in-Chief, put the French in indisputable control of the Ohio territory, but it did not end with Fort Duquesne: the French held Fort Crown Point and Fort Niagara and the following year they took Fort Oswego; following up in 1757 with the destruction of the important British stronghold on Lake George, Fort William Henry where, as by now could be expected, Montcalm's Indians massacred all the British prisoners of war.

Stirred by a bloodlust or scalping-fever, Indian tribes allied to the French went beyond Montcalm's objective, crossing the Canadian frontier and attacking the widespread homes of American civilians living in the west. One newspaper report would suggest that although such atrocities may not have been by French design, they met with at least some French approval. *The Pennsylvanian Gazette* described:

> '...villages laid in ruins, men, women and children cruelly mangled and massacred. Murders, butcheries and scenes of horror were reported from New York to the Carolinas. Thousands of refugees poured into the coastal towns. The Governor of French Canada, de Vaudreuil congratulated his Indian allies, believing "...there is no surer way to sicken the people of the English colonies of war and to make them desire to return to peace"'.

For the first few years, things looked bleak for the British in the North American theatre of war. They had some small successes – taking Fort Beauséjour and Fort Gaspareau three years earlier at the time of Braddock's four-pronged venture – but it was not until three years later and William Pitt's 'global strategy' pointed the way, that the tables began to turn.

Despite the premature opening rounds in America, the principal contenders in Europe were still at peace at the beginning of 1756; although espionage and preparations for war were the order of the day. Almost every detail of Edward Braddock's American mission had been known to the French before the General left England on his ill-fated expedition – and Britain was equally well informed of the French plan to ship three thousand fully trained reinforcements to Canada under the command of the Marquis de Montcalm.

Admiral Edward Boscawen, with eleven ships of the line and auxiliaries, left Portsmouth at the end of April, 1755, with orders to intercept the transport fleet before it could deliver its addition to the French military force in Canada. Much depended on the manner in which those orders were interpreted by Boscawen. To do less than prevent the French intention in its entirety would be to gain nothing worthy of the effort; to nibble at the problem by taking small bites at the enemy's strength would inevitably bring about a declared war in Europe for which neither side was fully prepared, either idealistically or materially.

The French transport fleet, under the command of Admiral the Comte Dubois de la Motte, comprising nineteen ships of the line and six frigates had something of a rough transatlantic crossing, and became split up by storms, high winds and mountainous seas by the time it reached the Newfoundland–Nova Scotia straits. The British fleet had made a landfall on the east coast of Newfoundland at Cape St Francis, where Boscawen learned that French warships 'full of soldiers' had been sighted by local coastal shipping. Moving down to the south-eastern point, Boscawen detached HBMS *Dunkirk*, Captain Richard Howe, with another British 64-gun ship, to reconnoitre, although heavy fog made long-range sighting impossible. Over the next two days there were brief tantalising glimpses of the enemy, which quickly vanished in the mists. The Admiral had brought the whole squadron out with a view to possible chase, and a couple of days later, on the 10th June, the fog lifted, and three French ships were in full view, six or seven miles on the lee bow.

Boscawen, hoping to lure them near, immediately hoisted French colours; but when he could not give coherent replies to the French interrogatory signals, they put on all sail and fled. They were the *Alcide*, the *Lys* and the *Dauphin Royal*. Captain Howe's *Dunkirk* led the pursuit and the story of the capture of the *Alcide* and *Lys* is quite in keeping with the spirit of the age, of Boscawen's sailing under false colours, and the belief that 'all's fair...etc.'. The *Dunkirk* out-sailed the 64-gun *Alcide*, came alongside and called on her captain, M. Hocquart, to shorten sail. Captain Hocquart, – who incidentally, had twice been taken prisoner by Boscawen during the War of the Austrian Succession – naturally refused the demand, hailing Howe and asking, 'Are we at peace or at war?' to which came the reply from HBMS *Dunkirk*, technically correct but morally as false as the colours, 'At peace! At peace!' – as she opened up on the Frenchman with broadsides. The action was over in a quarter of an hour. Perhaps Howe should be forgiven his deceitful part in the victory, as it is said that his Admiral had already hoisted the signal 'Engage!' before he went into action.

Later that day, another of the -64s, the *Lys*, struck her colours after a two-hour battle, and although the *Dauphin Royal* escaped into a providential bank of fog, it was captured a few days later. Many prisoners of war were taken in this unsatisfactory encounter. The *Alcide* had a ship's-company of 480 men, and the *Lys*, apart from her crew, was found to be carrying four companies of La Rein Regiment and another four of the Languedoc Regiment.

Although the action ended with the capture of three enemy warships, and the taking of prisoners of war reduced their fighting power by hundreds of naval and military men, the remaining, and by far the largest, part of the French fleet, reached Canada with its cargo of valuable warriors. By brilliant strategy, the Comte de la Motte had taken his ships through the Gulf of St Lawrence and the Canadians had received their reinforcements.

Both fleets could therefore claim a partial success – France almost to completion – in carrying out their given objectives; but Boscawen's famous, but comparatively unpraiseworthy victory – although wildly acclaimed by the British public – cannot be favourably compared with de la Motte's, and the Government ministers were less enthusiastic than the public. Lord Hardwicke, the Lord Chancellor realistically summed up the situation in Cabinet, when he said : 'We have done either too little or too much, the disappointment this news causes troubles me greatly.' But one thing was certain: the sending out of British troops under Braddock, and the French troops under Montcalm, to fight alongside their respective colonists, both in the spring of 1755, played a significant part in precipitating the war which was declared in the following year. Whilst the belligerent actions taking place three thousand miles away across the Atlantic in 1755 were obvious harbingers of war, the peace still held in Europe, at least for a short while yet. But news of the undeclared war and the breaking of the fragile Anglo-French truce in North America, sent ripples which quickly spread across another ocean, the Indian, where another delicate truce was about to be shattered.

The trouble in India was, on the surface, a commercial battle between two important trading companies: on the one hand a government-controlled enterprise, and on the other a private venture under royal charter – the Compagnie des Indes (the French East India Company) and the English East India Company. Both were of such immense importance to their respective nations, that political and imperialistic ambitions had long overtaken simple commercial interests.

The principal areas in contention were located on the western coast of the Bay of Bengal. Traditionally, the British were based on Calcutta in the north, although they had bases in Madras and Masulipatam to the south, and an important port on the Indian Ocean side of the sub-continent. Britain had received Bombay from Portugal, as part of Catherine of Braganza's dowry when she married King Charles II, in 1662. The main French trading centres were at Pondicherry to the south, on the Coromandel Coast – but they also had an important inland base, Fort Chandernagore, just above Calcutta, on the River Hooghly, an arm of the Ganges.

The Indian aspect of the Seven Years' War was to introduce another great name into our history – Clive of India – and an unforgettable *cause célèbre* of prisoner of war ill-treatment – the 'Black Hole of Calcutta'.

The rival British and French companies, backed by their countries, had long been jealous commercial opponents, but had recently set to work on fort-building and preparing for the inevitable opening of hostilities between their European masters, in much the same manner as their North American counterparts; but here a third party precipitated matters and brought them to a head.

The English company, which had been established in the first year of the seventeenth century and was an acknowledged agent of British imperialism, was confident in its well-established trade agreements with the Indian nawabs and nabobs; but that confidence was soon to be undermined. In June, 1756, the newly enthroned ruler of Bengal, the young and reckless Indian prince, Nawab Suraj-ud-Dawlah, who strongly objected to the English-built defences and fortification of Calcutta, made his objections felt, with devastating consequences.

Disregarding well-founded and long-standing treaties with the English Company, Siraj-ud-Dawlah made a surprise attack on Calcutta, sacking the city, capturing the fort and forcing the East India Company garrison to surrender. The details of that treacherous attack are largely forgotten in all but the history enthusiast's mind, but there can be few people who have never heard of the fate of the survivors of that onslaught. Although there are many versions of that story, even the least sensational of them is a horrible tale.

On the 20th June, the Nawab's prisoners – surviving defenders and Company employees – were herded into a part of the Company's own prison, known locally as the 'Black Hole'. One survivor, John Zephaniah Holwell, a senior East India Company official who, in 1758, published his narrative, *'The Black Hole',* tells us that one hundred and forty-six European prisoners were crammed into a foetid dungeon, eighteen feet by fourteen feet ten inches, locked in and battened down overnight. Most died from suffocation during that terrible night, and only twenty-three were found alive the next morning. Ever since, throughout the wars, the *Cachot*, or punishment cell in British prisoner of war depots and prison hulks (and, indeed, in military barracks), has been known as the 'Black Hole'.

Robert Clive had been sent out to India in 1743, when he was eighteen, to work as a clerk in the service of the English East India Company. Over the next few years he became deeply interested in the hostile rivalries between the English and French companies and their respective supporting Indian princes, and requested a transfer from the office to follow a military career. In 1751 he was set on the road to fame and fortune by his intervention in a struggle between the pro-French Chanda Sahib and the pro-British Muhammad Ali, at Fort Trichinopoly. Clive created a diversion by taking Chanda Sahib's base at Arcot, with a small force of only five hundred European and Indian troops, thus exhibiting an important superiority over the French alliances.

In the same month when the Nawab Dawlah was creating havoc in Calcutta, – June 1756 – Robert Clive fortuitously arrived in Madras, having been made a lieutenant-colonel in the Royal Army and Governor of nearby Fort St David; and at that same time, Admiral Charles Watson, Commander-in-Chief East Indies, was cruising off the Coromandel Coast.

News of the fall of the city reached Madras in August, and Colonel Clive sailed north with Admiral Watson early in October on a voyage of revenge and reprisal. The fleet comprised Royal Navy ships of the line with frigates and smaller craft belonging to the East India Company; carrying an army made up of about 900 European soldiers, 1,500 Indians and 500 sailors contributed by the Admiral. Calcutta was recaptured on the first day of the new year; and after a short break, it was decided to put a fine finish to the job by tracking down and challenging Suraj-ud-Dawlah, the villain of the piece.

Statistically, Colonel Clive's march towards Murshidibad, the Dawlah's capital city in West Bengal, near the Bhagirathi River, might suggest foolhardiness rather than a well-planned and heroic strategy. His army was tiny compared with expected opposition: in all it numbered no more than 2,700, the 700 being European and the remainder, Indian sepoys.

It was the wrong time of the year for marching, as the rainy season had begun – and the weather was to play a prominent part in the outcome of the conflict. The marching was done mainly by the Indians, the Europeans were transported upriver in naval long-boats; but whether they trudged through dripping jungles, squelched across muddy plains, or arrived by river, they wisely observed a sound gem of military advice, once expressed by Oliver

Cromwell as 'Put your faith in God, my boys, and keep your powder dry!'.

The confrontation between Robert Clive and the Nawab Suraj ud-Dawlah took place on the 23rd June, 1757, at Plassey, a small West Bengali village destined to go down in the history of Britain's fight for supremacy over France in India and the expansion of the British Empire. Yet, but for an act of God, and Indian inefficiency, the British would have stood no chance of victory. When Robert Clive saw what he was up against, he considered that the most he could hope for was to survive until nightfall, then retreat under the cover of darkness and fight another day.

The Nawab's military strength has been estimated as between seventy and one hundred thousand men, made up of foot soldiers, Pathan cavalry and French artillerymen who manned his fifty field-guns – nearly four times as many cannon as the British. This powerful force was backed up by more than fifty armoured war-elephants, camels, and yoked oxen to transport ammunition, provisions and move the guns. But although the Nawab and his armies were so numerically superior in men and cannon power they had neither luck nor the benefit of Cromwell's advice!.

Clive positioned his men on a prominence about a quarter of a mile above Plassey village, just out of effective range of most of the Suraj's artillery, and opened up with his own fourteen longer-ranged guns upon the vast mass of advancing Bengalis and Pathans. Despite the clashing of cymbals, the throbbing of drums and the trumpeting of elephants, the battle had begun in the morning in a desultory fashion, with the Nawab unsure which, if any, of his princely Indian allies would lead their troops against the British. Many of his high hopes were dashed and by late afternoon the combat was brought to a sudden end – not by numbers or gunnery, but by rain. The sky suddenly darkened as storm clouds gathered, and a heavy downpour dampened the enemy's gunpowder and their courage – the Indian troops, finding their weapons useless, about-turned and fled.

Great in significance as the Battle of Plassey undoubtedly was, Clive lost only seven men killed and thirteen wounded – although at least 500 of the Dawlah's troops, including many of his officers, were killed, and an untold number of his men wounded or taken prisoner.

Three months earlier, Colonel Clive and Admiral Watson had already fought and won a bloodier battle on their way to Plassey and the Nawab. They had decided to attack Fort d'Orléans at Chandemagore, the headquarters of the Compagnie des Indes in Bengal, using as justification the accusation that the French had given sanctuary to British deserters. A number of deserters had indeed gone over to the French, some of them even willing to take armed action against the British. Clive called upon Pierre Renault, the French Governor, to surrender, at the same time, '…making another shrewd move by getting word into the town – by notes attached to arrows – that British deserters who surrendered immediately would be pardoned and that any French officers who came over would be rewarded'.[3]

Pierre Renault ignored the call for surrender, regarding Clive's land force as no great opposition, and believing that Watson would never be able to bring his ships of the line far enough up the Hooghly River to pose a serious threat to the fort and the town. This was a reasonable surmise as old French ships had been ballasted and sunk in the approaches to Chandemagore. But Clive knew better. A French artillery officer with a chip on his shoulder had accepted the colonel's arrow-sent invitation to defect, and

came over to the British, bringing with him invaluable information that the blocking of the channels with sunken hulks had not been completed, and there was still a clear passage towards the town.

Clive, who was only too aware that his fire-power alone was insufficient to have much affect on the fortress, sent word post haste to Watson, whose squadron was well on its way upriver from Calcutta, and decided to make no attack on their main objective until his arrival.

Admiral Watson arrived off Chandemagore on the 20th March, and sent in two small warships to reconnoitre the reported gap in the underwater defences, before following closer in with his flag ship, the 70-gun *Kent*, ahead of two other powerful ships, the *Tyger* and the *Salisbury*.

The Chandermagore battle-proper started at sunrise on the 23rd March, with the land forces opening up with field-guns as the *Kent* and *Tyger* sailed past 'within pistol-shot' of the fort, with battle-flags flying and guns blazing. Broadsides from both vessels, fired at such close range hit d'Orléan with devastating effect; but the British did not have it all their own way. Although Watson himself miraculously lived through the two-and-a-half hours of slaughter, only one of his officers survived, and his second-in-command, Admiral George Pocock on the *Tyger*, '…was scratched shockingly [by splinters] and covered with blood from head to foot'. Their ships, too, suffered damage almost to the point of destruction, more than 150 cannon-balls hitting the *Kent* in hull, masts and rigging. To a great extent the Navy had borne the burden of the victory, the land forces sustaining comparatively few casualties as they marched in and took the town.

When after ten days the Chandermagore fortress had finally been forced to surrender, the French had not only lost many hundreds of dead, wounded and prisoners. Their town lay in ruins, most of their ships scuttled in the harbour or taken as prizes, and the warehouses, depots and magazines destroyed by the French defenders before capitulating.

By the time of the British victories at Chandermagore and Plassey the news of Britain's declaration of war upon France had reached India so they could be counted as legitimate acts of war. Over the following few years there were changes in the fortunes of war, but any future French imperialistic ambitions in the East were erased, it would seem forever.

A substantial treasure was taken from the two battles and shipped back to England. Clive himself had visited the Nawab's treasury at Murshidibad, where, although the deposed Suraj-ud-Dawlah had escaped with chests of jewels, he saw great heaps of gold and silver – receiving a personal thankyou gift of £180,000 from the new Nawab, Mir Jaffir.

Robert Clive returned to England for a period in 1760, where he was greeted by William Pitt as a 'Heaven-born General', fêted throughout the land, and rewarded with an Irish peerage – Baron Clive of Plassey – followed by an English knighthood a few years later. The vanquished Suraj-ud-Dawlah was later brought back to his capital city in irons, where he was assassinated by his own people.

Great Britain had finally declared war on France on the 18th May, 1756, and France responded in like fashion a few weeks later. The outbreak meant that a number of European powers were forced to decide who they would back in the forthcoming conflict. The ambitions of the two principal protagonists were overseas and colonial, whilst the interests of their possible allies were, in the main, local and European. The circumstances of this particular war dictated a change from the 'Old System' which had coupled Great

Britain with Austria and Prussia with France in past wars and now called for a complete reversal of alliances. This was appropriate at least from a religious point of view, with Protestant Prussia and Great Britain ranged against Catholic France and Austria. The final line-up was France, Austria, Saxony, Russia, Sweden, most of the German states of the Holy Roman Empire and (after 1762) Spain, versus Great Britain, Hanover and Prussia.

From the beginning of the Seven Years' War, King George II of England and Frederick the Great of Prussia were allies, to their mutual benefit. Frederick had taken the prosperous East German region of Silesia from Austria during the War of the Austrian Succession, and although a great power in his own right, he was aware of the need for a powerful ally, if he was to contend with the mighty military strength he would be up against, in the face of an alliance of Austria with France and Russia.

King Frederick had his own name for the Seven Years' War; he called it the 'Petticoat War', for he was, indeed, up against three powerful ladies: two Empresses and a king's mistress: Marie Theresa of Austria, Elizabeth of Russia and the French Madame de Pompadour. 'His malicious jests at Marie Theresa's piety, her husband's loose morals, Czarina Elizabeth's taste for vodka and virile aides-de-camp, and Pompadour's humble birth offended these powerful women and made them his implacable enemies'.

If Frederick needed Britain, George II, who was Frederick's uncle, needed Prussia no less. The British King had inherited the Electorate of Hanover from his father, George I, and the security of that German possession where he had spent his youth was of prime importance in his choice of allies. George II had proved himself personally courageous in time of war, by taking part in the Battle of Dettingen in 1743 – the last time that a British monarch made an active appearance on a battlefield. Despite his lifelong interest in all things military, and the fact that he possessed a keen political brain, George II more or less sat out the Seven Years' War, wisely leaving the planning to that brilliant strategist, William Pitt the Elder, who had early on seen that Britain should oppose France in her colonies and at sea, rather than in Europe.

As in every war we have ever fought, before or since, with so many hostile nations almost on her doorstep, Britain, both Government and public, was constantly concerned with the possibility of an invasion. 1756 was another year when all eyes were metaphorically on the Channel, and King George added to the defences of Great Britain by bringing over twelve battalions of his Hanoverian and Hessian troops from the Electorate. Although the French put up a frightening display of military might on the opposite coast, this was mainly show. William Pitt argued persuasively that there was little to fear – he hated the thought of Germans being employed to defend England anyway! – and it would seem that the apprehension of imminent invasion soon died down. Maybe the danger of reducing German military strength in Hanover was appreciated; or perhaps the cost of maintaining all these extra troops in England was as frightening – whatever the reason, the German mercenaries were returned to their homeland in 1757. Pitt did not view the security of Hanover as a prime consideration, believing that even if the Electorate was lost, it could be easily reinstated by arbitration at the conclusion of a successful war – but this was another opinion which he wisely kept secret from his royal master.

In spite of her indisputable maritime strength and reputation, Britain got off to a very poor start in European seas. Early in 1756, France had occupied the British naval base of Minorca in the western Mediterranean. Immediately the news reached London, England declared war on France, thus gaining points in the international popularity stakes; as the hostile action by the French so near home had made the opening of a war in Europe unavoidable However, Britain was to suffer further worrying incidents, miserable failure in actions against Rochefort in 1757, and St Malo in the following year.

To lose the island of Minorca was a blow to Britain's pride and its authority in the Mediterranean, necessitating immediate steps to rectify this calamity. The French had already repulsed the Gibraltar squadron, and now Admiral John Byng, second only in seniority to the First Lord of the Admiralty, was ordered to the Mediterranean, with a fleet of ten ships of the line to retake the island. Byng had many years' experience in Atlantic, Mediterranean and Home Waters operations; only six months earlier, he had captured the 74-gun *Espérance* in the Channel, which was too severely battered in the battle to be sent into a prize port. After taking off more than four hundred prisoners the French ship was put to the torch. One would have imagined him to be an ideal choice to reclaim the British naval base, and this he may well have accomplished, had he not been given the unseaworthy and undermanned fleet which set sail from Portsmouth on the 7th April, 1756, a few weeks before the actual declaration of war.

By the time the squadron reached Minorca, Port Mahon, the capital, had been captured and St Philip's Castle, the harbour fort, was under siege. The details of Admiral Byng's failure are less well known than its tragic – and scandalous – outcome. It is possible to argue either way, that he acted in a tactically correct manner by withdrawing after a brief battle to protect Gibraltar, or that he lacked aggression and courage; but what is unarguable is that his fate was a convenient cover-up of ministerial irresponsibility which had sent him to sea so poorly equipped in the first place.

When the news of the failure to recapture Minorca reached the Prime Minister, Thomas Pelham Holles, Duke of Newcastle, stormed, 'He shall be tried immediately, he shall be hanged directly.' Had the detailed despatch which Byng sent from Gibraltar been published in full, it is doubtful that he would have ever faced court martial; but the report was skilfully edited by neurotic ministers to remove any exonerating features in his favour, details which might reveal their contribution to the failure.

Admiral the Honourable John Byng, the son of Admiral George Byng (afterwards Viscount Torrington), was recalled to England and four weeks later arrested, fettered, and charged with doing 'less than his utmost' to relieve the siege of Fort St Philip. It was at first intended that he should be sent to the Tower of London to await his court martial, but he was eventually confined under a strong guard in a small barred room at Greenwich. On the 20th November, 1756, Byng was brought to the *St George*, lying in Portsmouth Harbour, where the trial was to take place.

The court martial dragged on for one whole month before a twelve-man court of admirals and captains. All of these he would have known, and whilst not all could be counted as friends or admirers, it is to be doubted that any one of them would have desired his capital punishment. From a strictly legal standpoint, Byng received a fair trial, but although he was expressly acquitted of personal 'Cowardice or Disaffection', he was found guilty of the principal charge of failing to relieve the besieged garrison at Port Mahon, or 'take, seize and destroy the Ships of the French King'. The penalty, under the 12th Article of War, was death – but the court unanimously thought it '…their Duty most earnestly to recommend him as a proper Object of Mercy'.

At first there were few people who believed that the sentence would be carried through to the bitter end, and he was in fact granted a two-week reprieve whilst the plea for mercy was considered. The pamphleteers and political cartoonists, French and English, had a field-day; but when it became apparent that politics rather than justice was the issue, protests came in from far and wide. William Pitt himself asked that he be reprieved, but George II was adamant that the admiral should pay for his failure with his life – to the private satisfaction of a number of his guilty ministers.

Admiral Byng, fifty-three, who had first gone to sea as a young lad of fourteen, was executed by a marine firing squad, on the quarterdeck of HBMS *Monarch* in Portsmouth Harbour, on the 14th March, 1757,[4] witnessed by senior naval officers, the *Monarch's* ship's company, and the hundreds of sailors who crowded the yards and rigging of ships in the harbour.

Newspapers, broadsheets, pamphlets and petitions had failed to save the Admiral's life. Pleas had also come in from abroad – Benjamin Franklin and even the Duc de Richlieu writing on Byng's behalf – and after all calls for reprieve had been disregarded, Voltaire, in *Candide,* cynically commented that the English found it necessary from time to time to shoot an admiral, in order to encourage the others – *'pour encourager les autres'.*

Once Byng had been satisfied that his courage and integrity was not questioned, he seemed to accept his fate, even refusing the efforts of his great friend Captain the Honourable Augustus Hervey, commander of the *Phoenix* at Minorca, to rescue him. Captain Hervey had spent a great deal of thought, time and money on the organisation of a carefully laid escape plan, whereby Admiral Byng was to be spirited out of the country. Hervey noted that Byng was well aware that he was suffering as a scapegoat in the midst of ministerial muddle, telling him that ''twas hard he should pay for the crimes of others with his blood that had never before been stained', but he would not run away. He may have lost a fight, but he never lost his courage: Horace Walpole wrote that as the admiral presented himself before the firing squad, which stood ready no more than six feet from him, he refused the offer of a blindfold, only allowing a handkerchief to be placed over his eyes when it was explained that his uncovered face '…might throw reluctance into the executioners', saying, 'If it will frighten them, let it be done; they would not frighten me.'

The story of the 'Tortoise and Hare' could be cited as a fair simile for Britain's record in most of her wars: she invariably won the race in the last few strides. Fraught with losses in North America, in parts of India, and Minorca nearer home, there was little to celebrate – but by the end of 1760, the prospect of victory could be glimpsed in the not too far distance.

Certainly the tables had turned in North America. In the first year of declared war the only significant action had been on Lake Champlain, by the Colonial Raiders under Major Robert Rogers. After that, for two years it was a case of attacks and counterattacks. When the tide changed, a great deal of the credit was owed to William Pitt, which was acknowledged at home and abroad. When, in November 1758, the French were ousted from Fort Duquesne on the Ohio Forks by General John Forbes, with his British and Colonial Army, Duquesne was renamed Pittsburg, in his honour; and it is small wonder that the Seven Years' War was widely known in Britain by another of its many names – 'Pitt's War'.

William Pitt had a genius for choosing the right military and naval men for the right jobs. He had given Clive of India an almost free hand in his field of war, and now in the struggle for Canada, he selected other names which would become great in British history. He appointed General Jeffrey Amhurst as Supreme Commander in North America. and in July 1758 Admiral Boscowen made a second and greater voyage to Cape Breton, delivering a British army. Together they took the great fortress at Louisbourg, thus closing the St Lawrence to the French and opening it up to the British.

Almost exactly a year later, the Siege of Quebec brought immortality to the name of another great British commander, General James Wolfe. Everyone will have some memory of the story of that great victory; of how the army, and a fleet under Admiral Charles Saunders laid siege to the capital of Canada, and how Wolfe's army of regulars scaled the Heights of Abraham, to meet the French army under Montcalm on the Plains.

Neither French nor British leader survived the battle. General Wolfe was mortally wounded whilst leading a bayonet charge, but lived just long enough to learn that he had won a great victory, and to utter his last words: 'Now God be praised, I die in peace.' The Marquis de Montcalm died of his wounds the next morning.

Quebec capitulated on the 17th September 1759, and when Montreal fell on the 8th September 1760, the war in North America was virtually ended, with Britain the masters of Canada and North America. The French were left with only one remaining possession, Louisiana – which they ceded to Spain in 1762.[5]

For the first half of the Seven Years' War the French Navy, which had started the war with sixty-three ships of the line and about half that number of frigates, had survived almost undamaged; but by 1760 it almost ceased to exist, its sea power depending almost entirely on privateers and letters-of-marque more than on royal ships of war. And France was as short of seaman as she was of ships – no less than 64,000 of the French prisoners taken by the British during the war were sailors.[6] Britain had struck a savage blow at the French economy by attacks on her merchant shipping and by warlike activities in the Caribbean sugar islands, capturing Guadaloupe in 1759, and Rodney taking Martinique in 1762.

The entry of Spain into the war on the side of the French in January of that year, bringing with her a navy of about a hundred vessels, looked like a tremendous boost to enemy strength; but with France now an inadequate maritime ally, weakness rather than strength was soon apparent. If anything, Britain gained by this late coalition, as it added one more nation's possessions to pursue legitimately.

On the 12th August, 1762, only seven months after Spain's declaration of war, Havana, her principal colonial possession in Spanish America, fell to British sea and land forces. Both countries paid dearly in death and injury, from action and disease; but the British survivors benefited financially from the proceeds derived from the fourteen men-of-war and nearly one hundred laden merchantmen taken as prizes. The two commanders, Admiral Sir George Pocock and the Earl of Albermarle each received £122,000 in prize money – each sailor received £3 14s 9¾d, each soldier £4 1s 8½d.

Nine weeks later, on the 6th October, Spain lost another of its treasure centres, Manila, the capital of the Philippines; and before 1762, that year of Spanish losses was over, Buenos Aires was also in the bag.

The 'Privateer' and 'letter-of-marque' vessels, so vital to the French diminished sea power, featured prominently in this and all the later wars, and were employed by all maritime nations. Many of those vessels and their captains, both English, French and their allies, earned fame, fortune and glory, and a niche in the history of the sea and sea-fights.

The terms 'Privateer' or 'Privateersman' – probably contractions of 'private-man-of-war('sman), which entered the English language in 1664, – were indiscriminately used to describe both the privately-owned, legally licensed vessel itself, and an officer or member of its crew. In a like manner, 'letter of marque' could be used to mean the ship or the document it carried.

As a high percentage of the prisoners of war taken at sea were the officers and ships-companies of privateers, particularly during the Seven Years' War and the American Revolutionary War, it may be as well to make a temporary diversion to answer, as clearly as possible, the question, 'Just what is/was a privateer?' and 'Was this just another name for a pirate?'

There has always been some ambiguity in the public mind concerning the difference between the privateer and the pirate. It is understandable that such confusion should exist, as it is an unfortunate fact that the line between the one and the other was sometimes very finely drawn. However much he is glamorized in film or stirring tales of adventure, everyone must know that the pirate, buccaneer or freebooter, even at his best, was little more than a fascinating but brutal plunderer of the innocent seafarer. The pirate and his ship's company cruised only for personal gain, with no pretence that even the tiniest degree of patriotism inspired or excused their bloodthirsty profession. In contrast, the privateer who acted true to his royal commission, was a legal and valuable addition to his county's regular naval force. So the great difference was, that one was lawful and the other lawless; that one would take prisoners of war, whereas the other was more likely to kill, ransom or make slaves.

And the difference between 'privateer' and 'letter-of-marque'? Both were vessels which carried identical documents which legalised their warlike activities. Nevertheless, although both were private ships of war, there was a distinct difference in their conditions of service. From medieval times licences or commissions, known as 'letters of marque' or 'letters of marque and reprisal', had been issued by the monarch or head of state of a nation to private ships, authorising them to take action against foreign shipping. These were normally granted only in wartime, but under certain circumstances, 'letters of reprisal' were granted to the captains and owners of merchant ships which had suffered damage or loss of goods at the hands of foreign aggressors in peacetime. In the latter case, the issuing of a licence was conditional upon the applicant supplying an accurate account of his losses.

The recipient of a letter of marque did not have to recoup his losses by searching out the original offender who had robbed him, the 'reprisal' was against the subjects of that nation and not the individual. Once he had been fully recompensed, his letter of marque was no longer valid, and if he continued to 'recoup' beyond the sum stated in his application to the Admiralty Court, his action could be adjudged as piracy.

By the end of the seventeenth century letters of marque were no longer issued in peacetime and the distinction between 'Letter of Marque' and 'Private man-of-war' was made plain – though still confused in common usage. Both were usually armed merchant vessels, although some privateers were privately built or substantially adapted for their specific use as men-of-war. The difference between the two categories was that the letter of marque ship was a merchantman which was hired – or commandeered – into State service; its crew paid, armed, fitted out and maintained, all at Government expense – whereas the privateer was expected to be self-supporting in every way.

The Privateer itself was exactly as its name implied, a privately owned, privately armed and crewed vessel, which had been granted a privateering licence/commission/letter-of-marque by the sovereign or Lord High Admiral of its country, authorising it to legally make war against a specified enemy. Unless armed with a letter-of-marque, any private ship which used armed force would not be regarded as a privateer, but as a pirate; – the vessel condemned and captain and crew liable to fines and possible capital punishment.

The privateer vessel was usually owned or part-owned by its commander and financed by a syndicate or consortium of businessmen and merchants. Their risk was only financial but the privateers themselves risked life and limb, for many did not survive their first cruise; but a successful cruise might bring in fabulous wealth in the form of what some might have regarded as ill-gotten goods.

The majority of privateersmen did not set out to gain glory by waging war against the enemy's navies. The governments of their countries did not normally contribute in any way towards their support or maintenance – in fact, some governments claimed a percentage of the booty! – so the privateers' main aim was to pay their own way, and prove to their backers that they had made a wise investment.

The rewards to the privateer came only after his captures, in the form of ships and goods – known as 'prizes' – had been adjudged by a Prize Court as fairly taken, condemned and then auctioned. Prize money was paid out not only to private armed ships but to naval vessels and one of the most prevalent complaints by the ordinary seaman from either service was their share in the pay-out.

There is an old privateer story which tells of an ordinary sailor whose ship was about to go into action. Briefly, he sank to his knees in an attitude of prayer and muttered a few words before dashing to his action-station. On being questioned by one of his shipmates after the action, he revealed his simple prayer; 'Dear God, let the enemy's cannon-balls be apportioned like our prize-money – the lion's share among the officers!'

A report in *Chambers Journal* records the distribution of prize money between four British frigates after their capture of the Spanish frigates *Thetis* and *Santa Brigida*, later in the eighteenth century. The share-out would have been a little different, and less, in the case of privateers, as there were owners and syndicates of merchants with fingers in the pie, but the following might indicate a reason for the sailor's fervent prayer:

Captains	each	£40,739 18s 0d
Lieutenants	each	£5,091 7s 3d
Warrant Officers	each	£2,468 10s 9½d
Midshipmen, etc	each	£791 17s 0¼d
Seamen and Marines	each	£182 4s 9¼d

The term 'privateer' does not describe a *type* of ship. They came in all shapes and sizes, from small coasters and luggers of fifteen or twenty tons, to fast man-of-war-like ships of five-hundred tons or more. Whatever their size, however, they would always appear to be vastly over-crewed. This is explained by the fact that they carried extra men, sometimes as many as twice the number required to crew the ship: often teenage boys, who could serve as 'prize crews' to man their hoped-for captures.

In the main, the defenceless victims of these fully-licensed and legal looters were the merchantmen with their valuable cargoes of provisions and materials. However, in fairness to privateers generally, it must be said that in their efforts to cut out merchant shipping from strongly escorted convoys, some of these para-naval vessels, under great commanders, put up valiant fights against the protecting naval men-of-war.

The privateer vessels of all the sea powers involved in all of the wars mentioned in the following pages, played their important part. Accordingly, the merchant fleets of all those nations were hard-hit by the hundreds of privateers which hunted seas on both sides of the Atlantic. Towards the end of the Seven Years' War, France was brought to the brink of economic ruin by blockades and British naval and privateer successes; and their efforts to employ the merchant ships of neutral countries, such as the Dutch, nearly brought Holland into the war. By 1759, the naval forces had taken over the capture and destruction of convoyed merchant shipping on the high seas and, except in the West Indies and coastal areas, the heyday of privateering in that particular war was, for the time being anyway, almost over. (It was, however, to return with a vengeance a decade later, with the American War of Independence. Privateering and the issuing of letters of marque was banned by most nations after the Congress of Paris in 1856.)

At that time in the eighteenth century privateering was generally accepted as a respectable, necessary and rather glamorous extension of a nation's regular naval services; but its ambiguous moral status was used by both nations in their never-ending propaganda tirades. The following extract from Robert Beatson's *'Naval and Military Memoirs'*, written not long after the close of the Seven Years' War is an example of what was probably some anti-French and pro-British exaggeration, sprinkled with flecks of accuracy:

> '…The enemy having swarms of small privateers at sea, captured no less than 330 of the British ships. It is to be lamented that some of their privateers exercised horrid barbarities on their prisoners, being the crews of such ships as had presumed to make resistance, and who were afterwards obliged to submit; conduct that would have disgraced the most infamous pirate; and it would have redounded much to the credit to the Court of France to have made public examples of those who behaved in this manner. I am afraid, likewise, that there was but too much reason for complaint of ill-treatment to the British subjects, even after they were landed in France and sent to prison. Of this, indeed, several affidavits were made by the sufferers when they returned to England.'

He then went on to paint in glowing terms Britain's great concern for her captive Frenchmen: '…the conduct of Great Britain was a striking example of their kindness and humanity to such unfortunate persons who were made prisoners of war. The prisons were situated in wholesome places, and subject to public inspection, and the prisoners had every favour shown them that prudence would admit of.'

He spoiled this rather idyllic picture of 'kindness and humanity',

when he went on to say that when prisoners were ready for exchange by cartel, they had been confined for so long that 'their clothes were reduced to a very bad state, many of them, indeed, almost naked, and suffered much from the inclement weather'; which would indicate that those to whom the prisons 'were open to public inspection', had not been very observant.

Many similar self-slanted reports and letters came in from over the Channel, and it can be assumed that the rank and file prisoner here or overseas had a hard time of it. The *Annual Register* in September 1758 tells of 'divers accounts published by gentlemen of credit in France which represent the usage of the poor prisoners there as intolerable,' and went on to say that 'the numbers reported to have perished by the wretchedness of their condition even exceeds those killed by sea and land'.

The Convention of Westminster in January 1756 ratified the alliance between Prussia and Great Britain, if and when war was declared. The sudden reversal of coalition was certainly not founded on bonds of friendship or family connections, but on convenience. Frederick had no love for his uncle and ex-enemy; and George II disliked his nephew's arrogance, referring to him as 'that proud, overbearing prince…' But both respected the other's abilities and national qualities in time of war. Frederick, with his highly trained and disciplined armies; himself one of the greatest generals of his age, and George, king of a prosperous Britain and with his Royal Navy the world's greatest sea power.

It is difficult to conjecture how Prussia would have fared in – or the outcome of – the Seven Years' War, but for that convenient coming together of their resources. Frederick's strange knack of upsetting both friend and enemy alike, by high-handed actions and indiscreet comments, his open contempt for Louis XV and his mistress would have made it hard to renew his old alliance with France. What with Marie Theresa itching for revenge over Silesia, and the Czarina definitely anti-Frederick, there was nowhere to turn except towards England. And both had much to gain.

Frederick's preoccupation with Austria and France allowed Britain to concentrate on her principal objectives overseas, taking only a comparatively minor part in most land operations on the Continent; but subsidising Prussia with financial aid to the tune of £200,000 annually. Keeping France as busy as possible in Europe was the name of the game, and one which took up so much of that nation's time, effort and a constant dipping into its meagre financial resources, that the French Navy was neglected beyond recovery.

Frederick the Great got off to a perhaps wise but controversial start by invading neutral Saxony, which brought international rebukes – including a feigned condemnation from his Britannic ally – all of which he justified by insisting that if he had not done so, Austria would.

Frederick's armies were always numerically inferior to those of the opposing forces; often by as many as three to one. They were, however, vastly superior in the quality of their make up; regular soldiers, with experience of previous wars; well trained and officered, and led by a remarkable military strategist – Frederick Hohenzollen himself. In battle after battle it seemed that he faced defeat, but somehow, more through brilliant military tactics than by luck, he pulled through. Over the years Prussia lost so many thousands of men through battle, disease and captivity, that the fruits of victory seem somewhat lean pickings – Frederick's major gain was no more than the confirmation of his possession of Silesia, for which he had fought for and won in the war of 1740–48.

It is well nigh impossible to form even a rough idea of the aggregate number of prisoners of war taken by the participating nations during the Seven Years' War. The two principal adversaries were engaged in hostilities on every known continent, America, Europe, Asia and Africa – and the high seas of the world. Even in the case of nationalities whose confrontations were mainly confined to the Continent, the numbers of prisoners of war taken were sometimes almost unbelievable. Over the years of that war, Prussia lost nearly a quarter of a million men to Austria alone, including 63,000 prisoners of war.

There was no consistency in the treatment of prisoners at that time. So much depended upon the part of the world where the captive found himself confined. Not so many years earlier the prisoner of war was as likely to be slaughtered as housed and, as we have seen, the soldier who fell into the hands of the Redskin allies of either side in North America, would be lucky to keep his hair or his head. Nevertheless, by that time in the mid-eighteenth century, a far more humane approach to prisoner of war management and treatment was taking place in the Western world. That is, on the part of governments and administrators, in the form of well-intentioned rules and regulations. Alas, these were as often as not flouted by a percentage of corrupt food contractors, prison guards and bribable officials. However idealistic the regulations from on high, it cannot be expected that the man in the street, whose equivalents to modern man's television, radio and sports days, were dog-fights, bear-baiting, the pillory and public executions, would invariably share our idea of what was reasonable or barbaric in the treatment of enemy captives.

The 'Parole System', which benefited a vast number of officer-prisoners and other special category captives, had been introduced, and was for the most part successful and generally honoured and respected; certainly in those early days before the French Revolution.

Prisoners of war were paradoxically both a gain and a burden. By their capture, the enemy suffered a loss to their striking force, but the captor had to find men to guard them, food to feed them, garments to clothe them, and places to house them. Over an almost unbroken period of warfare, from 1756 to 1815, we certainly had too many prisoners of war in Britain, but there was no real answer to the problem. There was never a sufficient number of our own men in foreign prisons for anything like a one-to-one exchange system to operate – and to return captives without exchange would have made a nonsense of having captured them in the first place – although both sides did on occasion return probably unwelcome cartels of prisoners to their homelands; but only if they were too old, wounded or sick to pose any future military threat!

From a logical standpoint, it makes it frighteningly understandable, though not forgivable, that in past ages combatants should have slain their captives on the battlefield or slung them overboard after sea fights; unless they could be put to use as turncoat additions to their armies or navies, as slaves, or were of sufficient importance to command a ransom.

As prisoners of war began to enter this country in the mid-1750s the old problem of secure accommodation once again reared its unattractive head. The old prisons and depots which had been used in previous wars were hurriedly called back into use: Portchester Castle, the Old Mill Prison near Plymouth, Stapleton near Bristol, and Forton Prison at Portsmouth, Liverpool Tower, and a number of other prisoner of war centres. Sissinghurst Castle in Kent was leased for the purpose, but was demolished after the war had ended. As many as 4,000 prisoners were housed in Portchester Castle at times, and on one occasion 5,000 were confined in the old King's House Barracks at Winchester.

Overcrowding sometimes made it necessary to board foreign war captives with our own civil prisoners; usually in debtors gaols, as, at that time and until the American Revolution, we 'exported' the majority of our felons, vagrants and political malcontents to the colonies.

By the end of the first year of the war, 1756, only about 7,260 prisoners of war had been brought into England, but the number grew as the war progressed, so that the average yearly number of prisoners in Britain during the Seven Years' War was in the region of 19,000: the figure for the penultimate year was particularly high, at 26,217; but by the Treaty of Paris in 1763, there were more than forty thousand men awaiting cartel[7] ships and freedom.

The rank and file prisoners, the 'broke-parole' officers, and officers who had refused to sign their *parole d'honneur* when captured, were distributed among the land prisons and depots, or sent to the few prison hulks then established. Officers who had accepted the conditions laid down in the parole form, and had pledged on their word of honour not to break them, lived a comparatively free internment in one or another of a surprisingly great number of villages and towns in Great Britain, until exchanged or the war came to an end.

ALRESFORD	CALLINGTON
HELSTON	SEVENOAKS
ASHBURTON	CHIPPENHAM
KINSALE[8]	SODBURY
ASHFORD	CREDITON
LAUNCESTON	TAVISTOCK
BASINGSTOKE	DUNDEE
NEWCASTLE	TENTERDEN
BECCLES	EXETER
OAKHAMPTON	TONBRIDGE
BIDEFORD	FALMOUTH
PETERSFIELD	TORRINGTON
BISHOPS WALTHAM	GOUDHURST
REDRUTH	WHITCHURCH
BRISTOL	GUERNSEY
ROMSEY	WYE

How these and many other selected towns in Great Britain reacted to the introduction of foreign additions to their communities between 1756 and 1815, and how captive warriors of a dozen or more nationalities – many of whom spent from a few months to as many as twelve years of privileged internment in English, Scottish or Welsh *cautionnements* – did or did not adapt themselves into these alien societies, is told in later chapters. The land prisons and depots, the prison hulks and their occupants, will be discussed in a like manner.

Throughout the Seven Years' War, there were recriminations and accusations between the British and French authorities regarding the conditions of confinement, provisions and treatment of prisoners. After reading through reams of complaint and counter-complaint, one can only conclude that all this correspondence was, in fact, more a paper-war between government departments of the two nations, each chalking up points to their own satisfaction; but it is to be doubted that the prisoners themselves gained much from their rulers' written attacks on each other. The Commissaries for prisoners of war of either nation seldom did more than exchange copies of the official regulations, as though the ideals envisaged therein for the treatment of the captives, had in fact been little cause for complaint – although it cannot be doubted, and should be understood, that captives would have felt duty-bound to lodge complaints against their enemy.

From the beginning of the war, King Louis of France had made one genuine, and point-winning, move by making a monthly grant, varying in amount according to rank or rating, to every French prisoner of war in British custody. This became known as the 'Royal Bounty' and came out of the monarch's privy purse. It was, like the similar allowances made to nationals by Denmark in 1807, and America in 1812, designed to provide extra food and such 'luxuries' as soap, coffee and tobacco – but with the French addiction to gambling, a good deal of it would have been dissipated at the tables![9] Part of the 'Royal Bounty' was also meant to provide for the needs of French prisoners fortunate enough to be included in exchange cartels.

This significant contribution towards the alleviation of French prisoner hunger and discomfort was enjoyed for three years; then, in 1759, all support from France, including the 'Bounty', came to an abrupt end. If this was a blow to the English administration, it was of course a greater one to the prisoners. Rumours, probably emanating from French sources, inferred that the British were to blame for the withdrawal of the King's generosity, but it is more than a coincidence that France was known to be near to the point of bankruptcy at that time. Nevertheless, in a letter dated a short while before the 'Royal Bounty' was discontinued, there is more than a suggestion that English duplicity – or perhaps malpractice on the part of the French Agents responsible for the distribution of the royal handout – had brought the cancellation of this boon to the prisoner of war standard of living.

Many French imprisoned in Portchester Castle describe the excessive length of their confinement, and an arrangement which enabled them to receive an aid of money from the King every month; after having exchanged the paper money and gold they had been given for copper coins named half-pennies, their supply was stopped and they were deprived of the King's aid.

Although constant warring had bred a natural animosity which had existed between England and France for centuries, it would seem that, once the enemy soldier or sailor was safely brought into captivity, a fair number of our countrymen felt some sympathy with his predicament. The *Brussels Gazette* for December, 1759, was somehow able to say: '...the animosity of the English against the French decreases, and they continue to hate only those French who are in arms. The English feel for their captives as men, and cannot but pity enemies in distress who are not in a capacity to hurt them.' This exaggerated generalisation of English enlightenment was accurate to some extent. Groups of thinking, well-to-do people, gentry, merchants and professional groups, throughout the wars willingly contributed in cash and kind, when particular prisoner of war suffering was brought to their notice.

Whilst that Belgian newspaper article was being printed, subscriptions were already being instituted in England for 'the clothing and comforting of the French prisoners during this rigorous season – unhappy brave fellows – who are totally neglected and abandoned by their own country'. There was a great response to this call, both in money and garments, and during that winter Frenchmen all over the country received gifts of suits and other clothing. Francis Abell gives some idea of the magnitude of some such subscriptions, when he tells of a Committee which met in London at the *Crown and Anchor* in the Strand, in that same year of 1759 when the 'Bounty' and French support of the prisoners ceased: '...the sum of £7,000 was collected. With this sum were sent to different prisons 3,131 great coats, 2,034 waist coats, 3,185 pairs of shoes, 3,054 pairs of breeches, 6,145 shirts, 3,006 caps, and 3,134 pairs of stockings'. Many letters of appreciation were sent, one from French prisoners on the prison hulk, *Cornwall,* at Chatham:

> '*Cornwall.* Man-of-War at Chatham 13.1.1760
> We, prisoners of war, on board the King's vessel *Cornwall* in the River Medway, acknowledge having received by grace of our good commander Guillaume Lefebre, second hand clothes comprising of one bonnet, a pair of stockings, shoes and a pair of pants [to each man]. We thank the English who have shown kindness to unfortunate people owning practically nothing, and before had no guarantee of protection against the severities of the season, and great suffering caused by the cold. Rest assured that our gratitude and recognition will not be forgotten.'

In that same year, Dr Samuel Johnson was called upon to write an introduction to a pamphlet in connection with one such London subscription; *'The Proceedings of the Committee Appointed to Manage the Contributions... for Clothing French Prisoners of War'.* Johnson was well aware that there were probably many who strongly objected to relief to the French, who 'urged that charity, like other virtues, may be improperly and unseasonably exerted; that while we are relieving Frenchmen, there remain many Englishmen [prisoners], unrelieved; that while we lavish pity on our enemies, we forget the misery of our friends.' The good Doctor thought that their argument must be examined, lest it be thought 'irrefragable'.

After disputing the allegation that 'Want was the effect of Vice', and that 'casual almsgivers were patrons of Idleness', he opined that not a single Englishman would suffer by charity to the French; directing the critics to remember the Scriptures, which command: 'do good to them that hate us'. If further proof is needed as evidence that all was not hatred between the belligerents, even in what was in many ways a brutal age, Arthur Bennett, in his *'Things Passed Away',*[10] quotes two instances where local peoples, English and French respectively, indicated that 'the spirit of chivalry in warfare was not extinct'.

In January, 1762, a French frigate, the 22-gun *Zenobi,* commanded by Captain de Sage, ran aground near Portland. Of its crew of 210 men, only seventy-one survived to reach the shore, and nearly all of these were wounded and naked. It is said that the local country folk attacked and would have killed them but for the intervention of Commander Travers of Portland, who had them taken to the town. From there they petitioned the Lords of the Admiralty, pleading that on account of their misfortune and distress they should not be treated as prisoners of war. Their plea was heeded, and it was ordered that they should be clothed and fed at his Britannic Majesty's expense.

Two months later, on the 21st March, a small English merchant ship was driven on shore at Harvre de Grace, and broke up into pieces. The crew were all saved and, although it is not stated that he knew of Commander Travers's gallantry, the Commandant of Harvre ordered that they should be quartered in a local coffee house, and allowed thirty sous a day during the short time before they were returned to England. We must not delude ourselves, however, by imagining that such inspiring records are anything more than exceptional. It is probable that only a small proportion of the population were involved in getting up subscriptions or sparing thought for the fate of foreign prisoners of war – far more may have reacted like the countryfolk around Portland.

Whilst thousands of men fought in actions on land and sea across the world, complaints concerning those whose fighting days were, at least temporarily, over, continued to flood to and fro across the Channel – and locally between the Sick and Hurt Office[11] and the prisoners and their Agents – the two prime subjects of discontent being food and clothing.

It was laid down that the food ration for the French (ideally) was to be the same as that allowed to the British naval seaman in weight and quality. On six days of the week the allowance was to be one-and-a-half pounds of fresh baked bread, three-quarters of a pound of fresh beef, and a quart of beer. There is some ambiguity over the promise of the equivalent of a British seaman's ration of 'fresh' beef – the sea-going English tar's beef was seldom fresh, was often substituted by putrid brined pork. His bread was seldom 'fresh-baked', more often hard-tack or ship's biscuit. On four of the six days the prisoners were allowed half-a-pint of peas, and on Saturdays they received either six ounces of cheese or four ounces of butter.

The French *'Table d'Avataillement'* for British prisoners of war differed in that one pound of meat instead of three-quarters was to be issued on four days of the week: 'beef, mutton or veal, without heads or feet', soup, salt and vinegar. On each of the other three days the allowance was a half pound of peas or beans, cooked in two ounces of butter. The beer was to be no less than one pint a day, and sometimes wine was served. So much for printed official regulations, which were no doubt originally laid down by conscientious officials intent on creating a basic – and affordable – diet, suited to men who would no longer be subject to an arduous life as soldiers or sailors. However, there was often a great deal of difference between the makers of the rules and those entrusted to carry them out. Many of the latter, at all levels of prison management and supply were the greatest contributors to prisoner of war suffering.

By 1762 the war was in effect over. In September, the Ambassador and the Plenipotentiary to the Court of France, the Duke de Nivernois, came to England to discuss the conditions of peace. Together with his twelve-strong party of French diplomats,

he landed at Dover and stayed at an inn in Canterbury overnight, before proceeding to London. It is said that they were 'shamelessly overcharged' by the innkeeper, who presented the Duke with a bill totalling £41 14s, 8d., for their tea, supper, lodging and next morning's breakfast. Their host would have been prosecuted but for the intervention of the Duke.

The end, when it came, was favourable to both England and Prussia. On the 10th February, 1763, the Franco-British Treaty of Paris gave North America and India to Britain thus establishing the latter as the greatest overseas colonizing power; and the Treaty of Hubertusburg, on the the 15th February upheld Prussia's possession of Silesia, which Austria had lost in the War of the Austrian Succession, 1739–1748.

But even after seven years the paper-war had not quite ended. There was still the question of certain international war-debts concerning prisoners of war to fight over. Robert Beaston had stated that 'the bad state of the finances of France did not permit that kingdom to continue the allowance they formally granted for the maintenance of their subjects who might become prisoners of war [after 1759]; but the nation who had acquired so much glory in overcoming them, had also the generosity to maintain such of these unfortunate men as were in her power at the public expense'; but this was not the whole truth.

We had, indeed, assumed responsibility for feeding and clothing our French prisoners of war for the last four years, but after the Treaty of Paris, France was presented with a bill for more than a million pounds, which the French Government hotly disputed. They contended that the profit gained from all the captures which our privateers had made under letters of reprisal before the war was declared, should have been more than enough to cover costs of supporting the French prisoners during the war. There was some justice on their side. We *had* taken more than one hundred French merchant vessels before war was declared, which in ships and cargoes must have been worth five or six million pounds. Nevertheless, in 1765 the French Ambassador offered £670,000, in full compensation.

The French were not the only losers in this long drawn-out war. The Indian tribes which were given – but often abused – freedom under the French policy of coexistence, were to lose their unique culture and way of life under a very different British/American policy.

Britain still had to find money to cover the many costs of fighting that expensive war which gained us America, and, ironically, it was her efforts to recoup by imposing a duty on tea, stamp duties and other taxes, which led to the war we shall be discussing next – THE WAR OF AMERICAN INDEPENDENCE.

---

1. Thomas Pelham Holles, Duke of Newcastle: Prime Minister 1754 to 1756 and 1757 to 1762.

2. Rupert Furneaux. *The Seven Years' War.* London.

3. Tom Pocock. *Battle for Empire.*

4. Admiral Byng's tombstone bears the inscription: *'To the perpetual disgrace of Public Justice, the Honourable John Byng, Admiral of the Blue, fell martyr to political persecution on March 14th of the year 1757, at a time when courage and loyalty were insufficient guarantee of the honour and the lives of naval office'.*

5. The vast area of the Mississippi Basin was held by the Spanish until 1800, when a reluctant Charles IV was induced by Napoleon Bonaparte to re-cede it to France. In 1803 the United States achieved the greatest real estate coup in history, the 'Louisiana Purchase', buying the colony from France for $11,250,000 – less than three cents an acre!

6. 'The Royal Navy had 97 ships of the line and 60 frigates; and in 1762 it still comprised 304 war vessels of all types.' Julian S. Corbett. *England in the Seven Years' War.*

7. The 'Cartel' itself was a written agreement regarding the exchange of prisoners between nations. The exchange itself was also called a 'Cartel'. A 'Cartel Ship' was an unarmed vessel which ferried exchanged prisoners to and from the specified 'Cartel Ports'.

8. Kinsale is the odd man out in this list as being the only Irish town mentioned. There is a record of 1,250 prisoners being there in 1759, but it is probable that they were awaiting transportation to England.

9. See Clive Lloyd's: *The Arts and Crafts of Napoleonic and American Prisoners of War 1756-1816*, Chapter 9: 'The Gamblers & the Brokers'.

10. Arthur Bennett. 'Things Passed Away.' Printed in the *Hampshire Advertiser*, 1918.

11. The Sick And Hurt Office was responsible, through its Agents in the depots, for all prisoners of war; duties which were later taken over by the Transport Officer in the early nineteenth century.

Chapter Two

The Americans:
The War of Independence 1775–1783

BETWEEN THE SEVEN YEARS' WAR AND 1815 THERE were very few years when there were no prisoners of war in Britain. They were generally referred to as 'French', even in those early times, though their nationalities ranged across the world, from the East Indies to the West. About the only exception to this prisoner of war nomenclature were captives from America.

From America? Most British people today have some memory from their schooldays of the War of Independence – of the Boston Massacre and the Tea Party; George Washington and Paul Revere; and the loss of the colonies – but that we were at war with America in Napoleonic times often draws a blank. Many more, both British and American, are amazed to learn of the presence of huge numbers of American captives in this country: in the depots ashore, aboard prison ships in the Medway, Portsmouth and Plymouth, or paroled to towns in England, Scotland or Wales.

They were here in their hundreds and, during the War of 1812, in their thousands. Many of these were impressed American seamen who were serving in the Royal Navy and had every reason to feel aggrieved when, at the outbreak of the 1812 war with their country, they were thenceforth considered legitimate prisoners of war. Many others were taken at sea – naval and merchant officers and their crews, and sometimes civilian passengers – but the greatest number were from captured privateers or letters-of-marque vessels. There were also, of course, soldiers and militiamen taken prisoner in battles on land.

Many hundreds of fine books have been published which have dealt with the above two wars from a multitude of viewpoints, but in general the subject of the prisoner of war has been neglected or given scant notice in their pages. These introductory notes, therefore, make no effort to present potted histories of the wars except to highlight appropriately my subject – the Prisoner of War.

Edward Channing, in his assessment of the military capacity of the United States at the beginning of the War of American Independence, calculated that the total population of America at that time was about three million, including about five hundred thousand negroes. Although almost all felt that their treatment at the hands of the British administration gave them good reason to fight, by no means all had any desire for war, and even less would have even dreamed of the possibility of an independent American nation. Congress had stated that the fight was not against the king – or even against England – but that their quarrel was with the government in power at that time, and their oppressive Acts.

Channing estimated that of the three million, only about 1,200,000 could truly be called rebels and that no more than a fifth of that number – say 240,000 – were men of military age. In a modern war about two-thirds of that number, say a hundred and fifty thousand men or more, would probably be available to serve at the front.

That was the estimate but, from all the states, Washington never had more than 30,000 land troops available to him at any time during the war. That was not, of course the country's total fighting strength. One of the reasons for such a small land force was that, in the absence of a navy, a great number, at least another thirty thousand, were soon engaged in privateering.

America was not without experience in the privateering game. Little more than a decade before, her fast privately owned armed-vessels and tough crews had been a valuable addition to Britain's sea-power during the Seven Years' War. As in that last war, so in this, most of the ships and men were from New England and the northern states. The New Englander speculators and the ship-owning merchants had much to lose through war, with almost complete loss of legitimate trade through blockades and embargoes; but although generally anti-war they were not anti-profit. Although the risks involved in privateering were high – financial for the investors and physical to the point of death for the seagoers – the fortunes which could be made through the sale of captured ships and cargoes were huge and irresistible. Soon they were involved in what, even then, some might have thought of as legalised piracy and whilst merchant ships and private schooners were being made warlike, plans were laid to establish a national sea-going force.

The first step in the establishment of an American Navy began on the 13th October, 1775, when the Continental Congress directed that two vessels – one of ten guns, the other of fourteen – should act as national cruisers, and early in the following month the Marine Corps was founded with two battalions. By the 13th December, it was decided that various shipyards should get to work on the construction of thirteen frigates which, it was expected, would be ready for sea late in the Spring of 1776. These vessels were well designed and built, but all manner of hold-ups, through blockades, shortage of materials, armament and manpower, resulted in only four of the frigates seeing sea service before 1777.

There was another type of vessel which, had it been successful, may have been looked at askance and with disapproval, judged, like the privateer, as downright irregular and ungentlemanly – the submarine! An interesting but little-remembered fact in the naval history of the War of Independence concerns such an American underwater craft. The American 'Turtle' was designed by David Bushnell of Connecticut, who demonstrated to a sceptical audience of military and naval 'experts' that gun-powder could be detonated under water.

The 'Turtle,' so-called because its shape resembled two joined carapaces, could dive and surface, travel submerged, and attach a large time-clocked mine to the underside of a vessel. As far as I can discover, the American 'Turtle' – operated by submariner Sergeant Ezra Lee – had the distinction of being the first submarine ever to be used in active warfare, in September 1776. It was unsuccessful in its attack on the British flagship, HMS *Eagle*, in New York Harbour and, in 1777 failed to destroy the *Cerebus* off New London – but it did, unintentionally, blow up a nearby schooner!

Just before Christmas, 1775, the Marine Committee appointed its first naval officers: Commander-in-Chief Esek Hopkins; four captains; five first-lieutenants; six second-lieutenants and three third-lieutenants. It is from the list of first-lieutenants that one name leaps from the page – John Paul Jones.

Jones was a complex, charismatic character, who became hated as a 'corsair, pirate and buccaneer' by his British enemy, but honoured as a great naval hero and courageous sea-fighter by his adopted country and her allies. Of particular interest in the context of this book, is the fact that John Paul was, literally as we shall see, a great fighter against unfair treatment of the prisoner of war.

In England his was a bogeyman name, to scare not just unruly children but the inhabitants of the coastal towns of Great Britain who were ever aware of the possibility of a French-Dutch-Spanish-American invasion. During his short, but heroic service as a American naval officer, he was fêted throughout the courts of Europe. Louis XVI made him a Chevalier of France and America, eventually, awarded him the Congressional Gold Medal.

His original name was John Paul, the Jones was adopted later – as was his nationality, for he was born a Scotsman at Kirkbean, Kirkcudbright, in July, 1747. The proximity of his home to the Solway Firth no doubt inspired his seafaring aspirations and at the age of twelve he was bound apprentice to a Whitehaven merchant in the American trade.

His elder brother, William, lived in Fredericksburg, Virginia, and the following year found Paul as a thirteen year old cabin boy, sailing towards what was to be his new homeland and fame. In 1766, his merchant employer's business having collapsed, he sailed as chief mate on a Jamaican brigantine in the slave trade; and after a couple of years of slaving, and a further four on other trading craft, he had become a master mariner and the proud owner of his own vessel in the West Indies. In 1773 he was back in Virginia, where his brother had died and he himself was far from affluent.

John Henry Sherburne[1], the Registrar of the United States Navy, came into possession of John Paul Jones's original letters and documents. Writing of that time in Jones's life, he said: 'It is probable that Paul, at this period, was suffering from pecuniary difficulties… he was living in America in a very retired manner, and about this time he adopted the name of Jones.' It is possible that Sherburne was being euphemistic regarding his hero's situation at that time, or Jones himself may have edited some of the truth from his papers. That truth could well have been connected with two unfortunate deaths.

In 1768 he had been given command of a merchantman, the *John*, and sometime in 1770, when the vessel was at Tobago in the West Indies, he had ordered the ship's carpenter to be flogged with the cat-o'-nine-tails, for insubordination. The carpenter, Mungo Maxwell, left the ship, but died later, it was said, of malaria, aboard another trading vessel.

However slender the connection between the flogging and Maxwell's death, John Paul's name was blackened. His reputation was further tarnished a couple of years later, when in command of the *Betsy* and again at Tobago, some of his crew mutinied. One mutineer attacked him with a bludgeon and in defending himself, Jones killed his attacker. A quick retreat from the islands and a change of name allowed him to escape trial for the killing – although, as a captain, he

may well have escaped any punishment for his action in the circumstance of mutiny. However, the bad luck of the carpenter and the mutineer was America's good fortune, as it brought him back there just in time to make his mark in his adopted country's revolution.

Right from the start of his career, John Paul Jones was discontented with many aspects of the newly-formed American navy. He was a prolific letter writer, addressing his recommendations and criticisms to Benjamin Franklin, Jefferson, congressmen and anyone else who might have influence for change. As a mere lieutenant, his harsh criticisms of many of his fellow officers, of the lack of discipline, the ill-trained crews and the deficiencies of the American navy in general, would surely have earned him a severe reprimand at least, in an older and more established navy.

John Paul had a reluctant admiration for the British Royal Navy and was conscious of how much America had to learn, but added the rider that 'I propose not our enemies as an example for our general imitation; yet, as their navy is the best regulated in the world, we must in some degree imitate them, and aim at such further improvements as may one day make ours vie with and exceed theirs.'

In September, 1776, he sailed as commander of the American, *Providence* – a sloop of twelve six-pounders – on a month-long cruise in search of enemy shipping. The voyage proved successful. The *Providence* took 'sixteen sail; manned and sent in eight, and sunk, burnt or otherwise destroyed the rest.' Busy as he was with his search for British prizes, his correspondence went on unbroken and, reading between the lines of his letters, one might suspect that he was less than satisfied with the rewards for his labours. Always the proud naval officer, Paul Jones looked down from the lofty height of his comparatively lowly rank, on privateering and all private armed-vessels:

> 'It is to the last degree distressing to contemplate the state and establishment of our navy. The common class of mankind are activated by no nobler principle than that of self-interest.
> 'This and only this determines all adventures in privateers; the owners, as well as those they employ; and while this is the case, unless the private emolument of individuals in our navy is made superior to those in privateers it can never become respectable, it will never become formidable; and without a respectable navy, alas America. In the present critical situation of human affairs, wisdom can suggest no more than one infallible expedient; enlist seamen during pleasure [peace], and give them all the prizes.
> 'What is the paltry emolument of two-thirds of prizes to the finances of this vast continent? If so poor a resource is essential to its independency, in sober sadness we are involved in a woeful predicament, and our ruin is fast approaching.'

Jones was probably right as far as prize-money was concerned. As he said; 'If our enemies, with the best established and most formidable navy, have found it expedient to assign all prizes to the captors, how much more is such policy essential to our infant fleet?' Without the privateers he so disparaged, however, America may well have remained as colonies for many long years after his time.

British merchant shipping was spread across the oceans of the world, much of it completely unprotected by war-ships or escorts of any kind. The job of the privateer was to search the seas and attack enemy vessels, usually merchantmen, wherever found; to claim both vessel and cargo as prize; incidentally causing as much distress as possible to the enemy's trade and commerce. Private armed vessels, of any nationality – for England, France and most other maritime nations had their letters-of-marque and privateers – depended entirely on their own efforts to subsist; they paid their own wages and provided their own and their owners' keep by their captures. They received no financial assistance from their governments, yet were at times the most effective part of their country's sea-power.

Unlike admirals, captains and military leaders commissioned in the national service of their countries, who were given titles, land and honours at the end of wars or even individual battles, few great privateers were given material recognition, although their names were known and resounded throughout the land.

The commanders, officers and crews of private armed vessels, operating under commissions or letters-of-marque were, in general, honourable and courageous men working in a hazardous trade; seeing far more action and facing far more danger than most men mustered into wartime service on land or sea. If successful their rewards could indeed make them wealthy men, but failure, in the words of an old letter-of-marque captain, brought them '…from their country? Nothing; from the enemy? hard knocks, prison ships and free lodgings as a prisoner of war in England'.[2]

The depredations of successful privateering were disastrous to British maritime commerce. By the end of the war in 1783, some one thousand five hundred vessels and their precious cargoes had been lost and the effect on insurance was almost equally ruinous. Quite early in the war the odds against a trouble-free passage of any length caused London underwriters to up their premiums to a massive twenty-five percent. Even short Channel voyages could call for rates of fifteen percent or more – for American privateers did not restrict their adventures to their own side of the Atlantic. Many cruised the English coast and Channel ports, taking their prizes into supposedly neutral Spanish havens, where captured vessels and their merchandise found a ready black-market. Of course not all privateers were fortunate in their chosen profession, and many a daring legalised buccaneer was forced to exchange his adventurous life with its hope of, if not fame, at least fortune, for a miserable prisoner of war existence in a makeshift barracks, an English prison depot or New York prison hulk.

It is perhaps not so surprising to learn that an American captured and brought to this country should have found himself viewed in a very different light from any other 'foreign' prisoner of war, considered as he was by many as a despicable 'rebel colonist' or 'renegade Englishman'. Consequently the non-commissioned American prisoner of war was often met with hostility and even cruelty, his keepers accusing him of insurgency and taunting him that the only way he could redeem his treachery would be to enlist in the British navy. Enlistment was a way out available to any able-bodied American who would put self-preservation before patriotism. The fact that after only a year of war, and despite some exchanges, there remained about one thousand American prisoners uncomfortably quartered in this country, proves that the majority stayed true to their country. Many other Americans were in prison camps ashore in America, or temporarily incarcerated in many other parts of the world awaiting shipment to Britain, whilst yet others were confined in even worse conditions on hulks like the infamous *Jersey* prison ship and her ugly sisters in New York Harbour.

Other than escape or enlistment, the only gateway to freedom whilst the war lasted was through the exchange system but, unless the exchange took place at sea, the prospect of rapid release was more often dreamed of than realised. Only in exceptional circumstances did British men-of-war permit exchange or parole at sea, but privateers often had good reason to do so. For one thing it released numbers of their countrymen back into active service and, perhaps of more immediate importance, it reduced the number of potentially dangerous prisoners of war on board their ship. Sometimes, when space aboard his vessel was of more importance than the $10 a head bounty he could claim for every British captive taken into a port, the American privateersman was known to release his captives without exchange. Searching through lists of prizes taken by American privateers, I found a few entries which, like the one quoted here, show that on some occasions British prisoners were offered another means of obtaining their quick release from captivity:

> 'Schooner **Mary**, of St Thomas, captured by privateer **Rapid**, of Charleston. Not having men to spare [for prize crew]: **Ransomed**.'

Ransom was not as rare as one might imagine. As we shall see, John Paul Jones ransomed prize vessels and also had great hopes of ransoming some of our coastal towns, such as Bristol, Leith and others; but he would never have parted with prisoners other than by exchange.

It cannot be denied that, at that period in history, the prisoner of war in Britain, had a very rough time of it – which is certainly not to infer that his British counterpart in France or the United States received kid-glove treatment. There was no deliberate government plan to make things unpleasant for our captive foe, but indolence and procrastination on the part of those in power, added to the general harshness and corruption of the age, made certain that he would have few pleasant memories of his stay in this country.

The housing of prisoners of war had always been a great and troublesome problem which, in spite of Britain's experience of almost continuous warring, had never been squarely faced, or received the attention which might have eased the situation for both administration and prisoner.

By the end of the Seven Years' War in 1763, there were about 40,000 prisoners of war in England, yet nothing was done to create a decent and humane system of prisoner of war management. They were crammed into unhealthily overcrowded hulks, shared filthy local gaols with civilian prisoners, or were kept in makeshift quarters in castle keeps and towers, hastily adapted large country houses, warehouses, and even caves. It should be remembered, however, that they were, at least, taken prisoner! Not so many years before, and for past centuries, most captured enemies would have been taken into slavery, thrown overboard or slaughtered on the battlefield; whilst a few nobles or men of substance may have been ransomed.

The day of the specially constructed prisoner of war depot, which could hold several thousand captives and operate under workable regulations and controls, was still in the future. It was not until 1782, and the American War was nearing its end, that Stapleton Prison, at Fishponds, near Bristol, was built; and the first great prisoner of war depot, Norman Cross, was not completed until 1797.

The position, therefore, at the outbreak of the War of American Independence was no better than before – in fact, much worse. In the first place, the Government rather expected a last minute escape from hostilities; and second was the fact that this war, more than any before it, made the problem of housing prisoners – whether civil prisoners or prisoners of war – more desperate than ever before.

From the time of Elizabeth I. there was no real need for large convict establishments in Great Britain – America itself was our penitentiary. The Act for the Punishment of Rogues, Vagabonds and Sturdy Beggars 1597, had introduced transportation as the sentence next in severity to the gallows. From then on, a hundred or more crimes, from the petty to the serious, could earn terms of seven, fourteen or twenty-one years' deportation to the American colonies. Now that we were at war with the keepers of this most convenient depository, transportation across the Atlantic came to an abrupt end.

Convicts, political and religious dissidents and other of Britain's unwanted subjects who would normally have been disposed of overseas, now more than filled this country's gaols and, for the first time, the harassed administration introduced civil prison hulks as a 'temporary expedient'.[3] With prison management almost unmanageable and prisoners of war arriving daily at our ports, it is not surprising that the American captives found hard lodgings in what, until recently, had been their motherland.

A few of the old prisoner of war hulks, such as the *Royal Oak* and the *St Rafael* at Plymouth, which had been used between 1756 and 1763, were brought back into service and were soon fully occupied. Any space in borough gaols which had not been taken up by 'Transportation convicts' – with nowhere to go! – was put to prisoner of war use; some inmates would even be able to make the unenviable boast that they had once spent time in notorious Newgate Prison.

Ebenezer Smith Platt, a captive merchant from Georgia, was fettered '…and placed in that part of the prison occupied by thieves, highwaymen, housebreakers, and murderers, with no allowance for food and clothes and must have perished but for private benevolence.' Whilst Ebenezer's case was not unique, I think it probable that he, and others who found themselves treated with such extreme lack of consideration, must have offended over and above his being thought of as a colonial insurgent.

John Howard, the great prison reformer, who tirelessly visited and reported on conditions in all types of civil and prisoner of war establishents and parole towns, found that many Americans were ill-housed and received provisions way below the quality and quantity specified in official regulations; but in most of the towns where there were also French captives, the latter fared even worse, sometimes through neglect by their own government representative, but more often through their uncontrollable addiction to gambling.[4]

In 1777, Benjamin Franklin complained to the British Ambassador in Paris of the treatment dealt out to his countrymen, of their poor rations and the 'most bitter accusation of all, that "stripes" [flogging], had been inflicted on some to make them commit the deepest of all crimes – fighting against the liberties of their country'.

Franklin's letter was passed on to London and he was given rather unconvincing reassurances that the matter would be dealt with. There was a good deal of comment in the newspapers and periodicals of that time, which left little doubt that the Americans had much to complain about. One commentator, writing in the *Gentleman's Magazine* in that same year, seemed insensible to the possibility that Americans might have genuine feelings of patriotism to their homeland, and considered that a gentler approach, plus a British seaman's ration, would soon overcome any feelings of loyalty to America:

> 'It must surely be a matter of some difficulty to dispose of such a number of prisoners as are daily taken from captured American privateers; some of whom have from 100 to 300 men on board, few less than 70 or 80; against whom the Americans can have no equal number to exchange. Were the privateersmen, therefore to be treated as prisoners of war, our gaols would be too full to hold them. What then is to be done? Not indeed to load them with chains, or force them with stripes, famine or, other cruelties, as the letter charges: to enlist in Government service; but to allow them the same encouragement with other subjects to enter on board the King's

ships, and they will have no plea to complain of hard usage.'

Surely he must have known that, for many of our subjects, the 'encouragement to enter' had come from the press-gang; that the food was seldom as good on the plate as its description on paper; and that pay was usually 'deferred'. Some of His Majesty's ships had been without pay for five years or more; sometimes because the money was just not available; more often as a security measure against desertion – in keeping with the cynical saying: *'Keep the Pay & Keep the Man!'*

There was one group of men who caused the prisoners far more suffering than the importunities of any enlistment officer or thoughtless taunting keeper: these were the corrupt contractors who were entrusted to supply their food, bedding and clothing. Throughout the period covered by this study, prisoners of war of all nationalities, including our own, were cheated by unscrupulous suppliers, whose greed and inhumanity was outstanding even in that brutal age.

A London newspaper, reporting on the plight of American prisoners in this country in 1778, made this very clear: '…their penury and distress was undoubtedly great, and was much marked by the fraud and cruelty of those who were entrusted with their government, and the supply of provisions'. It went on to say that the government could be found guilty only of omission, in not strictly overseeing these rogues, as the contractors who 'in their natural cruelty, considered their offices as only lucrative jobs which were created merely for their emolument.'

It was admitted that the Government subsistence allowance would indeed have been sufficient to sustain them, if honestly administered, 'yet the want of clothes, firing and bedding, with all the other various articles which custom or nature regards as conducive to health and comfort, became practically insupportable in the extremity of winter'.

No profitable fiddle was too low for the worst of the men trusted to see to the day-to-day needs of the prisoners. When John Howard visited Pembroke, in 1779, he found that they were cheating on the very straw used for bedding, by leaving it unchanged for long periods; and some of the prisoners who had small weekly allowances of a few shillings were docked 6d a week handling charge.

The Pembroke prison accommodation, which was guarded by militiamen, consisted of two old houses with a small airing yard 'twenty-five paces square', and two rooms in the Town Jail. One of these old houses held thirty-seven Americans, 'some without shoes or stockings, all of them scantily clad and in a filthy condition, whose straw had not been changed in seven weeks.' There was a small ill-equipped hospital which, at the time of the visit, was occupied by three Americans and nine Frenchmen and 'all lay on straw with coverlets, but without sheets, mattresses or bedsteads.'

Next door to the Americans' prison, there were fifty-seven French prisoners who were in no better state than their co-belligerents. Except for four lucky owners of hammocks, their bed was the floor. None of the prisoners could be other than filthy, as the airing yard was without water or sanitation and the Town Gaol, which housed another twenty Frenchmen, was also without water, and sometimes days would pass before supplies were brought in. Howard reported and the prisoners complained, but to little lasting effect.

Newspaper articles and official reports sometimes prodded the authorities into action and agents and contractors received a rap over the knuckles, the effects of which would last only a short while, for bribery and corruption flourished, and both the highly placed scoundrels and their underlings were into too good a racket for them to reform. Whilst officialdom was slow to act and often ineffective, however, when they did, published reports and prisoners' complaints attracted aid from what was, considering the age, a quite unexpected source. A surprisingly large number of the British public showed great generosity by contributing to subscriptions for prisoners' relief, and many hundreds of pounds were collected. Throughout the wars, charity committees were set up and subscription appeals published on behalf of French, Dutch, Spanish, American and other prisoners of war. There were also an equal number of subscriptions in aid of our own soldiers and sailors, held captive overseas.

Calls for help on behalf of the Americans were particularly well patronised. It may be that this can be explained by the fact that most of the latter prisoners of war were merchant-backed privateers. Bankers and merchants on this side of the Atlantic may well have been looking towards transatlantic business beyond the end of the war.

The majority of, but not all, American prisoners in England were seamen or ships' officers and mainly privateersmen. It could hardly have been otherwise, for the United States navy could boast only twenty-seven war-ships in 1776 and this number was reduced to twenty by the end of the war in 1783. During that same period the British naval strength had increased from two hundred and seventy to five hundred; but it should be remembered that France had entered the war in July 1778, followed by Spain in '79 and the Netherlands in '80.

This intervention provided a great deal of protection of the American coast, for Britain could not mount fully effective blockades on both sides of the Atlantic. Most naval action, therefore, was between the European navies whilst America relied to a great extent on her superbly manned private armed-vessels.

Privateers, both French and American, using Ireland as a base for their hit-and-run attacks, created havoc amongst our coastal shipping, but they had losses as well as gains and there was always a brisk traffic in prisoners of war. During the war more than 12,000 of our seamen were taken by American privateers and the impracticality of their all being shipped back to the United States was as obvious as the impossibility of our keeping all American captives in our inadequate prisons until the end of the war. So the exchange of prisoners went on all the time – but still our prisoner of war accommodation was always overcrowded.

Liverpool, one of Britain's principal ports for her own privateer fleet, was sure to be a centre for the reception of captives; but despite the fact that the town had experienced prisoner of war additions to its population, on and off since the beginning of the century, no special building had been adapted or built for their accommodation until 1776.

The old Tower at the end of Water Street, had been used for both civil prisoners and captives taken in past wars, and it was again used during the War of Independence. Such a place of confinement must have seemed a godsend to the ever escape-conscious Yankee rebels. Henry de Curzon, in a rare little volume on Liverpool,[5] described its shortcomings: 'This old building consisted of towers, houses, and buildings of various ages and indifferent features, with many walls, passages, turrets and dungeons, many windows – too many for a prison – and many doors, which were never repaired and very insecure.'

It was here that prisoners of war were housed, with felons and debtors, men and women mixed, singing drinking, gambling, and generally creating a pandemonium. Dr John Howard, in 1780, condemned it as a 'foul dirty place, a hotbed of diseases and unworthy of a great nation and of a town like Liverpool.' In 1776, with the expectation of an influx of American prisoners of war, the Transport Office – which was responsible for all prisoners of war in Britain –

showed some foresight by leasing an old gunpowder magazine, which had been used to store powder whilst ships were laid up or refitting in port. Now, 'instead of gunpowder, French and Spanish mariners and American insurgents were lodged there.'

It was surrounded by high walls and isolated in a field, but once adapted to its purpose it was a great improvement on the old Tower. The general conditions and the quality of the food were better than in most depots of that time. 1,432 prisoners saw the inside of the old powder magazine between 1778 and 1782, and the records show that only eighteen died whilst captive.

At this distance in time, it at first seems amazing that so many war-prisoners should have been kept in our ports and towns near the sea. Many hundreds of Americans and their continental allies were held captive in Portsmouth, Plymouth, Liverpool, Bristol and a number of other coastal prisons. It may have been convenient for exchange and cartels but equally it invited escape – not that the Americans needed the invitation.

This chapter – and many others – could quite easily be fully taken up with the story of escapes and escape attempts. It would seem that wherever there was an American, an escape was under way or a plan was being hatched. The Militia at the old Forton Prison, near Portsmouth, was kept on the *qui vive* at all times, but 1778 was a particularly busy, but unsuccessful, year for them. The year before, thirty had got away, but most were recaptured. These latter were so severely punished that their complaints were reported in the London newspapers; but their punishment did not deter others. Now large-scale escapes were being planned and attempted.

At Forton, fifty-seven Americans carried out a 'wooden horse' type of decampment and it would seem they got clear away: The *cachot* – the Black Hole or punishment cell – was beneath the sleeping quarters of their part of the prison and it was not too difficult for them to dig through to the cell below. From the *cachot* they excavated a tunnel which went under the outer wall. The hole in the floor was covered with a mattress and the excavated earth was secreted in the hammocks for which they hoped to have no further use.

There were numerous other attempts that year, including another planned mass exodus from Forton: On this occasion it was a Franco-American joint effort, and although the Militia who were camped nearby were alerted by the alarm guns, twenty-five had made their getaway before the arrival of the troops.

Farther round the coast, at Plymouth, was the old Mill Prison, renamed Millbay by the time it once again housed American prisoners during the war of 1812. We know a great deal of the everyday life at Mill Prison, from the memoirs of two young Americans[6] who spent part of their War of Independence within its walls, whose stories will be told a little later. For the moment we will record that the rebellious spirit which distinguished the Yankee prisoner from the French or captives of other nationalities, was as troublesome and worrying to their keepers there, as it was at Liverpool, Bristol, London and everywhere where they were detained.

Naturally restless, and impatient for freedom, the intensity of their mutinous activity was in part inspired by reports which circulated the prisons, of the activities in British waters of John Paul Jones. His successes were disturbing enough for the possibility of an uprising to be taken seriously, and many prisoners were transferred to inland depots and paroled officers were sent to towns well away from the coast. Thus it is appropriate that we should return to the story of John Paul Jones and his adventures in the *Providence*.

During that cruise he fell in with two British frigates, the 32-gun

Mitford and the *Solebay* of 28-guns, an encounter which could well have ended his career, but he managed to escape after an action with the last-named frigate which lasted several hours. He then proceeded to Isle Madame, off Nova Scotia, where he left devastation in his wake; burning vessels and destroying the buildings of the fishing industry there. On his return, he was promoted to the rank of Captain, given command of a small squadron, and immediately sent once more to sea. This time he was to proceed to Isle Royal and the main object was to obtain the release of American prisoners who were confined in the coal mines there.

Although he failed to achieve this objective, he left the whale and cod fisheries in ruins, and during the cruise took many prizes; and one of his captures added to his already growing fame. Although the vessel itself was of no great importance, its cargo was of great use to George Washington's ragged army which, at that time, was in dire need of clothing. His prize, the armed-vessel *Mellish*, out of Liverpool, was carrying 10,000 military uniforms, intended for the British army under General Burgoyne.

Among the communications with which Captain John Paul Jones continued to bombard Congress, was one which he addressed to the 'Secret Committee' in the Spring of 1777. By this time his ideas and opinions were highly valued and many of his suggestions adopted; but that the daring proposal that he should be sent to France – and from there attack the coast of England – should have been approved is indeed remarkable. It was typical of the courageous Jones that he should have proposed such a venture, but surprising that Congress should have made the equally courageous decision to reduce the tiny naval force which protected their own coast, to attack that of their enemy. He was given command of an 18-gun sloop, the *Ranger*, and a free hand: 'we shall not limit you to any particular cruizing station, but leave you at large to search for yourself, where the greatest chance of success presents.'

Before December, 1775, American ships flew the flag of whichever colony had commissioned or built it, but by that date the new navy had a new flag, which demonstrated the coming together of those colonies. The design of the Flag of the Continental Congress, or 'Grand Union', showed thirteen horizontal stripes, alternate red and white, and in the top left canton, nearest the mast was the British flag – the combined crosses of England and Scotland. On the 3rd December, John Paul Jones, on the deck of the *Alfred*, had had the honour of hoisting the new flag with his own hands.

On the day that Paul Jones was appointed to the *Ranger*, a national ensign, the Union Flag, came into being:

> **'In Congress**, June 14, 1777
> **Resolved**. That the flag of the Thirteen United States be thirteen stripes, alternate red and white; that the Union be thirteen stars, white in a blue field, representing a new constellation.'

When the *Ranger* sailed for France on the 1st November, her captain was the first man to hoist the Stars and Stripes, just as he had been the first to raise the Independent Standard at the beginning of the war. The French fleet under Count d'Orville was at Brest when he arrived there on the 14th February and, with the Union Flag flying from the *Ranger*, received its first salute ever made to an American ship by a foreign man-of-war.

Three weeks later he set out for his first voyage against Britain. There must be some psychological explanation for his having picked Whitehaven as the target of his first raid. That the reason why he chose the town where, only nineteen years before, he had begun the apprenticeship which led him to America, could be that these were waters and approaches which he remembered most clearly from his boyhood is too simple an answer. That he did so, however, makes understandable the hatred with which the British, and particularly the Scots, regarded him as a traitor, renegade and rebel.

He was delayed for some time by bad weather but spent the time sinking any craft unlucky enough to cross his path. Finally, on the the 22nd April, he landed at midnight with thirty-one volunteers and entered Whitehaven. They spiked the guns of the fort, set fire to ships in the harbour and part of the town was set ablaze – and Jones 'brought off three prisoners as a sample.'

The Cumberland Pacquet Extraordinary, for the 23rd April, reported that Whitehaven was saved from even greater disaster, by a traitor (or loyalist?) in the *Ranger*'s landing party who went ahead and warned the townsfolk:

> 'Late last night or early this morning a number of armed men (to the number 30) landed at this place, by two boats from an American privateer, as it appears from one now in custody. Whether he was left through accident or escape by design is yet uncertain. This much however has been proved, that a little after 3 o'clock this morning he rapped at several doors in Marlborough Street (adjoining one of the piers) and informed them that a fire had been set to one of the ships in the harbour, matches were laid in several others; the whole world would be soon in a blaze, and the town also destroyed; that he was one belonging to the privateer, but had escaped for the purpose of saving the town and shipping from destruction.'

Over the next few days, newspapers all over the country carried the dreadful news, some reporting the consternation of the east coast inhabitants; others deploring the lack of our national preparedness. One, obviously disgusted that the sentinals at Whitehaven had been in their guardhouse whilst their guns were being spiked, wrote scathingly;

> *'Gazetteer and New Daily Advertiser*, May 5, 1778.
> The people of Whitehaven, it is thought, can never recover from their fright; two thirds of the people are bordering on insanity; the remainder on idiotism; the defence of the harbour is left to the care of the old women, who declare that had they been called into power earlier, they would have preserved the town with their mop-sticks and cut off the retreat of the rebels.
> 'We hear that Dr ...., with about half a dozen Scotch physicians, is shortly to go to Whitehaven, to restore the inhabitants to their senses; but should these gentlemen not succeed it is determined that a Scotch architect be employed to build them a madhouse.'

Maybe because his character was that of a free-ranging adventurer and professional hero, the plight of his imprisoned countrymen was always present in the mind of John Paul, and one of his great plans was to find a means of 'striking a blow in their favour.'

On the very morning after the overnight attack on Whitehaven, he crossed the Solway Firth and landed at midday on St Mary's Isle, Kirkcudbright, not far from his own birthplace; intent on putting his plan into practice.

His wild but admirable idea was to capture a nobleman and hold him hostage against the release, exchange or better treatment of American prisoners of war in Britain. St Mary's was the seat of the Earl of Selkirk and it was to his mansion that Jones and the original landing-party proceeded to claim their hostage – only to find that the Earl had left the island on a visit to the mainland.

The disappointed Captain decided to return to his ship, but the men considered that they deserved some reward for the venture, saying that if the boot was on the other foot, Americans could not expect such gentlemanly treatment from the English. So, under strict orders to conduct themselves in an honourable manner, Jones left them under the command of his lieutenant and they went up to the Earl's residence.

It seems that they obeyed their captain to a great extent; and only the lieutenant entered the building, where he met Lady Selkirk who, with great dignity and composure, complied with his demand for booty, and parted with the the family silver – the plate of the House of Douglas.

The events and adventures of the past thirty-six hours would have been enough for most men's entire war, but by noon on the 24th April the *Ranger* was approaching Carrickfergus when she observed a British warship leaving the harbour. The 20-gun sloop *Drake,* with her Commander George Burdon, had received news of the Whitehaven disaster and had set out ready for action and revenge. It is an amazing fact that she was followed out of the harbour by five small vessels carrying sight-seeing passengers determined to witness what they hoped would be the defeat of the 'American pirate'.

Late in the afternoon the action between the *Ranger* and the *Drake* began. It was a short but bloody affair, the *Ranger* raking the British sloop as it passed across her bows, and when, after seventy-five minutes, the *Drake* – 'her sails and rigging entirely cut to pieces, her masts and yards all wounded and her hull very much galled' – struck her colours, John Paul Jones had achieved yet another 'first'. The *Drake* was the first British warship to be defeated and captured by an American.

After the battle, the two ships were roughly refitted, a prize-crew was put on board the *Drake,* and Jones with his prize and prisoners sailed round the north of Ireland and made for Brest, where they arrived on the 8th May. Five of the *Drake*'s 154-man crew had been killed, and another twenty wounded, and of the surviving prisoners, twenty enlisted in the American naval service. These turncoats were said to be Irishmen who had been pressed into the Royal Navy.[7]

On the same day that he reached Brest, the inexhaustible John Paul wrote a lengthy letter to the Countess of Selkirk. If an excuse is needed for setting it down here in its entirety, it is that its main theme is concerned with the subject of this book – the prisoner of war – and that it also reveals other aspects of the multi-faceted Captain. It is a cleverly composed, though somewhat indiscreet epistle, in which John Paul presents himself as a chivalric character. Whilst chatting-up the noble lady, he makes the outrageous excuse for his 'invasion', by suggesting that he would have been doing the Earl a service, had he been successful in kidnapping him!

'*Ranger*, Brest, 8th May, 1778.
Madam,
    It cannot be too much lamented, that, in the profession of arms, the officer of fine feelings and real sensibility should be under the necessity of winking at any action of persons under his command, which his heart cannot approve; but the reflection is doubly severe, when he finds himself obliged, in appearance, to counter such acts by his authority.

'This hard case was mine, when, on the 23rd of April last, I landed on St Mary's Isle. Knowing Lord Selkirk's interest with the king, and esteeming as I do his private character, I wished to make him the happy instrument of alleviating the horrors of hopeless captivity, when the brave are overpowered and made prisoners of war. It was, perhaps, fortunate for you, madam, that he was from home; for it was my intention to take him on board the Ranger, and to have detained him, until, through his means, a general and fair exchange of prisoners, as well in Europe as in America, had been effected.

'When I was informed by some men whom I met at landing that his lordship was absent, I walked back to my boat, determined to leave the island. By the way, however, some officers who were with me, could not forbear expressing their discontent, observing that, in America, no delicacy was shown by the English, who took away all sorts of movable property; setting fire, not only to towns, and to the houses of the rich, without distinction, but not even sparing the wretched hamlets and milch cows of the poor and helpless, at the approach of an inclement winter. That party had been with me, the same morning, at Whitehaven; some compliance, therefore, was their due. I had but a moment to think how I might gratify them, and at the same time to do your ladyship the least injury. I charged the two officers to permit none of the seamen to enter the house, or to hurt anything about it; to treat you, madam, with the utmost respect; to accept of the plate which was offered, and to come away without making a search, or demanding anything else.

'I am induced to believe that I was punctually obeyed, since I am informed that the plate which they brought away is far short of the quantity expressed in the inventory which accompanied it. I have gratified my men; and, when the plate is sold, I shall become the purchaser, and will gratify my own feelings by restoring it to you, by such conveyance as you shall please to direct.

'Had the earl been on board the *Ranger* the following evening, he would have seen the awful pomp and dreadful carnage of a sea engagement; both affording ample subject for the pencil, as well as melancholy reflection for the contemplative mind. Humanity starts back from such scenes of horror, and cannot sufficiently execrate the vile promoters of this detestable war:

"For they, t'was they, unsheathed the ruthless blade,
And Heaven shall ask the havoc it has made."

'The British ship of war *Drake*, mounting twenty guns, with more than her full complement of officers and men, was our opponent. The ships met, and advantage was disputed with great fortitude on each side, for an hour and four minutes, when the gallant commander of the *Drake* fell, and victory declared in favour of the *Ranger*. The amiable lieutenant lay mortally wounded, besides near forty of the inferior officers and crew, killed and wounded; a melancholy demonstration of the uncertainty of human prospects, and of the sad reverse of fortune which an hour can produce. I buried them in a spacious grave, with the honours due to the memory of the brave.

'Though I have drawn my sword in the present generous struggle for the rights of men, yet I am not in arms as an American, nor am I in pursuit of riches. My fortune is liberal enough, having no wife nor family, and having lived long enough to know that riches cannot ensure happiness. I profess myself a citizen of the world, totally unfettered by the little mean distinctions of climate or of country, which diminish the benevolence of the heart and set bounds to philanthropy. Before this war began, I had at the early time of life withdrawn from the sea service, in favour of 'calm contemplation and poetic ease'. I have sacrificed not only my favourite scheme of life, but the softer affections of the heart and my prospects of domestic happiness, and I am ready to sacrifice my life also with cheerfulness, if that forfeiture could restore peace and good will among mankind.

'As the feelings of your gentle bosom cannot be but congenial with mine, let me entreat you, madam, to use your persuasive art with your husband's to endeavour to stop this cruel and destructive war, in which Britain can never succeed. Heaven can never countenance the barbarous and unmanly practice of the Britons in America, which savages would blush at, and which, if not discontinued, will soon be retaliated on Britain by a justly enraged people. Should you fail in this, (for I am persuaded you will attempt it; and who can resist the power of such an advocate?) your endeavours to effect a general exchange of prisoners will be an act of humanity, which will afford you golden feelings on a death-bed.

'I hope this cruel contest will soon be closed; but should it continue, I wage no war with the fair. I acknowledge their force, and bend before it with submission. Let not, therefore, the amiable Countess of Selkirk regard me as an enemy; I am ambitious of her esteem and friendship, and would do anything, consistent with my duty, to merit it.

'The honour of a line from your hand, in answer to this, will lay me under a singular obligation; and if I can render you any acceptable service in France or elsewhere, I hope you will see into my character so far as to command me without the least grain of reserve I wish to know exactly the behaviour of my people, as I am determined to punish them if they have exceeded their liberty.

'I have the honour to be with much esteem and with profound respect, Madam, &c. &c.

To the Countess of Selkirk   JOHN PAUL JONES'

Nine months passed without reply and when one did arrive it was a message not from her ladyship but her husband. Passed to John Paul Jones via Benjamin Franklin, Minister Plenipotentiary for the USA to the Court of France, it said that if the plate was returned by order of Congress he would be pleased to receive it, but 'by a private person's generosity, the Captain's for instance,' he could by no means accept it. Two years later the silver, the property of Paul Jones, was still in France, awaiting the Countess' instructions.

The arrival of the *Ranger* and the *Drake* in Brest was as inspirational to his European friends and his American countrymen as it was devastating to his enemy; but it is fortunate that he was more a seeker of fame and glory than fortune.

Paul Jones had never received personal wages and despite the immense value of the ships and cargoes which he had captured, he was kept severely short of funds. The circumstances of capture, the details of ownership of vessel and cargo, all had to come before a Prize-Court before authorisation could be obtained for their sale. The American Commissioners in France protested that they too were short of funds, and the admiring French, who were not yet officially at war with England, had to tread a little carefully. Yet somehow he managed, though, understandably, not without complaint. In letters to the Commissioners he asked, were 'ships of war to depend on the sale of their prizes for the daily dinner of their men?' and said, 'I was left with 200 prisoners of war, a number of sick and wounded and almost naked crew and a ship, after a severe engagement, in want of stores and provisions, from the 9th May until the 13th June'.

During the month of June, 1778, Jones and Franklin were preoccupied with schemes for the destruction of the 'common enemy of France and America.' The idea was to concentrate, not on great men-of-war, but fast sailing ships which could carry out hit-and-run raids along the English and Scottish coasts causing alarm and confusion, until their 'infant navy' could one day 'dispute the soveignity of the ocean.' Whitehaven, despite the 'defending old ladies', was once more to be on the agenda, with a view to cutting off coal supplies to Ireland. Greenock and Glasgow were on the list for attack and 'perhaps the whole shipping on the Clyde'. Numerous other western coastal towns were to be threatened, and a small force was to be sent up the east coast to Newcastle to cut off fuel supplies to London.

The captured were not forgotten in the planning of these great schemes: Franklin laid particular emphasis on the taking of prisoners of war '...to complete the good work you have already made such progress in, of delivering, by an exchange, the rest of your countrymen now languishing in the gaols of Great Britain.'

Such small, Whitehaven-type, expeditions may well have been effective, and would have put a great deal of strain on Britain's coastal defences; but when, in July 1778, France formally entered the war, these plans were abandoned in favour of a much bolder one. The French Government, possibly inspired by the Franklin/Jones plans, decided that perhaps the time had come to attempt to achieve their centuries-old ambition – a full-scale invasion of Britain.

We shall return to John Paul Jones; to his continued efforts on behalf of the American prisoners of war, and his most famous sea fight – the historic battle between the *Bon Homme Richard* and the British 44-gun frigate *Serapis*; but for now we will go back across the Channel to Britain, where great numbers of French prisoners would soon be adding to the accommodation problem.

Straightforward exchange, on a one-for-one basis, could never have kept British prisons even comfortably occupied. In the case of the Old Mill Prison alone, 734 Americans had passed through its gates between June 1777 and March 1779, and Charles Herbert[8] tells us that, of that number, thirty-six had died; 102 achieved successful escapes; and 114 had joined the British forces. In the latter year, when Herbert was himself exchanged, there were still 298 there to bid him farewell. So only about a couple of hundred had been exchanged over that period.

Exchange at sea between private-armed vessels kept the numbers down, as did parole-exchange – where there was no simultaneous physical exchange, but was based on a promise: the parolee signed a paper which in effect said:

'I hereby promise on my word of honour to cause......... of his H.M. subjects to be set at liberty by way of Exchange; and should we not comply there-with, we are obliged when called to return as prisoner to.........'

Such an arrangement had been recognised since the Seven Years' War, but it would normally have only applied to officers; although the commander of a vessel with insufficient space below decks to store its captives, may well have accepted the signature and word of the defeated captain on behalf of both himself and his crew.

There had always been an agreement where, when it was impossible to exchange rank-for-rank, a number of junior grades would be accepted for one more senior officer; and, on occasion, a large number of other-ranks might be accepted in exchange for a commissioned officer.

There was one other variation on the above. Ransom – or exchange for cash or promise of payment. On the 12th March 1780, Britain and France issued a table of exchange of prisoners of war, which listed all military and maritime ranks and ratings and their ransom rates.

An Admiral or General was quoted at sixty men or £60; down to man-for-man in the case of a seaman or a soldier, or £1. A privateer captain was valued at four men, or £4; his crewmen or merchantmen at their equivalents or £1 each. I cannot imagine that this system was employed other than in exceptional circumstances, and doubt that Americans would ever have access to this route to liberty; one public subscription, or a single Paul Jones prize, would have cleared the land of our rebellious captured colonists.

The mere fact that 'exchange' existed was a disciplinary weapon, without which the prisoners would have been even more riotous and more intent on escape. Bad behaviour could lose a man his place on the exchange ladder; very bad behaviour would transfer his name to the bottom of the list; for an unsuccessful escape attempt, he might find himself transferred to the hulks or confined in the *cachot* on half-rations and even removed from the exchange lists altogether.

However, everything had its price, and the price of a place on the exchange list was high. But there are many records which show that business was brisk between buyers and sellers in this and future wars – the sellers being men in desperate need of cash, and perhaps some who preferred the comparative safety of captivity to the dangers of return to warfare – and possible recapture.

Many prisoners of war *had* been captured more than once. Among those who put pen to paper and preserved for us their war-time experiences as captives in a foreign land, was Commodore Barney, who was twice taken prisoner, in two different wars – on land in the War of Independence and at sea in the War of 1812. Another was the remarkable experiences of Andrew Sherburne, who went to sea as a young lad of fourteen and, by his seventeenth year, had been taken prisoner three times. It is worth while extracting some incidents from his little book, *Memoirs of Andrew Sherburne: A Pensioner of the Revolution. Utica. 1828*, which takes him from service in an American naval vessel ending in capture at Charleston; then in a privateer and capture off Newfoundland; transport to Plymouth and incarceration in Old Mill Prison and, finally, capture for a third time and imprisonment on the *Jersey* prison ship in New York Harbour.

Andrew Sherburne was born in Portsmouth, New Hampshire, the 30th September,1765; the year which saw the imposition of the Stamp Act which caused a storm of protest and riot which contributed to the outbreak of war when Andrew was ten. It was also the year of the formation of the Colonial Congress in New York, which made Britain conscious that the states could work together when aroused.

Andrew tells us that the young lads were all keen to become part of the later uprising:

> 'A martial spirit was diffused through the little circle of my acquaintances. As the men were frequently called together for the purpose of acquiring military discipline, their example was not lost on the boys. Lads from seven years old and upwards were formed into companies and, being properly officered, armed with wooden guns and adorned in plumes, they would go through the manual exercise with as much regularity as the men. If two or three boys met, their martial ardor showed itself in exercising with sticks instead of muskets.'

With his home not more than a quarter of a mile from the Atlantic shore, he witnessed how Portsmouth, New Hampshire, was becoming a bustling hive of war-related industry. With ships under construction as never before, privateers fitting out or returning to port with their prizes; with friends going off to sea or setting out to join the land forces, it is small wonder that, as 'standards waved on the forts and batteries, the exercising of soldiers, the roar of canon, the sound of martial music and the call for volunteers so infatuated me that I was filled with anxiety to become an actor in the scenes of war.'

With six months still to go to his fourteenth birthday, he made it obvious that if he could not go to sea with his parents' blessing, he would go away without it. His father, a 'high Whig' in favour of the war, but who disapproved of privateering, determined that if his son must go to sea it should be on a naval vessel. By one of those coincidences which delight the story-teller, the ship on which he was fated to serve was John Paul Jones's old ship, the 18-gun sloop *Ranger*, which had recently returned from Europe under another commander and was refitting and shipping a crew at Portsmouth, New Hampshire.

Andrew Sherburne, therefore, joined the crew of the *Ranger*, together with about thirty other young lads. The job of these boys was to act as officers 'waiters', stewards or servants, but each had an action-station, being quartered to a specific gun which he was to keep fed with ammunition when occasion arose.

Andrew's double job was waiter to the boatswain and carrier to the third gun from the bow. The *Ranger* was to be part of a small fleet – small, but a significant proportion of the American navy – comprising the frigate *Boston*, the *Providence* and the 20-gun *Queen of France*. They sailed in June, 1779, and young Andrew had his first taste of life as a sailor and, after a few weeks at sea, saw his first action. One morning, off the Newfoundland coast, he heard a shout from the lookout on the fore-topmast-head: 'A sail! a sail on the lee bow!', and then a further cry, 'another there! and another there!' They had encountered the homeward-bound Jamaica fleet of about one hundred and fifty merchant ships, escorted by a couple of line-of-battle ships, some frigates and sloops of war.

They manoeuvered to come astern of the fleet and the next few hours must have provided the young Sherburne with long-lasting memories, a mixture of exhilaration and fear, of unreality and pride. The Commodore on the *Providence* quickly made two captures, and before nightfall the *Ranger* came up with a three-decker armed-merchantman, the *Holderness,* laden with sugar, rum, coffee, cotton and allspice. She was well armed with 22 guns but was too under-crewed to put up much of a defence. After a few broadsides from the *Ranger*, she struck her colours, was boarded, the prisoners secured, manned by a prize crew and sent off to an American port.

The Americans spent an uneasy night surrounded by enemy ships, expecting to be discovered at any moment and anxious about the approaching daylight; but they were in luck, the morning was dark with thick fog and when it cleared they were alone, with no sign of the fleet – or their own consorts. That evening they captured a brig and the next morning were in hot pursuit of three merchant ships when a not unusual, but nevertheless interesting, event occurred – an example of 'sailing under false colours'. The *Ranger* had secured one of the vessels, manned her, and was about to put a prize-crew aboard a second, when they saw two frigates flying English colours, one in chase of their first prize and the other bearing down on the *Ranger*. The British captain of the second merchantman, showing great courage, made a bid for freedom, sailing his ship away from the *Ranger* and making for the protection of the oncoming British frigate.

His courage deserved a better reward, for when he hailed the frigate with the cry: 'a Yankee cruiser has taken one of the fleet!' the 'British' Commodore hauled down the English ensign and hoisted the American flag – it was the *Providence* and her companion was the *Queen of France.*

In July the expedition came to an end and the four ships set sail for Boston with their prisoners and the mercantile fruits of their exploits. They had taken ten vessels in all, of which two had been retaken, and it could be counted a successful cruise, both in terms of aggravation and loss to their enemy and profit to themselves.

When the *Ranger* returned to Portsmouth, New Hampshire for refit, Andrew returned home, just before his fourteenth birthday, and was able to proudly announce to his admiring family that, after the cargoes of the prizes had been divided up between the crews, his share was 'about one ton of sugar, from thirty to forty gallons of fourth-proof Jamaica rum, twenty pounds of cotton, about the same quantity of ginger, logwood and allspice – about seven hundred dollars in paper money, equal to one hundred dollars in specie'.[9]

Soon the *Ranger* and her consorts were once more made ready for sea and began what was to be an eventful cruise off Florida and the southern states. By February, 1780, they were off Charleston, South Carolina, when they found they were being pursued by a number of British men-of-war and managed to get into harbour over the shallows of Charleston Bar. This brought the chase to a halt and the British ships, which drew too much water for them to pass over the Bar, laid off for several days before lightening their ballast and entering harbour.

By this time other ships had joined the blockading vessels and British batteries had been established ashore and on St James's Island in the harbour. The *Ranger* was ordered close inshore to bombard the battery on the island, a task which kept young Andrew busy enough in the service of his gun to hide the terror which he admitted to feeling, but which he dared not expose to his shipmates. Sporadic ship-to-shore actions took place over the following few weeks, and all the time the blockading British vessels were increasing in number. It soon became obvious that their prime object was the capture of Charleston itself.

At the beginning of April the English land forces, under General Sir Henry Clinton, were within half a mile of the American lines of defence and the British fleet came closer in and anchored in preparation to bombard the city. The American squadron was of little use from then on, so crews and ships' guns were ferried ashore to reinforce the batteries and redoubts which, even so, were not strong enough to withstand a lengthy siege.

Andrew Sherburne, his officers and shipmates, were assigned to Fort Gadsden, which was constantly under attack and, 'the siege being closely pressed, balls and shells were continually falling within the city.' With supplies of food and other aids to resistance running out, and under constant shelling from both land and sea, Charleston capitulated on the 12th May 1780.

To the vast and varied store of experience garnered in the brief twelve months of his naval experience – the daily lessons in the hard craft of seamanship; cruises and captures and many near-escapes from injury or death on shipboard and on shore – Andrew Sherburne now added the unenviable one of 'prisoner of war'. At the outset he was luckier than the majority of the other Charleston captives. As was the usual practice, all officers who were willing to sign the appropriate form of agreement were paroled, and senior officers were allowed to retain their servants. Andrew, on the second cruise of the *Ranger*, had been assigned to the Master's Mate, Captain Powers, for whom he had high regard, and was therefore included in the captain's parole and was allowed the freedom of the town whilst awaiting an exchange cartel vessel to take them to Newport, Rhode Island.

During this wait they were short of food almost to the point of starvation: 'We were for several days entirely destitute of provisions, except muscles [*sic*], which we gathered from the muscle beds.' But more devastating than the lack of food was the

discovery that smallpox had broken out among the British military and was quickly passed on to many of the Americans – including Andrew, and his master, too, was ill.

At last, when they were recovered enough to travel, the officers and their boys set sail for Rhode Island in a poorly equipped vessel, in which the water became so foul that even the few comparatively healthy were laid low. So many were suffering from smallpox that, on arrival, they had to go through a fumigating process before being allowed to proceed further:

> '…it became necessary that we should be thoroughly cleansed, before we passed through the country. There were little smoke-houses erected on a remote part of the island for this purpose; to these we repaired, superintended by police officers; here our clothing were all unpacked and thrown about, and ourselves almost suffocated with a smoke made of oakum, tobacco, &c.'

Still very ill, the captain and his boy took a two-horse wagon from Newport to Boston, an agonising journey as the bumping and jolting over rough roads was much more uncomfortable than the worst pitching and tossing at sea. By the time they reached Boston, Captain Powers was desperately ill and was put to bed in the house of a friend – and Andrew was given the distressing news that, whilst he was serving on the *Ranger*, his father had died. And worse was yet in store for the ill and heartbroken boy: on the following day his 'second father', Captain Powers, passed away. The next morning Andrew gathered together his few belongings and decided to head for home. The Captain's friend gave him a few paper dollars to help him on his way and he set off alone on foot to face the sixty hard-going miles between Boston and Portsmouth.

After an exhausting journey overland, he arrived home in a sorry state; the effects of smallpox and dysentry and insufficient food laid him up for the next two months before he could return to a seafaring life. With little left from the profits of his first successful cruise, he now found himself, at fifteen, the family breadwinner; for he learned that his elder brother, Tom, had been so long gone on a voyage to the West Indies that there was little hope of his ever returning.

With the Portsmouth-built *Ranger* now a British prize, the merchants of Portsmouth – no doubt inspired by feelings of patriotism mixed with an anxiety to retrieve their personal losses – replaced her by a fine new 20-gun vessel, called the *Alexander*. The commander, officers and the majority of the crew, including Andrew, were ex-*Ranger*. She sailed in December 1780 and returned about four months later without encountering a single enemy merchantman or man-of-war.

Wandering around his home port, impatiently waiting for the *Alexander* to be readied for her second cruise, Andrew Sherburne was hailed by a young privateersman, with the invitation to take a short cruise in a fine schooner and make his fortune. Andrew was assured that he would be back in time to join the *Alexander* and, if he went with him as far as Old York port, about ten miles distant, and did not like ship or crew, he could return home all expenses paid. His new acquaintance was Captain Jacob Willis, commander of the Salem privateer schooner *Greyhound*. Andrew went along to see and was quite impressed with what he saw: 'She had been a bank fisherman, but being now finely painted, with a new and longer set of masts and spars, and having her ensign and pennant flying, she made quite a warlike appearance. She mounted four-pounders and being of about sixty tons burden.'

He knew that privateering had now become the order of the day and that many small vessels, some of less than twenty tons and crewed with less than twenty hands, had achieved as much success as larger ones. So he made a decision which he was only just lucky enough to live to regret.

At that period of the war it was far easier to obtain officers for a privateer than to assemble a crew. The fitting out of a vessel for this type of service was often centred round a captain – who sometimes was himself the owner, or backed by merchants – but the competition for seamen was great, and all manner of inducements were necessary. The *Greyhound* was no exception. She already had a full complement of officers but, apart from her new acquisition, the crew comprised only two or three ordinary seamen and twenty or thirty boys, some less than twelve years old. It may seem that their requirement was excessive in numbers for such a small vessel, but for an expedition to be successful it was necessary to have sufficient hands to man the prizes which were the objective of their cruises.

Before the *Greyhound* could make its first cruise it was essential that more seamen should be lured on board. Promises of a generous share in future profit must have been the prime attraction, but adventure as a member of a jolly macho company must also have been persuasive. Sherburne tells us of what must have been a typical enlistment enterprise. When they arrived at Old York, the captain:

> '...laid a plan to get up a frolic at a public house and suitable persons were employed to invite the lads and lasses for a country dance. Rum, coffee, sugar, biscuit &c. were taken on shore from the privateer for the purpose, and the frolic went on. Having but one fiddler and the company being large, it became necessary to have dancing in more than one room, I was selected by some of the officers to sing for some of the dancers; this suited my turn, for I was not proficient in dancing. Every art and insinuation was employed by the officers to obtain recruits.'

This was repeated on the following evening, but their Old York recruitment 'frolics' added only three more men to the crew. They picked up two more hands at other ports: Samuel Willis, a lad of Andrew's age and related to the *Greyhound*'s captain, at Cape Porpoise (now Kennebunkport), and another at Falmouth (Portland), and although still short of a full complement of experienced seamen, they made for Halifax, Nova Scotia.

This area had been a privateers' paradise, a source of prizes, prisoners and rich cargoes for the past three years or so; but the British were wise to the situation and had tightened up on security and the protection of their merchant ships. So the *Greyhound* was more often chased than chasing, and her crew began to recall the stories they had heard of the horrors of Halifax Prison. It was decided, therefore, to alter course towards the mouth of the St Lawrence and Newfoundland. As they passed through the islands they encountered a number of very small American craft, most of less than twenty tons, which seemed to be working together as a flotilla. It is probable that not all of them were made legal by commission of Congress or letters of marque, but were *picaroons*, small-time pirates, who plundered the small, usually undefended, British coastal settlements. Records other than Sherburne's memoirs mention these piratical raiders who never ventured far off shore and preyed on small townships on the American coast, often

with unnecessary cruelty.

Off St Peter's Island, near the entrance to Fortune Bay, the *Greyhound* made its first capture – a Newfoundland shallop[10] returning from St John's. The owner of the captured two-masted gaff-rigged vessel, was a free-lance English fisherman named Charlie Grandy who, after close questioning, told them that an English supply ship, a brig which provisioned the many English fishing ports, had recently entered Fortune Bay. Anxious to get under way in search of the brig, Captain Willis released their prisoner and his little craft and sent him on his way with a present of pork and bread. There is a hint that Americans did not always treat their captives with as much consideration as that received by Charley. Andrew tells us that they 'dismissed him to his great joy, for he fared much better than his countrymen generally did, when they fell into the hands of American privateersmen.' This action on the part of Captain Willis was to stand them in good stead in the not so distant future.

Their enquiries at the fishing ports produced no knowledge of the whereabouts of the brig, other than that it was 'expected'; so their sights had to be lowered and lesser game pursued. Two of the many shallops in the Bay were taken, with their cargoes of dried fish and oil, and prize crews were put on board. Only three men could be spared to man each vessel, for prizes of a much greater value would have to be taken to make the cruise a truly profitable venture. Captain Arnold, who was prize-master of the *Greyhound*, and in charge of both shallops, chose Andrew as his Mate on board the larger vessel and another young lad named James Annis made up the crew. They left the *Greyhound* to continue her cruise and set sail for Salem to deliver the prizes. With wind and weather against them, the two shallops were laid up in a small harbour for some time, and as the days passed by it became obvious that Captain Arnold was suffering some sort of mental collapse, losing all confidence in himself after leaving the privateer; one moment boisterous, the next in deep depression with an inordinate fear of becoming a prisoner of the British. It had been rumoured that he had once decamped from Halifax with a king's cutter – perhaps a good enough reason for his fears – but, whatever the cause, his condition became so bad that Andrew settled him into his cabin for the night and locked and barred the door.

Next morning the two boys saw that his door was swinging open and they could find 'nothing of the captain, his clothes all lay on deck except his waistcoat; his shirt lay on the top of his clothes and his silver buttons lay upon his shirt.' They called for the skiff from the other shallop and searched the bay in widening circles, peering through the clear shallow water until they reached the beach, then scanning the white sands for footprints; but to no avail. Captain Arnold's action had spared him the realisation of his worst fears by only a few days.

Not yet sixteen, it was now Andrew's duty to take charge of his little prize vessel and get it to the United States, virtually single-handed – for Annis was useless as a helmsman, knowing 'not a point of the compass' and had picked up only the most rudimentary knowledge of seamanship. They up-anchored and sailed next day but with Andrew at the wheel for most of the daylight hours and the whole of a night made miserable by the worries of his responsibilities, and haunted with thoughts of Captain Arnold's end. The succeeding day was no more pleasant, half of it spent in unsuccessful flight from a 20-gun armed-vessel, which fortunately proved to be American, but nevertheless meanmindedly plundered them of their fishing gear and nets and other paltry loot before allowing them passage.

By the fourth day Andrew was almost at the end of his strength. The night had seemed endless, with gale and high seas, the heavily laden craft making hard going and leaking badly. He never forgot the agony of those dreadful events:

> 'Our consort was about half mile ahead of us; the clouds looked wild and the ocean rough. We had lost our boat which was towing at our stern. At about sunrise we split our main-sail from top to bottom, and with difficulty got it down and secured it. At that moment we were obliged to put away before the wind, and scud under a whole foresail which was almost new. It would have been much in our favour if our foresail had been reefed, which would have reduced it at least a quarter part; but it was impracticable for one boy to get this sail down, reef it, and set it again; our foremast was now in great danger from having so much sail upon it, for the wind was not steady and blew in gusts and our foremast would bend like a whip.'

If the mast had gone over the bow there would have been no memoirs of Andrew Sherburne and no story to tell; but, with more than his usual share of luck, they came up to an island and both shallops passed safely over the surrounding reef and anchored in a small bay. Andrew now had the far more useful Willis aboard to replace Annis, who had joined Jasper Loyd and Samuel Babb on the other vessel. Loyd wanted to help patch up the mainsail, but Sherburne and his shipmate decided they had had enough and insisted that all five should crew one shallop and leave the other. Despite the threats and curses of the older man – who could not bear the thought of abandoning half of their prize – they stuck to their guns, and a compromise was reached: they would all man the second shallop and take the other in tow.

Soon after getting under way they found that a small schooner was overtaking them fast, for they were considerably slowed by the vessel in tow. All except Loyd were certain that they were in danger of capture, and begged him to cut their tow-line and run for it, but he refused. They were fired on and forced to heave to, the shots coming from long buccaneer pieces which had each been charged with eight or ten musket balls. Andrew was now about to become a prisoner of war for the second time: '... in a few minutes they were along side of us, and twenty men sprang on board with these long guns in their hands, loaded, cocked and primed, and presented two or three at each of our breasts... cursing us bitterly, and threatening our lives. We stood trembling and awaiting their decisions, not daring to remonstrate, for some of them seemed like perfect furies.' Finally, after their captain had pacified the rowdies, the prisoners and prizes were secured for the passage to Grandbank, the Newfoundlanders' home port.

One tends to picture the prisoner of war as an unfortunate soldier or sailor, confined to hard-lying accommodation in a dreary prisoner of war depot or prison ship – the main cause of his suffering coming from the uncertainty of the period of enforced idleness he would have to endure before his return to family, ship or regiment – plus boredom and the poor quality and insufficiency of victuals and clothing. However, in many cases the captive experienced far greater hardship during the journey to his designated place of detention than he ever met with on his arrival. The American Commodore Joshua Barney, captured by HMS *Intrepid* in 1780, had far less complaint of the time he spent on a prison ship and in Millbay Prison than he had of the fifty-three days

spent on HMS *Yarmouth*, which conveyed him and seventy other American officers from New York to Plymouth. They were stowed in an almost airless hold, no more than three feet high, and by the time they reached Plymouth, eleven of those officers had died; the rest were unable to stand and, after fifty-three days without light, all were temporarily blinded. The fact that transfer to a hulk was to be appreciated as an improvement says something about the horrors of their passage. Charles Herbert experienced a similarly terrible passage to England and arrived suffering from an infliction then called 'the Itch' which developed into smallpox.

Some of these 'deliveries' were as punishing on land as they were by sea. A quarter of a century later, Napoleon's captives – including thousands of British prisoners – were marched hundreds of miles to Verdun, which was the main entrepôt or prisoner of war distribution centre, before being assigned to Valenciennes, Charlemonth or one of the other French prison towns. Escorted by gendarmes or soldiers, they tramped from twenty to thirty miles a day, and at the end of each stage of their long journey, sometimes handcuffed or roped together in pairs, they were lodged in barns, hovels or common gaols. There are many records of such agonising marches: some tell of fleecing by rapacious inn-keepers and food vendors along the way; of the callous mockery and jeering of the townsfolk when they were paraded in the market square at the end of a hard day's slog – though in fairness it must be added that some met with compassion and kindness from peasants in the country villages through which they passed.

Bad as it was in the warm months of the year, winter added almost unbearable hardship; many prisoners reached the end of their march shoeless or ill-shod, and were only kept going by the ungentle persuasion of their gendarme guards. The prisons which received them at the end of such passages, whether over land or by sea, must have come as a welcomed relief, however foul or uninviting they were in reality.

The eventful transport of young Andrew Sherburne, from the time of his second capture until his arrival at his English prison, must rank with any of the above trials of endurance. When the five yankee prisoners were taken ashore at Grandbank the whole village turned out to witness this unusual event. Andrew described them as 'chiefly west countrymen, and Irishmen; rough, and quite uncultivated...there was neither a magistrate or minister among them; they appeared very loyal, however, to his majesty.' The crowd was not particularly menacing at this stage, and were kept in order by a dignified and obviously educated old English lady.

Andrew, always aware of the dangers of them being mistaken for picaroons or pirates if captured by the British, had kept Captain Arnold's copy of their privateers' commission or letter-of-marque although at that time he was himself illiterate and was not sure of the detail of its contents – and this he presented to the old lady.

All went well as she read it aloud, until she got to that part of the document which authorised them 'to take, burn, sink and destroy the enemy wherever he could be found either on the high seas or in British ports etc.' This, not surprisingly, caused an uproar and a demand for the summary execution of the five terrified captives but the tough old lady prevailed, insisting that they should be handed over to the British military authorities at Placentia, about a hundred miles away.

Next morning, after being deprived of their shoes and all other possessions, except the clothes on their backs, they were confined in the fish hold of a shallop which soon headed for the small port of Cornish. They were lucky to find that most of the small population were in the employ of the *Greyhound*'s first prisoner, Charley Grandy, who, to the disapproval of their guards, welcomed them warmly and fed them well that day and provided a good breakfast before their early departure next morning.

The five prisoners, with a seven man guard, armed with long muskets, landed a few miles up a river and then trekked some twenty miles through 'a most dreary wilderness', overland to Placentia Bay. Without shoes, feet and legs lacerated by brambles and undergrowth, they struggled on, the older Loyd helped along with a blow from a musket butt whenever he faltered. By nightfall they had reached a small port on the bay, but were still a few miles from their next official halt.

On arrival, the overlord of the port, a wealthy Jerseyman who owned a number of fishing vessels and had suffered in the past from the attentions of Yankee privateers, could see no good reason why they should not be executed then and there. After an argument with the guards who informed him of the consequence of such action, he went off in disgust, and they set about making a meal of corned codfish, boiled and served up on pieces of board, with saucers of sweet oil; eaten with the fingers and hard to get down in spite of their hunger.

The next day's march, although only five miles long, with their stiff limbs and cut sore feet was worse than the day before . Their way was over a cliff-top path with a steep drop to the rocks below, so they were relieved to reach another small harbour where they were put aboard a shallop, ready to sail to Placentia, a voyage of about seventy miles. The seven guards were left behind and the three-man crew of the shallop took over; armed with six loaded muskets – which were kept very much in evidence on the quarterdeck, where the prisoners were forbidden to go.

Placentia was a fairly large Newfoundland cod fishing station, with a broad beach and a mountainous background. The British fort and garrison to which the American prisoners were to be taken was situated in the north-eastern corner of the town. First they were examined by the commissary and a group of fair-minded men, who were shocked at the appalling condition of their feet and legs and gave them shoes and stockings.

After a while the skirl of bag-pipes was heard and they were 'taken into the custody of a sergeant's guard of Highlanders, in their kilts, plaids, Scotch bonnets, and checkered stockings, accoutred with guns, fixed bayonets, broad swords, &c.' who took them to the guard room of the fort. Though captivity can never be pleasurable, the next four months were probably the most comfortable that Andrew had experienced for a very long time.

The wife of Colonel Hawkins, the governor of Placentia, a young woman in her twenties who was the daughter of one of the Scottish private soldiers of the guard, took a great interest in the boys and was saddened that lads so young should be prisoners of war. It was probably by her influence that Sherburne and Willis were occasionally given a place in the crew of the governor's barge, as strokesman and bowman respectively; visiting the Colonel's small salmon fishery and islands where they collected wild fruits and berries.

They took great pleasure in showing their superior skill in boat-handling, when compared with the soldiers who made up the rest of the rowers, and on those occasions they ate well from the governor's kitchen – although at other times they were well guarded, the discipline strict and the food scant.

In September 1781 a 22-gun ship arrived in the bay. It was the *Duchess of Cumberland*, a recent addition to the British navy, for she was in fact the captured and renamed Massachusetts-built American ship *Congress*. Her orders were to escort a convoy of merchantmen bound for Britain, and on the way deliver the five Yankee prisoners of war to a prison ship at St Johns. There a large number of American prisoners were waiting for an exchange cartel to take them to Boston. They must have boarded the 22-gun vessel with high hopes of a short voyage to the Newfoundland capital, a speedy exchange and then the journey homeward-bound. You will have guessed that, with the misfortune-prone Andrew aboard, a different fate was in store for them.

During its stay at Placentia, a British sailor had deserted from the *Duchess of Cumberland*. This was no small thing for a vessel to lose an experienced seaman, especially during wartime and service overseas. A thorough but unsuccessful search was made through Placentia and so, under the assumed justification that the deserter was probably being hidden by an inhabitant of the town, a local resident was impressed into His Majesty's service. His name was Baggs and in him they had made a good choice. Baggs was a seaman with twenty years experience as captain of a shallop, with a fisherman's intimate knowledge of the coastal waters which no chart could equal. He was stationed with the experienced forecastlemen and was expected to take his turn at the wheel when the British ship sailed, about the middle of the month.

From the outset the weather was less than fair and daily it got worse. When Baggs relieved the helmsman at four o'clock on the third day, he became most concerned when he learned the course they were steering and opined that if they kept to it the ship would run aground within a couple of hours. It would seem that the ship's navigator thought they had already rounded Cape St Mary and the poor visibilty made the shoreline sightings impossible. Captain Baggs was urged by the worried crew to alert the duty officers, but his reception when he appeared on the quarterdeck was one of outrage. The British officers were affronted that an impressed fisherman should question their seamanship and threatened to boot him off the quarterdeck.

At about 5p.m. on the 19th September, 1781, the lookouts confirmed Baggs's fears screaming 'Breakers on the lee bow!' and 'breakers ahead!' over and over again, and the shouted orders from the quarterdeck: 'Stand by to about ship hard to lee foresheet! foretop bowline, jib and staysail sheets, let go!' But it was too late; the *Duchess* rounded to, head to the wind, and before the foretopsail could be arranged to gain the other tack, she was driven stern-foremost on to the rocks. At the moment of impact, as the transom smashed into smooth-sided crags which jutted up from the waves, the helmsman was flung overboard, but two seamen leapt from the taffrail and, by a miracle, landed on a small shelf high above the sea; another attempted to follow their example but was dashed to his death against the rocks. By the time that Andrew and his fellow captives reached the deck there was no hope for the *Duchess of Cumberland,* her hull pierced by underwater crags, her rudder smashed when she first struck, and the weather becoming ever more violent.

Andrew made a brave attempt to describe what must have been almost indescribable:

> 'A most terrifying scene was presented now to my view. The ship rolled so that her yard-arms nearly touched the water: the sea was breaking feather white all around us. Under the fog bank which hung

over the shore, we could discover the mountain, but could not see the top of it; the wind was heavy and increasing; the rain descended in torrents; the sea roaring like thunder, night coming on apace, some of the officers raving and swearing, some crying and others praying, some inactive and desponding, others active and courageous. The long boat was got out, but by time she struck the water, there came a heavy sea and crushed her against the ship's side, as quick as you could crush an egg shell in your hand.'

It seemed unlikely that any other than the two who had leapt ashore would survive and the five yankee prisoners were doubly at risk – in similar desperate circumstances where prisoners could not be securely held, and could present an additional danger to their captors, a council of the officers might well decide that they should be executed. In this case, however, with the ship fast filling with water and the prisoners few in number, the officers had more urgent matters on their minds.

Orders were given to cut away the masts and, as the fore, main and mizzen went over the side, the lightened *Duchess* cleared the rocks and was driven by the winds, careening dangerously towards the shore before grounding again. Held fast by jagged underwater crags which pierced her bottom, the rate of destruction increased as each wave slammed into her as it raged towards the shore. Swimming or floating ashore on debris was out of the question, but amidst the panic and confusion some were calm enough to secure a stout rope, about one and a half inches thick, to the stump of a mast and, after many attempts, float the other end ashore attached to a spar, where it was retrieved by the two men who had jumped from the transom at the outset.

Of the first four to make the attempt, three got within twenty feet of the beach but were swept from the rope onto the rocks and disappeared beneath the seas. After a few others had made successful clambers along the lifeline, Andrew decided it was now or never for him.

'I buttoned up my outside jacket, drew my shirt out of my trowsers. I had on my head an old fashioned Dutch cap, which went on very tight. As I could swim tolerably well, I flattered myself it would be in my favour, I took hold of the rope and fell into the water, but soon perceived that I could gain no benefit from the use of my legs, the water being in such an agitated state. The first swell and wave which run was in some measure obstructed by the ship, it however buried me for a short time. When the second sea came I was exposed to its whole violence; while it was running it seemed as if I should be pressed to death, and the time seemed exceedingly long. I was hanging by my hands and stretched as straight horizontally, as if I had been suspended in the air; but before the current abated, my right hand gave way, and was carried back in a moment. O, the multiplicity of thoughts that rushed into my distracted mind. One among the many was that the left hand would continue its hold until I should drown; another was that I must directly appear before my judge. I felt my left hand and arm faltering, and I expected to be immediately in eternity …God spared me. The undertow swept me under the rope; I hoved my right hand over the rope and gripped fast hold of the collar of my jacket and other clothes, and after taking breath made all possible exertion to draw myself towards the shore, before another sea should come. The third wave stretched me, but having my arm over the rope, I was better fortified, nor was it by any means so violent as the second, and when it went back it left me suspended by the rope, and I could almost touch the hideous rocks with my feet, but durst not let go my hold, because the men on shore could not yet afford me any assistance.'

At last he was helped ashore and lay for a long time helpless and exhausted.

By evening the small group of men who were safely on land had thought up an improvement on the strength-sapping way of getting men along the line. A particularly strong and courageous officer went back on board, hand over hand along the rope, and returned to the shore with the ends of a number of thinner ropes. For this his third hazardous trip he attached himself to a 'traveller' – a rope which went over the hawser and prevented him from being washed away if he should lose his grip; an idea which could have saved the lives of the first few who ventured and perished. Back on board each rope was tied round a man's body, leaving plenty of line for the crew on the vessel to pay out when he jumped into the water and the men on shore ran with their end to keep the line taut. More than a hundred were rescued in this manner before nightfall and darkness brought the operation to a halt; leaving about thirty, including Loyd and Annis, still on board the wreck.

They spent a frightful night of icy cold discomfort and rain, in the nearest thing to shelter they could find, a hollow in the cliff face some forty feet above the beach where they squatted or lay, sometimes three deep, until the dawn. The storm had abated and at low tide the rest of the survivors were able to scramble ashore. There was one woman aboard, the very pregnant wife of the ship's cook, who was carefully pulled ashore on the 'traveller' which passed over the original thick lifeline like a moving bosun's chair.

Immediate trouble and danger had by no means passed. The beach was backed by almost sheer cliffs and a mountain about five or six hundred feet high which they would have to negotiate to get anywhere. Aboard the wreck they found a couple of hundredweight of unspoilt bread and a like amount of pork; blankets enough to go round were retrieved from the hammocks below the gun deck; and some guns, hatchets and cutlasses were found undamaged in the arms-chest on the quarterdeck.

It was unthinkable that the cook's wife should attempt the climb from the beach, so a tent was constructed from sailcloth and a number of sailors and a surgeon's mate volunteered to stay with her and her husband.[11] After a meal of bread and raw pork, the survivors got ready to tackle the mountain. They were a still sizeable group, although about twenty of the one hundred and seventy ship's company had been lost, and in their weakened and bruised state few could have relished the prospect of rock climbing; though most of the seamen, with their experience of working aloft, would have had a good head for heights. A few heroes went first and prepared the way, banging crowbars and marlin-spikes into crevices and attaching ropes rescued from the rigging and lowering them to those below.

On reaching the summit they found themselves on a plateau covered with deep damp moss which stretched as far as the eye could see to the north, whilst a couple of miles to the southward there was a dense forest of spruce and fir trees. Towards evening they reached the edge of the woods where they made camp by layering branches and boughs on the ground to keep them above the wet moss, and there they spent a night made miserable by cold and damp; a fire made impossible by the soaked state of everything normally combustible. Captain Baggs who had been so unceremoniously dismissed from the quarterdeck of the *Duchess of Cumberland* only a few days before, was now treated with great respect by both captain and officers and consulted as to the best way out of their predicament.

The next day was spent in preparing for a long trek. The provisions and supplies rescued from the wreck were distributed among the survivors, officer, rating and prisoner of war each receiving an equal share. Early in the day, Captain Baggs and some of the officers set out on an exploratory survey of the coastline before deciding on the best way to shape their course to Placentia. The Newfoundland capital, St Johns, and therefore the cartel ship and the prospect of exchange, was too far away to be considered as an alternative. Andrew recalled that they had a tortuous march of about a hundred miles before them, over hard-going terrain, and it probably seemed like it to the tired and hungry marchers; but, according to my atlas, Placentia was nothing like so many miles away. By noon the following day, they had reached a point along the coast which Baggs said was called Distress Bay and it must have seemed to them that it could not have been more aptly named. Scattered for a mile or so along the shore was the wreckage of an American brig and, in the shallow inshore water, the bodies of fourteen men and a young lad who had once been her crew. Using barrel staves the British sailors dug a grave and gave them decent burial before combing the beach and wreckage for anything worth retrieving.

No provisions were to be found other than a tub of butter and – what in normal times would have been welcomed as a valuable prize – a number of hogsheads of West Indian rum. The British captain showed great wisdom in his decision that the rum should be confiscated, and both officers and men suffered the mortifying spectacle of gallon after gallon of the precious liquid gurgling into the sand.

After nine or ten days most of the survivors reached a small port not more than five miles from Placentia, where they were housed in outhouses and store rooms, and enjoyed hot Labrador tea sweetened with molasses, and feasted on ship bread and raw fish from the beach. Not all had made it thus far as some had lost the strength to carry on and were left by the wayside. The rest spent the night on the comparative luxury of a dry floor and the next day walked into the town which they had left only two eventful weeks before.

Captain Baggs was deservedly rewarded with a discharge from his impressment; fishing shallops were commandeered to convey the British officers and men to St Johns and the five prisoners of war found themselves once again in the Placentia guardhouse. So near and yet so far – the exchange cartel on which they had pinned their hopes had already left St Johns for Boston and the Yankees could only wait to see what Fate now held in store.

After a few weeks, a British 18-gun sloop of war, the *Fairy,* came into Placentia harbour to escort a small convoy of merchant vessels to Lisbon. Loyd, Annis and Babb were lucky enough to be assigned to short-crewed merchantmen and, if their ships made it across the Atlantic to Portugal, then fate had treated them kindly, for on arrival at neutral Lisbon they may well have been given their freedom.

Andrew Sherburne was less fortunate. He and his shipmate, Willis, were ordered aboard the *Fairy,* where they soon found that they were to be regarded as impressed members of the ship's crew rather than treated as prisoners of war. The prospect filled both of them with fear and revulsion and Andrew, in particular, felt that nothing worse could have happened to him:

'Willis and myself were destined to serve his majesty, on board the

Fairy, sloop of war, commanded by Capt. Yeo, a complete tyrant. I began to feel that my fate was sealed to serve his Britannic majesty on board a man of war all my days; a service I had detested from my infancy. Before I was six years old, I heard my parents speak of some of their friends who had been impressed on board of men of war… My father at that time lived on Frost's Point near the mouth of Portsmouth harbor, where we could see every vessel that went out and in. Our sailors and fishermen used to dread the sight of a man of war's boat, as a flock of sheep would dread the appearance of a wolf… Willis and myself were called upon the quarter deck, and after being asked a few questions by Capt. Yeo, he turned to his officers and said "they are a couple of fine lads for his majesty's service Mr Gray, see that they do their duty, one in the foretop and the other in the maintop.'

Willis replied that he was afraid to go up so high; that he was subject to fits; he was afraid he would fall down and kill himself. Andrew answered that he was a prisoner of war, and that he could not consent to serve against his country. 'With very harsh words and several threats, we were ordered off the quarter deck, and commanded to do our duty in the waist.'

The two lads went below in haste and tucked themselves away in the cable-tier where prisoners of war were often quartered. After a couple of days avoiding the disgrace of working for the enemy, they were rooted out by the boatswain's mate who, as we may say now 'blew his top', but Andrew described as 'raved like a bedlamite', and gave them both a thorough thrashing with his rattan cane and drove them on deck. It seemed that they would have to serve his majesty all the way to England, however unwillingly, but they were saved from truly active service through the thoughtful understanding of the ship's Carpenter, Mr Fox, who had witnessed their beating. As a warrant officer, he had a cabin and was entitled to two boys, or waiters, as general help and, warning them not to push their luck with Captain Yeo, offered to take them on in his service. Fox shared his mess with the Gunner and the Boatswain, and as their boys and the gunner's eight year old son shared the work, the two Americans had an easy, though rough weatherwise, passage to Plymouth.

Even if Andrew exaggerated the tyranny of Yeo over his crew, it would seem that he was typical of the worst type of British naval captain at a period when brutality was not unusual. There were many floggings with the cat-o'-nine-tails and a number of men were in irons for the whole trip. On one occasion six men were given twelve lashes over a bottle of spirit which none would, or could, admit bringing aboard; and if, as Andrew reported, the ship's cook was flogged for affront to a midshipman, Captain Yeo really did step out of line, for to flog a warrant officer, as was the cook, unless by decision of a court martial, was against naval law.

The *Fairy* reached Plymouth, England, in November 1781, and the two lads eagerly looked forward to their transfer to a depot ashore, thus regaining their status as prisoners of war, and the possibility of eventual exchange and return to their homeland. Andrew was surprised at the mixed feelings evoked by his first sight of England:

'…it excited some peculiar sensations to lift up my eyes and behold the land of my forefathers. I must admit that I felt a kind of reverence and solemnity, that I cannot well describe. Yet when reflecting on my situation, and bringing into view the haughtiness of her monarch and government; their injustice and cruelty to her children; I felt an indignant, if not a revengeful spirit towards them.'

Weeks went by with no sign of their being sent ashore. Time passed slowly, with little for them to do but wait and worry, observe the busy life of the distant dockyard – and to add to their knowledge of a sailor's life aboard a British man-of-war. They had already experienced the strictness and discipline at sea on board two of His Majesty's ships and now witnessed the surprising contrast in port at the end of a voyage!

The ship had not been a week in port, when almost as many women as men were on board; and the number every day increased. Until fifty years or more after Sherburne's enforced visit to Plymouth, it was usual for women to be allowed on board ships on arrival in port, at home or abroad. Portsmouth, Plymouth and Chatham were particularly infamous for the number, rowdiness and excesses of their sailor-loving – and robbing – dockside womenfolk. Of course, their presence on board was at the discretion of each commander, but it would have been a very tough, courageous and perhaps unwise, captain who denied his men this privilege. After all, the reason it was tolerated did not derive from a considerate understanding of the physical needs of men who had been cooped up – or as it was known, 'shipbound' – for months or even years at a stretch. Shore leave was a luxury seldom enjoyed, for the sailor once ashore could not always be relied upon to return.

The lengths to which Andrew's privateer captain had to go in order to scrape together a crew, was typical of a world-wide problem. Some admirals kept their men 'shipbound' for an almost unbelievable length of time: Admiral Penrose kept his crew confined to ship-board for seven years. So, although the spectacle of boats filled with noisy prostitutes and pin-money amateurs, often in their hundreds, shouting their wares and obscenities, caused some landlubbers to express their disgust with both the harlots and matelots alike, there was another side to the story.

Ships had to keep their full complement of men, particularly in wartime; most of the women would have had no other source of income and were ruled over by their boatmen pimps who rowed them from the shore. And if Jolly Jack did lose his head and self-control on the rare occasions when he did get shore leave, allowance could be made. As John Nicol[12] wrote:

> 'Did those on shore only experience half the sensation of a sailor at perfect liberty, after being seven years on board a ship without a will of his own, they would not blame his eccentricities but wonder he was no more foolish.'

The practice of allowing loose women to board naval vessels gradually died out – and the number of desertions increased.

As week followed week and the *Fairy* began to take on stores and provisions and was obviously making ready for sea, Sherburne and Willis became more and more apprehensive. It seemed probable that they were fated to serve the enemy until the end of the war, but once again their friend, the Carpenter, came to their aid. He advised them to put their case before the new and, he hoped, more sympathetic, captain. They were lucky in Captain Yeo's replacement, who told them he thought their plea was reasonable and that he would take up their request to become prisoners of war. Within an hour their names were called and they went below to bid a tearful farewell to Mr Fox.

The next stage in their journey to captivity was closer inshore, to what had been the old 74-gun, *Dunkirk,* but by that time was the reception hulk and guardship for Plymouth; Andrew called it the 'harbor admiral's ship'. All prisoners of war brought into the port had to pass through the *Dunkirk,* their names and details recorded by the admiral's clerk, then await decision from ashore as to their place of confinement; hulk, depot or parole.

The hulk was also the distribution centre for impressed men who were brought on board by the press gangs. Although most ships had their own gang, it seems that part of the local business of impressment was centralised at Plymouth and that ships short of hands could apply to the *Dunkirk* to make up their complements. The *Dunkirk* must have been a miserable hole in which to find oneself, filled as it was with discontented men; prisoners of war and impressed men who were themselves prisoners in a sense – many of the latter were merchant seamen who could earn about £2.50 a month on a merchant vessel, but as pressed naval men, less than a pound.

Long after the war had ended, the *Dunkirk* was still a prison ship, but of an even more unpleasant type than before – housing some three hundred and fifty civilian convicts. She was one of the early additions to the detested civil hulk fleet, which was instituted as a 'temporary expedient', to accommodate convicts who could no longer be transported to America or be found space in our overcrowded jails.

Sherburne and Willis were ordered into a ship's boat, accompanied by what would seem to be excessive security to guard two young lads – a midshipman with drawn sword, a sergeant and a number of marines with muskets and fixed bayonets. It seemed to them that each new move was worse than the one before and the *Dunkirk* was a veritable floating hell: 'being so near the shore, and there being so much passing and repassing from ship to shore, it was almost impossible to prevent their having spirits on board. There was, therefore, drinking, gambling, swearing, fighting, stealing, scolding, brawling, &c. &c. going on almost continually, and especially in the night.'

They were on the hulk long enough to become lousy, and to lose all the clothing not on their backs to thieves; but finally, in early January, their names were included in a roll-call of thirteen Americans who were to go ashore. Once ashore they were conducted by their escort to the Court of Admiralty, where they were to face another hazard – the ordeal by questioning to prove they were truly Americans.

Individually, they were called into a room and summoned before a bench of judges, 'elderly gentlemen, who all wore large white wigs', and examined in minute detail as to name, family origins, age with precise details of service on vessels naval and privateer; number of guns, captains' names and a dozen or more other searching enquiries.

When all had been interrogated, they had each to go through the whole thing again, with each question repeated and the answer checked by the clerk of the court against his original reply. One slip-up and the prisoner could find himself classed as a renegade Englishman who had served against his country and, at best, suffer the punishment of spending the rest of his seafaring days on board a British man-of- war.

The little group of Yankee prisoners having passed muster and convinced the judges of their American origins, were 'severally and individually' committed to Old Mill Prison – '…for rebellion, piracy, and high treason on his Britannic Majesty's high seas, there to lay during his Majesty's pleasure, until he saw fit to pardon or otherwise dispose of them.'

Daunting as this pronouncement may have seemed, Andrew was

filled with joy and relief, as they were marched the mile and a half to the depot; the first time they had felt firm ground beneath their feet since the eight-day march to Placentia. To most men the prospect of an indefinite length of time in an English prisoner of war depot would have been a fearful one, but for Andrew it was the fulfilment of a long-felt wish: 'I felt a high degree of animation that my prospects were so flattering. It was indeed a peculiar gratification to think of entering Old Mill Prison. At length we came to the outer gate, which groaning on its hinges, opened to receive us into the outer yard.'

There we shall leave him... at least for now. His memories and description of life in Old Mill Prison will be added to those of other prisoners during this and later wars; to tell the story of the depot which was to be known from the beginning of the nineteenth century as Millbay Prison (see Chapter 12. THE DEPOTS ON LAND: Millbay). And we shall meet Andrew Sherburne yet again, on the truly terrible *Jersey* prison ship in New York Harbour. After returning to America as part of a general exchange of prisoners earlier in the year, he was captured for a third time off the coast of Virginia, whilst serving as boatswain on the US letter of marque brig *Scorpion,* in November 1782. (See Chapter 7. THE NEW YORK PRISON SHIPS.)

The *Bon Homme Richard* and the *Serapis.*

When John Paul Jones left America in the *Ranger* and sailed for France in 1777, he had sailed with the promise of future command of a first-class American frigate to be called *L'Indien,* then under construction in Amsterdam. However, as so often in his career, Jones received less than was promised or merited. Britain made it plain to the Dutch that they would consider the matter a violation of Holland's neutrality and so, on completion, Congress presented *L'Indien* to Louis XVI and the frigate was taken into the French Navy.

The restless Jones, his mind full of ideas for creating havoc along the English and Scottish coastlines, was sure that a replacement would soon be found and continued to plan hit-and-run raids in fast sailing ships which could repel or outrun enemy frigates. He visualised the panic that such attacks would cause throughout the land, which '…would convince the world that their coasts are vulnerable, and would, consequently, hurt their public credit' or, 'If alarming the coast of Britain should be thought inexpedient, to intercept the enemy's West Indian or Baltic fleets, or their Hudson Bay ships, or to destroy their Greenland fishery, are capital objects.'

It was agreed that three fast frigates and two tenders should be put under his command immediately and that he was to have a free hand to sail under unlimited orders, and the Prince of Nassau volunteered to sail with him on his first expedition. He could hardly wait to get to sea, writing to everyone: George Washington, Benjamin Franklin, French ministers and the Prince, but once again he was completely let down. No frigates arrived and the Prince made other plans.

Instead, he was offered another command at L'Orient – an inferior force with armament insufficient to achieve any of John Paul's ambitious objectives – but even this came to nothing. Although he made all haste, he found that even this small force was under another command by the time he arrived. Frustrated and disgusted at his treatment, in desperation he volunteered for service under the Count d'Orvilliers in the French navy but this too was not possible.

John Paul Jones was recognised as an inspirational leader, a sea-fighter of great courage, resourcefulness and originality, by both America and his admirers in Europe; but to have given him an appointment in the French navy consistent with his rank, would have increased the jealousy, which already existed among some French officers, envious of his fame. Perhaps of greater importance was the ambiguity of his national identity. As a Scottish-born subject of George III, but fighting for the rebellious colonies, Paul Jones was classed by Britain as a traitor and a pirate. Even had he been born in America he would still have been regarded as a rebel colonist and buccaneer rather than bona fide belligerent.

A treaty of alliance between France and America was signed in February, 1778, and, although not officially at war until the declaration in July, the first sea fight between French and English vessels took place on the 17th June, a five-hour duel in the Channel between the French 30-gun frigate *Belle Poule* and HMS *Arethusa.* Only a few weeks later, a bloody but inconclusive battle was fought out between equally matched squadrons, each of about thirty ships-of-the-line and half as many attendant frigates, under the commands of Admiral Keppel and the Count d'Orvilliers.

Reports of these actions would have tried John Paul's patience to the limit. Although he could have had no complaint of his social acceptance during his months in France – applauded when he visited the opera and the guest of honour at a hundred balls, dinners and social occasions – each day ashore seemed a day away from glory. Letters, memoirs, chap-books, songs and newspaper reports, tell of his popularity in the courts of Europe, where he was lionised and regarded as a romantic hero, who could – and possibly did – take his pick of the prizes from among the high-born ladies of Paris. He was certainly not averse to admiration and his ambition for fame and honour was – as he himself admitted – 'infinite', but beyond wealth and all else, he valued the dreamed-of place in history he might achieve for himself through war and the sea.

An extract from a letter sent by an English lady in Versailles to a correspondent of the *General Advertiser and Morning Intelligencer,* dated June, 1780, and published the 7th September, reads:

> 'The famous Paul Jones dines and sups here often, a smart man of six and thirty, speaks but little French,[13] appears to be an extraordinary genius, a poet as well as a hero; a few days ago he wrote some verses extempore, of which I send you a copy. He is greatly admired here, especially by the ladies, who are all wild for love of him, as he for them, but he adores Lady .... who has honoured him with every mark of politeness and distinction.'

[The following verses were addressed to 'The Ladies who have done me the honour of their polite attention'.]

> 'Insulted Freedom bled; I felt her cause,
> And drew my sword to vindicate her laws
> From principal, and not for vain applause.
> I've done my best; self-intrest far apart,
> And self-reproach a stranger to my heart;
> My zeal still prompts, ambitious to pursue,
> The foes, ye fair! of Liberty and you.
> Grateful for praise, spontaneous, and unbought,
> A generous people's love, not meanly fought!
> To merit this, and bend the knee to beauty,
> Shall be my earliest and latest duty.'

If no worthwhile commission could be found for him on this side of the ocean he would have willingly returned to the American theatre of war, where he would be certain of a senior command, but he was assured by the American officials that the French Minister of Marine, M. de Sartine, had requested that he should stay for important work in the near future. Jones had heard all this before and, after having already spent a restless five months of disappointments, he informed Benjamin Franklin that he would write to Louis XVI personally, and that 'the Duchess de Chartres will, I am persuaded, undertake to deliver my letter into the king's hands.' The letter, written from Brest and dated the 19th October, 1778, was duly delivered by the Duchess and produced a surprisingly rapid response. Like the many similar letters which he had, with such tireless energy, written to just about everyone who might use influence on his behalf, it gave a history of his past achievements, his regret at unfulfilled promises and his ambitions for the future: to serve America, and to 'testify by my services my gratitude to your majesty, as the first prince who has so generously acknowledged our independence.'

Jones was probably less than impressed when, early in 1779, he was given an old converted East Indiaman, the *Duc de Duras*. Under a new name and the brilliance of her new commander, the ancient ex-merchantman was to replace the *Ranger* as the vessel which would forever be most closely linked with the name John Paul Jones.

John Paul had the *Duc de Duras* fitted out and practically rebuilt at Port L'Orient and did all that he could to turn the cumbersome old vessel into a weapon of war. He also changed her name to *Bon Homme Richard,* in honour of Benjamin Franklin's celebrated publication, *Poor Richard's Almanack* as *'a well-merited compliment to a great and good man, to whom I am under obligations, and who honours me with his friendship.'*

So the old *Duras* became the new 40-gun *Bon Homme Richard,* with an armament almost as strangely mixed as her crew: six 18-pounders on the lower gun deck; twenty-eight 12-pounders on the upper gun deck and eight 9-pounders distributed fore and aft. The motley crew was made up of Americans and eleven other nationalities, including French, Portugese, Dutch, Germans, Maltese and Malays (and there is little doubt that there were also English and Irish on board the American vessel).[14]

The *Gazetteer and New Daily Advertiser* for the 7th July, 1779, quoted a letter from an English officer, prisoner of war at Brest, who said that two hundred or more English prisoners had entered the American service, but *'Numbers of them, I am sure, would never have gone on board, but for the bad treatment they experienced in prison.'*

The *London Evening Post* of the 28th September, reported that the five hundred men on board the *Bon Homme Richard* included ex-prisoners of war, most of whom were 'English and Irish, many of them taken out of prisons at Brest and St Maloes, where any prisoner was offered his liberty to serve on board his [Jones's] fleet.'

In addition to the Commodore's 40-gun ship, the American squadron was to consist of the 36-gun *Alliance;* two armed merchantmen – the 30-gun *Pallas* and the *Vengeance* of 12 guns, and the 18-gun cutter, *Cerf.* The *Alliance*, a newly-built American frigate, should have been a valuable addition to John Paul's small fleet, but with Captain Pierre Landais, a Frenchman in the American service in command, she proved to be more a liability

than an addition to its strength. In April, Commodore Jones received his sailing orders from Benjamin Franklin and the Commissioners in Paris. He was, to have a free hand in general, but was to give particular attention to the taking of prisoners. Franklin urged him to 'complete the good work you have already made such good progress in, of delivering, by exchange, the rest of your countrymen now languishing in the gaols of Great Britain.'

Nearly two thousand men were to sail with the squadron, a good percentage of them a landing force which, it was originally intended, was to be under the command of General the Marquess Lafayette. They were to be provisioned with stores for a three months cruise – including a great deal of musketry, grenades and 'combustibles' – for the great aim was to 'alarm the coasts of Wales, Ireland, the Western ports of Scotland and the North Channel', landing shore parties within short marching distance of principal coastal towns, destroying ships in ports and harbours and holding the towns to heavy ransom against threat of burning. The busy shipping ports of Liverpool and Leith were to be prime targets and, after rounding the north of Scotland, to scour the North Sea for merchant shipping and the ultimate aim of meeting up with the yearly Baltic merchant fleet.

Therefore, with such great objectives, the American squadron, under the command of the Honourable Commodore John Paul Jones set sail from Port L'Orient on the 19th April, 1779, but without General Lafayette. At a late hour it was decided that he should remain in France, in preparation for a French-American-Spanish attack on the British mainland, which Franklin called 'the Grand Invasion'. Jones's raids were to provide a diversion in favour of the Grand Fleet of France and Spain and a French army was to storm the south coast of England. However, as we know, this 'grand invasion' was no more successful than past (and later) attempts since the twelfth century.

The *Bon Homme Richard* got off to a miserable start. Lafayette had warned John Paul to keep a keen eye on Captain Landais, of the *Alliance* whom he considered to be unreliable and a troublemaker; so when, soon after setting out, the *Alliance* ran foul of the *Richard* in the night, Jones was understandably suspicious. The old ex-merchantman came off second-best, but both were so damaged that they had to return to port for repairs. When the expedition was resumed on the 14th August, they carried with them experienced pilots with knowledge of the coast from Edinburgh to Harwich, most of them ex-prisoners of war, and pilots from Youghal and Galway, who had been prisoners in France but knew the coast of Ireland.

Where necessary, Jones was not above hoisting the English flag and signalling to the shore for pilotage, but he was usually fair enough to release the duped pilots after their work was done. Within a few days, at least four prizes had been taken off the southern coast of Ireland and the London newspapers had first-hand accounts, from an unusually reliable source, of the state of the American squadron, their intentions and their prizes. An express from Tralee informed them that seven English prisoners who had been recruited into the American service had escaped from the *Bon Homme Richard,* and landed from an open boat at Ballinskellig Bay, County Kerry, on the 23rd August. Their stories of Jones's strength in man- and fire-power, and his plans to raid and torch, caused an uproar which was echoed in English, Irish, Welsh and Scottish news-sheets for weeks to come. In fact, American manpower was somewhat further reduced by another misfortune in that same bay. Sixteen men with a Lieutenant of Marines were landed to recapture the absconding seven, but the squadron was blown out of Ballinskellig by an unexpected north-easterly gale, and they were left behind, to be captured by a detachment of the Kerry Legion.

On the 26th August, the *Pallas* and the *Cerf* were not within view and Captain Landais had gone off on his own arrogant way with the *Alliance*. Jones rounded southern Ireland and sailed north to Cape Wrath where he was rejoined by the *Pallas*. By the middle of September a fair number of prizes, from merchantmen to colliers, were taken; some were ransomed, some destroyed and others sent into French ports – and the *Bon Homme*'s collection of prisoners was growing apace. The Commodore had taken two more prizes in the Firth of Forth, and but for the insubordination of Captain Landais, who ignored his signals, and the effect that this had on the other French captains, he may well have succeeded in his plan to carry a raid into the Firth and put Leith itself to ransom.

It is perhaps not surprising that officers who had been trained in an old naval tradition, who had not previously sailed with Paul Jones, or had had no time to learn and understand his approach to warfare, should have found him difficult to take. There was a sort of accepted choreography about the naval battles, as opposed to privateering exploits, at that time, and traditions such as laying-up of ships-of-the-line in wartime during the winter months, were accepted by both sides. Departures from the norm were frowned upon and this would have made Paul Jones's tactics seem quite ungentlemanly and smacking of piracy – his methods also called for great individual courage and dedication. John Paul was certainly not a typical eighteenth century naval officer. As John Henry Sherburne, Registrar to the American Navy, said, when editing his hero's papers: 'Paul Jones should have been a companion for Nelson.'

'I HAVE NOT YET BEGUN TO FIGHT !'

After doubling Cape Wrath, the *Bon Homme* in company with *Pallas* and *Vengeance*, had sailed down the east coast of Scotland and arrived off the Firth of Forth on the 13th September. Jones had gained knowledge of British ships lying at anchor near Leith, from small vessels he had intercepted on the way, and was prepared for immediate action. He had a local pilot whom he had taken from a collier, but was frustrated by his French captains' reluctance to assist in his bold plans to attack. It took him well into the following day to convince them of the ease with which they might take both prizes and the town itself; but by that time the winds had changed unfavourably.

On the 21st September, three more ships were taken off Flamborough Head, which brought the number of prizes taken up to that date to seventeen. To many commanders of such a small force this would have been a more than respectable score, particularly when the alarm and discomfiture he had created in the towns along the coast was added as a blow against the enemy – and, in accordance with the wishes emphasised in his sailing orders, a great number of prisoners had been taken from the captured vessels – for possible exchange for American prisoners of war in Britain.

If nothing more had been achieved, there is little doubt that Jones would have reckoned his cruise, though profitable, an inglorious failure. Over the next two days the squadron was more or less reformed; on the morning of the 23rd, the *Pallas* and the *Alliance* rejoined the *Bon Homme Richard* and the *Vengeance*, and in the afternoon they beheld a sight as unbelievable as a mirage. On the horizon was a great convoy, the Baltic Fleet of forty-one merchantmen and their escort, carrying stores and materials for the depleted dockyards of Britain. The protecting warships were the new 44-gun frigate HMS *Serapis*, under the command of Captain Richard Pearson and the armed auxilliary *Countess of Scarborough* of twenty guns, under Commander Thomas Piercy.

The ships made ready for the inevitable contest, whilst on shore the chalk cliffs between Scarborough and Flamborough Head were dotted with crowds of spectators, who were to witness one of the fiercest and memorable sea-fights in history. Reports of the battle agree on all major points, whilst some details differ according to whether one is studying a British or American account. The following account, therefore, is a compound of contemporary and later descriptions from both sides of the Atlantic and Channel.

Captain Pearson, a well-seasoned and courageous commander, put his ships between the convoy and the Americans and, as the leading merchantmen came in sight of the enemy, the fleet 'tacked and stood in shore for Scarborough, letting fly top gallant-sheets as a signal for an enemy,' and the *Serapis* and the *Countess of Scarborough* also headed inshore to cover the rear of the merchantmen. The American *Richard*, should have been no match for the more heavily armed British frigate, only recently off the stocks and mounting twenty-two long 18-pounders, twenty-two long 12-pounders and with two long 6-pounders on her forecastle.

Towards evening the *Bon Homme Richard* and the *Serapis* were within musket-range of one another, Jones trying to gain the weather gauge and get into a position across the other's bow or stern, and thus be able to fire into the *Serapis* without risk of an answering broadside. However, the copper-bottomed English frigate was too fast for the less manoeuvrable *Richard* and the two vessels began an almost simultaneous bombardment. And so, just after 7p.m., the 23rd September, 1779, a close-fought and bitter battle began that was to last for three and a half hours, in full view of the cliff-top watchers.

Several broadsides had already been exchanged when an explosion on board the American ship almost brought about an early end to the battle. According to Richard Dale, the First Lieutenant of the *Richard*, her guns were old and two of the eighteen-pounders on her lower gun deck had 'bursted', blowing up the deck above, killing or wounding most of the gun crews and, in effect, putting all her heavy armament out of action. The American was so badly damaged and with only her 9- and 12-pounders left to fight with – and these not for long – that Jones decided that his only hope was to close with the enemy and attempt to board and force a decision hand-to-hand.

The *Serapis* continued to score with a number of hits 'between wind and water', and as John Paul attempted to close and grapple, the American's fourteen 12-pounders and most of her deck guns were dismounted or put out of action by the British cannonade. His first attempt failed, but on a second run, he rammed the bows of the *Richard* into the port quarter of the *Serapis* but, before he could board, a sudden gust of wind caused the vessels to swing one towards the other and come together, starboard to starboard, bow to stern. The mizzen shrouds of the *Richard* caught the jib-boom of the *Serapis*, which snapped, but the spare bow anchor of the latter caught in the after-gallery of the *Richard* and held the two ships fast together, their guns muzzle to muzzle.

Both American and British sources agree that John Paul himself dashed forward, calling for grappling-hooks, and grabbed a line to lash the bowsprit of the *Serapis* to his rigging. With the lower gun-deck out of action, the men who were not fighting fires were now on the upper deck and, as his only operative cannon were three-pounders on his quarter deck, the Commodore realised that he could not fight his enemy's ship with such unequal armament, but must now concentrate on weakening his enemy's manpower.

John Paul sent marksmen aloft with muskets, pistols and grenades, to pick off men on the deck of the *Serapis*. With grenades tossed from the tops onto her open deck, and snipers creating havoc among her gunners, the deck was soon cleared of all but the dead and wounded, the guns unmanned, and small fires breaking out in a number of places. But her powerful guns on the deck below were still blasting into the *Richard* and creating great damage. As the two ships had swung together, the British ship had closed the port-lids of her 18-pounder battery, as a precaution against boarders using the ports as a means of entry, but now, with the two vessels so closely lashed together, the guns were fired through the closed lids into the American, shattering whole areas of her ancient timbers into matchwood.

At this stage, at about 8.30 p.m., the odds were all in favour of the British, as it seemed that the heavy guns of the *Serapis* would soon send the *Richard* to the bottom, but at this critical moment a young American seaman, William Hamilton, crawled out along the *Bon Homme Richard*'s main-yard which overhung the British deck, and tossed a grenade through the main-hatchway and into the *Serapis'* gun room. The grenade fired 12-pounder cartridges and the resulting explosion was catastrophic, killing or wounding about forty officers and men and putting a number of guns out of action. A few minutes later another vessel, as unwelcome to the Americans as the British, came into the fray.

The *Alliance* which had so far played no part, now hove into sight firing indiscriminately and directing a broadside, not into the British frigate but hitting the *Bon Homme* below the waterline. With five or six feet of water in her hold and much of her upperworks on fire, she was in fact sinking and only kept afloat by the British ship alongside.

There have been many arguments, debates and theories as to the truth regarding Captain Landais' actions; Jones was in no doubt that the Frenchman was guilty of treachery, and John Sherburne backs up that accusation by citing the fact that the night was one of brilliant moonlight; that the scene was lit up from the fires on both ships; and that the *Serapis* was painted bright yellow whilst the *Richard* was painted black. Whilst there seems little doubt that the *Alliance* did fire on its consort, it is also true that the *Serapis* received some of her erratic fire and both ships were by now at the end of their tether.

At ten o'clock the battle had already raged for three hours and the American's position seemed hopeless. Her ensign staff had been shot away and her colours were touching the water. Many of the crew called on their Commodore to strike, and the Chief Gunner called out loudly for 'Quarter! Quarter! For God's sake, quarter!' Jones was furious and silenced him with a stunning blow on the head from his pistol, but the cry had been heard on the British ship. Captain Pearson called for confirmation of surrender, but John Paul grabbed his speaking-trumpet and shouted the words which are remembered two hundred years later, and are among the first things learned by cadets in the American Naval Academy today:

'I have not yet begun to fight!'[15]

With fire, rising water and shell fast putting an end to the *Bon Homme Richard*, the Commodore ordered that the 300 or more British prisoners of war should be released from the hold which could easily have presented an additional danger to the exhausted Americans; but Jones, with a great show of strength and authority, ordered them to the under-manned pumps, in a last effort to keep her afloat, convincing them that their alternative was to go down with the ship. And Jones still fought on. The Purser, who had been in charge of the three remaining deck guns, was shot through the head, and Jones took over a 9-pounder himself, twice loading and firing at the mainmast of his opponent.

It was 10.30p.m., and as the mast to which the British Captain Pearson had nailed his flag tottered, and with the *Alliance* taking a belated interest, now in a threatening position under her stern, the *Serapis* struck her colours. As the mainmast crashed over the side, the English captain and his first lieutenant were escorted onto the quarterdeck of the battered *Bon Homme Richard* to surrender their swords to John Paul Jones.

The *Countess of Scarborough* had struck to the *Pallas* earlier in the evening after a two hour battle, in which the *Alliance* is said to have taken some part – this time against the enemy. As far as the actual battle, the day went to the Americans, but the gallant officers and men of the British vessels had carried out their most important duty successfully – the escape of the merchant convoy without loss. This was recognised by the Government and Captain Pearson was rewarded with a knighthood for his part in the action on that memorable day. By the end of the encounter the fighting days of the *Richard* were over. A description attested by Lt. Dale, paints an almost incredible picture when it is realised that it refers to the victor.

> 'Abaft, on a line with the guns of the *Serapis* that had not been disabled by the explosion, the timbers [of the *Bon Homme Richard*] were found to be nearly all beaten in or beaten out, for in this respect there was little difference between the two sides of the ship; and it was said that her poop and upper decks would have fallen into the gun-room but for a few futtocks [the ship's ribs] that had been missed. Indeed, so vast was the vacuum, that most of the shot fired from this part of the *Serapis* must have gone through the *Richard* without touching anything. The rudder was cut from the stern-post, and the transoms nearly all driven out of her. All of the after part of the ship, in particular that was below the quarter-deck was torn to pieces, and nothing had saved those stationed on the quarterdeck but the impossibility of elevating guns that almost touched their object.'

The water was rising through her shattered hull throughout that night, but by the next day the crew, marines and prisoners were removed to the *Serapis*, but one report states the sad fact that the *Bon Homme Richard* 'sank with a number of her wounded on board.'

The triumphant John Paul Jones sailed the captured but crippled *Serapis*, with Captain Pearson and numerous prisoners, for Holland. That voyage was yet another test of seamanship and command, as the weakened squadron made its precarious way, in constant lookout for privateers or enemy cruisers. Jones arrived in the Texel on the 3rd October, to even greater renown; and more songs, pamphlets and broadsheets were sold in the streets to spread his fame. Although the Dutch were not yet officially at war with

Britain, and Sir Joseph Yorke, the British Ambassador at the Hague, was demanding that John Paul Jones be handed over to Britain for trial as a rebel and a pirate, the Commodore was able to report that he had 'authority, by unanimous resolution of the States, by order of the the Prince of Orange, to land as many prisoners as I please, to place centinals [*sic*] to guard them on the Texel, to haul up the drawbridge of that fort, and to take them from thence, whenever I think proper… Huzza! America!'

Benjamin Franklin wrote, 'I am uneasy about your prisoners, and wish they were safe in France; you will then have completed the glorious work of giving liberty to all the Americans that have so long languished for it in the British prisons, for there are not so many there as you have now taken.'

Sir Joseph Yorke bore an almost obsessive hatred and contempt for John Paul, and the latter's popularity in the neutral country to which he was British ambassador must have driven him mad. The French, Dutch and English newspapers reported the Commodore's every appearance at dinners, functions or on the streets of Amsterdam. He was described as of middle height, thin, strong featured with a swarthy complexion, dressed in American uniform with a Scotch bonnet edged with gold or, more often, with 'a roquelaure [hooded knee-length cloak] over his regimentals, with a large cape to it, edged with gold lace' – and all the book and print shops displayed the latest engravings of his portraits.

The question of exchange was by no means straightforward. John Paul's concern for the American captives in England was great and sincere, and he needed reassurance that his hard-fought efforts on their behalf would not be in vain. He wrote many letters seeking advice on the matter, and extracts from just two will show his concern. To the French ambassador at the Hague, the Duc de Vauguyon, he wrote:

'I would esteem it a particular favour to have your opinion on the measures that are most expedient to be adopted in this respect. Whether it would be consistent to set them at liberty here upon such security as may be obtained, that the English government will immediately expedite an equal number of Americans to France; for, unless such security as may be fully depended upon can be obtained, I think these prisoners must be sent immediately to Dunkirk.'

and to Benjamin Franklin:

'As I am informed that Captain Cunningham is threatened with unfair play by the British government, I am determined to keep in my hands the Captain of the *Serapis* as a hostage for Cunningham's release as a prisoner of war and with respect to the other prisoners, I would release them against Yorke's "security in his public character" of reciprocal treatment for the Americans.'

Sir Joseph's response was one of outrage, declaring that he would not listen to 'Scotch pirates and rebels.'

Captain Pearson and his officers were held prisoners on the *Pallas*, and Jones now received a letter from the ex-commander of the *Serapis*, asking for his release and charging him with 'a breach of civility'. Jones deeply resented this, and protested that he had shown only hospitality and consideration. (John Henry Sherburne, commenting on the letter, makes the snide remark that 'had not his naval conduct been more generally correct than his grammar, Captain Pearson would have been dismissed his Majesty's service long before he met the *Bon Homme Richard*.')

John Paul reminded Pearson that Captain Cunningham:

'…who has been a senior rank in the service of America, than yours in the service of England, is now confined at Plymouth, in a dungeon and in fetters. Humanity, which has hitherto superseded retaliation in American hearts, has induced me (notwithstanding the procedure of Sir Joseph Yorke) to seek permission to land the dangerously wounded, as well prisoners as Americans, to be supported and cured at the expense of our Continent…'

The irascible English ambassador plagued the Dutch government with demands for the restitution of the two British ships and all the prisoners, and demanded of their High Mightinesses the delivery unto the King, his master, 'of a certain Paul Jones, a subject of the king, who, according to treaties and the laws of war, could only be considered a rebel and a pirate.' The Dutch, however, insisted that their neutrality meant that they could not be the judge of the legality or otherwise of the taking, on the high seas, ships which did not belong to Holland, and that same consideration would be shown to any country, including England, whose vessels brought prisoners or prizes into the ports of their neutral republic. Yorke still insisted that their explanations did not apply in the case of John Paul Jones, as he and his squadron did not hold commissions from a sovereign state.

This was a delicate point for the Dutch to argue, without admitting the independence of the American states although at this tricky stage, France, already at war with Britain, came to the rescue as far as the ships and prisoners were concerned. The government bestowed French commissions on the squadron and its officers! This technically overcame the English ambassador's latest point; but John Paul would not accept the proffered commission, saying it would be 'dishonourable to himself and disadvantageous to America to change his flag.'

Except for one ship, the American-owned frigate *Alliance*, the squadron was now the property of King Louis XVI, and John Paul received orders from the French and American ministers to hand over his prisoners and his two hard-won prizes to the French ambassasdor. So the infuriated Sir Joseph Yorke learned that he had been outwitted, when the *Serapis* and *Countess of Scarborough*, with all the English prisoners of war on board, and escorted by the Dutch Fleet, left the Texel and set sail for France.

With Commodore Jones now given a deadline to leave the Texel, there was every chance that he would fall prey to the waiting British cruisers. With the combined fleet of France and Spain returned to Brest, Britain had ships to spare and two light squadrons could be seen cruising off Texel Island. John Paul's admirers and friends feared for his safety and were sure that, if captured, he would meet his fate in the Tower of London; others spread unlikely stories, such as: that he would sail with pockets filled with lead, determined never to be taken alive. Jones himself, whilst aware of the danger, seems to have spent his time writing poetry and light-hearted letters to friends: 'They have done me the honour' he wrote 'to place four fine ships, at each entry to this road, to give me a royal salute when I retreat. What regret I should have, if an ill-natured gale of wind should force them on shore before I am ready to receive the honour they intend to pay me.' He did not receive their salute.

One morning, in command of the *Alliance* and accompanied by a small Boston privateer of 10-guns, John Paul took advantage of a favourable wind and dashed from the Dutch port, avoided the waiting squadrons, and made for Port L'Orient where his great exploit had begun. Benjamin Franklin informed Jones that he had written to Pierre Landais, telling him that he was charged with a number of offences. Altogether twenty-five charges were laid against the Captain of the *Alliance*. Ten related to deliberate running foul of the *Richard*; disobedience to signals; 'impudent and arrant cowardice'; separation from the squadron; etc., etc. and fifteen other charges connected with: his conduct in the battle with *Serapis*; lack of attack on the Baltic fleet, etc. All of the charges were supported by officers, 'upon their words of honour as gentlemen', including officers of the *Alliance*. But Landais did not face a court martial. This would have been impolitic, as America owed so much to the French alliance. Captain Landais was thick-skinned enough to have taken the accusations without a blush. In fact, it is said that in later years he was known to boast that it was he, and not Jones, who caused the *Serapis* to strike.

That America's great naval hero John Paul Jones achieved greater contemporary acclaim in Europe than in the States may be explained by the fact that he was not the only great American captain. Men like Lambery Wickes, Gustavus Conyngham and John Barry, though great seamen, were completely overshadowed by the dashing, charismatic Jones, whose devil-may-care courage at sea and social graces ashore, made him Europe's darling. Created a Chevalier of France, Louis XVI also decorated him with the Cross of Military Merit, the only time it had been awarded to a foreigner; Marie Antoinette presented him with a bejewelled sword: Catherine the Great honoured him with the Order of St Anne and made him a Rear-Admiral in the Russian Navy.

Although Captain Pearson, the loser in the *Serapis – Bon Homme Richard* battle, received a knighthood from an appreciative Britain, the Scottish/American victor received no recognition equivalent to that of his vanquished opponent – although he was eventually awarded the Congressional Gold Medal. Neither was he given another sea-going command but was sent as a US representative to the Danish Court. After the war, he served in the Russian Navy in the war with the Turks.

John Paul Jones died in Paris on the 18th July 1792 and was buried in the 'Cemetery of the Protestants'. There he lay for more than a hundred years before his unmarked grave was rediscovered and his body, escorted by warships of a different age, was brought back to the country for which he had fought so valiantly. If John Paul was thwarted from fully realising his dreams of the glory of which he knew himself capable; he can at least look down with pride on his tomb in the Chapel of the Naval Academy of Annapolis: which is considered by some to be more magnificent than that of Horatio Nelson in St. Paul's Cathedral.

THE AMERICAN PRISONER OF WAR in Britain, like the captive of any other nationality, would have been unnatural if he did not resent his captivity, and saint-like if he did harbour at least some hatred for his captor, however compassionate the latter might have been. The truth is that though there was no official intention to make their incarceration harder than necessary, compassion did not feature highly as a qualification for the post of depot Governor, Agent, guard or sentinel. It took many years for the Briton to regard the American other than as a Rebel, and the American never quite forgot the high-handed arrogance which had forced them to break away from their mother-country. So the chips on their shoulders, though from different woods, brought about sufferings on both sides. In general, the Americans felt that they were ill-treated when compared with that experienced by the English prisoner in Yankee hands, and Franklin and Jones repeated the accusation often enough to convince one that they believed their own propaganda. It was true that, as we have read, English sailors were often left free to roam in ports where they were set ashore, and that many were only too ready to serve on American ships.

* There are a number of accounts of the Nelson-like **'I HAVE NOT YET BEGUN TO FIGHT'** – John Paul Jones's immortal words; but there are other versions of the surrender of the *Serapis*.

The nineteenth century British writer, Joseph Allen R.N., who was no fan of John Paul Jones, in his two volume *'Battles of the British Navy'* (Second Edition 1852), tells a different story:

> '…a ruse was tried, which, though natural and excusable enough in a privateer, is not to be justified in a national ship of war', and quotes from Captain Pearson's official letter which said that Jones made no reply to his call [to surrender] and that, as his [Pearson's] boarders entered the *Richard*, 'they discovered a superior number lying under cover with pikes in their hands to receive them, upon which our people instantly retreated… and returned to their guns.'

1. John Henry Sherburne: *The Life of Paul Jones from Original Documents.* The letters and documents, plus papers from the Department of State. Published 1825.

2. George Coggershall: *A History of American Privateers and Letters-of-Marque, 1821.*

3. See Chapter 5: 'THE CIVIL PRISON HULKS.'

4. See Clive Lloyd's: *The Arts and Crafts of Napoleonic and American Prisoners of War 1756-1816,* Chapter 9: 'THE GAMBLERS & BROKERS.'

5. Alfred de Curzon: *Dr James Currie and the French Prisoners of War in Liverpool.* A collection of Dr Currie's letters and reports concerning the Prisoners of War.

6. Charles Herbert: *A Relic of the Revolution*, published 1847. Andrew Sherburne: *Memoirs, etc.* 1828.

7. William Laird Clowes: *The Royal Navy: A History*, 1899. A somewhat indiscreet epistle, in which John Paul presents himself as a chivalric character. Whilst chatting-up the noble lady, he makes the outrageous excuse for his 'invasion', by suggesting that he would have been doing the Earl a service, had he been successful in kidnapping him!

8. Charles Herbert of Newburyport, Massachusetts: *A Relic of the Revolution*, published 1847.

9. During the war, paper money had plummeted to a mere seventh of its original face value.

10. Shallop: from the Old French *chaloupe*, Old Dutch *isloep* and Old English *slupon* (sloop).

11. Some days later, the marooned party were rescued by fishing boats visiting the cove – and by that time their number of survivors had increased by one.

12. Alexander Laing (Editor): *The Life and Adventures of John Nicol, Mariner.* Pub. Cassell 1937.

13. Paul Jones may have become more proficient in the language later, for he advised John Adams, then one of the Commissioners in Paris and later the second President of the United States, that the two best ways to learn French were: 'to take a Mistress or go to the Comédie'.

14. Eight per cent of the *Victory*'s crew at Trafalgar in 1805 were foreigners, of twelve different nationalities.

15. See also the note* above.

Patriotic Song.

Composed in Dartmoor Prison, 1814.

YE PARLIAMENTS of England,
　Ye Lords and Commons too,
Consider well what you're about,
　And what you mean to do ;
You are at war with Yankees,
　And I'm sure you'll rue the day,
You rouse the Sons of Liberty
　In North America !

You first confin'd our Commerce,
　And said our Ships shan't trade ;
You next impress'd our seamen,
　And us'd them as your slaves ;
You next insulted ROGERS
　While cruising on the main,
And had we not declar'd a war,
　You'd done it o'er again,

You thought our Frigates were but few,
　And Yankees could got fight,
Until brave HULL the *Guerriere*,
　'Took and banish'd her from sight ;
The next was your bold *Java*,
　The choice of British crew,
To fight us gallant Yankee Boys,
　They found it would not do.

The next the *Macedonian*,
　No finer ship could swim,
DECATUR took her gilt work off,
　And then he sent her in ;
The *Wasp* then took the *Frolic*,
　But nothing said to that,
The *Poictiers* being of the line,
　Of course she took her back.

You next sent out your *Boxer*,
　For to box us all about,
But we'd an *Enterprize*-ing Brig
　That beat your Boxer out ;
We box'd her up to Portland,
　And moor'd her off the town,
To show the Sons of Liberty
　The Boxer of renown.

'Twas next upon Lake Erie,
　Brave PERRY had some fun,
You own he beat your naval force
　And caus'd them all to run.
'Twas next on Lake Ontario,
　Which CHAUNCY knew before,
Again we beat your naval force,
　Some took, some drove on shore.

Champlain attests our valorous deeds,
　Again proud Britons cry
For quarter from our Yankee Boys—
　They cannot fight or fly ;
Your DOWNIE to M'DONOUGH yields,
　His decks deep stain'd with gore ;
Your coward PROCTOR's spirit fails—
　He quits Columbia's shore.

The *Congress* on the Brazil coast,
　Your commerce shall annoy,
The *President* and all her crew
　Go plough the ocean wide ;
The next our fine Ship *Essex*,
　She puts out all your lights,
A flag she wears at her mast head—
　" *Free Trade and Sailor's Rights.*"

Patriotic Song, American. Origin unknown.

Chapter Three
The American War of 1812
'The Forgotten War'

'THE WAR FOR FREE TRADE AND SAILORS' RIGHTS', or the 'Second War of American Independence', as it was also known, need not, and perhaps should not have taken place. Eventful though it was, it left only shallow impressions on the memories of either nation and, after very few years, it gained yet another appellation – 'The Forgotten War'. Britain may have asked for it, but certainly did not want it; which was made plain by her last-minute revocation of almost all the Orders in Council which had dictated the things which America was prepared to fight against. As we shall see, however, this softening of attitude arrived too late.

Although the war lasted for a comparatively short time, losses on both sides were expensive in ships, commerce and men – Britain claiming thousands of American seaman prisoners of war on the day that war was declared! One would have to dig deep to discover gains that were significant and worth fighting for to either nation.

With the outbreak of the Revolutionary War between Britain and France in 1792, the United States had been faced with a rather sticky situation. Some, mainly Federalist, Americans thought that their country should join the fray on the British side Others, true Republicans with bitter memories, felt that they should remember the part that France had played in their own quite recent revolutionary fight for independence. George Washington wisely chose neutrality.

Many treaties and agreements had been entered into between the US and her French allies during the War of American Independence, which now became a source of embarrassment and danger; as did some subsequent agreements with Britain. No effort had been made to rescind those treaties, including one entered into with the French in 1778, which permitted French privateers to bring their captures into American ports to dispose of their prizes – a permission from which most other nations were excluded. As these treaties had been made between the United States and the King of France, it could have been argued that, now that there was no king of France, they were invalid and would have to be re-negotiated or scrapped. But America was all too conscious of the possibility of her future need of a Continental ally, for them to risk such action.

At the same time, and confusingly, the President and his Federalist administration – though not the people – were largely pro-British and, during a brief period of peace in Europe a controversial Anglo-American trade/territorial/political agreement – far too complicated to discuss here – was prepared. This was the 'Jay Treaty', which was finally agreed upon in November 1794. A 'curate's egg' of a treaty as far as America was concerned, it did contribute to economic prosperity, but no other treaty was ever so unpopular with a large proportion of the population. Washington justified it by reasoning that: 'If this country is preserved in tranquillity twenty years longer, it may bid defiance in a just cause to any power whatever, such in that time will be its population, wealth, and resources', but many disagreed, one Republican newspaper labelling the Jay Treaty as 'the death-warrant to our neutral rights', and it was not far out.

The rage which the Jay Treaty aroused in France brought about another, and even more completely forgotten war, the undeclared 'Quasi-War' between America and France, which was waged between 1798 and 1801. The 'Quasi-War', which was almost entirely fought at sea, for the most part in the Caribbean, cost America many millions of dollars in ships and goods, but it was by no means a walk-over for the French. The Federal Navy and private armed vessels took over one hundred French privateers and defeated at least two French men-of-war.

The American privateers and naval vessels put up a very good show, recapturing at least seventy of her merchant ships which had been taken as prizes by the French. It has been estimated that the cost to America in ships and cargoes could have been as much as $20,000,000, but the cost to France could not have been much less. It is perhaps significant that, when the Convention of 1800 brought peace, the United States made no claim against France for her mercantile losses, and France reciprocated by rescinding those treaties mentioned at the beginning of this chapter, which were relics of the War of Independence.

Over the years between the two wars with Britain, America was never absolutely certain of where she stood; who was her friend and who was her foe. Some British vessels were captured and taken into American ports by the French, and the war which did not begin until 1812, might well have commenced some twenty years earlier. Washington's declared, but less than whole-hearted neutrality, did not ensure peace for his ships at sea. The American merchant marine was literally caught between two fires. Our ships of war and privateers were ordered to capture all American merchant vessels carrying goods to France: to sell both ships and cargoes as prizes, and to impress certain of their crews into the royal naval service of King George. And US merchantmen bound for British ports were in equal peril from the French privateers and men of war. At one time there were ninety-two American merchant ships held captive at Bordeaux and later, in 1810, Napoleon employed devious manipulations of maritime law to confiscate some two hundred 'friendly' vessels in Continental ports.

Amongst the tangle of events and frustrations which finally led to America's declaration of war against Britain in 1812, the most easily understood – and most deeply resented and detested by all Americans – was the British Navy's insistence on its 'right to Search and Impress', even in peacetime.

By a British Order in Council, American ships could be stopped at sea and searched for contraband and British subjects among their crews. Unfair as was this practice, the British were within their legal rights as they saw them. Impressment was by far the principal method of manning our navy – volunteers were few and far between – and the Royal Navy needed every able-bodied man it could lay its hands on.

It was hard work to get a crew together at any time – ships would sometimes be forced to lie in harbour for weeks or months before they could sail; but it was even harder to keep that crew complete once formed. The shockingly hard conditions of service aboard most of our men-of-war, the harsh discipline, the brutal punishments and often poor quality food, caused thousands of our seamen to abscond. Unwilling impressed men would often account for as many as three-quarters of a warship's company, many of them landlubbers drafted into a strange and terrifying watery world. The better pay and treatment on board an American merchantman – or ship of war – would have attracted many of these runaways; but then they stood the chance of recapture, impressment for a second time or, if adjudged a deserter, drastic or even capital, punishment.

In times of peace – and it should be remembered that we were not at war with the United States for most of the years of our struggle with France – a seaman of British or any other nationality was entitled to hire himself out to any foreign vessel, merchant or otherwise, whose country was not at war with Britain. So a Britisher legitimately employed and a British deserter might well be discovered on the same neutral ship and, under the powers provided by the Order in Council, both could be forcibly enlisted into the British naval service.

Had the impress-officers restricted their captures to 'deserters' and 'subjects', a war may well have been averted, but great numbers of Americans, six thousand or more, were taken into our fleets over the years until America belatedly said that enough was enough.

It was well-nigh impossible for any seaman to prove his nationality with evidence strong enough to convince a determined impress-officer in search of a crew. Few would have possessed a birth certificate, and it was not always enough to produce an official *'Proof of American Nationality Certificate'*. This document, which was introduced in 1796, described the bearer's essential personal details: name, age, place of birth, colour of hair, eyes, etc. Every American (and probably some Britons!) carried this 'protection' document, but it had to be believed for it to be effective. These certificates were so widely forged and sold in the ports for a dollar a time, that even the obviously genuine were disregarded together with the duds.

Thousands of American seamen who were caught in this unfair trap, served years as 'British' tars in our men-of-war. In January 1812, President Madison submitted to Congress a document listing the names of 6,057 American seamen said to have been impressed into the British Navy since 1809. Many saw action in sea battles great and small, and not a few were taken captive by the French. Finding themselves prisoners of war in a French depot ashore, where conditions were often far worse than they had experienced at sea, was too much for some. Pestered, bullied and cajoled by their French jailors to take heed of the only way out of their predicament, they submitted and entered the French naval service.

That the impressment of American subjects, together with the British blockades which cut off trade with legitimate markets, and the frequent confiscation by prize courts of American merchant vessels and their cargoes, were wrongs which greatly contributed to the declaration of war in 1812, is made clear by the following extract from a lengthy message which President Madison placed before the Senate and House of Representatives on the 1st June. At 4 p.m. on the first day of the war, the 18th June 1812, it was released for general publication in a special edition of the *National Intelligencer*. It was a bitter recitation of humiliations and impositions suffered over the years, accusing Britain of:

'…acts, hostile to the United States as an independent and neutral nation. British cruisers have been in the continued practice of violating the national flag on the great highway of nations, and of seizing and carrying off persons sailing under it; not in the exercise of a belligerent right, founded on the law of nations against an enemy, but of a municipal prerogative over British subjects.

'British jurisdiction is thus extended to neutral vessels in a situation where no laws can operate but the Law of Nations and the laws of the country to which the vessels belong. [It is a fact that, by the accepted laws of war, captured property (prizes) had to be adjudged by a competent tribunal, a Prize Court, which would decide its fate; but this was not so where 'the sacred rights of persons' were at issue. In place of such a trial, the rights of men were 'subjected to the will of every petty commander'.]

'The practice, hence, is so far from affecting British subjects alone, that, under the pretext of searching for these, thousands of Americans, under the safeguard of public law, and of their national flag, have been torn away from their country and from everything dear to them; have been dragged on board ships of war of a foreign nation, and exposed, under the severities of their discipline, to be exiled to the most distant and deadly climes, to risk their lives in the battles of their oppressors, and to be the melancholy instruments of taking away those of their brethren…

Washington June 1st, 1812　　　　　JAMES MADISON'

And so it went on, column after bitter column, citing injuries and indignities; from illegal blockading to accusations of British traders stirring up the Redskin 'savages on one of our extensive frontiers; a warfare which is known to spare neither age nor sex, and to be distinguished by features particularly shocking to humanity'.

President Madison was not exaggerating when he spoke of great numbers of his mariners being snatched into British fleets – and we shall hear later, in the words of some of those 'American-Englishmen', how one day they were serving in His Britannic Majesty's Navy, and on the very next became prisoners of war, the moment war was declared.

If the previous President of the United States, Thomas Jefferson, had dared the venture, he could have gone to war with Britain in 1807 with the full backing of a high percentage of his countrymen. In June of that year an English warship over-stepped the already hated imposition of 'stop and search at sea' with a giant stride. This action was illegal even when judged by its own laws, and was carried out in a manner which caused a wave of fury which swept throughout the United States; and simmered in the American mind for the rest of the century.

In June 1807, the British frigate HMS *Leopard* put into the port of Norfolk, where the United States frigate USS *Chesapeake* was preparing for sea. Whilst in harbour, some of the *Leopard*'s crew deserted and her captain took extraordinary measures to make good his loss.

On the 22nd June, both vessels sailed. The *Leopard* left first, lay in wait for the *Chesapeake*, and stopped her off the Norfolk Capes. The British captain insisted that his deserters were on board the American frigate and demanded their return. The captain of the *Chesapeake* denied the accusation and when he objected to his vessel being searched, the *Leopard* opened fire with broadsides.

Unprepared, the American frigate was in no state to put up a fight or even to defend herself; she struck her colours after three of her crew had been killed and about twenty wounded. After being boarded, four of the *Chesapeake*'s seamen were taken on board the *Leopard* and into British service.

Although thousands of neutral merchant vessels had been searched over the preceding years, this was the first occasion since 1798 that an American man-of-war had been boarded. Enraged America retaliated with nothing stronger than government recriminations and strong newspaper calls for action, and this was probably taken as proof that it would take a very great deal of provocation before America would take the risk of a second confrontation with Britain.

That year, 1807, was one of Decrees, Orders in Council, Embargoes, Blockades and counter-Blockades, none of which were of much benefit to the US, who was playing the part of piggy-in-the-middle in the international game of maritime commerce. A British Order of the 11th November, allowed the merchant shipping of America and other neutrals to enter French ports – but only after first going through an English port, off-loading all freight for examination, and paying all taxes and Customs duties in full, before continuing their voyages to France.

Drastic as it was, this did at least appear to be a concession on the part of the British, but it was made superfluous only a month later by Napoleon's Milan Decree of December 1807. This laid down that any neutral vessel which had passed through an English port before reaching France should be condemned and confiscated. His Decree went even further and banned the use of the English language on the Continent. This ridiculous prohibition would have affected American merchantmen in particular, who would have had to be desperate indeed to venture into a French harbour, whether they spoke French or no, or had or had not passed through an English port.

Thomas Jefferson came up with his own Embargo Act, also of December 1807, which complicated things still further. The *Chesapeake* affair earlier in the year, and the country-wide reaction of rage and the calls for revenge which it engendered, forced the President to do something positive. To divert the clamour for war, he introduced his Act, which prohibited the export of any American goods whatsoever by land or sea and involved blockading all along his coastline. He believed that cutting off British and French trade with America was the latter's greatest weapon of defence, but this gesture was more punishing to American shipping and commerce than it was to Britain or France. Tobacco prices rocketed in Europe, but hit rock-bottom in America, and left her cotton planters and wheat producers in a state of desperation. Once-prosperous and bustling sea ports were now filled with laid-up merchant ships, hungry jobless seamen and angry merchants – but the smugglers and embargo-breakers had a field day. Right from the start, some determined owners and daring captains found holes in the embargo, their ships leaving port before the prohibitions were officially promulgated, or under semi-legal excuses.

The American embargo of 1807 lasted for fifteen months, until March 1809, during which time the country was exposed to great commercial hardship. Even then, the Act was not repealed in all its aspects: American shipping was free to deal with all nations – other than Britain and France or their allies; but once the repeal had released port-bound vessels, a good deal of illicit Anglo-American and Franco-American dealing went on through neutral ports.

Over the next three years there were many complicated trade agreements and disagreements between the two countries – and several warlike occurrences which edged them towards hostile confrontation.

Early in 1811, a year before the official opening of hostilities, an English warship, HBMS *Guerrière* stopped and searched an American vessel off Sandy Hook, taking off one of her seamen under the Great Britain impressment laws. This time positive action was taken. The 44-gun frigate, USS *President* was sent off in pursuit, and on the 16th May sighted a British warship about ten miles off. By 8 p.m., as darkness began to fall, the vessels were less than a hundred yards apart, and after some hailing and a confusion of signals – which may have involved the hoisting of false colours – both ships opened fire.

The British ship was the 20-gun corvette, *Little Belt,* which could hardly have been mistaken for a line-of-battle ship, but a half-hour battle ensued, which left the corvette with her sails and rigging cut to pieces and almost completely dismasted. Out of a crew of 121 men and boys, the *Little Belt* lost a midshipman and ten men killed, and twenty-one wounded. The *President* suffered one man wounded. The details of this rather paltry victory were not generally broadcast to the jubilant American public, and it is perhaps understandable as it was generally regarded as *quid pro quo* for the *Chesapeake-Leopard* affair.

There were many puzzling ambiguities in mercantile law which needed clarification. Patriotism came a poor second in the hearts of some merchants and ship owners. Some American merchant vessels sailed into neutral ports under British licences – not strictly illegally until Congress made it so. Towards the end of 1812, the USS *Chesapeake* seized the American merchantman *Julia,* which was carrying goods of use to the British war effort into the port of Lisbon. The contested case was brought before a court, but it was not until the middle of 1813 that a decision was reached that such seizures were lawful. From that time on, any American traders transgressing the new law were condemned as enemy vessels.

But infringements of embargoes did not end with the blocking up of semi-legal loopholes. The most powerful professed reason for the declaration of war, much drummed up by the 'war-hawks', was the hated 'search and impress' policy of our Royal Navy. One might imagine that the eastern states, the principal home of American merchant shipping, would have been the most eager supporters of righting this wrong; but the opposite was the case. The prosperous New England merchants and ship-owners, foreseeing loss of trade and the end to that prosperity, protested that they were prepared to sacrifice a few ships (and men?) to preserve the peace – and, of course, the markets. On numerous occasions, before and during the war of 1812, the Federalist New England states openly considered secession from the Union and the creation of a Republic of New England. Nevertheless, when war did – officially at least – bring down the market shutters, the eastern states were the main beneficiaries of the immense wealth in goods and vessels brought in by Yankee privateers.

The American writer, W.E.Woodward[1] in his *A New American History*', says that most of the privateers' English prizes were genuine captures; but goes on to tell a darker story:

'... But a lot of them were not [genuine captures]. During the war there was a great deal of collusion between British and American merchants. A British exporter in secret partnership with an American owner of a privateer, would load a ship with goods which he knew would sell at high prices in the United States. The ship would sail, carrying clearance papers made out for the British West Indies, and at a certain place in the trackless ocean the American privateer would wait for her. Joyously, the captor and the captive would then turn their noses towards Boston, or Providence, or New York. Of course they were taking big chances. The British vessel might be seized by the wrong American, but that chance had to be accepted as a gamble.

'The same thing worked the other way; there was collusion between American shippers of wheat, tobacco and cotton, and British merchants. Stories are in print of American vessels that sailed forlornly about the Azores for days, waiting for certain privateers to appear.'

Similar un-American activities were taking place ashore. There was a good deal of trading with the enemy: 'droves of cattle and strings of wagons' laden with provisions were delivered to the British armies across the border in Canada. Towards the end of the war, Sir George Prevost, the Governor General of Canada stated that '...two-thirds of the army in Canada are at this moment eating beef provided by the American contractors.'

Blockades and threats of blockades were a frequently resorted-to strategy throughout the war and the years leading up to it. Some were carefully planned and successfully executed, whilst others were no more than 'paper blockades' of only propaganda value.

As in all other wars, before and since, propaganda based on fact, invention or exaggeration, was employed to keep up the morale of the contending parties. Both sides were constantly busily 'improving' the truth to uplift the sprit of their troops and seamen. (I have a letter in my collection dated the 14th December, 1798, from East India House, which gives a false report from Cairo of the death of Napoleon! It was not unusual for British admirals to proclaim that they had the American coast covered by well-nigh impenetrable blockades. Such statements may have been good propaganda and good for home consumption, but few could have taken them as literally true – it would have taken more vessels than we had on both sides of the Atlantic to have upheld such boasts.

The Americans took what they called these 'paper blockades', or 'burlesques', as something of a joke, and one privateer captain with a sense of humour entered into the spirit of this spreading of false news. Captain Thomas Boyle, commander of the privateer *Chasseur*, a large brig armed with sixteen long 12-pounders, who had achieved great success in the English Channel, capturing eighteen merchantmen and small armed vessels, composed his own lampoon of a 'paper blockade'. He had it printed and sent off a copy to London by a cartel vessel, with instructions that it should be prominently displayed in Lloyd's Coffee House in London:

PROCLAMATION
Whereas it has become customary with the Admirals of Great Britain, commanding small forces on the coast of the United States, particularly with Sir John Borlaise Warren and Sir Alexander Cochrane, to declare all the coast of the said United States in a state of strict and rigorous blockade, without possessing the power to justify such a declaration, or stationing to maintain said blockade. I do, therefore, by virtue of the power and authority in me vested (possessing sufficient force), declare all the ports, harbors, bays, creeks, rivers, inlets, outlets, islands and sea coast of the United Kingdom of Great Britain and Ireland in a state of strict and rigorous blockade. And I do further declare, that I consider the force under my command adequate to maintain strictly, rigorously and effectually, the said blockade. And I do hereby require the respective officers, whether captains, commanders, or commanding officers, employed or to be employed, on the coasts of England, Ireland and Scotland, to pay strict attention to the execution of this my proclamation. And I do hereby caution and forbid the ships and vessels of all and every nation, in amity and peace with the United States, from entering or attempting to enter, or from coming or attempting to come out of any of the said ports, harbors, bays, creeks, rivers, inlets, outlets, islands, or sea coast, under any pretence whatever And that nobody may plead ignorance of this, my proclamation, I have ordered the same to be made public in England.
Given under my hand on board the *Chasseur*,
THOMAS BOYLE'

Two days before America declared war on the 18th June, Britain revoked the Orders in Council which had plagued the US for so long, and which they were now prepared to fight against. Britain conceded just about every point – except, of course, their legitimate right of impressing British subjects serving on neutral vessels – but news travelled slowly in those days, and the possibly peace-saving gestures arrived too late.

On the 13th June, only five days earlier – and almost exactly five years after her unfortunate encounter with HMS *Leopard*, the USS *Chesapeake* re-entered the story – and the fate of her four impressed/kidnapped seamen became known:

Extract from the *Boston Chronicle*. 13 July 1812.
'The American seamen who were taken from the frigate *Chesapeake*, on the 22nd June, 1807, by the British ship-of-war *Leopard*, were this day, Saturday, June 13, 1812, restored to the same ship in the harbour of Boston. They were conducted on board by Lieutenant Simpson, a ...British officer, and received at the gangway by Lieutenant Wilkinson, of the *Chesapeake*, who made the following pertinent address:

"Sir, I am commanded by Commodore Bainbridge to receive these two American seamen, on the very deck from which they were wantonly taken in time of peace, by a vessel of your nation, of superior force".

'Midshipman Saunders conducted the men to Commodore Bainbridge, on the quarter-deck – the Commodore received them with these appropriate and truly American observations: "My lads, I am glad to see you – from this deck you were taken by British outrage – for you to return to it you owe gratitude to the Government of your country. Your country now offers you an opportunity to revenge your wrongs; and I cannot doubt that you will be desirous of doing so on board this very ship. I trust that the flag which flies on board of her, shall gloriously defend you in future".

'Three cheers were given by a numerous company of citizens and seamen, assembled to witness the interesting transaction. There were four men taken out of the *Chesapeake*; one, they tell us, has since died, two they now restore, and one they hung at Halifax.'

After five years of wrangling between the governments, three of the men who had been taken forcibly from the *Chesapeake* were finally acknowledged to be American citizens – although, sadly, one of them had not survived five years as a British tar. The unlucky fourth man had been adjudged a British deserter and ended his life at the yardarm. The two seamen who were returned to the

Chesapeake were indeed lucky. After five years of suffering one form of imprisonent and exile, they missed becoming prisoners of war and further exile by only five days.

The return of the *Chesapeake*'s men was obviously a belated act of appeasement, and there was another which carried a faint chance of the war ending within a few months. It had taken forty-one days for the news of America's declaration of war to reach London; and seven weeks had passed before Madison learned of the revocation of the Orders in Council. If the telegraph had been invented – who knows the outcome?

In September, Admiral Sir John Borlase Warren, British Commander of the North American Station, proposed that both sides should suspend hostilities whilst the lately arrived news of the rescinded Orders in Council were given further consideration. Congress was told that if negotiations failed, Admiral Warren was to concentrate his actions against the southern states, but was to negotiate with the disaffected eastern states of New England. He received his reply in October, which told him that negotiations of an armistice could never take place until all impressment from American ships was abandoned.

As Admiral Warren had at that same time published a call to 'all British seamen in the United States, urging them to return to their true allegiance. Not only would they receive full pardon; they would also be privileged to fight for 'the Preservation of the Liberties, Independence, Religion, and Laws of all the remaining nations of the world, against the Tyranny and Despotism of France,' it is not surprising that the war proceeded uninterrupted.

The United States' declaration of war was a blow which at first landed squarely on the Royal Navy. Britain was fully occupied on her own side of the Atlantic; endeavouring to blockade the whole of Europe; fighting on land and afloat in many parts of the world, and providing protective escorts for her merchant marine on the high seas. Now it was suddenly faced with the loss of a great number of our serving seamen. These were the Americans, volunteers and impressed men, who had chosen not to fight against their country and were now prisoners of war – a regrettable loss of useful sailors, who overnight had become liabilities to be fed, housed and guarded

There was little naval or military strength to spare from the vital struggle against Napoleon, which could be diverted to a new war on such a distant front. At first, on paper at least, the United States seemed even less prepared, and in no position to even consider confrontation with such an immeasurably more powerful nation. In 1802, Jefferson had reduced the regular army to not much more than three thousand men and it stayed that way until the *Chesapeake/Leopard* encounter dictated a rethink. Even then the number was raised to only a possible nine thousand or so, in April 1808; and three years later only half that number had been recruited.

Towards the end of 1811, the United States had been driven to the end of their tether. The Republicans, and even some Federalists, felt that the indignities and oppressions of the British were a slight on their achievement in winning their independence as a nation. Warlike attitudes and declarations might perhaps achieve respect, redress and concessions; if not, then war itself could be the only answer.

'Besides upholding independence and preserving republican institutions, war offered the prospect of significant political

dividends. A successful war would redound to the Republicans' advantage, while retreat would have just the opposite effect.

"The honour of the Nation and that of the party," said a Philadelphia newspaper editor, "are bound up together and both will be sacrificed if war be not declared."

"If War is not resorted to," added a Tennessee congressman, "this nation or rather their representatives will be disgraced."

"The War machine [must be] put in to active motion," said another Republican, "his deed, & this deed alone can save the character of the Democratic party & the Nation."'[2]

On the 4th November, a War Congress under President Madison was assembled to decide upon the manner in which Congress 'will feel the duty of putting the United States into armor and an attitude demanded by the crisis', brought about by the 'hostile inflexibility' of Britain.

By April 1812 it was decreed that an effort be made to build up the regular army to 35,000 regulars – offering a bounty of $31 and 160 acres of land as encouragement to each new recruit – and to call for 50,000 'one year' volunteers. The President also called on the states to supply 100,000 militiamen for terms of three to six months service. A formidable force, but only if the figures on paper could be realised in fact.

The American navy of 1812, appeared no more impressive than the land forces. After the War of Independence, the navy had been scrapped, but over the intervening thirty years a small force had built up, which distinguished itself during the Quasi-War with France; and its officers and men had gained invaluable active experience in that undeclared sea war. Comprising as it now did, less than twenty ships of war, it was, on paper, an insignificant opponent to King George's Navy which, at that time numbered about 700 warships – with perhaps as many again, under repair or laid up for one reason or another. But Britain's warships were active world-wide, and the US navy, although small in number, was not insignificant in strength. They had seven frigates, three of which were a match for any of their class in the world – and this they proved from the beginning and over the following years: their names and actions remembered when the war itself was forgotten. These were the *Constitution*, the *President* and the *United States,* each rated as 44-guns, (but often carrying far more in action) and the 38-gun *Congress, Chesapeake* and *Constellation,* the seventh and smallest, the 32-gun *Essex*. The first three of those frigates were truly magnificent vessels of their kind, much heavier-built than their British counterparts, but faster and more manoeuverable in action.

The American 44s were generally as much as twenty feet longer than the normal British frigates, and although classed as 44-gun vessels they often bore thirty 24-pounders, twenty-four 42-pounder carronades,[3] and two long 18-pounders, which made them 56-gun 'superfrigates' or, as they were sometimes described, 'line-of-battle-ships in disguise'. The ship's company of a '44' was about 475 men: eighty officers and non-commissioned officers, 65 marines; 145 ordinary and 180 able-bodied seamen, and a few young boys.

With their larger crews and greater firepower; their hulls protected by timbers 20-inch thick (a crew member of the USS *Constitution* once exclaimed, 'She must be made of iron!' when he saw cannon balls bounce off her side, after which she became known as 'Old Ironsides'. With their greater speed, it is small wonder that the Admiralty ordered that British frigates should never engage them in single combat.

In the first six months of the war the Royal Navy had been shocked and not a little humiliated by the success of these unexpected ships of war The victory of the USS *Constitution* over HMS *Guerrière* in the Gulf of St Lawrence in August; the capture of the *Macedonian* by the *United States* in October; and the defeat of HMS *Java* by the *Constitution* off Brazil at the end of the year. Both the *Guerrière* and the *Java* were too badly damaged to be brought in as prizes and, after their crews had been taken off as prisoners of war, the vessels were destroyed at sea. The *Macedonian,* however, was taken into New York, the very first time that a British man-of-war had been taken as prize into an American port. It was later adopted into the United States Navy.

There is a story that an officer from the USS *United States* was sent to Washington with news of the victory, taking with him the *Macedonian*'s flag. Finding on his arrival that a ball was in progress, he did a Sir Walter Raleigh, kneeling and laying the British flag before the feet of Dolly Madison.

Such great naval occasions, and the news of successful sea-fights between smaller warships – such as the US sloop *Wasp* over the English brig *Frolic* – proved great morale-builders to the nation. That the American navy achieved so much with so little in the early part of the war, may in part be attributed to that very smallness. The British Admiralty, with its great fleets, found it difficult to consider the United States Navy, with no battleships and built round a few frigates, as a serious opposition. It took until the middle of 1813 before such misjudgement was put to rights and something of British prestige was re-established by a naval success.

On the 1st June 1813, the captain of the British frigate HMS *Shannon,* Sir Philip Bowes Vere Broke, issued a challenge to Captain James Lawrence, the captain of the USS *Chesapeake*, to meet him in single ship-to-ship combat. The details of the ensuing fight have been described in too many books, paintings and prints for them to be repeated here. The *Chesapeake* came out from Boston Harbour, flying a pennant which read *'Free Trade and Sailors' Rights'*. After a short but vicious fight, which Captain Lawrence did not survive, the American frigate was defeated, and was sailed as a British prize to Halifax.

The Americans were certainly far better at building a navy than an army. In fact, the successes of the former assuaged national pride and cancelled out much of the embarrassment caused by the failures of the latter. To begin with they had, in addition to their small but powerful frigate force, about a dozen sloops of war and other small naval craft, though not all were fit for immediate sea service; but they tried at least one very adventurous naval experiment. In the first year of the war, Congress invested what was at that time a large fortune, in the development of a new form of warship and armament which, had it been perfected at that time, may have changed the face of warfare at sea by half a century.

Robert Fulton (1765–1815) a Pennsylvanian inventor, artist and canal designer, had experimented with steam as a motive power for shipping since the last years of the previous century. He had even designed and built a primitive form of torpedo – and the *Nautilus*, a submarine! In 1797 he went to Paris and submitted designs for the latter to the French Navy, describing it as a devastating underwater weapon to use against the British. This the French dismissed rather contemptuously, their opinion being that it was 'an atrocious and dishonourable way to fight'. Nevertheless, he built it, and in 1800 it was sent out against two British warships, but failed when it could not match their speed.

In 1804 he arrived in London with higher hopes but no more success. It was tried against two French vessels, but its slowness once again let it down. Even had it succeeded it is to be doubted that a British Navy, which had good reason to think itself already master of the seas, would have given it much priority.

Robert Fulton then returned to America, where he had a good deal of success building paddle-driven river steamboats, including the *Clermont* which paddled between New York and Albany in 1807.

Five years later, in 1812 and with America on the threshold of war he was back in the warship business. Against the frantic objections of the Federalists, Congress voted $500,000 to be spent on Fulton's type of innovation. This resulted in the building of the world's first steam frigate, the *Fulton the First*, a powerful floating battery, which was launched in October 1814. In length 145 feet and with a 52 feet beam, it was massively built from timbers five feet thick – and twice that thickness round the engine-room – she was heavily armed with carronades and all manner of ordnance. Stationed in the Long Island Sound the *Fulton* achieved more by its menacing presence than it was ever called upon to prove in battle.

Meanwhile, the *Nautilus* had reappeared, and actually went into action. Perhaps more actions of the kind may have taken place had not a consideration for prisoners of war become involved. Fulton's submarine dived below the British 74-gun ship-of-the-line *Ramilles,* and the American submariners drilled through the battleship's copper sheathing to fasten a torpedo to her bottom – but the fixing-bolt sheared off and the *Ramilles* survived.

Thomas Hardy, captain of the *Ramilles* was shaken by the attack on his great ship and Sir George Cockburn and Sir John Warren – two great British admirals particularly detested by the Americans as 'inhuman butchers' and 'a disgrace to humanity' – condemned Fulton's submarine and torpedoes as 'cowardly' and 'infernal'. Captain Hardy took no risks; every two hours the hull of the *Ramilles* was swept stem to stern with chains to dislodge anything which may have been attached by stronger bolts!

Dire warnings of revenge in the event of further departures from the accepted rules of civilized warfare were loudly declared. The warnings themselves skirted on the edge of those rules, by announcing that in future the ships of the fleet would carry American prisoners of war in their holds, so that any British ship which was sent to the bottom by their infernal machines, would be carrying their countrymen with it.

America, therefore, had to return to old and tried methods. Once again privateers and letters-of-marque came into their own. The authority to build up and employ a paranaval force was contained in the President's Act of Declaration, which said:

'BE IT enacted by the Senate and House of Representatives of the United States of America in Congress assembled, That WAR be and the same is hereby declared to exist between the United Kingdoms of Great-Britain and Ireland and the dependencies thereof, and the United States of America and their territories: and that the President of the United States [James Madison] be and he is hereby authorised to use the whole land and naval force of the United States, to carry the same into effect; and to issue to private armed vessels of the United States, commissions, or letters-of-marque, and general reprisal, in such form as he shall think proper, and under the Seal of the United States, against the vessels, goods and effects of the government of the same United Kingdoms of Great-Britain and

Ireland, and the subjects thereof.
June 18, 1812.   JAMES MADISON'

The sea-war actions in America's fight for independence had been fought with a navy made up of a small number of men-of-war and a vast number of privateers and letters-of-marque. Nevertheless, there was still a feeling amongst a proportion of American landsmen – and no doubt among merchant seamen who had come up against European privateers in the past! – that there was something dishonourable and degrading about this type of warfare. This prejudice which had existed, though to a lesser degree, from as long ago as the Seven Years' War, has been discussed in an earlier chapter;[4] but reiteration may be excusable, as the employment of private armed vessels was of such importance in this war.

The anti-privateer prejudice, which was shared by many throughout the world, was most often based on ignorance of the difference between a privateer and a pirate – and it is probable that even today there are many who think the two words synonymous. The difference was great: the swashbuckling pirate, the colourful buccaneer, the reckless corsair, was in reality the jackal of the seas. Hard-bitten and tough-living, brave sometimes but often cruel and ruthless, he knew few loyalties and preyed on all and sundry; on weaker vessels of other nations – and sometimes of his own.

No doubt there were privateers who, on occasion, acted in a piratical fashion – although Captain George Coggeshall, himself a letter-of-marque commander in the 1812 war, issued a challenge for anyone to prove even one single instance of such conduct.[5] These men and their vessels were commissioned by king, emperor or president, and bound under strict licence to a code of conduct, to act only against their country's enemies. Thomas Jefferson harboured no moral doubt in the matter of privateering as part of a nation's defence or offence. In a down-to-earth and commonsense article which he published the 4th July 1812, he asked:

'…What difference to the sufferer is it that his property is taken by a national or private armed-vessel? Did our merchants who have lost nine hundred and seventeen vessels by British captures, feel any gratification that the most of them were taken by His Majesty's men-of-war? Were the spoils less rigidly exacted by a seventy-four gun ship than by a privateer of four guns; and were not all equally condemned?

'War, whether on land or sea, is constituted of acts of violence on the persons and the property of individuals: and excess of violence is the grand cause that brings about peace.

'One man fights for wages paid him by the government, or a patriotic zeal for the defence of his country, another duly authorised, and giving the proper pledges, for his good conduct, undertakes to pay himself at the expense of the foe, and serves his country as effectively as the former…In the United States, every encouragement should be given to privateering in time of war with a commercial nation.

'We have tens of thousands who without it will be destitute of the means of support and useless to their country. Our national ships are too few in number to give employment to a twentieth part of them, or retaliate the acts of the enemy. By licensing private armed vessels, the whole naval force is brought to bear on the foe, and while the contest lasts, that it may have the speedier termination, let every individual contribute his mite, in the best way he can, to distress the enemy, and compel him to peace.'

The call went out through all the states for men and money; to build up their militias and find ships suitable for arming and putting them into service. There were already a few fast clipper-ships which could be fitted out immediately, and brigs and schooners were to be found in most of the Atlantic ports, vessels which had been employed for years in the dangerous trade with France and the West Indies. These ships had depended on their speed to outrun the British cruisers and their endless 'stop and search'operations. Then there were the pilot boats attached to most of the principal harbours. Already armed, the smaller with one large centre gun, called a 'Long Tom', a few other guns, and manned with crews 'of fifty to sixty men, a suitable number of muskets, sabres and boarding pikes, etc.' The larger pilot boats had the usual Long Tom plus twenty or so other guns and crews of one hundred and fifty or more men.

Early in July, one of the smaller pilot boats had been dispatched to Gottenburg, its important mission to warn all American merchantmen in the Northern European ports that they would soon be caught up in a war, and to order them to lay up until the end of hostilities.

The 'tens of thousands' of unemployed sailors of the Jefferson article were, of course, men flung out of work by American embargoes which, once again, confined all merchant vessels to port. US frigates were sent out to search for, and escort home, merchantmen still at sea – and to keep a retaliatory look-out for enemy vessels, commercial or naval, that came their way.

The port-bound vessels were stripped down and laid up, some for the duration of the embargo; but their crews were not idle for long. Letter-of-marque and privateer commanders had the pick of seasoned seamen to make up their ships' companies – often adding large numbers of landsmen and young boys, to act as boarding-parties and prize crews.

Some English newspapers carried the boast that, in six months, there would not be a single American ship left afloat; the London *Evening Star* disparagingly describing the US navy as made up of 'a few fir-built frigates, manned by a handful of bastards and outlaws.' But one article-writer with a longer memory, recalled the showing they had made thirty-odd years before. Just eight days before the declaration of war, his newspaper carried an article, part of which read:

The London Statesman. 10th June 1812.
'It has been stated, that in a war with this country, America has nothing to gain, but much to lose. In opposition to this assertion it may be said, with equal truth, that in a war with America, England has nothing to gain but much to lose.

'Let us examine the relative situation of the countries. America cannot certainly pretend to wage a maritime war with us. She has no navy to do it with. But America has nearly 100,000 as good seamen as any in the world, all of whom would be actively employed against our trade in every part of the ocean in their fast sailing ships of war, many of which will be able to cope with our small cruizers: and they will be found to be sweeping the West Indian seas, and even carrying desolation into the chops of the Channel. Everyone must recollect what they did in the latter part of the American War [of Independence]. The books at Lloyds will recount… what their diminutive strength was able to effect in the face of our navy, and that, when nearly a hundred pennants were flying on their coasts. Besides, were they not in the English and Irish Channels, picking up our homeward bound trade, sending their prizes into French and Spanish ports, to the great terror and annoyance of our merchants and ship owners.'

He went on to say that the Americans were likely to attempt deeds which a Frenchman would never venture, and that they would have the ports of our European enemy as well as their own, to retreat to with their booty. There was also the warning that American strength would probably be added to by British prisoners of war who might enlist in the service of the enemy: 'if much is also to be apprehended from the desertion of our seamen who will be met with every encouragement in the United States, by protecting laws made in their favour, perhaps large douceurs [douceurs: sweeteners, bribes] offered for their disaffection, and it is well-known the predilection which our sailors have for the American shores.'

None of these warnings and assertions can be described as mere scaremongering. Within two months, more than one hundred private-armed ships had been fitted out, and sailed in search of merchant prizes. Almost immediately both sides began to amass prisoners of war, in the case of Britain by the thousand. For many years American seamen had served in the Royal Navy, either voluntarily or unwillingly after being adjudged 'Englishmen'. Over the years, they had taken part in naval engagements against French, Spanish Danish and Dutch ships and some had died in the British service. But now, with President Madison's declaration of war, all Americans serving in British warships were given the option either to fight on – but now against France and their own country – or become prisoners of war. Some took the 'easy' way out and became, in the eyes of their compatriots, traitors – but, as the records of the Plymouth, Portsmouth and Medway hulks, and the great depot at Dartmoor clearly show, most chose captivity.

The number of Americans who experienced at least some time as prisoners of war of the British during the War of 1812, was about 20,000 – although there was never anything like that number of Americans in Britain at any one time. Most of the Yankee captives were seamen, and of these the great majority were privateers. The number of British prisoners taken was probably not much less, but as we know, not a few were released ashore, some of whom became 'Americans' or 'signed on' to serve in the enemy's naval or merchant vessels.

Escape – and death from the many prison-induced diseases and epidemics – reduced the numbers, sometimes significantly; but reduction through the exchange system was an ideal more often dreamed of than achieved. Thousands of prisoners *were* exchanged, but the many problems involved in its administration brought endless recriminations and accusations of unfairness.

The balance of prisoners of war actually held by Britain and the United States, a serious consideration as far as exchange agreements were concerned, was weighted heavily on the British side of the scales. This was not entirely dependent on the number that each country had taken, but on what happened to them once captured. Although prisoners taken by the British were sometimes temporarily held in depots or prison ships at Halifax, Nova Scotia and many other parts of the world, they were almost always eventually shipped to Britain. The British seaman captured by a Yankee privateer, on the other hand, stood a fair chance of being exchanged at sea or released ashore in America or a neutral port.. The number of prisoners taken by a privateer often greatly exceeded the number of its crew, and thus presented difficulties of security, provisioning, and overcrowding. It was natural, therefore, that they should take no great pride in amassing captives for longer than absolutely necessary.

Earlier in the war, Britain had agreed to an exchange policy of 'release on account', whereby prisoners of war were, on occasion, released against a type of parole certificate, signed on behalf of the receiving country. This promised to settle the account by returning a similar number of prisoners by a given date. Like many another best laid scheme, this was often abused, and it was abandoned by 1813.

Congress was well aware of the desirability of building up a stock of exchangeable prisoners, and sought to solve the problem of the imbalance by creating a bounty system which, in 1813, stood at $25 for every British prisoner of war delivered into a United States port. By the beginning of the following year, when it was estimated that the number was at least 2,000 in Britain's favour, the bounty was increased fourfold to $100. This huge increase caused much debate and objection before Congress was convinced of the importance of getting 'as many prisoners of war as we could, to balance accounts with the enemy, and enable us to redeem our fellow-citizens from captivity'.

The British Government was in full agreement with Congress that American privateers should keep their prisoners on board their vessels until delivered into a US port. It was decreed that no British prisoners off-loaded into neutral vessels or neutral ports should be considered as either paroled or 'exchanged on account', but had been granted free release. This surprising concurrence was no example of understanding and consideration between the two opposing nations; it was, of course, of decided advantage to Great Britain. The longer private-armed vessels suffered the inconvenience of prisoners cluttering up their limited space, and the more often they had to return to port, the less danger they would pose to British merchant shipping – and we held more than enough Americans to 'enable us to redeem *our* fellow-citizens from captivity'.

The usual procedure when a prize was taken, was for the most valuable part of the cargo to be taken on board the privateer. The prisoners, too, were taken on board or, if the prize crew was strong and large enough, kept below decks in the captured vessel until it arrived in an American port. It is not pleasant to imagine the fate of prisoners if privateer commanders – some of whom may have taken a number of prizes in a single cruise – had carried out to the letter their orders to 'sink, burn and destroy'. The fact that great numbers of captured British merchantmen were not sunk, burnt or destroyed is evidenced by the records of the American Prize Courts ashore. Some *were* put to the torch, but only where their auction value did not justify the expense of a prize crew to take them in. Other practical considerations for keeping them afloat, was that a successful cruise often resulted in a large quantity of valuable loot beyond the capacity of the privateer alone to store – and to have allowed captives to greatly outnumber the crew would have been most unwise.

One of the earliest published 'histories' of the War of 1812 made its appearance soon after the end of hostilities in 1815. Although entitled *The History of the War between the United States of America and Great-Britain'*, it was in fact a compilation of correspondence between the two countries, public documents and reports on the various battles on land and sea. It also listed by name and sundry details of the 1607 British vessels, mainly merchant, taken by American naval and private armed ships. The number of prisoners taken from those ships is stated as 11,797.

Some of the footnotes are as interesting as the more important of the facts. One refers to the very small but very successful Salem-built American privateer *Dart,* which counted among its captures the British brig *Diana* a number of times its size, '…and came into the harbor of Portland triumphantly mounted on the deck of her prize!!!'

Many prizes taken by either side were later re-taken – and some were captured for a second time. Another footnote records an extreme case of multiple capture: The asterisk against the British 16-gun *Invincible* captured by the Yankee privateer *Young Teazer* revealed the following:

> 'This ship was originally a French privateer [the *Invincible Napoleon*] and captured by H.B.Majesty's ship *Mutine* [16 guns]; re-captured by the *Alexander* of Salem; re-re-captured by H.B.Majesty's frigate Shannon, and re-re-re-captured by the *Teazer* of New York, and sent into Portland.'

A perusal of privateer records, British, French and American, make fascinating reading. They tend to show that, whilst many captives were deprived of personal possessions in a manner which could be judged piratical, they were, in general, fairly and sometimes even generously treated.

There is at least one instance where prisoners had every reason to bless rather than curse their captors. In December 1812, the New York privateer *Holkar* was cruising in the Atlantic off the Cape Verde Islands, when she overhauled and captured the 10-gun British brig *Emu,* out of Portsmouth and bound for Botany Bay. The *Emu* was a small transportation vessel with a crew of twenty-five, which was conveying forty-nine women-convicts to serve sentences of seven, fourteen or twenty-one years in Australia. The captain of the *Holkar* put his prisoners and female convicts ashore on the well-watered island of St Vincent (one of the Cape Verdes), with enough provisions to last them four months. He then sent the *Emu,* his prize, into New York. It would be nice to know the end of this unusual prisoner of war story. There were also instances where privateer captains displayed gallantry towards the fair sex. In August 1812, a New York newspaper reported under the proud headline, 'MAGNANIMITY':

> 'Arrived at New York on the 24th instant, the schooner *Industry,* Captain Renneaux, prize to the *Benjamin Franklin,* privateer. The *Industry* is laden with pickled salmon, worth about $2,000, and was captured near the Anglo-American coast, in order to prevent her giving information to some British cruisers of the *Benjamin Franklin* being in those seas.
> The owners of the privateer, on being apprized [*sic*] that the *Industry* belonged to a poor widow who had a family, promptly directed her [the ship and its cargo] to be restored.'

Another lady, Mrs Elizabeth Bell, of Nova Scotia, was a passenger on the schooner *Ann Kelly* when it was taken by the privateer *Dolphin,* and sent into Salem. Mrs Bell later sent a letter in which she 'begs leave to acknowledge, with much gratitude, the gentlemanly and humane treatment by the Captain and Prize-master of the *Dolphin,* in returning her $900, together with all her personal effects, etc.'

The prisoner of war in North America, whether Yankee or Britisher, had more to fear than mere imprisonment, unpleasant though that could be. There was always the possibility of ending up in the hands of the Red Indian allies of either nation – and the American prisoner stood in double jeopardy. It would seem that, as far as Britain was concerned, the 'rebels' had never been completely forgiven their sin of revolution. This was particularly so of those who claimed citizenship through naturalisation after the War of Independence, or had adopted America as their chosen place to live, without taking out naturalisation papers. Not that such papers would have vindicated the holder in the eyes of his mother country. Not until much later in the nineteenth century could a British leopard change his spots. According to the Common Law of England, if you were born a British subject, you died a British subject, without exception. Such an obdurate policy regarding nationality was against all the interests and ambitions of a new nation in need of new citizens, and was one of the many edicts worth fighting against.

The inflexibility of Britain's interpretation of its nationality laws was made plain early on in the War of 1812. Once it was realised that war was inevitable, there were reckless, over-confident Americans – carbon copies of the arrogance of those English who had described the US Navy as 'a few fir-built frigates, manned by a handful of bastards and outlaws.' Equally dismissive of British land forces, they contended that 'one American could whip five Britishers'. One 'war hawk' frontiersman from South Carolina, Senator John C Calhoun, announced to the House: 'I believe that in four weeks from the time a declaration of war is heard on our frontier, the whole of upper Canada and a part of lower Canada will be in our power'.

The first attempt to put this boast to the test failed miserably and caused a prisoner of war and 'nationality' row between Britain and the US which lasted to the very end of the war.

In October 1812, a 6,000-strong force of American troops and militia set out to oppose an army of 2,000 trained British soldiers and Indians, on the Canadian side of the Niagara River. The aim was to take Queenston Heights and then attack Fort George, some five miles northward. Though an apparent vastly superior force, its weakness lay in the inexperience and the lack of training of its men, as much as the stubborn singlemindedness of its senior officers. The American Army had no General Staff: generals were appointed by the War Ministry, then went their own way; which is precisely what happened on this occasion. The command at Niagara was shared by two generals – the Commander-in-Chief, General Stephen van Rensselaer, a militia officer, and General Alexander Smyth, a haughty army officer who, as a regular soldier, refused to take orders from a militiaman.

The Battle of Queenston was fought on the 13th October, 1812. A thousand or more Americans managed to cross the Niagara and succeeded in gaining the Heights where they drove off the British defenders, whose commander, General Brock, was killed in a gallant but futile attempt to retake the position. British reinforcements were on their way from Fort George and it was imperative that more men crossed the river to back up the American troops, who were now under the command of a young Lieutenant-Colonel, Winfield Scott.

Even without Smyth and his troops, Van Rensselaer commanded a great horde of New York militiamen still on the American side of the river and he ordered this force to cross over to Scott's assistance. They had a clear view of their countrymen, now gamely fighting a losing battle – which their aid might well have turned into a victory – but, probably daunted by the sight of the dead and wounded being brought back across the river, they refused point blank to pass over into Canada. Inevitably, Colonel Winfield Scott had eventually to surrender and was taken prisoner, along with about 950 of his brave American fighters.

It was the rough handling of just twenty-three of those American prisoners of war which brought about the long-drawn-out 'nationality' argument, and which created a furore on both sides of the Atlantic. Most of the twenty-three were Irish settlers, born in the British Isles, some of whom were already naturalised American citizens according to the laws of their adopted country. Now they learned that they were not to be treated just as prisoners of war, but as British subjects captured whilst serving on the side of the enemy. Segregated from their fellow prisoners and clapped in irons, they were shipped to England as traitors, there to face charges of treason, in that they had taken up arms against their Sovereign, King George III.

With a probable sentence of death hanging over their heads, the Irish-British/Americans entered an appeal, some pleading that they were naturalised citizens under a US Federal statute of 1790 and had wives and families resident in America. This would have had little effect, as Lord Bathurst, Minister of State for the Colonies, stated that as self-confessed British subjects by birth, 'they should be disposed of according to the pleasure of His Royal Highness the Prince Regent'[6] – but they were lucky in having a champion in their ex-commander. After his capture at Queenston, Lt-Colonel Wingfield Scott was paroled back to the United States, and sped to the Secretary of War in Washington with news of their predicament.

So began a game of international bluff-poker, played with prisoners of war as the chips, the stakes getting higher as the months and years of contention passed by. In May 1813, the US Secretary of War opened up the bidding, by instructing General Dearborn, the American commander on the Canadian frontier 'to put into close confinement twenty-three British soldiers, to be kept as hostages, for the safe keeping and restoration' of the twenty-three held in England.

Lord Bathurst immediately increased the stakes, by directing the British Commander-in-Chief in Canada, Sir George Prevost, 'forthwith to put in close confinement forty-six American officers and non-commissioned officers, to be held as hostages for the safe keeping of the twenty-three British soldiers,' adding 'that if any of the said British soldiers shall suffer death [in the event of the 'Americans' being found guilty of treason and executed], as many as may double the number of British soldiers who shall have been unwarrantably put to death, and cause such officers and non-commissioned officers to suffer death immediately.'

From this point on, the stakes went wild, neither side knowing who was bluffing or who held the best hand. Violently worded communications flashing to and fro between General Mason and Colonel Barclay, the resident commissioners for American and British prisoners of war respectively, each accusing the other of injustice and inhuman treatment of their charges. In an attempt to intimidate, the American Government was told that in the case of any retaliatory reaction to the treatment of renegade British subjects, 'His Majesty's armies and fleets on the coasts of America have received instructions to prosecute the war with unmitigated severity against all cities, towns, and villages belonging to the United States, and against the inhabitants thereof.'

At this point President Madison took a personal hand in the game, making it known that 'the United States could not be deterred by any considerations of life or death, depredation or conflagration, from the faithful discharge of its duty to the American nation'. General Mason was ordered to confine as hostages all British officer-prisoners of every rank in the states of Massachusetts, Kentucky and Ohio, to be held as insurance against British threats to 'exercise a severity unknown to civilized warfare, and outraging humanity.'

Things got worse. On the 24th June, 1813, a band of Indians led by a French captain, ambushed the American 14th Regiment at Beaver Dam. The Americans, fearful of their fate if they were taken by the Indians, surrendered to British reinforcements which arrived on the scene in the nick of time. Fifty-nine of the prisoners were declared to be British subjects, and followed the Irishmen to England to face trial for treason. America responded, of course, by segregating and locking up fifty-nine from among the 600 prisoners of war taken at the Battle of the Thames, near Detroit. By now the number of British officers and other-rank hostages held in close imprisonment by the Americans had grown to 128.

By the beginning of 1814, there was a break in the shuffling of unoffending captives from the status of prisoner of war to the deadly category of hostage. It was becoming essential that an answer be found to senseless tit-for-tat retaliation and threats. If one side had carried out the threat to kill even one hostage, retaliation may have set the whole system of exchange and the humane handling of prisoners of war, back a hundred years.

The man chosen to explore the possibilities was himself a hostage: the American Brigadier-General, William H Winder. Captured at the Battle of Stoney Creek in June 1813, Winder was lodged in close confinement at Beauport, near Quebec, but was granted a sixty-day parole from Canada to the United States, on the recommendation of Sir George Prevost, who he had convinced of his confidence to settle the dispute.

He arrived in Washington at the end of January 1814, where he laid his arguments, theories and suggestions before the Madison administration, but he returned to Quebec and imprisonment on the 22nd March 1814, a disappointed man, convinced that his mission had failed. However, the American administration had second thoughts, and President Madison authorised General Winder to arrange a convention with the British to investigate the matter of exchange.

The dangerous game was nearly over; the arrogant bluff of each nation was called, and the now-large kitty was evenly split between the two. Winder himself was exchanged and continued with the good work. By the middle of July all the 'retaliation hostages', British and American had been exchanged – except for the original twenty-three sent to England for trial in 1812 after the Battle of Queenston – and, as one might guess, the first twenty-three British prisoners held in America as their security.

The 'Queenston Twenty-three' remained in England, still untried, until the war ended. After the Treaty of Ghent, they were 'repatriated' to America, which indicated a great advance towards tolerance in the matter of nationality and naturalisation!

Only twenty-one of the ex-prisoners arrived in the cartel which brought them to New York on the 9th July 1815 – the other two having died from natural causes during the more than two and a half years of worrying incarceration. There they were met by Winfield Scott, now a general and the man whose initial efforts on their behalf probably saved their lives – for a number of British-Americans did end their lives on a scaffold or a yardarm during the war of 1812.

Many other Britons living in America over the war years who, though not serving in the US forces on land or sea against Britain, still came, strictly speaking, under the common law of England – the men always subject to the impressment laws, even in peacetime. Though safe from Britain's clutches, these people who probably thought of themselves as American through-and-through until the outbreak, now found that they were 'enemy aliens' under a United States law! Ten thousand or more British subjects lived, worked and settled as residents in towns and villages on the eastern seaboard, mainly around New York, but had never got round to changing their citizenship.

There was a good deal of confusion over their classification which gained them much sympathy from their American neighbours. But the law was the law, and though it seems that some 'carried on as usual' under friendly protection, many were sent to places at least forty miles inland from the coast. There they lived under a 'parole of honour', which allowed them to travel not more than five miles from their lodging.

These 'enemy aliens' were treated with consideration and compassion under the administration of James Mason, the Agent for British Prisoners of War in America. Although they did suffer a type of internment or open imprisonment for a couple of years or more, their predicament cannot be compared to that of the British *détenus*, confined by Napoleon in the fortress town of Verdun in 1803, under its corrupt governor, General Wirion. Some of those unfairly-taken civilian prisoners of war of the French spent as long as a decade within the walls of Verdun.

Despite the warlike confidence of the Americans during the run up to war, which led them to believe that their frontiers would soon be extended into British North America, it soon became apparent that there was far more likelihood of the contrary taking place. The poor showing at the Battle of Queenston was not atypical of the conduct of many militia regiments, some of whom were reluctant to cross the border from America into Canada. Desertion was commonplace; one large force deserting *en masse* although the enemy was still more than a hundred miles away. The one and only American victory on Canadian soil during the whole of the war, was the Battle of the Thames, in 1813 – whilst the British and Canadian armies achieved success after success from the very beginning, taking Detroit, Mackinac and Fort Dearborn, where modern Chicago now stands, in the first few months.

The story of Fort Dearborn is one of Indian treachery and barbarity. The Fort itself was garrisoned by a small force comprising three officers, a surgeon and fifty-four regular army soldiers under Captain Nathan Heald and some civilian families. In April they had trouble with pro-British Indians of the Potawatami tribe, who attacked buildings beyond the walls of the fort; but were quickly driven off by cannon-fire. Four months later, Heald received a dispatch from General William Hull, informing him that the small American outpost on Mackinac Island, between Lake Michigan and Lake Huron, had surrendered to the British, and directing that the garrison should abandon Fort Dearborn forthwith. General Hull's reasoning was that the loss of Mackinac had 'opened the Northern hive of Indians, and they were swarming down in every direction'.

The Potawaramis were still in the area, but Nathan Heald had been joined by Captain William Wells from Indiana who was reputed to have great influence with the tribe. With six-months supply of provisions to bargain with, they thought they had bought the Potawaramis over to their side, and 500 Indians agreed to escort and protect them when they evacuated the fort. True to his word, Heald handed over the goods, but, to the great fury of the Indians, he emptied the gunpowder and whisky barrels into the river, an understandable but in this case fatal move.

On the 16th August, 1812, the small column of American military men and a few civilians including children and three or four women, left the fort, but got no further than the nearby sand-hills, before their 'escort' opened fire. Heald and his regulars put up a fight, but finally agreed to surrender under a promise of clemency. To the Indian 'clemency' towards their prisoners was synonymous with carnage. Two officers and twenty-six soldiers, all twelve civilian men and twelve children were slaughtered (and the British were later accused of paying for their scalps!). A sickening postscript to this massacre. tells that 'certain warriors who had admired Wells's manliness, chopped off his head, cut out his heart, and ate it…'[7]

There is little doubt that the British would have invaded and been equally successful in the Northern States of America, had not President Madison who, on hearing of the failure at Lake Erie, ordered that all efforts should be concentrated on the building of ships on the Great Lakes. This decision made possible the great American naval victories on lakes Erie and Champlain, which halted an invasion on New York.

The British objective of occupying northeastern Maine, which 'at present interrupts the communication between Halifax and Quebec,' was achieved in the summer of 1814, when the garrison at Fort Sullivan, blew up the fort and surrendered. The inhabitants of eastern Maine were given the option of swearing an oath of allegiance to the British Crown, or leaving the occupied territory. Most accepted and enjoyed the welcomed additional business which the enemy's presence brought them until the end of the war.

At about that same time, British attention was once again focused on the Chesapeake. In 1813, Admiral Sir George Cockburn had earned the undying hatred of all Americans by his invasion of the Chesapeake. It is possible that he gloried in his evil reputation, for his mission was to convince the American people of the futility of waging war against Britain. This he demonstrated by capturing and destroying their shipping and dockyards in the Bay, and plundering and burning towns on its shoreline.

Whilst so doing, he got to know the geography and hydrography of the Chesapeake as well as any local pilot or scout. Now, in 1814, he was back in those waters. General Robert Ross and Admiral Cochrane were also intent on the Chesapeake, as a diversion and relief to the British defences in Canada, and as cover-up of a possible invasion of upper New York.

It is difficult to understand why the United States government had never given greater priority to the defence of the Chesapeake. Its extensive open coastline was vulnerable at so many points – the most obvious being two of the United States largest cities – Washington and Baltimore. They seemed to have learned little from the depredations of the previous year. There were some regulars and uncoordinated bodies of militia in the areas, and the principal sea defence was a flotilla of twenty-six gunboats, manned by a force of 900 sailors and marines. This flotilla was under the command of Commodore Joshua Barney, a veteran and hero of the War of Independence.[8]

Joshua Barney had been a renowned privateer captain during the Revolution, until his capture by HMS *Intrepid* in December 1780.

With seventy other 'rebel' prisoners of war, all American officers, Barney suffered the fifty-three day voyage from New York to Plymouth, in the hold of the 74-gun *Yarmouth*. On arrival he was first sent to a Plymouth hulk, then to Millbay Prison, from which he later made a thrilling escape to France.

By 1812, Barney had already been fighting Britain for longer than most of his countrymen After the outbreak of the Revolutionary War between Britain and France in 1792, he served as a commodore in the French Navy, carrying out many successful privateering attacks on British merchant shipping – and, as a 'French' officer of a French privateer, and sailing under French orders and decrees, probably more than a few American merchantmen were included among his prizes! In this latest war, he had already achieved fresh fame as a privateer, capturing eight prizes worth a total of more than £1,500,000 in ships and booty. His new assignment, though no less exciting was certainly less profitable.

In April 1814, he was cruising with some of his gunboats in the Bay – others were in Baltimore Harbour – when he met up with a superior British force, which comprised a 74-gun ship-of-the-line, seven gunboats and two schooners. Barney's flotilla escaped up the Patuxent River where it was bottled up for the next four months. Despite minor skirmishes with British vessels which ventured upriver as far as they could, and Barney's valiant efforts to get back into the Bay, as far as sea forces were concerned, the Chesapeake was just about defenceless.

To cover the British attack on America's capital city and the burning of the White House, I resort to a skeletal précis of a number of long and detailed descriptions of those events. By August there were two admirals, Cochrane and Cockburn, and General Ross, in the Chesapeake with a fleet of some twenty ships, transport vessels and auxiliaries.

On the 19th August, about 4,500 British troops, many of them veterans of the Peninsular Wars, were landed at Benedict, in Maryland, and a few days later met up with Admiral Cockburn at Upper Marlboro, roughly sixteen miles from Washington. From there they headed for Bladensburg, where they might cross the Potomac River, and march on Washington from the northeast. It would seem that at this point, the Commander-in-Chief, Admiral Cochrane, who was overseeing the operation from his ship in the Bay, may have lost a little of his nerve. On the 24th, General Ross received a message from the flagship, ordering him to retreat; an order which Cockburn and Ross chose to ignore, as they considered they had already passed the point of no return.

A good two years too late, the vulnerability of Washington caused the American authorities to belatedly spring into life. A number of bridges were destroyed, militia called out and added to by every untrained civilian who could carry a gun – and Commodore Barney was ordered to destroy his trapped gunboat flotilla to prevent its falling into enemy hands. On the same day that Ross received the order to retreat, seven thousand or so Americans gathered at Bladensburg, a suburb of Washington. President Madison, with some of his officials, arrived to offer unnecessary advice to his troops, and withdrew only just in time before the British army arrived on the opposite bank of the Potomac.

The American troops were deployed in three badly organised lines of untried country men and boys, only the third, and rear, line proving to be effective as a fighting force. The British troops had heard the explosions as the American gunboats were scuttled, and now Joshua Barney had strengthened that third line of militia with five or six hundred of his now shipless sailors and marines.

The defenders had neglected to destroy the one vital bridge over the Potomac, and by early afternoon the British brigades began to cross over. Outflanking the first American line, the British attacked the second, firing not only muskets, but directing rockets straight at the mass of largely inexperienced militiamen. Within a few minutes, the Yankee commander ordered withdrawal, and 'the countryside militia fled in a senseless panic, every man racing against his comrades on the Road to Washington.'[9] It is probable that all of these fugitives would have been killed or become prisoners of war, if Commodore Barney's small force had not stood firm, and covered their flight towards the capital. The British onslaught was temporarily halted by grapeshot from the naval guns which Barney had landed before destroying his gunboats, and was defiant until his ammunition ran out. The Commodore was himself badly wounded and, for the second time in thirty-four years, became a prisoner of war of the British. For many years after, the ignominious flight was remembered on both sides of the Atlantic – with either blush or sneer – as the 'Bladensburg Races'.

By the time the British marched into Washington, over roads strewn with discarded uniforms, baggage, guns and other equipment, most of the inhabitants, military and government officials included, had left the city. Madison had gone to Virginia and Dolly Madison, who left separately, first did a magnificent job by organising the rescue of the Cabinet papers and official treasures. It is said that although she left her personal possessions behind, she escaped with the residential silver spoons in a sack! When Admiral Cockburn and his officers entered the presidential, residence, then known as the 'Palace', at about 8 o'clock in the evening of the day of the battle, they found Madison's dinner cooked and ready to serve, so he and his party sat down to wine and dine.

The decision to burn Washington was not sudden and unplanned. Sometime in July, Admiral Cockburn had received a report from one of his officers, Captain Joseph Nourse, which stated that the Americans seemed so unprepared that, 'I do believe… it would require little force to burn Washington, and I hope soon to put the first torch to it myself.' And that is roughly what happened. Most public buildings went up in flames, including the 'Palace' and the Capitol; but it is something to the credit of the victors that private buildings were not included in that massive act of arson.

A sudden rainstorm saved the 'Palace' from complete ruin, though only the walls were left standing: 'cracked, defaced, blackened with the smoke of fire'. After the war it was restored and its smoke-blackened walls were painted white, which gave it the name we know it by today – 'The White House'.

Philip Freneau (1752–1832), the 'Poet of the Revolution', who had been a prisoner of war on British prison hulks in New York Harbour in 1780 – hence his long and bitter poem, *'The British Prison Ship'* – penned these lines in August 1814, whilst Washington was still smouldering:

> *'The veteran host, by veterans led,*
> *With Ross and Cockburn at their head –*
> *They came – they saw – they burnt and fled.*
>
> *They left our congress naked walls –*

Farewell to towers and capitols!
To lofty roofs and splendid halls!
To courtly domes and glittering things,
To folly, that too near us clings
To courtiers who – 'tis well – had wings

Farewell to all but glorious war,
Which yet shall guard Potomac's shore,
And honor lost, and fame restore.'

A month or more before the attack on Washington, the pros and cons of making Baltimore the next target had been discussed. The prospect of attacking Baltimore from the sea with ships-of-the-line was impracticable as ships drawing more than eight or ten feet of water would have had to stand at least five miles offshore from the town. To attack by land also had its drawbacks, as Admiral Cochrane considered it most unwise unless fairly large vessels could lay close in, to cover a possible retreat. Nevertheless, if Baltimore was to be attacked, it had to be one way or the other. Finally, Cochrane decided that an approach by water should be tried. This was probably due to the fact that, whilst he had an urgent desire to get his fleet out of the Chesapeake before too many of his seamen succumbed to yellow fever or malaria, seasonal storms confined them to the Bay. So if he had to remain, plans should be made to invade the city of Baltimore.

Baltimore was as strongly Republican and pro-war as New England was generally Federalist and against it. With its 40,000 population it was a large city by early American standards, with a Vigilance and Safety Committee which soon called up a strong defence force. The Committee drafted, armed and accoutred, every white man between the ages of sixteen to fifty into a home guard; and trenches were dug, palisades built and earthworks thrown up.

On the 12th September 1814, the British troops, under General Ross, the British commander, disembarked from their transports at North Point, about fifteen miles from the city. That morning they set off towards Baltimore with two howitzers and six cannon. After a march of about seven miles they came up with a force of some 3,000 Americans under General Stricker of the Baltimore Militia, most of them concealed behind a high palisade, their flanks protected by marshland on either side. General Ross urged his horse forward to assess the situation and had returned to lead an assault on the enemy, when a young American sharpshooter drew a bead on the General and shot him dead. Thereafter, no American sniper taken prisoner of war was ever shown quarter, but sentenced to death.

It was still only 10 a.m. on that first day, when Colonel Arthur Brooke, who replaced the lamented Ross, opened up with artillery fire, to which the Americans answered with their cannon. Although driven back a number of times to prepared positions, the Americans finally stood their ground and by early afternoon the two sides could only count their considerable losses rather than decide who had won. It was generally acknowledged that the city could not be conquered unless Fort Mc Henry, situated a couple of miles nearer the coast, had first been destroyed. The Fort was just within range of Admiral Cochrane's big guns, and at dawn on the 13th September five of his rocket-and-bomb ships opened up, and the Bombardment of Baltimore had begun.

The fort was garrisoned by about 1,000 men, under Major George Armstrong, who also commanded a shore battery and a small flotilla of gunboats, but Fort Mc Henry's cannon could not reach the attacking ships. It has been estimated that about 1,500 shells of one sort or another had been blasted at the fort, about a third of which scored hits on parts of the fortifications. The rest burst above the fort, the screeching Congreve rockets striking fear into the hearts of the defenders. Armstrong wisely kept his lookouts keenly on the alert throughout the bombardment. When Admiral Cochrane sent shallow-draft vessels closer in, and barges with landing parties amounting to twelve-hundred British sailors, both attacks were repulsed by a terrific barrage from the American fort, land batteries and gunboats.

During the bombardment from the sea, Colonel Brooke made another attempt on the road from North Point, but finding the Americans were now strongly ensconced behind a massive earthworks, and believing that he was facing at least 15,000 defenders armed with at least a hundred guns, he retreated after darkness had fallen. Over the next few days the flotillas began to leave the area. Cochrane left for Halifax and the main part of the fleet sailed for Jamaica – the Chesapeake campaign had ended.

After it was all over, the population of Baltimore heaved a deep sigh of surprised relief; then added to its general jubilation and heaping of praise on its defenders, by giving vent to its Anglophobia. Newspapers, pamphlets and broadsheets rushed out accounts which exaggerated both the achievements of its militia and the evils of the enemy. Hezekiah Niles, publisher of the *Niles Register* was particularly laudatory on the one hand and vehement on the other; dedicating one issue to militiamen who had lost their lives…'whose gallant hearts shielded the virgin from pollution, and the matron from insult; who preserved this city from plunder and conflagration and all the murdering business of war waged by a new race of Goths…'

He also spitefully recommended that a monument be set up on the spot where General Ross fell to the sniper's bullet: suggesting a long inscription, part of which read: '…the Leader of a Host of Barbarians who… devoted the Populous City of Baltimore to rape, robbery, and conflagration.' When Hezekiah Niles was aroused he could be far more irascible than this, but these two extracts should suffice.

Although many are unaware of it, every modern American is given a frequent reminder of the Bombardment of Baltimore. This fact comes about through a mission involving an American prisoner of war which, had it not occurred, the American national anthem would certainly have been different to the one we hear today.

Francis Scott Key, a Georgetown lawyer and officer in a volunteer artillery battery, had been sent on board the cartel ship, *Minden*, which was lying off Baltimore, to parley with Admiral Cochrane over the release of a certain prisoner of war. He was successful in his mission, but the British kept him on board until after the shelling had ceased. Key spent the night walking the deck of the British ship, observing with fascinated horror the bombardment of his countrymen ashore. Next morning, as the sky lightened, he could see the Stars and Stripes still proudly flying above the battered Fort Mc Henry and, thus inspired, he wrote his one and only, but immediately popular, poem, which recorded all that he had seen.

'*Oh, say can you see by dawn's early light…*; places one's imagination beside him on the deck of the *Minden* on that terrible night; '*And the rockets' red glare, the bombs bursting in air*' describes the British Congreve rockets and the mortar shells which shattered the darkness over the American fort.

The Star Spangled Banner'[10] was later put to music, set to the tune of an old English drinking song called *'To Anacreon in Heaven'*[11] and one hundred and seventeen years later, in 1931, it was to become the national anthem of the United States by Act of Congress. Many variations on Francis Key's original four-verse song were published, but the official version was prepared for the United States forces by the American composer John Philip Sousa. The second and third stanzas are usually omitted in the interests of peace!

'THE STAR SPANGLED BANNER

Oh, say can you see, by the dawn's early light
What so proudly we hail'd at the twilights last gleaming
Whose broad stripes and bright stars through the perilous fight
O'er the ramparts we watch'd were so gallantly streaming?
And the rockets' red glare, the bombs bursting in air,

Gave proof through the night that our flag was still there
Oh, say does that star-spangled banner yet wave
O'er the land of the free and the home of the brave?

On the shore dimly seen through the mists of the deep,
Where the foe's haughty host in dread silence reposes.
What is that which the breeze, o'er the towering steep,
As it fitfully blows, half conceals, half discloses?
Now it catches the gleam of the morning's first beam,
In full glory reflected now shines in the stream.
'Tis the star-spangled banner, oh, long may it wave
O'er the land of the free and the home of the brave!

And where is that band who so vauntingly swore
That the havoc of war and the battle's confusion
A home and a country should leave us no more?
Their blood has wash'd out their foul footstep's pollution.
No refuge could save the hireling and slave
From the terror of flight or the gloom of the grave,

And the star-spangled banner in triumph doth wave
O'er the land of the free and the home of the brave.

Oh, thus be it ever when freemen shall stand
Between their lov'd home and the war's desolation
Blest with vict'ry and peace may the heav'n-rescued land
Praise the power that hath made and preserv'd us a nation!
Then conquer we must, when our cause it is just,
And this be our motto "In God is our Trust"
And the star-spangled banner in triumph shall wave
O'er the land of the free and the home of the brave.'

Whilst Washington was being put to the torch and Baltimore was being bombarded, peace negotiations were already making their slow progress in Ghent, Belgium; and by the time the peace treaty reached America on the 14th February 1815, another memorable battle had been fought.

It may be remembered that after Baltimore, Admiral Cochrane's fleet had sailed to Jamaica. There it took on board several thousand troops, made available now that the war in Europe had ended and Napoleon was cooped up, safely it was supposed, in Elba. Most of the troops were battle-trained veterans who, under the leadership of General Edward Packenham, were destined to make an attack on Louisiana.

The Battle of New Orleans produced a new national hero, General Andrew Jackson, and an incredible victory which brightened the gloom of America's war. A fleet of about fifty British warships sailed to the Gulf of Mexico to prepare for attack on the Mississippi city, landing some 7,500 troops. Numerically, there was little difference between the attacking and defending forces; but Packenham's men were experienced regulars, whilst the American militiamen were mainly Tennessee and Kentucky backwoodsmen. Andrew Jackson was all too aware that, although most of his men were sharpshooters, and 'could hit a bear at 150 yards', they would not stay to face up to a bayonet charge, and though courageous, could never see the sense of facing a frontal attack without diving for cover. Jackson, himself a frontiersman, knew his men well, so when the British attacked, on the 8th January 1815, they found themselves facing breastworks and barricades made of cotton bales and scarcely a target in sight. Nevertheless, Packenham led his men forward into a deadly fusillade of musket fire which laid low his front line, only to re-muster his men and advance again. The British casualties numbered at least two thousand, including 289 killed including General Packenham. The Americans lost thirty-one killed and forty wounded.

The Battle of New Orleans was fought after the War of 1812 had officially ended. The news of Andrew Jackson's great victory arrived in Washington at almost the same time as the documents of the Treaty of Ghent, which confirmed that hostilities had ended on the 24th December 1814. Had Britain won the Battle of New Orleans, we could in theory have laid claim to it, as the ratification took some time to complete; but even if so, it would no doubt have been returned, like eastern Maine, through postwar negotiation.

1. W.E.Woodward: *A New American History.* Faber & Faber, 1938.

2. D.R. Hickey. *The War of 1812*, page 27.

3. Carronade: A short mortar-like armament firing heavy shot. Usually naval.

4. See Part I, Chapter 1 – THE SEVEN YEARS' WAR.

5. George Coggershall: *A History of American Privateers and Letters-of-Marque*, 1861.

6. Most of the quotes in this summary of the Queenston retaliation row are from the *American State Papers*, used by Ralph Robinson for an article in *American Hist. Review Quarterly Vol. XLIX.*

7. John K. Mahon: *The War of 1812.* D.R. Hickey: *The War of 1812.*

8. *The Memoirs of Commodore Barney.* Edited by Mrs Barney. Boston 1832.

9. John K. Mahon: *The War of 1812.* D.R. Hickey: *The War of 1812.* W.E. Woodward: *A New American History*

10. Francis Key's poem was originally called *Defence of Fort Mc Henry* but was changed to its present form when published as sheet music in 1814.

11. Anacreon *c.* 570 BC. Greek lyric poet who wrote chiefly on the subject of Wine and Love.

Chapter Four

The Last Invasion of Britain
Fishguard 22nd February 1797

THAT 1066 WAS NOT THE LAST TIME that Britain was invaded, is a fact almost completely forgotten after the passage of two hundred years. Its effect at the time, on both public and prisoner of war, is touched upon in a number of sections of this book. It brought about the Government's 'Restriction of Cash Payments' Order, which in turn caused the Bank of England to renege on its 'Promise to Pay', and the introduction of the One Pound Note for the very first time, which led to widespread forgery, and the resultant horrid sight of men and women hanging from the gibbet outside Newgate Prison. It caused panic throughout the land, and inspired a joyous spirit of insurrection and revolt among the many thousands of prisoners of war in hulk, depot or on parole in Britain at that time. This in turn necessitated the tightening of the screws of security, and the temporary suspension of that most

admirable prisoner of war privilege, the parole system. Of importance, too, in the present context, is the fact that it is an absorbing story of enemy captives taken prisoner on British soil and of adventurous escapes, embellished with touches of humour and romance.

To tell the story of 'The Last Invasion of Britain', we must first meet Colonel William Tate, a remarkable pro-French American, whose hatred of the British was so intense that it led him into an almost unbelievable adventure during the French Revolutionary War. That adventure resulted in his being remembered as a mixture

Above. The surrender of the French troops on Goodwick Sands on 24th February 1797.

From the painting by an unknown artist, in the Carmarthenshire Museum.

of hero and, to many British minds, an Irish-American renegade; but in many versions of the tale he emerges as something of a gullible laughing-stock.

Tate, a native of South Carolina, had already experienced some years of adventurous soldiering before his reputation as a military man of action spread to Europe – and gained him the rank of Colonel in the French Army. He had served as a Captain-Lieutenant throughout the War of American Independence, with a short break as a prisoner of war, captured by the British at Charleston and then exchanged; had been noticed with approval by George Washington himself – and with disapproval by a military court for unfortunate entries in the Company Account books! Already pro-French, he was later involved in expeditions against the Spanish in Louisiana and was given a roving commission to arrange Franco-Indian alliances with the Cherokee and other Indian tribes. One rather unusual gift within his power as enlisting officer of Indians in America, was that he could bestow military commissions up to the rank of captain in the French Army on collaborating Indian chiefs. Incidentally, it was said that the intensity of his life-long Anglophobia was made even greater by the fact that his parents had been killed by pro-British Indians.

The great adventure which brought him notoriety, if not fame, took place in February 1797; and earned him a now-almost-forgotten place in history as the man who, as *Chef de Brigade* of a small French army – the *Légion Noire* – led some 1,400 men in a raid on the port of Fishguard on the north Pembrokeshire coast, which became known as 'The Last Invasion of Britain'.

With Britain standing more or less alone, Spain and Holland having gone over to the enemy, and Austria about to make a separate peace; with the French Fleet refitting at Brest and our own Royal Navy in a mood of mutinous activity at Spithead and the Nore; and with rumours of a French invasion of Britain becoming more and more believable, British spirit was at a low ebb. A year before, in 1796, the Republican General Lazare Hoche, had led a large naval force and fifteen thousand troops bound for Bantry Bay, encouraged by the Society of United Irishmen who had called on France to release Ireland from British dominance: 'To subvert the tyranny of our execrable Government, to break the connection with England, the never-failing source of our political evils...'[1] This Franco-Irish dream was subverted, however, not by our naval superiority, but by the power of the storms which split up the French fleet of seventeen ships of the line with attendant frigates and support vessels and drove them back to Brest. Nevertheless, both the Government and the British public had every good reason to be on the alert and prepared for the worst; and when reports came in that a French force had landed at Fishguard, apprehension turned to panic, particularly among the more affluent members of Welsh society, many of whom headed inland with their goods and livestock. The first report of suspected enemy activity in the area was sent post-haste to the Home Secretary by an official of the Swansea Custom House, who had been advised by the Master of a sloop that suspicious-looking vessels had been observed about six miles north of Lundy Island. The Admiralty and Plymouth were also informed.

It is not hard to imagine the alarm, confusion and consternation ashore. What had been most feared was about to happen. Messengers were dispatched for military assistance, beacons were fired on the hilltops and those countrymen who did not make a dash inland, gallantly armed themselves with whatever weapon came to hand, from flint-lock to pitchfork. When the inhabitants of nearby St Davids heard of the French presence at Fishguard, they formed themselves into a home-guard force and demanded the keys to the cathedral, as they needed the lead from the roof to cast into bullets. After overcoming the objection that this would be a sacrilegious act as the lead was considered consecrated, it was divided among six blacksmiths who were kept busy converting it into ball shot. The bullets and all available powder in the district were distributed 'amongst those who bore fire-arms:- and thus accoutred, they proceeded *en masse,* clergy and laity, to meet the common enemy, at Pencaer...' Similar spontaneous forces were mustered from gutsy residents and sailors in a number of other small towns along the coast.

Later on that first day, a force of some fourteen-hundred men – and four women – were disembarked in sixteen boats from the French ships. As thousands of Welsh countrypeople watched from the cliffs and hill-tops, the intruders landed at Carreg Wastad Point, above Fishguard, bringing with them casks of ammunition and ball cartridges – together with hogsheads of brandy and two days' rations. Never before did such a ragtag and bobtail invading party hit an enemy shore. There were some six hundred well-trained and tested military men with a few Irishmen among them, but the vast majority of the other eight hundred were galley-slaves and convicted criminals – 'the most abandoned rogues' who had been cleared from the French jails and prisons; a ne'er-do-well brigade which France was only too pleased to dump upon British soil. Earlier, Tone himself had said: 'Saw the *Légion Noire* reviewed; about 1,800 men. They are the banditti intended for England and sad blackguards they are. They put me strongly in mind of the Green-boys of Dublin'.

After the French squadron, under Commodore Jean Castagnier, had off-loaded Tate's ruffian army, it lay off Fishguard for no longer than was necessary to see the last man ashore, before sailing back to France.

Finding their landings unopposed, the invaders began to settle in, commandeering local inns, houses and farm buildings, whilst Tate and his officers set up a headquarters at Trehowel, a little way inland. Many of the undisciplined invaders split up into small marauding parties, who set out to loot and plunder the by now deserted dwellings. In many of these houses they found quantities of salvaged port wine, and were soon toasting each other into a drunken stupor. More than one ordinary Welshman would later be able to claim that he had single-handedly captured a Frenchman or two, whilst the latter were under the influence! As we shall see later, Welsh women, too, played an important part in the defence of Fishguard; one in particular, a fearsome Fishguard heroine named Jemima Nicholas. Jemima, who became known as Jemima Vawr – 'Jemima the Great' – was described as 'a tall, stout, masculine female, who worked as a shoemaker and cobbler,' and 'felt imbued with the noble and patriotic spirit of Ancient Cambria:- she took a pitchfork and boldly marched to Pencaer, to meet the invading foe.' She came upon twelve Frenchmen in a field and, undaunted, advanced upon them. Whether it was her ferocious appearance, her obvious courage, 'or persuaded by her rhetoric', they allowed her to take them prisoner and to march them to the guard-house located in Fishguard Church.

France's expectation of their buccaneering American *Chef de Brigade* was a tall order indeed: 'The Expedition under Col. Tate has in view three principal objects: the first is, if possible, to raise an insurrection in the country; the second is to interrupt and embarrass the commerce of the enemy; and the third is to prepare and facilitate the way for a descent by distracting the attention of the English Government.' It is a fact that some of the French officers – who must have mistakenly identified the feelings of the Welsh with those of the Irish – were surprised and bitterly disappointed when, on landing, they were not welcomed with open arms!

Tate must have been more realistic. With the departure of the French vessels, which left him with his small army of largely undisciplined and untrained men, deserted in the midst of an unwelcoming and potentially hostile populace, he must have foreseen the inevitable from the very first day.

That Colonel William Tate was courageous cannot be doubted: he was about seventy years of age at the time of his great endeavour, 'a tall thin old man, dressed in a long blue Coat faced with Scarlet, blue Pantaloons, white waistcoat, Cocked Hat, and National Cockade.' But his capacity to dream great dreams must have equalled his courage if he really believed he could become another William the Conqueror; yet he did achieve one thing for which Napoleon would have envied him: for a very short time Tate stood master of a tiny piece of Britain.

The local militia regiment, the Fishguard Fencibles, were scattered and taken completely by surprise. Their commanding officer, Colonel Thomas Knox, was attending a ball at Tregwyn, a country mansion six miles off, when a mounted messenger brought him the news. The Tregwyn family and their guests hastily boarded their carriages and headed inland, and Knox hurried back to Fishguard and his militiamen. They had already begun to form themselves into some sort of defence force, and had been joined by worthy Welsh countrymen, proudly bearing their outlandish assortment of weaponry. This small force alone would have stood little chance against a stout and confident enemy, and they were greatly relieved at the arrival next day of Lord Cawdor, with his troop of Castlemartin Yeoman Cavalry and a detachment of Cardiganshire Militia, to augment Colonel Knox's Fencibles and his body of local volunteers.

From this point on the story reads more like a comedy than an invasion. Legend – and some French and British contemporary and later accounts – has it that many hundreds of Pembrokeshire women had joined the huge number of men who gazed down upon the invaders from the heights, and that, in their Welsh round black felt hats and their long scarlet cloaks, from a distance they had all the appearance of red-coated soldiers. General Tate did, indeed, report back to France that he had been faced by a large force of redcoats – although the Militiamen were dressed in blue! It was said that Lord Cawdor marched his motley force back and forth over the hills, using the same people over again, thus giving the impression that he had a great army under his command. General Tate fell for the deception and very soon he capitulated without firing a shot!

There are many versions of this story which seems too good to be true, but a number of eyewitness reminiscences of the occasion, indicate that the appearance of the red-mantled Welsh women played a significant part in the surrender – as evidenced by the two contemporary letters which end this chapter.

On Thursday evening, not much more than twenty-four hours after the landings, Colonel Tate had sent two French officers under a flag of truce, with a verbal and written offer to surrender, but only on certain conditions: that all prisoners of war should be repatriated to Brest – and that the British Government should foot the bill. His letter read:

> 'Cardigan Bay
> 5th of Ventrôse, 5th year of the Republic.
> Sir
> The Circumstances under which the Body of the French troops under my Command were landed at this Place render it unnecessary to attempt any military operations, as they would tend only to Bloodshed and Pillage. The Officers of the whole Corps are therefore intimated their desire of entering into a Negociation upon Principles of Humanity to surrender. If you are influenced by similar Considerations you may signify the same by the Bearer, and, in the mean Time, Hostilities shall cease.
> Health and Respect
> Tate, Chef de Brigade.
> To the Officer commanding His Britannick Majesty's Troops.'

A Council of War took place in an upper room of the old Royal Oak Inn at Fishguard, in the presence of Lord Cawdor, Colonel Knox, the Governor of Fishguard Fort, other senior military men and local dignitaries. The French conditional offer was laughed to scorn; and the officers were told that nothing less than unconditional surrender could be entertained, and that the surrender must take place by two p.m. on the following day at Goodwick Sands. In default of compliance with this ultimatum, Lord Cawdor informed them with intimidating exaggeration, the invaders would be attacked by the ten thousand troops he already had at hand – and the other ten thousand he expected to arrive on the morrow. At this, the French officers laid down their swords and pistols on the table, and signed a preliminary agreement. They were secured for the night in the Royal Oak, then early next morning were escorted, blindfolded, out of the town and back to their headquarters at Trehowel, bearing his Lordship's reply to Tate's letter:

> 'Fishguard
> February 23rd 1797
> Sir,
> The Superiority of the Force under my Command, which is hourly increasing, must prevent my treating upon any Terms short of your surrendering your whole Force Prisoners of War. I enter fully into your Wish of preventing an unnecessary Effusion of Blood, which your speedy Surrender can alone prevent, and which will entitle you to that Consideration it is ever the Wish of British Troops to show an Enemy whose numbers are inferior.
> My Major will deliver you this letter and I shall expect your Determination by Ten o'clock, by your Officer whom I have furnished with an Escort, that will conduct him to me without Molestation.
> I and &c.,
> Cawdor.
> To the Officer Commanding the French Troops.'

The number of fully trained men in Cawdor's military force was not much more than half that of the French invaders, but next morning the various British units were impressively deployed to give an appearance of greater strength than was the fact; some were drawn up on eminences overlooking Goodwick Sands where the surrender was to take place, whilst detachments of the Pembrokeshire Yeoman Cavalry and the Cardiganshire Militia took up position on the sands to receive the French troops. Every height and cliff-top was already crowded with ever-growing masses of witnesses to the great occasion, many armed with 'lances' of straightened scythes and other farm-implement weapons; the 'redcoat army' of scarlet-clad women, now numbered in their thousands, giving the impression that the whole country had risen up against the foreign invaders.

As the deadline approached with no sign of the French, a small party led by one of Cawdor's aides-de-camp under a flag of truce, went to the French headquarters at Trehowel, with the warning that tardiness in conforming to the stated conditions and time would result in them coming under a full scale attack. About half of the troops, probably the French regulars, were drawn up in good order and obeyed the order to 'open pans and shed priming', and soon their jail-bird comrades-in-arms made some effort to form themselves into a fairly respectable company.

At 2 p.m. on Friday, the 24th February, 1797, the beat of the French brass drums was heard, as the *Légion Noire*, defeated now and prisoners of war, crested the long hill which led down to Goodwick Sands, where they laid down their arms on the shore. Later in the afternoon the rank and file began the sixteen mile march through Fishguard to Haverfordwest, as a band played 'The Girl I Left Behind Me', which became known as 'Lord Cawdor's March'.

The spectacle of invasion and capitulation must have created never to be forgotten memories in the minds of both onlookers and defending servicemen. We read of disciplined French troopers, and also of ragamuffin groups dressed in old British uniforms, some dyed a 'rusty red', who laughed and sang as they were marched into captivity, and of others who ripped the national cockade from their helmets and cursed with cries of *'Au diable la République!'*

It is more than probable that had Tate not fallen for Lord Cawdor's bluff of vastly superior manpower – and had the Welsh women worn cloaks of a different colour! – his admittedly motley invading force could have reeked havoc on Fishguard, Haverfordwest, Carmarthen and other local towns and villages, before sufficiently large numbers of trained troops could have been drafted to the scene of conflict. As it was, most damage was caused by the looting and pillaging by mindless marauders. The Church record books and Registers at Llanunda and Fishguard were senselessly destroyed, thus obliterating volumes of local history up to 1797. At least one instance shows that all such sacrilegious acts could not be blamed on ruffian ransackers. The Commissary for Carmarthen was approached one day by a French officer on parole in that town, who offered him a silver Communion Cup and plate which, he said, he had purchased in Lanundee in France. However, an inscription on the Cup read *Poculum Ecclesiæ de Llanunda* which proved it to have been looted from Llanunda, one of the parishes where the records had been destroyed.

The accommodation of prisoners of war in Britain had been a problem for more than a century, and for a small coastal district in Wales to suddenly find itself saddled with an unexpected bag of something more than a thousand captives, the problem may have been insurmountable. But Lord Cawdor had ridden ahead to Haverfordwest on the Friday of the surrender and had organised the temporary housing of the hard-to-handle French mob, with all that same cool efficiency which he had shown over the last three days. On their arrival in the early hours of Saturday morning, 415 were somehow crammed into the County Jail and 520 were distributed between the three churches, St Mary's, St Martin's and St Thomas's. Others were confined in outhouses and store-rooms which had hurriedly been made as secure as possible – and that was not all; there were laggards yet to come. Late on Friday, drunken French soldiers straggled into Trehowel from the countryside, many in such a sorry state of over-indulgence and hangover that it was said that 'eleven carts were employed to convey them with their luggage, escorted by the Romney Fencible Cavalry and the Fishguard Fencibles, to prison in Haverfordwest'

It was essential that the Haverfordwest churches and other temporary accommodation be cleared as quickly as possible – St Mary's had already suffered considerable damage, and more would have been sure to follow – but the burden on the county was soon lifted, as the prisoners were marched off to Milford. There awaiting them were three brigs and other vessels with a strong escort of frigates to take them to the Plymouth hulks or local depots. A few of those in the county Jail were also included in the transfer to Plymouth, but the majority, perhaps as many as four hundred, were sent to the rather shaky security of the Golden Tower Prison at Pembroke, and, as we shall see, they were not there long before they proved just how shaky it really was.

So Tate's ill-fated attack on the British mainland ended in ignominy, with his men uncomfortably cooped up in prison ships, depots or small town jails; but what of the officers? Tate and his senior officers did not accompany their troops when they marched to the capitulation ceremony at Goodwick Sands, but bided their time at Trehowel where, it is said, they and their Colonel waited in a nervous and agitated state for the arrival of Cawdor. Maybe they feared that had they attended, they might suffer fatal retribution from the Welsh populace, whose homes and property they had violated and abused – or perhaps they were equally fearful of what fate may have held in store for them at the hands of their own men, few of whom would ever have volunteered to join such a death-or-glory venture.

Tate and his officers were sent on horseback to Haverfordwest, where they spent the night in the Castle Inn, and next day were taken under an escort of Cawdor's Yeoman Cavalry to Carmarthen. There they were lodged in the Ivy Bush Inn, until suitable accommodation could be found for them in the town's County Jail. It would seem that the French officers were allowed at least a few of the privileges of parole during the few weeks they were in the town, as they made such a bad impression upon it that appeals were made to Lord Portland, the Home Secretary, to have them removed. After about a month, they were marched to a transport vessel, and Carmarthen breathed a sigh of relief.

Colonel Tate and four of his officers – his French second-in-command, Le Brun, and three Irishmen – Captain Tyrrell, Lieutenant Barry St Leger and Captain Morrison – had already been taken to London, where they were to appear before a Privy Council at the Admiralty. The journey to London was long and nerve-racking – a letter from Lord Cawdor to his wife says that throughout the journey hostile crowds threatened the prisoners: 'The women were more clamorous than the men, making signs to cut their throats and desiring I would not take the trouble of carrying them further.' They also had other things to worry about, apart from the hostility of the public, and Tate doubly so. The Irish officers could easily have found themselves charged with High Treason and ended their adventure on the gallows; St Leger had indeed posed as an American for a while, obviously aware of the danger he was facing; although he did, in fact, have some qualification to be considered an American as he had lived in Charleston since the age of twelve.

There was a suspicion, too, that Colonel Tate was himself originally from the Emerald Isle, a native of County Wexford. Many contemporary documents exist which refer to the Colonel as Irish, as do a number of more recent writers, including Francis Abell; but there is no doubt that his life was lived as an American, and official documents in Paris give his birthplace as the United States: *'natif des Etat Unis de l'Amerique'*, *'Colonel aux Etats Unis son pays natal'*, *'habitoit la Caroline Sud,'* etc.

Much greater than his fear of a treason charge in England was the threat of being sent back across the Atlantic, where he would certainly have been imprisoned for offending against the laws of the United States, by his hostile action against a country with whom the United States were not at war, a very serious offence indeed, and one which Tate had committed more than once.

The Council found that there were grounds for charging the Irish officers with treason but, for complicated political reasons, they got away with the capital crime. Colonel Tate gave his *parole de honneur* and was allowed to live in comparative freedom – but for a short time only. News of his landing had spread rapidly to parole towns, depots and hulks throughout the country, creating a spirit of insurgence and a great increase in the number of escape attempts. The result was that the Government, fearing a general uprising of all prisoners, cancelled the privilege of parole, and parolees everywhere were transferred to depots or the prison ships.

Tate, hoist with his own petard, had to exchange the most comfortable of prisoner of war conditions for the most harsh of them all. For a second time the name 'Royal Oak' entered the history of his misadventure, but this time it was the *Royal Oak*, a prison hulk, moored in Portsmouth Harbour. It cannot be imagined that Tate and other officers would have experienced the worst aspects of prison ship life. Nevertheless, he was deeply shocked to find himself on one of the infamous English hulks. The records show that he immediately put his always active mind to work on schemes to improve his lot; writing to the Admiralty and War Lords, long letters containing propositions and improbable schemes which might earn him parole or exchange to France.

Some of his many letters to the Admiralty gently reminded them of his rank, and he applied for exchange-parole to go to France under one pretext or another. His most ingenious proposition was that his influence with the French government might achieve what all the efforts of our own Government had so long failed to do – obtain the exchange of Admiral Sir Sidney Smith, imprisoned in France. In a letter headed *'Royal Oak Prison Ship at Portsmouth.– 16th Prairial – 5th year of the Republic'*, he wrote:

> 'My Lords,
> If the consideration of Sir Sydney Smith's situation continues yet to exercise the attention of his Britannic Majesty's Ministers, I have to propose to your Lordships to obtain permission to go to France on my parole; & if (in a reasonable time) Sir Sydney shall not be released from confinement, then I shall be held to present myself in England …'

Untempted, the authorities had no reason to trust Colonel William Tate, the invader who sailed into Fishguard under false colours, or to grant him any favours. The Admiralty's reply was short but not very sweet. Captain Rawe, the Superintendent of Hulks at Portsmouth, was instructed to answer and acquaint him with the fact that '...their Ldshps cannot comply with his request.' His continued efforts did, however, bring him some success. For whilst his three Irish officers and his French second in command spent the next year and a half in the discomfort of *Royal Oak,* Tate was housed in Porchester Castle before being released to France on exchange-parole, on 24th November, 1798. He returned to Paris at least fully qualified as an expert in the British prisoner of war management, having experienced all four categories of the system: hulk, depot, parole and exchange – as well as a spell in a civil county jail.

Just about every depot and nearly every parole town has its story of wartime romances and some went too far in their efforts to assist their foreign romeos. Traitorous, misguided, love-struck, over-sympathetic, or just plain stupid, call them what we will, there were many young women, all over the country, willing to risk loss of reputation and punishment in the dangerous role of escape assistant. It is too much to hope that the feelings of these girls would always be reciprocated in the hearts of their captive boyfriends. Most, but not all, of these freedom-hungry men were more infatuated with their dreams of home than with the local womenfolk.

Whilst they could not but have felt gratitude towards these gullible girls, the majority took heed of yet another of their Emperor's maxims – 'The only Victory over Love is Flight' – and left their loves behind when peace and repatriation beckoned them home; but here is a story of escape and elopement which tells of two, at least, who found a happy ending.

After the abortive French 'invasion' of Fishguard, some four hundred of the captives were quartered in the Golden Tower Prison, near Pembroke, where discipline was slack, security poor and the buildings entirely unsuited to the purpose.

Some, with that adaptability typical of the French, quickly settled down to make the best of their predicament; some to produce the usual prisoner of war handicrafts for sale in the small depot market; but most, perhaps all, had dreams of escape and return to their homeland. The industrious craftsmen among them were always on the look-out for raw materials from which to make their profitable little artefacts. In this they were helped by some of the young Welsh girls who were employed in menial tasks about the prison, and who, quite openly and legitimately, brought in odds and ends of bone, wood and other scrap materials.

Two of these Welsh lasses soon fell deeply in love with young French captives and, 'not having the law of Nations or the high policy of Europe before their eyes', determined to help their lovers escape. As the idea grew it was extended to include all the prisoners in that part of the depot – about one hundred men in all. However lax the discipline, it was impossible for the girls to bring in shovels and spades or pickaxes, but an ingenious alternative was found. Each day they carried with them the shin bones of oxen and horses and passed them off as working materials for the bone carvers.

These were quickly converted into tunnelling tools and a burrowing operation was started, some of the excavated earth being scattered about the prison yards and some taken away by the girls in their covered pails. When a sixty-foot long passage had been dug under the prison, it only remained for the girls to keep watch until a suitable vessel came into the nearby harbour, then tip off the prisoners and the escape would be on. One dark night, thirty of the absconders and the two young women made their way to the harbour and boarded a sloop, only to find that the neap tide was against them and the coaster aground. But their luck never deserted them for long. As though Fate had decreed that one more act should be added to the Fishguard fiasco, a small pleasure yacht was lying at hand – a craft which belonged to Lord Cawdor, the British hero of the 'invasion' and the captor of the now fleeing men – who, it must be said, were putting up a better show on leaving England than they had on entering it.

After the crew of the sloop had been securely bound hand and foot and the navigational instruments, charts, water casks and provisions transferred to the yacht, the thirty men and two girls set sail for France. Next day there was a great commotion in the town. A prominent local figure, Dr Mansell, had notices posted up all over Pembrokeshire, which offered a reward of £500 (a huge figure at that time) for the return of the girls, dead or alive; but by that time the runaways were well out to sea.

Off Linney Head they met up with a coasting brig carrying corn, which they boarded, forcing the crew below decks and battening down the hatches. Having no further use for Lord Cawdor's yacht they cast it adrift and when, a few days later, its stern and other wreckage was washed up on the Pembrokeshire coast, the hunt was called off and the 'wanted' posters taken down; it being piously supposed that 'the vengeance of Heaven had overtaken the traitors.'

The Welsh girls meanwhile had safely reached St Malo, where they married their French admirers – what stories they must have had to tell their grandchildren. It is surprising to learn that during the short peace which followed the Treaty of Amiens, one of the couples returned to Wales and opened a public house in Merthyr Tydfil. With the recommencement of hostilities in 1803, they hurried back to France and there, for us, the story ends.

POSTSCRIPT

Many facets of the 'Last Invasion' story, however simply told, may read more like fiction or faction than depictions of actual happenings; but of some things we can have no doubt:

There really were women who landed with the invaders; two were officers' wives, the other two the wives of soldiers. During the period when parole was cancelled as a result of the invasion, these four women spent time on the *Royal Oak* hulk at Portsmouth, before being repatriated back to France.

The two Welsh girls really did hold patriotism in abeyance and helped their lovers – and twenty-eight of their comrades-in-arms! – to escape.

Jemima Nicholas certainly *was* a real life heroine, whom a grateful Government rewarded with a pension of £50 per annum, which she enjoyed until her death at the age of eighty-two. 1897, Queen Victoria's Diamond Jubilee year, was also the centenary of the event which inspired the Cambrian spirit which quelled the French intrusion. As part of the celebrations, an inscribed stone slab commemorating Jemima's brave achievements was erected in St Mary's Churchyard by public subscription.

And what of that most sensational, and to some incredible, ingredient in the Fishguard story: the presence of female 'Redcoats' which decided the day? Lord Cawdor did not deny it – neither did he confirm it – but two letters bear testimony to the large numbers of red-cloaked women who gathered on the hills above Fishguard. These letters could hardly be more contemporary, written as they were, only three days after the French surrender.

Mary and John Mathias wrote to their sister in Swansea:

'Narberth February 27 1797

Dear Sister

I write to you hoping that you are in good health as at present thanks be to God for it the French invaded near fisgard Last Wednesday wich put the Contry into Great Confusion because they wear 14 hundard and the Contry gathered from all parts of Pembrokeshire near four hundard Women in Red flanes and Squier [Squire] Gambel went to ask them were they to fight and they said they were and when they com near the french put down thair arns and they weas all tok presoners that time and are brought to haverfordwest Friday night Last not one kild But too of our men and five of the french by been to Bould please to give my love to my Brother and receive the same your self and we are wel so no more at present from your loving Brother and Sister John & Nary Mathius

We had no more than about four hundard men under arms qnd they thought the women to Be a Rigment of Soldiers and they 14 hundard abnd the Lord tok from our Enemes the Spirit of War and to him be the Praus.

God save the King'

— and on that same day, John Mends of Haverfordwest wrote to his Customs officer son John in Swansea. Although he miscalculated the number of men involved, the following extracts from his letter are persuasive evidence that he was an eyewitness, particularly so on the day of the surrender:

'Haverfordwest
February 27th 1797

Dear Son

I have the pleasure to inform you that the French Soldiers have all Surrendered themselves & Laid down their arms. There are several Causes assigned for their Surrender. The first is their Ships of War, which left the Coast immediately after they Landed the Troops and left them on the Shore with only two Days' victuals and without any Tents. The 2. Cause was owing to the vigilant alackrity, and spirit of the Welch, which came runing from all Quarters [of] the Country to oppose them and in about 48 hours they ammounted to about 7 or 8 Thousand men of all Sorts. Some well armed, others with Long pike staffs, others with Sythes straightened – Desperate weapon – others with pitch forks, and, above al, about 400 poor women, with Red flanel over their Shoulders, which the French at a Distance took for Soldiers, as they appeared all Red. This with as prospect of no more victuals to be had, intimidated the French Soldiers so much that they sent a Flag of Truce to our Gentlemen, with terms of Surrendering themselves, which was accepted. The terms was only to desire good usage and to keep their Clothes on their Backs, which was agreed to. They then advanced forward in Ranks & Laid down their arms in the Ground. They are all in Haverfordwest now, to the amount of 18 hundred Soldiers, all lusty fellows, and about 200 missing, Supposed to be Stragling about the Country in Search of Something to eat, as they are half Starved. And Early this morning their arms arrived in 50 Carts, amounting to about 19 hundred musquets & Bayonets, with the same number of Belts and Cartouches, Each containing 19 Rounds of Cartriges & Balls, and Several kegs of Gunpowder & Boxes of musquet Balls, with about 18 Brass Drums & Some Flags with the Tree of Libertty painted on them. Their fleet had some Irish Pilots on Board that conducted them to Fishguard Road out of reach of the Battery Erected there ....It was the Lord God's doing, and blesses be his name for it. The Lord be thanked and praised for eve & ever, Amen.

Dear Son John, my ernest blessing attend you and your Small family, & am your most affectionate Father,

John Mends.'

As a colophon, or tailpiece, to a piece of British history which, though significant at the time, was soon swept from all but local memories by news of great battles on land and sea, it is of interest to note that today's tourist industry has recognised its importance to the still-small coastal town of Fishguard. For the bi-centenary celebrations in 1997, two-hundred year old memories were revived, together with artefacts of the period, many of them genuine. The Napoleonic Association arranged a re-enactment of the French landings, and many other invasion-related activities took place.

There is no surrender document for tourists to peruse, as research on both sides of the Channel has failed to unearth such a manuscript. But the old Royal Oak Inn is still there, and a recent visitor to it was shown the actual table where the missing document was signed – although Colonel Tate never entered the Royal Oak or, for that matter, ever got to the town of Fishguard itself. A relic with a more reliable provenance – as it is mentioned in contemporary records – is still to be seen at Brestgarn Farm. One of the many intoxicated French plunderers entered the residence in search of loot, when he was disturbed by the movement of the pendulum, or the ticking, of a grandfather clock. Convinced that the wooden case of the clock was the hiding-place of the householder, the tipsy idiot raised his musket and fired. The holes can still be seen where his ball-shot passed through front and back of the casing. But perhaps the most impressive and instructive exhibit is the work of a modern group of Welsh heroines, who spent four years working on a tapestry 100 feet long by 20 inches deep, which tells the story in thirty-seven captioned panels.

---

1. W.T.W. Tone, ed. *Life of Theobald Wolfe Tone.*

Overleaf: Louis Garneray. French Prison Hulks in Portsmouth Harbour.

PART 2

THE PRISON HULKS

Chapter Five
The Civil Prison Hulks

'MAN took one of the most beautiful objects of his handiwork and deformed it into a hideous monstrosity. The line-of-battle ship was a thing of beauty, but when mast and rigging and sails were shorn away, when the symmetrical sweep of her lines was deformed by all sorts of excrescences and superstructures, when her white, black-dotted belts were smudged out, it lay, rather than floated, like a gigantic black, shapeless coffin.

Sunshine which can give a touch of picturesqueness, if not of beauty, to much that is bare and featureless, only brought out into greater prominence the dirt, the shabbiness, the patchiness of the thing.'

Francis Abell

ABELL'S DESCRIPTION OF A ONCE PROUD man-of-war degraded to the status of a hulk, could have been written only by a ship-loving member of a maritime nation, evoking as it does, feelings of pity for the vessel itself – as for a living thing doomed to a miserable old age.

A ship in its prime does, indeed, seem to possess a vibrant life and personality of its own and there are few sadder sights than the aspect of a vessel at the end of its days, left to rot in the breaker's yard; or put to some base use unworthy of its active past. Once converted for use as a prison ship, however, it is for the inmates that all sentiment and pity must be reserved. Many of these floating hells had spent their best days on the oceans of the world, had played their part in great naval actions or voyages of discovery; but many of the unfortunates condemned to them spent their best days, some their entire youth, in conditions of miserable discomfort and, one might decide, were subjected to a degree of unnecessary hardship and suffering.

That rotting and verminous hulks were no fit lodging for any man, much less the prisoner of war who was in no sense a criminal, is unarguable. But were they, as many Frenchmen – and later the Americans – were led to believe, the diabolical invention of a vindictive British Government, hell-bent on the destruction of its captives for reasons of economy and hate.

To discover a fair answer to this question it is necessary to tell something of the harshness of the age in which they were conceived, and the circumstances of their birth. It should be mentioned at the outset that the French, who were so self-righteous in their criticism of the English hulks, were themselves far more experienced as operators of floating prisons. The French Galley Corps was already notorious in the early years of the seventeenth century. The word 'galley' itself had become almost synonymous with slavery, savage imprisonment and forced labour in chains. Louis XIV had condemned many thousands of his own Protestant subjects – Huguenots who had not escaped the country in time – to serve at the oars with many more thousands of infidels. Admittedly, unlike the Moslems who were, indeed, called *esclaves*, the Christian oarsmen were known as *forcats* (convicts), but slavery by any other name.

As well as a prison, the galley was also a fighting ship; so, in addition to the muscle-straining punishment at the oar, the chained prisoner lived with the haunting fear of going down with his ship, still shackled to his bench. At the same time that the civil prison

hulk system was being debated in England, in the 1770s, there were still a number of galleys, complete with slaves, attached to the French navy at Toulon.[1]

The hulks, old line-of-battle ships and captured vessels unfit for repair and conversion for service under our flag, had long been adapted for worthwhile use in their retirement. As maintenance and rigging hulks, depot ships and isolation hospitals, they were well suited to their new employment. However, from time to time, superannuated vessels had been used for a purpose to which they were certainly unsuited – the accommodation of prisoners, whether civil or prisoners of war.

The old *Royal Oak* and a few other obsolete men-of-war moored at Plymouth, were stripped out during the Seven Years' War for use as prisoner of war depots and, even earlier, after the Jacobite Rebellion of 1745, there were prison ships on the Thames at Tilbury.

Apart from the comparatively few hulks which were prisons in the true sense, many more were places of a captivity of a different kind. Before the days of shore leave, in fact as late as the 1850s, our 'Jolly' Jack Tars were often lodged in depot hulks whilst their ships were in for provisioning or refit. At a time when naval discipline was maintained by the cat-o'-nine-tails, and flogging round the fleet a not unusual punishment, it was one thing to get a crew together and quite another to keep it intact within reach of shore.

Desertion was punishable by hanging from the yardarm, but even awareness of this barbarity could not ensure that impressed men and sailors grown weary of harsh treatment, once allowed on dry land, would be around when their vessels were again ready for sea. The ordinary sailor of that time did not see much of the world. At home or abroad it was likely that his only contact with the shore would be the bum-boats which came alongside with all manner of merchandise for sale.

Conditions on the floating barracks in which our sailors spent fitting-out time cannot, of course, be compared with the evils of the civil prison ships or the prisoner of war hulks, but they were bad enough for Admiral Sir John Napier to condemn them in these words: 'I would burn the whole of them, they are a nuisance; they fill up our harbours; they are nothing but a curse and the men hate and detest them.'

The romance of life at sea will be seen to be somewhat tarnished if we draw aside the veil of glamour and observe how often ships were used as repositories of 'free' ill-used humanity. The sailing ship was, indeed, a thing of beauty, but the unwilling seaman or landlubber press-ganged into Naval service was, in a very real sense, a captive, and can only have hated his ship as a prison – no matter how great its name. The galley-slave would surely have swopped his bench and chains for the foulest prison ashore.

From Elizabethan times until the middle of the nineteenth century, our convicts were brought aboard the transportation vessels and shipped to hard labour in the colonies thousands of miles away. For many, this journey by sailing ship was a sentence of death more harsh than the quick turning-off on Tyburn Tree. Of the 939 convicts transported to Norfolk Island in 1790, few could walk ashore unaided. 261 had died during the voyage and of the 500 who arrived in a state of chronic illness, fifty died soon after landing.

Anyone who has read John Prebble's *Culloden* will not easily forget the stories of cruelty and deprivation inflicted on the Scottish prisoners brought down to the Thames after the '45 Rebellion. The voyage from the Moray Firth to Tilbury was a three-week-long nightmare of suffering and deliberate cruelty. The prisoners, fit, sick and wounded, were herded in great numbers onto the ballast stones in the dark holds of leaky merchant coasters.

Lack of ventilation and a total absence of sanitation soon brought disease into these stinking pits, and many poor fellows died on the journey south. To typhus, starvation and the discomfort of swarming vermin, was added the inhuman treatment imposed by some heartless seamen-gaolers. 'They'd take a rope and tye about a poor sicks west, then they would hawll them up by their tackle and plunge them into the sea, as they said to drown the vermine; but they took specell care to drown both together. Then they'd hawll them up upon deck an ty a stone about on the leggs and overboartd with them. I have seen five or six examples of this in a day.'

Typical of these transport vessels was the *Jane of Leith,* and one of the prisoners, James Bradshaw of the Prince's Life Guards, used his last moments on earth to tell a largely unsympathetic public of the shocking conditions which he had experienced. In a speech which he made before his execution on Kennington Common, which ended with his swearing, 'upon the word of a dying man, as I hope for mercy at the Day of Judgement, I assert nothing but what I know to be true', he told of ' …several of the wounded who were put aboard the *Jane of Leith,* and there died in lingering tortures. Our general allowance was a half a pound of meal a day, which was sometimes increased to a pound, but never exceeded it; and I myself was eye-witness that great numbers were starved to death. Their barbarity extended so far as not to suffer the men who were aboard the *Jane* to lie down even upon the planks, but were obliged to sit on large stones, by which means their legs swell'd as big almost as their bodies.'

At the end of these terrible voyages, some of the Jacobite prisoners were sent to gaols ashore, whilst others were left on board their transports for weeks or even months. Even less lucky were those transferred to one or another of the truly dreadful Tilbury prison ships. The two descriptions already quoted are in the words of misused prisoners who would, understandably, be filled with bitterness and feelings of injustice. So now let us look at the findings of a surgeon, sent by the Commissioners for the Sick and Wounded, to report on the Tilbury prison hulk *Pamela*.

When the hatches which covered the hold were unbattened, he was met with 'such an intolerable smell, that it was like to overcome me, though I was provided with the proper herbs and my nostrils were stuffed therewith.' Some of the captives were too weak to climb on deck for this inspection, so a soldier was sent down to report on the state of things below. Perhaps the surgeon should have made his own investigations; he was certainly too sensitive to have made a good inspector. Even at second hand he was too shocked to repeat much of what the soldier had told him: 'To hear the description given by the guard who went into the hold, of the uncleanliness of the place is surpassing imagination, and too nauseous to describe, so that, together with the malignant fever raging among them and another odious distemper peculiar to Scotsmen, may terminate in a more dreadful disease.'

At least one naval vessel was used as a prison ship after the '45. The hold of H.M.S. *Furnace*, one of the ships sent to St Kilda in 1746 in search of Bonnie Prince Charlie, was the crowded, filthy, place of confinement for many of the Rebels taken in the islands. Some were kept there for as long as eight months, in conditions perhaps worse than those obtaining on the dreadful transports and on the convict prison hulks which will be discussed later. Here, too, on the *Furnace*, sick, hungry and lousy, the prisoners were at the mercy of a sadistic crew. They existed on 'only half-man's allowance in every respect' and the 'victuals were brought to the prisoners in foul nasty buckets, wherein the fellows used to piss for a piece of ill-natured diversion.'

It is strange that whilst the story of the Black Hole of Calcutta has survived from 1756 to the present day, equally terrible and not dissimilar atrocities which took place so much nearer home and such a short time before, should have been so completely forgotten.

It cannot be pretended that the public or the Government were ignorant of the facts. There was no planned prison ship system at the time. Prisoners were stored, rather than housed in any humane sense, in places most convenient to their captors. If they arrived overland and were packed into out-buildings or local gaols, they were in for a period of fettered suffering and neglect; but if their luck was really out, they came by sea and were left to rot in the holds of the *Pamela* or her sister hulks.

This long recitation of unpleasant facts has been included to illustrate, not only the accepted cruelties of the age, but to show that when an official prison ship system did come into being, there was already an abundance of evidence that floating prisons were a poor answer to the problem of housing either crook or captive – and that those who approved its inception must have been fully aware of the dangers.

The hulk as we shall come to know it through the following pages, did not make its appearance in any great number until the beginning of the last quarter of the eighteenth century. Events at that time inspired the Government to think up the 'Temporary Expedient' of fitting out decrepit old ships for the specific purpose of holding prisoners. Even then, the idea was only resorted to for want of a better means of relieving the burden on small prisons and gaols over-crowded with our own erring countrymen and, only as a secondary convenience, to house foreign prisoners of war.

There was little in the way of organised policing anywhere in the country. Even in London, where the incorruptible Henry Fielding – now remembered more as the author of *Tom Jones* – improved his small police force and established the Bow Street Runners, law enforcement was largely unsuccessful. In an age when a detected pickpocket or thief, whose haul had exceeded twelve pence, might expect to be clapped in irons and face the gallows; and there were hundreds of other 'crimes' on the Statute Book punishable by death or transportation, one might expect that Britain would have become the most well-behaved of countries; but the number of Britons who were publicly hanged or spent long years in the colonies, proves otherwise.

It was a period when 'nobody could feel himself unapprehensive of danger to his person or property if he walked in the street after dark, nor could any man promise himself security in bed'.[2] There was no public prosecutor and the onus was on the offended to prosecute the offender. But the shortage of suitable gaols, and corrupt prison management, was at the root of most of the evil. Newgate was already over six hundred years old and a hell-hole beyond modern imagination. The town gaols were, in the main, no more than unwholesome storehouses, into which offenders were swept from the streets and out of the public gaze.

Reformation of inmates was not a matter for consideration for many years to come, although it should be realised that vicious sentencing was not the product of a sadistic administration, but was intended as a deterrent – a sort of reformation by intimidation. Many, perhaps most, of the local gaols and prisons were privately owned, or leased from landlords who were often of noble birth or senior clerical gentlemen. From then on the gaolers made the rules. The conditions under which a felon spent his period of incarceration varied greatly – and directly in proportion to his financial state or access to helpful friends. Cash could purchase easement of the fetters which chained him to the floor, could furnish him with bedding and good food and anything else he could afford. Lack of it produced misery, semi-starvation and the strong possibility that the length of his sentence would be reduced by typhus or gaol-fever.

Before 1776, England had never felt the need for great prisons in which to quarter its felons and political malcontents. The sentence of 'Transportation' for periods of seven, fourteen or twenty-one years, had seen to it that these unwanted subjects were sent far away and off our hands.

During the reign of Queen Elizabeth I, the 'Act for the Punyshment of Rogues, Vagabonds and Sturdy Beggars (1597)', had decreed that transportation should be the sentence next in severity to death. If a convict returned to England before the expiry of his term of 'banishment out of the Realm', he risked landing on to a straight road to the gallows. Six years later, James I added branding to the punishment and ordained that incorrigible or dangerous rogues – men or women – should be branded in the left shoulder with a hot burning iron of the breadth of an English shilling, with 'a great Roman 'R' on the iron', before being shipped out of the country. An Order in Council specified the 'Places or Partes beyond the Seas' to which the branded convicts should be sent as 'The New found Lande, the East and West Indies, Fraunce, Germanie, Spayne, and the Lowe Countries or any of them.'

By the beginning of the eighteenth century, most transportees were sent to hard labour on the other side of the Atlantic. Reprieved capital offenders and those found guilty of minor offences, received sentences of fourteen and seven years respectively, and in 1717 a further scandalous amendment was added to the transportation laws – an Act of Parliament which amounted to the authorisation of the sale, or leasing, of convicts to the American plantation-owners for the period of their sentence.

Both gaolers and transport ship contractors had a field day, the latter purchasing their human cargo from its keepers and at the end of the voyage selling them on at a profit. It is hard to visualise an age when England was sending many hundreds of her subjects – many of them guilty of little more than vagrancy or political non-conformity – to be sold into virtual slavery overseas.

The convenient and profitable use of America, as a dumping-ground for the criminal and embarrassing political elements in this country, came to a sudden halt when the American colonies rebelled in 1775. At a stroke, the great prison on the other side of the Atlantic closed its doors – with the outbreak of the War of American Independence. One might ask if America was not also damaged by the shutting off of the convict labour on which the plantation owners had depended for so long. The answer is no. By that time America was importing many times the number of negro slaves each year than they had ever received of white transportees.

A decade was to pass before a replacement colony was decided upon – even farther away. Australia was to be the recipient of Britain's erring citizens. It was thought that Botany Bay, 'a series of beautiful meadows abounding in the richest pastures and only inhabited by a few savages might be an admirable destination for the savages at present a heavy charge upon their Lordship's at home.' However, until that decision there was no agreed place of banishment and no place to confine them on land until a solution was found. Nevertheless, the judges still kept to the Statute Book and continued to dole out sentences for any of the couple of hundred offences punishable by transportation.

The system of imposing vicious sentences for serious and petty crimes alike, now quickly began to catch up with itself. With nowhere else to send long-term prisoners, the local prisons and gaols were soon filled and over-filled. Faced with the urgent necessity of finding a quick answer to this problem of convict accommodation, the Government looked into proposed solutions and suggestions which ranged from the impractical to the downright outrageous. As with all wars, nobody expected the American Rebellion to last for long, and at first no great efforts were made to find a long-term answer to the prison problem. Soon it became obvious that things could only get worse, and one might expect to hear that a prison-building programme was immediately set in motion; but this solution does not appear to have figured large in their deliberations. It was not until more than seventy years had passed that Pentonville, and the fifty or more other prisons based on its model, was erected.

The old established convenience of transportation was not so easily abandoned. In view of Captain Cook's recent great discovery, it is possible that Australia was already being considered as a suitable substitute for America, as a journey's end for transportees. But Australia was a long way away, and the present convict accommodation situation was becoming desperate enough for serious thought to be given to even the wildest propositions.

Consideration was given to the establishment of a penal settlement on an island in the Gambia River, many miles from the coast. With only a guard-ship downstream, convicts could be left to fend for themselves – and the climate and the generally unhealthy atmosphere would have made certain that few of the 'settlers' would live out their full sentences. Although this was attractive from an economic point of view, this and similar ideas were found to have hidden and insurmountable snags.

The prize for inhuman ingenuity must surely be awarded to Sir Frederick Eden, who seriously suggested in Parliament that the problem might be solved quite simply, by establishing an exchange system between the British Government and the Mohammedan Barbary pirates of the North African Coast. His idea was: that the convicts who could not easily be accommodated in our prisons, should be offered in exchange for 'more Christian captives' held as galley slaves by the Algerian corsairs!

With nothing approaching a permanent solution in sight, and matters getting worse daily, it was decided that further thinking time could be gained only by resorting to some sort of 'temporary expedient'. The choice fell to the 'temporary' employment of old vessels which could be stripped down to the hull and anchored in the Thames. That this was recognised from the beginning as less than ideal, even in the short term, can be gathered from the fact that the implementing 'Hulks Act' was designed to last for one year only. Or it could be that the Government expected that the rebellious colonists would be suppressed within that short time span, and our transport ships would once more be back in business, after the expected defeat of the American Colonies. Had it lasted only twice that long there would be a short, but still terrible, tale to tell; but, like so many permanences which begin as temporary measures, the civil prison hulks were to be an ugly scar on our rivers and harbours for many years to come. Introduced as a 'temporary expedient' in May, 1776, and operating by August of that year, they were not abolished until 1857.

The 'Temporary' Expedient.

The convicts who were to be sent to these hulks were, of course, men – and women – who would hitherto have been put to hard labour overseas. Now, for the first time, they were to be put to hard work during their terms of imprisonment in England. Up to this time prisoners had seldom been employed in works of public utility, or in any other way of usefully spending their time. The short-term prisoner in an English gaol lived out his sentence in morale-destroying idleness, usually ironed or double-ironed and often chained to the floor of his cell at night. Thus, the introduction of the civil hulks coincided with the introduction of the sentence of hard labour in this country. It was enacted that any man whose crime would normally have earned him a transportation sentence – had there been anywhere to send him – 'shall be punished by being kept at hard labour in the raising of sand, soil and gravel and cleaning the River Thames, or any other service for the benefit of the navigation of the said river.'

On the surface, this was progress of a kind. The great prison reformer, John Howard,[3] had been advocating prisoner employment for many years and seems to have welcomed the innovation, at least in principle, as a reformatory influence upon the convicts. He could not possibly have foreseen the corrupting and demoralising influence of the hulks, to which the convict was returned at the end of each day's 'reforming' labour. Neither could he be expected to have foreseen the callous indifference of the authorities now that the problem could in the main be shelved.

Once the decision regarding the 'temporary expedient' had been resolved and the few details of the experiment determined, the Government heaved a sigh of relief and farmed out its responsibilities into the hands of private enterprise. This meant that at least one out-of-work transportation contractor found quick re-employment, and in a business not so very different from his late profession. That man was Duncan Campbell. His years of experience in the transportation trade ensured the right degree of hardness of heart and immunity from feelings of compassion,

necessary to his new assignment.

Campbell's official title was 'Overseer' but, as he owned the vessels which would house the convicts, was in charge of their labours ashore, had managed to secure the contracts for supplying their food and clothing – and to a great extent could make his own rules and regulations – he was in effect their lord and master in every respect.

When we look into the economic aspects of his new venture, it is hard to credit that Duncan Campbell would have taken it on if he believed in the temporary nature of the exercise. In his previous occupation as shipper of transportees, he would have received at least twenty pounds a head for his human cargo, and may well have made a number of Atlantic crossings each year. Added to this, there were charges on the Government and, like many other contractors, he had probably retained a proprietory interest in the service of each delivered convict during his term of labour in the colonies.

Now, as hulk-master and owner, he was to be allowed £38 a year for each convict placed in his care. Multiply this by three hundred – the approximate capacity of his first two hulks – and we arrive at a not inconsiderable sum by the values of the times. There were also other sources of profit of which he would have been fully aware. If, in his capacity as supplier of victuals and clothing, he was as unscrupulous as some, perhaps most, of the contractors to the prisoner of war hulks, whom we shall meet later, he had the opportunity to further line his pockets at the expense of bellies and backs. From later reports of the wretched, underfed and ragged appearance of his charges, it would seem that he did see the opportunity and grasped it with both hands.

Nevertheless, from his legitimate rewards he was expected to provide, adapt and maintain the hulks; appoint and pay a staff of twenty officers and guards on each ship, and meet the hundred-and-one expenses involved in the initiation of such an enterprise. It is hardly likely that Campbell would have considered this a viable proposition, if he expected it all to fold up at the end of twelve months.

As it was, he lost no time in converting two vessels, an old East Indiaman called the *Justitia,* which he owned, and an old naval frigate, the more aptly named *Censor,* which he had purchased from the Admiralty. By August, 1776, only three months after the Act had received the Royal Assent, the two hulks were moored in the Thames off Woolwich, and were ready for their first unfortunate lodgers. From gaols and makeshift prisons all over the country, convicts were brought down to the Thames in irons, and distributed between the two vessels; about 125 to the *Justitia* and 185 to the *Censor.*

On arrival, any money that they had was taken by the captain for safe-keeping and the Quartermaster took the clothes they arrived in and condemned them. They were then issued with ship-dress of coarse checked shirt, canvas trousers, a brown jacket, footwear and stockings. The 'condemned' garments were supposed to be slashed and burned, but anything saleable usually ended up in the hands of the old-clothes traders, who purchased them from the quartermaster or the captain. Although there was no uniform as such, they were supposed to wear the issued slops; but from early days, the canny Campbell allowed friends and relatives of the convicts to supply them with garments – thus saving on the expense of clothing them himself.

The newly arrived convict had to keep his eye on every little article which he was allowed to retain, personal things like combs, belts and other odds and ends; for, after he had run the gauntlet of the official robbers who had relieved him profitably of any tradeable clothing, he had to contend with companion convicts and not rely too much on the honour which is supposed to exist among thieves.

Each day, those who were fit enough were rowed ashore and kept at various tasks in and around Woolwich Dockyard, some raising ballast, others working hand-operated pile-drivers and yet others building embankments or working on roads in the Dockyard itself. They toiled encumbered with 'Fetters on each leg, with a chain between, that ties variously, some around their middle, others upright to the throat. Some are chained two and two; others, whose crimes have been enormous, with heavy fetters'.

Their taskmasters were guards with cutlasses drawn, who saw to it that there was no talking and that they worked as well as men could weighed down with chains and irons. It seems that not all worked and neither were they made to, so long as there were sufficient volunteers; but those who did so laboured silently and well, 'being induced thereto by one only hope, viz., that of obtaining their liberty by good behaviour… all is discretionary with their keeper… The greatest liberty [during their working hours] allowed them is that of being permitted to go to a neighbouring ditch within the boundaries to drink.'[4]

We have read much of the unfeeling attitude towards suffering misfortune at that time. It is, therefore, not surprising to learn that, at a time when sightseers turned out in their thousands to witness a public execution, and pie-sellers, jugglers, fiddlers and side-shows helped to make it a festive occasion, the miserable spectacle of fettered men labouring in the mud was soon high on the list of musts for Thameside visitors.

Duncan Campbell had been given no specific directions as to the conversion of his vessels, or the manner in which the prisoners should be lodged. This left him a free hand to arrange for the accommodation of a maximum number of inmates, at a minimum of expense and consideration. After removing all unnecessary rigging and masts, and building shed-like structures on the upper deck, the decks below were cleared of all encumbrances which might take up valuable convict space and the landward portholes were permanently blocked up; the seaward grilled with iron bars. The officers lived in the stern cabins; and the single lower deck, with a head room of no more than six feet, was the living, eating and sleeping area for all the convicts on each hulk.

All the shipboard hours were spent in these cramped ill-ventilated quarters, with nothing to occupy their minds or time but complaints, or the reliving of past crimes and escapades. There was no division or classification of the prisoner according to his crime. Young lads in their early teens were cooped up with old lags and villains of every description. Alas for John Howard's dreams of reformation. Any good which may have come from convict employment ashore, was quickly undone through the association of the hardened criminal and the first-offender in these floating 'seminaries of profligacy and vice'.[5] Tricks of a dozen criminal trades could be learned from experts in each and every field. Small wonder that the Thames hulks became known to the newspaper-reading public by a name derisively bestowed – 'CAMPBELL'S ACADEMY'.

A short extract from a long poem written by a prison ship convict in 1815, (nearly forty years after the 'temporary expedient' had been introduced) when conditions, though still foul, were somewhat improved, shows that the hulks were still academies for criminal instruction:[6]

> 'Here arts of fraud are taught, here leagues are made,
> Of blackest guilt, and plans of mischief laid.
> The young offender with amazement hears
> The sins and outrages of riper years;
> But soon familiar grows with every crime –
> A veteran of vice whilst in his prime.
>
> Confine not youth in this abandoned place,
> To herd with everything both vile and base,
> Let Justice rather strike her victim dead
> Than send him here the path of sin to tread.
> Where vice unblushing tells her grossest tale
> And images obscene are made for sale.'

On Sundays, and when the weather made the boat trip ashore impossible, all labour ceased; but work was generally preferred to the stinking, crowded prison deck. These were days of miserable discomfort rather than rest; but however unpleasant the days, the nights were even worse. The prison deck, cramped enough when its occupants were on their feet, became an even more poisonous and inadequate accommodation when the tight-packed bodies stretched out to try to sleep.

The sleeping arrangements were deplorable from every viewpoint – comfort, morals and health. Hammocks had at first been tried, but without success. This is hardly surprising. The hammock is a treacherous cot, which even the rookie sailor has to learn to master – as for the landlubber in his chains and shackles – never! So they were soon replaced by wide wooden boards, ranged along the bulkheads on either side and used as mess tables during the day. Each of these shelves was the sleeping place for six men lying side by side, allowing about twenty inches shoulder space per man, one blanket shared between each pair.

Disease, and the vermin which helped it to spread, was the inevitable outcome of such conditions. This fact should have been foreseen by a man of Campbell's past experience – he had once admitted 'upon an average of seven years, [of transporting convicts to the plantations] the loss of convicts in gaol and on board will be one-seventh.' Yet he failed to include even one medical officer among his original staff appointments, much less a sick-bay or hospital quarters.

By the Autumn of 1776, when the 'temporary expedient' had been in existence for no more than a couple of months, gaol fever and dysentery had begun to take their toll of the inmates of the *Justitia* and *Censor*. Hastily constructed 'hospitals' were introduced, but these were no more than small forward areas of the prison decks, 'where they had nailed up a few boards to separate the healthy from the sick.'

John Howard recorded in 1780, that out of 632 prisoners on the two hulks, 116 were dead within nineteen months – and Campbell himself admitted 176 had died in two years.[7] Had there been any genuine examination of the situation regarding hulks as prisons at the end of the first year, the Hulk Act would have had to be repealed, and an alternative found. There was no lack of evidence that the system was rotten at the roots. The Admiralty would certainly have made known the fact that, at the same time that all this was going on in the Thames, as bad or worse was happening across the Atlantic, in the English prisoner of war hulks we had moored in the Hudson, off the City of New York since 1776.[8]

The untiring efforts of John Howard and a few like-minded men who deplored the evils of the British prison systems in general and the prison hulks in particular, resulted in a number of improvements over the years. By 1779 there were nearly twice as many convicts on the Thames hulks, as a second deck had been opened up or added to each vessel; but in some respects the conditions were better than before. On an earlier visit, Howard had commented on the poor quality of the prisoners' rations, particularly the ships' biscuit, which he found to be 'mouldy and green on both sides'. He had noted their down-beaten and ragged appearance, 'many had no shirts, some had no waistcoats, some no stockings, and some no shoes.'

Three years later, the mouldy ships' biscuit had been replaced by bread and most of the prisoners were reasonably clad and shod. Reports which told of the atrocious state of the 'Academy' had probably earned Duncan Campbell a belated rap over the knuckles and forced him to do something about his wilful neglect. Left to his own interpretation of his duties, his disregard for matters of health and sanitation would have made certain that few of his charges survived to the end of their lengthy sentences.

Largely due to the reformers' representations, two much-needed vessels were added to the Thames prison fleet. One was a receiving ship, the *Reception,* in which newly arrived convicts were examined by surgeon and kept under observation for three days before their imprisonment on *Justitia* or *Censor.*

Until the introduction of the receiving ship, convicts had been drafted direct to the prison hulks, whatever the state of their health. This meant a constant re-introduction of disease, and a form of typhus had raged throughout the whole of those first three years. Now, the spread of the disease was somewhat halted by sending infected new arrivals from the *Reception* to the second, and equally important, addition – a Hospital ship. The latter vessel was in fact the original *Justitia,* which had been replaced by another hulk which took over her name.

These were, indeed, great improvements, but improvements in a still rotten system. Laudable as were the efforts of the men who brought about these changes, it is possible that recommendations rather than down-right condemnations, may have helped to perpetuate a misconceived experiment which should have been abandoned on the evidence of its first disastrous year.

Coincident with the improvements at Woolwich, more hulks were being planned for elsewhere. It would seem that in spite of his manifest unsuitability, Campbell still had something of a monopoly in the convict-labour trade. Assisted by the Deputy Overseer, his brother Neil, the unpleasant family business had spread to Plymouth and Portsmouth. His new prison fleet was no less unwholesome than the Woolwich prototype. We hear of men who died from no other discoverable cause than hopelessness and depression of spirits. We hear of the most terrible overcrowding, where as many as seventy convicts were confined in a space no more than seventy feet by eighteen feet. Also, Black Holes, or punishment cells, in the bowels of the hulks, where troublemakers and would-be escapers were kept in darkness, half-naked and half-starved, with only a little straw to lie on.

John Howard still continued to send in his critical reports. He urged that 'the mode of confinement and labour in the hulks is too severe for the far greater number of those who are confined in them. At the same time, there is no proportion of punishment to the several offences, and consequently no distinction of guilt; which many legislators have long lamented as an evil which wants to be remedied. I must repeat my complaint that such an assemblage is entirely destructive to the morals of the young convicts.' And some of them were very young. Among the 'assemblage' on board the *Lion* hulk at Gosport, there were boys of only ten years of age.

The 'temporary' nature of the prison ship system was by now completely forgotten. As the number of prisoners increased over the years, so did the number of hulks. The confinement of war prisoners and other national problems occupied the minds of our statesmen, and little thought could be spared for an alternative means of accommodating felons – until transportation again came to the rescue – in 1787.

In the May of that year, the first Botany Bay Convict Fleet assembled at Spithead and made ready for the long voyage to New South Wales. This did not mean a reduction in the number of hulks and certainly not their abolition. Transporting convicts to Australia was a different proposition to sending them on the much shorter passage to America. Convicts awaiting transportation were sent to the hulks or confined in Newgate until their transports were ready and, for many, this could be a very long wait. Some spent three or four years on the hulks before they were included in an Australian draft – and the term of their sentence only counted from the day they were actually transported! Archbishop Whateley[9] wrote:

> 'The sentence of Transportation does not, as a stranger might suppose, imply some description of punishment, but several different ones such as, (besides actual removal to New South Wales) imprisonment in a House of Correction, confinement on board the hulks, etc., with the greatest uncertainty as to what description of punishment really does await each criminal.'

The civil prison hulks disgraced our great river and our harbours for eighty years. All who knew the facts regarding the system must have been conscious that it was a failure, other than in its basic use of convict-caging. As a source of labour it was neither cheap nor efficient; as a deterrent to further crime, a complete flop – more men emerged from the hulks as hardened villains than were ever reclaimed into decent society.

Why, then, was the expedient never improved and perfected over that long period, or abandoned at an early date? The answer to the first half of the question is that it was well-nigh impossible, as the inherent obstacles were insurmountable. As to the latter, three-quarters of a century had to pass before a more civilised view of crime and punishment was considered, and officialdom was persuaded of the importance of reformation as well as storage and punishment in the treatment of offenders. It was then, for the first time in this country, that a major building scheme for prisons ashore got under way.

In 1802 the Government assumed the responsibilities which should never have been relinquished in 1776. From that time on it provided the vessels which were to be converted, and appointed the officers and staff to manage them. Prisoners were more or less segregated according to the seriousness of their crimes; and there was some improvement in medical facilities. After another ten years, in 1812, a chaplain was appointed to each hulk, and later still, evening classes were started in most of the vessels and some even had small libraries of religious books. Whilst it may be doubted that many souls were saved, it makes a pleasant break in this chapter of human misery to note that, in the unlikely setting of a prison hulk, a number of illiterates were taught to read and write.

A far cry from 'Campbell's Academy', but much of the original evil remained to the very end. In 1825, a Dane who had been a prisoner of war and had experienced the discomfort of a floating war prison at Chatham fifteen years earlier, was sentenced to transportation to Van Diemen's Land for life. Like most transportees, he was put on board a Thames hulk to await the fitting out of a transport vessel for that long voyage. His name was Jorgen Jorgensen and in his memoirs, written ten years later, his recollections reveal that many of the horrors still remained after fifty years of civil hulk existence:

'In October, 1825, I was removed from Newgate to the hulk *Justitia* [the third of that name since the days of Duncan Campbell], which was lying at Woolwich.

'The moment a convict passes over the gangway of a hulk, he is searched for money or other articles of value; he is then taken below, and entirely stripped, is subjected to an ablution, has his hair cut off, and a prison-dress put on; irons are placed on his legs, and next morning he is sent to hard labour in the dockyard. A very few, as a matter of great favour [bribery?], are permitted to wear a slight bezel on one leg and are exempted from dockyard labour. I was one of those thus privileged.

'All communication with the rest of the world is cut off, no person is allowed on board, a visitor must stand on the platform by the side of the hulk, and can only speak to a prisoner in the presence of an officer. Any money or articles given to a prisoner must be handed over to the chief mate; all letters, even from members of Parliament, to a convict are opened, and if the captain does not choose to deliver them, he need not do so. In like manner, letters from convicts to friends, relations and others are inspected, so, should anyone complain, he only exposes himself to vengeance and punishment.

'When a House of Commons committee of inspection visits the hulks, everything seems in admirable order, and when the unfortunate men are asked if they have any complaints to make, the reply is invariably in the negative, for woe betide him who should dare to open his lips except to say that the treatment on board was most humane and kind.

'The superintendent of a hulk is styled captain and the subordinate officers are called mates, although none of them are seafaring men, being simply promoted turnkeys. I have seen the captain knock a poor fellow down with one blow merely for not getting quickly out of his way when passing forward on the deck. Redress is impossible, for all is mystery and secrecy...

[Jorgensen opined that from what he had seen of his fellow prisoners, the majority deserved some strong punishment, but...] '...but the whole system tended unequivocally to make them sycophants, hypocrites, and ten times more the children of darkness than they were before. Only those amongst them were appointed to petty offices who would betray their fellow-convicts, not in matters of great crimes or attempts to escape, but in such little trivialities as the unwarrantable possession of an inch of tobacco, or a little tea and sugar, or half a loaf.'

The end came on the morning of the 14th July, 1857, when smoke was seen rising from the forepart of the last of the civil hulks, the *Defence*. The 300 or more convicts were quickly transferred to a nearby hospital ship before the whole vast hulk went up in flames.

The Times reported that there was the 'probability of the fire having been caused by a spark from the pipe of one of the convicts picking oakum, although the regulations of the establishment strictly forbid the use of tobacco, which regulation, however, it is said, is relaxed in the case of certain invalids.' If so, then at least one good thing resulted from smoking!

As a means of punishing our social enemies the hulks were inexcusable; can we then be surprised that our national enemies found them unforgivable?

'THE PRISON HULK'
By a Convict. 1815.

'When evening o'er the ship her shadow throws,
With aching heart I hear the hatches close.
On the same deck confined a varied crew,
Employment various at their choice pursue
No keeper nigh their conduct to behold;
Free are their words, their actions uncontrolled.

'Here works are carried on of lawful trade,
Here implements of fraud and vice are made;
The coiner's hammer sounds upon the ear,
And picklock keys are manufactured here:
Here sleepless gamblers pass in play the night,
Dispute for petty stakes, and swear and fight.

'The purchased slave, his daily labours o'er,
Fatigued with toil, perhaps with lashes sore,
Enjoys at least some respite from his woes,
When on his bed his weary limbs he throws,
And sinking in night's friendly shade to rest,
Sleeps undisturbed, and in his dreams is blest.

'Not so the convict, 'midst the horrid din
Of oaths and strife, in this sad house of sin;
Not e'en though penitence and prayer should close
His eyes in hope, and promise him repose.
He knows not rest: the horrors of the night
Mix with his dreams, and rouse him with affright.
If hopeless then of sleep, the book he seeks
Whose pages comfort to the sinner speaks,
And if, in Christian charity and love,
His fellows he admonish or reprove,
The laughter loud and ridicule prevail –
Loose jests and wanton song his ear assail;
Then some more daring than the rest deny
Their Maker, and the wrath of heaven defy,
And glory in their crimes, and deeds unfold
Which blanch the cheek, and make the blood run cold.
Nor dwells their converse on the past alone:
Here deeds of future wickedness are sown;

'Here arts of fraud are taught, here leagues are made
Of blackest guilt, and plans of mischief laid.
The young offender with amazement hears
The sins and outrages of riper years;
But soon familiar grows with every crime –
A veteran in vice while in his prime.

'Confine not youth in this abandoned place,
To herd with everything both vile and base,
Let Justice rather strike her victim dead
Then send him here the path of sin to tread
Where vice unblushing tells her grossest tale,
And images obscene are made for sale.

'Place not the boy with those who know not shame,
With some whom nature shudders e'en to name;
Then better doom him to the lion's den
Than to this cursed abode of wicked men.'
(Quoted by Captain Vernon Harris in 'Dartmoor Past and Present.)

THE CIVIL HULKS 1776–1857

WOOLWICH

JUSTITIA. One of the first two hulks established under the 'Hulks Act'. May 1776. An old East Indiaman. Over the following eighty years, two other hulks were given that name.

CENSOR. The second of the original civil hulks. An old frigate, purchased from the Admiralty.

CERES. An early receiving ship at Woolwich.

DEFENCE. Fitted out at Portsmouth and brought to Woolwich. Officially the last civil hulk. Destroyed by fire on the 14th July, 1857.
GANYMEDE and **LEVEN.** The former a large hulk with a smaller close by. In most official returns, both hulks were counted as one.

HEBE. A small hulk which, together with the **WYE**, took convicts after the **JUSTITIA** became too decrepit for further service.

LEVEN. Overflow hulk alongside the **GANYMEDE**.

RETRIBUTION. Old 32-gun man-o'-war, captured from the Spanish. A second hulk of that name, based at Sheerness, was broken up in 1834.

UNITE. Hospital ship. A captured French frigate. Housed the survivors of the fire which destroyed the **DEFENCE** in 1857.

WARRIOR. At various times in company with **DEFENCE**, **WYE**, **UNITE**, **JUSTITIA** and **HEBE**. Broken up 1856/7.

WYE. Hospital ship. Originally at Chatham, later Woolwich.

SHEERNESS

BELLEROPHON. 74-gun Man-o'-war. The ship which brought Napoleon to Plymouth in July, 1815. following his defeat at Waterloo. Served as a hulk from 1816 to 1825. In 1823 the **BELLEROPHON** was a special hulk for convict boys.

RETRIBUTION. A second hulk of that name.

ZEALAND. Established as a hulk about 1810.

CHATHAM

CANADA. Hospital ship to the **CUMBERLAND** and the **DOLPHIN**.

CUMBERLAND.

DOLPHIN. In October,1829. There was an attempt to sabotage the **DOLPHIN**. About four hundred convicts were rescued and some were put into the **CANADA** hospital hulk.

EURYALUS. Was one of the only two frigates in Nelson's Fleet at Trafalgar. After the death of Nelson, Admiral Collingwood took his flag from the disabled **RESOLUTION** to the **EURYALUS**, which then took the **RESOLUTION** in tow. When the boy convicts – between three and four hundred – were removed from the **BELLEROPHON**, at Sheerness, they were transferred to **EURYALUS** at Chatham.

FORTITUDE. Prison hulk.

WYE. Hospital ship. Later moved to Woolwich.

DEPTFORD

DISCOVERY. This is the **DISCOVERY** which sailed with Captain James Cook on the **RESOLUTION** in 1776; on what was to be his last voyage. He was killed in the Sandwich Islands in 1779. In 1824 she was put to use as a convict hulk at Deptford, and was broken up at Woolwich in 1834.

PORTSMOUTH

BRITON. Hospital ship to **STIRLING CASTLE** and **YORK**. The **BRITON** was the only hulk left at Portsmouth after 1852, as a hospital to the new prison ashore at Portsmouth.

CAPTIVITY. Prison hulk on which the first school was started in 1813. In 1825 a second hulk of the name **CAPTIVITY** was towed round to Devonport.
HARDY. Prison hulk moored at Tipner, Portsmouth area. Taken out of service in 1834.

LAUREL. Prison hulk.

LEVIATHAN. Prison hulk. In the 1830s it had a small library with books available to certain prisoners.

STIRLING CASTLE. Prison hulk. Until early 1840s at Devonport, then moved to Portsmouth.

GOSPORT

LION. Prison hulk. An old East Indiaman, established as a hulk at Gosport in 1820, and broken up in 1848.

YORK. Prison hulk. Established at the same time as the **LION**, in 1820 and condemned and demolished by convict volunteers in 1848.

LANGSTONE HARBOUR

CERES. At first a receiving ship at Woolwich and later moved to Langstone Harbour, Portsmouth.

FORTUNEE. A captured French frigate. Converted and moored in Langstone Harbour.

PORTLAND. Prison hulk at Langstone Harbour. Portsmouth.

PLYMOUTH

CHATHAM. An old 70-gun warship, she was one of the earliest prison hulks at Plymouth in the 1780s. Did not serve for long and was replaced by the **DUNKIRK**.

DUNKIRK. An old 74-gun ship, and at one time the largest prison hulk in service. Replaced the **CHATHAM** in the 1780s. During the War of American Independence, the **DUNKIRK** was the guardship at Plymouth and the receiving ship for prisoners of war. First of the hulks to segregate different classes of criminals and crimes.

DEVONPORT

CAPTIVITY. Prison hulk. Brought from Portsmouth to Devonport in 1825. The second hulk of that name. Demolished in 1834.

IRELAND

ESSEX. Prison hulk for both felons and political prisoners. Anchored in Kingstown Harbour. 1826.

SURPRISE. Prison hulk. Anchored in Cork Harbour 1826. By 1838 nearly 11,000 prisoners had passed through these two comparatively small hulks, most of them transported or transferred to the Bermuda hulks.

BERMUDA

ANTELOPE. Established in 1824; the first hulk to be based in Bermuda for the reception of particularly incorrigible types of offender.

DROMEDARY. One of the three other hulks which made up the original Bermuda prison fleet.

COROMANDEL. Prison hulk. There was constant trouble on all these hulks, mutiny, disease, etc.

WEYMOUTH. Prison hulk. Taken out of service in 1836 and later replaced by the **MEDWAY** and an attendant hospital ship.

MEDWAY. The last prison hulk to join the fleet. Between the four hulks they could accommodate about 1,500 convicts.

TENEDOS. The hospital ship to the prison fleet.

The Bermuda prison ship fleet at Ireland Island, existed for thirty-eight years, and was still operating for some years after civil hulks in England were no more.

One other hulk, a prison hospital ship to the convict establishment at **GIBRALTAR** lasted even longer, until 1875.

1. P.W. Bamford: *Fighting Ships & Prisons.*

2. The Solicitor General. 1785.

3. John Howard, 1726–1790. Philanthropist and prison reformer, Howard was himself a prisoner of war of the French in the beginning of the Seven Years' War, 1756.

4. *The Scots Magazine.* July, 1777.

5. Patrick Colquhon: *Roots of Evil.*

6. The complete poem appears at the end of this chapter.

7. John Howard: *State of the Prisons, 1775–76,* and

Appendix, 1780.

8. See Chapter 7, THE NEW YORK PRISON SHIPS.

9. Richard Whately, 1787–1863. Archbishop of Dublin.

Chapter Six

Part One

The Prisoner of War Hulks

'It is difficult to imagine a more severe punishment; it is cruel to maintain it for an indefinite period; and to submit to it prisoners of war who deserve much consideration, and who incontestably are the innocent victims of the fortunes of war.

'The British prison ships have left profound impressions on the minds of Frenchmen who have experienced; an ardent longing for revenge has for long moved their hearts… '   BARON DE BONNEFAUX

THE PREVIOUS CHAPTER HAS SHOWN THAT THE proliferation of hulks as places of detention, came about only after 1775, at which time Britain was faced with an almost insoluble problem – the extreme shortage of prison and gaol space available in which to house her civil prisoners.

It was, therefore, inevitable that as the Government could find no better method of confining its felons and political offenders than the hulks, it should sooner or later resort to extending the 'temporary expedient' of prison ships, to cover the internment of our enemy captives, both at home and overseas (see Chapter 7, THE NEW YORK PRISON SHIPS).

Nevertheless, many of our own people, prominent men amongst them, had deep-felt objections to the whole idea of prison ships, however well maintained and managed. Sir William Napier, historian of the Peninsular Wars, detested the hulks, and – perhaps conveniently forgetting our convict transportation system – considered them a punishment 'far beyond that inflicted on the most infamous felons, who are only shut up for a few months.'

He did, however, suggest a more humane, though not very practicable alternative. 'What', he asked, 'was to hinder these honourable and brave men from being placed in one or two of our western islands which they could have cultivated, and from whence they could not have escaped, if all boats had been forbidden to approach the islands save for an armed vessel or two to guard the coast?'

The records are filled with Government Orders, Tables and Lists, which set down in minute detail provisions to ensure the fair treatment of the prisoner of war; most of which had been agreed upon between the warring governments. These rules and regulations were undoubtedly well-meant on both sides of the Channel, and only the most cynical could imagine that they were no more than bureaucratic cover-ups for a cruel disregard for enemy captives. Nevertheless, how ever good the intentions, their implementation left much to be desired; and few British prisoners who had experienced the dungeons of France, or foreigners the hulks of Britain, could ever forgive their captors.

It is true that the Transport Board appointed travelling inspectors whose job it was to visit the prison ships and report on what they discovered. Some were conscientious men who reported honestly and told often grim stories of neglect and suffering. But these honest men were up against so many vested interests – the crooked contractors, suppliers of food, soap, clothing, bedding and other

necessities and the purser who augmented his small pay at the prisoners' expense.

Corruption was prevalent at all levels of society, and among the hulk-inspectors there were those who never gave an unfavourable report after their investigations; but as we shall see, there were some clean-ups and improvements: when bad agents were dismissed, dishonest contractors lost their contracts, and, of equal importance, efforts were made to save the worst type of prisoners from their own follies. However, there could never be a complete solution to such a fundamentally bad system.

One prison ship commander left the authorities in no doubt of his opinion of the state of things on the Europe hulk at Plymouth, to which he had been appointed commander in 1796. In November, Lieutenant Gardiner wrote to The Lords of the Admiralty:[1]

'I beg to state for their Lordships' information the wretched situation of at least 300 of the Prisoners now on board the *Europe* under my command, they are destitute of almost every Article of Clothing and all that many have is a miserable piece of dirty old Hammock sewed round their bodies without Shoes, Stockings, Shirts, without so much as a covering to the head or a handkerchief to the neck and to compleat their misery they have not had an ounce of Soap issued to them these three weeks and upwards.

'The Surgeon of the *Europe* has represented to me that the Prisoners are becoming sickly and that he is apprehensive that some Serious Disorders may ensue if Clothing is not issued to them at this inclement Season of the Year; and hopes that their proportion of soap might be continued to keep them clean.'

As the *Europe* was classed as a seven-hundred-prisoner hulk, it would seem probable that the unwashed destitute 330 were, in the main, that part of the crew who had lost any clothes and possessions they might ever have had to the gambling tables; but the conscientious and humane Lieutenant Gardiner went on:

'I trust their Lordships will believe me when I assure them that I have used every argument and endeavour in my power to obtain relief for these miserable Prisoners before I would presume to trouble their Lordships upon the subject, but sorry I am to add that all my endeavours have not only been in vain but very unsatisfactory........................

'Finding the Prisoners in this wretched state, I have made very diligent and minute inquiry to find whether they had any Clothes issued to them, from an Idea that they might have made an improper use of them [selling to obtain stakes] but strange as it may appear to their

Lordships I cannot find by the Prisoners nor the joint testimony of the Officers of the Ship that any Articles of Clothing has ever been issued to them.'

(It would be interesting to know whether their Lordships enquired into the conduct of Gardiner's predecessor as commander of the *Europe*.)

Many other British censures could be recited here; and the bitter criticisms and recriminations of the men (and a few women) who had suffered the trials of life on board a floating prison, will suffice to tell the story. That story, garnered from the memoirs, diaries, letters and complaints of prisoners – French, Dutch, Danish, American – covering more than half a century, leaves one with a vision of hell on water; a blot on those pages of Britain's history. Even when the more reasoned reminiscences of prisoner memoirists are balanced against the exaggerations and bitter tirades of their unforgiving brothers; when the records of to-and-fro complaints and justifications between the warring governments have been examined; and the reports of fair-minded men like John Howard and other contemporary observers are carefully perused; one can be left with only one conclusion – that the prisoner of war hulk was an abomination.

But it does not follow that, as the French would have it, there was a devious plot on the part of the Government to severely punish, as well as confine, its prisoners of war. The administration can be rightly criticised for not making greater efforts to root out the corruption that certainly added to the suffering, by clamping down on the unfair contractors and those captains, agents and overseers who neglected their duty and treated their posts as sinecures.

Greater foresight may have led to the creation of shore-based prisoner of war establishments in the early days, but once the unexpected and almost unimaginable flood of captives hit our shores, it is hard to see an alternative to increasing the use of hulks. Some efforts had been made. The huge wood-built Norman Cross Depot at Peterborough had been built solely for the confinement of war prisoners in the last years of the eighteenth century, and was capable of holding between six or seven thousand captives. The great stone-built Dartmoor Depot, with its seven prisons and yards, opened its doors to a like number in 1809; and in the north there were the Scottish Depots at Greenlaw and Valleyfield. But even the many acres of space within these vast depots were insufficient to make the hulks less necessary – in fact, had those depots not existed, there is little doubt that the prison ship fleets would have greatly increased countrywide.

There is little doubt that ships have been put to use as prisons throughout the centuries in many parts of the world; either as a temporary means of conveying captives to shore-based confinement away from the possibility of enemy liberation, or as superannuated ships stripped down, converted into more permanent establishments, and moored in rivers and harbours. In the early 1750s two hulks were already moored at Plymouth, the *Royal Oak* and the *San Raphael* (or *San Rafael*), and both of these hulks were still operative during the War of American Independence a quarter of a century later.

It may be appropriate at the beginning of this chapter to relate the story of a happening on one of these earliest of prison hulks: At whatever period in the history of war, thoughts of escape would have occupied the minds of most prisoners, whether their confinement was on land or afloat. An important factor in the well-planned escape was the possession of passport papers and money – and, as we shall discover, in most if not all prison hulks, there

were skilful forgers of documents and bank-notes.[2]

The *Royal Oak* was no exception. In 1759, a mass escape was planned by a group of her inmates, and passports and paper-money had been forged to assist in their escape to France; but before they could be delivered, the plot and the forgeries were made known to the Captain of the hulk. The would-be absconders were certain that they knew the identity of the informant, another Frenchman named Jean Maneaux. Five of them decided on revenge: 'they got Maneaux into an obscure corner of the ship, tied him to a ringbolt, and gave him sixty lashes with a rope to which was fastened an iron thimble as thick as a man's wrist. He got loose, and fell back; they jumped on him till they broke his neck, then cut his body into small pieces, and conveyed them through a waste pipe overboard. The next day twenty-seven prisoners were arrested, and one of them pointed out the actual murderers.'[3] In April, the five were tried and executed.

The name of the other early Plymouth hulk, the *San Rafael*, crops up in one of two accounts of prison ship escapes, which, though separated by thirty-two years, are suspiciously similar in detail. It may, of course, be that the second event was a copycat venture inspired by long-remembered reports of the first – or they may have been two completely unconnected happenings.

Francis Abell tells us that, in 1778, two French prisoners from the *San Rafael* escaped and swam out to a lighter laden with gunpowder. They boarded the lighter and, after overpowering the one man left in charge, swept down through all the ships in the Hamoaze, rounded Drake's Island, and 'got safely away to France, where they sold the powder at a handsome price'.

The second account, I found among many interesting entries in the log of Captain Edward Hawkins, one-time Superintendent of the Plymouth Prison Ships. An entry for June, 1810, records that a number of French prisoners from the hulks were put to work on board a powder ship, the *Union*, moored in the Hamoaze. It seems that the majority of the British crew had been given overnight leave and had departed for an enjoyable night ashore. Only a minimal number were left to guard the prisoners, so it was not surprising that the latter took advantage of the situation, overcame their keepers, cast off the *Union* from her moorings, and sailed away to France!

The use of the ship-as-prison on a large scale did not feature as vastly important in our system of prisoner of war management until the beginning of the nineteenth century – with the dreadful exception of the British prison ships in America, twenty years earlier (see Chapter 7, THE NEW YORK PRISON SHIPS).

There had been a few additional vessels to cope with Yankee, French and other continental captives during the American war; but over the twenty-two years of warfare which followed the outbreak of the Revolutionary War with France, in 1793, the prison ship fleet grew to the more than sixty vessels which were regarded with fear and remembered with hatred by their inmates.

A few of the many thousands of prisoners who endured months or years on one or more of the hulks listed below, left memoirs, journals or diaries which provide the material for this chapter. All were genuinely convinced that they were the victims of a system inspired by the fiendish cruelty and vindictiveness of the English. Napoleon perpetuated that belief on many occasions, particularly in his address to the army before the Battle of Waterloo: 'Soldiers, let those among you who have been prisoners of the English describe to you the hulks, and detail the frightful miseries which they have endured.'

However, most of these reminiscences told of the good with the bad, whilst some others are so filled with exaggeration and vengeful bitterness that, whilst interesting in providing us with details of individual vessels, are historically useless.

PLYMOUTH

LA BRAVE	*ROYAL OAK****	*SAN RAFAEL*
SAN NICOLAS	*HECTOR*	*GENEREAUX*
L'OISEAU	*BIENFAISANT*	*PRUDENT*
PANTHER	*EL FIRME*	*VANGUARD*
SAN YSIDRO	*GANGES*	*PRINCE**
*LE CATON***	*RENOWN***	*EUROPE***

DUNKIRK Reception hulk and guardship.
SAN SALVADOR Receiving ship.

**PRINCE* (98) Prison ship only from December 1807 to April,1808.
**Hulks at one time or another employed as Hospital Ships.
****ROYAL OAK* renamed *ASSISTANCE* (see Portsmouth).

PORTSMOUTH

ASSISTANCE	*CAPTIVITY*	*CROWN*
ARVE PRINCEN	*DIAMOND*	*GUILDFORD*
KRON PRINCESSA	*NEGRO*	*PORTLAND*
PROTHEE	*SAN ANTONIO*	*SAN DAMASO*
*SUFFOLK***	*VENGEANCE*	*VETERAN*
VIGILANT	*PRINCESS SOPHIA*	*WALEMAR*
*MARENGO**	*PEGASUS**	

*Hospital Ships. ***SULTAN* renamed *SUFFOLK* 1805.

CHATHAM

BAHAMA	*BELLIQUEAUX*	*BRISTOL*
BRUNSWICK	*BUCKINGHAM*	*CAMPERDOWN*
CANADA	*CAPE ST VINCENT*	*CORNWALL*
CROWN PRINCE	*EAGLE*	*GLORY*
GELYKHEID	*HERO*	*IRRESISTIBLE*
NASSAU	*ROCHESTER*	*SAMPSON*
SOUTHWICK	*SANDWICH*	*VRYHEIT*
*FYEN**	*TRUSTY**	

*Hulks at one time or another employed as Hospital Ships.

The vessels which ended their days as prison ships had, in the main, once been powerful ships of war of the 60- to 90-gun class. Many of them had reached old age in the service of Britain, their feats celebrated in the annals of the Royal Navy. Others – French, Dutch, Danish and Spanish men-of-war – were prizes taken in great sea fights. The Spanish 80-gun *San Nicolas*, at Plymouth, was captured by Nelson in the Battle of Cape St Vincent in 1797; the Dutch 72-gun *Vryheid*, at Chatham, had been the flagship of Admiral de Winter at the Battle of Camperdown in that same year; The Superintendent's hulk at Plymouth, the *Brave*, was the former French 90-gun, *Formidable* captured after escaping from the Battle of Trafalgar. The pre-capture histories of the foreign contributions to our prison ship fleet could constitute an interesting book in its own right.

Four British ships which were later to become Chatham hulks

had a less than glorious event to add to their service records – the Mutiny at the Nore. The *Nassau*, *Eagle*, *Belliqueaux* and the *Sandwich*, were among the dozen or so men-of-war anchored in the entrance to the Thames when, in 1797, the mutiny which had started at Spithead spread to the Nore. The chief mutineer, Richard Parker, an educated 'lower deck lawyer', who was once a Midshipman, had been court-martialled and demoted in 1793 – and dismissed as insane in 1794. Surprisingly, he had somehow managed to re-enlist and had now appointed himself 'President' of the rebel delegates council.

The *Sandwich* (90), was at that time the principal ship on that station and carried the flag of Vice-Admiral Buckner, and the arrogant Parker determined that nothing less than the *Sandwich* itself should be his revolutionary headquarters. On the 23rd May, he struck the Admiral's flag and hoisted the red flag of mutiny in its stead. It flew for only three weeks. By the 14th June, the rebellion was over and a large number of the mutineers were imprisoned on the *Eagle*, moored in the Medway. Over the next few months, more than four hundred of the rebels faced trial, and received sentences of gaol and or flogging – some were awarded the terrible punishment of flogging-round-the-fleet. Richard Parker was court-martialled and sentenced to be hanged at the yard-arm of his erstwhile 'flagship'. On the 29th June, he was executed on the *Sandwich* – and twenty-nine of his principal followers suffered a similar fate.

At almost exactly that same time in 1797, the *Royal Oak*, which had by then been moved from Plymouth to Portsmouth, was adding some colourful characters to her complement of captured inmates. In May of that year, the American Colonel William Tate, Chef de Brigade of the French *Legion Noire* – and antihero of the Fishguard landings[4] – arrived on board together with his French second in command, Le Brun, and three Irish officers. His ineffectual invasion force of about fifteen hundred, had been made up of six hundred convicts from the French galleys, 'still wearing irons', and the remainder included about the same number of selected civil prisoners impressed from the gaols of France – all in all, a sorry, undisciplined and rather insulting bunch to send on an invasion of Britain! After the surrender, this strange assortment was distributed through the few Portsmouth hulks or housed in prisons ashore.

The *Royal Oak* received its share – including four women taken prisoner at Fishguard with their husbands, two officers and two soldiers. Colonel Tate was shocked to find himself on a prison ship, and wrote many letters to the Admiralty, gently reminding them of his rank, and applying for parole to go to France under one pretext or another. His most ingenious proposal was that his influence with the French government might achieve what all the efforts of our Government had failed to do – obtain the exchange of Admiral Sir Sidney Smith, imprisoned in France.

In a letter headed 'Royal Oak Prison Ship at Portsmouth.–16th Prairial – 5th year of the Republic', he wrote:

> 'My Lords,
> If the consideration of Sir Sydney Smith's situation continues yet to exercise the attention of his Britannic Majesty's Ministers, I have to propose to your Lordships to obtain permission to go to France on my parole; & if (in a reasonable time) Sir Sydney shall not be released from confinement, then I shall be held to present myself in England… '

However, the authorities had no reason to trust Tate, the invader who sailed into Fishguard under false colours, or to grant him any favours. The Admiralty's reply was short but not very sweet. Captain Rawe, the Superintendent of Hulks at Portsmouth, was instructed: '…answer and acquaint him that "...their Ldshps cannot comply with his request."'

Some of the more extreme and sensational of the allegations made by French memoirists regarding prison ships, were later refuted by some of their own countrymen. In 1815, the 'broke-parole', General René Martin Pillet, published his *'L'Angleterre vue à Londres et dans ses Provinces, pendant un séjour de dix années'*, in which he said that 150,000 French prisoners had died in our hulks from deliberate ill-treatment, and other exaggerated statistics, easily dismissed by official British and French figures. The next year another French General, Jean Sarrazin, published *'Tableau de la Grand-Bretagne'*, which demolished almost every accusation; even adding a stones-and-glasshouses reply to Pillet's diatribe on British corruption (which may have contained some truth), by reminding him: 'Have we not seen that General Wirion [General de Gendarmerie and Commandant over British parolees], at Verdun, in France, blow out his brains, after having employed the funds destined for the British prisoners, to his own private purposes… and being unable to protest his innocence.'

Nevertheless, extracts from Pillet's book will add to our knowledge of the *Brunswick*, the hulk to which the General was sent after breaking his parole at Arlesford, and first spending some time in Norman Cross Depot. Two other French 'broke-paroles', Colonel Lebertre and Captain (later Baron) Charles Dupin were both, perhaps understandably, given to overstatement. Lebertre, who had also been paroled to Arlesford but later earned a place on the *Canada* prison ship at Chatham in 1811, wrote:

> 'Men sensual and hardened by pleasures. You who in full Parliament outrage your victims and declare that the prisoners are happy. Would you know the full horror of their condition, come without notice beforehand; dare to descend before daylight into the tombs in which you bury living creatures who are human beings like yourselves; try to breathe for one minute the sepulchral vapours which these unfortunates breathe for many years, and which sometimes suffocates them; see them tossing in their hammocks assailed by thousands of insects, and wooing in vain the sleep which could soften for one moment their sufferings.'

This hard-hitting and indignant declaration has the ring of truth about it – justified when one learns that he had just read a report addressed to the British Parliament by J.W. Croker, Secretary to the Admiralty, which said he had visited the hulks at Portsmouth, where the prisoners were 'comfortable and happy and well provided with amusement.' Colonel Lebertre's book also contained the hammock plan of the orlop deck of the Chatham hulk, *Brunswick*.

Captain Charles Dupin's memories, though often fascinating, cannot always be relied upon wherever he has the opportunity to further blacken England's name. He would have been taken more seriously had he stuck to the facts and figures, which were bad enough without elaboration. In a post-war report to the French Government, Dupin described the hulks on the Medway:

'The Medway is covered with men-of-war, dismantled and lying in ordinary. Their fresh and brilliant painting contrasts with the hideous aspect of the old and smoky hulks, which seem the remains of vessels blackened by a recent fire. It is in these floating tombs that prisoners of war are buried alive – Danes, Swedes, Frenchmen, Americans, no matter. They are lodged on the lower deck, on the upper deck, and even on the orlop deck… Four hundred malefactors are the maximum of a ship appropriated to convicts. From eight hundred to twelve hundred is the ordinary number of prisoners of war who are heaped together in a ship of the same rate.'

It is understandable he should have somewhat over-stated his case; but Dupin's lengthy report laid on layers of complaint with an outsized trowel. His description of the 'hideous aspect' of the prison fleet was fair enough, but, whilst from time to time there was terrible but unavoidable overcrowding, he certainly exaggerated the convict/prisoner of war ratio – we know from the records and the journals of Superintendents of the dozen or so hulks on the Hamoaze, and the hulks at Portsmouth at about that time, that the average number on each prison ship was about seven hundred.

Another two Frenchmen, the Baron de Bonnefoux and Ambroise Louis Garneray, captured on the same frigate in 1806, contribute greatly to the picture of prisoner of war life in a floating prison. Garneray's *'Mes Pontons – neuf années de captivité'*, is filled with detail and has its share of anti-British criticism, but is a more pleasant read and in places highly entertaining. Garneray was a remarkable and admirable character; a born story-teller whose more amazing tales should, perhaps be seasoned with a little salt. But, in general, his is the most reliable source of prison ship information among the French writers. However, the French did not have a monopoly in recollections. We have the Americans, Josiah Cobb, the 'Greenhand'; Benjamin Waterhouse, 'The Young Man of Massachusetts'; Charles Andrews, and a few others, who will tell their part of the story as it progresses. The account of the Danish, Norwegian and Swedish prisoners on the hulks, based on the diary of Jens Krog – *'Prisonen Danske og Norske Krigsfanger i England 1807–14'* and Kaptein Paul Kaals', *'Pa Kapertokt og i Prison 1808–1810'* – will take up a separate chapter.

Louis Garneray was born in Paris on the 19th February, 1783, and christened Ambroise Louis, but is always referred to by his second forename. Born into a family of successful artists, it had been intended that he, like his father and three younger brothers, should become a painter. He did receive some early training from his father, Jean François, but from a very young age Louis was lured by the spirit of adventure and the call of the sea. Encouraged by an old sea-dog cousin, Beaulieu Le Loup, who commanded a vessel called *La Forte*, the thirteen year old Louis pestered his parents until they capitulated and let him go. He joined the *La Forte* which was being fitted out for a voyage to India, as a 'novice', or ship's boy, who would have to jump to it, whatever he was asked to do. Louis would have been forewarned that he would have to learn the tricks of the sailor's trade from tough, hard-bitten and often brutal, seaman – not least, his captain cousin who, he was given to understand, had been ordered 'to throw the boy overboard at his first sign of weakness, so as to preserve the family name'. Tough as it was, he never regretted his choice between art and seafaring; although even in his first months at sea he had experienced what was literally a baptism of fire – his first sea battle: 'the decks awash with shellfire, the wounded wailing in cannonfire smoke'.

Louis grew up fast. His next ten years were packed with all manner of adventure; the taking of merchant-ship prizes, action in many sea fights; always the hazard of the elements, and survival of shipwreck on more than one occasion. Over those years he served on at least ten different vessels, sometimes as quartermaster's mate in the French Imperial Navy, at others as a lieutenant on privateers in the Indian Ocean, in company with such exotic characters as the famous Breton corsair Captain Robert Surcouf, known as *'le Roi des Corsaires'*. By that time Louis had graduated to become a typical all-round privateer officer, competent and fearless, identifying himself with that select brotherhood of corsairs known as *'Les Frères La Côte'*; but at the time of his capture he was back in the Imperial Navy.

Garneray's last ship was the frigate *Belle-Poule*, and his last day of life as a free mariner was the 13th March, 1806. On that day the *Belle-Poule*, in company with the *Marengo*, were captured off the Azores, by a British squadron commanded by Admiral Sir J. B. Warren. Garneray and his fellow prisoners were taken aboard the *Ramilles* and some weeks later they were landed at Portsmouth – their 'home' for the best part of the following nine years. It is sad to think that this talented, adventurous young man, with his love of ships and the sea, should have been doomed to spend the rest of his youth on a very different type of vessel – 'a black, shapeless sarcophagus' – the prison hulk *Prothée*, and later, on the *Crown* and the *Vengeance* at Portsmouth.

Undoubtedly, many thousands of lives were blighted by even short periods spent in marine prisons. That Louis Garneray should have endured so many years without ever losing his dream of freedom by exchange, escape or parole, shows a man of indomitable courage, who made the best of what could have been completely wasted years. He says, in his memoirs *'Mes Pontons'*, that he vowed to himself that he would never have an idle hour in any day of his captivity; that he would not be diverted by the gambling or any of the low life that existed on every hulk, but would seek out men who could improve his mind. Louis studied mathematics, improved his English and took fencing lessons from prisoner instructors on board the *Prothée* 'with the object of tiring my body'.

It must be admitted that, in each of his three pontons, he was more privileged than any other prisoner on board, that his lodging was better, and his ability to supply himself with additions to his rations was greater. But it should also be said that none of these things were obtained through influence, but through ingenuity in turning his versatile mind and hand to anything which would stimulate his interest or bring him in a sou.

Louis Garneray was no less dismayed than his shipmates by his first sight of the *Prothée*, whose 'monstrous shape made me think of some vast dark tomb.' Every Frenchman had heard of the hulks; but the reality of the worst of them could never have been visualised.

' …the escort party led us up on deck and flung us without warning into the midst of the pitiful, horrifying inhabitants of the *Prothée*. Picture an army of corpses emerging from the grave, hollow eyed, bent, unshaven, their faces wan and grey, their bones only half covered in yellow rags. Picture this, and you will still have only a feeble impression of what met my eyes when I saw my future companions.'

Soon he was grabbed, stripped of his uniform and pushed into a cold bath, before being issued with his prisoner uniform. This outfit of coarse material consisted of orange-yellow trousers, shirt and waistcoat, all stamped with the large black T.O. mark of the Transport Office. There was no fitting; the trousers ended at his knees and the waistcoat did not meet up across his chest. Prison issue varied from place to place and over the years, but it usually included a yellow T.O. jacket, a grey or yellow cap, two pairs of stockings and a pair of shoes, all of which were expected to last at least eighteen months. As if the yellow garb and large T.O.s would not make a would-be escaper easily spotted by the guards, at least in daytime, the waistcoat was often of bright red material. Each prisoner was treated the same, be the officer or rating. Only those with money or valuables for barter could improve on the basic food ration, clothes and bedding of hammock and flock or straw-filled mattress.

After Garneray had undergone a close questioning and 'signing-in', which took note of every personal detail of prisoners, from rank or rating to birthmarks and scars – he was taken to the 24-pounder gun deck and left to lay claim to a sleeping place among the four hundred prisoners on that deck: 'I cannot find words to fully describe the feelings of disgust and nausea which assailed me… I felt a heavy and stifling fog choking me – a cloud of deadly germs of every disease about to corrupt my blood. Fortunately, the shock soon wore off and after half an hour between decks I became, if not accustomed to the stifling atmosphere, at least able to cope with it.'

It was pitch-dark, but glimmers of light which filtered through the iron-grilled portholes soon revealed the impossibility of finding space to sling a hammock among the great mass of prisoners who had already staked their claim. At first he felt resigned to the inevitability of sleeping on the deck of this dirty, evil-smelling dungeon, but then appealed for help and advice from the most presentable figure he could find amongst the pale-faced mob which crowded the deck, clad 'in the most indescribable assortment of rags. Even the most squalid beggars of Spain could give no idea of the tattered state of my companions.' His adviser, a shoemaker who earned enough to keep himself well-fed, assured him that he could solve his problem.

Garneray was about to learn one of the greatest facts of prison ship life – the importance of money – though strength of character was undoubtedly the greatest. He found it quite unbelievable that any man would sell his very living space, but very soon the cobbler came back to him with a thin and hungry-looking infantryman. The soldier had recently 'inherited' one of the best sites on the deck, but was induced to part with it by the thought of being able to eat well for a few months. Garneray, ignorant of property prices on the hulk, willingly allowed himself to be grossly overcharged, and the soldier went off with three gold louis – and the helpful cobbler pocketed his fee of forty sous.

Louis was delighted with his purchase, which he found to be beside a porthole, with plenty of space for his hammock and a small table and bench for his exclusive use. Living space, like everything else in prison or on hulk, had its price, and although the triumph of the capitalist over the needy may be reprehensible, there was no wiser way for a newly arrived prisoner to spend his money. Such buying and selling is mentioned in a number of memoirs: Colonel Lebertre at Chatham, paid 120 francs for a tiny plot in the battery of the *Canada* hulk, but did not have Garneray's luxury of an air vent.

Louis' description of the Portsmouth hulk itself, in terms of basic layout, is almost identical with that of Baron de Bonnefoux at Chatham – and not so different in essential details from the *Jersey* and her sister ships at New York in the 1770s.

The visual contrast between the 'brilliant' active man-of-war and its blackened static cousin could not, as Captain Dupin noted, be greater. During the eighteenth century and well into the nineteenth, British men-of-war were painted a gleaming yellow all over, above a broad black band at water-line. This was the general approach, although some Admirals adopted individual trade marks by painting their ships red, black or blue; Nelson's vessels were distinguished by their all-over black and white chequer-board pattern.

When the combined French and Spanish Fleet was sighted before Trafalgar it was noticed that some of the French ships were similarly painted with yellow, red or white bands along their black hulls. The ever-diligent Nelson ordered that the iron hoops which banded the masts of his ships should be painted bright yellow, for easy identification amid the smoke and confusion of close battle.

But whether bright yellow or dismal black on the outside, the interior architecture was never designed for the comfort of either free seaman or prisoner of war. The head-height between decks was never more than six feet, and often less - only four feet ten inches in the orlop-deck of the *Brunswick* at Chatham. Cracked heads were so frequent that some believed the malicious rumour that there was a greater incidence of madness among sailors than among landlubbers ashore. If the rumour was indeed true, a dozen more believable reasons could be cited.

In theory a ship which had been stripped down to accommodate seven hundred prisoners, should have provided more space than that available to the crew of that same vessel when in service as a man-of-war. The full ship's complement would have seldom been less in number, and much of the deck space would have been taken up by guns, anchors, cables, masts, rigging and all manner of ship's furniture. With all those obstacles out of the way and the sleeping decks furnished with no more than two benches which ran the length of the decks and four athwartships, there was, in fact, more space. But the 'free' *vessel* did not have the problem of providing a dormitory for six or seven hundred men at one time – the larboard and starboard watch-keeping system, which meant that the use of sleeping space could be staggered over the twenty-four hours, would have seen to that.

Garneray says that the *Prothée*'s open upper or well-deck was the prisoners' main place of exercise and access to fresh air, a relief from the stagnant atmosphere of the decks below. It was about 44 feet by 38 feet in area and had long been known as the 'Parc'. The only other open-air part of the hulk where prisoners could forgather was the fo'c'sle, but this was unpopular on days when the wind did not favour them and the thick black coal smoke from the forward chimneys soon cleared the deck.

The British naval complement, numbering about thirty, and the military force, were accommodated fore and aft of the hulk. The naval complement of each hulk at that time would have been made up roughly as follows:-

> Lieutenant and Agent; Surgeon; Gunner; Boatswain; Carpenter; Cook; Purser; Master's Mate; two Midshipmen; fifteen to twenty Seamen; Purser's Steward; five or six Boys.
> After September 1813 the Transport Office added a Second Lieutenant to the staff of each hulk.

The officers, their staff and servants, were housed in the stern, and the garrison forrad. The military guards and sentries – who would have been replaced by other units from time to time in the interests of security – amounting to between forty and fifty men, were under the command of a Lieutenant of Marines.

Between the guards and the prisoners was a strong bulkhead of hardwood, studded with 'thousands of large-headed nails, very close together, forming a wall of iron'. As on the *Jersey*, observation holes were cut through this barrier, for the guards to oversee their charges – and use as gun-ports in the case of mutiny or riot. The commander of the *Prothée* was a naval lieutenant, with a master as his second in command. About twenty sailors were kept busy, manning the hulk's boats, securing and raising the port and scuttle covers morning and night, and the hundred and one tasks associated with such a large ship's maintenance.

The number which made up the British garrison on the *Prothée* was similar to that of most prison ships; as were the security arrangements. The hulks were not scattered, but moored stem to stern or broadside on, so that the guards on one ship could operate a certain amount of additional surveillance over neighbouring hulks.

By day, three sentries patrolled the gallery which went completely around the hulk, just above the water-line. It had a lattice-work floor which made it difficult for a would-be escaper to hide beneath a sentry's beat. A guard was stationed on each of the gangboards and another at the foot of the ladder. On the hulk itself, a guard took up position on the fo'c'sle and on the quarterdeck a group of eight or ten fully armed soldiers were on the alert to cope with any sort of trouble.

The actual fabric of the hulk and the two-inch-thick iron grilles which covered the portholes and scuttles, were examined every day. At six o'clock in the evening in summer and two in the afternoon in winter, a patrol equipped with iron bars sounded the wooden walls of the prisons and tapped the bars of the grilles. An hour later, a body of soldiers with fixed bayonets and loaded muskets, descended to each deck and drove the prisoners up to the upper deck to ensure that none had escaped.

At night, the number of gallery sentries was increased to seven, and watches made up of an officer, a sergeant, a corporal and a party of sailors, made their rounds throughout the night, disturbing it with the monotonous cry of 'All's Well.' every fifteen minutes. Despite all this, escape would have been the most fervent hope of most captives, and ingenious – and sometimes hare-brained – schemes were hatched on every hulk. Many courageous attempts were made, and most failed; but, as will be told, some achieved what must have seemed the impossible and got clean away.

Altogether, about seven hundred or so prisoners were lodged on the gun- and orlop-decks, each measuring about 140 feet by forty feet wide. Fire was a terrible hazard, as there was only one official companion-way, or ladder, between the 'Parc' and the gun-deck; although the prisoners had cut a secret aperture between the well-deck and the deck below.

The only light and ventilation to the gun-deck was from the portholes – or what had been gun-ports – and depended on the brightness or the dullness of the day. The illumination on the orlop-deck was even worse as the only source of light was through narrow slit scuttles. At night these air-holes were closed up and only opened in the morning – at six o'clock in the summer and eight in the winter. Garneray says that the warders who carried out the task, opened the vents with great caution; the horrible atmosphere resulting from so many sleepers was so foul that 'as their work was done they [the warders] retreated hastily to avoid the pestilential stench'.

Colonel Lebertre, too, told of the terrible condition of the sleeping decks at Chatham, after a battened down night of ten or twelve hours.

He said that many of the prisoners walked naked in the stifling and foul atmosphere in which a candle could not burn, and that the soldiers whose job it was to open up the hatches in the morning were almost overcome by 'the sudden outrush of reek from below'.

As a matter of appropriate interest at this point, I shall interpose the reassurances of the British translator and commentator on Captain Dupin's previously mentioned devastating report on prison ship conditions, that such conditions did not exist:

'In the first place, the most roomy and airy ships of two or three decks were selected to be fitted up as prison-ships. Every thing within them that could encumber any part of the space, or prevent a free circulation of air, was completely cleared away. A post-captain of experience and humanity superintended the whole at each port; and each ship was under the command of a steady lieutenant. Instructions for the commanding officer were printed, and posted in a part of the ship to which every prisoner had free access. By these instructions the commanding officer was directed to muster the prisoners twice a week: to take care that the person's, apparel and bedding were kept perfectly clean; that the decks were scraped and dry-scrubbed with sand; that they were seldom allowed to be washed in the summer, and never in the winter months and that a due circulation of air was admitted into every part of the ship – *That in the mornings the lee ports be opened first, in order that the prisoners might not be subject to a too sudden change of temperature, or be exposed at once to a through draught …*' [author's italics]

So much for the instructions. Sincere, and almost paternal, as they seem to be, the writer, replying to Dupin's 1816 report when the war was over, must have known of the hundreds of proofs that they were largely ignored, or almost impossible to fully implement; and Dupin must have known of the self-imposed sufferings of the semi-naked down-and-outs whom it was almost impossible to save from themselves.

The lower decks, unimaginably squalid during the night, took on a different aspect by day. Once hammocks had been stowed and opened vents had cleared the miasmic fug, the decks became a busy place of industry; a marketplace of hawkers and vendors; the working place for a dozen little manufactures. 'Some were working in wood, some making chessmen or ships from meat bones, some were plaiting straw for hats or slippers, or knitting nightcaps'

In the middle of the deck masters of dancing, fencing and quarter-staff were offering lessons for as little as a penny an hour; and there were the 'school-masters', officers and educated men who did their best to teach the mysteries of geometry and algebra in such an unlikely classroom.

If the hulks were abominable, the greatest abomination to be found in them was the fatal addiction to gambling, which reduced so many to the point of starvation. Without these desperate losers, the most sought-after trader on board would have been out of business – the ratatouille-merchant. He was in demand at all hours, doling out portions of his unappetizing-looking concoction to the most hungry in exchange for cash, barter or, in some rare cases, promises.

Food, wherever served, is often less tasty and nutritious than its description on the menu would have one expect – and nowhere was this truer than of the victuals supplied and dished up on the hulks. Many on the *Prothée* and other hulks believed that 'food gave the English their best opportunity to vent their spite upon us' – ridiculous as an accusation of Government or Transport Board intent, but understandable if aimed at the sharp practice of the many who cheated them in both the quantity and quality of their provisions. Even then, callous avarice rather than nationalistic spite was behind the heartless double dealing.

Garneray said that the prisoners were also short-changed in their rations by the fact that 'the English pound has only fourteen, not sixteen ounces'; but surely, he must have learned that it was the 'Pusser's Pound', not the 'English', which was short by two ounces. It was an old tradition in the Navy that pursers retained their 'eighths' as a perquisite; hence, the 'Pusser's Pound' or 'Pusser's Perks' – and if they could get away with it in the British fleets, what chance had the prisoner of war? Whatever the degree of illegality, only accomplices would know – for the purser kept the books.

The official allowance for each prisoner, on five days of the week, was one and a half pounds of bread, 'entirely of wheaten flour'; half a pound of 'good and wholesome fresh beef, with a sufficient quantity of cabbage or turnips, onions and salt'. On the other two days they were supposed to receive one pound of 'good salt cod, or herrings, one pound of potatoes'. If the contractors and pursers had honoured the specifications in all respects, there could be no excuse for loud complaint. Whilst no one could have got fat on such a ration, nobody would have starved. In fact, the wartime armies and navies of France or England would not have fared much better. A seagoing British sailor would have considered 'bread of wheaten flour' a rare luxury, and 'good and wholesome fresh beef', the stuff that dreams are made of; accustomed as he was to salt beef and pork of indeterminate age; his 'bread', ship's biscuit, was often worm- and weevil-eaten.

On the *Prothée*, their week was divided into five days when meat was issued and two fast, or meagre, days. 'Each of us were allowed a ration of a pound and a quarter of black bread and seven ounces of cow meat. We had soup at midday which we made from a ration of three ounces of barley and one ounce of onions between four men, but as often as not we went hungry.' They had breakfast of dry bread – which was sometimes 'not fit for a dog', when the bakers had used salt water to economise on salt. The next meal was soup with a little bread in it at noon – if the ingredients arrived – the meat they saved for supper. Monday and Friday were the 'meagre' days: Louis said that those fish days were the most unpleasant, for the salt herring was so foul that it was seldom eaten, but 'sold back to the contractors, who would bring it back to us on the following Friday, and again buy it from us at twopence a ration. With the twopence we would buy butter or cheese. I am convinced that some of those red herrings saw ten years service in the Navy.' The cod was almost as bad but just edible when re-boiled for a long time, so, in the absence of herring, it had to serve both days.

If the 'salt herring' story was a lone accusation of low jobbery, one might doubt its veracity, but it was by no means unique. Captain Daniel Woodriff, Agent at Portsmouth, was unusual in that he always carried out the distribution of clothing on time; but it was alleged that much of it was bought back through his secretary – shirts for which the Government paid three shillings were re-purchased from the prisoners at one shilling and resold. Considering the thousands of prisoners in the Portsmouth area, and the number of times the trick could be repeated, great sums of money were misappropriated – at a cost to both captive and Government.

A great part of the working day of all prison ship commanders was taken up with food and clothing related problems. It would seem that most dealt with them fairly, but the lackadaisical attitude, and even self-interest and corruption, which existed at some levels of the Transport Office itself, must have left many commanders frustrated. Many of the complaints were of the quality of the bread issued, which was often officially declared 'not fit to be eaten'. It was ordered that a specimen loaf 'of whole wheaten meal actually and bona fide dressed through an eleven-shilling cloth' should be sent to all prisons as a model of their rightful issue.

The Board went further and occasionally sent a directive to the commander of a hulk where the quality had been in question:

> 'I am directed by the Board to desire that you will immediately forward to this office by coach a loaf taken indiscriminately from the bread issued to the prisoners on the day you receive this letter.'

So somebody was trying. That ruling was made in 1804, but the 'model' loaves sent to the *Prothée* and her prison sister ships must have long been lost, as black sea-water bread was still being supplied many years after. As will be told later, one sample of a bad loaf, sent as directed to the Transport Office, served a double purpose. Not only did it show the poor quality of the bread, for secreted within it was a petition of complaint against the ship's commander.

Much depended on the particular investigating commissioners. Branch Johnson recorded extracts from a number of reports which makes his point. Commissioner Rupert George, who became Chairman of the Transport Office and was later knighted, once visited the Chatham hulks as an inspector and, wearing rose-tinted glasses, reported:

> 'I found the *Sandwich* in which there are 708 men, of whom 18 are in Sick Berth, in the most perfect state of cleanliness, and the Provisions, viz., Bread, Beef, and Soup, very good of its kind; the Meat, the Lieutenant informed me, is much better than the Ship's Company is supplied with from the Victualling Office.'

If the lieutenant had forewarning of Sir Rupert's visit, he may have employed the old service ploy of 'painting the coal' to impress the inspectors – and succeeded with this particular Commissioner, who was never inclined to scratch too far beneath the surface in search of trouble anyway. The report continued:

> 'The Violence of the Wind prevented me from visiting the other Prison Ships, which I have no doubt are in a State at least equal to the *Sandwich*, as she is the oldest Ship and has the greatest Number of Prisoners on Board.'

Commissioner George was not alone in turning a blind eye to prisoner of war discomfort, but there were others who respected their office and did an honest job of investigation. One, W.A. Otway, examined the grievances of neglected prisoners at Chatham in 1796. In despair, the inmates of the *Bristol* and the *Hero* had threatened mutiny if their case was not looked into. Their principal complaints were that their Agent, Mr Dyne, had systematically defrauded them in their provisions; that they had not been issued with soap for more than a year and that he accepted bribes to substitute names on the exchange lists. Dyne rejected every allegation but was nevertheless dismissed.

In that same year Otway and another commissioner named Johnson, were involved in another nasty case. 1795 had been a very harsh winter and West Indian and other black prisoners in Portchester Castle had suffered particularly badly. The two Commissioners decided that the unventilated decks of the hulks, which were a suffocating evil at night for most prisoners might well prove a boon to captives from tropical countries:

> 'We have directed all the Blacks and People of Colour in health at Portsmouth to be removed into the Captivity and Vigilant Prison Ships [at Portsmouth], being the only ones now ready, the warmth and comfortable situation of the Spaces alloted to them between the different Decks we trust will prevent the effect the cold had hitherto had on them at the prison…[it] is truly melancholy, being rendered Cripples for Life by the loss of Toes, Fingers etc., etc., some are even deprived of both Feet. …many others I apprehend will meet a similar fate if detained in this Country, as it is absolutely impossible to guard People of that description from a climate so different from their own.'

Otway and Johnson must, in their day, have been the *bêtes noires* of crooked Agents and contractors. The following is an adverse report which could not have helped the career of the Agent at Plymouth in the early 1800s:

> 'We visited the *Bienfaisant*, *Europe*, and the *Prudent* Prison Ships; on board the former are Dutch, and in the others French Prisoners, these last were in general much in want of Necessary Cloathing and bedding, tho' it appeared that the Commanders of the Ships had made repeated application to the Agent for their being supplied… The Dutch prisoners are in want of only a few articles of clothing which they shall be supplied with directly. The particulars of the unpardonable negligence of Mr White, the Agent, in seldom visiting the Prison Ships, and the consequent inattention of the Stewards to their duty, we shall not trouble their Lordships with.'

On a number of occasions Contractors' Bills were introduced in Parliament, aimed at cleaning up the abuse of contracts. A significant Bill was that of April 1778, which called for restraint on Members of Parliament or their representatives from holding any contract issued by the Admiralty, Treasury, or Ordnance Board unless that contract had been first offered at public bidding. It passed its first and second reading – but was defeated by two votes in the House of Lords!

To return to the *Prothée* and Ambroise Louis Garneray… Despite the best part of a decade as a prisoner of war, spent almost entirely on prison ships, Garneray's highly detailed reminiscences of those years are the most unsensationally written, the least recriminatory and, however colourful his story-telling, the most believable, of all ex-prisoner writers. Not that there was anything placid or complacent in this young Frenchman's make-up. Louis had no reason to love or like the English and makes that very plain in his memoirs, but he never allowed his memory to be warped to the same extent as the Anglophobic General Pillet, Captain Dupin, and others of their kind. He took on the challenge of the hulks with all the spirit and resourcefulness that he had displayed as a naval and privateer officer; nothing could dampen his energy, neither captivity nor the misery and depression he saw around him over so long a period.

Soon after his arrival Garneray was surprised to meet an old shipmate, Quartermaster Bertaud, who had served with him in the privateer *La Confiance*. They had memories to share of great adventures in the Indian Ocean; of the occasion in October 1800, when the *Confiance*, under Captain Surcouf and Lieutenant Garneray, captured the English East Indiaman *Kent* in the Bay of Bengal – and particularly of the prize money that was realised from the sale of its valuable cargo.

Bertaud had already been a captive for two years and the *Prothee* was his fourth hulk; so he was fully qualified as mentor on prison ship survival. When he described the down-and-outs, who formed a community of their own and occupied a segregated corner of the lower deck, Garneray felt that he must be joking or at least exaggerating. In fact, societies of down-and-outs, known as 'Raffalès', 'Les Misérables', 'Rough Alleys' and other names, existed in every shore depot and prison ship. Without the whole story of prisoner of war gambling, which reduced these pitiable creatures to their state of abject poverty, near-starvation and nakedness, we, too, might find it difficult to credit the existence of such societies – I have, therefore, dealt with the subject in a separate chapter – 'The Gamblers and Brokers' (see *The Arts and Crafts of Napoleonic and American Prisoners of War 1756-1816*).

The *Prothée* had its own prisoner-controlled 'courts of law' to protect it from the desperate, the degenerate and criminal elements on board. A committee of usually eight or ten was elected by majority vote, who looked into and settled disputes and petty infringements of their rules of conduct. However, criminal cases were tried before the whole body of prisoners, convened from gun- and orlop-decks. Garneray had an early introduction to the existence of one such court.

Louis had spent sleepless hours on his first night on board, dreaming up escape plans which would never have worked, so he was up early, and found that there was a great milling around of excited prisoners. There had been a robbery during the night. It transpired that the victim was Private Picot, who had sold his berth to Garneray only the day before for three louis. A little later the abject Picot was approached by a down-and-out who said that he could reveal the name of the culprit, but at a price; for if proved wrong it would mean a duel – 'and duels are punished by death'. The price was set at five francs, two francs down, but the unhappy Picot who had been rich for the day, did not have a penny. Louis came to his aid and gave the informer the two francs, who turned the money over a few times in his hand, flicked it in the air with his thumbnail and, once satisfied that it was not counterfeit, knotted it with great care into the tail of his ragged shirt.

A few minutes later a medical orderly named Chiquet was dragged before the committee. Garneray was called to testify that the three louis had existed in the first place and the court ordered that the accused be searched. Chiquet had had no opportunity to hide the loot and the gold was soon discovered. His advocate put up an eloquent case for the defence, spoiled somewhat by the half a dozen conflicting excuses which Chiquet put up to explain possession of the coins. Garneray says that the court was run with extreme correctness, although 'it was much more expeditious than justice usually is'. The judges consulted together and sentenced the accused to be given thirty lashes – to be administered there and then. His shirt was stripped off and he was tied to a stanchion, hands above his head. The prisoners burst into song with a loud rendition of the *Marseillaise* to smother his cries from the ears of the guards above; but half way through his punishment Chiquet passed out. The flogging was halted, but the shouts of the mob insisted it continue, and only after the twentieth stroke was the flogger told to call it a day. Chiquet was cut down unconscious and was left in a dark corner of the deck to recover as best he could.

Over the next weeks Bertaud revealed that he had been working on an escape plan with a Captain Thomas, but the plan, though not the planners, had been betrayed to the guards. Bertaud and Louis were persuaded to help the Captain with an alternative plan which

meant that they would be left aboard, but if it succeeded and the Captain got back to France, he would arrange their exchange for two British prisoners in that country.

Each morning the water boat came alongside and a prisoner working-party brought the full barrels inboard and lowered the empty ones into the boat by crane. The idea was that Thomas should be hidden in a marked barrel overnight and next morning his two accomplices would be extra careful in lowering it into the boat to be ferried ashore. The plan was no crazier than many others attempted, even in recent wars, and Thomas got clear away. Bertaud and Louis gave up any escape plans of their own, confident that the Captain would honour his word,

The next two days were hell, imagining that at any moment a recaptured and battered Captain would be delivered back on board. After that they just waited patiently, joyfully expectant of a place on a cartel ship bound for France; but after a month they were forced to believe the Captain had broken his promise to them, as so many other French officers had done to the English.

From that moment of realization, their every thought was tuned to escape. By this time Louis' money had run out and there was no chance of bribing guards, of employing help, or buying tools of any kind. Their only course was to resort to that most common of prison ship avenues of escape – a hole through the ship's side. Officers imprisoned on a New York hulk had toiled over such a hole through the oak counter of the Gun Room many years before, and Tom Souville, the famous escaper, made more than one hole through the *Crown*, at Portsmouth. Tom and his helpers had made saws from barrel-hoops and gimlets from a fencing foil; Louis and Bertaud made two small saws out of knife blades and somehow created a mallet, a gimlet and a chisel.

They chose the darkest corner of the lower deck and began the quite fantastic task of cutting a man-sized hole through the two-feet thickness of the *Prothée*'s hull, not far up from the waterline. The first operation was the most delicate – to remove a square 'bung' or 'lid' the size of the finished hole, which could be replaced at the end of each session of hard work. They had no doubt that within a few weeks they would finish their task, leaving only a 'skin' of oak to be cut through at the moment of escape. Their only real worry was the money which was needed for a number of items: clothes to exchange for their T.O. outfits, tarred canvas to make carrying bags, food and a little cash to see them on their way once they had reached the shore.

Hours of thought produced a bright, but mad, idea from Bertaud. The semi-literate Breton asked Louis if he could write, to which the latter replied that he could, but for the obvious absence of paper and the necessary implements. Bertaud revealed his plan, and despite Louis' complete lack of faith in the idea, the upshot was that they pledged their meat ration for the following three days for twelve sous. With the money they purchased a large sheet of paper, a pen and ink. Garneray had a very fine hand and drafted the following notice to Bertaud's dictation:

'A CHALLENGE TO THE ENGLISH !
Long live French Brittany !
I, Bertaud, seaman, born in Saint-Brieuc, being tired of the idle boast of the English that they are the best boxers in the world, which is a lie, hereby declare that I will fight any two of them, in any style, but no kicking. In order to show his contempt for the boasters, he, Bertaud, will take ten blows with the fist before the fight begin wherever his opponents chose, then he will thrash them. He

stipulates however, that so soon as he has received the ten blows, and before he begins to fight, he shall be given two pounds to compensate for broken teeth. Done on board the *Prothee* where Bertaud is depressed to the point of death.'

The Breton confessed that he had not the slightest hope of winning a fight against the two, but felt that forty shillings and freedom were worth a few broken teeth.

The boast was the talk of everyone on the hulk, both French and English and one day Louis received the message that the commander of the *Prothée* wished to see the writer of the notice. He confessed and feared his punishment when taken by guards to face the Lieutenant.

The commander enquired whether Bertaud could really box that well, and whether he was really that strong. Louis replied: 'Commander, he is known throughout the French Fleet, and as to boxing, that is beside the point, he can kill a man with a single blow. At Bourbon I once saw him crush a negro's head as though it had been hit by a shell.' No wonder that, to Bertaud's bewilderment, no one took up the challenge.

The commander found these 'facts' interesting, but said that he had really sent for him as he admired his penmanship and asked whether he would like to instruct his ten-year-old daughter for a fee of one shilling a lesson.

Louis and Bertaud could not believe their luck and the lessons began the very next day. As the weeks went by, the two friends kept strictly to their rations with no luxuries, and gradually built up their store of cash to forty-five shillings – enough for them to set the date of their escape. At last the day they had dreamed of dawned and that night they removed all their clothes and packed them carefully into the waterproof bags which they had made. When it was dark enough, they crept along the deck to their escape-hatch and, within a few minutes, had cut through the last thin layer of wood which stood between them and the warm June night air. Bertaud claimed the honour of going first by right of longer tenure on the hulk, shook hands with Louis and slipped through the hole.

Louis was about to follow when he heard the challenge, 'Who goes there?' followed by a musket shot. Louis lay flat and peered through the hole, and saw that his friend was in a hopeless position. The rope which held the canvas bag strapped to his back had caught on a large nail in the ship's side as he fell, and now as he hung suspended, the alarm was raised and the river was lit up with sentry lights from the *Prothée* and the nearby hulks. Louis could hear the commotion on the deck above and the shouts from the boats as they made for the helpless Breton. After a while he heard more distressing sounds; the dull thud of musket butts, cries of pain and the splash as a body hit the water. Then silence. The distraught Garneray, unable to aid his friend, could only accept that he should save himself, and only just crept into his hammock as soldiers descended with muskets, bayonets and sabres to drive all prisoners onto the upper deck for roll-call and questioning.

Louis had little faith that Bertaud could have survived the beating and a possible musket shot, but next day made careful enquiry of an English sailor, as to the 'fate of the poor devil who had tried to escape the night before'. The unsympathetic sailor returned an insulting reply, but the persuasion of a shilling elicited the information that 'the dog of a Frenchman got three thrusts from a bayonet, one in the ribs and two in his backside - and a good sabre cut which nearly split his head in two – but at the moment the dog still breathes'.

Garneray purchased his shilling's-worth of news regularly over the next three months, though knowing full well that the sailor would probably give him false news of Bertaud, even if the latter was dead; but deep inside he knew that he would meet up with his friend again. Meanwhile he carried on with his writing lessons and studied mathematics under one of the *Académiciens*, as the prisoner schoolmasters were known.

We know that there were prisoners who conducted classes in a number of academic subjects on all the hulks and in the prisons ashore. Language lessons were popular, particularly English and French – for many of the so-called 'French' prisoners were natives of a dozen or more nationalities which made up the armies and navies of France – and many illiterate captives learned to read and write during their long years of captivity. Baron de Bonnifoux, on the Chatham hulks, taught mathematics, drawing, French and English – and later published an English Grammar. The greatest obstacles to learning on the hulks were lack of space and an over-abundance of noise. Also the professor-prisoners were usually poverty-stricken, for they could not command the prices obtained by the teachers of the martial arts or the traders, who regarded the academics with some amusement and not a little contempt. Daytime instruction was difficult and ingenuity had to be employed to make it possible in the comparative quiet of night, wherever space allowed. Tom Souville on the *Crown*, Garneray on the *Prothée*, and others described how the problem of night-time study was overcome, in words so similar that the dodge must have been practised in most prisons from early days:

'Grease and fat from their meagre meat ration was saved for use as lamp oil, which was placed in the shell of a horse-foot oyster equipped with wick of twisted cotton threads. This small light was suspended from the deckhead over their study table, which was walled around with a "tent" of canvas and blankets. All lights below decks were forbidden after curfew and infringement of the order was rewarded with as much as three days in the cachot, or Black Hole, on two-thirds ration. A worse outcome of discovery was the petty-minded destruction of their pens, pencils, slates, inkpots, books and paper. But they were seldom caught, as the prisoners had their ways of avoiding detection, which often involved petty bribery.'

Day and night, rules were constantly broken – by the forgers and coiners, the makers of the interdicted straw hats, and the perpetrators of other ignored proscriptions. So over the years codes and warning signs and sounds of approaching danger had become established. Internal cautions were usually simple man-to-man-down-the-line tip-offs like a whispered 'Alerte.', or 'Ohe.', or hand signals; but there were also quite sophisticated systems of communication between prison ships. Carpenters, who had their benches on the upper deck or fo'c'sle, conducted a signalling system which sounds like a cross between semaphore and the morse code.[5] Individual letters of the alphabet were transmitted by hammer beats and by changing the angles and positions of their work benches or stools. Louis said that students had to be keen, to endure the air inside the 'tent', which soon became polluted by the smoke from their improvised lamps and the tobacco pipes of the scholars; but that those hours of study were amongst the happiest periods of his imprisonment.

He did not take up mathematics merely as a means of killing time, but rather to improve his knowledge of navigation and add to his chances of gaining a captain's certificate when his captive days were over. Also, perhaps, to bring that day nearer. He had heard through the prison ship grape-vine that his old captain, Robert Surcouf, was fitting out and arming privateers, and thought that if he could contact him, Surcouf might be able to arrange for him an 'exchange at sea'.

There was a strict rule that all letters had to be left unsealed and passed by the British authorities before being posted ashore – and try as he might to avoid the censors, Louis' letters were all seized and destroyed. Had he been able to contact his old privateer chief, the latter would probably have been pleased to arrange the exchange of his ex-Lieutenant for an English captive.

'Exchange at sea' was not all that uncommon, though more often arranged by French than British captains. The procedure was simple enough – a captured English or French officer or officers would sign a form of parole d'honneur prepared by the captor, promising to return a like number of French or English prisoners of equal rank when he reached home. The paroled men would then be put ashore or sent home on an early cartel and, in theory, the promise would be honoured with alacrity. That was the theory, but the frequency with which it was dishonoured meant that, by 1812, it was declared illegal.

Garneray did not restrict his activities to teaching the Lieutenant's daughter and studying mathematics, but involved himself in a number of profitable pursuits. His early art training came to his aid in one instance. He had noticed that the craftsmen who made a good income from the creation of amazing works in straw marquetry with which they covered caskets and work-boxes, used only geometrical patterns or design motifs of flowers and birds. Louis became fascinated with their craft and introduced, probably for the first time, designs which incorporated ships and marine motifs, for which he was paid three sous apiece.

He so completely occupied himself that he was no longer plagued by thoughts of escape, but worked hard and prayed and trusted that the war would soon end. Then, one September morning, his old friend Quartermaster Bertaud reappeared upon the scene!

Bertaud was still weak and his head wounds hardly healed, but boasted that a Breton head was too hard to be smashed by a mere Briton. Delighted as he was at Bertaud's return, Louis was less than pleased to learn that his hard-headed friend had spent every minute of his convalescence thinking of his next escape attempt. Louis told him that after their last attempt – and the shock of Bertaud's narrow scrape with death – his own ardour had somewhat cooled.

For a number of weeks Garneray carried on with his various occupations, feeling relieved that he was not involved in hole-making and escape planning. He was therefore apprehensive when Bertaud asked that they retire to the bench under Louis' hammock, for a quiet chat. He was asked how would he reply if someone said to him: 'Garneray, the hole is ready; the gear is ready. Let's go.' Not knowing how far Bertaud's plans had matured, he said that in such an event he could only gladly cooperate – never dreaming that the attempt was to be made that very night.

Everything had been prepared. Two shoulder-bags were ready, each containing rum, a couple of biscuits, and a dagger-like sharpened file. The Prothée was moored bows-on to Portsmouth, in the central of three channels divided by huge mud-banks which extended into Portsmouth Harbour. Bertaud had thererfore added an ingenious addition to their escape gear – pairs of boards (patins), which they could attach to their feet, if need be, to negotiate the foul expanses of mud. It was now mid-winter and as a protection against the bitter cold of the water, they appropriated most of the lamp-oil, stored for use in the school-masters' 'tent', and greased themselves from head to foot.

Garneray was the first to grasp the rope and lower himself through the hole. Half paralysed by the shock of the icy water, expecting musket shots and the scene to be illuminated at any moment, as it had been on the first attempt, he did not move until Bertaud whispered: 'Swim slowly and cautiously – and don't make any noise.'

After half an hour of steady but exhausting swimming, they reached a mud-bank to the right of the Prothée, and after laboriously fitting their mud-boards – and each fortified with a slug of rum – they crossed the mud to the channel on the Gosport side.

Once again they were swimming, with the tide slowly sweeping them towards the mouth of the river and a landing point. Chilled to the bone, and in a darkness so deep that they could scarce see each other, their situation was becoming desperate. More than once Garneray was at the point of giving up, saved only by the superior strength of the Breton, who, to his own cost, kept him afloat. Within minutes of being supported, Louis was once again asking to be held afloat so that he could take a drink of rum. Bertaud replied with taunts like, 'Don't you think I'm made of flesh and blood just the same as you, Louis?' but helped him nonetheless.

Soon they were both too numb to swim, and Bertaud suggested they turn on to their backs to conserve their strength. Whilst this did rest their tired limbs, and made for easier access to the warming rum bottle, they soon became disorientated and after a while realised that they were not heading for land. Swimming again, they found the currents had taken them well into Portsmouth harbour. Disappointment and fatigue almost brought their venture to a watery end; but Bertaud, whom Louis, honest memoirist as he was, always gave full credit for having saved his life and infusing the will to carry on, instructed: 'Empty your bag of everything and tie it round your neck – your patins will keep you afloat.' Louis obeyed. Dumping biscuits and clothes into the sea, and securing the boards to his bag, he turned onto his back and lapsed into semi-consciousness, aware only of a terrible pounding in his head and piercing pains through both his temples. He was revived by a cry from Bertaud, who shouted the magical word, 'Land!' and at that same moment, Louis' head struck what he thought was a rock with such violence that he thought his skull was cracked.

It was not a rock with which Louis had collided, but a ship's side, a realisation which gave him renewed strength. Within minutes they had located a ladder, but Bertaud was less thrilled than Louis, thinking that it would almost certainly be an English vessel, saying that from the vantage point of the deck they should locate a landing point ashore and then take once more to the sea. Garneray was horrified at the prospect, saying that it would almost certainly lead to death. Bertaud muttered 'At least death is better than captivity!' but followed Louis as he climbed silently onto an unguarded deck. Unguarded, that is, except for a large dog which welcomed them with a continuous loud barking which soon brought half a dozen seaman rushing onto the deck. The two shivering Frenchmen were taken aft to the captain's cabin, relieved to find that the seamen who escorted them were not speaking English.

'Who are you?' the captain asked, in very poor English, and when he was answered with, 'Two Frenchmen, escaped from the hulks, captain; who trust that your feelings of humanity will allow you to grant them refuge', flew into an indignant rage. 'Escaped from the hulks and you dare to board my ship and beg hospitality.

From me, a Danish captain, my country an ally of England. You must be mad.' They asked him to at least give them some old, cast-off clothes and let them rest awhile; but he replied that he did not care to be their accomplice, and rose to call for an escort to take them back to the *Prothée*. The Breton, who had allowed Louis to do all the talking, suddenly grabbed a knife from the captain's table, and flinging himself at the hateful Dane, knocked him down and held him there with a knee on his chest, hissing 'One word and you're a dead man!'

After tying up the now submissive Dane, Louis, who by now was completely exhausted, asked what next? well-knowing that he would be asked to face the sea, the mud and the cold again. As he feared, his companion was determined to carry on, but understood when Louis said, 'Listen, Bertaud, I have suffered as much as I can take – I have no courage left – leave me to be taken back to the *Prothée*' – and tried to persuade his friend to do likewise. Bertaud shook his hand, then, knife in hand he rushed from the cabin onto the deck and, before the sailors could stop him, jumped over the side and into the sea.

Garneray pleaded with the freed captain to lower a boat to look for Bertaud, who answered that: 'The bandit insulted me and struck me. So why should I send a boat to his aid?' At four o'clock in the morning the naked, perished, and distressed Louis was rowed back to the *Prothée*, where he was thrown into the cachot, half-dead from exposure. It is unlikely that he would have survived the night had there not been a heap of wood-shavings, left by carpenters who were repairing the Black Hole, with which he covered himself.

At least, that is the story more or less as Garneray told it; but many Danes have resented the fact that Louis described the heartless Scandinavian captain as Danish. Carl Roos[6] said that, by that time, Denmark was at war with England and Garneray must have been mistaken in the captain's nationality; who must have been a Swede. It is a fact that Sweden was an ally of Britain except between 1810 and 1812.

Late the next day, after only one terrible night, he was released from the Black Hole and returned to his place on the gun-deck, aching and shivering until some sympathetic prisoners collected together some old clothes to cover his nakedness. Feeling warmth for the first time in many hours, he dozed off into an hour's fitful sleep. When he awoke, he saw that the portholes on the starboard side were crowded with prisoners, gabbling and pointing. 'What's all the excite-ment?' he asked, with fear in his heart, and was told, 'We're watching the crows.'

Finding a space between the staring prisoners, Louis was sickened by the sight which met his gaze. At the edge of the mud-flat which surrounded the *Prothée* was a naked body, half out of the water, left there by the tide. Garneray rushed on to the upper deck and approached an officer who was surveying the scene through his telescope, and pleaded with him to send out a boat as his friend might still be alive, but was told, 'We'll take a look at low tide'. At low tide, two hours later, a boat-party from a nearby hulk, the *Veteran*, pulled away from the ship's side and rowed towards Bertaud's corpse.

Horror and fury were added to distress when the watching prisoners realised that there was no intention of picking him up. A rope was tied to his leg and the horribly disfigured body dragged through the mud to the hulk's side, where it lay till next day before being towed to the Hospital ship *Pegasus* and eventual burial.

The tragedy of Bertaud's end weighed heavily on Louis' mind and as days passed the more hopeless and dejected he became. He had, of course, lost his teaching job, and the straw-marquetry worker, who had paid him for his nautical designs, had been transferred to another hulk. Soon his cash began to run out and he was reduced to subsisting on his bare ration. Lethargy and despondency had ruined many prisoners of the hulks, but a stroke of good fortune rescued Garneray from utter and dangerous depression. Newspapers were one of a number of prohibited importations into the hulks, but the middle-deck prisoners had arranged for a local paper to be smuggled in on a regular basis – at three times the issued price – and there was great excitement when the first copy arrived on board. Some had heard Garneray speak in English to the guards and knew that he had served in British India, so he was invited to become their official reader and translator.

He allowed himself to be persuaded and was conducted to a clearing on the deck with expectant cheers ringing in his ears. Although he could understand English fairly well, his command of the written language was too slight for genuine impromptu translation; but once he had taken on the task, his 'translations' were delivered with great panache, however little the accuracy. His audience were deeply impressed with his erudition and voted him a daily 'reader's fee' of six sous.

Garneray's spirit and his mastery of English grew over the following months, and he regained his old determination never to admit an idle hour into his day. His greatest desire was to take up drawing and painting again, and this became possible after three months of frugal budgeting of his 'reader's fees'. Each day he spent four sous on food and put two aside for the eventual purchase of art materials. At the end of three months he had nine francs, in return for which an English merchant – either through a bumboat trader or by arrangement with the guards – delivered a small box of colours, brushes, pencils and a number of large sheets of paper.

The Garneray 'masterpiece', which set him on the road to success as a prison ship artist and changed his captive life, was the portrait of one of the *Prothée*'s garrison, an English soldier, who Louis made 'uglier', if possible, than the original, but which was acclaimed a prodigious success. With reluctance, he allowed one of his messmates, a hat-maker, to show it to the soldier. A crowd of prisoners gathered round, expecting fury and indignation, but the soldier was delighted and asked how much he could buy it for. He was told 'Two shillings' but said that as a hard-up soldier he could offer no more than sixpence. The business-like Garneray stuck to his price, which was finally agreed to – if he added a meerschaum pipe and an umbrella (a gift from the soldier's wife, Betsy) to the portrait. Soon, a Garneray portrait was a must for nearly all the garrison and the naval complement of the *Prothée*, and he was doing a brisk business; at sixpence for a sketch and a shilling for a faithful likeness, sometimes selling as many as two or three a day.

Over the next two years, Louis became wealthy in the terms of his environment, and his painting ability had become known ashore. The purser of the *Prothée* had set himself up as an art dealer and, with the permission of the commander, had installed Garneray in a small cabin under the starboard side of the quarterdeck. The Purser may have been an art-lover, but he was also on to a good thing, making much more than his 'Pusser's Eighths' from Garneray's work. From every four paintings which were sold to the Portsmouth dealers, the purser claimed the price of one. I like to think that some of the Garneray paintings in my collection, which illustrate this volume, may have been executed in that little studio under the quarterdeck, almost two hundred years ago.

Success inevitably breeds envy – particularly in such a closed society as the hulk, where the very lowest and starving mingled with the comparatively well-fed by day and were housed only a deck's-thickness away at night. Louis Garneray became a victim of such jealousy. One morning in 1809, three years after his capture, he was suddenly transferred to the next hulk in line, the *Crown* (*la Couronne*). We shall return to the story of this atypical prisoner of war and his next six years of captivity but first we shall interpose more generalities of what Abell called 'prison ship sundries'.

Over so many years, the inhabitants of Portsmouth, Plymouth, Woolwich and the Medway Towns, must have become so used to the miserable and depressing sight of prison hulks, both civil and prisoner of war, that they hardly noticed them. However, just as sightseers had crowded the banks of the Thames in the early days of the civil hulks, to gaze upon fettered convicts labouring in the mud at Woolwich, so the English gentry were equally fascinated with the sight of our foreign captives in their floating prisons. We have many records of visits to the hulks by the ladies and gentlemen of nearby towns – and a number of records of how the prisoners regarded those elegant gawkers. They could not understand how educated, civilised men could take such morbid pleasure in witnessing the discomfort of their unlucky captives. (Perhaps, in fairness to the 'callous British', the French might have reminded themselves of the many thousands of their fellow countrymen who had so recently turned out to celebrate the activities of 'Madame Guillotine')

Colonel Lebertre was particularly shocked that the prison-ship-viewing parties to the Chatham hulks were not restricted to men only:

> '...even the women visitors displayed a truly striking indifference to our plight. They could be seen sitting for hours on end; staring at the prisoners on the Parc [the upper deck]. Such a scene of misery as would acutely effect a Frenchwoman, did not make them shed a single tear. On the contrary, an insulting laugh could often be seen on their lips. The prisoners can recall only one instance of a woman fainting at the sight...'

However, not all boat trips out from the shore were heartless sightseeing tours. Memoirs tell of British visitors welcomed as ticket-buying patrons of the prison ship theatres; of generous donations of costumes and props from groups of ladies; of some sympathetic hulk commanders and their wives; and of subscriptions which were got up for the benefit of not only our own men in France but foreign prisoners in Britain. All manner of prisoner of war entertainment was well patronised wherever it was staged. Garneray was much involved in at least one memorable stage production, and Jens Krog described in detail productions on the 'Danish' hulks at Plymouth and Chatham (see *The Arts and Crafts of Napoleonic and American Prisoners of War 1756-1816*, Chapter 10, THE ENTERTAINERS).

The Portsmouth waters were particularly hulk-ridden. At the same time as the prisoner of war hulks, which came under the authority of the Admiralty or the Transport Office, there were at least a dozen civil hulks – a few moored at Gosport and Langstone Harbour – which housed convicts serving terms of hard labour or awaiting transportation. In fact, two Portsmouth prisoner of war hulks, *Captivity* and *Portland*, were handed over to the Home Office in 1813, and changed their surveillance from captives to convicts.

Incidentally, as a civil hulk, the *Captivity* was the first to include a school in its conversion, for the instruction of young felons, some of

whom were very young. Youngsters were to be found, too, among the prisoners of war inmates of most hulks – boys as young as nine or ten. In most cases, these lads had been captured on privateers or letters of marque vessels, which often included as many as twenty or more boys in their crews – to act as servants to the officers, to serve a gun in action, or form part of the prize crews of captured merchantmen. At one time the *Prothée* itself had more than one hundred and twenty boys among its charges, fifty of them under twelve years of age. The *San Ysidro*, further round the coast at Plymouth, had over three hundred boys on board in 1801. It is said, we hope with truth, that these young captives were often included in early exchanges; although we know that not all survived their captivity.

There are few records of a hulk which had a bad reputation – either for trouble and riot, complaints, or an inordinate number of escape attempts – where the officer in charge was not known to be a bad and inconsiderate commander. It might be supposed that the conduct of his charges may have driven him to what seemed like tyranny; but wherever a tyrant was replaced by a reasonable commander, the prisoners responded appreciatively. He could be strict as long as he was fair, but the faintest sign of nationalistic prejudice or contempt for his prisoners spelt trouble for him, deep unrest throughout his vessel, sometimes even to the point of rebellion – although, of course, in the long run it was the prisoners themselves who suffered most from a badly-run ship.

One might wonder why any naval officer should want to become a prison ship commander, and might well suspect that they had no choice in the matter; that their appointment was a sign of displeasure on the part of their superiors. It is therefore not surprising that many prisoners should have believed that these men were deliberately chosen from the worse type of Francophobes to add to their sufferings.

That belief had no foundation in fact, but, as we shall see, the conduct of some commanders makes that belief understandable. General Pillet went even further. He not only believed that the commanders were chosen from the lowest dregs of the Navy cast-offs, but that their staff and crews were picked from an even lower human stratum – men who had been found guilty of capital crimes and had been sent as marines to the hulks as an alternative to the gallows.

As a matter of fact, the would-be-commander who applied for the post would usually find himself at the tail end of a long queue of applicants. To qualify he had to have a good service record and to have served for at least ten years as a lieutenant. We know that some of the successful applicants were men who had been partially disabled in action, and it may be that there were some who, after a decade of active service, were attracted by the comparative safety of harbour service, away from the dangers of the deep.

The basic monetary reward was not all that attractive – about fifty shillings a week, plus staff allowances – but like most official appointments at that time, there would have been a number of legitimate perks which would have added to his income. The great difference in serving as an officer on a proud man-of-war to commanding a squalid floating prison and overseeing six or seven hundred miserable men, would have brought out the worst in all but the best of them. With unavoidable daily evidence of corruption and the fortunes made by crooked contractors, it would have taken a remarkable character to come out of it entirely untainted.

Commissioner Otway who, you will recall, gave honest

assessments of offending prison ship agents, sounded resigned to the inevitable when he reported from Plymouth: ' ...on inquiry into the Characters and Conduct of the various persons employed at the Prison and on board the Prison Ships, they seem to be as fit for their respective Situations as under the Circumstances can be expected.'

The *Bahama* hulk at Chatham was a typical example of the coincidence of a brutal commander and constant trouble. For the whole of the period that she was under the command of Captain Milne, an unpleasant and much-hated character, both he and the prisoners lived on a knife-edge of rebellion. Many of his prisoners were privateer officers, tough corsair captains of the 'Frères la Côte' type, who would not take easily to threats and bullying. The Baron de Bonnefoux, captured with Garneray on the *Belle-Poule*, was one of those who described Milne as a coarse and drunken bully, who frequently invited low-life visitors from ashore to join him in drunken carouses on the *Bahama*. It seems that the Lieutenant was seldom sober, and when a fire was accidentally started on the hulk during one of his particularly riotous revels, the tipsy Milne gave orders that if the fire spread towards the prison decks, the prisoners should be shot rather than allowed to escape.

The Baron was as disgusted with the British commander as he was with the lowest level of his fellow-countrymen who appalled him with their depravity:

> 'There existed neither fear nor reserve, nor modesty, among that class of prisoner which had not been endowed with the benefits of any degree of education. The most perverted immorality, the most shameful offences against decency, the most ignoble cynicism, the most disgusting behaviour, was rife amongst the prisoners – and this in a place of misery, a still greater misery beyond imagination.'

Conditions on the *Bahama* were made unbearable by Milne's methods of trying to maintain discipline, punishing the prisoners with the cachot on the slightest pretext, and hitting them where it hurt most – in the stomach. His idea that semi-starvation would dampen rebellious spirits achieved exactly the opposite result. Not only did it further inflame the already deep hatred for their captors, but brought trouble between the prisoners themselves – hungry men are never the most sociable or well-behaved.

Bonnefoux was involved in one revolt against the commander, who had put everyone on half-rations as a general deterrent against escape attempts by the few; an order which might easily have resulted in massacre. All prisoners strong enough assembled on the 'Parc' and disobeyed all orders to disperse, threatening mutiny if they were not given proper food. Milne, crazy with fury at such effrontery, and as usual in his cups, gave the order to fire into the tight-packed mass of several hundred captives, but the garrison officer wisely ignored the order – thus preventing a slaughter worse than the infamous 'Dartmoor Massacre', and saving Milne from historic detestation by both British and French. Bonnefoux himself saved the day by approaching Milne and his staff and convincing the sozzled commander that he could not win against so many hungry and determined men. So the prisoners were fed and Milne lived to make other days unpleasant.

That took place in 1808. Three years later a similar protest on another hulk ended in tragedy. The *Sampson*, a sister ship to the *Bahama* in the Chatham prison fleet, was probably the most execrated of all English-based prison hulks, and the most difficult to manage. This was the ship to which *mauvais sujets* were sent,

incorrigibles not only from other hulks, but from depots and prisons ashore. Broke-paroles who had betrayed their word more than once; recaptured escapers; groups of 'Raffalès' too depraved or unmanageable even for a 'decent' prison hulk; men who were persistent troublemakers and rabble-rousers; all these were transferred to the *Sampson* and a few other chosen hulks. The commander's job must have been an unenviable one. With hundreds of desperate and potentially dangerous men to control, something of an iron hand was doubtless called for, but tact was also called for – and often missing. The commander of the *Sampson* had the same blind idea of prisoner psychology as the heavy-handed Lieutenant Milne; believing that if he punished everyone whenever there was trouble, the majority of the prisoners would do his job for him and deal with the miscreants. Deprivation of full rations and access to bumboat merchandise were his most powerful weapons.

Sergeant-Major Beaudouin, in his *Carnet d'Etapes*, said that half the time they were given food 'the very dogs would have refused', that the meat often looked as though it had been dragged through the mud, and further verified Garneray's statements regarding the putrid salt fish served up on 'meagre' days. When even these sparse and unsatisfactory provisions were reduced 'as a disciplinary measure', it is small wonder that the *Sampson* became the scene of disorder and rebellion. On a number of occasions the prisoners, who believed that the English thought that anything was good enough for Frenchmen, had refused to eat the rubbish supplied by the contractors, and one such refusal brought about the dreadful confrontation of the 31st May, 1811.

The commander of the *Sampson* had once again resorted to half-ration punishment for all prisoners, and on that day they refused to accept what they were offered. There are several accounts of what happened then, but, like Abell and Johnson, I quote Beaudouin, who was on the Chatham hulks from 1809 until the end of the war:

> 'The English allowed them to exist two days without food. The prisoners resolved to force the English to supply them with eatable provisions. Rather than die of hunger, they all went on deck and requested the captain either to give them food or to summon the Commandant of the anchorage. The brute replied that he would not summon the Commandant, and that they should have no other provisions than those which had been served out to them two days previously. The prisoners refused to touch them. The tyrant then said: "As you refuse to have this food, I command you to return below immediately or I will fire upon you." The prisoners could not believe that he really meant it and refused to go below. Hardly had they made this declaration, than the Captain gave the word to the guard to fire, which was at once done, the crowd being fired upon. The poor wretches, without any means of defence, crowded hastily down, leaving only the killed and wounded – fifteen killed and some twenty wounded. Then the Captain hoisted the mutiny signal, which brought reinforcements from the other ships, and all were as jubilant as if a great victory had been won.'

Beaudouin continued, 'I do not believe that there is any Frenchman who hates this nation more than I do; and all I pray for is that I may be able to avenge myself upon it before I die.' Beaudouin's hatred is understandable as was that of British prisoners who suffered under brutal gaolers in the worst of the French prisons. He may, however, have been wrong in the number killed: other reports state less, including one from a French officer on the *Brunswick*, which speaks of 'this massacre, in which six Frenchmen were killed and six seriously wounded', but did repeat the accusation that the English gloried in their action.

The *Crown* at Portsmouth was another hulk which, like the *Bahama*, owed its bad name to a drunken commander, whose idea of commanding would have been a disgrace wherever he served. The following account of his prison ship management will prove the disastrous effect of a bad commander on every aspect of prison ship life.

Garneray was shattered by his sudden transfer to the *Crown*. Everything had been going so well for him, his shipboard life so organised, that he had placed his whole hope of freedom on eventual exchange rather than risk the hazard of a third escape attempt. He could not imagine how he had in any way offended: 'Only a long time later did I learn, and with sadness I confirm it here, that I was the victim of the jealousy of my fellow unfortunates who, hurt by the opulence and relative well-being I enjoyed, denounced me as a leader of escape plans and also accused me of financing them from my own pocket'.

Within an hour of receiving the order, a dinghy came alongside and took him to the *Crown*, moored ahead of the *Prothée*'s bow. There is a saying in all navies that 'the last ship is always the best', and it was certainly true in this case. He was pleased to meet up with men who had served under him on *La Confiance* or with him in India; but soon found that he had joined them in a ship seething with discontent.

Collective punishment was the order of the day. Both innocent and offenders alike, newcomers included, were forbidden any contact and communication with the shore. This meant that the market-boats, which provided the prisoners with 'luxuries' to augment their bare rations and the hundred and one commodities – important as much for personal use as to stock the little businesses on board – were not allowed alongside.

Other prisoners have left descriptions of the character of Lieutenant Ross, commander of the *Crown* and there is little doubt that he was generally hated by the French. However, Tom Souville's biographer, Henri Chevalier, wrote that Tom said that Ross was a 'martinet, although not bad at heart'; but it should be taken into account that, although Souville had been a prisoner on the *Crown* three times, in 1797, 1809 and 1812, and that Ross was commander on the last two occasions, Souville had never stayed captive long enough to develop the passions of some longer-serving prisoners. It may be that Tom's assessment of Ross's character was influenced by the latter's words on meeting him after one of his many attempted escapes:

Among the prisoners on the *Crown* were soldiers taken at Guadeloupe and in May 1809 word came that all these men were about to be exchanged. Tom Souville and a shipmate, Captain Havas, talked two of the soldiers into selling their exchange papers – and made an excellent job of disguising themselves as men who had seen service in the tropics; complete with moustachios and dark tanned skin. They were included undetected in the cartel group, but on reaching the jetty they were shocked to find Lieutenant Ross ready to conduct an inspection of his departing guests. He spotted Havas and Souville and almost immediately wished that he had not acknowledged the fact. Souville had been involved in so many escape attempts that his return to the *Crown* could only mean more trouble. Lieutenant Ross then made this amazing statement, ' …although I must do my duty and take you before Commodore Woodriff, I shall recommend that he lets you go – if I don't you'll sink my ship with your constant hole-boring through her timbers.'

Ross was true to his word, but earned for himself a reprimand for poor security surveillance – and Tom Souville and Captain Havas were sent back to the *Crown*, to start another four-week spell in the Black Hole, on reduced rations.

Except as regards the commandant's character, Souville's recollections and descriptions of prison-ship life tie in well with those of other *Crown* ex-prisoners. He also made mention of a few French women who lived on the hulk: 'women of very low class, extremely coarse and crude.' There are other records of female prisoners which show that by no means all were of that class. One French lady hand-delivered a letter from T.B.Thompson of the Navy Office to Commissioner Bowan of the Transport Board in 1813. It read:

> 'The Bearer is the wife of a Captain Douditt a French prisoner of war at Chatham whom I took the liberty of writing to you about some time ago. She wishes to be allowed to live on board the Prison Ship with her husband. Pray do me the favour to see her, and hear her wishes with a favourable ear if you can.'

Commissioner Bowan saw Captain Douditt's lady and wrote to the Secretary of the Transport Board to the effect that 'if the Board have no objection, I think the Lady may be indulged'.

Of all the comments and criticisms of Lieutenant Ross, Garneray's was the most devastating in his description of the detested commander:

> '[He was] our absolute master after God, and the most terrifyng figure one could imagine. His appearance was in perfect keeping with his mean, cruel, vindictive and overbearing character. Imagine a small man, just short of five feet, enormously solid, like a bear, with a hideous square head set on a monstrously thick neck. Red hair, grey-blue eyes, a thin, hooked nose, a mouth which opened from ear to ear, lips always twisted by a kind of nervous tic, a skin the colour of mahogany and atrociously pitted by the smallpox – such was his portrait.
> 'To his other physical attractions add that his right hand had been amputated as the result of a wound incurred in a duel. His profound scorn for the French and his implacable hatred of them were doubtless the qualifications which won him the command of the hulk.'

If Ross was really as physically disadvantaged as Louis describes, perhaps he could be pitied as much as detested: Souville's biographer says that Captain Ross was 'a fine old man who had lost an arm at Trafalgar; but that he did hate the French'.

The *Crown* carried the usual proportion of desperate gamblers, down-and-out 'Raffalès', forgers, and industrious workers in bone, wood, plaited straw and hair; but far more than its fair share of escapers. There were few who would not cooperate in any sort of escape plan. Even the makers of saleable artifacts, a group most often content to work and wait out the war, were willing to risk the dangers involved in getting away from this particularly hated prison. By cutting them off from the bum-boats and therefore markets ashore, they had nowhere to sell their work. There was, of course, an inboard market. The sentries, guards, sailors, and some officers on all the hulks were eager to buy prisoner-of-war-work cheap to re-sell ashore; but Ross had created such animosity and anger between the French and their English overseers that the prisoners refused to sell to their persecutors.

Lieutenant Ross was subjected to enough aggravation and humiliation to make any man vengeful, whether he had brought it upon himself or not. The prisoners went out of their way to antagonise him, always referring to him disrespectfully as the 'Turnkey', and showing their contempt in a dozen different ways. This, plus ever-increasing escape attempts, led him to demonstrate his authority beyond all fairness, so that by the time Louis arrived his tyranny was at its height.

The showdown came one morning, when Ross came onto the snow-covered quarterdeck in a towering rage, having heard through an informer that a number of prisoners had made their getaway overnight. All the prisoners were driven on to the upper deck by armed soldiers, who made a futile attempt to count them. After the first count it appeared that twelve had got away, after the second check the number increased to seventeen. The prisoners were having the time of their lives, despite the cold. As on the *Prothée*, the carpenters had made secret accesses between decks and store rooms, and could control and confuse the count at will. Ross, guessing that he was being fooled, decided on a petty revenge by taking his officers off to breakfast, leaving the hungry prisoners on deck in the hail and snow.

It was four hours before they returned and some of the prisoners were in a terrible state, some unconscious on the deck or held up by friends. Counts and recounts went on till evening when it was decided to start again on the following day. The prisoners could have saved themselves further torture by manipulating the count, but they had a double incentive to carry on. It gave more time for the six men who had actually escaped, and a great opportunity to drive the Lieutenant, and his almost equally-hated officers, completely mad. Sometimes the tally was a great number short, and at the very next count that same number too many, and all the time there was a whistling and a derisive cheering.

On the third day they were surprised to see that the 'Parc' had been divided up by a maze of wooden partitions, and the *Crown* was surrounded by boats from the other prison ships. On the quarterdeck the Commodore of the hulks and Captain Woodriff, the Agent-General, were seated with the officers of the *Crown*, and watched as the prisoners came up from below to be counted into the pens, ten at a time. Even so they managed to cheat and by sundown they thought they had won, and looked forward to another day of cat-calling, whistling and rumpus; but they were in for another surprise. At daybreak they were awakened from their hammocks by soldiers, driven up on deck, and loaded into the flotilla of armed ships' boats which lay alongside the hulk. Under heavy guard they were carried off to the *San Antonio* hulk, moored ahead of the *Crown*. An accurate head count was then an easy matter as each boat unloaded its cargo of captives – and Lieutenant Ross was informed that he had lost six of his boarders.

The next day they learned at what cost they had defied the commandant, and how highly priced he valued his humiliation. Back on the *Crown*, they found that their tools and furniture had been smashed and books gutted, their pages torn in tiny pieces and littering the decks like snow. Garneray's colours had been ground into the deck, his canvases ripped to pieces, his brushes and pencils broken and useless. Added to this, and possibly in fear of the reaction to his wanton destruction, Ross had made an addition to the guard – a huge Newfoundland dog.

For many days the inmates of the *Crown* seethed with impotent rage and venom, planning everything from the torture and murder of Ross to a general uprising – but having to resort to the small satisfaction of smashing up anything that came to hand and shrieking revenge. Finally it was the most innocent of their guards which

suffered the cruellest fate – they poisoned the commandant's dog!

Ross, at his wit's end from frustration and the embarrassment of constant chivvying and barracking – which could be overheard on all the nearby hulks – offered terms which were considered more insulting than acceptable. So bitter confrontations continued in this battle which neither side could win and which each lost in its own way: the prisoners through hunger and discomfort – on one occasion they were brought to heel when the anchorage fire-fighting boats were brought alongside to pump icy water through the portholes and scuttles into the sleeping decks; and another when two prisoners were killed by guards – and the commander whose reputation as a drunk and a tyrant was by now the talk of the prison fleet, a gossip which had filtered through to the Transport Board.

At last he realised that he must do something to pacify his unruly mob, and, thinking that an improvement in provisions would succeed where deprivation had failed, called on the crooked mess contractors to cooperate to that end. Without success. The enraged but crafty Ross then decided to place the entire blame for all the troubles on the uncooperative contractors by eliciting the aid of the prisoners themselves.

First he rescinded his bumboat order and allowed the traders to bring their wares to the *Crown*, and relaxed his strict though ineffective discipline. He then summoned a party of ten prisoner representatives to his cabin, where they were invited to draw up a detailed statement of all their complaints against the 'scandalous behaviour of the contractors'. The prisoner-representatives took full advantage of the invitation, preparing a devastating report of their sufferings at the hands of the contractors – and did not forget to add a hypocritical note of the kindness and consideration shown by Lieutenant Ross in allowing them to present their case.

They then created a most profitable item of 'prisoner-of-war-work'. Calling into play the Transport Board order regarding the 'Model Loaf', so long ignored by the contractors, they selected the most inedible example of what they actually received, to accompany the complaint. But first the inside was scraped out to hold a second report which told the truth of the infamous conduct of Lieutenant Ross and his principal officers. Then the loaf was skilfully invisibly mended and crated for onward transit to the Transport Office in London.

The Commandant's gentleness did not last for long, but during that period of forced and false friendliness, Garneray, whose efficient preparation of the petition against the contractors had been noticed by Ross, was appointed official interpreter to the hulk. Also during that period of comparative calm, a number of events occurred which must have lightened the air of almost perpetual gloom which hung over the *Crown*.

The most notable of those events concerns another boxing match. Unlike Bertaud's boastful proclamation on the *Prothée*, this time it was a British challenge to French boxing skills.

The arrival of any boat which came alongside the hulk was always a source of inquisitive interest. The civilian clothes, uniforms and costumes of the visitors with their women and servants, brought a breath of the outside world to their miserable prison. One boat which was spotted approaching the *Crown* one fine morning in 1809, caused a particular flutter of curiosity. It carried a wealthy titled English colonel, well-known ashore for his sartorial elegance, his sporting interests, his gambling and high life-style; but it was not this gentleman who captured the attention of the captives. Standing in the bow was the Colonel's servant, a negro of truly herculean proportions, dressed in the most impressive livery they had ever seen.

It transpired that the Colonel was touring the hulks in search of opponents brave enough to take on his black champion, who, as he was very big and very black, was known by the sobriquet of 'Little Whitey'. If a challenger could be found, the fight was to take place a week or so later, before a ringside audience of Hampshire gentry. Win or lose, the challenger was to receive a purse of twenty pounds – with a guarantee that, should he be killed, the money would go to his next of kin – but it seemed unlikely that one would be found from among the poorly-fed prisoners who watched as the enormous negro strutted arrogantly on the quarterdeck. There is little doubt that any number of opponents could have been found who would have taken him on with sword, rapier, knife or pistol, but to oppose him with fists seemed less courageous than suicidal.

There was, however, a quiet unassuming Breton, noted for his strength and past successes as a village wrestler, who was willing to fight for such a purse. Robert Lange was not much more than five feet six inches in height and except for noticeably well-muscled arms, was of slight though athletic build.

Lange, accompanied by the interpreter, was taken before Lieutenant Ross and the Colonel, who expressed surprise that he should even consider taking part in what would so obviously be a mismatch – warning him that Whitey had already killed three Frenchmen in his many previous bouts. The interpreter imparted this information to Lange, expecting him to retract his challenge, but he seemed if anything even more determined. He was presented with an advance of two pounds and was promised a meal of first-rate food and drink – perhaps in the tradition of the condemned man's choice of his last meal, but more likely so that he would be fit enough on the day to provide good sport for the Colonel's visitors.

During the following week the ship's carpenters were busy building staging in the space between the mainmast and the quarterdeck, bedecking it with flags and bunting. This was to provide seating for the ladies and gentlemen from Portsmouth and Gosport. There was a great deal of interest among the betting fraternity ashore, and as gambling was second nature to most French men, few prisoners could have resisted a flutter. There may have been a few 'loyalty' bets on Robert Lange to win, but most of the betting, both French and English, was not on whether he would be floored or killed, but on the number of punches he could take before meeting either of those sad ends.

About two o'clock in the afternoon of the contest a dozen or more boats approached the *Crown* with their loads of fashionably dressed ladies and their escorts, and a little later loud cheers welcomed the arrival of the Colonel and Little Whitey. After the visitors had been courteously greeted by the commander and shown to their seats in the stands, he returned to the Colonel to arrange the preliminaries for the match.

The Colonel and Whitey presented a most impressive sight, enhanced by the Colonel's dog, a magnificent Great Dane. Robert Lange had not yet made his appearance and Ross sent for him with the words, 'The illustrious Whitey should not have to wait for a Frenchman'.

Whilst they waited, Whitey began to strip off his elaborate livery to flattering exclamations of admiration for his magnificent torso – soon balanced by groans of disappointment when the challenger came into view. Whitey's arm was 'thicker than an average thigh' and his chest twice the size of most men's, whilst Lange's

comparatively puny frame and short stature made him the source of amusement to many of the visitors, whilst others thought they had been exposed to one of the Colonel's practical jokes. Robert slouched over, hands in pockets, shoulders hunched, a quid of tobacco bulging his cheek, and only straightened up when he realised with annoyance that Whitey's laughter was loudest of all.

The two combatants were called together for the formality of shaking hands and a cheer came from the visitors followed by a roar of anger from the prisoners when Whitey said: 'Shake this hand with great respect, a hand which has floored and killed a number of Bretons.'

When this was translated for Lange, the words had a fantastic effect on him, his eyes blazed with fury, his face contorted with rage, as he strode forward and clasped the negro's hand. There was complete silence as the two faced one another motionless, for so long that it soon dawned on everyone that something unexpected was taking place. At first those nearest noticed a wince of pain on Whitey's face, then a grimace as he bit his lip and appeared to swoon, then with a great cry he tried to release his hand from Robert's grip; but, as blood dripped from the finger-tips of Whitey's crushed hand, the normally quiet Breton still imposed the torture and shouted, 'That hand that killed Frenchmen will not scare babies in future!'

The 'fight' was over, Whitey admitted defeat. The prisoners went crazy with jubilation, shouting 'Long live France! Long live Brittany! Long live Robert Lange!'. The Colonel took the whole fiasco in a sportsmanlike manner, apologising to his guests and suggesting that they left the French to their triumph. Congratulating Robert on his great strength as he gave him his twenty pounds, he could not forebear to say that had he boxed Whitey, Robert would certainly have been beaten and probably killed. Lieutenant Ross was livid with a fury which had to be suppressed until the visitors left the hulk. Before leaving the ship, the Colonel asked Ross to have his Great Dane brought to him – but that is another story, the details of which will not be recorded here. Sufficient to say that when it was learned that the hound had been lured down to the orlop-deck by the down-and-outs, the general opinion was that it would have become the equivalent of 'legs of mutton, a few beefsteaks and a stew', long before the Colonel left the ship.

Once the ship was clear of guests, the short truce between captors and captives was irretrievably broken. Over the following week the situation got worse than ever before, the guards behind the massive hardwood barricade manning their loopholes at all times, and the scuffles which broke out between prisoners and soldiery sent in to control them resulted in injury on both sides. The prisoners used tables, benches and anything moveable that came to hand to build their own barricades to shut themselves off from the musket-manned loopholes – and Ross's threats became more and more extreme, warning them that he had every right to hoist the red flag of mutiny and shoot the lot of them.

The prisoners took him seriously and many regretted that their petition to the Transport Board had not produced a peaceful solution to their complaints. Weeks had passed by and they had long decided that their second and secret report had gone undiscovered, that the loaf which contained it had been cast aside unexamined – or that their complaints had been read and ignored. Then one morning an admiral's barge came alongside the *Crown* and Lieutenant Ross received a number of gold-braided officers on board. Fearing the worst, no one could guess the reason for the visit, but were relieved that at least there would be a respite from trouble, threats and violence whilst these dignitaries were on board. After some time it was made apparent that their petition had been read: all ten signatories to the 'loaf-letter' were summoned for questioning before a board of enquiry which went on late into the evening. Less than a week after the investigation, Lieutenant Ross left the *Crown* to a last farewell of hoots, whistling, derisive jeers and cheers.

It must be admitted that we have seen Lieutenant Ross through French and prejudiced eyes. Garneray saw him as a monster, Souville as a French-hating hero of Trafalgar. Like every man, he must have had his good as well as bad points, but it cannot be denied that he was a bad prison ship commander. If his physical presence was only half as unprepossessing as the French described him he would have started out at a miserable disadvantage, and if he lacked an air of authority and strength sufficient to naturally command the respect of great numbers of disgruntled men, then inner feelings of frustration and helpless anger may well have driven him to excessive drinking and heavy-handedness.

Reports of drunken commanders are by no means confined to prisoners' memoirs: Transport Commissioner A. Boyle, reporting in 1813 on the *Guildford*, lying two hulks astern of the *Crown* and the *Suffolk*, moored in the line of hulks to her port hand, noted: 'Lieutenant Hartles of the *Suffolk*, I found extremely drunk at 10 o'clock and I understand that is generally the case with him. Lieutenant Pedin, 2nd [Lieutenant] of the same ship, is also a most Drunken Character.'

It would seem that Lieutenant Voller, second in command of the *Guildford*, did not restrict his sinning to toping, but was guilty of darker offences. Boyle reported: 'Lieutenant Voller, 2nd of the Guildford, who is absent on leave, I should recommend to the Board to be immediately discharged for reasons unnecessary to point out in a Public Letter, but which I will communicate on my return'.

Conditions on the *Crown* improved under its new commander, but Ross had left a long-lasting mark on the health of its inmates. Periods of reduced rations and poor quality provisions, added to the constant trouble, general discontent and indiscipline which had left the lower decks in a state of stinking filth and vermin, resulted in a greater incidence of sickness and mortality higher than the norm.

At the best of times, with full rations and a commander who could control the worst excesses of his crooked contractors, any hulk was still a hazard to health. The dreadful overcrowding and foul atmosphere of the lower decks during the night, and the sudden drop in temperature in the morning when hatches and scuttle-covers were raised, has been described earlier; but the poisonous odour which plagued them was not just the inescapable result of hundreds of largely unwashed bodies crammed into a small space. The stench which rose up from the holds located in the lowest part of the hulk, where stagnant bilge-water water impregnated with all manner of filth over months or even years, lay beneath the ballast which balanced the vessel, was an ever-present threat to well-being.

Until the middle of the nineteenth century British ships, both naval and merchant, had always been ballasted with stones, rock and sand and their crews, no less than prisoners, were afflicted by all the ills resulting from constant dampness and the foul vapours which rose from the bowels of their floating home. That is, of course, unless they were blessed with a hygiene-conscious captain who was willing to take on the not inconsiderable task of shifting and cleansing the

ballast and pumping out the bilges on a regular basis – but it would have taken a most remarkable hulk commander to make such an effort with six or seven hundred prisoners on board. When any effort at all was made, it was more often in the form of an issue of vinegar to use as a disinfectant for sprinkling the decks – though fumigation was sometimes employed. To this end, brimstone and or vinegar was heated over burning braziers, thereby producing acrid sulphurous fumes which were believed to neutralise the poisons of the noisome atmosphere of the lower decks.

There are records of prison ships being temporarily cleared of all prisoners whilst they were scoured out and disinfected, (as happened in 1783 in New York, when the *Jersey* prison ship underwent the treatment – with catastrophic results), but more often they were left until things had gone too far and the hulk was so rotten and filthy that it was taken out of service. In 1811 the *Crown* itself was decommissioned.

It is arguable whether a comparatively clean prison ship was a much more healthy abode than one where the decks were seldom washed. Branch-Johnson in discussing the dirt, vermin and unhygienic conditions on the hulks, quoted Transport Office Commissioner H. Towse, who after visiting the Chatham hulks in 1806, commented: 'The Prison decks [were] washed on alternate days, which I conceive too frequently'. Branch-Johnson viewed this comment critically, but Commissioner Towse may well have been right from some points of view.

Until holystoning and hot-sand-cleaning of wooden decks were introduced into Royal Navy ships, it was more or less accepted that sailors would suffer from catarrh, congestion of the lungs and other respiratory troubles and agues, to some degree – and crippling rheumatism. These complaints could be laid at the door of the high degree of humidity in which they lived and worked, caused as much by frequently scrubbed decks as the constant sea-water soakings that went with the job. In good weather or in the tropics the upper decks would have lost their dampness quickly enough, but the lower decks were never completely dried out and men served and slept in an atmosphere of perpetual dampness. What was true of naval vessels was doubly so of the hulks, where ventilation was virtually non-existent, ports were closed and hatches battened down. Prisoners in unwashed hulks were probably less liable to suffer from breathing troubles and rheumaticky joints – although perhaps more vulnerable to skin diseases; but these afflictions were as nothing to the fevers and epidemics which hit the prison ships from time to time.

Scurvy, the scourge of the free sailor for centuries, had been to a large extent overcome, except on very long voyages, by the discovery that fresh vegetables and citrus fruit added to the diet kept scurvy at bay. Doctors had known of this preventative measure for almost a hundred years, although still ignorant of the fact that the cause of the disease was the lack of ascorbic acid (Vitamin C) in the diet – but it took many years for that knowledge to be put into practice, and then only on the best-run ships.

The most dreaded of prison ship ills was typhus. Typhus, or 'gaol fever' was a disease of filth, which occurred wherever people were crowded together in unhygienic conditions; in civil habitations where dirt and malnutrition reigned; in armies, navies and prisons; in fact anywhere where sustained personal cleanliness was impracticable and a regular change into fresh clothing would have been a luxury.

One of the earliest European epidemics attacked Spaniards in the armies of Ferdinand and Isabella in the late fifteenth century, and typhus was endemic throughout Europe from the sixteenth to the end of the nineteenth century. Napoleon lost many times the number of men in Russia to typhus than were lost in combat; of the quarter of a million men who set out on the march through Poland, only 90,000 reached Moscow.

Doctors at that time – and indeed until the beginning of the twentieth century – were ignorant of the true means by which the disease was spread. They believed that typhus and other fevers were caused by the noxious odours so often mentioned in the last few pages. This was a universal belief; judges and officials who came in contact with the offenders who had been kept in foetid gaols or hulks before coming before the bench, carried posy-holders which contained nosegays of herbs and flowers to ward off 'dangerous smells'. (I believe this old practice is perpetuated in the small nosegay-holders which are part of a judge's regalia today.)

The villain of the piece, as we now know, was not the smell but the louse, and lice which abound wherever there is filth, on unwashed bodies and in unclean clothes. Gaol fever broke out on the civil hulks within weeks of their establishment, in 1776, introduced by felons delivered up from verminous gaols ashore. The prison reformer, John Howard, suspected that there was something more than just dirt and pungent odours which caused and spread typhus. In his State of the Prisons.1777, he says:

> 'If it were asked, what is the cause of gaol-fever [typhus]? it would in general readily be replied, "the want of fresh air and cleanliness." But as I have found in some prisons abroad, cells and dungeons as offensive and dirty as any I have observed in this country, where, however, this distemper is unknown, I am obliged to look out for some additional cause for its production.'[7]

At least he did not entirely blame the stench as the conveyor of the disease. Had he suspected the louse he would have achieved even greater fame; but he came to a different conclusion:

> 'I am of the opinion that the sudden change of diet and lodging so affects the spirits of new convicts, that the general causes of putrid fevers exert an immediate effect upon them. Hence it is common to see them sicken and die in a short time… the gaol-distemper is always observed to reign more in our prisons during winter than summer; contrary, I presume, to the nature of other putrid diseases… the Ruffians enclose themselves in hot rooms, [as prisoners of war on the hulks were unwillingly enclosed in a stifling atmosphere below decks and] dislike the fresh air, even before the cold months commence… [and because they spent most of the day in] utter inactivity, immersed in the noxious effluvia of their own bodies.'

In the above, John Howard is quoting a physician in a Russian military hospital in Moscow. John Howard died in the Ukraine in January 1790, after contracting camp fever – a type of typhus – whilst visiting military hospitals.

The true facts regarding typhus were not discovered until the early years of the twentieth century when the American pathologist Howard T. Ricketts isolated the causitive organism of typhus (rickettsia), in 1909, and revealed that it was transmitted by the body louse. Later that same year he died after contracting typhus during his research.

The unpleasant subject of diseases and their treatment will have to occur a few more times in this chapter, but for now we shall return to the *Crown* and our old friend, Louis Garneray, who was soon to be transferred yet again – and was himself soon to experience the horrors of the fever and a prison ship hospital.

After the departure of Ross, Garneray began to settle back into his various profitable occupations, painting and acting as interpreter, although the latter took up little of his time as the new commander was himself fairly fluent in French. But Louis had little chance to establish himself as securely as he had on the *Prothée*, for after only a few weeks he was sent 'on loan for a few days' to the commander of the *Vengeance*, five hulks astern of the *Crown*, who had lost his interpreter. Those 'few days' were, in fact, to last the next four years.

As official interpreter, Garneray arrived on board the *Vengeance* as a privileged prisoner, entitled to a very small room of his own on what used to be the 18-pounder gun deck, aft of the well deck. Although low in funds, he was still wealthy compared to most of his fellow prisoners (for whom, in his diary, he expressed pity), and as it became obvious that his 'temporary' post was hardening into a permanency, he determined to once more set himself up as a painter. This he achieved by an arrangement with the Purser, who rented him a cabin on the starboard side of the poop deck for use as a studio. The story of his work as a marine artist, his introduction to the Portsea picture dealer, Abraham Curtis – who at first brought him prison ship prosperity and was later to cause him so much trouble – we shall learn about elsewhere (see *The Arts and Crafts of Napoleonic and American Prisoners of War 1756-1816*, Chapter 7, 'THE ARTISTS').

Conditions on the *Vengeance* were no better than on the average hulk. The elderly commander, whilst a great improvement on Ross and his kind, still ran a prison where bad provisions and gambling produced an orlop deck population of 'Raffales' and *manteaux imperiaux*, whose filth and vermin ensured that the hulk was never completely free of diseases and fevers. Garneray was at first comparatively shielded from unhealthy communication with the rest of the captives, but no one was completely immune.

About six months after his transfer to the *Vengeance*, a medical officer from the Transport Office, Dr Weiss, arrived to select prisoners for exchange from among the great number of ailing men on board. Garneray, like Charles Dupin and many other French writers, seem to have been convinced that these doctors chose only very sick men and incurables to send back to France, in exchange for English prisoners in health. Garneray said that we made a great show of our humanity in returning twelve thousand prisoners since the beginning of the war, but that because of their condition we were, in fact, guilty of almost that number of murders. Probably the majority of prisoners believed this to be true, and were terrified at the prospect of being included in exchange cartels where they might be infected by their sick fellows; some so terrified that they considered refusing (or selling.) their exchange opportunity.

Taking the period 1803 to 1814 (when about 122,500 prisoners were brought to this country – and according to official records, 10,341 died in English prisons and hulks) Charles Dupin came up with the following exaggerated figures:

The number who died in English prisons 12,845
Returned to France in a dying state 12,787
Returned after 1814, their health
       more or less debilitated 70,041

If Tom Souville is to be believed, Dr Weiss was something of a sadist with a very unpleasant sense of humour. Stories of his 'accidentally' dropping a false list showing names of prisoners who were to be exchanged, which was later revealed as a cruel hoax: and of a sick and old one-legged French sailor who had been captured with his son, both of whom had been prisoners on the hulks for six long years. Weiss had genuinely informed him that he was to be exchanged, playfully tapping his wooden leg with his cane and commenting 'Ah,ah, see where an argument with the British has got you.' The old man, delighted at the prospect of returning home, was profuse in his thanks, and pleaded that his son might be allowed to accompany him. Dr Weiss looked thoughtful for a moment then said: 'Only a monster would separate father from son, you must surely stay together.' Their joy and thanks were turned to misery when Dr Weiss then took his leave: 'Au revoir, my friends. You will agree that I have kept my word. We shall meet here again next year.'

However, Dr Fuller, the regular medical officer, attached to the *Vengeance* was a man of a different calibre and much respected by the prisoners. He detested Weiss and his despicable humour and let him know it. During the rounds of the sick, Fuller spotted a seriously ill seaman who had been captured in the Floridas; Weiss considered he was malingering, but was visibly shaken when the younger doctor diagnosed yellow fever, a horrible disease attended by retching and vomiting. Weiss was only too pleased to leave the hulk and the vicinity of the dreaded fever, leaving Fuller to deal with the anxious prisoners who were all aware that a spread of the disease was almost certainly unavoidable. Fuller tried to reassure them, telling them as would have most doctors, that yellow fever was common, treatable and not contagious.

Inevitably, within a short time the fever spread through the hulk, but, with the use of 'quinine and restoratives', Dr Fuller successfully dealt with the great majority of cases – so much so that a lyricist aboard composed a comic song called 'Messieur Vomito'.

The ever-recurring accounts of hardship, malnutrition, sickness and death in depots and on prison ships, the reader might well give some credence to the prisoner's belief that deliberate neglect and malice towards Britain's captive foes was at the root of their ills. It should be remembered, however, that great numbers of captives were delivered to depots or prison ships already in a poor state of health. Many were imprisoned whilst still recovering from unhealed wounds. Others had been captured abroad and had spent time in terrible foreign prison camps before enduring the sufferings of a battened-down sea voyage to imprisonment in England. Some arrived suffering from malnutrition and all manner of diseases, often verminous and unwashed. Officially they were supposed to be bathed immediately on arrival aboard the hulk, as has been mentioned of the *Prothée*'s reception of the *Belle-Poule* captives at Portsmouth in 1806. But this bathing, though intended as an important hygiene precaution, was often a death sentence to the bathed.

An example of the all too rigid attention to the above rule took place in Portsmouth towards the end of 1811. Prisoners taken by the Spaniards when the French division led by General Dupont capitulated at Baylen in 1808, had been imprisoned on the island of Cabrera for a full two years of unimaginable suffering. Subjected to great hardship and starvation, great numbers died on the island before the survivors were handed over into British hands and shipped to Portsmouth. There they were distributed among the hulks, the *Vengeance* being allocated thirty of the pitiable Frenchmen. Their boat came alongside and a dreadful sight met the gaze of the hulks inmates: 'The poor wretches, lying in the bottom of the boat, cried aloud in their agony and tossed in the delirium of fever; thin as skeletons, pale as corpses, scarcely covered, although the cold was intense, by their miserable rags… of these thirty only about ten had strength enough to get on board.'

The hulk's doctor was horrified, saying that they were full of contagious fevers and that they should be in hospital; that he could not with conscience allow them aboard, otherwise, within a fortnight, the *Vengeance* would become a morgue. He was right, of course, and the commander sent a boat to the *Pegasus* hospital ship requesting that its captain prepare for the reception of the thirty men. The unfortunate prisoners lay in the boat for the best part of an hour before the message came back from the *Pegasus*, saying that the hospital was so crowded that there was no facility to bathe new patients and that they could only be received if they were bathed before admission. Against the good sense of the doctor, the thirty men were hoisted aboard the *Vengeance* and carried to the wash house, where they were stripped and plunged a number of times into baths of ice-cold water. They were then ferried over to the *Pegasus*. It is not recorded how many of the survivors of the torments of Cabrera's prisons, survived this hygienic hospital treatment.

The *Pegasus* was an ugly hulk. Once a French 64, she had been captured in 1780, and thereafter used as a prison or hospital ship. Her silhouette was made more grotesque by all manner of accretions; wards, cabins, mortuaries, added to her upper decks. It is said that from a distance she looked less like a prison ship than a huge Chinese junk. Many Portsmouth prisoners were soon to discover that the *Pegasus* was no more attractive when viewed from within. True to the doctor's warning, the fever introduced by the Cabrera unfortunates struck the V*engeance* with a vengeance.

Louis, although better fed and more sheltered from most infections and contagions in his poop deck cabin, eventually became ill. Feverish and afflicted by violent headaches he passed out, coming to briefly to find himself amongst other sufferers being taken by boat to the *Pegasus*. He again lost consciousness, awakening in a delirious state in the wash house of the hospital ship. The sight of the huge tubs of icy water and his memory of the cruel dowsing of the Cabrera captives, cleared his mind sufficiently for him to be able to shriek objections to the treatment. He was lucky again, in finding another old crew-member among the French assistant handlers who, for old time's sake – and no doubt because Louis was in funds – saved him from the dreaded tub. Fignolet, the handler who had served under him, managed at a price to secure for him a single bed in a healthy spot (ordinary patients were often forced to share, two or more to a bed). Fignolet also purchased supplements to his diet, so Louis lived to serve out more time on the *Vengeance*.

Each hulk or hospital ship was supposed to carry at least one French doctor, but when they were appointed they were seldom treated as anything more than assistants. The general quality of patient care in those days was very low, whether in armies, navies, prisons or prison ships. There was no official rating of sick-bay attendant staff until 1833. John Laffin, in his *Jack Tar*, wrote:

'The comfort of patients always depends on the nurses, and naval nurses – at least until late in the nineteenth century – were untrained and rough. Men who were not much use anywhere else on a ship became sick-bay attendants. Some were 'loblolly boys', young seamen serving in the sick-bay, who got their name from the lemonade they made and served. A few nurses were women, legal or *de facto* wives of seamen, but they were not trained and many had little gentleness or femininity.'

Much of the 'nursing' on the prison ship hospitals was carried out by prisoners. These were men who had volunteered or been transferred to serve as general helpmeets and odd-job-men and found 'nursing' was part of their job, usually encouraged by better provisions and petty privileges. The ailing prisoners usually regarded them with some dislike, thinking of them as sellers-out to the enemy and referring to them as the 'undertaker's men' – as one of their tasks was the removal of corpses to the morgue as quickly as possible, to make room for the next delivery from one or the other of the hulks.

Official regulations stated that a doctor assigned to duty on a hospital hulk should consider himself a member of its permanent staff and make it his full-time practice. He was expected to live on board, but it was found that, in all the three prison fleets, this was largely ignored, most of them more interested in their private practices ashore.

Even as late as the last year of the war there was little improvement in hospital ship management. Francis Abell recorded the following report:

'States of the *Renown* Hospital Ship at Plymouth for February 1814:

Staff: 2 Surgeons, 1 Assistant Surgeon, 1 Matron,
1 Interpreter, 1 Cook, 1 Barber, 1 Mattress-Maker, 1 Tailor, 1 Washerwoman, & 10 Nurses.
Received: 141. Discharged 69. Died 19. Remaining 53.

Fever and dysentery have been the prevalent complaints among the prisoners from Pampelune [Spain], whose deplorable state the Board of Inspection are in full possession of. (Among these were some forty women 'in so wretched a state that they were wholly destitute of the appropriate dress of their sex'. Two British officers' wives collected money for the poor creatures and clothed them.) Pneumonia has recently attacked many of those ill-conditioned men termed Romans [Dartmoor down-and-out prisoners sent to the hulks because there was no way of reforming them from gambling and the unpleasant habits which had reduced them to that state], many of whom were sent here literally in a state of nudity, an old hammock in the boat to cover them being excepted.'

Even the most caring of surgeons and staff must have found their task uninspiring when dealing with 'Romans' and 'Raffales', but there was no excuse for the conduct of a considerable number of them. The records abound with complaints of just about every one of the hospital ships. The Transport Board was inundated with accusations regarding all the Portsmouth floating hospitals, the *Pegasus, Vigilant, Marengo, Princess Sophia*, all came in for bitter criticism; the principal surgeon of the *Vigilant*, at Portsmouth, and the complete medical staff were all replaced; Dr Kirkwood of the *Europe* at Plymouth, who usually slept ashore, was found guilty of culpable neglect and lost his post, in 1810. However, one Frenchman, at least, had reason to thank a British prison ship doctor. The following letter from a French 'broke-parole' officer, whose offence had landed him on one of the worst of the Gillingham hulks, was addressed to a lady of influence in 1812, together with a medical certificate from the doctor of the *Trusty* Hospital Ship at Gillingham:

'My Lady: H.M.S. *Sampson*
I am afraid of taking advantage of the human kindness and gentle compassion which has always made you take pity on unfortunate prisoners, but, Madame, an unlucky person, without friends or benefactors, seeks refuge under the auspices of generous people who condescend to pity him, and you have kindly taken part in my ills. Then allow me once again to implore you to use your influence in my favour, providing that this influence is not contrary to your personal leisure. It is now two years that I have been confined to this prison, so injurious to my health, which is more delicate and weak than ever before. It is now six or more years that I have been a hopeless prisoner, with a destiny so dark and so little deserved.

'If I have not merited to die, and no one wants to inflict death upon me, I must be allowed to return to the world to seek solitude, and to where I could then live in a peace which would be more suited to my feeble constitution, to withstand unhappiness, and to prove to you, my lady, that when I committed the crime for which I have so much endured, it was much more out of lack of experience than out of malice.
1812.   Jean-Auguste Neveu'

Sometime at the beginning of 1810 the elderly commander of the *Vengeance* retired, and was replaced by a much younger officer, Lieutenant Edwards, who took over the hulk for less than two years before being given command of a corvette at the end of 1811. We hear only praise of Edwards who, whilst conscientious and tough when necessary, showed an understanding of the plight of men who had no way of knowing how long their loss of liberty would last. There was an almost immediate improvement in their sustenance and rules were interpreted with common sense and fairness; whenever it was wise to do so, the decision going in favour of the prisoners. Over the period of Edwards' command we hear of a complete change of attitude on the part of the captives; there were fewer escape attempts and security was more easily maintained. Gambling had been officially abolished, (though how can you stop the addicted punter, when two flies on the wall can be wagered on as effectively as the crown and anchor board?). It was impossible to reform the *raffelès* down-and-outs who still occupied the lowest decks, but they became less troublesome. The hulk was cleaner and healthier than ever before – to the once-unbelievable extent of prisoner volunteers helping the naval deckhands with their chores.

There was, of course, the odd hiccup in this peaceful co-existence. One in particular concerned an alleged Order from the Council of Regency (which I cannot trace) dated the 6th March, 1810. This Order was on the subject of reducing the number of escapes – by employing the vicious threat of hanging two innocent prisoners for every one who made a successful getaway. If such an order had been sent to every hulk and depot, it can be imagined that it would have caused something like fa general uprising. But the order, or the rumour of it, was believed well enough on the *Vengeance* for a group of officers to petition the Council, describing themselves under their signatures as: 'Officers of the French Army, in captivity since the violation of the Capitulation of San Domingo.' It is almost certain, however, that the Order, if order there was, was never implemented.

T.J. Walker mentions that the incidence of escapes from Norman Cross, *c*.1805, was so great that prisoners caught in the attempt were to be immediately executed; but, once again, there is no evidence that this ever came about – although a number were shot dead in the course of recapture.

Until the end of 1812, prisoner life on the *Vengeance* had so changed that, as well as all the usual little industries and businesses, the hulk had its sing-song entertainments, concerts, and even plays. Lieutenant Edwards had allowed the prisoners to build a small theatre right aft on the orlop, at a point where the deck was lower and allowed a headheight twice that of the orlop proper. The remarkable story of the first, and last, performance of 'The Corsairs Bride' is told in *The Arts and Crafts of Napoleonic and American Prisoners of War 1756-1816*, THE ENTERTAINERS.

Garneray's career as artist and interpreter progressed to the point where he considered himself as happy as any captive could be. That is, until Lieutenant Edwards left the hulk to pursue a more active role in the war at sea. Louis himself was not at first affected by the change in command, in fact his financial prospects improved five-fold, when a visiting Portsmouth picture dealer came aboard soon after, and informed him that he was being robbed by Abraham Curtis, the dealer who handled his works.

The new commander was no fit successor to Edwards and within weeks all the old evils began to creep back; the contractors resumed their cheating ways; gambling was back in fashion and all the recent good work was undone. Louis was still official interpreter, but found himself mysteriously out of favour with his new commander, a mystery only solved when he learned that the latter was the cousin of the now vengeful Curtis.

Although no one who had spent so many years on the hulks can be described as 'lucky', Garneray was always more fortunate than his fellow captives. The Portsmouth picture dealer, Smith, contacted the French artist Colonel, Baron Louis François Le Jeune, on parole at Ashby-de-la-Zouch, and solicited any influence he might be able to bring into play on his fellow artist's behalf. The Baron, although enjoying the privilege of parole, was in an ambiguous position as a 'parolee'. He had never given his parole in the first place and whether he was even a prisoner of war of the English was in doubt, as he had been taken by Spanish brigands and only later handed over to the British. However, Baron Le Jeune did have influence and used it.

Louis Garneray was granted release on his parole of honour to Bishops Waltham at the beginning of 1812. So we shall leave Louis for many pages, and look at the Medway hulks which, within a few months of Louis' parole, would be receiving prisoners of a different nationality taken in a brand new war.

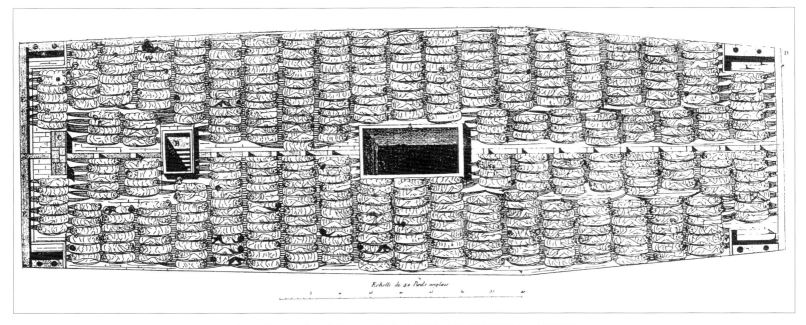

ORLOP DECK OF A PRISON SHIP AT CHATHAM KENT

HAMMOCK PLAN
Length of deck: 125 feet. Beam: 40 feet.
Height: 4 feet 10 inches.
Number of Prisoners: 460.

---

1. Before the 1st January, 1810, the prison ships came under the Admiralty and only the prisoners came under the Transport Board's authority.

2. See *The Arts and Crafts of Napoleonic and American Prisoners of War 1756-1816*, Chapter 11, THE FORGERS AND COINERS.

3. Captain Edward Hawkins' Papers: Edited J. Rudland Hearn. Cornwall Records Office.

4. Stuart Jones: *The Last Invasion of Britain*, 1797.

5. Semaphore was invented in 1794 by a Frenchman, Claude Chappe. Samuel Morse developed his Code in the 1830s.

6. Carl Roos: *Prisonen, Danske og Norske* ... based on the captivity of Jens Krog from 1807 to 1814. Garneray does not give an exact date to the second escape attempt. It may have been early 1807, before the bombardment of Copenhagen, and the captain may have been correctly described as a Dane.

7. In warmer countries fewer layers of clothing would be called for; and therefore less breeding grounds for lice.

Chapter Six

Part Two

The Prisoner of War Hulks

A MAN-O'-WAR'S SONG

1.
Now our ship is arrived
And anchor'd in Plymouth Sound
We'll drink a health to the Whores
That does our ship surround

2.
Then into the boat they get
And alongside they came
Waterman call my Husband
For I'm damb'd if I know his name

3.
Then up steps a nimble Jack tar
He hearing what was said
Aft on the Quarter deck he goes
And humbly bows his head

4.
Sir my Wife's alongside
Will you please let her in
Yes, my lad says he
But see she's got no Gin

5.
My Wife she never carries any
You scoundrals I won't take your word
Midshipmen search that boat
Before she comes on board.

6.
Then up the side she comes
And down the bay she runs
It's ten to one to me
She's a bladder or two of Rum

7.
Then down steps nimble Jack tar
Jonny have you got any thing
With that she up with her smock tail.
And hauls out four Bladders of Gin

8.
Come I'll go fetch some beer
That we may have some slip
The Devils may damb them forever
For we can sling them yet.

Finis.   Anon. 14 January 1779.

THE AMERICANS

THE WAR OF 1812, or 'The War for Free Trade and Sailors' Rights' – sometimes called the 'Second War of American Independence', and, only a short time after its end, 'The Forgotten War'– was declared on the 18th June, 1812.

Although the British Government had made a last minute bid to avoid the conflict, by rescinding just about all of the Orders in Council which had brought matters to a breaking point between the two nations, there was one upon which they were immovable: one of the primary causes of this second outbreak of hostilities between the United States of America and Great Britain, was the latter's practice of 'recruiting' men into the Royal Navy by impressment; insisting on its right to stop and search merchant ships for British subjects among their crews. Britain, confident of her supremacy as a sea power, refused to acknowledge that the deck of an American merchantman was national territory.

This hated 'right' was never relinquished. Congress made an attempt to discourage searches by introducing an Act which prohibited British-born seamen from serving in American ships, but without much success. More than a quarter of a century after the War of Independence, the memory of the Yankee as a 'Rebel' still lingered on, and it was a difficult thing for a young, fit and healthy merchant seaman, who had caught the eye of a British impressment officer as a likely lad, to prove that he was, indeed, a born-and-bred American. The status of 'naturalised American' was not recognised, however long the accused had been settled in the country of his choice. Under English common law, anyone British-born remained a British subject for the rest of his life and could never swear allegiance to any other country

In theory, there was no legal reason why a Briton should not serve on an American merchantman, or any other foreign vessel, if the two countries were not at war – but if discovered he was nevertheless a sitting duck for service in His Majesty's ships. Every true-born American seaman usually carried an 'identity card' (the 'scrip' mentioned in the following song) which was meant to confirm his nationality; but, though read, it was usually disregarded.

Once war was declared, the adjudged 'Englishman' faced a double jeopardy: if he resisted too strongly he might well be accused of being an army or navy deserter – a crime punishable by death – so they usually went quietly. Not without cause, the American developed a fierce hatred of what he considered the high-handed injustice of the British impressment system – and a strong taste of that bitterness can be detected in this song, sung by a group of American prisoners of war on the *Crown Prince* prison hulk moored at Chatham, on the Fourth of July, 1813:

'THE IMPRESSMENT OF AN AMERICAN SAILOR BOY
A SONG

The youthful Sailor mounts the bark,
And bids each weeping friend adieu;
Fair blows the gale; the canvas swells;
Slow sinks the uplands from his view.

Three mornings, from his ocean bed,
Resplendent beams the God of day;
The fourth, high looming in the mist,
A war-ship's floating banners play.

Her yawl is launch'd; light o'er the deep
Too kind, she wafts a ruffian band;
Her blue track lengthens to the bark,
And soon on deck the miscreants stand.

Around they throw the baleful glance;
Suspense holds mute the anxious crew –
Who is their prey? – poor sailor boy.
The baleful glance is fix'd on you.

Nay, why that useless scrip unfold?
They damn the "lying yankee scrawl,"
Torn from thine hand, it strews the wave –
They force thee, trembling, to the yawl.

Sick was thy heart, as from the deck,
The hand of friendship wav'd farewell;
Mad was thy brain, as, far behind,
In the grey mist, thy vessel fell.

One hope, yet, to thy bosom clung,
The Captain mercy might impart;
Vain was that hope, which bade thee look,
For mercy in a Pirate's heart.

What woes can man on man inflict,
When malice joins with uncheck'd pow'r;
Such woes, unpitied and unknown,
For many a month, the sailor bore.

Oft gem'd his eye the burning tear,
As mem'ry linger'd on past joy;
As oft they flung the cruel jeer,
And damn'd the "chicken liver'd Boy."

When sick at heart, with 'hope deferr'd,'
Kind sleep his wasting form embrac'd,
Some ready minion ply'd the lash,
And the lov'd dream of Freedom chas'd.

Fast to an end his miseries drew;
The deadly hectic flush'd his cheek;
On his pale brow the cold dew hung,
He sigh'd, and sunk upon the deck.

The Sailor's woes drew forth no sigh;
No hand would close the sailor's eye;
Remorseless, his pale corpse they gave,
Unshrouded, to the friendly wave.

And, as he sunk beneath the tide,
A hellish shout arose;
Exultingly the demons cried,
"So fare all Albion's REBEL foes."'

Written by JOHN DE WOLFE of Rhode Island.

Some of our naval historians have put up convincing arguments in justification of recruitment by impress; that our men-of-war had to be manned; that it sometimes took months to get a crew together; that in time of war it was the duty of every man to serve his country, however enlisted, etc. However, the strict discipline and punishments which were designed to keep a crew together once formed, generally had just the opposite effect.

Volunteers were few and, despite the risk of vicious punishment, desertion was rife. Admiral Nelson once calculated that, between 1792 and 1803, more than forty thousand sailors deserted from the British fleets – and when a man absconded he had to be replaced from somewhere. Men were garnered in from all over the world, merchant seamen, recruited captives, landlubbers and 'Mayor's men'. The 'British' crew of the *Victory*, for example, on that great day at Trafalgar in 1805, included a sprinkling of sailors from at least a dozen nations.

However great the Navy's needs and however reasoned the argument when the policy was applied to our native subjects, it cannot be expected that an American, naturalised or native-born, would be sympathetic when it applied to himself.

The tyranny of unfair impressment into the British Navy is decried in the memoirs of a number of American ex-prisoners of war, where stories are told of deprivation of food and floggings dealt out to reluctant recruits. Typical of these complaints is that of Benjamin Waterhouse, in his *Journal of a Young Man of Massachusetts*:

'The British had been in the habit of pressing the sailors from our merchant ships, ever since the year 1755. The practice was always abhorred, and often resisted, sometimes even unto death. We naturally inferred that, with our independence, we should preserve the persons of out citizens from violence and deep disgrace; for, to an American, a whipping is a degradation worse than death.

'Since the termination of the war with England, which guaranteed our independence, the British never pretended to impress American citizens; but pretended the right of entering our vessels and take from them the natives of Britain and Ireland, and this was their general rule of conduct:- they would forcibly board our vessels, and the boarding-officer, who was commonly a lieutenant, completely armed with sword, dirk, and loaded pistols, would then muster the crew, and examine the persons of the sailors, as a planter examines a lot of negroes exposed for sale; and all the thin, puny, or sickly men, he allowed to be Americans – but all stout, hearty, red-cheeked, iron-fisted, chestnut-coloured, crispy-haired fellows, were declared to be British; and if such men showed their certificate of citizenship, and place of birth, they were pronounced forgeries, and the unfortunate men were dragged over the side into the boat, and forced on board his floating prison. Not a day in the year, but there occurred such a scene as this; and to our shame, be it spoken, we endured this outrage through the administrations of Washington, Adams and Jefferson, before we declared war, to revenge the villainy.'

Many hundreds of American seamen, mainly but not all impressed from merchant vessels, were serving in our ships of war right up to the outbreak Some had served for as many as ten years, fighting alongside our men in actions on the high seas; and a number had already experienced the misery of capture – as prisoners of Napoleon. However, once war was declared they were given the choice of one of two unpleasant options: to continue to serve in the British Navy – but now against their native land – or resign themselves to an indeterminate period as prisoners of war in Britain. The majority of them chose imprisonment

So, from Day One of the War of 1812, there were American prisoners of war in British hands; men not fairly captured in action, but men who, only the day before, had been fighting on the British side against France and her allies. It is difficult to imagine an alternative, but one might expect to find that they were given preferential treatment – as was shown to the Danes and Norwegians[1] – that they were included in early exchange cartels, or that some sort of limited system of parole was created as a reward for past services; but, if anything, they were more closely secured than our more natural enemy, the French. It must, however, be reported that the British Government was meticulous in seeing that the new prisoners were paid all back pay and all prize money due to them for their service in British ships.

Americans who qualified by rank were paroled, but the rest and the seamen were sent to the hulks or the depots ashore where some were to be held until long after the war had ended and the French had gone home. Had the US seamen been exchanged for a similar number of British prisoners in the first place (in the manner adopted by Nelson in the case of the Danes) at least some of the gaps in our warships' crews could have been filled – and the Government would have been spared the huge expense of housing, guarding, clothing and feeding so many men over a long period. With the expansion of the wars and greater demand on its ships and men, the Navy could ill-afford the reduction in experienced seamen. Recruiting officers tried every inducement, from generosity to cruelty, to lure the Yankee prisoners back into the British service and, as we shall hear, continued to do so over the following wartime years. The first Americans actually captured – as opposed to the impressed men who surrendered – arrived in England within weeks of the commencement of hostilities. The majority were seamen, officers and ratings taken at sea, mainly on small privateers or letters-of-marque vessels. A little later, soldier and sailor captives who had been confined in the Main British prisoner of war depot in North America, Melville Island off Halifax, Nova Scotia, arrived after unbelievable Atlantic crossings in the holds of men-of-war.

On arrival they were examined and sent to land prisons or the hulks; some to Portchester Castle and other depots, but most, and least fortunate, found themselves on prison ships. Between the late summer of 1812 and the spring of 1813, there were roughly 900 Americans on the hulks at Chatham, about 700 at Plymouth, and a hundred or more at Portsmouth – and all the time the number was growing, as warships returned to English ports, delivering up

surrendering Yankee seamen who had been members of their crews. Although anxious at the loss of seasoned seamen, a reasonable captain would have understood any man's reluctance to fight against his native country; but many American prisoners remembered that they went into captivity cursed as 'damned rebellious villains, unfit for his majesty's service!' Officers of the US Navy, commanders and first lieutenants of privateers with more than fourteen guns at the time of capture, captains and first mates of merchantmen and non-combatants, were offered parole, and on acceptance were sent to Ashburton, Reading or one of a few other parole towns.

Among the first of the American captives to arrive in England in 1812, was Charles Andrews, who spent the whole of his war as a prisoner in Britain and, like a few others of his countrymen, left a record of his imprisonment. The manuscript – *A Prisoner's Memoirs of Dartmoor Prison* – was signed by sixty-two of his fellow prisoners, who attested to the accuracy of his narrative and believed – inaccurately – that his was the only journal kept at the 'Depot on the Moor'. Charles Andrews' description of the reception of prisoners into the hulks is so similar to that of the French memoirists as to make detailed note unnecessary; each man was issued with 'a very coarse and worthless hammock, with a thin coarse bed-sack, with at most not more than three or four pounds of flops or chopped rags, one thin coarse and sleazy blanket…', and so on. The greatest difference in their reception was the closeness of the examination and cross-questioning that each prisoner had to undergo, to ascertain that no English seaman among them was masquerading as a Yankee.

When the American captives arrived there were only nine hulks moored in the Hamoaze off Plymouth, *La Brave, Hector, El Firme, Genereaux, L'Oiseau, San Ysidro, San Nicholas, Ganges, Vanguard*, with the hospital ship *Le Caton* still moored off Saltash. The *Bienfaisant* and the *Europe* were brought back into service in the autumn of 1813.

From the log of the Superintendent of Hulks, Captain Edward Hawkins, we learn that there were already Americans among the six-thousand prisoners on the hulks at Plymouth; Americans who had been captured when serving on French ships prior to the 1812 war. His log also records that a percentage of the captives other than the French – Prussians, Saxons, Italians, Austrians, Hungarians, Poles, Spaniards, Swedes, and Americans – to name but a few in that mixed bag of nationalities which went to make up our prisoner of war population – applied to enter the British Service. The Swedes who had been reluctantly forced into war with Britain by Napoleon between 1810 and 1812, always volunteered for service in the merchant marine rather than our men-of-war. Later in 1812 when Sweden became our ally once more, these men were safe from criticism from their own country or Britain.

Captain Hawkins lived on the hulk *La Brave*, which until the spring of 1812 held almost entirely Danish prisoners until the majority of the latter were transferred to the hulks at Chatham, leaving only those Danes and Norwegians captured whilst in the service of France.

This left the *Brave* free to accommodate the incoming Americans, and she and the *Hector* became the principal 'American hulks' on the Hamoaze. The principal 'American' hulks at Chatham were the old *Nassau* and the *Crown Prince*, the latter being all-American except for a hundred or so Frenchmen, some Portuguese and a few Danes. Other groups were confined elsewhere among the Chatham prison fleet of fifteen hulks; three hundred and sixty-one Americans being put on board the *Bahama* in January 1814.

From the very beginning, the Americans proved more troublesome than the French had ever been. Their one thought was of escape and the majority made next to no effort to come to terms with their predicament. Having been used to generous allowances of incomparably better and fresher provisions than the British sailor, the Yankee seaman who had suffered weeks in the hold of a transport ship, exposed to poor quality prisoner of war rations, was in a sorry state by the time he arrived on board his designated hulk. If the bitter Charles Andrews is to be believed, 'most of them were destitute of clothes and swarming with vermin', and it is not surprising that fevers and illnesses soon became endemic:

> 'Every ship has a physician attached to it, who is ever to be on board, and when any prisoner is sick, he is to repair immediately to a certain part of the ship for medical aid: but seldom has any attention paid to him till the moment of dissolution, the doctors paying but little attention to the sufferer, although a prisoner is seldom or never suffered to expire on board; for as the moment of death seems inevitably approaching, the prisoner is moved to a ship nearby, which is called a hospital ship [*Le Caton* or *Renown*], where, if he happens to survive the removal, he receives much better treatment and attention; but when once removed to that ship, they may bid adieu to their fellow prisoners, and most to sublunary things, for not one out of ten ever recovers.'

The prisoners were expected to assist the crew in some of their everyday duties; to haul inboard the water casks, coals, provisions and the hundred-and-one items essential to the maintenance and running of a prison establishment, housing as many as seven hundred captives, plus the British officers, crew and garrison. They were also supposed to clean the decks where they lived and slept but even if carried out conscientiously, which was seldom, none of these duties would have taken up much time or employed many hands. The boredom and idleness, which undermined the spirits of all but the strongest characters, were probably as debilitating as their meagre basic diet of often poor quality food.

The wisest of all Government regulation concerning the prisoner of war, was that which permitted prison markets and even encouraged prisoners to develop any talent they possessed, to keep themselves profitably employed – and to a great extent, out of trouble. The French had always taken full advantage of the opportunity to manufacture and market all manner of popular articles of 'prisoner of war work'. Andrews, however, who would have suspected the motives behind any considerate act on the part of the British, saw even this as a phoney gesture; considering that certain conditions attached to the privilege provided an excuse for some American sailors who entered the British services!

There were, indeed, a few necessary restrictions – to straw-plaiting for instance – but the reasons were promulgated together with the Act, and the well-informed Andrews would have been well-aware that no unfairness was involved. The story of the great economic importance of straw-plait and hat-making as a cottage industry to a number of English counties, and the necessary Act which prohibited its production by prisoners, (see *The Arts and Crafts of Napoleonic and American Prisoners of War 1756-1816*, Chapter 4, THE STRAW WORKERS).

Most sailors, on the hulks or in land depots, could have soon mastered the craft of Straw-plait had it been permitted, and Andrews wrote:

' …by strict attention to the business, [they] could have earned six or eight pence sterling per day: but this was not permitted. And we considered this prohibition a contrivance of the agent's government to induce the prisoners to enter his majesty's service. Their situation was now so abject and wretched, that they were willing to embrace any opportunity where there was the least prospect of bettering their condition, however repugnant to their feelings or sentiments; although their country's interest was ever nearest their hearts, yet, through the faint hope of ameliorating their condition, and some day or other returning to their native land, their wives and families, some of less fortitude were induced to join in arms against their country. *It could not be a crime; for self-preservation is the first law of nature*'.

In all my reading, Charles Andrews' justification for turncoats stands alone. The more than five thousand Americans who were set free after the war would not have agreed with his sentiments, and we shall hear of the depth of their disapproval as told in other American memoirs.

The American Agent for the American prisoners of war was Reuben Beasley, a man who deservedly earned the unforgiving hatred of all his unfortunate charges. Eden Philpotts, in his *Farm of the Dagger*, described Beasley as 'either a knave or a fool, and never have unhappy sufferers of this sort endured more from a callous, cruel, or imbecile representative'. Evidence abounds, in the recollections of men who suffered from his neglect whilst prisoners in hulks, Dartmoor and elsewhere, to show that Philpotts in no way exaggerated the shortcomings of Beasley.

He lived in London and, it would seem, visited the Chatham hulks on only one occasion – and seldom replied to the hundreds of letters of complaint and pleas for help addressed to him by his distressed countrymen. Beasley's unfeeling disregard for his duties, resulted in a general feeling among the captives that their country had abandoned them, and led to either rebelliousness or abject despair.

By April 1813, the restless discontent and disturbances among the American captives, at Plymouth in particular; their escapes and open threats and boasts of plans for future getaways, had become a cause of serious worry to the Transport Board. Captain Richard Pellows, the British Agent for the prisoners of war at Plymouth, was instructed to prepare the Americans on the *Brave* and *Hector* for transfer to Dartmoor Depot, about seventeen miles away. The great prisoner of war depot on Dartmoor had only been opened in 1809, but its reputation as a hell-hole was already known world-wide wherever there were enemies of Britain.

On the morning of the 3rd April, the first of the prisoners to be transferred from the *Hector* were ordered up on deck with their hammocks and belongings and told of their destination. Charles Andrews who was included in this first batch, tells of the horror with which the Yankee captives received the news that they were to march to a prison the very name of which made the mind of every prisoner shrink back with dread, and startle at the thought, for fame had made them well acquainted with the horrors of that infernal abode, which was by far the most dreadful prison in all England, and in which it was next to impossible for human beings to survive for long. Of course, most of them did.

It is somewhat surprising that Dartmoor should have been more dreaded than the hulks – the latter having been in ill-famed existence for more than half a century longer than the Depot. Paradoxically, the records show that the worse types of troublesome captives were sent from Dartmoor and other depots to the hulks as a punishment. Other records reveal the at first puzzling fact that a number of inmates did, indeed, prefer the hulks, and endeavoured to gain transfer from Moor to prison ship by request or wile; but a second thought might suggest that the real reason was that far more successful escapes were accomplished from the prison ships than from the Moor!

> 'Two hundred and fifty dejected and unhappy sufferers, already too wretched, were called, each of whom received a pair of shoes, and his allowance of bread and salt fish. Orders were then immediately given, for every man to deliver up his bed and hammock, and to repair forthwith into the different launches belonging to the ships of war, which were alongside the ship, ready to receive them. The prisoners entered, surrounded by the guards and seamen belonging to the *Hector* and *La Brave*. We landed at New Passage, and were placed under the guard of soldiers, equal in number to the prisoners! Orders were then given to march at half past ten in the morning, with a positive injunction that no prisoner should step out of, or leave the ranks, on pain of instant death. Thus we marched, surrounded by a strong guard, through a heavy rain, and over a bad road, with only our scanty allowance of bread and fish. We were allowed to stop only once during the march of seventeen miles. We arrived at Dartmoor late in the after part of the day, and found the ground covered with snow. Nothing could form a more dreary prospect than that which now presented itself to our hopeless view. Death itself, with the hopes of an hereafter, seemed less terrible than this gloomy prison.'

By June, Dartmoor had received further drafts of Americans which aggregated to at least five hundred men from the Plymouth hulks alone, but by that time the hulks were being refilled with Yankee captives at an alarming rate. The *Hector* alone was overcrowded with no less than seven hundred Americans, and Captain Pellows was kept busy, searching for space to accommodate the overflow of his troublesome charges. Some were transported by man-of-war to the Chatham hulks; others were added direct to the ever-growing American population at Dartmoor; and another two hundred faced a march far more daunting than that endured by Andrews and his fellows of the first draft.

These men were assigned to Stapleton Prison, near Bristol, one hundred and forty miles away. This journey was to be made on foot and was scheduled to take no more than eight days. They were given the usual warning of the seriousness of breaking ranks during the march, and told that the guards had orders to dispatch anyone who attempted to escape. Each man was to receive a travel allowance of one shilling per day, from which they were expected to provide their own food, drink and lodging. Although it cost each prisoner three pence a night to lie on a bed of straw in barns, farm outbuildings or areas in public buildings, it would seem that they managed well enough on the remaining three-quarters of their one shilling allowance.

This first march to Stapleton set out on the 30th June 1813, and was followed by another two hundred and fifty Americans from the *Hector* five days later. This distribution of Yankee prisoners of war over a wide area was the result of a genuine apprehension that the restless and reckless 'Sons of Freedom' might band together in a desperate effort to regain that freedom.

Charles Andrews was himself a prison ship captive for only a short time, but he was still kept well informed of conditions and goings-on in hulks and depots throughout the war. Although all letters were strictly censored, newspapers prohibited and incoming communications monitored, it is plain that a long established grapevine of up-to-date information was in operation. After he was uprooted from the *Hector* and settled into Dartmoor, he was in receipt of regular news-flashes from his fellow countrymen, not only from Plymouth, but the Portsmouth and Chatham prison ships.

However, we do not have to depend on those second-hand accounts of the Yankee prisoner of war hulks on the Medway. We have that other memoir, *A Journal of a Young Man of Massachusetts*, a very full and descriptive account of American and French prisoner of war life on the Chatham hulks. The author, Benjamin Waterhouse, was a young New England doctor who had been invited to join a privateer being fitted out in Salem docks in December 1812, as ship's surgeon.

Waterhouse had no burning ambition to go to sea, and was driven by no great feelings of loyalty or patriotism – in fact, before his capture, he had a great admiration for the English, their culture and achievements. Raised in a 'federalist' family, he was well-read in British history, and held a profound respect and admiration for what he had read of and heard of the bravery and honour of our soldiers and sailors. He knew all our old patriotic ballads, and expressed the thought that there must have been a tenth muse – a British mermaid – which inspired our sailors' songs.

(Many of our national songs were parodied by the Americans during the wars – *Rule Britannia* became *Rule Columbia*; *God Save Great George, Our King* was sung as *God Save Great Madison*; and so on – until September, 1814, when Francis Scott Key wrote *The Star Spangled Banner*. Francis Key was a Georgetown member of an artillery battery, who had gone on board the cartel ship *Minden*, during the bombardment of Baltimore, to parley with the Admiral over the release of an American prisoner. He was successful in his mission, but was kept on board until after the shelling, spending the night on deck during the bombardment. As the sky lightened he could see the Stars and Stripes still flying above the battered Fort McHenry and, thus inspired, he wrote his one and only, but immediately popular, song. Incidentally, the *Star Spangled Banner* which, one hundred and seventeen years later, in 1931, was to become the American national anthem, was set to the tune of an old English drinking song called 'To Anacreon in Heaven'.[2]

Waterhouse admitted that he joined the privateer with no more noble aim than to 'enjoy a pleasant cruise and make a fortune'. It transpired, however, that his cruise was seldom pleasant, that he certainly made no fortune, and within a very short time he had reason to become disillusioned of his romantic beliefs in British gallantry and sense of fairness. Even at the time of imminent capture he had felt relieved that the United States was fighting Britain and not France, confident that he would be treated with fairness whilst in British hands, but shuddering at the thought of being a prisoner of the French:

> 'The French are a people marked by nature, as well as by custom, a different nature from us. Their language is different, their religion is different and so are their manners. All these things have conspired in making a wall of separation between us and that lively people. But it is not so with the English. Our language, religion, customs, habits, manners, institutions: and, above all, books have united to make us feel as if we were but children of the same great family, only divided by the Atlantic Ocean.'

Unlike most prisoner of war diaries or journals – some of which were written many years after the events which they record – the *Journal* was published in 1816, within months of the cessation of hostilities. Benjamin Waterhouse's name does not appear on the title page, which describes him as 'Late a Surgeon on board an American Privateer' and 'WRITTEN BY HIMSELF'.

It has been conjectured that some of the journal may have been a compilation of the stories of a number of ex-prisoners rather than the work of one man; but there is something so immediate and personal about it, plus the fact that it was officially registered in Massachusetts on the 6th March, 1816 (only twelve weeks after the last prisoners had left Dartmoor), that it is hard to believe that it could be the hurriedly collated, edited and printed memories of several men.

The cruise of the little four-carriage-gun privateer schooner lasted only four and a half months. They had sailed along the Brazilian coast, for the most of that time flying British colours and wearing British uniform – a trick which, they said, they had learned from 'our elder brothers in deception' – but had taken no worthwhile prizes. They were homeward bound when, off Martha's Vineyard on the 20th May, they came up with two vessels in the mist which they took to be merchantmen and likely prizes. They hoisted the American colours and were immediately met by broadsides from the two 'merchantmen' – which were, in fact, His Majesty's frigate *Tenedos*, and the brig, *Curlew*. Waterhouse and the rest of the ninety-man crew were taken on board the frigate, which later delivered them to the prisoner of war depot on Melville Island, Nova Scotia. After about three months of misery in the island prison, one hundred prisoners picked from various captive crews were put aboard a man-of-war, the *Regulus*, for a hard-lying delivery to imprisonment in England.

Reports of the trans-Atlantic transportation of prisoners of war, and even shorter voyages, where the lowest decks or holds of men-of-war provided their accommodation, are always disturbing and sometimes horrifying. It is understandable that the young man from Massachusetts and his fellow-prisoners should imagine that none before had suffered as they did on that crossing; but I have read, and believed, many reports of far worse conditions and treatment. Although their below-the-waterline quarters in the *Regulus* had scant ventilation, it was fitted out with large bunks or berths, whereas many consignments of prisoners had to try to sleep on the stones of a ship's ballast – but this provision seems less a luxury when we learn that six men were to share each bunk.

The transport had recently brought British soldiers out to America, and amongst the dirt left behind were rags of bedding alive with myriads of fleas. At first the vermin drove them to distraction, but during their voyage of forced idleness, flea-hunts became competitive and a source of amusement. The crowded and unhygienic conditions of captivity made flea-bitten discomfort a commonplace to be dealt with as a daily chore. Joseph Valpey, an American privateersman prisoner, who kept a journal of his adventures and captivity, was inspired when watching a flea/louse-hunt in Dartmoor Depot to venture into verse:

1.

'*In Yellow dress from head to foot*
Just like a swarm of Bee's
From Morn to Night you'll see a sight
Of Hunting lice and flea's

2.

They skip and crawl most ravingly
And pass from man to man

If they could speak – you'd hear them say
Now catch me if you can

3.

The other Morn as I walked out
To take the pleasant Air
I saw a Louse whose Magnitude
With Horror he made me stare

4.

Old Trafalgar³ he pinned him fast
And killed him for his Crime
Saying Yesterday was your's my Louse
But now the day is Mine!'

And before leaving this itchy subject, it should be mentioned that captive craftsmen made what must have been a best-selling item of prisoner of war work for sale in the depot markets and the hulks – the 'flea-trap'.

The food, too, was far worse than they had complained about in Nova Scotia. At intervals during each day, one man from each mess of six, was called to the galley by boatswain's pipe to collect their unsavoury meals: including the hated Burgoo, the Pea-water Soup and smoked fish. Bad bread and ship's biscuit feature prominently in most stories of Jack Tar's hardship in the age of sail. The bread which was served to the prisoners on the *Regulus* would not have surprised any free sailor in our foreign service naval vessels, but came as a shock to the Yankee captives. It was old, hard, powdery 'like rotten wood' and alive with worms. Some could not face it; some ate it up as quickly as possible; some picked out the worms and ate the tasteless crumbs which remained; others, after long discussion, decided that, as the worms had eaten the best part of the bread, they should, like the birds, eat the worms. The sailor of any period has always needed a sense of humour to help him endure his unnatural way of life; and just as the torment of the fleas had been turned into an amusement, so with the rotten bread. There was one bright spark who cried out: 'Retaliation, by God! These damned worms eat us when we are dead, so let's get at them first!

When the *Regulus* left Halifax, Nova Scotia on the 3rd September, she sailed in company with another man-of-war, the *Melpomene*. A number of prisoners on that vessel had more serious worries to occupy their minds than the quality of their accommodation and provisions. These were the American soldiers of Irish birth who had been captured in Upper Canada. They were men who had left Ireland for much the same reasons that the forebears of Americans had left England. Many of them had married in America, but were now on their way to face trial and possible execution as traitors.

Battened down below, Benjamin and the others had little knowledge of what was going on above them during the voyage; but an occasional event was made known to them. The *Regulus* had retaken an English brig which had been captured a few hours earlier by the United States Frigate *President* and put under the command of an American midshipman. The *Regulus* set a course to keep well out of the way of the renowned 44-gun American heavy frigate, and later fell in with the 74-gun HMS *Bellerophon*, which, only a couple of years later, would bring our most famous prisoner of war, Napoleon Bonaparte, to England, and would end its days as a civil hulk for convict boys at Sheerness, but now it sailed in search of the *President*. The news from the outside world they natural than the prisoners should spread the word that the suspect and receiver was their unloved commander? So that the yarn could be neither proved, nor disproved and the suspect absolved, rumour added that influential friends had intervened, the farmer recompensed, and the commander's involvement covered up.

The story, however, does not end there. One Sunday morning, as the Osmore family were getting into a boat to go ashore, probably to church, an American lad went up to a porthole and shouted 'Baa! Baa!' Osmore, who was aware of the false gossip, would have saved himself days of trouble and riot, had he ignored the feeble jibe; but he took it as a deadly insult and ordered that the port cover should be closed down, thus depriving some messes of light. The angry Americans forced it open and the enraged commander ordered marines to re-close it, and spike it firmly-shut. Once again the port was forced, and jammed open with a heavy oak bench, as prisoners in every part of the ship took up a Baa-baaing, 'sounding like an immense flock of sheep, that might have been heard a full mile away'.

His family outing forgotten, Osmore had the still-bleating Yankees driven off the forecastle and the 'pound', or 'Parc', forced below and battened down; only the cooks in the galley were allowed to remain, and one mess representative allowed on deck to collect water from the scuttlebutts. The market boats, on which they depended to supplement their rations, were forbidden to come alongside. After two long days of discomfort and unbolstered provisions, the President of the twelve-man Committee somehow managed to get a message to the Agent and the Commodore, who came aboard to sort out the dispute.

Lieutenant Osmore lost the day: it was decided that his punishments were too great for the 'crime'. The hatches were unbattened, the bum-boats were soon alongside, and life on the *Crown Prince* returned to normal – although thereafter Lieutenant Osmore seldom came on to his quarterdeck unheralded by at least a few subdued 'Baas'.

On at least one other occasion, the Americans genuinely suspected Osmore of dishonesty, this time towards the prisoners. They had learned from Captain Hutchinson that they were entitled to good soft bread from the contractor, unless the weather made delivery impossible; in which case hardtack would be served and should be accepted. Hutchinson further informed them that if the contractor failed them without good reason, a ruling existed which stated that he should forfeit one half pound of good bread to each man (about 300lb at that time). Of late they had been served more hard than soft bread and the now-wiser prisoners were forced to conclude that all past forfeitures had gone into Osmore's pocket rather than their stomachs. On the next appearance of hardtack, it was refused and the heavy-handed commander told them they could eat it or go without until they did so. The journal describes this confrontation in strange words:

'Our commander then swore from the teeth outwards, that if we did not eat his hard bread, we should have none; and we swore from the teeth inwardly, that we would adhere to our first declaration, and maintain our rights.'

Then followed the old routine of marines driving everyone below, ladders drawn up, hatches closed down – but this time the captives were so enraged and rebellious that Osmore lost his nerve and sent the female members of his family ashore for safety. This time it was he who contacted the Commodore, telling him of his fears of mutiny and requesting a reinforcement of marines. After a few days the Americans found it hard to hold out against hunger, and would have welcomed even the hardest of ship's biscuit. Even the most stubborn found their resolution cooling: 'to lay such an embargo on our own bowels was, to be sure a pretty tough piece of self-denial; for we found, in all our sufferings, that bread was the staff of life.'

They were on the point of voting on the subject of starvation or hard biscuit, when the Commodore and Hutchinson arrived to investigate this latest contest between obdurate commander and stubborn prisoners. To Lieutenant Osmore's chagrin, battle honours went once again to the Americans, who acknowledged their good fortune in having 'two honourable [British] gentlemen' who dealt fairly with complaints.

As July approached, the spirits of even the most dejected of hulk-bound Americans were raised at the prospect of celebrating the birthday of their nation. Everyone was animated and full of ideas of how to spend the contents of the kitty to which every mess had been contributing. The 'luxuries' and extras which would be added to their basic rations were simple enough; but on the day of their celebration their feast would seem as grand as any town hall banquet. Application was made to the British Agent for an additional allowance of porter and beer, and this was approved; but he had not the authority to allow them to hoist the American Flag. Disappointed, they petitioned the Port Commodore, who gave all hulks permission to fly their national flag – but no higher than the top of the ship's railings. Some of the prisoners had musical instruments and one persuasive Yankee had borrowed a British drum and a fife, so all was set for a great day of feasting, drinking and patriotic jubilations.

Early on the morning of the Fourth of July, 1813, the prisoners crowded onto the 'pound' and forecastle of the *Crown Prince*, and the strains of 'Yankee Doodle' could be heard throughout the Chatham prison fleet. The *Nassau* and other Yankee-bearing hulks were saluted with such loud cheers and songs that the rumpus could be clearly heard ashore. The whole forenoon was noisy with music, song and hurrahing and the sound of the borrowed fife and drum (which bore the arms of His Britannic Majesty), as the Americans drank toast after toast to 'Success to the American Cause' – in good English porter and beer.

At noon, silence was called for an Address to be read. The orator was a Yankee sailor who had been impressed into the British Navy before 1812, and had reached the rank of boatswain of a frigate by the time of his surrender. He mounted a rostrum and delivered a distinctly inflamatory oration, which was listened to in respectful silence, save when particularly powerful and anti-British points roused them to loud cheers and applause.

It is pleasant to note that the prison ship officers took everything in good part and seemed to appreciate the orator's valiant efforts: 'even Osmore, our jailor, grinn'd horribly a ghastly smile'. After the Address, the prisoners descended to the decks below, where the dinner had been prepared and fell to, with 'a zest and hilarity rarely to be found among a large collection of prisoners.' Waterhouse, who could seldom resist a biblical reference, ended his own description of the jubilant captives enjoying their celebration with: 'If, like the captive Jews on the Euphrates, we had hung our harps upon the willows of the Medway, we took them down on this joyous occasion…!'

Similar celebrations took place on other Medway hulks. Those organised by the *Nassau* were particularly well conducted. The

Oration was so carefully composed and well-delivered, that a number of the local gentry who had been invited on board, lent a sympathetic ear. It later went into print, first locally in England and later in Boston, Massachusetts, and I reproduce it here, in spite of its length, as it makes interesting and relevant reading:

'AN ORATION DELIVERED BY PERMISSION ON BOARD THE *NASSAU* PRISON SHIP AT CHATHAM
On the FOURTH of JULY, 1813.
By an American Prisoner of War

My Fellow-prisoners, and beloved countrymen,

WE ARE assembled to commemorate the ever memorable Fourth of July, 1776, when our forefathers, inspired with the love of liberty, dared to divest themselves of the shackles of tyranny and oppression: yes, my friends. On that important day these stripes were hoisted on the standard of Liberty, as a signal of unity, and of their determination to fight under them, until America was numbered among the nations of the globe, as one of them; a free and independent nation.

'Yes, my countrymen, she was determined to spare neither blood nor treasure, until she had accomplished the grand object of her intentions; an object, my friends, which she was prompted by Heaven to undertake, and inspired by all that honour, justice and patriotism could infuse; her armies were then in the field, with a WASHINGTON at their head, whose upright conduct and valorous deeds should be held sacred in the breast of every true-born American:- Let his heart beat high at the name of WASHINGTON! Sacred as the archives of Heaven! For he was a man of truth, honour and integrity, and a soldier `fostered by the gods to be the saviour of his country,

'The struggle was long, and arduous; but our rallying word was, "Liberty or Death!" Torrents of blood were spilt; towns and villages were burnt, and nothing but havoc, devastation and destruction was seen from one end of the continent to the other; and this was not all; but, to complete the horrid scene, an infernal horde of savage murderers was prompted by our enemy to butcher our helpless wives and children! Then did our fathers' hearts swell in their bosoms, and they were ten-fold more resolved to break the yoke of the tyrant.

'I recite these things, my countrymen, that you may know how to prize your liberty, that precious gem for which your fathers fought, wading in rivers of blood, until it pleased the Almighty to crown their arms with success; and, glorious to relate, America was acknowledged free and independent by all the powers of Europe. Happy period! Then did our warriors exult in what they had so nobly achieved; then commerce revived and the thirteen stripes were hoisted on the tall masts of our ships and displayed from pole to pole; emigrants flocked from many parts to taste our freedom, and the other blessings Heaven had bestowed upon us; our population increased to an incredible degree; our commerce flourished, and our country has been the seat of peace, plenty and happiness for many years. At length the fatal blast reached our land! America was obliged to unsheath the sword in justification of her violated rights, Our ships were captured and condemned on frivolous pretensions; our seamen were dragged from their lawful employment; they were torn from the bosom of their beloved country; sons from their fathers; husbands from their wives and children, to serve with reluctance for many years, under the severity of martial law. The truth of this many of you can attest to, perhaps with an inward pining and a bleeding heart! My countrymen! I did not mount this rostrum to inveigh against the British; only the demagogues; the war-faction I exclaim against. We all know, and that full well, that there are many honest, patriotic men in this country, who would raise their voices to succour us, and their arms too could they do it with impunity. The sympathetic hearts of the good, feel for the oppressed in all climes. And now, my countrymen, it is more than probable that the land of your nativity will be involved in war, and deluged in blood for some time to come; yes, my friends, that happy country, which is the guardian of everything you possess, that you esteem, near and dear, has again to struggle for her liberty. The British war-faction are rushing upon us with their fleets and armies, and, thinking to crush us in a moment. Such infatuation! They have forgotten Bunker's Hill! They have forgotten Saratoga, and Yorktown, when the immortal WASHINGTON with his victorious army chased them through the Jerseys, under the muzzles of their ships' canon for protection! They have forgotten that the sons of America have as good blood in their veins, and possess as sound limbs and nerves as they; strange infatuation! I repeat it, if they presume to think that eight millions of free people will be easily divested of their liberty; [take] my word for it, they will not give up at the sight of their men-of-war or their redcoats; no, my friends, they will meet the lads who will play them the tune of 'Yankee Doodle', as well as they did at Lexicon, Bunker Hill. Besides, my countrymen, there is a plant in that country (very little of which grows anywhere else) the infusion of which stimulates the true sons of America to deeds of valour. There is something so fostering in the very sound of its name, that it holds superiority wherever it grows; it is a sacred plant my friends, my friends, its name is LIBERTY, and may God grant that that plant may continue to grow in the United States of America, and shall never be rooted out so long as it shall please Him to continue the celestial orb to roll in the azure expanse.

'Ah! Britons! Had your councellors been just, and had they listened with attention. And followed the advice of the immortal William Pitt, Britain and America might have been one until the present hour, and they united, in time might have given laws to the inhabitants of this terrestial ball. Many of you, my friends, have voluntarily embraced this loathsome prison, rather than betray your country, for by the laws of your country, to aid or give any assistance to an enemy, is treason, is punishable with death. I therefore hope that your country will reward you abundantly for your toil. And one and all let us embrace the icy arms of death, rather than cherish the least symptom of an inclination to betray your country. Some have done it, who have pretended to be Americans, so far as to shield themselves under the name. Whether they were real Americans or not, it is hard for me to say; but if they were, they have put their hand to the plough, and not only looked back, but have gone back. I have not the least doubt that they will meet their reward; that is, they will be spurned by those very people that laid the bait for them. Such characters will be forever condemned, and held in detestation by both parties. Therefore all who feel the tide of true American blood flow through your hearts, I hope never will attempt to flee from the allegiance of your country. It is cowardice, it is felony; and for all those who have done it, we may pray that the departed spirits of their fathers, who so nobly fought, bled, and fell in the conflict to gain their Liberty, will haunt them in their midnight slumbers, and that they may feel the horrors of conscience and the dread of the gallows!

'Also that they will have no rest, but like the dove that Noah sent out from the Ark, be restless until they return to the allegiance of their country. And now, my countrymen, let us join in unison to correct our own morals, let us be sober; let us be vigilant over ourselves whilst in this situation. And although it is not in our power to assist our countrymen in the present conflict, yet if we are good the powers of Heaven will fight for us, for the good must merit God's peculiar care. The powers of Heaven fought for us; they assisted us to gain our Liberty, we had no navy, or none of any consequence, yet Great Britain lost more line-of-battle-ships in that war than she did with France, although France is a great naval power. And we should be thankful to God for all the blessings He hath bestowed upon us from time to time, and in particular for the blessing of that unity which we are recently informed prevails among our countrymen in America; united they stand, nor will powers of hell will be able to overthrow them.

'And now let us appeal to the God of Saboath, that is, the God of armies – let us appeal to Him who holds the balance, and weighs the events of battles and of realms, and by His decision we must abide. And may He grant us health, peace and unity in this our disagreeable situation; and let us join in concord to praise the Ruler and Governor of the Universe. Amen. Amen.'

This worked so well that after a while the same ploy was tried again. Two men slipped into the water and swam off; but the second man, overcome by nerves and the coldness of the water, stopped swimming and was spotted by a sentry as he turned to try to clamber back through the escape-hole. The guard was turned out, the general alarm sounded through the fleet, and the swimmer was dragged back on board. The river was soon dotted with boats searching for the other man, but there was no report of his recapture. Next day his body was found on the marshy shore.

Many are the tales of such brave escapades, of success and failure, but three Medway escape attempts which did not use the hole-though-the-hull method are worth relating here:

In June, 1814, three prisoners had escaped by concealing themselves in empty water tanks which were taken ashore for refilling. As this was achieved through the purchased cooperation of the corporal of the guard, many more may have made this their vehicle to freedom, had not one of them crowed over his success. He wrote a satirical note to the commander, Lieutenant Osmore, thanking him 'for his tenderness, humanity and extreme kindness', and stupidly boasted of his method of escape. It is not too heart-breaking to hear that he was soon recaptured.

Another employed a similar method by hiding in an old worn-out copper boiler which was being sent to the dock for replacement He got safely to the dockyard, but after wandering about for some time without discovering an exit, was apprehended by dockyard police. Terrified by the thought that he might be impressed on to a British man-of-war, he confessed and was returned to the hulk.

The third example is truly remarkable, as it was carried out with great daring in broad daylight. Four Americans from the *Irresistible*, the Commodore's ship at Chatham, noticed that the jolly-boat,[5] with oars inboard, and lying alongside the gangway, was guarded by only one sentry. The leader of the four was an American Indian of the Narraganset tribe, a man of great strength and stature, who seized the sentry, disarmed him and threw him from his post on the staging, into the jolly-boat below. All four were soon pulling away for the shore 'with all the agility of so many Nantucket whalemen', running the gauntlet of musket fire from all the hulks within range as they passed through. Soon boats manned by marines set out from all the nearby ships and gave chase, pouring continuous fire at the fugitives – despite the fact that their boat was ballasted with a semi-conscious British sentry. By a miracle, only one of the Americans was wounded and the other three leaped ashore and made for the open fields. They soon outdistanced the more heavily-clad and encumbered marines and may well have got away but dozens of countryfolk poured out from houses, farms and brickyards to join in the hunt. The captives on the Chatham hulks had a grandstand view of this memorable event and, whatever their nationality, cheered and shouted-on the courageous Yankees. But eventually they were hounded to exhaustion by their military and civilian pursuers – except for the Narraganset Red Indian. It might perhaps be forgivably unpatriotic to wish to hear that he got clear away, but though he outran them all, 'skipping over the ground like a buck'; he leaped a fence and cracked an ankle on landing, so was forced to surrender. The four were rowed back to captivity amidst the loudest cheers that had been heard on the Medway for many a day.

In the late spring of 1814, the war had ended for the French, some of whom had been prisoners since 1803. The land depots and parole towns were being cleared of their unwilling guests, the roads and tracts leading to the coast jammed with marching men, carriages, coaches, carts and transports of every kind. The prison ships were also busy decanting the French prisoners and their continental allies into dozens of boats, ferrying the freed though defeated ex-captives to the cartel ships.

Louis XVIII had passed through Chatham in May. Only the tops of the carriages could be seen from some of the hulks, but the sound of saluting cannon fire from London to Sheerness brought joy to the hearts of the British. The French, of course were in a quandary of ambiguity, feelings of relief at the prospect of freedom battling, for many, with despair at having to don the white cockade in place of the tricolour. The Americans, too, could not have enjoyed the celebrations any more than the French, although many felt a greater natural affinity with the Englishman, whilst hating him as a gaoler. They would have hated their gaolers even more, had they known that many months of agonised waiting were to pass before they returned to their homeland.

Charles Andrews' journal has told of the drafts of Yankee prisoners being sent from Plymouth and Portsmouth to Dartmoor and other depots. A similar operation had been under way at Chatham since the middle of 1813, though transports were held up during the worst periods of infectious and contagious diseases, for fear of introducing further evils into Dartmoor, which already had its share of illnesses. A group of one hundred and fifty set off by sea for Plymouth and Dartmoor, but soon after leaving the Medway it was found that many were suffering from measles and was turned back at the Nore.

The Americans at Chatham were as appalled at the thought of being sent to the Moor as the Plymouth prisoners had been. Men who had spent their days planning escapes and boring holes in hulks, now expressed sincere regret at leaving their floating prisons; of having to face another transport; another line-up on deck or depot yard, to be examined and possibly insulted as renegades. 'Dartmoor' was a dreaded word.

Waterhouse was as apprehensive of the 'untried scene' as any, and the thought of leaving the Medway, lent it a certain beauty:

> 'The Medway, though a small river in the eyes of an inhabitant of the New World, is a very pleasant one. The moveable picture on its surface, of ships, tenders and barges, is very pleasing, while its banks are rich and beautiful…The picture from the banks of the river to the top of the landscape, is truly delightful, …and beyond anything I ever saw in my own country; and owing to the hedges, which are novelties in the eyes of an American.'

The river was busier than ever before, with boatloads of guarded prisoners heading for transport vessels; and tenders filled with seamen and marines who would soon be bound for America, often playing 'Yankee Doodle' as they passed the American hulks – shouting boasts that now the French were beaten, they would soon polish off the Yankees: and receiving in return dire warnings of the dreadful fate that awaited them on their arrival in the States!

Spirits were low on the no-longer-crowded prison ships. The Americans were miserably uncertain of their immediate, or even distant, future – and the bungling Lieutenant Osmore, who had learned nothing during his overseeing of Yankee captives, unnecessarily brought about one last mini-mutiny.

About thirty Dartmoor-bound draftees had been detailed to make ready to depart early on the following morning. They had to return their hammocks, correctly lashed, to the store-shed on the upper deck before leaving in the tender. This they did, but learned that there was a postponement and the tender would not be alongside until the next morning.

Later in the day they applied to Osmore for the return of their hammocks and bedding, but the heavy-handed commander replied that it would be too much trouble, and they should make do as best they might until next day. With only bare boards for their bed they decided if they could not sleep, then neither should Osmore, nor anyone else for that matter.

After the commander had retired at about ten o'clock, they uprooted heavy oak benches, tied ropes to them and dragged them round the deck, dashing them against the bulkheads, shouting, yelling and shrieking like mad things. Using the benches as battering-rams, they brought crockery crashing down on the marines' side of the cockpit, which brought the marines onto the scene. Osmore came out of his cabin and called upon a senior Committee member to quell the rioters but was told they were completely beyond control. His threat to give the order for the marines to fire, was greeted with 'Fire then, and be damned!', and he accepted defeat, retreating to his cabin – but not to sleep. They collected all the pots, pans, kettles, coppers and tins, tying them into jangling bunches and trailing them round the decks; accompanied by war-whoops and cheering; pausing for intervals long enough for Osmore to doze off, before starting the terrible uproar all over again.

Next morning the tender came alongside and Lieutenant Osmore superintended the departure of the tired but happy Yankees, who gave him a last farewell 'Baa! Baa! Baa-ing', continuing the bleating until the *Crown Prince* was well out of sight.

On the 15th September, 1814, the *Crown Prince* was cleared of all her remaining prisoners. For some reason they were not not yet to be sent to a land prison, but were put on board the *Bahama* hulk, farther upriver. Life had become easier on the almost empty hulk they had just left, so the change was not for the better. About three hundred Americans were already on the *Bahama*, living in a state of dirt and disorder. There was a Committee made up of a few decent men, but too few and too weak to control the vice and gambling which obtained on board. 'I never saw a set of more ragged, dirty men in my life, yet they were disposed to sell their last rag to get money to gamble with.'

Some of the newcomers joined the gambling fraternity within a few days, whilst others joined those who kept themselves occupied with those profitable crafts which we more often associate with the industrious French: making watch-cases, snuff and tobacco boxes from bone, and even building small model ships.

A fair number of the American prisoners were soldiers who had been captured at the beginning of the war, and most of these were included in the rough, tattered and vicious mob which spent all their time at the tables. In general, the American sailor considered the soldier as a member of a lower class than himself; at least, any captured before the end of 1813, after which the standard was improved by the inducement of a bounty of a grant of land at the end of the war – which encouraged farmers' sons and men of good family to enlist.

The Duke of Wellington had described our soldiery in less than complimentary terms during the Peninsular Wars, but Waterhouse's description of his country's first army recruits was downright heartless and cruel:

> 'They were, many of them, intemperate men, void of good character and good constitution. The high-flying federal clergy, among other nonsense, told their flocks that the war would demoralise the people; whereas it had the contrary effect... It absolutely picked all the rags, dirt and vice, from our towns and villages and transported them into Canada, where they were either captured, killed, or died with sickness, so that our towns and villages on the Atlantic, were cleared of idlers and drunkards, and experienced the benefit of their removal.'

After not much more than a couple of weeks on the *Bahama*, about a hundred Americans were ordered into gun-brigs which were anchored alongside and, on the 2nd October, they sailed down the Medway, passed Sheerness and headed for the Nore, where the transport, the old Dutch 64-gun *Leyden* with others of their countrymen aboard, awaited them. They rejoiced in the rumour that they would find a cartel ship at Plymouth which would carry them home – but that was not to be.

The voyage round the coast on the *Leyden* was only slightly less unpleasant than they had experienced on the *Malaga*, but they were in for the biggest surprise of their captivity on arrival at Plymouth. Next morning boats came alongside filled with women, 'generally, healthy, rosy looking lasses.[6] Their number increased every hour, until there were as many on board of us as there were men. In short, every man who paid the waterman half a crown had a wife'. This invasion by female boarders would have been no surprise to Jack Tars in general, for every home-coming ship was greeted in this manner; but many of the American captives had seen little sea-time before their capture, and although they may have read of such exotic happenings involving dusky maidens of the South Seas, it was the last thing they expected in an English port. Waterhouse crammed a great deal of moralising in his journal throughout its length, and one might expect him to point the Plymouth episode of tarts and tars as another example of the low standards of the British. But in one remarkable passage he indicates that two-and-sixpenny temporary 'wives' were also available to the prisoners!

> 'Yes, Christian reader! In this religious island, whereof George the 3rd is king, and Charlotte the queen, the young females crowd the prison ship, and take for husbands the ragged American prisoners, provided they can get a few shillings by it.'

It would be easy to dismiss this as fiction, remembering the strictness of the dour captain of the *Leyden*, who discouraged fraternisation between captives and crew – and had had a marine flogged for selling a little of his own tobacco to an American. But why should Waterhouse have included a complete fabrication in a book published at a time when thousands of his fellow prisoners, and potential readers, were returning home and would have laughed inaccuracies to scorn?

As well as a first edition of the *Journal*, I have a second edition in my collection: published later in 1815, in which I rather expected the prostitute story to be omitted; but, although there was a good deal of revision and editing, it remained unaltered.

As the *Leyden* lay off Plymouth, the two-months-old news of the burning of the City of Washington reached the prisoners, and many of the Yankees felt sure that their next transport would be a States-bound cartel ship; for surely, with their capital captured, America must be defeated and their war at an end; but they learned that their destination was Dartmoor (where most would spend at least the next six months before release).

For many of the two hundred men who were ferried ashore it would be the first time they had set foot on terra firma for at least a year; and for some who had served on our men-of-war, many years longer. One such old-timer spoke of nostalgia as their boats passed through the harbour. Among warships on the stocks was a new man-of-war, 'pierced for 120 guns', called the *Lord Vincent*, in honour of Admiral Sir John Jervis. The American had played his part, as an impressed seaman, in the Battle of Cape St Vincent against the Spanish, on the 14th February, 1797; and his nostalgia must have been tinged with a sense of unfairness as he recalled that Sir John had been rewarded with an earldom, whilst he was now heading for Britain's most feared prison.

Once ashore, the marines handed their charges over to a lieutenant and a double file of soldiers for the march to the 'Depot on the Moor', but first any who had money enough refreshed themselves with cakes and ale, purchased from old ladies bearing foaming jugs and laden baskets, who eagerly awaited such deliveries of captive customers. Thus refreshed, they tramped the long miles with all the trepidation of the drafts described by Andrews a year and a half earlier.

Charles Andrews, Benjamin Waterhouse the 'Young Man of Massachusetts', Josiah Cobb the 'Green Hand', and a few others continued their journals in the Depot on the Moor, where we shall leave them until Chapter 19, DARTMOOR PRISON; and return to Louis Garneray and the prison ships at Portsmouth.

It will be remembered that we left Ambroise Louis Garneray at a time when his prison ship captivity on the *Vengeance* had come to an end. Through the influence of the Portsmouth picture-dealer Smith, and the French Colonel, Baron Louis François Le Jeune, he had been granted parole to Bishop's Waltham in Hampshire. Now he could look forward to dry land under his feet, and association with free – though enemy – civilians for the first time in many years. But the story of Louis and the hulks does not end at this point, so we shall follow him ashore.

Knowing the resourcefulness with which he had adapted himself to the restrictions and hardship of prison ship life, one might expect that he would exploit with delight the freedom and privileges presented by this very different type of captivity. Bishop's Waltham was a pleasant small town, where the inhabitants had grown used to having captive foreign officers in their midst for most of the past half century; their town having being one of the first *cautionnements* established at the beginning of the Seven Years' War. The townsfolk profited by their presence both financially and culturally, and would have met many colourful and famous military and naval characters over the years. Admiral Villeneuve and his staff were sent there after Trafalgar; and the more infamous than famous Anglophobe, General Pillet, spent time in the town in 1808, before his misdeeds earned him a spell on the *Brunswick* hulk at Chatham.

Bishop's Waltham was ideally situated for Garneray's needs; no more than fifteen miles inland from Portsmouth, in easy reach for Smith to collect his paintings. Yet, right from the outset of his life ashore, his memoirs are filled with complaint and criticism: 'When I arrived under escort at the little village to which I was assigned as my place of residence, I was disillusioned to find twelve hundred Frenchmen, of all ranks…' Here he was exaggerating the number of parolees by seven or eight hundred; they would not all have been French, and the 'all ranks' was misleading. Although himself a privateer lieutenant, Louis had been captured as a quartermaster's

mate in the French Navy, and was himself in Bishop's Waltham only by special dispensation after being spoken for by a titled and much respected French officer.

He went on to complain that the officers were living in a group of 'wretched, tumble-down houses' for which they were charged such an exorbitant rent by the English landladies that one year's rental would have bought a whole house. As for himself, he managed to get, for ten shillings a week, 'not a room, but the right to put up my bed in a dirty room shared by five other officers'. Next day he found better accommodation by striking a deal with an old Waltham lady who rented him a garret where he could set up his studio. He now had better quarters both for working and living than he had ever had since being taken prisoner – but daily found cause for new complaint.

Garneray, like any other parolee, had to pledge his word of honour by signing a declaration that he would not escape from, or plan against, his captors, and would observe a few simple restrictions. As is more fully explained in Chapter 21, PAROLE D' HONNEUR, acceptance of the parole rules was a reasonable exchange for the advantages offered; and as no one had to accept parole, it was expected that, once a man had put his signature to the *parole d'honneur* document, he would not forfeit his reputation by breaking his word.

I believe that in writing so critically of the townsfolk, and by listing far too many alleged unfairnesses to be repeated here, Garneray was trying to prepare his readers for the time when he would break his word of honour – perhaps hoping to convince them that his written promise as a gentleman was abnegated by the unfairness of the British. Had he escaped from hulk or depot he could be regarded as a hero; breaking his word to his captor – and incidentally letting down Baron Le Jeune who had guaranteed him – Louis, who we had much reason to admire became just another 'broke-parole'.

Nevertheless, for the next few months, he carried on a profitable business from his garret, supplying Smith with paintings for his Portsmouth gallery. Then one fine morning Louis, with two friends, a corvette captain and a major of dragoons, decided to dine at a farm about a mile along the turnpike – the limit of their parole. They set off along the high road, then decided on a high-spirited breach of the rules by cutting across the fields to the farm; Louis jumping ditches and generally enjoying his outing, until he fell and sprained his ankle. Lagging well behind his friends, he suddenly heard shouts for help and a cry of pain from the other side of a hedge.

Hobbling up as fast as he could, he saw that a farm labourer had been trimming a hedge, but, on seeing the two officers out of their parole area, had attacked them with his bill-hook. The major had been dealt a serious blow to his arm and the captain, who could make himself understood in English, came to his aid, protesting and placing himself between the two, trying to reason with the countryman, only to receive two terrible cuts to the head, which knocked him to the ground.

Garneray armed himself with a broken bough, but the attacker took to his heels, returning later with a menacing group of country people armed with pitchforks and guns. However, they were shocked by the bloodstained scene and the condition of the two Frenchmen, and listened sympathetically to Louis' account of the cowardly attack: after which they made a litter from their pitchforks and carried the wounded men back to their lodging.

The hedger was within his rights to apprehend or report any

parole offender, indeed would have been entitled to a cash reward for so doing; but such brutality went beyond all bounds. The savagery of the attack caused great indignation among both prisoners and townsfolk; a group of senior officer prisoners deciding to get up a petition of strong protest to the British Government

Garneray then went on to tell the possible, but improbable, story that he had been warned that if he translated the petition, he would earn the displeasure of the Transport Board; but did so nevertheless. If he was in trouble at all, it is far more likely that he would have been answerable to the local Agent for the relatively minor offence of leaving the turnpike to go into the fields. But Louis says that as he was leaving the meeting after delivering his translation, a pretty little twelve-year-old English girl, who he already knew, beckoned him to follow her to her grandmother's broken-down cottage. The old lady, for whom Garneray had painted a portrait of the young girl without charge, told him she had overheard two constables discussing their orders to arrest him. It was on such grounds that he made his decision to escape – and a truly remarkable escape it was. Returning to his lodging, he stuffed a leather money-belt with the gold and banknotes he had earned by his art, and after buying a fine pair of pocket-pistols from an ensign, headed for the open road. Walking confidently down the middle of the road, he stopped a diligence and was lucky enough to get an inside seat. His idea was to hide in Portsmouth and on finding that the coach was heading the other way, he got off at the first stop. Pretending to be suffering from a violent toothache, he wrapped his supposedly swollen jaw in a black scarf, which not only hid much of his face but also muffled his accent when he spoke. He then entered the inn, dined, and asked that he be awakened an hour before the first Portsmouth coach left the next day.

The chambermaid roused him at five o'clock in the morning, and the coach arrived just as he was finishing a good breakfast and a glass of port. He was in Portsmouth by nine o'clock and by eleven had located Smith. The dealer was, of course, less than delighted to see him, as their business had gone well from Bishop's Waltham, but stood by him as a good and profitable friend. Smith was taking a terrible risk in aiding a 'broke-parole', as detection could have meant transportation to Australia for seven or fourteen years. Louis was given a room in the attic of the dealer's home, equipped with easel, canvases and all the necessary paraphernalia to continue with his painting – although he made it clear that he would continue his escape to France at the first opportunity.

Confined as he was to the house, Smith made all the enquiries on his behalf, assuring Louis that he had a contact through one of his gilders, whose cousin made a living by smuggling contraband goods – and men – across the Channel. Garneray's delight at this news was very short-lived: next day Smith brought him the story that, on his way to the gilders, he had met up with an old friend, a merchant navy captain and, in an exploratory but apparently disinterested way, brought up the subject of prisoners who escaped from the hulks and the cupidity of the traitorous smugglers who aided them. He then passed on what, he said, were the captain's comments, 'I wouldn't worry if I were you,' he said, 'the number of prisoners who actually get to France is very small indeed. Remember that the penalty for aiding escapers is death, so if the smugglers sense any danger they do the usual thing – dump the contraband overboard. Some of them even go so far as to slit the throats of escaping prisoners, once they've been paid. Of course,

some are more reputable and work for the Transport Board: they take the money the prisoners have paid for their passage, steal their belongings and then turn them over to the Board, who then pays them the reward of five pounds a head.'

Incredibly, Louis Garneray spent almost a year penned up in that Portsmouth house, painting and earning,[7] seldom venturing out during the daylight hours, and becoming ever more depressed. By April 1813, he could stand the life no longer, too downcast and ill to paint, and willing to take his chance with the worst of smugglers. Smith, no doubt realising that his French goose had laid its final golden egg, at last agreed to contact his gilder's smuggler cousin.

The cousin knew of three recently escaped and hidden prisoners who were only waiting for funds from France to reach them through paroled friends, before they could make their getaway. The three, Labosic, Mercadier and Vidal, who, like Louis, had at one time sailed with Captain Surcouf in the Indian Ocean, were delighted to hear that he would advance them the money to expedite the escape of all four.

It was arranged that the Frenchmen should meet up with the escape agents in the room at the inn where the three had been hiding out. Louis was the last to arrive and found everyone in high spirits, the Frenchmen already three sheets in the wind, were being encouraged to drink up, from pewter tankards of gin. He was invited, but declined, to join what was a drinking competition between the English and French, which the latter had already lost.

The skipper of the small sailing boat which was to carry them across the Channel, whose name was Jeffries, gave him careful instructions as to where they were to rendezvous between ten and eleven o'clock that night. The ruffian appearance of Jeffries and his crew, their rough speech and untrustworthy appearance, convinced Louis that the merchant captain's warning of the previous year had been no exaggeration, and if he could have safely returned to Smith at that moment he would not have hesitated.

He did his best to sober up his companions before they left the inn, but when darkness came and they set off they were still unsteady. Each had obtained a pistol, one had a cutlass and Louis still had his pocket-pistols, but except for Garneray none would have been capable of defending himself.

They found the boat in a little creek near Portsmouth, at the base of a cliff. Jeffries met them and greeted the three tipsy men with, 'Oh! Oh! Obviously gin is not your usual drink, but a few hours sleep and fresh air will wake you up!' and a few minutes later they were leaving the creek and heading out to sea, with a brisk south-west sea wind helping them on their way.

In pitch-black darkness Louis sat whilst his companions slept, certain that the next moment could well be his last; and when, an hour or so later, he heard mutterings and someone creeping towards him, he challenged loudly so that it was known that he was very much awake. After another hour on tenterhooks, Louis was relieved to see the moon appearing through the clouds for short periods. Feeling more secure when he could see the smugglers before him in the bows, he said he would listen, when Jeffries said there was something of great importance which they must discuss – so long as he came no nearer to him.

Jeffries asked did he not think that ten pounds a head for risking his neck was cheap for such a service? Louis agreed, but said that it was not he who had fixed the price, but would nevertheless agree to up the price to fifteen pounds. But Jeffries had not finished. He said that if, when daylight came, they were to encounter a British ship, it would be advisable for the prisoners to look less Frenchified and more like English sailors, and that he had all the necessary gear below – which he could offer at a bargain price:

'Let's see now, what would you need? Shoes? Four pairs, say ten pounds sterling. Hats, six pounds. Jackets, forty pounds. Trousers, twenty pounds. Cravats, five pounds. That comes to eighty-one pounds, but let's call it eighty. What do you think?'

Garneray told him what he thought – and as it was obvious that matters were coming to a head, he tried to rouse the others by dipping his hat in the sea and dousing them with cold water. Keeping one pistol in his grasp he repeated the water treatment until his fellow countrymen began to sit up. But he had concentrated so intently on the men in the bows that he had forgotten the helmsmen in the stern. He was bending over the gunwale when he was struck a heavy blow on the head and another on his shoulder, which knocked him into the bottom of the boat. As he lay there he saw the flash of a knife, and instinctively fired the gun in his left hand, putting a bullet through the head of the helmsman, who fell dead on top of him.

When he recovered it was daylight, and a frightening sight met his gaze. Lebosec lay beside him, his chest and shoulder bloody from deep cutlass wounds. In the bottom of the boat were two dead men, the helmsman and Jeffries, who had been struck down by a cutlass stroke from one of the Frenchmen. He asked where were the other two crewmen and was told that 'they found their way over the side, with very little help from us', which was probably a polite way of describing their exit and demise.

Garneray, who had been stunned and lost a good deal of blood, fell into a deep sleep for some time, until Mercadier woke him to give him the good and the bad news: they were off the French coast above Cherbourg – but bearing down on them was a British corvette; and fifteen minutes later they were once more prisoners of war.

When Ambroise Louis Garneray was brought back to England, he was sent again to the *Vengeance* hulk; but to a very different accommodation to that which he had left so many months before. He returned to spend weeks of solitary confinement on short rations in the damp and dirt of the Black Hole. There had been some sort of inquiry into the attempted escape and injury and death but it would seem that there was little sympathy for smuggler escape agents, and the enquiry was soon abandoned.

Once out of the *cachot*, hungry and hard-up – for although Smith held money for him in Portsmouth, there was no way of contacting the dealer at that time – he began to sketch and work again. It was not long before Abraham Curtis, the picture dealer cousin of the hulk's commander, heard that he was back on board, and was pleased to arrange for him to regain his cabin – in return for painting at a very low price. Once again he began to find his feet, was able to eat well and live in greater comfort than most of his fellow prisoners – and perhaps better than many of the British crew.

His long experience of prison ship life and the privileges which his talents had earned him, took him through to the end of 1813 without great incident. But the early months of 1814 were a miserable time for all French prisoners of war. Britain was rejoicing at a whole succession of French defeats, and some thoughtless, ignorant or deliberately cruel members of the ship's company taunted the French with insults and contemptuous remarks, perhaps hoping to taunt them into violent reaction. If that was their aim, they succeeded with Garneray. He became involved in an upset with the hulk's boatswain and a drunken sailor, who had been particularly insulting. In the ensuing fight there could only be one loser: Louis found himself once again in the foul *cachot*.

After only five days in the miserable hole, the gaoler roused Louis at an early hour and told him, 'You may go! You are free! The war is over!'

'Tarts and Tars'
Admiral Hawkins' comments on the subject.

It is well known that immediately on the arrival of a ship of war in port, crowds of boats flocked off with cargoes of prostitutes. Having no money to pay for their conveyance, the waterman takes as many as his boat will hold, upon speculation, and hovers round the ship until she is secured at her anchors and the necessary work done, when he with others, is permitted to come alongside. The men then go into the boats and pick out each a woman (as one would choose cattle), paying a shilling or two to the boatman for her passage off.

'They then descend to the lower deck with their "husbands", as they call them. These women are examined at the gangway for liquor which they are constantly in the habit of smuggling on board. Hundreds come off to a large ship. The whole of the shocking. disgraceful transaction of the lower deck is impossible to describe – the dirt, filth, and stench; the disgusting conversation; the indecent beastly conduct and horrible scenes; the blasphemy and swearing; the riots, quarrels, and fighting which often takes place where hundreds of men and women are huddled together in one room, as it were, and where, in bed (each man being allowed only fourteen inches breadth for his hammock, they are squeezed between the next hammocks and must be witness to each others actions; can only be imagined by those who have seen all this. A ship in this state is often, and justly, called by the more decent seamen "a hell afloat". Let those who have never seen a ship of war, picture to themselves a very large low room (hardly capable of holding the men) with 500 men and probably 300 or 400 women of the vilest description shut up in it, and giving way to every excess of debauchery that the grossest passions of human nature can lead them to; and they will see the deck of a 74-gun ship the night of her arrival in port.'[8]

1. On 27 April, 1816, President Madison laid a statement before the House of Representatives which listed names and details of 1,775 impressed American seamen taken into His Britannic Majesty's Service and after 1812 treated as prisoners of war.

2. Anacreon born *c*.570 BC Greek Lyric Poet: who wrote chiefly in praise of Wine and Love.

3. 'Old Trafalgar' was a shipmate and fellow prisoner.

4. If detected or recaptured, the hole-makers were made to pay for the necessary repairs to the damaged hulk, by instalments deducted from their rations.

5. Jolly-boat: a clinker built ship's boat, smaller than a cutter.

6. See 'Tarts and Tars', at the end of this Chapter, and 'A

Man-O'-War's Song'at the beginning.

7. The dealer could not have sold paintings under the 'broke-parole' Garneray's real name, which may explain why many of his works were once attributed to 'Hoppey Turner' and other invented names.

8. Lloyd; *The British Seaman*. p.224.

UNITED STATES OF AMERICA,
District of Maine—ss.

Portland, *May 28* 1814

No. (▬▬▬▬)

To all who may see these Presents,

GREETING:

WHEREAS *George Gilliard* a Prisoner of War to the *United States of America*, hath this day engaged on his Parole of Honor, " that he would not commit, say or communicate any matter or message detrimental or hostile to the Government, Laws, Authority or Interest of the United States, and that he would ~~repair without delay, and by the usual rout, to~~ *main* *in* the Town of *Portland* in the County of *Cumberland* within the District, and there remain a true Prisoner of War on Parole, and would not go without the limits of said Town unless he may obtain permission from the Marshal of this District, or some officer authorized by the President of the United States for this purpose."

These are therefore in the name of the **President of the United States,** to require and request of all officers, civil and military, within the United States, that they suffer the said *George Gilliard* ~~repair to~~ *maining* the Town of *Portland* ~~there~~ to remain a Prisoner of War on Parole, without let, hindrance or molestation, and to exercise towards him all kindness and hospitality—while he conforms to the engagement made by him as aforesaid.

Given under my hand and seal, at Portland, the *twenty eighth* day of *May* in the year 1814 and of the *thirty eighth* year of the Independence of the United States of America.

To all officers, civil and military, } within the United States. }

For the MARSHAL.

Stephen McLellan

American Parole of Honour document given to a British Prisoner – George Gilliard in 1814.

Chapter Seven

The New York Prison Ships

'Two Hulks on Hudson's stormy bosom lie,
Two farther south, affront the pitying eye –
There, the black *Scorpion* at her mooring rides;
There, *Strombolo* swings, yielding to the tides,
Here, the bulky *Jersey* fills a larger space,
And *Hunter*, to all hospitals disgrace –
Thou, *Scorpion,* fatal to thy crowded throng,
Dire theme of horror and Plutonic song,
Requir'st my lay – thy sultry decks I know,
And all the torments that exist below!'

PHILIP MORIN FRENEAU 1752–1832.

THE ENGLISH PRISON SHIPS, WHICH STOOD OUT SO starkly in their miserable and threatening greyness against the background of brightly painted men-of-war, on the Thames and Medway and off Portsmouth and Plymouth, left a life-long mark, mentally and often physically, on many of the thousands of prisoners who had suffered in them – at any time between the Seven Years' War and the end of the Napoleonic Wars.

They were, fairly or unfairly, considered proof of England's vindictive and cruel attitude towards her captives, not only by our enemies, but by some of the more enlightened of our own people; and they were, indeed, a blot on our seascape and maritime history. Records, reports, letters and memoirs in half a dozen languages tell of the horrors of those floating hells; but there were others, if anything more hellish, which are by comparison more or less forgotten – the English prison hulks off the City of New York.

Before entering into this record of suffering, and what might seem to be wanton cruelty, towards prisoners of war who were regarded by their captors as rebels and insurgents, a fair balance should be struck by acknowledging that many British prisoners were as badly treated by the Americans – who regarded them as oppressors. For the Americans, too, had *their* 'floating hells'; the prison ships at Boston, in the harbours of Connecticut and on the Hudson. Even if we discount by fifty percent the complaints and accusations from either side, there would still remain sufficient undeniable hardship to justify their bitterness.

My reference for this chapter depends entirely on official records, newspapers and the written recollections of a few eighteenth century American seamen – and a sailor-poet; all of whom had good reason to remember. These were men who were captured during the American War of Independence and never forgot the horrors of that experience. Among those sailors were

Ebenezer Fox, Thomas Andros, Thomas Dring, Alexander Coffin, Christopher Hawkins and our young friend, Andrew Sherburne, whose previous captivities are recorded in an earlier chapter. Another was the American poet and journalist, Philip Morin Freneau, who became known as the 'Poet of the American Revolution'. All these men spent their floating captivity in one or another of these deadly prisons, most of them on what must have been the most dreadful and disgusting of all prison hulks, the old *Jersey,* moored at the Wallabout, 'a solitary and unfrequented place off the Long Island shore.'

Philip Freneau was born in New York City in January, 1752 and began writing anti-British satire from about 1774, when restless American feelings were building up towards the outbreak of war. His political burlesques, his tirades against Tory Loyalists and neutrals, and his lampooning of King George, quickly made his name. In 1778 he joined the New Jersey Militia, but before the year was out, he turned to sea service and was captured by the British two years later, on the privateer *Aurora*, in the West Indies. On his release in 1781, with the ordeal of captivity to add to his already extreme hatred of Albion, he wrote his poem, *'The British Prison-Ship'*, a long and bitter harangue in verse; as miserably dark, depressing and full of suffering as the prison hulk itself.

Ebenezer Fox was born in Roxbury, Massachussetts, in 1763, and at seven years of age his father put him out to work for a local farmer. He did not enjoy this work, and at the age of twelve he decided to run away to sea and headed for Providence, Rhode Island, with an equally adventurous young friend. On arrival, they split up to search for a job among the vessels of all types and sizes which crowded the port – and he never saw his friend again. After a day or two Ebenezer found a job as cabin boy on a small trading vessel which was ready to set out for Cape François in Santa

Domingo. It was only a short voyage and The War of Independence was declared whilst they were at sea and on their return journey with a cargo of hogsheads of molasses. They were just off Providence, their port of delivery, when they were fired on by a British cruiser.

They had no means of defence and, while the captain remained on board, young Ebenezer and most of the crew avoided capture by jumping overboard and swimming to the shore. After another short voyage he returned home and was apprenticed to a barber, but when his unheroic master was called for military service, he persuaded the not-yet-sixteen years old Ebenezer to take his place in the fight for freedom. So young Fox became a militiaman attached to an American army force which was preparing to attack New York. However, General Washington called the whole thing off, and Ebenezer, who preferred sailoring to foot-slogging, signed on for sea service in the 20-gun ship *Protector*. The latter was built by the state of Massachusetts to protect merchant shipping and to take on any British war ship against which they might have chance of success.

On the 9th June 1780, they met up with the *Admiral Duff*, a huge old East-Indiaman of more than a thousand tons, now fitted out as a British 32-gun letter of marque in the West Indies trade. She was flying the British ensign, as was the *Protector* – the latter employing the 'false colours' ploy frequently used by both sides. They were within musket range before the American colours were displayed and a one and a half hour battle ensued, which ended when fire aboard the *Admiral Duff* reached the magazine and she was completely destroyed.

On a second voyage, this time to the West Indies, they captured an English sloop which they sold in Porto Rico, together with its cargo – which included fourteen negro slaves. They were to take two more prizes before their luck ran out. Towards the end of November, 1780, the *Protector* was captured by two English ships (both showing French colours); the double-decked 40-gun *Roe-Buck* and the *May Day* of twenty-eight guns, and the American prisoners were transported to the New York prison fleet.

Ebenezer Fox was placed aboard the *Jersey* in November 1780. Like others, he said that able-bodied and seaman-like Americans were often accused of being Englishmen and were forced to serve on British warships. In vain would the comrades of a selected man attest to his being a native-born American; tell the place of his birth, etc. 'It was all to no purpose. Sailors they wanted, and have them they would, if they set law and gospel at defiance!' He bemoaned the fact that many an American citizen was forced on board a ship of war and 'compelled to fight against his own country'.

In spite of his professed indignation, he himself succumbed to the persuasions of an English recruiting officer. By the autumn of the following year he was serving as a foot soldier in the British 88th Regiment, stationed in Jamaica. In June 1782, he and four other Americans inducted into the British Army, somewhat cleared their consciences, when they made off with a native boat and set sail, first for Cuba and thence to Santa Domingo (Haiti) where they once again joined the fight for their independence, by joining the crew of the American frigate *Flora*.

Thomas Andros was one of the many young lads whose adventurous spirits – inspired by the sight of triumphant prize crews bringing captured merchant vessels and their valuable cargoes into the port of New London – led them to rush to join privateers and private armed vessels. He joined the *Fair American*, a privateer brig, specially built to prey on British merchant shipping. She mounted sixteen carriage guns and was additionally well-armed: 'the quarterdeck, tops and long boat were crowded with musketry, so that in action she was a complete flame of fire'. The *Fair American* got off to a flying start as within a few days she captured an English brig and Thomas Andros was a proud member of the prize crew put aboard to take her into New Bedford. However, Thomas's career as a privateer was short-lived. Within a week his seafaring days were over, when the English brig was recaptured by the frigate, *Solebay*, on the 27th August, 1781.

Thomas Andros was in his seventeenth year when he was captured. Later, we shall hear how, though seriously ill, he made his getaway and, after many hair's-breadth escapes from recapture through British-controlled Long Island, was back in New London by the end of October of that year.

Master's Mate Thomas Dring, who was born in Newport in 1758, had the misfortune to be captured twice by the British, and experienced imprisonment in two of the New York hulks. In 1779 he was confined in the inappropriately named *Good Hope* in the North River opposite the city of New York. He escaped in October, was recaptured but later exchanged; sailed again, in May 1782, as Master's Mate on the maiden voyage of a privateer, *The Chance*, a smart little craft which mounted twelve six-pound cannon. She sailed out of Providence, Rhode Island with great hopes but less luck; after only a few days *The Chance* was chased and captured by the 26-gun *Balisarius*, and the sixty-five American sailors were placed in irons and taken aboard. Next day the British man-of-war added two more prizes to her bag, a merchant schooner and another twelve-gun privateer. The officers were left aboard the prize ships, but their crews, also in irons, were added to those already in the cable tier. Captives were not always fettered, but with more than a hundred and thirty prisoners crammed below, it was probably an unavoidable precaution, as she made all haste for New York.

After Andrew Sherburne's imprisonment in England, he was returned to America by exchange cartel. There he met up again with Richard Tibbits, who had befriended him in the Old Mill Prison at Plymouth. Tibbits, who was now mate of the letter of marque *Scorpion,* invited him to join the ship as boatswain on her cruise to the West Indies. The *Scorpion* had no better luck than *The Chance.* She first had a narrow escape when chased into the harbour of Monserrat by a British brig, and was then captured by the 40-gun *Amphion* off the Virginian coast, only a couple of days from home. The thirteen crewmen and a hundred other American prisoners spent an uncomfortable two weeks on the cables in the bowels of the *Amphion* before adding their number to the already overcrowded hulks.

There is no evidence that any of these men ever met on board the *Jersey*. Thomas Dring was exchanged a few weeks before Sherburne arrived on the hulk in November 1782 and for a very short while Andros and Fox were on the *Jersey* at the same time. Furthermore, their memories coincide in most major details of the hulk itself and conditions of the prisoners' life on board.

They have left us their memoirs in a variety of forms. Ebenezer Fox's account of his adventures in the Revolutionary War was published by his son Charles: Andros' narrative was in the form of five letters written to a friend: Thomas Dring, who in later years became a merchant captain, left a sixty page manuscript which was edited and published after his death. Andrew Sherburne's prison ship memories are included in his little book which, as we have seen, told of his two previous captivities. Christopher Hawkins' journal was printed just as he wrote it and delightfully unedited, 'somewhat faulty in orthography and the use of capitals'. Christopher was indentured to a farmer until 1777, and then, like Ebenezer Fox, broke his apprenticeship and swapped farming for privateering. He was just thirteen years of age. Alexander Coffin's brief account was in the form of two letters, which told of imprisonment in land-based gaols, two periods on the *Jersey,* and finally a spell on the *John* hulk.

If only one memoir had survived, it might well be suspect of exaggeration, and that hard-lying and poor rations had affected the memory and soured the description of prison ship-life; but there can be no doubt that conditions on board those decaying old monstrosities could not have been much worse, even had they been planned as torture chambers. And we can be sure that every one of our memoirists believed that much of their sufferings had been deliberately inflicted. That accusation could take up a whole volume of argument without arriving at a complete refutation of the American premise; and here only a few points need be made.

From the outset, the rebellion of the Colonists had brought into question the standing of the American captives: should they be treated as prisoners of war or as criminals? It was generally felt that their case was not covered by international usage; that it was a domestic affair, and that the Government should deal with them as rebellious subjects offending against the Crown. They were certainly regarded as rebels and renegades rather than as members of a national military force; and letters of marque and privateersmen were classed as picaroons and buccaneers anyway. Even men holding American naval commissions from Congress, men like John Paul Jones, were invariably spoken of as pirates or traitors.

The authorities were faced with a difficult decision. It was obvious to all that, in the forthcoming fighting, on land or sea, prisoners would be taken by both sides; and the likelihood of reciprocal treatment of British prisoners by the American Agents and gaolers could only be guessed at. So the quandary was not resolved definitely one way or another, but with one which allowed for 'options to be exercised as circumstances dictated'.

By 1777, Parliament gave the North administration extraordinary powers to deal with the problem. Lord North proclaimed that these wide ranging powers would allow officers of the Crown to confine American prisoners anywhere in the King's dominions. He said that his ministry reserved all powers of punishment, and that he meant to punish, for treason or piracy, rebels taken in arms on land or sea; but that such offenders would be tried at the pleasure of the Crown. Which meant that, for most of the war, no Yankee prisoner knew for certain how he would be categorised – as traitorous criminal, renegade or prisoner of war.

And so it was, until towards the end of the war. At the beginning, the ratio of British to American prisoners had been so overwhelmingly balanced in Britain's favour, that consideration of the consequences of retaliation was slight. But towards the end, Washington – whose armies were taking British and Hessian captives in great number – was in a better bargaining position as regards exchange and conditions.

The treatment experienced by the American captive depended largely upon where he found himself imprisoned. Many of the British serving on the American continent and the American

Loyalists, genuinely considered that rebels did not qualify for prisoner of war status or treatment and should be dealt with out of hand – and within the hearts of those 'rebels' who suffered the worst type of confinement, there built up an undying bitterness.

If, on the other hand, the Yankee captive was sent to England, he was comparatively lucky. Often his voyage would have been worse than his eventual imprisonment; but before being sent to the Old Mill Prison at Plymouth, Forton Prison near Portsmouth or perhaps one of the two hulks on the Hamoaze, he would have to face a Court of Admiralty. There he would be closely questioned by the court and the judge would pronounce his always daunting sentence; which usually ran along the lines of:

> '…………………is committed to…………………prison: for Rebellion, Piracy, and High Treason on his Britannic Majesty's High Seas, there to lay during His Majesty's pleasure, until he pardons or otherwise disposes of you.'

This sentence, though certainly terrifying, was, in most instances less drastic than it would seem. The object of the trial was more to sort out 'genuine' Americans from Englishmen who had enlisted in the Yankee service. Any unfortunates so discovered could look forward to a very rough future: close civil imprisonment, the gallows, or an unspecified number of years on one of his Majesty's ships of war.

Although all prisoners of war, wherever captured and confined, would have had much to resent and complain about – though many suffered most from their own self-destructive habits – the inmates of the English depots and hulks never experienced the horrors endured by the Americans and their allies who were incarcerated in New York – 'the Prison-house of the Revolution' – whether on the prison ships in the harbour or the almost equally awful prisons ashore.

Until well into the nineteenth century, there was a general indifference to the treatment of criminals, as opposed to prisoners of war. If, therefore, the rebellious colonists had been collectively classified as the former, there may well have been stories of even greater hardship and suffering than those which follow. From the beginning of the war there were convict hulks on the Thames which were far worse than any prisoner of war depot; and soon after the hostilities ended the transportation of convicts from Britain to Australia and Van Diemen's Land began, which continued until 1868. The records of those eighty or more years of vicious floggings with cat-o'-nine-tails, executions and sadistic treatment of men – and women – for petty infringements of the harsh camp rules, make depressing reading; but are mentioned here as a reminder of a brutal age in which prisoners, whether civil or of war, were confined, and endured barbarities brought about as much or more through ignorance and indifference, than sadism or deliberate brutality. Australia had its hulks. In the mid 1800s there were five convict hulks at Hobson's Bay, in the port of Melbourne. On these vessels the ill-fed convicts were weighed down with chains and leg-irons, put to hard labour in the quarries ashore, and subject to all the punishments which commandants and gaolers had invented and practised over all those years: 'Tube-gagging and spread-eagling, the bludgeon-handle jammed in the mouth in tobacco searches, the loading with irons, the beatings …'

A warship stood guard hardby these hulks, guns charged and ready, and orders for action in the case of mutiny. Had such an uprising occurred their troubles would have been over, for men laden with twenty or thirty pounds of iron, would have had little chance of survival on a sinking hulk.

Returning, however, to America and the New York hulks…The filth, the vermin, the inadequate protection against summer heat or winter cold, the necessary strictness of guards and sentinels; the ever-present threat of sickness and death from the many diseases endemic in such overcrowded prisons; all these things and a dozen more, inspired complaints, protests, petitions and the threat of insurrection.

Some guards, but not all, were guilty of brutality and thoughtless acts of cruelty, but much of the blame could be aimed at the Agents and Commissaries who were charged with prisoners' welfare.

Perhaps the job of dealing with many hundreds of discontented men, and the almost as many things which contributed towards that discontent and misery, was beyond the capabilities of their British overseers and local agents – and the procrastination of the long-winded committees set up to eradicate the evils, brought frustration rather than solution.

Neither can the whole of the blame for captive discomfort be laid at Britain's door. The Continental Congress had no worthwhile system regarding the incarceration and care of prisoners of war, whether British or American. Admittedly, they had not the hundreds of years of war-and-prisoner experience of the British; but they could have kept a much more caring eye on their own captive countrymen. The American prisoners on the hulks were in a particularly invidious position, first as rebels rather than prisoners of war in the normal sense, and then, as the vast majority were privateersmen, there was ambiguity in the eyes of Congress as to their status as servicemen.

For clothing and bedding they had largely to depend on whatever they could hang onto at the time of capture. There was no regular British policy to issue or replace garments or bedding to seamen prisoners of war at that time – still less to rebel prisoners. Some garments and blankets were donated by a few caring people ashore, and Congress spasmodically encouraged the Commissaries to set up subscriptions to supply the most needy.

As winter approached, the necessity of warm clothing and blankets became desperate, and caused a terrible atmosphere of distrust between the captives. Knowing that want of protection from the cold could mean death, no man could afford to trust his neighbour. Those with cash could buy bits and pieces from men desperate for food or a chew of tobacco: others stole, bartered or gambled for even the tattiest of coverings.

THE *JERSEY* AND HER CONSORTS

Most of the British prison hulks and their attendant hospital ships which were moored in East and North Rivers at New York, and the few on the Hudson, were floating disasters; but one, the *Jersey,* was far worse than any hulk on either side of the Atlantic, then or after. In nearly all memoirs of life in floating prisons there is mention of prisoner of war activities and occupations, which helped to lighten the burden of their otherwise idle days. There are, however, few records of such activities on board the America-based hulks: it would seem that the only occupation was an endeavour to survive.

Soon after the Battle of Long Island, in August 1776, the prospect of dealing with huge numbers of American prisoners of war had to be faced by the British occupying force. When, in November, the Battle of Brooklyn and the fall of Fort Washington added almost

another 3,000 to their score – plus perhaps another thousand citizens who had made their patriotic feelings too obvious. So what to do with something like five thousand rebellious captives?

The same problem of housing prisoners, which had so plagued the British Government in their efforts to accommodate both civil and enemy captive at home, now duplicated itself on the American continent.

Accommodation-hunting officials were sent forth with authority to commandeer any suitable – and often unsuitable – buildings in which to house them: which resulted in the establishment of some very unusual 'prisons' indeed. The number of rebel prisoners grew rapidly, and the searchers' task was made even more unlikely of success by the great fires which destroyed about a quarter of New York in the Autumn of '76.

Therefore, in desperation, as land-based accommodation became more and more scarce, the Government resorted to the same unsatisfactory solution which they had arrived at in England to house their civil prisoners – the 'temporary expedient' of prison ships. Superannuated and wormy old men of war, depot ships and transports were very quickly stripped down and, with little superstructure and rudderless, were moored in the rivers off the City of New York.

Over the war years the New York prison fleet grew to a recorded twenty-five hulks, though never to that number at one time. Some were employed as prisons proper and others as hospital or receiving ships, but they sometimes exchanged their usage from prison hulk to hospital ship or vice versa, during the course of their service.

My research through official records, newspapers, journals and even poems, has turned up the following names, and there may possibly have been a few more:

WHITBY	*STROMBOLO*
SCORPION	*GOOD HOPE*
HUNTER	*GLASGOW*
FALMOUTH	*PRESTON*
GOOD INTENT	*WOODLANDS*
SCHELDT	*BRISTOL PACKET*
PERSEVERANCE	*CLYDE*
FELICITY	*LORD DUNLACE*
FREDERICK	*JOHN*
MYRTLE	*KITTY*
JUDITH	*GROVNOR*
CHATHAM	*PRINCE OF WALES*

and, the most remembered of them all, the infamous *JERSEY.*

From elsewhere could be added the many British men-of-war, which themselves served as 'prison ships' until their captives could be transferred to depots, prisons or hulks – and were therefore genuinely 'temporary expedients'.

The first duty of a warship was to carry out its mission against the enemy, and only after that had been accomplished could it take on a secondary task, as transport for prisoners of war. The custom of conveying captives from all parts of the world to England, for incarceration in land-based depots, the hulks – or, once there, given their parole – meant that some endured agonising voyages into captivity. The American prisoners suffered particularly badly because of the huge distances they were carried: battened down below decks in the cable tier, sometimes in irons – unless they were lucky enough to be sent to the receiving hulks at St John's, Newfoundland, or Halifax, Nova Scotia, there to await the cartel ship and exchange.

In other ports of the world there was a scattering of hulks. After the fall of Charleston, South Carolina, in 1780, two hulks, the *Torbay* and the *Pack-Horse* were moored in the harbour. A number of others were stationed in the West Indies, such as the *Peter*, at St Lucia, where they were employed as prisons or receiving ships, and captives were held awaiting warships to transport them to more permanent prisons, on the American coast or Britain.

The earliest of the New York prison ships was an old converted transport vessel called the *Whitby*, which was established as a hulk on the 20th October, 1776 and moored in the Wallabout Bay. She was already crammed with prisoners when she arrived on station. Many were army men (although later the hulks were used almost exclusively for sailors), naval men and privateersmen and, unlike most other prison ships, she carried a number of politically offending civilians.

Even with the introduction of that first hulk, the likelihood of a high death rate from diseases resulting from overcrowding, filth, vermin and poor quality provisions, must have soon become apparent. The Trumbull Papers tell of the already unhealthy condition which pertained, after only seven weeks into her prison ship service:

'***Whitby* Prison ship, N.Y.**, Dec. 9, '76. Our present situation is most wretched; more than 250 prisoners, some sick, and without the least assistance from physician, drug or medicine, and fed on two-thirds allowance of salt provisions and crowded promiscuously without regard to color, person or office... Only 2 at a time allowed to come on deck to do what nature requires, and sometimes denied even that, and use tubs and buckets between decks, to the great offence of every delicate cleanly person, and prejudice of all our healths.'

From the autumn of the previous year until May, 1777, the *Whitby* was the only prison hulk in the Bay, and during those few months she left her mark on the Long Island shore: Some hundreds of American prisoners had died and had been buried in the sandy bank near Remsens Dock.

It is probable that the bones which were recovered in such unimaginably great number after the war, and were 'credited' to the ill-famed and better-known *Jersey* alone – included those of the many who did not survive their confinement on the *Whitby* and her later ugly sisters. In May, two more ships were moored near the *Whitby* and most of her inmates were transferred to them – and took their pestilences with them; thus ensuring that disease and death would be with the prison fleet until its own demise in 1783.

The *Whitby* did not survive her first anniversary; she went up in flames in October, 1777. A number of the Wallabout hulks were destroyed by fire, and there was a popular belief that the captives themselves were the incendiaries; men so oppressed by their hopeless situation that they were willing to wager their lives against the possibility of escape or transfer to depot, prison or stockade on land. The *Good Hope* hulk, the prison ship from which Thomas Dring had escaped in October, '79, went the way of the *Whitby*, five months later:

'*Rivington's Gazette,* March 8. 1780.
Last Sunday afternoon, The *Good Hope*; Prison ship, lying in the Wallabocht Bay, was entirely consumed after having been wilfully set on fire by a Con't man, named Woodbury, who confesses the fact. He with others of the incendiaries are removed to the Provost [New Jail. N.Y.]. The prisoners let each other down from the port-holes and decks into the water.'

Although we have the names of the component vessels of the New York prison fleet, our detailed knowledge of individual hulks is, in most cases, fragmental – garnered snippets from newspaper reports, letters, advertisements, official documents, petitions and exchange lists. But from these mites of information we can gather something of their histories. Such scraps as: 'December 14. 1778. The *Jersey* Hospital-ship lies at Franklin, near Tomie's Wharf, East River', which locates the *Jersey* in her previous employment before later becoming a prison ship in the Wallabout Bay. There is even one rare example of a captive's favourable comment – although admittedly from a man who was no longer on board:

'*New Jersey Gazette*. Aug.23.'80.
Capt. Grinnel, who made his escape from the *Scorpion* prison-ship, at New York, on the evening of the 15th, says: "more leniency is shown to the prisoners. There are 200 in the *Strombolo*, and 120 in the *Scorpion*."'

And the following extract from the remembrances of a Lt. Catlin, mentions the *Glasgow*, and one of the 'church prisons' ashore:

'Taken Sept. 15th, '76, confined with no sustenance for 48 hours; for eleven days, had 2 days' allowance, pork offensive to the smell, bread hard, mouldy and wormy, made of canail and dregs of flax seed; water brackish, I have seen $1.50 given for a common pail full...'

About the 25th December, he together with 225 men was put on the *Glasgow* to await exchange. They were aboard for eleven days. The food was no better than before and 'had no fire for sick or well... 28 died through ill usage and cold.'

The terrible conditions of prison ship life was no secret to the American public. The many hundreds who had been exchanged or escaped, brought their stories of suffering with them when they came ashore – sometimes exaggerated and understandably bitter narrations – and the newspapers quoted smuggled letters and reported official recriminations. What is surprising is that, although there are records of subscriptions on their behalf, and instances of individual charitable generosity, the hulk-bound prisoners received so little help from their fellow countrymen.

'*New London*, June 16, 1779.
Our prisoners on board the prison-ships suffer beyond description, being turned down in great numbers below decks, where they are compelled to languish in stench and dirt.'

The following newspaper quote from a smuggled letter is typical of the information which was available to the press and public at that time, and incidentally tells us of something of the conditions on – and an escape from – one of the lesser known hulks, the *Falmouth*:

'*Connecticut Gazette*. May 25th, 1880.
I am now a prisoner on board the ship *Falmouth*, in N.Y., a place the most dreadful; we are confined so we have not room even to lie down all at once to sleep. It is the most cursed hole that can be thought of...

I was sick, and longed for some small beer while I layed unpitied at death's door, with a putrid fever, and though I had money, I was not permitted to send for it... I am just able to crawl about. Four prisoners have escaped from this ship. One having, as by accident, thrown his hat overboard begged leave to go after it in a small boat, which lay along side. A sentinel with only his side-arms on, got into the boat. Having reached the hat, they secured the guard and made for the Jersey shore, though several armed boats pursued, and shot was fired from the shipping.'

Details of the disposal of the hulks when they were too rotten to cope with their tasks, or made superfluous after the war, exist in public records and newspaper advertisements. They also tell of the selling-off of gear no longer needed when vessels were originally stripped down:

'*New Haven*, August 23, 1779.
TO BE SOLD. The sails and the rigging of the ship *Good Hope*. Masts, spars and yards, good as new.'

'*Gaine's NewYork Gazette*, July 1. 1780.
FOR SALE. The remains of the Hospital prison-ship, *Kitty*, as they now lie at the Wallebocht, with launch, anchors and cables.'

The Naval Store-keeper's Office. Dec. 4, 1780.
'NOTICE, is hereby given, that on Wednesday, the 13th instant, will be offered for sale at this office at twelve o'clock, the Hulls of his Majesty's sloops the *SCORPION* and *HUNTER*, and of the *STROMBOLO* fire ship, now lying in the North River.
Wil.FOWLER.
On the 14th, the sale result: NOT SOLD.'

'*Rivington's Royal Gazette*. August 16, 1783.
[two and a half weeks before the war ended.]
FOR SALE. The Hulls of the *Perseverence* and the *Bristol Packet*, Prison Hospital Ships, as they now lie in the Wallebocht.'

Odds and ends of information like these are the tiny rewards for many hours of research, but without them, and the more substantial documentary relics of the *Jersey,* it would be difficult to write more than a sketchy outline of those seven years of floating prisons in New York Harbour.

The newspaper extract above, which tells of the unsuccessful attempt to sell the *Hunter, Strombolo* and *Scorpion*, in December, 1780, is of particular interest, as it and other scraps of information help to explain how all three continued to appear in the story of the New York hulks long after that date.

The old *Jersey* in her days of glory, had been a proud 64-gun line-of-battle ship. A typical British man-of-war, with imposing rampant-lion figurehead and carved and ornamented aftercastle, she had shown the flag in many parts of the world, for thirty years or more. Built in 1736, on the bottom of her predecessor of the same name, the *Jersey* had seen many naval actions and had survived a bloody battle with the 74-gun French ship the *St Esprit*, off Gibraltar in 1745; but by 1770 her best days were in the past. From then on she was put into less adventurous service, as a naval hospital ship in Britain. Six years later, the War of American Independence brought the *Jersey* one last ocean-going voyage – in company with a fleet of transports taking Hessian mercenaries to America – arriving just before the battle of Brooklyn. No longer fit for active service, stripped of her guns and most of her rigging, she was at first anchored in the East River off the Fly Market at New

York. There she was put to still honourable employment, at first as a store or depot ship, provisioning vessels fitting out for patrols and voyages, and then as a hospital ship once more. And so she remained for the next three years, but as the British cruisers took more and more American prizes, nearly all of them privateers and letters of marque, the use of hulks to house the prisoners became common practice.

There were already prison ships at St John's, Newfoundland, and the *Good Hope* and other hulks were on the North River near New York – and now, in 1780, the *Jersey* was recruited into the prison service and quickly began to earn her evil reputation. From the outset the *Jersey* was a floating health hazard, and that this was recognised almost from the start, is shown by the fact that she was quickly removed from her inshore anchorage in the East River, to what was to be her last mooring, about three-quarters of a mile east of the Brooklyn Ferry and about a hundred yards off the Long Island shore. This move was in no way made with consideration of the prisoners' health in mind, but to prevent contagion and infection creeping ashore.

As a prisoner of war hulk, the *Jersey* presented an even grimmer aspect than she had as a depot ship. Rudderless, and with little left of her rigging other than the bowsprit and, on the stern, a flagstaff which was used for signalling to the shore. The gibbet-like derrick on the starboard side did nothing to enhance her appearance. This was, however, a very important piece of equipment, as it took on board the water casks and the vast amounts of stores and provisions necessary to sustain so many men, however meagre their allowances.

All the gun-ports and port holes had been filled in with heavytimber, and were replaced by twenty-inch-square unglazed windows, cut through her sides. These were made secure by two stout iron bars, one horizontal and the other one upright. A 'barricado', ten feet high, had been built across the quarter-deck and protruded for a few feet over each side. This protective wall was designed to separate the guards from their charges, and was pierced with musket apertures across the whole width, so that any suggestion of riot or rebellion could be quickly brought under control.

The space between the forecastle and the quarterdeck was roofed-in with spars and booms to form an area known as the Spar Deck. This temporary deck above the upper deck provided some protection from both rain and sun. On either side were gangways guarded by sentries, and others were stationed by the accommodation ladder on the port side which ran from gangway to water level. The ship's officers and crew were remote from the prisoners, and the only time the latter may have glimpsed them was as their boat brought them to the hulk or took them to the shore. Their entry to the ship was via the stern ladder on the starboard side; the officers heading for their accommodation under the quarterdeck and the crew to steerage.

The ship's company was not large; the Captain and his First and Second Mate, his Steward and Cook, and ten or twelve seamen. The prisoners' cook was one of their own number, sometimes appointed by themselves, and was in the employ of the British for a small reward – until he became just too unpopular with his fellows or was exchanged.

The hundreds of captives – who could spend time on deck during the day – were confined to the middle and lower decks at night. Thomas Dring described the middle but never ventured to descend to the lower deck during his five months on the *Jersey.* 'Our chests, boxes and bags were arranged in two lines along the deck, about ten feet distant from the sides of the ship; thus leaving as wide a space unencumbered in the middle part of the deck, fore and aft, as our crowded situation would admit'.

The long narrow strip running the length of the deck on either side, between prisoners' boxes and bulkhead, was where the messes got together for their meals. Each small mess area was jealously guarded territory, and it was usual for at least one member to sleep on the chests or boxes which concealed their goods as a precaution against thieving and skullduggery by their neighbours. At night, the centre of the deck was a jam-packed, unhealthy sea of bodies and hundreds of pieces of bedding, blankets, hammocks and clothing; but each morning everything had to be taken to the upper deck or, if the weather was good, laid out on the Spar Deck for a much-needed airing.

The *Scorpion* had been a 14-gun sloop-of-war in Lord Howe's fleet in the early days of the conflict. In 1779 she had been in Sir George Collier's squadron which lay off New Haven, and set fire to the local towns of Fairfield, Greenfield and Norwalk. The following year the *Scorpion* had been debased to the category of Prison ship, anchored in the North River, with a captive population of about three hundred. But when, for some reason, she and other vessels were put up for sale at the end of the year, and the Naval Storekeeper failed to find a purchaser, the *Scorpion* was fitted out as a hospital ship to the *Jersey* on the Wallabout.

The *Hunter* was also a sloop of war which had seen better days and was added to the prison fleet at about the same time as the *Scorpion* and *Strombolo*, as a hospital/medical depot ship. There was one unique feature about the *Hunter* which must have stood out in the midst of the depressingly sombre fleet – her bright pink-painted stern.

The *Strombolo* had once been a fire-ship, which arrived in America in 1776, in a fleet which included the *Jersey.* For a short time she, too, became a prison ship – and got off to a bad start: one of her captives, Captain Silas Talbot, tells a possibly propagandist anti-British tale: 'The prisoners confined on board the *Strombolo* prison-ship, anchored in the North River, having been irritated by their ill treatment to rise one night on their guard, the commander being on shore, several, in attempting to escape, were either killed or wounded. The captain got on board just as the fray was quelled, when a poor fellow lying on the deck, bleeding, and almost exhausted by a mortal wound, called him by name, and begged of him, "for God's sake, a little water", for he was dying.' The captain was said to have shone a light on his face and exclaimed, 'What! is it you, damn you? – I'm glad you're shot. – If I knew the man that shot you, I'd give him a guinea.'

Silas Talbot had been a prisoner ashore in New York's Provost Jail, before being sent to the *Strombolo*, from which he later escaped. Making a clean getaway, and swearing that he would avenge himself upon the enemy, he immediately rejoined the army and, at the end of the war, recorded, and/or boasted, 'eight large and 127 small notches' on his rifle stock.

From the earliest days of their establishment, the New York prison ships were known to be hell-holes, unfit for the incarceration of even the vilest criminal offender – although prisoners of war were not normally considered to have committed any crime; or merit greater punishment than deprivation of their liberty whilst at war with their captors; but, as we have seen, during this particular

war, the ambiguity of the American prisoner status and the 'optional' powers meant that protest was seldom rewarded with improvement.

In a later war, Napoleon was to use fear of the cruelty of the English hulks to inspire his troops to fight hard and not get caught; and it can be imagined that many an American lad, eager to serve his country or become a legalised buccaneer by boarding a privateer, must have had his ardour for enlistment somewhat dampened by the general belief that to be sent to the New York hulks was really a sentence of death – as for many it was. Freneau's grim poem (see page 134), which was published in 1781, and added to the rumours and harrowing tales told by men who had escaped or been exchanged, would have caused bitter resentment, at least throughout the eastern seaboard – for, with few exceptions, only sailors were held prisoner on the New York hulks.

Intimidating as the hulks were by rumour and appearance, few prisoners could have imagined, even in their wildest nightmares, the conditions they would meet within; but, if the wind was in the right (or wrong) direction, a sense other than sight might give them some forewarning of what they might encounter; for a dreadful stench would reach them long before their delivery boat reached the hulk's side – a smell which never completely left the nostrils of their memory. Thomas Dring, who had already been a prison ship captive, wrote: 'We had now reached the accommodation ladder, which led to the gangway on the larboard side of the *Jersey*; and my station in the boat, as she hauled alongside, was exactly opposite to one of the air-ports in the side of the ship. From this aperture, proceeded a strong current of foul vapour, of a kind which I had been before accustomed, while confined on board the *Good Hope*, the peculiarly disgusting smell of which, I recollected after a lapse of three years. This was, however, far more foul and loathsome than anything I had met with on board that ship, and produced a sensation of nausea far beyond my powers of description.'

The amount of comforts a prisoner could bring with him to the hulks depended entirely on the circumstances of his capture. If his vessel had surrendered to a superior force without a fight, and his possessions had been salvaged more or less intact, then the fate of his goods depended on the personal character of his captors. Of course, many lost almost everything when their ships were destroyed; but others lost whatever they could not cling onto to unprincipled thieves. Men like Sherburne and Dring, with previous experience as prisoners of war, were more chary and hid money and things of value in boots, hats, coat linings, etc. and wore their clothes in layer upon layer to thwart the looters. Usually, if they managed to get as far as the prison ship with their few possessions, they were allowed to keep them, except for weapons of any kind; though money, too, if unwisely declared, was likely to be confiscated. Although safe from enemy confiscation, they still had to keep a beady eye on the more desperate or unscrupulous of their fellow captives.

After climbing the gangway ladder to the upper deck, the prisoners were hustled through the barricado door to the area on the guards' side of the partition, and lined up for examination. Often a boat would arrive from the shore carrying officials and the notorious David Sproat, the Commissary of Prisoners of War. This man was an American 'Refugee', (a derogatory term used to describe American 'Loyalists', or 'Tories' as they were also known), universally detested for the 'cruelty of his conduct and the insolence of his manners'.

David Sproat, Commissary-General for the American prison ship captives, had been a Philadelphia businessman before joining the British in 1776. As the man to whom all complaints and grievances were addressed, his was the name which was most cursed when only unfavourable results were forthcoming. Journals and memoirs remember him as an unfeeling monster, responsible for much of the prisoners' great suffering. They did suffer, and perhaps he could have been more effective on their behalf; but he was part of the hard-hearted attitude adopted by both sides, and was working in the middle of a political juggling act. After reading many of the long and reasoned letters which he wrote to both the British and Washington – and the frustratingly discouraging replies – I conclude that he was much less bad than he was painted.

If, after their details had been recorded – name, ship, rank or rating, date of capture, etc. – and the examining officers were satisfied that there were no British sailors or deserters among them – they were directed through the door on the starboard side of the barricado onto the upper deck, and down through a hatchway, well guarded by soldiers, to the middle deck. As the prisoners were kept on the upper deck for most of the daylight hours, the newcomer would most likely be driven below during the hours of darkness – and the descent of the hatchway ladder would introduce him to the greatest shock of his captivity. No lamps or candles were permitted below decks, the only light the dim glimmer which filtered through the lattice of the hatchway grill, or through the air-ports on either side of the hulk.

All descriptions of that first night speak of the difficulty of putting into words the terrible conditions which they found below: 'passing down the hatch way, which was still open, through a guard of soldiers, I found myself among the wretched and disgusting multitude, a prisoner on board the *Jersey*. The gratings were soon after placed over the hatchways, and fastened down for the night; and I sat on the deck, holding my bag with a firm grasp, fearful of losing it among the crowd. I had now ample time to reflect on the horrors of the scene, and consider the prospect before me. It was impossible to find one of my former shipmates in the darkness; and I had, of course, no one with whom to speak during the long hours of that dreadful night. Surrounded by I knew not whom, except that they were beings as wretched as myself; with dismal sounds reaching my ears from every direction; a nauseous and putrid atmosphere filling my lungs at every breath; and stifled and suffocating heat, which almost deprived me of sense, and even of life.'

Dring had bundled himself up with as much extra clothing as he could bear, but now had to unburden himself of much of it for fear of blacking out, and 'was willing to hazard their loss, for a relief from the intolerable heat. Thus I passed the first dreadful night, waiting with sorrowful forebodings for the coming day. The dawn at length appeared, but came only to present new scenes of wretchedness and woe. I found myself surrounded by a crowd of strange and unknown forms, with the lines of death and famine upon their faces.'

After eight o'clock in the morning the prisoners were allowed to spend time on the upper deck, where daylight revealed what darkness had hidden – worst details of the evils which the *Jersey* had inflicted on its inmates; sights 'more disgusting and loathsome, met my view. I found myself surrounded by a motley crew of wretches with tattered garments and pallid visages, who hurried from below, for the luxury of a little fresh air.' All were verminous, and Dring himself was lousy after that very first night on board.

Newly arrived captives stood out in stark contrast to men who had preceded them by even a short time. Foul air, poor food, filth and fever made their effects obvious in a very short time, and in days or weeks the healthy and vigorous sailor soon lost the robust look that ocean breezes and hard exercise had given him, and took on the pallor of his fellow-captives. The newcomer, looking around him, 'saw but too faithful a picture of our own almost certain fate; and found that all which we had been taught to fear of this terrible place of abode, was more than realised'.

All prisoners suffered hunger for at least the first twenty-four hours, for to draw food they had to be a member of a 'mess', each of which was made up of six men. If he was in the know, or tipped off by an old-timer captive, he might advantageously join an established mess which was short of one or more members. This was easier than one might suppose, for, almost from the begining, disease and death made vacancies a daily occurrence. Once formed, each mess was allocated a number, and one member was elected to represent it and answer to that number whenever it was called. He had to be alert, for the hulk's regulations were inflexible – no number, no food.

Each morning the mess representatives would assemble near the Steward's Room, which was situated in the after-part of the hulk. At nine o'clock sharp, the Steward and his assistants would begin the lengthy business of calling out numbers, and passing out rations through the window of the store – and whatever was offered had to be accepted without complaint. The seaman prisoner was allowed a ration two-thirds that of a British sailor, and his army counterpart ashore received that same proportion of a British soldier's allowance. This ration was based on the assumption that a captive would need less food than an active serviceman. It ignored the fact that few free sailors or soldiers could have remained healthy without the opportunity to suppliment their ungenerous diet; a diet seriously deficient in scurvy-combating fruit and vegetables. And when considering quantity, it should be remembered that weight was in 'Pursers Pounds' – 14-ounces, for pursers were permitted to retain their 'eighths' of all issued rations, as their perks.

If the rations had been in fact as they were described on paper; if the quality had been as good as laid down in government regulations; if the cooking had been carried out in a proper manner, and under anything like hygienic conditions – then, perhaps, there would have been less complaints, illnesses and deaths, resulting from what was supposed to be nutriment. As it was, some of the food and its preparation, was potentially poisonous. Ebenezer Fox recorded the laid down bill of fare:

SUNDAY:	One pound of Biscuit. One pound of Pork. Half pint of Peas.
MONDAY:	One pound of Biscuit. One pint of Oatmeal. Two ounces of butter.
TUESDAY:	One pound of Biscuit. Two pounds of Salt Beef.
WEDNESDAY:	One & half pound of Flour. Two ounces of Suet.

THURSDAY:	One pound of Biscuit. One pound of Pork. Half pint of Peas.
FRIDAY:	One pound of Biscuit. One pint of Oatmeal.
SATURDAY:	One pound of Biscuit. Two pounds of Salt Beef.

The Galley was at the opposite end of the hulk from the Stewards Room, under the forecastle. It was better known as the Great Copper, and there was indeed a great copper there, with a capacity of about three hogsheads, about 150 gallons, set into a brickwork surround about eight feet square. The bread – also called biscuit, hard tack, sea cake, and many less complimentary names – was described by each of our memoirists:

Ebenezer Fox:
'The bread was mouldy and filled with worms. It required considerable rapping on the deck before the worms could be dislodged from their lurking places in the biscuit.'

Thomas Andros:
'Our bread was bad in a superlative degree. I do not recollect seeing any which was not full of living vermin; but eat it, worms and all, we must, or starve.'
(Master's Mate Dring's description was very similar.)

Andrew Sherburne:
'It consisted of worm eaten bread, and salt beef. It was supposed that this bread and beef had been condemned in the British navy. The bread had been so eaten by weevils, that one might easily crush it in the hand and blow it away.'

Philip Freneau poeticised on the ship's biscuit:
'Hunger and thirst, to work our woe combine
And mouldy bread, and flesh of rotten swine'.

Andrew Sherburne and others may not have known that bread served up to British naval seamen was often no better. Admiral Reigersfeld, in his *'Life of a Sea Officer'*, wrote of ship's biscuit at roughly that time:

'… it was so light that when you tapped it on the table it fell almost into dust and thereout numerous insects called weevils crawled, they were bitter to the taste and a sure indication that the biscuit had lost its nutritious particles; if instead of these weevils, large maggots with black heads made their appearance, then the biscuit was considered only in the first stage of decay; these maggots were fat and cold to the taste, but not bitter.'

So much for the staff of life.

After each six-man ration had been collected, it was sorted into the portion which they wished to be cooked that day, and tagged by a long string to a tally bearing the appropriate mess-number. The cook was usually a prisoner of long standing who, because of the opportunities afforded by his occupation, could not be counted among the emaciated. The clanging of the Cook's Bell was the signal for a great dash to the galley, and soon there were hundreds of tallies hanging over the side of the brick surround of the great square cooking pot – with each mess representative keeping an eagle eye on his own tallies.

The Great Copper was divided into two sections by a metal partition through its centre. Into one compartment went the peas and oatmeal, which were boiled in fresh water; but into the other – which was corroded and poisonous – went the meat, which was cooked in polluted salt sea-water taken from alongside the ship. Ebenezer said that, being so close inshore, the *Jersey* was embedded in the mud and that he could not remember ever seeing her afloat. All the filth accumulated among upwards of a thousand men was dumped overboard daily, where it remained until carried away by the next tide; and the tide at that point did not generally rise more than two or three feet. Thomas Dring attributed his survival, in an environment where many thousands had perished, in great part to the fact that he never once ate food which had been cooked in the Great Copper.

It is probable that the quality, quantity and preparation of rations was no better on other prison hulks than on the *Jersey*; in fact, in at least one case, it was at least as bad. Alexander Coffin said of his time on the prison ship *John* (which must also have had a 'poisonous' meat copper'):

'All the time that I was on board this ship not a prisoner eat his allowance, bad as it was, cooked, more than three or four times; but eat it raw as it came out of the barrel. These, Sir, are stubborn facts that cannot be contraverted't.'

Coffin was convinced that many of his fellow-captives (and he himself) were deliberately poisoned. He wrote in one of his letters of the death of a young Boston lad named Bird:

'… that he was poisoned we had no doubt, as his body had swelled very considerably, and two hours before, he was to all appearance, as well as any of us. Many, shortly after, went off in the same way, among them my cousin, Oliver C. Coffin. I did but just escape the same fate…'

Soon after, Coffin was exchanged – or 'bought off' as he described his release – and arrived home in Nantucket in a very distressed state. 'I felt extremely ill… My body swelled to a great degree, and my legs were as big round as my body now is, and affected with the most excruciating pains.' His bitterness led him to the conviction that his captors would go to such overt, uncertain and unpleasant lengths to dispose of individual captives, and asked: 'Is it possible… for any person to form any other opinion than that there was a premeditated, organised system pursued to destroy men they dare not meet openly and manfully as enemies?'

George Washington, professed to believe that the treatment of American prisoners was a deliberate plan to render them unfit for active service after exchange. As early as January 1777, he was writing to Sir William Howe in protest at the terrible condition of 'rebel' prisoners received in exchange for healthy British captives. He concluded: 'If you are determined to make captivity as distressing as possible… let me know it, that we may be on equal terms, for your conduct must and shall mark mine.'

The 'freshness' of the fresh water was the subject of constant complaint. The water, brought to the hulks by tankers from New York, was often foul by the time it got to the captives – 'water which would have discomposed the olfactory nerves of a Hottentot'. Why, they reasonably asked, when there was fresh running water on Long Island, only a cable's length away, was it ferried from the city at great expense? They could only conclude that it must be a deliberate attack on the constitution of the prisoners.

Rations were the same in quantity and quality for all captives on board the *Jersey* irrespective of rank, officers and ratings alike. Naval captains and senior officers would have been given the opportunity to give their pledge of honour and be placed on parole ashore, perhaps in America or sent to England; but there were many junior and privateer officers on the hulks, and they had at least one advantage over the common sailor. Even among the prisoners it was accepted that officers should be entitled to any privileges that were going; and perhaps the greatest perk on the hulk was admission to the Gun Room, which was situated in the extreme after-part between decks, and in pre-hulk days had been the ship's store for small arms, cutlasses and pistols. This area was reserved for the use of officer-prisoners, and Thomas Dring, a Master's Mate and therefore an officer, discovered this advantage within a few days of his incarceration and was welcomed into this officer-only company.

Although Gun Room rations were in no way better, the cooking arrangements were a great improvement and healthier. By an agreement with the cook, which probably involved some sort of incentive, a number of spikes and hooks had been driven into the brickwork surrounding the boiler, from which to suspend the concave-bottomed tin kettles in which the officers boiled their pork or beef. Each officer-mess saved as much fresh water as they could from the pint-at-a-time they were allowed to dip from the scuttlebutt[1] on the upper deck. As soon as they were allowed on deck in the morning they would hurry to the Galley with fresh water and any scraps of wood they had managed to scrounge from the cook's assistants – and probably slivers of oak from the decaying hulk itself. Once there, they could make their little fires and stew their salt meat, whilst the Great Copper was boiling its vile mixture for the less privileged. So it must be admitted that Thomas Dring owed his comparatively good health less to his greater awareness of the threat of the Copper, than to his ability to do something about it. He was not unappreciative of his good luck:

'But, terrible indeed was the condition of most of my fellow captives. Memory still brings before me, those emaciated beings, moving from the Galley, with their wretched pittance of meat; each creeping to the spot where his mess was assembled; to divide it with a group of haggard and sickly creatures.'

Whether cooked in salt water or fresh, neither could make the meat ration itself appetising. Beef was the most often supplied and, the 'bill of fare' might suggest, in generous quantity. But 'beef' seems to have been more a generic term, covering anything that was not pork. Contractors and sutlers [pursers] were often a greater enemy to both naval servicemen and prisoners of war than their declared foe.

Until the second half of the nineteenth century jobbery and corruption reigned at every level, to an almost unbelievable degree. Often in store for many years, the beef was so steeped in salt that it was said that even cooking in sea water seemed to reduce its salinity. So what went into the Copper could have come from ox, ass or horse, at best: 'its color was of dark mahogany; and its solidity would have set the keen edge of a broad-axe at defiance to cut across the grain', and yet, 'like oakum, it could be pulled into pieces one way in strings, like rope-yarn.'

References to its toughness and age can be taken quite seriously: it is known that a type of scrimshaw was carved by our sailors from beef 'so black, tough and solid that it could be cut and polished into model ships, ornamented buttons and snuff boxes.'

The cooking fire was lit at seven o'clock in the morning and, as it was fuelled with often damp green chestnut, there was no telling when the pot would come to the boil. However, the cooking time allowed was as fixed as any other prison ship rule; at the second sounding of the Cook's Bell, that was it – whether half raw or overcooked. If the latter, beef emerged from the Copper shrunken to as little as half its size; if the former, only a desperately hungry man could have faced it. The promised pork was often omitted from the ration and, when issued, was no great luxury. Although less susceptible to shrinkage, it was as soft as the beef was hard and was even less satisfying to the eye, having 'the appearance of variegated fancy soap.'

Mondays, Wednesdays and Fridays, were meatless days, (as was the practice in the British Navy, where they were known as 'banyan', or fast days) and on those days 'burgoo' took its place. Burgoo, mush – or 'hasty pudding' as the Yankees called it – was made from oatmeal and water and, on the rare occasions when molasses could be added, presented what was the most palatable item in their dreadful diet. The two-ounce butter allowance, though mean in quantity, still brings to mind a milky creaminess, but nothing could be further from the truth. It was, in fact, a rancid, smelly substance known as 'sweet oil', and the nearest it got to bread was when it was used as an adhesive to knead together the crumbs and dust of dry, worm-eaten ship's biscuit. It was, however, put to other uses; on the *Good Hope* and other hulks where lights were allowed below decks after sunset for an hour or two, 'butter' was used by prisoners to fuel the bulkhead lamps. On the *Jersey*, however, where no light or fire of any sort was allowed at night, the 'butter' was often given to the hungry French prisoners who occupied the lower deck, in conditions which even the Americans could only imagine, for few ever ventured down the hatchway ladder which connected their deck with the 'foreign' deck below.

The reasons, speculations and excuses given for the poor quality of prisoner rations, were many – and the theories, surmises and sometimes scandalous rumours, even more. The most popular belief amongst the prisoners was that the contractors, in cahoots with the agents and the commissaries, were selling their fresh provisions to the British warships – of which there were many in the harbour – and feeding them on ancient salt meat and mouldy bread which had travelled the world. It may well be that this did happen on occasion; and it is true that there was always a toing and froing of provisions between arriving and departing vessels. It was not at all unusual at the end of a long voyage, for casks of salt beef or pork, which had been on board for months or even years, to be transferred to a ship ready for sea.

Naval Stores, which supplied both prisoner and free mariner, seldom held a large stock of fresh provisions. The villain of the piece was the unscrupulous contractor, who was without conscience whether dealing with friend or captive foe. There was no way of knowing what the huge salt beef casks, once opened, might reveal: Irish salt horse mixed in with beef, nails, meatless bones and hooves, and other (we hope not literally) foreign bodies.

Every prisoner, not only on these hulks but wherever prisoners were subjected to bad victuals, had contempt for the food contractors and their associates, and put nothing below their grasping avariciousness. John van Dyk, who was a captive on the *Jersey* when she was anchored near the Fly Market, in the Spring of 1780, said that he and his mates felt sure that the purser robbed them – even of the peas in their soup:

'...one day, called pea day... I received the allowance for my mess, and behold brown water and fifteen floating peas – no peas on the bottom of my drawer – and this for six men's allowance for 24 hours. The peas were all on the bottom of the kettle [the Great Copper]; those left would be taken to New York, and I suppose, sold.'

An interesting article, recently published by the New York Historical Society, contains the following off-beat theory:

'The poor quality of the rations may have been partially due to the love and illicit passion between General Sir William Howe, who commmanded British forces in the area, and a certain Mrs Loring, who was married to the British army's sole "vendue-master and auctioneer". In other words, as historian Will Brownell tells us, the General was having an affair with the wife of the man who had the responsibility of providing the prisoners with life's necessities.

'According to Brownell, Mr Loring was able to pillage the commissary, to sell food officially intended for the prisoners to the public at profitable rates, and to purchase rotten provisions for the prisoners' consumption. This cozy arrangement allowed Mr Loring free reign over foodstuffs in return for allowing General Howe free reign with Mrs Loring [!].'

And the Tory, pro-British Judge Thomas Jones wrote that, Mrs Loring was 'the illustrious courtesan' who lost for Sir William 'the honor, the laurels and the glory of putting an end to one of the most obstinate rebellions that ever existed.'

At one time the prisoners were allowed a rum ration each day. John van Dyk witnessed an at least temporary cancellation of the privilege: 'We, for some short time, drew half a pint of rum for each man. Once Captain Lard [Laird], who commanded the ship *Jersey*, came on board. As soon as he was on the main deck of the ship, he cried out for the boatswain. The boatswain arrived, and, in a very quick motion, took off his hat. There being on deck two half hogshead tubs where our allowance of rum was mixed into grog, Captain Lard asked, 'Have the prisoners had their rum today?' 'No, sir,' answered the boatswain. Captain Lard replied, 'Damn your soul, you rascal, heave it overboard.' The boatswain, with help, upset the tubs of grog on the main deck. As an old sailor, I can imagine his feelings as he reminisced: 'The grog rum ran out of the scuppers of the ship into the river. I saw no more grog on board.'

On all the hulks based on English rivers and elsewhere, with their prisoner populations of French, Danish, American and many other nationalities, and in the depots and prisons ashore, in addition to rules laid down by the authorities, there were always byelaws by which the captives governed themselves. The value of these internal regulations has been acknowledged by captors and captives alike and the worse the conditions the more important were some of them. And so it was on the *Jersey*. I have no evidence that these by-laws were ever posted up, but it would seem that they were known to all, even those who did not choose to live by them. It is certain, however, that they had been written down, and were probably preserved and passed down through successive officers; for relevant parts were read out by the 'Judge' – usually the oldest officer of the Gun Room – whenever a prisoner was punished for their violation. They were designed to keep some sort of discipline

in an atmosphere where trouble was always brewing; to punish crime and immorality and to preserve as much self-respect as possible among the inmates.

The sentence for betraying a prisoner to the guards in any way was, like murder, death; and high on the list of very serious offences was the stealing of food from another mess or individual. Smoking between decks was a danger to all, and anyone detected by the guards would have been guilty of a serious breach, of both their own by-laws and the British rules governing the ship; for it would mean that the culprit had had with him the means of lighting his pipe below decks. The comparatively few who could afford to buy tobacco could only obtain a light as a favour from the cook to the British officers' mess. Many smokers who queued up for their turn at his taper, believed that the smoke from their pipes not only helped to blot out the ever-present stench of the hulk, but protected them from disease, as it 'appeared to purify the pestilential air' by which they were surrounded.

Thomas Andros, who witnessed the enforcement of the prisoners' rules, said of them, ' ...in severity they were like the laws of Draco. Woe to him that dared to trample them under foot.' and told of the proposed punishment of a suspected trampler, Spicer, a Sailing Master's Mate.

'A Captain Young of Boston, concealed hiself in a large chest belonging to a sailor going to be exchanged, and was carried on board the cartel, and we considered his escape as certain; but the secret leaked out and he was brought back, and one Spicer of Providence, being suspected as the traitor, the enraged prisoners were about to take his life. His head was drawn back, and the knife raised to cut his throat, but having caught a hint of what was going on below, the guard at this instant, ran down and rescued the man.'

Young Thomas Andros did not think that the evidence was strong enough to take a man's life and he was not among those who voted for his death; but Spicer was either not guilty and a born loser or an unrepentant villain. Another prisoner, Christopher Hawkins – who was captured on the Providence brig *Marianne* in 1781, wrote of Spicer's involvement in another, and similar case. It may be that his judges decided to get him for his first betrayal at all costs.

A young prisoner who had served as a cabin boy was hidden in a sea chest, (the coincidence of method need not seem surprising, there cannot be many other ways in which an extra body can be smuggled by prison boat onto a cartel ship) and, like Captain Young, was discovered and returned. Spicer was again condemned and 'paid for his treachery with the forfeit of his life.' When evening was coming on, and the prisoners were going below for the night, he was knocked down the hatchway to the bottom of the steps below, into the arms of those who had been waiting for his fall and who 'fell upon him, cut off his ears and mangled his body in a most shocking manner, and to such a degree that he died of his wounds in a day or two after.'

There is one report of a prisoner stealing food from a mess, where the crime was reported to the British commander of the *Jersey*. 'This officer decided that the delinquent should be punished by all the members of the mess who had suffered by his pillage.' This seemed like a wise decision, but his punishment would have been less 'Draconian' had the miscreant been awarded a British flogging.

'The accused was tied across a water butt on the upper deck – his posteriors were laid bare... The mess-mates who had suffered by his pilfering, and six in number, were arranged around him.' (He was to be thrashed with an oar-shaped length of wood and each of the six were to take their turn.) '… one of the mess took the instrument in hand (it was very heavy, and as much as one man could conveniently wield) – and inflicted six strokes with the ponderous weapon, apparently with all his might – the sufferer groaning at every stroke – blood appeared before the first six were administered – a second man took the instrument and with no less mercy than the first, inflicted six more strokes – the blood and flesh flying ten feet at ev'ry stroke – during this period the defaulter fainted, but was resuscitated by administering water to him – a third man took the instrument in hand and inflicted six more strokes though not as severe as the first. The officer before mentioned then interposed and observed to the enraged mess-mates that they were too severe with their fellow. He had again fainted. No more blows were given and the horrible looking man was untied and fell down on deck. He was again resuscitated but still lay prostrated on the deck, not being able to rise. Beef brine was thrown upon his wounds but he appeared to be senseless...'

It is not surprising to read that he did not recover from his vicious beating.

Most prisoners entered the hulks with at least a little money and some with what would have then been considered a good amount. If a man was frugal and eked out what he had with care, he might well avoid becoming one of the skeletal throng which crowded the decks around him, until released either by exchange or escape – and if he was lucky enough to escape any of the numerous and deadly diseases which plagued the hulk. There were two sources from which he could purchase the small items which made all the difference to prisoner of war existence, one was through the Sutler or Purser, and the other the bum-boat which was allowed alongside on alternate days.

The Sutler's small shop was on the starboard side under the quarterdeck, and goods were passed to the buyer through a window cut through the bulkhead. Nothing was priced, except for 'ardent spirits' (strong liquor, such as rum and whisky) which was priced at two dollars a gallon. All else was left to the honesty, or otherwise, of the Sutler: the purchaser stated what he required, handed over the amount he wished to spend, and was given what he had to accept as his fair due.

A welcome break in the miserable dullness of the prison ship day, came when the market boat put out from the shore with its load of simple merchandise. It was rowed by two boys and, filling the stern sheets with her enormous bulk, was a wonderful old market-woman who was known to the prisoners as Dame Grant. This much-loved vendor brought the monied-ones soft bread, fruit and other desirables, such as sugar and tea, etc., 'all of which she had previously put up into small parcels, from one ounce to a pound in weight, with the price affixed to each, from which she would never deviate'.

Dame Grant was their one dependable contact with the shore and accepted their shopping lists for items which she did not herself carry, such as needles, threads, combs, pipes and tobacco. She never let them down – or ever forgot to impress on them that the price she charged them was 'at cost'. The shoppers were of course the lucky few, and some remembered with sympathy the 'faces of hundreds of half-famished wretches, looking over the side of the ship into the boat, without the means of purchasing even the most trifling article before their sight'. As the prisoner of war has no period of sentence and can but pray for the war to end, only the most unimaginative could have failed to foresee the day when, with money spent, they too might join the host of envious watchers.

However, Dame Grant's bum-boat business did not last out the war, and 'at length she did not make her appearance for several days – and her approach was awaited in extreme anxiety. But alas, we were no longer to enjoy this little gratification. Her traffic was ended. She had taken the fever from the hulk, and died; if not in the flower of her youth, at least in the midst of her usefulness; leaving a void which was never afterwards filled up' – leaving the field to the mercies of the Sutler.

Andrew Sherburne recalled that during his imprisonment on the *Jersey* late in the war, market boats came out every day from New York whenever the weather allowed and, as in Dame Grant's day, fresh food was the most sought-after of their offerings. Andrew's long-winded description of his favourite 'sausage' shows how much such rare delicacies were valued and remembered by poorly fed men: 'The livers delicacies were valued and remembered by poorly fed men: 'The livers of sheep, cattle, &c. were well boiled, chopped fine, seasoned with pepper and salt, and filled into the small intestines of those animals; and a piece from seven to nine inches long, sold for sixpence, New York currency; six cents and a fourth. The most of my money went for those meat puddings, and for bread'.

The bum-boats came out from hard-by the ferry stairs at the lower end of the Fly (or Vlie) Market, which was then the principal market of New York City. It was there that the Brooklyn passenger-craft picked up and landed their fares and unloaded their market freight. Consequently, there was always a good variety of goods available to the captive with cash – except in the worst months in the year.

The Yellow Fever, which had carried off Dame Grant, was always a deadly threat to the prisoners on board the *Jersey* from the first few months of the hulks' establishment off Long Island. Dysentry, typhoid and many other diseases, infectious and contagious, spread rapidly among men crowded together in such close proximity. Breathing in a foul polluted air, half-starved and plagued by vermin, few could have escaped at least one of the many evils which could afflict them. When Thomas Andros arrived there were about four hundred captives on board and the number of dead removed from the hulk each day was already horrifying enough; but within a very short time the number of prisoners had risen to something like twelve hundred – and the mortality rate rose disproportionately higher.

At first there were two hospital ships hard by the *Jersey* and after a while others were added to the prison fleet. The four, for which we have some more detailed record than just the name, are the *Scorpion*, the *Strombolo*, the *Hunter* and the *Frederick*. Strictly speaking, for most of its service, the *Hunter*'s main purpose was to act as a depot hulk, a sort of dispensary for medical stores and equipment, supplying the other three. There, too, lived the Doctor's Mates, and the boat's crews who were kept all too busy ferrying the sick and dying from the prison hulk to hospital ship. Once again, as with the government's Official Contracting Obligations in the case of food, the establishment of these hulks was well intentioned, but in practice there were some terrible shortcomings. It cannot be doubted that there must have been some dedicated staff on these vessels of meagre mercy, but there was a number of despicable creatures among the 'nurses', whose actions are not pleasant to relate.

Compared with the *Jersey*, the hospital ships must have seemed like an escape from Hell – at least to Limbo – but many captives, perhaps the majority, were beyond all help by the time they were ferried over for treatment. Although no less repulsive in outward appearance than the prison hulks, the conditions on those ships were in some ways better. They were smaller and not so crowded, the hatchways were sometimes left open at night, (though patients well enough to be cynical felt the reason must be that they were considered too weak to escape) and there were even wind-sails, which helped to circulate fresh air through the decks below.

It is not unusual to read, in reports relating to illness and mortality among prisoners at New York and elsewhere in the world, that often the fittest-looking and apparently strongest of men were the first to go. In most contemporary reminiscences this is remarked upon as a fact. 'Such men [of strong and robust constitution] were subject to the most violent attacks of the fever; and were also its most certain victims', and, 'The most healthy and vigorous were first seized with the fever and died in a few hours'. More than once we hear of a new arrival being warned, by wrecks of men who had been prisoners for some time, to look out for themselves as 'Death has no relish for such skeleton carcasses as we are'. Among the 'foreigners' who lived in the squalor of the orlop deck – or 'dungeon' as it was known – there were many who survived two years or more of every variety of human suffering, and despite their wretched appearance, seemed well. 'The faces of many were covered with dirt and filth; their long hair and beards matted and foul: clothed in rags and with scarcely sufficient supply of these to cover their disgusting bodies. They had, as they expressed it, "been through the furnace, and become seasoned"'. But the answer may be that these survivors from among the thousands of their fellows who had died, had something inbuilt in their physical make up which would have saved them whether well-fed and robust or half-starved and 'skeleton carcasses'.

Nevertheless, Tom Andros believed whole-heartedly in the theory, and blessed the fact that his own constitution 'was less muscular and plethoric' than his fellows – and it is true that he was one of only three or four of the thirteen-man crew of the *Fair American* who survived more than a month or two of imprisonment on the hulk. But his lack of plethora did not provide complete protection and, though later than his shipmates, Andros eventually contracted yellow fever, at first in a mild form. It would have been a miracle had he escaped entirely, for very soon the hospital ships were filled and the healthy and diseased were forced to share their cramped between-decks accommodation.

An area was set aside to segregate the most desperately ill from their fellows, until death or hospital ship vacancy released them from the hulk. In Andros' time this area was located in the forepart of the lower gun deck, where all the captives lay down for their awful night's attempt at rest. In almost complete darkness, disturbed by the murmers and complaints of the afflicted, and either stifled by stinking heat or frozen by gusts of cold winds through the unglazed ports, there was another unhealthy horror – which turns our stomachs now, but which they learned to accept – the large tubs in their sleeping quarters, placed around the hatchway to the 'foreign' deck; 'for the occasional use of prisoners during the night, and as general receptacles for filth'. Soon there were two hundred or more sick and dying to be carried to the upper deck each morning; and every morning there were bodies to be removed from among the 'healthy' on the deck below.

Having avoided infection for so long, Andros had had plenty of time to observe its effect on those around him. He noted the delerium, the derangement and the unquenchable thirst, particularly at night, which often led them to stumble around blindly over the forms of cursing men – crying for water. It is obvious from Thomas's letters how much this affected him, but when smallpox invaded the *Jersey* – and never completely left it – he became really terrified. Before the onset of fever he had slept amongst – and helped nurse – some of the smallpox victims at all stages of their affliction, but now, understandably, his every thought was for his own survival: 'For I was now seized with Yellow Fever, and should unavoidably take the natural small pox with it; and who does not know, that I could not survive the operation of these two diseases at once?' With hospital ships full and no chance of inoculation, he almost resigned himself to his fate.

Until that time, he had pinned his hopes on an early exchange, but now his dream had taken a complete about turn – and the arrival of a cartel was his greatest fear. Thomas had no doubt that exchange would put paid to any hopes he had had of survival, and make his death more certain. He based this on his conviction that the 'inhumanity of the English' would be demonstrated by their exchanging 'Americans as had but the breath of life in them, and were sure to die before they reached home', for sound and healthy Englishmen – and that when the cartel ship arrived, 'numbers would be put on board and sent home with me from the hospital ships, whose flesh was ready to fall from their bones in this dreadful disease'. Had there been any truth in his belief in British fiendishness, one might well believe that the captain of the cartel vessel would have had something to say about it; and that the latter would have been as scared of a ship load of diseased passengers, as Andros would have been to be among them.

Nevertheless, terror gave Thomas courage. He chose escape, and the possibility of a cleaner death from a sentry's bullet, rather than the more ghastly possibilities on cartel or the *Jersey*. Although very ill, he did escape and made it back to New London; but that is another story.

Seven months later, when Thomas Dring arrived, smallpox still raged aboard the *Jersey*. One of the first sights he met on coming up into the light from the deck below after his first night on board, was a man suffering with smallpox:

> '…and in a few minutes, I found myself surrounded by many others, labouring under the same disease, in every stage of its progress. As I had never had small-pox, it became necessary that I should be inoculated; and there being no proper person on board to perform the operation, I concluded to act as my own physician. On looking around about me, I soon found a man in the proper stage of the disease, and desiring him to favour me with some of the matter for the purpose. He readily complied… the only instrument which I could procure for the purpose of inoculation, was a common pin. With this, having scarified the skin of my hand, between the thumb and fore-finger, I applied the matter and bound up my hand. The next morning, I found that the wound had begun to fester; a sure symptom that the application had taken effect'.

Many of the crew followed their Master's Mate's example; but not all with such successful result. The first member of the crew of the *Chance* to die from the foul disease was the youngest. Palmer was just twelve years old. He had served as an officer's waiter on the privateer, and Dring, whom the lad looked up to as his protector, admitted him to the privilege of the Gun Room. Young Palmer had been inoculated by their do-it-yourself method but with sad consequences.

There were many youngsters among the vast numbers of prisoners taken during the war. It was not unusual for lads to start their naval, merchant or privateering careers at a very early age, some as young as eight. Fox and Sherburne were only seventeen years old when they survived the old *Jersey*, and thousands of young boys experienced the hardship of the hulks, and a high percentage of them would have perished in those dreadful prisons.

For some time, a 'hospital' area had been prepared aft on the upper deck of the *Jersey* and bunks had been made where prisoners who felt the onset of illness could lie until found by one of the 'nurses' permanently aboard. It also saved them from being trodden on by the hundreds who packed the upper deck during the day. It was remarked that such was the throng, that it was common for men to lie out along the bowsprit to escape the crowded deck. The Spar deck was the only place were they could walk, along narrow walkways which were so narrow that the prisoners had to regiment themselves into shoulder-touching platoons, all facing the same way and turning about at the same time. These walking aisles were the only exercise they could enjoy until the guard shouted his hateful cry; 'Down! rebels! Down!' just before sunset.

From all accounts, the nurses were the dregs of prison ship life. They were themselves prisoners of war and had either been found suited for their work by a natural lack of finer feelings, or had become callous by daily association with death and suffering. Each day a medical officer was rowed over to the *Jersey* from the *Hunter*, to inspect the upper deck sick-bay and, if space was available, the worst cases would be rowed across to a hospital ship. The *Jersey* nurses then came into their own; for when a patient left the hulk, all but the most essential of his possessions became the property of this unholy gang – unless he returned. The odds were against this occurring, for it has been estimated that between ten and twelve thousand men died in the short time of that small prison fleet's existence.

At one time – the summer of 1782 – the number of prisoners of war on the *Jersey* was about one thousand; all were sailors and the great majority of them American. There were, of course, seamen of many other nationalities captured on American ships – samples from that cosmopolitan society which make up ships' crews, particularly merchantmen. And some representing America's allies, French, Dutch and Spanish captured when their own national vessels were taken as prizes.

With new deliveries of captives – 'fresh fish' in prisoner parlance – constantly arriving alongside, even exchange, escape, enlistment in King George's forces, evacuation to hospital ships, or death, could ever have reduced the numbers sufficiently to provide the space, cleanliness and the conditions necessary to turn the disgrace of the New York hulks, into an acceptable prisoner of war accommodation.

Administrations of all the warring countries, and their lack of conscientious attention to international rules of prisoner of war treatment, were certainly at fault. Wholesome rations and tougher control of the crooked contractors could have eased the prisoners' lot, preserved something of his health, and saved many lives. The most effective solution, had it been possible, would have been a more rapid system of exchange, thus saving the expense of

imprisonment on all sides, but there was never an equal balance in the numbers of captives for this to have worked to everyone's satisfaction. This imbalance was in some part due to the fact that when American privateers brought British prisoners – usually merchant seamen, or British privateersmen – into port, many of those ports could not, or would not, afford any sort of prison building to house them, and they were left to fend for themselves. Had the Americans retained them all as captives for potential exchange, many of their captive countrymen may have lived out the war. As it was, only some British captives were exchanged, some just settled in as 'Americans'; but many more enlisted in the service of Yankee privateering. And there is some sad evidence that there was a certain reluctance to exchange on the part of the American service authorities.

Ebenezer Fox and Thomas Dring tell us independently, that in 1782, a committee of officer-prisoners got a petition, via David Sproat, through to General Clinton, the British commander at New York, requesting permission to acquaint George Washington with their plight. Perhaps surprisingly, permission was granted, as was the further request that one of their number should personally present their message to Washington. They were permitted to choose three representatives to report to the British Embassy, where a passport was granted.

Captain Aborn of the *Chance* and its Surgeon, Joseph Bowen, and one other officer delivered the memorandum with its plea for the speed-up of exchange and improvement in their food and conditions. The document was signed by the Committee, in the name of all the prisoners on the *Jersey*, and a copy was made for General Clinton.

General Washington felt that the problem was outside his sphere of influence, but did not dodge the issue. In a carefully worded, but accusatory, letter to Rear Admiral Digby, with a diplomatic threat of reprisal in its tail, he said:

'Head-Quarters, July 5, 1782

SIR:-

By a parole granted to two gentlemen, Messrs. Aborn and and Bowen, I perceive your excellency has granted them permission to come to me with a representation of the sufferings of the naval prisoners at N.Y. As I have no agency of naval matters, this application is made to me on mistaken grounds. But curiosity leading me to inquire into the nature and cause of their sufferings, I am informed that the principal complaint is, that of being crowded, especially at this season, in great numbers, on board of foul and infectious prison-ships, where disease and death are almost inevitable. This circumstance, I am persuaded needs only to be mentioned to your excellency, to obtain that redress which is in your power only to afford, and which humanity so strongly prompts. If the fortune of war, Sir, has thrown a number of these miserable people into your hands, I am certain your excellency's feelings for your fellow men, must induce you to proportion the ships (if they must be confined on board ships) to their accommodation and comfort, and not by crowding them together in a few ships, bring on disorders which consign them by half-dozens in a day to the grave. The soldiers of his Britannic Majesty, prisoners with us, were they to be equally crowded together in close and confined prisons, at this season, would be exposed to equal loss and misery.

Washington'

In reply, Admiral Digby put forward the suggestion that – as the number of British sailors in American hands was minute compared with the host of seamen prisoners on the hulks and elsewhere – American seamen should be exchanged for British soldiers. This proposition had been mooted many times by many on the American side, from Sproat to the prisoners themselves. However, Washington thought that to receive his Yankee privateers, most in poor condition, in exchange for trained British or Hessian soldiers, was a bad deal and against the continental interest; he told the Continental Congress: 'It ought to be considered that few or none of the naval prisoners in New York or elsewhere belong to the Continental service.'

His message to the prisoners declared that he intended to place their case before Congress. It expressed his sympathy, and his regret that his authority did not extend to the marine department. His message, and the details of the petition, were read to the mustered captives, jam-packed on the Spar deck of the *Jersey* and on the other hulks.

They must have been encouraged, and given some hope, by the knowledge that their terrible predicament was known on shore, which must have seemed worlds away. But nothing short of exchange and release from the hulks could appease the prisoners who, at the time of Washington's letter to Digby, addressed a heartfelt cry for help to their fellow countrymen, in the form of a letter which they smuggled out to a newspaper:

> *'New-York Gazette.* 17 June, 1782
> You may bid a final adieu to all your friends and relatives who are now on board the Jersey prison ships at New York, unless you rouse the government to comply with just and honorable proposals. What is to be done? Are we to lie here and share the fate of our unhappy brothers who are dying daily? No, unless you relieve us immediately, we shall be under the necessity of leaving our country, [by enlisting in the British Forces] in preservation of our lives.'

It would seem that there was no great public response to the above pitiful plea. Henry Ondsedonk noted: 'There appears to have been no systematic plan of the citizens of New York for relieving prisoners. We have scattering notices of a few charitable individuals.' This is difficult to understand, as there were many organised subscriptions in aid of American prisoners in England, throughout the war.

Nevertheless, the official petition yielded some immediate, but not long-lasting improvements. The bread was of better quality, there was butter instead of the nauseating 'sweet oil', and windsail ventilation freshened the middle and lower decks of the *Jersey* but only during the day. At night, when it was most needed, it was removed so that the gratings could be put in place and secured – and in a very short while the sleeping accommodation became almost as noxious as before. An even greater relief came about when some of the sick were sent ashore to sick-quarters on Blackwell's Island and their number was added to from time to time; but nothing could clear the pestilence from the hulk.

Towards the end of the war the *Jersey*, crammed to the gunwales with prisoners, was further lightened of her unmanageable load. Between two and three hundred were transferred to other nearby hulks. This was something of a relief for the *Jersey*, but for one group of prisoners it was a frying-pan-into-the-fire experience: John van Dyk, captured again in February, 1783, and on the *Jersey* for a second time, found himself in a group which was ferried over to the prison ship *John*, where the treatment was if anything worse than that dished out on the monster they had left; an opinion echoed

by Alexander Coffin. The *John*, being an ex-merchantman was, of course, much smaller than the old sixty-four-gun ex-ship-of-the-line. It had no ports, small hatchways, was battened down overnight, and 'all exonerations were of course made below.'

Although the prisoners in general received little aid from nearby New York, some were remembered by individuals who had themselves been prisoners. One example of this extends the story of the petition to George Washington: the three officer-messengers who delivered the petition to the General did not return to the hulk, but were given their parole to live in comparative freedom on Long Island. Not long after, Captain Aborn was allowed to return home, still bound by his word of honour until officially exchanged; but before he left he came back to the *Jersey* – at least as far as the head of the gangway (from a natural fear of infection). He had come to collect letters home and the names of the thirty-five members of his crew they knew to be surviving at that time – from the original sixty-five crew of the *Chance*. He left with his promise to do everything he could to arrange an exchange for his men. And he kept his word. It was not long before a cartel sloop arrived with forty English prisoners on her deck. The latter were ferried off to New York and Tom Dring and his shipmates left for home, together with five lucky prisoners who had never known the *Chance*, but had been 'enlisted' for this farewell roll-call.

There is a sad postscript to this otherwise happy account: a few of the *Chance*'s crew were left behind. As the cartel passed Blackwell's Island, Dring and his shipmates could see some of their friends who had been sent ashore among the sick. They stood there with their bundles, hoping to be picked up by boat; but the cartel did not stop.

There had always been some effort, slight as it was, to prevent the *Jersey* from becoming weighed down under its own filth. Cleaning utensils, buckets, scrubbing brushes etc., and vinegar were supplied, but most prisoners were in no condition to work, or could not face what looked like fighting a losing battle. Some from among the fittest were in regular employment at the pumps, to keep the hulk afloat – and there was also an official Working Party.

The Working Party was made up of a couple of dozen carefully chosen prisoners under the orders of the 'Boatswain' – a prisoner-officer from the Gun Room – who was changed each day. To become a member of the Working Party was, to the ordinary seaman, almost as big a perk as the Gun Room was to an officer. They not only received a half-pint of rum each day, but a full daily ration, (their normal 'bill of fare' was therefore increased by fifty percent to that of a British sailor's allowance). Another great advantage was that they were allowed to enjoy the luxury of fresh air, hours before the hatchway was opened for the others to ascend.

Of course, their job was no sinecure and they worked hard for their privileges. The day started with a scrub-down of the prisoners' walkways on the upper deck, the spreading of the canvas awning, and working the derrick which hoisted the water casks, provisions and wood fuel, from the boats which lay alongside. Then, after the mass of prisoners had brought their hammocks or bedding on deck, the Working Party went below to help or carry the sick and disabled up to the 'hospital' bunks, there to await the arrival of the surgeon from the *Hunter*. Then below again to bring up the bodies of any who had died during the night, and wash down that deck. Their most unpleasant task was the carrying up and emptying of the latrine tubs, which stayed on deck until evening.

There is no doubt that the Working Party was invaluable to the hulk and it would be impossible to visualise the state of things without it; but twenty or so men could only touch the surface of the filth of the living space of a thousand men.

A few months before the end of the war, in 1783, there was one official attempt at disinfection. The *Jersey* was temporarily evacuated and all its prisoners were housed on a number of transport vessels, whilst the hulk was washed and scrubbed and sprinkled with vinegar. The organisation of this well-intentioned operation was as shoddy as usual. The transports were so crowded that there was insufficient room for each man to lie down under cover, and when hit by a violent storm they were in a state of soaking distress for days before they were returned to the old prison ship. Once back on the hulk, so many became seriously ill that the hospital ships were again soon filled and the 'hospital' areas had to be re-established on the *Jersey* – and the Working Party resumed its dreary task of clearing the middle and lower decks of the sick and the dead.

*

At this point we will leave the unhappy story of the old *Jersey* prison ship and, before returning to tell of her end, take a look at the Hospital Ships which featured in the dreadful seascape of the Wallabout.

The Hospital Ships.

All who left memories of their captivity, wrote of the Hospital ships, and had seen hundreds of sick men ferried to them from the main hulks – and watched the boats with bodies and burial parties which left them daily on the short trip to interment on the Long Island shore. However, only a few of them could write with knowledge of them from within.

Over the years a number of hulks were adapted for use as hospital ships, primitive in their facilities, but some more worthy of the prefix 'hospital' than others – and all liable to be used as prison ships when called upon: the *Boston Packet, Perseverance, Kitty, Scorpion, Strombolo* and the *Hunter.*

The poet, Philip Freneau was captured in May, 1780, and was first introduced to the hulks when put on board the *Scorpion* whilst that vessel was still a prison ship. He was later transferred to the *Hunter*, which was at that time a hospital ship on the East River. His memories of these two vessels are perhaps better conveyed by an extract from his poem *'The British Prison Ships'*, than by his description of happenings on board:

'The various horrors of these hulks to tell,
Where want and woe, where pain and penance dwell;
Where Death in ten-fold vengeance holds his reign,
And injured ghosts, yet unavenged, complain,
This be my task –
Hail, dark abode, what can with thee compare –
Heat, sickness, famine, death, and stagnant air.
Pandora's box from whence all mischiefs flow,
ere real found, torments mankind anew.
Swift from the guarded decks, we rushed along,
And vainly sought repose, so vast our throng.
Three hundred wretches here, denied all light,
In crowded mansions, pass th' infernal night.
Some for a bed their tatter'd vestments join;
And some on chests, and some on floors, recline.
Shut from the blessings of the evening air,

Pensive we lay, with mingled corpses there.
Meagre and wan, and scorched with heat below,
We looked like ghosts, ere death had made us so.'

Freneau wrote his poem soon after his release from captivity, and the complete poem, though extremely long, seemed to sum up, in comparatively few words, all that fellow-captives had laboriously set down in many pages of memoirs years later.

When I first read it, I felt convinced that he must have suffered longer and greater than any other prison hulk captive whose recollections I had studied. That is, until I discovered a small book which he had written on the 14th July, 1780, only two days after he had been released from the hospital ship *Hunter*. This rare little volume, less than forty pages in length, was titled, *'Some Account of the Capture of the Ship "AURORA"'* and revealed that Freneau spent only twenty-two days on the *Scorpion* and twenty days on the hospital ship *Hunter*. Those weeks of captivity marked his sensitive poet's soul with an indelible hatred and bitterness – and a feeling of personal affront that he should have been made prisoner of war at all. And yet he was a fairly captured privateer.

At a time when he was editing a magazine in Philadelphia, Freneau had obtained letters of marque from Congress, and built and fitted out what was in effect a privateer, the 20-gun *Aurora*. On the 25th May, 1780, they set off down the Delaware, ostensibly as a trading vessel with a cargo of tobacco for St Eustacia in the West Indies. Whilst still in the river, the *Aurora* captured an enemy sloop, but the next day was chased by His Majesty's frigate, the *Iris*. After an hour-long unequal battle, 'the frigate hulled us several times. One shot went betwixt wind and water, which made the ship leak amazingly.' So ended Philip Freneau's short career as a privateersman.

Squires, the prize master from the British frigate, and his crew came aboard and ordered the prisoners aboard the *Iris*, but Freneau insisted that he was a passenger on private business and therefore not subject to capture. Although owner, he was entered in the *Aurora*'s books as Third Mate and his gun position was listed, but nonetheless protested it was all a mistake. His whole concern was for himself and would seem to have had little compassion left over for his unfortunate crew. In fact, he simply could not believe that he should have to accompany them in the same boat which took them to the frigate.

'I was cruelly seized and driven down the sides, in the sight of Squires, into the barge, among the common sailors, and could not get liberty to go to my chest to put on anything, so that I had to go on board the frigate in my common ship clothes.' [The *Iris* already had the crews of two other prizes stowed away, when the newcomers were ordered below]. 'When I got between decks I thought I should have been suffocated with the heat. There were about one hundred prisoners forward, the stench of whom was almost intolerable – so many melancholy sights, and dismal countenances made it a pretty just representation of the infernal region. I marched through a torrent of cursing and blasphemy to my station, viz., at the blacksmith's vice, where the miserable prisoners were handcuffed, two and two.'

Freneau was lucky enough to be vouched for by a Loyalist officer of the frigate's crew, and so was excused handcuffs – which would have been 'a cursed disgrace, which I hardly knew how I should get clear of'– and allowed to 'come over among the gentlemen'. Feeling quite cocky now, he was sure that when they reached New York he would be paroled to Long Island, and was more worried about his inability to appear well dressed whilst on the *Iris*.

When the frigate reached New York and anchored in the North River, the Commissary's boat came out and took Freneau ashore, where he learned that his parole had been refused. Still insisting that he was a non-combatant, and cursing the fact that he had ever even seen a ship, he guaranteed $10,000, through friends ashore, that if granted he would stay within the limits of his parole but to no avail. Freneau was conducted on board the *Scorpion* where he found conditions even worse than he could have imagined. Almost suffocated with heat and stench, he did not think he would survive the first night; 'but human nature can bear much more than one would at first suppose.'

On the 3rd June there was a great panic A storm blew up and with the rolling and tossing of the *Scorpion*, some of the prisoners way down in the cable tier thought they were sinking, as water gushed in through the lower ports – and made for the main hatchway. Freneau sketched a lively word picture of hundreds of men crying out, cursing their luck, begging for God's mercy, and all making for the main hatchway – where sentries and guards were beating heads with the flats of their swords and muskets.

Next day, and by then safe in the knowledge that there had been no real danger, he shows his superiority of his courage to that of the common man, when he wrote: 'To such ridiculous distress does the fear of death reduce the generality of mankind when they apprehend it to be nigh.'

Freneau also left us with a record of an escape from the hulk, and its aftermath, which will be related elsewhere. The *Scorpion* was coming to the end of her life as a prison hulk, and six months after Freneau's short imprisonment she was fitted out as a hospital ship.

On the 22nd June, Freneau, finding himself 'taken with a fever', reported sick and was sent to the hospital ship *Hunter*, lying in the East River. He must have expected the transfer to improve his lot. If so he was to be disappointed. Although the *Hunter* had only recently been put into service, she was already filthy, her decks leaking so badly that 'the sick were deluged with every shower of rain.' His description of life between decks could have been used for any of the other hulks, prison or hospital – sickness, dirt and death. But the food sounded better. The pound of bread was edible and the meat ration was one pound of fresh beef each day. Unfortunately, although an improvement, the fresh beef was generally heads or shanks, which 'would just answer to make soup.' – and on alternate days a barrel of spruce beer was sent on board.

A Hessian doctor came on board at eight o'clock each morning and seems to have tried to do a good job, administering whatever remedies were available. His conscientiousness was not encouraged when three of Freneau's crew stole his boat one morning and made their escape. For some days he refused to board the *Hunter*, and sick prisoners, seeing him pass by to other hulks, called out for blisters, but he shouted back that they should put tar on their backs, which would serve as well as anything else.

Two or three of the *Hunter*'s patients died each day, and as Freneau's fever did not improve he felt he might soon be included in the daily count. But when the German doctor eventually resumed his calls, Freneau 'had a large blister put on my back which helped me amazingly'. On the 12th July, 1780, a cartel vessel came alongside and cleared the *Hunter* of her sick prisoners; and Freneau went home to write his little volume.

As we know, the *Hunter* was put up for sale at the end of the year,

was left on the naval Storekeeper's hands, and became a medical store ship in 1781.

Andrew Sherburne was twice sent to Hospital ships – the *Frederick* and an unnamed other – during the last months of the war. The majority of the prisoners would have known very little as to the internal layout of these vessels, or of the treatment of captives under their care; but they could have guessed the quality of the nursing from the example set by the 'nurses' on board their floating prison. Andrew began his imprisonment on the *Jersey* at the end of 1782, and the hulk was, as usual, in the grip of all manner of diseases. A week or so later he witnessed the arrival of the crew of the captured 30-gun American frigate, *Chesapeake* – and once again we hear the story:- 'the younger, the fitter, the more likely to be struck down'. The frigate's crew numbered about three hundred, many of them 'green hands' – young lads whose only experience of the sea had been the few days before their ship was captured. The contrast between their lives on shore, the unaccustomed hardship of naval service, and the horror of the *Jersey*, must have hit them hard – and they died like flies.

Although himself only just seventeen, Andrew had 'been through the furnace and seasoned' by hard experience; but in January '83, he, too, became very ill. Just after his arrival on the hulk, he had been amazed to spot his uncle, James Weymouth, amongst a fresh batch of prisoners. This was the second time they had come together as captives. Weymouth had been captured with Andrew at Charleston, nearly three years before, and this time had been taken when returning from a voyage to the West Indies. Now it seemed unlikely that they would meet up for a third time, for Andrew was by this time very ill and was awaiting transportation to the *Frederick*. The older man was able to give him a couple of dollars and an emotional farewell but expected never to see him again.

The *Frederick* was a small hulk and its facilities, such as they were, were already over-stretched. A hundred or more sick men were distributed over half that number of beds – two men to a bunk. Apart from the ship's British naval officers, the staff consisted of guards, cooks, storemen, etc. and nurses – whose number worked out to about one nurse for every ten patients. These dozen or so attendants, the majority of whom were prisoners, probably received a small emolument from the government, and would have been entitled to better rations and other privileges. Physicians came over from the *Hunter* for short periods every few days, but it seemed to Andrew that they seldom administered much in the way of medication.

The *Frederick* was far from clean, but there were a few luxuries which were never to be found on the main hulk: a small sheet-iron wood-burning stove gave off some heat between decks; a daily ration of flour bread – though badly baked and often made from musty flour; and a gill (one quarter of a pint) of wine each day. But the greatest boon came from ashore – 'A company of good citizens in New York, supplied all the sick with a pint of good Bohea Tea, (well sweetened with molasses,) a day, and this was constant. I believe this tea, under God's providence, saved my life, and the lives of hundreds of others'. In the eighteenth century 'Bohea' was made from the best black China tea. Andrew's bunk-mate was a young Massachusetts man named Wills. Andrew himself was at a very low ebb and Wills in an even worse condition. Their bunk '…sat fore and aft directly under the ballast port, opposite the main hatchway. Wills was a very pleasant young man, of a serious turn, and was persuaded he should not live. At this time my mind was very fluctuating, and occasionally deranged. My bed-fellow was running down very fast; but I was not, at that time, aware of it… He appeared to have his reason until he was speechless, and finally died, stretched across me.'

Andrew, who was too weak to move, called for nurses to help him, but he said they gave him 'hard words', and he never forgave the fact that they left him for half an hour before Wills' body was taken away.

'The death of a man in that place, and at that time, excited but little notice; for a day did not pass without more or less deaths. I have seen seven dead men drawn out and piled together on the lower hatchway, who had died in one night on board the *Frederick*'.

The nurses, of whatever nationality, were remembered with more bitterness and contempt than was aimed at their less-than-gentle British captors. Not just Freneau and Sherburne and, one can imagine, all survivors of the Hospital ships, but men on the *Jersey* and other prison ships, who had much to recall of the depravity of their loblolly attendants. Thomas Dring told of the end of Robert Carver, Gunner on the *Chance*. Gunner Carver had lain himself on an upper deck bunk to await removal to a hospital ship, and when Dring found him he was sitting up, dressed in all the clothes he owned, with his overcoat over all, and his hat between his knees. The weather was fiercely hot and the man was delirious, so Dring removed his greatcoat and placed it as a pillow under his head and went off to fetch him a drink. When he returned after only a few minutes, he saw one of the nurses with Carver's greatcoat over his arm. Both Carver and Dring were officers, so there was no argument about its return; but neither was there an apology. The thief just said that it was a perquisite of the Nurses, the only one they had; that the man was dying anyway, so what use was a coat to him? Sadly, Robert Carver did not live long enough to prove him wrong, and died before he reached the Hospital ship.

The nurses lived in the steerage and worked among their charges only during the day, for on the *Frederick*, if not on the *Scorpion*, the hatches were battened down soon after sunset. After that, no attention was available to the sick or dying other than the voluntary kindness of convalescing invalids. Most nurses were scavengers of the lowest order, claiming anything which fellow sufferers had not been able to retrieve from a deceased's effects – and they went even further. If a man had had a good head of hair, that too was taken as a perk, shaved off and sold ashore. Andrew was on the *Frederick* at the worst time of the year. If the heat was intolerable in the warmer months, the cold of winter could be fatal. There were many instances where men who, already ill, lost toes and feet to frost bite or their lives to the cold (negro prisoners of war in the depot at Portchester Castle, in Hampshire, England, also suffered the loss of fingers and toes in freezing weather). It may be difficult to believe that this is not an exaggeration, but many non-prisoner records and newspaper reports bear testimony to the fact:

'*New London*, Christmas Day, 1778.
A cartel arrived here from New York with 172 American prisoners. They were landed here and in Groten – greater part sickly and in most deplorable condition, owing chiefly to the ill-usage in prison-ships, where numbers had their feet and legs froze.'

And from the same newspaper:

'*New London*, February 16, 1780.
15 prisoners arrived here, who three weeks ago escaped from the prison-ship in the East River. A number of others who escaped about the same time from the ship, some of whom being frost bitten and unable to endure the cold, were taken up and carried back, one frozen to death before he reached the shore.

After the death of Wills, Andrew had two blankets and his greatcoat to help him fight the cold at night, and a small sack of straw on which to lie. 'I suffered extremely from the cold. I have frequently toiled the greatest part of the night, in rubbing my feet and legs to keep them from freezing; and while I was employed on one, it seemed as though the other must absolutely freeze'.

The uncaulked seams of the ballast port beside his bunk let in wind, rain and snow, but the latter was sometimes welcome, to help quench the thirst from which they all suffered, particularly at night. The tiny stove was of little help, it was usually screened by the 'peevish and surly fellows' who huddled round it; 'I never got the opportunity to set by it; but I could generally get the favor of someone near it to lay a slice of bread upon it, to warm or toast a little, to put into my wine and water.'

With the dollars his uncle had given him he got a nurse to buy him a few things from shore, a pint tin cup, a spoon, some oranges and a pound or two of sugar, for which he would have had to pay over the mark. The cup was one of his most valued possessions, although often he had to plead hard to get it filled with water before the hatch was slammed shut at the end of the day. Both on the *Jersey* and the hospital ships, and probably on all the prison fleet, thirst was remembered more than pain; Andrew was frequently so dry that he could not swallow his bread, and traded it for water – at times of desperation up to three days allowance for one tin cupful:

'I was under the necessity of using the strictest economy with my cup of water; restricting myself to drink such a number of swallows at a time, and make them very small… I became so habituated to number my swallows, that for years after I continued the habit, and even to this day I frequently involuntarily number my swallows'.

To have survived wartime privateer and naval service, smallpox, shipwreck, three captivities and the unnamed complaint which brought him to the *Frederick*, Andrew Sherburne must have had the constitution of an ox. Against his own expectations he recovered sufficiently to be returned, still unfit, to the *Jersey*. He found that Richard Weymouth had become ill during his absence and that he too had been sent to a Hospital ship, and could discover only one member of his crew, a young lad of his own age, who told him that their gunner, Daniel Davis, had come to a miserable end through fever and severely frozen feet.

It can be understood that the two young lads should spend much of their time lamenting their fate and when, a few days later, they were put aboard the transports whilst the hulk was undergoing her aforementioned long overdue cleansing, they must have felt that nothing more could go wrong. However, their terrible time on the transport brought Andrew low again, and he was on board a hospital ship once more. He was sent to the same ship as his uncle, and found the older man in a very sorry state; unavoidably he must have been lousy and his hair was so tangled as to be uncombable; but, for a consideration, a 'kindly' nurse shaved his head – accepting his saleable hair as payment. Andrew said that he had but 'little recollection' of the state of his mind during some of the time he spent on hospital ships and could not remember the name of the second one. I cannot think that it could have been the *Scorpion* – *Scorpion* was also the name of the 8-gun letter of marque on which Andrew had been captured, and I am sure his memory would have been jogged.

Andrew often spoke of prisoners who were affected mentally to greater or lesser degree by their suffering. He had said that his bunk-mate, Wills, was 'occasionally deranged', and that during his own sickness he 'was delirious a considerable part of the time.' Back on the *Jersey*, there were men who had suffered great mental strain after months, and even years, of captivity, and were just existing without giving much intelligent thought to their surroundings, or remembering how long they had been in captivity.

Seventeen years old Christopher Hawkins, on the same hulk in 1781, said that 'ev'ry prisoner was infested with vermin on his body and wearing apparel.' One day he observed a prisoner on the forecastle, with his shirt in his hands, picking off the vermin and putting them into his mouth. A number of prisoners had told Christopher that many were in the habit of acting in this way, but until now he had not credited it. He was fascinated, and later asked the man his name; to his question, 'How long have you been a prisoner?' he took some time before answering, 'Two years and a half, or eighteen months.' Hawkins was sure that he had no certain knowledge of the period of his captivity, and thought it was but one case 'from perhaps an hundred of others similar.'

Andrew Sherburne and his uncle never went back to the old *Jersey* again. Whilst they were on the second hospital ship, peace was declared and, still sick but with joy assisting their recuperation, they returned as free citizens of a new nation, to Providence, New Hampshire.

Back with the Prison Ships.

Previous chapters have made it plain that the American was never a submissive prisoner of war. Whilst the French were more industrious in other ways, and often made the best of their captivity, the American employed as much energy in efforts to regain his freedom. In the English depots and hulks the Yankee prisoners were a constant thorn in the side of their gaolers – their every thought concentrated on escaping and planning escapes, or at least devising escapades which kept their spirits high and their keepers tormented.

Doubtless the men who were sent to the New York Hulks were of no different fibre and their instinct to abscond no less. The military force which guarded the many hundreds of prisoners on *Jersey* was minute. The ship's crew may be disregarded. Apart from them, there was a resident guard of a dozen or so superannuated marines, unfit for active service, backed up by about thirty soldiers from one or another of the British regiments based on Long Island, who acted as sentinels. Each week this soldiery was relieved by a party from a different regiment.

Numerically there was nothing to stop a general uprising on the hulk itself at any time. There would certainly have been something of a massacre initially, with marines and soldiers sniping through the loop-holes of the barricado, but such a small force could not have held out for long. So, despite the bloodshed, it is likely that some hundreds of Americans could have reached the shore. But what then?

Long Island and the New York coast had been well and truly in British hands since August, 1776, and even a large – mainly unarmed – rampaging army of freed Americans would have been quickly overcome by reinforcements from the regiments close by. Even those who avoided immediate recapture could have no expectation of assistance or sympathy from their fellow Americans, inhabitants of Long Island. Almost without exception, Long Islanders were fiercely pro-British Tories, or Loyalists.

Whilst a large scale attempt would have been doomed to failure, it was not difficult to get as far as the shore, individually or in small groups; and there were many getaways and attempted escapes from the *Jersey*. The story of most of these must remain a mystery as they were usually planned with great secrecy within individual messes; but we do know the detail of some which were successful – and of others which were not. Only in exceptional circumstances did a member of the ship's company, guards or soldiers, come among the prisoners, so the disappearance of a complete mess would not be noticed, perhaps for weeks or months – and we have noted the prisoner's 'by-law' sentence for conveying such information to the enemy.

One fairly large, but only partly successful breakout, was recorded by Ebenezer Fox. At sunset, after all prisoners had descended to the two lower decks for the night, the main hatchway was closed and bolted down. In the hatchway was a small trap door, watched over by just one sentinel and when there was a call for water, only one man was allowed on deck through the small opening. The guard, with fixed bayonet, made sure that no one followed up the ladder as the prisoner made his dip in the scuttlebutt.

On this occasion an Irish soldier, nicknamed Billy the Ram, admitted a strong, and plausible, captive on to the deck and closed the trap door behind him. The sailor asked Billy's advice as to how he might enter the British service, and rewarded the helpful and gullible sentinel by laying him out with a single blow to the back of the head. The trap door was opened and soon thirty or more men were over the side and in the water. The noise of the escaping men aroused the guard and soon the boats were got out and shots were aimed at the flashes of phosphorescence in the darkness, where the swimmers disturbed the surface of the sea.

Only about half were brought back to the *Jersey*, most of whom were wounded, and the others were either shot, drowned or got away. The recaptured would have returned as heroes to their fellows but they would have suffered for their adventure: for some time at least they would have been put in the bilboes – leg-irons which anchored their feet to a long iron bar, and – a worse part of the punishment – their meagre ration would have been cut by a third for at least a month.

Thomas Andros escaped against all the odds. Both his courage and desperation must have been great to have even contemplated escape whilst suffering from yellow fever. He at first planned to leave through a gun-port which the prisoners had worked on and opened, and swim to the shore; but he sensibly decided against the attempt. In his weakened condition he could never have swum to the shore. Others had left by the same exit, as can be inferred from his remark that once he was in the water, he would almost certainly be shot, 'as others had been'.

He got to the shore by a far easier means; Mr Emery, the Sailing Master included him in a working party going ashore for water. Although Mr Emery was a British officer and had not aided escape, he was probably in serious trouble when the boat returned without Thomas. Getting away from the hulk was the easy bit: from then on he faced adventures and sufferings which could be a volume in themselves. He struggled through marshland and forests, slept rough and half-starved, saw recaptured prisoners being marched back to the *Jersey* – and conjectured how much better chance they would have stood had they travelled alone. Thomas schemed and lied his way through days and weeks of enemy territory, occasionally enjoying kindness from folk who at least pretended to believe his assumed identity – a young surviver from an English vessel out of New York, driven ashore by an American privateer.

At last he arrived at Sag Harbor, at the east end of Long Island, where he met up with two other decampers from the *Jersey*. After a short but complicated voyage across Long Island Sound, he arrived home in New London, one hundred and fifty miles from his point of departure. There, he gave in to his illness and the mental and physical bruises of his painful journey, and it took long months of nursing before he recovered.

There was one officer-only escape plan which went sadly wrong. The scheme was to cut a hole through the oak planking of the hulk's counter, (that part of the stern aft of the rudder) big enough for a man to drop through. This was an ambitious undertaking with the tools they had at their disposal – just one gimlet and their jack knives. Only the inmates of the Gun Room were in on the enterprise, and very few held any hope for its success. The enthusiasts were led by a young Master's Mate from Philadelphia, named Lawrence, and no argument could weaken his determination, or that of the few men who were willing to follow him.

The plan was discussed over and over again in the Gun Room and the more often the pros and cons were weighed against each other, the more often the balance fell towards the latter – but the work still went on.

The escape attempt was open to all, but notwithstanding the desire of every man to leave the misery of the hulk, only Lawrence and three other officers were willing to face the bold adventure. Although few had any faith in the outcome, every man in the Gun Room was willing to contribute, by working on the four-inch thick iron-hard oak of the counter. They laboured in shifts, digging and scratching away at the solid wood with their knives; screened by a blanket from prying eyes, and making as little noise as possible; working from seam to seam until there was only a thin skin of oak left on the outside, and clearing the caulking from the seams to a similar depth.

At last, all was prepared, and the four waited, with their clothes tied across their shoulders, while the last thin layer of wood was cut away, the oaken plug removed, and the aperture revealed. At midnight, one after the other they dropped into the water. They had chosen a very dark night and the plan was that they should swim together to the shore, but their escape ended almost before it began – and it could have been prevented weeks before without bloodshed and tragedy.

The hulk's officers and guards had had wind of the attempt from early days, but had let the men toil their way through the solid hull without putting a stop to what could only be wasted effort. Now they lay in wait under the hulk's quarter, with boat's crew at the oars and soldiers with muskets at the ready.

As the four swam away from the ship's side there was a burst of fire which awakened the sleeping prisoners throughout the hulk – and told the officers in the Gun Room that their worst fears were realised. After a short while there was activity on the deck, the gratings were raised 'and the guards descended, bearing a naked and bleeding man, whom they placed in one of the bunks; and having left a piece of burning candle by his side, they again ascended to the deck, and secured the gratings'. This was the first time that prisoners had seen a light between decks, and it was obviously only put there now as a warning to the captives, and to exhibit an example of what could happen to any who might be similarly foolhardy.

'The wounded man was my friend Lawrence. He was severely injured in many places, and one of his arms had been nearly severed from his body by the stroke of a cutlass'. He told his friends this had happened deliberately as he clung to the gunwale of the boat and asked for mercy. They were denied the usual access to a measure of water during the night, so Lawrence's wounds could not be cleansed and no medical aid was sent below. Next morning the hatchway was not raised until ten o'clock and by that time he was past all help. Nothing is known of the fate of the other three officers but it is doubtful that any survived.

The members of the Gun Room 'received not the least reprimand', and the hole in the stern was repaired without comment; it was probably considered that the candle-lit scene of Lawrence's demise would stay longer in the memory than any other type of punishment.

One other officer-escape story has a happier ending. It was not unusual for visitors to come out from New York to 'gratify themselves with the sight of the miserable tenants of the prison-ship; influenced by the same kind of curiosity that induces some people to travel a great distance to witness an execution'. Those were the words of Ebenezer Fox; and Thomas Andros, who was on board at about the same time said: 'Once or twice, by the order of a stranger on the quarter deck, a bag of apples was hurled promiscuously into the midst of hundreds of prisoners crowded together as thick as they could stand'. The ensuing scramble can be imagined and, as Andros said, 'this instead of compassion was a cruel sport'. It is true that these were the observations of imprisoned men, who could be justified in attributing the worst motives to the perhaps innocent actions of people who viewed them; but at a time when bear-baiting and public executions were the television of the age, it is probable that to many there would have seemed nothing wrong in watching prisoners of war, and considered it as no more than an interesting spectacle. This was certainly true of the other side of the Atlantic: When civil hulks came into being in Britain, in 1776, convicts were employed on the foreshore of the Thames where, with chained fetters on each leg and watched over by guards with drawn cutlasses, they worked in the river mud, constructing the docks for Woolwich Arsenal – and this soon became recognised as one of the sightseeing spectaculars of London. The following story, however, shows that visitors were not always unwelcomed:

One fine morning a beautiful yawl, manned by four oarsmen and a helmsman came alongside. A number of gentlemen from New York were admitted aboard and shown great courtesy by the officers of the hulk. After securing the yawl to the fore-chains, the boat's crew were curious enough to also venture aboard. The splendid little craft was gazed at with a professional eye and much admired by the seamen prisoners, especially so by a group of American officers sitting in the forecastle; a captain and four mates who had been captured only a few days before. As usual, a sentry was pacing the length of the deck and executing smart about-turns at the end of each short march, before retracing his steps, usually at a measured tread. 'Whether upon this occasion any one interested in his movements had secretly slipped a guinea into his hand, not to quicken, but to retard his progress, was never known', but his back was turned long enough for the four officers to lower themselves into the yawl, and with four mates as oarsmen and the captain at the helm, the boat was away at a speed greater than its arrival. By the time the soldier became aware, the boat was well away and he missed with his shot, either intentionally or through nervousness at the prospect of an examination of his part in the affair.

One result was that for some time after, whenever visitors came aboard the hulk, prisoners were sent below until they had left. There is a humorous, but apocryphal, ending to this tale: the whole guard was called out, and both visitors and ship's company were staring in astonishment at the getaway. 'The guards were firing as fast as they could load their guns,' and 'the captain in the yawl left the helm, and standing erect in the stern, with his back to the *Jersey*, bending his body to a right angle, he exhibited the broadest part of himself to their view, and with a significant gesture directed their attention to it as a proper target for the exercise of their skill.'

Philip Freneau's account of an escape from the *Scorpion*, tells of action more open and violent than the norm. A large trading schooner was anchored quite close astern of the hulk, and the night after the 'storm and sinking' panic, a party of about thirty-five prisoners determined on escape. At that time of the year, July, the prisoners were allowed to stay on the upper deck until nine o'clock on that particular hulk, although most went below well before that time. As the clock neared nine o'clock, the deck was almost clear, 'except for the insurgents, who rushed upon the sentries and disarmed them in a moment; one they tied by his neck stock to the quarter rails, and carried off his marquet with them, the rest they drove down with their arms into the cabin, and rammed the sentry-box down the companion in such a manner that no one could get up or down.

Once the sentries had been secured, they manned the ship's boat and boarded the schooner, where they had another fight on their hands, the crew trying to keep them off with hand-pikes. 'The wind blowing fresh at south and the flood of the tide being made, they hoisted sail and were out of sight in a few minutes.'

Freneau had wisely stayed below during the rioting, and was given the details by some of the rebels who could not find room in the boat. One morsel of information pleased Freneau greatly: he particularly disliked the prison ship steward, a man named Gauzoo – 'the most brutal of mankind' and 'impossible for words to give his character... the most vile and detestable of mortals'– and during the fracas a Yankee mutineer, one Murphy had relieved Gauzoo of his silver-hilted sword and made off with it. As soon as the *Scorpion* was once again in the hands of the British – or Germans, for all the guards were Hessians – the sentries were placed at each of the hatchways. Freneau says that they fired fore and aft among the prisoners with pistols and marquets, but, 'By the mercy of God, they touched but four, one mortally; another had his great toe shot off.' The next morning the Deputy Commissary came on board and the wounded were put in irons and ordered to lie on deck. In the afternoon one of the wounded died and his irons were struck off and he was shipped ashore for burial.

Not surprisingly, there was a tightening up of security and, for the rest of her life as a prison ship, all the captives were driven below strictly at sunset and the grog allowance was withdrawn.

There are other stories of escapes which could be told, and throughout the war there were newspaper reports of escapes – and recaptures – usually short; but no matter how brief they tell their story: like the one below, which in a few words tells of a fortunate Yankee who got away quickly and so escaped the many horrors related in the preceding pages:

> '*New London Gazette*. Nov. 8, '76
> Yesterday arrived E.Thomas, captured Sep.1, carried to N.Y., and was put on board the *Chatham*. He escaped Wednesday se'ennight.'

No one knows how many men escaped from the *Jersey*. It probably ran into several hundreds over the whole period of her inglorious existence; and how many died during the actual operation of their escape; were struck down by disease they had carried with them from hulk to shore; or did not survive the rigours of their trek through Long Island; were recaptured by soldiers from British, Hessian or Refugee regiments; or were impressed into the service of King George on land or sea: these are figures which no amount of research can reveal with any accuracy.

Neither shall we ever know how many prisoners of war died from the multiplicity of diseases which the prison ships engendered, exacerbated by corruption and the supply of rotten food and the politics of exchange. We do know that an unimaginable number – estimates of ten or eleven thousand are probably exaggerated, but certainly many thousands – left their bones in the banks by the Wallabout during its years as a disrespectful graveyard.

We have seen that the Working Party had a number of advantages – extra food, a tot of rum, etc., but it had another perk – terrible and unpleasant by normal standards, but a valued perk nonetheless. As members of almost contiguous burial parties, they were of the few who had the opportunity to set foot on dry land and breathe fresh air, for however short a period. After they had performed their morning duty of putting the sick into bunks on the upper deck, they answered the sentry's call 'Rebels! Turn out your dead!' and brought up the victims of the previous night, and placed them on the gratings or the spar deck. A signal was then made to the *Hunter* from the flagstaff on the stern, and her boats, after making their rounds of the other prison ships, would come alongside. There was little in the way of ceremony. No coffins were supplied, but if a blanket could be found or spared, and a caring shipmate was prepared to sew him into it, the deceased might be sent ashore with at least a minimum of decency; but there were not always blankets to spare or shipmates left who knew him.

When the *Hunter*'s boat came alongside, the body was lowered into it on a stretcher-like board, which was then retrieved. It was accepted that little could be expected in the way of respect for the dead: (I noted that in one memoir, it was considered thoughtful that when there were a number of bodies, they were lowered into the boat one at a time). It would seem that one hulk, at least, used hammocks to cover its dead when they were shipped ashore. But Alexander Coffin tells a grim story of one particular burial collection whilst he was a prisoner on the *John*. In a letter which he later wrote to the Chief Editor of the *Medical Repository*, he described how, every morning, a large boat came from each of the hospital ships and carried bodies to the interment site. He then went on to say:

'A singular affair happened on board one of these hospital- ships, and no less true than singular. All the prisoners who had died after the boat had gone ashore, were sewn up in hammocks, and left on deck till the next morning. As usual, a great number had thus been disposed of. In the morning, while employed in loading the boat, one of the seamen perceived motion in one of the hammocks, just as they were about launching it down the board placed for that purpose from the gunwale of the ship into the boat, and exclaimed, "D—n my eyes, that fellow is not dead", and, if I have been rightly informed, and I believe I have, there was quite a dispute between this man and the others about it. They swore he was dead enough, [!] and should go into the boat; he swore he should not be launched, as they termed it, and took out his knife and ripped open the hammock, and behold, the man really was alive.'

Alexander Coffin could not resist including in his letter his own very unmedical theory to explain the man's recovery:

'There had been heavy rain during the night, and as the vital functions had not totally ceased, but were merely suspended in consequence of the main spring being out of order, this seasonable moistening must have given tone and elasticity to the great spring, which must have communicated to the lesser ones, and put the whole machinery again in motion [then, remembering who he was writing to, added...]…You can better judge of the cause…'

The resurrected prisoner's surname was Gavot, and Coffin went on to tell us – 'He [Gavot] went to Rhode-Island in the same flag of truce [cartel ship] with me about a month afterwards.' Coffin was sure of his story, but realising that it was sensational enough to be disbelieved, said that 'Capt. Shubael Worth, of Hudson, was master of the flag, and will bear testimony to the same fact.'

There was never a shortage of eager volunteers who offered their assistance to the official interment parties, 'It was high gratification to us to bury our feet in the sand, and to shove them through it, as we passed on our way'. When all was ready the carriage boats, and the burial party boat with its guard of soldiers, pushed off for the shore. They made for a small wharf which had been built as a landing stage for a tide-mill owned by an old man named Remsen, known to the prisoners as 'The Old Dutchman'. His house and barns were on a hill which sloped down to the tidal shore where there was a small hut. Spades and hoes were issued to the prisoner-gravediggers from the hut and the corpses were put into hand-barrows and wheeled to the burial place.

Everything was done in a great hurry, the guards never allowing sufficient time to dig a proper or deep enough grave. Once a vacant spot had been selected, a trench wide and long enough for a mass grave was scraped out of the sand, and the bodies quickly laid in it. Thomas Dring, who had received permission to attend the burial of his friend, Gunner Carter, said that the guards paid no more respect to the dead prisoners than they would to dead animals:

'They scarcely allowed us time to look about us; for no sooner had we heaped the earth above the trench, than the order was given to march. But a single glance was sufficient to show us parts of many bodies exposed to view; although they had probably been placed there, with the same mockery of interment, but a few days before.'

If, in the case of the *Jersey*, officialdom and its minions showed little respect for the enemy dead, it showed even less respect and consideration towards men who might soon join them. It was possible to see from the hulk, part of the strip of sand where these makeshift funerals took place. Thomas Andros never lost the memory of this barbarity:

'…a boat loaded with dead bodies, conveying them to the Long Island shore where they were very slightly covered with sand. I sometimes used to stand and count the number of times the shovel was filled with sand to cover a dead body. And certain I am that a few high tides or torrents of rain must have disinterred them.'

These are not just prisoner of war horror stories. A teenager farm-worker, Jerimiah Johnson, who lived near the miller wrote:

'The whole shore, from Rennie's Point to Mr Remsen's dooryard, was a place of graves; as were also the slope of the hill near the house; the shore, from Mr Remsen's barn along the mill-pond to Rapelye's farm. The atmosphere seemed to be charged with foul air from the prison ships and with the effluvia of dead bodies washed out of their graves by the tides. The bodies of the dead lay exposed along the beach, drying and bleaching in the sun, and whitening the shores.'

That men should compete to visit such a place and find it less noisome than the prison ships, speaks volumes against the policy of using hulks as housing for prisoners of war. A touching little story tells of a returning burial party who were given permission by their Hessian guard – who were usually more inclined to grant little favours to the Yankees than the Loyalists or British – to take up a few small turves of grass and carry them back on their reluctant return to the hulk. 'The pieces of turf which we carried on board, were sought for by our fellow prisoners, with great avidity: every fragment being passed from hand to hand, and its smell inhaled, as if it had been a fragrant rose.'

The end of the war was the end of the old *Jersey*. The last one thousand four hundred American prisoners of war were released from her grasp and her working days had come to an end. A barely floating pit of contagion and by now too rotten to be moved, she was left to decay. With no captive hands to work the pumps and the seams of her worm-eaten timbers ever widening, she sank; and with her the thousands of scratched and carved names which covered her inner planks, disappeared beneath the waves.

Twenty years later, in 1803, the bank of the Wallabout was removed during the building of the Brooklyn Navy Yard. A vast quantity of bones was retrieved and an application was made to Congress, requesting that they be re-interred wth honour and a monument erected on the spot.

This was not approved, but in 1808 the bones of the Prison Fleets' victims were buried under the direction of the Columbian Order of New York (Tammany Hall) and the cornerstone of monument was laid, inscribed:

'IN THE NAME OF THE SPIRIT OF THE DEPARTED FREE'

TWO LETTERS FROM A PRISONER IN THE OLD *JERSEY* PRISON SHIP

The following two letters were written by Captain Stephen Buckland, a native of East Hartford, Connecticut, and captain of a privateer which was captured by the British Brig *Perseverance*, on the 2nd April, 1782. Buckland, his officers and crew were all confined in the old *Jersey* prison ship.

Three weeks after his capture he sent a short but reassuring letter to his wife, playing down the full awfulness of his confinement:

> 'To Mrs Mary Buckland   *Prison-Ship of* New York
>   *April 22nd, 1782*
> MY DEAR:
> *Before this comes to hand you will doubtless hear of our misfortune. I have nothing to write, but that we are all well, except some have got the small-pox. Poor Michael was drowned by the oversetting of the boat, and several others in great danger.*
> *I hope it won't be long before will get home by some means or other. Give yourself no uneasiness about me, I live very well, and*
>   *Remain your ever affectionate*
> *Mrs Buckland*   *STEPHEN BUCKLAND'*

Two weeks earlier, he had written to his brother-in-law, Aaron Olmsted. This letter was also brief, but it would seem that there was no opportunity to dispatch it for some time (and that conditions were getting worse), for he appended a longer postscript which told more of the true situation in which they found themselves on the hulk. The postscript was dated the same as the letter to his wife: April 22nd –

> 'To Aaron Olmsted,   *On board the Prison-Ship,* New York.
> *Capt. Gideon Olmsted,*   *April 9th, 1782*
> *and Abraham Miller.*
>
> SIRS:
> *Before this comes to hand you will doubtless hear of our fate. We were taken on the 2d inst., by the Brig* Perseverance, *Ross Commander Ezekiel Olmsted is slightly wounded, but will be well in a few days. All the rest are well. Poor Michael was drowned by the*

over-setting of the boat, and several others narrowly escaped. Our situation you can guess. If you can do anything for us, should be glad.

If you get any person to exchange for any of us, you must get him or them paroled, and send them in on condition that they get the persons exchanged that you send them for, or to return; for you send ever so many in a flag, they will not be exchanged for us. Remember me to my family and friends.

>   *I remain, Sirs, yours,*
>   *STEPHEN BUCKLAND*
> P.S.
> *April 22nd, Esq, Legerd was on board yesterday, and informs us that there will be no exchange for privateers-men, that he had got liberty to take twenty prisoners only, that they were taken in merchantmen. Our situation is truly distressing, especially our people, for they were stripped of everything, even to the buckles out of their shoes, and the buttons out of their shirts, hats coats and jackets. Many of them have got the small-pox, and must all have it that han't had it, and not a farthing of money. You would do well to inform their friends that if they are inclined to send them any relief they may if an opportunity presents.*
> *There is on board this ship about seven hundred prisoners, and increasing almost every day. You can easily guess what a life we must live, and hot weather coming on. At present we are as well as can be expected. What provision we get is very good. It is an excellent place to prepare a man for inoculation. Lieut. Warner stayed in the brig that took us and had the promise of being set ashore. I hope he has got home before this.*
> *If you can think of any way by which you can get us out, should be very glad. For my part, I cant think of any at present, but to make the best of a bad bargain.*
>
>   *STEPHEN BUCKLAND'*

The story ends sadly. Aaron Olmsted made all haste to visit the *Jersey* 'under a flag, to ascertain what could be done to relieve or mitigate the sufferings of his relatives', only to find that Capt Buckland had died on the 7th of May, aged thirty-six, and that his (Aaron's) 'slightly wounded', brother, Ezekiel, had died at about the same time. The twenty-six year old Ezekiel, realizing that his end was near, sent his gold sleeve buttons to the girl he had hoped to marry.

---

1. Scuttlebutt: water-butt on deck with hole in top for dipping from.

Chapter Eight

The 'Danish' Prisoner of War Hulks

'The smallest dory there was to hand
he chose for the Skagan trip.
Sail and mast he left on land –
such gear he thought best not to ship.
He reckoned did Terje, the boat would steer
though seas ran somewhat a-beam.
The Jutland reef was the devil to clear –
but worse, he'd the English blockade to fear,
Its look-out's eagle-eyed gleam.

'The boat was sighted, a challenge was heard,
and the handiest route was barred;
The dawn-breeze flickered and hardly stirred –
so Terje went westwards, hard.
They lowered their jolly-boat over the side
he heard how the sailor men sang –
He pressed on the boards with his feet braced wide,
he rowed till the waters seethed to the stride,
And blood from his fingertips sprang.'

HENRIK IBSEN. *Terje Vigen.*

SEVERAL VERY INFORMATIVE MEMOIRS IN THE FORM of journals and diaries have survived, which record the experiences of Scandinavian prisoners of war in Britain – in closed prison, prison hulk or on parole. Informative, that is, to those who read Danish, but so far none has appeared in English.

A surprising number of paintings and sketches also survive, and although there were no 'Danish Louis Garnerays' among those northern prisoner-artists, their works add much to our knowledge of their prisons. This is particularly true in the depictions of the prison hulks, where close scrutiny reveals small details immediately, which pages of description would have made less clear – although it must be admitted that the charming naivety of some of these works tends to divert the mind from the misery and sufferings of men confined in the worst of those floating depots.

As we have said in an earlier chapter, the Danish prisoners in general received better treatment, better allowances, in fact were thought of as a different type of prisoner from the French – more hostage than prisoner of war.

The Scandinavians were also particularly fortunate in two of their civilian countrymen living in this country, who diligently looked after their interests: the Danish Consul-General in London, Jens Wollf, and the Reverend Ulrik Frederik Rosing, Minister of the Danish Church in Stepney and the prisoners' Agent.

This does not mean that they did not suffer, and sometimes suffer badly. Some spent as much as seven long years on prison hulks, years which would have dragged by in depressing uncertainty, even had the conditions been twice as good. But it may be a reason why so many mementoes in the form of portraits of their prisons have been preserved in Denmark to this day, compared with the few similar artefacts to be found in other countries.

Above. Painted by a Danish Prisoner. Prison Hulks in Chatham Harbour.

It is only to be expected that any man who kept a diary of his captivity would have filled its opening pages with his feelings of the shock and horror experienced on his entry into the claustrophobic world of the prison hulk. How they adapted to this violent change in their fortunes varied according to the individual character – and to some extent to their nationality. In some it brought out the best and in others the worst – to an almost unbelievable degree.

It is also to be expected that those ex-prisoners of war who wrote their memoirs many years later, sometimes towards the end of their lives, would remember those wasted years with bitterness and – whilst not necessarily guilty of exaggeration – would tend to recall the darkest moments to which their captivity had subjected them, rather than the brighter story of how they overcame the vicissitudes of the closed prison and survived. And there *were* bright spots.

Jens Krog, Johan Federspiel, Hans Dam and others, all of whom had recorded the hopeless terror of the first days, later told of celebrations, of plays performed; of profitable prisoner of war industry; of happy days – as well as days of hunger and misery. And all this on what had at first appeared impossibly overcrowded hulks.[1]

The American, Benjamin Waterhouse, who was seldom very complimentary towards men of any nationality other than his own, nevertheless mentioned that some prisoners, of whatever nation, employed themselves profitably. He was particularly down on the feckless French, though giving them a grudging credit for their skill and craftsmanship in turning out delicate little artefacts in bone, hair, wood or straw, for sale to the British public. In this field of prison of war activity on board the *Crown Prince* hulk, he had no praise to spare for the Dane or Hollander:

> 'Here we see the thick-skulled plodding Dane, making a wooden dish; or else some of the most ingenious making a clumsy ship; whilst others submitted to the dirtiest drudgery of the hulk, for money; and there we see a Dutchman, picking to pieces tarred ropes, which, when reduced to its original form of hemp, we call oakum; or else you see him lazily stowed away in some corner with his pipe.'

There can have been little difference in the accommodation and basic conditions under which the prisoners of different nationalities fared. All prison hulks were at one time or another visited by foul diseases; all had their share of good and bad inmates: and it was pot-luck whether a particular hulk was commanded by a compassionate commander or one of those few well-recorded drunken brutes who disgraced their commissions and their country. But the general tempo of everyday prison-board life differed, sometimes greatly, according to the national characteristics and temperaments of the prisoners. The Scandinavian captives were comparatively easy-going and down-to-earth. with little of the high spirited and excited exuberance of the French, or the troublemaking rebelliousness which typified the American prisoner. They had their troublemakers, ne'er-do-wells and down-and-outs: they had their gamblers too, but the Nordic punters seldom went to the damaging extremes taken by the gaming-mad French.

The number of Danish prisoners brought to Britain after the first Battle of Copenhagen in 1801, had been comparatively small – although a great number had been freed by Nelson after the battle, on a kind of parole: They were to be counted as 'exchange-prisoners' or 'prisoners theoretically already exchanged' – and therefore in debt to Britain for that number – if the two countries were ever involved in a future war. But even these comparative few were released with

the signing of the Treaty of Amiens in the following year. Over the four years following the reopening of hostilities between France and Britain in 1803, Danish merchant sailors captured on vessels adjudged by 'right of search' to be carrying cargoes of use to the enemy – or serving on French ships at the time of capture – were brought into British prisons. However, these were still too few in number to be segregated, and were bundled in with the dozens of other nationalities to be found in Napoleon's forces, and collectively classified as 'French' prisoners of war.

That is, before 1807. Then, with trouble once again brewing between this country and the Northern Powers, Britain jumped the gun and detained men who might well have been classed as political prisoners, but could in no way be fairly labelled prisoners of war, since no war had been declared. After the signing of the Tilsit Treaty in July 1807 – which inspired the second attack on Copenhagen and secured for Britain the Danish fleet, which would certainly have been added to Napoleon's strength had the French beaten them to it – all Danish vessels in English ports (or apprehended at sea) were placed under embargo, their bewildered crews confined to their ships and uncertain of their future.

Perhaps it was better that they did not know, for many of these men were to remain imprisoned until the end of the Napoleonic War in 1814.

Unfair as it must have seemed to the individual captive – *and* to many Englishmen – the apparent small-mindedness of the Government in detaining these men was not without excuse and some justification. Napoleon's Continental System, or Berlin Decree, and later the Tilsit Treaty, made 1807 a threatening year for Britain. Bonaparte's 'System' was aimed at 'the stomach of his enemy' by ordering 'a continent-wide blockade of the British Isles by closing all ports within the Empire to shipping of British origin'.[2] It was a threat with holes in it, as France could not equal our sea-power, but on the 7th January, 1807, Britain responded with Orders in Council which forbade all neutrals From trading with France, thus, not only Danes but many other foreign prisoners fell into our hands.

As more and more merchantmen were brought into British ports, their crews must have become increasingly disturbed; uncertain of their standing as neutrals and wondering when next they would see their homes and families. Wherever large groups of men are held against their will, whether as impressed sailors, enlisted troops, and prisoners civil or captured in war, the general atmosphere will tend to be one of discontent, resentment, anger and despair. So it might be expected that the Danes, a friendly but not the most extrovert and high-spirited of people, would have been particularly downcast and depressed. But not all spent their hours of detention in negative complaint and distress. When Johan Christian Federspiel, a Danish sailor, whose ship had been seized in the late summer of 1807, was brought into Plymouth, there were already eighty Danish vessels flying the British 'Embargo flag' at the mainmast. In his memoirs, he says that on arrival the captain disappeared ashore and was not seen again, (probably making his escape with help from English friends or merchants – or he may have been granted some sort of private pre-war parole).

Some enterprising members of the crew took full advantage of the captain's absence, almost immediately entering into the smuggling business. Their vessel was carrying a cargo of coffee and rum and, although the Customs men had been increased as the number of detainees grew, they were soon doing a roaring trade with the Plymouth receivers, apparently undetected.

Federspiel tells us something of their *modus operandi*, describing how ox-bladders were filled with rum and hidden in their hats, and the ingenious way in which the coffee reached their customers. Each smuggler wore two pairs of trousers, the legs of the inner pair tied tight at the bottom with string and filled from hip to ankle with coffee beans. Over the weeks during which their business thrived uninterrupted, Johan and his mates became rich enough to throw riotous parties on board – and enjoy the pleasures of Plymouth and its surroundings. The secret of their success is explained by Federspiel's note that the British Customs officers seemed to enjoy the shipboard parties as much as any Dane.[3]

The above escapade was probably not unique. Many a man must have chosen to live on the edge, rather than be immersed in gloom at the prospect of long incarceration. One merchant officer detained at Plymouth stayed with his ship, but only long enough to dismantle enough of her saleable fittings to finance his successful escape.[4]

Amongst those Danes unfortunate enough to suffer pre-war capture was a young Danish seaman, Jens Krog, who, though a simple and unlearned youth, produced a remarkable journal of 180 closely written pages; meticulously kept throughout a long imprisonment which took him on board six different prison hulks. A non-smoking, non-gambling young man of calm disposition, with deep feelings on the subjects of fairness, honour and patriotism, his fellow captives would probably have regarded him as something of a sobersides. It seems he never once contemplated the possibility of escape, and would have been horrified at the thought of obtaining rapid and dishonourable release by volunteering to serve in the British naval or merchant marine.

A 'fly-on the-wall' diarist, Krog recorded details of the restricted world around him in an objective manner, seldom mentioning personal details and using the personal pronoun 'I' only a couple of times throughout the whole manuscript. He counted, and resented, each and every day of his captivity, finally recording that he had been away from home for 'seven years, six months and nineteen days' of which he had spent '6 years, 5 months and 22 days as a prisoner of war… during which time I was not thought worthy of putting my feet on dry ground.'

Jens Christian Hansen Krog was born at Kolding on the fjord of that name, in 1787. In the late summer of 1807 he sailed as a deck-hand on a Danish brig, *De Tre Brodre* (*The Three Brothers*), which was commanded by his uncle, Captain Christian Krog.

The Three Brothers was bound for Oporto, carrying a cargo of flax; but in the Channel she was stopped and boarded by an English privateer, the *Lion*. This took place on the 28th August, 1807, and although Admiral Gambier's fleet was deployed and ready for the attack on Copenhagen by that date, and many of our land forces were already ashore, the bombardment did not commence until the 2nd September – and the Danes did not declare war on Britain until nearly ten weeks later.

The brig, with its officers and crew, was brought into Plymouth on the following day and added to the growing number of seized merchant ships which were anchored in the eastern harbour. Jens Krog tells us that, like all the other vessels, they had to fly what he called the 'King's Mark' at their masthead, as a sign that they were embargoed; the 'King's Mark' being an ensign displaying the emblem of a 'fouled anchor' (where the anchor chains are wrapped round the anchor itself). Each hostaged vessel was also allocated a number, which was painted prominently on its bows. When Krog arrived his ship was given the number 20: by the beginning of October, he noted, the number of Danish and Norwegian merchant vessels held at Plymouth had risen to 203.

Scandinavian ships in other British ports were similarly held; so, country-wide, it has been estimated that 335 vessels were detained, their interned ships' companies anxiously awaiting news of their probable fate from their Consul-General in England, Jens Wolff.

They had not long to wait. Denmark declared war on the 4th November, and the Danish 'détenus' then faced a sterner type of detention. These probably illegally-held men were, from that date, retrospectively and unfairly classed as prisoners of war. Even the British Government itself seemed unsure of that classification and these early prisoners suffered from that indecision. Denmark maintained that such a seizure of ships and men was contrary to international law, and the argument went on and on for many years, during which time the unfortunates remained on the hulks as 'remand' prisoners.

A great number of prisoners, later legitimately captured after the declaration of war, were included in exchange cartels over the years; but, despite international pleas and counter arguments, many of those many hundreds of unfairly-taken merchant sailors were never granted the privilege of exchange, because of the ambiguity of their position as captives – the innocent and unwarlike victims of diplomatic arguments left unresolved.

The long job of emptying the detained Danish merchant ships and re-categorising their inmates from hostages to prisoners of war, began on the 12th November. They were first sent to 'Receiving Ships' which were usually hulks adapted for the purpose – or 'stone frigates' (shore based centres) – where they faced a lengthy process which involved the recording of minute personal details of every man, before he was allocated to one or another type of imprisonment.

Officers of the rank of Captain and First Mate were usually granted the privilege and advantages of parole, as were civilian passengers, supercargoes and merchant representatives. All naval and military officers were allowed a servant to share their parole, as were some, but not all, merchant captains and chief officers. These servants were usually young boys, of which there was a great number in many of our prisoner of war depots – some as young as ten or eleven years of age. These were lads who had served in a similar capacity on their own ships; but doubled up as powder-monkeys to serve the guns on naval vessels, or to act as prize crews in the case of privateers.

Captain Christian Krog, the uncle of the diarist Jens, was paroled to Reading, and his detention was comparatively short-lived. On the 5th October, 1809, all the Danish parolees in Reading, about two hundred in number, were released by an amnesty which was part of the celebrations of the 50th Jubilee of George III's reign. But the ordinary prisoners were not so lucky; being at first distributed between a number of the Hamoaze-based prison ships, but after September 1809, all the Plymouth Danes were confined on board the Superintendent's hulk, *La Brave*. The Superintendent of HMS Prisons and Prison Ships at Plymouth was, at that time, Captain Richard Matson and the *Brave* had been specially fitted out to cope not only with 700 or more prisoners, but to house the Superintendent, his staff, family and servants – plus the ship's company and garrison.

It was not until the 16th December that Jens Krog and his shipmates were processed, condemned to the hulks, and sent to HM Prison Ship *Prince*, moored on the Hamoaze at Plymouth. Jens noted in his diary on that first day:

'16th December 1807. In the morning, at the break of dawn, we were taken from our Danish ships and brought aboard the three-decker, The *Prince*, lying in the dock and we were Prisoners of War. How long it is going to last God only knows'.

It would be superfluous to record Krog's description of the general layout of the hulks in any detail, as this has been dealt with in previous chapters: Garneray, Greenhand, Waterhouse, Bonnefoux, and others have all supplied written descriptions and some artistic depictions of the manner in which old warships had been stripped down and converted into grim prisons. Nevertheless, the Danish hulk-portraits reveal items of interest generally omitted in such works by other prisoner-artists.

A number of the French memoirists mention a gallery, a few feet above water-line, which was patrolled day and night by sentinels, but I have yet to see this gallery featured in a French or English drawing or painting – including Garneray's own canvases and drawings. This omission is somewhat puzzling, for it appears in more than one of the Danish works. The colourful little drawing of the *Samson* at Chatham, with its fluttering flags and washing hanging out to dry, clearly shows railed galleries, and platforms extending a number of feet beyond bow and stern, each with its red-coated armed guard. That same picture and others also depict screened raft-like landing-stages chained to the hulk's side, into which a stairway from the upper deck descends: some also show derricks for hoisting supplies and water-casks aboard, and one or two show canvas cylinders which doubtless descended as air-vents to the decks below, a luxury denied to most early hulks.

The old three-decker Plymouth hulk, *Prince*, once a 98-gun ship-of-the-line, to which Jens Krog and the crew of the *Tre Brodre* were first sent, was employed for only a short time as a prison ship. It entered the service at the end of 1807 – so Krog and his shipmates, arriving on the 16th December, must have been amongst the earliest of its customers. They were, therefore, spared the horror of the many whose first experience of captivity was the overcrowded, filthy and often disease-ridden interior of a long-established floating prison.

By the end of January the number of prisoners on board, not all of them Danish, had risen to 980, but was reduced to 780 within a few weeks. At that time the Hamoaze prison fleet would have housed about 6,500 captives, and the British hulks' officers, ships' companies, guards and supernumeraries, would have totalled at least another thousand. After less than three months, on the 7th March, 1808, the Danes were transferred to the *Panther*, where they were to stay until April of the following year. The *Prince* itself, however, was decommissioned a month later, in April 1808, and so disappears from our story.

Jens Rasmussen, who was sent to the *Panther* in February, found that he had arrived at an unfortunate time. There was a clamp-down on all prisoner of war privileges, the commandant acting in an autocratic manner; enforcing every petty restriction, forbidding outgoing mail and destroying incoming letters. Rasmussen, who was almost certainly guilty of exaggeration regarding the destruction of mail, was of the opinion that the iron-fist strictness was the result of some Danish military success at that time, for he admitted that, by the time Jens Krog arrived a month later, that same commander was a changed man, allowing all the freedoms within his power.

Over the following years, Jens and his fellow captives were to experience many changes of prison ship location. On the 24th April, 1809, they were put aboard the Superintendent's hulk, the *Brave*, but for only four months, until the 3rd September. Those four months must have been hard to bear: Krog says:

'It will soon be so filled with men here that it will become impossible to stand. Already it is so uncomfortable that everybody is trying to shove everyone else out of the way. And not everyone can find space for his hammock and has to sleep on the sea-chests ranged along the sides of the deck. If we have to live like this, many will become ill through the unhealthy smells that are created among so many people in such a small space.
'We were over 900 men. So it was a very welcomed thing when we were moved to the *Bienfaisant*, where a detached group of 200 of us were shown a place on the upper deck, where there was quite a lot of space, light and fresh air.'

The Danish occupation of the upper deck of the *Bienfaisant*, was only achieved by the French being officially committed to the dark, miserable depths of the lower deck. The northerners, however, were to enjoy the luxury of light and fresh air for only a short period; after which they were returned to the *Brave*. By that time, Captain Richard Matson had been succeeded by Captain Edward Hawkins, and we know that the new Superintendent of the Plymouth Prisons and Hulks held a sympathetic appreciation of the ambiguous situation of the Danes who had been detained pre-war on merchant vessels. He made many allowances because of their predicament, and it was he who permitted a small stage to be constructed on the *Brave*.

Even so, Krog, tells of a dispensation, the like of which I have not discovered elsewhere; the creation of an, at least verbal, 'lower-deck parole of honour':

'23rd May, 1810. Today two men went ashore and when in the afternoon they came back, the Captain promised that, as they returned without making any attempt to escape, two people each day would be given permission to go ashore, if the weather permitted.'

However, it could not be expected that all Danes – or any other group of captive men – would have proved unselfish enough to resist the temptation, and some did escape, to the detriment of the remainder; thus ending a humane gesture from a compassionate – though when deserved, tough – commander.

Captain Edward Hawkins was a shining example of everything a great governor of prisoners should be. Tough enough to deal with the most mutinous of uprisings, and at the same time appreciating why men should rebel against the restrictions of captivity. We have read of commanders of individual hulks whose ineptitude – and sometimes drunkenness – deservedly brought trouble on their heads, but Edward Hawkins had more than just one hulk to oversee and control. Besides the *Brave* and eleven other hulks, he was also Superintendent of HM Prisoner of War Depots ashore at Plymouth, including Mill Prison, which sometimes housed as many as five thousand captives. The many thousands of prisoners on the Plymouth hulks came from at least a dozen different countries and not all were as easy to handle as the Danes.

That Captain Hawkins' fairness was appreciated is shown by the fact that, in December 1810, a group of Danish merchant captains and chief officers (who had been on the *Brave* before transfer to a parole town) presented him with a three-piece silver tea-service, each piece engraved with the legend, in Danish and English: 'Humanity softens the Miseries of War – *Mennefkierlighed lindrer Krigens Ulkker*'. The base of the tea pot was engraved with the personal inscription:

> 'To Captn. Edward Hawkins of the British Navy. This small mark of
> Esteem and Gratitude, Sentiments universally produced by his
> disinterested kindness towards the Danish Prisoners under his Care
> is respectfully presented by a few of their Countrymen.
>
> London. November 1810.'

Jens Krog's second period on the *Brave* lasted for almost two years, then, on the 5th January, 1812, an Order from the Transport Office directed that all the Danes were to be removed from Plymouth. Crowded into the lower deck of the transport ship, *Diamond*, to be dispatched on the week-long voyage to the prison fleet at Chatham, the prisoners were without hammocks and were expected to sleep on what they called 'plank-beds'– six men to a plank.[5] Spending even the daytime in semi-darkness, the only light filtering through the few unbattened but grilled gun-ports, conditions were almost unbearable; and they counted themselves lucky when an outbreak of fever made it necessary to clear the ship and transfer them to another vessel. Their next transport was a frigate, the *St Fiorenza*, where they were still stowed below but were allowed refreshing periods on the upper deck during the daylight hours.

In 1807, there were eleven prison hulks at Plymouth, plus the hospital ship *LE CATON*. They were:

LA BRAVE	*EL FIRME*	*SAN YSIDRO*
SAN NICHOLAS	*GENEREUX*	*HECTOR*
L'OISEAU	*BIENFAISANT*	*EUROPE*
PANTHER	*PRINCE*	

Over the next five years Jens Krog was to experience imprisonment on four of the Plymouth hulks already mentioned, plus two more after being transferred to hulks in the prison fleet at Chatham in 1812, where he was doomed to wait out the rest of the war. A great number, perhaps the majority, of the eight thousand or so Danish and Norwegian prisoners of war taken over the following seven years, would have experienced, if only for a short period, the unpleasantness of our floating prisons. Many of their officers were housed on prison ships before being sent to the open prison of one of the English parole-towns[6] – and by 1812 all the Danish occupants of land depots, including those who had been confined at Greenlaw in Scotland and the English depots, were concentrated in the Medway hulks.

One much captured Danish officer who recorded his memories of the hulks was a young lieutenant, later to become an Admiral, named Hans Birch Dahlerup, whose wartime experiences as a prisoner are dealt with at greater length in the chapter dealing with parole and the parole-towns. Dahlerup was thrice-paroled to Reading, in 1808, 1810 and 1813, but each time he, and other officers like him, had to spend a short period in a prison ship whilst the official documents for their *parole d'honneur* were being prepared.

Lieutenant Dahlerup was a lad of eighteen years when his ship, Denmark's last ship-of-the-line, the *Prinds Christian Frederik*, surrendered in March 1808. Years later he still had vivid memories of the first sight and approach to the *Bahama*, recalling that, 'as we came closer, we all started to shiver' as they neared the heavily barred gun-ports, through which the French down-and-outs, 'dressed like galley slaves, put out their arms towards us… their look was wild and some were even naked to the waist'.

Jens Rasmussen, an able-seaman who, like Hans Dahlerup, was captured when the *Prinds Christian Frederik* was taken, also wrote, in a manner common to just about all prisoner of war accounts; of his first impression of his prison hulk, of his shock at the sight of the French deadbeat, verminous long-haired, ragged, hollow-cheeked wild-men, who rushed to plead for bread from the newcomers. And, of course, Rasmussen, as a crew member, would have had a longer and closer contact with everyday life on the hulk than his lieutenant.

Lieutenant Dahlerup, an officer and therefore presumed a gentleman, would never have to suffer direct contact with the French 'wild-men' – or, for that matter, his own well-behaved captive fellow-countrymen – unless he broke his parole of honour. He wrote of his first spell on the *Bahama*:

> 'We officers who had to wait here on board for the arrival of our
> passports from London [parole documents], so that we could travel
> to Reading which was to be our place of parole, were treated very
> politely, and shown an empty room under the quarter-deck, where
> later some chairs were supplied; and for the night we were each
> given a mattress and a blanket on the floor.'

On the occasions of his second and third temporary confinements to that hulk over the next five years, he was quartered in the *Bahama*'s hospital, which he describes as:

> 'A room on the lower gun deck, which was sheltered off with very
> strong and double thickness timbers, and occupied almost half of the
> length and breadth of the lower gun deck.
> 'It was very roomy and airy; but, unfortunately, it was filled up with
> very sick people, most of them suffering from consumption, from
> which several died near me.'

He conjectured that many of them died through a combination of sorrow, boredom, home-sickness and hopelessness; that a number had spent what might have been the best years of their lives in idleness, without work or even fighting to maintain their spirits.

Another Scandinavian occupant of the *Bahama* was a Norwegian ship's pilot named Schow, who had already been a prisoner of war in the East Indies for two years before reaching Chatham. Although an experienced captive who had known the discomfort of dirty, unhealthy, overseas depots, he was still astounded at the below-decks filth and vermin of the English prison hulk. He, like so many others, told of the foetid atmosphere that struck him as he descended into the dark lower-deck where he must compete for a resting place. Hammocks were slung so close together that it was impossible to pass through without stooping and, in places where they hung two-deep, only by crawling on hands and knees.

All manner and classes of men were herded together into these crowded hulks: from children and youngsters to old and seasoned naval and merchant sailors; soldiers, privateersmen, 'broke-parole' officers – and non-combatants, who spent years in this worst type of prison, for no other reason than the misfortune of being swept up in the general confusion of war.

The expense of guarding, feeding and clothing many of these prisoners must have been more harmful to Britain than release could ever have been. The name of one such unprofitably and unnecessarily held prisoner of war is remembered to this day in Norway and Denmark by almost everyone, as a national hero – immortalised by Henrik Ibsen in his epic poem, 'Terje Vigen'.

The real-life Terje Vigen was a Norwegian[7] who lived on Fjaere, a desolate spot on the south coast of Norway, near Grimstad. He was a born sailor who, as a youth, lived a rip-roaring sailor's life of voyages and adventure, carousal and wenching, when he and his shipmates hit the shore with money in their pockets.

After falling in love and marrying a local girl, he continued his seafaring – and some of his old wayward habits – until, on his return from one voyage, he found he was the father of a baby daughter, Anna. It was said that, from that moment, the devil-may-care Terje became sober and responsible, gave up his beloved long sea voyages, and settled down to life as a hard-working local seaman and family man.

This change in his circumstances came about at the time of the attack on Copenhagen which brought about the war which then brought the British blockades which cut off supplies of food to Norway. Things got worse and worse until, by 1809, the situation was desperate:

'The tale's still told of what people bore,
where want and distress combine.
Cruisers from England blockaded each port,
on land there was dearth far and wide;
The poor people starved, and the wealthy went short,
two powerful arms were no longer support
Where death and disease ruled outside.'

Terje was determined that his little family should not starve and decided to set out for Denmark, where he might obtain corn and provisions. A courageous and powerful man, he chose – as the verse which heads this chapter tells us – to row to Denmark in a small open dory: a flat-bottomed, high-sided, fishing boat. This meant a dangerous crossing of the Skagerrak to Fladstrand, near Skagen at the tip of Denmark:

'Then trusting to Fortune's grace profound
he smartly took to the oars,
At Fladstrand, reaching there safe and sound
he gathered his precious stores.'

After loading his 'precious stores' – just three casks of barley – Vigen set out to face the torturous effort of rowing back to Norway and his hungry family: 'He slaved on the thwart for three nights and days, this brave and powerful man,' and on 'the fourth, at dawn, by the sun's first rays, a blurred, misty view he could scan'. He was within sight of home; but, as he thanked God for his success, he saw that an English warship lay in Hesnes Sound.

Ibsen, with a poet's licence, said that 'it was Lyngor happening once more': Lyngor is a harbour north of Grimstad, near Terej's home town, where Norway's last frigate was destroyed by British warships – but that was three years later, in 1812. And this time the prize was just a small rowing boat, powered by one exhausted civilian oarsman. Terje Vigen was captured and watched as his boat was stove in and sank with its pathetic but invaluable freight beneath the waves.

Terje Vigen was taken to Chatham, where he spent the next five miserable years on a prison hulk. He was released at the war's end, in 1814, 'his shoulders rounded, his hair turned grey', and returned to Norway with other Norwegian prisoners on a Swedish cartel ship – to find that his wife and daughter were dead, and were buried in a pauper's grave.

In after years, Terje became a renowned local pilot, guiding vessels through the treacherous waters near his home with a skill which increased the widespread fame which his tragic personal wartime story had already brought him.

A story is told, apocryphal, I fear – although I would not like to express my doubts to any Norwegian or Dane bigger than myself – that one day he encountered a small English yacht in distress, its occupants in mortal danger. On board were an English lord, his wife and infant daughter. This brought memories of his own dead wife and little Anna, and the long years he had spent in English prison ships, flooding back into Terje's mind. (the poet says that the lord was that same officer who had captured Terje Vigen and sent his precious 'barleycorn casks' to the bottom, so many years before!).

At first he saw this as divine vengeance for all the sufferings that had been so unfairly thrust upon him; but after much soul-searching, he overcame his longing for revenge and brought them safely to the shore.

Henrik Ibsen met Terje many years later, at the time he was writing his famous poem, and described him as a white-headed, 'remarkably grizzled', but high-spirited and greatly respected old man. It is said that a tombstone still marks his grave on Fjaere.

'In Fjaere Churchyard I saw a plot
that lay in a weathered sward;
It looked all neglected, a mean, sunken spot,
but kept still its blackened board.
It read "Thaerie Wiighen" in white, the date
his final repose had been.
He lay to the sun and the winds' keen weight,
and that's why the grass was so stubborn-straight
But with wild field-flowers in between.'

By the end of 1808 the prisoners began to receive a Danish State allowance, which was a great boon, and the Copenhagen newspapers were able to report that: 'this help from the Mother Country has been received by the prisoners, and has saved many of them from taking a drastic step.' This ambiguous statement could have been taken as referring to suicide, or perhaps taking the dangerous risk of an escape attempt; but I feel sure that it meant something far more serious than either of those options – the possibility that they might enter the British armed forces.

The allowances varied according to rank. Officers who had not taken, or not been offered, their parole, received six pence per day and the ordinary prisoner got twopence. The paroled officers did much better: naval officers, 4/-; skippers and chief mates, 9d; servants and boys, 6d.

This strengthening of Danish buying power would have been much envied by the French; but was received with gratitude tinged with dissatisfaction by the Danes. An entry in Krog's diary for the 26th September, 1809, includes a copy of a letter addressed to the King of Denmark which regrets that, whilst they want to express their gratitude, they regret that they cannot thank him as much as they would wish, as the captains and chief officers, who already live more comfortably on the hulk than themselves, were given an allowance three times that of the ordinary prisoner.

A similar letter, or petition, was written on the *Bahama* at Chatham, and signed by hundreds of prisoners. Neither reached the king, but a reply came from their Consul-General, Jens Wollf, which told them in effect, that if they were dissatisfied the inequality could soon be levelled by stopping all allowances! There were other occasions when the fact that sums of money were donated for the benefit of specific groups of prisoners, caused minor riots. In both land prison and prison ship memoirs there is mention of sums of money being directed towards the 'the deserving poor'. Captain Kaald at Greenlaw near Edinburgh and Krog on the *Brave* tell of the fury which such directives aroused, resulting in the money being snatched and distributed equally. No doubt this apparently mean-minded reaction came from the knowledge that many of the pitied among the hard-up prisoners had become the 'deserving poor' through gambling and profligacy.

Apart from the State allowances, Jens Wollf in London and Pastor Rosing in London and Copenhagen, worked hard for the captives, setting up a fund built from subscriptions donated by the public, ship-owners and businessmen. The kitty was distributed whenever it amounted to £200, (4,000 shillings[8]), thus an estimated two thousand prisoners would each receive a hand-out of two-shillings periodically. Apart from church collections, each ship under the Danish Flag was asked to contribute one or two pounds according to their ability to do so, and there were other unusual sources of income. Paroled Norwegian officers bought tobacco, shirts and other clothing for distribution to closed-prison inmates, but only to Norwegians – as the Danish officers had similarly wished to look after their Danish own.

Another method of adding to the fund comes as a surprise: examples of that rarity, Danish Prisoner of war work, were shipped to Denmark for sale – which is at odds with Benjamin Waterhouse's generalisation of the 'thick-skulled plodding Dane' making primitive artefacts and, in at least one instance, was wide of the mark when he described the 'most ingenious making a clumsy ship'.

On the 30th March, 1810, the Danish newspapers announced that a bone model of a three-decker, 106-gun warship was to be put on exhibition, and later sold, in aid of the prisoners of war in England. Admission tickets were 48 Danish shillings each, and there would be a number of other specimens of Danish prisoner of war work on view and on sale.

The model had been made at Greenlaw Depot, in Scotland, and purchased in the prison market by Andreas Feldborg, a man who did much for the relief of his prisoner of war fellow countrymen. The exhibition raised some 3,000 Rix Dollars and the ship model was later featured in further fund-raising efforts.

In 1811 a specially commissioned ballet was staged in Copenhagen in aid of the captive Danes and Norwegian captives in Britain. It was a great success and ended with the playwright Hans Kristian Knudsen coming on to the stage carrying that same prison-made model ship.[9]

A number of Danish-Norwegian authors and some historians have written on the subject of their war with Britain. The Norwegian author, Constantin Flod, in his book *Under Kaperflag* ('Under Captured Flag?') which was published towards the end of the nineteenth century, included a good deal of information regarding the life of the Northern prisoner of war, gathered from memoirs and official records.

But the first Dane to put a prison ship memoir into print was Neils Martin Neilsen, a young ordinary seaman, who published his little book in Copenhagen in 1821. His vessel was taken in the English Channel very early in September 1807; no doubt detained under the Embargo Act which came down heavily on neutrals dealing with our enemies' ports – and he would not have known of British action against Copenhagen at that date. As we know, many merchant sailors so taken were persuaded to serve on British ships,

so when Neils and a number of his countrymen soon found themselves in London, they legitimately signed on to a British ship being fitted out for a voyage to China.

Soon after, when he discovered that war had been declared, he made the courageous decision to inform his captors that he could not serve against his country's enemy, and would rather be put aboard a prison ship if, in spite of the fact that he was captured before the war, they would not grant him his freedom.

He was taken at his word and was given no other choice than the prison ship; but before he was delivered to his floating prison, he made his escape and managed to join a Norwegian merchantman.

Captured for a second time he was sent to the prison hulk, *Buckingham*, at Chatham. Neilsen suffered the shock common to all prisoners of war on their first close-up contact with a hulk, particularly if their future place of confinement proved to be a well-established prison ship of mixed inmates, where all the dirt and evils had had ample time to develop and mature. 'The sight of the ship where so many of my unhappy brothers stood in their prison clothes and looked through the iron grids on us, distressed my heart…'

But that was just the outside. Had it been possible for him to see an article published in *The Times* on the 16th December, 1807, at almost exactly the same time that Neilsen was being introduced to the hulk mentioned, he would have been forewarned of what to expect within. It said that a delivery of French prisoners [of the losing-gambler down-and-out class] transferred from Norman Cross to Chatham, had arrived 'semi-starved and almost naked, having lost their rations and food through gambling'. That their condition was hardly likely to improve on the *Buckingham* is clear, for *The Times* went on to say: 'On board the *Buckingham*, where there are nearly six hundred prisoners, are a billiard table, hazard tables, &c; and the prisoners indulge themselves to play…'

Neils Neilsen may have been the first to publish his memories of the hulks, but the 'Journal' kept by Jens Krog is unique in its detailed unsensationalised observations of prison ship life on the Plymouth and Chatham hulks. About fifty years ago a descendant, Carl Roos, published *Prisonen, Danske og Norske Krigsfanger i England 1807–1814*[10], which was built round Krog's journal, supplemented with quotes from Garneray and others. Considering the conditions under which they were written, the one hundred and eighty pages of Jens Krog's original 'Journal' are remarkable examples of beautifully controlled penmanship. Carl Roos was convinced that Jens first made diary notes from which he composed his 'Journal', but was equally certain that the final work was carried out on board the hulks. This is borne out by the fact that it was written on stout English writing paper, watermarked 'R.T.1807' (Rose & Turner 1807) with a title page which (translated) reads:

Plymouth
Journal
kept on board the Prison Ships
Panther & Bienfaisant

& Brave & Prince.
Chatham
H.M.Prison Ship **Nassau**, *Fyen*
On the reverse of the title page Krog inscribed:
'*This book has been written to pass the time in my long, boring, idle hours, by me*, J.C.Krog.'

Surprisingly, another Danish prison ship journal has survived, much of which was written at that same time, using Krog's work as its model. The writer was a young sailor, H.S.Engels, who shared the last two years of his captivity with Jens Krog, first on the prison ship *Nassau* and then the *Fyen.* They also shared some of the entries in their journals.

Engels, who came from an island in the Baltic, was captured when his ship, the *Lille Sophie,* was taken off Cadiz on 22nd October, 1807. After a short spell of imprisonment at Gibraltar, he was brought to the hulks at Plymouth, where he stayed until January 1812, when he was moved to Chatham and the *Nassau* hulk. His journal is a much smaller work than Krog's, consisting as it does of no more than fifty pages. It is obvious that they must have become close friends, for copies of petitions to the Prisoners' Agent, news items and quotations from English newspapers, are to be found in both journals, almost word for word, containing the same misspellings and mis-translations. Engel's journal adds little that Krog does not already tell us – and towards the end he dwelt mainly on the details of his own failing health.

Jens Krog patiently kept a day-by-day account of all that went on around him: the behaviour of both prisoners and the British guards and sailors. At first he has an unshakeable confidence that their release will come about through French-Danish victory; satisfied that every bit of news obtained through Danish sources is as true and reliable as British news reports and rumours were sure to be false.

It would seem that the Scandinavians had less difficulty in obtaining contact with the outside world through English and foreign newspapers than captives of other nationalities. Throughout his journal Krog quotes extracts and sometimes whole articles from the English and foreign press. Amongst entries for 1808, there are news items culled from six-week-old Norwegian periodicals and, from then on, fairly regular reports of happenings on the Continent, passed on by the Agent and other visitors to the prison ships; or – and to be taken with a pinch of salt – culled from our English newspapers and magazines.

However, the chosen subject matter of these extracts was not always concerned with the progress of the war. Some items would no doubt have entertained his fellow captives; such as the story of the English military man who sold his wife in the market place for five shillings and a pint of gin; of blacks who captured an American ship and ate its crew; of riots in London and Manchester and an attack on the Prince of Wales; of the assassination of the Premier, Spencer Percival, and choice snippets of scandal in high society – but the entries which gave Krog most joy were any which told of even the slightest success over the English.

Louis Garneray had earned a few sous from his French comrades by translating newspapers which had been smuggled aboard the hulks at Portsmouth; but it would appear that smuggling was unnecessary in the case of the Danes. At first the papers had been obtained through the good offices of the hulk's baker, but after April 1811, newspapers and magazines were delivered to the hulk every Saturday – as the prisoners had taken out subscriptions direct!

When in the summer of 1813, at a time when Denmark was in a state of bankruptcy, the allowances were temporarily halted, the news-hungry among the prisoners sold their salt-herring rations in order to renew their subscriptions. Of course there was news which saddened as well as some that cheered, but Jens Krog was not convinced that the war could be lost until almost the end.

After 1809, there was also what might be called a small 'circulating library' for the Danes and Norwegians. No doubt Pastor Rosing had a hand in its institution. 'Library officers' were paid a monthly fee to ensure that the valued books were not mishandled and did not go astray: collecting them in to re-circulate every eight days, and later to exchange with other hulks. The books were bought from Danish funds, contributed by Copenhagen bookshops, or donated by the public. As they were at first mainly history books, naturally politically slanted towards the North, with titles like, *The Occupation of Copenhagen* and *The Bombing of Copenhagen,* the British authorities must be given some credit for allowing its rules to be bent to admit such works on board – for even letters to and from the prisoners were subject to censorship. Later there was a wider range of subject matter and ordinary school books were sent in for the instruction of the youngsters on board.

If the latter contained some of the song books included in the normal Danish school curriculum, we were certainly allowing the importation of anti-English propaganda. Between 1801 and 1807 books of specially composed patriotic songs had been issued to schools which depicted the British as cruel robbers and marauders of the worst possible type. But, as the British prisoner of war, James Macdonald, found in Jutland, despite the Danish Government propaganda of hate for the enemy, there was little evidence of its effectiveness towards himself or his fellow prisoners. And in this country, Dahlerup, Jorgensen, and other parolees at Reading tell of strict Government restrictions, the breaking of which could bring a reward of one guinea to the informant, but which were seldom enforced, the rewards never claimed.

It was, however, very different for men like Jens Krog, whose only contact with Britons was through bum-boats or uniformed representatives of the Government, working to strict orders. This was also true of prisoners in the closed land depots – except for the comparative few who came in contact with the public through their prisoner of war work stalls in the prison markets. Krog felt that the indifference to the type of books included in their library, as well as other dispensations and tolerances, were merely further evidence of British arrogance and conviction of its invincibility!

No doubt the captive captains and other officers on the hulks would have kept an eye on the young boys who had been members of their crews, may have helped to instruct them in maritime matters, or even have employed them as servants. But there were so many young Danish lads under fourteen years of age on board the prison ships, that it was the older prisoners themselves who put it to the Agent that a well-organised school would be a blessing. The authorities caught on with enthusiasm, and were keen for all youngsters to receive something of an education – whether they liked it or not!

The result was that a letter from Pastor Rosing in London arrived, addressed to all the Danish and Norwegian prisoners in Plymouth:

'Dear Fellow Countrymen,
In this, the poor conditions you have had to suffer for so long, no doubt it must be pleasant to hear that the very young people among you have the chance to occupy themselves with learning, to get to know their God and grow up as educated human beings. The means to implement this are near at hand; one of your fellow prisoners has volunteered to teach these young people, and we are lacking nothing except classroom space.

'I shall be very surprised if you are not willing to contribute a small amount of space for this purpose. You can imagine the benefit these young people will derive if kept busy studying, instead of sitting around in boring idleness.

'If you are conscious of all the efforts your King and Country are making on your behalf, you will realize that it is your duty to make this contribution for the good of the young. The school will be open for two hours a day, and when that time has elapsed, those who have contributed must be allowed to return to their space.

'If it cannot be decided where this school should be sited, let Fate decide, by spinning a coin. I trust that this small request will not be in vain,

Your Fellow-Countryman

London. 3rd August 1810   U.R. ROSING'

The school opened for the first time on the *Brave* on the 13th August, and became a great success. A blackboard, paper, pens, candles and books were bought with Danish funds, and there were soon a number of additional instructors, who were each to receive £1 a month. The main subjects taught were, religious instruction, history, mathematics and, of particular interest, English both written and spoken. Papers were marked, and there were regular examinations and prize-giving days; but boys will be boys, and so there were some truants. To some the idea of school on a hulk must have seemed like a second imprisonment, but they were not permitted to dodge unpunished. At the beginning of 1811, a notice was posted up on the ship which said that many young boys were not turning up for their religious education and in so doing they were letting down not only themselves but the good Pastor Rosing. Therefore it was now proclaimed that any boy who did not turn up for lessons, would forfeit his bread ration for that day, and that bread would be given to those who studied and worked hard. The notice ended with the teachers saying that they hoped this drastic measure would help them to realise where their duty lay.

We know that most hulks and all land prisons had always had their 'professors', who charged a small fee to instruct adult prisoners in all manner of arts, sciences and skills. The French were particularly keen on fencing and dancing; the Americans on a variety of subjects, including boxing; and the Danish prison ships at both Plymouth and Chatham also had their 'professors'. Hans Moller, a prisoner on the *Brave*, was encouraged by Pastor Rosing to set himself up as instructor on navigation, sending him a copy of a book on the subject, published in 1781, called *Skatkammer eller Sturmande-kunst,* by Christian Carl Lous, the standard work taught in the Naval Academy in Copenhagen.

The shortage of such books was a bugbear, overcome to a great extent by making handwritten copies of the complete works. Some beautifully executed examples of this self-help and dedication to learning under adverse circumstance, are still preserved in Danish museums. One particularly fine example of this rare and unusual type of prisoner of war work, was executed by a seventeen year old youth, Ditley Friedrich Grube, who was a prisoner on the *Irresistible* at Chatham between 1807 and 1809, and is based on Lous's *Skatkammer*.

One outstanding 'professor' of navigation on the *Bahama* at Chatham, was Sven Torstensen, who is said to have trained over two hundred students in the art during his time on the hulk; and was so valued for his work that his wage was five times the usual one pound a month. Hans Dahlerup, recalling one of his short stays as a prisoner on the *Bahama*, wrote: 'In the morning, when the lower gun-deck had been aired, small tables or benches were dragged to the open gun-ports and prisoners, young and old, occupied themselves with their books and papers. Quite a number of captains and mates passed their time, and made some money, as teachers of

writing, language and other subjects.'

The prisoners dressed according to their means, which covered a wide range from comparative prosperity to poverty; the optimists among them probably keeping their best clothing carefully tucked away in the hope of early release, and making do with a mixture of the detested prison clothes and civilian everyday wear.

The issued 'slops' – or clothing – varied little over the years of the Napoleonic Wars and nor did the prisoners' opinion of it. Whichever nationality mentioned prison garb, it was described with disgust as 'hideous' and 'stigmatising' in appearance, and usually of the poorest quality that the contractors could get away with.

It was laid down that the basic issue was to be a coat, waistcoat, breeches, a pair of stockings, two shirts, a woollen cap, a neckerchief and a pair of shoes. These items were to be renewed every eighteen months – at least, that was their allowance on paper: in fact, some never received a complete kit in the first place, whilst others went years without replacement.

The Scandinavians would have been provided with much the same gear as that described in previous chapters by French and Americans, with occasional slight variations. Neilsen, Federspiel and Krog, spoke of bright yellow jackets and trousers marked with T.O. in black below a broad-arrow mark, the latter a symbol which once marked all convict clothing and Government stores. This emblem worried Neilsen at first because he had heard said that the broad-arrow was used to indicate ships or goods which had been condemned! and Federspiel thought that the T.O. signified an English term meaning 'taken out [of action]' but of course it was really just the initial letters of 'Transport Office'

Whilst yellow or orange was the usual colour, I have read of issues of grey coats and breeches to some ships and depots, and of red waistcoats and striped shirts, Neilsen says that they were given wooden shoes, but these were nothing like Dutch clogs; the American Charles Andrews called them 'list' shoes, one-and-a-half inch thick wooden soles with uppers made from 'list', strips of canvas or other material. He described the cap as knitted from inch-thick stuff more like coarse rope yarn than wool. Often a whole delivery would arrive all of one size and a fit would be purely by chance.

The better-off of the officers whether on prison hulk or on parole, and anyone else who could afford bespoke tailoring, would have had no difficulty in obtaining materials; and even in the prison ships a skilled tailor was not hard to find. Nobody wore the hated 'uniform' who could possibly avoid it – we read of prisoners being fined 5/- or a few days' ration, for making long trousers or jackets out of issued hammocks – and some of the prison clothing would have been remodelled into wearable attire. Everything in the way of raw material was highly valued on a prison ship, so the hated yellow was not wasted. Some would have been contributed to re-clad the naked down-and-outs – or, like the unloved salt-herrings, would be sold back to the contractors, who would sell them again to the Government, who would re-issue them to captives… and so on, *ad infinitum.*

Much of the general facts of prisoner of war life to be found in Jens Krog's journal, we are already familiar with from late eighteenth and early nineteenth century memoirs; written by Continental and American captives, usually with far more venom and exaggeration than the fair-minded Dane would ever express. Although Krog was very positive in his hatred for his captors, he never allowed his bitterness to unbalance his level head.

Although a youngster, he understood why men should want to drink and gamble, annoy their keepers, seek revenge, and above all attempt escape. He also appreciated why the British had to maintain a strict discipline to deal with such actions. He noted – and probably preached – that the prison ship authorities did not reserve their harshness for dealing with captive offenders, but displayed an equal, or perhaps greater, degree of strictness and brutality towards their own people.

He tells of an English soldier of the guard who had violently attacked a Danish prisoner, who was put in irons and later suffered two dozen strokes of the cat-o'-nine-tails; and of another who wounded a fellow sentry and was given the same number of lashes.

The prisoners were sent below whilst such punishments were carried out on the deck above, except in the case of one soldier who habitually returned to the hulk hopelessly intoxicated, making life unpleasant for everyone. After each drunken debauch he had been heavily flogged, but made light of the punishment. Finally, after all else failed, he was sentenced to a great number of stripes, stripped and laid over a sea-chest on the upper-deck to receive his flogging. There is a suggestion that he was beaten not only on his bare back, but also backside, for it was said that he suffered much more from embarrassment than from the strokes of the 'cat'.

During his five years of prison ship captivity, Jens Krog had plenty of escape attempts to record, and a few successes, and would have understood the sentiments of the adventurous French ex-privateer/corsair, Ambroise Louis Garneray, when he asked: 'If you shouldn't think of the possibility of escape, what else is there worth thinking about?' Whilst he understood, he considered the runaways less heroic than selfish, knowing as they did, that their success would bring down harsh restrictions on those left behind. Krog was not sorry when bully-boys who sought personal glory by playing useless tricks on the British – even on good commanders like Edward Hawkins – were caught and punished, or were undetected and their shipmates threatened with punishment if they were not exposed; yet he despised anyone who informed, however despicable the offenders. Informing was to him a deadly sin. Although himself a teetotaller, with a regard for the French only slightly higher than he held for the English, he was disgusted when a Dane betrayed a group of French prisoners who had organised the smuggling of booze into the hulk, and was pleased to see the informer sentenced by the prisoners' own court.

These internal, prisoner-run courts were as much to be feared as British justice. Krog tells of a whole range of punishments, from freezing out of prisoner society – being 'sent to Coventry' – to fines and heavy floggings. Extreme cases of uncleanliness were dealt with practically, by stripping and painful scrubbings. Three men on the *Panther* in 1808, were so dirty and lice-ridden that they were stripped, their clothes destroyed, their hair shaved off, their bodies scrubbed; after which they were given twelve cuts of the 'cat'. Whilst drubbings and floggings were the most usual sentences for theft, humiliation was used as an addition punishment if food was involved. A man who stole bread had his hands strapped behind him, the bread fixed to his back, a placard on his chest stating his crime, then led by a halter through the jeering prisoners on the gun-deck. With nowhere to hide in the closed world of the prison hulk, such a punishment must have had a long-lasting effect.

Jens Krog spent the last two years as a prisoner at Chatham, first on the *Nassau* then the *Fyen*. The natural bitterness of captivity was added to by the fact that both those hulks had once been Danish men-of-war. The *Nassau* had in fact been the *Holstein*, the only Danish ship-of-the-line to be brought back to England after the first bombardment of Copenhagen in 1801, and the *Fyen*, which retained her own name, was a 74-gun man-of-war taken in the second attack in 1807.

Towards the end of the war there was some attempt on the part of the British Government to make a distinction between Danish and Norwegian prisoners of war. As already mentioned, Norway had been united with Denmark for nearly four hundred years, but that unity was not to last much longer. The Consul reported that the Government were considering releasing all Norwegian prisoners but that they were delayed by political disturbance in their home country. Meanwhile they were transferred to a special hulk. Jens Krog tells us that 700 or more were taken out of the *Fyen* at Chatham at that time; and a letter signed by fifteen Norwegian parolees at Reading, says that 800 Norwegians held in Britain had refused to accept a British offer of release, conditional on their adoption of Swedish nationality. Nevertheless, Norway was handed over to Sweden a few months later.

On the 25th January, 1814, the prisoners were told that the war was as good as over, and that they would soon be homeward bound, but two months went by before the peace was ratified. Yet another month passed before the Danish Agent came aboard, on the 10th May, bearing the glad tidings that they really would soon be given their freedom; and amid great rejoicing and many hurrahs, the Danish Flag was hoisted beside the British Ensign. Nine days later an order was posted which proclaimed that 'any prisoner in possession of cash to the value of £2 should be freed at once.' So, at last, on the 6th June, twenty-five-years-old Jens Krog and 132 of his countrymen who could rake together the above mentioned sum regained their freedom.

After his return to Denmark, Jens Krog resumed his seafaring life, and pursued a steady-going, successful life consistent with the character he revealed throughout his diary; becoming a merchant captain and farmer (through his marriage into the family of Carl Roos). An old aunt remembered him in his later years, as a much respected old man who walked with a permanent stoop, which he said came about through five years spent on the hulks, where the hammock-hung lower gun-deck made it impossible for a man to walk upright.

He died in 1862, and one of his last wishes was that his coffin be surrounded by many coloured candle-lights – which he had brought from England on his return from captivity nearly fifty years before.

---

1. See *The Arts and Crafts of Napoleonic and American Prisoners of War 1756-1816*, Chapter 10, THE ENTERTAINERS.

2. A.S. Britt: *Wars of Napoleon.*

3. Johan Christian Federspiel: *Journal.* Roskilde. 1841.

4. Hans Schlaikier.

5. Plank-beds: these would have been like the mess-table sleeping 'shelves' on the first Civil Hulks.

6. See Chapter 21. PAROLE D'HONNEUR.

7. Danish and Norwegian prisoners were collectively classified as 'Danish' in many official prisoner of war lists. Sometimes Finns, Icelanders and Swedes were also listed under that general heading. From 1442 the two countries were united under Danish kings, until 1814, when Norway was awarded to the Swedish crown. It was not until 1905 that Norway became an independent monarchy.

8. Before decimalisation, the English pound equalled twenty shillings.

9. This treasured bone model is preserved in one of the Royal Palaces, at Rosenborg.

10. Carl Roos: *The Prison, Danish and Norwegian Prisoners of War in England 1807–1814.*

Chapter Nine

The Danes and the Battles of Copenhagen 1801 and 1807

LATE IN 1800 A CONFEDERATION OF THE NORTHERN Powers, Russia, Prussia and Sweden, met with the object of persuading – or demanding – Great Britain to give up its long-assumed right to search neutral vessels for contraband materials of war. This 'right' was universally resented, but firmly defended by its instigators – and was later to prove an important contributory cause of the war between America and Britain, 1812–1815. The Northern Powers had tried to achieve their aim for many years without success. Enforcement of the right to board and examine

their cargoes – condemning anything which Britain considered contraband – deprived them of profitable commerce with France and her allies. A coalition had been formed in 1780 which was to operate under the title of the First Armed Neutrality; but, like many treaties and coalitions between nations, it soon began to weaken

Artist unknown. The Bombardment of Copenhagen, September 1809. British Forces under the command of Admiral Gambier and Lord Cathcart.

and fall apart. By 1787 Sweden had withdrawn and six years later Russia signed a treaty which fully recognised Britain's right of search over neutral shipping.

In the first year of the new century, the Northern Coalition was provided with good reason to set up a Second Armed Neutrality, by an extreme example of British enforcement of the much disputed right. On the 25th July, 1800, the 40-gun Danish frigate *Freja*, was convoying six merchantmen, two fair sized ships, two brigs and two galliots, when she was intercepted by a small British squadron of five warships off Ostend. The squadron was commanded by Captain Thomas Baker in the 28-gun frigate, HMS *Nemesis*, who hailed the *Freja*, announcing his intention to board the convoy and search for contraband. Captain Krabbe, the Danish commander replied that any attempt to do so would be vigorously resisted; nevertheless, a boat was lowered, crewed by a Midshipman and four hands. Whether the *Nemesis* or the *Freja* was the first to fire depends on whether one quotes from the Danish or the British account, but a short but spirited action took place, which ended with the damaged *Freja* striking her colours after about twenty minutes. The British lost four men killed, two on the *Nemesis* and two on the *Arrow*. The *Freja* also lost two men, and each of the three warships suffered a number of wounded.

The *Freja* and her convoy were escorted into the Downs, where the problem of sorting out the intricacies of the situation was left to the British Vice-Admiral commanding, Skeffington Lutwidge. It was decided that, until matters were sorted out, the Danish frigate could fly her national colours and that a diplomatic mission headed by Lord Whitworth should be sent forthwith to Copenhagen – accompanied by a squadron of ten men-of-war under British Vice Admiral Dickson, to 'support the negotiators'.

Although a London meeting was arranged to go deeper into the matter, Britain had not the faintest intention to give up the right of search. However, by the end of August it had been agreed that the *Freja* and any damaged vessels in her convoy should be repaired and refitted at British expense, and that Danish merchant ships in the Mediterranean should be allowed warship escort, but only as a safeguard against North African corsairs – they would still be subject to interception and inspection by British men-of-war.

Denmark had been fairly easy to mollify, but now Russia added her strength to the argument, mobilising her army and navy, laying an embargo on all British ships in Russian ports, and calling for a renewal of the coalition. The erratic Czar Paul, who had so recently been an ally of Britain, had fallen for the persuasions of Bonaparte, who had judged the Russian monarch's character accurately and seduced him with a magnificent present: Napoleon returned to him several thousand Russian prisoners of war – in much better condition than at the time of their capture. They looked well-fed, were fitted out with smart new uniforms, were armed with good muskets, and were delivered with the flattering note that these men were far too valiant for France to hold them captive.

Beside Sweden and Russia, the probably-reluctant Denmark (which then included Norway) was dragged into the Second Armed Neutrality of the Northern Powers, December 1800.

Britain responded with immediate and overwhelming action, culminating in the Battle of Copenhagen, which broke the new Armed Neutrality of the North, brought about the destruction of the Danish fleet, and earned a viscountcy for Admiral Nelson.

This first Battle of Copenhagen – there was another in 1807 – has been mentioned in a thousand books, sometimes dealing with the battle in minute detail, sometimes only briefly; but all re-tell the story of Nelson's disregard of the orders of his Commander-in-Chief, when Admiral Hyde Parker hoisted the signal to 'Discontinue the Action'[1]: Horatio said to his officers who had observed it: 'I have only one eye – I have the right to be blind sometimes' and, with telescope to blind eye, 'I really do not see the signal'.

On the 12th March, 1801, Admiral Sir Hyde Parker in the 108-gun *London*, with Vice-Admiral Nelson as his second-in-command in the 98-gun *St George*, and Rear-Admiral Thomas Graves in the 74-gun, *Defiance* sailed for the Baltic with twenty-one ships-of-the-line and about thirty smaller craft. They carried on board a military force comprising the 19th Regiment, two rifle companies of the 95th Regiment and a certain amount of artillery. It was estimated that in the Baltic Sea at that time they might have to face besides Danish warships, about twenty Russian and a dozen Swedish ships-of-the-line. By the 21st of the month the Fleet was anchored off Kronenburg near the entrance to the Sound, where it was to await an important communication from the Danish Government: Denmark had been given a forty-eight-hour deadline to decide whether it would agree to leave the Confederation and open up the Danish ports to British shipping, or try its strength against the British fleet.

The gallant but cautious Admiral Parker was deeply disappointed to receive the Danish rejection of an offer which would have maintained the peace: the Danes probably trusting that the fleets of their partners in the Northern League would hasten to their aid, outnumbering and deterring the British fleet. However, the Russian and Swedish fleets were, at that time, icebound and inactive in their harbours. Sir Hyde Parker's orders from England were to do all in his power to persuade Denmark to withdraw from the Armed Neutrality of the North and, if successful, to sail and attack the Russian Fleet at Tallinn.

It was a week, however, before the order came to weigh anchor. Nelson himself was impatient at the delay, but put the time to good use by moving his flag from the 98-gun *St George* to the 74-gun *Elephant*, which drew less water, and got together a squadron of ten selected ships, likewise of shallow draft. At 6 a.m. on the 30th March, with Nelson commanding the van, the whole fleet moved into the Sound in line ahead. After about an hour the Helsingor (Elsinore) batteries opened up, shelling the British ships as they passed, but the range was too great to do serious damage, and as the guns of the forts on the Swedish side were silent, the British ships-of-the-line crossed over, nearer inshore on that side, completely out of harm's way. Nelson's bomb-vessels, however, were effectively shelling Kronenburg and Helsingor, throwing in more than two hundred shells and causing much devastation.

Towards afternoon they anchored off the Swedish island of Hveen, some fifteen miles from Copenhagen, where the three Admirals and a few other senior officers boarded the lugger, *Lark*, to reconnoitre the enemy defences – which they found to be daunting.

There were eighteen Danish ships-of-the-line forming a line of defence stretching a full two miles from the entrance to Copenhagen Harbour, which was guarded by the powerful Trekoner (Three Crowns) Batteries, southward to the Island of Amager. Besides many smaller vessels, formidable shore batteries were backed up by armed hulks and fire-ships, strategically placed in the treacherous channels of the approach. The two Trekroner Forts, which were equipped with furnaces for heating shot, were built up on wooden piles: one mounting thirty-eight long 36-pounders and the other thirty long 24-

pounders. The Forts were further strengthened by the presence of two blockade-ships, the *Elephanten* and the *Mars*. Copenhagen was by no means lightly defended.

A council of war was called for that evening on board the London, where Admiral Parker and other doubters presented discouraging opinions, but Nelson offered to lead the ten sail-of-the-line and a flotilla of smaller vessels, in an attack on the Danish capital. The smaller vessels comprised five frigates, four sloops, seven bomb-vessels and two fire-ships. His proposal was accepted.

As darkness fell Nelson wisely made a further detailed reconnaissance of the Danish lines of defence and discovered that all the buoys had been removed from what were at the best of times dangerous waters. The rest of that night was taken up with rebuoying of the Outer Channel.

On the morning of the 1st April, the fleet moved up to within six miles of Copenhagen and anchored off the north-western tip of the Middle Ground – a shoal which extended outside the King's Channel along the whole seafront of the city. Most of the Danish block-ships, gun-vessels, praams[2] and radeaus[3] were anchored or moored in this channel. In the early afternoon, the signal to weigh anchor was hoisted on board the *Elephant*, to great cheering from all the ships' companies, and the Vice-Admiral's squadron sailed into what was the commencement of the Battle of Copenhagen proper.

Leaving Parker and the remainder of the fleet at anchor, the squadron of twelve ships, (the Admiral had given Nelson two more line-of-battle ships to add to his selected ten) and auxiliary craft, amounting in all to about thirty-six sail, passed down the Outer Channel which ran to the west of the Middle Ground, parallel to the King's Channel. The Vice-Admiral led in the *Amazon* (38), which was acting as pilot-ship, followed by his flagship, *Elephant*, and with a fair and favourable north-west wind was anchored off the southernmost tip of the Middle Ground by 8 p.m. At that point the leading British ship was anchored no more than two miles from the first defending ship in the Danish line. Nelson's stratagem in forming a squadron of shallow-draft ships was soon to prove itself, but even now he took further precautions: the Vice-Admiral's flag-captain, Captain Thomas Hardy (of 'Kismet' or 'Kiss me' fame), set out with a cartographer and a leadsman in a small boat to sound the channel for depth of water and obstructions, bravely venturing up dangerously close to the Danish fleet – in fact passing completely round the block-ship or floating battery, the *Provesteen*. Before midnight, Hardy reported his favourable findings to Nelson, who had by that time returned to the *Elephant*.

At 8 a.m. on the 2nd April, signals were made to all captains,[4] giving them their stations in the forthcoming battle. The wind, having swung round overnight to become a brisk southeaster, could not have been more in their favour – but they were less lucky in the expertise of their pilots. The *Edgar* led the squadron into the King's Channel and headed north, but the *Agamemnon* who was to follow her could not round the point. The latter ship was replaced by the *Polyphemus*, but the pilotage troubles did not end there. Although the *Bellona* and the *Russel* managed to round the point, they both failed to clear the Middle Ground and were stranded within gunshot-range of the enemy, so close together that the bow-sprit of one crossed the deck of the other The flagship was the next to round the point, followed without mishap by the remaining ships.

Nelson's plan had been that all the ship-of-the-line should station themselves opposite the enemy ships and drop their stern anchors, whilst the frigates were to challenge the ships at the entry to the harbour, and attack the southernmost of the Danish fleet. This meant that the main lines of fighting ships would not be more than four or five hundred yards apart. There had also been a plan for the 49th Regiment and five hundred sailors to storm the largest of the batteries, but, with a quarter of the squadron aground, new strategies and on the spot changes had to be considered.

Firing had commenced by mid-morning as the British ships-of-the-line reached their stations, but with the absence of the *Agamemnon* – and the *Russel* and *Bellona* flying distress signals – it meant that some British ships were each soon engaged with more than one enemy vessel. Strong currents prevented the gun-vessels or the 24-gun *Jamaica* from getting close enough inshore to play much part in the action. The *Amazon*, which was anchored with three other frigates opposite the Trekroner Batteries, also suffered great damage. Although the Danish ships were taking a considerable bashing from the British line-of-battle-ships, Admiral Parker had observed or had been informed of the misfortunes of part of his fleet, and hoisted his famously-ignored signal to discontinue the action.

After the engagement had already lasted four hours, the Danish ships which could still do so continued to fight valiantly, but gradually their firing slackened and by 2 p.m. had almost ceased, most having struck their colours. However, the final surrender was not easily achieved. The Danish ships which had struck were being fired upon by their own shore batteries, yet they in turn fired on any British boats which approached with prize crews to take possession of vessels and crews. An example of this peculiar behaviour was experienced by the flagship *Elephant's* boat, which was fired upon when it set out to take possession of the 62-gun *Dannebrog*, which had already lowered her colours and was on fire. The flag ship and the *Ganges* had little option than to re-open fire until the Danish ship drifted off in flames and later blew up.

Nelson was reluctant to react, as some victors may have done, by sending in fire-ships to put his uncooperative prizes to the torch, and instead decided to attempt negotiation. He sent an aide-de-camp, Commander Sir Frederick Thesiger, ashore under a flag of truce, with a letter addressed to Frederick, the Crown Prince of Denmark, who met him near the sally-port of the Citadel.

Lord Nelson's letter read:

> 'TO THE BROTHERS OF ENGLISHMEN,
> THE BRAVE DANES.
> Vice-Admiral Lord Nelson has been commanded to spare Denmark, when no longer resisting. The line of defence which covered her shores has struck to the British flag. If the firing is continued on the part of Denmark, he must set on fire all the prizes that he has taken, without having the power of saving the men who have so nobly defended them. The brave Danes are the brothers, and should never be the enemies, of the English.'

Although Nelson's sentiments were no doubt sincere as regards saving Danish (and British) lives, there is little doubt that he realised the great benefit of a truce which would give him time to extricate his own ships from their tricky situations in the Channel. This was a wise move, for by the end of the battle at least six of his big ships were aground; his own ship the *Elephant* and the *Defiance* having grounded whilst moving from their stations in the line.

His 'Brothers of Englishmen' letter was no soft-soaping of the Danish royalty. Nelson was always forthright in his likes and dislikes: he detested the French, disliked the Italians who were, in his opinion, a nation of 'fiddlers and poets, whores and scoundrels'; had little time for the Irish and even less for the Spanish. Yet he had a sincere regard for the Danes, perhaps because like many East Anglians, Nelson was a descendant of the Vikings – his forebears were Scandinavian and had borne the name of Neilson.

Although the guns of most of the enemy line-of-defence ships were now silent, the *Indosforethen*, *Holstein* and *Hoelperen* continued the battle until silenced by the *Defiance*, *Monarch* and the *Ganges*. The great Trekroner Forts, which had been reinforced with 1,500 men, were also still blasting away – it had long been decided that the original intention to storm them was unrealistic; but they too ceased firing when it was learned that the Danish Adjutant-General, Lindholm, had set out under a flag of truce with Prince Frederick's reply to the Vice-Admiral's note. The Crown Prince required clarification of Nelson's precise intentions, and was told that the object of bringing hostilities to a close was inspired by British feelings of humanity; that wounded Danes should be taken ashore; that the unwounded should be cleared from the surrendered ships and be considered prisoners of the British. Finally, that Nelson could burn or carry off his prizes as he saw fit.

By next day all the grounded British ships had been cleared of the shoals, and those prizes which could be moved were brought out clear of the harbour. Except for the *Holstein* which was brought back to England when the fleet returned, all of the prize ships were condemned and destroyed. Most of the prisoners taken were returned to Denmark on the understanding that they were to be considered 'exchange-prisoners', that is, held on account against British captives who might be taken in any future conflict.

So ended The Battle of Copenhagen, which the Danes had fought valiantly, but which had resulted in the loss of their fleet and about six thousand men, killed, wounded or captured; the British losing 255 killed and 685 wounded. But memorable and glorified as it was to become in our naval history, it was a battle which, had Admiral Parker procrastinated a week or two longer – or Marconi been born a hundred years earlier – need never have been fought.

Czar Paul of Russia, the prime instigator of the second league against the British right to detain and search, had been assassinated on the 24th March, a week before the first shell was fired against the Danes, and with him died the Second Northern Coalition of Armed Neutrality.

Compared with the many thousands of prisoners of other nationalities at that time – generally referred to as 'French' – there were few Danish prisoners of war confined in Britain as a result of the 1801 battle of Copenhagen, and those soon regained their liberty with the signing of the Treaty of Amiens and the all-too-short peace of 1802. However, many Scandinavians spent years in British prison ships, depots or parole towns after the second raid on Copenhagen and the capture of another Danish fleet in September 1807. This second attack on a people for whom we felt no hatred or ill-will, came about through a set of circumstances not dissimilar to those which inspired that first attack six years earlier – and once again a Russia Czar was deeply involved.

After the assassination in 1801 of Czar Paul, who at the time had been pro-French, his successor, the young Alexander I, favoured the British cause and so ruined Napoleon's dream of a Franco-Russian invasion of India. Fancying himself as the saviour of Europe, Czar Alexander sent his armies into many battles, from which they usually emerged defeated; nevertheless he literally stuck to his guns until 1807. On the 14th June of that year the Russians were badly beaten, and lost half of their armed manpower, at the Battle of Friedland, which forced Alexander to the conclusion that Napoleon would make a better friend than an enemy. The Czar gave up the heroic image of himself as the great liberator against France and, two weeks after the Russian defeat, the two rulers met on neutral territory to discuss the future.

The meeting, which ended with the signing of the Treaty of Tilsit on the 7th July, was held on a great raft on the River Nieman, where Bonaparte and Alexander had discussed many aspects of their new relationship – whilst the King of Prussia, who also went over to the Emperor but was treated as a junior participant, waited on the Russian bank of the river to learn the outcome.

All European ports were to be closed to British vessels. Denmark, Austria and Portugal were to be pulled into the alliance and a great Northern Fleet was to combine to wrest from Britain the command of the seas – and, of course, plans to end the British Orders in Council which backed His Britannic Majesty's Navy in its authority to 'stop and search' were hotly discussed.

On receiving the news of the Tilsit happenings and an unfounded rumour that the Danish fleet was ready for sea, to join in an imminent French invasion of Holstein, the Government once again took amazingly quick and bold action – for as Francis Jackson, the British plenipotentiary to Denmark, wrote: 'We may see another attempt at a Northern Neutrality, which I hope and trust another Nelson may arise and destroy'.

With the possibility of being faced with about sixty or seventy ships-of-the-line in the North and Baltic Seas alone if they procrastinated, and the knowledge that Bonaparte was trying to bully Denmark into lending him her warships for the duration of the war, Britain once again got its blow in first. On the 19th July, only twelve days after the signing of the Tilset Treaty, Francis Jackson was dispatched to Copenhagen to present the Danish Crown Prince with an ultimatum from Foreign Minister George Canning, demanding that the Danes hand over their fleet to the British Navy or face the consequences of refusal. It was not, however, couched in the harshest of terms: the demand read:

> ' …to consent to deliver up the Danish fleet to the British, and to their carrying it away, to be held in deposit for his Danish Majesty, to be restored with all its equipments, in as good a state as it was received, as soon as the provisions of a general peace should remove the necessity which had occasioned the demand.'

In addition, if accepted, the Danes would be offered an alliance with Great Britain and £100,000 a year would be paid as rental for their fleet – plus the biggest argument for acceptance: that the ultimatum was to be backed up by a powerful British fleet and 30,000 men.

Thus Denmark was once again exposed to quandary, one faced by many weak countries without sufficient strength to preserve their neutrality in time of great wars and, forced to choose, stood only a fifty-fifty chance of having chosen wisely whichever way they jumped. For a second time in six years, the Crown Prince, convinced by his meetings with Napoleon that France would eventually emerge the victor, rejected an offer which could have prevented the Bombardment of Copenhagen and the surrender of another Danish fleet.

On the 26th July, 1807 Admiral James Gambier sailed from the Yarmouth Roads with a fleet of seventeen ships-of-the-line and

155

twenty-one smaller warships and set course for the Baltic. During the following weeks more men-of-war caught up with the fleet until it totalled twenty-five major fighting ships and more than forty frigates. The British military commander was Lieutenant-General Lord Cathcart, and convoys of troop-carrying transports followed the fleet with his army of 30,000 men, more than half of them German mercenaries.

The Danish Government had already received warnings of trouble, early in 1807, from their Consul-General in England, Jens Wolff. Wolff had become disturbed by rumours of British intentions contrary to his country's interest, and was even more convinced by an anonymous (though signed 'Howard') letter, which he received on the 2nd June. The letter, which probably came from an official of some importance among the many British sympathisers, read:

'It is the opinion of some well-informed persons, that the expedition now fitting out in this country is intended for the purpose of taking possession of Copenhagen and the whole island of Zealand – of which your Government should certainly be informed in time to prepare accommodation for the said troops etc.
Wishing for peace among all mankind, I am etc

Howard'.

Wolff forwarded this message post-haste to the authorities in Denmark and requested guidance as to the advice he should offer to the commanders of Danish vessels in the British ports. With the unforgettable memory of Nelson's so recent victory as evidence of Britain's determined action when aroused, the Consul-General was amazed at the reply, which he received from the chargé d'affaires on behalf of the Danish Government. He was assured that the rumours were 'without the least foundation', and was told to 'calm down the frightened merchant captains'.

With no alternative but to act in accordance with his orders, Jens Wolff dispatched printed notices to the 'frightened captains', instructing them that they 'must be obedient and do as the British Government tells you to do; keep your crews quiet and avoid mutiny, etc.' Thus some three hundred Danish and Norwegian vessels and their crews were, in effect, captured or held hostage. Meanwhile the British merchantmen in the north had been ordered by their Consul to quit Danish ports.

Admiral Gambier and General Cathcart found the defences of Copenhagen itself were much the same as Nelson had found them in 1801. The harbour, which divided the town, was covered by the Trekroner Forts, the Citadel and the Arsenal battery which altogether mounted a total of 174 guns – mostly long 24- and 36-pounders – and about 25 mortars. The floating defences comprised sixteen sail-of-the-line and twenty-one frigates – many of them unfit for battle. In addition there was the block-ship *Mars* (64), three 74-gun ships which were on the stocks, two floating batteries, and about thirty small gun-boats. The country's main military body was in Holstein, and the Danish Governor of Copenhagen, General Peyman, had less than six thousand regulars, four thousand seaman and a similar number of civilian militia, or home guard, with which to defend his city against a vastly superior force.

A surprising, and seldom mentioned, fact concerning the defence of Copenhagen in 1807, is that the Danes seriously considered attacking the British Fleet from the air!

The French had their *Aerostatier Corps*, or *Ballon* units, formed at the end of the eighteenth century and the use of balloons for

offensive reconnaissance played an important part in the victory of the French over the Austrians at the Battle of Fleurus in June 1794. Had certain technical difficulties not arisen, they might well have been employed in the planned invasion of Britain. It was proposed, in 1808, that one hundred huge Montgolfier balloons should be constructed; each three hundred feet in diameter, with 'baskets' capable of carrying one thousand men, two cannon, twenty-five horses, and two-week's rations – not to mention the great quantities of fuel required to supply hot air during long, slow flights. This was thinking on a grand scale, but far too grand to be realised at that time, and the idea was abandoned.

The Danes were by no means as ambitious, but got nearer to achieving their aim. They did build and test-fly a great airship-like balloon, propelled by broad-bladed 'paddles' operated by oarsmen – or airmen – which was capable of being steered. With this they intended to bomb the British fleet as it lay deployed off the city. Had they succeeded in this imaginative scheme, an unforgettable page in naval (and airforce!) history would have been written; but insufficient power of propulsion and the vagaries of wind and weather reduced it to a mere fascinating footnote.

On the 16th August, at five o'clock in the morning, the first British division under Major-General Sir Arthur Wellesley (later Duke of Wellington), landed on Danish soil, at Vedboek Bay. The invaders pushed towards Copenhagen and by the end of the month had routed the Danish defenders at Kjoge, capturing 1,500 men and sixty officers and a large quantity of arms and stores. Other divisions disembarked at Skodsborg, north of the city, and Kjoge Bay in the south. Once ashore and marched to their appointed stations, officers and troops were involved non-stop in setting up army headquarters in the outskirts of the city, in the complicated logistics of constructing shore batteries and fitting them out with ordnance, and providing provisions for both troops and prisoners. The distribution of the British siege-works and Gambier's fleet, is clearly shown in the illustration to a broadsheet published in London on the 28th September, 1807.

By the beginning of September the fleet was deployed and the mortar and howitzer batteries ready for action; but, although there had been attacks on the batteries and their protecting flotilla by Danish praams and gun-vessels, and one of our armed merchant transports, the *Charles*, had been destroyed, the British Commander-in-Chief gave the Danes one last chance to surrender. The Danish General Peyman declined and, at 7.30 on the 2nd September, the batteries opened up and within minutes Copenhagen was in flames. For three more terrible nights the Danes held out in spite of the hundreds of shells and Congreve rockets which blasted into the burning city. One eye-witness said that, five miles away, the night-sky was as bright as day, and his vessel shook with reverberations from the distant guns – but on the evening of the 5th, General Peyman flew a flag of truce and begged for an armistice. Instead, articles of surrender were drawn up, which were signed and ratified on the morning of the 7th September.

The naval and military losses on the British side, from the commencement of hostilities, were surprisingly small for such an action: fifty-six killed, 175 wounded and twenty-five missing – and these casualties came about, almost to a man, in skirmishes and small actions before the bombardment commenced. The Danish losses were more serious, about 500 in the skirmishes, and at least 1,500 killed and wounded within the fortifications – including women and children, whom the Danish general had neglected to evacuate during the many opportunities afforded by Gambier and Cathcart's patience before the last offer of a peaceful surrender had been scorned. In addition to loss by death and injury there must also be included the large number of prisoners of war. The Danish loss in ships and material was immense. More than seventy ships, including seventeen men-of-war were handed over to the British Navy, plus the three ships on the stocks in the dockyard. Two of these were taken to pieces and shipped to England, the third destroyed by fire – as were the block-ships, which would probably not have survived the voyage to Britain.

An interesting sidelight, only learned some time after the battle, reveals that the British may well have been deprived of the floating fruits of their victory. It was later reported that the Crown Prince had sent an order instructing General Peyman that if the fleet had to be sacrificed it should be burnt rather than surrendered – but the courier was captured by a British patrol and destroyed his dispatches.

On the 21st October, the fleet with its prizes left Copenhagen, homeward bound. Many of both British and prize ships carried stores claimed from the vanquished country, but it required a follow-up of ninety-two heavily laden transport vessels to convey the balance of the easily-won goods and equipment back to England. A Naval State Paper of May, 1808, estimated that the value to the Naval and Victualling Office of these Danish stores totalled £274,851.11s.9d.

An interesting footnote tells us that any of the stores which were adjudged unfit for His Majesty's Service, 'were delivered to the Commissioners for Danish Affairs'.[5]

After the loss of its fleet and much of its capital city, Denmark not surprisingly, though perhaps unwisely, declared war on Britain, on the 4th November. This was countered with British Orders of Reprisal (the forcible seizure of vessels, men and goods, as an act of retaliation) against all Danish shipping; and the 74-gun *Vanguard* with a flotilla of frigates was left to patrol the Northern seas. There was already a fair number of Scandinavian prisoners in England as a result of existing British Orders in Council which forbade neutrals to trade with France; and another, issued late in 1806, which forewarned that neutrals who failed to carry a British permit or licence would be subject to capture on the high seas.

Out of context, these British demands may sound high-handed in the extreme; but, for all our mastery of the seas, Napoleon was master of just about all the ports of Europe, and his 'Continental System' was aimed at closing all those ports to British shipping and commerce, and the blockading of Britain itself. Caught between these two great adversaries, little Denmark, an unhappy participant in warfare but now an ally of France, was deeply involved in the struggle, her shipping, naval and mercantile, fair game for British cruisers and privateers.

With his Consulate in England closed down with the declaration of war, Jens Wolff's name may well have disappeared from the story; but he pledged his time and not a little money to the cause of Danish and Norwegian prisoners of war. With great dedication he supported that cause over a number of years, even to the point of personal bankruptcy. He immediately asked questions of the British Government regarding prisoner of war allowances. After 1801, the prisoner of war allowance to Danish officers had been: Captains, Chief Officers and others, 3s.6d., 2s.0d. and 1s.3d. per day respectively; but now, in 1807, they were reduced to 1s.6d.,

1s.0d. and 9d. In protest, Wolff wrote to the Finance Minister Perceval, that, if the amount was not increased, he would have to open up a public subscription in England, asking the British people to contribute what their Government refused.

The Treasury increased the amount as far as they could, but reminded him that the allowance to the seized Danes was twice that doled out to French prisoners of war.

As prisoners of war the Danes received better treatment than captives of other nationalities, whether confined in land prison, prison ship, or enjoying the many privileges of the open prison of a parole town. Some contemporary British writers placed them in an entirely different category to the normal prisoner of war, thinking them more akin to the English *détenus* unfairly detained by Napoleon after 1803. Except in the case of officers and men of the Danish Army, Navy or privateersmen, it is true that a great proportion of them had not been captured in actual warlike action. Most were sailors – and some passengers – taken from the three-hundred merchant vessels, entrapped in English ports in 1807, just prior to and after Denmark had been pushed into a declaration of war against Britain.

Captain Edward Hawkins, Superintendent of the hulks at Plymouth viewed them in a quite different light from the French and their allies. Entries in his diaries and log-books concerning the 750 Danes on his hulk, *La Brave*, often refer to them as 'hostages'. The British public in the parole towns seem to have treated them more as wartime guests than captives; exhibiting nothing like the hatred they might have felt (but seldom showed) for our traditional enemies, the French; or the ambivalence of our attitude towards the American prisoners of war – torn between regarding the latter as our trans-Atlantic cousins or as renegades and rebels.

Danes of all ranks were certainly better-off financially than prisoners who had to depend on their basic prisoner of war allowance. The Danish Government made a regular cash allowance to all their captive subjects, usually paid into London banks and distributed through Danish officials, such as the Reverend Ulrik Rosing who was pastor to the prisoners at Plymouth from 1801 to 1811.

At the end of 1807, the number of Danish prisoners of war in Britain stood at 1,840 and remained at about that level in the following year, although large numbers had been returned to Denmark in exchange agreements, whereby a similar number of British prisoners should have been repatriated to this country. The figure in 1809 had risen to 3,574, but in October of that year the majority of paroled Danes were freed by the General Amnesty which was granted to celebrate the 50th Jubilee of George III's reign.

Over the years of war from 1807 to the end of hostilities, seven years later, between seven and eight thousand Danish prisoners of war were confined in various depots in England and Scotland, but, as we shall see, the majority ended up on the Plymouth, Portsmouth and Medway hulks.

Although generally referred to as 'Danes', these captives should, with greater accuracy, be called Scandinavian. The 1,350 Scandinavians recorded and described in the prisoner of war lists for the Scottish depot at Greenlaw, between 1807 and 1811, were mainly Danish, but among that number Norway, Finland, Sweden and Iceland were represented.

Many crews of vessels captured in the northern seas were sent to Scottish prison depots. We read of ships which were wrecked or driven on shore by storm or high seas; of others which struck their colours in combat or submitted to an obviously superior force. After the Danish privateer schooner *Roling* was captured by the sloop HMS *Snake* in 1809, off the North Cape of the Arctic Circle, the forty-five members of its crew were put ashore, probably at Leith, and marched to Greenlaw, one of the three depots at Penicuik.[6]

Whilst we have a several memoirs which tell of Danish and Norwegian officers and their servants who spent their period of imprisonment in parole towns in England and Scotland, and a few journals kept by less fortunate captives who were sent to the prison hulks, there are far fewer remembrances left by Scandinavian prisoners who were confined in closed land prisons or depots. There is, however, the journal of Captain Paul Andreas Kaald.

Kaald was born in Trondheim, Norway, in 1784, and went to sea when he was fourteen and had reached the rank of Chief Officer by the opening of hostilities in 1807. He was fortunate enough to escape capture in that year, but in August 1808, whilst serving as Captain of the *Den Flinke* ('The Good One'), he was forced to strike to two British brigs, one the *Basilisk* and the other a prize vessel taken from the Norwegians, formerly the brig *Tordenskjold* now renamed and adopted into the Royal Navy.

The renaming, conversion, refitting and re-use of captured vessels would alone make an interesting study and fascinating volume. Some saw service against their original nationality, others became prison ships, rigging hulks or depot or hospital ships. Captain Kaald's own vessel had itself once been a prize taken from the British and renamed *Den Flinke*.

We read that the *Flinke's* ship's company were relieved of most of their possessions by the captors, and that it seemed likely that their captain would lose even his precious journal. A young British midshipman took possession of it for a purpose which Kaald preferred not to put into words, but it was rescued before no more than one half page had been so dishonourably employed. Kaald and his men were taken to Greenlaw, the Scottish depot at Penicuik, south of Edinburgh. There they were lodged in a prison building where 252 captives were already housed. Kaald was directed to a room already occupied by twenty-eight officers, amongst them some old friends and ship-mates, including the commander of one of his previous vessels, Captain Richelieu. Already grossly overcrowded, Kaald found the only available space for him to settle, sleep and eat his food, was by a door to what he called the 'piss-tub'.

In May, 1809, after many months of this distasteful lodging, he and Captain Richelieu were moved to another small but less crowded room to share with only five other officers. Kaald's crew were later transferred to the Chatham hulks, and he later heard that many of them had succumbed to recruiting officers' persuasions and signed on to British vessels fitting out for the East and West Indies. Captain Kaald was himself too honourable to take such a course – or even to grasp the chance for escape when offered the opportunity to sign a parole document when asked to attend as a witness in a court case in Edinburgh. Much of the information in his journal regarding Greenlaw is contained in the section which discusses the land depots.

There were few military men among the Northern prisoners and, with thousands of experienced naval and merchant seamen so near at hand, they were obvious targets for British naval recruiting officers forever on the lookout for likely lads. Whilst comparatively few Danes were tempted into serving in our men-of-war – from reasons of national loyalty or daunted by our Royal Navy's reputation for brutal discipline – a fair number were willing

to swap the misery of prison for service on British merchantmen. Where French captives shared a place of imprisonment with their Danish allies, the willingness of so many of the latter to serve the enemy caused much ill feeling between the two nationalities. As MacBeth Forbes put it:

> 'There were constant quarrels between French and Danish prisoners which necessitated their being kept apart. The French had not unnaturally from the invincible prestige of their arms formed a high opinion of themselves, which implied a correspondingly low opinion of other people'.

Relationships were particularly bad in some of the Scottish depots, where in one case the Scandinavian 'traitors', as they were termed, 'had been prevented leaving Greenlaw Prison by an Insurrection of the French Prisoners'. The Transport Board and the local Agent acted quickly, issuing orders for 'removing all the refractory French Prisoners under a strong Guard as soon as possible', and later told the Agent to 'separate the Danes who volunteered for His Majesty's Service but afterwards refused to leave the Prison [through fear?] from the French Prisoners as soon as possible'.

The French and the Danes were separated, but a newspaper report at the time indicates that the Danes came off second best by that separation, as they headed for the Portsmouth hulks:

> '*The Edinburgh Evening Courant.* 6th April 1811. 300 Danish prisoners were marched into Leith yesterday forenoon from Penicuik, under an escort, to be embarked on board the *Romulus* frigate for Portsmouth. We understand that the constant quarrels betwixt French prisoners and these men is the reason for sending them thither.'

Francis Abell tells of one 'traitor' who succumbed to the persuasions of a British recruiting officer – then conducted a prosperous business by his apparent disloyalty. This was a man named Wipperman, a Danish clerk on HMS *Utile*, who profited from the rewards he received from the British for enticing his captive fellow countrymen into our merchant navy. It was only when one of them accused him of false pretences in the matter of some money and a watch, that his British paymasters learned that he was similarly false in his dealings with them. He was luring the prisoners with promises of help and advice on how to desert and escape at the first opportunity after entering the service of their enemy.

Wipperman may have been guilty of the initial charge of false pretences but – as he was not bound by any parole of honour – in offending against his captors he was serving his country well. However, 'He was severely punished, and his exposure brought to an end an extensive crimping[7] system by which hundreds of dangerous foreigners had been let loose from prison ships...' As we shall see, when discussing the 'Danish hulks', renegades were held in contempt by their fellow prisoners and were often punished for the betrayal of their country's cause; but they were seldom shown the same violent punishments which the Americans and French inflicted on offending fellow countrymen.

The Transport Office and its Prison Agents had, over long years of experience, learned that it was unwise to put implicit faith in any prisoner of war, even when bearing the hallmark of 'gentleman' by signing his *parole d'honneur,* or wearing the cloth of the clergy. French officers had injured the parole system almost beyond repair, and their 'Resident priests' had often provided the un-churchlike service of smuggling and dealing with illegal mail for the prisoners: the Bishop of Moulins at Norman Cross Depot had done nothing to improve that clerical image (see Chapter 22, PAROLE IN ENGLAND). So although a Danish pastor was allowed to visit the prisoners on the hulks at Chatham, it was with the proviso that 'he does not repeat the old offence of talking upon matters unconnected with his mission and so cause much incorrect inferences'.

Denmark and other allies of the French also copied their master's disregard for the honourable system of exchange. In 1808, when there were only 1,796 Danes in this country, Denmark was in debt to Britain for no less than 3,807. It is doubtful that they ever held anywhere near sufficient British prisoners to clear up the discrepancy, even had they wished – it is more likely that the number included the 'held on account' prisoners released by Nelson after the first Battle of Copenhagen, seven years earlier. Although Denmark did reduce the balance over the years, that country was still a couple of thousand in arrears in 1814.

The British prisoners taken by the Danes were almost all seamen. Some were crew from men-of-war, landing parties captured in boats belonging to the attacking frigates and ships-of-the line; but the majority by far were the officers and crews of transports and merchant vessels, most of them taken in the Sound or the Kattegat to the north of the city of Copenhagen.

William Chambers, the Scottish writer and publisher, visited Copenhagen some years after the bombardment, but whilst the memory of the bombardment and the presence of British prisoners was still painfully fresh in Danish minds. These memories he recorded in a short article which he published many years later in his famous *Chambers' Journal*[8]. Chambers was always fair-minded in his judgement of the qualities of his fellow man, whatever his nationality; it can therefore be taken as an unfortunate fact that the behaviour of a large number of our prisoners in Denmark was at least as bad as that of the worst type of prisoner of war in Britain.

Before being marched to depots at Randers and other towns outside the capital, the English prisoners were first sent into the still-smoking ruins of Copenhagen, where one might expect them to have been roughly handled and abused by captors embittered by the damage inflicted on their city; but it would seem that the Danes treated them with fairness and humanity. The Danish Government allowed each man one shilling a day with which to buy provisions, which could not have purchased more than the bare necessities in Copenhagen, where food prices had sky-rocketed in a very short time. Once they had been sent off to one or other of the country depots, where food prices were dramatically lower, their allowance was reduced from 1s. to 5d. per day. No one could have got fat on the goods which that small sum could supply, particularly as they had to be purchased through contractors and, as Chambers reported, 'we may perhaps safely assume that the Commissaries did not neglect to squeeze a considerable profit out of the aggregate of the small allowances'; but the food, however small the portions, was fresh and wholesome.

Although the bread would have appeared strange to the prisoners – black and made from rye, but nourishing – it was a great improvement on the weevil-eaten hard-tack often issued to the free British tar and to some prisoners of war. Pork, beef, fish, pea-soup, etc. made up the rest of the British prisoners' provender, but in insufficient quantity to appease the appetite of the British sailor. Of course, extra food and small luxuries were available to anyone with

sufficient money, but as sailors were infrequently paid – usually at the end of a voyage or commission which may have lasted years, if they were lucky – most would have been hard up at the time of capture. There were few opportunities of earning pocket money by producing odds and ends of 'prisoner of war work', owing to the generally impoverished state of most of the Danish countryfolk, their only possible customers.

More than three hundred prisoners were sent to the Randers Depot, near the coast on the other side of the Kattegat. They were housed in a two-floored brick-built barrack, each floor consisting of one large room. Some slept in hammocks but there were insufficient for all, so some made do with straw bedding on the floor. Wood-burning stoves were supplied, but the unhealthy cramming of some hundred and fifty men into one room caused miserable stuffy discomfort and ill-health. Although there were exercise yards at Randers, there were long periods when they were confined indoors both by day as well as night, and bad ventilation inevitably resulted in a stinking atmosphere and sickness: ' …on the whole, they were on short allowance of fresh air, a deprivation which sailors, of all men, feel most severely, as they are accustomed to spend their lives inhaling the pure open sea-breezes'. Additional suffering was caused by the lack of suitable clothing to protect them from the worst of the icy northern climate, a suffering which the by no means affluent Danish town and country folk sought to alleviate by contributing all the clothing they could spare, and even supporting subscriptions to purchase extra food to supplement their meagre ration. It is remarkable that a people who had themselves suffered two attacks on their homeland which many Britons, including General Gambier himself, found it hard to justify, should have found it in their hearts to aid their captured invaders.

Chambers was told that:

> '....as a body, our captive fellow-countrymen behaved very ungratefully towards the sympathising Danes, whom they robbed and outraged on several occasions in a most discreditable manner. Nor was their conduct to one another any better. The life they led in prison reflected little honour on their country in any respect. They were perpetually quarrelling, fighting, gambling and occasionally misconducting themselves so outrageously that the severe punishment of ringleaders became absolutely necessary to restore anything like order. The quiet, phlegmatic Danes were scandalised and amazed at the behaviour of their incorrigible captives, and were much more anxious to get rid of them on any terms than to keep them, for, as nearly all were penniless sailors, they of course brought no money into the country, but cost it money to keep them, which Denmark could ill-afford.'

He was told that 'they were not ashamed to beg regularly and importunately of the poor country-people or visitors' to their prison.

Not a pretty picture of the British prisoner of war, but it could have been based on the conduct of only a proportion of their number, perhaps even a minority; for, as with our football hooligans today, the majority is often stigmatised by the actions of the few, and bad news and scandalous occurrences last longest in the general memory. The better-behaved spent their time in a manner common to men crowded together in forced idleness; spinning yarns and tall stories; singing patriotic and more questionable songs; writing, and reading the few books available; and adapting odds and ends to improve their comfort, Many admirable and adventurous characters made valiant attempts at escape from Randers and the other country depots, but with limited success. When recaptured they were sentenced to floggings inflicted as punishment and discouragement to other bold types, and security restrictions were tightened as a general punishment to all.

Gambling was always the greatest cause of trouble and suffering amongst prisoners everywhere, and even here, where most English prisoners could not easily afford the smallest wager, they would stake their pay, their rations of food in advance and even the clothes off their backs. No mention is made of there having been an elected prisoner-controlled 'law-court' to punish trouble-makers and criminal elements among them. As we shall see, such courts were a commonplace among Danish, French and American prisoners of war confined in most English depots and most prison hulks. In the absence of such disciplinary committees, there was much disorder and fighting at Randers, often caused by the frequency of theft among them – 'the law of *meum* and *tuum* being held in little respect'.

Most of the British prisoners held by the Danes at that time were released by exchange within a year to eighteen months of their capture. But the joy of any among them who were fit and healthy sailors would have been soon depressed by the discovery that they had escaped the discomfort of the Danish frying-pan only to land in the uncomfortable fire of a British man-of-war. On release they were delivered to the British vessels cruising the Sound, where they were invited to join His Majesty's Navy – or were impressed into it anyway.

Not all of the prizes taken at Copenhagen were destined to reach safe anchorage in England. A number of the smaller captured vessels met with storms and adverse winds which drove them ashore on the Dutch coast. The British prize crews were taken prisoner and marched the hundreds of miles to the French war prisons in northern France. Other ships which did make it were renamed and saw service as patrol vessels or with English fleets.

On the evening of the 29th November, 1808, HMS *Crescent*, left Yarmouth with essential supplies including clothes and slops for the Baltic Fleet. The next week was one of storm and darkness, with no sight of sun or moon, depending entirely on their pilots, who in turn depended entirely on guesswork and soundings. By the 5th December they stood off the coast preparing to round the Scaw (Skagan) of North Jutland, the pilots assuring Captain Temple that they were a good ten miles offshore. They were in fact less than two miles from land when they crashed on to rocks off Lonstrup, at ten o'clock that night. For seventeen hours captain and crew put up a valiant fight to save the *Crescent*, jettisoning her guns and cutting away her masts and sails: the captain declaring he would not leave the ship 'while a man could live upon her deck, and accordingly sacrificed himself to his duty'. Of the crew of two hundred and seventy-four men, Captain Temple, three lieutenants, a second lieutenant of marines, eight midshipmen, two hundred men and six women, all perished on that night.

On the 9th December, the survivors were brought into the village of Aalborg, about forty miles inland south-east of Lonstrup, where a number of British prisoners of war were already held. An eye-witness said that 'never was there a more wretched set of human beings as the poor remains of the *Crescent's* gallant crew' – they were the Master, the First Lieutenant of Marines, four midshipmen, the boatswain and about fifty seamen and marines. A pitiable sight as they were marched into the town, some had 'neither hats on their heads, nor shoes on their feet. Some had one boot and some one

shoe, some jackets of their own, and some Danish jackets or great coats lent them in charity by the peasants or the soldiers'.

The Danish government had gone out of its way to encourage a nation-wide hatred against their British enemy, but although the whole population of Aalborg lined the streets, not 'a harsh word or illiberal reflexion' was heard. This showed remarkable restraint, for, added to their understandable resentment and rage after the bombardment of Copenhagen and the capture of their fleet, was the fact that the wrecked British ship had only recently been part of that fleet, one of the Danish frigates taken at Copenhagen in September, 1807, then adopted by the Royal Navy and renamed HMS *Crescent*. Even the most saintly of the onlookers must have felt that Divine vengeance had delivered their ship back to its country, with enemy prisoners alive and dead.

Over years of searching for prisoner of war related data, I have made a number of 'finds' so remarkable in their improbability and coincidence that I now begin to think of such discoveries as 'meant-to-be', rather than just luck. One such occurred in the very week I began to tackle the rather difficult task of gathering together information regarding Scandinavian prisoners of war and British prisoners held by the Northern Powers. In a local second-hand bookshop I came across a little unbound booklet of eighty pages, written by the eyewitness referred to in the above account of the wreck of the *Crescent*. It was the *Journal of James Macdonald*, which he wrote whilst a paroled prisoner of war in 1808, and was printed in the form of fifteen letters in 1810.

James Macdonald was a Scot who had business connections with Denmark and Norway and had lived in Copenhagen for a while in 1804. His little memoir shows that he had a wide knowledge of northern agriculture and strong political opinions, particularly concerning the 'unjust' war between Britain and Denmark. He also had a high opinion of his own importance.

Macdonald found himself a prisoner of war in Jutland, a survivor of a shipwreck only a couple of weeks before the *Crescent* met her end. He does not make plain his business on board the small British ship, *The Johns*; but presumably expects us to deduce his standing from the manner in which he instructed the doomed vessel's commander, Captain Hutton, and the arrogance he showed towards Danes of lesser importance – referring to the Danish corporal, who later guarded him when a prisoner, as his servant.

On the 20th November, 1808 *The Johns* was off the North Jutland coast when, at about two o'clock in the morning, the helmsman sang out that he could see a light and land ahead.

'We all ran in our shirts to ascertain the fact, and, not withstanding the coldness of the wind, did not dress... until the whole crew unanimously declared they could see the light, and also the hull of a British ship' which carried the light at her mizzen top. This 'ship' could have been, but wasn't, the bomb-ship HMS *Fury*, which was expected to be lying off the Scaw reef at that date, and the captain made the fatal error of ordering the helm to 'steer close to the stern of the man-of-war'.

Macdonald tells of how he entreated Captain Hutton to beware of false lights, kindled as decoys to lure English and Swedish vessels on to the rocks, and appealed to the crew to back him up, as he could 'see objects at a great distance', but all to no avail. It transpired that the light was neither the *Fury's* mizzen-lamp, nor a false light on the shore. It was in fact the Scaw light at Skagen and, at three o'clock on that bitter morning, *The Johns* 'followed' it on to the shore and disaster.

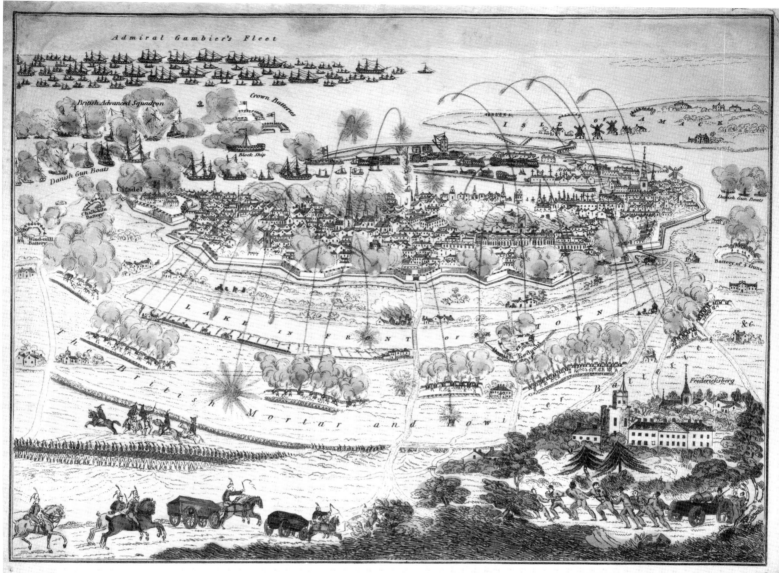

The **BOMBARDMENT** of **COPENHAGEN** and **SURRENDER** of the **DANISH FLEET**,
To the British Forces under the Command of Admiral Gambier, and Lord Cathcart, September 7, 1807.

James Macdonald paints himself as the hero of the hour – as he may well have been – whose calm selflessness saved all ten of *The Johns'* ship's company from a watery grave. With no chance of saving the vessel, 'its cabin filled with water and all the pumps choaked, a scene of horrible confusion followed'. The captain having 'lost his recollection a good deal' and with all around him the panicking crew, what else could Macdonald do but take over? When a young boy began to cry and whine that all was lost, and others lost hope on hearing gunfire from the shore (which was in fact a signal that help was at hand), he 'calmed' the youngster and the crew by promising that anyone who uttered a single complaint would be thrown overboard immediately!

He then called all hands together to prepare themselves to bravely await the dawn and proceeded to conduct a short service of prayer:

'The effect produced by the performance of this religious duty was truly astonishing. They recovered their spirits, and even had the presence of mind to dress themselves in their best clothes (a most fortunate circumstance for them), and to conceal what little money they had, as they expected to be plundered the moment their Danish enemies could approach the ship's sides.'

With the sea breaking over the shattered vessel and a south-east wind chilling their bones, they waited out the rest of the night. At daybreak they found that they were within half a mile of the shore, 'amidst horrible breakers, a furious current, sand-banks and the remains of wrecked vessels'. Rather unnecessarily – as the shore was lined with villagers and soldiers and one abortive attempt had already been made to launch a boat – a distress signal was hoisted. Unfortunately it was late in the afternoon, with the sun setting, before a boat rowed by nine stalwart Danes got within fifty yards of *The Johns*; the seas too rough and the wind too strong to come alongside. We should not be surprised to learn that Macdonald, alone among the benumbed crew, was strong enough to cast a rope attached to an oar which was picked up by the rescuers. Suffering from the freezing cold, hunger and thirst, there were probably never men more anxious to become prisoners of war; but after three had been conveyed along the line to the boat, it returned to the shore, leaving with the promise to return, if possible, on the following morn.

That night, Macdonald ordered the men into the ratlines to climb above the level of the waves washing over the decks:

> 'After prayer, I directed them to separate, desiring some to go into the fore-top, and others into the main-top; with the captain, his son and a boy, I climbed into the main-top and three others got with difficulty into the fore-top. The sea made a breach over me as I was getting into the shrouds, knocking me down, carrying off my shoes and stick and afterwards I lost my hat…'

Later, his right leg and arm were badly damaged when he collided violently against the top-mast whilst saving the cabin-boy from falling. That night was spent keeping one another awake and moving to prevent slumber and inevitable freezing to death. As dawn approached Captain Hutton's condition deteriorated and he lapsed into semi-consciousness, muttering 'the morning sun will rise, but not to us,' as his nineteen year old son wrapped his own great-coat round his father's shoulders.

However, at six in the morning, after a long night of agonising hopelessness, the wind dropped sufficiently for the rescue boat to venture alongside and take on board the near-frozen prisoners.

> 'At length we got clear away from the ship, and made for the shore. The steersman felt my cheeks, hands and feet, and instantly took off his hat, gloves and jacket, into the sleeves of which he thrust my feet; his hat he put on my head, and with one of his gloves, which were of fur, and not divided into fingers, he covered both my hands.'

When they reached the Skagen shore they were escorted by a guard of eight soldiers and a corporal and taken to an inn, where they were given hot coffee, eggs and bread and a place to sleep. Macdonald says that his exertions had finally left him in a worse conditions than those he had helped; his arms and legs 'all black and blue, and much bruised', whilst his companions, after three days reduced to the brink of despair, were soon in high spirits. So, fatigued and dejected, he tried to sleep, but was aroused from his 'state of stoical apathy and indifference' by the arrival of the town's chief magistrate, who showed more interest in details of *The John's* cargo than of his shipwrecked prisoners. Nevertheless, he was induced to send a boat to rescue what he could of their personal possessions from the wreck.

Macdonald, who had been given the landlord's bed – the latter sleeping on the floor – later that evening sent for Captain Westenholz, chief of the military force in the town and requested that he remove the guard of twelve men from the inn, as their constant noise and chatter disturbed his rest! It was, of course, beyond the officer's power to do so, but he did manage to quieten them down. Macdonald also asked for the return of his clothes and papers, retrieved from *The Johns*, and was pained to hear that all his papers had to be sent to Copenhagen.

By the 24th he was sufficiently recovered to write Letter 1. of his journal, which began: '*Skagen or Scaw, a Village in North Jutland, November 24, 1808.* Confined here in a Danish prison, I have abundance of time to commit to writing what I can remember of the last four most unfortunate days of my life.' On that same day he also wrote letters seeking the special treatment which he considered his due, not only to a contact in Copenhagen, where he obviously had business interests, and General Bardenfleth, Commander-in-Chief in North Jutland, but to the King of Denmark himself.

Although Macdonald uses most of his eighty pages to describe his own feelings and experiences as a privileged prisoner of war, and neglects to tell us much of the fate of his shipmates and other inferior British prisoners or their prisons, the story is worth telling as personal prisoner of war records of this arena of war are rare indeed.

On the 29th, the prisoners were considered recovered enough to set out on the long journey to the prisoner of war depot at Randers, where, it will be remembered, the 300 Copenhagen prisoners had been sent in 1807. Captain Westenholz commandeered farm-carts to take them on the first leg, to the village of Flagstrand; with two prisoners and a peasant driver travelling in each cart, the little convoy escorted by five foot-soldiers and three mounted dragoons. To assist with communication, a German-speaking corporal of the guard was appointed to travel with Macdonald, who understood that language – the corporal who our hero thereafter referred to as his servant.

They travelled through an icy landscape with not even a tree, bush or blade of grass to break the monotony, but to seaward thirty-five wrecks were counted in less than five miles. A few cottages or shacks were dotted here and there, badly constructed from the remains of shipwrecked vessels. The village of Flagstrand, about twelve miles from Scaw, was the first overnight stage for the prisoners, but some miles before they reached that point, Macdonald became ill through trying to digest the dark Danish bread, a coarse mixture of rye, barley and fish-bones pounded into a paste and baked, which William Chambers had remarked on as abhorrent to the digestion of the English prisoners at Randers. Therefore, whilst the others moved on, Macdonald and his guard spent the night in a peasant hut.

He arrived at Flagstrand next day and stayed there until the 2nd December, then was advised to hurry on towards Aalborg, where the Commander-in-Chief, General Bardenfleth, would expect him to be with the rest of *The Johns'* ship's company. There are intimations in his journal that Macdonald had many social contacts in Denmark, Norway and Sweden – sometimes referring to the Commander-in-Chief as 'my friend General Bardenfleth'. Very late that evening he had only reached the seaport town of Saebye, where his patience was tried by the burgomaster, who kept him waiting in the cold streets before finding him 'an unpleasant lodging'.

That night must have vied with his night in the shrouds on the wreck, as the most worrying and intimidating of James Macdonald's captivity. The landlord and landlady were both already three sheets to the wind on brandy, but had just set him down before a miserable supper of 'bad fish and four greasy potatoes', when six half-drunk masters of Danish privateers, accompanied by their mates and companions made a noisy entrance and set themselves down at his table.

As he sat surrounded by twenty or more fierce-looking, mustachioed and bewhiskered desperadoes, each clad in a fur jacket with a brace of pistols in his belt and a cutlass at his side, he must have doubted his chances once they learned that he was British. 'They looked alternately at me and at each other and

162

evidently suspected that I was a spy. I was anxious to remove this idea, lest they should despatch me in self-defence.' Outwardly calm but inwardly quaking, he told them of his painful past ten days and said that he carried letters from Flagstrand to the magistrate of Saebye, and that that gentleman was awaiting their delivery. He told them that his corporal had gone to look for a horse and cart for the next day's journey to Aalborg, and managed to persuade one of the privateers to conduct him to the magistrate's house.

With some difficulty, he persuaded the magistrate to join him for a drink at his lodging and kept him talking and drinking in his bed-chamber next to the room where the privateers were noisily merry-making and singing, until midnight. Afterwards, alone in his room, with no lock to its door, he heard whisperings through the thin wall on the other side of the room and, listening, thought he heard words like 'damned English', 'baggage', 'gold', 'cutlass' and 'spy'. Lighting a candle, he went to the room where the captains were still laughing and singing, but their companions were gone; probably to the room whence came the whisperings which had so unnerved him. Certain that he was in dire danger, Macdonald confessed his worries, and was reassured that the privateers would watch out for trouble, after which he returned to his chamber. Nevertheless, he was determined not to sleep, keeping the candles burning and listening to every creak and noise in the house.

About two in the morning he saw the door slowly opening and, expecting a murderous ruffian with pistol or cutlass, was relieved but suspicious to find that it was the landlord, miraculously recovered from his complete intoxication of a couple of hours earlier. He said he had come to request that the candles be extinguished, as the police did not permit lights after midnight. 'Well,' said I, 'put them out, but remember that if anything happens to any part of my baggage in your house, both you and your lodgers shall be broken on the wheel, for my name and journey are already known at Aalborg and Copenhagen, and you shall be made responsible for anything that may happen.' Brave words, but he did not sleep a wink for the rest of that night.

A bad night was followed by an equally bad day. Heavy snowfall, sleet and frost made it necessary to travel in a cart fitted with runners. It was Macdonald's first experience of sleigh-riding, and not a happy one, twice being tipped into snow-drifts and once, more seriously, into two feet of water as they crossed a stream: 'No sooner did I get out of the water, than all my clothes froze round my body, even to my neckcloth, which had on its surface a crust of ice an inch thick,' He lodged that night at a small inn, still twelve miles from Aalborg, where he found Captain Hutton had left his dog, 'Chance', which afterwards stayed with him during the remainder of his journeying.

Macdonald and his 'servant' reached Aalborg on the 4th December and he was gratified to find that his friend, General Bardenfleth, had arranged for his reception at a comfortable lodging in the town. One of the oldest towns in Denmark, Aalborg was a busy port, as it is today, on the south side of the Limfjorden arm of the sea which formed its harbour. Ships sailed from there to Norway laden with corn, and at that time was the base for a fleet of twenty-six Danish privateer vessels. So far in this chapter we have recorded the capture of many Scandinavian vessels, but the presence in Aalborg harbour of some twenty merchant prizes taken from Britain and Sweden, was proof that success was not all one-sided.

James Macdonald hoped to stay in Aalborg until he received the reply from the King which would decide his fate and, as we know, he was there to witness the arrival of the survivors of the wreck of the *Crescent.* He tells us that the sailor and marine prisoners were sent under guard to a large building which had been converted into a prison, and the officers paroled and billetted in three town houses. Two young midshipmen were quartered in the same place as Macdonald, and gave him a disturbing account of aspects of the shipwreck. They told of how one distraught young woman wrapped her baby in her cloak and gave it to an officer, pleading with him to forget her and save the child, and how, soon after, she was washed off the deck with her husband; and 'the officer and child soon found the same watery grave'. A sad story, but another was truly harrowing.

Two boats had left the ship in an effort to carry an anchor to windward and towards the shore, but the current took them to leeward and only one regained the wreck:

> 'The captain ordered as many as it could safely carry to go aboard that boat, and try to reach the shore. Twenty-two rushed into it, and three times that number threw themselves into the sea in hopes of being admitted with their comrades. The latter were obliged, in self-defence, to push them from her into the sea, and to see them drowned before their eyes. Some of the stoutest, and who were expert swimmers, got to the boat's side before she could clear the wreck, and with their half-frozen hands laid hold of her sides and stern, and that in such numbers that she must soon have sunk if they had not quitted their deadly grasp.
>
> 'This was the most horrid scene of all. The people in the boat cut off the hands and fingers of their unfortunate shipmates with their knives: and one saw his father and brother served in this manner. He offered his place in the boat to his father, and wished to die for him, but it was too late; the latter sank in his sight...'

Macdonald had an easy, even pleasurable, stay in Aalborg, dining with the General and his officers, and entertained by the gentry of the town to balls and evening entertainments. He found the Danish ladies 'neither so elegant nor so handsome' as the English, and felt that the dress of women of the lower classes was probably designed to 'render their charms as harmless and unattractive as possible'. Wrapped from head to hip in layers of clothes, which concealed lips, eyes, neck and all the female features which he found attractive; swathed in cloth below the waist to such bulkiness that from a distance they looked like 'moving hogsheads'. He seemed to suggest that the Jutland menfolk would seldom find need to be reminded of the scriptural edict which begins: 'Whoever looks upon a woman...'

Above all else he was impatient to hear from the Danish monarch, whose permission he had sought to be allowed to return to England or travel to Sweden. Despite Captain Westenholz and his word of honour, Macdonald's private papers had not been returned from the capital and however well he was treated by the Danes he found that 'delays and mistakes are vexatious, and the more peculiarly so because time is so precious, and the season for returning home is in all probability lost'. He was also alarmed by the soaring cost of living in Denmark since 1807, typified by the price of common necessities in Aalborg:

> 'Meat is from sixpence to ninepence per pound, of eighteen and a half ounces; bread is certainly dearer than in London... a goose costs seven shillings and sixpence; a fowl, a very scarce article, and bad at the best, two shillings and four-pence; and a small fishy-tasted duck one shilling and tenpence. Cloths, linens, paper, books, leather, stuffs of all kinds, for whatever species of apparel, male or female, are at least eighty percent dearer than in London, supposing they could be procured equally good here...'

Another difficulty was the almost total absence of coinage in Jutland since the war. Anyone who could lay his hands on hard cash hoarded it, so that if one shopped for small items, such as a penny loaf, with grey paper dollars he could expect no change, but must buy a full dollar's-worth or leave the balance on deposit with the vendor.[10]

After nearly three weeks in Aalborg General Bardenfleth advised Macdonald that it would be better if he went to Nijborg in the Island of Funen, and there await the decision of Copenhagen, as he would be nearer to his only passage to freedom at that time of the year, the Sound between Elsinore in Denmark and Helsingborg in Sweden. He was to travel with the officers of the *Crescent* and would pass through the prison town of Randers. Before leaving, he visited the sailors and marines from the *Crescent* and other English and Swedish captives in the town, and found that they were well-quartered, with clean rooms and bedding: and permitted the luxury – seldom allowed to common prisoners of war in England – of occasional walks in the town under escort. The allowance to a sailor or marine was eight-pence a day, whilst merchant masters and naval petty officers received about two shillings.

Time after time, in reports by Chambers, Macdonald and others, we hear of the general generosity of the Danes towards their captives, although false propaganda was constantly fed them that their countrymen, prisoners of the British, were starved and ill-treated into serving in our navies. Many letters were cited as evidence of our cruelties and the horrors of the hulks, but when asked to produce the evidence, the recipients said that the writers had begged that they not be shown, lest they be exposed to even worse ill-treatment.

The parolees set out on the nine-day journey to Zealand, with an escort of a captain, two sergeants and four soldiers. They travelled as usual in open country carts, tolerable but uncomfortable in the summer, but a miserably cold means of transport in a Danish December. Often they had to descend and tramp through the snow beside their carts, to stimulate the circulation and prevent loss of toes or feet from frost-bite.

Their first overnight stop was to be the village of Hobres, six and a half Danish miles (just over thirty English miles[10]) from Aalborg. This village, like many others, was run down by the constant call on them to supply accommodation and carts for soldiers and prisoners on government account, and could only scrape together a bit of warmed-up veal and the hated rye bread for a late night meal. The disappointed Macdonald said that it was impossible to 'conceive the apathy and frozen indifference of a Danish landlady' in a country village.

They arrived at Randers, a town of between four and five thousand inhabitants, on the 24th December, where they caught up with English prisoners who had started out from Aalborg and Viborg a week before them and had probably had to march at least part of the way. With eighty or more men to settle in, the prisoner of war authorities in the town were kept busy but were able to find good accommodation for Macdonald and his seven officer companions.

Although he appreciated his comfortable bed, and each day took him another step towards the prospect of freedom, the Scot was seriously pained in the pocket: 'the supper for eight [British] persons, including three bottles of weak wine; and for a cup of coffee and a bit of biscuit, which was the breakfast of each of us, we are charged twenty dollars !! …at eight it would still be dear'.

The journey from Randers to the Belt, the strip of water which separates the Island of Funan from the Jutland mainland was completed in good time, as they passed through pleasant countryside almost clear of snow and the Belt itself was clear of ice. At Snoghoj they were to embark on a packet-boat to cross over to Middlefahrt and it was there that Macdonald met with his first instance of 'downright intentional rudeness' from a Dane. The officer in charge of embarkation was packing the passengers, carts and baggage into the craft 'like so many pigs and was rough and boisterous' when, Macdonald. in the presence of a hundred or more onlookers, told him that he and his group were English sailors, and considered he was jeopardizing the safety of both vessel and passengers.

Macdonald was amazed when his 'temperate remonstrance' produced a violent response. He was told that he knew his duty and would do it in spite of English arrogance, that Macdonald should remember his situation, that he was not entitled to objections, reasonable or otherwise, and should not adopt bullying airs. Our hero says that he calmly made a reply before the Danish crowd, to the effect that, had an English officer taken advantage of his accidental power, to add insult to misfortune and used ungentlemanly language to a prisoner of war, he 'would be ruined in his character and scorned by everyone as a coward'. If he did, indeed, make such a heroic speech, he was lucky to get away with it; and one might spare some sympathy for the Danish officer.

The crossing took only half an hour; but long enough for it to be observed that the vessel sailed like a tub, her sails were ill-set and the Danish sailors were 'slow, clumsy, and fresh-water like – the fellows trimmed her like land-lubbers'.

After leaving Middlefahrt, they travelled the thirty miles by cart to the capital of Funen, Odensee, where Macdonald was invited to the home of General Bardenfleth's son, who was a staff captain of dragoons in the city. Until recently there had been a number of Spanish prisoners of war in Odensee, and one Spanish officer was at Bardenfleth's house when Macdonald arrived, but most had left with their commander, the Marquis de la Romana. He learned that the townsfolk would prefer any number of British or Spanish prisoners in their town rather than accommodate their Gallic allies who abused their hospitality, the French officers demanding better wines and food than the landlords could afford or obtain and insulting their womenfolk with lewd and indecent suggestions. From Odensee they were to go to Nijborg, where they were not allowed the freedom they had so far experienced, being carefully watched over by security guards every minute of their stay, as the place was a fortified barrack town. However, the stay was short; next morning they were to cross the Great Belt from Funan to Zealand.

The prospect of another crossing, caused Macdonald to muse philosophically on the wisdom of the Greek sage who said, 'never go by sea if the journey can be made by land', dreading all the possible sufferings: perhaps seasickness, cheating boatmen, 'squalling children, squeaking pigs, filth and abominations innumerable' and – a self-pitying exaggeration of his own case – 'as was our hard fortune, all these miseries, combined with hunger, thirst, want of sleep'. The following night they were assembled in the cold and frosty streets at Nijborg at two in the morning and sat in open carts until six o'clock, before moving off into a freezing north-east wind to the embarkation point, only three miles but an hour away.

He was right in anticipating a second miserable crossing, longer and more uncomfortable than the first. About eighty passengers and prisoners were bundled onto the sloop which was to ferry them on the nine-hour voyage to Zealand. The deck space, with its two-feet-thick collar of ice, was jam-packed with luggage, cargo, pigs, horses, cattle, carts and shivering bodies; but it is unlikely that Macdonald himself suffered the worst discomfort. He had dined well enough on salt-beef, ham and bread, but was shocked that the sailors had not brought fresh water aboard: 'for my brandy was now useless to me' without water, 'I was consequently compelled to endure all the horrors of thirst during the nine hours of our painful voyage'. Neither could he have been much inconvenienced by his crammed-in fellow-travellers, as he records long discussions with the captain on a number of subjects. Not that he had forgotten the oversight which had deprived him of his diluted brandy, 'I had only the poor consolation left me of scolding the sailors, [who] bore my ill-humour very well, and endeavoured to excuse their carelessness...'

Although James Macdonald's journal was presented in the form of fifteen letters by its editor in 1810, those 'letters' were neither written, addressed nor sent to individuals, but, as he wrote to his publisher after his release, were aimed at giving as wide as possible publicity 'to circumstances so honourable to [the Danish] nation, and which may eventually soften the spirit of mutual hostility, which at present subsists between the two countries, and procure for the Danish prisoners in Britain as kind a treatment as the circumstances of the times permit'. So, despite his annoying arrogance, it must be admitted that his heart was in the right place. The only passage in the whole journal intended for the eyes of one particular person, appears in the half a dozen opening lines of Letter X, written when they arrived at Roskilde on the 31st December.

'In this town... I conclude the year 1808, a prisoner. Little did I expect to pay it such a visit, when, half a dozen years ago, I left this melancholy place, with no intention of ever seeing it again; and little didst thou expect it, my dear, far distant friend, when on the 10th of October last, thou wert pleased to dedicate thy life to the happiness of him who loves and esteems thee.'

The city of Roskilde, at the head of the fjord of that name, had been the capital of Denmark and the seat of Danish kings until the fifteenth century. The cathedral was, and still is, the royal mausoleum, where the Danish kings and queens were buried from the earliest to modern times. Understandably, this was another town where even parolees had little freedom. The explanation for this strict surveillance was that fighting had taken place there in the early days of the war in 1807, in which many brave Danes had met their end, and that as the city was now full of soldiers, they might insult or show violence towards any British prisoner who walked its streets. Typically, Macdonald took umbrage at what he considered a slight and an unnecessary restriction. The prisoners were due to leave for Copenhagen the next morning, but when he found that he was to spend the night with twenty-eight other prisoners of war in one room and under guard, his anger knew no bounds. Finding that the officer in charge spoke fluent German, and considering knowledge of that language to be 'a criterion to distinguish persons of education', he had no doubt that the Dane could be prevailed upon to provide them with more rooms and beds, and permission to roam through the town, or, if neither wish could be granted, to see that they were conveyed to Elsinore that very night. Macdonald was amazed at the commander's reaction: 'He took it highly amiss that I seemed dissatisfied with anything he chose to do, and asked me, if I suspected him to be ignorant of his duty.' The Scotsman's reply we can guess.

He could have been proud had he remembered that he was a privileged prisoner of an unmalicious enemy, then shown discretion and for once kept his mouth shut. Instead he took pride in his contribution to the long, serious dispute which ensued, (but which the publisher mercifully decided to omit from the printed version of the journal) and found himself in Copenhagen quicker than he thought – under escort as an offending prisoner of war or, as we would term it, a 'broke-parole'.

The 1st January 1809, found him once more addressing a petition to the King of Denmark asking for his release and permission to continue on his journey to Sweden and freedom. It is possible that influential businessmen supported his petition, or perhaps the Danes valued his absence greater than his detention; for by the 5th of the month he was in Elsinore, awaiting passage across the Sound to Helsinborg, in Sweden.

It is difficult to imagine our ally, Sweden, being only three English miles from our enemy, Denmark, separated only by that narrow strip of water. The batteries on either side were no more than three and a half miles apart, but, if the wind was right and a ship could maintain about five knots, and could keep more than half that distance from the opposite shore there was little danger from enemy cannon. Nevertheless, on the 7th January the Swedish man-of-war brig, *Wenta Litet,* became trapped in a drifting ice field which carried her towards the north. Although she immediately struck her colours, the Kronborg Castle battery opened up and did considerable damage. The Swede gallantly returned the fire, lobbing seventeen shells into the town before the Castle called off the cannonade, destroying the town gallows and striking the roofs of houses near to Macdonald's quarters.

During the time that he was delayed in Elsinore, the Oresund Sound had become ice-bound and unnavigable, and when, on the 12th January 1809, the last day of his captivity, he made the crossing, he made the 'voyage' by 'ice-boat'. Ice-boats were employed to carry both mail and passengers from island to island or mainland during very severe winters. They were stoutly built, in much the same way as traditional boats, but with sledge-like keels, heavily reinforced with iron. These were dragged over the ice by teams of men fitted with harness and safety-ropes, who drove ice-poles before them to test the firmness as they progressed over their treacherous passage – and the ice was not firm everywhere. Not infrequently they sank through soft patches and all hands struggled to pull them back to the boats by their safety lines, but there were many reports of ice-boatmen being drowned or crushed to death. between ice-floes. Such tragedies occurred more often on long hauls, such as the eighteen or nineteen miles across the Great Belt between Funen and Zealand.

Macdonald's ice-boat voyage was comparatively short in distance, but it took six hours for six strong Danes to cover the three miles and deliver him to the Swedish shore without mishap. His unusual mode of travel from captivity to freedom certainly gave him something to write home about.

Stories of those Scandinavians who spent at least some part of their captivity on the ill-famed English prison hulks, and of their more fortunate brethren who were granted the great privilege of parole, are told elsewhere in this book.[11] This short chapter set out to explain just how Danes came to be brought as prisoners to this country in the first place. I shall end it with a tale of 'English' mariners, captured by the 'French' on a 'Danish' ship which the 'British' had recently captured at Copenhagen.

The unhappy fate of two of those English prisoners of war is related in the diary of John Wetherell,[12] himself a prisoner of the

French for eleven years, most of them at Givet, one of the four great French fortress prisoner of war depots, These two, Henry Haywood and Robert Gale had been officers on that Danish prize which foundered on the Dutch coast.

Henry Haywood, a young English officer who had been Master's Mate of HBMS *Alfred* (74) before being given command of one of the Copenhagen prizes, found that life as a prisoner of war at Givet – at any rate for one of his rank – was not unbearably unpleasant. Like other junior officers, he had the privilege of a kind of semi-parole, whereby they were allowed to stroll through the streets and ramparts of the old walled town and mix freely with the townsfolk, but accompanied by a gendarme who was responsible for their timely return to the depot. Haywood and his young midshipman friend, Richard Gale, had settled in well enough to have found regular girl friends, whom they had met among the farmers and peasants who crowded the morning market at the gates of the prison.

The two couples, with their gendarme escort, often enjoyed excursions into Petit Givet, the smaller of the two parts of the town which straddled the River Meuse. Once outside the prison walls, it was customary for the gendarme to be made comfortable in a tavern, with a bottle of his favourite wine and a promise that the prisoners would report back to him in time for the evening muster. One day, early in January 1808, Haywood and Gale set off for an afternoon out with their girlfriends, after depositing their French overseer, La Marque by name, in his favourite inn and assuring him that they intended to spend an hour or so of the evening in Petit Givet. However, encouraged by the girls, their real intention was to bend the rules slightly and meet them in the little village of Ransend, about three miles distant on the other side of the river, where a harvest festival dance and fair was in progress.

They tipped the keeper of the Port Ransend Gate five francs and passed onto the road which led to the bridge, after telling him that they would be gone for no more than an hour. The gatekeeper would not have doubted their truthfulness for a minute, as it was a point of honour not to miss a muster: to do so would mean that all officer parolees would suffer loss of the privilege, for a short or longer period according to the seriousness of the offence.

On their way towards the bridge they had the misfortune to meet with an English Royal Marine named 'Pegleg' Wilson, who acted as the servant and cook to the officer prisoners. Elderly captives or cripples were allowed to walk out from the prison each day and Wilson was entitled to go beyond the gate or roam the town and ramparts, as he had lost a leg whilst serving as a marine on the English frigate *Minerva*, during the action which resulted in her capture off Cherbourg – the diarist, John Wetherell noted at the time that 'a pitty it was that it had not been his head'!

Wilson was invited to accompany them to the dance, but instead, the troublemaking marine sought out La Marque and told him that his charges were beyond the gate. The gendarme was so enraged that one might guess that he had over-slaked his thirst at the inn. The two young officers had stopped to watch some stone cutters at work on the bridge when the gendarme soon caught up with them. John Wetherell wrote:

> 'Haywood was the first that approached him and in his Merryway of talking says to La Marque, "Come let us go together and have a little amusement in the Village." La Marque drew his sword, Haywood made a halt and was in the act of lifting his arm in self-defence when La Marque made a desperate Stroke at his head with all his might and split his head entirely in two so that he lay dead at his feet. Gale seeing him strike Haywood was in the greatest amazement and ran to the Gendarme begging for mercy when the bloodthirsty rascal up Sword and Cut Gale down the right side of his head face and breast.'

Gale was taken to hospital but expired that same night and was buried with Haywood in one grave on the following morning. The shocked friends of Haywood and Gale made a vengeful search throughout the prison for the peg-legged Wilson, but the Commandant had wisely sent him up to Charlemont and thence to a distant depot. The murderous La Marque was confined for a few days but, after something of a mock trial, he was acquitted, and transferred to the prisoner of war depot at Arras. However, news of his villainy had followed him.

Towards the end of 1808, a group of prisoners were transferred from Arras to Givet and brought with them the satisfying news that, during a masquerade at carnival time, La Marque was 'run through the heart' by someone dressed 'in the character of a French Drummer' – but was most probably an English officer.

---

1. Whilst signal No. 39 (Discontinue the Action) was flown by the Commander-in-Chief, and Nelson did *not* strike his own signal, No. 16, (Close Action), some historians do not believe that he was ignoring an order, but that the Admiral had hoisted No. 39 so that commanders whose ships were badly damaged during the battle could retire without being accused of cowardice.

2. 'Praam': a flat-bottomed vessel.

3. 'Radeau': a raft-like floating battery.

4. Among the captains who commanded sail-of-the-line in Nelson's squadron at the Battle of Copenhagen were men whose names are well remembered today. William Bligh commanded the 54-gun *Glatton* which lost 18 killed and 37 wounded in the battle. Everyone remembers

him as captain of the *Bounty*, but few know that he also served with distinction at the Battle of Camperdown as captain of the *Director* in 1797. He was appointed Governor of Australia and was promoted to Vice-Admiral in 1814.

5. *Naval Chronicle*. Volume XIX, page 493. 1808.

6. Ian MacDougall: *Prisoners at Penicuik.*

7. A 'Crimp' is a person who lures, forces or entraps men into military or naval service.

8. *Chambers' Journal*. Volume I, page 333. 1854.

9. The Danish mile was equal to about four and three-quarter English miles. Under Danish law, peasants were required to make their own farm carts available to

transport prisoners of war from place to place, at the rate of one Danish mile an hour. Some time-based remuneration must have been involved as it is said that they seldom arrived until hours after the estimated time of arrival.

10. In 1804 the Danish dollar was worth about four shillings and sixpence sterling. In 1808 it was devalued to about two shillings and fourpence.

11. See Chapter 8, THE DANISH HULKS and Chapter 22, PAROLE IN ENGLAND.

12. John Porritt Wetherell's memoirs existed as a three-volume, one thousand page manuscript for more than a century, until its publication in 1954.

Chapter Ten

The Peninsular War

FRANCE INVADES PORTUGAL; FRANCO-SPANISH ALLIANCE BROKEN;
THE BATTLE OF BAYLEN 1808; THE SPANISH HULKS AT CADIZ;
THE FATAL ISLE OF CABRERA.

THIS CHAPTER TELLS OF CAPTIVITY even harsher and sometimes even more horrific than the tales told of the worst of the English hulks, or the New York prison ships during the War of American Independence. It deals briefly with the second half of the first decade of the nineteenth century, when Portugal, Spain, France, and later Britain, were involved in warlike circumstances which led up to the Peninsular War.

Nelson's glorious victory at Trafalgar in 1805 had not only overcome the French naval strength, the Spanish Fleet, which Napoleon had depended upon in his long-laid plans for a descent upon England, was almost completely obliterated, its remnants lying to rot in the Spanish ports.

That great battle had gained for Britain the title of 'Queen of the Seas', but between that year and 1807, Napoleon had defeated

Austrian, Prussian and Russian armies and was virtually 'Monarch of the Continent', or nearly so, for only England stood in his way. However, neither were content. Our naval superiority had relieved us from the fear of imminent invasion of England; but Napoleon's Berlin decrees had closed practically all European ports to British subjects, ships and trade. Businesswise, this was bad for both nations, for the closed ports would have welcomed the trade in British-made goods; as much as the latter would have been delighted to supply them; but their time was taken up with blockades and counter blockades.

Portugal, Britain's oldest ally since the Middle Ages, objected to the French decrees and decided to ignore them, as did Sweden. The

Letecaire. Desolate French Prisoners on the Island of Cabrera.

thwarted and enraged Emperor could not tolerate such resistance to his ordinance, so on the 28th July 1807 an ultimatum was served on the Portuguese and, in October 1807, the Treaty of Fontainebleau was signed by France and a reluctant and resentful Spain. This called for a joint invasion of Portugal, which would have denied British shipping its last point of entry into a European trading port. The Tsar of Russia, now allied with Bonaparte, was left to deal with Sweden.

The signing of the treaty was on the 27th of October but a full week before that date the French General Jean Andoche Junot, without forewarning or declaration, had already marched through Spain and crossed over the border into Portugal with a French invading force of some 30,000 troops, many of them untrained recruits.

Junot was acting under ill-conceived orders from the very top, when he set out on his long march to Lisbon. He was first to head for Salamanca and then proceed on a punishing march to Alcantara, over primitive roads made almost impassable by the most terrible climatic conditions imaginable. At Alcantara he was to take command of a detachment of similarly untrained, and largely unwilling, Spaniards. Many of his original army had been left in the rear during the long and painful marches which had brought them thus far, but now, with his Spanish reinforcement, the General's army was again about 25,000 strong. However, they still had two hundred miles to negotiate, through mountains as inhospitable as the fierce peasants who inhabited them. The invaders were short of so many things, usually thought essential to the successful outcome of any military operation, such as ample ammunition, sufficient provisions and, of equal importance, information. Junot had no certain knowledge as to how he would be received when he arrived in the capital with his ragtag army.

He had learned that, in November 1807, the royal family was still in residence; that Portugal had a standing army of about fifteen thousand regular troops, and that life was going on at its usual laconic pace. But he had no clue as to whether or not he would have to fight before declaring Portugal a French occupied territory.

That nightmare two hundred mile slog through the mountains literally decimated the Franco-Spanish army: some fell by the wayside from sheer exhaustion, disease, desertion, or fell victim to the savage peasantry, and, inevitably, there were stragglers. Horses died in their hundreds, and large quantities of powder and cartridges were made useless by the torrential rains. When Junot finally reached Lisbon, his 25,000 strong force had been whittled down to only 2,000 exhausted French grenadiers. He arrived just in time to see the Portuguese fleet disappearing over the skyline, carrying the royal family and court into exile in South America. It had long been recognised that Queen Maria I was mentally unfit to rule, and her eldest son, John, Prince of Brazil, who had ruled in her stead since about 1790, was left behind as Prince Regent of Portugal. With the fleet had gone several thousand of the nation's most important men and families and, to Junot's bitter disappointment, also the contents of the Treasury.

The intruders found little resistance, though of course, no great welcome, and there was no overt trouble until the Portuguese flag, which fluttered above St George's Castle and a few other official buildings, was hauled down and the tricolour took its place, that some spirit of patriotism rose up and rioting, and rowdiness broke out, but was soon subdued.

Propaganda or rumour had been sown along the route of Junot's march, suggesting that the French were advancing on Lisbon to protect the Portuguese from a British invasion of their country. There had, indeed, been an English fleet lying off the port in September 1806 but a stern letter from Napoleon to the timorous Prince John listed a number of anti-British actions which the Regent should bring about immediately. The Prince lost no time before consulting the Admiral, and sighed with relief as our fleet – for the time being – sailed away.

It is most tempting to carry on the story of Junot and the French, Spanish and Portuguese, but for this chapter it is unnecessary, for the moment, to go further than the above as far as Portugal is concerned. It is now necessary to return to Spain to pick up the other half of the tale, of how the war which lasted another six years, came about.

Napoleon had little respect for his Spanish ally and although he could see her possible usefulness in closing the last hole in the Continental System – hence the Fontainbleau Treaty – his treacherous intention was to enter Spain under the guise of a friend and protector, and invade her when the time was right. This underestimation of the courage and possible strength of the Spanish people was one of the greatest misjudgments of his long and brilliant military career and played a significant part in his downfall several years later. At that time he could have had no doubt that the conquest of Spain and Portugal would soon be added to his unbroken chain of victories. Spain had been prosperous, with a golden stream of wealth flowing in from her South American possessions but the loss of her fleet had stemmed that flow and the British navy in the south Atlantic had its source well blockaded. Consequently, Napoleon's Iberian ally was financially weak, with a royal family which he despised and was determined to replace as soon as possible. The country was run, not by the Bourbon king, Charles IV, but by the Queen's reputed boyfriend, Manuel Godoy, the 'Prince of Peace'[1], who had virtually ruled for the past sixteen years. The trio had no faith or feeling for Ferdinand, the eldest son and heir apparent. But by now it was an unhappy country, hardly likely to rise in revolt against the most powerful man in the world. It is understandable that the Emperor should have taken Spain so much for granted. A great achiever himself, he spared no sympathy for failures. He had pulverised the Prussian armies at Auerstadt and Jena in the autumn of 1806, and had lost all respect for their Emperor, Frederick Wilhelm. However, he had retained sufficient appreciation of the qualities of the Russian Emperor, Alexander I, whose armies he had also recently defeated, but was now entrusted to stop up the Swedish gap. When, on the 25th July 1807, the Treaty of Tilsit took place on a raft on the River Niemen, Napoleon and Alexander were in deep discussion for hours, whilst the Prussian Emperor and his officials were left waiting on the river bank in the pouring rain.

At about the same time that General Junot was preparing to set out on his unheralded invasion of Portugal – October 1807 – the Spanish Court had moved to El Escorial, the vast monastery situated about twenty-six miles to the northwest of Madrid, where the ruling family had taken residence in the royal apartments. Ferdinand found quarters in another part of the great building, but was not to enjoy the isolation from his unloving parents for long. They were, unintentionally but as usual, aiding the French Emperor in his dynastic plans, by chipping away at their own already crumbling image, with intrigues and bitter accusations. An anonymous (Godoy?) letter alleged that the Prince, along with

Spanish and French conspirators, were negotiating a marriage between him and a member of the Bonaparte family. Worse still, he was said to be planning to usurp the throne and assassinate his parents. Charles IV was not just disturbed, but terrified. The Prince was arrested and imprisoned within the monastery under a strong guard, his personal papers impounded and scoured for evidence of his crime. None was found, but the deeply disturbed King wrote a craven appeal to Napoleon, begging for his advice and protection against his wicked son and heir. He also named some of the alleged conspirators, including the Marquis François de Beauharnais, the French Ambassador. The Emperor's reply must have left the King doubly terrified, couched as it was in terms of extreme anger; not with Ferdinand, but with Charles for daring to suggest that his Ambassador was in any way involved. He said that the Prince was now under his protection, and if he heard another word against him, France would declare war on Spain.

The confused and corrupt Spanish Government was falling apart and was, of course, weakened by its division into at least three distinct leaderships: Charles IV, Prince Ferdinand, and Godoy. Each had his own followers and it was not long before there were demonstrations and rioting in the streets. As often as not, these outbreaks were rows between Godoyist and Ferdinandist partisans, rather than anti-French disturbances. Prince Ferdinand and his father had each sought backing from the French, to help deal with their particular problems – although the latter were probably responsible for the state of affairs in the first place.

Napoleon had been preparing for sizeable numbers of trained soldiers to be sent into Spain. They were to enter under the pretext that they should join up with General Junot, in the event of his invasion of Portugal. The Emperor was confident with the way things were progressing. Unabashedly appreciative of his own greatness – he once corrected Talleyrand, his Foreign Minister, saying that he should not be thought of as a reincarnation of the great Bourbon king, Louis XIV, but of the even greater Charlemagne – he would not have blushed had he also heard himself called the greatest nepotist in history. The fragmented state of the Spanish Government fitted perfectly with his plans to found a Bonaparte dynasty, built upon his siblings, relatives and friends. Impatient as he was to bring to fruition any of his ambitions, he had only a short while to wait for the Spanish royal family to bring about its own downfall. In spite of his threatening letter to King Charles, Godoy and Maria-Luisa had the accused aristocratic followers of the Prince arraigned before a panel of Spanish judges who wisely found them not guilty.

Maria Luisa described her eldest son more than once as 'very ugly', but waxed enthusiastic when speaking of her favourite son, the Infante Don Fransisco, who bore. 'a most indecent likeness to Manuel Godoy.' She had no greater liking for Ferdinand's wife, Maria Antonia of Naples, and once described her as ' …this slut who fans the flames, my daughter-in-law… that off-scouring of her mother (the Queen of Naples), that poisonous viper, that animal bursting with spleen and venom in place of blood, that half-dead toad, that diabolical serpent.' The young Princess Maria Antonia died from tuberculosis in 1806, and now the Prince of Peace seized a possible main-chance, by suggesting that the Crown Prince should marry Maria Teresa of Bourbon, who happened to be the sister of Godoy's wife. Ferdinand's reply was explicit: rather than be related to Godoy, he would prefer to be a widower or a monk for the rest of his life.

In November 1807, whilst all this in-fighting and family quarrels kept the Spanish authorities busy, the French had quietly and – by ignoring the terms of the treaty – illegally, sent another army over the Pyrenees into northern Spain. These 25,000 men were under the command of General Dupont, of whom we shall soon hear more, at the Battle of Baylen. In January 1808 another 30,000 men arrived at Navarre, to be followed in February by General Duhesme and a force of 14,000 more, who headed for Barcelona. Although the higher ranked officers must have been aware of the underhand trickery by which they intended to conquer Spain, the French rank-and-file and the Spanish populace, at least the countryfolk, were still under the impression that they were genuine allies of Spain; but once the troops began to move into strategic positions, both peoples woke up to reality.

Aware that the Spanish Army was as disorganised as the Government; and with no expectation of a serious resistance from the country's gentlemen and peasants, the great leader brushed aside any advice on the subject as a waste of words: such things might occur, but would be immediately put down. The Duke of Otranto once proffered his opinion that Spain might be stronger than was generally supposed and he received the Emperor's ungrateful retort: 'What are you talking about? Every reflecting person in Spain despises the government; the Prince of Peace is a scoundrel who will himself open the gates of Spain for me. As to the rabble… a few cannon shots will quickly disperse them.'

Evidence of discontent and anger among the Spaniards was growing louder daily. Frustrated by the Emperor's constant reassurances that he was their friend and protector – then often acting in a manner contrary to their interests – the revolutionary feelings of the Spanish people now focused against their erstwhile ally with an intensity of dislike which bordered on hatred. Without warning, rebellious uprisings broke out, and fighting of a type outside the experience of many of Napoleon's senior staff and most of his troops, their officers and NCOs. Some Spanish historians give such an exaggerated degree of importance to the part played by guerrilla warfare, street-by-street and house-by-house fighting, that it might appear that Spanish peasants and townsfolk might have saved Spain from Napoleon's grasp, without the help of Britain or Portugal; although they did grant some credit to their own regular army. It is true that there were heroes – and heroines – among the 'civilian soldiers'; their achievements perhaps marred by the inevitable carnage which followed their successful clashes. The cruelty with which they perpetuated their atrocities was matched only by the French.

Had these scattered insurrections been confined to one or two areas, there is little doubt that the French could have contained them as minor mutinies, but once started they spread like wildfire throughout the whole country, and war was now inevitable. Manuel Godoy, whose loyalty to Spain or devotion to Bonaparte switched sides at the drop of a hat, according to his own personal interests, had ordered the return of what was left of the Spanish troops who had been part of the French invading force under General Junot, who was isolated in now neutral Portugal. Some were detained by Junot as prisoners of war or hostages, but most got back to rejoin the main Spanish army.

Bonaparte would have received the news of Spain's defection and defiance with anger and amazement at such effrontery; nevertheless he immediately sent more soldiers and a number of senior officers to Bayonne, where they were to come under the command of Joachim Murat, Napoleon's brother-in-law, from his headquarters at Vitoria.

In early 1808, the French army in Spain under Murat totalled some 90,000 men. The army of Spain would have been about 100,000, but these figures alone cannot be compared, as the latter were confused and to a certain extent undisciplined. Many Spaniards whose future prospects were reduced by the financial state of the country, had joined the forces more for their personal chances of advancement, than patriotism – although it was unlikely that they would reach very high rank (or even become officers), unless they were titled or came from aristocratic lineage. The great difference lay not so much in numbers, but in the fact that only one side had a great war leader. Godoy's ambitions were too centred on himself rather than his country for him to ever be regarded as great, and the public realised it. Ferdinand now became the people's favourite and the Prince gloried in the warmth of the cheering crowds when he arrived in Madrid, on the 24th March, 1808. A week earlier King Charles IV had abdicated; in favour of 'my most beloved son, the Prince of the Asturias (Ferdinand)', Godoy was put under lock and key, and Ferdinand VII succeeded to the throne of Spain. Godoy, whose popularity had dropped to zero, faced charges of treason, and had he not been in prison, may well have been lynched by the boisterous mob; but of one supporter he could be certain.

Ex-Queen Maria Luisa immediately began a series of more than a dozen letters to France, which were repetitious in so much as they each carried the same requests and a warning. Her first and most fervent plea was that the Grand-Duke of Berg (Murat) might 'intercede with the Emperor to safeguard the life of the Prince of Peace…' Her second plea, garnished as was the first, with hypocritical words of friendship and appreciation of the Emperor's kindness and generosity, intimated her wish to leave Spain; ' …our one desire is that the Grand-Duke obtains permission from the Emperor for the King, my husband, myself and the Prince of Peace to live together, all three in some place beneficial for our health, without authority and free from intrigues…' Maria Luisa then ended with the unmotherly warning: 'Of my son, we can never hope for anything but miseries and persecutions. Both to the public and the Emperor, he has began and assiduously continues to misrepresent that innocent and passionate friend of the French, the Grand-Duke and the Emperor – the poor Prince of Peace…'

The reign of Ferdinand VII, the Bourbon king of Spain, came to an abrupt end when Charles, Maria Luisa and Godoy made their earth-shattering declaration that Ferdinand was illegitimate and therefore not in line for the throne. Napoleon quickly resolved the matter of the monarchy without bothering the Spanish people. To aid the fulfillment of his deep laid plan, rather than the result of the ex-queen's pleading letters, Codoy was released from prison and sent secretly to France. Charles IV, Ferdinand VII and Maria Luisa, were summoned to meet the Emperor at Bayonne, where the two kings were required to officially hand over the rights to the crown. In return they were promised generous pensions and property.

On the 9th June, 1808, Bonaparte presented the Kingdom of Spain to his eldest brother, Joseph.

By the spring of 1808, the inhabitants of Madrid had rebelled against the French occupation and their attempt to decide who should rule Spain. The Prince of Peace, once the most fêted, but by now the most hated aspirant, was detained by the French in France, and the majority of all classes shouted in favour of Ferdinand as the country's possible saviour – but did not approve of the rest of

their royal family being sent into exile. Napoleon had given no sign of acceptance or otherwise of Ferdinand as the new king – and was silent about his own amazing move, which he would make five weeks later. Apprehensive of the fate which might lay in wait for their country and their futures, the lack of reliable information engendered rumours, false reports and troubles, whether from actions taken by the French, or their own shaky government. Uncertainty lit the short fuse of Spanish tempers in many parts of the country. Most of these were small, though often violent, incidents; some would have been Spaniard against Spaniard, scuffles between *ferdinando* and *godoyistas* groups of anti-French patriots, whose one wish would have been to chalk up a Frenchman. However, rioting in Madrid and its environs during April and May 1808 was far more serious and opened up the doors to full-scale war.

Rebelliousness and violence had broken out in the busy city streets with ever more frequency. The 1st May was a typical day of restlessness and muttering; among a dozen other reasons for angry discontent, was a series of rumours, the answers to which were of immense importance to the populace. Rumours such as – the French intended to bring back Godoy; the French were considering Charles IV's efforts to rescind his abdication and return to Spain; King Ferdinand VII was to be deposed, etc., etc.– plus a few truths. One of those truths was that an order had been revived which stated that all remaining members of the Spanish royal family were to be sent to Bayonne forthwith.

Next morning, the 2nd May, a huge crowd had assembled outside the palace at Aranjuez, where carriages awaited the embarkation of the young Prince Francisco de Paula and other members of the royal family, for their journey to the frontier. By the time the passengers emerged, the temper of the mob had grown to fever-pitch, and a group of foolhardy rioters was setting about a French officer of Murat's staff. The Grand-Duke Murat, however, was already observing the mêlée from his nearby headquarters, and arrived on the scene within a few minutes, with a detachment of the Imperial Guard.

Ordered to put a stop to the fracas, the Guard's first volley of musketry shot left a dozen Spaniards dead on the pavement. The unwounded fled for cover; but the sound of action, and cries of 'Death to the French!' brought more citizens than ever on to the streets, but this time armed with anything of use as a weapon. Any lone Frenchman encountered on the street was as good as dead. Farm and domestic implements were most in evidence, although a few had muskets or pistols, and little ammunition. The crudely armed civilians did not stand a chance. Murat had an army of some 10,000 men under canvas in the surrounding countryside, and columns from the camps were soon streaming in on foot or horseback, towards the Puerta del Sol, or city centre. Some of these had to pass through Calle Mayor, where the tall buildings provided ideal points from which the guerrilla snipers could pick off the French soldiers as they passed below although the odds against the civil heroes were incalculable. The Junta de Gobierno decreed that none of the Spanish military, officers or men, should become involved in the uprising of civilians. However, the courageous actions of two young Spanish officers and forty troopers are immortilised in the history of that tragic day.

The officers, Deoiz and Valarde, of the Madrid Garrison were in charge of the Arsenal at Artillery Park. They could have avoided danger and death without losing honour but disarmed the small

French contingent and opened the gates to a mob in search of weapons. Pouring volleys of grape shot into the advancing French troops, they repulsed two attacks, in a four-hour-long battle, during which they captured the commander of the second column, Colonel Montholon. By the end of the morning, Murat's troops in the city had grown to a force of between one thousand five hundred, and two thousand trained guardsmen, who brought to an end the gallant stand at the Artillery Park. Deoiz, Valarde and their small force of Spanish regulars were all killed, as were some of the civilians who joined them. The French then systematically reduced the crowds of desperate revolutionaries into straggling bands of bloodied and exhausted men and women.

By 2 o'clock in the afternoon, all but the seriously wounded, those who were not fleet of foot, or those unwise enough not to have got away to safety whilst the going was good, were rounded up by the French cavalry and infantry, together with the civilians from the Arsenal – said to have originally been about 500.

The Madrid uprising became known as the *Dos de Mayo* (2nd of May), and is one of the most celebrated dates in Spanish history. Although the insurrection may in some senses be deemed a failure; in others it might claim success as an inspiration which helped to win a war. The story of its heroic defenders and the heartless cruelty perpetrated by the French on that and the following day, soon reached every corner of Spain, inspiring resistance and feelings of revenge against their hated oppressors. It may also be a part-explanation, or excuse, for the inhumanity of the Spanish towards the thousands of soon-to-be-taken French prisoners of war. The men and women who had been caught in the round-up, were not treated as prisoners of war, but as offenders against an order made the day before by Marshal Murat. All rioters taken 'with arms in their hands' and a range of other offenders including vendors of weaponry, were to be summarily executed by firing squad.

There was little time for any sort of fair trial. To be accused was to be found guilty, and those religious Spaniards were granted no last rites. The slaughter was sickening, even to some Frenchmen; General Maximilien Foy wrote: 'Among those who were condemned who had not fought, and whose only crime was having had about them large knives, or other sharp instruments... ' Interpretation of the Murat order was loose, and in the case of some of those men who were captured in their homes, the knives and sharp instruments were the tools of their trades. It was said that to carry even a pair of scissors might invite a sentence of death – in fact, a young girl was executed during the fight for the Madrid arsenal. The firing squads were kept busy throughout the night and well into the following day, the 3rd May.

After any war politics and discretion make it almost impossible to estimate the number of casualties with any accuracy, each country tending to decrease their actual losses, and exaggerate their gains. This was also true of the Madrid insurrection. Murat reported that he had lost only eighty men, whilst his contemporary, Sir William Napier, put the figure of French dead as 750. In order to sustain the spirit of the inhabitants of Madrid, the Gobierno Junta declared that only 150 had been killed although the French paper, *Monituer* reported that 2,000 Spaniards had been slain.

******

We have now laid down the bare bones of the incidents, events, and ambitions which led to a six-year-long war, which Spain and Portugal did not want, which France lived to regret, and Britain was fortunate enough to eventually win.

The Peninsular War, 1808–1814, must be the most written-about campaign in our military history. The mighty endeavour to record those action-packed years, was undertaken by Major-General Sir William Napier. None could have been more suited to the task. He was eye-witness to much of what he wrote; for he was present, and fought, in a number of the great battles in Spain, under his friend and hero, Sir Arthur Wellesley. Napier's famous work, *History of the War in the Peninsular*, was written between 1828 and 1840, and was published in six volumes. Since then and to this day, historians have reviewed the story from all manner of viewpoints; military, political, nationalistic, etc. Others have written detailed books on individual battles, or used the war as a background for fiction based on fact. Details of places, time, dates, terrain, contemporary happenings, important or mundane, even the weather and minutiae down to the tiniest detail may be culled from this mountain of information. All this is invaluable to researchers, writers, and the designers of life-sized and tabletop war games. It is rather disappointing, therefore, to find that most references to servicemen below the level of officer, are presented only as numbers. For instance, ' ...forty men were killed, sixty-five wounded, and one hundred and twenty were taken prisoner', without describing how they were imprisoned, or how they were housed or treated. In fact, it is unusual to find in the indexes of many good war books reference to 'prison' or 'prisoner of war'.

Fortunately, I have in my possession two journals or memoirs left by two French soldiers. The latter, whose names were Gille and Quantin, were taken prisoner in the first major battle to take place in Spain, early in the period covered by this chapter, 1806–1810, and at a time when many of the Spanish people were still uncertain where they stood; were they, as the treaties said, allied to France, or were they being invaded? These two Frenchmen, were captured and imprisoned, not by the British but by the Spanish, at the Battle of Baylen, in 1808. As far as I know, their memoirs have never been published in Britain.

Louis-François Gille's memories were first published anonymously. Francis Abell refers to him as *Philippe* Gille in his notes on Portchester Castle, but a later edition of the memoirs, with a new foreword and title-page, reveals that Philippe was the editor of his father's reminiscences: '*L-F Gille. Les Prisonniers de Cabrera. Mémoires d'un Conscrit de 1808'.* Collected and published by Philippe Gille. The diaries of Quantin are bound together in one small volume: '*Trois Ans En Espagne.'*

Despite his harrowing march on Lisbon, General Junot had somehow achieved a great deal in a very short time. France now occupied Portugal. The Braganza dynasty was officially ended, and Junot, king in all but name, had created a new government over which be acted in the style of a benign dictator. He was welcomed by many Lisbon dignitaries and titled gentlemen for political or business reasons but the public viewed things differently. Misled, like the Spaniards, by Napoleon's assurances that, as he was protecting them from the perfidious English, he was showing them friendship, the Portuguese people began to awaken. When, a few weeks later, news of the 'Dos de Mayo' spread through the whole Peninsular, a new and dangerous spirit was aroused.

Towards the end of 1807, French troops in the Peninsular numbered about 60,000 men, quite apart from General Junot's invaders in Portugal. They were held in reserve, mainly in Bayonne.

To the puzzled distress of their Spanish ally, two French divisions had crossed the frontier, and by the 12th February, 1808, had occupied the cities of Pamplona and Barcelona. From the Spanish Government protests were met with yet another dose of Napoleonic honeyed words and false promises. They were already booked to receive a slice of Portugal, but now they were promised the whole country – but only after signing away impossible-to-accept sacrifices of territory and other conditions. In effect, Spain and France were now at war, although only one country seemed to realise it. However, the Spanish people could not be hoodwinked indefinitely.

With their own royal family exiled, and their government headed by a king enthroned by their oppressor, rebellion reigned in the form of large and small uprisings throughout the land, most of which were fairly quickly dealt with, but had the virtue of keeping many units of the French armies busy. Most of the provinces were preparing for rule by juntas, or local governments, and on the 25th May the province of Asturias declared war on France.

During that same month, Murat brought another army out of reserve and into play. It was a hotchpotch army of 25,000 men, under the command of General Dupont de l'Etang, which had arrived in Iberia in November 1807. Dupont had already distinguished himself in three of Napoleon's victorious battles; but this was his first experience as Commander-in-Chief. It was a great career opportunity, for he was aware, that whilst his Emperor had no time for failures, he could be generous in reward for outstanding military service. Juno was to be given a dukedom for his work in Portugal, and Dupont had been waiting impatiently for a chance to exhibit his skills. Perhaps he would receive a marshal's baton, or even greater glory.

His orders were to make the long march south, to subdue any insurrection in Cordoba, Seville and the port of Cadiz – which was blockaded by the Royal Navy. In fact he was to occupy Andalusia.

On 24th May, 1808, the 2nd Army of Observation of the Gironde, an incongruous mixture of 13,000 men; tried and untried troops of French, Swiss and other European nationalities, left Toledo and headed south. Napoleon's personal lack of respect for Spain as a worthy belligerent, led him, not for the first time, to send armies of ill-matched make-up into situations which called for experienced warriors and careful planning. General Dupont's fighting force was made up of two divisions, the second under General Honore, Comte de Vedel.

The first division of about 8,000 men, comprised only one battalion of seasoned French veterans – Seamen of the Guard – a great number of youngsters who, like Louis-François Gille, had been caught up in the revived Conscription Act of 1807, and other disparate units. Vedel's division was made up of six battalions from Reserve Legions, and about a thousand Swiss mercenaries, in all, just over 5,000 men.

Fighting and short-lived battles were taking place all over Spain; against regular Spanish troops or, just as painfully, against vengeful and ferocious peasants. The French plan was to first establish a good line of contact with France; and experienced generals were given orders to take strategic towns, cities and ports. Jean Baptiste Bessières, Duke of Istria, was to be responsible for keeping the Madrid highway free from blockage in the interest of communication, and to capture Santander. Bon Adrien de Moncey, Duke of Conegliano, was to take Valentias and the Cartegena naval base, where he should join up with Philibert Duhesme who would be coming down the coast from Barcelona.

There was already talk of inhuman treatment of prisoners, of atrocities and even torture; but for the first two weeks of their expedition, Dupont's army met with no hostilities or hold-ups: in fact, most of the towns and villages were eerily silent, deserted by their inhabitants. The French had crossed plains, uplands and, by the beginning of June, had left the Sierra Morena behind and entered the plains of Cordoba.

On the way to the city, Dupont encountered token aggressions which were quickly suppressed, but found on reaching the outskirts, that a gallant conglomeration of Spaniards, almost equal in number to his own attacking force, who were prepared to defend their homes and city. The battle, was fought on 7th June, at Alcolea Bridge, only a short distance outside the city walls. It did not last long; the disorganised defenders being put to flight and into hiding.

Dupont had succeeded in his task so far, and the Caliphate of Cordoba was occupied by the French – but at the cost of thirty-two men killed and eighty-seven wounded. Military historians have noted what the General should have decided to do next. Anything would have been better than what transpired: there was 'no excuse for the pillage, rape and murder, which continued unabated for two days.

Cordoba was one of the richest cities of Spain; its churches and palaces were treasure houses of paintings, tapestries and metal-work; and the treasury alone was sacked of no less than ten million reals in coin. Officers and men alike took part in the systematic looting; and when the French retreated nine days later they left with five hundred wagons piled high with the spoils. The atrocities set in train prompt Spanish reprisals: isolated parties of French wounded and foragers were set upon and tortured to death. General Foy, most reliable of French historians, in condemning the conduct of Dupont's army, goes on to relate how a French officer, Brigadier-General Reme, was surprised and captured and then boiled alive. According to another account he was strapped down and sawn in two.' The binding of a man between two planks, and sawing him in half, became a frequently used reprisal by peasant torturers. In fact, the pillaging of Cordoba appears to have set the pattern for the brutalities perpetrated by both sides.

Our diarist, Louis Gille, who was one of the quartermasters, in the Second Division, under Vedel, had now been in the army for only one year. He had made the first notes for his journal on the first day of his call-up in Paris in 1807, and continued to record everything that caught his eye, for the next six years. The battle at Cordoba had been fought on the 7th June, at which time Louis Gille had already been in hospital for a week at Toledo. On hearing the ghastly news, he was inexperienced enough to regret that he had missed the action. But within a fortnight he had seen enough mindless slaughter to last a long time

By mid-June Louis had recovered and rejoined his unit at Andujar, where both divisions were preparing to make further progress. Dupont, however, had come to realise that his army was in a perilous situation. The Spanish regular army had been reorganised into four divisions, each led by a general, under Commander-in-Chief, General Francisco Xavier de Castanos, who now had a fighting force of some 33,000 troops. Andalusia was in passionate revolt against the invaders; Cadiz was firmly defended by the Spanish, who had also captured the French warships – remnants from Trafalgar – which had been blockading the port since 1805, and had taken 3,000 French seamen prisoners. Once the Spaniards were convinced of the duplicity of their supposed ally, friend and protector, the Emperor, their hatred of the French knew no bounds – and international agreements designed to protect prisoners of war went largely disregarded.

Dupont had every reason to be apprehensive. Although he had received two units of reinforcement from Madrid, his line of communication with the capital had now been broken. Examining the circumstances, the general had to accept the probability that his dream of becoming a marshal had met with a rude awakening; that his expedition had come to an end, and he could go no farther south. He took his army back to Andujar, hoping there to plan a way out of this serious predicament. He then came up with some plans and moves which – with the benefit of informed hindsight and from the depths of a comfortable armchair – we might consider were less than brilliant. He began by splitting up the two divisions and sending General Vedel off to intercept a Spanish army which, he believed, was waiting in the mountains to frustrate the French effort to retreat to the north. Vedel was to proceed to and hold the town of Baylen. Dupont then, amazingly, settled down in the town for a whole month, awaiting reinforcements from who knows where. Next he split up his own army of 20,000 men into three groups, one of which he posted in Andujar itself, and the others in two small towns, La Carolina, and a place he would never forget, Baylen. Had he kept his armies undivided he would have had a fighting force which had gained a great deal of experience in a few short months, and was large enough to deal with anything which the Spanish Commander-in-Chief, General Castanos, might throw at him. (It was said that the reason that he did not follow Vedel was because of wagon-loads of treasure from Cordoba; but that was just a rumour.)

Louis-François Gille marched with Vedel's 2nd Division, which caught up with its infantrymen and cavalry at Madrilejos on the 19th June, and that evening a regiment of Swiss mercenaries added to the crowds of troops quartered in the little village. Both cavalry and the Swiss had seen action: hundreds of peasants and 'brigands' had attacked, some with sabres, and there were many casualties. The next day they set out through ever more dangerous terrain. Gille wrote: 'Before we got to Manzanares (in the plain of La Mancha) we encountered a small French troop who gave us the bad news that the sick which General Dupont had left in the town had their throats slit. There was a unanimous cry of "Vengeance!" from all of us, even the general shared our sentiment.

'Finally we arrived at this city which had been the stage of a dreadful attack. It was hard to suppress the fury of the soldiers. A messenger from the town was sent to the general, telling him that the authorities were on their way to give him the keys to the city. The authorities were the mayor, his adjuncts and many other dignitaries, including priests of the city. They begged the general to listen to them and to be assured that the residents of the city had not participated. It was apparently two bands of peasants. Despite intervention from the monks, the peasants continued with their savage rampage.' General Vedel calmed the townsfolk by reassuring them that he would not make reprisals against them, and soldiers would remain in their lodgings overnight.

Next day, 'my sergeant-major fell ill and we were obliged to leave him at the hospital' and 'I accompanied him to this terrible place where the doors had been hacked with axes and the blood of our comrades was splattered on the walls. I really did not want to leave him there but I had no other choice.'

'I went down into the courtyards and the garden of the hospital and there I was confronted with a hideous sight. About fifty cadavers were lying there; they had not yet been buried. Now I witnessed the savagery they had been exposed to. They had been bludgeoned, cut up with axes, their heads hanging off. Some had been put in boiling oil, others in fire. Their bodies were so charred that a man of five and a half feet looked more like a man of three feet. I left in a state of shock to return to my lodgings. I was about half way there when I heard the piecing yell of a woman. She was in the middle of a group of French soldiers. They were taking her to prison. Near to her was the mutilated body of a dragoon officer who had been killed the previous day and she and the rebels had not had time to bury. I did not enquire what became of the woman.'

For the following week Vedel's troops, conducted by Spaniards who had been persuaded, or forced, to guide them through the mountains, marched on toward the Sierra Morena. The ominous silence as they passed through deserted Valdepenas and El Viso, on the road to Jaen, were obvious warnings that danger lay somewhere ahead, confirmed by the sudden desertion of the Spanish guides and baggage handlers, who left behind them their horses and some beef, about three miles after leaving El Viso. The attack, when it came, was from peasant guerrillas, sniping from above the gorge through which the French were passing. Though tired and hungry, agile French sharp shooting riflemen scaled the rocky slopes, did battle with and overcame the attackers. They took a number of Spanish prisoners of war who were peremptorily executed.

Gille tells us that

'In front and to the left of the town 1500 peasants were positioned. Many cultivated areas on the right bank were full of men. The remainder were spread out in the mountains, forming a kind of amphitheatre behind the town, the highest summit of which was crowned with a fort guarded by troops and a line of peasants. Our soldiers, although exhausted regained their strength at the first shots fired by the Spaniards. We advanced strategically, our weapons in our arms, the First Battalion veering to the right of the fields, the Second in the centre and the Third to the left. The Spaniards organised themselves on the ridge and then discharged their bullets mercilessly. We gave them no time to re-load. We advanced rapidly towards them, our bayonets crossed. They little expected our swift retaliation so they fled chaotically. The First and Second Battalions were equally successful. They cleared the fields of the peasants trying their best to hide there, driving them into the mountains and overwhelming them after chasing away the Spaniards.

'Among the horrors of war, there are many which are too repugnant to recall. However, since I have set out to document all that I saw, I will recount this incident, painful though it is, the more so because I witnessed it'.

He went on to tell of a Spanish mother who, on a generous impulse, sent her six-year-old son with some food to one of a group of French soldiers near her home in the town. Excited, the boy with his little parcel held before him ran towards the soldier, who raised his musket and shot him dead. Gille does not say so, but the twenty-year-old soldier, who was killed on the following day, must surely have mistaken the gift as a possible booby-trap.

The next day, the 2nd July, the battle continued. By eleven o'clock the Spanish strength was reinforced by a 5,000-strong army, led by General Castanos. Firing went on incessantly throughout the day, and possession of the town and fort changed hands more than once. The Spanish artillery and the French howitzers destroyed a number of buildings in the deserted town.

Firing recommenced at daybreak. Spaniards were everywhere, including townspeople who had not joined the general exodus. Castanos' army, which included amongst its cavalry a unit of the Queen's Dragoons and several regiments of its main cavalry. Farther away were large groups of guerillas, and even greater numbers of peasants who would eagerly volunteer if required. Every spot which might provide cover was likely to be used as a hideaway for a rifleman; in fact, on that very morning, a wing of one of Vedel's battalions came under deadly, well-controlled rifle-fire, which came from monks shooting from their monastery windows.

Unfortunate Portugal was well and truly caught between two fires: to stand by her old alliance with England, or give in to the importunities of an impatient Napoleon. The Prince Regent let it be known that he preferred to make a plea for continued neutrality. General Lannes, the French ambassador until 1805, had already put a price on such a possibility – British shipping to be forbidden entry into any of the country's ports, and monthly payments of one million livres. This brought about demonstrations and complaints, which only toughened the already hard-hearted General, who then demanded a further sixteen million livres, to be paid over the next sixteen months. And that was not all: decrees from the Emperor ordered General Junot to take possession of the property left by the 15,000 Portuguese who fled to Brazil. The French army and, more discreditably, its officers on their own behalf, then took to sacking the churches of their gold and silver relics. It was a pattern which was to be repeated throughout the Peninsular War and, together with the savagery of the French troops in the country districts, soon brought Portugal to a state where all that was lacking to fan the smouldering flames of revolt was effective leadership.

Ammunition in Vedel's battalion was becoming scarce and three companies of light infantry were sent to retake the fort. As they left a major brought the news that unknown troops were entering the plains. At first they were thought to be French reinforcements but were soon found to be an addition to the Spanish contingency, which would make them numerically double that of the French. Despite the disparity the insurgents were quickly put to flight when some bodies of French cavalry knocked out a battery of a dozen or more pieces of Spanish artillery which had been plaguing them. Many lives were lost on both sides. Once again we hear of the cries and prayers of the wounded, who the French had to leave behind, few of whom would be lucky enough to be treated as prisoners of war. The decision to leave suffering men to almost certain death was never taken lightly. Space was found wherever possible in carts and wagons, for wounded men fit enough to survive the painful trundling over rough and rocky roads; and there were many cases where cavalrymen gave up their mounts to the wounded.

The companies which had taken the fort were now ordered to vacate it yet again and, as silently as possible, return to the main body of the French division which was encamped on the plateau. Three hundred had been killed during the three-day battle, and 150 were wounded, leaving only about 840 to creep down the mountain as quietly as possible, to rejoin their comrades, who were ready to set off towards Baylen. They did not need a guide, as a few burning buildings in the distant town lit their way.

At daybreak, they entered Manjibar, where foraging parties were sent in to search for food, but some put self before provisions and foraged for riches. When the call 'To arms!' was sounded, and the rush was on to rejoin their ranks, some were so laden with loot that the road became littered with castaway bundles of valuable silks, velvets and even overweight objects made of precious metals, which would have impeded their return to duty. After crossing the Guadalquivir they rested for a while before completing what had been the long and painful march to Baylen, where they arrived on the afternoon of the 4th July.

Whilst all this was going on, General Dupont was still in Andujar. In the absence of his 2nd Division, his army numbered no more than 17,000 and he could have come up against a Spanish force of at least 33,000 regulars and many irregulars under regular officers. However, early in July, aid in the form of a third division, commanded by General Jacques Gobert, had been sent from Madrid, to watch over the approaches to Baylen. By mid-July Dupont had decided to restore his scattered division and retreat towards the mountains; but a wasted month had passed by and Castanos' comparatively large Army of Andalucia was by now not very far to the south of Andujar.

Many versions of the simple story of the Battle of Baylen may be found in a large number of books. After studying them, one may conclude that there was no great glory attached to it; that it produced no unforgettable heroes to decorate the history of its occurrence; and that the victory came about through luck rather than memorable manoeuvres or brilliant leadership. Castanos and Dupont were brave experienced soldiers, each devoted to his cause and his country, but neither were great strategists.

To know what happened next we need to refer to Charles Esdaile who wrote:

> 'In brief, whilst part of the Spanish army pinned Dupont down at Andujar, two divisions would cross the river south of Bailen and descend on his rear, whilst another force composed largely of new levies worked its way around the French forces from the west before attacking from the north. Finally, a further two thousand levies would move around Dupont's eastern flank and attempt to block his retreat through the Sierra Morena. By all normal rules, this was madness. As Castanos had little idea that Dupont had received reinforcements, the Spaniards were running the risk of being defeated in detail, for Dupont could easily have united his forces and struck at the various Spanish detachments in turn. Even if he remained as passive as the plan required, neither of the two main Spanish forces was really strong enough to defeat either Dupont on the one hand or Vedel and Gobert on the other. However, for once fortune favoured the Spaniards.

> 'Operations began on 14th July, when the division of General Reding (Teodoro Reding von Schwiz mercenary, in the service of Spain), appeared on the southern bank of the Guadalquivir at the ferry of Mengibar and attacked the French outpost that had been stationed there. Not much came of this other than the fact that Vedel hastily rushed most of his men to support the detachment posted to watch the river, but on the 15th July Castanos feinted against Andujar. Shaken by the Spanish demonstration, Dupont therefore sent orders for Vedel to send him some assistance. In doing so, he made it quite clear that his subordinate need only send a brigade and, further, that he should continue to watch the river. Unfortunately, misled by a rather feeble show on the part of Reding, Vedel left only two battalions at the river and marched for Andujar with almost his entire division. Thus began a chain of misadventures…'

The first was an uncomfortable surprise for Jacques Gobert when, at daybreak on the 16th July, the sadly reduced French force of only 4,000 troops was faced by Teodoro Reding, who had returned to the Guadalquivir with an army of more than twice that number. The Spanish noticed that the majority of French troops, who had been positioned in front of Manjibar, had departed. Not doubting success, they attacked what remained. Louis Gille was amongst that small army which was almost indefensible. He says:

> 'It was only when they teamed up with a part of their division under Gobert that they tried once more to rally their forces. The enemy, assured of victory, had spread consternation among our ranks and brought encouragement to their own. General Gobert, galvanized by personal courage and a duty to the soldiers he commanded, had it in his mind to settle the score with a charge of the cavalry. He led a regiment of cuirassiers into battle and threw caution and fear to the wind. Three times he penetrated the Spanish lines'.

Finally he was shot in the head and thrown from his horse. His last words were for his country and the men he commanded.

Although the death of Jacques Gobert had a depressing effect on the survivors, the French army was in a better state than it had been for some weeks. Dupont was still in Andujar, and was now the commander of a force, though split, almost as powerful as it had ever been. Vedel's battalions and other reinforcements had built it up to a numerical strength far in excess of either Castanos' or Reding's armies. Had he had a worthwhile intelligence service to keep him informed of his superiority, he might have tackled them successfully, one at a time; then head south, and eventually win his coveted baton – but he did not do this.

Once again he began to divide his army. On 17th July, the day after the victory over General Gobert, Dupont sent a detachment of cavalry to General Vedel, together with orders to oppose Reding and, after defeating him, occupy the town of Baylen. The following day Vedel arrived to find, to his surprise, that there was no one to fight: there were citizens, peasants and traders; so seeing no sign of a military presence to oppose, carried on to La Carolina.

Our young memoirist Louis-François Gille writes:

> ' …arrived at 8 o'clock in the camp of General Dupont which then numbered 30,000 and who were only separated from the Spanish troops by the river and whose lines occupied all the elevated areas. We were dog-tired but happy to be reunited with the First Division. After regaining our strength a little, we planned to get some well-earned rest, when we were ordered to take up our arms. General Dupont, gave the order to General Vedel to beat a hasty retreat, and have his troops overwhelm the enemy and clear the mountain passes. I was ignorant of the reasons why General Dupont was prevented from leaving the same time as us. I dared hazard a guess, but the consensus was that many of his company had amassed large amounts of treasure en route, and it took longer to pack it all up. Whatever the reason, at 9 p.m. we were back on the Baylen road.'

At last, and too late, General Baron Dupont decided that it was time to move out of Andujar. Meanwhile, vast Spanish armies, under Castanos and Reding were converging on the area where the Battle of Baylen was soon to take place. French observers from the hills above the River Guadalquivir could see their enemy amassed in great number on the southern bank and obviously preparing to cross over.

General Castanos, the Spanish Commander-in-Chief, was to lead the attack on Dupont, who had given himself the hopeless task of defending Baylen, La Carolina, and Andujar, which involved a number of small clashes which were nevertheless, expensive in blood, sweat and ammunition. By the 19th July, the French army was as ready as it ever would be to vacate Andujar. A vanguard had been sent ahead the day before, and now the six-mile-long main body of troops set out at a painfully slow pace, their progress impeded by the five hundred wagons and oxcarts which made up the baggage train in their midst; weighed down by loot and ill-gotten treasure and wounded men.

Dupont had made another costly error of judgment, in that he felt sure that his dangers lay behind him, and that only Castanos' army was on his tail and that his advance would be unopposed. He had, therefore, formed his rearguard with hand-picked men and his vanguard with young reserves. This mistake was made plain when, somewhere to the west of Baylen, his comparatively weak vanguard was faced with a stronger force of General Reding's divisions positioned above them in the hills. With great, but foolhardy, courage, the Frenchmen attacked, but were soon beaten back by the Spaniards, with great loss of life.

Dupont's main column caught up with his battle-worn vanguard early next morning. Although his troops were in no fit state for action, having marched all night over rough, exhausting tracts, the general decided to carry on the fight. He brought up batches of well trained troops from the rear, who put up a good show, before being repulsed by the insurgents. In a last desperate effort of assault, Dupont called up his last reserve of trained men, the Seamen of the Guard and four battalions of Swiss mercenaries. This final heroic attempt was shattered by the Spanish artillery. Dupont had fought his last battle and had himself been wounded in the hip. His Division had already lost about 1,800 men and when he learned that his rearguard was under attack, and that he was virtually surrounded, he sent his aide-de-camp to General Reding to discuss the terms of a possible armistice, truce or capitulation.

The French 2nd Division under General Vedel had left La Carolina at about this time. This army of about eleven thousand men had arrived there half starved and without provisions and, as usual, they were expected to live off the land. However, Quartermaster Gille found little available other than an abundance of ripe figs, so early next morning the 19th July, they were back on the road to Baylen. Since daybreak the sound of cannon and shot reminded them that they were marching to the assistance of their Commander-in-Chief. Gille, based on his one year long experience and interest in military matters – but perhaps echoing the opinion of some of the more seasoned warriors, amongst his comrades – was beginning to doubt the wisdom or intent of General Vedel:

> 'It is not the business of a soldier to second guess the plans and strategies of a general. However, the conduct of he who commanded our division was such that it would cause a man of the world less accustomed to making decisions of this nature to reflect. Whatever the instructions General Vedel received did he have the authority to interpret them himself? Should he have been deemed guilty by his inaction when it was in his power to assist his superior and to facilitate his passage? Such were the questions posed which invited answers unfavourable to him.'

He noted other incidents which led him to his conclusion; that Vedel might sometimes slow down a bit when called to the scene of war.

> 'By 5 p.m. we were in sight of Baylen. A large number of Spaniards

were positioned in elevated areas. We immediately went into battle, and in a short time had them fleeing for their lives. There were more than 10,000 of them. The French Eagle then shone brilliantly where five minutes before the Castilian flag had been waving in the wind. We pursued those fleeing, with dragoons and soldiers on horseback. More than 1,800 were impeded by a hillock which was situated on the right of the town, on top of which was a chapel. The enemy defended the approach stubbornly, but despite its efforts it fell into our power. Our young soldiers revelled in this victory, crying "long live the Emperor!"'

They had taken 1,000 prisoners, and their jubilation increased when they saw a small party of Spaniards – an officer and a few soldiers, all mounted – coming towards the French line, under a large white flag. The gleeful Frenchmen thought the enemy were suing for peace; but the opposite was the case. To their horror, they learned that General Dupont – who had lost about 2,000 men killed or wounded, plus 800 Swiss mercenaries who had gone over to the Spanish – was considering surrender.

Vedel decided to await official orders from his Commander-in-Chief and during the cease-fire, gathered together all the Spanish prisoners he had taken, and who would soon be regaining their freedom. Vedel and his army had not surrendered and after a few days' wait, he took his troops into the mountains, heading northward and 'homeward'. However, on the 28th July the details of the Capitulation Document which Dupont had signed, revealed that it covered all troops under his generalship, so the 2nd Divison was recalled to Baylen forthwith. All quartermasters were ordered to copy out the terms of the surrender and to keep their comrades informed.

The effects of Dupont's defeat at Baylen were widespread and profound. The news that, for the first time, a whole French army had been beaten in open combat – and by ill-equipped and untrained Spanish peasants – seemed incredible to the people of France and at first to most Spaniards. Once established as a fact, however, it inspired uprisings and resistance all over the country and throughout those parts of Europe which Napoleon had thrashed so soundly.

Both the French and Spanish were guilty of waging a dirty war against each other. Who was to blame for introducing atrocity, torture and summary execution into the hostilities, depends on the nationality and persuasiveness of the author one is studying. The French were occupying a country they had entered treacherously, under the guise of a friend and ally, and the Spanish were proud of their fearsome peasantry who had contributed courage and blood in the defence of their country.

Why, however, did the British leave the story of those two hell-holes, the hulks at Cadiz and the Isle of Cabrera, out of *their* history of the war? As we shall see, the British had nothing to be proud of, as they ignored the possibility of saving the lives of thousands of French prisoners of war.

So many unpleasant happenings occurred during those first seven months of the Peninsular War; Napoleon's duplicity; the sadistic cruelty of the Spanish peasantry; the piratical sacking of towns and churches by the French and the general neglect of prisoners of war. After all that, one might expect that the Capitulation agreement (Full details of this agreement are given at the end of the Chapter. See 'CAPITULATION AT BAYLEN 18th JULY 1808'.) would be full of recriminations and vengeful demands; but there was none of that. In fact the twenty-one clauses were couched in terms more

respectful and even generous, than a defeated invader might reasonably expect.

Summing up the surrender document; nearly all prisoners, officers and men, were to be repatriated to France. All men too wounded to travel would be nursed and returned to France on recovery. Senior officers were allowed to keep part of their booty, after returning the church silver, taken at Cordoba and elsewhere. Vedel's troops were not to be counted as prisoners of war but would be treated as such until they returned to France.

The Spanish authorities could not have honoured their promises, had they ever wished or intended to. They were quite unprepared for the accommodation and victualling of the thousands of men caught up in their unexpected victory. We know that Spain approached the Royal Navy, through Admiral Collingwood, suggesting that they supplied the transportation of the prisoners. As a token of cooperation with their new ally the Admiralty reluctantly agreed, but some of the juntas objected to the repatriation of any Frenchman before the war had ended. Consequently, two years of inhuman imprisonment were to pass before the comparatively few survivors were picked up from Cabrera and brought to England. On the actual day of surrender, when General Dupont was handing over his sword to Castanos he was reported as saying to the Spanish Commander-in-Chief: 'You may well, General, be proud of this day; it is remarkable because I have never lost a pitched battle until now – I who have been in more than twenty'. Castanos is credited with the instant reply: 'It is the more remarkable because I was never in one before in my life'.

The Spanish general was indeed a lucky man. His victory over the hero of the battles of Ulm, Halle and Friedland, owed more to the latter's procrastination and miscalculations, than to tactical or numerical superiority. The Emperor, whose confidence in his assessment of Spain's essential weaknesses, was also a contributor to this unbelievable humiliation. In a towering and unforgiving rage, he came down heavily on Dupont and a few of his officers:

'In all the history of the world, there has never been anything so stupid, so inept or so cowardly. From the very dispatch of General Dupont one can see perfectly that everything has been the result of the most inconceivable incompetence'.

The rumour that the outcome of the Baylen débâcle had been influenced by the importance given to the 500-waggon baggage train of loot and pillage, was not confined to Gille's memoirs and the opinions of his comrades. Napoleon himself said that Dupont and some of his officers had displayed more interest in the spoils of war rather than the safety of their men.

When General Vedel imparted the news of the surrender to his chief officers, it was received with a mixture of shock, elation at the thought of repatriation, shame and defiance. General Poinsot said he was willing to head the brigade and make for the Sierra Morina but was warned that, if he attempted to do so, he would be shot. Nevertheless, quite a number of infantrymen and cuirassiers who in small groups had guarded the highroad got together, reached Madrid and re-joined the main French army stationed there.

The first count of prisoners after Baylen came to just under 18,000 men who had laid down their arms (Charles Esdaile gives the exact figure for 23rd July, 1808 as 17,645) and there were many more to follow including detached units and stragglers who later brought the number up to about twenty-two thousand.

With no suitably secure accommodation to house such large numbers of prisoners it is a wonder that there is no story of great uprisings or mass escape attempts. A two-fold explanation could be that, firstly, the majority of the prisoners, officers and men, fully believed the clause in the surrender agreement which promised they would be homeward bound as soon as transport vessels could be obtained; and secondly, that although escape was easy, it was unwise; individuals or small groups of absconders would have been lucky to survive even the first night.

The 26th July was a great day for the Spanish and one of great misery for the French captives. The remnants of Dupont's defeated army and Vedel's comparatively intact Division were marched in from the battlefield, and were lined up on the plain outside Baylen, in as good military order as circumstance allowed. Present, too, were the armies of General Castanos and General Reding.

According to the clauses, all French troops in Andalusia were to go to San Lucar and Rotta, so that they could be transported on Spanish ships to the French port of Rocheport, where they would be freed with all their equipment. This was all very convincing and reassuring, but had the regular Spanish Army harboured anti-French feelings as deep as the genocidal hatred exhibited by the peasants, it is to be doubted that any prisoner, other than a few officers, would ever have returned to France.

By the early years of the eighteenth century, the lot of the prisoner of war was improving beyond all recognition. Gone was the disposal of the ordinary prisoner, either by post-battle slaughter or committing enemy sailors to the waves after sea fights. The practice of using some prisoners of war as slaves to their captors, or as saleable as any other merchandise, was becoming less frequent; but ransom never really died out. By the beginning of the nineteenth century, the treatment of prisoners of war had become a matter of international concern. Basically the modern humane approach was to remove him from the fight, to place him in secure accommodation, and at the same time protect him until the war ended or he was exchanged. The captives in this unorthodox war, were not to enjoy this enlightenment. The Spanish authorities and populace were at least a hundred years out of date, as the prisoners of Baylen were soon about to discover.

In fact, the Spanish regular soldiers who made up the escorts, spent much of their time protecting the prisoners from the inhabitants as they marched through. the villages and towns. There are many records of jeering crowds of hate-filled Spaniards, who hurled not only threats and epithets but sometimes stones, as the hungry and footsore captives passed by their dwellings.

'We stopped in an olive grove near Baylen where we were given a ration of bread… It was too dangerous to stay overnight in the interior. We made our way towards Rosa, where we were to pick up transportation to France. We passed through the towns Torrenjinian, Cabra, Alcandete, Bayena, Puente de Gouzale and Moren where we stopped a while. I was surprised that we made it thus far because, despite the precautions taken by the Chief of Staff of the Spanish Army for our safe passage, many French soldiers fell under the swords of exasperated Spanish peasants.'

'From afar the sight of our column of soldiers brought entire communities from their houses, not out of curiosity but because they wanted to slit our throats. Throughout we were followed by shouts of threats and abuse. Women, who I believe ordinarily have an inherent pity for the underdog, were more ferocious than the men.

'In favour of the Spanish, I have to acknowledge that it is to the firmness and tenacity of those who were assigned to escort us, that we owe our very existence.'

Whilst in Moren, they had been joined by a detachment of French soldiers, which included recovered wounded who had been hospitalized at Manzanare – among them was Gille's old friend, Sergeant-major Laucotte – but they also learned that all the wounded who had been left behind at Baylen had been massacred whilst under escort on the way to Villa-Horta.

Like the Second Division, Dupont's battalions were directed towards Rota and San Lucar. They were some days behind Vedel's men and stayed a while in the town of Lebrija, where the inhabitants were just as anti-French as elsewhere. The officers, who were not short of cash, spent 'the days and nights in excesses and pleasures,' which was 'scandalous to the townspeople, who were resolved to put a stop to it.'

A French colonel, observing a large crowd converging onto the town centre, roused his officers from their lodgings in the town. It will be remembered that the French officers had been allowed to keep their swords and pistols, and this lightly armed force was stationed before the large parole building. They waited until the peasants, led by a number of monks, and crying 'Death to all Frenchmen!' came in close. The officers opened fire with their pistols; but the odds were too great. They soon ran out of ammunition and, with only swords to defend themselves, were soon overwhelmed.

Only one man, whose name was Chavenbourg, managed to escape. All the rest were mercilessly slaughtered.

'The body of the Colonel was torn into shreds and fought over. While some of the victors shared the spoils of their victims, others went to the barracks where the soldiers were. Forty-six of them succumbed to the same fate as their superiors. Their rage not yet assuaged, they ran to the lodgings of the sub-officers and ordered them down into the courtyard. There, they were made to kneel in lines opposite one another. The monks passed through the lines with a crucifix which each was told to kiss… Then, from a given signal by the monks, the peasants who were armed with hammers and hatchets beat the poor souls to death.'

At this point the local authorities had seen enough. A detachment of Spanish troops surrounded the executioners and carted them off to the town gaol, which no doubt saved the lives of the remaining prisoners.

References to priests and monks as the instigators of hatred and barbarity towards the French captives occur more than once in the memoirs of men who took part in those terrible marches. J. Quantin, captured at Baylin, served in the Second Division of Dupont's army, under General Vedel. He said that much of the hatred which he witnessed, was inspired by the priests who 'instilled both cruelty and superstition in the populace.' The French, they said, were blood-thirsty monsters and heretics. They even re-wrote the Catechism, (Full details of this Catechism are given at the end of the Chapter. See 'CATECHISM'.) and convinced the peasants that 'God smiled upon any Spaniard who killed a Frenchman'.

Although Quantin and Gille were both in the same Division and would later be sent to the prison ships at Cadiz, ending their Spanish incarceration amidst the horrors of Cabrera, it would seem that they never met. Or if they did, had no reason to mention that they both kept journals of their experiences. Quantin only began his short memoir after his capture at Baylen and he does not mention his rank, whereas Quartermaster Gille was a sub-officer, a fair step away from the rank and file, as far as accommodation and messing were concerned.

Both must have been good looking lads, and possessed a certain amount of charm, if their romantic musings were ever reciprocated by the Spanish beauties they mention – and some officers' wives, it seems found Gille particularly attractive. The latter had learnt enough Spanish to be frequently called upon as interpreter, and had impressed the governors of some towns sufficiently for them to make generous offers, if he would turn his coat and stay in the town until the end of hostilities. Attendance at meetings with French and Spanish officers and high ranking local dignitaries kept Gille well informed – except for the one important question: when would the cartel ships arrive to repatriate them to France? Not one Frenchman had returned home in accordance with the capitulation promises. The 'repatriation' clauses may well have been sincere from the start; or the exact opposite, included only as an encouragement for General Dupont to sign the documents of surrender without months of wrangling and detail, knowing that they could dishonour them at a later date. Whichever, the dream of home and freedom kept many thousands of prisoners of war with nowhere to go, in a reasonable state of mind and patience.

In September, patience was encouraged when it became known that General Dupont and 180 of his officers had been shipped to France. Given a choice, the General may have preferred to be shipped anywhere other than to France. For a man who had fought with distinction in many famous battles and had won fame as a national hero, to be brought home in disgrace, was a tragedy. The Count Pierre Dupont de L'Etang, Great Eagle of the Legion of Honour, General and Commander-in-Chief of the 2nd Army of Observation of the Gironde, was arrested and taken before his beloved, but terrifyingly unforgiving, Emperor. Dupont was court-martialled and dismissed the service.

As the year drew towards its close, all but the most hopeful of prisoners realized that the cartel ships might never materialize; but after five months of apparently hapless marching, living off the land; often half-starved and famished, the dream was too beautiful to be completely abandoned however hard the hardship. In December the governor of Teba requested the assistance of Louis Gille in the translation and promulgation of an order from the Seville Junta. Gille gloried in such tasks, and carried them out so well that all his comrades benefited from his popularity. His own privileges were almost unbounded: he was permitted to visit captives taken at Baylen and now imprisoned in Campillo, Canete, and other small towns and villages within a few miles of Teba. The governor had lent Gille a Spanish town sergeant named Manuel, and given him his own horse for the tour. They found that the French prisoners at Teba fared better than their comrades in the camps they had visited. This they attributed to the humane attitude of the Teba governor towards the defeated foe under his care.

The prisoners were overjoyed when they learned that the instructions from Seville which Gille had translated were, in fact, orders that all French prisoners should be prepared to transfer to the Port of Cadiz within a few days.

Louis Gille was less certain that the great day was at hand. Not for the first time, the kindly Governor had tried to persuade him to stay behind and work for him. He could not reveal their final destination even had he known it, but dropped heavy hints, urging him to let his fellow prisoners go ahead, and saying 'You will be much happier here'. Gille was not even tempted, explaining that nothing could persuade him to desert his comrades or betray his country.

On the 21st December, they bade farewell to the Governor and townsfolk, then set off next morning to Olbera. By the 23rd they had reached the unwelcoming town of Argonales, where hostile crowds greeted them with a hail of stones and calls for French blood. In the afternoon, Gille was closely questioned by the governor and a local lawyer. He had no objections to the interrogation, though he was puzzled that some questions were repeated a number of times:

Where were you born? Where did you live? Why did you join the army? etc. etc. Little did he know that he might be answering for his life. It seems that his written translations had been so good, that it was rumoured he was really a Spanish deserter masquerading as a Frenchman. He was complimented by the officials and invited to dine with them.

Early on the 24th, they arrived at Bornos and were led to a convent which served as a barracks, and were reunited with some companies of the 4th Legion, and soldiers from the Imperial Guard. Next day, before they could leave:

> 'We were told to bring our bags, then four at a time we were taken into a room… Eight armed men were stationed around the room and near to the door, and eight other unarmed men were awaiting orders. At a given signal our bags were taken from us and the clothes we were wearing, even the shirts on our backs, were searched. All our effects were ransacked. Our belts were taken off us and the gold and silver in them emptied on the table. Nothing escaped search by these greedy men. Our epaulettes, gold badges and even the hunting horns embroidered on the edges of our uniforms were picked with large needles to make sure there was no gold hidden underneath. These Spaniards extended their inhumanity to tearing to shreds strips of linen covering the wound of one of our comrades in case he was secreting something of value. Watches, jewelry all were removed from us. It was impossible to save anything. However a subsistence amount of money was returned to us which they calculated to a cent.'

Other detachments from General Vedel's division had followed much the same course as that described by Gille. Quantin, the diarist, in one of them, recorded the wide variety of receptions as they passed through the villages and towns; from blood-thirsty hatred to rare cases of generosity and even kindness. They were travelling a few days ahead of Gille and had had no trouble at Bornos; but were given a bad time of it in Xeres, the last stop before Cadiz. The Spanish 'searched us for weapons and then strip-searched for hidden ones. This was the prelude to further outrages which they were to impose upon us.'

As hard as it is to credit the fact that a makeshift Spanish army should have defeated a French force, led by battle-seasoned generals, in open warfare; it is even less credible that the majority of the 17,500 prisoners were hoodwinked by false Spanish promises. That most of the captives were fooled until the last minute, is indicated by a note in Gille's journal for the 25th December, 1808: 'At two o'clock in the afternoon we left for Puerto Santa-Maria. The thoughts of seeing our homeland again brought joy to our hearts and helped us forget that same morning we had lost all our possessions.'

A few companies from the Dupont/Vedel army had already arrived at Cadiz and were looking forward to embarkation and the longed-for repatriation. As Gille, at Santa-Maria, was writing his cheerful entry on the 25th December, his fellow prisoners were boarding launches which, they believed, would ferry them into Cadiz Harbour for embarkation onto cartel ships. No words can describe their sick horror and disappointment when the launches arrived at a long shallow stretch of water to find that they were, indeed, to embark, not on to transportation vessels which could carry them to freedom, but on to one or other of a group of antiquated, one-time fighting ships. Static now, stripped of most of their masts and rigging and converted into prison hulks, they lay moored bow to stern like a line of tethered coffins – and they did not deny their looks – the outcome of neglect and starvation, heat and cold, on the hulks and on the Island of Cabrera, resulted in the miserable fact that fewer than half of the prisoners of Baylen ever left Spain alive.

Cadiz could already boast more than one prisoner of war shore establishment, the San Carlos Barracks and the Isla Leon. For the past three years a fairly large contingent of French sailors, officers and ratings of the Rosely Squadron, had manned the remnants of the French fleet which had survived Trafalgar in 1805, under the protection of the Spanish. Now, in June 1808, no longer an ally Spain was their captor, and the 3,676 French seamen were imprisoned in the nearby San Carlos barracks.

Later in the year, the prisoner of war population was increased by at least 18,000 when Dupont's defeated army was added to their number. The new arrivals were divided between the prison ships in Cadiz Bay and San Carlos Barracks.

THE CADIZ HULKS AND THE ISLE OF CABRERA

RUFINA, TERRIBLE, ARGONAUTE, MIHNO, HORCA, EL NINO, LIEVRE, VAINQUEUR, VIELLE CASTILLE, VENCEDOR.

For a country which, less than a year before, had been allied to France and its empire-building Bonaparte, to suddenly find itself jailor to over twenty thousand of its recent ally's soldiers and sailors – plus camp-followers – was to confront it with problems which it found almost impossible to solve. That the Spaniards were capable of converting a Cadiz hulk into an accepted standard of prisoner of war accommodation, is a fact, as they did just that – but only once.

Moored a few hundred yards away from the other nine prison ships, was one of the old French warships in the prison fleet, which had been adapted as an 'officer-only' prison. The French writer, Philippe Masson, in his *Les Sépulcres Flottants, prisonniers Français*, quotes from the *Memoirs* of the future Vice-Admiral Baron Grivel, who, ignoring the terrible conditions prevailing in the ordinary hulks, had only fair memories of his time on board the *Vielle Castille*. Although he had only hearsay knowledge of the English hulks, he condemned them as 'floating tombs' and 'a far cry' from their Cadiz counterparts.

The British Government, after much discussion, had 'solved' the problem of housing our civil offenders and, later, war prisoners, at the outbreak of war with America in 1775 by introducing the prison hulks as a one year 'temporary expedient' – which lasted for eighty years!

From the beginning, at home or abroad, the hulk was a detested blot on the local seascape. Except for a splash of colour from the national flag or ensign, prison fleets were very much alike: sepulchral, black and depressing: that is, from the outside. If comparisons are to be made, it must be said that, although the British prison ships left much to be desired, they were commanded by Royal Navy officers of some seniority – most of whom carried out their difficult duties fairly – whilst the Cadiz hulks, from just about every aspect, were disgusting.

From the comfort of the *Vielle Castille*, the Anglophobic Grivel and his fellow officers were safe from the verbal and physical attacks they had experienced ashore. They had generous rations and access to good bread, meat, vegetables, fruit and wine. It would also seem that they were not short of recreations and diversions; fencing, float-fishing, draughts, musical concerts, all are mentioned; but one of the most popular distractions was when a prisoner entertained his fellows by recounting his wartime adventures.

Discipline was strict and rank respected. A number of captured French colonels were granted special privileges including superior rations, and were accommodated on the poop deck. These senior officers acted as judge and jury in all matters concerning the hulk and all dealings with the Spanish Commandant.

Grivel would have had to be half blind, hard of hearing and have lost his sense of smell, not to have known something of what was happening in the rest of the hulks. Without those disabilities he could not have avoided, almost daily, seeing bodies being thrown from the hulks into the Bay; sound travels well over water and complaints of foul odours were being made from the town. It would seem that he was far more interested in denigrating the British, than exposing the sufferings of his fellow Frenchmen.

> 'On board the *Vielle Castille* we were at liberty to go up on board for fresh air, and I can say that life on the ship was not at all intolerable. Certainly, the Spanish are cruel but not in the same way as the British who are odious and whose behaviour towards their prisoners is calculatingly bad. It is inconceivable that a country which believes itself to have global supremacy and tries to convince other countries that it has, should retain such barbaric practices.'

I may have been unfair to Baron Grivel by portraying him (as a rather self-centred man, who it would seem did little to help the lower ranking less fortunate prisoners; but it should be remembered that he was only one of a whole hulk-full of officers who, it appears, also did nothing on their behalf. One officer, a Swiss named Amedee de Muralt, did however tell of the 'Boat of the Dead', which went round the hulk fleet collecting bodies, the Spanish sailors attaching long lines to arms or legs and towing them to the shore for disposal.

Although the *Vielle Castille* was primarily an 'officers hulk', there would have been a number of non-commissioned men on board. Most of these would have been servants or batmen. Officers of seniority, were allowed servants – sometimes more than one.

One Baylen captive who had been conscripted into Dupont's Reserve Legion, at the same time as Louis Gille in 1807, was Louis-Joseph Wagre, a talented and wily lad, who wangled his way aboard the 'officers only' hulk. There, he set himself up as laundryman to his gentlemen captive customers; his payment? an agreed percentage of their food and pure clean water rather than cash. For a while he prospered, then suddenly fell seriously ill from one of the many ailments to which unfortunate prisoners on other hulks often succumbed. However, L-J Wagre was fortunate; coming from the privileged hulk, he was brought to a shore hospital and made a full recovery; in health but not in business for when fit he was transferred from the hospital to the terrible hulk named the *Terrible*.

The Cadiz prison fleet was as miserable and daunting to the onlooker as any other; but if we can believe even a fraction of the reminiscences of the few captives who recorded something of their everyday existence, it is a wonder that any survived the cruel neglect and unnecessary hardship which obtained on board most of those floating hells.

Memoirs left by officers are a different matter and, like Grivel's, usually speak of a very different world of experience. That the diarists who, in spite of the truly abominable conditions of their imprisonment, outlived the horrors of the hulks and the cruelties of Cabrera, may have owed some part of their survival to their memoirs.

On Christmas day 1808, Quantin was put on board the ex-French *Argonaute* already fully overcrowded.

'1900 of us were crammed in a small space, without hammocks or any type of bed and lacking at times both bread and water. Death was rampant. Old soldiers died alongside young men scarcely out of their mother's arms. Epidemics raged and it was not unusual to hear in the evening about the death of someone who had been alive and well that same morning. There were all around us the dying and the dead. For the first no assistance was given and for the second no coffins or resting places were provided. Cadavers were strewn about, which was a cruel reminder that this was our fate also. The priests were our most relentless enemies, more barbaric than the vile people of Cadiz, who had cut Governor Morla's throat when he tried to protect the French prisoners. The priests rejoiced in our plight and loved to heighten our distress. Those wretches! Ministers of God, peace and humanity. They bowed to their lower natures and were led by demons which engendered hatred in them. The atrocities to which we were exposed on the ship was a result of the influences the priests and monks had on the Spanish… When the sea was rough the decks were flooded and we were soaked and without shelter. There we squabbled over small portions of rice or beans which we sometimes had to wash in sea water before cooking. It seemed the Spanish were continually searching for more pain to weigh us down. If we had been deprived of water for a day or so they would bring us bread, and if we had been without bread they would make a point of bringing us water. Never did we have the two at the same time. The Spaniards, and the monks when they were on board, never missed an opportunity of insulting us as they passed by us on the deck. Sometimes to taunt us they would show us the bread and then quickly take it away.'

Quartermaster Gille arrived at Cadiz two days after Quantin, on the 27th December, with another delivery of Baylen prisoners:

'We found launches awaiting us. When we had been allowed to purchase small amounts of bread from merchants, we were put on board the launches with their flags flying and within minutes we watched the shore recede in the distance. Seven or eight large vessels, with neither masts or rigging, arranged in a line occupied the middle of a large basin of water. It was evident before long the fate which awaited us. We could clearly tell that these vessels which we came to know as hulks would be where we were going to stay. Finally we arrived at one of the hulks which was called *Vainqueur*. It was an old French vessel, took about forty men on board. Once on board, we were once again searched… As night approached we looked for a suitable place to rest our heads. Everyone went below decks. Curiosity led me to the officers' quarters which was on the poop deck. There I found a small place overlooking the bridge which I stayed in for my duration on the hulk. It was a useful place. My bread when I had it was safe there and it was like my own little office which was useful because I was secretary of storekeeping which is a very important position.

'We were installed on the hulk on the 27th and it was not until the 30th December that we received any provisions. It is not difficult to imagine the hardship we endured during those first three days. It was a cruel death for many. About 1,824 men were piled into this vessel over a period of eight days. Hammocks were unknown. It was only after some time that eight sailors were put on board to maintain the vessel and then some (hammocks) were made from cord and twine.

'How happy I was to have my own little area. [which he later shared with his best friend, Golvin.] I was alone and as a result clean while my unfortunate comrades, sleeping on top of one another, were plunged into filthy conditions which made them prey to the most wretched misery. Such a situation could not exist for long without something causing great anxiety. Provisions came very rarely. I would say that they came only about twice in the space of three months. When we had bread we did not have vegetables and we rarely had them both at the same time. We had no wood for a fire or water to cook them. Our provisions consisted of rice, dried broad beans, haricots and peas. These were not enough to sustain us. The lack of food plus the bad air on board ship combined to cause epidemics which claimed many lives. The first to succumb were the most robust, such as the cuirassiers and the dragoons, who most needed food.

'For three weeks everyday we saw between 30–40 of our comrades die. Some took 24 hours to die. They had no assistance and the poor wretches did not even have a drop of water most of the time. The Spanish contributed to this treatment in the cruellest fashion. It was the women in particular, as hard as it is to believe, who were the most sadistic. Elegantly clad women from the highest strata of Cadiz society would walk among our cadavers spread out over the bay. They would strut around the hulks and enjoy the sight of our suffering. Joyfully shouting abuse that we would soon all have our throats slit. But what more did we have to fear? Would it have been a kindness, a quick prompt death would have been a happy alternative to the evils we endured.

'It was truly an upsetting sight to see the birds of prey swooping down to peck at the remains of our comrades and see their flesh torn right under our eyes. Even more disturbing was the fact that before some of them had taken their last sigh, the birds were upon them. One can only imagine how we felt in being reduced to having to guard the dead when no-one came for five to six days to take them away. I counted as many as 98 at one time… to deal with the constant sights of horror we tried to become inured by delivering ourselves to games and exercises on board. However, illnesses took their toll and we were never surprised to learn that the following day death had claimed one of those we had been playing with the day before. We had been reduced to such a numb level that, rather than bemoan the death of one of our friends, we rejoiced knowing that he was out of his misery… To maintain order we set up a commission of under officers. They were five or six men who qualified as overseers. They watched the water supplies to see that the soldiers did not appropriate them. It was ridiculous; we had about seven bottles of water for each sixteen men per day and a barrel reserved for cooking vegetables. When there was only half a barrel left we saved that for the sick. We meant by sick those who were put in the ranks of the abandoned… famine overtook us. Several days passed and we had once again not received any bread or vegetables. Any water we had was a great help. We used it to cook straps, braces and the skins used for making haversacks. The stems of plants were not forgotten. We had already eaten all the dogs on board. We had no other options than to eat every possible resource. Despite the taste of these unusual foods, every man, even the fussiest, was happy to be able to nourish himself.'

One surgeon said that the delivery of provisions was very lax, particularly the bread ration, which was often a week overdue and of poor quality: 'The bread was black and had earthy substances in it. Biscuits full of worms, meat dirty and decomposed by decaying matter, fat which was yellow and rancid, spoilt cod and rotten beans'. To convert these unappetising ingredients into anything even remotely edible, cooking was essential, and cooking needed wood – which was almost as rare as good clean water.

The same surgeon described those who could not resist the temptation to drink from the old barrels of brackish and highly polluted water which were kept in the stinking hold. The general conditions of filth, ill-health, starvation, misery and vice, was common to all the Cadiz hulks except for the *Vielle Castille.*

Louis Gille says that the barbarous cruelty of the Spaniards, had driven some of the prisoners well beyond the end of their tether, and determined to attempt to escape. One of them decided to jump into the foul and contaminated water, and swim for the shore but a suspicious sentinel brought him back to the prison fleet. 'Which ship do you come from?' he was asked by an officer. 'The *Vencedor*, sir' he replied and was returned to that hulk. He was greeted by a comrade as he came aboard, who was asked to join the small group, which presented itself to the captain on the bridge. There was no inquiry, or trial of any kind, and both prisoners were taken down to the launch, and there they were shot dead.

Masson has quoted from an officer, Castil-Blaze, who had experienced incarceration in both the opulence of the 'officers-only' hulk and the squalor of one of the other Cadiz prison ships. The senior officers were noticeable, he said, by their 'three chins, ruddy complexions and pot bellies'; describing the rest of the foul fleet which had become 'places of suffering and death', their starving occupants, 'roaming shadows of men'.

Exhaustion, overcrowded and vermin-infested conditions all were ideal for the development of 'fevers on board' and in particular typhus. Men became feverish, delirious and had attendant agonizing deaths. Dreadful heart-wrenching cries and awful contractions followed the stiffness and misery of tetanus. Confusion ensued and some believed they were being stabbed to death by the Spanish who were always ready to kill them. They recalled many of their comrades ending their lives at the hands of the Spanish in the billeting at Andalusia, and they thought the same thing was happening to them. Others thought that the vessel was under attack from the forts of Cadiz and was on the point of sinking or being consumed by fire.

The numbers of dead was staggering. Every day on each ship between ten and twenty men perished, and this increased at one time to thirty to forty. On the *Argonaute* records reveal that eight hundred men died in one month. The sick and dying were always isolated in a section reserved only for what became known as 'place of the abandoned'. On other hulks they were piled high on the gun deck called 'the kitchen'. As soon as a man fell ill he was thrown into this area so that even if he was not dead he had to die alongside those who had already perished. His comrades were fearful that they might contract whatever he had, so he received no help but was left to face death alone in barbarous conditions.

With such widespread reports of inhumane treatment of the French prisoners by the Spanish authorities, who put their charges to the torment of starvation and deliberate cruelty; there is little doubt that the Spanish were the worst example of prisoner of war management. All the memoirs, letters and reports tell of the lack of hygiene and general neglect which brought about epidemics, and were a danger not only to the French prisoners but to the residents of Cadiz and the public at large.

Denis Smith, in his book *The Prisoners of Cabrera,* introduces a young French sailor-prisoner, who was in the same age group as Gille and Quantin and, like them, was a dedicated memoirist. Henri was a patriotic young lad, who longed to play a part in his country's great adventures in Europe. Unwilling to wait the long years before conscription called him to the colours, Henri Ducor, in 1801, then just twelve years of age, joined the French Imperial Navy as a naval cadet and was sent off for training. Graduating as a seaman, he was posted to the two-decker 80-gun French warship, the *Argonaute.* After some active time in the West Indies, the *Argonaute* returned to home waters, but was later blockaded in the harbour of La Coruna, a port in northern Spain. At the first opportunity the French vessel escaped and joined the Franco-Spanish fleet at Cadiz, where it was being brought up to scratch by Vice- Admiral Villeneuve, under the Emperor's orders. This fleet was originally conceived as the backbone of Napoleon's greatest ambition – the invasion and occupation of Great Britain. A powerful French army was building up at Boulogne, and the French navy greatly increased in strength by its absorption of the Spanish fleet.

At that time, the summer of 1805, Napoleon became displeased with his Admiral, cruelly accusing him of over-cautiousness and even cowardice. Villeneuve had also been informed that another senior officer (Admiral Rosily) had been dispatched to replace him. Villeneuve may have thought his career was at an end and he had nothing to lose, or that he might reclaim the approval of his Emperor by some brilliant manoeuvre of naval strategy, before the arrival of his would-be successor.

Whatever his reasoning and plans of action, his decision to face up to the already famous Admiral Lord Nelson was doomed to failure – and what a failure! The story of the Battle of Trafalgar has been told ceaselessly since the day of its happening – the 21st October, 1805.

The fleets of France and her ally, Spain, were virtually swept from the seas; except for a few vessels which escaped towards the end of that greatest of sea battles. One of those was the *Argonaut*, in which Ducor, now aged sixteen, was still serving when it made its narrow escape:

' …This latter ship (*Colossus*) as she neared the enemy was going to pass the stern of the French *Swiftsure* which, to avoid being raked, turned towards her so the *Colossus* ran past her starboard side, firing as she went and soon was locked alongside the *Argonaute* which lay to leeward. The British ship's starboard battery had nearly silenced the Frenchman's port one within 10 min and the *Argonaute* looked nearly ready to surrender, but the ships drifted apart, though not before the French ship was well raked.'

David Lyon   *The Age of Nelson.*

The *Argonaute* survived a number of attacks by British ships, but with a few Spanish vessels, and three French men-of-war they finally limped into Cadiz harbour and, at least temporarily, safety.

Although, Henri and his shipmates had narrowly missed becoming prisoners of war, they were to experience a different sort of captivity. For the next three years they were to suffer house – or ship – arrest protected by their Spanish ally, but confined to the harbour by a British blockading squadron which they could plainly see.

In 1808, the alliance between Spain and France began to crack and was soon to be broken. There were uprisings all over Spain, brought about by the duplicity and insincerity of Napoleon, in particular his act of supplanting the Spanish Bourbon monarchy by establishing his brother, Joseph Bonaparte, as King of Spain.

Thus the allies were now enemies, and Spain was at war with France. The French, who had enjoyed the safety of Cadiz for three years, were now literally between two fires; the British waiting to pounce if any attempted to escape; and the gun emplacements on the shore, where the Spanish gunners had swung their artillery inland, to cover the harbour and the French ships. Surrender was inevitable, although the French would not at first submit, but, after a drubbing from the shore batteries, capitulated on the 14th June, 1808. Ducor found himself a prisoner of war on a hulk in Cadiz harbour.

The 'Rosely Squadron' captives numbered over three-and-a-half thousand sailors, who were imprisoned ashore for a short period. However, when the Convention of Andujar was signed on the 20th July, and General Dupont surrendered, the seamen, both officers and men were transported to the prison ships in the harbour, and a large proportion of the eighteen thousand soldiers took their place in San Carlos on nearby Isla Leon.

Many of the residents of Cadiz and its environs bore a hatred for the French which went far beyond the natural feelings between foes. They had a strong conviction that the hulks were hell-holes and disease-ridden death-traps; and the harbourside of their city stank. By the Spring of 1809, some among the more enlightened members of the local junta realized that if nothing was done to sanitize the hulks, where seriously ill men lived alongside the healthy, their maladies were almost certain to creep ashore. Furthermore, if a significant number of townsfolk had suddenly gone down with a 'hulk disease', riots or a massacre may well have ensued. However, it took until the end of 1809 before the threat to the public had been removed – and the terrible conditions under which prisoners had lived and died – some from no more than a lack of reason to live – were looked into with a degree of success. The local authorities appointed inspectors to see to it that the immense task of disinfection of not only the filthy hulks, but also the half-starved, ill-shod and verminous prisoners themselves, was not carried out in vain. Hammocks and camp-beds were distributed and, where possible, dirty ragged clothing destroyed and replaced.

These improvements, though less inspired by a Spanish turn towards humanity than by fear of infection from their French prisoners, were none the less of great importance. The Junta had opened two hospitals at San Carlos – the Nueve Poblacion and the Seguand Aguada. They were off to a good start; but, beaten by sheer numbers, and only a nationwide effort might have solved the problem. The best of juntas had not much influence outside its own domain. Three or four old frigates, including the hulk *Terrible*, were converted into hospital ships in Cadiz Bay. A witness aboard one of these frigates testified that only thirty mattresses were in use to serve two hundred sick and suffering prisoners. The 'repugnant demons' whose job it was to undertake the collection of the dead, were just as unreliable as ever and the atmosphere below decks was too nauseous to describe.

Most of these efforts came about too late for the first thousands of captured Baylen soldiers who filled and overfilled the prison ships in December of the previous year,1808.

By March 1809, these men had endured three months of precarious existence on the hulks, still unsure of the Spanish intention regarding their future destiny as prisoners of war; then news arrived that a convoy of prisoners was to be sent to Mallorca and another to the Canary Islands. Having experienced the bitter disappointment of broken promises and the insincerity of clauses in the Capitulation document, the Cadiz captives may well have lost all faith in rumour. Although disease was still rife, and the odds against survival were astronomical, there were some born survivors who had personal interests which overcame despair, and, like the memoirists, would clutch at even the weakest straw rather than give in. Few could know that the reduction of the disease-carrying Frenchmen, was to protect Cadiz residents, a few of whom had been caught up in the tail end of a local epidemic.

Without the jottings of prisoners like Gille, Quantin, Ducor and other diarists, the life of the captive serviceman below the rank of officer would be lost to social history. This is particularly true of the Peninsular War, as they are hardly mentioned in French, Spanish or British official records. A few, sometimes a very few, reliable memoirs have survived the wars which make up this book. Some are so bitter or prejudiced as to be unreadable; others too political and one-sided; or, in rare cases, vainglorious. Reasonable exaggeration, is understandable – what the reader may dismiss as hyperbole, the captive-diarist, in crowded depot or filthy hulk, may genuinely have thought that, if anything, he was guilty of understatement.

The unenviable adventures of Gille and his fellow memoirists do not end here. His confidence in believing that this new mystery voyage would be more successful than past disappointments, may be thought admirable or pitiable, but they still had amazing and terrible stories to impart.

THE ISLE OF CABRERA

The rumoured convoy began to materialise in March 1809. The hopeful prisoners spent happy hours watching from their hulks, as the harbour became busy, with supply vessels scuttling in and out of the entrance, servicing the rapidly growing convoy.

After four weeks of preparation, the prisoner of war fleet was ready to sail. It comprised sixteen transport vessels, protected by one Spanish frigate, the *Cornelia*, and four British ships of the line – HMS *Bombay*, HMS *Norge*, HMS *Grasshopper* and HMS *Ambuscade*.

The senior Spanish presence was Don José Rodriguez de Arias, captain of the *Cornelia*, whose sailing orders detailed the distribution of the prisoners after reaching Palma de Majorca, particularly mentioning Cabrera. But once in the Mediterranean, the British navy would have a strong say in the fate of the prisoners; for Vice-Admiral Lord Collingwood was now commander-in-chief, based at Port Mahon in Minorca.

It is amazing that so many among the thousands of prisoners still believed they were being repatriated. Henri Ducor dismissed the fact that the conditions on the transports, were not much better than the hulks, exclaiming, 'But what a difference! What a future opened up! We were going to be returned to our country.'

Nothing could dampen the spirit of the prisoners, who felt that this latest transfer must surely lead to their promised freedom. Embarkation was a time of such celebration that Louis Gille, on the prison ship *Vainqueur*, devoted only a few lines to describe a happening which nearly ended as a catastrophe, ' …we watched the approach of the hulk *El Nino* who had broken from her mooring cables, and came swinging into ours. The wind and the elements brought her on fast and collision could not be avoided. The shock to the two vessels was considerable, but the *El Nino* survived.'

Believing that nothing could be as terrible as the Cadiz hulks, Quartermaster Gille wrote:

'It became increasingly clear that we were going to be transferred to a vessel which would take us to the Balearic Islands. Everyone was ready in an instant and vying to be first on board the transport launch in case they were left behind on the fatal hulk. Finally we were boarded and away from our miserable life on board the hulk. In no time we were sailing towards the shipping lanes, which to our amazed eyes looked like an immense forest of masts. The air resounded with the lighthearted songs of the French prisoners. We arrived at the spot where all the vessels which were part of the convoy were gathered, and we stopped alongside a vessel with three masts which was called *Prince Royal*, or No. 10. Our share of prisoners totalled 508. I was responsible for reporting this figure to the Captain and ascertaining that it was correct.'

The Cadiz hulks were by no means cleared by these two convoys. Some five or six thousand captives still disgraced the city, and the spaces left by the Mediterranean-bound transports were quickly occupied, although a start was made to clean up the hulks.

Enthusiastic as he was, young Gille went aboard a sick man:

' …right from the beginning of my task I was uncomfortable with the continuous movement of the vessel. I took a break by going out on to the bridge to get some air. I tried to get back to work but I really could not and had to abandon it completely. My discomfort grew and I assumed that I was suffering from the same sea sickness which had affected so many of us. However, I was wrong. I had a fever and I was sickening with something. I lay in a string hammock which I had brought with me from the hulk. I was happy I had done this otherwise I would have had to sleep on the floor like some of my comrades, and I know I would have felt worse. The 508 men on board occupied only one third of the ship. The rest was reserved for the captain and his crew.

'Those who were accommodated in the ship's hold were so squashed, that throughout the entire voyage they had to rest and sleep sitting up or leaning against one another.'

Quantin, who sailed in the transport ship *Enero*, confirmed Gille's comments on the unnecessarily scant accommodation allowed to the prisoners. He also briefly mentioned two escape attempts from the Cadiz hulks which I had not discovered elsewhere. A group of young Frenchmen, from a land prison and possibly sailors, arrived in the Bay and were put upon a hulk, but 'tried to make a break of it back to their comrades, by swimming to the shore, but most did not make it' and were shot when recaptured.

The second incident involved the 'officers only' hulk, the *Vielle Castille*. During a storm which filled the Bay, some of the officers cut the cables and managed to get her underway, 'and ran for freedom under fire. Many of them made it.' I am still searching for more evidence! The remarkable young French matelot and memoirist, Henri Ducor, made an 'escape' with a difference. Surreptitiously, he transferred himself from the French Imperial Navy into the Grand Army. After six years a sailor and still a minor, Ducor was certainly not the sort of seaman who wished he had never joined. On the contrary, his one worry was that the war might end before he could prove himself before his idol, Napoleon and his country.

Among the chit-chat and stories which kept the lower mess-deck abuzz, grew the rumour that the soldiers sailing with the convoy for Majorca and Minorca, stood a greater chance of repatriation than the seamen sent to the Canary Islands. So, after a deal of benefit to both parties, Henri, exchanged his sailor's uniform and identity for that of a dying French soldier – a cavalryman.

The transport ships which left Cadiz under convoy on the 3rd April, 1809, reached the Mediterranean after some hard sailing; then headed towards appointed destinations with their contingents of prisoners: 1,000 to England, 1,500 to the Canary Isles, 3,500 to the Balearics and 4,500 to Cabrera.

The 1,000 bound for England, would have included French and Swiss officers of distinction, who would be sent to one of the many parole towns in Britain. The prisoners sent to the Canary Islands were almost entirely sailors, (the advice given to Ducor, which caused him to change from sailor to soldier was true in parts but did not bring him repatriation).

More than half of the 8,000 Dupont's soldiers included in the convoy, were the unluckiest of the unlucky, heading, as they were, for conditions and cruelty, more dreadful than even those experienced sufferers could possibly imagine.

It would have been unusual, during the age of sail, for sea voyages of any length, to take place without any event or mishap – and the transport of the Cadiz prisoners was no exception. Gille and the other diarists tell of terrible storms, delays and near catastrophes. Transport vessel No 10, the *Prince Royal*, was involved in a collision at the very beginning of the voyage. Louis Gille says that at 5 p.m., when they were weighing anchor, an English vessel under sail, bore down on them. 'His bowsprit came towards us and curled itself round the shrouds on the port side'. The damage was bad enough to prevent them leaving Cadiz until noon the following day; when they left in pursuit of the convoy, which stood out at sea to await them. They entered the Straits of Gibraltar on the 6th April, to be met by seas which grew rougher by the minute, and lightning flashed across the skyline, leaving them in no doubt that they were soon to be met by very bad weather.

'Our fears were soon to be realized. The night became dark, the waves resembled mountains which threatened to break up our ship, and sometimes they seemed as if they were going to raise us up to the clouds, and then drop us into a deep abyss. In the midst of the disturbance of the elements the captain and his crew, fearful of the imminent danger ahead, abandoned their maneuvers and were concerned only with communicating with God. All of a sudden a fierce wind descended upon us. Our mizzen mast was broken above the maintop and it fell with an enormous bang on to the bridge.

'At that moment which seemed to be the last one of our lives, the fall of the mast caused our vessel to reel and fortunately we had the presence of mind to cut all the rigging attached to it, and which would have weakened the vessel and dragged it down. Frenchmen nearby seized the Spaniards hatchets and set to work. We had a horrifyingly anxious night. The force of the wind carried us away and we found ourselves hopelessly distanced from the rest of the convoy.'

After a terrible night they found themselves on a rocky coast, which turned out to be the Barbary Coast, where had they known it they might have been taken into slavery by Barbary pirates. However, the present situation was dangerous enough, barely escaping death and destruction on the jagged rocks, and miraculously floating into calmer waters – in spite of a terrified and useless Spanish crew. On the 8th April, their hopes improved with a change in the weather. In the afternoon, they were gladdened by a cry of 'Ship ahoy!' which proved to be one of the escort fleet, who first challenged them, then delivered a shot which destroyed the mizzen mast. Finally No. 10 was towed into the port of Malaga, where they met up with half of the convoy, while the others lay in Gibraltar.

Quantin on the *Enero*, transport No. 2, attested to the ferocity of the storm, and to the misfortunes of No. 10. The reformed convoy continued on its voyage and eventually reached the Balearic Archipelago in the Western Mediterranean:

> 'We dropped anchor off the town of Palma (capital city of Majorca), which was situated in a large harbour… we were under the impression we were being dropped off on the large island, but the transport vessel set sail and took us, a sad and sorry lot – the army of General Dupont – to an island called Cabrera which was only about 8 leagues away.'

There, over a period, between five and six thousand of Dupont's men were disembarked – or rather dumped – on a desert island no more than two miles wide and three miles long, and virtually forgotten.

> 'Men exhausted, starving and miserable to the core of their being. We were sparsely clad and there was no shelter from the heat of the day nor the cold of the night.'

Cabrera, or Goat, island with its background of 'craggy mountains and shaggy rocks', was devoid of any sign of comfort or accommodation for this large influx of weary men – and some women.

Had Spain still possessed a navy, both military and public would have been delighted to see it used to honour the capitulation, and clear every French prisoner from their country. However, this would never have been agreed to by the Royal Navy or the British monarch – even Napoleon could see no sense in setting free a large recently captured army; who would soon be fighting again against Spain.

It seemed that the only buildings were a couple of derelict fishermen's huts and an ancient fortress high on a rock overlooking the port. This was soon taken over as lodging for some of the officers whilst others encamped in tents. For the ordinary soldier, however, there was no cover or protection. Prisoners fit enough to forage or build, were soon hard at work constructing temporary shelters from the blazing sun.

Gille, who had not fully recovered from his illness, had lost his clothes during a period of delirium and stepped ashore naked, until his friends lent him a great coat, and supported by Golvin he caught up with the rest of the company. Most of that first night, was spent in a long march in a vain search for some sign of habitation.

Next morning, they returned to the beach where they found a great pile of copper pots, saucepans, tin dishes and other eating utensils, which they had used on the transports, and indicated that the prisoners would probably remain on the island for some time.

The retreating transports had left behind no provisions, and it was not until the second day that a supply vessel arrived.

> 'We were treated just like we had the plague. The Spaniards did not allow us to approach the shore until they had deposited the provisions, which we had to share among ourselves. The next voyage brought with it tents for the officers. A launch came out to offer us various merchandises. A terrine full of vinegar served to hold the pieces of money we threw them because they wanted to receive nothing directly from our hands.'

Many of the prisoners had begun to sicken soon after leaving the transports, whilst many others, like Gille brought their illnesses and diseases with them. Reports of the conditions in Cabrera were received in Palma, and a complaint that there was no one there to administer the last rites to the dying. The authorities acted promptly, and, on the 18th July, 1809 dispatched a priest to the island – although food and medical attention might have been better for the starving wretches. Father Damian Estebrich, ' …was between forty and fifty, small in stature with an unpleasant face. He had the features of someone who was guarded and up-tight'. He was reluctant to take up the responsibilities of his new task, believing the Spanish gossip, that 'he had been sent to preach to a bunch of savages'. Instead he was welcomed and accepted by the prisoners; in fact they eventually built him a chapel.

What this house of God could have looked like architecturally must be left to the imagination, with so many men endeavouring to create shelters for themselves, on an island with next to no building materials. The average edifice was only just large enough for one man to occupy; only the most pessimistic of French prisoners could imagine living under such abominable conditions for any length of time. Their main concern was the reliability of the supply ships, which were supposed to deliver their provisions at regular intervals. On those days thousands of eyes would have been fixed on the horizon, sometimes causing days of misery and hunger, when they did not arrive. Worse still was the deprivation of good clear water, as the only source of fresh water was one fountain, and an untrustworthy well, the water from which made the desperate prisoners ill.

> 'We were abandoned to our own resources and left to fend for ourselves… we all started to build shelters with branches of shrubs. We didn't plan on building anything substantial as we were sure that the Spanish government were not going to keep us very long in this place. [Gille continues to say] What I built as a shelter was exactly the length of my body. I could only sit or lie down because of the lack of elevation I have given myself. This dwelling served me for seven months.'

Despite the wretched conditions in which they found themselves, the French rarely missed an opportunity to create some sort of diversion to ease their misery. On Cabrera they set up a theatre in an old cistern. Quantin was given a role in a play called *'Sophie and M. Vautour'*, '…this distraction was wonderful for our spirits and became an important use of our time… for in general each day followed another with a uniform boredom and tedium.' He also tells of the misdeeds and corruption on the island:

> ' …theft was the most common crime among the miserable inhabitants of Cabrera. Thieves were all soon brought to justice. When the criminal was caught in the act, or proven guilty, he was beaten without any kind of trial. Rousseau with his "All men are born good!" A post was erected which was for attaching thieves to die, under the blinding and cruel heat of the sun. Most offenders preferred a bloody execution to this. It was in the distribution of the provisions that profound misery was manifest among the men. When they were distributed the men were like vultures, ready to pounce on any piece of bread which fell to the ground.'

The prisoners knew nothing at all of the events taking place in Europe; there was no communication with France and they felt they would be there for life. However, in late July, small boats arrived from Mallorca to take some of them to Gibraltar. On the 29th July, 1810, 800 men, including Gille and Quantin, left the island, not to go home but to be transferred on to a British vessel for England and further imprisonment in Portchester Castle. They were replaced with new prisoners from Catalonia. 'The joy at leaving was only lessened by the sight of those standing on the shore, seeing favourable winds taking our vessel far from that terrible place.'

It was not till early 1815, that the final 3,700 prisoners were liberated and returned to France. In the opinion of the Majorcan authorities, that from 1809 to 1814 some 11,800 prisoners were transported to Cabrera, of these from 3,500 to 5,000 prisoners, some forty percent had perished on the island. The French calculated that some 10,000 men had perished and they may have included those who died on the Spanish hulks.

The last prisoners burned and destroyed everything they could; their own shelters, the supply shed, the cistern theatre, nothing was left. It was '…as though all these things were accomplices in our torments, and their destruction an act of revenge demanded by our ill-feeling'.[1]

MADAME JUNOT AND THE REGENCY

General Junot' wife, who later became the Duchess of Abrantes, when her husband was elevated to the Dukedom, may have been beautiful, but exposed a cruel unpleasant streak in her nature when she took pleasure in describing the Prince of Brazil and his wife the Infanta Carlota of Spain. Of Carlota she said:

'Picture to yourself, reader, a woman four foot ten inches high at the very most, and crooked, or at least both her sides were not alike; her bust, arms, and legs, being in perfect unison with her deformed shape. Still, all this might have passed off in a royal person, had her face been even endurable; but, good Heavens! What a face it was! She had two blood-shot eyes, which never looked one way, though they could not absolutely be accused of squinting – everybody knows what I mean… The dress of the Princess of Brazil was in discordant unison, if I may so express myself, with her person… This dress, which was wretchedly ill made, very imperfectly covered an enormous bosom, and a chest all awry, while diamond brooches ornamented the sleeves, whose extreme shortness displayed a pair of arms which would have been much better concealed… The exquisite beauty of these jewels, combined with the extreme ugliness of the person who wore them, produced an indescribably strange effect, and made the Princess look like scarcely belonging to our species…'

And of the Prince Regent she wrote:

'I had not then seen the Prince of Brazil, therefore I could not laugh as I afterwards did, when I beheld his corpulent figure, clumsy legs, and enormous head, muffled in a hussar uniform. His negro hair, which by the way was in perfect keeping with his thick lips, African nose and swarthy colour, was well powdered, and pomatumed, and tied in a thick queue. The whole was surmounted by a shako, ornamented with a diamond aigrette, of great value… I call up my recollection of him, at those gloomy moments when my spirits require to be rallied by a hearty laugh!'[2]

'*En route* we found a large number of mutilated French bodies, some of whom had been buried alive. Others had had their fingures cut off so that they could not help themselves and there were those whose tongues and teeth had been yanked out and others who were horribly mutilated with their body parts stuffed in their mouths.'[3]

CAPITULATION AT BAYLEN 18th JULY 1808.

Their Excellencies the Count of Tilly and the Count Castanos, Generals in Chief of the Andalousia armies for the General Count Dupont, Great Eagle of the Legion of Honour, Commandant of the 2nd Observation corps of the Gironde, giving orders to an army to gloriously defend itself against an enemy which is infinitely superior and all pervasive.

General Chabert, Commander of the Legion of Honour, fully entrusted with power by His Excellence the General in Chief of the French Army and the General Marescot, Great Eagle of the Legion of Honour, are agreed on the following articles.

Article 1 French troops under orders of General Dupont are prisoners of war, excluding the division of General Vedel.

Article 2 Vedel's division and other troops who are not mentioned in the first article are to evacuate the Andalousia region.

Article 3 Troops referred to in Article 2 will conserve all their baggage and to avoid any trouble while marching they will surrender all their artillery and any other arms to the Spanish who will return it to them when they embark.

Article 4 Troops referred to in the first Article will leave their camp and be afforded all honours of war due to them, each battalion having two canons at their head. Soldiers rifles are to be deposited 400 toises [six and a half feet] from the camp.

Article 5 General Vedel's troops and others will stack their arms on the front of the bandiere [?]. A verbal acknowledgement will be drawn up by the officers of the two armies and everything submitted will be restored to them as agreed in Article 3.

Article 6 All French troops in Andalousia will go to San Lucar and to Rota. Their daily journeys shall not exceed 4 leagues, with necessary rests so that they can be transported on to Spanish vessels with their arms and equipment at the Port of Rochefort in France.

Article 7 Superior officers will take charge of their arms and soldiers their sacs.

Article 8 French troops will embark as soon as they arrive and the Spanish army assures a safe crossing without any hostilities.

Article 9 Lodging, provisions and forages during the march and the crossing will be provided by the superior officers and will be assigned according to rank and in accordance with Spanish troops in times of war.

Article 10 The horses of the officers, generals and staff major will be transported to France and nourished befitting in times of war.

Article 11 Superior officers, generals, will keep a chariot and wagon, the officers of staff major a chariot, without being subject to inspection or examination.

Article 12 Chariots from Andalousia are excluded from the previous article. These will be examined by General Chabert.

Article 13 To avoid the difficulty of transporting horses by sea (mentioned in Article 12) the said horses will be left in Spain, sold as agreed by both French and Spanish Commissioners and the former receiving the proceeds.

Article 14 The wounded and sick of the French army in hospital will be treated with the greatest of care and then escorted and transported to France as soon as they are cured.

Article 15 In many places, notably the attack on Cordovia, many soldiers, despite orders from their generals to the contrary, looted which is a natural occurrence in towns taken under attack. The officer general will take all measures to locate and return all sacred vases taken in the attacks.

Article 16 All civil personnel attached to the French army will not be viewed as prisoners of war and thus will enjoy during the repatriation all advantages commensurate with their position.

Article 17 French troops will start to evacuate Andalousia on the morning of 23 July. To avoid the intense heat marching will be overnight, conforming with the daily stages of travel according to the chiefs of staff of both the French and Spanish armies. This will be done while avoiding the passage of troops in the towns of Cordovia and Seville.

Article 18 The 3,000 French troops will be escorted during their march by troops from the Spanish line. This will be done in columns of 300. The officer generals will be escorted by detachments of cavalry.

Article 19 The troops will be accompanied by French and Spanish Commissioners who will arrange for food and lodging *en route*.

Article 20 The present terms of this capitulation will be carried by an officer escorted by Spanish troops to His Excellence the Duke of Rovigo, Commander in Chief of the French army in Spain.

Article 21 It is understood by both armies that additional articles may be added to this should something have been overlooked or omitted or which could be advantageous to the French troops in Spain.

Signed By
Xavier, the Count of Castanos.
General Chief of Staff Dupont, Count of the Empire, Great Eagle of the Legion of Honour, Commander of the 2nd Observation Corps of Gironde.
General Vedel, Commander of the 2nd Division of the Army Corp.

CATECHISM

Chapter I

Question: Tell me my child who are you?
Answer: Spanish by the grace of God.
Q. What does it mean to be Spanish?
A. It means a man of worth.
Q. How many things are there of importance to a Spaniard?
A. There are three. Christian, Catholic, Apostolic Roman. We must defend our religion, our country, King and to die rather than be defeated.
Q. Who is your King?
A. Ferdinand VII.
Q. How much should you love him?
A. Most passionately and duly meriting his virtues and his sufferings.
Q. Who is the enemy of our happiness and well being?
A. The Emperor of France.
Q. What kind of man is he?
A. He is a rogue, ambitiously greedy, an embodiment of all evils, the destroyer of all that is good and the holder of all vices.
Q. How many natures does he possess?
A. He has two – one devil and one human.
Q. How many Emperors are there?
A. In reality there are three deceptive persons.
Q. Who are they?
A. Napoleon, Murat and Godoy (Prince of Peace).
Q. Is anyone more evil than the other?
A. No, my Father they are all equally evil.
Q. What is the essence of Napoleon?
A. Sin.
Q. What is the essence of Murat?
A. Napoleon.
Q. And Godoy?
A. The intrigue of both of them.
Q. What is the character of the former?
A. Egoism and tyranny?
Q. And the second?
A. Thievery and cruelty.
Q. And the third?
A. Cupidity, treason and ignorance.

Chapter II

Q. What are the French?
A. They are ancient Christians and modern day heretics.
Q. What has brought them to this point?
A. False philosophy and a corruption of morals.
Q. How does Napoleon profit from these?
A. One feathers his ego and the other is an instrument of iniquity which he uses against his fellow man.
Q. When will his atrocious tyrannies come to an end?
A. They are fast coming to an end.
Q. From where does this optimism stem?
A. From the efforts which are the embodiment of our country and fatherland.
Q. What is the fatherland?
A. The union of several states governed by the same laws.
Q. What punishment awaits a Spaniard who falls short of his duties?
A. Infamy and a natural death reserved for traitors and civil death for his descendants.
Q. What is a 'natural death'?
A. The deprivation of life.
Q. What is a 'civil death'?
A. The confiscation of all worldly goods, the stripping of honours which the King accords all his valiant and loyal citizens.

Chapter III

Q. Who is he who has come to Spain?
A. He is Murat, the second person in this infamous trinity.
Q. What are the principles he employs?
A. To steal, deceive and oppress.
Q. What doctrine is he trying to spread?
A. The depravation of all morals.
Q. What can deliver us from such iniquity?
A. Union and taking up arms.
Q. Is it a sin to assassinate a Frenchman?
A. No, my Father it is a worthwhile act which will deliver our homeland from these insolent oppressors.

Chapter IV

Q. What is courage?
A. A force of the spirit which calmly seeks out prudence and the chance to be victorious.
Q. Does subordination have to be used to acquire it?
A. Yes, because it is the soul.
Q. To whom is subordination due?
A. To all the leaders.
Q. Who is the most cherished and revered anong us?
A. He who joins courage to the principles of honour and a disinterested nature.
Q. Who are they who claim honours without meriting them?
A. They are ignorant egomaniacs, useless people who do not know the meaning of obedience.
Q. What are we doing when we go into battle?
A. We are increasing our Fatherland's glory, defending our comrades and saving our country.
Q. Who should take up arms?
A. All those who can, those chosen by the Junta and those less useful to the public.
Q. What are the obligations of the others?
A. By contributing to the success of the war by a display of ardent patriotism and returning to it what the gods rendered to them.
Q. What should he do who has nothing to do?
A. He can arm himself and pray to God for the prosperity of the Spanish armies and to occupy himself well in his chosen field and in this way he will be contributing towards the good of the cause.
Q. From what do we derive our happiness?

A. From God, the loyalty and adroitness of our leaders and from our obedience and our valour.

Chapter V

Q. What are the politics of Spaniards?
A. The maxims of Jesus Christ.
Q. What are those of our enemies?
A. Those of Machiavelli.
Q. What does it consist?
A. Egoism.
Q. What followed?
A. Self love, ruin and destruction of one's comrades.
Q. What motives did these tyrants employ to deceive the people?
A. Seduction, baseness.
Q. Are these means legitimate to overcome a crown which does not belong to them?

A. No, on the contrary these are atrocious and we have to courageously stand up to a man who made himself a sovereign by such unjust and abominable means.
Q. What happiness should he expect?
A. What the tyrants can not give us.
Q. What is that?
A. The certainty of our laws, the free expression of our sacred culture, and the re-establishment of our monarchy in accordance with regulations of Spain and those of Europe.
Q. But have not we always had this?
A. Yes my Father but degraded by the indolence of the authorities which govern us.
Q. Who should regulate and enforce these laws?
A. A united and true Spain which is unthreatened by the yoke of foreigners.
Q. Who is behind our striving to be great?
A. Ferdinand VII who we wish to see among us for eternity.

---

1. Louis-Joseph Wagre: *Mémoires des Captifs.*

2. Laure Junot (Duchesse d'Abrantes) *Memoirs.* 8 vols., London.

3. *Espagnols dans L'île de Cabrera, etc.* Paris, 1833. Henri Ducor. *Adventures d'un marin de la Garde Imperiale, prisonnier de guerre sur les pontoons.*

POSTSCRIPT

The first draft of this chapter was written some time ago, after my daughter, Stephanie, translated my copy of Gille's *Memoirs*, J. Quantin's *Three Years in Spain*, and later, the French writer, Philippe Masson's book on floating prisons. I suddenly realised that, despite the thousands of books on so many aspects of the Peninsular War, the story of prisoners of war on the hulks at Cadiz and the island of Cabrera, had never been published in the English language.

I had the smug satisfaction of knowing that, when my book was published, it would include at least one account which a journalist might describe as a 'scoop'. However when, a week later, I decided to finish the chapter, it came as a momentary disappointment to find that I had been pipped at the two-hundred-year-old post by an American, Denis Smith. Actually, I profited as his research in the Spanish archives added much to my knowledge.

Chapter Eleven

Women:
Their Absence and Their Presence

A FORMER GOVERNOR OF A GREAT PRISON, SIR BASIL Thomson, described the prisoner of war depot as 'an overcrowded city without women', a community with its own laws and a society made up of every social class, from the officer of the Grand Armée, to the Sanscalotte from the Fauboug St Antoine. 'It is not surprising,' he said, 'that monstrous growths should be produced'. Dr T J Walker, the historian of Norman Cross Depot, made a carefully worded reference to the unnatural world into which the prisoners of war were forced to live, some for many years.

In the course of discussing the efficiency and self-sufficiency with which prisoners organised their prison communities, particularly the French with their own elected courts and magistrates, Walker says:

> 'These communities differed from every other community of human beings (except perhaps the inmates of monasteries) in being deprived of any participation in the two essential factors on which the bare existence of every animal race depends – viz. the provision of the actual necessaries of life, food and, in the case of man, clothing, for the preservation of its own generation; and the reproduction of its kind, to insure a future generation.'

And that is about as much detail as can be found in most of the books, memoirs, and official documents, which tell us so much about most other aspects of their captive lives. The question most often asked is – 'Were there any women in the prisons?' The answer is – 'Yes,' but it has to be qualified by saying that although the number was small, it has to be split into at least four categories. The first was made up of females who were actually captured in or after actions on land or sea, most of whom would not have experienced very long periods of 'durance vile', before being paroled or shipped back to the Continent. In the second category were those remarkable creatures who had applied for and gained permission to share their men's uncomfortable captivity, in crowded depot or dreaded prison ship. The third were female civilian members of the prison staff. The fourth and largest category, the wives of British officers, who frequently lived on board the hulks or, in the case of shore depots, in houses within the prison area. The wives of soldiers and militia guarding the prisoners were often likewise housed. There were other women who followed their husbands into captivity, but these were the wives of paroled officers, who could usually enjoy a comfortable lodging or, if they could afford it, buy a house.

This may give the impression that, with so few female captive and voluntary prisoners of war, the vast majority of the prisoners may never have even seen a woman, perhaps for many years; but this would be misleading. The bum-boats which were the floating markets which supplied the inmates of the hulks with 'extras' and small luxuries, were mainly run by women, some of whom were remembered as great characters. On occasion, the land-based prisoners could view – with disapproval – the Agent's guests with their fine ladies, who had come to see what the captive enemy looked like; and, of course, there were the wives and children of the depot staff. From the upper floors of some of our larger prisons, it was possible to catch a glimpse of life beyond the prison walls; and prisoners whose airing ground abutted the market square, could have enjoyed the day-long view of the hustle and bustle, as crowds of local shoppers bargained on the other side of the high metal palisading. However, all these were cases of looking but no touching. The only closed-prison captives with the opportunity of any physical contact with the public, male or female, were the 'trustee' prisoners who sold prisoner of war work from their stalls, or bought provisions and merchandise for resale in the inner markets. Inevitably there were romances, and more than one instance where a market girl helped her foreign romeo to escape.

Although we may read in journals and memoirs, of women prisoners of war, in the true sense of the term, living in closed prisons ashore or on the hulks, verification of their onetime presence is not always easy to find. This could be the fault of a busy masculine Register keeper who may have felt 'she's only a woman, and may not be here for very long': or maybe she only existed in the imagination of an ex-prisoner diarist. Nevertheless, there is enough evidence to show that they did exist, though never in great number. It is not so surprising that details of the girls who voluntarily joined their husband's or lover's imprisonment in hulk or shore depot, should seldom be found in official records. To be named in the depot muster book meant that that person was entitled to official rations – and it is unlikely that the Government was ever that generous.

The short story of one French couple, who shared the husband's confinement in Liverpool's old Borough Gaol early in the Seven Years' War, did not come to a happy ending. Joseph Le Blan, an ordinary prisoner, wrote a brief note to his brother, bearing the sad news of his wife's death:

> 'De Livrepool: Ce 21 Septanbre 1757.
> Mon cher frere je vous dis ses deux mot pour vous dire que ma tres cher femme a quitte ce monde pour aller a lotre monde; je vous prit de priyer pour elle et.de la recommender a tous nos bons paran.
> Je suis en pleuran votre Serviteur et frere
> Joseph Le Blan

The famous French escape artist, Tom Souville, was less than complimentary in his assessment of the women who were on the Portsmouth prison hulk *Crown* in 1797; he described them as 'de basse extraction et extrêmement grossières'.

In February of that same year, 1797, the Fishguard affair,

commonly remembered as 'The Last Invasion of Britain', had occurred, but soon came to its farcical end. Women, both Welsh and French, played star parts in versions of its history (see Chapter Four). There was the tall and fearsome-looking Fishguard heroine, Jemima Nicholas, who single-handed (in which was a pitchfork!), captured twelve Frenchmen, and delivered them to the guardhouse. Soon after the landing, crowds of Welshwomen sightseers had gathered on a hill-top near Cawdor's troops and the French, seeing them arrayed in their red capes and black bonnets, took them to be Redcoat reinforcements and surrendered.

Four hundred of the fifteen hundred prisoners were stowed away in Golden Tower Prison at Pembroke and most, in a manner typically French, settled down to make the best of it. However, some young Welsh girls were employed in menial tasks about the prison, and two of them fell in love with two young prisoners, who were deeply involved in the planning of a sensational mass breakaway. Aided by the two love-struck girls, a number of prisoners and their collaborators made a clear getaway and the couples were later married in France.

The rest of the Fishguard 'invaders' were distributed in various prisons, including four French women whose names appear in the register book of the *Royal Oak* prison hulk at Plymouth: two were officers' wives, the other two the wives of ordinary soldiers.

Penny, in his *Traditions of Perth*, mentions that there were women among the four hundred prisoners who arrived in Perth from Plymouth in September 1812; the first to enter the newly opened great Perth Depot. There is also the Portchester Castle story of a young French girl who, distraught on hearing that her sailor lover had been captured and was a prisoner in the Castle, disguised herself as a young lad and signed on as a privateer. This is not quite as improbable as it may sound, there being many well-documented records of women – including English women – who served their country as soldiers or sailors, some with great distinction. John Nichols wrote that all the information which came to their ears on HMS *Goliath* during the Battle of the Nile, came from the women and the boys who carried the gunpowder from the magazine to the guns. There were quite a number of women who were wounded on that day, and at least one died of her wounds.[1] When, in 1847, the Naval General Service Medal was struck, there were many female applicants. Although they had proof of their presence on that occasion, the decision rested with Queen Victoria, who finally decided against – for if the precedent was once created, many more women would be applying!

Louis-François Gille, tells of a pro-French Polish girl, who was captured by the Spanish at the beginning of the Peninsular War. She put up a valiant fight, until her horse was killed beneath her, and she became a legitimate female prisoner of war. ' …her head and chest were covered with scars. Her regiment recommended for her to be awarded The Legion of Honour because she had shown such courage on the battlefield'.

However, we must now return to the Portchester she-privateer. Her vessel was captured soon after she signed on, and she, too, became a prisoner at Portchester. For some months her sex was undetected, until she became ill and was taken to hospital, where her secret was soon discovered. She suffered no punishment for her deception; in fact it was said that she was sent back to France, with a promise that her boyfriend would soon be exchanged for an English prisoner.

In February 1814, among the many prisoners taken at Pampelune

were some forty women; a report from the hospital ship *Renown* at Plymouth stated that 'they were in so wretched a state that they were wholly destitute of the appropriate dress of their sex'. The wives of some of the British officers set up a subscription to clothe them decently.

If such tales of females in the land depots are hard to credit, to hear of women actually living on the hulks might seem unbelievable; but Richard Rose[2] in his excellent study of Ambroise Louis Garneray as author and painter, says:

> '…the fact that a few women can be identified on the registers of some vessels lends authenticity to Garneray's general account of prison life, if not to his narrative of particular events… The registers of the hulks provide a similarly small amount of official information about women and occasionally children associated with prisoners… So far as can be deduced from the details of when and where persons were captured, most women in the hulks seem to have been the wives or camp-followers of soldiers, rather than sailors, and were generally taken prisoner with their men during some large scale action or surrender of troops. Wellington's successes in Spain appear to have swept up a number of Spanish women who passed through the hulks.'

So far, no one has tackled the enormous task of researching the registers of all the prison hulks, so we may never know just how many women suffered that unpleasant experience. Richard Rose, who made a special study of Portsmouth hulks associated with his subject, Louis Garneray, found that of about 1,200 captives who passed through the *Crown* prison hulk, between 1806 and 1814, only two wives of soldiers were actually recorded, 'Some 2,400 prisoners passed through Garneray's hulk, the *Vengeance*, between 1806 and 1814; amongst these Therese Chapelle, the wife of a drummer, Annette Paquet, a corporal's wife and Catherine Chaumay, described as a 'Girl' in the register are the only females named.' The 'Girl' was released on the 25th March, 1809, and the two women on the 25th April, 1810. They had been on the *Vengeance* for two years.

We have already noted that it was not unusual for the families of British officers to live in the depots, whether on land or afloat, but it is probable that a certain number of female outworkers were employed in most establishments as cooks, washerwomen and so on. The wives of depot officers, senior officers at least, would doubtless have needed a few female servants, although most would have been served by selected male prisoners.

The staff lists for hospitals and hospital ships usually included a Matron; and where nurses are mentioned they might be of either sex, French or British – loblollies who assisted the medical officers. The list of staff appointments at Dartmoor Prison in 1809, called for one hospital Matron and one Seamstress. Elizabeth Arnold was Matron on the hospital hulk *Pegase*, at Portsmouth in 1810, where a seamstress was also employed. Thus it may well be that all those depots with hospitals were allowed to take on similar female employees.

It may be of interest to make a quick comparison between the life of the average prisoner of war and the 'free' British soldier or sailor. It was not until the first quarter of the nineteenth century that the harsh shipboard life of the ordinary naval rating began to improve. Before 1797 and the great Spithead Mutiny, his lot had been little better than that of the prisoner of war. Sometimes his food was not as good as the depot ration and, if he happened to step out of line, a callous flogging would remind him not to do whatever he did again. His pay was unbelievably scant, and often paid out in dribs and drabs, or withheld, sometimes for years. And freedom? All he was likely to see of the world was what could be seen from the deck of his ship, or through the scuttle; for shore leave was seldom granted. Once a ship's company had been formed, every effort was made to keep it together; hence the cynical withholding of pay – 'keep his cash and hold your man' – and the banning of shore leave, so as not to invite desertion. It also explains why each man was allowed the consolation of 'one gallon of beer and half a pint of rum' per day.

Of course, there were some enlightened commanders who endeavoured to run their ships efficiently but without cruelty, their crews treated as men, rather than as members of a low sub-species of the human race – which some tyrannical commissioned Royal Navy officers believed them to be.

The English ships of war really were prisons of a kind, and the inmates, other than commissioned and warrant officers, were almost as womanless as the prisoners of war – except on some special occasions. When a voyage or commission ended and they were heading for a home port, there was much rejoicing on board, for a tradition which dated back to mediaeval times would be re-enacted on arrival in port.

Admiralty Regulations had been emphatic for centuries that –

'No women be ever permitted on board, but such as are really the wives of the men they come to; and the ship be not too much pestered even with them. But this indulgence is only tolerated when the ship is in port, and not under sailing orders.'

(National Maritime Museum HAW/8)

No Admiralty law was ever more completely ignored.

The arrival of large warships in harbours such as Plymouth, Portsmouth and some other ports at home and abroad, brought about an air of excited gaiety, both on shore and on board. A vulgar pantomine-like ceremony was about to unfold, which has been reported in many books and diaries, both civil and prisoner of war. The latter could only have viewed the scene from transport vessels which were bringing them to England, or cartel ships which were taking them home. However, whether envious or disgusted, few ever forgot it and some recalled it in their memoirs.

The Admiralty did not stick rigidly to their Regulation for good reason. Jack could be pushed just so far but no farther, so if he could not go to the women on shore, they would have to come to him on board. Otherwise the dreaded word 'Mutiny!' would sooner or later be heard.

Many senior officers strove to enforce the 'no women' rule. Admiral William Hawkins and others produced a pamphlet anonymously, in the hope that the Admiralty would bring the practice to an end It read:

'It is well known that immediately on the arrival of a ship of war in port, crowds of boats flocked off with cargoes of prostitutes. Having no money to pay for their conveyance, the waterman takes as many as his boat will hold, upon speculation, and hovers round the ship until she is secured to her anchors and the necessary work done, when he with others, is permitted to come alongside. The men then go into the boats and pick out each a woman (as one would choose cattle), paying a shilling or two to the boatman for her passage. Then they descend to the lower deck with their husbands, as they call them. These women are examined at the gangway for liquor which

they are constantly in the habit of smuggling on board. Hundreds come off to a large ship. The whole of the shocking, disgraceful transaction of the lower deck is impossible to describe – the dirt, filth, and stench; the disgusting conversation; the indecent beastly conduct and horrible scenes; the blasphemy and swearing; the riots, quarrels, and fighting which often takes place where hundreds of men and women are huddled together in one room, as it were, in bed – each man being allowed only fourteen inches breadth for his hammock, they are squeezed between the next hammocks and must be witness to each others actions; can only be imagined by those who have seen all this. A ship in this state is often, and justly, called by the more decent seamen 'a hell afloat'. Let those who have never seen a ship of war, picture to themselves a large low room (hardly capable of holding the men) with 500 men and probably 300 or 400 women of the vilest description shut up in it, and giving way to every excess of debauchery that the grossest passions of human nature can lead them to; and they will see the deck of a 74-gun ship the night of her arrival in port.'[3]

Most of the women stayed on board until the vessel received new sailing orders, sometimes for days; then, before the ship could be readied for sea, it had to be cleared of the female intruders. Jack Nastyface[4] described the scene on HMS *Revenge*:

'The word was now passed for the women to stand by to go on shore the next day. It is not the happiest moment of a sailor's life when he has to part with his Nancy, but grieving's a folly and upon these occasions they generally throw grief and temporary affection over the taffrail as commodities they do not take to sea with them. The boats being ready alongside, some of our men, being full of frolic and fun, had bought bunches of onions and turnips, and would very politely offer a few of the onions to those ladies who could not contrive to get up a cry at parting without their aid... a dozen or two (of the sailors) had plunged themselves into matrimony during the time we were in harbour.'

Not all of the women left the ship, as commanders sometimes allowed a few of the 'married' women to sail with their new husbands – and share their rations. These women would have useful jobs to do, though they may not have known it at the time; their action-stations were to help the young boys to carry powder to the guns, and to nurse wounded seamen.[5]

Prisoners of war of many nationalities published their recollections of imprisonment in Britain, but I know of only one who mentioned prostitutes and of their sexual service ever being available to prisoners of war: and had it appeared in a memoir written many years after the wars, I would have dismissed it as sensational memoir-padding. It was, however, penned by the American privateer surgeon, Benjamin Waterhouse, in his *Journal of a Young Man of Massachusetts*, which he published in 1815.

The voyage round the coast on the *Leyden* was only slightly less unpleasant than they had experienced on the *Malaga*, but they were in for the biggest surprise of their captivity on arrival at Plymouth. Next morning boats came alongside filled with women, 'generally, healthy, rosy looking lasses. Their number increased every hour, until there were as many on board of us as there were men. In short, every man who paid the waterman half a crown had a wife'. This invasion by female boarders would have been no surprise to Jack Tars in general, for every home-coming ship was greeted in this manner; but many of the American captives had seen little sea-time before their capture, and although they may have read of such exotic happenings involving dusky maidens of the South Seas, it was the last thing they expected in an English port. Waterhouse crammed a great deal of moralising in his journal throughout its length, and one might expect him to point the Plymouth episode of tarts and tars as another example of the low standards of the British. However, in one remarkable passage he indicates that two-and-sixpenny temporary 'wives' were also available to the prisoners!

> 'Yes, Christian reader! In this religious island, whereof George the 3rd is king, and Charlotte the queen, the young females crowd the prison ship, and take for husbands the ragged American prisoners, provided they can get a few shillings by it.'

It would be easy to dismiss this as fiction, remembering the strictness of the dour captain of the *Leyden*, who discouraged fraternisation between captives and crew – and had had a marine flogged for selling a little of his own tobacco to an American. Why though should Waterhouse have included a complete fabrication in a book published at a time when thousands of his fellow prisoners, and potential readers, were returning and would have laughed inaccuracies to scorn?

Besides a first edition of the *Journal*, I have a second edition in my collection published a year later in 1816, in which I rather expected the prostitute story to be omitted; but, although there was a good deal of revision and editing, it remained unaltered.

1
Now our ship is arrived
And anchor'd in Plymouth Sound
We'll drink a health to the Whores
That does our ship surround

2
Then into the boat they get
And along side they came
Waterman call my Husband
For I'm damb'd if I know his name

3
Then up steps a nimble Jack tar
He hearing what was said
Aft on the Quarter deck he goes
And humbly bows his head

4
Sir my Wife's alongside
Will you please let her in
Yes, my lad says he
But see she's got no gin

5
My Wife she never carries any
Scoundrals I won't take your word
Midshipmen search that boat
Before she comes on board

6
Then up the side she comes
And down the bay she runs
It's ten to one to me
She's a bladder or two of rum

7
Then down steps nimble Jack tar
Jonny have you got any thing

With that she up with her smock tail
And hauls out four Bladders of gin

8
Come I'll go fetch some beer
That we may have some slip
The Devils may damb them forever
For we can sling them yet.

'A Man-o'-War's Song'. Anon. January, 1779

The infliction of celibacy upon thousands of male captives in our prisoner of war establishments, was an unavoidable additional hardship. It was a subject not often openly discussed, as it would have involved the mention of homosexuality, (although the word had not been invented at that time: two words based on the old French, sodomy and buggery, were sometimes used, but euphemisms such as 'unclean acts', 'unnatural practices', 'crime against nature', 'infamous vice', etc. were usually preferred.) – and the offence a capital crime until 1861.

Of all the deprivations which must have changed the life and character of the captives – in some cases permanently – the loss of freedom, the insufficiency of food and clothing, etc. – the most important must have been, at least to the heterosexual male, the absence of women in his life. It is probable that the majority of the prisoners stood up to even this privation valiantly; but most French and American memoirs make it obvious that many succumbed to circumstance, particularly among the *Rafellès* on the hulks and the *Romaines* and *Misérables* in the depots on land, who were capable of just about every vice known to man. Depot records of Black Hole punishments reveal that this was so, once the euphemisms have been translated.

Yet I know of only two plain outspoken references to homosexuality by prisoner memoirists; they also tell of male prostitution. One was a sailor, Lieutenant J. Mesonant, a prisoner on one of the Chatham hulks, who wrote *Coup d'Oeil Rapide Sur Les Pontons de Chatam*, ('A Quick Glance at the Chatham Hulks'), a short but descriptive book, which records his observations and comments on his life on board: the other was a French soldier, captured in Spain. Mesonant wrote:

> 'Theft was infrequent on board the hulks. However, there was another more common vice which was generally widespread among men subjected to five, seven or nine years of rigorous incarceration and deprived of all pleasures associated with freedom. If this vice, too terrible to name, was not already shameful in a man, it was even more unspeakable in the dreadful and dishonest way it was exercised in deplorable conditions which caused men to abandon all shame and modesty.
>
> 'The active party, with flagrant liberties taken by him, often displayed unnatural brutalities while the passive party would not blush at selling his favours, too repugnant to describe. Such bargaining was for a couple of sous or a ration of herrings.
>
> 'Such actions were beyond redemption. Only the lord above and his mighty wrath, rained down as it did on Sodom and Gomorrha, could have any effect and then it might have touched both the guilty and the innocent.
>
> 'However, if ever this vice was in any way excusable, could it not be in this instance when men young and at the height and mercy of natural ardent passions, succumbed to their baser natures when deprived of not only natural physical but also their freedom which they saw waning every day. In the final analysis what does it really matter! Is this just not another drop in the torrent of evils which

wartime imposed on men in captivity.

'In the space of eight months on board the hulks I only saw two punishments, one for sodomy and the other for spying.'

The second outspoken diarist was the French soldier, J.Quantin, who was captured during the Peninsular War, and spent the first three years in Spain, at first enjoying a semi-parole period in a pleasant Spanish town. Then his group of prisoners were sent first to the terrible Cadiz hulks and after a while to even worse imprisonment on the island of Cabrera⁶. In his journal, 'Three Years in Spain', Quantin tells us that there were women on the island, some of them very attractive, but although they were outnumbered by men about two hundred to one, '…none were ever insulted or abused'. However, there were liaisons: he went on to tell of a young Polish woman who had, somehow, become the 'property' of a French Lancer, who later sold her to a Light Infantryman, who in turn sold her to a Dragoon. 'The beautiful young woman equally loved all who possessed her'!

Quantin arrived in England, and ultimately Portchester Castle, in September 1810. Among the many interesting observations on life in the Depot which made up his memoir, are his comments on the subject under discussion.

'Maybe at this point, while on the subject of the conduct and peculiarities of the prisoners, I should mention a certain vice which arose in the prison and brought with it unpleasant incidences. This vice, in the past adored by the Greeks and still today held in high esteem in many Asiatic countries, occurs almost always in places where men are gathered together without the presence of the opposite sex. At Porchester, where we were more deprived of women than on the island of Cabrera, it was rampant. As a result there were many scandalous episodes which triggered emotions such as hatred, jealousy, scandalmongering, slander and a whole host of other vices which are enemies to the spirit, destructive in nature and disquieting to the human mind. It was difficult for men involved in this distasteful business to stop when it was a question of them gainfully benefiting. However, it has been my intention to inject some cheerfulness into these Memoirs and I have always tried to remain pure, and even though I am totally adverse to this vice, I feel that it is sufficient for me to acknowledge that it was one of the established vices of prison life. I am writing this to explain this and to also engender repulsion in my readers as I profess to feel myself.'

To write of the lady wives of paroled officers in a raunchy chapter such as this has become, may seen rather out of place; but I've started so I'll finish.

There was nothing that the authorities could do to relieve the monk-like existence of the ordinary prisoner in his 'no women' town; but it does emphasise the enormous gulf between the rank and file captive and the parolee, who, as we shall see, was often spoilt for choice.

The rules and restrictions involved in the privilege of parole were few and easy to keep. Briefly summed up, they warned: don't wander beyond one mile along the turnpike road from your lodging; don't cause trouble; don't attempt to escape. The majority honoured their word, but, during the Napoleonic period in particular, quite a large number of French officers and gentlemen did dishonour their word, and fled back to France. The officer who settled into one of the often delightful parole villages or towns in England, Wales or Scotland, were in an ideal position for a prisoner of war to find himself: he was sheltered from the dangers of battle,

retained a high percentage of his freedom, could send for his wife to join him, or if unmarried, court and possibly marry a British girl.

Just about every rank of military, naval, privateer and merchant officer, was represented in one or other of the hundred or more parole centres spread throughout the country. From General to sous-lieutenant, Admiral to gardes-marine (midshipmen), some officers of privateers and merchantmen, and gentlemen and lady passengers – all were represented. Parole towns varied in popularity according to their geographical siting and facilities which might occupy the idle time of men who had been so recently active. Towns like Bath, Reading, Cheltenham and sometimes London, headed the list; but these were almost exclusively reserved for very senior and wealthy officers, their servants and aides.

General Lefèbvre-Desnouettes, Officer of the Legion of Honour; General of Division, a very senior officer, was granted the almost unheard of privilege of taking with him two Imperial Guardsmen as servants when he was sent to Cheltenham, where he lived with his wife, until he broke his parole in May 1812.

It is surprising to read that so many Napoleonic senior officers had broken their parole pledge – an act which would have brought disgrace in previous wars. When the usually dour Transport Board acceded to Admiral Count Linois's request that his wife be allowed to join him at the fashionable city of Bath, they added a compliment to his conduct: '…which has formed a very satisfactory contrast to that of many officers of high rank, by whom a similar indulgence has been abused'.

Many officers sent for their wives and luxuries from home, and their addition to the local populations, often added a sparkle which enlivened the society of some rather dull inland towns and villages. The parolees themselves were, in the main, amiable men of education and ingenuity, good company and excellent raconteurs; so they were much sought after by the local gentry who invited them into their homes and, unknowingly, sometimes into their families.

General d'Henin, one of the senior officers captured at San Domingo in 1803 was sent to Chesterfield in Derbyshire. He was a popular figure in the town, and married a Scots 'lady of fortune'. They lived in Chesterfield until 1814, then went to Paris. The General returned to war during the Hundred Days and lost a leg at Waterloo.

Another senior officer prisoner, captured at San Domingo was the black General Marienier who was brought to Portsmouth, where he disembarked with his four wives!

The inhabitants in general accepted and respected them from many viewpoints. The shopkeepers and business men appreciated their patronage, the landladies as their tenants; and as a result of the long drawn-out wars, most *cautionnements* suffered a serious shortage of young men, so when drafts of anything between one and three hundred fascinating strangers marched into the market square of village or town, there would have been a great fluttering of female hearts, and dreams of romance. Understandably so, for these captives were figures from another culture, different in dress, manners and personality from any one the English women and maidens had ever encountered; even more so to the Scottish lassies of the newly established border town *cautionnements* after 1811. Although most of the officers were French, there was a wide choice of other nationalities, Italians, Spaniards, Poles, the perhaps less exotic Dutch, Danes and Germans, and later the very different Americans. We have a number of descriptions of the young French officers: one newspaper[7] said '…they were frivolous, as many of them wore ear-rings, and one, a Pole, had a ring through his nose'. Hospitable and, as many of them were well-to-do, always ready to organise a party, concert or ball. They spent some time on their personal appearance, Macbeth Forbes[8] said that they were always immaculately dressed, 'usually attired in white trousers or breeches and jackets', and on special occasions, 'were resplendent in gaily-coloured coats, frilled at neck and cuffs, and long white stockings'.

A description by Mrs Roberts of Chesterfield was similar, but perhaps more disapproving (as she had described some of their wives as 'very dingy, plain looking women'): 'Their large looped gold ear-rings, their pink or sky-blue umbrellas, the Legion of honour ribbons in their button holes; their profuse exchange of embraces and kisses in the public street; their attendant poodles carrying walking sticks in their mouths; and their incessant and vociferous talking…' An intriguing picture of fighting men, but small wonder that some down-to-earth Americans, like Benjamin Waterhouse, considered all Frenchmen as effeminate in their manners.

The records abound with stories of affairs and marriages between parole-town girls and captive officers – In Ashby-de-la-Zouch, for instance, between 1806 and 1814, fifteen local girls married Frenchmen.

Some of those glamorous suitors from other lands played havoc with the hearts of more than one of the local beauties, and some of those beauties were pursued by more than one suitor. This caused quarrels and jealousies, and more than one duel was fought, but none, as far as I can discover had a fatal ending. Having no swords or guns, the duellists concocted dangerous-enough weapons: canes or walking-sticks were fitted with razors or knives, or metal from barrel hoops sharpened and fashioned into make-shift swords. One bloodless duel, between contenders for a girl's favours, went on for over an hour before being stopped; but as duelling was one of the few prisoner of war offences which came under civil laws, the contestants were each sentenced to a month in the County Gaol.

There were, of course, womanisers in the worst sense of the word, but most were high spirited and romantic gallants, like Louis Garneray's old friend and shipmate, the Baron de Bonnefoux who, like the typical sailor that he was, had at least one girl friend in each of his *cautionnements*. The inhabitants of Thame, in Oxfordshire, both gentry and townsfolk, were genuinely sorry when, as the result of his involvement in an altercation with local rowdies, he was transferred to Odiham, in Hampshire. Amid the sad farewells, he was presented with a lock of hair by 'la jeune Miss Harriet Stratford aux Beaux yeux bleus, au teint éblousissant, à la physionomie animée, à la taille divine.'

Odiham had even more attractions for the Baron and his friends with far more facilities for the parolees to fill in their idle hours. Besides almost nonstop invitations to banquets, balls and soirées, where they would meet pretty and beautiful girls, the town had its Philharmonic Orchestra, clubs and a theatre. All in all, they could not have expected, or even wished, for more; but Bonnefoux accepted a one too many invitation. An English friend named Danley tempted him into a reckless escapade, by suggesting that they should venture many miles outside his parole limit, and visit Windsor. The Baron could not resist the venture, during which they saw the King. No one saw them leave or return. That was in June 1807, and although there had been a faint rumour that a prisoner

had been in the crowd which watched the King pass by, but no one was under suspicion. Then, in September, a widow – who may have had some interest in Bonnefoux – discovered a billet-doux he had written earlier in the year, addressed to her nurse, Mary. It read: 'To-morrow, I shall have the grief of not seeing you, but I shall see your King'. The infuriated widow denounced him, and he was ordered to be removed to the *Bahama* hulk at Chatham.

Whilst awaiting transport to the Medway, the Baron escaped and lay hidden for three days before setting out for the coast with another of his lady-loves, Sarah Cooper, daughter of a local pastry cook, who guided him as far as Guildford. There, he ordered a coach to take Sarah back to Odiham, and there we shall leave him, as the rest of his story is told elsewhere in this book (See 'Prisoner of War Hulks').

The saddest story of parole town romances is that of one French officer who was paroled to Andover. He found accommodation in a fine house in West Street, and soon after, fell deeply in love with the daughter of his landlord. She rejected him and, broken-hearted, he went out to the garden-house, opened a vein, and committed suicide.

The names of two prisoners, Duchemin and Viollet[9] are of particular interest to me. Both were paroled to Wincanton, both married Wincanton girls, and both stayed in this country when the war ended. In 1804 Louis Michel Duchemin was Comptable Agent on *La Torche*, a corvette in the French Imperial Navy. *La Torche* was captured off St Domingo in August 1805, and on reaching England, Louis was paroled to Wincanton early in 1806.

On a wall in my study, is his framed bi-lingual 'Certificate of membership of the French Lodge, LA PAIX DESIREE', founded in the town by the prisoners a few years before. This rare Freemasonry document was produced by a Wincanton printer named Clewett, and on the 4th February, 1808, Louis Duchemin married the printer's daughter, Elizabeth.

Next to the Certificate is a vellum extract from the Parish Register, which records the marriage. It was transcribed in 1812, probably by fellow prisoner, Deben Aine, who signed it. It also recorded the baptism of a Duchemin daughter, Louisa Elizabeth, on the 9th March, 1809.

The Italian soldier, Alberto Viollet, was not an officer but one of the lucky young lads who, as servants, were allowed to share their senior officer masters' parole. He, like Duchemin, was one of the very few parolees who was not sent to the Border Towns in 1811. The surname, Viollet, had for some reason been changed to Biolotti, which I discovered during a research trip to Wincanton, when I met one of Alberto's descendants – which led to my meeting a number of the Biolotti family, when they visited me a year or so later.

After the war Alberto Biolotti established a hairdressing business in the town. He married two English girls, and outlived them both. He died in 1869, aged ninety-two.

The Governments of both England and France were concerned at what might be referred to as over-fraternizing. Wincanton had been virtually cleared of parolees principally because of possible uprising; but the pamphleteer, George Sweetman, considered it had also been cleansed, because irresponsible affairs between local girls and prisoners had shown that 'our small town was becoming a veritable hotbed of vice.'

However, the French were more drastic than the English, although the girls were warned that they were playing with fire:

'…some of them (the parolees) have made overtures of marriage to women in the neighbourhood, which the magistrates very properly, have taken pains to discourage', was typical of the messages promulgated throughout the parole towns. This was sound, but unromantic advice, and Antoine Bret's 'The first sigh of Love is the last of Wisdom', proved itself over and over again.

As the following note will show, the British authorities were as concerned for the daughters of the gentry, as they were for the daughters of the shopkeepers or landladies. Some time in 1804, the Board were keeping a covert eye on General Pageot, who had been paroled to Ashbourne, and was thought to be 'paying his addresses to a Lady of Respect' in the area. The suspicion was well founded; the General already had a wife and family in France. Such interferences were considered necessary, as France's heartless ruling on mixed marriages, was available to anyone who wished to take advantage of it. The French Government did not recognise such marriages as binding, and when the war ended, English wives were sent back to England when their transport reached the cartel port of Morlaix. Many of the Frenchmen settled with their wives in England or Scotland, but there were many others who followed their Emperor's dictum, that: 'The only victory over love is flight', and fled; often leaving not only a destitute wife but children. Although the latter were technically French subjects, the deserted mother and offspring received no maintenance money from the Continent, their subsistence was paid for by the British Government. Illegitimacy was another matter, and a nationwide and constant worry. Quite early on in the wars the offending prisoner partner, where known, was held responsible under the civil law, as shown in the following instance. In 1805, a Colonel de Bercy got involved with a girl in the Oxfordshire parole town of Thame, and was 'in difficulty' when he found she was pregnant. The Transport Office 'declined to interfere, but said that if the Colonel could not give sufficient security that mother and child should not be a burden on the rates, he must be imprisoned until he did.'

A hard up French naval officer, Le Forsiney, who was responsible for the condition of an Odiham girl, would have certainly gone to prison, had not the wealthy Count de Bonnefoux come to his aid with the necessary 600 francs.

The French never had the same degree of worry over the outcome of Anglo-French relationships. With their comparatively few captive English officers, and the concentration of these in just the one fortified parole town, there was nothing like the widespread goings-on so prevalent in all the British *cautionnements*, at least, not during the Napoleonic period. Some English wives joined their paroled husbands, and that there must have been some romances, is shown by the occasional duel between Englishmen over a French girl. However, when, in 1803, Napoleon unfairly created hostages by detaining a large number of British travellers who had been touring the Continent during the short Peace of 1802, the face and pace of Verdun changed. It became the wartime home of both officers and *detenus*. J.G.Alger[10] estimated that amongst them were 'five dukes, three marquises, thirty-seven earls and countesses, eight viscounts, seventeen barons, and forty-one elder sons and other heirs – two-thirds of the House of Lords at that time,' plus a few hundred other *detenus* wealthy enough to travel. These grand men with their grand ladies and their servants, soon turned Verdun into a fashionable and prosperous English-like town. The gentry had their clubs and societies, and after a while sent home for their coaches, horses and hounds: the ladies had a fine up-market shopping place, called, not coincidentally Bon(d) Street.

That, however, is another story (see Chapter 21, PAROLE D'HONNEUR).

CAMP FOLLOWERS

As mentioned earlier, the presence of women in our war prisons in any noticeable number, would indicate that they were followers of soldiers recently captured in battles on land or transport vessels, within a reasonable distance of the British coast. Most foreign soldier captives were eventually incarcerated in our hulks or depots, whilst the women would have been repatriated, except in exceptional cases. The great majority would have been non-combatant camp followers of the troops.

There was a great difference in preparing an army or a navy for a voyage or expedition. A well-provisioned ship was in many ways self sufficient, something like the market of a small village or even town, in that it carried all manner of stores and victuals to sustain a large number of men; though the ship-borne goods most often were more sufficient in quantity than in quality. Whereas, armies particularly the French, usually lived off the land, sometimes purchasing provisions from farmers and peasants, or perhaps more often by pillage and devastation.

To many readers the term 'Camp Follower' is taken as a synonym for 'prostitute', but there is more to it than that. In most cases the number of male followers far exceeded females. Although prostitution was an important and thriving business, there were many other services and trades needed by the fighting forces. Non combatant skills of all kinds were available; for the most were connected with the production, collection and distribution of food for the thousands of hungry fighting men.

Quartermasters, like Louis-François Gille, were of great importance in the food chain. They were sent ahead of their divisions to locate likely foraging grounds, undefended farming areas, and sources of supply by purchase. Much of this produce was handled by experienced civilian contractors, merchants, middlemen and suppliers, many of whom had lost their businesses at the outbreak of war and now followed the troops. Gille said: 'since armies travelled on campaign for long periods and were expected to live off the land, civilian traders and suppliers normally moved with them, as did numbers of wives, companions, laundresses, prostitutes, and even children. Armies on the road were substantial travelling towns.'

Both Louis Gille and J.Quantin, also an officer diarist, Charles Frossard, were prisoners on the hell-hole of Cabrera in the Balearics, and commented on the small group of women who were there, and who shared the hardship of that dreadful place.

The American writer, Denis Smith, in his book on the prisoners of Cabrera found a number of references to women in Captain Charles Frossard's journal 'Prisonnier des Espagnoles: mémoires du capitaine Charles Frossard' (published in *Historama 305, 306 Paris*) some of which is included here. There were about twenty women, and some five or six of these ladies were the legitimate wives of French officers, and no doubt would have shared their husbands' quarters in the old castle. The remainder would have endured a very much harder life, having already spent time on the hulks at Cadiz, after the Battle of Baylen. These camp followers, who may have been market women or cooks, now finding themselves on a desert island, without provisions to deal in would have been lucky to find work as servants to the officers' wives. Some, therefore may have reluctantly turned to prostitution. This was not always against the wishes of their lawful or sometimes temporary husbands, 'who agreed to surrender their marital rights in return for a share of their income'. Frossard, says there was a good deal of wife swapping and dealing on the part of the men. Some women were sometimes treated as pieces of property; a Polish widow whose husband had died in a Spanish prison camp, was young, blond and attractive and now lived with a Polish non-commissioned officer. She was eventually sold by her new husband to a dragoon sergeant for sixty francs. Even stranger, Gille tells us of another Polish women, who was offered in a lottery at four sous per ticket!

> 'La Jacquette (who lived with a gunner named Jacquet) had been a wine and coffee merchant, and a seamstress as well. She was young and pretty and distributed her affections widely in the camp. She carried on many affairs and was sought by many officers, all of whom she tried to satisfy. One day she tried to drown herself because one of her lovers had left her for another woman. Afterwards, the most remarkable thing was that she demanded to see the one she said she loved best, and insisted on going with her husband to persuade him to return to her…the officer showed his gratitude by taking his sweetheart away with him to England. She left her Jacquet on Cabrera.'

Not everyone approved of the conduct of these women and their consorts. Quantin wrote that none of these women were ever abused, but there is at least one story which says otherwise; La Denise, a pretty brunette wine supplier, whose husband Sergeant Denis of the light infantry kept a watchful eye on her. For a long time she rejected the advances of many would-be suitors, but finally she gave in to their importunities, for which she was repeatedly thrashed by her husband. Battered and bruised, she was out of circulation for a time but her husband never did learn how many times he had been cuckolded.

The most vehement objector to women on the island was Father Damian Estelrich, the only cleric on Cabrera, who plagued the officials in Palma to remove them all. The official reply was that there was no proof that these women were not married as, like so many other prisoners their papers had been lost. So they stayed on Cabrera until 1810, when the British Navy transported nearly all of the French prisoners to English depots, principally Portchester Castle. Father Damian would still not have been happy, for we read that after the clearance, fresh prisoners arrived – with their complement of women followers.

POSTSCRIPT

Amongst Father Damian's papers was a list of the names of some of the first women on Cabrera:

Tiny Maria Murviosa, of Versailles.
Madame Bela, calling herself the wife of Guime.
Maria, calling herself the wife of sergeant Martin.
Cristina, calling herself the wife of sergeant Cosin.
Cristiania, German, calling herself the wife of grenadier sergeant Carvet.
Sofia, a German widow.
Maria, sergeant Galiaco's woman.
Maria, sergeant Dionisio's woman.
Fat Maria, a sergeant major's woman.
Rosa the Pole, Antonio Bordange's whore.
La Jacqueta, after a certain Jacquet.

Artist unknown. Seamen and their women dance to a one-eyed, one-legged fiddler, while others gamble or read letters.
© NATIONAL MARITIME MUSEUM, LONDON

1. Peter Kemp: *The British Sailor*. Dent, 1970.

2. Richard Rose: *The Floating Prisons*. Conway Press, 2003.

3. Christopher Lloyd: *The British Seamen*.

4. Jack Nastyface: *Nautical Economy, or Forecastle Recollections of the Last War*. Nastyface is thought to be the pseudonym of William Robinson, a seaman who joined the Royal Navy via the press-gang but in his writing always referred to himself as a volunteer. The award was for their help in dressing and attending the wounded at the Battle of the Nile, 1st August, 1798.

5. John Nicol: ' …the boys and the women who carried the powder. The women behaved as well as the men…some of the women were wounded, and one woman belonging to Leith died of her wounds. One woman bore a son in the heat of action.' Four women were entered in the muster book of HMS *Goliath*, the first women to be so honoured, as it entitled them to two-thirds of a seaman's ration. The award was for their help in dressing and attending to the wounded at the Battle of the Nile, 1st August, 1798.

6. See Chapter 10. THE SPANISH HULKS and THE ISLAND OF CABRERA.

7. *The Southern Counties Courier*.

8. Macbeth Forbes, 19th century banker and researcher.

9. J.M.Duchemin. See 'Parole d'Honneur' and Violet or Biolet, 'Parole'.

10. J.Godsworth Alger: *Napoleon's British Visitors*. 1904.

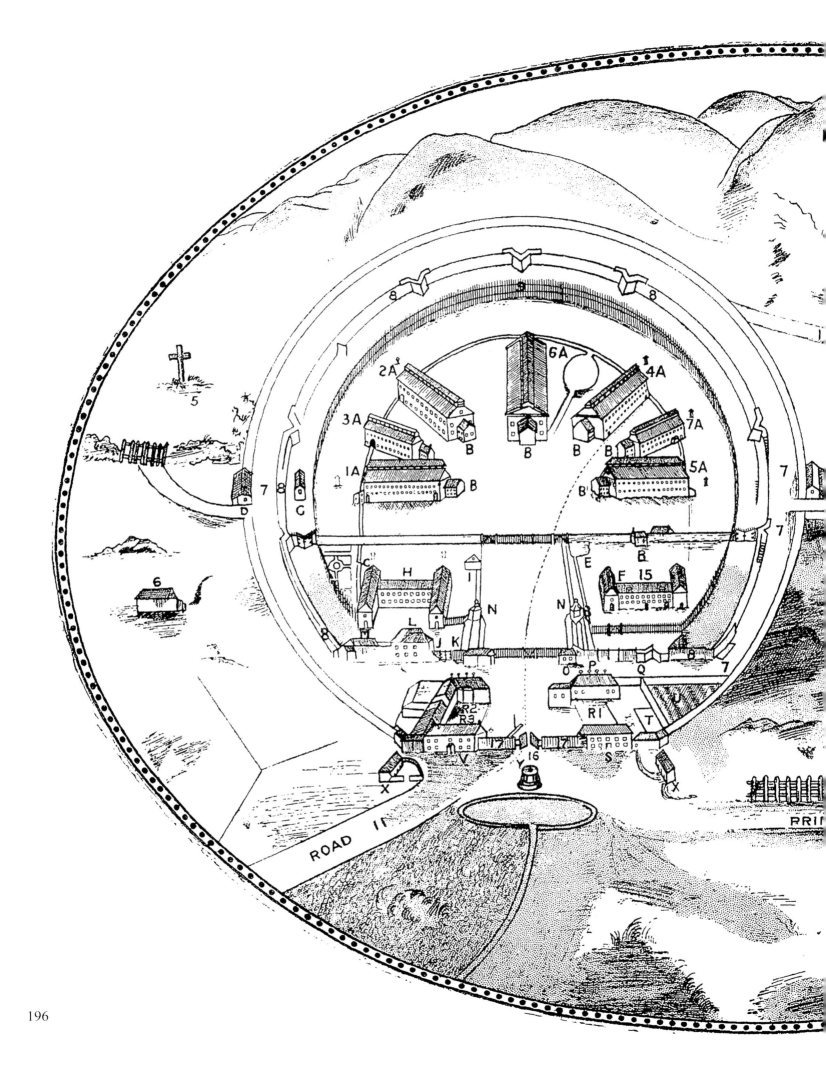

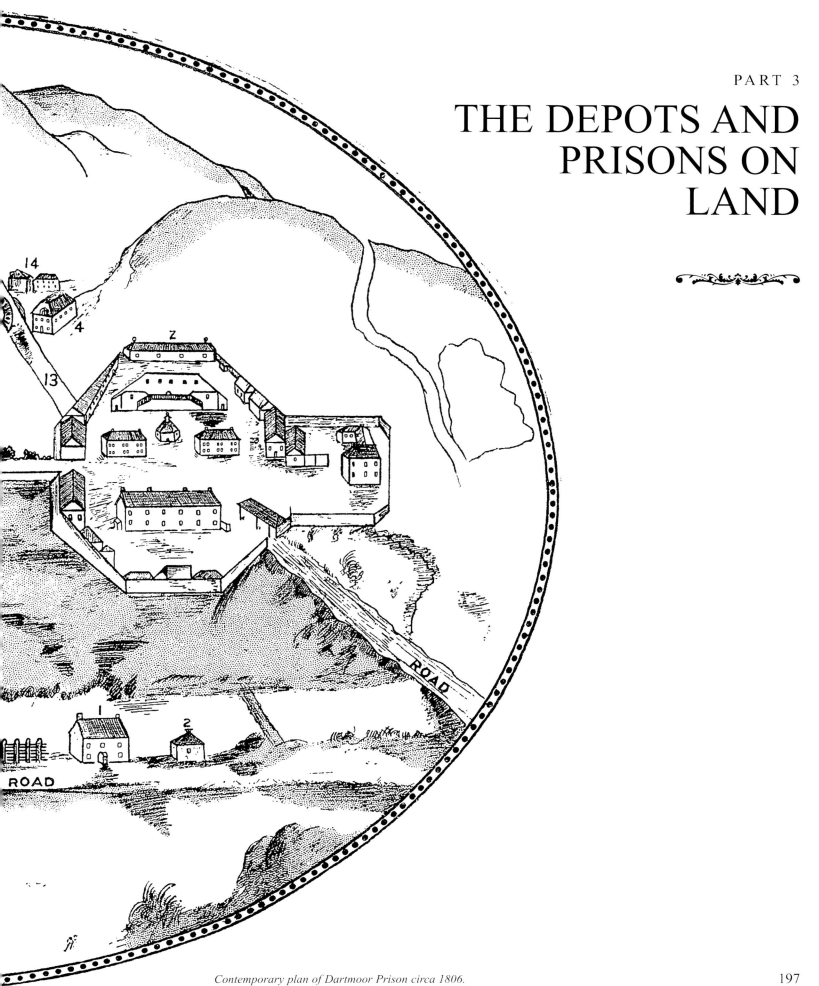

PART 3

THE DEPOTS AND PRISONS ON LAND

Contemporary plan of Dartmoor Prison circa 1806.

Chapter Twelve

The Depots and Prisons on Land
A Preview

CHATHAM	KIRGILLIAK	PORTCHESTER CASTLE	TYNEMOUTH
DARTMOOR	KNOWLE (Bristol)	ROSCROW	VALLEYFIELD
EDINBURGH CASTLE	LIVERPOOL	SHREWSBURY	WINCHESTER
ESK MILLS	MILLBAY	SISSINGHURST CASTLE	YARMOUTH
FALMOUTH	NORMAN CROSS	SOUTHAMPTON	
FORTON	PEMBROKE	ST GEORGE (scot)	
GREENLAW	PERTH	STAPLETON	

IT CANNOT BE DENIED THAT THERE WERE TIMES IN our history when the non-paroled prisoner of war in Britain had a very rough time of it, whether confined in prison ship or on land – which is certainly not to infer that his British counterpart in France or the United States received kid-glove treatment. There was no deliberate governmental plan to make things unpleasant for our captive foe, but indolence and procrastination on the part of those in power, added to the general harshness and corruption of the age, made certain that he would have few pleasant memories of his stay in this country.[1]

Recriminations between the two countries regarding the treatment of prisoners of war were endless. Many have such a ring of truth about them as to indicate that the Commissioners of the Transport Board and their French opposite numbers probably believed their own exaggerations – which were often taken as gospel by journalists and writers of the time. The following extract from Robert Beatson's *Naval and Military Memoirs*, written not long after the close of the Seven Years' War, is an example of what was probably some anti-French and pro-British exaggeration, sprinkled with flecks of accuracy:

> 'The enemy having swarms of small privateers at sea, captured no less than 330 of the British ships. It is to be lamented that some of their privateers exercised horrid barbarities on their prisoners, being the crews of such ships as had presumed to make resistance, and who were afterwards obliged to submit; conduct that would have disgraced the most infamous pirate; and it would have redounded much to the credit to the Court of France to have made public examples of those who behaved in this manner.
>
> 'I am afraid, likewise, that there was but too much reason for complaint of ill-treatment to the British subjects, even after they were landed in France and sent to prison. Of this, indeed, several affidavits were made by the sufferers when they returned to England.'

He then went on to paint in glowing terms Britain's great concern for her captive Frenchmen:

> '...the conduct of Great Britain was a striking example of their kindness and humanity to such unfortunate persons who were made prisoners of war. The prisons were situated in wholesome places, and subject to public inspection, and the prisoners had every favour shown them that prudence would admit of '.

He spoiled this rather idyllic picture of 'kindness and humanity', when he went on to say that when the French prisoners were ready for exchange by cartel, they had been confined for so long that 'their clothes were reduced to a very bad state, many of them, indeed, almost naked, and suffered much from the inclement weather'; which would indicate that those to whom the prisons 'were open to public inspection', had not been very observant.

Many similar self-congratulatory reports and letters came in from over the Channel, but it can be assumed that the rank and file prisoner here or overseas had quite a lot to complain about. The *Annual Register* in September 1758 tells of 'divers accounts published by gentlemen of credit in France which represent the usage of the poor prisoners there as intolerable,' and went on to say that 'the numbers reported to have perished by the wretchedness of their condition even exceeds those killed by sea and land'.

The housing of prisoners of war had long been a troublesome problem which, in spite of Britain's experience of almost continuous warring, had never been squarely faced, or received the attention which might have eased the situation for both administrators and prisoner. By the end of the Seven Years' War in 1763, there were about 40,000 prisoners of war in England, yet little had been done to create a decent and humane system of prisoner of war management. The few shore depots and hulks which had been set up as exclusively prisoner of war establishments were soon filled and overfilled, and the unfortunate remainder stowed away in the most unlikely and unsuitable places. Many were forced to share the horrors of filthy borough jails and lock-ups with our civilian prisoners: debtors, felons, and miscreants awaiting transportation.

At the other end of the scale – though often without much improvement in conditions and comfort – quarters were found for prisoners in castle keeps and towers, hastily adapted large country homes, warehouses, and even caves. It should be remembered, however, that they were, at least, taken prisoner! Not so many years earlier, and for past centuries, most captured enemies would have been taken into slavery, thrown overboard or slaughtered on the battlefield; whilst a few nobles or men of substance may have been ransomed.

The day of the specially constructed prisoner of war depot, which could hold several thousand captives and operate under workable regulations and controls, was still in the future. It was not until the American War was nearing its end, that Stapleton Prison, at Fishponds, near Bristol, was built; and the first great prisoner of war depot, Norman Cross, was not completed until 1797 followed by Dartmoor in 1809, and Perth in 1812. The great Scottish depot at Valleyfield, capable of accommodating 10,000 prisoners, did not open until the following year.

Therefore, the position at the outbreak of the War of American Independence was no better than before – in fact, much worse. In the first place, the Government rather expected a last minute escape from hostilities. Second was the fact that this war, more than any before it, made the problem of housing prisoners – whether civil prisoners or prisoners of war – more desperate than ever before.

From the time of Elizabeth I there was no real need for large convict establishments in Great Britain, which might be converted for prisoner use in time of war – America itself was our penitentiary.

The Act for the Punishment of Rogues, Vagabonds and Sturdy Beggars 1597, had introduced transportation as the sentence next in severity to the gallows. From then on, a hundred or more crimes, from the petty to the serious, could earn terms of seven, fourteen or twenty-one years' deportation to the American colonies. However, now that we were at war with the keepers of this most convenient depository, transportation across the Atlantic came to an abrupt end.

Convicts, political and religious dissidents and other of Britain's unwanted subjects who would normally have been disposed of overseas, now more than filled this country's gaols and, for the first time, the harassed administration introduced civil prison hulks as a 'temporary expedient'.

With prison management becoming almost unmanageable and prisoners of war arriving daily at our ports, it is not surprising that the American captives found hard lodgings in what, until recently, had been their motherland.

A few of the old prisoner of war hulks, such as the *Royal Oak* and the *St Rafael* at Plymouth, which had been used between 1756 and 1763, were brought back into service and were soon fully occupied. Any space in borough gaols which had not been taken up by 'Transportation convicts' – with nowhere to go! – was put to prisoner of war use.

A number of American 'rebels' spent some of their captivity in London's civil prisons such as Wellclose Square, the old Savoy and Coldbath Fields Prison – some inmates would even be able to make the unenviable boast that they had once spent time in notorious Newgate Prison.

Ebenezer Smith Platt, a captive merchant from Georgia, was fettered 'and placed in that part of the prison occupied by thieves, highwaymen, housebreakers, and murderers, with no allowance for food and clothes and must have perished but for private benevolence.' Whilst Ebenezer's case was not unique, I think it probable that he, and others who found themselves treated with such extreme lack of consideration, must have offended over and above his being thought of as a colonial insurgent.

John Howard, the great prison reformer, who tirelessly visited and reported on conditions in all types of civil and prisoner of war establishments and parole towns, found that many Americans were ill-housed and received provisions way below the quality and quantity specified in official regulations; however, in most of the towns where there were also French captives, the latter fared even worse, sometimes through neglect by their own government representative, but more often through their uncontrollable addiction to gambling.

In much the same way that prison hulks had been introduced as a one-year experiment to solve the problem of housing our civil prisoners after 1775 – a *'one*-year temporary expedient' which lasted *eighty* years! – equally makeshift and unsuitable measures were employed to accommodate prisoners of war on land. That neither the civil nor prisoner of war accommodation problem was ever satisfactorily solved is evidenced by the fact that, throughout the whole period of the wars under discussion, the number of prison ships rapidly increased – although, *pro rata*, it was far more costly to confine prisoners in the hulks than in a land depot. One official estimate calculated that the annual running cost of a hulk which carried an average number of prisoners (700) was £5,864, whilst the great depot at Dartmoor, capable of holding almost ten times that number, was £2,862!

There were, of course, inbuilt and from some aspects insuperable handicaps which stood in the way of an adequate answer, such as the smallness of our island home. Unlike France which could, with comparative safety, tuck away her English captives in walled fortress towns, situated deep within the interior of her larger land area, there was nowhere in the British Isles far enough from the sea to similarly discourage escapes and uprisings.

In theory, the problem of prisoner of war accommodation and maintenance, may have been lessened, if not solved, by the employment of an internationally approved, but often misused or neglected, part of the established prisoner of war system. The reduction in numbers by the intelligent use of the Exchange system would have thinned out the populations of the hulks, depots, and even the parole towns, and would no doubt have improved the conditions for all classes of captive. Some attempts were made from time to time. One British proposition was that French and English captives should be traded man for man, rank for rank, until the French prisons were cleared of British captives. At that time in the war, April 1810, when there were about 10,000 British captives in France, this would still have left a residue of some 40,000 French prisoners in British hands. In return for these we asked for Portuguese and Spanish sailors or soldiers of equal rank to those captive Frenchmen.

So near to a solution for both countries – and so near to freedom for some 100,000 men! – but it was not to be. Bonaparte was finicky about the nationalities of the non-French who were to make up the balance. His optimistic alternative suggestion was that we should first release four Frenchmen for every one Englishman, the balance to be made up with captives of three other nationalities. He can hardly have imagined that his proposal would be accepted – four Frenchmen for one Englishman! – perhaps he thought that one of his own assessments of comparative fighting quality had not crossed the Channel:

'Whilst as a fighting unit, you might set against **one** Frenchman **one** Englishman, you would need **two** Prussian, Dutch, or soldiers of the Confederation.'

199

Napoleon was not the only national leader to be choosy in the matter of prisoner of war exchange. George Washington could have obtained the release, and probably saved the lives of hundreds, perhaps thousands, of his countrymen, had he been willing to part with his British and Hessian captives in exchange for American privateers, many of them condemned to the dreaded British prison hulks in New York Harbour.

In earlier times, the accommodation problem, though it existed and was worrying, had not reached the danger point it was later to assume. A number of prisoner of war camps, or depots, had existed in various parts of Britain from the beginning of the period of our study. Parts of Portchester Castle, Edinburgh Castle, Sissinghurst Castle and the Old Tower Prison at Liverpool, were all established war prisons by the outbreak of the Seven Years' War. Sissinghurst was leased for that purpose in 1756, but its existence as a prisoner of war depot ceased permanently at the end of that war. The other two castles already had some experience of managing foreign captives from even earlier wars. A few other castles were considered for conversion into depots; in fact, a part of Pendennis Castle, near Falmouth in Cornwall, was adapted to house some American prisoners during the War of 1812, and Frenchmen captured in the Peninsular Wars: but most edifices escaped that fate. Kenilworth Castle, in Warwickshire, which could have provided accommodation for 'some thousands of prisoners', which would 'reflect Honour on the British Nation' was considered and rejected. Two rooms in Dumbarton Castle were, however, the temporary close prison of the French trouble-making and Anglophobic General Simon, after he broke his parole and escaped from Odiham in Hampshire. Another Scottish Castle was rescued from what would have been considered desecration by Viscount Henry Dundas. This was the Royal Palace at Linlithgow. Sir Walter Scott mentions this fact in one of his *Waverley* novels:

'They halted at Linlithgow, distinguished by its ancient palace, which, Sixty Years since, was entire and habitable, and whose veritable ruins, not quite Sixty Years since, very narrowly escaped the unworthy fate of being converted into a barracks for French prisoners. May repose and blessings attend the ashes of the patriotic statesman [Viscount Dundas], who, amongst his last services to Scotland, interposed to prevent this profanation!'

Apart from the prisons already mentioned, our foreign captives were housed at the Old Mill Prison at Plymouth – which was specially re-built to house prisoners of war and was later renamed Millbay – Forton Prison at Portsmouth, Fish Ponds at Stapleton near Bristol and a few strong houses in other parts of the country. As the wars progressed the need for more and more holding space became acute. By the end of 1756, the first year of the Seven Years' War, the number of prisoners brought to Britain was not much in excess of seven thousand, but the figure for 1763 had increased six-fold. This figure, though small when compared with later years, was still a matter of concern and called for action.

Professional prison-hunters were employed to travel throughout Britain and – in the absence of a well-planned prison-building programme – had some success in carrying out the task of locating properties, piecemeal, for conversion into places of confinement for small, and sometimes fairly large, numbers of prisoners. From Cornwall in the south and up country into Scotland; they commandeered or hired farms, out-buildings, and private houses. In Cornwall, as early as the Seven Years' War, a stoutly walled

mansion and a number of farm buildings had been adapted to provide two prisons – one at Kergilliack, the other at nearby Roscrow. The old Esk Paper Mills at Penicuik in Scotland also became a depot, which grew in capacity and importance and towards the end of the wars, became the great Valleyfield Depot.

Space was also found in some military establishments, such as Hillsea Barracks at Portsmouth, Tynemouth, Edinburgh, and Winchester. However, with the exception of Chatham and the Kings House Prison at Winchester, which sometimes housed as many as four to five thousand captives, these would be better described as receiving houses or distribution centres, where prisoners stayed for a short while rather than depots proper.

One might imagine that the prisoner who found himself in one of the 'selected' and converted buildings was fortunate, compared with a fellow captive imprisoned in a scruffy and insanitary borough gaol or a hulk. However, according to one famous eye-witness, the evangelist John Wesley, who visited one such conversion, an old disused pottery, at Knowle on the Bristol road, there could not have been much to choose between their fates: Wesley noted in his *Journal*:

Monday, October 15, 1759.
'I walked up to Knowle, a mile from Bristol, to see the French prisoners. About eleven hundred of them, we were informed, were confined in that little place, without anything to lie on but a little dirty straw, or anything to cover them but a few foul thin rags, either by day or night, so that they died like rotten sheep. I was much affected, and preached in the evening, Exodus 23, verse 9.'

It should, however, be remembered that, by that time, in 1759, the French prisoners had recently been deserted by their own government, with its refusal to contribute towards their upkeep, and the withdrawal of King Louis' Bounty. Such disastrous states of affairs did exist from time to time, but they seldom came about through deliberate neglect or sadistic punishment. A reasonably well-treated captive was always easier to manage and control, than a man seething with nationalistic hatred and longing for revenge. Such extreme cases as the one observed by John Wesley came about through financial crises in the captives homeland – or, and more often, through gambling and profligacy taken to extremes by certain groups to be found in every depot or hulk.

The effects of imprisonment, on both captives and their keepers varied widely, according to many circumstances. Nationality was certainly a general distinguishing feature – the easy-going Dane, the dour Dutchman, the high-spirited but adaptable Frenchman, the dangerous-if-provoked Spaniard, and the bitter and troublesome American. National characteristics played a heavy part in the histories of some of the depots and hulks. As we shall see, Dartmoor Prison was a prime example of the manner in which the atmosphere of a depot could be completely changed by a comparatively few prisoners of a different race.

For the first four years of its unholy existence, the administration of the Depot on the Moor had been fairly trouble-free – although, like any other depot, plagued by petitions, complaints and escape attempts. With a prisoner population which varied from five to eight thousand 'French' captives (which included, of course, allies of several nationalities), the garrison was seldom called upon to supply more than five hundred soldiers and guards, and the Agent, officers and officials were generally treated with at least token respect. Yet, after the Americans arrived in 1813, hatred and rebellion replaced tolerance; which resulted in misery, official blunders and, finally, tragedy. And, the garrison was increased to between twelve and fifteen hundred – plus a few pieces of artillery – to oversee from fifteen hundred to five thousand Americans.

The French and English Governments' allowances to prisoners were almost identical. Ships' Captains, Mates, Sailing Masters and Surgeons, received 3d. per day; Bosuns, Carpenters and Petty Officers, 2d.; Everyone below those ranks and ratings received 1d. per day. Equivalent ranks in the military received the same amounts. From time to time official bounties helped to bolster up their pocket money, as did a generous public and societies, who came to the aid of our unwilling guests, by organising and contributing to subscriptions and appeals for second hand clothing. Despite this help, there were periods when French allowances and bounties completely dried up and the prisoners were reduced to near starvation and nudity. Such occasions put a terrific strain on the agents and the running of the depots. At the best of times as many as ten percent of them would have been in a similar condition of malnutrition and nakedness resulting from gambling fever.

The rations issued to the prisoners of both countries varied little over the years, although ingredients differed slightly, in order to suit the individual tastes of the French and the British prisoners. Apart from occasional shortage brought about by crop failure or other natural calamities, the quality and quantity depended entirely on the honesty of the provision contractors and the depot authorities, and either or both were quite frequently brought to book. The main complaints were of unacceptably poor quality and short weight – the French could never understand, or forgive, our 14-ounce pound!

Basically; the menu would have read:

Days	Beer quart	Bread lb.	Beef lb.	Butter oz.	Cheese oz.	Peas pint	Salt oz.
Sunday	1	1½	¾	—	—	½	¼
Monday	1	1½	¾	—	—	—	¼
Tuesday	1	1½	¾	—	—	½	¼
Wednesday	1	1½	¾	—	—	—	¼
Thursday	1	1½	¾	—	—	½	¼
Friday	1	1½	¾	—	—	—	¼
Saturday	1	1½	¾	4	6	½	¼
Total	7	10½	5¼*	4	6	2**	2¾

* sometimes mutton or other meat   ** or greens in lieu of peas

An early French diet-sheet stated that French naval sailors should receive at least: 18 oz. of Bread; ½lb. Beef (once a week); ¾ pint Wine; 4 oz. of Lard (three days a week); 4oz. of Gruel or Beans or Other Vegetables; 2oz. of Rice; ¼ of Oil; ½ pint of Broth.

On Wednesdays or Fridays there was often a change of diet, and fish was substituted for meat. Whether this was a welcome treat, or inspired revulsion, depended on the locality of the prison, and the age of the fish by the time it arrived there. It may be remembered that unacceptable consignments of fish caused trouble on the hulks; some of the salt herring was so inedible that the prisoners connived with the contractor to buy it back at a very low price, so that something more appetising might be found in the bum-boat markets which came alongside. Many believed that those same herrings were delivered and rebought a number of times whilst the

swindle lasted. Prisoners in Cornwall complained to the Board, that a surfeit of pilchards replaced their meat ration far too often.

Tea was expensive and available to only the better-off English families, and was not included in the diet of the healthy prisoner, although both tea and coffee could usually be purchased by the prisoners in the depot markets. However, the ailing prisoner in a depot hospital was entitled to a pint of tea morning and evening, plus the generous issue of one pound of white bread, one pound of mutton or beef, a pint of rich soup and a quart of malt beer.

The small daily poundage, shown on the above diet sheet, when multiplied by the number of prisoners in Britain, added up to the immense annual tonnage of produce needed to feed our captives, at least to subsistence level; but there were many more who had to be catered for including the militia, guards, sentinels, the garrison and some categories of depot staff. Some idea of the vastness of the quantities involved, may be gathered from food-and-drink-related statistics quoted by Dr Walker: the 'Account Books of the Oundle Brewery' showed that, in 1799, the total amount of beer supplied to the Regiments quartered at Norman Cross alone, was 4,449 barrels, each of 36 gallons, quite apart from the 'Small Beer' which they supplied to the prisoners. As to the beef, a butcher once calculated for Walker that, taking the average bullock as weighing 850 lbs, it would take five or six of that size *per day* to feed the inmates of such a depot. *The Times* for the 14th August, 1814 stated that about £300,000 a year had been spent by the Government in Yakley, Stilton and Peterborough in the provisioning of Norman Cross.

If the official regulations regarding provisions and rations had been strictly observed by all concerned in their production and supply, the only legitimate complaint might have been of its meagreness in quantity, based as it was on two-thirds of that of an active free sailor.

By far the most frequently criticised item on the prisoners' menu was the bread, which could vary from hard tack, ships' biscuit, black rye bread, to soft white wheaten loaf. The complaints were seldom of non delivery or short weight, but were more often a question of quality; for the prisoners, particularly the French, were fussy about their staff of life.

An early petition addressed to the Transport Office by 'The General Body of French Officers confined in Roscrow Prison', and also signed by the officers at Kergilliac, complained of just about everything, from the Agent to the bread. They said that they had sent him a sample of 'the bread delivered to us, or rather rye, flour and water, cemented together, and at different times as black as our shoes.' Sometimes the discontent over bread deteriorated into serious confrontations with guards and Agents.

A short while ago, whilst researching aspects of Norman Cross in the Kings Lynn Archives, I was side-tracked by an article which told of bread riots in the town, after a series of poor harvests at the end of the eighteenth century. The shortage of wheat had a disastrous effect on the quiet little town. The price of the quartern loaf (weighing four pounds) was sixpence (2½p) in 1794, but had risen to 1s. 2½d. in the following year, reaching a peak at 1s. 7½d. in 1801. Few working class families could afford such inflation, particularly if the breadwinner was a farm labourer, whose weekly pay would have been no more than 9s. 6d. By the end of 1795 the townsfolk were driven to desperation. Fearing the result, the Corporation called in the East Yorkshire militia to keep the poor rioters under control.

After reading this, my sympathy towards the prisoner

complainers waned a little; to think that they should query the quality of their allowed 1½ lb. of daily bread, without working for it, whilst the agricultural workers went without. However, sober thought reminded me that the prisoner was paying for his bread with his freedom.

Individually, much depended on strength or weakness in the character of the prisoner, his occupation or rank in the forces, and his everyday life before the outbreak of the wars. For instance, the initial shock of captivity must have been harder for the conscripted landlubber – who may never before have seen the sea – than it was for the professional seaman, be he naval or mercantile, who was often away from his family for long periods, sometimes as long as two years; and this must have equally applied to the military in the case of hardy Regulars and what we used to call 'Hostilities Only' soldiers.

The most enlightened feature in the British scheme of prisoner of war management, was the introduction of the depot markets (see Rules and Regulations *Article 9.* below). Without their inspired existence, there would have been little to relieve the debilitating boredom of long hours of unproductive idleness. However talented, only the most dedicated of artists or craftsmen would have spent the soul-destroying days, weeks months or years of an imprisonment of unknowable duration, in producing work for which there was no outlet. The depot market provided just such an outlet, for the prisoners were permitted, in fact encouraged to produce works of art or craft, or manufacture a wide range of saleable artifacts which might appeal to the visiting public. As well as local inhabitants, visitors came from far and wide, some to buy or sell, others to experience the rather exotic atmosphere of the markets, and see for themselves real live, foreign captives, and wonder at the quality and beauty of much of their work.

The sale of prisoner of war work was carried out by trustee-prisoners, sometimes the originators of the articles for sale, but more often representatives selling on behalf of groups of *industrialists* within the depot. So only a small percentage of the prisoners actually enjoyed the privilege of mixing with men and women of all classes, catching up with the news and the progress of the wars; and buying vegetables and other goods in bulk, for resale in the prison yards. Whether or not the prisoners had experienced the freshness and even gaiety of the market, every prisoner benefited by its existence. A prisoner of war community living at subsistence level and zero cash flow would soon become one of strife and trouble, ever-increasing escape attempts, and add to the already large numbers of down-and-outs who disgraced our prisons.

As we shall discover as the following pages conduct us through the land prisons of Great Britain, the markets were as important to the local trades people, farmers and suppliers of provisions, as they were to the prisoners of war. Many a town and village owed its prosperity to a depot in its vicinity, a prosperity which declined or disappeared with the end of the wars in 1815. Princetown in Devon grew up with the building of the great Dartmoor Depot and almost died when the war prison closed its gates. And the Scottish potato growers of Perth were almost bankrupted by the loss of the prisoner of war trade when that huge depot closed.

The main market was usually set up in a square or fenced-in area sited near the main gate, of the prison; although, in the case of some of the smaller depots, business between prisoner and local trader or casual purchaser was restricted to bargaining through small apertures in the metal fence or prison wall. In some cases, British officers and soldiers of the garrison found a profitable sideline by acting as wholesalers of prisoner of war work, delivering it to local towns with larger markets; in much the same way as Louis Garneray's paintings were disposed of through the Portsmouth picture dealers.

However, the market was not the only source of wages – and comparative wealth. The staff whose job it was to keep the prison clean, to light the lamps, cook the food, to attend the sick and, to a large extent, maintain the fabric of the prison itself and its buildings, was largely recruited from among the prisoners themselves. So almost anyone fit and industrious enough, stood a good chance of gainful employment and, if he managed his small income wisely, relief from poverty and hunger.

Most successful applicants wore the tin-plate cap-badge which designated their occupation – 'Sweeper', 'Baker', 'Gardener' etc. – with pride. Hospitals were allowed one prisoner attendant to every ten patients, at the going rate of sixpence a day. Cooks – one for every 400 prisoners – received 4½d a day; whilst sweepers – one to every hundred captives – Barbers, Carpenters, Gardeners and categories far too numerous to mention, earned 3d, per day.

Discipline, though not harshness or insensitive authority, was essential to the smooth running of all depots, large and small. In order to make this plain to our foreign captives, rules and regulations were posted up, in English and in French, in the yards and prisons. These notices, which would have changed only in detail over the wars, not only informed them of the dire consequence of transgressing, but also informed them of the privilege of the Market:

By the Commissioners for conducting His Majesty's Transport Service, and for the Care and Custody of Prisoners of War.

RULES TO BE OBSERVED BY THE PRISONERS OF WAR IN GREAT BRITAIN, IRELAND, &c.

1. The Agent's Orders are to be strictly obeyed by all the Prisoners; and it is expressly forbidden, that any Prisoners should insult, threaten, ill-treat, and much less strike the Turnkeys, or any other Person who may be appointed by the Agent to superintend the Police of the Prison, under pain of losing turn of Exchange, of being closely confined, and deprived of half their Ration of Provisions, for such time as the Commissioners may direct.

2. All the Prisoners are to answer to their Names when mustered, and to point out to the Agent any Errors they may discover in the Lists, with which he may be furnished, in order to prevent the Confusion which might result from erroneous Names: and such Prisoners as shall refuse to comply with this regulation shall be put on Half Allowance.

3. Should any damage be done to the Buildings by the Prisoners, either through their endeavouring to escape, or otherwise, the expense of repairing the same shall be made good, by a Reduction of the Rations of Provisions of such as may have been concerned; and should the Aggressors not be discovered, all the Prisoners confined in the particular Building so damaged, shall contribute by a similar Reduction of their Rations towards the cost of the said repairs.

4. Such Prisoners as shall escape from Prison, and be re-taken, shall be put into the Black Hole, and kept on Half Allowance, until the expenses occasioned by their Escape are made good; and they shall moreover lose their Turn of Exchange, and all Officers of the Navy or Army so offending shall, from that time, be considered and treated in all respects as common men.

5. Fighting, quarrelling, or exciting the least Disorder is strictly forbidden, under pain of a Punishment proportionate to the Offence.

6. The Prisons are to be kept clean by the Prisoners in Turns, and every Person who shall refuse to do that Duty in his Turn, after having received Notice of the same, shall be deprived of his Rations, until he shall have complied.

7. The Prisoners are from Time to Time to inform the Agent of the Clothing or other Articles which they may stand in need of, and have Money to purchase; and the Agent shall not only permit them to purchase such Articles, but also take care that they are not imposed on in the Price.

8. The Prisoners in each Prison are to appoint Three or Five, from among their own number, as a Committee for examining the Quality of the Provisions supplied by the Contractor; for seeing that their full Rations, as to Weight and Measure, are conformable to the Scheme of Victualling at the Foot hereof; and if there should be any cause of Complaint they are to inform the Agent thereof; and should he find the Complaint well-founded, he is immediately to remedy the same. If the Agent should neglect this part of his Duty, the Prisoners are to give information thereof to the Commissioners, who will not fail to do them justice in every respect.

9. All Dealers (excepting such as Trade in Articles not proper to be admitted into the Prison) are to be allowed to remain at the principal gate of the Prison from six o'clock in the morning until three in the afternoon, to dispose of the Merchandise to the Prisoners; but any of the Prisoners who shall be detected in attempting to introduce into the Prison Spirituous Liquors, or other improper Articles, or in receiving or delivering any Letter, shall be punished for the Abuse of this Indulgence, in such Manner as the Commissioners may direct.

Other notices were displayed which informed the prisoners of their right to make objects for sale in the markets, except for a few prisoner manufactures which were proscribed as being in unfair competition with some local trades and professions. Examples of the latter such as bonnet or plait-making in the straw-working districts, where straw plaiting was the cottagers' only source of income, were forbidden. A further factor was that foreign plait and straw head wear were taxable, and although the Government classed the prisoner product as 'imported', the impossibility of collecting the duty constituted a loss to the Revenue! Other, less widespread, prohibitions effected specific locations; but the depot authorities waged a general war on the widespread producers of pornographic or erotic work of any kind.

The visiting public were warned of the serious consequences of illegal dealing with the prisoners and the drastic punishments dealt out to any involved in escape attempts. They were also advised to watch out for sharp practice when dealing with the foreign vendors, and to keep a keen lookout for forged paper money and counterfeit coins.

From this short introduction, we can now move on to a closer examination of Britain's land prisons and their development over the period of this study. The stories of the major establishments, such as Porchester, Norman Cross, Dartmoor, etc. will be dealt with individually, and the minor depots fitted in where appropriate.

These histories are the outcome of reading a great number of books, all of them now out of print – many of them written a hundred years or more; official documents; contemporary newspapers, and the transactions of local history societies; and original research. French, Danish and American diaries and journals; were invaluable, as were the works of three Britons, Sir Basil Thomson and Dr T. J. Walker who, in 1907 and 1913 respectively, each wrote books on single depots in which they had particular interests. There was, also, of course, Francis Abell who, in 1914, tackled the subject of the prisoner of war in Britain as a whole – an exhausting task which I timorously attempt to emulate and update.

---

1. It must be said, however, that the often squalid condition of some PoW accommodation and the complained of meagre food rations, was used by recruiting officers and jailers – with the tacit approval of the Government, or at least the Admiralty – as a strong incentive for prisoners to turncoat and serve in the Royal Navy.

An Outside View of PORTCHESTER CASTLE, in HAMPSHIRE. Dedicated to the Officers of the Militia
Engrav'd from a Drawing taken on the Spot by an Officer.

Chapter Thirteen

Portchester Castle
and
The Old Wool House 'French Prison'
at Southampton, in Hampshire

'The defences of Portsmouth Harbour form an impressive series extending from the Roman period down to the present day, and until the sixteenth century Portchester Castle was the main fortification.'

English Heritage: 'Guide to Portchester Castle'.

AFTER NEARLY TWO THOUSAND YEARS, Portchester Castle still presents an impressive appearance of one-time power and strength, situated as it is on a promontory that juts out into the upper reaches of Portsmouth Harbour. Now little more than an interesting tourist attraction, it had assumed many and varied guises over the course of its long history.

Its first incarnation was as a Roman fortress, built in the second half of the third century AD, on a nine-acre site. It was a daunting deterrent to barbarian would-be invaders from Germany and Denmark – and to back up anti-piratical activity in the English Channel where marauders not only preyed on other shipping, but sometimes descended on coastal towns and villages. Another important consideration was that, from its lofty eminence above Portsmouth Harbour and the Solent, a protective eye could be kept over the Roman fleet when in port. For these reasons and its powerful armaments, the fortress was well maintained and occupied for most of the period up to the decline of Roman Britain.

It would seem that, after the departure of the Romans, Portchester became more important as a well-protected Saxon settlement, than as a fortress. Traces of timber-built wattle and daub dwellings would indicate a domestic rather than a military occupancy – that is, between the fifth and the ninth centuries, but archaeological evidence suggests that, early in the tenth century, it was re-fortified and militarised against Viking attacks on the south coast of Britain.

At the beginning of that century, in about AD 904, King Edward the Elder had taken possession of the fort, which he had received in exchange for nearby Bishop's Waltham; so Portchester became a *burh,* or *Royal* Borough, one of the many such strongholds that were thus created as defence against the Norse invaders.

When William the Conqueror arrived in England in 1066, the already ancient fortress was still in a good state of preservation, its ten-feet-thick walls of coursed flint rising to thirty feet high in places, and hardly marked by the passage of time. Many alterations and dramatic additions were carried out in the eleventh and twelfth centuries. The Normans built a Castle and Keep in the north-west corner of the huge site – hence, Portchester *Castle,* as the fortress then became known – its courtyard enclosed by a high stone wall (the Inner Bailey), could only be entered through a stone gate-house built over the moat which protected that inner wall.

The Norman church, situated in the Outer Bailey diagonally opposite the Keep, nearly in line with the eastern entrance, dates from about 1130, and was built on the site of a Roman *sacellum,* a small shrine or chapel. It was built to a cruciform plan, with arched windows and doorways, originally for the Augustinian monks of the Priory within the Inner Bailey; but as they soon after moved to Southwick, it became Portchester Parish Church and, as such, has to a great extent survived to the present day. Particularly noteworthy is the stone arch of the doorway in the western front of the church, which is sculpted with typically Norman ornamentation.

During the Mediaeval period, Portchester Castle and its outbuildings underwent a number of changes and conversions. To some extent it was maintained as a still powerful stronghold, but the changes also provided for another phase in its history – as a Royal residence. Its proximity to the Channel enabled monarchs and their households to enjoy the security it offered on their arrival in Britain, or when preparing to leave on armed intrusions or royal visits to the Continent. It was also a convenient stopover for royal parties who hunted in the Forest of Bere. Many significant changes were made over the years: Henry I increased the height of the Keep by adding several storeys, which led to it becoming known as the Great Tower; Henry II stayed there more than once, using a strong-room in the Keep to store bullion, which he later shipped to Normandy.

When the Hundred Years War with France came to an end, very late in the fourteenth century, King Richard II went on a building and spending spree demolishing some of the buildings in the courtyard of the Inner Bailey, and replacing them with a Royal Palace – at a cost of £1,700! Apart from Royal and official quarters, there were many other buildings distributed over the nine-acre site: storehouses for armour and armament, workshops and kitchens; provisions and accommodation to provide for the sometimes large number of troops who were assembled there before embarking for service overseas. In the 1340s, King Edward III mustered a military force of 15,000 men, who were to seek, and find, glory at Crécy; and, some three quarters of a century later, Portchester was Henry V's rallying point before his departure for Agincourt, in 1415. By the end of that century, however, Henry VII moved the Royal Navy away from Portchester to the newly established Royal Dockyard at the entrance to Portsmouth Harbour – a move that deprived Portchester Castle of much future glory.

Henry VIII built a chain of forts along the south coast to guard Britain against invasion, but Portchester was not even considered or mentioned as a ready-made link in that chain; although during the war with France, in 1563, it took on yet another of its many facets; as a military hospital for the treatment of sick and wounded combatants in that war. Queen Elizabeth I made a number of visits to the Castle, and was last entertained there in 1601; but, by that time, other and more modern installations, built for the defence of fast-growing Portsmouth during the sixteenth century, had lessened the importance of Portchester as a fortification.

Neglect followed by decay ensued, and in 1632 the Castle was sold to Sir William Uverdale; with a covenant that the Crown should retain the right to lease it whenever national interests prevailed. So, on a number of occasions, Portchester Castle was called upon to assume the last – and to us, in the context of this book, most important – of its many roles in history: as a place for the incarceration of our foreign captives – a Prisoner of War Depot.

*****

It may be thought that I have devoted an inappropriate amount of time and space to descriptions of Portchester Castle over the ages, but must justify that extravagance, by a reminder that it was by far the most ancient building in Britain to be adapted for use as an imprisonment depot for many thousands of prisoners of war. Also, that it had been leased by the Government for that purpose both before and a little after the period of our study. England was almost continuously at war from the mid-1600s to 1815, most often with the French, although a great number of other nationalities became involved at one time or another. The 'Sick and Hurt Office', which, until the late eighteenth century, was responsible for the welfare of wounded seamen and the overseeing of prisoners of war, considered Portchester as well suited to their requirements in both those responsibilities. In 1644, a decade after Uverdale bought the Castle, it was used as a barracks to accommodate about four thousand dragoons, mounted infantrymen, of the Parliamentary Army; and eight years later it was being fitted out as a military hospital to care for the wounded in the first Dutch War. Hostilities were mercifully short-lived and its services were never fully called upon. However, during the Second Dutch War – 1665–67 – Dutch prisoners of war were kept in the Inner Bailey, the majority in the Castle Keep, although, unsuitably as it may seem, others were housed some distance away across the Outer Bailey in the old Norman church. This unholy adaptation of a sacred edifice did not last for long. Some of the Dutch captives set fire to part of the church, causing serious damage, which went unrepaired for nearly half a century. It was eventually restored by work carried out between 1706 and 1710, funded by a grant from Queen Anne's Bounty, which the queen set up at the beginning of her reign for the maintenance of poor clergy, and other ecclesiastical purposes. The old Norman church features in a number of prisoner of war occurrences and stories.

During the War of the Spanish Succession, 1701 to 1714 – which overlapped Queen Anne's War (1702–13) – Portchester Castle was once again a prisoner of war depot, this time housing mainly Spanish rank and file captives and some French officers. By that time, the buildings within the Inner Bailey were in a sorry state of disrepair, and became progressively worse, so that it is not surprising that by the outbreak of the next long war, the War of the Austrian Succession, 1740–49, many and bitter were the complaints of the overcrowding of something like 2,000 prisoners into the Great Tower. Halfway through that war, in 1745, large airing grounds, or exercise yards, were laid down in the Outer Bailey, where the prisoners could socialise. They were, in the main, Spaniards and Frenchmen and some Poles. The latter were seamen, and some of these spent only a very short time in the discomfort of the Castle. It is said that at least fifty of the Polish sailors turned their coats, and immediately volunteered to serve in the English Navy. Unlike prisoners of later wars, particularly the Republican and Napoleonic, many of whom spent as long as five, ten, or twelve years in captivity, few of the captives taken in the mid-1700s would have spent much more than a year before being exchanged for a British prisoner held in France or Spain.

We have now, at last, reached the first conflict of immediate interest relative to our present study – the Seven Years' War, 1756 to 1763; but before leaving the Portchester/Roman connection, a rather fascinating coincidence should be mentioned. Among the officers appointed to oversee the security at Portchester Castle, was one young captain who would one day become famous as a world-wide authority on Roman history.

Edward Gibbon was nineteen when the war broke out in 1756. Educated at Westminster and Oxford, he published the first volume of his great work, *The Rise and Fall of the Roman Empire*, twenty years later, in 1776. When he was twenty-two, he joined the Hampshire Militia, and was posted to Portchester Castle where, for some time, Captain Edward Gibbon was in command of some two-hundred and thirty militiamen, who served as the guards and sentinels who watched over the prisoners of war. In the first year of that war, the prisoner population in Britain was just over 7,000, but, although the exchange system still worked reasonably well, the numbers grew until, at the end of the war, in 1763, there were more than 40,000 captives due for repatriation. Captain Gibbon would have been responsible for the superintendence of about 3,200 prisoners at Portchester. In his autobiography[1], he recalled that conditions there, for both prisoners and their military overseers, were far less than ideal: '…agreeable for the officers, who boarded in a neat private house and lived very well, but it was very bad for the men…The prison was very loathsome and the men's barracks not much better'.

On paper, at least, the Castle must have seemed well qualified for conversion into a great war prison, capable of housing many thousands of our captives. Nine acres of land and buildings, enclosed within massive and towering stone walls, together with a good deal of past experience in prisoner of war management, should have made it an ideal site for such an establishment. However, by 1756 and the outbreak of the Seven Years' War, not all of those walls and gateways were sufficiently well maintained to make this possible. In previous wars, only a small proportion of the available space had been used to accommodate captives; mainly within the Inner Bailey and the Castle Keep. Large numbers were crammed into such unhealthily small spaces, that it was occasionally necessary to transfer many hundreds of Portchester prisoners to other war prisons.

In the 1740s, a thousand or more were sent to a converted building in Southampton, which became known as 'The French Prison'. This was the old Wool House, near the Town Quay, built at the end of the fourteenth century. It was appointed by royal charter as one of the very few medieval warehouses and weigh-stations, which were allowed to export wool to the Continent. The appalling conditions at Southampton's 'French Prison' were as bad, perhaps

worse, than those pertaining at Portchester at that time; and when disease struck, it spread like wildfire. It is recorded that more than a hundred prisoners died there in a single week, carried away by jail-fever – typhus, as it is now called – a highly infectious disease, caused by filth, and spread by lice or other vermin.

The old Wool House is now Southampton Maritime Museum. Well worth visiting, not only for its maritime relics and to admire its ancient oak and chestnut timbered roof, but to observe evidence of the presence of our unwilling guests of more than two hundred and fifty years ago. Some have left their names, and sometimes the date of their incarceration, carved or scratched into the beams and stanchions of what was once their prison. Prison graffiti is always fascinating, recording as it does, a man's desire to make his mark in history, however insignificant. Many such marks may still be seen on the walls and beams of the Great Tower at Portchester Castle, particularly in the uppermost storey (and there are traces of a never-brilliant mural on the wall of a lower floor).

With the outbreak of the Seven Years' War, it again became necessary to make similar transfers of prisoners from Portchester, as the Depot was not adapted sufficiently for it to be classed as a major war prison – that is, until the great transformation which took place twenty years after that war had ended. In 1761, 2,000 prisoners were marched under strong guard to Forton Depot – or the old Fortune Prison, as it was then known – at Gosport, just a few miles from Portchester.

The official records of all depots abound with petitions and individual letters of complaint, addressed through the Agents to the Transport Office. Stories of insufficient food, of crooked contractors, of overcrowded accommodation, and a thousand other grievances were delivered to the Commissioners in a non-stop flow. Many were founded on fact – though often helped along by a touch of hopeful exaggeration – and where possible the Government endeavoured to put matters right. Much of these mountains of paperwork was submitted less with the hope that it would improve the prisoners' lot, than to ruin the smooth running of their captors' administration.

However, some missives were the work of selfless prisoners whose reasonable recommendations would have been advantageous to both prisoner and captor alike. One such remarkable man was the French Captain Fraboulet who concerned himself with certain important omissions at Portchester Castle. Fraboulet, who had served on board the French East India Company's frigate *Astrée,* submitted a number of reports to the Government, mainly concerning medical matters. In 1756, he complained bitterly that there was no hospital at Portchester, and that prisoner-patients had to be transported in carts over rough roads to Forton Hospital, many of them dying in transit or soon after arrival. Those who survived often found themselves bedded in wards where both the convalescent and the dying were housed together.

Some ailing Portchester prisoners, who were sent to nearby Fareham Hospital, were not much luckier. For although it was only two miles distant from the Castle, the wooden wards were situated hard by the unhealthy mud flats and marshes that bordered the river. Fraboulet did his best to improve the lot of his fellow prisoners, pleading with the Government to provide medical facilities at Portchester, and even taking unpopular measures when he thought it was for his countrymen's good. He was in charge of the distribution of the (French) King's Bounty, and decided that it should be shared only among healthy prisoners, and 'no more to invalids, as they spend it not properly, bribing sentries and attendants, and all who have free access and egress to get them food such as raw fruit, salt herrings, &c. [both of which, he believed, brought on a flux of the blood]. His efforts to do away with gambling and gaming tables were similarly unappreciated by the prisoners.

Surprisingly, he reported that the food rations were, in general, of a high standard, but was less complimentary about that of the small beer, the weakness of which, he said, was another thing 'apt to cause a flux of the blood'. For many years each prisoner of war was issued with what would seem to be a generous allowance: two quarts of beer a day – but the quality seldom matched the quantity. Such complaints were common to all depots. Nearly half a century later, during the Revolutionary War, British NCOs of the Garrison at Norman Cross backed up a complaint from the prisoners, that the food was unfit for human consumption, and added that 'the water they had was much better than the beer.'

The Seven Years' War ended in 1763, and for the next twenty years the Castle was used only as a storage place for provisions and military equipment. During that time, the War of American Independence, 1775–1783, had come and gone. A large number of American prisoners had been brought to England during that war, nearly all of them captured at sea; officers and men of the new American navy, merchant service, and privateers. None of these 'renegades', 'rebels' or 'traitors', as they were regarded at that time in Britain, were sent to Portchester; most were committed to Forton, Millbay near Plymouth, Stapleton near Bristol, Liverpool and a few other depots.

In 1784, a year after America had won her independence, work was commenced at Portchester Castle which, by the outbreak of the Revolutionary – or French Republican – War in 1793, had converted it from a makeshift, overcrowded and insecure place of confinement, to something like the specially designed depots which were to follow in later years. The ancient walls were repaired where necessary, and the once-deep moat which encircled those walls was dredged and cleared of the accretion of silt, plant-life, debris and rubbish, which had built up over the ages. The Keep had undergone considerable changes, in size and adaptation; its prisoner accommodation was spread over five storeys, and Portchester now had at last got the hospital that the French Captain Fraboulet had advocated at the beginning of the Seven Years' War. A number of prison blocks were under construction in the Outer Bailey, and many auxiliary buildings, including a Barracks for the soldiers who served as sentries and guards. It is interesting to note that, at some time during the Revolutionary War, the young Arthur Wellesley – who would later became Lord Wellington, the Iron Duke – was for a while officer of the guard at Portchester. The Parish Records reveal that the wives and families of some of these men lived in married quarters within the Castle walls.

During the Revolutionary War the Depot, which was growing all the time, was the somewhat improved wartime home for captives, mainly French and Dutch, taken in battles on land and sea. The sailors came from ships captured during Lord Howe's victory of the 'Glorious 1st of June, 1794'; Admiral Duncan's defeat and capture of the Dutch fleet in October 1797, and other less remembered sea fights, plus privateers and captured merchantmen. The soldiers had served in land engagements on the Continent or as far away as the West Indies.

They were not all rank-and-file servicemen, these soldiers and sailors. Some were of very high rank and, men of distinction, who, at least in the eyes of their captors, had disgraced themselves by breaking their parole, or word of honour in one way or another. Among these gentry of the closed prison who spent at least some time at Portchester, were the black General Marienier, who was captured at San Domingo and sent to England – accompanied by his four wives; the Irish-American, General William Tate, *Chef de Brigade* of the French *Legion Noir*, composed mainly of galley slaves; the rabid General Pillet and a surprising number of other senior officers.

The prisoner capacity of the renovated Depot eventually equalled that of the super-depots. In 1795 the prisoner population at Portchester was 4,769, which increased to an official maximum of 7,000 by 1810.

By that time the exchange system had broken down to a serious degree, so that even the much-improved depot could not cope with the thousands of prisoners flooding in to Portsmouth and other southern ports; and further tailor-made depots were either planned or dreamed of.

Unlike Norman Cross Depot, in what was then the county of Huntingdonshire, which could accommodate a similar number of prisoners to that of Portchester, but has left us only one contemporary prisoner of war memoir – and that apocryphal – there are a fair number of first-hand accounts to help us visualise prisoner of war life in the Portchester Castle of nearly two hundred years ago. Apart from official documents, we have the memoirs of French prisoners, the recollections of some British military men; newspaper articles, etc. and a number of Portchester stories collected by Francis Abell.

One of the most unusual but interesting of these was penned by an English officer who wrote under the name of *'The Light Dragoon'*. His observations on British prisoner management – or mismanagement – could not be more critical, or more first-hand, as he had served as an officer of the Portchester Depot guard. He says:

'Whatever grounds of boasting may belong to us as a nation, I am afraid that our methods of dealing with the prisoners taken from the French during the war scarcely deserves to be classed among them. Absolute cruelties were never, I believe, perpetrated on these unfortunate beings; neither, as far as I know, were they, in any pretence whatever, stinted in the allowance of food awarded to them. But in other respects they fared hardly enough. Their sleeping apartments, for instance, were very much crowded. Few paroles were extended to them. It is past dispute that when the parole was obtained they were, without distinction of rank, apt to make a bad use of it. While their pay was calculated on a scale as near the line of starvation as could in any measure correspond with our nation's renown for humanity. On the other hand, every possible encouragement was given to the exercise of ingenuity among the prisoners themselves by throwing open the Castle yard once or twice a week, where their wares were exhibited for sale, amid numerous groups of jugglers, tumblers, and musicians, all of whom followed their respective callings, if not invariably with skill, always with most praiseworthy perseverance. Moreover, the ingenuity of the captives taught them how on these occasions to set up stalls on which all manner of trinkets were set forth ... bone and ivory knick-knacks, fabricated invariably with a common pen-knife, yet always neat, and not infrequently elegant [whilst many of the simplest knick-knacks, such as apple-corers and pipe-tampers were no doubt fashioned by the use of a 'common pen-knife', the producers of the more 'elegant' manufactures, such as ship models, clock-cases and the more elaborate of the games boxes, would have required more sophisticated tools.]'

However, by far the most detailed descriptions of everyday life as a captive in Portchester – at least in the years following the improvements and expansion of the Depot, at the beginning of the nineteenth century – are to be found in the memoirs of two French prisoners, Saint-Aubin and Gille, who may well have known one another, as they were captured during the same battle in Spain and were certainly in Portchester at about the same time.

At this point I must put right one of the very few errors I have ever found in Francis Abell's researches. He quotes freely from Philippe Gille's 'Mémoires d'un Conscrit de 1798', but in digging into root sources, I discovered that Philippe Gille was never a prisoner of war at Portchester Castle or, for that matter, anywhere else! The Napoleonic Wars had ended many years before his birth. The prisoner memoirist was, in fact, Philippe's father, Quartermaster Louis-François Gille, of the French First Reserve Legion.

Abell's mistake might be explained by the fact that, when the book – the correct title of which is 'Les Prisonniers de Cabrera. Mémoires d'un Conscrit de 1808', – first went into print, the title was followed by the words 'Recueillis et publiés (collected and published) par Philippe Gille', but there was no mention of the prisoner's name.

Philippe had presented his father's papers with much respect and little personal comment; just as they had been left thirty years earlier; but he hid the author's name within a cloak of anonymity. It is probable that some readers thought, like Abell, that Philippe himself was the hero and author of the work; but a later edition sorted out the confusion.

Louis-François Gille and Saint-Aubin (Abell never mentioned the forename of the latter, or the title of his memoirs, so perhaps he had worked from translated extracts), were among an almost incredibly large number of French soldiers, taken prisoner at the very beginning of the Peninsular Wars; when the French General Dupont surrendered, with 20,000 men of the French Imperial Army, at the Battle of Baylen in July 1808.

After a long and fruitless effort to discover whether or not the memoirs of Saint-Aubin had ever gone into print, my problem was solved by a particularly helpful librarian at the London Library. It transpired that although it had not been published in its own right, it was included in a small two-volume journal, written by another French soldier who had been captured at Baylen. That was the good news, the bad was that no library in this country possessed a copy of the work. However, two weeks later the London Library informed me that a copy, which they had borrowed from a French library at Strasburg, awaited my perusal, (and my daughter's translation!)

The journal, 'Trois Ans de Séjour en Espagne dans l'intérieur du pays, sur les Pontons à Cadiz et dans l'Ile de Cabrera' by Joseph Quantin, published in Paris in 1823, tells of his own captivity and that of fellow prisoners; and the second volume contains the memoirs of M.P.Saint-Aubin (as we shall henceforth know him).

In the reminiscences of Louis Gille, he tells something of the horrors of his first experience of captivity. Soon after they were captured, the twenty-year-old Gille and many others were crammed into the overcrowded Spanish prison hulks at Cadiz. He was himself sent to Hulk No.27, which, he says, was already the

dreadful depository for more than one thousand eight hundred unfortunate prisoners of war.

That experience was bad enough, and the captives could hardly have imagined that worse was yet to come. After some time, spent in these floating hellholes, they were moved to the unforgivably dreadful prison island of Cabrera, where, if they survived, they were to await transportation to England.

Eventually a number of British ships arrived and lay off the island to embark their share of the huge transportation. Louis Gille, who found himself on board HMS *Britannia*, was probably typical of all those fellow prisoners who had been delivered from the hell of Cabrera. He was overwhelmed by the contrast between the filth and starvation of the Spanish prisons and the scrupulous cleanliness of the naval vessel, and the generous daily allowance of food and drink (six prisoners received the equivalent of four British sailors' rations). He said, 'The cruel and ferocious treatment by the Spaniards was followed by the compassionate consideration of the British soldiers and sailors.' A rare compliment indeed! Gille's list of provisions supplied on board, shows that the praise was not exaggerated. The families of many of our servicemen would have envied the prisoners their menu:

> 'We had a bottle of Tafia rum to drink, beef or pork five times a week, vegetables the other two days, in order to balance the bitterness of the saltiness. We had a bowl of oats for which we had enough brown sugar. And we often did not use all that we were given. We also had pudding which we made ourselves. For this we were given good quality flour and dried raisins.'

They arrived in Plymouth Harbour late in the summer of 1810 – more than two years had passed since their capture at Baylen. Plymouth, and England in general, came as something of a surprise to Louis Gille:

> '20th September. …we dropped anchor. Immediately the townspeople started to approach the ship, but were stopped, as the health officials had not yet visited the ship.
> 'The following day they came and declared that the ship was clean, and we began to disembark in great number. At this point merchandise of all kinds were offered to us. I could hardly believe my eyes. Merchant fisherwomen in black velvet robes, hats garnished with flowers, approached us. I could not believe that such luxury existed in England.
> 'I had noticed that since our entrance into the English Channel, they took more precautions with us, because we were so close to France. They were frightened, perhaps, that we would revolt and jump ship, especially so during the thick fogs.'

After five days at Plymouth, they sailed round to Portsmouth, where the bleak sight of so many prison ships moored in the harbour must have filled them with foreboding.

> 'We could see the hulks in the distance, I shuddered at this sight. The memory of those in Cadiz and the suffering on board the *Vancedor* came rushing back to me in colours so sinister that I was overjoyed when I discovered that we were going to disembark next morning and then be put into a prison on land.

Their destination was Portchester Castle, where they were received on the 28th September, 1810. The officers were given their parole – and two shillings a day – and the rest of the prisoners were marched into the depot where, one by one, they were questioned and their details entered in the Depot Register – Gille's number was 5765. They were then issued with 'a sleeved vest, a waistcoat and yellow trousers, a blue and white cotton shirt, a canvas hammock, a padded mattress weighing about two pounds, a woollen blanket – and some pieces of tarred cable the length of one's arms'.

The newcomers were greeted by the usual hordes of already resident prisoners, who crowded around with their questions; 'Where do you come from?', 'What is your regiment?', 'Where and when were you captured?' Also, of course, any news of the progress of the war. In return, they were given information and advice to help them settle into their new confinement – and also the solution to the mystery of the usefulness of those pieces of tarred rope. They were to be made into hammock-clews, the short lengths of cord at the head and foot of the canvas bed, by which it could be suspended from the hammock hooks in their sleeping quarters. Louis-François Gille was directed to the second floor of the Keep, or Great Tower, where he found that the hammocks were slung in four tiers, one above the other. New arrivals, like him, had no choice but to sleep on the highest level, which was accessible by climbing a wooden framework built for that purpose. It would have taken a soldier some time to become accustomed to sleeping in a 'matelot's cot': it is easy to fall out of a hammock – as I can bear witness – and to crash from such a height, as Gille said some did, would have been serious indeed; unless some unfortunate dozing prisoner on a lower tier broke his fall.

Had the Baylen prisoners not been transferred from the Peninsular to an English depot, but had been left to the untender mercies of the Spaniards, a great number of them would doubtless have sworn undying hatred for all things English; like the Anglophobic French General Pillet, who, as already noted, could count himself a Portchester old boy, though his stay in the Depot was rather short. Those parts of the journals kept by Gille and Saint-Aubin which deal with their experiences as prisoners of war would certainly have been written in a different and darker spirit; whereas, they make good and informative reading, critical when needs be, but always fairly balanced. For instance, Saint-Aubin complained bitterly of the poor quality of the provisions, especially the bread, and says that it was quite insufficient on account of the avarice of the contractors; but adds that, at least, it was always regularly distributed. Gille made similar complaint and couched it in similarly reasonable terms: 'Prisoners in England receive their supplies regularly; unfortunately, as I have said before, the rations were scarcely enough'.

Every morning, at five o'clock in summer and six o'clock in winter, the depot bell announced the arrival of the soldiers and turnkeys, who would open the doors and call the prisoners into the yard for a head count. They were not allowed to return to their halls for two hours; which gave them ample time to wash and enjoy an airing, after a long night spent in the stuffy atmosphere of their crowded sleeping quarters. At eight o'clock the bell rang again and the distribution of the bread began. As there were often as many as 700 men in each of the Portchester prison buildings, this distribution could take as long as half an hour or more and as the bread was distributed by weight, a keen eye was kept on the scales – the proceedings were watched over by a committee of prisoners, the members of which were different every day

A similar scrutiny was kept at midday, for at that hour, the most important of the day, the soup and meat were shared out, together with other items of food, which varied according to the day of the week. For this division of rations, the prisoners were divided into *plats,* or messes, of twelve men, each *plat* was again subdivided, and each had two *gamelles,* mess-tins, or soup-pots to receive their rations. At sunset the bell clanged again, the jailers and soldiers went through the evening head count, all were obliged to be within doors and lights were put out.

Louis-François Gille settled in remarkably quickly, making notes of all that was going on around him, as he had done since his very first day in the French army; notes which would be published many years later as his *Mémoires.*

> 'Portchester Castle is situated on the water, deep in Portsmouth Harbour. The sea bathes the northeastern side of the castle. We were never taught of its origins and history… but I always thought it was the work of the Romans. Its solidity, its type of construction all pointed to this. It was square in shape, its walls forty feet high, fifteen to eighteen feet in thickness, with foundations ten feet deep.
>
> 'There were two towers, one large and one small. The larger was six storeys high and divided into two parts. Each floor was fitted out to accommodate the hammocks of twelve to thirteen hundred prisoners.
>
> 'Near the tower were the remains of a Gothic chapel whose vaulted arch was completely destroyed, the only vestiges remaining being sections of wall through which one could see windows in the shape of Gothic arches.
>
> 'The small tower, which had a signal area on top housed some of the depot guards.
>
> 'In the great courtyard [airing ground] which served as an exercise area for the prisoners, and which they called the grand *pré,* there were nine wooden buildings, each of which could accommodate about three hundred prisoners. They called these prisons *casernes.* There were several pumps in the courtyard, each with a basin, where prisoners could wash their clothes and themselves. The water which flowed from the taps was good and clean, and the only drink freely available to the captives. It took me many days to get accustomed to the sight of so much water wastage and turn a blind eye to it. How our poor comrades at Cabrera would have enjoyed what we were wasting.
>
> 'The prison property was maintained in all parts by the prisoners themselves, who received three pennies a day from the Government (three centimes in our money). In each of the halls there were two barbers, who were both treated equally. Their job was to shave the prisoners every week. In separate buildings there were kitchens where twenty Frenchmen were kept busy at seven cauldrons, to produce sufficient soup each day for 700 men. The master chef received one shilling per day, his assistant half a shilling, and the others three pennies.
>
> 'Apart from these, a dozen or more prisoners were given jobs as ground workers [in Portchester and some other depots, prisoner kitchen-gardeners grew vegetables, to help eke out the non-too-generous rations] and the hospital employed a large number of captives in the form of cooks and wig-makers {barbers}. Despite the paucity of their pay, these occupations were eagerly sought after, and were only obtained by favour or bribe.'

The Portchester markets were centres of great activity. Anyone fit enough and inclined to work would have had little difficulty in finding gainful employment, either as a freelance trading in any talent he might have, or in one of the workshops, such as that which was set up in 1810 to make shoes for the prisoners – and probably for the soldiers: a large number of shoe buckles were unearthed during a recent excavation.

There were manufacturers of straw hats (a forbidden industry), stockings, gloves, purses and braces. There were cunning artisans in bone who made tobacco boxes, domino sets, chessmen, ship models of all kinds (especially men-of-war), as well as the most artistic ornaments and knick-knacks. A model of a man-of-war, only one foot in length, is said to have been sold for £26. There were tailors, goldsmiths, shoemakers, caterers, *limonaidiers,* and comedians of the Punch and Judy and marionette class. There were professors of mathematics, of drawing, of French, of English and Latin, of fencing, of writing, of dancing, of the *baton,* and of *la boxe.* Saint-Aubin was amazed by the fact that many prisoners who had arrived at Portchester unable to read or write, *'...en sont sortis la tête et la bourse passablement meublées.'*

Louis François Gille had more than one iron in the fire of prisoner of war industry. He gave lessons in painting to the prisoners, at the usual fee of one franc fifty centimes per pupil per month, but also made artificial flowers that were sold in the market – and he could knock out a tune on a violin, made for him by another prisoner of war.

The majority of the works of art and craft, and the activities of the *lecturers* and entertainers, was carried out inside the prison itself or in the airing grounds, and therefore out of sight of the visiting public. The breadth and scope of prisoner ambition depended much on the understanding and wisdom of the depot Agent, and in this respect Portchester was blessed with one of the best, in the person of Commander William Patterson

We know, for instance, that he made possible a first-rate prisoner – created and managed a theatre at Porchester, within the Castle Keep; which rivalled the theatres in Portsmouth. (See *The Arts and Crafts of Napoleonic and American Prisoners of War 1756-1816,* Chapter 10, THE ENTERTAINERS.) He also provided a suitable site for the working of a French prisoner of war Masonic Lodge in Portchester Castle, into which Louis-François Gille was initiated on the 24th June, 1812. He noted:

> 'A Society, known for several centuries by the name of Freemasons, was established in the prison. The commandant had permitted the members of this association to meet, for the celebration of their mysteries, in a vault quite secluded'.

One should not, however, imagine that Portchester was blessed with none but industrious, gifted and untroublesome inmates, far from it. Like other depots, it had the equivalent of the *Rafellès* and *les Misérables,* two hundred of whom, half-naked and more than half-starved occupied the top storey of the Keep. These were the unlucky gamblers and ne'er-do-wells to whom trouble-making was a way of life; duels, fights, and vicious rows were frequent, sometimes even leading to murder.

Of all the long list of arts, crafts and professions practised and mastered, by prisoners of war, perhaps the most surprising is that of thread lace-making. Saint-Aubin went into some detail on the subject, showing that it was much more than a pocket-money-making occupation. It was said that the thread lace industry was introduced into Portchester Depot by a French prisoner who, before becoming a soldier, had lived and worked in a lace-making district of his homeland. After setting up in business at the Castle, he began to take on pupils and, in less than a year, there were 3,000 prisoner lace-makers, most of them working for French *capitalists,* each of whom employed fifty to sixty workers. This lace was reputed to be of such quality, and was so eagerly purchased by the local families and traders, that the English lace-makers protested at this unfair

foreign competition. The complaint was upheld by the authorities, and its manufacture within the prison was forbidden. The work of suppression was carried out by troops who were sent in to smash the machines, and destroy all lace in stock or in course of production.

As a life-long collector, I have seen or possessed examples of just about every known type of prisoner of war work – except for even a single specimen of prisoner-produced machine-made thread lace-work. I discussed the matter with experts, and made enquiries at many museums, including the Victoria and Albert in London, but without success; the consensus thought it was most likely a myth, or a bit of memoir-packing; but I cannot believe that Saint-Aubin, with so many things around him to describe, would have found it necessary to go into so much detail about something which did not exist.

Francis Abell felt that the prisoner lace industry must have been unique to Portchester Castle, but I have found several references to its production elsewhere. Dr T. J. Walker lists lace-making among the comparatively few employments prohibited to prisoners of war at Norman Cross Depot, as the prisoners, with free board and lodging supplied by the Government, had an advantage over the local lace workers, whose livelihood depended upon the craft.

I next came across another reference, brief though it was, whilst reading the reminiscences of an American privateer officer, which inferred that the craft was pursued by French prisoners at Stapleton Depot, near Bristol. The reference was, in fact, just one word; but at this point I shall introduce a short history of the man who wrote it, as we shall meet him again in other chapters of this book.

George Little, born in Roxbury, Massachusetts, on the 18th September, 1791, was for many years a merchant captain, sailing the oceans of the world – a career which was temporarily interrupted by the Anglo-American War of 1812. In his book *'Life on the Ocean, or Twenty Years at Sea',* (Boston, 1845*),* Captain Little tells us that he arrived in Norfolk, Virginia, a few weeks after war was declared. There, he found the people wild with patriotic excitement; flags and ensigns waving; the docks and shipyards buzzing with activity, fitting out the privateers and letters-of-marque which were to play such an important part in the progress of that war. Seeing little chance of finding a berth as a merchant service officer, and perhaps stirred by the beating of drums, colours flying, and loud calls for enlistment in one service or another, he chose one for which, hitherto, he had always expressed abhorrence.

On the 20th July, 1812, the twenty-year-old George signed on as first lieutenant of a gloriously named privateer, the *George Washington*, a swift and beautiful 120-ton schooner. His fellow lieutenants and prize-masters came from backgrounds similar to his own, but the crew of eighty was a motley gang of desperadoes of all nationalities, 'scraped together from the lowest dens of wretchedness and vice.' He took an instant dislike to his captain who, though courageous, was a 'rough, uncouth sort of chap. ...fit only for fighting and plunder.'

George Little's initiation into the world of the privateer was something of a crash course. Two days after becoming her first-lieutenant, the *George Washington* was under sail and heading for the Spanish Main, where she was to cruise and intercept British merchantmen dealing with local ports. Over the following weeks Little was involved in sea fights and chases almost daily; taking prisoners and prizes which were dispatched under prize-masters to American ports. On two occasions he had personally led boarding parties on to captured British vessels; and had narrowly escaped

An Inside View of PORTCHESTER CASTLE, in HAMPSHIRE, Dedicated to the Officers of the Militia
Engrav'd from a Drawing taken on the Spot by an Officer
The Property of Mr Thistlethwayte

with his life from Indians, after leading a foraging party ashore on the Carthagena coast – and he had by now decided that enough was enough. After delivering a Spanish prize to the port of Carthagena at the beginning of September, George and the second lieutenant obtained their discharge from the privateer, and left with their share of the prize-money – about eight hundred dollars each.

Pooling their newly acquired wealth, they purchased 'a fine coppered schooner' and succeeded in getting freight and passengers for a voyage to New Orleans. On arrival, eleven days later, they found that the likelihood of finding employment for their schooner at New Orleans was as remote as it had been at Norfolk. By October, George, who had vowed never again to follow the 'nefarious' work of privateering, and his friend found berths on two of the three large letters-of-marque fitting out in the port.

On the 8th October, 1812, the 200-ton letter-of-marque sailed for Bordeaux, with George as first lieutenant. This second cruise was to show none of the financial success of the first; most of the time being chased, rather than doing the chasing.

On the morning of the 21st October, they came up with an English frigate, against whose guns they would have stood little chance; but, luckily, they were to windward, and ran for their lives. They were chased for the rest of that day until nightfall, then altered course, and eluded the enemy under cover of darkness. After a couple of days of comparative ease, a British sloop-of-war was spotted two miles to windward, and another hectic chase ensued. By keeping away right before the wind, so as to bring the sails of the sloop-of-war all on one mast, the letter-of-marque outpaced its pursuer.

They were by now heading up towards the Grand Banks, and a good lookout was kept for British cruisers, as well it might. On the 5th November, as they were scudding along under a reefed foresail in a westerly gale, they saw an English seventy-four laying to, no more than a mile ahead of them – but that was by no means all. Bearing down on the weather quarter was a British frigate and, soon after, another vessel under full sail appeared over the horizon on the starboard bow. The Americans were not yet ready to surrender their schooner, and after ditching half of their armament, decided to take the desperate risk of being blown out of the water, by crossing the bows of the seventy-four to get to windward, then make a dash for it. This they did, without damage from the small amount of gunfire from the man-of-war. In a short space of time, the schooner had a reefed squaresail set and, as Little put it, 'our noble craft was running off at the rate of twelve knots', with the sloop-of-war giving chase, but already two miles astern.

Four days later, they entered the Bay of Biscay and, by the 13th November, were only half a day's sailing from their destination, Bordeaux; but the voyage was doomed from the start. The gales had died down, and by sunset that evening, and for most of the night, they were in a flat calm. Daylight revealed that they were at the mercy of three vessels, an 18-gun ship and two brigs, with English ensigns fluttering from their peaks. A breeze had sprung up, but flight was impossible and within twenty minutes, the letter-of-marque struck her colours. Boarded by her captors, the American officers and their crew were taken prisoner.

George had been uneasy during the night of calm, and a forewarning of disaster had inspired him to be prepared for it. So he had spent some of the sleepless hours sewing the seventeen gold doubloons of his current means into a flannel shirt, which he wore at the time of his capture. It transpired that the three vessels were Guernsey privateers, their ships' companies comprising about one hundred and seventy typically rough tough privateersmen, who quickly plundered the American crew of everything worth stealing.

The Yankee letter-of-marque was sent under a prize-crew to the Channel Islands for condemnation, and the prisoners divided between the two brigs, to be delivered to the nearest receiving centre ashore. However, the American captain and George, his first lieutenant, were put on board the 18-gun privateer, where it was intended they should stay until it had completed its cruise on the coast of Portugal and Spain. During the time they were aboard, they were treated with respect and consideration, but just three days after their capture, a cry from the masthead of 'Sail ho!' heralded their deliverance.

The newcomer was a 'large rakish-looking schooner, evidently American by the 'set of her masts, cut of the sails, and color of the canvass'. The Guernseymen, overjoyed at the prospect of taking another American prize, were less elated when it was revealed that she was what we would now call a Q-ship – a man-of-war disguised as a merchantman. Both vessels were prepared for action and, after a day and night of running and pursuit, they exchanged fire; the American opening up with her forward division and the British ship replying with her stern-chasers. Thus began a running fight, but late in the morning the British flag was hauled down, and the Guernsey privateer became a prize to the mystery ship, the *Paul Jones* privateer of New York. George Little, though overjoyed to be free, was depressed to witness further evidence that the American crew were at least as depraved as their British counterparts, looting everything they could lay hand on; even including, though perhaps unknowingly, the contents of the sea-chests belonging to George and his captain.

The *Paul Jones* already had a first-lieutenant, so it was suggested that George Little should become one of the six prize-masters in the privateer's full complement. He jumped at the chance, imagining himself commander of a fine prize-ship taken from the British, and sailing it home to the United States.

By the last week of November, they had reached their cruising ground in the Azores, or the Western Islands, as they were known. They soon took two English prizes, a brig that was sent to the States and a small schooner. But the captain of the schooner had whetted their piratical appetites for larger prey, by telling them that a large convoy, the Lisbon and Mediterranean merchant fleets, were readying to sail from England.

With the prospect of untold wealth and plunder in the offing, storage of the imagined booty was of prime consideration. Space was far more important than prisoners, so the Americans released all their captives on to the captured schooner, and bade them steer for the nearest island, Terceira.

The *Paul Jones* then left the Azores and made all haste for Lisbon; but before reaching their new hunting ground, they had taken their most valuable prize ever. She was a large British brig, out of Cork and bound for Cadiz, with a cargo of Irish glass, linen and many other desirable commodities.[2] After a forty minute battle she surrendered, and was sent to the States under a prize crew.

The following day, the privateer came up with an American merchantman, also bound for Lisbon. George Little, had a strong suspicion that she might be sailing under a British licence. She was boarded and, on examination of the ship's papers, this suspicion was confirmed. This meant that the American ship could be considered a legitimate American prize; so the vessel and her officers were sent off to the States, her crew being added to that of the *Paul Jones*.

At crack of dawn, on the 4th December, they got their first glimpse of the great merchant convoy, far off to the leeward. The privateer captain, made over-confident by recent successes and noticing that the naval escort vessels were in the van – against the advice of all his officers – had decided to sail in amongst the merchantmen in daylight and cut out one, maybe two, vessels from the fleet. A mad, though apparently courageous enterprise, the privateer was soon within pistol-shot of a mouth-watering prize, but by that time, guns and visual signals were being made to alert the fleet that it was under attack. The response was immediate, and the privateer was once again on the run, this time chased for six hours by a naval frigate and a sloop-of-war. The frigate was soon dropped astern, but after some hours of hot pursuit, the sloop came within range and let fly with her bow-chases. This action saved the *Paul Jones* for the act of yawing to get her guns to bear and firing, slowed the British sloop sufficiently for the privateer to make yet another getaway.

Some days later, by which time the privateer should have been nearing the end of her cruise, the captain made another unwise decision, which brought about that end, sooner than expected. He decided to make for the Irish Channel in an attempt to intercept the West India Fleet, which they did – to their cost.

On the morning of the 14th December they found themselves in thick fog, which lifted every now and then to reveal that they were providentially in the midst of the merchant fleet, a privateer's dream, with so many prizes to choose from. A fine British prize was quickly taken and a prize-crew put on board, with instructions to stay in the convoy until night, then leave under cover of darkness.

As a reward for boarding and capturing the ship with only five men, George was granted the privilege of selecting the vessel which, as prize-master, he would command on his way back to the States. He had already made his choice and selected his crew, and now only awaited the fog to rise before boarding her; but when it did it revealed that an English frigate lay on their starboard bow, no more than a musket-shot away. So ended George's dream of a triumphal homecoming. The situation was hopeless, but in spite of objections, the captain insisted on making a run for it.

In his memoirs, George recorded details of all the chases and manoeuvres mentioned so briefly above; in the fascinating but now archaic language of the days of sail. He thus described the last hours of the cruise of the *Paul Jones*:

'All opinions and remonstrances were thrown away upon the captain. Every sail was got ready, the helm put up and in a few minutes she was under a cloud of canvass before the wind. It was not long before Captain T saw his egregious error, for it will be evident to every seaman, that we were now running nearly in a line to meet the frigate. The latter, quickly perceiving our mistake, kept her wind, and as there was no time now to be lost with us, the helm was put down, and the privateer brought to the wind; in the act of doing which, she gave us another division of her eighteen-pounders, which cut away the fore-gaff, the slings of the fore-yards, and riddled our lower sails, and, to add to the difficulty, our manoeuvre gave the frigate the weather-gage of us – the principal sail, too, had become useless from the loss of the gaff. The next discharge from the frigate cut away the main-topman-lift. There being a heavy sea in at the time, the main-boom got command of the quarter deck and carried away the bulwarks from the tafferel to the gangway. The frigate then overhauled us without any difficulty and opened a most murderous fire with the marines. We were unable to haul down our colors, from the fact that the topman-lift having been shot away. Seven men killed, and fifteen wounded, lay on our decks; and notwithstanding

Porchester Castle and Barracks. Hampshire

the frigate must have perceived that we were so much cut up that we had no command over the privateer, and that she lay like a log upon the water, nevertheless, she poured into us her quarter deck caronnades which, striking us amidships, nearly cut our craft in halves. It was about four hours from the time we fell in with the frigate until the time of our capture and in about one hour after, all of our crew were snugly stowed away on board of the frigate.'

George Little's service as a privateer officer had lasted for only sixteen action-packed weeks, during which he had been captured three times, once by the Indians, and twice by the British; but this time there was no escape. The privateer crew and officers were taken on to the frigate; the former confined in the cable tier, the latter, with a plank to sleep on, against the wardroom bulkhead.

Only the captains, first lieutenants and surgeons of privateers were granted parole. Had George been captured whilst on his previous privateer or letter-of-marque, he would have qualified for that privilege, and seen out the rest of the war from a lodging in an English or Scottish parole town or village. Unfortunately, his rank of prize-master meant that he would share the same type of imprisonment as the rest of the crew; although he, and the other

seven *Paul Jones* officers, would no doubt enjoy a slightly better accommodation.

Two days later the frigate was at anchor in Plymouth Harbour, and all the prisoners were off-loaded on to one of the prison hulks, an old seventy-four, which was rapidly filling with prisoners from many parts of the world. There were already three hundred and fifty Americans on board and when, after four weeks, that number had risen to six hundred, it was decided to distribute the Americans amongst designated depots ashore. They were dispatched in parties of one hundred prisoners, guarded by two hundred foot soldiers and fifty dragoons.

George Little and his party made up one of the drafts destined for Stapleton, near Bristol; which meant an exhausting march of one hundred and thirty miles. It was January 1813, and many of the cold and underfed Americans found the trek hard-going, and had to be conveyed to their prison by wagon. However, at last they arrived at Stapleton, where the footsore Yankees joined the three thousand French prisoners of war already in the Depot – and we get nearer to the one word that was the excuse for the mini-biography above.

George says that after three months in the place, the naturally

213

improvident American prisoners presented 'a sad spectacle of wretchedness and misery'. Most of them were penniless, some after losing their few possessions – and often their food and clothing – at the gaming tables, but they could not bring themselves to do any sort of labour to alleviate their self-imposed suffering. Unlike the majority of the French:

' …The fact that the French prisoners were allowed a market outside of the first wall; and as the whole of these men were industrious, and brought themselves systematically some pursuit, they manufactured a variety of articles, such as lace, straw plait for bonnets, bonework of almost every description, instruments and music and miniature ships, &c. &c., which were bought up by the country people or exchanged for their produce.'

The memoirists recorded many details of the day-by-day and routine happenings within the *grand pré*. Saint-Aubin noted that, every so so often, there was a great clean up of the prison buildings. All prisoners had to vacate their quarters whilst this giant 'spring cleaning' took place. Hammocks and bedding were brought out for a good airing in the yards – and doubtless the prison dormitories were cleared of rubbish, and sometimes disinfected. It was also an opportune time for the security 'tappers' to go round the walls and floors of the empty rooms, sounding for possible tunnelling or other excavating which might result in escape attempts. This may seem to be a ridiculous precaution. No wall, however high, was impossible to climb or scale, and the histories of other depots are rife with stories of attempts to prove this fact, often successfully; and most of the ground floors and airing yards of those prisons were riddled with subterranean passages and tunnels. However, one can well imagine that any would-be absconder who proffered an escape plan based on the undermining of Portchester's Roman-built massive stone walls – ten feet thick and from ten to thirty feet high – would be dismissed as a dreamer or an idiot. Yet *'The Light Dragoon'* tells of just such an attempt, and a large one at that, involving a great number of prisoners. I find this hard to believe, although the English officer must have based his story on some happening, as he tells it with confidence and obviously believes it himself. Abell did not query it, so, authentic or not, I repeat it here. *'The Light Dragoon'* wrote:

'It happened one night that a sentry whose post lay **outside** [my emphasis] the walls of the old Castle, was startled by the sound of a hammer driven against the earth under his feet. The man stopped, listened, and was more and more convinced that neither his fears nor his imagination had misled him. So he reported the circumstance to the sergeant who next visited his post, and left him to take in the matter such steps as might be expedient. The sergeant, after having first ascertained, as in duty bound, that the man spoke truly, made his report to the captain on duty, who immediately doubled the sentry at the indicated spot, and gave strict orders that should as much as one French prisoner be seen making his way beyond the Castle walls, he was to be shot without mercy. Then was the whole of the guard got under arms; then were beacons fired in various quarters; while far and near, from Portsmouth not less than from the cantonments more close at hand, bodies of troops marched upon Portchester. Among others came the general of the district, bringing with him a detachment of sappers and miners, by whom all the floors of the several bedrooms [on the ground floor, of course,] were tried and who soon brought the matter home to those engaged in it. Indeed, one man was taken in the gallery he was seeking to enlarge, his only instrument being a spike nail wherewith to labour. [A very

unresourceful miner! We know from the hundreds of records of escape attempts, from castles, depots, hulks, and commandeered civil jails, that the ingenuity of the prisoners produced efficient tools for their every need, including excavation. Even prisoners taken in the 'Fishguard Affair'– many of whom were described by their commander, as 'rogues and brigands', scum dredged up from the French jails – carried out a successful mass escape, tunnelling their way out of the Golden Tower Prison near Pembroke, using shovels and picks fashioned from the shin bones of horses and oxen. The plot thus discovered was very extensive and must, if carried through, have proved a desperate one to both parties.] For weeks previous to the discovery, the prisoners, it appeared, had been at work, and from no fewer than seven rooms, all of them on the ground floor, they had sunk shafts 10 feet in depth, and had caused all of them to meet at one common centre whence the many chambers went off. These were driven beyond the extremity of the outer wall, and one, that of which the sentry was thus unexpectedly made aware, the ingenious miners had carried forward with such skill, that in two days more it would have been in a condition to be opened. The rubbish, it appeared, which from these several covered ways they scooped out, was carried about by the prisoners in their pockets till they found an opportunity of scattering it over the surface of the great square. Yet the desperate men had a great deal more to encounter than the mere obstacles that the excavation of the castle at Portchester presented. Their first proceeding after emerging into the upper air must needs be have been to surprise and overpower the troops that occupied the barracks immediately contiguous, an operation of doubtful issue at the best, and not to be accomplished without a terrible loss of life, certainly on one side, probably on both…'
[He then went on to point out the fact that getting beyond the walls of the Castle, by whatever the means, was only one, and probably not the most daunting, obstacle they would then have had to face.]

Rather surprisingly, there is another story of excavation under the great walls of Portchester Castle. Sometime in 1797, the Agent was tipped off that the prisoners had almost completed a tunnel, which ran from one of the prison blocks, under yard and wall, to the outside world. It was planned that, after lights out, a company of guards should descend upon the prison and capture the miners in the act. The raid was successful and a number of workers were captured in the tunnel. However, there was more to come. That same evening, the alarm was sounded in another part of the prison, where the soldiers found prisoners attempting to escape through a hole they had made through the wall.

The miserable failure of two such courageous efforts in one day caused anger and rioting among the remaining prisoners; to a degree which may well have unnerved some of the guards and sentinels. The singing of patriotic songs of defiance, shouting and cursing, demonstrating and dancing, 'Lights out!' was ignored, and the uproar went on throughout the night. At the end of their tether, the military authorities decided it was necessary to use extreme force. The order was given to fire ball cartridges in to the midst of the prisoners, by which many were seriously wounded. By the next morning, the situation was, if anything, worse, the rioters were even more defiant and abusive, taunting their captors beyond endurance. One prisoner was shot in the back whilst trying to escape through a skylight in the roof – whether from the troops or his rioting brethren, is not known – and another was shot through the heart.

Most troubles and offences involving prisoners were judged by the depot Agent, the Transport Office, or the prisoners' own internal courts; but in the case of murder, forgery, duelling, or the violent death of a prisoner of war, these were always investigated by a civil court in the nearest county town. Almost invariably, in cases where a prisoner had been killed by a sentinel, guard or trooper, the magistrate or coroner would bring in a verdict of 'Justifiable Homicide'.

Escape and the planning of escape, was probably the prime preoccupation of most war-prisoners' minds, particularly during those war years when international recriminations brought the exchange system almost to a standstill. That excellent carrot which dangled the dream of freedom before the captive's eye, had been a greater aid to depot management and security than all the Black Holes or additional sentinels and guards could provide. The most severe part of punishments for attempted escape or recapture, was the deletion of the culprit's name from future exchange lists – and with that last hope shattered, the only alternatives were, a dispirited resignation to make the best of it until the end of the war, however long the waiting, or, in desperation, make even greater efforts to escape.

As many and as varied types of escape plans were hatched at Portchester as at any other depot, but the number who made completely successful getaways was low indeed; for, as the '*Light Dragoon*' said, it was but one thing to get out and avoid recapture by troops posted on the outside off the walls, but 'moreover, where this was done, there remained for the fugitives the still more arduous task of making their way through the heart of the garrison town of Portsmouth and seizing a flotilla of boats should such be high and dry upon the beach' [obviously, a lone absconder would have stood a better chance than a mass breakout of prisoners]. Worse even than this remained, for both the harbour and the roads were crowded with men-of-war, the gauntlet of whose batteries the deserters must of necessity have run.

Every type of escape plan was put to the test, by just about as great a variety of prisoner, from ordinary soldiers and sailors to senior officers of army and navy. Hiding away in contractors' delivery vehicles, rubbish wagons, and even dung carts; concealing themselves in barrels or empty water tanks; boldly posing as British officers, traders or country folk, their costumes obtained through market dealers in second-hand clothing, or smuggled in by girlfriends – or for hard cash. All these things and many others were tried, as well as the traditional tunnelling and climbing. Some succeeded though the many failed; but, as in any other profession, there were just a few who became famous in their chosen field, of escapology. Such men as Tom Souville, who escaped from the *Crown* prison hulk at Portsmouth and whose adventures were celebrated in his hometown, Calais, by naming a street after him the *rue Tom Souville*. Then there was the Houdini-like Petite, who was captured, escaped and recaptured a number of times, whilst on the run from the great Scottish depot at Perth, until finally disappearing from the records and, we hope, reaching his home in France.

Portchester Depot, too, had its own escape expert, a strange character who, it would seem, had far more interest in escaping for escaping's sake than any burning desire for freedom. The Revd J. D. Henderson, in his short history of Portchester, wrote:

'One, Francis Dufresne, who was confined here for more than five years, escaped again and again, despite the vigilance of his guards. He seems to have been as reckless and adventurous as any hero of romance, and the neighbourhood was full of stories of his wanderings and the tricks he resorted to obtain food.

'Once, after recapture, he was confined in the Black Hole, a building still to be seen at the foot of the Great Tower, called the "Exchequer" on plans of the Castle. Outside walked a sentry day and night, but Dufresne was not to be held. He converted his hammock into what sailors call a "thumb line", and at the dead of night removed a flat stone from under his prison door, crawled out, passed with silent tread within a few inches of the sentry, gained a winding stair[3] which led to the summit of the Castle wall, from which he descended by the cord, and, quickly gaining the open country, started for London, guiding himself by the stars. Arrived in London, he made his way to the house of M. Otto, the French Agent for arranging the exchange of prisoners. Having explained, to the amazement of Otto, that he had escaped from Portchester, he said: "Give me some sort of a suit of clothes, and a few sous to defray my expenses to the Castle, and I'll return and astonish the natives."

'Otto, amused at the man's cleverness and impudence, complied, and Dufresne in a few days alighted from the London coach at Fareham, walked over to Portchester but was refused admittance by the guard, until to the amazement of the latter, he produced the passport by which he had travelled. He was soon after this exchanged!'

Sheer devilment and the enjoyment of baffling his custodians seems to have been Dufresne's sole object in escaping. For a trifling wager he would scale the walls, remain absent for a few days living on and among the country folk, and returning as he went, so that he became almost a popular character even with the garrison.

1812 was a particularly worrying year for Britain. On many occasions over the war years, there had been rumours and alarming predictions of imminent invasion from France. The panic which followed William Tate's laughable 'invasion' of the small Welsh town of Fishguard, in October 1797, was never far beneath the surface of men's minds, even fifteen years later, particularly in the southern coastal towns of England. Now, with credible reports of Napoleon building up a powerful army and naval force at Boulogne for such a purpose, it seemed less a question of *were* we going to be invaded, than *when*.

Captors' discomfort was, of course, prisoners' joy. The latter would have been well informed of the situation through the prisoners' nation-wide grape-vine, through smuggled news-papers, or friendships struck up in the depot markets – and were fully prepared to play their part in their own deliverance.

The thousands of inmates in depots on shore and afloat, and parolees in towns and villages all over the country, were encouraged, by certain senior officers to believe that a general uprising of prisoners of war would prove a significant contribution to a glorious French victory – and, indeed, it may well have done so, had things gone to plan. With the great majority of our regular troops and sailors fully occupied overseas, it is difficult to imagine how we could have resisted a huge invading force from across the Channel, plus something like seventy thousand ex-prisoner fighting men who awaited their arrival.

Britain was saved – and not for the last time – by an enemy leader's decision to invade Russia first. With a large portion of the Boulogne soldiery detached to reinforce the ill-fated Grand Army, the idea of an invasion of Britain collapsed; and the disappointed prisoners gradually settled down to resume their long and weary wait for the war to end.

It ended sooner than they might have expected and with a result the antithesis of their dreams. Bonaparte's catastrophic expedition into Russia and inglorious retreat from Moscow, and then the entry of the Duke of Wellington's army on to French soil in 1813, heralded the beginning of the end for their beloved Emperor.

Early in the following year, 1814, the Allied armies were victorious in France and marched upon Paris. With the abdication of Napoleon, his retirement to Elba and the signing of the Peace Treaty of Paris on the 30th May, 1814 the thousands of prisoners, wherever confined, regained their longed-for freedom; but for many perhaps for most, this was not an occasion for unalloyed jubilation. However great the joy of liberation, it was dampened by the downfall of their heroic leader and Emperor – and some may have had reason to worry and wonder what life would be like under their new sovereign, Louis XVIII.

It was ordered that all depots should replace the tricolour by displaying the white flag of the Bourbons in the prison courtyards, in honour of the new regime. As the stories of all the depots show, this was one of the most resented of all orders. At Portchester, no Frenchman could be found willing to hoist the flag, and that it was eventually raised by a British trooper; and it is said that an English officer, who unwisely visited the Castle wearing a white cockade,

was greeted with 'hisses, groans, and even stone-throwing', and was only rescued from further abuse by Agent Patterson – who later criticised the officer for his indiscretion.

The continental prisoners had all been repatriated by June 1814, but for the next eighteen months Portchester Castle remained a prisoner of war depot, though now on a small scale, housing prisoners taken in the American War of 1812, who were not released until January 1816.

Most of the timber prisons and barrack buildings were demolished and the materials put up for sale. Portchester Castle had, by now, completed its long stint of national service as a prisoner of war camp – although part of the Castle was used for a while as a prison of a different kind – the inmates were deserters from our own army and navy.

For some time, a number of war-wounded and injured soldiers from the Peninsular Wars were housed in a building that had been converted into a hospital, but in 1819 the gates and doors of Portchester Castle were finally closed, and the Government returned the property to the descendants of William Uverdale.

PORTCHESTER CASTLE TODAY

In the same way that the visitor to a natural history museum may stand awestruck before the mighty remains of a giant dinosaur, his imagination fleshing out the skeleton until a living moving creature enters his mind, the visitor to Portchester, confronted with the immaculate remains of the Castle and Keep, which lie there like the timeless bones of history, may conjure up visions of junketing in the royal apartments, or the misery and suffering of prisoners of war of later years, crammed into those self-same rooms – depending on which track he is listening to on the audio-guide, now issued to each visitor.

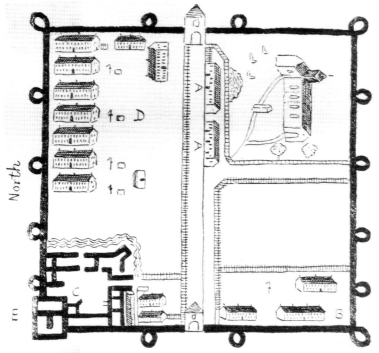

PLAN OF PORTCHESTER CASTLE, 1793.
A. Kitchens. B. Hospital. C. Black Hole. D. Caserns.
E. Great Tower.

---

1. *Miscellaneous Works of Edward Gibbon.* Edited by John, Lord Sheffield.

2. The brig's cargo was rich indeed. A prize-crew delivered her safely to the United States, where vessel and cargo realised nearly $400,000 at auction.

3. I recently clambered up that same steep and narrow winding stonestairway, built in Norman times. It is not for the unathletic or claustrophobic!

Three contemporary water-colour views of Portchester Castle by the British Captain Durrant. Pictures 2 and 3 also show the Castle Market in progress.

Chapter Fourteen

Millbay Depot
Old Mills Prison, the New Prison & later Millbay, near Plymouth, Devon

THE OLD MILL, OR OLD MILLS PRISON, which was later renamed Millbay, was probably the earliest establishment to be reserved exclusively for the confinement of war prisoners. Situated on high land between Plymouth Town and Plymouth Docks, it was so-called because a number of windmills had once occupied the site. However, that must have been in the distant past, as the records tell that it was already a centre for the detention of prisoners of war by the time of the War of the Austrian Succession – 1740 to 1748 – and that in 1745 the 'French prisons at Old Mills' were badly damaged by fire.

Old Mills Prison comprised four principal buildings. The largest was the two-storey Long Prison, appropriately so-called as it was 132 feet in length by 20 feet wide. Apart from the prisoner-occupied buildings, there were numerous smaller structures, the offices of the Commissary, the Keeper and the Agent; and, of course, huge kitchens and cookhouses. At first, unlike Forton Depot, there was no separate building for captive officers, an omission not rectified until 1778.

The large main courtyard, or airing ground, was 252 feet long by 156 feet wide, with a water pump by the inner gate and a lamp post in its centre. The whole prison complex was surrounded by inner and outer walls, with a twenty-feet space between the two. The outer wall varied in height from ten to fourteen feet, and was built of stone, topped by a barrier of broken glass set into the mortar to discourage escapers who might plan to climb over rather than burrow under it. The massive main gate was heavily reinforced with metal, but the inner gate and lofty palisading was sturdily constructed from wood.

Guards patrolled the prison walls and yards, and with its longer experience in the confinement and controlling of wily, and sometimes desperate, foreign captives, one might expect that security would have been tighter than in many smaller depots and escapes rarer. Yet there were many spectacular breakouts from Old Mill throughout its existence as a prison.

During the Seven Years' War, when thousands of French, German, Austrian and Russian prisoners were housed there, the guards and militias were kept on their toes by the prisoners' constant dashes for freedom. On one occasion in 1760 a particularly ambitious large-scale mass escape was attempted by burrowing under the prison walls. One hundred and fifty captives experienced a brief period of freedom, but within a very short time most of them had been rounded up and awaited their turn in the *cachot*; only sixteen had made a clear getaway.

The authorities were also kept busy with other prisoner of war problems during that complex war of strange alliances – for to be allied did not necessarily make them friends. In 1758, Saxon prisoners at Plymouth who had been captured earlier in the war – King Frederick had taken Saxon prisoners even before war had been declared! – pleaded to be separated from one of their co-belligerents, or sent to another depot, 'as they were ostracized and even reviled by the French'.

Segregation by nationality was not unusual in prisoner of war management. As we shall see, the Americans were quartered away from the French at Forton, but rather because of the ambiguity of the former's status as prisoners of war, than from incompatibility, and this applied to Old Mill and anywhere else where Americans were held. In both Old Mill and Forton, the American blacks were housed apart from their white countrymen – at the request of the latter.

There was a hospital within the prison walls – or rather a medical centre with a nursing staff and visiting doctors – which dealt with the lesser sicknesses. Only serious cases, such as smallpox, were sent to the Royal Hospital situated about half a mile north-west of the prison.

The prisoners in general had little faith in the visiting doctors, who had but one universal remedy for all illnesses: *Doctor Ball's Infallible Cure of All Manner of Diseases'*, which was a mixture of 'salts, jalap, conserve of roses and balsam'. One prisoner recalled seeing a sick-parade, where one man said 'Doctor, I have a violent pain in my Head', another said, 'I have a sour Stomach' and a third, 'Doctor, I have a violent Fever on me every night'. Each was advised by the Doctor, to 'keep taking the Mixture'! Although most accepted any sort of British medical treatment as better than none, there were many who preferred to treat – and even inoculate – themselves. This lack of confidence in the Old Mill doctors of that time and the medical care generally available, was summed up by the following entry in the journal of a captive during the War of American Independence:

'This morning we are informed that the chief doctor [the chief surgeon at Old Mill] is dead. He died suddenly; I believe that there are not many in prison who will mourn, as we have no reason to expect that we can get a worse one.'

Only the very sick were admitted as in-patients and most of these were sent off to the Royal Hospital after a few days. This large Hospital was housed in a group of three-storeyed buildings, divided into ten sections, each of six wards. Each ward, which was designed to receive about twenty-five prisoner-patients, was furnished with double-decker beds or bunks, so the Plymouth Royal Hospital could accommodate about 1,500 men.

Whether due to their arrogance or ignorance, few depot doctors or surgeons are mentioned with gratitude or respect in prisoners' memoirs. More often we read of 'brutes' and 'monsters' and there is little doubt that some deserved to be so called. There were those who gloried in their rank, but treated their post as a sinecure; visiting their patients rarely, until pulled up sharply by the Sick and Hurt Office or the Transport Board. There must have been others who, armed with only the meagre medical knowledge of the day, found the job of watching over the health of thousands of men a hopeless task.

However, for quite a long period, Millbay Depot had a hospital of which it could be proud, headed for most of the Napoleonic Wars by a remarkable man. George (afterwards Sir George) McGrath MD, a resident of Plymouth, was blessed with a personality and devotion to his profession which endeared him to both public and prisoners alike. That his good work was appreciated is shown by the following epitaph in St Andrew's Church:

'A follower of the immortal Nelson – in all things he did his duty: as an Officer with zeal, as a Citizen with dignity, as a Friend with devotion.'

Probably, his most amazing achievement as a man and a doctor, was when he supplanted the hated William Dykar as Chief Surgeon at Dartmoor Hospital, and won the admiration of the American prisoners at a time when the relations between the two countries were at their lowest ebb. For this he was honoured by both Britain and The United States.

The conditions and everyday happenings in the Old Mill Prison during the War of American Independence, were basically the same as those experienced by the Yankees sent to Forton Prison, near Gosport in Hampshire, or other depots. Wherever British captors held Americans captive, there was sure to be trouble. Although the majority of the British public would have regarded these Americans as renegades and their seamen as pirates, which caused bitterness and concern, a surprising number of English people showed compassion for their unhappy transatlantic cousins. On more than one occasion, subscriptions were organised, which produced quite large sums of money, on their behalf and bundles of second-hand clothing were collected and distributed among needy near-naked 'Rough Alleys'.

On reaching England the captives were assigned to one or another of a few depots; and the records would suggest that no sooner were they within the prison walls their only dream was of getting under or over them. There was a theory that their escape-mania came about through uncertainty of their fate: whether they would eventually stand trial as 'rebels and traitors', or be released as prisoners of war when hostilities ended. However, when, after thirty years, we were once again at war with America, the prisoners were just as escape-obsessed, although they were no longer in fear of the gallows.

Our principal source of specific information regarding prisoners in England during the War of Independence comes from the writings of two young New Englanders, Charles Herbert and Andrew Sherburne. They never met as prisoners in this country, for Charles Herbert was included in an exchange cartel and returned to America before Andrew Sherburne was brought to Plymouth as a captive Yankee rebel at the end of November 1781.

We also have *The Memoirs of Commodore Barney.* Joshua Barney was a famously successful privateer captain who was captured in December 1782 and sent to Old Mills where he stayed just long enough to plan and achieve a sensational escape. Barney was a remarkable and courageous character whose story reads more like fiction than fact. After the Ghent Peace Treaty of 1783 – and only months after his escape from Old Mills – Joshua Barney returned to Plymouth; but this time he arrived on the USS *George Washington*, as a representative of the United States Government.

A decade later, during the Revolutionary War between England and France, Barney was serving as a Commodore in the French Navy, preying on British merchant shipping, but when America declared war on Britain in 1812, he was back in the American naval service. In August 1814, whilst putting up a gallant defence of Bladenburg as the British were advancing to capture and burn the nearby city of Washington, Commodore Barney was badly wounded, and once again became a prisoner of war.

Charles Herbert was just nineteen when he joined the brig *Dolton* at Newberryport, Massachusetts, his hometown, in November 1776. After only forty-one days as a sea-going sailor, Herbert became a prisoner when the *Dolton* was captured by the 64-gun man-of-war, HMS *Reasonable*. He was stationed on the main-top when the brig was taken, but having heard that prisoners were often robbed of all good clothing other than that on their backs, he made a rapid descent and dashed below to break into his sea-chest – 'putting on two shirts, a pair of drawers and breeches, and trowsers over them; two or three jackets, and a pair of new shoes, and then filled my bosom and pockets as full as I could well carry.'

This immediate reaction to capture was a typical example of his active mind. As his journal, *A Relic of the Revolution,* shows his talent as a carpenter, shoe-maker, carver – in fact as a jack of all trades – and his natural instinct for business, served him well during his time as a prisoner at Plymouth. His ability to earn for himself extra food, clothing and small luxuries, made his life as a captive bearable. It also tended to make his memoir more credible, written as it was with moderation, less laced with bitterness and exaggeration than many prisoner reminiscences of that time.

Herbert was, however, no fawning Anglophile, and could robustly complain when unjustly treated. All of the Americans had every reason to complain of their transportation to England. All the common sailors, Herbert amongst them, were lodged in the suffocating, overcrowded, cable-tier of the *Reasonable*, their only bed the anchor cable itself. After twenty-seven days of discomfort, they arrived at Plymouth and the prisoners were transferred to the cable-tier of the 64-gun *Bellisle*, where their nocturnal comfort was slightly improved by the laying of planks and boards over the bare cable chains.

After nineteen days, on the 7th February, 1777, they were again removed, this time to the HMS *Torbay*, but by now most of the crew of the *Dolton* were in a poor state of health. The day before the transfer, Charles Herbert had noted in his journal:

'February 6. We begin to grow very sickly, and twenty or thirty of us are suffering with the itch [the 'itch' was often a forewarning of smallpox yet to come], and we are all dreadfully infested with vermin. I make a constant practice to examine my clothes every day, when we are permitted to go upon deck. I often find them swarming with these.

'We are informed that the Admiral was heard to say, that no favor was to be shown to us, on account of our orders' [the orders common to all letters-of-marque, to 'sink, burn and destroy' enemy vessels].

On the *Torbay* they were to experience another dreadful variety of accommodation. On this vessel, they were concentrated in an area between decks, 'partitioned off, like a sheep-pen, and takes in two side-ports [portholes] only', and too small for all to lie down at one time. At the mercy of winter weather, insufficient bedding, blankets, and clothing, nearly everyone was sick, some from colds and chills, others wracked with rheumatic aches and pains and a growing incidence of the 'itch'.

A few days later they were lucky enough to make one last move from ship to ship, to the 74-gun HMS *Burford*, where they were to receive considerate treatment for the first time since their capture. They were brought aboard on the 13th February, and on observing that most were dressed in rags and many of them almost naked, they were informed by a lieutenant that although it was generally accepted that rebel captives were likely to be 'robbed and plundered', the commander of the *Burford*, Captain Boyer, would arrange for their wants to be seen to. They were to be quartered with plenty of room between-decks, and allowed upon deck, twenty at a time. Charles Herbert welcomed the latter privilege as much as any as, away from the darkness of the cable-tiers, any who could would be able to read and write. His entry on the 17th February, 1777, read:

> 17. 'Very stormy. To-day we had delivered to us, by the purser of the ship bedding and clothes. I received a shirt, and bedding, consisting of a *flock bed and pillows,* a *rug,* and *blankets.* Some who were almost naked, had nearly a whole suit given them. When they gave us the shirts, they told us to take off our old ones and throw them overboard, "lice and all".'
>
> 'Our beds are a great comfort to our sore bodies, after lying fifty-five nights without any – all the time since we were taken – sometimes upon hard cables, sometimes upon boards laid over the cables, and at times on a wetdeck, with nothing to cover us but the clothes on our backs. Now we have good bedding for our comfort, thanks be to God! *And a good friend,* for we are told that the captain of the ship, whose name is Boyer, gave us these clothes and beds, out of his own pocket.'

On the 25th the master-at-arms of the *Burford* called for a volunteer joiner, and Herbert immediately volunteered, reporting on deck with a shipmate as his assistant. In the absence of the ship's carpenter, they were given the freedom of his bench and tools. They soon got down to work and made a table to the full satisfaction of the master-at-arms, afterwards rewarding them with 'a bag to put our clothes in, half of a salt fish, a quart of potatoes, six biscuits, and butter to eat with our fish, besides a good hot supper.' In addition, they were given news from the outside world.

They heard that, of the nine seriously ill prisoners who had been sent ashore to the Royal Hospital ten days earlier, one had already died and others were dangerously sick. They also had access to an English newspaper, in which they saw for the first time in print, the details of the Act of Parliament, passed by 112 to 35, which denounced them as traitors; decreeing that they be sentenced to prison, 'there to lay, without bail, until the first of January, 1778, then to face trial'.

Herbert and his shipmate found fairly regular work in the carpenter's shop, a privilege which gave them a sort of parole on board the *Burford.* Despite the fact that they, and all other members of the *Dolton's* crew, were treated with fairness, the general state of health onboard grew steadily worse, mainly due to their past sufferings as captives in the depths of men-of-war – conditions

certainly far worse than most prisoners of war experienced on the dreaded British prison hulks.

More and more sick men from the *Burford* were being hospitalized ashore and, on the 12th April, 1777, nearly four months after the capture of the *Dolton*, Charles Herbert was one of the eight men sent to the Royal Hospital on that day, all of them suffering from an advanced stage of the 'itch'.

The religiously kept record of his two-months' stay in various wards of the Royal Hospital, is remarkably free from criticism of the staff, food or conditions; on the contrary it contains examples of that rarity in prisoner memoirs, compliments concerning the considerate treatment by the British of their captive patients. Twenty-four of his shipmates were in the hospital at that time, some with smallpox and the rest with the 'itch'. The 'itch' was treated with a sulphur-based ointment, and each morning and evening they were dosed with large spoonfuls of sulphur mixed with honey and cream tartar. Their food ration depended on diet at various stages of their illness; but the basic full allowance was generous enough: bread, a pound of beef (or mutton), a pound of potatoes, greenstuff, and three pints of beer, each day. If they could afford it, it was also possible to purchase tea and milk (in later years, a morning and evening issue of tea would be included in the basic diet). Herbert shared a spacious ward – capable of administering to twenty-five men – with seventeen fellow sufferers, mainly men with whom he had sailed. Captives from a number of other American privateers and merchantmen were distributed throughout the many wards and buildings of the large hospital complex.

Although no mention was made of escape attempts from the man-of-war transports, there were frequent reports of escapes from the Royal Hospital. As a number of these were from the 'itch' and smallpox wards, these absconders presented a far greater threat to Britain as carriers of a dread disease, than they ever had as rebels.

After a week of considerable pain and discomfort, Herbert was informed that the 'itch' had developed into smallpox:

> April 30. ' …he told me I had the small-pox and ordered the nurse to remove me immediately into the small-pox ward, which she did. After I got there, I was ordered to strip off all the dirty clothes I had upon me. I washed myself in warm water, and put on a clean linen shirt, a woollen gown, waistcoat and drawers, and turned into bed with clean sheets.'

Although seriously ill – his flesh feeling as if it was 'raked up in a bed of embers', his head 'swollen very much', and his eyes 'so blind that I could scarcely see daylight' – he kept a detailed daily record of his time as a smallpox victim. Fortunately, we have no space for it here! At least six Americans died from the disease in Herbert's part of the hospital, but by the 24th May he had recovered sufficiently to be sent to the recovery ward.

On the 5th June, Charles Herbert and eleven other ex-patients were considered well enough to be discharged from hospital. Four of them, privateers from the *Charming Sally*, which had been taken after the *Dolton*, were delivered to the *Blenheim*, but the remainder were taken under guard to the 'Fountain Tavern', Plymouth, which was the usual seat of judgement where Americans underwent the lengthy and complicated inquisition which would decide whether they were rebels to await trial, non-Americans, who could be impressed in the Royal Navy, or British deserters, who would be lucky not to face the hangman. Charles Herbert was lucky, and was merely found guilty of high treason, and sentenced to prison.

When Herbert and the other Americans returned to Old Mills, they found that the food allowance was less than they had been receiving at the Royal Hospital, and Herbert complained that he had 'a continual gnawing' at his stomach, and 'only seven pence' in his pocket, all that was left of the money he had before going into hospital. He soon observed that some of the prisoners were busying themselves in various occupations: making ladles, chairs, small caskets; in fact anything which might be saleable in the weekly Sunday market held in the courtyard between the outer and inner gates of the prison. On most weekdays a number of visitors would be admitted into the outer yard, Americans who had come to Britain before the Revolution, and now came to talk with their captive countrymen, often donating quite large sums towards their relief. However, the majority were local inhabitants and gentry, among them sympathetic visitors who bought prisoner-made artifacts small enough to be traded through the gaps in the slatted metal inner wall; and fascinated gawkers who came to see what savage Yankee rebels and vicious Frenchmen looked like.

Charles Herbert soon set himself up in business, making boxes and punch ladles for an established prisoner-carpenter in return for wood from which he made articles for sale in the prison market. His small boxes brought from ninepence to a shilling a piece, and by means of this industry he sometimes made as much as five shillings (25p) in a week.

Observing the generally generous and amiable nature of the visitors, a few of the woodworkers got together to make a 'Charity Box' which was set up at the main gate, and bore the inscription: '*Health, Plenty, and Competence to the Donors*'. This was successful enough for a treasurer to be appointed, but after a few weeks the takings dwindled – the prisoners believing that the guards literally had a hand in it – so that when it was taken down for the last time, the final share-out was only five farthings a man.

There was no time during the American occupation of Old Mills, when the authorities were not preoccupied with escapes. Somewhat neurotic guards and sentries became hypersensitive to any unusual noises or happenings; any strange tapping, scuffling, scratching, banging or thumping, was often enough to raise the alarm. A great lighting up of lanterns ensued throughout the prison yards and a bell or bugle called forth the guards with bayonets fixed. As often as not it would be to a false alarm; and did nothing to reduce the uncomfortably tense atmosphere in the depot.

In July, 1777, when a fresh outbreak of 'itch' and smallpox hit the depot, a number of patients under treatment escaped through a drain which led from the hospital to the river bank. It was not obvious how they had made their getaway, so all the remaining patients in the ward from which they had escaped were put on half allowances until someone revealed the bolthole. After three days of under-nourishment, someone informed the Agent, and full rations were restored. Quite a few of those hospital cases were men who had inoculated themselves with matter taken from smallpox sufferers at an advanced stage of the disease – although it had been promulgated that the doctors would treat anyone who applied.

The majority of the Americans were housed in the Long Prison, and so many escape attempts by burrowing and digging were reported that parts of the buildings must have resembled warrens rather than a place of confinement. Charles Herbert was involved in the preparation for one mass breakout, although he did not himself make a bid for freedom:

> 'July 20. Last night we made a breech in the prison wall, and began to dig out, which we expect will take near a fortnight to accomplish, as we have near eighteen feet to dig under ground to get into a field on the other side of the wall.'

The tunnel was excavated just large enough for one man at a time to crawl through it. The dirt was temporarily crammed into their sea-chests, and when each night's work was over, the hole was covered with the original stone and daubed with lime to match the rest of the wall. On the 5th August, thirty-two men passed out through the tunnel, only eleven of them being re-captured and brought in by 'five-pounder' bounty hunters. That twenty-one should have got away caused consternation among the guards and officials. For a period musters and counts were called two or three times a day and night searches were frequent, as were examinations of sea-chests for dirt, tools or other evidence. The searching of chests must have been particularly nerve-wracking for Charles Herbert. It was forbidden for prisoners to keep uncensored diaries and journals, so the daily notes which he made were secreted in his boots until they could be added to his journal, which was hidden in the false bottom of his sea-chest.

The occasional newspaper was smuggled in, but as often as not there was little to raise their spirits or hopes. Exaggerated accounts of British victories; stories that the Americans had laid down their arms and false reports of the death of George Washington; all these things caused great depression and pessimism. Herbert wrote: 'should they [the British] conquer the country [America], or even get the upper hand of it, we are positive that the gallows or the East Indies will be our destiny.' Small wonder that their most concentrated occupation was digging for liberty.

Before the boon of British public subscriptions and American Government allowances, which began in 1778 and made such a difference to the wellbeing of the Americans in Forton and Old Mill, there were many bitter complaints regarding their food. In an age when back-handers and rake-offs were the order of the day, it was inevitable that all prisoners would suffer to some degree at the hands of unscrupulous contractors and distributors, and many of their complaints are to be found in Herbert's journal. However, the most strident need some explanation:

> August 31. ' …it is enough to break the heart of a stone to see so many strong, hearty men, almost starved to death through want of provisions. A great part of those in prison, eat at one meal what they draw for twenty long hours, and go without until the next day. Many are sorely tempted to pick up the grass in the yard, and eat it, and some who pick up old bones in the yard, that have been laying in the dirt a week or ten days, and pound them to pieces and suck them. Some will pick up snails out of the holes in the wall, and from among the grass and weeds in the yard, boil them and eat them, and drink the broth. Often the cooks, after they have picked over our cabbage, will cut off something of the butt-ends of the stalks and throw them over the gate into the yard, and I have often seen, after a rain, when the mud would be over shoes, as these stumps were thrown over the gate, the men running from all parts of the yard, regardless of the mud, to catch at them, and nearly trample one another under feet to get a piece.'

There is no reason to doubt the above observations; but it is unlikely that Herbert or the majority of his fellow captives were ever driven to such desperate measures. The 'many' who competed for muddy cabbage stalks, were more probably the down-and-outs at the very bottom of the lowest level of prisoner society, Americans who in a later war with Britain would be known as the 'Rough Alleys'. Had all been in the same dire straits, it is unlikely that old bones would have lain undiscovered 'in the dirt a week or ten days' – and snail-hunting sounds more like a pursuit of French rather than Yankee prisoners.

Apart from 'Rough Alleys', there were men made hungry by their unsuccessful escape attempts. The Black Hole was always fully occupied and had a waiting list of offenders who were temporarily housed in parts of the Long Prison, all of them faced with forty days on half rations – anyone detected helping them in their distress being similarly deprived of sustenance. Civilians, guards and escape agents, involved in prisoner breakouts were, understandably, more harshly punished than the escapees themselves.

In 1778, a building in the Old Mill complex, was set aside as an officers-only prison – but it got off to a poor start. At the end of January, five American officers – four captains, Henry and Eleazer Johnson, Offin Boardman, Samuel Treadwell and a Mr Deal – determined on escape and involved two Old Mill sentries in their plans. The officers possessed sufficient good quality civilian clothing to fit out not only themselves but their British accomplices; the latter deciding to accompany them in their flight. The two soldiers unwisely left their regimentals and firelocks at their sentry posts, which made their desertion almost immediately apparent. Four of the officers made their way to London, but on the 14th March, Samuel Treadwell was brought in and committed to the Black Hole. By that time the two English sentinels had been captured and had stood trial for desertion and assisting in the escape of rebel prisoners. One was sentenced to be executed by firing squad, the other to suffer seven hundred lashes.

After the trial, handbills and pamphlets were distributed, which announced the sentences as warnings against the 'heinousness of their crime of deserting their colours and carrying off rebels with them.' This provoked another example of the often encountered ambivalent attitude of some British people towards rebels and prisoners of war – and of those who helped them to escape. Plymouth Dockyard workers and sailors on shore from men-of-war gathered in a mob to collect all the handbills they could lay hands on, and burnt them in the town. Some time in April, Captain Boardman and Mr Deal were recaptured and escorted back to Old Mill, but it would seem that Henry and Eleazer Johnson made a clear getaway.

This escape attempt had cost the life of one soldier and a vicious flogging of another; but the recaptured officers got off lightly, spending only seventeen of the normal forty days confinement in the Black Hole before being released back into normal prison life.

In most escape attempts which involved officers, the power of the pound was greater than a dozen diggers. Although many were recaptured, most had walked out through the main gate, rather than crawled or climbed. Dressed in British uniforms or clothed as visiting gentry, conducted by bribed English accomplices and with guineas to buy professional escape agents, their recapture was usually the result of sheer bad luck, or the double-dealing of informers.

It is rather surprising that would-be escapees, officers or other-ranks caught in the act of absconding were not dealt with in a more draconian fashion. According to the records, few days went by without the discovery of newly started excavations, clear evidence of the route of successful escapees, or shortages when the muster rolls were called. Yet, if anything, security grew weaker. In fact, after General Burgoyne returned to England on parole of honour after his surrender at Saratoga, the 17th October, 1777, it was learned that the soldiers, both at Old Mills and Forton were ordered not to fire on prisoners attempting escape. They were 'to fire only clear powder to alarm the guard; and they were not to strike any of us, nor offer a bayonet to us: thus their rigour has abated since Burgoyne has been taken.'

Therefore the digging, scaling and bolting went on, even after well-founded rumours were spread that Americans might soon be exchanged for British prisoners held in France. Eventually, even the level-headed Herbert, who had taken part in many digs, but had never before included himself among the absconders – now made his own bid for liberty.

By the middle of 1778, with France now entering the war under a twenty-one year treaty with America, Plymouth, both inside and outside of the prison, became a hive of activity. Warships massed in the harbour made ready for sea, as press-gangs ruthlessly sought to make up their crews – even the prison lamp-lighter was gathered in – and preparations were in hand for the reception of expected French prisoners of war. Orders came down from London, that a three-storey building with its own yard at Old Mill should be repaired, and kept separate from the American captives – although American masons and carpenters worked on the building repairs, and four American sail-makers were employed to make hammocks for its future inmates.

By September there were more French prisoners of war in Old Mills than there were American rebels. Between four and five hundred Frenchmen were sent to the newly prepared prison, whilst only 330 Yankees occupied the Long Prison – and that number was reduced when thirty-six of the men petitioned for the King's pardon, so that they could enlist in the Royal Navy. A few weeks earlier, Admiral Keppel had sent in his recruitment officers in a desperate search for much needed volunteers from among the prisoners. The remaining 294 did not resent the loss of those turncoats, as the majority of them were from the troublesome element who often made their life a hell with their drunkenness and general lawlessness. A few were 'Old-Countrymen' – English/Americans awaiting trial – and some were just unthinking youngsters. After receiving the pardon, which read something like:

> 'His Majesty has been graciously pleased to grant a free
> pardon to thirty-six men, by name..........................
> resident in Old Mill Prison, upon condition that they
> serve, and continue to serve in His Majesty's Navy.'

twelve were put on board HMS *Royal George* in Plymouth Dockyard, the remainder to HMS *Russell* lying in the Sound.

All through October and November rumours of cartels and exchanges excited the optimistic, even though their hopes had been so often dashed. The correspondence, which was somehow regularly maintained between the Portsmouth and Plymouth prisons, told of Benjamin Franklin organising passports for the Americans, and ships being made ready to take them all to France. Everything but thoughts of packing up and leaving went by the board; routine cleaning of the living quarters and yards was neglected; and Old Mills Depot was once again an unhealthy place to be. It was a long time since the prisons had been disinfected by 'smoke pots', and the whole prison was 'foul, and smells very offensive'. A new disinfectant, 'oil of tar', was liberally spread throughout the prisons, but the smell of this curing agent was just as disagreeable as the stench from filth and neglect which it overpowered.

The New (French) Prison was soon overcrowded, and a high percentage of its occupants were seriously ill, most of them suffering from 'spotted fever', which they had brought with them from the East Indies, and carried with it a high mortality rate. A new hospital was being adapted for the Americans, as their original one was later to be taken over by the French. At the same time foundations were being laid for the building of a large new hospital within the prison walls, as the Royal Hospital would soon need all its wards and beds to cope with British and captive servicemen wounded or infected in the now extended war.

The French prisoners were almost as great a problem as their American allies. The fit, and some of the sick amongst them, showed just as much energy as escapologists; although in their case the depot guards and militia proved less reticent to use their firearms to prevent escapes. However, the biggest problem was space; something like two hundred Frenchmen were marched out of Old Mills and put on board a seldom-mentioned Plymouth prison ship the *Cambridge*.

Charles Herbert had little to celebrate when the 17th November, 1778 came round. It was his twenty-first birthday; there was no sign of the promised exchange cartel; there was no sign of the war ending; and he had been an untried rebel for nearly two years – and the Act which held him in this invidious position had recently been renewed. To add to his depression, he learned from an article in a smuggled newspaper, that the British brig, *Fortune*, had become one of the most successful of privateers, and over the past two years had brought in an unmatched treasure in prizes. The *Fortune* was, in fact, the renamed *Dolton*, the brig in which he had been captured in 1776!

Six weeks later, on the 28th December, after a miserable Christmas, an escape plan on a truly heroic scale got under way. Had it been completely successful, the American section of Old Mill would have been left virtually empty, at least temporarily. The prisoners had been working on a tunnel for the past month, which descended nine feet to a point where it went for fifteen feet under a road to another vertical hole, which came up into a garden. Huge quantities of earth had been removed, but as almost everyone was in on the scheme, hundreds of small quantities had been carried in pockets, hats or wherever, and deposited in every hole and corner of the yard. A number of large stones encountered during the excavating, were piled in various parts of the living quarters, hidden under hammocks, stacked high, or draped with old clothes and blankets. The work could only proceed on alternate days, when the militia took over as sentries from soldiers of the 23rd Regiment; as the former had proved themselves more susceptible to bribes and were less wide awake.

Eventually the great day, or rather night, arrived. The order of exit was decided in a democratic manner; Herbert noted: 'While I now write, we are dividing ourselves into companies, to cast lots who shall go first, so as to give every one an equal chance that intended to go; except three that dug the hole – they are to go first.' He was realistic about the possibility of success, even in the early stages of the breakout, 'on account of there being four walls to get over, each about eight feet high, after we get into the garden, and before we get into the road.'

Two men who had volunteered to stay behind, took charge of the lists to make sure that the men entered the hole in correct order – and Charles Herbert was included in the first company to leave. After negotiating the excavations and scaling the four walls, which 'they went over like greyhounds', Charles and five companions struck out inland and made for the country. A few miles outside Plymouth they headed, as they thought, towards Teignmouth – about thirty-six miles from their prison – where they hoped to find someone who, at a price, would sail them to France. The day was bitter cold, and so overcast that they lost their sense of direction, as they kept away from public roads and scrambled across fields, over hedges and through ditches until they were hopelessly lost.

They calculated that they had travelled about twenty miles before they stopped, exhausted, to rest under the lee of a haystack and await the dawn. Daylight revealed that they were close by a high road which led to a bridge – where a milestone revealed that, although they were now indeed on the road to Teignmouth, they were still only three miles from Plymouth! They pushed on along the road for a couple of miles until about seven in the morning, then, seeing that the countryfolk had begun to stir, they left the road and crossed a field to the cover of a thick hedge.

There they lay for nine hours, 'wet, hungry, and almost chilled to death with the cold; lying all the time in one position, longing for the night to come.' When it did come, and Herbert stretched a cramped leg to rise, there was a sharp crack and his knee went out of joint. It was while one of his fellow absconders was endeavouring to reset it, that a group of about ten farmers, flails and clubs in hand, and an armed soldier, came upon them. The captors were no doubt delighted by their 'five-pounds-a-head' windfall, and were not bullying or unkind to the unfortunate Yankees. They were, in fact, escorted to a small nearby village, where each was given a glass of good brandy and a halfpenny cake, before being handed over to the militia for the march back to Old Mills Prison.

One hundred and nine went out through the hole that night, and the number may well have been double that figure, had not a young boy prisoner become stuck on one of the eight-foot high walls. His cries for help alerted the guards, and the prisoners who may have followed retreated to the upper floor of the Long Prison, whilst their bolt-hole was resealed.

Small numbers of the retaken were brought in daily over the weeks, until eighty-seven men were on half-allowance, in the Black Hole or punishment block; but twenty-two was still a large number of successful escapes to have taken place in one night. The only consoling thing for the Americans was the thought that, under the 'five-pounder' reward rule, it would have cost the Government £435 to bring in the recaptured eighty-seven.

1779 started as miserably as the previous year had ended. So many men were on half-rations that there were insufficient on full allowance to help out their hungry brethren. The preoccupation with thoughts of food led to many diary entries. We read that during the first week of the new year, many a hungry eye had been cast on an officer's dog which frequented the yards; but on the 7th January it had been reprieved by a donation of food, given in at the gate. This was the earliest of a number of 'dog-dinner' stories I have encountered in memoirs; predating Louis Garneray's story of the visiting Colonel's Great Dane on the *Crown* prison hulk at Portsmouth by thirty years.

The reprieve of the Old Mills dog was short lived. The following week, the poor hound was quartered and shared out:[1]

'January 9, 1779. …[it] was dressed so neat, and being so fat withall, that if I had seen him in a butcher's shop I should have thought it to be a young lamb… We had a bag of potatoes given us, to eat with our venison. Some stewed theirs, others roasted it; and I must confess I made a tolerable meal out of some of this roasted dog, with potatoes dipped in its dripping. Rats have been eat in this prison often before.'

Next day they were told that a cartel vessel had arrived in Plymouth and that the Americans would be exchanged for as many Britons captured by American privateers as were held in France; and that the Old Mills prisoners would go on board according to their length of time in captivity. At that time there were 298 Americans (and 392 Frenchmen) in Old Mill.

Finally, after two years and four months in captivity, Charles Herbert was granted his longed-for exchange, on the 15th March, 1779. That part of the journal which recorded the passage of the cartel to France has been lost, but we know something of Charles Herbert after his arrival at Nantes. Correspondence between Benjamin Franklin and the Scottish-American hero, Commodore John Paul Jones, often indicated that the capture of British prisoners was of more importance than any other sort of prize-taking. John Paul had a passionate desire to see the release of all Americans held in British prisons, by exchange or any other means, made it known that any ex-prisoners would be welcomed into his fleet.

Two months after their release, Charles Herbert and seventeen of his old *Dolton* shipmates, sailed for L'Orient, where Jones's squadron was anchored: the 40-gun *Bon Homme Richard*, the frigates *Alliance*, *Pallas* and *Vengeance*, and the 18-gun cutter *Cerf*. There they joined the American-owned and built *Alliance*, a particularly fast frigate, which Franklin considered ideal for the taking of 'privateers and a number of prisoners, so as to continue the cartel, and redeem all our poor countrymen'. It had been named by Congress to celebrate the treaty between France and America, and handed over to a French commander (under Paul Jones), the famous – or infamous – Captain Landais.

After the great victory of the *Bon Homme Richard* over the *Serapis* a number of captured British vessels were sent to Bergen in Norway, then part of the kingdom of Denmark, and Herbert and his comrades were among the prize crews which sailed them there. After successfully delivering the prizes to Bergen they sailed in a small galleon to Dunkirk and thence travelled overland by horse and wagon to Paris.

On reaching the French capital, they were welcomed by Benjamin Franklin at his residence in Passy, a few miles from the city. They were well fed with breakfast and dinner, shown the gardens and taken on a tour of the town, where they twice saw the King and Queen of France with their retinue of nobles. Before they left Paris to begin their three hundred and sixty mile march to L'Orient. Dr Franklin paid their expenses and gave each man a silver crown piece as a parting gift and memento.

Charles Herbert sailed for America in the *Alliance* early in June and arrived back home in Newberryport after almost four years, on the 23rd August, 1780. He never returned to the sea; became a block-maker, and three years later married a local girl by whom he fathered fourteen children. That he never forgot his years as a rebel sailor, privateer and prisoner, is shown by a family reminiscence: that he valued as 'a sacred treasure' the crown piece presented to him by Benjamin Franklin, until the day he died – the 4th September, 1808.[2]

Andrew Sherburne, born in Portsmouth, New Hampshire, in 1765, joined the American Navy six months before his fourteenth birthday – and had been captured twice by the British before reaching the age of fifteen. The story of his adventures and sufferings before arriving at Plymouth in the *Fairy* in November, 1781, and his eventual imprisonment in the Old Mills, has been related in a previous chapter of this book.[3]

His little book, *'Memoirs of Andrew Sherbourne. A Pensioner of the Navy of the Revolution. Written by Himself"*, was published in Utica in1828, when Andrew was sixty-three. His recollections confirm stories of the horrors of the verminous *Dunkirk* prison ship moored on he Hamoaze at Plymouth. It would be better described as a reception ship for prisoners of war, and a distribution base for impressed men; although many prisoners spent short, but unforgettable, periods on board, whilst awaiting transfer. Like Charles Herbert, he told of the nit-picking thoroughness of the Courts of Admiralty, still held at 'The Fountain Tavern' in the town, where old judges 'in large white wigs' cross-examined them as to their origins.

Like so many before him who had suffered imprisonment afloat and under constant fear of impressment, he was genuinely happy to enter the prison on shore in January 1782. He recalled the groaning of the hinges as the great metal gate swung open to admit the prisoners and their military escort. A number of local traders were already busy in the yard before the inner gate; purveyors of all manner of permitted goods – and probably a few illegal ones – which they traded with the prisoners through the inner fence. There were milkmen and other vendors, including one old lady – who Andrew came to know as 'Old Aunt Anna' – who dealt from her large handcart, drawn by a boy, which supplied 'bread, butter tobacco, needles, thread, and every other article for which they might call.' It was probably 'Old Aunt Anna' who used to sell Charles Herbert his daily breakfast of bread and milk during his periods of affluence, and supplied him with tobacco and bread wholesale, for him to retail in the inner yard.

Once the inner gate had been opened, and they had been ushered in through a cordon of soldiers with fixed bayonets, prisoners from every corner of the great yard descended upon them in search of news or acquaintances. Twenty or more were from the Piscataqua river region of New Hampshire, but Andrew was the only new arrival from that area and had sailed before any of them, so he received far more news than he could give.

They welcomed him with a penny roll and a halfpennyworth of butter, and brought him old clothes and stockings, so that he could divest himself of a shirt infested with 'contemptible animals' which he had 'unavoidably brought from the *Dunkirk*.'

Andrew was lucky in his friends. A number of them were officers and were educated men who, conscious that Andrews was still a very young lad – and having seen so many boys go from bad to worse in the prisons – decided to take him in hand. At that time Sherburne had had only six months schooling, and was only semi-literate and numerate – although he could read the New Testament at a painfully slow pace and had ploughed his way through *Roderick Random*, but he had never written a word in his life. He applied himself to his lessons, and the dedication of his tutor, Richard Tibbets, changed the course of his life.

During Andrew's comparatively short stay in Old Mill, he found the food passably good, except in quantity. The bread, which they supposed was composed of 'rye, oats, barley and peas', was generally known as 'Brown George' and varied in quality from time to time. The prisoners were divided into unusually small messes, four men to a mess. He thought he remembered that they were allowed twelve ounces of bread and twelve ounces of meat per day, but it is more likely that their provisions were weighed out in fourteen-ounce 'pusser's pounds'.

Andrew has left a very full account of the jealously fair distribution of food at meal times:

'There had in time past, been serious difficulties about the division of the beef. The beef is weighed out to the cook; in the gross, and an allowance is made for the turn of the scale to each mess it is, therefore, divided into as many lots as there are messes; as equally as possible. The messes in rotation, send one of their number into the cook room every day. The mess which sends the man is called the Blind mess. This man superintends the division of the beef, which is stuck on the long iron skewers while raw. This blind mess, has its part by weight, without bone, and a sufficient quantity of fat out of the common stock to fry in. The blind mess generally calculated to have a feast on this day, something like a Yankee thanksgiving.'

There was no door between the cookhouse and the main yard, just a serving hatch through which the bowls of soup were passed. The meat was brought round through the Commissary's yard, between the inner and outer walls of the prison, and delivered to the cooks. Whilst the man from the blind mess superintended the cookery, and cooked the special portion for himself and his messmates, another ritual took place:

' …another man of the same mess, is blindfolded and kneels down over the tub of meat and one of the cooks who is not a prisoner, begins to call the numbers of messes in order. These numbers are one day called forwards, and the next day backwards.

'When the cook calls a mess by their number the blind[folded] man, with his forefinger, touches a lot of the meat, and notwithstanding all their punctiliousness, some lots will be worth as much again as others.'

Those who considered that they had drawn the short straw on a particular day, would wait until all messes had been called, when odds and ends remaining in the tub were 'judiciously divided' among them. When all the fair-play formalities were completed, and the meat was being delivered to the messes, representatives from each mess formed up in two ranks in front of the cook's serving hatch to collect their soup. The bowls, which were numbered on the rim and held two quarts of broth, were passed from hand to hand until a man recognised his mess number, took it, stepped back and delivered it for division between himself and his three messmates.

Whereas Charles Herbert had, in the main, limited his description of prisoner of war industry to his own efforts, Andrew Sherburne has more to say about the industrious among his fellow captives. He mentions proprietors of coffee stalls, makers of wooden spoons, punch ladles, knitting sheaths, stay-busks and those princes among prisoner of war workers, the makers of bone ship models. The names of some of these wonder workers and description of their output, will be discussed in a later chapter (see *The Arts and Crafts of Napoleonic and American Prisoners of War 1756-1816*, Chapter 5 (Part 2), THE SHIP MODEL MAKERS).

Those workers whose energies were centred on escape, carried on their exhausting employment until the end, usually by excavation. However, one variation which led to the successful flight of twelve Americans, occurred during Andrew's time at Plymouth. After hours of painstaking work, the iron grating which covered the window above the door in the west end wall of the Long Prison had been loosened but left in place. On the given day, the window was opened, the grating was removed, and a loose beam was passed through at an angle, just far enough to reach beyond the north wall of the 'necessary yard' (the heads, or toilet yard). Hammocks were strung together and fastened to the end of the beam, to make for easy descent onto the outside road. After their departure, the beam was withdrawn and carefully replaced, and the grating reinstalled, by accomplices who stayed behind.

Andrew Sherburne did not have a long experience of life as a rebel prisoner in England. About the last third of that time was spent in Old Mill Prison Hospital, having been laid low, physically and mentally by some mysterious ailment which was never definitely diagnosed.

He had arrived at Old Mill in January, 1782, and in March the Government had decreed that the revolutionaries were to be accepted as prisoners of war. The fear of trial for treason or piracy no longer hung over their heads, and King George's pardon was no longer necessary before they could be exchanged.

Andrew was still seriously ill when the joyful news arrived that cartel vessels were arriving in Plymouth Sound; doubly joyous when they learned that they were not to be exchanged in France, but shipped home to America. One vessel, the *Lady's Adventure*, was to sail for Boston and two more to other American ports. By special dispensation from the senior doctor, he was released from hospital bed into the care of the officers who had helped to educate him.[4]

Throughout the wars, the French had produced reports of British atrocities inflicted on prisoners of war. Some were accusations of brutality, expressed in terms which exceeded mere exaggeration to the point of being ridiculous. They spoke of the horrors of the prison ships; of prisoners starved to death to conserve provisions; of English doctors who took the pulse of their French patients whilst wearing gloves, or applied the tips of their swagger-canes to the patients' wrists. These calumnies were published mainly in France, probably to inflame even greater hatred against their captors.

It would seem that the French authorities began to believe their own propaganda, for, in 1798, the Directory sent a government official, M. Vochez, to England to see for himself. He was allowed free access to the prisons and hulks at Plymouth and Portsmouth without hindrance. He was surprised to find that the mortality rate on the ill-famed hulks was amazingly low, and found that all of the most extreme accusations were 'gross misrepresentations', and promised to acquaint his Minister with the facts when he returned to France. He did, however, find much to complain of in the quality of the provisions supplied to the depots, and emphasised his displeasure by bringing a legal action against the most outrageous of the food contractors, accusing them of short weight and inferior quality. In this he had the backing of some fair-minded Admiralty inspectors, but although Vochez proved his case and there was a short period of improvement at Old Mills and elsewhere, such lucrative swindles were never suppressed for long.

After the beginning of the (French) Revolutionary War in 1793, prisoners of war taken from France and her allies were brought into England in their hundreds and thousands and although the great new depot at Norman Cross had opened its gates in '97, it was never easy to find space to house our captive guests. In 1799, a few months after M. Vochez had returned to Paris, work began on the almost complete rebuilding of Old Mill Prison, which greatly increased its capacity to about five thousand. After its completion the new depot was renamed Millbay.

In 1802, Millbay, like all other depots, on land or afloat, was virtually cleared of prisoners, only to be refilled with a new captive population in the following year. Millbay was by now one of the larger depots, but in essentials little had changed; except that the Agent and the military had even greater burdens to bear as more and more prisoners flooded in. Sub-standard provisions and shortage of clothing were the principal grievances, and there is some evidence that the Commissary, or the Agent, conscientiously followed up some of those complaints. In 1806, a group of Spanish prisoners at Millbay, brought a successful case against a local firm of dishonest contractors, who suffered a painfully heavy fine.

Those Spanish complainants were possibly survivors of Nelson's great victory at Trafalgar, although most Spanish prisoners were sent to prisoner of war camps at Gibraltar. The huge Trafalgar catch of nearly five thousand Frenchmen was shipped to England, where the 210 officers were paroled to Wincanton or Crediton. The 4,589 other-ranks were first sent to a distribution centre, from whence they were apportioned to Forton and the nearby Portsmouth hulks; the prison ships at Chatham. Those sent to Plymouth were housed in Millbay or scattered among the eight hulks on the Hamaoze.

Perhaps the most colourful, if not the most convincing, description of life as a prisoner in Millbay, is to be found in *Le Négrier* ('The Slave-trader'), a little book by Édouard Corbière, a French privateer sailor. Corbière was only fifteen when his ship, the *Val de Grâce*, struck her colours without a fight, to HMS *Gibraltar*, in 1807. It was useless for the French privateer to put up any defence against the mighty 80-gun *Gibraltar*, and the embarrassment of unresistant submission was followed by further indignity. The British ship-of-the line sent off a longboat with the necessary block and tackle equipment , and hoisted the tiny *Val de Grâce* on to her deck, lock, stock, and barrel.

Francis Abell made a summary from a translation of that part of Corbière's memoir which told of his time at Millbay, and may be paraphrased as follows:

Édouard Corbière began with a scathing attack on the British war prisons in general, some of which must have been based on hearsay; saying that only those who had experienced life in an English war prison could realize the depths of utter depravity into which men could sink. Life on board a privateer would have inevitably resulted in a degree of worldliness beyond the ken of a landlubber lad of his age, but to be thrust into a society of largely undisciplined prisoners must have been traumatic indeed. He found that most aspects of life in Millbay were ruled by the 'Government of the *Pre*' which held despotic sway over anything which they presumed to judge; officiating over the many duels which were fought (in spite of the British law which forbad duelling between prisoners), and settling with an iron hand disputes in which they might have a vested interest. The everyday disputes and offences, such as stealing and general trouble-making were dealt with by the more democratically elected internal courts, common to most depots and hulks, but the *forts à bras* probably did some good by

controlling their own unruly brethren.

The regular 'Courts of Justice' were held 'within the space of twelve hammocks', walled in by a curtain of blankets. The elected President was usually a chief *maître d'armes,* literacy being an important qualification, as he had to read out the charge and the verdict. The sentences were usually announced in stripes, as flogging was the normal punishment, but their powers were unlimited. Nine out of ten offences involved pilfering, vicious gambling, excessive blasphemy, or the heinous crime of stealing another man's food ration; but there was the occasional *cause célèbre.*

Corbière recounted one serious and horrific case which came before the Court. A scheme was in hand which went so far beyond the dreams of any previous escape attempt, that it might be better described as an uprising. A tunnel of amazing length had been dug out which, when completed, stretched for 532 yards to an outlet into a meadow. At that time there were about five thousand prisoners in Millbay and the plan was for one party to overcome and disarm the guard, so making it possible for the whole prison to be cleared of captives.

Had it not been for a French traitor named Jean Caffé, who sold information to the British authorities, escape on a truly grand scale may have succeeded, at least in part. On the evening of intended departure, the long tunnel was packed with more than a quarter of a mile of men waiting for the off; but when the first men emerged from the outlet, they were confronted by a troop of Scots soldiers – and a disconsolate cry of *'Le trou est vendu'* echoed back through the tunnel.

Jean Caffé was a rather pathetic creature, a witless deadbeat who had owed his existence to the consideration and charity of his fellows. Pathetic or not, his crime was so unforgivable that his punishment was proportionately terrible. He was dragged before a gathering of all the prisoners, his head was shaved, and he was flung down on to a table and pinioned. A prisoner who had once been a professional tattooist entered the scene to carry out his part of the punishment; pricking and branding his forehead with the inscription:

'FLETRI POUR AVOIR VENDU 5000 DE SES COMARADES DANS NUIT DU 4 SEPTEMBRE 1807'

And that was not all. Caffé was taken to a well, thrown down and large stones tipped after him, until his cries were silenced. Corbière says that the informer's execution brought no punishment from the authorities, the British commandant opining that he deserved his fate.[5]

If another part of Corbiere's account can be fully believed – it makes a good story, anyway! – both he and Ivan, the captain of the *Val de Grâce,* made their escapes from Millbay in a spectacular fashion. At the time of his capture, Ivan had not long returned to his ship from a ball in Calais, and was still in his dancing gear when brought before the captain of the *Gibraltar* to hand over his sword – and in that same rig he entered Millbay. The entrance of the handsome Ivan, elegant in his fancy clothes of silk stockings, breeches, ruffles, and laced coat, caused much amused comment amongst the prisoners; but some of the comments went beyond good-natured chaffing. One of the most powerful of the *forts à bras* so angered him with taunts of 'armchair sailor' and 'carpet knight', that a fight ensued which ended with a severe battering of the taunter – and acclaim for the victor. That first day in Millbay, established Ivan's position in the prison hierarchy, and earned him a triumphal progress round the airing ground and his election as a *Chef de Pré*.

From the start, Ivan became a popular and respected character among the great mass of prisoners. The young Edouard hero-worshipped him to a rather worrying degree, and Ivan's romantic good looks had already caught the eye of Mrs Milliken, the attractive young wife of the depot's Purser. We are left to guess how far the affair went, but she bought him presents and was clearly smitten. Corbière, himself, must have been something of a pretty-boy, for of all the boys in the prison – and there must have been hundreds – he was chosen to work in the Purser's office in the outer yard, returning to the prison each evening. It was said that he was chosen to save him from the 'wild, wicked world' of the war prison, but he soon became a pampered novelty, indulged by Mrs Millikin, her servant Sarah and visiting friends. The favourite amusement of these ladies, was to dress him up in female attire, and the young privateer, who must have had a rather wide streak of femininity in his make-up, says 'they were good enough to say that, except for my rolling gait... I should pass for a distinguished-looking girl.'

After a happy period of un-prisoner-of-war-like luxury, his happiness was shattered one morning when Mrs Milliken gave him the news: Ivan had escaped! Any feelings of gladness for his captain and idol were smothered by the devastating disbelief that his friend should have left him behind.

A few days later 'a young lady' left through the back door of the Milliken home, and stepped out on to the road to Plymouth. Corbière remembered the next few hours as the worst in his adventurous life. Completely lost and ogled by intimidating strangers, 'she' was on the point of finding a way back to the Purser's house, when an old Jew with a sack on his shoulder came close and whispered his name. It was Ivan!

Édouard followed his captain friend to a safe house, where he was told the plan of escape – which, in both cases had been masterminded by Mrs Milliken but... to curtail a long account ...they had intended next day to set off towards Bigbury, about fifteen miles further round the coast, where they might contact a smuggler to take them across the Channel. Ivan had provided himself with thirty one-pound notes of bribery-money; forgeries manufactured in Millbay for which he had paid a genuine guinea (we know that this is not at all an improbable part of the story – see *The Arts and Crafts of Napoleonic and American Prisoners of War 1756-1816*, Chapter 11, THE FORGERS AND COINERS). However, next morning circumstance changed the plan. Somewhere not far outside the city limits, they spotted a small empty boat riding at anchor close inshore. They swam out to it and were soon under way, heading for anywhere, as long as it was far from England. After days of suffering from lack of water and provisions, they were sighted and picked up by the *Gazelle* out of St Malo. Courbière described their saviour as a French *'aventurier'* and in her they sailed for Martinique.

Although the possibility of escape loomed large in the dreams and ambitions of many prisoners of war, some would have tried to make the best of the situation, and put their time to as good as use as possible, and many settled in to what might be a long wait for freedom. Amongst the many activities which took place within Millbay Prison was the working of its own French prisoner of war

Masonic Lodge. That a Lodge under the name *'Des Amis Réunis'* – Reunited Friends – was operating in 1809 is known from a Masonic Certificate issued in that year. Another confirmation of its existence, is an endorsement on the reverse of a Certificate issued by a Lodge in the Island of St Domingo to a French Master Mason, François Lescamela:

> *'Vu à la R..'. les amis Réunis à L'o de Mill -prison, Plymouth le 4e Jour du 4e Mois de l'an de V .'. L .'. 5809. Séanetenante.*
> *Gme. Brousse.*
> Inspected at the Lodge of 'Reunited Friends' held at the Mill Prison, Plymouth, the 4th day of the 4th month of the year of the True Light 5809; In open Lodge.'

Guillaume Brousse was a French surgeon and Master of the Mill Lodge, Plymouth.

In 1812 the prison buildings were again extended, to accommodate a further 2,000 prisoners and every inch of hammock-space was needed. When the United States declared war in that year, some Americans were sent to Millbay, although most were sent to the Medway, Portsmouth and Plymouth hulks, Stapleton, and, later, to Dartmoor Prison.

With so much building and extension going on at Millbay over the years since 1799, one might imagine that by 1812, conditions would have improved and become less hard for the prisoners. Henry Woollcombe, however, in his *History Of Plymouth*[6] writing early in that same year, indicates otherwise:

> 'The present buildings are in a miserable state, but we understand they are to be removed immediately and rebuilt on an improved plan...There is a great deficiency of fresh water. Gambling and vices of a more heinous nature prevail in this prison; no public worship is performed here. Happily the children have been separated and sent home from this hot-bed of vice and corruption.'

The history of the American prisoners of war in Britain, who had been taken in the Anglo-American War of 1812, is told in the chapters on the prison ships and Dartmoor Depot. It is mainly one of bitterness and hatred, so it is pleasant to include an exception to that generalisation. A fine example of the acknowledgment between captive and captor, of gallantry and courage on either side was evidenced when a brave American officer died in Millbay, in 1813.

Lieutenant W.H.Allen, had been first lieutenant of the USS *United States*, in that famous action on the 25th October, 1812, when the American frigate captured the British frigate HMS *Macedonian*. He so distinguished himself on that day, that he was promoted and made captain of the 10-gun brig USS *Argus*. In August 1813, the *Argus* was cruising off the Irish coast in search of English prey, when she encountered a brig of similar fire power, HMS *Pelican*. On this occasion the English vessel was victorious, and Captain Allen was seriously wounded, losing a leg in the action. When he was brought to Millbay, where he died, it was remembered that, after the capture of the *Macedonian* a year earlier, the many British prisoners had testified to his humanity and kindness. He was buried with honour, as one Plymouth newspaper reported:

> 'The Funeral Procession as it moved from the Mill Prison to the Old Church, afforded a scene singularly impressive to the prisoners, who beheld with admiration the respect paid by a gallant, conquering enemy to the fallen hero. 500 British Marines first marched in slow

time, with arms reversed; the band of the Plymouth Division of Marines followed, playing the most solemn tunes. An officer of Marines in military mourning came after these. Two interesting black boys, the servants of the deceased, then preceded the hearse. One of these bore his master's sword, and the other his hat. Eight American officers followed the hearse, and the procession was closed with a number of British Naval officers.

'On arrival of the body at the Old Church, it was met by the officiating Minister, and three volleys over the grave closed the scene.'

It would be difficult to walk through modern Plymouth today without encountering reminders of incidents in the city's abundant history; but it would be even more difficult to find reference which records the fact that many thousands of foreign captives filled its prisons and its prison ships, between 1756 and 1814. Except for a few street names – Millbay Road, and Millbay Dockyard etc. – and a few prisoner of war relics in the town museum, their story has been lost in the mists of time.

However, amongst the numerous memorials on Plymouth Hoe, there is one tiny uninscribed, and largely unnoticed, granite cross, set flush with the surface of one of the pathways. Of this I may have remained unaware, had I not been browsing through a back number of *The Officer Magazine*.[7] The cross marks the spot where, in 1797, three Irish Marines were cruelly executed. 1797 was a year of uncertainties and worries for Britain and its peoples. The Fishguard Affair, had convinced many that a full-scale invasion from France was imminent; the Bank of England Restriction of Cash Payments, which caused a loss of faith in paper money; and a restlessness among the downtrodden, inspired by the revolutionary spirit in France. This was the year of the Spithead Mutiny which quickly spread to the Nore and along the south coast.

A number of sailors were hanged at Plymouth, or suffered an unbelievable number of lashes. Four Irish marines, McGennis, Lee, Coffy and Branning, brought the troubles ashore, with a plan to free the French prisoners of war at Millbay Depot, but were reported to the authorities by a young drummer boy, who had heard them swearing oaths to that effect.

McGennis was sentenced to receive 1,000 lashes and transportation to Botany Bay for life. The other three were to be shot, their sentences to be carried out on the 8th July, 1797.

'On that day 10,000 troops from the Plymouth area were assembled in a hollow square at the place of execution, along with a huge crowd of civilians. At exactly noon McGennis was brought from the Citadel and received the first 500 of his 1000 lashes. Then, at half past one, Lee, Coffy and Branning were brought out. It was a grim procession, led by a Royal Marine band, their instruments draped in black crêpe, playing the *Dead March from Saul*. Each prisoner was preceded by his coffin, and on reaching the place of execution, the men knelt to pray. Lee was attended by the Rev. Dr. Hawker, Coffy and Branning by Fr. Thomas Flynn.'

After they had prayed, they were ordered to kneel on their coffins; a Royal Marine officer then covered their faces as the firing squad moved into position. Coffy and Branning were killed instantly by the first discharge, but Lee was still alive until an officer approached and delivered the *coup de grâce* with his pistol. The troops were marched away, and the bodies put into their coffins and removed. A short while later, Father Thomas Flynn had the small cross placed at the spot where the three men died. This was a courageous action for it was he who founded the Roman Catholic church at Devonport, the first since the Reformation, which put him in a rather invidious position.

*****

Towards the end of the nineteenth century Millbay was converted into a military barracks, but during the Crimean War (1853–6), thousands of Russian prisoners of war were confined within its high walls.

*****

1. The story of the dog-eaters reached the London newspapers and caused something of a furore. Prisoners were questioned through the Agent as to the truth of whether or not they resorted to such an extreme through near starvation. A number of tales of similar unappetising feasting are told, featuring dogs, horses, rats, snails and small birds, not all of which can be dismissed as memoir padding.

2. Charles Herbert made the last entry in his Journal in August 1780. His work remained in manuscript until 1847, when it was published under the title: *A Relic of the Revolution*.

3. See Chapter 2. THE WAR OF AMERICAN INDEPENDENCE.

4. In November of that same year, 1782, Andrew, who was not yet eighteen, became a prisoner for the third time, and found himself on the terrible prison hulk *Jersey*, in New York Harbour. Sherburne had joined the letter-of-marque brig, *Scorpion*, where the Mate was Richard Tibbits (who was Andrew's tutor in Old Mill) and sailed for the West Indies. The *Scorpion* was captured by HMS *Amphion*.

5. This story of tattooing as a punishment for disloyalty, or informing is not unique. We will read of Americans carrying out similar atrocities on men whom they considered traitors.

6. Henry Woollcombe's *History Of Plymouth* remains in manuscript and unpublished.

7. *The Officer Magazine.* November/December, 1994, page 23.

Chapter Fifteen

Forton Depot
The old 'Fortune' Prison at Gospel, Hampshire

FORTON DEPOT, SITUATED ABOUT A MILE from Gosport, and two miles from Portsmouth, was one of the early civil prisons which were first brought into use to deal with the overflow of war prisoners which increased as the Seven Years' War drew towards its end. In 1761 some two thousand French captives were marched in from Portchester Castle, so the adaptation must have been pretty well established by that time. Few descriptions of its appearance in those early years have survived, but some details can be garnered from the diaries, journals and memoirs of American and French prisoners who occupied it during the War of American Independence and later wars.

Several manuscript diaries and memoirs which contain references to everyday life of the prisoners and to Forton Depot itself, are preserved in American libraries and historical societies. Two are the works of American diarists, Timothy Connor and Jonathan Carpenter[1], who, like the Danish diarists Jens Krog and H.S.Engels on the British prison hulks, obviously dipped into each others' journals on occasion.

Early entries mention Forton as comprising 'two large spacious buildings', separated by an extensive exercise yard. This ties in well with the Commissioners for Sick and Wounded Seamen[2] – colloquially known as the 'Sick and Hurt Office' – assessment that Forton Depot was 'capable of containing 2,168 prisoners with a sufficient airing ground for that number'. In fact, one diarist mentions another three-quarters of an acre of level ground which they used as an additional airing yard. One of the buildings was reserved for captive officers and the other for the men – almost all of them sailors and privateers – with one part set aside for 'under-officers' or NCOs. The crews were separated from their officers, at the latters' request, and they certainly had better accommodation than their men. Their rooms were spacious and fitted with fireplaces, whilst the common sailors' prison had only one fire place, which the prisoners could use 'alternately'!

The officers also had a covered night latrine tub which was emptied for them daily – which indicates that they were also allowed servants in the depot, as they would have been had they

---

Above. View of the market at Forton Depot. Artist unknown.

been paroled. However, the men were each provided with a hammock, a coverlet, straw bedding and a straw pillow; but one prisoner, Nathaniel Fanning complained that the beds and pillows 'were full of knits [*sic*] and lice.'

Some further subdivision of available space must have taken place once France and Spain entered the war – in 1778 and 1779 – as the Americans were then segregated from continental prisoners. This was made necessary by Britain's complicated reasoning that Americans were not yet admitted to be 'foreigners' and – until March 1782 – were not even categorised as 'prisoners of war'; but were officially regarded as rebels, renegades or pirates! An Act of George III[3] made it clear that Americans taken in arms were to be classified as criminals guilty of 'the crime of high treason' and those taken at sea 'guilty of piracy'.

The ambiguous status of the American, as prisoner of war or traitor, has been discussed in a previous chapter, and he certainly had far more to worry about than just his loss of freedom, the quality of his prison sustenance, or the condition of his prison: technically, at least, his life hung in the balance. On arrival at Portsmouth or other ports of landing, the prisoners were taken on board guard-ships and brought before tribunals for close examination, after which they were committed to Forton, Old Mill or elsewhere, each man bearing with him a warrant which branded him a criminal awaiting sentence for his crimes of:

> ' …rebellion, piracy and high treason on his Britannic Majesty's high seas, there [Forton] to lay during his Majesty's pleasure until he see fit to pardon or otherwise dispose of him…'

Thus leaving him in a state of anxiety and terror as to his ultimate fate. In such circumstance it is small wonder that a fair number took what they were persuaded was the only way out of their predicament – turned their coats and joined the Royal Navy. Nathaniel Fanning, in his *'Memoirs of an American Naval Officer'*, said that a great deal of pressure and threat was used to intimidate Americans into defecting. Both during the passage from their place of capture, and afterwards on the guard-ships at the time of their questioning, they were cajoled or bullied, and only sent to the Depot if all persuasion failed. Fanning and his shipmates were told: 'You are a set of rebels, and it is more than probable that you will all be hanged on our arrival at Portsmouth', and that as they neared the port, their attention was drawn to a warship in the harbour and they were told, 'There is she on board of which you are to be hanged.' Those that did defect were not immediately sent to serve on a British man-of-war. They had first to wait, sometimes for quite a long period, until they had received the King's pardon, and only then were they allowed to fight for Britain against their homeland.

The waiting was a time of danger at the hands of their fellow captives. On the 22nd January, 1777, a committee of 'officers and Seamen and others' drew up an agreement that any American found to have volunteered to join the British Navy, should suffer thirty-nine lashes, and have one ear cut off. (During the War of 1812, a defector was sometimes tattooed on the forehead with a '**T**' for 'Traitor'.)

Compared with prisoners of war of any other nationality, our transatlantic cousins had a hard time of it from the outset. Not knowing whether they were heading for a prison or the gallows, some had experienced a long punishment of uncertainty even before they reached England. Many had been taken as privateersmen in the Channel or off the British coast, but others had experienced nightmare voyages across the Atlantic, stowed deep in the bowels of a British man-of-war, often after weeks or months in prison camps in Nova Scotia, or in the prison hulks off New York. Jonathan Carpenter spent some time on a prison ship moored in Rhode Island Harbour before he and his fellow captives were sent to England. Their transport was the 28-gun *Andromeda*, the prisoners 'put in irons and crowded Down between Decks, half Starved like Poor devils'. Not all transported prisoners were 'put in irons', and when they were it could seldom have been as a punishment. This harsh treatment was more often used in a small vessel, as a protection against uprising and possible mutiny. Timothy Connor, who was transported on the large 74-gun *Terrible*, did not mention irons, but also complained of being half-starved, during the two months on three-quarter rations he spent as a prisoner on board. 'Sometimes we had nothing but burgout and peas without salt, butter or meat; only what we begged from some of the sailors, as it happened there were some of our countrymen on board.' – so they were lucky that at least some of their countrymen had defected.

Timothy Connor had begun his short career as a privateer when he joined the crew of the private armed brig, *Rising States*, off Cape Cod, in January 1777. They headed for the Azores in search of merchant shipping, then for European waters, arriving in the Bay of Biscay early in March. There they made their first two English captures which they manned with prize crews and sailed into French ports for condemnation and auction. Full of confidence, they headed northward into the English Channel, where they took their third and last prize, a British sloop – before sailing into trouble and the end of their adventure.

Connor's journal account of their capture by HMS *Terrible* might be written off as boastful, when he said that the tiny *Rising States* 'got out our own stern chases, and began firing…', were it not for the entry in the British battleship's log, which recorded that '…she hoisted American Colours…she fired two stern Chases'. Connor was probably also right when he considered that the reason they were not blown out of the water was that they had on board the English prisoners from their own three prizes.

For most of those who had been captured in American waters, the worst period of their captivity was over by the time they reached Forton, at least physically; but mentally they suffered the uncertainty of their standing until the last months of their war. That they were pleased to get ashore from the British men-of-war was mentioned in many a memoir. Carpenter wrote that when he was sent to Forton, he 'rejoiced at the Opportunity to go to Prison'; and another memoirist, Caleb Foot, said that the difference was 'like coming out of Hell and going into Paradise.' Encouraging words for the depot garrison, had they but heard them; but the iniquitous position of the American made it hardly surprising that the history of Forton should contain more than its fair share of Yankee escapes and escape attempts. The Forton alarm guns becoming all too familiar to the inhabitants of Gosport and Portsmouth.

The guards and local militia at Forton Prison was kept on the *qui vive* at all times, but 1778 was a particularly busy, but unsuccessful, year for them. The year before, thirty Americans had got away, but most were recaptured. These latter were so severely punished that their complaints were reported in the local and London newspapers; but their punishment did not deter others. It could well be that those newspaper reports inspired the generous public contributions which poured into a subscription which was organised in support for the Americans later that year. On Christmas Day, 1777, Timothy Connor wrote: '…now the people begin to use humanity throughout England. There are subscription books opened in many parts of England for our relief.'

Most of the donated money went to the Forton and Old Mill depots, and surprisingly large sums were raised. In Cornhill, London, £800 was subscribed in 'less than an hour,' and a 'meeting of Middlesex justices raised £3,815. 17s. 6d.' The first distribution of small sums in Forton began in January of the following year, and continued on and off until at least 1782. However, such generosity did not discourage escape, in fact it may have been essential to the successful accomplishment of many a getaway. 'Blind-eye' bribes on the inside, and the payments to cross-Channel smugglers, all had to come from somewhere.

Throughout that war, individual and large-scale escapes were constantly being planned and attempted. It was at Forton in '78 that fifty-seven Americans carried out a 'wooden horse' type of decampment, and it would seem they all got clear away. The *cachot* – the Black Hole or punishment cell – was beneath the sleeping quarters of their part of the prison and it was not too difficult for them to dig through to the cell below. From the *cachot* they excavated a tunnel which went under the outer wall of the depot. The hole in the floor was covered with a mattress and the excavated earth was secreted in the chimney and in the hammocks for which they hoped to have no further use.

Almost all of the large-scale escape plans were based on excavation – known to the prisoners as 'mining for elopement'. A member of one such team of American 'elopers', Luke Mathewman, has left us a few technical details of a Forton getaway:

> 'Over or through the roof of the prison, at the top, there are ventilators for extracting the foul air from the prison; they are about eighteen inches square, and come through the ceiling that forms a cockloft; these we removed, and getting through the holes of the ceiling, and laying on our backs, passed the bags of dirt we had dug in undermining the prison, and stacked them on the ceiling. In this manner we dug; the first hole was about 40 feet, in which we were found out. The next we attempted we were more fortunate; we dug 42 feet; the method of calculating was ten bags to a foot, and a 100 bags was usually a night's work.
>
> 'At length we broke up in the cellar kitchen of an old woman, who, being frightened, fell backwards, but recovering, called "the guard! the guard!", however, we soon gagged her, and about sixty got out of the hole.'

There were numerous other attempts and successes that year, including an uprising supposedly against the callous treatment of prisoner-patients by the hospital doctors and staff – during which eleven Americans made their getaway. Only a fortnight later another planned mass exodus took place. On this occasion it was a Franco-American joint effort, and although the Westminster Militia, who were encamped on a nearby common, were alerted by the alarm guns, twenty-five had made their getaway before the arrival of the troops.

Almost from the start of this outbreak of break-outs, the Admiralty had made an expensive misjudgment in its security plans. The usual reward for the recapture of an absconding prisoner was about half a guinea, but in July 1777 the reward was increased to £5 for every American returned. Overnight it created bands of Hampshire bounty-hunters, who became known as 'five-pounders'.

Many escapers were returned, but if anything the escapes increased in number. The wily Americans had soon realised that they were on to a good thing, and were soon planning escapes which were never meant to succeed! In cooperation with their English hunters they would escape, hide for a few days, then be brought in by their 'captor' – to split the reward fifty-fifty. Sometimes a guard had to be brought into the subterfuge – despite the three-way split – five pounds was a considerable sum at that time. The CSWS (Commissioners for Sick and Wounded Seamen) lists 536 escapes from Forton alone between June 1777 and April 1782, but does not break that figure down to show success and failure or if it also includes men who had escaped more than once.

The degree of anxiety caused by the Yankee absconders is illustrated by the fact that the security unit which had guarded the depot in 1777 had been made up of only ten militiamen, had grown to two officers and sixty men by mid-1778.

It would be interesting to know how such a plague of security-breaking was dealt with. One of the above stories tells that the escape route was via the Black Hole, but one might imagine that a whole block of those unpleasant punishment cells would have been needed to deal with the rebellious 'rebels'. If such a block existed, it was not recorded by any of our diarists, though Fanning, Foot, Carpenter and Connor mention the Black Hole more than once.

A notice board which detailed privileges and punishments was permanently on display in the airing ground. The two principal punishments were 'Closer Confinement' and 'Reduction of Allowances'. The prisoners would probably have considered the second to be the greater punishment. 'Closer Confinement' meant, of course, the Black Hole – except in the case of murder, when the culprit was usually sent to the local lock-up or county gaol until his trial. The prisoner who was sent to the Black Hole – described by Connor as 'a very small room with neither bed nor bedding to lie on, but the soft side of a good plank' – had to exist on half the regular ration. This would not seem too much to endure for a short spell, but the would-be escaper who was brought back to Forton could face a long period, even as long as forty hungry days, in his comfortless cell – and it did not end there. As in other depots, the half-ration part of his sentence could be extended until all expenses involved in his recapture had been recovered, and until any damage to Government property had been paid for.

From all that has been written so far, it may seem that the Americans spent all their time boring through, digging under or climbing over prison walls. Indeed, there was probably no one who would not have confessed that his greatest ambition was to escape to France, and from thence homeward. However, Forton did, in fact, have its own social life, limited though it may have been. The prisoners were allowed out of their buildings each day, but not 'till the sun was half an hour high' and they were encouraged to spend as much of the daylight hours out of doors for their health's sake. To encourage this, a large open-sided gazebo-like structure, complete with seats, was erected in the middle of the exercise yard.

Like almost all British depots, they had the great privilege of an open market. Situated inside the main gate, and open between nine in the morning until two in the afternoons, they could buy from English vendors any little luxuries they could afford and, of equal importance, they were allowed to sell any artefacts they were capable of making. Thus, for all but the indolent, there was plenty to keep both body and mind active: exercise and games, planning escapes, plaiting straw and other saleable pursuits, penning complaints and writing letters home for example. Memoirs tell us that the latter activity was made possible for a number of prisoners who had entered Forton as illiterates, by their attendance at one of the little schools which were regularly held in the main prison building. Reading, writing, arithmetic and navigation were taught in those classes, and two Frenchmen in the officers' prison who had set themselves up as language masters, taught French.

Although the depot must have had its sick bays from the beginning, probably staffed by attendants and with a visiting doctor, it was not until 1777 that a hospital building was erected, well clear of the prisons, with beds enough for one in eight of the prisoner population. Before that time the sick had been sent to the naval hospital in Haslar at Gosport. Most depot hospitals earned more brickbats than compliments, but their presence was much better than their absence, although, as we have seen, complaints against this one were convincingly used as a cover for a multiple escape attempt – and in 1782 John Howard reported its wards were 'not clean'.

John Howard's visit to Forton in 1779 revealed that there was a great difference in the living conditions of the Americans and their captive French allies. There were 251 prisoners in the American part of the depot and 177 Frenchmen who were living in under-nourished squalor. Their meat ration was of poor quality, the bread loaves were underweight (perhaps victims of the 'Pusser's pound'!), and 'the straw in the mattresses had been reduced to dust by long use, and many of them had been emptied to clear them of vermin. The floors of the hospital and sleeping quarters… were dirty and offensive.' The probable explanation was that, whilst the Americans were supported by extra allowances from their Government and recent British subscriptions – and perhaps because similar treatment might have induced a mini-revolution to add to their larger one! – the French were for the most part dependent on their basic ration. This meant that they were in the hands of the crooked contractors – callous rogues who could not have operated without the connivance of depot officials.

Howard advised the French to complain through official channels, but was told that all communications, in and out of Forton, were examined by Newsham, the Agent, so complaint was useless. Connor, speaking of a visit of the Commissioner to the Americans in Forton 'to Rigtifey out Grivernces', said 'non of us Culd get an Opportunity to Speek to him on account of the Agent, the Doctor and the Clerk keppet Close by His Side.' So the French probably had reason to doubt the efficacy of any complaint. It was indeed part of Agent Newsham's job to intercept and censor incoming and outgoing mail, and to keep a close check on the news coming in from the outside world; but if memoirs are to be believed, he either neglected those duties, or they were too easily circumvented. It seems that, through friends and visitors to the market, they ran an efficient unofficial postal service, even receiving letters from their countrymen who had escaped to London or France. The diaries verify that the Americans were kept well supplied with news and newspapers – even sending helpful (bribed) messengers into Gosport and Portsmouth to fetch them – and news came in with each delivery of newcomers to the depot.

John Howard recorded the total number of American prisoners sent to Forton between mid-June 1777 and early November 1782

as amounting to about 1,200, though there were seldom more than 400 at Forton at any particular date. Only sixty-nine died there during those years.

An American prisoner-population similar to that at Gosport was housed in the Old Mill Depot at Plymouth, and smaller numbers were from time to time confined near to their places of landing for short periods. It would seem that lack of clothing was of the greatest concern when they first arrived. Most had been robbed of their sea-chests when first captured and possessed only the tatters they stood in, minus silver buckles or anything of value which may have caught the captor's eye. By the winter of 1777 the Government did supply bare necessities of clothing and continued to do so spasmodically until 1782 when, on the 25th March, the American captives were acknowledged to be 'prisoners of war' for the first time. From that time on the clothing situation grew so serious that the 'Sick and Hurt Office' suggested that if the American Government did not clothe their subjects, we should send them all home! What with British subscriptions, which brought each prisoner from 6d. to 1s.2d. per week – the officers received double – plus some second-hand clothing, and American aid organised by Benjamin Franklin, Minister Plenipotentiary for America in Paris, the American who did his best to make ends meet probably suffered less than most prisoners of war.

As Britain did not recognise America as a sovereign state, no official 'prisoner of war' exchange system could operate, but the Admiralty turned a blind eye to arrangements between Franklin and an English Member of Parliament. This informal cartel was delayed by all manner of hold-ups, French passports and the Royal pardon, and it was not until June 1779 that 119 jubilant Americans left Forton for France, and a like number of British prisoners returned to England. Another small number were exchanged in the following year, but formal exchange only took place after they were admitted to be prisoners of war, in March 1782, when they were all sent across the Atlantic to be exchanged for British prisoners in North America.

It is said that when the exchanged prisoners left Forton to join the cartel ship they were escorted by an English band which played 'Yankee Doodle', and that after exchange the Americans chanted a Forton Prison song:

> 'In Support of the thirteen states
> For which we endured Captivity
> The Motto now that cures all fates
> For me is Death or Liberty
> For me is Death or Liberty
> And let's be resolute and brave
> See how just our cause appears
> For Independence we shall have
> If we fight for it fifth [fifty?] Years.'

Any prisoners taken after march 1782, were sent to France on the 3rd March, 1783.

With the departure of the Americans, Britain enjoyed a decade of brittle peace, that is until the spring of 1793, when she joined the European coalition in its battles against Revolutionary France. By July, when there were already nearly a thousand French prisoners in Forton, the guards were kept as busy as they had been during the previous war. A report to the Admiralty at that time informed their Lordships that:

'The French at Forton continue extremely restless and turbulent, and cannot bear their captivity with moderation and temper though they are exceedingly well supplied with provisions and every necessity their situation requires. A sailor made a desperate attempt to disarm a sentinel through the bars of the compartment where he was confined (the Black Hole?).

'The sentry with great exertion disengaged himself, and fired at the offender, but wounded unfortunately another prisoner, not the aggressor. Friday se'nnight, the guard discovered a plot by which several prisoners had planned an escape over the wall by tying together their hammocks and blankets. The sentry on duty fired in at the windows, and hit one of the rioters, who is since dead. Three French prisoners were dangerously wounded while endeavouring to escape from Forton. One of them with a drawn knife rushed upon a guard, a private of the Anglesea Militia, who fired at him. The Frenchman seized him by the coat, whereupon the guard ran the offender through the body.'

The above report makes it clear that the guards were now permitted to deal with escape attempts with a far heavier hand than the Americans had felt ten years earlier. There is only one record of an American being killed by a guard at Forton, and that was a personal contention between the victim and a militia corporal. It is doubtful that there was ever an official order which directed guards to fire on fleeing Yankees.

In April, a particularly alert guard patrolling the space between the palisade and the outside wall, was conscious of a strange scraping sound which seemed to come from beneath his feet. Investigation revealed two loose boards in the sleeping quarters, which covered the entrance to a tunnel already twenty-seven feet long, which went under the palisade and was heading for the outer wall.

We have one recollection of Forton Depot which cannot be omitted. In his *Souvenirs Militaires de Doisy Villargennes',* the young French Sous-Lieutenant Adelbert Doisy de Villargennes, of the 26th French Regiment of the Line, tells of a visit to the Forton Depot in 1811.

He had been taken prisoner after the Battle of Fuentes d'Oñoro on the 3rd May, and must have been one of the most fortunate of prisoners from the beginning to the end of his captivity.

After a short time in hospital, where he seems to have been befriended by just about every British officer he met, he was sent to Fort Bellin at Lisbon, where prisoners were held until transported to England. At Fort Bellin, which was garrisoned by the 26th *English* Regiment, the '26' on his cap-badge and uniform was observed, and he became more an honoured guest than a captive. In his memoir he described his delivery to England as 'a very pleasant ten days' voyage to Portsmouth. 'I fared well during the voyage, a quantity of delicacies having been provided for my use by my over-hospitable hosts of the 26th [British] Regiment.'

All this kindness and generosity from the enemy would seem to have injected Doisy with such a massive dose of Anglophilia that he judged the merits of the British prisoner of war system entirely upon his own spoilt treatment – describing his unfortunate countrymen on the prison hulks as 'refractory and incorrigible'.

Doisy landed at Gosport with sixty other prisoners, and was himself lodged in the officers' building to await his official *parole d'honneur* papers and transfer to a parole town. Meanwhile, he and his fellow officers were allowed to leave Forton for a few hours each day, and to wander about the town.

Describing one of their wanderings, he tells us: 'Walking on the road encircling the prison – the prison was large enough to contain upwards of five thousand men, and was guarded by two regiments of militia – I was startled to hear a loud cry of "Mon lieutenant!" Those who accompanied me turned quickly about, when the same voice repeated "Mon lieutenant!" joining my name to the cry.'

It transpired that the hailing came from his foster-brother, Germain Lamy, an other-rank soldier who had been claimed into the 26th Regiment by his sous-lieutenant relative. At Doisy's request Lamy was attached to his company, but after the Battle of Busaco there was no answer when his name was called at muster. Villargennes, on whom had 'devolved the sad duty of announcing to his mother the news of his premature end', was naturally overjoyed to find him 'well and hearty'. After approaching the Governor of Forton Depot with his story, he was given permission to spend the day inside the prison.

His account of that visit, in which he says: 'I ought here, in truth and in justice, to combat an erroneous belief relative to the harsh treatment of prisoners of war…' carries on in a spate of Pro-British exaggeration which misleads the seeker after truth at least as much as the writings of the Anglophobic General Pillet or General Simon:

'Although a prison, in reality, it more resembled a huge barracks wherein reigned the most perfect order under a severe but humane rule. We did not hear sobs of despair, we did not see sadness in the eyes of the inmates, but on the contrary all around there was peals of laughter, or patriotic songs resounding. My foster-brother [Germain Lamy] led me towards a comfortable corner which he occupied with a friend. There I noticed a decent looking bed, and some other modest furniture which they might have bought with their own money. The kitchen occupied a neighbouring compartment, and was used by 200 men, and the smell issuing from it did not indicate that the inhabitants were starving. I stayed to dinner. I would not go so far as to say that the meal was delicious, but the dishes were sufficient and of good quality, and although served on pewter dishes and plates, with knives and forks of the same metal, they were accompanied by such a friendly reception that the memory of that dinner has always been a pleasant one for me. Wine or liquors found no place on the table, the rules of the prison not permitting their use, nevertheless we were not reduced to drinking cold water, for we had an abundance of that most excellent ale which England alone produces.'

Doisy goes into a fair amount of detail regarding the Forton prison market, which he says was held twice a week. He may have used Germain Lamy as a means of describing some of the profit-making activities of the industrious amongst the prisoners, or perhaps Germain was indeed something of a jack-of-all-trades. As the son of a basketmaker, he knew enough of the craft to join a group whose products found a ready sale to British visitors to the market, not only for their cheapness but the quality of the French workmanship. Lamy then went into the straw-plait business, and here Doisy helps to perpetuate the myth that prisoner of war straw-work was made from Government-supplied raw material. He says that 'straw in considerable quantity was furnished to the men for their bedding', and that Germain, who had learned the art of plaiting and straw hat and bonnet making, was soon making more money than his old father could at home. That profitable enterprise was ended by the Government ban designed to protect the English cottage industry.

In an unbelievably short time, Lamy was working in another industry: the manufacture of bone 'work-boxes, combs, different

233

kinds of toys, more especially models of boats and ships.' De Villargennes says that his foster-brother showed him the model of a fully-rigged frigate, its cordage made from human hair, which necessitated 'on his own part and that of his partner six months' assiduous labour, and for which I afterwards learned, they obtained the handsome sum of £40 sterling'.

From the above it is obvious that Forton was typical of most land depots at that late stage in the Napoleonic Wars, in that a proportion of its inmates were sufficiently resigned to long captivity to learn new crafts and occupations.

A few facts concerning the history of Forton at that time might tend to smudge the idyllic picture painted by young de Villargennes. At no time during that war was Forton a healthy place of confinement. In 1794, an epidemic had caused the deaths of 200 French inmates in one single month. The number of prisoners was ever on the increase over the following years, bringing overcrowding, dirt, disease and pressures on what was, by today's standards, a primitive medical service.

After the Battle of Trafalgar in October 1805, Forton received a proportion of the four and a half thousand rank-and-file French captives brought into the English depots. They must have found it generally less pleasant than Doisy described, for in 1806 the high level of ill health in the prison brought about a Government inquiry which censured and replaced the chief surgeon. Furthermore, five more years brought about no great improvement as in November 1810, only a few months before Doisy paid his visit, the Forton Depot Hospital sick list recorded 800 names, and once again a surgeon was superseded.

Surely the observant Doisy could not have spent a day in the prison without noticing, or at least hearing of, the *raffalès,* the semi-naked, half-starved, down-and-out victims of their own gambling addiction, who roamed the yards of every depot. That Forton was no exception can be seen from a letter which was sent to the French Commissioner for Prisoners of War in England, from an earlier surgeon at Forton Hospital. It read in part:

> 'Several prisoners have been received into the Hospital in a state of great debility owing to their having disposed of their rations of provisions for a week, a fortnight, and in some instances for a month at a time. We have felt it our duty to direct that such persons as may be discovered to have been concerned in purchasing any article of provision, clothing or bedding, of another prisoner, should be confined in the Black Hole, and kept on short allowance for ten days and also be marked as having forfeited their turn of exchange.'

In 1811 there had been so many escapes from the parole town of Wincanton in Somerset that all the parolees were removed from the place, those of the rank of captain and above being sent to Forton to await embarkation to the Scottish Border towns – where Doisy was very soon after to find himself. Germain Lamy, like his officer foster-brother, was released at the peace of 1814, returning to France with about £150, with which he bought a smallholding. He died of cholera in 1832.

As the record of Forton Depot was one of attempted escapes and successful getaways for the whole of its wartime existence, it is appropriate that we should conclude with one last story in which three fatally ham-fisted Frenchmen – Jean Marie Dauze, François Relif and Daniel du Verge – managed to get out of the Depot without detection. Their subsequent actions, however, led to profitless murder and execution. Subsequent investigations revealed that one of them at least, perhaps all, had earned sufficient money from the sale of prisoner of war work – bone boxes, lace, toys and other artefacts – to buy a suit of good clothes and cover the expenses of escape. Convincingly disguised as a visitor to the Depot market, he (they) mingled with the English crowd and left with them when the market closed in the afternoon.

The three Frenchmen met up at the Point at Portsmouth, where they chartered a pilot and boatman named George Brothers, to take them to a ship off Spithead. Brothers must surely have known that he was becoming involved to some extent in an escape attempt or, if they were masquerading as officers, in parole-breaking. He did not have long to wait to learn the truth. On the way to Spithead they revealed that their real destination was France, and proposed that he take them there.

George Brothers flatly refused and, panicking, signalled to nearby ships and watchers on the shore. That signal signed his death warrant – and theirs. They attacked him with knives, stabbing him sixteen times and, casting his body overboard, set sail for France. It would seem that their seamanship was no more skilful than their planning. Pursued by a veritable flotilla of small craft for some miles, they were eventually overhauled and taken on board HMS *Centaur.*

Examination revealed that, besides knives, they had between them a considerable sum of money, one of them having thirty silver crown pieces concealed about his person. The 'Brothers Murder' caused a sensation of outrage, both inside Forton and among the British public beyond its walls. Many of the latter attended his funeral, in Kingston (Hampshire) churchyard. Francis Abell says that the prisoners at Forton 'expressed their abhorrence of the crime by getting up a subscription for the murdered man's widow and children, to which it is said one of the murderers contributed £7.

Relif, Dauze and du Verge were hanged at Winchester in 1813.

1. Connor. *Journal: New England Hist. Register XXX. 1876.* MS. Vermont Hist. Library.

2. The duties of the CSWS were later taken over by the Transport Office.

3. 17 Geo c 9. 1777.

Liverpool, The Old Tower Prison.

Chapter Sixteen

Liverpool
The Borough Gaol, The Old Tower Prison, The Powder Magazine & 'The French Prison'

FROM THE MIDDLE OF THE EIGHTEENTH CENTURY until the end of the Napoleonic wars – the long heyday of wartime privateering – Liverpool was one of Britain's principal centres for her own licensed and privately armed fleets. For much of that time, it was also a natural centre for the reception and confinement of foreign captives, themselves mainly taken whilst serving in privateer and letter-of-marque vessels.

Syndicates of merchants, bankers and businessmen – patriots in a sense, but primarily non-altruistic and high-stake gamblers – invested a good deal of their wealth in the purchase and fitting out of all manner of ex-merchant vessels, from tiny ten-tonners to vessels of five-hundred tons burden, armed and equipped to take on large enemy merchantmen and sometimes even men-of- war.

Historically, the three great British privateer ports in the eighteenth and early nineteenth centuries were Bristol, London and Liverpool, where successful investors made their fortunes from the prizes brought in for condemnation and auction. Those same three ports had vied with each other from the late sixteenth century until the abolition of the traffic in human beings, for supremacy in African exploitation and the slave trade – with Liverpool eventually gaining that unenviable distinction.

With Ireland just across the sea and a haven for the French and American privateers who preyed upon our merchant shipping and worried our coastal towns, the importance of a defensive and offensive force of Liverpool-based armed vessels could not be exaggerated. But despite the fact that the town had experienced prisoner of war additions to its population since the beginning of the eighteenth century, no special buildings had been built or adapted for their accommodation until 1776.

This was to some extent understandable, for unlike prisoners taken by our men-of-war and eventually brought to Britain, privateersmen were often quickly exchanged, at sea or by semi-parole[1], which was economical both in that much-needed seamen were soon returned to active service and their captors were spared the expense of housing and feeding them. Not only men, but privateer vessels and private merchant ships were sometimes released by their captors, but in return for ransom. The French privateer lugger, *Le Comte de Guichen* was particularly successful in her predations off the Manx coast. By the beginning of the 1780s, the latter had captured eighteen prizes, most of which had been sent under prize crews into Cork for eventual auction, but some were ransomed: the *Spooner* out of Glasgow for 1,800 guineas, a Ponteferry vessel for 500 guineas and a couple of colliers for 350. However, on the 7th May, 1781, *Le Comte de Guichen*, with its 16 guns and 10 carronades and swivels, came to the end of its prize-winning run, when it struck to the British man-of-war *Aurora*, after a fourteen hour chase.

The prisoners brought to Liverpool from earlier wars, such as the Austrian Succession, had been comparatively few in number, and were inconsiderately forced to share their captivity with our civilian offenders, in the Liverpool Borough Gaol or the old Tower Prison.

Richard Brooke, in his '*Liverpool from 1775-1800*' considered the old Borough Gaol 'a most ill-judged place of confinement because of its contiguity to Coast and Shipping, and the facilities afforded for escape of prisoners in case of appearance of an Enemy.'

The brilliant achievements in 1779, of the Scottish-American hero, John Paul Jones, had given coast-dwellers – and many Yankee prisoners – good reason to believe that the rumours of an uprising and invasion might be more than just a nightmare possibility. Richard Brooke says that the prisoners in the Borough Gaol were, in general, 'ill-clad and appeared dispirited and miserable, and the mortality among them was considerable; the hearse was constantly in requisition to convey from the Gaol the corpse of some poor Frenchman to the public cemetery at St John's Church, (where they were buried unmarked in a special corner set apart for felons and paupers).'

The Old Tower Prison at the end of Water Street, between Tower Gardens and Stringer Alley had a long history of housing civil prisoners and war captives together in its unhealthy depths. It was used during the Seven Years' War, and again during the War of American Independence. Such a place of confinement must have seemed something of a godsend to the ever escape-conscious Yankee rebels, for security was at an all time low. Alfred De Curzon quoted a contemporary description of the shortcomings of the Tower as a stronghold: 'this old building consisted of towers, houses and buildings of various ages and indifferent features, with many walls, passages, turrets and dungeons, many windows – too many for a prison – and many doors, which were never repaired and very insecure.' There are records of a number of escapes from the Tower, and it is a wonder that there were not more; some 'went out through windows and walked quietly away among the citizens, the more easily because the prisoners were allowed to work for town merchants, to receive their envoys and be visited by friends.'

For all its outside appearance of menacing impregnability, the old Tower Prison was no more than a collection of semi-derelict buildings, yards and out-houses, which altogether covered no more than three-quarters of an acre. The conditions within were below the standard which even the worst offending criminal might expect, yet prisoners of war were housed there, with felons and debtors, men and women unsegregated, singing, drinking, gambling, and generally creating a pandemonium to which, it would seem, the inhabitants had become accustomed.'

With the outbreak of the Seven Years' War in 1756, the probable arrival of hundreds, perhaps thousands, of prisoners of war into this country, made it necessary to extend the old Tower accommodation. This was achieved by Admiralty purchase of the ballroom and other buildings at the bottom of Water Street, which were fitted out –

' …in a most commodious manner, there being a handsome kitchen with furnaces, &c., for cooking their provisions, and good lodging rooms both above and below stairs. Their Lordships have ordered a hammock and bedding (much the same as used on board our men of war) for each prisoner, which it is to be hoped will be a means of procuring our countrymen who have fallen into their (the French) hands better usage than hitherto. Many of them having been treated with great inhumanity.'

A story of one Seven Years' War privateersman who made Liverpool his home when the war ended, is one of escape, prisoner of war work and romance. The hero was Felix Durand, a French captive who was sent to Liverpool and the old Tower Prison. As a broad generalisation, the French prisoners were most remembered as addicted and profligate gamblers, or as ingenious and skilful artisans, who worked all manner of materials into artefacts for sale in the prison market. Felix was of the latter ilk and soon gained a reputation for excellent craftsmanship.

Not all the local visitors to the market came to buy souvenirs or gawk at the prisoners; some brought with them articles for repair, from small pieces of furniture, broken pottery, and all sorts of damaged treasures. It was one such repair job which was to prove of great significance in the life of Felix Durand.

One day a lady visited the market square with a curiously wrought box or casket which had been damaged beyond the abilities of the local craftsmen to restore. Enquiring among the talented Frenchmen in the square, she was directed to Durand, who took on the job but warned that it was likely to take him a long time to complete.

The box was the property of Mrs P. the wife of an ivory turner and carver with premises in Dale Street, who was part-owner of the English privateer *Mary Ellen*. Over the weeks which followed, Felix became acquainted with the ivory carver and his family through their visits to the market, even carrying out small trade commissions for him.

The repair of the damaged box was nearing completion when Durand – and at least one member of the ivory-worker's family – became involved in a fairly large scale escape attempt, by fifteen men, including Felix, from Liverpool Tower. The escape was well planned, at least as far as getting out of the prison, but once beyond its walls most of them would be at a loss, having little money or food; no knowledge of the local topography and hardly a word of English. Eventually, they were likely to be recaptured after aimless wanderings, or return to the Tower voluntarily when driven by hunger. However, Felix Durand had wisely planned to strike off on a course of his own. He said:

'I am a Frenchman, fond of liberty and change, and I determined to make my escape. I was acquainted with Mr P. in Dale Street; I did work for him in the Tower, and he has a niece who is *tout à fait charmante*. She has been a constant ambassadress between us, and has taken charge of my money to deposit with her uncle on my account. She is very engaging, and when I have had conversation with her, I obtained from her the information that on the east side of our prison there were two houses which opened on to a short narrow street. Mademoiselle is very kind and complacent, and examined the houses and found an easy entrance into one.'

The fourteen-man team began to work on their escape route by dislodging stones in the east wall, secreting the mortar under their beds. To make the disturbed stone less obvious to the occasional turnkey who might call in on a tour of inspection, they committed one of their team to bed and covered the window grating with a blanket, pretending that bright light inflicted great pain on the 'patient'.

In the early hours of a wet and windy night, when the hole in the wall was just large enough for a body to pass through, they all left the room, and dropped in to a yard. They quickly made their way according to plan to a cellar beneath the window, and passed through a number of passages until they reached a kitchen, where they made what they hoped would be their last prison supper, a feast of bread and beef.

They heard a clock strike two as they got beyond the outer wall, having first sent a scout ahead, who reported that there was 'not a soul to be seen anywhere, the wind rushing up the main street from the sea'.

Once outside, they split up into groups and scattered, but Durand, whose objective was to meet up with a certain French priest in Dublin, went on alone. He 'passed the Exchange, down a narrow lane facing it [Dale Street], in which I knew Mademoiselle dwelt, but did not know the house; therefore I pushed on till I came to the foot of a hill. I thought I would turn to the left at first, but went on to take my chance of four cross roads. In less than an hour he had reached the outskirts of Liverpool at Townsend Mill and, as the clock struck three, arrived at what was then the little village of Wavertree, where he drank from a brook and ate some bread.

He came to the quaint little village of Hale early next morning, just as an old lady came out of her cottage to take down the window shutters. Felix Durand, whose poor English would have betrayed him, took on the role of deaf-mute as he strolled over and took the shutters from her and stacked them away. To the old woman's amazement, he then took up a broom and proceeded to sweep the yard; filled the kettle from the pump; then raked the cinders from the grate and reset the fire.

As all this took place in complete silence, and from a few gestures from Felix, the old Lancashire cottager was easily convinced of Durand's affliction. After his long night's walk and recent exertions, he collapsed onto a settle and soon fell fast asleep.

Durand awoke to an excellent cooked breakfast which he gratefully devoured, and was enjoying a moment of relaxation when the sound of approaching horses brought his deception to an end. Alarmed, the 'deaf and dumb' Frenchman, leapt to his feet and fled the cottage.

He got as far away from the cottage as quickly as possible, and later in the day came to a barn, where two farm workers were threshing wheat. The Frenchman was once again a wandering 'deaf-mute', and as he was obviously exhausted, the threshers allowed him to rest in the barn. He tells us that in one corner of the threshing room there was a quantity of fresh straw, and some of this straw he was beginning to weave into a 'dainty basket' when the farmer came into the barn. With laudable feelings of pity for the weaver's sorry state and affliction, and appreciating his craftsmanship, the farmer invited him home for a meal. Before dinner Durand presented his little basket to the daughter of the house; then after a splendid repast, looked around for some way to repay this hospitality.

There is no reason to doubt Durand's story, either in broad outline or in much of its detail, but if the boast of his efforts to recompense were even half true, the farmer and his family would have had to be idiots if they failed to guess that he was more likely to be an escaped French prisoner of war, than a multi-talented, deaf and dumb, English tramp!

Felix said that when dinner was over, he looked around for jobs to do, occupying the afternoon by restarting a stopped clock with the aid of an old skewer and a pair of pincers; repaired a china figurine; mended a chair; cleaned an old oil painting; adjusted a lock, reshaped its key, and fed the pigs!

Durand was offered accommodation in the barn for the night; but, the farmer's daughter having cast an admiring glance towards the unusual visitor, her jealous boyfriend had no compunction in sending him on his way. He wandered the hamlets and villages for many weeks, making a fair living by selling baskets, and as repairer of almost anything; his skill and apparent disability ensuring that he found a kindly reception wherever he went. However, it was inevitable that, sooner or later, his caution and luck would run out. It happened that one day he was standing by a tree famed for its great size and beauty, when a group of visitors approached. Among them was a young lady who waxed quite lyrical in her admiration – in beautifully expressed French. The Frenchman could not resist joining in with a comment in his mother-tongue – and immediately blew his cover. The young lady looked amazed and exclaimed, 'Why! This is the very same dumb man who was repairing broken vases up at the Hall yesterday!'

Felix Durand's days of freedom were over for a while. He was recaptured and imprisoned, first in Ormskirk Gaol then transferred to the Liverpool Tower Prison, from which he might well have made a perfect escape. However, Felix, whose good fortune in being chosen from among the craftsmen in the Tower Prison market to repair the 'curiously wrought' but broken box, had brought him the friendship of a British family, did not stay locked up for long.

After a very short time of close confinement in the Tower, he was paroled into the care of the ivory carver and his family, through the influence of a Liverpool Member of Parliament, Sir Edward Cunliffe.

Felix took up residence in Dale Street and when, in September of the following year, he married the *tout à fait charmante* niece, her uncle made him a partner in the turning and carving business. Mr and Mrs F. Durand lived and worked in Liverpool for many years after the Seven Years' War had ended.

Twenty years later, the Tower Prison and its extension was still in use, but was now occupied by Americans as well as continental prisoners. When Dr John Howard visited it in 1779, some of the gloss had worn off, and he condemned it as a 'foul dirty place, a hotbed of disease and unworthy of a great nation and of a town like Liverpool'. Four hundred and fifty-three French and fifty-six Spaniards were packed into five small rooms cluttered by three tiers of slung hammocks.

In 1776, with the expectation of an influx of American privateer prisoners into Liverpool, the Transport Office had shown some foresight by leasing the old Gunpowder Magazine on Brownlow Hill, which had been used to store powder, whilst ships were laid up or refitting in the port. Now, 'instead of gunpowder, French and Spanish mariners and American insurgents were lodged there'.

The Magazine was a large brick building surrounded by high walls, situated near present-day Russell Street, but was in those days isolated in a field. Once adapted to its purpose it was a great improvement on the old Tower Prison and the Borough Gaol. The general conditions and the quality of the food were perhaps a bit better than in most other depots at that time. Between 1778 and 1782, about 1,432 prisoners of war saw the inside of what was once the old powder store, and the records show that only eighteen men died whilst held captive there. When the weather was fine they would have found the airing yard the most pleasant place to be. It was spacious enough, even in 1779, when there were 509 men using it for exercise or occupied themselves in a dozen different and sometimes profitable activities. Night time was a different matter. Hammocks were slung close together three-deep, and such cramped conditions caused a great deal of quarrelling and fighting, most often between the French and the Spanish.

With the end of The American War of Independence, in 1783, the short lived 'Magazine Prison' was demolished; but only ten years were to pass before prisoner of war space was again a priority, with the outbreak of the Revolutionary War with France, in 1793.

Luckily for the Admiralty and the Transport Board – if not for the local authorities – in 1786, the Corporation of Liverpool had begun to build a new civil Borough Gaol, at a cost of £30,000. It was situated in Milk House Lane near the Leeds Canal. From the beginning of the new war with France, in 1793, this civil prison was taken over by the Transport Office on a six years' leasehold; but as they were quite a few years out in their estimate of the probable duration of the war, the Government had to re-negotiate the lease in 1799. Meanwhile the old Tower Prison was given a new lease of life as the city's repository for its civilian criminals and debtors.

From 1793, the new Liverpool Borough Gaol, by then a prisoner of war depot, became generally known as the 'French Prison'. It was built to the plans and ideals of the great prison reformer, John Howard – I believe that Milk-House Lane was later renamed Great Howard Street in his honour. When finished it was to comprise six three-storey prison buildings, 106 feet in length, 47 feet wide and 23 feet high, each standing within its own fenced-off courtyard; and two single-storey buildings, forty-eight feet by twenty, were erected as kitchens for the prisoners. However, when first taken over only three of those prisons were ready for complete occupation. In fact building was still going on when war was resumed in 1803, after the very short Peace of Amiens – and it was not described as completed until 1812!

We know, however, that all six prisons were to some extent operational by the late summer of 1797. In September of that year, Sir Rupert George, one of the Commissioners of the Transport Office, was making a tour of the English land prisons and came to inspect 'The French Prison' at Liverpool. A rather long extract from an exceedingly long Report to the Board, told of his visit:

'*Transport Office the 20th September, 1797.*
Gentlemen,
…Thursday, the 24th [of August] I reached Liverpool but was prevented by indisposition from visiting the Prison till Thursday the 7th instant. This is a most compleat and substantial prison, in a detached situation to the northward of the Town, and commands a beautiful prospect; it consists of six large detached buildings in which Prisoners are confined, exclusive of a large building in the centre, two storeys of which are appropriated to the purpose of a Hospital, and the lower storey to an Agent's office, Officer guardroom, store rooms, etc.
    'The Prisoners do not sleep on the ground floor in any of the buildings: they are lodged in the second and third storeys, which principally consist of a number of cells each nine feet by seven, and ten feet high, on an average about five inhabit each cell.
    'At the end of three buildings there are six large rooms fitted with hammock posts and rails, these rooms are 11 feet high and contain two heights of hammocks.
    'There are six court yards, which are used by the Prisoners for

airing ground, and also another separate from the rest as an airing ground for the sick. The Prison has a plentiful supply of good spring water raised by six pumps and is surrounded by a stone wall 20 feet high, one hundred and thirty-seven yards long from north to south, 124 yards from east to west, and 455 yards in circumference.
    'There were confined in the Prison 1,265 French Prisoners and 85 Spanish, of whom 21 French and 4 Spanish Prisoners were sick including seven who had the itch [a disease akin to smallpox], three or four hundred of them have been in Prison since the year 1793, whose Cases I commend to the Board's notice' [for possible exchange?].

The Spanish prisoners had prepared a petition for him to present to the Transport Board, in which they humbly requested to be separated from the French owing to frequent disputes and fights among them. After calculating that the cost of compliance with their petition would amount to no more than three pounds and sixpence, Sir Rupert recommended that it be granted.

The prisoners' provisions had been submitted for inspection and found generally satisfactory, although he agreed about the poor quality of the boiled 'pease and small beer', which resulted from the hardness of the water, and for this he 'directed a proper remedy'.

'The Prisoners are indulged with an oven of their own in the Prison to bake bread, as well as a space or ground in cultivation as a kitchen garden; and as they make a considerable sum by the sale [in the prison market] of toys and trinkets of their own fabrication, they live in a manner so plentiful that I was told the poor people of the neighbourhood almost regard them with envy.
    'Strangers being admitted into the prison, which they generally are at the discretion of the officer of the guard, is attended with much inconvenience, and often produces discontent among the Prisoners from their incautious expressions, it would therefore be very desirable that some check be put to this practice, if not totally prohibited.
    'As this prison is so secure, I do not see that any danger can be apprehended (notwithstanding its situation is so near a sea port of great trade and opulence)' from filling it if necessary, and it would contain nearly five hundred more than are at present confined.
                                                    I am, &c., &c.
                                                    Rupt. George.'

The 'strangers' referred to in the above letter would have been privileged guests who were allowed into the inner prison yards, and should not be confused with the great crowds which thronged the prison market place.

Records exist of the complaints of prisoners of many nationalities who objected to being exhibited to the gentry with their wives or lady friends, many of whom acted like visitors to a zoo.

In 1798 a House of Commons inquiry was instigated to look into the possibly exaggerated complaints and false accusations regarding the British treatment of French prisoners of war. This inflammatory propaganda was denied in a Report which was published in May and contained what may have been a misprint or a slight exaggeration. In September, Sir Rupert George had stated that there were 1,265 French prisoners, and a small number of Spaniards, in the depot. However, a Colonel Stanley, who contributed to the Report, had recently been to Liverpool, '*where 6,000 were confined*'. He found that they were generally well treated, and the officers among them had 'every indulgence, three billiard tables, and that they often performed plays'.

Richard Brooke also mentioned the activities of captive thespians at Liverpool Prison.

'Amongst the amusements some of the French prisoners during their confinement here performed plays in a small theatre contrived for that purpose within the walls, and in some instances they raised in a single night £50 for admission money. Many of my readers will recollect that with the usual ingenuity of the French the prisoners manufactured a variety of snuff-boxes, rings, trinkets, crucifixes, card boxes and toys which were exhibited on stalls at the entrance of the Gaol and sold for their benefit.'

Every depot and prison ship has its stories of half-starved, half-naked men, who slept without hammock or bedding. There were good Agents and there were bad, but any official who brought about such a state of affairs through deliberate neglect of his charges would soon have been out of a job – and possibly out of the Royal Navy. Some diarists have denigrated the type of men who became depot Agents, describing them as superannuated, service failures or naval chuck-outs. In fact, the post was eagerly sought after, and the successful candidate had to have at least ten years' seniority, and a clean record. As I have noted so many times, gambling was the root cause of destitution and loss of self-respect. There can be no doubt that most of those stories of prisoner of war sufferings were not in any way exaggerated or untrue. Men did die from malnutrition and exposure in our prisons; and it is natural that the French officials should have taken up the cudgel on behalf of even the most degenerate among their countrymen. However, when reading their recriminations, it is rare to find even a hint that the accusers were aware that they were protesting about a self-destructive minority, rather than prisoners of war in general.

In 1798, *The Liverpool Courier* printed a letter which the London *Times* later commented on as 'emanating from some sanguinary Jacobin in some back garret of London'. It was aimed at the heartstrings of the British public – who were often generous contributors to the frequent prisoner of war subscription appeals – but also as an anti-British recrimination. There was no qualification that the 'prisoners in the dungeons' were often habitual offenders who sold their clothes and provisions in order to gamble, or recaptured escapers. They could indeed have been sentenced to as long as forty days in the Black Hole; but many of the unlucky losing punters would have been better off and better fed on half-rations during their time in the *cachot,* than as a 'free' man in the yards, and at the mercy of the gamesters and the relentless 'brokers'.

The pro-French article read:

'*Liverpool Courier* 12 January 1798
The French prisoners in the dungeons of Liverpool are actually starving. Some time ago their usual allowance was lessened under pretence of their having bribed the sentinels with the superfluity of their provisions. Each prisoner is allowed ½lb of beef, 1lb bread, &c. and as much water as he can drink. *The meat is the offal of the Victualling Office* – the necks and shanks of the butchered: the bread is so bad and so black as to incite disgust; and the water so brackish as not to be drunken, and they are provided with straw. The officers, contrary to the rules of Nations, are imprisoned with the privates, and are destined with them to experience the dampness and the filth of these dismal and unhealthy dungeons. The privileges of Felons are not allowed them.

Philanthropos'

Things were becoming extremely bad for the prisoners, and some Members of the House of Commons were sufficiently disturbed by the 'Philanthropos' article and similar reports for an order to be made that a Commission should be sent to Liverpool. The inquiry which followed was conducted by the Mayor and Aldermen of Liverpool, who produced a reassuring report in the following May. It stated little more than that the conditions in our prisons were superior to those endured by the British captives in France; that the French prisoners were well fed and their officers had three billiards tables.

The building of the Howard-inspired prison had brought about improvements for prisoners and their keepers. There were fewer complaints of overcrowding and filth; the water was pure and the recreation grounds spacious; in fact, the Liverpool prisoners were probably a little better off than the inmates of many other British depots. As the century neared its end, however, international disagreements, economies, and pig-headedness on both sides had gone on with little regard for the men who would live or die by their decisions.

As they became aware of the terrible situation of the captives in their Borough Gaol, private people attempted to help them by collections and gifts of cast-off clothing; but this could only be of temporary aid to the few. There was also a group of very distinguished gentlemen who got together and formed a semi-secret society of corespondents, which it thought might find an answer to the international quandary. The leading spirit was a Scottish doctor, with a home and surgery in Liverpool, who had strong feelings about the unfair treatment of the French prisoners in the Borough Gaol, as much neglected by their own country as by their captors. Dr James Currie MD, FRSA, (1756–1805), philanthropist, editor[2] and medical specialist kept up a correspondence on the subject with like-minded friends, which included Sir Joseph Banks and other famous members of The Royal Society, all of whom dedicated time and money to assist 'poor destitute people'. Copies of thirty-three of his letters, replies and reports lay unpublished for 120 years, until in 1926 they were discovered by a researcher, Alfred de Curzon[3], who put them into print. This now rare little book of letters supplies first-hand descriptions of the town's prisons, observations on the inmates, and such sincere concern for the suffering Frenchmen that one might think that, rather than seekers after fairplay, Dr Currie and his associates were a group of devoted Francophiles.

A letter dated the 29th October, 1800, from M. Louis Guillaume Otto, the Commissioner or Agent, for French Prisoners of War in England, reveals, in just three words, that he understood that much of the suffering of certain French prisoners was self-imposed.

'My letter from Liverpool states that the number of deaths during the past month has greatly exceeded that of four previous months, even when the depot contained twice the number of prisoners. This sudden mortality which commenced at the close of last month, is the consequence of the first approach of cold weather, all without exception failed from debility. The same fate awaits many more of these unfortunate beings, already half starved from want of proper food, and obliged to sleep upon a damp pavement or a few handfuls of rotten straw. Hunger and *their own imprudence,* deprived them of their clothes, and now the effect of the cold weather obliges them to part with a share of their scanty subsistence to procure clothing. In one word, their only hope is a change in their situation or death.'

It is obvious that the French Commissioner was not referring to the Liverpool captives *en masse*, but, almost exclusively to those who had descended to the bottom rung of the prisoner of war social ladder through gambling and general improvidence. It was also on behalf of these pitiable dead-beat creatures that Dr Currie and his friends addressed the authorities between 1800 and 1801.

In the wars prior to 1793, the expenses involved in maintaining the prisoner of war, his provisions, some of his clothing, etc., were borne by his captor; the bill to be settled between the two nations when the war had ended. In fact this practice continued for the first few years of the Revolutionary War; but then an important change took place which decreed that henceforth the French would be responsible for their captive servicemen in Britain, and likewise, the British would provide for their fellow countrymen in French prisons – with a periodical settling of accounts.

England naturally welcomed this arrangement, the British prisoners in France being only a fraction of the number of Frenchmen held in Britain; but it was a blow to the French Treasury. There were complaints and wrangling from the start, and when, in February 1798, the British Government submitted a bill for settlement, which covered the expense of maintaining the French prisoners, the *Directoire* was hard pressed to find the cash. At that time, the prisoners had already cost France 1,185,000 L. and a ruinously high exchange rate caused severe financial alarm.

On the 7th December 1799, the *Consulate,* the newly formed French Government, took a step which was bound to cause more trouble, complaints and counter-complaints – the prisoners on both sides suffering, whilst their masters squabbled. Without prior warning or discussion, Napoleon decided to abandon all responsibility for the French prisoners of war in this country, transferring the burden, and the fate of the prisoners on to British shoulders; stating that 'it was up to the captor to entertain his victims.' This was not only high-handed but also a serious threat to both prisoners and the British Government; for every depot in the land would be affected. *The Times,* for 20th December, 1799, reported:

> 'The late decree of the French *Consulate* withdrawing all further supplies for the maintenance of their prisoners was extremely sudden and unexpected; as only a few days before M.Perigeaux the Banker remitted to Mr Hammersley 60,000 L. on this account with a promise that the payments should be more regularly made in the future.'

Before that extreme measure taken by the *Consulate*, the provident prisoner could make ends meet and the industrious among them lived quite well; but, cut off from all aid from France, their future looked bleak. The British Government economised by drastically reducing the food ration. The bread issue was reduced by a third to one pound each per day, meat to eight ounces; they were allowed half a pound of cabbage or other vegetables, but no cheese, butter or beer. Unless he had money the prisoner's only drink was water.

The winter of 1799/1800 was severe and clothes were scarce. Before the later introduction of the saffron Transport Office prisoner garb, the French had supplied almost all of the clothing for their captured countrymen. Now, with prisoners all over the country suffering from lack of protection from the icy weather, the worried depot Agents called on the London-based French Commissioner Otto, pleading for assistance in finding a solution to what for many would be a matter of life and death. Liverpool was no exception. Lieutenant Ebenezer Fisher RN, the Agent, wrote, 'There are some few here in extreme want of clothing and they have no friends capable of making them any remittances to enable them to purchase; which circumstance obliges me to represent their

situation to you and to say in their present situation it is not in their power to keep themselves free from vermin.'

Otto's reply regretted that he could not help by supplying the desperately needed clothing, but offered the rather unhelpful advice that, if England could not afford to feed or dress its captives adequately, perhaps they should be put to outside work locally, whereby they might earn their own living and purchase their own food and clothing. Imagine the consequences of such large bands of foreigners competing for jobs, against our local labourers and craftsmen!

Few Liverpool inhabitants could have been entirely unaware of the prisoners' plight. Newspapers and the gossiping of off-duty guards and prison staff, would have kept the interested well informed: and security was in some respects lax.

Although generally considered a good Agent, Lieutenant Ebenezer Fisher did not keep a strict watch over visitors to the inner prisons of his depot. Local dignitaries, official and unofficial inquirers, some with an anti-British axe to grind, others, genuine philanthropists, who were ashamed that prisoners of war should be neglected in such a life-threatening manner no matter who was to blame; all found easy entry. This inattention earned poor Ebenezer a rather threatening rap over the knuckles from the Transport Office. It seems that John Shaw, Mayor of Liverpool, had made an unofficial and unannounced visit to the French prison and sampled the provisions, which, on that day were even worse than usual. He sent his findings to the Transport Board, who informed Fisher:

> 'We have this day received a letter from the Mayor of Liverpool informing us that he had visited the Prison accompanied by another Magistrate, and upon inspecting the Provisions they found that the beef intended for the Prisoners in Health was not of a sufficiently good quality equal to what is stipulated in the Contract. We are much concerned in receiving such a Statement from the Magistrate, because it certainly implies a degree of blame which we trust will be avoided in future.'

Ebenezer Fisher took the rebuff badly, and wrote to the Transport Board in an effort to excuse his apparent neglect, saying that the offending batch of beef was only a very small part of the whole, which was otherwise of good quality and that he would certainly have spotted it himself in his usual personal daily inspection of the prisoners' provisions, had he not been occupied elsewhere on that particular day.

The Transport Office Commissioners had also written to the Mayor, telling him that the present distress of the French prisoners had been occasioned by 'their own imprudence' and want of clothing, and not by the insufficiency of their daily ration, 'which certainly affords more nourishment than a considerable part of the labouring class of the Inhabitants of this Country can at present procure'.

Agent Fisher would have been even more disturbed had he known that Dr Currie often visited the depot incognito, during the last few months of 1800 and the beginning of the new century. Currie obtained reports on the condition of the ill-fated Frenchmen, supplied first by his good friends, Dr Carson, and Dr Cochrane, who were in charge of the Hospital within the prison walls. The two doctors were taking something of a risk to their positions in the prison service, by passing on the confidential information regarding the French captives at Liverpool to private people; but, unselfishly, they put their enemy patients first and continued to do so. The doctors did, however, communicate with the French Commissary General, Otto, the Transport Office, and other authorities from time to time during that worrying period. In fact, one of the first letters in the 'Currie collection' was sent from Dr Cochrane to Louis Otto. There is no doubt that Cochrane, was a good and humane doctor with great devotion to his task. He was described as a 'more timorous' character than his partner, Dr Carson, and was circumspect in his assessment of some possible solutions to the predicament of his charges. For instance, he was opposed to public subscriptions got up by the good people of Liverpool. He considered that the regularly issued ration was sufficient to sustain an imprisoned man, and whilst such generosity would be appreciated by the average prisoner as a welcomed windfall, it would do nothing towards reforming the distressed and starving band of losers – now numbering about 400 – many of whom would eventually come under his medical care.

Cochrane's letter, which gave Otto a factual but unemotional account of the situation in September 1800, read as follows:

> 'Since the time the French Government threw the maintenance of their Prisoners of war on this country, the universal allowance has been one pound of bread, half a pound of beef and half a pound of vegetables made into soup daily.
>
> 'The provisions have been and continue to be regularly issued out at that rate and of as good a quality as can be afforded.
>
> 'Many of the Prisoners by remittances from France, or by their own industry, have added considerably to this, and of course live better. Others from want of this aid, or what is generally the case, prompted by the destructive principles of *gambling*, have sold their clothes to each other, and win their rations for a fortnight to come either to add a temporary gratification to their appetites, or to furnish the means to play. The consequence has been that numbers have not only been ruined but their bodies so impoverished by want, that all those who have been admitted into the Hospital have been of this description, some of whom were too far gone to recover notwithstanding they were indulged with the best Diet (which is a very liberal one) and supplied with wine, porter etc., according to their necessities. To put a check to this evil, if possible, the strictest orders were issued by the Agent and Surgeon to prevent the sale of the clothes and provisions; the gambling tables were destroyed, the Prisons directed to be visited often by the turnkeys, to detect the private practice of it, and the buyers of provisions or clothes, when found out were confined… in short every precaution possible has been taken to hinder the evil consequence that were foreseen to happen and are still continued.'

At about this time, M. Otto received a joint letter, signed by Doctor Cochrane and Agent Fisher, delivered via the Transport Office. It informed him that the British Transport Office felt that it 'did not ly [sic] with them' to supply new clothes for the French prisoners. Acting, as they said, from principles of duty and humanity, they urged him to take whatever steps were appropriate to send a fresh supply as quickly as possible, before the beginning of the cold months ahead, which would otherwise bring sickness and death.

Surprisingly, and almost incidentally, the second half of the letter reveals that there was already a stock of clothing at the Depot, large enough to solve a good deal of Liverpool's troubles, but it was bound to the storeroom shelves with lashings of French and English red tape.

> 'There remain in the storehouse here about 500 jackets and 400 trousers belonging to the French Government which were furnished by Mr Vochez and for which the Agent granted a receipt to Mr Foster the former Agent. Please inform if these in meantime may be delivered among the most needful, and if you will be accountable for them to Mr. Vochez.'

Otto, who had suggested that the prisoners might be found public or private employment to enable them to purchase their own requirements, now came up with another unacceptable idea. It was not new, having previously cropped up in this and other wars, *'If we could not afford to keep them, why not send all French prisoners back to France, on parole?'*

The reasons why this was impracticable are too many to be cited here; but Dr Currie and his associates, who were more devoted to the alleviation of avoidable suffering than to politics, saw some sense in the proposition. They did not believe that many lives would be saved over that winter by one-off public subscription, or by re-clothing the naked and near-naked prisoners. An absolute necessity was an increase in the food allowance, but one unlikely to be granted. James Currie, in letters to Government Medical Commissioner Dr Garthshore, Sir Joseph Banks FRS and Dr Cochrane, detailed why he advocated parole as the answer to the nation-wide problem of under-fed and dying French prisoners of war. (He also requested that they would treat his correspondence as confidential, but the authorities were no doubt kept informed.) He expressed his admiration of their various endeavours on the sufferers' behalf, but said:

> 'I do not see how it could be done by private subscription in the present state of our own Charitable Institutions and the general distress of our poor. For my part, I should think the best measure would be to discharge these miserable deserted men on their parole, by which the provisions they would have consumed would be added to the stock of our own people, a circumstance that would far over balance any injury they could do us, even if, in breach of their parole, they were to take up arms against us. But all this is between ourselves.'

By now, December 1800, there were far more sick prisoners than the Hospital could comfortably accommodate. The number needing attention and treatment crept up daily; but new entries could only be accepted as beds were vacated, by recovered patients or some poor devils who had died. The newcomer may well have thought he had gone straight up to Heaven: to a warm bed and good food. The allowance for the prisoner of war in health was laid down by the Admiralty. However, the diet for the hospitalised prisoner came under the authority of the 'Sick and Hurt Office', which was a generous one, usually prepared with superior ingredients, plus a few luxuries, such as tea and porter!

Chief Surgeon Cochrane and Dr Carson carried out their herculean task with great dedication, knowing full well that many of the men who were 'emaciating daily', would be entering the establishment only to die. Not all of the sufferers had been *raffalles,* or down-and-outs. Some were ordinary hard-up, God-fearing men, for whom the nutritional value of the reduced rations was just not enough. During the summer months they had parted with bits and pieces of clothing in order to obtain a little extra food and perhaps tobacco; which was reputed to assuage the worst pangs of a man's hunger. Now it was a case of food for odds and ends of covering.

We have heard, and will hear, of crooked contractors who robbed hungry men by supplying bread and other provisions way below the contracted standard, in both quality and quantity. However, after the economies made necessary by France's abandonment of her captured subjects, it would have been difficult for the contractor to make a profit, honest or dishonest. The contract had gone to the lowest bidder, who received only 5d. (just over 2p.) per man per day to supply beef, bread and vegetables, and only when the price of wheat had risen to 10/- a bushel, was he allowed a further three farthings – or three-quarters of an old penny – per head.

Protests of Governmental meanness and inhumanity were heard from both home and abroad, and critical articles in our opposition evening newspapers, were pounced upon by an unshamefaced France, for distribution to her armies. The prison doctors and the band of benefactors continued with their letters and reports, the gist of which, they hoped, would be discreetly passed on to Otto, the Transport Board and 'Sick and Hurt Office', Lord Melville, the Secretary for War and others. The words 'suffering', 'naked', 'starvation', 'sickness' and 'death' sprinkled the pages, and ideas which might produce economies in a more civilized manner were propounded. For instance, every time a prisoner died it cost this country nearly one pound sterling to bury him, and Currie reasoned that 20/- would have been better spent on woollen garments, thus saving the Government the expense of coffin and grave (and, incidentally the prisoner's life). A powerful point which, unfortunately, does not stand up to statistical analysis.

Dr Currie could never quite understand why the Government could not bypass M. Otto in the matter of French clothing already in the Borough Prison, indemnifying the Commissary by promise of settlement after the war. Or why the Admiralty forbade the acceptance of clothing paid for by public subscription, or by private donation. The items were actually in the depot stores, but Agent Fisher, backed by Dr Cochrane, was unwilling to release them without definite Government approbation.

Both of these men were caring officials, who helped the prisoners as far as their positions would allow. In fact the 'timorous' Dr Cochrane went farther. Alarmed and frustrated by the ever worsening condition of the captives, he had the courage to take upon himself the responsibility of instructing the contractor to increase slightly the prisoners' rations.

The effect on the recipients was immediate, but brought the wrath of the authorities on to the good doctor's head. The 'Sick and Hurt Office cancelled the extra ration after a few days – and all expenses involved by the incident were billed to Dr Cochrane personally.

The average number of prisoners at Liverpool was about 2,000 and, by the end of the first year, 1799, of France's refusal to support them, 103 of that 2,000 had died and forty 'invalids and children', most of whom were not expected to survive had been shipped back to France.

In a letter to Dr Garthshore, the young Dr Carson, noted that the high mortality came about during the last four wintery months; for the rest of the year, the monthly average would have been about three or four. Now, in November, twenty-one Frenchmen had died; and between the 1st December, 1800 and the 15th, another twenty–four miserable souls had passed away in the Prison Hospital.

It is perhaps understandable that for reasons of national pride, neither side would want to be the first to back down on any point of contention. In this case, however, it can only be said that both France and Britain were equally guilty of murder by neglect. Dr Currie was deeply worried, and, on Christmas Eve 1800 he, too, wrote to Garthshore, telling him:

'I have examined the state of the prisoners myself and can positively declare that they are dying of cold and hunger. Thirty-one have died in the present month and there are 250 more that will in my judgment be dead before the end of January. If relief is not obtained speedily, some other steps must be taken, though it would be most painful and injurious to bring this subject before the public at present.'

He added that he was utterly bewildered by the fact that, in a Christian country like England, the Agent (Ebenezer Fisher), whose appointed task included the welfare of his charges, should be able to refuse to allow those dying men the relief gladly offered by private charities. Could he be carrying out Government instructions? As was the case with most of his letters, it ended with a request that Sir Joseph Banks be kept informed of its contents. A great deal of letter circulation went on between Currie and his friends, many of whom, like himself, were Fellows of the Royal Society, of which Sir Joseph Banks was President, and had contacts and friends in very high places. Unfortunately, Sir Joseph passed on to Sir Gilbert Blane, one of Currie's long letters.

So much for influence! Three days later, Sir Joseph received a lengthy missive from Sir Gilbert Blane, MD, Chief Government Medical Inspector and President of the Naval Medical Board, decrying the fact that private people were meddling in the affairs of the Government. There is much in Blane's report which might be considered reasonable, had there been even a suggestion that he had any sympathy for its suffering subject matter. I reproduce it here in all its coldness :

'Dear Sir Joseph
I have been favoured with your letter enclosing one from Dr Currie respecting the situation of the French prisoners at Liverpool.

'While I give the Doctor full credit for his humanity and good intentions, I must at the same time remark that as the *whole case* cannot be known but to the executive government of the country, there is a certain degree of delicacy and reserve due from private individuals who comment on these measures, as they must be imperfectly informed, and this is more particularly becoming, as it is no part of the character or conduct of this country to exercise cruelty towards persons in that infortunate situation. I have particular cause to know this in my publick situation, the only intimation given to us relative to the sick from the Board of Admiralty being "to treat them in the same manner as British seamen".

'I do not pretend to know the whole merits of the case, nor have any right to inquire into the reasons of Ministers for what they do, but enough if the circumstances come to my knowledge to acquit them of blame, and tho' I did not know so much, I think I should rather say to myself "there must be reasons I do not know" than hastily accuse government of inhumanity.

'With regard to the quality of provisions, I do not think it too small for men who do not labour. A few years ago, I took an exact amount of what I ate and drank, and my usual quantity of solid food was exactly the same as is allowed to the prisoners, viz: one pound and a half of solid food. Their meat is indeed weighed before dressing, and mine after but they have peases, cabbage or potatoes over and above my quantity.

'As to the clothing I think I can safely affirm that it has not been withheld on the account of the barefaced breach of faith but which the French Government gave up the maintenance of their own prisoners, but because in all time past, it has been the rule for the respective countries to clothe their own people, the only exception to this being the period at which all intercourse was suspended in the time of Robespierre. We at this moment clothe our people in France (and were the Russian prisoners there till very lately) and supply them with such additional food and other articles as are necessary for them. Mr Otto, the French Commissioner admits all this, and as he does not make complaints nor remonstrances, it is pretty plain that he does not think the blame due to us. The fact is that the most urgent representations have been made on this subject to the French Government by ours, and we had a good right to expect that they would sooner or later be listened to. I have no reason, however, to think that our government begin compleately to despair of this and that the prisoners will be clothed at our own expence. There are at this moment two commissaries, one belonging to the Transport Board, another to the Medical Board on a visitation to one of the depots of prisoners in order to ameliorate their situation as far as it is proper and practicable, and it will soon be seen whether our government and that of France are most alive to the calls of humanity even to Frenchmen. Dr Currie asks how the clothing belonging to the French Government comes not to be distributed to the Prisoners. The clothing alluded to belongs to the contractors who have never been paid for this, anymore than for other articles, which have been actually consumed and expended.

'The greens were substituted for the pease for the most humane and salutary purpose, and this affords me an opportunity of mentioning to you a circumstance which I think will appear curious and interesting to you as one versant in nautical medicine which you could not avoid being in your circumnavigation. It is that at Portchester and Norman Cross the true sea scurvey broke out under the use of fresh meat and farinaceous food without the least particle of salt provisions. Our Board advised a substitution of greens for pease which had the most salutary effect, and as it was a general order, it extended to Liverpool. Hence the cabbage complained of by Dr Currie.

'When the Dutch have been separate from the French they have been much more healthy with the same rations and the French were healthy in the summer months, which proves that the late sickliness and mortality have not been owing to the want of provisions but of clothing and to their losing their victuals and clothes to each other at play. The vice of gaming has however prevailed among them at all times and by no means confined to the present season of distress as alleged by Dr Currie.

'With regard to Dr Cochrane our Board has seen his conduct as a confidential servant of the public in a very reprehensible point of view for communicating as he did with regard to the grievances of the prisoners with those who were strangers to the service instead of trusting to the representations which he made to us and which we communicated to the Board of Admiralty. The Boards in town were well acquainted with the sufferings of the prisoners and I apprehend I have accounted for them not being sooner relieved. We also thought Dr Cochrane highly to blame in adding to the allowance without any authority, and such authority could not have been granted even by the Admiralty, these matters being regulated by the King and Council. Such a liberty would have been unwarrantable even on a foreign station, but to the highest degree improper in England where a few days would bring an answer by post. In the present hour of national distress it is with a bad grace in my opinion that any one pleads for such indulgence to prisoners of war.

'With regard to the bad quality of the provisions, if such are ever served to the prisoners, it must be the fault of the Agent on the spot who has directions to return upon the contractor what is not of a proper quality; and I must here remark that Dr Currie has taken up some very incorrect information when he affirms that the prisoners are maintained by a contract to the lowest bidder. The truth is that the contractor for prisoners in health at Liverpool is paid according to the certified market price of provisions. Contracts are indeed frequently given to the lowest tenderer, but he is bound to find satisfactory security for the performance of it.

'There is still another great inaccuracy which has escaped Dr Currie. He says some of the prisoners have been there for seven years. Now it appears from the books of the Transport Office that there are only four men who have been in captivity more than four years, and if there has been any hardship or injustice in this respect, it is imputable to the French Commissioner who has the selection of those who are preferred for exchange.

'I have much respect for Dr Currie as a physician, a man of research and of considerable literary talents, and am sorry that truth and justice

have obliged me to say so much on the subject of his letter to you.
Believe me with great esteem and regard
Dear Sir,
Your most faithful and very obed. humble servant   Gil. Blane
Sackville street, 27th Dec 1800'

He added a postscript which was meant to make clear the wisdom of the Government in discouraging acceptance of public benevolence. His own opinion was that

' …the French Government when hearing of this might be confirmed in their neglect of the prisoners to whom this might ultimately be a great detriment, for it could hardly be the intention of those who thus intermeddled to find them ample general permanent supplies.'

As the busy Sir Joseph had passed one of Currie's long letters on to the President of the Medical Board, the unofficial work of investigation by the sympathisers, was now in the open, at least as far as the authorities were concerned, and the offenders were castigated with various degrees of severity according to their standing. The heaviest censure fell upon Dr Cochrane, as a servant of the prison service. In letters to Sir Gilbert Blane, Dr Currie defended himself boldly, protesting that Blane should accuse him of expressing himself in unguarded language, which might suggest that he was critical of the Government of his country. Indignant, the doctor reminded Sir Gilbert that the letter was a private one, meant only for the eyes of Sir Joseph Banks: 'therefore, my terms were not so measured or guarded as they would have been had they been employed in a representation to a public Board, or to the world at large.' He said that it never crossed his mind that the executive power of any board acting under it could knowingly suffer men at their mercy to perish of hunger or cold. Yet the men were perishing from one or the other or both combined. Having heard of it, he felt that as an act of no less patriotism than of humanity, to make the truth known without disguise in the only quarters accessible to him. 'Every thing depends on the truth of my representations: and this is now on the point of being investigated. If they are founded in truth *in the essential points* the evil is not a slight one.' If found false, he was willing to take the blame.

He also sprang to the defence of Dr Cochrane, as did Dr Carson. Dr Currie told Blane that the details given him by Cochrane regarding the state of affairs at the depot and hospital were not secrets, as officers and men of the guard or any other prison attendants could confirm, and the sexton of St John's Church knew the number of fatalities from the number of coffins he had to purchase for their burial. Both doctors expressed their earnest hopes that no permanent inconvenience or displeasure be held against their 'worthy and humane friend'.

It would seem, however, that the labours of 'Intermeddler' Currie and his friends had not been completely in vain. On the 30th December, Sir Gilbert Blane informed Sir Joseph that the Transport Board had ordered that a general supply of 'clothing' should be sent to the French prisoners in the Borough Gaol, and two Commissaries – one from the Transport Office, Mr Ambrose Serle, the other from the Medical Board, Dr Johnson, were to proceed to Liverpool forthwith. And at about that time, a small amount of firewood had been allowed into the prison by private donation, during the worst winter weather in the first months of 1801. By this time most of the poorly clad and naked prisoners had been fitted out with some sort of clothing. On the 1st January, 1801, the Lords of the Admiralty received a letter from the Secretary of State for War, Henry Dundas which brought the long-awaited news of relief for the French captives. Two weeks later, the newspapers made the facts general:

The Times. 14th January 1801. Extract.
'Since the French Government does not reply to the observations of our Government, about the prisoners, H.M. can no longer consider them simply as French prisoners... But as destitute fellow creatures, abandoned by that Government, and as such having no hope left but from the compassion of this country... The King... has commanded me to have clothing sent as soon as possible to the depots, and rations delivered onto these poor men.'

The two commissaries had arrived at Liverpool on the 6th January and, already biased against the critics, found to no one's surprise, that everything was in perfect order. The food ration had been restored two days earlier, and the naked clad, so when the prisoners were questioned individually, they wisely made no complaint. M. Otto had at last ordered the distribution of the clothing already in the depot store. These were only jackets and trousers, but other necessary items were ordered, except for footwear which was made in the prison, by the French shoemakers, at one shilling a pair. These were known as List-shoes; very thick wooden soles and uppers made from material not leather. Shoemaking was a legitimate prisoner of war work, but it was well-known that issued clothing often ended up as list-shoe uppers. This brought about the order that footwear which matched the wearer's garments, should be seized and confiscated.

We have been able to tell the story of the Liverpool captives in particular and in some detail, through Alfred de Curzon's discovery of the Currie Collection of letters and reports. However, it should be remembered that this sad tale was only a comparatively small item in the larger story of a nationwide year-long crisis. The problem was not peculiar to Liverpool; and there were probably other selfless 'Curries', 'Carsons' and 'Cochranes' in many parts of the country. It is possible that, even among the Liverpool philanthropists, there were some who used charity work as a cover for political or even revolutionary ends; but, even if incidentally, they aided helpless men who were technically their enemy.

To end on a cheerful note. Any prisoners of that dreadful period, who managed to survive for the following fifteen months, would find themselves homeward bound for France after the Peace of Amiens in 1802.

The French Prison, or Borough Gaol, was barely half full by the time the Treaty of Amiens ended the Revolutionary War, on the 27th March, 1802. Only twelve hundred prisoners were left to join the waiting cartel ships in the harbour, and, as far as we know, they were the last of our unwilling guests to occupy Liverpool's prisons.

Apart from general research, Francis Abell studied every writer of Liverpudlian history available to him in 1914; mostly nineteenth century[4] but could find no reference to captives taken in the new war, which lasted from 1803 to 1815. Likewise this author, at the beginning of the twenty-first century, made a similar effort; but with no better result. So we must take it that, although Britain was always short of prisoner space, Liverpool was, for some reason, never again a war prison city. Perhaps the reason was that it was claimed back and put to the use for which Howard originally designed it – a civil gaol.

---

1. The sooner a small privateer could be rid of prisoners, the sooner the vacated space would be available for captured booty. Prisoners were sometimes put ashore on a nearby friendly coast, after the two captains, captor and captive, had signed an agreement (often dishonoured) that a like number of prisoners would be released by exchange.

2. One great task which he tackled was editing the life's work of Robert Burns, in aid of Burns's widow.

3. Alfred de Curzon. *Dr Currie and French Prisoners of War in Liverpool 1800-1801.* Published 1926.

4. Picton, *Memorials of Liverpool*; Stonehouse, *Recollections of Old Liverpool*; Richard Brooke, *Liverpool from 1775–1800*; Gomer Williams, *Liverpool Privateers.*

Chapter Seventeen

Norman Cross Depot
In Huntingdonshire (now Cambridgeshire)

'NORMAN CROSS is the name given to that part of the parish of Yaxley, in the county of Huntingdon, where that great old thoroughfare of England, the Great North Road, along which coaches might drive four abreast, is crossed by the Peterborough Road.

'In one corner, bounded by those two roads, is a large piece of pasture land, some forty acres in extent, which the Government purchased in 1796, for the purpose of erecting barracks on it for prisoners of war, then multiplying fast, and for large numbers of soldiers to guard them.'

The Revd Arthur Brown:
'The French Prisoners of Norman Cross'

APART FROM DARTMOOR, STILL A PLACE OF confinement to this day – though now its inmates are civil prisoners – the great Depot at Norman Cross is the most well-documented of prisoner of war establishments; though scarcely a trace of its seventeen years of wartime existence now remains to be seen.

It is strange to relate that, whilst we have quite a number of memoirs which record the daily lives of 'French' and American prisoners of war who spent time as captives in the 'Prison on the Moor' during its comparatively short period of six years as a depot, no similar journal or diary by a prisoner relating to Norman Cross, either published or in manuscript, has so far been discovered. That is, none that can be ascribed with any certainty to a known Norman Cross prisoner of war; but there is a manuscript in the Scottish Records Office, written by an unnamed French prisoner, captured

at sea in August 1809, which is worthy of consideration. Dr Walker, the historian of Norman Cross Depot, writing a hundred years later, was of the opinion that it was written by a Mr Bell, an Oundle schoolmaster, who had once been employed in the Depot. One might well wonder why he should have written it in French, as it was only after many years had passed that it was published in English. Contemporary local belief had it that the story had been given to Bell by the French prisoner himself, so it could be that the schoolmaster was the original translator rather than the author. Be that as it may, it was a story so well told that it was reprinted in journals and magazines over the years.

Neither Governor, Agent, nor any other official has left anything like a full record of his period of office – although some authentic

Above. Norman Cross – The Block House.

details of Norman Cross may be found in a few well-researched prisoner-of-war-based works of fiction, such as, D.K.Broster's *Mr. Rowl*, and *The French Prisoners of Norman Cross* by the Revd Arthur Brown[1] – and, in his famous book *Lavengro*, George Borrow, the author, linguist and traveller, included a long and vivid, though unfair and prejudiced, boyhood memory of the treatment of his friends among the foreign prisoners of war at Norman Cross, in 1812.

Despite the absence of even a single volume of prisoner of war reminiscences of this Depot – apart from the anonymous contribution previously mentioned – a great mass of detail was to be garnered from the mounds of documents in the Public Records Office, the British Museum, in local archives, newspaper files, diaries, letters, personal recollections and tradition; and to this end a distinguished Peterborough doctor began his researches, more than a century ago. In the early days of his explorations and inquiries, there were still quite a few older folk among the locals who had personal memories of visits to the prison markets, and younger people who remembered the stories which had been passed down through their families.

In 1894, Doctor Thomas James Walker delivered a short lecture based on his findings up to that date, at an exhibition of Napoleonic prisoner of war artifacts, held at the Peterborough Assembly Rooms. Encouraged by its reception, he carried on his exhaustive rummaging through official and local records and, after almost ten further years of diligent research, published his discoveries in 1913: *'The Depôt for Prisoners of War at Norman Cross, Huntingdonshire, 1796 to 1816'*.

Norman Cross, Yaxley or Stilton – Depot, Camp, Barracks or Prison – all names by which this great prisoner of war establishment was known, in one permutation or another, in official and private documents, was considered as a possible site quite early in the seventeen-nineties.

The violent happenings in Europe; the French Revolution in 1789; Louis XVI's declaration of war against Austria in 1792; his downfall and execution, all led inevitably to the French declaration of war against Britain in 1793 and exposed once again the dire lack of prisoner of war accommodation in this country.

As mentioned elsewhere, garrison towns, military centres and great barracks had never been regarded as important necessities in Britain, as our fighting was carried out almost exclusively on foreign soil or in battles on the high seas. Internal security and defences were mainly left to the Yeomanry and local Militias – the Local Defence Volunteers (LDV) or Home Guard of that period. Now, the probability of an influx of large numbers of prisoners who would soon overflow the available secure accommodation on land and the comparatively few hulks at that time already converted for use as floating prisons, was a worrying one. The prospect of that overflow of warlike captives being confined in insecure 'warehouse prisons', thus putting too great a strain on the militias, which would have inevitably led to uprisings and mass escapes, called for immediate action.

In 1793, the very first year of the Revolutionary and Napoleonic Wars, the introduction of the Supplementary Militia Act directed that the then huge sum of two million pounds should be committed towards coping with the problem. A Barrack-Master General was appointed, whose task it was to commission the conversion of buildings thought suitable for the incarceration of foreign captives, and the erection of barracks and depots to house both prisoners and their overseers. A large percentage of the allocated money was committed to the building of what was later often described as the first establishment to be specially designed and built to accommodate prisoners of war. This description is essentially true. Norman Cross was certainly the first really great depot, and was designed to accommodate 7,000 or more prisoners – although the old Fish Ponds Prison near Bristol, later known as Stapleton, had been converted and almost completely custom-built towards the end of the War of American Independence, in 1782

A fairly clear idea of the layout and appearance of the Depot can be gathered from Dr Walker's researches and descriptions, and from four plans which have survived (illustrated and described), together with a number of contemporary watercolours and drawings. The plans cover many years of alterations and additions to what was at first expected to be an important but short-lived establishment. Whilst there was no doubt that such accommodation was an urgent necessity, no one expected that, except for two very brief intervals, it would be fully operational for the next eighteen years.

More revealing and informative than any two-dimensional plan, was an amazingly detailed model of Norman Cross Depot, showing it as it was when the war ended, in the last year of its existence. It was executed by M Foulley, a French prisoner of war, after he had returned to France in 1814. Foulley spent four years and three months as a Norman Cross prisoner, and perusal of the key plan to his model, makes obvious the fact that he must have made reams of notes regarding all aspects of his prison, its civil and military staff and captive occupants, in preparation for this masterpiece of ex-prisoner of war work. Overall, it was not an exact scale-model, but the *casernes* were made to a scale of approximately 170–1; which gives some idea of the size of the completed model: each of the sixteen prison blocks measured about seven inches in length.

The model may still survive somewhere, but so far I have been unable to locate it. We know that it was on display in the Musée de l'Armée in Paris until the First World War as Dr Walker obtained a photograph of it from the Director of that Museum and reproduced it in his book in 1913. Francis Abell may well have actually seen it, as he described it in some detail: 'Not only are the buildings, wells, palisades, pumps, troughs, and other details represented, but tiny models of prisoners at work and play are dotted about [most of them clad in yellow T.O. and broad arrow issue clothes], and in front of the chief, the eastern gate, a battalion of Militia is drawn up, complete to the smallest particulars of arms and equipment.' M. Foulley took a few, perhaps understandable, liberties in his model-making, depicting the outer wall of the Depot as a rectangle, rather than an octagon; and basing the details of buildings outside of the prison on guesswork or misinformation. But it is the only plan or model which shows that the prisoners had their own theatre, situated in the centre of the south-eastern quadrangle.

In 1796, the Government purchased forty-two acres of land from an Irish peer, the Earl of Carysfort (later Lord Carysfort of Norman Cross). The site could not have been more wisely chosen. 'The situation was exceedingly healthy, being at the highest point of the road sloping up for a mile and a half from what was then Whittlesea Mere. It was not too near the sea, to make escape more easy, yet near enough to Yarmouth, Kings Lynn and Wisbech to facilitate the landing and transport of prisoners to their destination. It was on the Great North Road, only seventy-eight miles from London, and near enough to towns to obtain provisions with ease and in abundance.

It was in fact selected by the War Office on all these accounts, from amongst several other eligible sites in the kingdom.' Good fresh water in plentiful supply was another qualifying factor: over the years more than twenty wells had been sunk, some as deep as a hundred feet. However, above all other considerations, speed of construction was of the essence. Dartmoor was to take four years to erect, built as it was of granite, but prefabrication in wood was the more rapid and economical method employed in the case of Norman Cross, which was almost complete in as many months.

Work began at Norman Cross in December 1796 The prisons and most other buildings were prefabricated in London, under the direction of William Adams, Master Carpenter to the Board of Ordnance. His craftsmen fashioned substantial wooden frameworks at a feverish rate, which were quickly carted up-country to the site of the future depot. There they were received by a great workforce of some five hundred carpenters and labourers, who erected the skeletal frames on to footings of hard-core or stone, before cladding them with overlapping weather-boarding. These men worked in shifts day and night, seven days a week, so that the job went on non-stop – and none were employed who had not previously agreed to work on Sundays, when called upon.

On the 13th February, 1797, the rather procrastinating Barrack Master General, applied for the order to start the building; but the Transport Board had beaten him to it by some months as, by the 4th of February, surveyors had pronounced the first stage of the prisons, the administrative offices, outbuildings and the military barracks, for the most part completed! It is hard to understand how the Barrack Master General could have been unaware of the progress made in such a nationally important matter; but it must be admitted that he was responsible for depots and converted buildings all over the country.

During the following weeks, various alterations were made to the original plans and constructions. Some prison buildings were reallocated for use as hospitals; the resultant loss of prisoner-space being made up by adding another storey to each of the remaining prison blocks. An interesting item unearthed by Dr Walker in his searches, was a bill for a six month supply of coal to Norman Cross Depot, which was for the sum of £390. This was a surprisingly large fuel expense, as only the hospitals were fitted with fireplaces, and then sparingly – the prison blocks were not supplied with artificial heating of any kind, it being generally supposed that the natural body-heat emitted by so many thousands of men would suffice. A more generous reason may have been that the authorities were conscious that the confinement of so many men in wooden buildings, penned in by wooden fencing, presented an obvious fire hazard. If so, they had not long to wait to prove their point But for the prompt action and fire-fighting ability of the Depot's military men, we might well be reading of the destruction of Norman Cross Depot in the great fire of 1798. In October, two straw-thatched huts adjoining wooden buildings went up in flames, whether the work of arsonists or accidental was never discovered. With the wind in their favour, the soldier-firefighters managed to subdue the flames, probably using the 'chain' method of passing buckets from man to man, from the water source to the point of conflagration. Nevertheless, a lesson had been learned; soon after the event a fire appliance was delivered to Norman Cross; a rather magnificent horse-drawn fire-engine; which may still be seen in Peterborough Museum.

The prison buildings, the airing yards, and the surrounding walls took up some twenty-two acres, which were positioned roughly in the centre of the forty-two acre site. A bird's-eye view of the original layout would have revealed that the Depot was enclosed by an octagonal outer wall of stout wooden palisading; but some years later, in 1807, the wooden wall was replaced by one of brick. As can be seen in the various plans, the Depot was designed from a focal point at its very centre, where four roads crossed. At that point there stood a feature unique to Norman Cross Depot – a strongly armed octagonal wooden Block House. Radiating out from that central point were four quadrangular yards, each about three and a half acres in extent. In each of these yards were four red-tile-roofed, two-storey prison buildings, or *casernes*, each of them measuring 100 feet in length by twenty-two feet in width, all facing eastward. Within, the ceilings were rather lofty, that of the lower storey being twelve feet high, and the upper eight feet six inches. There was good reason for this apparent generosity of air space. Each of these chambers served as living room, dining hall or dormitory, according to time of day; and the height was necessary to provide the maximum hammock space at night. Hooks to take the head clews at one end of each hammock were affixed at regular intervals into rails along the length of wooden walls of each prison building. Eight feet out from each long wall and opposite each hook were floor-to-ceiling posts or stanchions, into which were driven hooks to take the foot clews. From this it is relatively easy to picture the upstairs and downstairs chambers, each of them one hundred feet by twenty-two, with lines of wooden pillars no more than two feet apart, eight feet out from either wall; thus leaving a clear space six feet wide, which ran the length of the building. When stretched to the limit, each of the twelve buildings in the three quadrangles dedicated to rank and file prisoners could sleep about 500 as they slung their hammocks one above the other, three tiers deep on the ground floor and two deep on the upper. Each tier would accommodate fifty sleepers – when occupied, the hammocks would have been no more than a few inches apart. This may seem like cruel overcrowding, but the hammock-space allowed to the captives was no less than that allowed to Royal Navy seamen at that time – and no worse than that experienced on some vessels during World War II, particularly on troop ships!

Walker calculated that, over the eighteen years of its existence, the average number of prisoners to be held in Norman Cross must have been about 6,000.This means, of course, that, from time to time, the Depot must have been seriously overcrowded. Nevertheless, specially designed as it was, the accommodation was probably a decided improvement on just about every other depot in this country and there were some periods when the prisons were half empty. In the early days of the Revolutionary War, when the exchange system was working at its best, many hundreds of British prisoners and an equal number of our foreign captives, had been exchanged and returned to their homelands. The number of prisoners of war in Britain in 1799 was just under 26,000, and only 3,038 were confined in Norman Cross. There were other years when, for one reason or another, the prisoner population in the Depot was down to a particularly low level – for a time in 1804 it had dropped to about the 3,000 mark; but as the second half of the war dragged on, the number of prisoners flooding into this country rapidly increased to the point when other super-depots had to be built.

The space between the front of each *caserne* and the back of the one before it, was enclosed at each end with a high gated palisade fence, thus providing each prison with an inner yard some one hundred feet by seventy feet in area. During the day, after early morning muster, the gates were opened into the main airing yards, which allowed the inmates of all four prisons in a particular airing yard to indulge in exercise, sport, trade or intermingle socially with their fellows. Then, in late afternoon, they would be returned to their inner yards for evening muster, the gates being locked for 'lights out' at sunset.

The freedom of the airing yards, whilst of the most humanising importance to the prisoners, was not so much a privilege as a must. In accordance with Transport Office Regulations, all captives had to spend the hours between sunrise and sunset out of the prison blocks and in the fresh air of the yards, except when the weather was particularly inclement. Sick or ailing prisoners were usually granted special dispensation from this otherwise strict regulation.

Securely fenced-off areas in each of the airing grounds enclosed a courtyard wherein were situated two turnkeys' lodges, and other small official buildings, stores, and a cookhouse. The south-eastern of these courtyards, to the right of the southern entrance to the Depot, on the Peterborough Road, was similarly the site for two turnkey lodges, etc., but in addition contained the administrative centre and the Agent's offices.

Long experience of prisoner of war management dictated that priority should be given to the inclusion of a punishment block in the planning of the new depot. This, the *cachot* or Black Hole, was situated in the south-western courtyard, close by the turnkeys' lodges. It comprised a dozen tightly barred lock-ups, designed for discomfort, wherein serious wrong-doers were committed to periods of solitary confinement, plus a stomach-punishing reduction in their rations, with only the occasional luxury of a short period of exercise in its tiny heavily stockaded airing yard. The most incorrigible, or violent offenders were sometimes clapped in irons – a requisition form in the Norman Cross archives requests delivery of two dozen pairs of handcuffs.

In the north-eastern quadrangle two – and in later years three – of the four blocks originally intended for the confinement of prisoners, were converted into hospitals. One section was reserved for the treatment of officers and other distinguished prisoners; and part of another block was used as living quarters for the doctors, matron and medical staff. There were a few other buildings in that yard, including the very necessary ones of medical storerooms and a mortuary – which was hidden away behind the prison blocks.

After the 22nd December, 1799, the Transport Office or Board became answerable for just about everything concerning the housing, provisioning, transport, transfer, exchange, etc., of prisoners of war – *in health*. However, all depot hospitals and their patients remained under the auspices of Chief Surgeons, who were still responsible to another and much earlier authority – the 'Sick and Hurt Office'. As far back as Samuel Pepys, himself one of its Commissioners, it had been the overseeing authority for all prisoners of war in Britain, in sickness *and* in health.

The Sick and Hurt Office was the colloquial name for *'The Commissioners for Taking Care of Sick and Wounded Seamen and the Exchanging of Prisoners of War'*. This lengthy title gave little idea of the scope of its duties, for, until December 1799, it had encompassed all the jobs which the Transport Board had taken over – plus the medical duties which it continued to undertake.

There was only one legitimate way out from each quadrangle of the prison yards and that was through a gateway between the two turnkey lodges located on the inner side of the fences which enclosed the courtyards. Directly opposite these were gates which exited on to the main roads between the stockades and the outer walls of the Depot.

As can be gathered from the preceding notes, the basic layout of the Depot was brilliantly conceived for its purpose and, had it been built in stone or brick, it may well have thwarted the ambitions of many an ingenious escape specialist. However, built as it had been, of wood as an urgent 'temporary expedient', security depended more on physical deterrents, such as diligent sentries and strong detachments of guards, than on timber stockades, however well constructed. Cannon were mounted at strategic points and the octagonal Block House at the centre of the site, with its swivel cannons and musket slots, which overlooked all four prison blocks, was an ominous reminder that riots and uprisings could be quickly suppressed.

The outer wooden stockade wall – later replaced by brick – which was just over three-quarters of a mile in circumference, was patrolled by companies of militia or regular troops drawn from the two regiments which were accommodated in the Eastern and Western Barracks. These regiments were regularly changed in order to discourage a too close association between guards and prisoners, which might lead to bribery and collusion in escape attempts, or assistance in carrying on forbidden trading in straw-plait, pornography or other illicit employments. Every prisoner of war establishment in this country practised this precaution, but as can be learned from the many instances quoted throughout this book, no matter how many stripes, and worse, were inflicted on guards who were detected in their treachery, the financial rake-offs must have been great indeed, for no war prison ever found a complete answer to the problem.

After darkness fell, the outer wall was illuminated by lamps set at regular intervals along its length, and at all hours of the day and night strong detachments of guards were posted at all the main entrances. However, all this show of military strength was confined to the outside of the prison yards, and no sentries or guards were posted within. The only prison officials within the quadrangles were the turnkeys who, incidentally, lived in their lodges during their duty shifts, and a few others who came and went, such as store-keepers and cooks; but their workplaces were safely situated within the palisaded courtyards already described. There were of course, times of unrest and insurrection when companies of troops were sent in with loaded muskets and fixed bayonets to quell disturbances. To a very great extent, however, the everyday life of the prisoners of war within the yards, their protection from troublemakers and ne'er-do-wells, depended on policing by prisoners elected from among their fellows, who, with few exceptions, conducted their internal courts and administration of justice with great seriousness and fairness.

The only description we have of the Depot as seen through the eyes of a confinee, is to be found in the manuscript in the Scottish Records Office mentioned earlier, which professes to be a first-person narrative of capture, imprisonment and escape from Norman Cross Depot (1809–1811).

> 'On the 1st of August 1809, a day I shall ever have cause to remember, I went on a pleasure excursion, in a small vessel belonging to my father, from Marseilles to Nice. At this time the coast of France was strictly watched by English cruisers; and to elude

these we kept as much as possible close inshore. This precaution was, unfortunately, useless. When off the Isles of Hyeres, we were observed, and chased by an English cutter, which soon came up with us. Resistance was of course useless, and, foreseeing the result, we at the first shot yielded ourselves prisoners. Before going on board the enemy's vessel I concealed about my person as much money and other valuables as I could; and of this property I was not afterwards deprived. We were, indeed, treated with less severity than we had reason to expect. On the day after our capture, we were removed, with many other prisoners, into another vessel, with orders to make the best of our way to England. What my sensations were on being thus torn from my beloved country, my friends and relations, may be easily conceived.

'In a few days we arrived on the coast of England, and were immediately ordered round to an eastern port – Lynn in Norfolk – whence we were forwarded, to the number of some hundreds, in lighters and small craft, to the depôt of prisoners of war at Norman Cross – I think about fifty miles inland. Arriving at Peterborough – a respectable-looking town, with a handsome cathedral – apparently a gay and thoughtless set, we were marched to our destination. On reaching Norman Cross, we all underwent the usual scrutiny by the inspecting officers; and an exact description was taken of each individual as to his age, size, colour of hair and eyes, &c., which was entered in a book kept for the purpose. All these preparations gave a fearful presentiment of what we were afterwards to expect, and raised emotions in my breast of a nature I cannot define, but which several times whilst the examination was going on, made me shudder with a kind of horror, not at all lessened on our admittance into, and review of our prison. The English had here upwards of seven thousand prisoners of war, of one nation or another, but chiefly Frenchmen. I will endeavour to describe a few particulars of the place, as well as I can recollect, which may at the same time also serve to illustrate my escape from it.

'The whole of the buildings, including the prison, and the barracks of the soldiers who guarded us, were situated on an eminence, and were certainly airy enough [*this was something of an understatement, as many complaints were made of life-threatening exposure to the cold; though those who suffered most would have been the half-starved and half-naked deadbeats who had sacrificed their food and clothing to the gambling tables*] commanding a full and extensive view over the surrounding country, which appeared well cultivated in some parts; but in front of the prison, to the south-east, the prospect terminated in fens and marshes, in the centre of which was Whittelsea Mere, a large lake, of some miles in circumference. The high road from London to Scotland ran close by the prison, and we could, at all hours of the day, see the stage-coaches and other carriages bounding along the beautiful roads of the country with a rapidity unknown elsewhere, and the contrast afforded by contemplating these scenes of liberty continually before our eyes, only served to render the comparison more harrowing to our feelings.

' There was no apparent show about the place of military strength, formed by turreted castles, or embrasured battlements; in fact it was little better than an enclosed camp. The security of the prisoners was effected by the unceasing watch of ever-wakeful sentinels, constantly passing and repassing, who were continually changing and I have no doubt that this mode of security was more effectual than if surrounded by moated walls or by fortified towers. Very few, in comparison of the numbers who attempted it, succeeded in escaping the boundaries, though many ingenious devices were put in practice to accomplish it. However, if once clear of the place, final success was not so difficult.

'The space appointed for the reception of prisoners consisted of four equal divisions or quadrangles; and these again were divided into four parts, each of which were surrounded by high palisades of wood, and paved for walking on; but the small ground it occupied scarcely left us sufficient room to exercise for our health, and this was a very great privation. In each of these subdivisions was a large wooden building, covered with red tiles, in which we ate our meals and dwelt; these also served for our dormitories, or sleeping places, where we were nightly piled in hammocks, tier upon tier, in most horrible regularity.

'A division of another quadrangle was allotted to the officers, who were allowed a few trifling indulgences not granted to the common men, amongst whom I unfortunately was included. In another division was a school, the master of which was duly paid for his attendance. It was conducted with great regularity and decorum, and there you might sometimes see several respectable Englishmen, particularly those attached to the duties of the prison, taking their seats with the boys to learn the French language. Another small part was appropriated as a place of closer confinement or punishment to those who broke the rules appointed for our government, or wantonly defaced any part of the buildings, or pawned or lost their clothes; these last were put, I think, upon two thirds allowance of provisions, till the loss occasioned thereby was made good; and I must confess this part was seldom without its due proportion of inhabitants.

'The centre of the prison was surrounded by a high brick wall, beyond which were the barracks for the English soldiers, several guard houses, and some handsome buildings for both the civil and military officers; whilst a circular blockhouse, mounted with swivels or small cannon, pointing to the different divisions, frowned terrifically over us, and completed the *outside* of the picture.'

He then went on to describe many interesting aspects of a prisoner's life in the depot, and details of his adventures before completing his successful getaway and arrival in Marseilles; some of which will be included later in this chapter.

The first batch of 934 prisoners arrived at the new Depot on the 26th March, 1797. They were delivered by barge to Yaxley from Lynn, at a charge of 1s.10d. per man, under the superintendence of Captain Daniel Woodriff RN., who was at that time responsible for the reception and distribution of prisoners of war to Yarmouth, Hull and Lynn. Woodriff later served as Agent at Norman Cross from 1799 until the temporary cessation of hostilities in 1802; then, during the short Peace of Amiens, he was made captain of the 42-gun HMS *Calcutta* which, after resumption of the war a year later, was captured by the French, and he himself became a prisoner of war, paroled to Verdun.

By the 18th May, eight weeks after the first arrivals from Lynn had passed through the main gate, the number of prisoners had risen dramatically; officially, 3,393 had been added to the original intake, but a few less than that number actually arrived: three had escaped and seven died in transit.

The victual allowances for prisoners were often much more generous on paper than they were in fact. Sustenance at 7d. a day for men in transit may not seem much, but was supposed to represent a pound of bread or ship's biscuit, and three-quarters of a pound of beef; but what with corrupt contractors, the 'pusser's pound' and the fact that the weight included bone, it was often less than sustaining. One might expect to learn that the carefully planned depot got off to a good start, with the prisoners being served provisions as clean and fresh as the new buildings, but from the outset there were bitter complaints about the quality of the food provided. It would seem that the complaint of one prisoner, who said that 'the beef and bread were so bad that they were not fit for a prisoner's dog to eat', was not just an unfair grouse made by an habitual captive fault-finder. British soldiers and NCOs of the Depot Garrison sympathetically attested that, 'as fellow creatures they must allow that the provisions given to the prisoners were not fit for them to eat, and that the water they had was much better than the beer'.

The responsibility for protecting prisoners against sufferings imposed by unscrupulous contractors, cooks and numerous others who had a finger in the prisoners' pie, lay primarily at the door of the depot Agents. The first of these to be appointed to watch over Norman Cross inmates was John Delafons, who was appointed to that important position on the 18th March, 1797 – but resigned eight days later, on the 26th March, the very day that the Depot opened its doors to its first reluctant visitors. Delafons was superseded by another civilian, James Perrot, who had been transferred from Portchester Castle and reigned at Norman Cross from the following month until January 1799. After that time, the appointment of Agent to any prisoner of war depot in Britain was given almost exclusively to naval officers, usually post-captains of not less than ten years seniority; and, as we know, Captain Woodriff RN took over at the Cross until April 1802.

Captain Woodriff was at sea when the war broke out anew in 1803, and the post was held by Captain Thomas Pressland RN from June of that year until August 1811. Fifth in the line of succession was Captain John Draper RN one of the fairest and most highly regarded of depot Agents. He served for only eighteen months, until his death in February 1813, but during that short time he earned the appreciation and respect of his captive charges. In St Peter's Church, Yaxley, there is a marble tablet which for ever attests to their esteem for his humanity and consideration towards them:

> 'Inscribed at the desire and the sole expense of the French prisoners of war at Norman Cross, to the memory of Captain John Draper R.N., who for the last 18 months of his life was agent to the depôt, in testimony of their esteem and gratitude for his humane attention to their comforts during that too short period. He died Feb. 23, 1813, aged 53 years.'

Captain Draper was given a military funeral, attended by officers and men of the Garrison and the Depot guard. The Revd Arthur Brown, in his little book on Norman Cross, wrote: '[The prisoners] addressed a petition to the commandant that some of them might be allowed to attend the funeral at Yaxley Church, a request which Major Kelly granted with the greatest readiness, and was much touched by the concluding words of the petition, that he need not be afraid of incurring any risk by letting them come out for the occasion, because, wild as many of them were, there was not a single man amongst them that was such a *mauvais sujet* as to take advantage of the opportunity to attempt his escape.' The prisoners justified Major Kelly's dangerous trust, and were as good as their word. The last Norman Cross Agent was Captain W Hanwell, who carried on the good work until August 1814.

Not all of the prisoners were common soldiers and sailors. There was a separate *caserne* for non-commissioned officers, which was probably a bit more spacious and comfortable than that which their rank and file countrymen endured. Also, within a fenced-off subdivision of the south-eastern quadrangle, was the Officers' Prison, where 'broke-paroles' – and officers who had honourably refused to sign their *parole d'honneur* in the first place – were quartered. Norman Cross was opened in good time to receive its share of officers who, though individually unoffending, were deprived of the comparative freedom of parole, and experienced close confinement for short periods. The Government took this step on more than one occasion: at times when the French were known to be preparing for invasion or the general restlessness of the prisoners of war and the increase of escape attempts were particularly worrying. 1797, the first year of Norman Cross Depot's existence, was one such a time. The Fishguard affair in February, which really was an actual French landing on British soil, however ineffectual, convinced the Government and many of our countrymen that it was just a foretaste of danger, with a full-scale invasion soon to follow.

On the 25th November, 1797, all English parole towns were cleared of their prisoner populations, and most of the parolees sent to Norman Cross. Some would not have had far to travel, as about a hundred officers were lodged in Peterborough and its surrounding villages; but others were marched, some for hundreds of miles, into their first taste of real close captivity. Over the years, the Norman Cross Officers' Prison was to know just about every rank of officer captive, naval, merchant and military, from cadet to general – plus a few distinguished civilian gentlemen, passengers on ships at the time of capture. However, the most senior – and incidentally the most troublesome – of all French military prisoners, General Donatien-Marie-Joseph-de-Vimeur Viscount de Rochambeau, and General Jacques Boyê were given special accommodation. As a result of their repeated disregard for their given word of honour, they were not allowed to communicate or mix with other captive officers in the official Officers' Prison, however senior. Until they were again granted parole in March 1806, they spent eighteen months in specially adapted and strongly guarded wards in the Military Hospital within the confines of Norman Cross Depot.

As was the case in all prisons, the greatest relief from boredom and depression at Norman Cross must have been the Depot Markets. They provided a profitable means of disposing of any of their works which might appeal to the British public, and thus produced an income by which they could add the odd luxury to their monotonous and often frugal diet; provide warm clothing against the discomforts of the winter months – and, in some cases, build up the kitty in an escape fund. The story of the prison markets is, to a great extent common to all depots. Some were, it is true, no more than trading slots through prison walls or palisades, or a bumboat moored alongside a prison hulk; whilst some, large prisons such as Norman Cross, Dartmoor, Perth, Valleyfield and the like, rivalled the local town markets in both size and prosperity. Talented or industrious prisoners could avoid most of the hardships experienced by the unresourceful or profligate among them; and the markets of the great depots created thriving businesses and wealth to British growers and dealers from nearby town and villages; blessed as they were with a captive clientele of thousands with nowhere else to shop.

As I have shown in my other book, (*The Arts and Crafts of Napoleonic and American Prisoners of War 1756-1816*, Chapters 2 and 3, PRISONER OF WAR MARKETS), both prisoners and dealers were fully aware of the do's and don'ts of the marketplace, and equally aware of the punishments doled out on detection of infringements. The appropriate clauses of the strict but reasonable Government rules and regulations – which forbade a number of illicit manufactures and activities – were prominently posted up in all trading areas. Article 9 read:

> '**9.** All Dealers, (excepting such as Trade in Articles not proper to be admitted into the Prison) are to be allowed to remain at the principal Gate of the Prison from six o'clock in the morning until three in the Afternoon, to dispose of their Merchandise to the Prisoners; but any

of the Prisoners who shall be detected in attempting to introduce into the Prison Spirituous Liquors, or other improper Articles, or in receiving or delivering any Letter, shall be punished for the Abuse of this Indulgence, in such Manner as the Commissioners may direct.'

Other promulgated rules and regulations detailed what was meant by 'improper Articles'. Prisoner-produced pornography was greatly frowned upon by the authorities, and there was much concern that if it was not completely stamped out, the evil French pornographers would ruin the morals of the countryfolk! As early in the life of the new Depot as 1798, an Order was made and displayed with the warning:

'Obscene figures and indecent toys and all such indecent representations tending to disseminate Lewdness and Immorality exposed for sale or prepared for that purpose are to be instantly destroyed.'

There are many records of the military being sent in to break up those prisoners' workshops which were producing obscene 'toys', indecent writings and erotic illustrations, which indicates that the production and popularity of such material was widespread. The most harshly punished of prisoner of war offences was the forging, or passing off as genuine, false paper money, for both were capital crimes. Many prisoners of war in England were hanged for forging no more than a single One Pound note.

Nearly all prohibitions were common to all depots, such as the fabricating of prisoner of war artifacts from Government issue materials; blankets, hammocks, bedding, wood from the prison structures, etc. However, some bans were enforced in the interest of particular local trades and professions. In the case of Norman Cross it was the manufacturing of straw-plait and the making of straw bonnets. This was a reasonable enough prohibition, as straw plaiting was a cottage industry upon which many Huntingdonshire families depended to survive. The Government, too, had an interest; it contended that, technically, the prisoner-made plait should be regarded as a taxable foreign import, and that the Revenue was thus being deprived of its dues. This might have been a legal ploy to help protect the cottage plait-makers; and as the tax was uncollectable, the only alternative was to punish the prisoner plaiters and the local dealers who encouraged them, and destroy the illegal plait. (see *The Arts and Crafts of Napoleonic and American Prisoners of War 1756-1816*, Chapter 4, THE STRAW WORKERS)

The market was the greatest privilege granted to prisoners of war in Britain, and yet was the most abused. None of the contraband activities were ever completely wiped out; but the blame for this could be more fairly aimed at the wealthy civilian dealers who met the workers in the markets, and guards who were their go-betweens.

Despite this, and the indisputable fact that the privilege of the market made for a too close fraternization between inhabitants and prisoners, to the detriment of security, it is probable that the privilege prevented the majority of the captives from contemplating riots and great uprisings. It is known that the mere threat to close the market, was often enough for troublemakers to be handed over to the authorities by their wiser and better behaved brethren. It was said that some prisoners, perhaps men who had found a comfortable niche in the prisoner-of-war work industry which fed the market, sold their turn on Exchange Lists, rather than return to their war-torn homeland – although a more cynical view suggested that they preferred to spend the war years in the comparative comfort of a depot, rather than face re-enlistment in their Emperor's Army or Navy, with the prospect of wounds or death – or a second spell of captivity, perhaps in the prison hulks.

There were five markets in all at Norman Cross, the principal one, indirectly supplying the other four prisoner-run inner markets, one in each of the quadrangles. At one time the main market was open on three days each week, but some records state that it was open every day, except Sundays. There is room to doubt that there was never a Sunday market, at least at Norman Cross. An extract from a near contemporary article in a local publication suggests otherwise:

Crosby's Complete Pocket Gazette. Yaxley. 1818.
'...Barracks were erected on a very liberal and excellent plan for the security of French prisoners who were confined here during the late war, and employed themselves in making bone toys, and straw boxes, and many other small articles, to which people of all descriptions were admitted on Sundays, when more than £200 a day has been frequently laid out in purchasing their labours of the preceding week. It is capable of containing 7 or 8,000 men, and has barracks for two regiments of infantry.'

It is written rather ambiguously, for it might suggest that the market only opened one day a week, or that the prisoners only sold their work on the Sabbath.

The market day began at six o'clock in the morning, when the local dealers and their merchandise were checked into the Depot through the Eastern Gate, on to a paved courtyard within, which was the prison Marketplace, In the centre of this area they rapidly set up their shops, stalls, benches and tables, which were soon laden with all manner of goods in great quantity; from greengroceries, provisions and secondhand clothes to tobacco, coffee and tea. A little later, an inner gate was opened to usher in elected prisoners from each of the four prison squares, who represented their unprivileged fellows. Some were commissioned to act as sellers of their fascinating works of art and craftsmanship, and others as buyers in bulk to stock up the prisoner-shopkeepers in the inner markets. The tables on which were exhibited prisoner of war-created artefacts for sale, were ranged around the periphery of the marketplace, up against the wall and wooden fencing which cut it off from the rest of the prison.

If the reader is able to inspect the prisoner of war collection at Peterborough Museum or can visualise the works illustrated in this book as they once were – each labelled with its price and the maker's name; a colourfully-clad Frenchman singing the praises of his wares in an equally colourful mixture of French and English – then it becomes easier to understand why these foreign manufactures in bone, straw, wood and other recycled materials, remained popular with the British public for as long as there were prisoners to produce them.

One may be sure that some pieces were bought as acts of charity towards men who, though our national foes, were in a pitiable condition. Whilst other inexpensive odds and ends, such as pipe tampers or apple-corers, would have been purchased and kept as souvenirs fabricated by a captured enemy. However, the large number of pieces, often delicate and fragile, which have survived undamaged for two hundred years or more, show that they were treasured for their quality and beauty, and for that air of mystery which still clings to them to this day – how could they possibly have been created from such materials, without the finest of tools, by men existing in such primitive conditions as the crowded depot or the prison ship?

At ten o'clock in the morning, when the local and prisoner vendors were ready for the commercial battle of the day to begin, the main market at Norman Cross was opened to the visiting public. The latter could then enjoy their excursion into a foreign environment until three o'clock in the afternoon.

Both Francis Abell and Dr Walker, working at the end of the nineteenth century, found evidence that Norman Cross was far from escape-proof, though the majority of the planned getaways were thwarted in the attempt, most of the courageous escapees being soon recaptured. In fact, the percentage of successful escapes from Norman Cross was less than from most other depots. This was due to several factors; it was sited farther from the coast than many others; the training of its military strength was superior to the general standard and it would seem that the inhabitants of the surrounding countryside were particularly keen bounty-hunters. It is also probable that even among local people who were deeply involved in illegal dealings with prisoners in the Depot market, there were some who were not above adding to their ill-gotten gains, by betraying prisoners whom they had helped to escape – in return for the ten-shillings-a-head offered for their recapture. The cost to this country in reward money was slight indeed because, as the recaptured absconder was well aware, it would ultimately be he himself who paid for his own recapture. Amongst the many warnings prominently posted up in every depot, was one which informed him that '…any prisoner who shall be taken attempting to escape shall have his ration reduced, until the amount saved by such reduction shall have made good any expense incurred in his recapture.'

All the usual methods of quitting the Depot were tried; tunnelling, climbing, bribery, etc., plus individual ingenious efforts, which were swiftly communicated to other depots through the prisoners' grape-vine, thus inspiring copycat efforts elsewhere. Dung-cart getaways are mentioned in the records of a number of war prisons, as are other unusual means of transport beyond the confining walls. In the 1797 register of Dutch captives received at Norman Cross, is a four-word example of one such exit. Against the name of Jan Cramer, sailor, captured after the Battle of Camperdown, is the laconic note: 'escaped in a Chest'.

Another favoured stratagem was 'disguise', a ploy probably popular with all liberty-seeking prisoners in all wars – many exciting tales are told of its employment in escape attempts from stalags during The Second World War. The secondhand-clothes dealers who came miles to shout their wares in the depot markets, were never without purchasers. One of the most ardent ambitions of a prisoner in funds, was to get out of his hated sulphur-yellow prison-issue – and there were some who had more than sartorial elegance in mind. From time to time, prisoners disguised as local residents, farmers or stall-holders, tried to leave with the visiting public when the market closed for the day. Well-worn cast-offs were an excellent camouflage, but odds and ends of old military uniforms, jackets, breeches, caps, which might be transformed into look-alike regimentals, were always in demand. The Dartmoor records tell of three prisoners who had each bought complete secondhand, but genuine, British military uniforms in the depot market. Their acquisitions were reported to the Governor, who told the prisoners that he was not questioning their intent, but must regretfully confiscate their purchases – issuing to each a signed receipt and assuring them that their goods would be returned when the war was over!

A paragraph in a nineteenth century military magazine tells the story of a prisoner whose careful 'disguise' preparation was *almost* perfect:

FRENCH INGENUITY
'A French Prisoner in Norman Cross Barracks had recourse to the following stratagem to obtain his liberty: He made himself a complete uniform of the Hertfordshire Militia, and a wooden gun, stained, surmounted by a tin bayonet. Thus equipped, he mixed with the guard (consisting of men from the Hertford Regiment), and when they were ordered to march out, having been relieved, Monsieur fell in and marched out too. Thus far he was fortunate, but when he arrived at the guard room, lo! What befell him. His new comrades ranged their muskets on the rack, and he endeavoured to follow their example, but as his wooden piece was unfortunately a few inches too long, he was unable to place it properly. This was observed, and the unfortunate captive obliged to forego the hopes of that liberty for which he had so anxiously and so ingeniously laboured.'

Although successful escapes from Norman Cross were very few and far between, attempts and rumours of attempts kept the Depot officials and military staff constantly on their toes. Abell, who most often showed a great deal of sympathy for our captive French foes, was stating no more than unprejudiced truth when he reminds us:

'…that the rank and file and not a few of the officers, of the French Revolutionary Army and Navy, who were prisoners of war in Britain, were of the lowest classes of society, desperate, lawless, religionless, unprincipled men who in confinement were a constant source of anxiety and watchfulness, and at large were positively dangers to society. If a body of men like this got loose, as did fifteen on the night of the 5th April, 1799, from Norman Cross, the fact was enough to carry terror throughout a countryside.'

It would seem that even when 'a body of men like this got loose' *legally* – by exchange – their presence in a town might be intimidating to local inhabitants.

Early in 1799, the Mayor of Lynn was disturbed by the large number of freed French prisoners who, unsupervised, jubilant and no doubt unruly, ranged through his town. Each would have possessed a genuine (we hope!) passport, and we can imagine their high spirits as they awaited the cartel vessels which would soon take them on the short Channel crossing, to their homeland.

A letter, written a year or so after the Depot's opening, proves that even this specially designed establishment suffered from the same difficulty as all other land prisons and prisons afloat: they had no rapid and fool-proof method of establishing the exact number of prisoners within their walls at any particular moment. The wily prisoners who were well aware of this, made life hell for their captors. On the 8th August, 1798, the Depot's first active Agent, James Perrot, wrote to Captain Daniel Woodriff:

'If you remember, on returning from the barracks on Sunday, Captain Llewellin informed us that a report had been propagated that seven prisoners intended to escape that day, which we both looked upon as a mere report; they were counted both that night, but with little effect from the additions made to the numbers by the man you brought from Lynn, and yesterday morning and afternoon, but in such confusion from the prisoners refusing to answer, from others giving in fictional names, and others answering for two or three. In consequence of all these irregularities I made all my clerks, a turnkey

Norman Cross – The Cooking Ovens.

and a file of soldiers, go into the south east quadrangle this morning at five o'clock, and muster each prison separately, and found that six prisoners from the Officers' Prison have escaped, but can obtain none of their names except Captain Dorfe, who some time ago applied to me for to obtain liberty for him to reside with his family at Ipswich where he had married an English wife. The officers remaining have separately and conjunctively refused to give the names of the other five, for which I have ordered the whole to be put on half allowances tomorrow. After the most diligent searches we could only find one probable place where they had escaped, by the end next the South Gate, by breaking one of the rails of the picket, but how they passed afterwards is a mystery still unravelled.'

It is possible that an 'escape chapter' could be compiled which cited a story, or stories, representing each of the eighteen years of the Depots existence; but much of this would be repetitive. So just a few examples must suffice.

Until the rebuilding of the outer wall in brick – in 1807 – the wooden fence which surrounded the prison must have seemed an open invitation to any adventurous spirit and a number took up the challenge. It was, in fact, one mass attempt to defeat the timber structures in that year, which called for a team of bricklayers to erect a more daunting obstacle. Long after lights out, on the 25th September, 1807, no fewer than five hundred prisoners made a concerted attack on the stockade which surrounded their quadrangle smashing a whole length of it to the ground. Their intention was, of course, to repeat their onslaught when they

reached the outer wooden fence; but a strong force of soldiers, militia and guards drove them back inside their inner yards. Strangely, not a shot was fired; but between forty and fifty suffered serious wounds from bayonet thrusts.

Three years earlier an even more serious uprising had taken place. With the Treaty of Amiens in March 1802, Norman Cross had been completely emptied of its prisoners, and much of its stores, equipment, land and buildings had been leased or sold off. All this had to be hastily clawed back on the resumption of hostilities in May of the following year, and Norman Cross reopened its gates on the 18th June. By late 1804, only about fifty percent of the Depot's prisoner capacity had been taken up, but the 3,000 or more troublesome captive occupants were in a rebellious state of mind. Even though the Agent and the military Commandant had only half the possible number of prisoners to control, the situation was disturbing enough for special precautions to be taken.

Any prisoner attempting to escape was to be summarily executed! (Although on occasion some prisoners did lose their lives whilst making a dash for freedom, there is no evidence that any recaptured escapee was ever subsequently shot or hanged for that offence alone.) All 'implements and sharp edged tools' had to be given up; and each prisoner was allowed just one knife – presumably for use at mealtimes or as a working tool. Even these had to be handed in each evening, to be kept under lock and key in the Guardroom overnight. That this was not an example of nervous over-caution was shown a few years later, when a thorough search of the Depot gathered in some seven hundred daggers and knives, none of them of prisoner manufacture; which made it obvious that they had been smuggled in from outside.

At least one would-be absconder *was* executed at Norman Cross, but in his case he was found guilty of a far more heinous crime than merely attempting to escape. For the latter offence the very worst he could have suffered was sentence to the prison hulks; but a local newspaper gave the details of his sorry case:

> *Stamford Mercury.* September 15, 1808.
> 'Early on Friday morning last Charles François Maria Boucher, a French officer, a prisoner of war in this country, was conveyed from the County Gaol at Huntingdon to Yaxley Barracks where he was hanged, agreeable to his sentence at the last assizes, for stabbing with a knife, with intent to kill Alexander Halliday, in order to effect his escape from that prison. The whole garrison was under arms and all the prisoners in the different apartments were made witnesses of the impressive scene.'

But to get back to October, 1804. The rioting began one morning and intensified as the day wore on. One London newspaper reported the incident as follows:

> *The Times.* October 15, 1804
> 'An alarming spirit of insubordination was on Wednesday evinced by the French prisoners, about 3,000 at Norman Cross. An incessant uproar was kept up all the morning, and at noon their intention to attempt the destruction of the barrier of the prison became so obvious that the C.O. at the Barrack, apprehensive that the force under his command, consisting only of the Shropshire Militia and one battalion of the Army of reserve, would not be sufficient in case of necessity to environ and restrain so large a body of prisoners, dispatched a messenger requiring the assistance of the Volunteer force at Peterborough. Fortunately the Yeomanry had a field day, and one of the troops was undismissed when the messenger arrived. The troop immediately galloped into the Barracks. In the evening a tumult still continuing among the prisoners, and some of them taking advantage of the extreme darkness to attempt to escape, further reinforcements were sent for and continued on duty all night. The prisoners, having cut down a portion of the wood enclosure during the night, nine of them escaped through the aperture… Five of the prisoners have been re-taken.'

Considering the large number of rioters involved, the number of getaways seems small indeed; but it speaks wonders for the efficiency of the Agent, Commandant, guards, sentinels, garrison and local military backup.

Another outcome of this large but badly organized uprising, was the discovery next day of an escape tunnel in another part of the prison. It was nearing completion, and must already have cost a fair number of prisoner-excavators a great deal of time and effort. *The Times* reported that '…it was found that they had undermined a distance of 34 feet towards the Great South [!] Road, under the fosse which surrounds the prison, although it is four feet deep.' Had the tunnel been completed, it must have been a far better way out than any amount of crude bashing down of wooden fencing.

'In transit escapes' were not uncommon, despite the fact that a would-be escaper on the march stood a greater chance of being shot, than a prisoner attempting to escape from the Depot. Mention has been made that three had escaped from a batch which reached Norman Cross just after it opened and later in the year another prisoner, on the way from Yarmouth, made his getaway at Norwich. There was always a toing and froing of prisoners on the march;

some entering prison for the first time; others, usually more desperate characters, heading in the opposite direction, transferred from the Depot to tougher incarceration. These latter were usually multiple offenders and ne'er-do-wells who had tried the patience of the Agent and the Transport Office just too far.

In August 1809, one such group, comprising thirty Norman Cross desperadoes, under an escort of the Westminster Militia, were bound for Chatham and the dreaded hulks. It is not surprising that men faced with an indefinite period of confinement on a prison ship should have sometimes risked their lives to avoid such a fate. Their great leader, Napoleon, had put fear of capture into their hearts, by describing condemnation to the hulks as not much better than death.

By the 18th August, the thirty prisoners had marched in stages about seventy miles and had reached London, where they were bedded down for the night in a stable at Bow. Next morning twelve were missing. It is not known how many got clear away, but they would have stood a better chance of disappearing in the maze of London streets than in the Huntingdonshire countryside.

It may well have been fear of the hulks which drastically cut short the life of one brave young Norman Cross prisoner. Twenty-eight years old Jean de Narde, whose father was a Notary Public of St Malo, had escaped from the Depot, and by the time he reached East Dereham, about sixteen miles from Norwich, he had travelled some sixty miles towards the coast and a possible passage home. However, on the 6th October, 1799, he was recaptured at East Dereham and lodged for the night in the Bell Tower of the local church. No doubt deeply distressed that all his planning and efforts should have come to naught, and fully aware that he could not hope to enjoy even the meagre comforts of Norman Cross again – but would end up for who knew how many years on a Chatham, Portsmouth or Plymouth prison ship – he determined to make another bid for freedom. It was as he climbed down from the Tower that he was shot by a soldier of the guard.

He was buried in the churchyard and in 1857, more than half a century after Jean de Narde's death, the vicar of East Dereham and a few others raised a tombstone to his memory, which reads:

> 'IN MEMORY OF
> JEAN DE NARDE
> SON OF A NOTARY PUBLIC
> OF ST MALO
> A FRENCH PRISONER OF WAR
> WHO HAVING ESCAPED
> FROM THE BELL TOWER
> OF THIS CHURCH
> WAS PURSUED AND SHOT
> BY A SOLDIER ON DUTY
> OCT 6, 1799
> AGED 28 YRS.'

T.J. Walker tells a few similarly sad tales of 'in transit' prisoners who lost their lives in vain bids for freedom. On the 4th February, 1808, a consignment of captive French privateersmen, under an escort of the 77th Regiment, were nearing the last stage of their march to Norman Cross Depot. They were lodged for the night in a stable outbuilding in the yard of the Angel Inn at Peterborough. One of them made a desperate dash for it, and was shot dead by a guard. The subsequent inquest brought in a verdict of 'justifiable homicide'.

Another party of prisoners was crossing the Nene Bridge at Peterborough, when one of them threw caution to the winds, jumped over the low wall of the bridge, and plunged in to the river. He was killed as he broke surface, by a shot from an escort's musket. No doubt his death, too, was written off as 'justifiable'.

The anonymous memoirist of 1809 had expressed his impression that the Depot was adequately secured by the 'constant watch of ever-wakeful sentinels', whose diligence was probably more effective than 'moated walls' or 'fortified towers'; but, in the eighteen months he spent in captivity, he must have learned that not all of those watchful sentinels were incorruptible. Nevertheless, he did not resort to bribery when he made his own getaway. He inferred that it was not so much neglect or ill-treatment on the part of his captors which inspired his carefully planned escape, but rather the mental distress brought about by his daily witnessing the disgraceful scenes among large groups of his fellow prisoners, 'men lost to all sense of honour and shame'; whose conduct made miserable the lives of those who, like himself, had tried to cope with the already great hardship of imprisonment. This, plus the improbability of exchange, and the fact that there was no sign that the war would ever come to an end, strengthened his determination to make his bid for freedom; 'for death itself was to be preferred to the misery of delayed hope, which I daily endured'.

For the most part he worked silently and alone, avoiding suspicion among his fellow prisoners, for his was to be a one-man adventure. Too many large-scale, and often ingenious, attempts had come to naught through the failure of some individual who proved the weakest link in the carefully forged chain of escape. It was, however, necessary to elicit the help of a particular fellow-prisoner in his scheming. He still had a fair sum of the French gold which he had hidden about his person on the day of his capture, in 1809, some of which he now turned into English money. Soon, his escape-kitty amounted to about five pounds in English silver, a small hoard of copper coins, a few gold guineas, between twenty and thirty *louis-d'ors* and other gold coins. The exchange of French to English coinage he achieved through those industrious workers amongst his comrades, who supplied the Depot Market with ever-popular prisoner of war artefacts. Some of these craftsmen were wealthy by prisoner standards, the most brilliant, prolific and thrifty among them would possibly return to their homes when the war ended, with more money than they could have earned over a similar length of time in their civilian occupations.

One of these latter, who had sold his wares for some years in the Depot market, was particularly versatile and successful, and had already amassed a fortune of some £800. His versatility went beyond the bounds of the legitimate categories of work permitted, indeed encouraged, by Government regulations; for, in return for a *louis-d'or*, he supplied a fine example of his penmanship – a beautifully detailed copy of a map of part of England, complete with a recommended escape route. On this the name of every town and village along the way was indicated, together with the distances between, as it headed towards the Norfolk coast. A helpful note advised that once there he should look out for a certain escape agent, or some bribable skipper who might ferry him to France or Holland – even giving the probable whereabouts of a particular smuggler, who would be sure to help – at a price!

Most depots would have had their cartographers who, it was said, supplied getaway maps of England for as little as twenty francs. Dr Walker draws our attention to the fact that some of the buildings depicted in the Washingley Plan of the Depot are named – incorrectly, it so happens – in Franco-English; which might suggest that it may once have served as an escape accessory.

Many weeks were spent in learning all that he could of the country which lay beyond his prison walls, and in gathering together all the things he might need on his dangerous venture. These included a good knife, warm clothes, stout shoes, and a hook-ended rope with which to scale the outer brick wall. He had at first been concerned at not possessing 'false papers', but was relieved to learn that passport or proof of identity were not needed to travel in this country.

He seems to have had little doubt that he was physically up to the task of getting out of the prison building itself, finding a way through the stockade which surrounded the yard, then scaling the lofty outside wall. His chief concern was the large number of guards and the frequency of their patrols, noting the times when sentries changed posts and when the patrols were replaced by fresh detachments of soldiers from the barracks.

For some time he had laboured on a bolt-hole at the foot of the wooden ground-floor wall of his prison block, under a table at which his map-maker friend habitually sat at a bench, creating his little prisoner-of-war-work masterpieces. The latter had also volunteered post-escape assistance by promising to answer to the absconder's name at morning and evening musters, at least until one of the frequent head counts revealed that someone was missing.

The weeks went by with agonising slowness before a favourable opportunity presented itself; then, in mid-February, 1811, the great day – or rather night – arrived. A heavy fall of snow had been followed by a violent storm, with raging gale-force winds and a torrential downpour of driving rain. Instinctively, he knew that he would never have a better chance than this. With the pockets of his coarse blue-cloth seaman's jacket and trousers bulging with escape accessories, which by now included a tinder box, a small dictionary and a few biscuits, he crept beneath the work-table and, screened by his seated fellow prisoner, prised loose the boards of his escape-hatch and crawled into the yard. Once through, he carefully replaced the outside weather-boards, then made for a recently delivered pile of faggots, where he concealed himself. Wet through and benumbed by the cold, he stayed there long enough to assess the movements of the patrols and sentries. He knew that the changing of the guard took place at nine and again at midnight and that the diligence of their watchfulness tended to peter out during the hour leading up to the changeover. This night of atrocious weather made this even more likely; he could hear the chattering in the distance and could imagine that the sentinels had sought the comfort of their boxes. Therefore, as the clock struck eleven, he left the woodpile and headed through the jet-black night to the wooden fencing of his quadrangle. Just as he had calculated, this proved no great obstacle, but he was now to face the third and most daunting stage of his venture, the scaling of the distant outer wall. He could see the rows of lamps which burned at intervals along its crest, but these proved an aid rather than a hazard, as the areas of darkness between the arcs of yellow light appeared even more impenetrable by contrast.

This part of the operation, too, went off without a hitch. The hook held fast at the first cast of the rope, and the bold young Frenchman was soon lying flat along the top of the wall. At this point the memoir takes on dramatic detail which, true or exaggerated, adds some excitement to what might so far seem a run-of-the-mill, or depot, escapade. We read that, just as he was about to pull up the rope to make ready for his descent and first step outside his prison, he heard the door of a sentry box open and a soldier emerge from its shelter and begin to pass and repass directly below him. Wet through, half-frozen, miserable and terrified, he was on the point of giving up in despair, when the sentry put comfort before duty and re-entered his box slamming the door behind him. Quaking, but relieved, the Frenchman made a rapid but silent descent, gulping down a first great breath of freedom as his feet hit the ground.

Not expecting to encounter patrols *outside* the prison walls, he was shocked when distant lamplight revealed a picket of half a dozen guards heading straight for the spot where he crouched in darkness by the roadside. Hardly daring to breathe, he waited for what seemed the inevitable, hardly believing his luck as they passed him by unnoticed. His nerve restored, he crossed the boundary ditch, fosse, or moat, and found himself on the high road, and made for what he knew to be northward.

Heading into the wind and rain, after an hour or so he reached a crossroads where, he later remembered, a 'London and York' stage-coach stood outside the door of a well-lit hostelry. Keeping to the cover of the hedges, he carried on, passing through small villages and crossing a number of bridges until, as a church clock struck three in the morning, he came to the fair-sized town of Oundle. Scurrying through its unlit and deserted backstreets he came to a field on the outskirts of the town in which stood a rather ramshackle hovel, which offered temporary shelter. Pushing open the door, he entered what proved to be a cattle-shed, its floor invitingly covered with fresh dry straw; a cow tethered to a manger, its calf in a nearby pen. After changing his soaking stockings and resting awhile, he milked the cow into his upturned cap and supped on biscuits and rich warm milk. He dared not sleep for fear of pursuers from the Depot, or the early arrival of the farmer. Therefore, as a weak and watery sunrise heralded the new day, he crept from the cow-shed and made for a distant haystack, situated well away from roads or footpaths.

On arrival at the field, he tucked himself into a crevice where the stack had been cut into, and settled down to study his map for the first time since his departure from the Depot. He was not too disturbed to find that he was well off track, in fact he decided to deviate still further from the recommended route. He would head eastward where, he calculated, he might reach the coast within the next couple of days and perhaps find some cooperative and bribable skipper, who would return him to his homeland. By noon, the sun had strengthened and, 'although a February sun in England is very different from a February sun in the south of France', it lulled him into the first sound sleep he had enjoyed since the beginning of his adventure. It was afternoon by the time he awoke and set out in as straight a line as possible. He had cut himself a stick or staff to help him on his way, as he strode through hedge and ditch, in the direction which he imagined would take him to the sea and freedom. Avoiding dwellings and roads, he strode on, filled with self-congratulatory confidence, eating the last of his biscuits as he walked. Warm, and with his clothes now dry, he proceeded for some hours on what was more akin to a country stroll than a desperate flight from captivity. Then, suddenly, as he topped the crest of a small mound, his gaze met a sight which filled him with horror and dismay. There before him, just a few fields away, was a

line of red-tiled buildings which he was never likely to mistake. He was heading back to Norman Cross, no more than half a mile away.

Sick at heart, he fell to the ground and some minutes passed before he recovered his composure: then, taking to his heels 'as if pursued by a whole legion of devils', he fled, and never stopped until he reached the cow-shed which had first given him shelter. This time there was no warm milk to sustain him; the cow and calf had gone, so he settled down in the dry straw to recover from his exhausting and ill-fated day. It had begun to rain soon after he reached the shed, and this continued throughout the night, so that when he looked out next morning it was to see that the meadows which surrounded the hovel were now sheets of water where the grass had been. This was a comfort rather than a worry; surely, he reasoned, it made less likely the approach of pursuers. Once again, and even then not for the last time, his optimism and too easily recovered confidence almost brought an end to his gallant venture. Luckily, he reserved enough caution to realize that if someone did visit his hideout, whether farmer or military, he would be caught like a rat in a trap. Looking around him, he noticed that an old gate and some hurdles had been stored on the beams which supported the rafters at the far corner of the hovel, and this platform he covered with a deep layer of dry straw. He decided that the rest of the day should be spent planning a fresh course to the coast. Settled in to the comfort of his elevated makeshift bed, he once more studied his map; for, chastened by his recent terrifying experience, he vowed that, from that moment on, he would not veer by an inch from the course recommended by his captive map-maker friend.

He spent the rest of that day perched among the beams, keeping a watchful eye on the nearby road and what he could see of the town, through a small hole he had made in the roof. It was well that he kept watch, for at noon his heart missed a beat as he saw three soldiers crossing the bridge, no more than a hundred yards away. By their uniforms he knew that they were from one of the regiments which supplied guards for duty at Norman Cross. With all the appearance of men acting on information received, two of the soldiers climbed over the gate and, with bayonets fixed, advanced on the hovel. However, after entering what seemed to be an empty stable, they walked round once then left, one of them disinterestedly thrusting his bayonet overhead a couple of times, through the hurdles and straw, before leaving. Tucked safely away to the side where rafters and beams met, the fugitive escaped all harm.

As soon as darkness fell, he left his refuge and, with place-names and distances between well planted in his memory, he set off through the unlit streets of Oundel, recrossed the bridges, and headed for Wansford, some nine miles distant on the road to Peterborough. At about three o'clock in the morning he reached Peterborough, entering the town with almost as much trepidation as he had felt when, eighteen months earlier, he and a hundred or more fellow-prisoners had straggled through its crowded streets, on their way to Norman Cross and close imprisonment. After at first losing himself in a bewildering 'labyrinth of streets and lanes' he came to the bank of the river Nene, and a road as straight and long as the eye could see in the semi-darkness. With the river on his right and an immense tract of fenland on his left, he could spot danger from a mile away. Once again his confidence was restored as he pictured the river by his side 'rolling along to the ocean which was to waft me home.' He was, however, to meet up with many more adventures before the dawning of that happy day.

He had by now been without food for more than forty-eight hours. It was the wrong time of the year for the traveller to hope to live off the land, though even a turnip would have been a luxury. He had to find something to eat, even if it meant taking risks. Travelling by night meant little chance of spotting anything edible on the way, so he broke his promise to himself, never to travel during the daylight hours and, after a short rest in a barn soon after dawn began to light the sky, he continued on his journey. Except for the sounds which floated across the water from lightermen hailing one another, and from the passing horse-drawn barges close in to the towpath, he encountered no one. According to his map, the next fairly large town was Wisbech, another sixteen miles further on his route. He reached the town just as it was getting dark, and found it to be a small shipping port though still a long way from the coast. He nervously observed a number of seamen as they passed him by, but was comforted by the fact that they were clothed in similar fashion to himself. Relief was followed by alarm when, by the light of the lamps, he saw several soldiers in the street – and decided to get clear away from the place as quickly as possible. After passing through the toll-gate at the edge of town, he walked and ran for some miles, through several villages before again reaching the bank of a navigable river, with marshland stretching to his left.

At about ten o'clock he came to a village comprising only a few small houses, the last of which, well away from the others, was built into the slope of the bank and was a shop with lights burning in its front windows. That it was a waterman's supply business was shown by the merchandise on display; candles, bread, cheese and all manner of chandlery. The sight of bread and cheese must have played havoc with our escapee's gastric juices; but we shall let him tell of the alleviation of his hunger, in his own words. The shopkeeper, he noted, was something of a jack-of-all-trades, fortunately he was also a silent one:

'Whilst I was deliberating with myself how to act, a waterman as I judged from his dress, passed by me at the door, and throwing himself onto a chair, and made a sign… by drawing his hand across his face, and chin, as if he wanted shaving. He never spoke a word, but the shopkeeper appeared perfectly to understand his meaning, and placing a cloth, which was none of the cleanest, over the fellow's shoulders, made preparations to perform that service.'

Finding that the chandler – whom he described as 'a little, thin, spare bodkin of a man, about seventy years of age' – was also a barber – he decided that he might well look a less suspicious character, if he too was clean shaven. He continued:

'I kept my eyes upon them both, with the hope of profiting by what I saw, and carefully noted that, after being shaved, the man threw two copper coins upon the counter. He then walked to the window and took down a loaf of bread and two or three red herrings, then drawing a mark with his finger across a piece of cheese, it was cut off and weighed out to him. For these he threw down a silver coin, a half-crown, receiving some small change in return; and, tying up his purchases in an old handkerchief, departed in the same silent surly mood as he had entered.'

Spurred on by hunger, and determined to emulate all he had observed, the young Frenchman strode into the shop and, with a boldness he did not feel, flung himself into the chair which the waterman had vacated.

'The same cloth was put round my neck, I was lathered the same, and shaved the same, and the same sum of two coppers was thrown by me upon the counter. I now began to feel courageous, and went up to the window to lay in a stock of provisions, which I intended should last me the whole of my journey.'

He had almost convinced himself that the old man was dumb, perhaps even a deaf mute, when the latter muttered a few words – which went unanswered, as his customer's knowledge of the English language was almost nil. He just whistled as he carried on choosing his purchases, handing two half-crowns to the shopkeeper, and waiting for his change.

'Well, imagine my ecstacy on leaving the shop, which I did completely unsuspected, with two loaves of beautiful white bread, some excellent cheese and three or four herrings…, and to crown all, some tobacco and a pipe.'

Back on the riverside road, he picked and ate from his precious bundle, which he clutched to his bosom with as much delight 'as ever did a mother her first-born'. Later that Saturday night, he rested in an isolated barn, where he broke his long fast, demolishing nearly a whole loaf and a huge chunk of cheese.

Invigorated and refreshed, the next couple of days took him through wide open flat, rather desolate countryside, where he reckoned he could see for thirty miles around him, the villages spread wide apart, and only the occasional farmhouse dotted here and there. However, he then came to the end of the riverbank road and to the town of Downham, where he arrived about midnight. According to his prison-produced map, there were two roads out of Downham which led to the coast – the recommended one, which went through the small towns of Swaffham and Fakenham; the other by way of the considerable seaport town of Lynn – which was to be avoided at all costs.

Although it had started to rain, he decided to carry on, keeping as close as possible to the advisory notes which were attached to the map, turning right or left through the winding streets of the town as instructed, then taking what he felt sure was the right road to Swaffham. He had sorted out what remained of his provisions, stowing them away into his various pockets according to size, and was in high spirits when, as dawn broke, he saw that he was nearing a large town. Those high spirits should have sunk to zero when he realised that he had once again taken the wrong road, and the town he was entering was Lynn, the very place he was cautioned to avoid. However, instead he tried to look on the bright side; after all, he was still free, despite 'trifling disappointments,' and might even find something of advantage in his latest misfortune:

' …and so far from feeling this wandering from my direct road of any consequence, I rather rejoiced at it, and foolishly resolved to endeavour to get a passage to Holland at this place, without going farther. Perhaps I was encouraged in this resolution by the sight of the harbour and shipping, now gilded by the rays of the morning sun, and the knowledge that it was this port we were brought prisoners to on our first arrival in England.'

He was right to judge his decision as foolish, but was at least sensible enough not to enter Lynn by daylight; marching on for a mile or so beyond the town, before bedding down for the day in a haystack. His plan was to reconnoitre the town for a night or two, before testing his luck. Rather nervously, he approached the town gates at about eleven o'clock, and found that, to his amazement, there was no sign of even a single guard or sentinel at his post; and that the gates had the appearance of never being closed. This lack of security caused him to theorise that a single French privateer might have sailed up the harbour and burned not only the shipping but the town itself. As he wandered about the town he encountered only a few old watchmen who 'cried the hour', and a soldier who stood guard at an hotel, which, he decided, was probably the local military headquarters.

Encouraged by this apparent lack of security, he resolved to enter the town at an earlier hour on the following night. Therefore, after resting during the day, he ventured into Lynn late in the evening, whilst there were still a number of people on the streets. Some of the shops round the market square were still open but, as they closed, the shoppers wandered off homeward, leaving him to himself. Settling down on a bench by the nearby quayside, he was enjoying his solitude, reflecting on his venture to date and looking out across the harbour, when a party of a half dozen sailors, headed by an officer in naval uniform, suddenly appeared and passed close by. His relief was great, as each sailor carried a stout stick and the officer his sword; but they had not gone far before they stopped, looked back, then returned to where he sat. One of them tapped him on the shoulder and said something to him, which the Frenchman, despite his lack of English, understood to mean that he should go along with them. He dared not answer, and seeing him hesitate, the most ruffianly-looking of the party grabbed him by the collar of his jacket and began to pull him along. He still had the walking stick which he had made for himself at Oundle and now, in a mixture of desperation and hopeless despair, he struck out to left and right with it, which brought two of the sailors to their knees. Almost simultaneously, he received a blow which sent his stick flying from his hand, and another to his head which felled him to the ground. Raised to his feet, he was half marched, half dragged, through several streets towards a small inn, where the officer gave instructions to one of his men, who beckoned his captive to follow him into a small room; whilst the officer and the others set off in another direction.

The sailor, who seemed a decent type, took a seat by the fire and, inviting his charge to do likewise, tried to encourage him to break his silence. The sailor eventually gave up, and occupied himself with a tot of rum and a pipe of tobacco.

The Frenchman was as bewildered as he was distressed. He had taken it for granted that his captors were some sort of escapee-hunting naval police, so why was he not in jail rather than seated by a fire in an inn. Perhaps at any moment the officer might return to lead him in chains to some dreadful dungeon. If he had considered for a moment that the naval party might be a 'press gang', or even known what the term implied, he would have had yet another worry to torture his aching head   It would, however, have been interesting to know how he would have responded if given the choice of serving in King George III's navy, or returning to Norman Cross, the Black Hole, and probably the hulks!

He had more time than was needed to study the room in which he was confined; for, apart from the two chairs, there was only a large oak table with leaves which nearly reached the floor, and a sashed window which opened on to the street, the latch of which, he noted, was unfastened. If only his guard would go to sleep; but the sailor, whilst no longer talkative, was ever on the alert.

Suddenly, loud noises, quarrelling and a violent scuffling broke out in an adjoining room, the sailor guard being repeatedly called for by name. After a short period of uncertainty, the latter snatched up his stick and made for the door, uttering admonishments which probably amounted to; 'Don't dare move a muscle.' Obviously, it was now or never, and the prisoner made a dash for the window, flung up the sash, and was about to climb out in to the street, when he heard his guard returning. Thinking that all was up, and fearing the wrath of his captor, our enemy hero dived beneath the table. Hidden behind its large leaves, he could imagine his keeper taking a quick look round the apparently empty room, with its window wide open, then heard him scrambling through and the pounding of his feet as he sped in what he thought was hot pursuit.

The trembling prisoner crept from his hiding place, and kept an eye on the sailor until he turned a corner, then he too leapt out, and ran as fast as he could – in the opposite direction. He ran himself into a state of near exhaustion, his mind in a muddle, one minute congratulating himself on yet another stroke of good luck, the next cursing his stupidity in taking risks which landed him in such dangerous situations. His headlong flight through the dark streets, lanes and alleys, left him completely lost; all he wanted now was to find the town gates and seek refuge in the comfort of his haystack bed. But his present contretemps was not yet over. Emerging from an alley, he was shocked at the sight of the naval officer and party, who had reformed, a short way off and seeing him immediately gave chase. Dashing back the way he had come, he could not have got far, had he not providentially noticed ahead of him the door of a small house, slightly ajar.

> 'Unperceived by anyone, I entered the house, and safely closed the door, holding, with breathless suspense, the latch in my hand. In a few minutes I heard my pursuers passing in full cry after me, clattering and shouting most terrifyingly. It was the last time I ever saw or heard them… For I verily believe that, had I been taken, it would have broken my heart: as it was, I sank exhausted upon my knees, almost fainting with agitation and terror.'

As he regained something of his composure, he realised that he was not alone. A little old lady was sitting by the fire, a cat on her lap and one hand on a wire, which must have led to a bell in the adjoining house Although she appeared rather frightened, she did not sound the alarm; the pitiable condition of the young man, and the shouts of his pursuers, gave her pause for thought. Putting a forefinger to her lips, she made a shushing sound and listened until she was sure the hunters were not returning, then got up and approached him. Shaking a tiny fist in the direction they had taken, she cried 'Press-gang! Press-gang!' with anger in her voice; to which he repeated 'Press gang' without the faintest idea of what it meant.

He was still on his knees inside the door, too weakened by running and panic to stand; his senses reeling from the cruel blow to the head he had suffered at the hands of the naval gang. The old lady, seeing the wound and his general state of debility, brought him a tot of brandy, but before he could accept it he had lapsed into unconsciousness. He had no idea how long he had remained in that state, but when he revived it was to find his head being bathed, and the brandy held to his lips.

The old lady, who, for the rest of his life he always recalled as his 'guardian angel' or 'second mother', helped him to the table where she had placed a pillow for his head and, urging him not to talk – which suited him perfectly – left him to rest.

Norman Cross – The Quadrangle.

Next morning he awoke to find her preparing his breakfast, for which he showed his thanks by appreciative gestures, but still had not spoken. Knowing that he was still too ill to continue his journey, and appreciating the unfairness of accepting the repeated kindnesses of this good woman by keeping her in ignorance of his true position as an escaping enemy prisoner of war, he resolved to throw himself upon her mercy. Tearfully, with a mixture of hope and apprehension, he struggled with the few words of English which he knew, and stammered that he was a foreigner, a stranger, and begged her to take pity on him. She seemed unperturbed, thinking him to be a foreign sailor from one of the ships in the harbour who had had the misfortune to fall in with a press-gang. Sensing that she still did not understand, he continued: 'un pauvre Frenchman – un prisonier François.' For a moment her beneficent countenance changed to one of dismay and consternation, which convinced him that all hope was lost. With a typically French show of emotion, which might well have melted hearts far harder than that of the kindly old lady, he fell to his knees, pleading that she would not betray him. Rummaging in his pocket for the dictionary which he had included in his escape equipment, that he might find the odd, more telling word, and placing every penny of his money on to the table before her; he anxiously waited to hear his fate.

She did not betray him, and neither would she accept his money. With the help of the dictionary and sign language they learned a lot about each other and their families over the following week. Her husband, a merchant captain out of Lynn, had died some years ago,

and her children and grandchildren were all dead, except one, a grandson who was a prisoner of war in France. He had been taken captive whilst serving as mate on a ship bound for St Petersburg, and was, she thought, a prisoner in the fortress city of Verdun.

After the first day, the fugitive was removed in to a little back parlour, which opened on to a small high walled yard. There, safely locked away from detection by casual callers or neighbours, he was well fed and nursed with tender care, so that, slowly at first, he regained his health and strength. He could not understand why he, a runaway prisoner, was not allowed to pay for his keep or even contribute towards his food, but all offers were waved aside. There was just one way, she said. that he could repay her. She had not heard from her grandson for more than two years, which sorely grieved her and if, when her foreign guest succeeded in reaching France, he would help her beloved grandson, she would feel more than adequately rewarded. Deeply touched, he swore that he would do all in his power to fulfill his promise; perhaps through family influence, he might effect an exchange; that he would see to the Englishman's comfort at whatever the cost – and even assist in an escape attempt if that were the only answer.

At the end of seven days, he was fit and confident enough to tackle what should be the last stage in his great adventure. In this, too, his benefactress came to his aid – she fitted him out with a complete suit of civilian clothing; two spare linen shirts, stockings and a hat; all of which had belonged to a deceased son. His own seaman-like garb and checked shirt were destroyed. Having transformed his outward appearance, she then provided for the inner man, by preparing packages of bread and meat and a small bottle of brandy. Once more he tried to pay, but she just said, 'Put it to my grandson's account.' All that she would accept as mementoes of their amazing week, were a ring of only sentimental value, which his mother had given him, and which he had worn on a ribbon round his neck ever since his capture, and a few small Spanish coins she could use as whist counters.

They parted early next morning amid emotional farewells we can leave to the imagination. His way out of town and the route he was afterwards to take, had been carefully planned and, in his English guise, he passed unnoticed through the market-day crowds to the eastern gate. From there on, his journey was a pleasant and uneventful one. The day was fine, and, after so many miserable nights of marching through darkness he could now enjoy walking in the sunshine. A few miles beyond the village of Gaywood, he reached a hill where he sat on a mile-stone for pensive moments, as he took a last look back at Lynn, a town he would always have reason to remember.

Next morning he set off at sunrise on what his map told him should be the last day of his journey – just twenty-five miles to go! He was determined to get to that part of the coast where he might find his recommended contact before nightfall; he would know that much sooner whether he had been over-confident in expecting a happy outcome to his adventure or whether it would turn out to be a great success. That last leg began on a spirited high, filled with confidence inspired by the sight of ships and the sea, and visions of his homeward voyage. However, as he got nearer to his objective, his mind became haunted by a thousand doubts and fears: what if the man who held his fate in the balance betrayed him or for some reason refused to assist him? Perhaps he was at sea, ferrying some other runaway to France; perhaps his treachery had already been detected and he was even now languishing in gaol! – or maybe he was dead, for smuggling and escape-running was a dangerous game.

With no more than a mile or so to go, he had to put fears and worries to the very back of his mind, and rehearse all the identifying details he had learned – landmarks and signs, passwords and answers, etc.– which would lead him unmistakably to the right house and right confederate. The coastal road had taken him out of sight of the sea for a mile or two but now it took him to the brow of a high cliff which towered over a few fishermen's cottages on the beach far below. Away from the rest, at the entrance to a small creek where a boat was moored, stood the house of his hopes, the description of which had been drummed into him by his map-making fellow-prisoner at Norman Cross. Yet it was one thing to recognise it, but quite another to find a way to get to it, for there seemed no way down from the cliff top.

The light was beginning to fail and he wondered where he would spend the night, when, about half a mile further on, he came to an opening in the cliff face. At some time a landslide had sent great quantities of earth and rock crashing to the beach, but now provided a rather dangerously sloping road, which he bravely tackled, his feet sinking ankle deep in the fine white sand as he neared fishermen's cottages and the one he was bound for.

'I kept my eyes fixed on the window of the house, from which I was not far distant, till I saw a candle lighted and the shutters closed; and it by now being quite dark, with a palpitating heart and high expectations… I approached the door. The well-remembered sign of three oyster-shells over the window assured me that I was correct as to the house, and a mark over the door, of which I had been particularly cautioned to take heed, told me that the master was at home. Indeed, had not this mark appeared, I was to have turned away, and waited for a more propitious opportunity. Encouraged by all these signs in my favour, I lifted the latch, and, as I was instructed, stepped boldly in and closed the door after me.

'A man in sailor's dress, with a hair cap on his head, and huge boots turned over his knees, was sitting at a small round table smoking his pipe, with a can of grog before him. A woman, apparently superannuated by age and infirmity, was spinning flax with a spindle by the fire; and close by her, on a stool, half asleep, sat an arch-looking boy, about twelve years of age, also in a sailor's jacket and trousers, and cap.'

Although the Frenchman had to go through the rigmarole of passwords and signs, he was himself immediately quite certain that the sailor was the genuine article. As the former entered the cottage he had raised two fingers above his head and made a sign, to which he received the countersign and a few words, to which he boldly replied with a sentence he had learned by rote. He had previously been informed of the Englishman's appearance, so was fully convinced when he noted the deep scar which cleft his forehead from right to left, and the silver ring he wore on his thumb – a custom based on 'some superstitious notion prevalent among seafaring people.'

After a meal of beef and bread, they sat and talked well into the night. Jack (for that was the sailor's name – and the only name to be found in the whole of the French memoir!) spoke fluent French, and explained that, as arranged, a boat would soon be arriving to ferry the fugitive to Holland. As the smuggler listened to the story of escape from Norman Cross to the arrival at his cottage, he smoked pipe after pipe of strong tobacco, and knocked back glass after glass of grog, disappointed that his guest could not keep up with him; but finally the Frenchman was taken to an upstairs room which was to be his hideaway.

He was shown an iron bar which was to be put in position after the door was closed; given a new password should anyone demand admission to his room, and, as 'a last assurance of your safety,' his attention was drawn to a cunningly concealed recess in the wall where, if need be, he could hide himself. Jack told him, either truthfully or at least reassuringly, that, 'one of your generals knew its dimensions well, for he was in it when every house in the hamlet was filled with redcoats in search of him. They were within two inches of him; and the old woman held a lighted candle for them as they searched.'

Several days were spent in that little room, with no more to do than contemplate the ocean through a spy-hole, and pray for the sight of the vessel which surely must soon come to his rescue. Some evenings he was invited to join the family in the living room below, where Jack held forth with yarns of the sea and shore. He had an inexhaustible stock of tales of adventure, of smuggling and hair's breadth escapes: for, as he said, he had 'been at sea ever since I was no higher than a marlin-spike.'

At last the day of departure arrived. At about twelve o'clock, on a particularly bright star-lit night, a small boat, which the watcher recognised as the coble which had been moored at the head of the creek, came into the shore hardby the house. It was rowed by Jack and a stranger, with the boy at the tiller. Within minutes our memoirist was hurried into the boat, followed by Jack, who grabbed an oar and, with the other man, pulled away with all their strength. Once clear of the shore, they settled down to a steady stroke, but it was a full two hours before they rendezvoused with a small sloop, which had lain-to to await their arrival.

The Englishman, Frenchman and the Dutch skipper retired to the cabin, where business details were speedily concluded. After this, Jack and his more than satisfied customer, went back on deck, exchanged genuine farewells and parted with a hearty handshake. The Frenchman had developed a genuine liking for the rascally old salt, and had rewarded him beyond all expectations; adding a golden guinea for the old lady, his mother, and another for the young helmsman, his son.

There is little more to tell of this escape from Norman Cross. Although every voyage of a smuggler's vessel was fraught with perilous possibilities, this one was comparatively uneventful – except for sighting several English cutters which looked like giving chase – and once nearly running aground when keeping too far inshore, in order to avoid small English cruisers! In the evening of the second day all worries were put to rest, for they had reached the safety of the Texel. There the Dutch skipper was paid his ten *louis-d'ors*; plus a voluntary five, to be shares amongst the crew.

Next morning, the successful absconder went ashore and, after posting off news of his escape to his parents, immediately set out for Paris. He was detained in the capital for only one day, to be debriefed by order of the French Minister for Marine. Then, free as a bird, he purchased a seat in the first available diligence which would take him to Marseilles, and the waiting arms of his family.

Postscript:
The remarkable old lady, whose compassion had played such an important role in the young Frenchman's escape from captivity, was never forgotten. Exposing herself to the dangers of aiding an escaping prisoner of war, by nursing, feeding and hiding him for a week, her only reward had lain in the promise that similar help might be given to her grandson, in the prison of Verdun – but it was not to be. Enquiries soon revealed the sad fact that he had been wounded whilst involved in a mass escape attempt, and had later died of his wounds. She was informed – and then there was silence.

Four years later the war had ended, and the French family commissioned a visitor to Britain to call in at Lynn and seek out the lady to whom they owed such heartfelt gratitude. He carried with him letters which invited her to live with them in France for the rest of her life; or, should she choose to stay in England, sufficient funds would be remitted to provide her with an annuity of £50. But when he arrived in Lynn, it was to find that she had been dead for some years.

When hundreds or thousands of men, from many differing levels of society, find themselves thrown together for any length of time, there always occurs a natural sorting out, and a breaking down into strata dictated by common backgrounds, interests, beliefs, talents, education or inclinations: musicians gravitating towards musicians, craftsmen towards craftsmen, religious towards other believers, for instance, and, unfortunately gamblers towards gamblers.

That this was true in the case of all British prisoner of war prisons on land or afloat, is shown in memoirs and documents which describe everyday life in a number of those depots. We have an abundance of detail in the case of Dartmoor – from both the French and the American points of view – and Scandinavian prisoner journals which tell of their life on the hulks.

Basil Thomson, one-time Governor of Dartmoor Depot, listed the names given to the various grades of prisoner of war society, from apex to the depths – from *Les Lords* to *Les Romains*, or 'Romans'. *Les Romains* formed the lowest class of prisoner in Dartmoor (although it was possible for some to sink even lower down the social scale within that category. The lowest class on the hulks, equivalent to the 'Romans', were *Les Raffalès*, and the very lowest of these, the most filthy, degraded and verminous, became known as *Les Manteaux Impériaux*. The lice which swarmed on the single blanket which they wore, poncho-like, to cover their nakedness, inspired the impolite allusion to the embroidered bees on Bonaparte's Imperial Mantel. The given names differed according to period and depot; at Norman Cross, more than a decade before Dartmoor came into being, the desperate and incorrigible blots on the prison-scape were given the sobriquet of *Les Misérables*.

The men who adopted this hopeless and self-destructive mode of living, came originally from every other class, from the educated to the ignorant, from the well-to-do to the hard up; but two things they had in common which plunged them into a sub-class all their own – they were all gamblers and they were all losers. They staked first their money, then their possessions, followed by their clothing and then, the final folly, their food. Their story is a terrible one.

The reports and complaints which periodically accused Britain of being hell-bent on killing off her admittedly all too many prisoners of war, usually originated from perfectly true descriptions of groups of men living in conditions of starvation, semi-nudity and squalor – although it was well-known that the sufferings of these poor fellows was self-inflicted, or could be more fairly blamed on the evil 'brokers' among them who prospered by their improvidence. After the following notes on the health, sickness and mortality of prisoners at Norman Cross, I shall append an accusatory extract from a book written by that arch-Anglophobe, General Pillet, one of the most senior of French officers to spend time at the Cross.

Norman Cross was always regarded as a 'healthy' depot, despite the fact that the War Memorial in the prisoners' burial ground, states that '1,770 soldiers and sailors, natives or allies of France', had died there during the seventeen years of its occupancy. Had it not been for a strategy employed by the authorities, many more hundreds may have been added to the number on that Memorial. Often, when prisoners developed serious illnesses, or were sufficiently incapacitated to make them unlikely to be of any further military use to their country, they were returned in cartel ships to their homelands, often without exchange agreements. Of course, amongst these would have been men who had arrived as prisoners still suffering from wounds, and others who brought illnesses and diseases with them. However, the most likely to be transferred were from groups of desperate losing gamblers who were reduced to the state of trouble-making physical wrecks. They were sent elsewhere *en masse*, often to the hulks.

No definite figure can be given for the number of prisoners who passed through Norman Cross between 1797 and 1814, but it was probably in the region of 30,000. Neither is it possible to arrive at a meaningful calculation of the mortality rate. The official figure of 1,770 is misleading for such a purpose, as 1,020 of the poor fellows had passed away in just six months; between November 1800, and May 1801. Epidemics struck the Depot from time to time over its long existence, but no others with anything like the terrible ferocity as that of 1800–1.

As might be expected, the first and worst smitten, were *Les Misérables*. Already weakened by under-nourishment, ill-clad and with next to no protection against the November chill, they dropped like flies when hit by what was probably typhus or enteric fever. The hospital soon filled to overflowing and the medical staff were faced with a quite impossible task. There was no suggestion of deliberate neglect on the part of the carers. Even if the nursing facilities had been doubled, lack of hospital space and primitive knowledge of the diseases involved, meant that the death toll would inevitably be great.

As mentioned earlier, when a prisoner became ill, he came under the authority of the Sick and Hurt Office and the prison surgeons, rather than the Transport Office, the Depot Agent or the military staff. Conscientious records were made of all deaths, and the details were communicated to both the British and French authorities. Dr Walker read through many hundreds of those certificates, which gave a great deal of information regarding the deceased – name, age, when and where captured, etc. – although the entry in the last column was often far from explicit and read: Cause of Death: *Debility*.

Unlike the *Romains* at Dartmoor, the *Misérables* at Norman Cross retained their hammocks (they would have been sleeping on the floor had their canvas beds been of any value to the 'brokers'!) and those hammocks became the death beds of many who succumbed to the dreadful fever.

Whilst there is no certifiable prisoner of war memoir to tell us about *Les Misérables* and their miserable existence, it is worthy of note that the escapee of 1811 says that he risked the hazards of escape to get away from daily witnessing the conduct of 'men lost to all sense of honour and shame'. And it would seem that he was not alone in his revulsion. Captain Woodriff's reports and Transport Office documents indicate that large groups of destitute losers were ostracized by the other prisoners and were segregated in part of *Caserne* Block 13. With every bed – and probably the floor – of the hospital occupied, many infected prisoners were confined in close proximity to the healthy, with dire results. In the first months of the epidemic, twenty-nine dead or dying *Misérables* were removed from their hammocks in that appropriately numbered *Caserne* 13. In a single day, the first day of January 1801, nine men of that class died in their hammocks, and appended to the sad entry in the death register was the following note:

> 'These men being in the habit of selling their bedding and rations, died of debility in this prison, there not being room in the hospital to receive them.'

Norman Cross was never again to experience such an appalling period of sickness and death, and could regain its reputation as a 'healthy depot'. The total mortality among all classes of prisoner over the eleven years of the second part of the war, 1803 to 1814, was 559; the lowest number of deaths in one whole year being eighteen, in 1804.

The rabid General Pillet would have scoffed at these figures, and at anything else complimentary to our management of French prisoners of war. However, to be fair – something of which Pillet could never have been accused – the General did have a smidgen of justification for his undying hatred of the British; though none which could excuse the vitriolic exaggerations and falsifications which he crammed into his book: '*L'Anglerre, vue à Londres et*

dans ses Provinces, pendant un séjour de dix années, dont six comme prisonnier de guerre.'

General René Martin Pillet, Adjutant Commandant, Chef de l'États-Major of the First Division of the Army of Portugal, was badly wounded and captured at the Battle of Vimiera in 1808, and seems to have genuinely believed that, under Article 2 of the Convention of Cintra, he should never have been taken captive. (Article 2 decreed that no Frenchman should be considered a prisoner of war; should keep his arms; and be shipped out of Portugal by the British). However, he and many others were taken prisoner, and on arrival in England he was paroled, first to Bishops Waltham then to Alresford, where, because of his high rank, he was granted some privileges over and above those enjoyed by other officer parolees. Yet he refused to be bound by any of the rules which regulated and made the parole system possible. With complete disregard for his given word of honour, he escaped from his parole town, on the 22nd March, 1810. He was aided by an expert, one of the most famous of escape-agents, Captain Richard Harman (one of the many aliases of Thomas Feast); but he had only got as far as Hastings before he was recaptured. Many troublesome 'broke-paroles' were heavily punished for their dishonorable conduct, but General Pillet was sent to the Officers' Prison at Norman Cross. Harman was at first held in Horsham Gaol, then suffered a worse punishment – he was drafted into the Royal Navy. Pillet made himself as unbearable as possible during his time at Norman Cross, until his conduct exhausted the patience of the Transport Board, and he was transferred to the *Brunswick* prison hulk at Chatham.

He published his scurrilous work of misinformation in 1815, and misjudged the gullibility of his readers, both French and English. Writers of both nations issued books and pamphlets of criticism and refutation of many of his accusations. Having experienced all three types of prisoner of war incarceration, hulk, depot and parole, he could have reported some indisputable facts regarding less than satisfactory conditions and treatment in each category – but he could not leave a bare fact alone without exaggerating and sensationalizing it. For instance, when he related the story of Lord Cawdor's visit to Portchester Castle, he said that his Lordship returned to the courtyard where he had left his horse, only to find that the animal was missing. Pillet said that the starving prisoners had taken it away, killed it – but he could not resist adding that they *had eaten it raw!* The 'Norman Cross' extract from his book which follows illustrates his equally incredible mishandling of statistics:

> 'I have seen at Norman Cross a plot of land where nearly four thousand men, out of seven thousand in this prison, were buried. [for Pillet this was only a mini exaggeration. In an earlier extract, he had stated that *'a hundred and fifty thousand Frenchmen have been killed, in the midst of torture,'* in the British prison ships. This was quite ridiculous, as there were not 150,000 prisoners of war in the whole of Britain. One commentator on Pillet's inaccuracies, calculated that, if we were to take the mortality rate of French prisoners of war as ten percent, the General's figure would suggest that 1,500,000 were confined to the hulks alone – and as only about half of our captives were sent to prison ships, our French prisoner population must have been in the region of 3,000,000!]
>
> 'Provisions were then expensive in England, and our Government [the French], it was said, had refused to pay the balance of an account due to the prisoners. To settle this account all the prisoners were put on half rations, and to make sure that they should die, the introduction of food for sale, according to custom, was forbidden. To

reduced quantity was added inferior quality of the provisions served out. There was distributed four times a week, worm-eaten biscuit, fish and salt meat; three times a week black, half baked bread made of mouldy flour or of black wheat. Soon after eating this, one was seized with a sort of drunkenness, followed by violent headache, diarrhoea and redness of face; many died from a sort of vertigo. For vegetables, uncooked beans were served up. In fact hundreds of men sank each day, starved to death, or poisoned by the provisions. Those who did not die immediately, became so weak that gradually they could digest nothing. [He continued with descriptions of ill-treatment which, the translator considered too disgusting to repeat.] Hunger knows no rules. The corpses of those who died were kept for five or six days without being given up by their comrades, who by this means received the dead men's rations.

'I myself took a complaint to Captain Pressland. Next day the officers of the two militia battalions on guard at the prison and some civilians arrived at the time of the distribution of rations. At their head was Pressland who was damning the prisoners loudly. The rations were shown, and, as the whole thing had been carefully rehearsed beforehand, they were good.

'A report was drawn up by which it was shown that the prisoners were discontented rascals who grumbled at everything, that the food was unexceptionable and that some of the grumblers deserved to be shot, for an example. Next day the food was just as bad as ever… Certainly, the prisoners had the chance of buying provisions for themselves from the wives of the soldiers of the garrison twice a week. The women, however, bribed to ruin the prisoners, rarely brought what was required, made the prisoners take what they brought, and charged exorbitant prices, and as payment had to be made in advance, they settled things just as they chose.

'I have been witness and victim, as prisoner of war, of the false oath taken by the doctors at Norman Cross. They were supplied with medicines, flannel, cotton stuffs, &c., in proportion to the number of prisoners, for compresses, bandages, and so forth. When the supply was exhausted, the doctor, in order to get fresh supply, drew up his account of usage, and swore before a jury that this account was exact. The wife of the doctor at Norman Cross, like that of the doctor of the *Crown Prince* at Chatham, wore no petticoats which were not made of cotton and flannel taken from the prison stores. So with the medicines and drugs. The contractor found the supply ample, and that there was no necessity to replace it, so he shared with the doctor and the apothecary the cost of what he had never delivered, although it appeared in the accounts he had renewed their supplies.'

[Ignoring the fact that, at Norman Cross, as at many other depots, French surgeons, themselves prisoners of war, worked alongside their British counterparts, he tarred the Depot hospital with his intensely black brush.]

In an age of rake-offs, back-handers and bribery, it would have been easy to find genuine instances of corruption. Captain Pressland, the Norman Cross Agent, himself admitted to jobbery on one occasion, in that he had regularly deducted two and a half percent of all moneys passing through his hands for payment to prisoners. He got off with nothing more than a severe rebuke; and it is more than probable that some doctor's wife may have received a 'perk' in the form of a petticoat fashioned from hospital materials. However, it was going far too far to suggest that all instances of dishonesty could be blamed on the British Government's cruel hatred of its French prisoners of war.

The Treaty of Paris in the spring of 1814, and Napoleon's retirement to Elba, brought an end to the long drawn out war, and the white flag of the restored Bourbons fluttered over prison yards throughout the land. The 4,617 inmates at Norman Cross, who only yesterday were prisoners of war, were now free men. The prospect of a speedy return to their homeland and their families, must have filled every heart with joy – although many, perhaps the majority, must have experienced bitter regret at the downfall of their beloved Emperor. The celebrations were great as party after party marched or were driven – for some could afford it – to the coast and freedom. They were remarkably well-behaved, although there was the odd report of some getting too intoxicated to proceed for some time. Charles Dack, an early curator of Peterborough Museum, collected newspaper cuttings relating to the departure of the prisoners:

'11th April, 1814. The joy produced among the prisoners of war at Norman Cross by the change of affairs in France is quite indescribable and extravagant. A large white flag is set up in each of the quadrangles of the depot, under which the thousands of poor fellows, who [have] been for years in confinement, dance, sing, laugh, and cry for joy, with rapturous delight.

'5th May, 1814. The prisoners at Stilton Barracks [Norman Cross] are so elated at the idea of being so soon liberated, that they are all bent on selling their stock, which they do rapidly at 50% advanced prices. Many of them have realized fortunes of from £500 to £1,000 each.

'9th June, 1814. Lynn. Upwards of 1,400 French prisoners of war have arrived in this town during the last week from Stilton Barracks, to embark for the coast of France. Dunkirk, we believe, is the place of their destination. In consequence of the wind having been hitherto unfavourable, they have been prevented from sailing, and we are glad to state that their conduct in this town has hitherto been very orderly; and although are continually perambulating the street, and some of them indulging in tolerable libations of ale, we have not heard of a single act of indecorum taking place in consequence.'

Dr Walker quoted an extract from an article in *The Times* for the 19th August, 1814, which referred to the last prisoner left in the Depot on that date:

'Of the great body of Prisoners of War, who were lately at Norman Cross Barracks, at this time only one single prisoner remains, and he, in consequence of illness preventing him his removal.'

The unfortunate fellow did not survive to return to his native land. The doctor found his name in the Norman Cross Register, on the last Certificate of Death to be issued. He was Petronio Lambartini, a soldier in the Italian Regiment of the French Army. Petronio was the last of the 1,770 who were interred in the Prisoners' Burial Ground near the Great North Road.

Postscript

After the last detachment of freed prisoners had left for the coast and home, in August 1814, the story of Norman Cross as a war prison came to an end. No captives taken during the hundred days which ended with the Battle of Waterloo in 1815 were sent there; and, unlike the great depots of Perth and Dartmoor – which were converted and became two of our principal civil prisons – its wooden buildings were soon demolished and the materials and stores later disposed of by auction. On the 30th October, 1814, Captain W Hanwell, the Agent, handed over the now empty Norman Cross Depot to the Barrack Master; but two years went by before the sale took place. The October, 1816, auction of the site and a wide range of contents lasted thirteen days and was no greater financial success than that which had taken place fourteen years earlier. In 1802, hammocks had been sold for 1s.3d. each (about 6p.), and in the present sale, the whole paving of the Depot Market

Norman Cross Model. *Unique model of the block house at the Norman Cross depot for prisoners of war in Huntingdonshire.* Height: 13in.

went for £20. As well as the site itself, all manner of items were on offer; fixtures, fittings, furniture, all remaining stores and odds and ends, large and small, most lots being knocked down at give-away prices. At the end of that two-week-long auction, the grand total taken amounted to only £11,060 4s 4d. Much of the wood from the dismantled prison buildings was used in the erection of houses and outbuildings in Peterborough and its surrounding villages, some of which survived well into the twentieth century. Francis Abell, writing in 1914, remembered one such house which, perhaps with good reason, was known as 'Bug Hall'!

THE NORMAN CROSS MEMORIAL

During the seventeen years of its occupation by prisoners of war

(1797–1814), many thousands of captives of many nationalities, but mainly French, had passed through the gates of Norman Cross Depot. From time to time, some were exchanged for British prisoners held in continental prisons; others who were repatriated were invalids too sick to present any future danger to Britain as enemy soldiers or sailors. There were also the fortunate thousands who regained their freedom when the Depot was cleared during the short Peace of 1802 and at the cessation of hostilities in 1814. However, there were unfortunates whose fate it was to spend eternity in the country of their captors.

In the early nineteen hundreds, by which time nothing remained to be seen of the once great prisoner of war camp and barracks at Norman Cross, Dr T J Walker, its historian, suggested that a memorial should be raised in memory of those who died in the prison over those long years of warfare. The idea was taken up by the Entente Cordiale Society who commissioned a memorial which thereafter became a landmark for travellers on the Great North Road. It was situated quite near and facing the road, at the top of a field which sloped down to the prisoners' burial-ground. The design was warlike but simple and respectful; a huge bronze eagle, with wings outspread, settled at the top of a tall stone column which rose out of a squared base, carved with a design representing the wooden palisading which once surrounded the prison and its quadrangles.

It was unveiled on the 18th July, 1914, by Lord Weardale. The inscription read:

IN MEMORIAM:

This column is erected AD 1914 to the memory of 1,770 soldiers and sailors, natives or allies of France, taken prisoners of war during the Republican and Napoleonic Wars with Great Britain, AD 1793–1814, who died in the military depot at Norman Cross, which formally stood near this spot, 1797–1815.

DULCE ET DECORUM EST PRO PATRIA MORI
Erected by
The Entente Cordiale Society and friends on the initiative of the late
W H Sands Esq. Honorary Secretary of the Society.

For three-quarters of a century the column with its emblematical eagle stood as a memorial to victims of an almost forgotten war. Then, in 1990, it was vandalised and the great bronze eagle stolen. For a few years their resting-place was left unmarked until public subscription provided a new bronze eagle modelled by animal sculptor Sally Arnup. This looks down from atop the original column, now resited nearer the site of the prison, at the junction of the A1 and the A15.

1. Arthur Brown. Rector of Catfield. *The French Prisoners of Norman Cross.* Hodder Brothers. D.K.Broster. *Mr Rowl.* Heinemann, 1924.

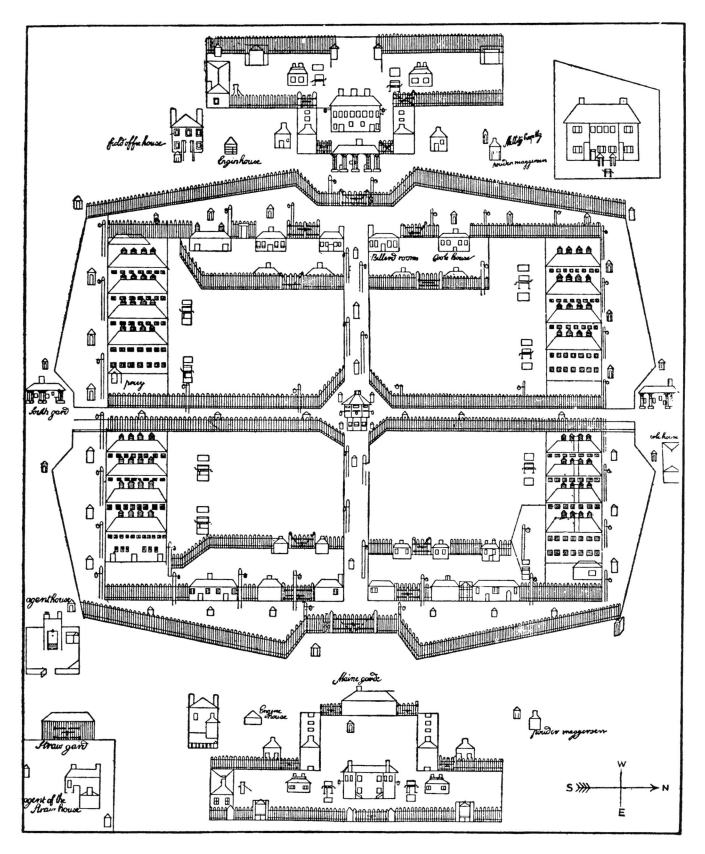

The Washingley Plan of the Norman Cross Depot, East Elevation 1797-1803.

Chapter Eighteen

Stapleton Depot

Redcliffe Back Prison, Knowle Pottery Prison, & Fishponds Depot at Stapleton near Bristol

THE SPECIALLY BUILT FISHPONDS DEPOT for prisoners of war at Stapleton was not finished and ready for occupation until 1779. Before that date, during the Seven Years' War and in the opening years of the War of American Independence, fairly large numbers of war prisoners had been housed in the small prison in Redcliffe Back and in the French prison at nearby Knowle, which had once been the old Pottery Works. Abell says that prisoners also filled the caverns under the cliff itself and that tradition had it that the crypt of St Mary Redcliffe was employed to house some of the overflow.

When, in 1775, it was proposed that Redcliffe Back Prison should be re-opened, the news brought an uproar of disapproval from residents in the town. John Durbin, the Mayor of Bristol at that time, was particularly apprehensive at the prospect of 'Yankee rebels' being confined within the town itself. It was certainly not an ideal place of confinement for war prisoners as it was difficult to guard and a danger to public health if typhus or other 'prison diseases' should break out among the captives.

The converted Pottery Works prison, situated about a mile outside Bristol, which could accommodate more than fifteen hundred prisoners, was no more ideal than Redcliffe in those early days. John Wesley, the founder of Methodism, visited Knowle in October, 1759, where he found more than a thousand French prisoners, many of them living in dreadful conditions, 'without anything to lie on but a little dirty straw' and nothing to cover them 'but a few foul thin rags, either by day or by night so that they died like rotten sheep'. He did his best to help these destitute Frenchmen by organizing subscriptions and the distribution of clothes and bedding; but like so many humanitarians before and after him, Wesley's efforts largely met with frustrating results.

When he next visited Knowle, exactly a year later, he found that those who had survived the winter were as naked and destitute as before he had come to their aid – rations, bedding, clothes and money had been lost to the gamesters or had gone in repayments to the money-lenders. Suffering caused by the French addiction to gambling was never completely wiped out, and it is probable that John Howard was only reporting on the 'decent' inmates at Knowle when he went there twenty years later, in 1779. He found the prisoners busying themselves in creating saleable artefacts, comfortably housed, their food good, and compared the Depot favourably with Millbay near Plymouth.

Bristol, like Liverpool and Plymouth, was one of the principal reception ports for prisoners of war arriving in England, particularly privateers, but it had no great depot to deal with its share of the expected thousands of enemy captives: American, French, Spanish and Dutch. Efforts to rectify this omission began in 1778, with an Admiralty advertisement for a suitable building

'not nearer than twenty miles from the coast with a good water-supply and a large airing-ground, walled and fenced'.

I am indebted to a study by Dorothy Vinter for information concerning the procuring and leasing of the site and many other interesting details of the new depot at Stapleton[1]. John Howard's records of his visits, contemporary newspapers, and Francis Abell's research add to our knowledge of its early days. However, for a first-hand description of prisoner of war life in the Depot during the War of 1812, I shall refer to the memoirs of a young American sailor, George Little, when we come to that point in its history.

It would seem that there was only one reply to the Admiralty's 1778 advertisement, and that came from a Bristol distiller, Nehemiah Bartley, who offered a site in the parish of Stapleton, 'three miles south-west of Bristol, near the banks of the River Frome'. The site, which measured about three acres, was leased by Bartley for £75 per year, and this was extended by another two-and-a-half acres, which were leased by the distiller at an additional annual rental of £6.

A number of buildings were already there at the time of the leasing; a barn and waggon-house, a granary and dairy, stables and store houses, plus a courtyard, gardens and orchards, and 'part of a dwelling house. Some of these buildings were later put to use as prisons for particular categories of prisoner, such as non-paroled officers and petty officers.

When completed, the Fishponds Depot at Stapleton comprised a two-storeyed prison house built of stone, 256 feet long by 45 feet wide, each floor divided in two along its length, thus providing four extremely long and narrow prisons. Another and important specially-built building was the prison hospital. The prison buildings and airing ground were, like most other depots, surrounded by a substantial inner fencing, beyond which was the great outer wall, 'on which stood sentry-boxes in pairs facing each other'. Captain Little, writing of his experience as a Stapleton prisoner some twenty years later, also mentioned the sentry-topped outer wall:

> 'The yard, in the form of a circle, is surrounded with a strong wall, say fourteen feet in height, on the top of which, at intervals, are cannons planted, and a sentinel stationed at each gun; outside of this wall runs a ditch twenty feet broad. Sentinels are so posted around the yard, both day and night that it is almost impossible to effect an escape from the prison'.

That Stapleton was more escape-resistant than most other depots, is certainly true, but that it was not as escape-proof as George Little supposed, will be shown later.

The transformation of Nehemiah Bartley's site into a substantial prisoner of war centre was carried out at a cost of £3,000, and, when extended over the following years, it grew into one of Britain's largest war prisons. Between 1799 and 1800, it was enlarged by a London contractor, and in 1805 a new prison building project was completed which added 3,000 to the Depot's capacity, which meant that it could then accommodate between five and six thousand captives – the equivalent capacity of eight prison hulks.

Although the building of the new depot was well under way when France once again declared war on Britain in 1778, and was completed by the time Spain had joined the fray in the following year, its prisons were still empty at the end of 1779. The Admiralty had planned that a division of Spanish prisoners should be transferred from Redcliffe Prison to Stapleton in the autumn of that year, but the Glamorganshire Militia, who were to have escorted them on the march to the Depot, were reluctant to leave their comfortable winter quarters at Redcliffe.

It was planned that in April 1780 about twelve hundred prisoners should be transferred from Millbay at Plymouth and Forton near Portsmouth, to relieve the pressure on those overcrowded depots. However, an understandable hitch delayed its achievement in full.

The one hundred and fifty prisoners from Redcliffe had eventually arrived as Fishpond's first reluctant guests early in 1780, and were followed by five hundred captive Spanish merchant sailors who had made the long trek from Forton. The balance of the twelve hundred, comprising four hundred from Millbay Prison and three hundred Dutchmen – Holland entered the war in 1780 – were expected at about that same time, but typhus had broken out at Plymouth and danger of the disease being spread as the captives passed through the west-country villages and towns, brought about a postponement of their draft.

Vinter, whose searches through Admiralty papers revealed many interesting facts, says: 'When these latecomers arrived by sea [from Plymouth], the Dutchmen brought their own bedding with them, as well as a hundred and twenty-three large sea-chests. The admiralty was angry at the expense incurred in transporting all this gear by waggon from Shirehampton [on the Avon, near Bristol] and a rule was made that in future only 20 lbs per man should be allowed. This they would have to carry themselves, exception being made for those who were ill or wounded.'

From Spain's entry into the war in 1779 until its end four years later, two thousand three hundred and thirty-nine Spanish sailors saw the inside of one or other of the Bristol prisons. However, in 1780, between one and two thousand Spaniards were exchanged in a cartel agreement between Britain and Spain. Just about all of the Spaniards were sailors, but some were exchanged for British soldiers.

Within two or three years of its construction, the 'new' depot was already something of a mess, and no credit to the Admiralty appointed Agent, James Jones. As we know by now, corruption was rife at almost every level of administration, and it would appear that Fishponds was no exception. Crooked contractors, lack of official supervision over them, meant that prisoners rations were often deficient in both quality and quantity. It is remarkable that James Jones was not only the Agent but a contractor. He was a generally disliked and distrusted civilian: it was only later that the post of Depot Agent went exclusively to experienced Naval officers of the rank of lieutenant or above. An accusatory cartoon, published at about that time, shows Jones suffering for his alleged negligence, or worse.

When John Howard visited Fishponds in 1782, he found the bread was of poor quality, and that the seven hundred and seventy-four Spaniards and thirteen Dutchmen were living in rooms which were filthy and never cleaned. He also felt that prisoners suffered worse treatment at Stapleton, where they were comparatively out of sight, than they would have experienced at Redcliffe, as in the latter case their condition would have been observed by the citizens of Bristol.

During that particular war, which ended in 1783, there were very few escape attempts, and only one prisoner, a Spaniard named Manuel Sceberia, got clear away. A number of others did escape, but all were sooner or later recaptured. One Spaniard who made his attempted getaway at the same time as Sceberia was shot dead by a sentry as he tried to scale the outer wall; and another, Miguel de Asalde – who had tunnelled under the wall – enjoyed three months of freedom before being marched back to Stapleton and the Black Hole.

With the approach of the Treaty of Versailles, and the end of the American war, foreign prisoners from depots all over the country were gathered together into larger groups, to facilitate release when the treaty became ratified.

> 'The Falmouth prisoners joined those in Plymouth, those in Yarmouth went to Deal, and many Dutchmen travelled towards Bristol from Shrewsbury. The military escort which conducted them, via Kidderminster and Tewkesbury, was a detachment of the 1st Regiment of Dragoons. These prisoners having joined the French, Spanish and Dutch already in Stapleton, the united group, six hundred in all, was sent to Winchester, and the empty jail [Stapleton] was closed.'

The main prison and most of the outbuildings remained empty for the whole of the decade which passed before France again declared war on Britain. Three years after its closure the Admiralty purchased the Stapleton Depot outright from Nehemiah Bartley for £1,029, after turning down the latter's asking price of £1,750 as 'a very extravagant demand'. A vast amount of stores and equipment had been sold off at knockdown prices; hospital beds, seven hundred hammocks and surgical instruments and the property itself was advertised for rental.

The 'two very long, spacious and airy buildings [the prison and the hospital] with seven or eight tenements close adjoining, six acres of land, a courtyard and a good water supply with five or six pumps' were offered to but refused by two Government departments, and no private speculator was ever tempted. However, sometime in 1785 the prison hospital was put to use as a sort of reformatory for young offenders: The Marine Society took it over, at a nominal rental of £10 a year, as a school to train, and then apprentice, 'poor boys, young vagrants and criminals to the Sea Services'. Among the subscribers to this admirable cause, were the marine artist Nicholas Pocock, and the poet Robert Southey.

With the outbreak of the Revolutionary War with France in 1793, Stapleton was quickly prepared for the reception of a new influx of foreign captives. Many of the prison officials picked up where they had left off ten years earlier; the Bristol doctor, Thomas Shute, was chief surgeon to the prison hospital as before; and Viscount Bateman was in charge of security at Fishponds, as he had been in its previous incarnation.

It is surprising to find that James Jones was once again appointed Agent to the Depot, despite his less than pristine reputation. His salary would have been about 30s. a day (roughly £550 a year) plus free accommodation, a stationery allowance and some other expenses. Whether he fulfilled his office honestly or strayed, the task of Agent was no sinecure. Vinter says that the Lords of the Admiralty admitted that at Stapleton it was a 'painful and troublesome task'.

'Prisoners up to every subterfuge, dishonest contractors, overbearing stewards, bribed porters, drunken turnkeys, all needed his most watchful supervision, and frequent affronts from his military colleagues who tried to usurp his authority were hard to tolerate. Cut off by a long journey from London, whether by sea or land, he had often to tackle big problems unaided, but on minor points Admiralty regulations arrived by every mail coach'.

Lord Bateman, who was Colonel of the Herefordshire Militia, must have found his security task daunting, as the great outer wall, which stood fourteen feet in height when he left a decade earlier, was now only seven to eight feet high and 'was without mortar so that a man may put his foot between every stone'. Where six or seven feet of massive stone wall had disappeared to over the years can only be imagined, but rebuilding must have been a priority. Perhaps that urgency made for hasty and poor quality construction, for the great gale which hit the prison in 1804 brought down a whole stretch of it. Never was Stapleton subjected to a greater threat of breakouts; riots took place which necessitated the Bristol Horse Militia bringing in a reinforcement of fifty or more troops from the city. We can be certain that the second rebuilding of the wall was of more substantial workmanship – it may be remembered that the American prisoner, George Little, described it twenty years later as back to its original height of fourteen feet, and virtually escape-proof.

The first prisoners to enter the newly opened prison, in April 1793, were about one thousand Frenchmen, brought by sea from the Forton Depot at Portsmouth. They would have had the advantage of clean and ample space for a while, and Colonel Bateman, who viewed the French with more approval than he had for the Spanish, protected them by refusing admission to thoughtless gawkers, saying 'Humanity even to our enemies should prevent their being exhibited to an idle mob, like wild beasts at a fair'.

The layout of the establishment in 1793 was much as it had been in 1779, just the one long prison building, the hospital and adapted buildings already described, but over the next three years which brought so many thousands of prisoners into Britain, Stapleton became as inadequate as many other depots, and began to suffer the dirt and evils which inevitably resulted from unhealthy overcrowding.

In 1794 there were seldom more than eleven hundred prisoners in the Depot at any one time, but two years later that number was almost doubled. The Agent, James Jones, had been replaced by Samuel Span who, although wealthy, was equally dishonest and lasted only a short time. The new Agent was Robert Allard who carried out his office with honesty and efficiency. It was Allard who complained of the overcrowding in 1796, but was induced to accept charge of an additional six hundred French prisoners and ninety officers. The latter would have needed only temporary accommodation, until parole arrangements could be made. Besides that contingent, which had been captured in Ireland, Agent Allard was expected to find room for some of Lord Abercombie's thousands of West Indian captives, including a number of French

Creole officers, who had to be found special quarters apart from the established Officers' Prison. Allard demonstrated his resourcefulness by confining some two hundred prisoners aboard their transport vessel until more suitable accommodation could be found ashore.

1797 was one of the most nerve-racking of the 'invasion' years; which created public panic and prisoner escape-mania in every depot and parole town in the country. General Tate's invasion at Fishguard in February, though in fact a farce, caused fiscal damage which lasted for years (see *The Arts and Crafts of Napoleonic and American Prisoners of War 1756-1816*, Chapter 11, FORGERS & COINERS), and Government concern, inspired not so much by the Fishguard fiasco itself, but awareness of the possibility of a more successful invasion attempt and war on British soil. Just as important was the very real fear of a general uprising of prisoners of war. All parole was discontinued and those already enjoying its privileges were marched to the nearest depot and housed as ordinary prisoners.

The upheaval at Fishponds and Bristol generally, was as great as elsewhere. The Stapleton share of ex-parolees amounted to more than two hundred, from the parole towns of Chippenham, Carmarthen and Tiverton. The regular troops and men of the local Militia had been hurriedly summoned to Fishguard and their place taken by the recently enrolled and inexperienced (Bristol) City Volunteer Corps. Abell quotes a tradition that when the troops and Militia left Stapleton it was found that insufficient arms remained to equip the Volunteers. It was said that 'all the mop-sticks in Bristol were bought up and furnished with iron heads, which converted them into very respectable pikes.'[2]

During this period of anxiety, an April issue of the London *Times* came up with an outrageous suggestion which might have reduced the number of guards required at Stapleton. The idea was that a percentage of the prisoners might be lowered down the Duke of Beaufort's coal-pits at Kingswood!

We have dwelt too often on the fact that a whole class of prisoners, in particular among the French, were their own worse enemies, but there were times when all prisoners suffered from neglect by their own country. The warring countries were expected by international agreement to provide clothing for their captured nationals. However, after the beginning of the Revolutionary War, supplies from France began to dry up. On the 22nd December, 1799, the French Government made it official that in future no clothing would be provided for the French in Britain, a decision which caused suffering to even the most provident. The state of things at Stapleton was made known to the public by two respected Bristol citizens – Thomas Batchelor, the Deputy-Governor of St Peter's Hospital, and Thomas Andrews, cabinet-maker and Poor-Law guardian, who published a record of their visit to the Depot in 1800. The scandalous state of prisoner accommodation at Bristol – or perhaps rumours of the forthcoming report – may have brought about the building programme which took place in that same year.

A few months earlier, in September 1799, the Transport Office invited tenders for the construction of an entirely new prison capable of holding at least a thousand more captives. The deadline for completion was December 1800, and the building was to be 'equal in strength and extent to the present one, to be placed between it and the hospital yard. The contract went to a company called Sanders of Pedlar's Acre, Lambeth, London, with a strict emphasis on the delivery date. One condition of the contract was that no Sunday labour was to be employed, and when the work was delayed by the loss of a ship carrying Baltic timber for Stapleton, Sanders pleaded in desperation for permission to carry on working through the Sabbath. The Transport Board refused this request, but instead gave the rather unusual permission to employ (and presumably pay) a 'reasonable number' of prisoners, as unskilled labour to complete the job. By the time it was completed, the new prison and its fittings, 'including hammock posts and iron lamp-brackets', had cost, £3,000, a similar figure to the original conversion twenty years earlier. The Batchelor/Andrews report had read as follows:

'On our entrance we were much struck with the pale, emaciated appearance of almost everyone we met. They were in general nearly naked, many of them without shoes and stockings, walking in the Courtyard, which was some inches deep in mud, unpaved and covered with loose stones like the public roads in their worst state.

'Their provisions were wretched indeed; the bread fusty and disagreeable, leaving a hot, pungent taste in the mouth; the meat was beef, of the very worst quality. The quantity allowed to each prisoner was one pound of this infamous bread, and half a pound of carrion beef weighed with the bone before dressing for their subsistence for 24 hours. No vegetables are allowed except to the sick in the hospital. We fear there is good reason for believing that the prices given to the butcher and the baker are quite sufficient for procuring provisions of a far better kind.

'On returning to the outer court[yard] we were shocked to see two poor creatures on the ground leading to the Hospital Court; the one lying at length, apparently dying, the other with a horse-cloth or rug close to his expiring fellow prisoner as if to catch a little warmth from his companion in misery. They appeared to be dying of famine. The majority of the poor wretches seemed to have lost the appearance of human beings to such skeletons were they reduced. The numbers that die are great, generally 6 to 8 a day 250 have died within the last six weeks.'

This horrific but well-intentioned account was probably only a bit exaggerated when it came to the *quality* of the provisions; but that no vegetables or variations on beef such as pork or fish, were ever issued, is less believable. Regulations regarding rations were posted up in all depots – and prisoners of war were notorious complainers! Neither is it easy to visualise Stapleton as an inferno-like hell of between two and three thousand near-naked sufferers. Nevertheless, it served its purpose. An official investigation of the accusations was set up, as was a public subscription which called for clothes and cash. At this point the British Government intervened, and took full responsibility for prisoner of war clothing; directing that the public subscriptions should be returned to the donors, saying: 'His Majesty can no longer consider the men as French prisoners but as destitute fellow-creatures.'

The Government-supplied suits were produced at a cost £1.2s, each, but would have had little resale value for the gamblers to trade in to the 'brokers'. These garments were the universally-hated, **TO** outfits, comprising a jacket and trousers in brilliant sulphur-yellow. The prisoners were also issued with a shirt, shoes, stockings, a woollen cap and a neckerchief.

Not surprisingly, the Commissioners found that all the accusations 'were unfounded: that only 141 out of 2,900 had died during the whole year of 1800, and that the chief cause of misery, disease and death was the profligacy of prisoners or the niggardliness of the French Government. Batchelor and Andrews later decided, or were persuaded, to withdraw their allegations; but a year later a letter received by the Transport Board might suggest that they really did see what they had described; without perhaps realising that they were describing, and listening to, only that part of the whole who found it profitable to present themselves. The letter was written by Lieutenant C Ormsby, the first of the naval officers who were to replace civilian appointees as agents at Stapleton and elsewhere:

'Numbers of prisoners are as naked as they were prior to the clothing being issued. At first the superintendents were attentive and denounced many of the purchasers of the clothing, but they gradually got careless. We are still losing as many weekly as in the depth of winter. The hospital is crowded, and many are forced to remain outside who ought to be in.'

Four years later, in 1804, the year of the great gale, an even larger expansion took place. With the resumption of hostilities the year before, captives from all the nationalities which made up Napoleon's armies and allies flooded into Britain in even greater numbers. Two more long prison buildings were added to the Stapleton establishment, capable of housing another three thousand prisoners. It would seem that some economy was shown in filling in the storm-stricken section of the outer wall. To save the cost of building in stone, rows of quicksets (fast-growing hedges, usually of hawthorn) were planted within wooden palisading and the deterrent of the twenty-foot moat or ditch, which George Little later mentioned, was dug out beyond the wall.

By now, Fishponds Depot at Stapleton could be counted as one of the principal depots in Britain, inferior only to Norman Cross and, later, Dartmoor and Perth. However, as fast as its capacity was increased, even faster was it occupied and unhealthily overcrowded. A description of the conditions within the sleeping quarters of those four prisons would seem more appropriate to the orlop deck of a prison ship. Hammocks were slung with the usual eighteen-inch space between, but in three tiers. The barred windows were close-shuttered from the outside at night; and when the guards removed the shutters in the morning, they would have met with the blast of hot foul air from within – so often described in memoirs of the hulks.

Louis Garneray, on the *Prothée* hulk at Portsmouth at about that same time, told how the barred scuttles which were the only source of daylight and fresh air, were shuttered and bolted at night. He said that the warders who carried out the work of opening them, did so with great caution: 'as their work was done they retreated hastily to avoid the pestilential stench.' John Howard was once asked what protection he took to avoid infection when making his visits to such foul places. He replied: 'I trust in Providence but I never enter a prison before breakfast [presumably until after the air had cleared] and in an offensive room I seldom breathe deeply.'

During daylight hours, the inner yards with their little shops and stalls, all manner of enterprises and recreations, provided relief from the misery of the nights. It was, however, the opportunities provided by the main daily prison market which afforded a lightening of the burden of captivity for the many talented or industrious enough to profit from its privileges. Almost anything was resorted to which might relieve days, and in some cases years, of grinding boredom and idleness. Great numbers of over-hopeful, foolish, or desperate men chose gambling, with often disastrous and sometimes fatal results. Others used up the time writing, drawing, or carrying out menial tasks about the inner yards and prisons of the Depot; and it is more than probable that wherever thousands of men were herded together, some would have enjoyed the companionship of pets.

Every depot had its important wild cat population of mouse- and rat-catchers, and some of these, and even some rats and mice, may have been tamed or befriended by the captives. We know that bets were laid on 'rat-races' in Dartmoor Depot. Dogs were also sometimes mentioned, but more often as items on the menu than as pets! The French privateer Louis Garneray, told of cooked Great Dane on the *Crown* prison ship at Portsmouth; and the American Charles Herbert made a note in his journal of how much he had enjoyed roast hound at Millbay Depot in 1779 – euphemistically describing it as 'venison'. There is also the apocryphal story of the gargantuan appetite of the Polish prisoner, Domery, who devoured 174 cats in one year at Liverpool!

It is therefore reasonable to suppose that there may be a darker story behind the record of canine pets at Stapleton. It was well-known that the prisoners kept a large number of dogs, but no one knew just how many until officials investigated a report that, for some unknown reason, a cur had been thrown down one of the prison wells – a serious health risk. After the inquiry, it was decreed that all prisoner pets in the Depot should be put down – and no less than 710 were destroyed! There are many references to, *Raffalès* and other down-and-out captives having dined off rats, so it is quite possible that many of the Stapleton 'pets' were in fact bred for the table.

This is by no means a sensational and unwarranted assumption: Transport Office Commissioner, Sir Rupert George, one of the committee investigating the Batchelor/Andrews report, said, 'The beef and vegetables are boiled in very good soup, seven quarts to each mess of six men', but admitted that 'in a few instances the prisoners have seized dogs within the prison and made soup of them.'

As well as all the little wonders of craftsmanship and ingenuity to be found wherever prisoners of war, the French in particular, were confined, just about all of the illegal and punishable pursuits were to be found at Stapleton – straw-plait, erotica, forgery, etc. When semi-derelict outbuildings were being demolished in 1809, an illicit still for producing forbidden spirituous liquors was revealed; and in 1812 the equipment for turning out counterfeit coinage and false bank-notes was discovered.

Despite the harshness of the punishment for forging paper-money – which was death – Stapleton, like all the other depots, displayed notices warning the public who visited the prison market, to watch out for false notes and coins. The Stapleton penmen did produce passable bank-notes, but their speciality was the production of passports, which at times took on the proportions of a wholesale business (see *The Arts and Crafts of Napoleonic and American Prisoners of War 1756-1816*, Chapter 11, FORGERS & COINERS). As the forged bank-notes were usually of low denomination, whilst passports could command a good price, the latter was the more profitable occupation – and the punishment more lenient.

Like all of the Depots, Stapleton had its problems with pornographers. All manner of erotica was being produced and purchased: drawings, paintings, automated vulgar 'toys' in bone and wood, and suggestive carvings and snuffboxes. In 1808 William Wilberforce appealed to John Birtill, secretary of the Society for the Suppression of Vice, to look into the matter. The concern was serious enough for the Mayor and the Duke of Portland (the Lord High Steward of Bristol), to become involved.

The outcome was that as a result of the market being closed long enough, non-offending prisoners were induced to betray the perpetrators, who were then sent to the Portsmouth hulks.

With the exception of those who have left memoirs or journals, or are named in connection with some famous action or memorable event, prisoners of war are seldom written or spoken of as individuals, but more often collectively, as part of the make-up of a number – say 500 Frenchmen, 200 Americans, 50 Spaniards and so on. Nevertheless, at Stapleton, as in other depots, there were some whose names have survived. Many of these were officers, most of whom were there for the discreditable reason of having broken their *parole d'honneur*. In many cases they deserved this deprivation of their privileges, but in others they were the victims of official nit-picking attention to the rules of parole.

Colonel Thiéry, who had been paroled to Oswestry, was sent to Stapleton for the parole offence of writing to the Comtesse de la Frotté, his niece, without first submitting his letter for censorship by the Agent. It is of interest to note that two of his nephews, who had been born in England, were serving in the British forces, one as an officer with Wellington, the other as a naval officer.

Thiéry did not accept his punishment without complaint, but contended that he should be allowed a servant and separate accommodation. He also wrote another letter, but this time to the Transport Board, which translated read:

> 'The troubles which overwhelmed me en route were revolting. The scoundrels sent by your laws to Tyburn are no worse treated. Such behaviour towards a prisoner of war, a Colonel at that, is horrific, and I reproach the English all the more because I have extended such kindness to those prisoners who have come under my power.
>
> 'If the French Government was apprised of this dreadful treatment, and gave orders of reprisal towards English prisoners in France… the English Government might then order its guards to treat its prisoners with more regard, moderation, and humanity.'

He was released from Stapleton soon after and was probably allowed to renew his parole.

Colonel Thiéry was not the most senior broke-parole French officer in Stapleton at that time. There was General Bron, who had broken his parole at Welshpool, but was permitted to send to France for his wife to share his imprisonment at Stapleton. She was given accommodation in one of the houses in the courtyard between the inner and outer wall. Another of equal rank to Thiéry was Colonel Pavetti, who had committed the far more serious breach, by planning an escape and endeavouring to obtain possession of a forged passport through the French Madame Carpentier, who dealt in such criminal matters in London.

There were a number of other distinguished prisoners who spent part of their captivity in Stapleton Depot. Abell makes brief note of a Frenchman named Cartigny who had experienced life as a captive on the prison hulks at Plymouth, in Stapleton, and later Dartmoor. His posthumous claim to distinction was, that he had taken part in the Battle of Trafalgar at the age of fourteen, and was the last French survivor of the great battle, until he died at the age of 101, in 1892.

In the early days of the Bristol prisons there were very few successful escapes, but as Stapleton Depots expanded and the number of captives increased, so did the incidence of attempted breakouts. All the usual methods were employed: tunnelling, climbing, disguise and bribery. Most were small-scale attempts, too similar to those which took place in so many other depots to be repeated here – although, in October 1800, twenty-five got out by crawling through the prison's main sewer. Reward notices were posted up in Bristol and nearby towns and the public became very 'escaped-prisoner-conscious'. Vinter records an occasion in 1804 when a deaf Bristol citizen was fired upon in Milk Street when he failed to obey a pursuer's challenge. Americans were renowned for their dedication to bids for freedom, and it is not surprising to find that during the short time they were in Stapleton several attempts were made. At least one, Rufus Lockwood, a Connecticut privateer, got clear away.

Investigation into the proliferation of escape attempts, revealed at least one surprising fact – that it was advantageous to make the bid for freedom on a rainy day! The authorities found that the sentries were in the habit of putting up the shutters on either side of their boxes when it rained, thus limiting their vision to dead ahead. It was suggested that the shutters should be replaced by glazed windows.

There is little mention of any general observance of religious matters by prisoners in the British depots – there is, however, record of French prisoners, homeward bound from Perth Depot in 1814, cashing in by selling most of the hundreds of New Testaments which had been donated by the Edinburgh Missionary Society. Officers in the parole towns, particularly in Scotland, complained of the dreadful dullness of the English and Scottish sabbath day. Francis Abell says that 'it is surprising to read [although he doesn't say where] that, notwithstanding the utter irreligion of so many French prisoners in Britain, in more than one prison, at Millbay and Stapleton for instance, Mass was never forgotten among them.' In the absence of a priest, a French naval officer, captured at San Domingo, read the prayers and conducted the Mass at Stapleton. An Altar was painted on the wall and 'two or three cabin-boys served as acolytes, as they would have done had a priest been present…'

In 1813, the second year of Britain's second war with America, about four hundred Yankee sailors were brought to Stapleton. They were the crews of the captured privateers, *Paul Jones*, *Fox*, *Zebra*, *Leo*, and *Tom* among them the aforementioned Captain George Little.

George was born in Roxbury, Massachusetts in September 1792, and was just twenty-one years of age when he found himself in Stapleton. His father was serving with the United States navy and was usually far from home for most of George's childhood, so the youngster was farmed out to the family of a maternal uncle in that same town. There he was given a strict Presbyterian upbringing and a good education. As a lad, his mind was set on following an adventurous life at sea, and his first ship was the *Dromo*, a 26-gun, six hundred ton, Yankee *contrabandista* – a cross between a smuggler, a privateer and a pirate. George had put in a good deal of sea time and was an experienced mariner by the time of his capture, whilst serving as a junior officer of a privateer.

The privateer reached its wartime cruising-ground off Terceira, in the Azores in November 1812, and within a few days had taken her first two prizes, an English brig and a small schooner. A prize-crew was put aboard the brig and she was ordered to the United States, but its crew and that of the smaller vessel were in luck. The captain of the schooner happened to, or deliberately, let slip that a convoyed fleet of merchantmen was due to leave Lisbon, bound for Britain. Ambitious for greater prizes, and valuing their space

greater than their presence, the privateer released all its prisoners into the schooner, and watched as it sailed away to Terceira.

Three days after arriving in their new cruising ground off Lisbon, they captured a much larger British brig after a brief action. It was out of Cork and bound for Cadiz, with a rich cargo, consisting of Irish cut-glass, and other valuable merchandise. She was manned and ordered to the United States, where she arrived safely, and the vessel and cargo sold for nearly four hundred thousand dollars.

Their next capture was an unusual one – a large American vessel, bound for Lisbon. Guessing that it might be sailing under a British licence, in which case she could be counted a legitimate prize, a diligent search was made which eventually unearthed just such a licence. All the ship's company, except the officers, enlisted to serve in the privateer, and their ship was despatched to an American prize port.

At the beginning of December the combined Lisbon and Mediterranean merchant fleet was sighted. George Little rightly doubted the wisdom of their captain, whose plan was to get among the escorted merchant fleet during the daylight hours. George's fellow officers shared his concern, but the captain was obdurate, and 'the privateer ran down amidst the fleet, hauled up alongside of a large ship, and engaged her at pistol-shot distance.' Had this taken place at night, they would have succeeded in gaining at least one prize, but the foolhardy action alerted the convoy, and a frigate and a sloop-of-war were soon bearing down upon them. After a six hour flight they had been chased miles away from the merchantmen, and the pursuers returned to their guardianship of the fleet.

Over the following week they had another narrow escape from capture, when they came up with a large vessel to windward, with its 'main topgallant-sail set, and her fore and mizzen topgallant-masts down' and bales of cotton lashed on the quarter. As they closed, Little went aloft with a telescope and soon came to the conclusion that she was a decoy – or what we would now call a Q-ship – a man-of-war disguised as a merchant vessel. Once more the privateer was on the run. Within a quarter of an hour, the frigate was under a cloud of sail and in full chase.

Both vessels were making about eleven knots, and the Yankees could be thankful for the slight getaway advantage they had whilst the pursuer set her sails. The Americans lived with the prospect of being captured or run ashore for the next four hours, but as evening fell and the sky clouded over, they escaped into the blackness of a moonless night. The privateer 'was luffed to on the starboard tack, every sail lowered, and nothing was to be seen except her hull and poles' when daylight came with no sign of the enemy.

Their next move was to make for the Irish Channel where, fortuitously, they found themselves in the midst of the West Indian merchant fleet, which had recently sailed from Cork. The weather could not have been better from a privateering point of view, thick fog which one minute closed down and the next lifted to reveal possible prizes. On the morning of the 14th December, Little and five of his men boarded and captured a fine large brig and put a prizemaster and crew on board – but that was to be their last capture of the war. Soon after, the fog lifted again, to reveal not a new prize but their captor – a frigate not more than musket-shot distance off the starboard bow. After four hours of chase and a murderous battering from fore-guns, eighteen-pounders and quarterdeck carronades, the American was cut to ribbons. Unable to strike her colours through loss of rigging and yards, it took an extra pounding, which left seven men dead and fifteen badly wounded.

The more senior American officers were well treated, but George and his prisoner shipmates were, as was usual, stowed into the cable tiers. George Little does not describe how the Yankees treated their British captives – except when, for their own convenience, they released their prisoners in the Azores – but they were probably no more gentle than their British captors. He says: 'We were robbed of nearly all our clothing, and as roughly used as if we had been pirates.'

The English frigate added to its collection of American prisoners next morning, by re-capturing the prize brig taken from the West Indies fleet. As the warship came up with her, they found the prizemaster and his crew blind drunk, having spent the night in celebration instead of making all haste to America.

Two days later the frigate reached Plymouth Harbour, where all the prisoners, except for the captain, first lieutenant and surgeon who were entitled to parole, were put on board one of the prison ships, where three hundred of their countrymen were already uncomfortably housed.

After four weeks the number had grown to six hundred and it was decided to transfer them, and Americans from other Plymouth hulks, to depots ashore. George Little was included in one of the drafts which were marched to Stapleton, and he may have exaggerated the strength of its escorting troops:

> 'The number of prisoners contained in each escort was one hundred, guarded by two hundred foot soldiers and fifty dragoons. Our march was severe, as we had to perform a distance of from fifteen to twenty-five miles per day. Many of the prisoners broke down from fatigue, and consequently had to be carried in wagons. Seven days brought us to our journey's end, when we were put into a strong prison, with three thousand French prisoners.'

The chance of their being exchanged was almost nil, largely due to the cat-and-mouse game which was being played between Britain and America over twenty-three Irish/British/American prisoners who had been shipped to England to face the capital charge of treason. (See Chapter 3, THE AMERICAN WAR OF 1812.)

The Americans were prisoners in Stapleton for only a few months before being transferred to Dartmoor where it was considered they would be more strictly overseen, and where the very setting was daunting to the would-be escaper. Many years were to pass before Captain Little wrote his book, *Life on the Ocean*[3] but it would seem that he never forgot a moment of that unpleasant stay in Stapleton.

He had seventeen Spanish gold doubloons at the time of his capture, but, in typical privateer fashion, he was at first open-handed, sharing some of it with his brother officers. When he arrived at the Depot he had forty dollars which, he calculated, would last him no longer than six months – as the Government allowance 'was so small and miserably bad that, without other means of subsistence, no man could exist.'

> 'In three months after our entrance into this prison, the American prisoners presented a sad spectacle of wretchedness and misery. Naturally improvident, and at the same time restless, always planning schemes to effect their escape, they could not bring themselves to any species of labour; many of them, too, coming from the worst grades of society, with habits imbibed from those haunts of wretchedness, soon lost, by gambling, what little means they had. [George then went on to tell the old, old, story of self-imposed hardship, disease and starvation.]
> 'Many sickened and died, others became almost frantic with hunger, and that most abominable vice, theft, was perpetuated upon one another with impunity.
> 'I have actually seen one hundred or more of these half starved wretches scraping out from the piles of offal thrown from the prison, potato and turnip skins, and whatever they could find to masticate, to satisfy their raging hunger.'

The industrious among the Americans soon caught on to the opportunities of the daily market, run mainly by the French. George Little recorded a fact observed in many other depots: that there were some among the well-established French craftsmen and traders who, though prisoners of war, seemed content with their lot, having saved 'one to two thousand guineas' – and there were some who would have liked the war to last longer! George himself took up the craft of straw-plaiting for bonnet-making – a strictly illegal manufacture at that time, which carried heavy penalties to the detected, particularly the guards, who had to smuggle the straw in and the plait out. As George said: 'riches could not flow in abundance through this channel', but by working hard he could make at least one shilling a day, which quite easily kept the wolf from the door.

Others of his countrymen, who had carving or model-making talent, quickly followed the French example of making good use of what would otherwise have been unprofitable and soul-destroying idleness. No well-conducted American need ever have starved. There were any number of ways to add to the basic allowances, and the United States Government allowed each man six shillings and eight pence per month, with which to purchase coffee, tobacco or extra food.

When, in 1814, the Treaty of Paris brought almost final peace between England and France, the two thousand French prisoners at Stapleton left for home – but the Americans remained. It would have been uneconomical to maintain a garrison at Stapleton to guard no more than four hundred Yankees, so they were transferred to Dartmoor, where thousands of Americans had already been sent from the prison hulks and other depots. [We shall meet George Little again, albeit briefly, in 'The Depot on the Moor'.]

The French were released in order of their capture – some who had been detained since 1803 being the first to leave. Most of the invalids and sick, who numbered nearly four hundred, left when fit enough to travel; two of the last three being transferred to Bristol Royal Infirmary. The very last French prisoner to leave Stapleton, Jean Jacques Declerc, was admitted into Fishponds Poorhouse in July 1814.

The buildings and acreage were never again used to house prisoners of war, but were put to many different uses over the years. During the outbreak of cholera in Bristol in 1832 it became an auxiliary of St Peter's Hospital; but for most of the remaining years of the nineteenth century it was taken over by the Bristol Poor-Board as a workhouse.

---

1. *Transactions of the Bristol & Gloucester Archaeological Society*. Volume 75. 1956.   D. Vinter: *Prisoners of War in Stapleton Jail near Bristol.*

2. In 1939, the LDV (Local Defence Volunteers, later known as the Home Guard), similarly short of arms, had drilled with broomsticks and pitchforks.

3. George Little. *Life on the Ocean or Twenty Years at Sea.* 1847.

Chapter Nineteen

Part One
Dartmoor Prison
'The Prison on the Moor' Princetown Devon

'The War Prison (at Dartmoor) was an overcrowded city without women; with its own laws, its schools, manufactures and arts, its workshops where coin could be counterfeited and Bank of England notes forged. In a society composed of persons drawn from every social rank, from the officer of the *Grand Armée* and the negro general from Hayti to the *Sansculotte* from the Faubourg St Antoine, it is not surprising that monstrous growths should be produced.'

Sir Basil Thomson: former Governor of Dartmoor Prison.

THE STORY OF DARTMOOR DEPOT IS A CURIOUS ONE, which poses many questions. Why was such a wild, inhospitable and remote place as the Moor chosen as the ideal site for a great prisoner of war depot, designed to house thousands of our luckless foreign guests? Deliberate punishment, or the physical discomfort of the confinees, was never a consideration when making such a choice.

Why was it so stoutly built, more like a fortress than a prisoner of war establishment? Less than a decade earlier, Norman Cross Depot, in Huntingdonshire, had been purpose-built, economically and quickly, and almost entirely from wood. It was constructed from prefabricated sections, made up by teams of carpenters in the south, and delivered to the site, a method which made it possible to speedily – and again economically – dismantle it when the country was once again at peace.

With such an example of careful planning and clear thinking before them – and with the cons so outweighing the pros in the case of Dartmoor – one might imagine that the Commissioners would have poured scorn on the possibility of a prison ever being built on the Moor. The urgent necessity to supply additional prisoner-space, was as great in 1805 as it had been in 1797; but the site-selectors involved in the Dartmoor project, must have feared that the war might last forever. Whereas Norman Cross was built and occupied in a little over four months, the Prison on the Moor took almost as many years to complete, built, as it was, of granite – at a cost of about £135,000.

Could it be that such a huge sum of money was being invested by a far-seeing Government, who foresaw the day when the depot might be converted into a much-needed civil prison? Nothing could be further from the truth.

Although Britain was in dire need of additional prisoner of war accommodation, the problem of housing our civil prisoners loomed almost as large. With the loss of America as a dumping-ground for our transported criminals and political malcontents – and Australia so far away – Dartmoor might well have been considered as ideal for post-war conversion, had it been sited almost anywhere, other than the climatically cruel, thirty acres of boggy moorland, finally chosen. When the war ended, the massive granite pile remained unoccupied and left to rot, until 1850 when it was at last converted from prisoner of war depot to penal establishment.

The credit, or blame, for the creation of Dartmoor Prison, must go chiefly to a Mr (later Sir) Thomas Tyrwhitt, who was a friend of, and former Secretary to, the Prince of Wales. In 1780, Tyrwhitt was appointed Auditor to the Royal Duchy of Cornwall, and, in 1805, Lord Warden of the Stanneries of Devon and Cornwall. He was twice a Member of Parliament; for Okehampton from 1796 to 1802 and Plymouth from 1806 to 1812, after which, he served as Gentleman Usher of the Black Rod, and was given his knighthood.

Although Tyrwhitt was a Northerner, he had a strange but genuine affection for bleak and lonely Dartmoor, dreaming that one day he would transform parts of that wasteland into a bustling Utopia of prosperous farms and homesteads. Ambitious and optimistic, between 1785 and 1788, he poured a fortune in money and hard work, into the building of his own home – Tor Royal – with extensive farm lands: ignoring the old Dartmoor curse: *'If you scratch my back, I'll break your heart.'*[1]

Inspired by Tyrwitt's enthusiasm and tenacity, a few other farmers followed suit, laying out areas as future agricultural farmland and building themselves dwellings with stone from his quarries. However, Thomas Tyrwhitt could never have been satisfied by the founding of a small scattered community of farmers. The epicentre of his vision was the establishing of a Dartmoor town, which he would one day call Princetown, in honour of his friend and master.

Before the last quarter of the eighteenth century, there were no roads or habitations in that part of Dartmoor, just rough pathways and pack-horse tracks; but in 1772, the Government ordered that a real road, for wheeled traffic, be made, across the Moor from Moretonhampstead to Tavistock. As Sir Basil Thomson says: 'But for this road Dartmoor Prison would never have existed.'

By the turn of the century Tyrwhitt had turned the old track to Two Bridges into a road fit for wagons, carts and carriages; had built roads to his home at Tor Royal, and a start had been made on what would later be Princetown. However, by this time he was forced to realise that the old Dartmoor curse was no idle boast. Beaten by poor soil and harsh climate, his taming of the Moor and prospering from imagined fields of waving wheat and flax had largely come to naught. It seemed that all his hopes and efforts had been in vain. He had built a small number of cottages, an inn called 'The Plume of Feathers' and at Okery Bridge, a mill, but was by now badly strapped for cash, without which those achievements would be left to decay without ever being occupied – and the Moor would return to its uninhabited desolation.

Tyrwhitt was saved by a circumstance of national importance. In the summer of 1803, Britain was once again at war with France, the hulks and depots ashore were rapidly filling with prisoners of war, and the 'prison-hunters' were already out in search of convertible buildings, or a site for a new prison. The opportunistic – and perhaps desperate – Thomas Tyrwhitt determined to promote his area of Dartmoor as the ideal site for a war prison; speedily adjusting his dream of a happy, idyllic community of gentlemen farmers and their workers, he replaced it with the vision of a great stone structure – which would be remembered as a nightmare by thousands of men from many countries; and was reviled almost from the time if its inception.

Although several other Devonshire locations were recommended and investigated as suitable sites, it is probable that they were never really in the running. With the future King of England as his patron, and easy access to the ear of many people in high places, it is likely that the job had gone to the Lord Warden at the outset, however weak his claim.

In July 1805, the Transport Board sent representatives to Tor Royal, to meet Tyrwhitt and the architect, Daniel Alexander, in order to discuss the final positioning of the proposed depot. A newspaper reported:

> *Bristol Mirror* July 13th 1805
> 'The Prince of Wales is about to erect, at his own expense, a chapel at Princetown in the forest of Dartmoor, under the direction of Thomas Tyrwhitt Esq., Lord Warden of the Stannaries. Mr Tyrwhitt has suggested to the Government the propriety of erecting a building near the above for the deposit of such prisoners of war as may be brought to Plymouth, which can without difficulty be conveyed up the river Tamar and landed within a few miles from the spot. It is said that this plan will be acted upon forthwith, and barracks built for the reception of a proportionate number of troops.'

Such a mammoth task as the building of a great war prison, gave rise to a great deal of official correspondence, and necessitated the calling of many meetings. Much of the time was spent in attempting to justify the choice of location and the material from which the prison was to be built. The question as to why, at a time when the country was in such a poor state of financial health, granite was to be used to erect a building which, might well be of only temporary use, received the surprising explanation that, in this case, stone was cheaper than wood! Much of the granite required could, they said, be taken from the Moor for nothing; whereas the Plymouth price for timber was quoted at £12 a load, and difficult to obtain even at that inflated price.[2] 'Nothing', was a rather misleading word, for the granite had to be quarried and carted and to this end stone-cutters and Cornish stone-masons had to be brought in at considerable expense. There would also be a great difference in the time and cost between the handling of wood and that of stone; and time should have been of the essence (it is of interest to note that labour took up three-quarters of the final estimate).

Their justification for location was often no more convincing. The report in the *Bristol Mirror* stated that '…prisoners of war as may be brought to Plymouth, which can without difficulty be conveyed up the river Tamar and landed within a few miles from the spot.' Had this been practical, or even possible, many thousands

of hapless captives would have been saved from the rigours of the seventeen mile march from Plymouth, over some of the most rough and exhausting moorland tracks.

Many and laudatory were the claims for its siting: it was ideally situated, well away from our nearest naval arsenal: its very isolation was an additional security against mutiny and uprising of the prisoners: that no healthier spot could have been chosen than its elevated position on the Moor.

That last statement must have been made by a medical officer who had visited Dartmoor only during the pleasant months of the year; but it was not as outrageous as it might seem. In the second half of the nineteenth century, when it had become a civil prison, the 'healthy' aspect of Dartmoor was the subject of a number of conferences. An early Governor Captain Vernon Harris, in his short but interesting booklet, *'Dartmoor Prison – Past and Present'*, wrote: 'Many [convicts] are sent to Dartmoor for health's sake: for early stages of chest complaints the climate is most efficacious'; and in the twentieth century, it was considered as a possible convalescent gaol for lags recovering from respiratory troubles. Let us, however, return to the prisoners of war. When the warm weather of summer waned, and the miseries of fog, rain, snow and ice took over, there would have been little that was healthy about Dartmoor, and to have crammed men who had committed no crime, into a cold, dank, unheated stone place of confinement, was a cruelty, mainly brought about by ignorance and neglect, rather than deliberately inflicted.

Close scrutiny of the financial side of the logistics resulted in much chopping and changing, in design, detail and, of course, price. The Admiralty, a department of which was the Transport Board, was shaken to the foundations when it received the architect's first estimate for the proposed depot. Daniel Alexander, the official architect, had worked it out, literally to the last penny – £86,433. 13. 4d.

The plans were hastily redrawn, the actual prison area reduced from 23 acres to '15 acres 2 roods', and a new estimate submitted – £70,146. 4s.10d.

Only four Plymouth building companies competed for the work; the highest tender being a Government-shaking £115,331. The next-highest applicant protested that he could make no more than ten percent from his figure of £84,828; but, as might have been expected, the contract went to the lowest tender. Isbell, Rowe & Co., to their lasting regret, came up with the unrealistically low price of £66,815 – more than £3,000 less than architect Alexander's revised estimate.

On the 20th March, 1806, Thomas Tyrwhitt laid the foundation stone of that massive granite edifice which would bear an evil name from that day to this; the French prisoner of war author, M. Catel, referred to it as 'A Receptacle of Human Flesh'; Sir George McGrath, Chief Medical Officer at Dartmoor from 1814 until 1816, when the last of the Americans were repatriated, called it 'The Great Tomb of the Living'; and when Sir William Joynson-Hicks visited the prison in his official capacity as Home Secretary, in 1927, three-quarters of a century after it had been converted for use as a civil penitentiary, he was no more complimentary, describing it as 'A Cesspool of Humanity'.

However, what was to be something of a hell for the future prisoners of war and their overseers, was a godsend for Tyrwhitt and his dreamed-of village of Princetown. The influx of builders, labourers, stone-cutters and all manner of craftsmen, together with suppliers and traders, shopkeepers and agricultural workers, made certain the rapid growth of the small township, and guaranteed its prosperity – at least, for as long as the war lasted.

In the early days of the Depot's history, its remoteness shielded its faults and horrors from the public at large; though some newspapers wrote critically of the state of affairs on the Moor. In 1811, the *Independent Whig* carried an article deploring the unsuitability of the place as a depository for 'six or seven thousand human beings, deprived of their liberty by the chances of war.' After reading that article, Lord Cochrane, the MP for Westminster, took up the matter before the House of Commons. Criticizing the Government for ignoring his past complaints, (asserting that it was afraid to lose what little character it still had), he put forward many reasons why Dartmoor was a misconceived and cruel folly; also significantly pointing out that the prison had been built for the convenience of the town, and not the town for the convenience of the prison.

An impressive, and mildly eulogistic, memorial to the Dartmoor Dreamer, may still be seen in St Michael's, the Parish Church at Princetown. The inscription reads:

'Sir Thomas Tyrwhitt, Knight, late of Tor Royal, Lord Warden of the Stannaries, and many years Usher of the Black Rod, died February 24, 1833 aged 71. His name and memory are inseparable from the great works in Dartmoor, and cannot cease to be honoured in this district.'

Many people, however, would have shared the opinion of a Mr Baring-Gould[3] who, speaking of Sir Thomas and his chosen spot on the Moor, said:

'It is on the most inclement site that could have been selected, catching the clouds from the South West, and condensing fog about it when everything else is clear. It is exposed equally to the North and East winds. It stands over 1,400 feet above the sea, above the source of the Meavy, in the highest as well as the least suitable situation that could have been selected; the site determined by Sir Thomas, so as to be near his granite quarries.'

The parsimony of the Government in choosing the lowest tender, without sufficient investigation into what they were likely to get for their money, and the contractor's ruinously undercutting quote, were both responsible for the holdups, snags and discontent, which haunted the site from start to finish. It is a wonder that any builder should have wanted the contract, as it contained a clause which would enable the Admiralty to terminate it at a moment's notice, should peace be declared!

For some reason, it was at first proposed that stone-workers should be brought down from Yorkshire, but Alexander discovered that, although 'the masons in the country were beginning to rouze', he could get enough Cornish masons to carry out the work – and that they were paid a lower wage.

Isbell, Rowe & Co. began the actual building work in the winter of 1806 and within a few weeks the company's problems began with a vengeance. Labour costs had risen by 20%, and even the Cornish masons had 'begun to rouze'. It may be that there was good reason why the Cornish stone-workers had earned less than their Yorkshire brethren – or perhaps the understandably worried contractor had pushed them too hard for them to produce their best work. Whatever the reason, the standard was poor.

Ex-Governor Basil Thomson, writing in 1907, said: '…the haste

with which the masons set to work may be judged from the state of the rough walls today, when they are but a century old, and have been repeatedly pointed and braced to hold them together'.

Isbell and Rowe suffered frustration and financial agony for the whole period that the prison was under construction, and had good reason to believe in the potency of the Dartmoor Curse. Even before Tyrwhitt laid the foundation stone in March 1806, a letter to the architect, dated November of the previous year, mentioned that 'This hath been a hindering week, the sun hath scarcely made its appearance, and we can safely say that £120 hath been lost this week in wages'; but worse was yet to come. The price of timber now entered the ring, and a verbal battle which ensued between contractor and the Admiralty brought all building work to a halt.

By 1806, the cost of wood, much of which was imported, had doubled, partly owing to the blockading of the Prussian ports. The contractor's prices had been based on £5 a load, so they wondered who would be responsible for the balance. They might have guessed! The Admiralty at first refused to budge, and only after long and tiresome bargaining did they offer to allow a deduction equal to the import duty on the timber. However, Isbell, Rowe & Co. stuck to their guns courageously. They issued a strike-like ultimatum and told the architect that, in order to save their families from ruin, they would dismiss their workers forthwith, and leave the unfinished, in fact just started, prison for someone else to complete.

The strategy, if strategy it was, caused the Admiralty to think again, and a compromise was reached. Devonport Dockyard would supply the required loads of timber at a reasonable rate. Thomson said that ships' timbers and 'oaken knees' could still be seen among the roofing-work in one of the prisons during his time as Governor.

The architect had promised that Dartmoor would be ready for occupation by the end of 1807, but by September of that year, another problem had brought about another serious hold-up. The wagon road over which the contractors brought their materials to the main gate and on to the site, was in such a sorry state as to be virtually impassable.

A representative of the Transport Board who was sent down to assess the situation, found that 'the road that was to run past the gate was nothing but a deeply-rutted cart track, about which were scattered temporary huts for the work-men', and that the prison roofs were still being slated; the Agent's house and those of the other depot officials were just bare walls; 'the barracks had not got beyond the foundations; and the yards were so littered with material of all kinds that the water-courses had not been begun'.

He added that 'to put prisoners into such buildings in the depth of winter would be cruel', and that they could not be ready before the end of the next summer. Although even this was wishful thinking!

The work staggered on from crisis to crisis throughout the whole of 1808, and it was not until May 1809, that the great Dartmoor Depot was considered sufficiently finished to receive the first of the captives for whom it had been built. The Government had long ago realized that they had gained no bargain by accepting the lowest quote. The costs had already risen to more than £74,000, and building and repair work was still going on in 1812.

The first Agent of Dartmoor war prison was appointed in October 1808, in preparation for the opening in the spring of the following year. He was Post-Captain Isaac Cotgrave RN, a strict disciplinarian who had been the Agent at Plymouth. He held the post until December 1813 and his staff were as follows:

DARTMOOR PRISON STAFF 1809

Captain Cotgrove R.N.	Agent
William Dykar	Surgeon
William Dickson	Ass. Surgeon
	1 Dispenser
	10 Turnkeys
	3 Hospital mates
	3 Labourers
	1 Matron
	Foreman of Works
	1 Seamstress
	1 Plumber
	1 Steward
	1 Carter
	1 First Clerk
	1 Mason
	1 Market Clerk
	1 Blacksmith
	1 Extra Clerk
	1 Navigator[4]

It is not difficult to picture the turmoil which must have attacked the prisoner's mind, when he learned that he was going to be transferred to the Depot on Dartmoor. Although still empty in the spring of 1809, it had been so long in the building, that the bitter recriminations of the workmen and humanitarian critics from all levels of society, that it was already indelibly branded as a place of hardship and cruelty – even before its first inmates arrived and could confirm or deny that description.

Napoleon sought to 'inspire' his troops by warning that capture by the British could mean confinement in one of their dreaded prison ships; but we know, from French and American diaries and memoirs, that some captives who had suffered imprisonment on one or other of our infamous hulks, were reluctant to swap the devil they knew for the rumoured horrors of the Prison on the Moor.

On the 24th May, 1809, the first batch from a division of 2,500 foot-sore French prisoners began to arrive at Dartmoor. They would have been divided up into drafts of about one hundred prisoners, each party escorted by a like number of militiamen under the command of a regular officer. Most would have come from the overcrowded Plymouth hulks, Millbay Prison, and perhaps a few from Portchester Castle. The rough cart track which connected Plymouth with the prison must have soon become well-worn, for by the end of June the prisoner population had grown to 5,000. Weather-wise, these early arrivals were lucky: even the gloomiest parts of the Moor were not foggy, misty, windswept and rain-sodden for the whole year round. The French prisoner of war author L.Catel, created a meteorological howler when he wrote:

'...for eight months of the year it [Dartmoor] is a *vraie Sibérie* covered with unmelting snow. When the snows go away the mists appear. Imagine the tyranny of *perfidé* Albion in sending human beings to such a place!'

In commenting on this calumny, A.J.Rhodes, author of *'Dartmoor Prison'* goes slightly over the top in the opposite direction:

'There are periods when Nature smiles and the great expanse reflects her most genial moods, when during the summer and autumn the desolate hills and valleys become rich in colours of golden gorse, purple heather, pink ling and green bracken, when the sun shines, and bracing breezes are a tonic both to the body and soul.'

An early and uncritical description of the new prison, written and published within a few months of its opening, may be found in Risdon's *Survey of Devon* (1811):

'It is probably the finest of its kind. An outer wall encloses a circle of about 30 acres. Within this is another wall which encloses the area in which the prison stands; this area is a smaller circle with a segment cut off. The prisons are five large rectangular buildings each capable of containing more than 1,500 men; they have each two floors, where is arranged a double tier of hammocks slung on cast-iron pillars; and a third floor (the 'cockloft') in the roof, which is used as a promenade in wet weather. There are besides two other spacious buildings; one of which is a large hospital and the other is appropriated to the petty officers, who are judiciously separated from the men. In the area likewise are sheds or open buildings for recreation in bad weather. The space between the walls forms a fine military road (nearly a mile in length) round the whole, where the guard parades, and the sentinels, being posted on the platforms, overlooking the inner wall, have complete command of the prison without intermixing with the prisoners.

'The segment cut off from the inner circle contains the governor's house and the other buildings necessary for the civil establishment; and into this part of the ground the country people are admitted, who resort to a daily market with vegetables and such other things as the prisoners purchase to add to the fare that is provided for them, and which they buy at lower rates than they could generally be procured for at the market towns. The barracks for the troops form a detached building, and are distant from the prison about a quarter of a mile. The number of prisoners that have been lodged here [at any one time] has been from five to seven thousand, and the troops employed to guard them not more than from 300 to 500.'

The prison buildings, which were situated in the eastern half of the site, were originally five (later seven) in number and, radiated out from a centre point roughly into a half circle. Both boundary walls were stoutly built of stone; but the inner wall was twelve feet high, whilst the height of the outer was no more than eight feet, and thus constituted a security risk. In the early days, the safety of the Depot depended largely on the discipline, alertness – and trustworthiness – of the sentinels and guards. The sentries were posted at regular intervals on 'peaked bastions', platforms on top of the wall, which were reached by stairways outside the wall. From their elevated vantage points the sentries could, collectively, keep the prisons fairly well covered. It was not until 1812, and the prospective coming of the Americans, that the outer boundary was wisely raised to twelve feet in height (one can imagine Yankee escapers pole-vaulting the mere eight foot obstruction to their flight!) and an alarm system was installed. This was a simple enough device, with wires attached to a large number of bells running around the top of the walls, so that if touched even lightly, the resultant clamour would immediately call out the guard. The building work on the wall was carried out by *Les Laborieux*, who would have been pleased to receive the few pence a day paid by the Government.

Within the two stone walls was a third, but this time one of metal. A high wrought iron palisade, with granite supports, surrounded the prisons and airing yards, thus preventing the prisoners from getting nearer than five metres from the inner wall, whilst not obscuring the vision and aim of the sentries on the walls.

It was not at all usual for prisoners to be employed outside the walls of their prison; in fact, it contravened the strict Government rules against the practice. Nevertheless, there is evidence of their work in some parts of the country – but nowhere near as much as attributed to them.

The British and French governments differed on the subject of prisoner of war employment. Conscription, which had swept most of France's male population into the French Army or Navy, had drained off much of its civil labour force. Bonaparte, therefore, was only too pleased to be able to set his British captives to work on public projects; saying that only our natural stinginess and cruelty prevented us from doing likewise, thus allowing our French prisoners to earn a little money. The truth was three-fold: that we had no shortage of civil labour (except in remote places like Dartmoor); that the privilege of the Prison Markets, allowed the prisoners to earn according to their industry and talent; and that the British Government was saved the cost of military surveillance over outside working parties.

That was the rule, but Dartmoor was one of the exceptions to it. A large number of prisoners must have been employed in heightening the outer wall, (by 4 feet, times the width of the wall, times a mile). But they also built or rebuilt parts of their own prisons – and a few houses and the Parish Church at Princetown. All of this must have been carried out under the approval of the Transport Office, who would have covered that approval with a covenant: that all the pay due to the builders and labourers should be withheld until the completion of the work; and should even one of the group escape the whole of their earnings would be forfeited.

One of them, a member of such a working party, did escape. Captain Vernon Harris, predecessor of Basil Thomson as Governor, wrote of this remarkable event in his *Dartmoor Past & Present,* a pamphlet which he published for private distribution:

'A prisoner of about thirty years of age, who had acquired some knowledge of mason's work, was employed with several others in building the Rectory house in Princetown. They were engaged upon the breastwork of a flue intended for open fireplaces; and as soon as the work had been brought to a convenient height, a recess was formed in the thickness of the wall corresponding to the space occupied by a man's body. The outer face being filled in with thin stone selected beforehand for the purpose. The flue, after being carried above the recess at the original thickness, was rendered in mortar, care being taken to leave sufficient openings for air and observation. During the afternoon of the day fixed upon for the attempt, the prisoner concealed himself in this hiding-place, and it was built up by his companion. They took so much pains to ensure a creditable appearance as to draw forth the commendations of the instructor, who complimented them upon the improved face put on the work. The man being missed at evening roll-call, strict search among the buildings was made. The general opinion among the guard was that the prisoner must have eluded the vigilance of the sentries posted round the house during the day. As night drew on the prisoner observing that all was again quiet, easily removed the green work, with which he was surrounded, and succeeded in making off without attracting attention. The condition of the wall on the following morning, pointed clearly to the stratagem that had been so successfully carried out.'

Although it is to be doubted that they would have accepted the compliment gracefully, it must be said that, from the captors' point of view, the majority of French captives made ideal prisoners of war. This does not mean that they knuckled down to draconian discipline, or toadied up to their captors in any way – they could hate with the best of them! However, whether they found themselves in a well-governed depot which attempted to honour the international agreements regarding the treatment of prisoners of war, or were confined in a verminous hulk under the tyranny of a drunken captain, in an amazingly short space of time they settled down to face their predicament as a community, rather than a group of unfortunate individuals. Their committees and courts concerned themselves with almost every aspect of prisoner of war life, from personal hygiene and the cleanliness of the prisons, to the trial and punishment of wrongdoers.

The French prisoner, L Catel, in his *La Prison de Dartmoor* – or *The Historical Story of the Misfortunes and Escapes of French Prisoners in England under the Empire, from 1809 to 1814,* described how the prisoners organized their self-governing society.

The inmates of each of the prisons cast a vote to elect one of their number as *Commissaire de Salle,* who would be responsible for the good conduct of his share of the prisoners – which could vary from a thousand to fifteen hundred men. He also had the power to convene courts and summon witnesses and juries. The five – later seven – *Commissaires* were responsible to an elected *Président,* who was himself responsible to Cotgrave, the Agent. The Agent was only involved when a problem got too much for the *Président,* or was outside his jurisdiction, such as murder, forgery or escapes.

Therefore, to a great extent, the captives governed themselves. Had the French not possessed that talent for making the best of their imprisonment, great depots like Norman Cross, Perth and Dartmoor would have needed to double the size of their garrisons. Dartmoor itself illustrates the point. Before 1812, the number of troops employed there to control as many as 7,000 men, varied from 300 to 500, but when the Americans came, the guard increased to more than 1,200 – and a detachment of artillery stood by until the end of the war.

Thomson described the Depot as a city run by prisoners and, as with all other towns and cities, its population was made up of a very wide range of citizens, the good, the bad, and even worse. Catel says that the French prisoners based their society on the principles of equality and fraternity, although the fact that the class system had not been abandoned was all too obvious in some cases. The French names for some of the classes have been mentioned in other parts of this book, *Les Lords* and *Les Laborieux* for instance. The lowest form of prisoner of war life, the down and outs of the prison ships, were *Les Rafallès*; but had they been transferred to Norman Cross, they would have been called *Les Misérables*; and if to Dartmoor, *Les Romains*. So let us sort this out from the top, from prisoners dressed in bespoke attire, down to poncho and nakedness.

Les Lords were the aristocrats of the Depot, men of means, who could draw on their own accounts, or received allowances from abroad. Some were wealthy merchant or privateer officers, others were commissioned officers who had never signed a *parole d' honneur,* and some who had but later broke their word.

Les Capitalists were entrepreneurs who employed some of their fellow prisoners from the following group.

Les Industrialists or *Les Laborieux* describes the most admirable of categories – the workers who used their energies and talents to improve their lot, and make bearable the misery of incarceration. Their industry ranged from creating artefacts for sale in the prison market place, to cookhouse aids or sweepers of the yards, who were paid a small wage by the Government.

Les Indifférents, uninspired and idle men, who 'made do' on

Government rations and issues – and probably still wore the detested 'TO'- branded, sulphur-yellow prison garb.

Above this point, most of the prisoners were manageable and, except for escape attempts, of little trouble to the authorities. However, below it were men who brought hell upon themselves and their fellow captives – and were responsible for much of the squalor for which the British prisoner of war system was blamed.

Les Minables were only a step or two away from the bottom of the heap. They were the inveterate gamblers who lived for – and sometimes died from – their addiction to cards, dice and the gaming tables. The losers usually sank into the squalor of one or other of the last two grades. Gambling fever was about the worst disease a prisoner could contract. Often fatal, it plagued every prison on land or afloat, and was the bugbear of the Transport Board and Government. (The story of the terrible effect that extreme gambling had on all depots, is told in *The Arts and Crafts of Napoleonic and American Prisoners of War 1756-1816*, Chapter 9, THE GAMBLERS & BROKERS.)

Les Kaiserlics were probably as objectionable as their rivals in infamy, but I cannot say what kept them afloat just above the bottom.

Les Romains were, then, the lowest of the low; but there was yet another, and even more disgusting category, for which some *Kaiserlics* and *Romains* may have qualified. It is doubtful that there was ever any prisoner of war who had never felt the bite of bug, flea or louse; but there were some deadbeat losers who had long given up the fight against filth and vermin, and had no further to fall. These were the *Manteaux Impériaux,* who were given that grand soubriquet by an unfeeling but witty observer, who professed to see a sartorial similarity between the prisoner in his louse-laden poncho and a portrait of Napoleon in his Imperial Mantle – embroidered with a thousand tiny bees.

Les Romains, as the English and the Americans called them, were a well-documented band of villains, who had developed their infamous way of life into an exclusive society of vice and viciousness. All prisoner of war establishments had a version of such groups of forsaken men, though none who gloried in it, as did the many hundreds at Dartmoor. It may be that it took the coincidence of French prisoners and their addiction to gambling to bring about such a disastrous state of affairs.

The authorities had endeavoured ceaselessly to save them from themselves and the unscrupulous among their fellows, but to no avail. It would seem that *Les Misérables* at Norman Cross were of a lesser constitution than the Romans: although they retained their hammocks and a few possessions, they died like flies when an epidemic hit their depot, whereas the Romans, who slept on cold stone floors survived.

Ex-Governor Thomson gathered together and published a great deal of information from French and American sources which, told of the daily life and predations of the Romans.

T.J.Walker, when preparing his book on Norman Cross, could find no such detailed records regarding *Les Misérables*, and requested that he be allowed to include the work on the Romans as a parallel case. Thomson kindly agreed and Walker reproduced it *verbatim* – which I, to a much lesser extent, shall do here.

To the sociologist there can be nothing more significant than the fact that a body of civilised men, some of them well educated, will under certain circumstances adopt a savage and bestial mode of life, not as a relapse, but as an organised proceeding for the gratification of their appetites and as a revolt against the trammels of social law. The evolution of the 'Romans' was natural enough. The gambling

fever seized upon the entire prison, and the losers, having nothing but their clothes and bedding to stake, turned these into money and lost them. Unable to obtain other garments, and feeling themselves shunned by their former companions, they betook themselves to the society of men as unfortunate as themselves, and went to live in the cockloft, because no one who lived in the more desirable floors cared to have them as neighbours. As they grew in numbers they began to feel a pride in their isolation, and to persuade themselves that they had it by their own choice. In imitation of the floors below, where a *Commissaire* was chosen by public election, and implicitly obeyed, they selected some genial, devil-may-care rascal to be their 'General', who only held office because he never attempted to enforce his authority in the interests of decency and order. At the end of the first six months, the number of admitted Romans was 259, and in the later years it exceeded 500, though the number was always fluctuating. In order to qualify for admission, it was necessary to consent to the sale of every remaining garment and article of bedding to purchase tobacco for the use of the community.

The communism was complete. Among the whole 500 there was no kind of private property, except for a few filthy rags which were donned as a concession to social prejudice. A few old blankets with a hole in the middle were held in common, to be worn like a poncho by any whose business took them into the yards. It would seem that the 'General' kept a cache of musical instruments and odds and ends, for use on ceremonial occasions.

In the Capitol itself, everyone lived in a state of nudity, and slept naked on the concrete floor, for the only hammock allowed was that of the 'General' who slept in the middle and allocated sleeping-places to his constituents. A rough sort of discipline was maintained, for whereas 500 men could sleep without much discomfort in three tiers of hammocks on a single floor, the actual floor space was insufficient for more than a third of that number of bodies lying side by side. Therefore, at night the cockloft must have been an extraordinary spectacle, with the concrete carpeted with nude bodies, all lying on the same side, so closely packed that it was impossible to get a foot between them. At nightfall, the 'General' ordered 'fall in', and the men ranged themselves in two columns facing one another. At a second word of command, alternate files took two paces to the front and rear and closed inward, and at the word 'Bas!' they all lay down on their right sides. At intervals during the night, the 'General' would cry 'Pare à viser!' (Attention!), 'A Dieu, Va!' and they would turn over.

From morning to night, groups of Romans were to be seen raking the garbage heaps for scraps of offal, potato peelings, rotten turnips, and fish heads, for though they drew their ration of soup at mid-day, they were always famished, partly because the ration itself was insufficient, partly because they exchanged their rations with the infamous provision-buyers, the 'brokers', for tobacco, with which they gambled. Pride was certainly not a failing of which they could be accused. There was always a foraging few lurking in the alleys between the tiers of hammocks on the floors below in search of scraps. If they spotted a man peeling a potato, a dozen or more of these wretched men would surround him, begging for the peel. They would form a ring round every mess bucket, like hungry dogs, watching the eaters in the hope that one would throw away a morsel of gristle, and fighting over every bone. Sometimes the continual state of starvation did its work, and the poor wretch was carried to the hospital to die; generally the bodies of the Romans acquired a toughened fibre, which seemed immune from epidemic disease.

Very soon after the occupation of the prison the Romans had received their nickname, and had been expelled from the society of decent men, for we find that on the 15th August, 1809, five hundred received permission to pay a sort of state visit to No. 6 prison. At the head of the procession marched their 'General', clad in a flash uniform made of blankets, embroidered with straw, which looked like gold lace at a distance. Behind him capered the band – twenty grotesque vagabonds blowing flageolots and trumpets, and beating iron kettles and platters. The ragged battalion marched in columns of fours along the grass between the grille and the boundary wall, without a rag on any of them but a breech clout, and they would have kept their absurd gravity till the end, had not a rat chanced to run out of the cookhouse. This was too much for them; breaking rank, they chased it back into the kitchen, and the most nimble caught it and, after scuffling for it a neighbour, tore it to pieces with his teeth and ate it raw. The rest, with appetites, fell upon the loaves and looted them.

The guard was called out, and the soldiers marched into the mêlée with fixed bayonets; but were immediately surrounded by the naked mob, who disarmed them and, in high spirits, marched off with their 'prisoners' towards the main gate, with cries of 'Vive l'Empereur'. Awaiting them, at the head of a strong detachment of troops was Captain Cotgrave.

The 'General' of the Romans then delivered a mock heroic speech to the Agent. Striking a pose, he said, in effect,

> 'Sir, we were directing our steps to your house to hand over to your care our prisoners and their arms. This is only a little joke as far as your heroic soldiers are concerned, who are now as docile as sheep. We now beg you to order double rations to be issued as a reward for our gallantry, also to make good the breach we have just made in the provisions of our honourable hosts.'

The naked Romans were driven back to their cockloft with blows from the flats of musket butts, and the 'General' was rewarded for his gallantry – Captain Cotgrave gave him eight days in the Black Hole!

For some time after their humiliating experience, the guards were hypersensitive on the subject, and would drive off any Roman that neared them with bayonets at the charge, whenever it was necessary for them to go amongst the prisoners. Some Romans may have already been down-and-outs at the time of their being called to the colours, but a few were young men of good family, who received quarterly remittances from home. When it arrived, the naked Roman would borrow clothes and collect his money from the Agent's office. After contributing a pound or so for the General to buy tobacco or potatoes for his less-lucky brethren, he would clothe himself decently, and settle down as a temporarily reformed character, on one of the lower floors. However, within a week or two the gaming-tables would have claimed his twenty-five louis and a suit of clothes, and he would have returned to the cockloft and his old friends.

On the 8th October, 1812, the bakehouse burned down, and bread was sent in by a local contractor. The quality was so poor that it was rejected, and the whole Depot went without for twenty-four hours. This was particularly distressing for the Romans, who scurried off to try their luck at the offal heaps. A French prisoner who was there at the time, later recalled the happenings of that day and, if his recollections can be trusted, tells a story even more revolting than that of the foul rat soup. He says that when the Romans reached the offal heaps, it was to find that a two-horse rubbish wagon was

already being filled with the ill-smelling mounds. During the altercation which followed, some of the famished wretches fell upon the horses with knives, killing them both and cutting into the carcasses: some, it was said, eating their portions raw! All this was too much for the non-Roman onlookers, who drove them back to their lofty dens.

Filthy, shameless, a disgrace to their country and its fighting forces, the inhabitants of the cocklofts did little to offend their fellow captives, other than by their ceaseless begging and scrounging and, of course, their objectionable presence in the Depot. As time went by, however, and the Romans grew in number, their depravity grew deeper. From being miserable losers and moral delinquents, who may have evoked a certain amount of pity in the hearts of the compassionate – particularly if the latter had ever thought 'there, but for the grace of God, go I' – they became violent and a vicious threat to the whole prison population.

Captain Cotgrave tried as hard as, but with no more success than, other depot agents, to suppress the sale of food and clothing for betting stakes. It was, and still is, impossible to stamp out gambling – a spinning coin is just as effective as the finest gaming-table – and it would have been almost as difficult to stop prisoners buying and selling between themselves – even if it did mean that one of them would go hungry next day. Nevertheless, some of the worst offenders among the purchasers were put into the Black Hole for ten days – in spite of their protests that they had done nothing against the rules.

The Agent answered their complaint by letter, which read:

To the Prisoners in the Cachot for Purchasing Provisions

The orders to put you on short allowance from the Commissioners of His Majesty's Transport Board is for purchasing the provisions of your fellow prisoners, by which means numbers have died from want of food, and the hospital is filled with sick not likely to recover. The number of deaths occasioned by this inhuman practice occasions considerable expense to the Government, not only in coffins, but with the hospital filled with those poor unhappy wretches so far reduced by want of food that they linger a considerable time in hospital at the Government expense, and then fall a victim to the cruelty of those who have purchased their provisions to the disgrace of Christians and whatever nation they belong to.
The testimony of your countrymen and the surgeon prove the fact.

Cotgrave also tried to lure them back into the normal world by giving them a fresh start, re-clothing groups of them, only to find that on the very next day they were walking the yards, once again in a state of semi-nudity. Captain Cotgrave then decided to attack from another angle; he posted up throughout the prisons a 'Notice to the Prisoners in General'. This called upon the well-conducted among them to note the 'infamous and horrible practice' of the 'brokers', who preyed upon the 'evil conducted' among their fellow prisoners. He warned that, on the first appearance of a recurrence of 'this odious and abominable practice', he would close not only the main Marketplace, but the prisoners' shops and stalls in the inner markets. This was an idle threat: to have closed the main market for any length of time would have caused unrest, perhaps even a general uprising.

However, the prisoners in six of the seven prisons were relieved when, in 1812, all of the Romans were banished to No. 4 prison which, by then, stood cut off and alone. It was reasonable to think that with no one else to deal with, the problem might be solved. Bedding and blankets, clothing and hammocks, were supplied to them, either from Government stores or contributions from generous fellow prisoners. But all to no avail. They were soon seen to be selling their newly-acquired possessions through the bars of the prison's gates. For the moment we shall leave them but return to the subject after the arrival of the Americans in 1813.

A large number of nationalities were represented among the thousands of prisoners at Dartmoor, but none coped with captivity with the adaptability of the French. All were co-belligerents who had fought for France, but it would seem that the hand of fraternity and equality was seldom offered in reciprocation. In fact, there were times when segregation was the only answer to troubles between the allies. Sergeant-Major Philippe Beaudouin was not alone in his dislike of the Spaniards, decrying 'their tendency to use the knife rather than words', and adding that 'they were bone idle, dirty traitors, gamblers, and as dishonest as magpies'. The Scottish depot at Greenlaw in Midlothian, separated the Danes from the French, and sent them down to the hulks at Chatham and, as we shall see, the Americans were shut off from the French when they reached Dartmoor.

Trusting in its remoteness on the Moor and the strength of its design and layout, it was rashly said that the new prison would be escape-proof, a boast which was very short-lived. It should be remembered that the captives who were sent to Dartmoor early in 1809, were already experienced prisoners of war, who had spent long enough on hulks or in shore establishments to have learned that not all British sentries, guards and turnkeys were incorruptible.

In July 1809, only eight weeks after the Depot's opening, two Frenchmen made their bid for freedom. They had bribed four sentries of the Notts. Militia, giving eight guineas to each soldier – a rather high price for such assistance at that time. The escapees were soon recaptured, and would have sampled some time in the Depot's brand-new Black Hole. The soldiers were brought to trial and confessed to their crime. Two were condemned to be shot and the other two would each have received several hundreds of lashes.

We have read of all manner of escapes from other depots, where, once past the sentinels, guards and patrols, and beyond the fences and walls of their prison, the absconders stood a fair chance of making a successful getaway. Although all escapers had a price on their heads – at one time ten shillings (50p), rising later to as much as £5 – as a reward for each man recaptured, many of our countrymen had a certain amount of sympathy for the courageous fugitives and would not have cashed in on their misfortune. However, not all felt this way towards our disarmed enemy. In the vicinity of some of our larger depots, were some who formed themselves into bounty-hunting parties and there were, of course, the unprincipled and unpatriotic escape-agents, who could often provide something like a door-to-door delivery service – if the money was good enough.

In Dartmoor's early days, the would-be escaper had few of these advantages. He still had corruptible troops who might get him through the three barriers of his prison and on to the wilderness beyond, but from then on he was in much the same position as escapers from Portchester Castle. It was said, in effect, that getting out of Portchester was the easiest bit; the hardest was running the gauntlet of a harbour crowded with men-of-war and the Portsmouth batteries.

The Moor itself was Dartmoor's 'men-of-war and batteries', and there were few inhabitants from whom to seek kindly assistance.

Such sympathy may have been withheld anyway, for they showed little regard for the French prisoners except as purchasers of their goods in the Depot Marketplace. In his book, *The Farm of the Dagger*, Eden Philpotts has one of his characters, a typical Dartmoor native, say:

> 'Dartymoor's bettem they deserve anyway. I should like to know what's too bad for them as makes war on us. 'Tis only naked savages, I should have thought, as would dare to fight against the most civilized and God-fearing nation in the world.'

Without a guide, disorientation could set the runaway on to a wandering path to death from exposure and starvation, or loss in the treacherous bogs and marshes of the moorland.

Nevertheless, there were many attempted, and some successful, escapes from Dartmoor. If the escapee had cash he stood a better chance than one who had to depend on courage and ingenuity alone. Disguise of one kind or another featured prominently in many stories of these escapades: see *The Arts and Crafts of Napoleonic and American Prisoners of War 1756-1816*, THE ENTERTAINERS (Chapter 10) where two prisoners acted their way to freedom; and THE MARKETS (Chapters 2 and 3) which tells of the importance of the second-hand clothes stalls to the escape planners. All of these things cost money or local friends in the market-place. If the getaway was from Plymouth, coach fares and possibly bribe-money would also be needed.

The very first escape from Dartmoor Prison, which took place only five days after the first prisoner arrived in May, 1809, employed a very economical disguise technique. A French naval surgeon named Sevegran and Auvray, another naval officer, devised an escape plan based on disguise, darkness and a steady nerve. They had observed that a detachment of fifty militiamen were marched into the prison each evening, to assist the turnkeys in their work in getting the prisoners into their appointed prison blocks. Determined to join this militia for a very short time, Sevegran and Auvray, got down to the making of 'army' overcoats and Glengary caps (which would not have passed muster by daylight) from blankets and other bits of material.

One particularly dark evening, after the prisoners had been locked up for the night and the troops were about to leave the prison, they calmly attached themselves to the end of the column and passed through all three gates. They dropped out of line before the militia reached the barracks, then made for the road to Plymouth, seventeen miles away. Next morning they reached the port where, as the two Frenchmen spoke good English and they were not short of cash, they bought their tickets and boarded the coach to London.

It was some time before their departure was noticed, as fellow officers had covered for them by confusing the turnkey at the morning head count. That evening the same simple subterfuge was tried again. Three French officers, Cherabeau, Vasselin and Keronel were successful in joining the militia lock-up squad as it marched out of the Depot. The column was almost through the third and outer gate, when the gate-keeper hailed the tail-enders with some salutation or query. Receiving no reply, he merely grumbled: 'All these lobsters are deaf, with their caps down over their ears.'

Another interesting 'costume escape' came about when the doctor's house needed repair. The Gallic charm of the French prisoner who was sent along to carry out the work, so impressed a maidservant that she conspired to get him one of the doctor's uniforms. Dressed as a naval surgeon, he passed the guard and eventually reached France. Some time later the surgeon received a letter from the Frenchman, and a package which contained a silver-headed cane and a snuff-box, which he had 'borrowed'. We do not know what happened to the girl.

Catel, who gives us so much detail of the everyday life of the Dartmoor captives, tells a very long – and in places improbable – story of four men who made a successful escape, dressed in the second-hand uniforms of English naval officers. They were three Frenchmen, Messieurs Gamier, Revel and Borel, and William Grenwoth, an American, who was captured whilst serving in a French naval vessel. Catel, whom we know could exaggerate (remember his 'eight-month-long' Dartmoor winters!) tells a thrilling tale of tunnelling under the Depot's walls and the adventures of the quartet after leaving the prison.

Whatever type of escape plan was resorted to, the most successful usually depended to some degree on bribery, and this could become quite expensive. Although the going rate for assisting the enemy was seldom more than two pounds a head, the original conspirator often had to call into the scheme other sentries or guards, perhaps from each gate. This sometimes brought trouble and punishment to all concerned. Evidence which shows that honour is not always to be found among thieves – or whatever bribe-takers are called – is confirmed in the escape-records of this and some other depots. Disgruntled soldiers, who were willing to betray their country at a price, but were dissatisfied with their proposed share of the escape-money, quite often took another route to reward and, showing no thought for prisoner or messmates, turned informer to the authorities.

Whilst the thwarted or recaptured prisoner could expect no greater punishment than a spell in the *cachot* and a reduction in rations – unless he suffered the rare misfortune of being shot whilst attempting escape – a wide variety of penalties could be handed out to the escape-aiding Britishers, according to circumstance. Fine, flogging, transportation, even death, could be the outcome. In March 1812, a 'moorsman', Edward Palmer, was given twelve months' imprisonment and fined £5, for obtaining a 'disguise' for a French escaper. Also, at the other end of the scale, was the luckless Irish militiaman who helped three prisoners to escape, then found that they had paid him with false notes. Both were life-threatening offences and he was hanged in 1812.

Security was a day and night preoccupation, and when a prisoner was detected in the very act of attempting to escape, sentries or guards were expected to shoot to kill. As has already been recounted in the stories of other depots, the trooper involved would know full well that the subsequent inquest would almost certainly bring in a verdict of 'Justifiable Homicide'. All cases of the violent death of a prisoner were brought before the local coroners and, almost from the start, Dartmoor kept those gentlemen busy. Apart from escape-related inquiries, there were other calls upon their services. Suicide was not infrequent at most social levels – we know that over the years a number of desperate Romans died that way, usually by hanging themselves from the hooks which had once held their hammocks. Deliberate killings and altercations which ended with deaths, brought charges of murder. Disputes involving insults or matters of honour, which the American prisoner would most likely settle in the Anglo-Saxon manner by a properly arranged boxing match or a fist-fight, whereas the volatile

Frenchman would resort to duelling – often with fatal results. In February 1810, barely a year after the Depot opened, Mr Whiteford, the Plymouth Coroner, stated that the number of inquests held over that short time, far exceeded the total number held by him over the past fourteen years.

Duelling between prisoners of war was strictly forbidden by British law, but not by the French. Earlier in the wars, fencing masters were allowed to practise their profession with real foils, and their lessons had a good following. However, many foils were made into dangerous weapons by removing the buttons, then used in serious duelling. As a consequence, whilst fencing instruction was not banned, they had to do without foils!

As we shall see, duelling was bound up with pride and honour, and Frenchmen often risked their lives for petty reasons. To achieve their aim they needed weapons and all manner of substitutes were concocted in place of the real thing: knife-blades, razors, etc. Not all duels proved fatal. Thomson wrote of one contest between two inmates of the Petty Officers' Prison, which left the winner in some disgrace. On the 15th August, 1809, a special occasion was being celebrated by something of a festival by members of the *Cautionnement*. The high point was a procession, headed by a band and led by an eighteen year old youth proudly bearing the tricolour. A *maître d'armes* named Souille, who had already spent three years as a prisoner of war in England before the Peace of 1802, felt slighted. He believed that the honour of bearing the national flag should have been his, and tried to wrench it from the youngster's grasp. Understandably, the lad defended himself and his flag, giving the older man a thorough drubbing in the process. He was immediately challenged to a duel. As he knew nothing of the arts of fencing or swordsmanship, whereas the *Maitre d'armes* was trained and experienced, the young man's seconds decided that the duel should be fought with razor-blades set into wooden handles. The youth courageously set about his foe, but as he dashed in, Souille delivered a slashing stroke to his right hand which nearly severed his forefinger, and brought the unfair match to an end.

On the 8th April, 1812, two French prisoners fought literally to their deaths. Using improvised daggers, they fought with such ferocity and inflicted such serious wounds on one another, that both died before reaching hospital. The Coroner's jury brought in a verdict of 'Homicide by Accident' A fatal duel which took place in the cockloft of No.4 prison, when the war was nearing its end, illustrates how cheaply a man's life could be lost to petty pride. In June 1814, two fencing masters who were old friends, were comparing the achievements of their star pupils. The friendly chat suddenly turned sour, descending into argument and anger, and ending in a scuffle The loser, Jean Vignon, challenged the other to a duel to settle the matter. The outcome was that Vignon killed his adversary, an act for which he never forgave himself. He was brought before the court at Exeter Assizes, charged with the crime of manslaughter, and sentenced to six months' imprisonment.

An unusual case, in which neither victim nor defendant was a prisoner of war, came before the Coroner in 1809. On the evening of the 8th October, a group of prisoners found that the turnkey had forgotten to lock one of the doors to their prison. When the night got very dark they crept out into the yard, but were almost immediately challenged by a sentinel on the wall. Receiving no reply, he fired in their general direction, which sent them scurrying back into the prison. However, the musket shot had raised the alarm and fifty troops dashed into the yard with Captain Cotgrave at their head. After the search which then ensued, the Agent, satisfied that no one was missing, was about to leave, when one of the soldiers spotted a figure creeping along the wall. They brought him down with a shot through the head but when they got to him they found they had executed one of their own men.

Between the main prison area and the 'segment cut off from the circle' of the inner wall, in which were the houses of senior staff and offices, there were two other walled yards, with metal palisades similar to those which kept the rank and file away from the inner wall. In each of these was a spacious prison building, one the Hospital and the other, the Petty Officers' Prison. The latter was rather misnamed, as its occupants were, in the main, commissioned naval offices or their equivalents in the merchant or privateer services, most of whom had broken their parole or were guilty of some other offence against the regulations. Among its inmates it was more appropriately known as *Le Petit Cautionnment,* or 'Little Parole'. It was also home to officers of lower rank who were not entitled to the privilege of parole: and because of the French system of enlistment all manner of trades and professions were represented. Most were not short of cash, some were of independent means and, if they could afford it, servants, cooks and cleaners could be hired from the main prison for threepence a day.

The difference in living conditions enjoyed by the inhabitants of the *Petit Cautionnement* and that of those on the other side of the fence, could hardly have been greater. As well as being comparatively spacious and having its own airing yard, with a separate cookhouse and servants, and sweepers to carry out the menial tasks – which meant better eating and more comfortable sleeping – it really did provide a 'little parole'. Some officers, but not all, were granted the privilege of being allowed to go out through the gate and, for a limited time and distance, stroll along the road outside the prison.

Not all of the inmates of this rather elite prison had offended individually. Some who would normally have qualified for full parole privileges, lost out through international tit-for-tat wrangles.

Napoleon had a positive dislike for British midshipmen amongst his prisoners, thinking of them as unruly young gentlemen. The French guard-marines, the rough equivalent in rank to midshipmen, were given their parole and lived in towns all over the country. Our middies were all sent to Verdun, where they were granted a sort of subsidised parole, whereby the French Government could claim a sum of money if they misbehaved. They did misbehave, and in 1811, General Courcelles packed them off to the closed prison at St Vannes. England responded by sending all garde-marines into depots on land.

A.J.Rhodes who, with Job-like patience, scanned through all the local news sheets of the period, when researching for his book on Dartmoor, came up with the following report of the arrival of the Depot's share of the ex-parolees:

The Plymouth and Dock Telegraph, 16 November 1811.
On Tuesday last an officers' guard belonging to the Somerset Militia proceeded to Launceston for the purpose of escorting all the French prisoners of the rank of midshipman on parole at that place to the prison at Dartmoor. The number of prisoners so sent off amounted to 37. Their removal has been occasioned by the order of the French Government to imprison all midshipmen amongst the British prisoners of war in France.

The organisation of the *Petit Cautionnement* and the conduct of its occupants, was watched over by their own internal 'police', who ruled in cases of dispute or law. They would have featured in the sad little story which follows.

It was reported one day that an officer's shirt had been stolen, and a thorough search was made through the chests of all the officers. The culprit was soon identified and brought before a tribunal. The court of elected prisoners, comprised 'a president, two assessors an *accusateur* (Prosecutor), a *greffier* (Clerk of the Court) and a defending counsel. The latter did his best, but the accused was found guilty. The penalty for his crime should have been expulsion from the *Cautionnement,* but the court, possibly thinking they were being merciful, allowed him to stay. The sentence was: that he be debarred from voting in any future elections, and from becoming a member of any mess; that he should not hold conversation with any of his fellow officers except when absolutely unavoidable. Disgraced and humiliated, he took to his hammock and refused all food. He was later taken to the Hospital where, after a few days, he died.

As the war dragged on, the same old problem of prisoner accommodation raised its worrisome head. Two great prisoner of war depots had been opened in Scotland – Valleyfield in 1811, and Perth in 1812 – but drafts of captives still arrived at the gates of already filled Dartmoor. By the middle of 1812, the Depot was so overcrowded that even the most fastidious of men might have found themselves lousy and living in unavoidable squalor. Such dreadful conditions heralded an inevitable outcome. In the autumn of that year, Dartmoor was struck by another epidemic and this time it was 'Gaol Fever', or Typhus. The Hospital was soon as crammed as the rest of the unhealthy prison so where to bed the overflow? The treatment of officers, even those who had broken their parole or other Government regulations, was always superior to that of the ordinary prisoner; but, unexpectedly, in this case the needs of the sick were given priority over the privileges of the elite. The *Petit Cautionnement* next door was to be converted into an auxiliary hospital, and the uprooted officers were transferred into the main prison and were expected to make the best of it. The stark difference in their new mode of life and the loss of the comparative freedom of even a part parole, was hard to take. They were no more welcomed into the hard-lying society of the yards, than they were keen to join it. They had the advantage of knowing that theirs was only a temporary discomfort, and that there were none who could not improve his sustenance by purchasing in the markets. However, there was one group who sought to regain some of their lost privacy. They bought second-hand hammocks, cutting them up and sewing the pieces together to make screens or curtains, to surround any small area they could occupy as sleeping quarters in the crowded prison.

In the walled-in yard, opposite the Petty Officers' Prison was the Hospital, which might have been the envy of every other depot. Portchester Castle, which had acted as a prisoner of war establishment, on and off, since the seventeenth century, had had to wait until the end of the eighteenth century before it was given its own medical quarters.

In the Hospital enclosure was the Matron's house, and a number of small buildings – the Receiving House, the Pharmacy, a Wash-house and a Bath-house. If the food was as good and generous on the plate, as it was on the Diet Sheet, then the patients did well. The prisoner on full diet was to receive:

1 pint of Tea, morning and evening
16 ozs. of White Bread.

16 ozs. of Beef or Mutton.

1 pint of Broth.

16 ozs. of Greens or good sound Potatoes.

2 quarts of Small Beer, besides Barley Water acidulated with Lemon Juice.

For prisoners suffering from debility or 'capricious in appetite', the surgeon could use his discretion and substitute Fish, Fowl, Veal, Lamb or Eggs, in place of Beef or Mutton.

From the staff list, it may seem that the medical team was rather scant. Two Doctors, three Medical Assistants, a Dispenser and a Matron seems hardly enough to watch over the health of five to seven thousand prisoners, but the list is misleading. We find that wherever there were war prisons, captive doctors, mainly French, and men with medical knowledge, worked alongside their British captors, and prisoner-loblollies nursed the patients. Therefore, theoretically, Dartmoor had a prison hospital of which it could be proud but there was one drawback – the appointment of Dr William Dykar as Chief Surgeon.

With prisoners coming in from all over the world, often after weeks of crowded confinement in the holds of naval transports, or confined to the orlop deck of a prison hulk, it was inevitable that all manner of disease and sickness should be rife – smallpox and fevers were endemic to prisoner of war bases and epidemics were not infrequent.

Dartmoor's first year was its worst – and may well have been its last. The mortality rate rose to such a horrifying level that serious consideration was given to transferring the captives and closure of the Depot. There were about 5,000 prisoners there at that time, but between November 1809 and April 1810, 500 had died of a virulent type of measles.

William Dykar, of whom I have never read a complimentary word, was accused of taking no notice of illness until it was too far gone for treatment, and of 'refusing patients admission to hospital until the last moment: for fear, he said, of spreading the disease'. Known as a brute and heartless, one French source says that, at the height of the epidemic, he stored coffins in the hospital, within sight of the patients. Yet Dr Dykar remained Chief Surgeon until he was superseded by Sir George McGrath, in 1814.

There was one other and surprising building in the Hospital yard. Tucked away in the top left hand corner was the *cachot*, 'Black Hole' or 'Dungeon', as it was sometimes called. It was ridiculously small for its purpose, and so badly built, that many escape attempts achieved at least the minor success of getting out of the building. In 1811, when a great deal of building work was being carried out by the prisoners, they were employed to construct their own enlarged punishment cell. The new *cachot* was twenty feet square, with wide windowless walls and a vaulted roof, the only daylight coming through two six inch by four inch slits high up in the wall. It was built from granite blocks, those used in the floor each weighing a ton or more. The wooden door was reinforced with metal plates on both sides. When we consider that the *cachot* was without heat and normally without straw or bedding, summer or winter, perhaps it is not so much surprising as strategic, that it was located in the Hospital yard.

A Dartmoor record lists the names and offences of many men who were committed to the Black Hole in 1812 and 1813. The most frequent offences were attacks on sentries and turnkeys, who were often seriously injured by stone-throwing prisoners. Typical offences include:

February 24th, 1812.

Louis Constant and Olivier de Camp. For striking a sentinel on duty.

August 15th, 1812.

A. Creville. For drawing a knife on a Hospital turnkey.

September 24th, 1812.

S. Schamond For throwing down a sentinel and attempting to take away his bayonet.

The list for 1813, included some very dark deeds:

March 13th, 1813.

P. Boissard. For striking a turnkey and threatening to murder him at the first opportunity.

April 6th, 1813.

F. Le Jeune. For being one of the principal provision buyers [Broker] in the prison and for repeatedly writing blood-thirsty and threatening letters.

April 10th, 1813.

M. Girandi and A. Moine. For being guilty of infamous vices.

The paved square between the Hospital and the Petty Officers' Prison was the Market Place; the one contribution from the British Prison System, which painted Hope into the grim picture of Dartmoor and some other depots. Without it the even more colourful inner markets could not have existed, and depression and trouble would have taken the place of industry and enterprise. It was not only the talented but also those menial workers who earned by the sweat of their brow who profited by having an outlet for anything they might produce. The prisoner shop keepers and stall holders of the prison yards, the entertainers and even the gamesters profited by the steady flow of ready cash which circulated throughout the depot. The local merchants and food producers, also, appreciated the captive custom, and in general, both sides played fair. All in all, the phenomenon of the prison markets is one which some other countries might well have emulated (see Chapters 2 and 3, *The Arts and Crafts of Napoleonic and American Prisoners of War 1756-1816*, THE DEPOT AND INNER PRISON MARKETS).

Originally all cooking facilities were centred in one building, but by 1812 each prison block had its own cookhouse added to the side of the original building. These were no small galleys as each had its Chief Cook, his Assistant, and a number of helpers who worked at the five or six huge copper cauldrons, which boiled up each day hundreds of gallons of necessary, but generally disliked, soup or broth.

There was little variation in the basic food and drink ration issued to prisoners of war over the years as far as quantity and ingredients were concerned. Quality, however, was a different matter. So much depended on the honesty or otherwise of the people involved in supplying the raw material, and the prisoner-cooks who turned it into meals for the always-hungry thousands. With so many mouths to feed, an honest contractor could make a fair fortune, and many did. To win a contract with a large depot meant big business. However, some were in a hurry and cheated, by giving short measure or substandard, sometimes even rotten, merchandise – quite often in cahoots with members of the depot staff.

Dartmoor Depot was mainly supplied with food by Tavistock companies, and the records show that, true to type, some of the bread suppliers were brought to trial, charged with fraudulent dealing. Contractors were committed to a bond with the Government for £3,000 to keep to the terms of the contract. In 1812, a Tavistock baker, named Hageman, was brought before the Magistrates and fined that large sum. His co-offenders were given long prison sentences.

There were certainly a few corrupt food suppliers to Dartmoor Depot, but compared with many other land depots and probably all the prison hulks, the food at Dartmoor was said to have been good, but never sufficiently filling. The rations were not niggardly and no one would have died of starvation had they, like *Les Indifférents*, depended upon them alone, without extras. Except for the Romans and the most sorely out of cash, everyone could have afforded the occasional luxury from the well-stocked shops and stalls in the inner markets.

The almost unchanging nature of the table of ingredients could have meant months and years of monotonous eating, but the French being the French, would have made their eating more interesting by the expert use of herbs and spices. However, not all additions were appreciated.

Monsieur Catel tells a story of one mealtime at which he was present. Even when pruned of its obvious hyperbole, it would seem hard to stomach – in more ways than one – were it not for the many similar hunger tales throughout the wars. The mess representatives had come in from the kitchens with their soup buckets, and were beginning to dish out, when one man dipped into his bucket and jumped up, holding a dead rat by its tail. Immediately the men dredged through the other buckets, landing heads, tails, legs and bodies, 'in such number that they would have furnished limbs for fully a hundred animals.'

Catel said that although the prisoners swore vengeance on the cooks, the majority, including himself, were so hungry that they dined on the foul soup. The Chief Cooks, when taken to task before the *Commissaire* explained that it was just an unfortunate oversight. It was usual for the coppers to be filled with water and left overnight, ready for the cooks to fill up with meat and vegetables and light the fires, first thing next morning. On this occasion they had forgotten to put the covers on the coppers before going to bed.

So far, this has been a tale of misery, of inhumanity in selecting the site in the interest of a small group of people, rather than the health and comfort of men who had already suffered the loss of their freedom; of hunger and starvation; of jam-packed overcrowding and insanitary conditions. All true, though some of the worst hardships were self-inflicted – a Roman was a Roman by choice – and some of the overcrowding was also by choice. When the two smaller prisons (Numbers 2 & 6) were built, the floors were made of wood which made them warmer and more comfortable, unlike the concrete and stone of the other five *casernes* and so attracted more than they were designed to accommodate.

Nevertheless, it is surprising to find that prisoner of war memoirists and visitors to the Depot spoke of a general air of cheerfulness and, in some cases, even gaiety. A great deal of this spirit can be accredited to the influence of the markets, which made it possible for prisoners to make and spend money. Dartmoor's was one of the most colourful in the country; with its buskers, hawkers and pedlars, sparkling displays of prisoner of war work on offer to the public; shops and booths of the local farmers and traders, and the stalls of dealers up from the coast, with their bundles of all manner of merchandise.

Although depots like Stapleton and Portchester, with comparatively large populations from which came visitors to their depots, Dartmoor, for all its remoteness, was always busy. The prisoners could enjoy quite a range of recreations and diversions. If sportsmen they might play or watch football, a game something like 'Fives', or if so inclined, take classes in any of a dozen different subjects taught by the professors of the Depot. They had a fine theatre which changed its shows regularly, glee clubs and music societies.

For the first three years, there had been free communication between all prison yards, now seven in all, which was worrying to the authorities. The thought of between seven to eight thousand rioting prisoners in some future uprising, gathered together in one area, called for action. So two walls were built, one either side of No.4 prison which greatly reduced the number who could assemble in any place at one time. It also isolated No.4 which made it possible to segregate the Romans from the decent prisoners of war. By the spring of 1812, the Transport Board must have foreseen the probability that Dartmoor would eventually be adding Americans to its prisoner population; for there was a general tightening up on security in the Depot.

It is often something of a mystery why countries should have resorted to warfare to settle their differences; but, in this case, it would seem that America had no alternative. Britain and the United States had been at peace since 1783 but the Royal Navy had retained its hated right to 'stop and search'. Thereby, American merchantmen could be stopped, boarded and searched for contraband and British subjects or deserters. Any seamen so detected were then impressed into His Majesty's Navy, or sent to England for trial. By such methods did the Navy stock up its ships' companies; and many thousands of Americans unfairly adjudged 'British' were serving on our men-of-war at that time. Mainly in an effort to abolish this obviously unfair practice, President Madison declared war on Britain on 18th June, 1812: The 'War for Free Trade and Sailors' Rights' had begun.

As soon as the declaration of war reached England, all American sailors serving in the British Navy, whether volunteers or impressed men, found themselves faced with a quandary: they were given the choice of continuing in the service of King George – and fighting against their own country – or immediately becoming prisoners of war. The majority chose the latter option.

In the first months of the war, most of the American prisoners were confined in the hulks at Chatham, Portsmouth or Plymouth, and by the time they were transferred to Dartmoor the reputation they had earned as escape-obsessed trouble-makers and rioters on the prison ships, had preceded them – and struck apprehension in the hearts of the Depot authorities. This is understandable, for many of the Yankee captives were tough, devil-may-care characters, taken whilst serving on privateer or letter-of-marque vessels – and to add them to the 5,000 Frenchmen already there could only spell danger; so segregation was called for. Had the authorities but known it, the Yankees had fears of their own: Charles Andrews, the American prisoner-historian of Dartmoor Prison, wrote that when the first draft was told of their destination and were ordered on deck:

> '…with their hammocks, baggage &c., in readiness to march to a prison, the very name of which made the mind of every prisoner shrink back with dread, and startle at the thought; for fame had made them well acquainted with the horrors of that infernal abode; which

was by far the most dreadful prison in all England, and in which it was next to impossible for human beings long to survive.'

On the hulks and elsewhere the American prisoners had, from the start, been treated with less consideration and trust than the French, and at Dartmoor they were to fare no better. This unfairness, whether inspired by nervousness or respect for their captives' dedication to freedom, or the fact that many Britons of every class, still thought of the Americans as 'renegades and traitors', even a quarter of a century after they had won their independence, it marked the Americans with an unforgiving bitterness.

By March 1813, there were about 1,700 Americans on the hulks: 700 on the *Hector* and *Le Brave* at Plymouth, 900 at Chatham, and 100 at Portsmouth; and some others spread over a number of land prisons. Soon after, the Transport Office ordered that all Americans be transferred to Dartmoor, and so, on the 2nd April, the first detachment of 250 hungry, weary and neglected prisoners were brought ashore from the two prison ships moored in the Hamaoze at Plymouth, to begin the uphill seventeen-mile march to the Depot on the Moor. On the 18th May and on the 1st June drafts of 250 and 100 Americans respectively, arrived from the *Hector* at Plymouth.

The first sight of their new home was enough to convince them that everything they had heard of the horrors of the place were true. That was just from the outside, inside must have inflicted even greater misery as they endeavoured to find living and sleeping space in one or other of the always-damp and overcrowded prison halls. They were, however, allowed to mix freely with the non-too-welcoming French, and had access to their well-established markets in the prison yards. Surprised at the existence of the French theatre, the sideshows, schools, gambling tables, food booths and coffee shops – and workshops where craftsmen produced all manner of prisoner of war mementoes for sale in the main market-place – the Americans could never really understand how so many of the French captives could have settled in comfortably enough to have created this microcosm of their homeland in 'The Great Tomb of the Living'.

Charles Andrews, an American who spent almost the whole of the 1812 war as a prisoner wrote, with a mixture of admiration and wonderment:

> 'Whether they are constituted by nature to endure hardships, or so long confinement has got them wonted to live in prisons, I will not venture to say, but they really seem easy under it, live well, and make money to lay up. They drink, sing and dance, talk of their women in the day time, and, like Horace, dream of them at night; but I have not heard of any issue from these visionary conexions. But the Americans have not that careless volatility, like the cockles in the fable, to sing and dance when their house is on fire over them.'

So, for a very short while, the first Yankee prisoners to arrive enjoyed the diversions of the busy world of their French allies.

Then, after only four weeks, they were dealt another stinging blow. On the 1st May, 1813, the Transport Office informed Isaac Cotgrave that all American prisoners were to be transferred to the isolated No.4 prison. On the hulks they had been able to trade with the bum-boats which came alongside each day, but here in their cut-off *caserne,* there was no market of any kind – and it is to be remembered that Cotgrave had considered the closing of the markets as one of the most powerful punishments he could impose. However, the greatest shock must have been to find that they were

sharing No.4 with 900 naked, half-starved monsters, the French Romans.

Charles Andrews, who was one of the first draft of Americans on the 2nd April, tells of the shock they experienced on first encountering the Romans. In his book, '*The Prisoner's Memoirs' or Dartmoor Prison 1852*', he says:

> 'In this prison were about nine hundred of the most abject and outcast wretches that were ever beheld. French prisoners, too wicked and malicious to live with their other unfortunate countrymen: they were literally and emphatically naked; having, neither clothing or shoes, and as poor and meager in flesh as the human frame could bear. The mind cannot figure to itself any thing in the shape of men, which so much resembled the fabled ghosts of Pluto, as these naked and starved French prisoners. Much of the misery and wretchedness of these creatures was owing to their imprudence and bad conduct.'

Bitter complaints and appeals to Reuben G. Beasley, the American Agent for American Prisoners of War, produced no more succour from that gentlemen – described as a 'callous, cruel, or utterly inefficient, imbecile representative' – than he had offered the American prisoners on the hulks. With even less privileges than those normally enjoyed by the vilest class of French captives – who deserved their segregation – and with no admission to the markets, the Americans' only recourse was to deal with the French stall-holders from other prisons, who sold them food etc., through the bars of No.4's gates – at anything up to 25% above current prices. The Romans, too, were discontented, resentful at what they considered an invasion of their own private territory, and the Americans deeply and bitterly resented the Transport Office insult which, in effect, categorized them as equals with the lowest type of French ne'er-do-well.

There was bad blood and trouble from the outset. After about two months of miserable monotony in No.4, a great date in United States' history gave the Yankees something to celebrate. Two national flags were dredged up from someone's baggage, and although Agent Cotgrave had refused their request to celebrate Independence Day 1813, the two flags were soon fluttering, one at either end of the yard. Captain Cotgrave took this as a serious affront to his authority, and brought in the guards who overcame the Americans who defended one of the flags, and bore it away. However, the Stars and Stripes still flew defiantly at the other end of the yard, until the evening. Once more the troops were sent in and, finding themselves resisted for a second time, opened fire wounding two American defenders. Their national flag hauled down, thus ended the celebration of their Day of Independence.

The quarrels and upsets of the few weeks of unwelcome cohabitation in *caserne* No.4, had developed into a mutual hatred between the embittered Americans and the verminous Frenchmen, which made a violent conclusion inevitable. The Romans brought the matter to a head by waging undeclared war upon their foe. Late in the afternoon of the 10th July, six days after the Independence Day fiasco, taunts and insults developed into what might have become a serious confrontation, but was cut short by the arrival of the turnkey and troops to lock up the prison for the night. It would seem that the Romans spent more of that night planning rather than sleeping; for as soon as the doors were opened, the Romans surged into the yard, intent on trouble.

Soon after, the unsuspecting Yankees began to drift into the airing yard, to find the Romans waiting for them, armed with clubs, stones, sticks, knives and anything which could be used as a weapon; declaring their avowed intention to kill every American they could lay hands on. The Americans had been caught absolutely unawares and only about 120 had actually entered the yard before they realised that retreat back into the prison was impossible, as was the chance of any of their comrades trapped inside, would be able to dash to their rescue.

With nothing but their fists and feet to inflict retaliation, the Yankees gave a good account of themselves; but luckily the affray was quickly spotted by sentinels, from their observation posts above the inner Wall.

The guards made several charges into the ill-matched mob, laying about them with musket-butts and flats of bayonets, until order was eventually restored, but not before forty of the prisoners had been badly injured and carted off to hospital.

Cotgrave, in his official report to the Admiralty, loaded the blame squarely on to the Americans, and who should say who was right and who wrong. The Americans were, it is true, notorious troublemakers, and Captain Cotgrave was there on that day – but so, too, was Charles Andrews. Andrews went to a great deal of trouble to assure his readers that his journal was a straightforward ungarnished narrative of his captivity, prefixing it with a warrantee attested to by sixty-two signatories, many of them officers, all of whom had been prisoners at Dartmoor. There can be found some minor mistakes and doubtful passages in his work; but if we endeavour to strip away his deep anti-British bitterness and his agonising hatred of the two Dartmoor Agents, Cotgrave and Shortland, we are left with a fine example of prisoner of war history.

Like Catel, he sometimes exaggerated but, unlike that French memoirist, seldom arouses suspicion of inventive padding; and his was a somehow different Anglophobia to that of General Pillet, who penned his calumnies with scant regard for truth. Andrews made it plain that he detested Captain Cotgrave, declaring that 'the name of Isaac Cotgrave, Agent at Dartmoor, of cruel memory, will ever be engraved in odious characters on the minds of every American who witnessed his unparalleled cruelty'. Andrews blamed him for all their sufferings, amongst other things, for sticking to the rule that prisoners should muster for head counts outside in the yards, however inclement the weather; and imprisoning then in No.4. However, that was to forget that Cotgrave was a regular Royal Navy post-captain of more than ten years' seniority (the minimum requirement for anyone to be given the governorship of an English depot), trained from midshipman to captaincy to maintain order by exacting discipline, whether at sea or as governor of a great war prison. They had earned their isolation by their conduct before reaching Dartmoor and were probably in No.4 by direct order from the Transport Office.

A great improvement was carried out at that time, as a direct outcome of the Yankee-Roman clash. A wall twelve feet in height was built, bisecting the yard of *caserne* No.4 thus preventing future clashes between the Americans and their French antagonists, who were confined to the first floor and cockloft of the prison. Also, at the end of that same July, some of the 610 Dartmoor Yankees had an impossible dream come true: 120 of them were included in an unexpected exchange list and were sent to Chatham, where a cartel ship awaited their embarkation. Apart from the 490 in Dartmoor, about another 1,800 were scattered between Stapleton and other English depots, including a few still on the hulks.

The conditions in No.4 grew progressively worse and most of the prisoners were near paupers. The majority were as addicted to chewing-tobacco as the French were to gambling, and the price of tobacco had risen to 5s.6d. per pound in the outside market. The French dealers at the gate had upped the price to three chaws or plugs of tobacco for 2d., and the most addicted would now and again barter their ration of very poor quality beef in exchange for a chaw, or two, the Frenchmen knowing that they could convert the sub-standard viand into a delicious ragout, which might double their profit.

However, worse was yet to come. The mortality rate so far had been normal to good, but only a few days passed before more misery entered the infamous No.4 in the form of small-pox. Terrified by the deadly disease, and having little faith in Cotgrave's goodwill, and none at all for the abilities of Dartmoor's chief medical officer, Dr William Dykar, the prisoners were in deep despair. They already knew that, no matter what was wrong with them healthwise, Dykar would be reluctant to send Americans into his hospital, openly saying that he had served as a surgeon during their War of Independence, and knew that they were all a crowd of malingerers and shirkers, who would not be given the chance to impose on him again. He further justified his decision by declaring that were he to send segregated American patients into the hospital 'such numbers would breed every kind of pestilence and disease among the French prisoners.'

The distraught Yankees tried, yet again, to spur the lackadaisical Beasley into action with a broadside of petitions and letters of complaint; some pleading for him to act urgently to ease their distress, and many other letters, which they asked him to forward to the United States Government – which, of course, he did not do.

However, early one morning at the end of August, a rumour began to circulate that Reuben Beasley was to visit his fellow countrymen that afternoon. The American prison was agog with expectant anticipation; hands and faces – though perhaps not bodies – were scrubbed cleaner than they had been for months; the yard was given a special sweep-up; the writers spent the morning listing the communal grievances and the official speakers polished up their short orations. They need not have troubled.

Beasley arrived at the prison at the head of a retinue of clerks and guards and, for the first time, saw his neglected countrymen in their sordid prison setting: row upon row of gaunt but hopeful men, clad in ill-fitting sulphur-yellow Government issue clothing. Muttering something about his surprise at seeing how great was their number(!), he said that he could only tell them that they must not expect better conditions at that time; that there was no way he could help them financially; and that the exchange system had been completely halted, as far as Americans were concerned for a year.[4]

The desperate Americans had no other recourse in their searching for fair play, than to keep up their battery of letters and petitions to Agent Beasley, 'representing with pardonable exaggeration, that numbers were dying daily and that the survivors were swarming with vermin; that they were defrauded of their rations, and that, unless he came speedily to their aid, they must either enlist with the enemy or perish.' These letters were delivered, via a bribed guard, but were not even acknowledged.

Disgusted with their American Agent and feeling let down by their own Government, they let it be known that they were seriously contemplating enlisting in the Royal Navy, *en masse*. The realisation of such a threat would have brought joy to the Admiralty and British enlistment-officers in general, for a great number of enlisted or impressed men were urgently needed as replacements for the Americans serving in the Royal Navy when war broke out. This is not to suggest that cruelty, discomfort and hunger were ever deliberately employed in order to persuade men to turn their coats. However, no American would ever have doubted that this was exactly what was happening – and the threat would have caused consternation in the American Government particularly as a number of No.4 Americans really had signed on to serve in British men-of-war. (Charles Andrews gives the names and details of fifty-nine men who succumbed to the temptation). The prisoners did not hear from Beasley until January of the following year.

In the late summer of 1813, Stapleton Depot was preparing to transfer all 400 of its American captives to the distant Depot on the Moor. At Stapleton they had mixed freely with the French, and some of the normally work-shy American prisoners found profitable employment in the yards. The proceeds from this enabled them to supplement their meagre rations by purchases from the market, so the provident and strong-willed among them, who could steer clear of the wily French gamblers, were comparatively well-off; but we read that in many cases their cash was lost to the gaming tables almost as soon as they had been paid. The prisoners had been divided into four drafts, each of one hundred men, and the first of these were to set out on the 20th September, the other three to follow on at weekly intervals. Prisoners from the *Hector* and *La Brave* had arrived foot-sore and tired after their seventeen-mile uphill trek from Plymouth, but their journey was as nothing compared with the one-hundred-and-ten mile march from Stapleton to Dartmoor.

Apart from Charles Andrews' recollections of his Dartmoor days, we have the works of three other American memoirists: Captain George Little, Josiah Cobb ('Green-Hand') and Benjamin Waterhouse. Their books have been out of print for at least one hundred and fifty years, but still make fascinating reading.

George Little, who was included in the fourth draft from Stapleton, describes the wearisome nine-day march in his book: *Life on the Ocean, or Twenty Years at Sea,* and tells of some who dropped by the wayside and were carted to the prison in wagons, and of exhausted men who were only too pleased to arrive somewhere, even the disreputable Dartmoor.

George was a young merchant captain who, for hostilities only, had served as first-lieutenant in privateers and letters of-marque on both sides of the Atlantic. It was his bad luck to be serving as a prize-master when the privateer *Paul Jones* was captured a few months earlier, as it prevented his being granted parole. In his short but hectic career as a privateer officer he was twice captured by the British and had spent some months on board a Plymouth hulk before being sent to Stapleton Prison. He was certainly not a typical privateer, in fact regarded them as little better than pirates, until the lack of work in the merchant service at the beginning of the war, caused him to enter what he had always considered a 'nefarious occupation'. He did not sensationalise even his most thrilling adventures, but his book exhibits a Wellington-like lack of respect for a whole swathe of his fellow Americans.

George had nothing but disdain for most privateers, contending that their captains often had more courage than wisdom, and the ships' companies, vile and quite beyond the pail. Of the crew of his first privateer, the *George Washington*, he said they 'were a motley set indeed, composed of all nations; they appeared to have been scraped together from all the lowest dens of wretchedness and vice and only wanted a leader to induce them to any acts of daring and desperation.' Later on, when the *Paul Jones* had taken a British prize, he describes the action of the American crew:

> 'Now a scene of plunder and robbery was perpetrated, by the privateer's crew, which beggars all description; every article of clothing and stores, which they could lay their hands upon, were taken without any ceremony. The crew were a perfect set of desperadoes and outlaws, whom the officers could neither restrain nor command'.

He goes even further and says that, except for those Americans who had given themselves up from British men-of-war, and were at that time confined in Portsmouth, there were still about six thousand on the hulks who were, for the most part 'a perfect set of outlaws and desperadoes, having no doubt, been selected from the most miserable haunts of vice in all the sea ports within the United States.' He moderated this a little by continuing, 'It must not be understood, however, that all came under this description of character, for there were some among that number, an honor to the profession of a seaman.'

Nevertheless, he intimates that at that time, the loafers and troublemakers ruled the roost. He gives as an example something which I have not seen mentioned in the other journals, he says: 'If a man who had been an officer manifested a disposition to keep himself aloof from these miscreants, he was almost sure to be mobbed, and if he had kept a taut hand and good discipline on board of his vessel, on entering these prisons, he was generally tied to the whipping-post and flogged.'[5]

Meanwhile, during the autumn and winter of 1813, a number of changes had taken place, mainly for the better. The authorities had not forgotten the viciousness and vice of the Romans in No.4. Commissioners of the Transport Board held an inquiry where General Stephenson was of the opinion '…that the prisoners who call themselves the Romans, should be removed and live like human beings, in some place where they can be kept under strict surveillance'. Therefore, on the 16th October, 1813 the scarecrow group of Romans was mustered at the gate, all decently clothed, and marched to Plymouth where they were conveyed to one of the hulks, and kept under close confinement, until the war with France ended in the following year.

1. Sir Basil Thomson, former Governor, says in his book, *Dartmoor Prison, 1806 to 1932*, 'If Dartmoor did not break Thomas's heart, it emptied his purse, for it is recorded that he lost a fortune on the moor and died a poor man.'

2. In contradiction to this statement: the unfortunate contractor whose tender had been accepted, had been assured that all the timber he would need for roofing, etc. would always be available at £5 a load. Almost immediately after signing the contract, the price shot up to £8. 8s!

3. S.Baring-Gould: *Devonshire Characters and Strange Events.* 1908.

4. Sir Basil Thomson wondered what would be 'the duties of this curious appointment' of a navigator. I suggest that he may have been responsible for water-courses and ditches as a 'navvy', a slang term for the Irish labourers, known as 'Navigators', who dug canals.

4. The stalemate over exchange came about because Britain was holding a number of Americans in bondage, claiming them to be deserters or renegade Englishmen. If found guilty they would be sentenced to death. On the other side, Commodore Rogers, commander of the US frigate *President*, held a number of Britishers in close confinement as hostages whose fate depended upon that of the Americans.

5. This seems to me to be an incident magnified into a generalisation.

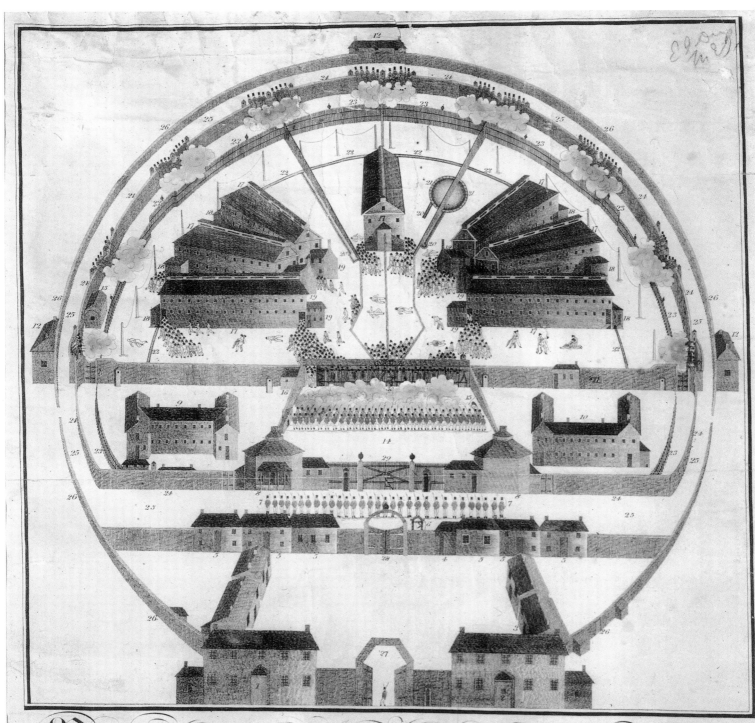

Massacre OF THE **American** PRISONERS OF WAR *at* DARTMOOR PRISON *on the* 6ᵗʰ *of* APRIL 1815, *by the* SOMERSETSHIRE MILITIA

Explanation

1. Surgeon's House 2. Shortland's House 3. Shortland's Office 4. Turnkey's Lodge 5. Clerk's Houses 6. Alarm Bell 7. Rear Guard 8. Store Houses 9. Hospital 10. Barracks 11. Hole in the Wall 12. Grain Houses 13. Cachot or Black Hole 14. Market Square 15. Shortland ordering the Military to fire 16. Receiving House 17. Prisons 18. Privies 19. Cook Houses 20. Fresh Water for use 21. Bathing Pond 22. Run of Water for cleaning Privies 23. Iron Railing 12 feet high 24. Inner Wall 15. do. 25. Military Walk 26. Outer Wall 13 feet high 27. Outer Gate 28. 2ⁿᵈ Gate 29. 3ʳᵈ Gate 30. 4ᵗʰ Gate

Chapter Nineteen

Part Two

The Americans and the Dartmoor Massacre

JUST BEFORE CHRISTMAS, THE AMERICANS WERE cheered by the news that Captain Cotgrave had resigned, and a new Agent, Captain Shortland R.N. had been appointed. Captain Shortland, though tough and enough of a disciplinarian when duty called, approached his considerable task with a softer touch than his predecessor; getting off to a good start, by staging the morning head-counts under cover when the weather was wet or excessively cold.

He listened to their tales of woe; of the despicable conduct of their Agent, Beasley, and their feeling that the country for which they had fought had now deserted them. The Captain advised them that he should handle any future communications between them and Beasley, and promised he would contact the American Government with copies of all the prisoners' unanswered mail. He also ordered that two of their number should be allowed to visit the main market twice weekly. This was an almost unimaginable concession, particularly for those lucky enough to have even the most meagre purchasing power.

It is possible that Beasley may have kept his Government informed of the prisoner of war situation in England; if so, perhaps he also helped to bring about the promises made in the only letter he had ever written to them:

'Fellow Citizens,
I am authorized by the Government of the United States to allow you one penny-halfpenny per day for the purpose of procuring you tobacco and soap, which will commence being paid from the first day of last January. And I earnestly hope it will tend towards a great relief in your present circumstances.

I likewise would advise you to appoint a committee by which means you can convey to me any intelligence through the Board of Transport.'

After a while, their hard-up Government granted them another penny per day, with which to buy tea or coffee. This seemingly small amount of money was paid out monthly to every American prisoner of war and 6s.8d. was a life-saver for many captives.

Whether the suggestion regarding a committee originated with Beasley, or came from Shortland or the US Government, it was sound advice. During the short period after their arrival in April, when the Americans had enjoyed the freedom of the yards, the intelligent amongst them had observed the virtues of the French system of self-government, and were now determined to create something like it for themselves. Suitable men were elected by ballot, some to invent a code of conduct, others to sit in judgment on their erring fellow prisoners. In the absence of any way to earn money, stealing was rife amongst the mishmash of Yankee seamen, most of them white but with a fair sprinkling of negroes. The Committee's court was constantly in session, trying cases of theft or any of a dozen other offences, and handing out appropriate sentences from a strictly laid-down table of punishments – sometimes as fierce as twenty-four lashes. Or more.

With their prison lives completely changed by the US Government allowances – two pounds of potatoes could be bought for only 1½d. – the Americans became a little less famished and a little less troublesome. Believing that, at last, petitions might sometimes bear fruit, they requested that Congress authorise Beasley to arrange an issue of much-needed clothing, to replace the rags and tatters which they had worn since their capture. Furthermore, although colour had not raised its unpleasant head in the past, the whites now petitioned that the blacks be found other quarters, as they were 'dirty and thieves.'

Their request was granted, and on the 22nd February, the then ninety negroes were banished to the recently vacated abode of the Romans; the first and top floor of *caserne* No. 4. – together with 'such whites whose conduct and habits rendered them unfit to associate with men of their own colour'.

'Dirty and thieves' may, perhaps with more justice, have described another category of American prisoner, the 'Rough Alleys'. George Little has told of the disreputable characters who made up the crews of many of the privateersmen, and no doubt some of these ruffians belonged to a class which might be thought of as the 'American Romans'. They seldom descended to such depths of depravity and vice as their French counterparts, but were no less a thorn in the sides of their decent fellow prisoners. How these bully-boys came to be called 'Rough Alleys', or 'Rough Allies' is not known. No one is certain how their name should be spelled, or how it originated: though Josiah Cobb thought it might be based on the term, 'rough house'. Waterhouse described them, as a company of plunderers, 'who were such a band of villains as could be collected in the United States'. Like George Little, he said that to see their filthy condition and lawless capers, made him ashamed to admit that they, too, were American.

The Rough Alleys were the scourge of the Dartmoor markets; indiscriminately plundering American stall-holders or, if the opportunity presented itself, English traders in the main market square. They loafed and lazed in their hammocks, when not out scrounging or inspecting the offal heaps, except when aroused by their war-cry, 'Keno!' which would set them all rampaging through the yards in search of whatever was happening. All memoirists have left their comments on these rogues; including a young privateer who came to Dartmoor in October 1814, and sadly died at sea in March 1816, on his homeward journey. Joseph Varley left a little unbound journal, which he wrote in his own quaint style, omitting even the tiniest hint of punctuation. I came across this small rare book on a recent visit to America – only 300 copies were published by a descendant more than a hundred years after his death. In it he theorised how a certain number of Americans had sunk to the depths of the Rough Alleys, saying that he thought the rot had set in before their captivity:

' …while those that had money when they had there Liberty would stay on Shore Until every Cent was gone and then would be Obliedged for to put to sea again without a penny for to help them selves and then they would get Captured by there enemy and sent to this place and the first thing that they would do would be for to sell off what few Clothes they had and then they would be tempted by the help of the Devil for to steal from there Mess mates and Fellow prisoner's and then there backs would be Brought to disgrace.'[1]

Rough Alleys, like all other prisoners, came under the juristiction of the Committee and the inner courts. On occasion the most outrageous amongst them, men like Sodom and Gomorrah[2], were put on trial and sentenced to a few dozen lashes; but there was no chance of redemption. Had too great an effort been made to reform them by punishment, it may well have resulted in an American Civil War inside the Depot.

The blacks were, in fact, well organised and resourceful, controlled and watched over by a strict leader, 'Big Dick', and his cohorts. Benjamin Waterhouse, who we have already met on the Medway hulks, in his book, *Journal of a Young Man of Massachusetts*, described their leader as a 'Black Hercules', a veritable giant of a man, 6ft. 7in. tall and with a physique in keeping with his height. He was an impressive character, quite apart from his stature, and his word was law in the widest sense. Big Dick was prosecutor, judge, and executioner, and ruled his subjects with a rod of iron, often literally; when, immediately after passing sentence, he belaboured the miscreant with one such rod. Wearing a huge bearskin cap and with a large club in hand, he made a daily round of his community, visiting and examining every berth for cleanliness. Anyone offending by their dirtiness, drunkeness, or acting in a discreditable manner, were first given a warning, then, if necessary, a thorough beating.

Although most 'trembled in his presence', there were a few of his brethren, courageous or mad enough to attempt to depose him, but none succeeded. One night, whilst asleep in his hammock he was attacked by three or four of his unruly subjects, but springing up he caught the smallest of his assailants by the ankles, and swinging him like a human club, floored the next one to come forward.

Dick and his two principal henchmen, Chaplain Simon and Deacon John, were religious – at least on Sundays – and keen observance of the sabbath was demanded of all American blacks. All the gambling paraphernalia was hidden away till the morrow and that part of No.4. became the Black Church for the day, with much singing and preaching. Both of Big Dick's assistants preached with gusto and hell-fire and were highly respected by the black congregation; for Simon enjoyed the reflected glory of having once been in the service of the Duke of Kent. And they hung on Deacon John's every word, for, as he had told them, he had a close association with the Archangel Gabriel, who had visited him in prison, and prophesied the destruction of the evil Dartmoor Depot.

The winter of 1813/14 was said to have been the worst for half a century and the middle two weeks of January being the coldest in living memory. The rain and frosts persisted almost non-stop; then in January it began to snow. By the 19th the drifts were from five to ten feet high, and the supply road from Plymouth was closed, even the wagon tracks to the depot's provision stores were impassable. The streams which flowed through each of the prison yards, and were the only water supply for the prisoners had frozen solid. Ice and snow completely cut Dartmoor off from the rest of the world for a number of days at a time. Inside the prison buildings, the granite walls were dank and glistening with

condensation. No form of heating was supplied, except in the Hospital; although we know that some of the better-off French inmates, had provided themselves with small oil-burning stoves[3]. It is a wonder that any survived. At that time, Dartmoor was figuratively bursting at the seams, with 9,000 prisoners somehow crammed into what was designed for the accommodation of 7,000, and we must add to this the 1,500 prison staff, guards and troops, all of whom had to be fed and watered. Ten days' supply of salted rations, which were in the snowed-in provision storehouses, were only made available after Captain Shortland had gathered together a working-party of 200 prisoners, guards, and civilian volunteers, who dug for a whole day to get to the stores, and until the thaw, the Dartmoor thousands slaked their thirst with melted snow.

Despite the terrible weather it did not cool all ardent desire to escape. At midnight on the 19th January, eight Americans, having observed that the number of sentinels and guards had been reduced, the Agent probably thinking that the weather itself was guard enough, decided to try their luck. With an improvised ladder, they began to climb the boundary wall, when one of them became entangled in the alarm-bell wires. The troops brought seven of them back to the guardhouse, where they were kept under strict surveillance. Somehow, the eighth man, ill-clad for such an adventure, struggled on through the snow. Sometime during the second day, he came to a small cottage, where the occupants, realising that he must be an escaped prisoner bound him and escorted him back to the Depot. All eight were sentenced to ten days in the Black Hole, on reduced rations.

With the arrival of the new year, it became obvious that the long war, which with only one short break, had now dragged on for more than twenty years was slowly coming to an end, in Britain's favour. The allied victories and progress in France, had made it obvious that Napoleon's days were probably numbered, and thousands of French prisoners would soon be going home; but the war would not have come to an end for the Americans. However, the prison life of the latter was lightened and completely changed by another wise decision of Agent Shortland. He opened wide the gates of prison No.4, allowing the 1,200 scruffy and deprived Yankees to mix with the French and enjoy with them the privileges and diversions of a Dartmoor they hardly knew existed. There must have been among them a percentage of the lay-about and dead-beat class, who would later become known as the 'Rough Alleys'; but the majority took advantage of this opportunity to use their hands, minds, energies and time to improve their lot, rather than bathe in bitterness and dreams of escape.

There was plenty of employment on official projects and, in the markets, a wide scope for anyone with talent. Captain Shortland had already set French prisoner-artisans to work on repairs within the Depot, but he now allowed quite large parties to work beyond the prison walls. A new church was under construction at Princetown, the builders being French prisoner stone-workers and their labourers. Much of the interior was finished by American carpenters and wood-carvers. Visitors to Princetown can inspect their work to this day.

No doubt a strict military watch would have been kept over the outside workers, but in reality the biggest safeguard against attempted escape, would have been the watch the prisoners kept on one another. The same warning which had been issued to earlier outside working parties was again posted up: the workers were paid every three months, and the aggregated sum owing to all the workers would be forfeited if one of them tried to abscond.

Having been confined to the miseries of prison No.4, and an airing ground only half its original size, the inmates appreciated this semi-freedom, and eagerly tried to emulate the industrious Frenchmen in their market ventures, learning the illicit craft of straw-plaiting (by which they could earn between 1d. to 3d. per day) and the manufacture of a whole range of saleable articles, from hair bracelets, list shoes and bone ship models.

Some quickly became adept and could begin to spend as well as sell. After the luxury of extra food and drink, came visits to the second-hand clothes stalls, where gradually they could replace the remnants of the clothes they had been captured in, or the abhorrent yellow Transport Office issue. Eventually they attained a decent appearance, and became more acceptable to their French fellow prisoners and to one another.

The Americans were kept informed of happenings in the outside world through several sources. From a friendly – or bribable – Scottish Militia unit, which had recently taken over the guard at Dartmoor, they received newspapers; and by some means were in regular correspondence with their countrymen on the hulks at Chatham and the other prison ship ports. Some of the news was unpleasant to their ears, particularly articles which predicted that once the French war was over, Britain could concentrate on America and revert it to individual British Colonial states.

The third week of March 1814, saw the establishment of a coffee booth in the yard of No.4, selling its coffee-like beverage at a penny a pint. Its immediate success inspired other Yankee entrepreneurs, who had earned a little cash or received money from home, to start up small businesses as purveyors of potatoes, sugar, tobacco, and all manner of odds and ends. Except for the loafers, or the American equivalent of *Les Indifférents,* nearly everyone was gainfully employed, including the young American boys, many of them under thirteen years of age, who worked as waiters or servants to the French officers.

Towards the end of April, their smuggled London newspapers featured official reports of the Allies' entry into Paris, and that a treaty of peace was being prepared. This made certain that the French prisoners, some of whom had been imprisoned in Britain since 1803, would soon be freed. Their reaction to the news was much the same as in all the other depots: genuine sadness at the fate of their beloved Emperor, and joy that their long captivity was coming to an end.

On the 30th May, 1814, the peace between France and Great Britain was announced, and the Treaty of Paris had been ratified. The Depot was visited by French officials, who advised them on the subject of their departure and of the wisdom of wearing the white cockade of Louis XVIII, when their turn came to leave Dartmoor; but most declared that they would rather stay in prison than swear allegiance to any other monarch than Bonaparte. Andrews says they expressed these feelings by destroying the white flag of the Bourbons, and by all wearing the tricolour cockade, whilst the prison dogs ran through the yards with white cockades on their heads. Noble and genuine sentiments; but as the days crept by, and they waited for the ratification of the Treaty of Paris, thoughts of freedom, home and loved ones, must have diminished their devotion to what was now a lost cause.

On the 20th April, 1814, the first batch of 500 freed Frenchmen set out to march, or ride, to the cartel ships at Plymouth, followed a week later by a draft of 1,000. Smaller drafts left the Depot every five or six days until all the French had been released; but before they left there was one last regulation to observe. As they neared the gateway to freedom, each man had to hand in his hammock and bedding, before being checked out. One poor fellow in the last draft could not comply, having lost those essential articles (whether by theft or to the gaming tables), was removed from the draft. In hopeless distress, he cut his throat at the prison gates.

It was said that, in one draft, as many as twenty French-speaking American officers escaped as 'Frenchmen'. Somehow, they had gained knowledge that the Dartmoor mortality records were badly kept and not up to date, and when the list of departing prisoners was called, they answered to the names of men long since dead and buried. Two more drafts left with their complements of Yankee absconders before the ruse was discovered. Other successful escapes were achieved under disguised nationality. When an Order came instructing that any subject of an Allied Power, taken prisoner under the American flag, should be released, it was a gift to the lively sons of the brave. Everyone familiar with a foreign language, even if only a sentence or two, presented himself at the Agent's office as a Russian, a Prussian, a Swede, or a Dane – with a New England accent.

The poor French lad who brought his life to an end, when he missed the last draft to Plymouth, was one of the 1,198 French prisoners who would never leave Dartmoor. That figure covers all causes of their death; accident, duelling, suicide, starvation, or the many different illnesses and diseases resulting from the overcrowded, damp, unhygienic condition under which they had to live. One might suppose that there would have been plenty of fellow prisoners, perhaps even the Committee itself, to have seen to it that, when one of them died, he would have been given a decent burial; but there is very little evidence that this was ever general practice. It appears that they were buried without religious rites, in shallow graves, in a field near the Depot and there they lay, unhonoured and unnamed (except in the Depot Records), for nearly half a century.

Then in 1845, Rachel Evans, a prison visitor, discovered that cattle and horses had so churned up the ground, that the bones of dead prisoners were 'left to whiten in the sun'. In 1865 Dartmoor, by then a civil prison, demolished its piggery and the animals were turned out into the field. The pigs soon began to root up bits of coffin-lids, coffins and bones. Captain Stopford, the Governor, decided to do something about it and had two fenced areas within the prison walls laid out as cemeteries – one for the French and the other for the Americans. As many bones as could be recovered from the field were divided into two unequal piles, (the Americans who died in Dartmoor numbered 280) which were buried in their appropriate plots. He also erected in each of the two graveyards, a granite memorial inscribed with French or American details and the motto *'Dulce et decorum est pro patria mori'.*

Over the years, the French *Industrialists* had perfected tools, gadgets and machines, with which they had produced the myriad of saleable articles for the markets. Before leaving Dartmoor, they put these treasures up for sale. Everything was snapped up by Americans who could afford them, as were the shopkeepers' booths and stalls, lamps and signboards, though the latter would have to be Anglicised – or Americanized. One surprising transaction was the sale of the French theatre, which included costumes, scenery, props and some interesting mechanical effects. To the chagrin of the whites, the American negroes beat them to it, and re-established their purchase in the cockloft of No.4 prison. They staged Shakespeare and heavy dramas successfully until the end of the war. (See Chapter 10, *The Arts and Crafts of Napoleonic and American Prisoners of War 1756-1816*, THE ENTERTAINERS)

The American-managed markets were soon as colourful and entertaining as they had ever been under the French. As more and more Yankees arrived from Chatham and Stapleton, the old air of destitution changed to one of prosperity. All of the Depot employments vacated by the French, cooks, builders, sweepers, etc., were now available; schools teaching navigation, seamanship, and any number of academic subjects sprang up. Big Dick's boxing academy, and similar ones in the white prisons, were at least as popular as the fencing classes had been – but there were no fewer gaming tables than before! With the prospect of steady employment, and 6s 8d a month only the profligate suffered.

The 4th July, 1814, was vastly different from the Independence Day of the previous year. Shortland had given permission for the celebration to take place and a number of the Garrison officers visited the yard as spectators. It all began with what should have been an entertaining happening. The previous day, two sailors, Thomas Hill and James Henry, both of the United States brig *Argus*, had a difference of opinion, which they thought could best be settled by a boxing match to decide the matter The bout took place at 9a.m. on the 4th in the prison yard of No. 4, and soon after it started Hill struck Henry a blow which felled and killed him. It was later decided that he should be charged with manslaughter at the August Exeter Assizes, where the verdict was 'justifiable homicide', and he was returned to the Depot.

The day started with the unfurling of the national flag, on which had been inscribed the slogan: *'ALL CANADA or DARTMOOR PRISON FOR LIFE'*, which amused the guards, but offended the officers. Andrews says that, at eleven o'clock, 'British officers belonging to the garrison, colonels, majors, captains, clerks, turnkeys, and a great number of soldiers assembled on the walls to hear an oration composed by a Yankee sailor.'

At two in the afternoon they sat down to their celebratory dinner, of the finest soup and best beef that their money could buy. There was no lack of liquid refreshment. They had gained permission to buy two hogsheads (50 gallons each) of porter, and had smuggled in several gallons of rum, so their country's great day must have ended in good fellowship and song.

At the end of the Napoleonic Wars, nearly all depots on land or sea, had come to the end of their usefulness as prisoner of war establishments; except for those holding Americans destined for Dartmoor, which were not cleared until October. Perth Depot became a civil gaol, but most closed down, never to open again as prisons. Some, like the great Norman Cross Depot, were completely demolished, and disappeared from the landscape within months of the end of hostilities. But Dartmoor was unique. Directly it was emptied of thousands of French prisoners, as many thousands of Americans from Stapleton and the prison hulks took their place.

From the end of 1812 to the closure of the Depot some two and a half years later, the Agent, sentries and guards were constantly on the alert. No other captives were ever as escape-obsessed as the Americans. No matter how much their conditions and general treatment had improved, or how successful they became in their various occupations, their hatred for any sort of confinement was claustrophobic. They tried every kind of getaway attempt, and were still working on a complicated and energy-sapping scheme of mass

escape, up to twelve weeks before their war with Britain ended. It may be remembered that the French prisoner, M.Catel, had written the story of a French escape by tunnelling, which I had found too fanciful and improbable to quote, unlike the following tale of American tunnelling which is too well documented to be doubted.

Early in August 1814, a group of American officers in No. 6 *caserne* had completed their plans for escape on a truly grand scale. Every depot had its story of attempted mass escape, but this ambitious scheme went far beyond anything ever dreamed of, and would involve almost every prisoner in Dartmoor.

The idea was to excavate underground passages beneath not one but three *casernes*, simultaneously: Nos. 4, 5 and 6. At that time No.5 was temporarily empty – although large drafts of American captives were arriving almost daily – there were 1,200 in No. 4 and 800 in No. 6. (there were at that time about 3,500 Yankees in Dartmoor, the number constantly mounting). The importance of silence was impressed on everyone involved; Bibles were procured, and every man in those two prisons was sworn to secrecy, on pain of death to any who uttered a word concerning that enterprise. As an added precaution a committee of secret agents, spies in fact, was formed to watch out for loose-talkers or men too friendly with prison authorities or staff.

The plan was to sink shafts twenty feet deep in each of the three prisons, at which depth the tunnels would be well below road level. They were then to strike out horizontally for some two hundred and eighty feet, to converge at a point outside the boundary walls. The entrance shafts were designed with ingenious, not easily discovered, covers; but the horizontal tunnels were wide enough for four men to work abreast.

The tunnellers worked in shifts – by day in Nos. 4 and 6, and in the empty No. 5[4] at night. The excavated soil was disposed of by surface workers, mostly through the fast-flowing open sewage conduit which ran through the rear of all the prisons. Some of the rather sandy soil ended up as 'plaster' on the rough stone walls of the officers' quarters: they had been permitted to buy in quite large quantities of lime and whitewash, having convinced the Agent that it was in the interest of hygiene.

By the end of August, they were within a few yards of the wall, so it is anticlimactic to have to report that such an imaginative endeavour should fail at a point so near its completion; but with so many prisoners in the know, it was hardly surprising. It was also well that this audacious venture came to naught, as it could hardly have succeeded without a great deal of bloodshed. The ringleaders had instructed that once outside the Depot, the fugitives, armed with daggers forged by the prisoner blacksmiths, were to head for Torbay where they believed they would find sufficient fishing boats to carry them across the Channel. They were to give no quarter, no one was to be taken alive.

On the 2nd September, 1814, Captain Shortland, attended by a strong force of guards, paid an unheralded visit to prison No. 5, where he told the conspirators that he had heard of their plot and had come to find the entrance to the tunnel. The prisoners did not help, and it took some time and much tapping with crowbars, before the cunningly concealed entrance was revealed. Although it was known that the officers in No. 6 were somehow involved, there was no idea that there were tunnels in their prison and in No. 4.

None of the guards or officials ventured into the tunnel but followed the Agent's order, to fill the entry shaft with stones and cap it off. Shortland did not punish the offenders with any great severity; little more than by reducing their rations to two-thirds until all damage to the prison had been paid for. He was, however, puzzled at the huge amount of earth which had been excavated and asked how they had disposed of it. He was politely answered: '…each man ate his portion, to make up for his scant food allowance.'

It did not take long before the thwarted Yankees were back in absconding mood. They reasoned that they could not have been betrayed by one of their number, for had that been so, Shortland would have known about the other two and the location of the shaft cover in No.5. The planners got down to work again. Big Dick and his black Americans were ordered to carry on with their digging in No.4 and report progress every forty-eight hours. In addition, a party from the officers' prison was to examine the possibility of breaking into the horizontal passage in the still-empty No.5 by sinking a new shaft into it, as the old one was now filled with stones.

This second attempt was as ill-fated as the first. This time the betrayer was a prisoner named Bagley, a native of Portsmouth, New Hampshire. One day, after visiting the burrowers in No. 5 *caserne*, he went into the yard and, in broad daylight, strolled over to a turnkey and engaged him in conversation. After a few minutes Bagley and turnkey went out through the gate and headed for the Agent's house.

Shortland did not believe the traitor's excuse for informing on his fellows. The untrustworthy wretch said that it was a matter of conscience, which led him to risk his own life, in order to save that of the Agent and others; which was the murderous intention of the conspirators, before they made their getaway. Bagley was awarded two guineas and the Transport Office gave him a passport to go wherever he wished.

Captain Shortland had been plagued almost to the point of persecution, with showers of complaints, petitions, escape attempts and sheer time-wasting cussedness; but had never felt physically threatened by even the worst of the Yankees. Nevertheless, with the prison filling so rapidly – in November another 5,000 prisoners had been added to the restless Dartmoor population – he had to tighten up on discipline and security in general. This did not endear him to his American charges, not only the newcomers but men who owed him a debt of gratitude for the changes he had brought about after the retirement of Isaac Cotgrave. He had restored the privileges denied them by the latter; did as much as any man could to correct the erring ways of Reuben Beasley; had seen to it that any sick Yankee was admitted to hospital – the despicable Chief Surgeon Dykar had gone – replaced by Dr (Sir) George McGrath, who became as respected by the prisoners, as Dykar had been detested. All in all, Captain Thomas Shortland would seem to have been a compassionate governor, who conscientiously carried out an often thankless task It is therefore to be regretted that his handling of an unfortunate and tragic happening at the very end of Dartmoor as a prisoner of war depot, should have caused him to be remembered as a monster by all Americans of the period. Shortland once said to a friend: 'I never saw or read or heard of such a set of Devil-daring, God-provoking fellows, as these same Yankees. I had rather have the charge of 5,000 Frenchmen, than 500 of these sons of liberty; and yet I love the dogs, better than I do the damned frog-eaters.'

Among the thousands of American prisoners, there were some whose exact status as prisoner of war was in some doubt; as was that of the United States brig *Argus*. In the summer of 1813 her hunting ground was mainly off the Channel ports, but on the 14th August she encountered the British brig *Pelican*, off the coast of Ireland. The two brigs were evenly matched but the action which ensued led Theodore Roosevelt to condemn it as the 'least creditable of all American single-ship battles'. The superior accuracy of the British gunnery and the fact that the American captain, W.H.Allen, had lost a leg, soon forced the *Argus* to strike her colours. When the prisoners had been brought ashore, one of them, named Robinson, denounced seventeen of his messmates as deserters from the Royal Navy. This was a capital offence, and the accused men (which included Hill and Henry, the contestants in the 4th July boxing match) were tried for their lives. The court acquitted them on grounds of insufficient corroboration of the accusation, and they were sent to Dartmoor.

The US brig *Argus* features in another Dartmoor story. On the 20th November, 1814, two American prisoners arrived from Plymouth. It was soon known that earlier in their experience as prisoners of war, they had been amongst the few (seventy-nine in all) who had enlisted in the service of King George III. Learning of the signing of the Treaty of Ghent, they applied as citizens of the United States, for their discharge from the Royal Navy. Returned once again as prisoners of war, but opulent and boastful, they flaunted their prize-money before their disapproving fellows.

One afternoon, after a good deal of carousing, they crowed a little too loudly, revealing how they had earned their ill-gotten gains. By a quirk of fate, they were serving on the British brig *Pelican*, when the *Argus* was defeated, so their reward was blood-money rather than a prize.

The two turncoats were immediately seized, and an impromptu 'court' was called to decide on their punishment. At first it was felt that the only sentence should be death, possibly by flogging; but it was then decided that the wretches should carry a mark of betrayal for all to see. They were bound, face-upwards, on to tables, and needles and Indian ink were prepared for their branding. They were then tattooed with a large **U.S.** for 'United States', on one cheek, and with **T** for 'Traitor' on the other. The two offenders were then sent to hospital, with a note advising the Surgeon to keep them there. One died in an effort to remove his disfigurement, the other was 'blistered', which only resulted in him returning to prison with the brands still clearly marked, but in scars rather than tattoos. Three members of the 'court' were sent for trial at Exeter Assizes, but were acquitted.

Twenty-four Americans had been confined in the Depot since 1810, two years before their war had begun. These were men captured whilst serving under the flag of France. They had been ceaseless in their efforts to be freed as subjects of a neutral state, but to no avail.

When, in 1812, America declared war, and these prisoners found that in Reuben Beasley they had an agent of their own nationality, they petitioned him immediately, asking to be quartered with their fellow countrymen. His reply was that 'having entered the service of a foreign power, they had divested themselves of every shred of nationality,' and that whilst he felt that the British Government had no right to hold them, he could not himself accept them as American prisoners of war. So, without funds or allowances, for the whole of the following year, they survived on the charity of their fellow Americans. They were not released as 'Frenchmen' in 1814, and it was not until the 24th March, 1815 that the American

Government decided to accept them and grant them the same monthly allowance as the others.

In August 1814, another American who had fought on the French side a few years earlier, arrived at the prison. His name was Simeon Hayes, of Baltimore, and this was the second time he had entered Dartmoor as a prisoner of war. His first experience of captivity came about when the French privateer on which he served was captured off Bordeaux. After a spell on the Moor, he was exchanged for an English prisoner in France. When the American war broke out, he joined the *Surprise* on a privateering cruise in the Pacific. Among their modest successes, was capture of a small merchant schooner, and Hayes, together with three other privateers, were put on board as prize crew. Their instructions were to keep in close touch with the mother vessel; but at first sight of a British frigate in the offing, the *Surprise* was off under full sail, with the frigate in hot pursuit.

Hayes and his shipmates, John Miller, an Englishman, James Rickor and Elisha Witten, both of Massachusetts, had to face up to the fact that, except for her cargo of oranges, there was nothing edible aboard the schooner. When a few days later they fell in with a brig, they determined that, by fair means or foul, they would capture it. Hoisting a distress signal, they waited for the brig to come to their aid; then, as she neared, opened up with the schooner's four six-pounders. The brig outsailed them and escaped, but later that day, the homeward-bound British frigate, *Ceres*, appeared on the scene, took the four men aboard and put a prize crew on board the schooner. On examining their prize, the British sailors found burnt-out matches in the open hold, where the four careless gunners had thrown them – unfortunately near the powder store. It did not take much of a jump to conclude that the Americans had intended to blow up the vessel. They were clapped in irons, and suffered the forty-two days voyage to England and Dartmoor, on a diet of six ounces of bread a day.

On reaching the Depot they learned that, without trial or further inquiry, the Admiralty had decided on their sentence: they were to be kept in solitary confinement in the Dartmoor *cachot* until the end of the war – a truly terrible punishment. The severity of such a cruel and open-ended sentence had a disastrous effect on the whole prison population. The other prisoners could only display their outrage to the authorities around them, and this they did without fail, so that guards, sentries, turnkeys and perhaps even the Agent, became nervous, edgy and, eventually, trigger-happy.

The four *cachot* prisoners probably owed their lives to the corruptibility of their jailer, an Irishman named Carley, and the generosity of fellow Americans. The latter supplied the bribes and cash for Carley to smuggle in food to supplement the scanty rations. The *cachot* was cold and damp, the only window a small grill through the stone wall, just below the vaulted roof. So they existed in a gloomy half light until the daylight faded, then darkness till next morning; but, after four months of this hell, the jailer obtained for them a regular supply of candles.

After six months, they were each allowed to walk beside an armed sentry every day for half an hour. Whenever the four took their daily exercise, huge numbers of prisoners crowded the railings to watch and call out encouragements.

The 13th February, 1815 was a Sunday, and Carley, a devout Roman Catholic, had gone to church to attend Mass. Hayes, Mills, Rickor and Whitton were walking up and down the beat with their four sentries. The usual crowd of prisoners had assembled when, just as the sentries were turning at the end of the beat, Hayes jumped for the railings, scrambled to the top and dived into the crowd of prisoners on the other side. Screened by the mass of bodies, he was first hidden in No. 1 prison, then transferred to No. 4 where he was 'metamorphosed into a darkie'. Next day a head count was made at all prisons, each man passing singly through a door where they were checked by, of all people, Mr Carley; who, of course, saw no one who resembled his lost prisoner. It is probable that Carley would never have betrayed Hayes, but he was so berated by his Commandant, presumably for going to church without permission, thereby losing one of his charges, that from then on he searched the yards constantly for him in an effort to restore his standing with his superior officer.

The yards were kept under close scrutiny and Shortland ordered that if the prisoners did not produce Hayes by a certain date, the market would be closed for ten days. His threat was promulgated throughout the prisons by 'criers' who shouted, 'Shall the prisoner, Simeon Hayes, be given up to be sent to the *cachot*? Aye or No'. The market was closed, but this only made the six thousand prisoners more resolute and even less controllable. Meanwhile, Hayes was having a whale of a time, constantly changing his appearance, at one time chatting with turnkeys whilst dressed as a professional jester; but he was not without narrow escapes. Shortland had found a prisoner who, at a price, was willing to betray him and said, correctly, that Hayes was in prison No. 5. Marching into No. 5 yard with a troop of sixty men, the Captain found his way jammed with cavorting prisoners, blocking the stairways and floors with their high-spirited prancing and dancing. A bright turnkey thought of a ruse and blew on his horn, which was the method of calling prisoners into the yard, to hear important announcements. Within minutes the prison was cleared, then Shortland and his men searched the building, prodding floors and walls with their bayonets; but they found no trace of the fugitive.

Returning with his troops to the yard, Captain Shortland found their way was once again blocked by nearly two thousand prisoners, and ordered them back into the prison. Despite his vow that they would be kept in the yard without food and water until Hayes was recaptured, no one budged; in fact the crowd grew denser, as men from other prisons learned that a 'baiting of redcoats' was about to take place.

With bayonet-pricks, the small company of soldiers somehow managed to cram the majority into the passage between prisons Nos. 5 and 6. Tempers had reached a touch-paper point, made worse when a young lad threw a stone with great force, which luckily only grazed the Agent's cheek. It was said that the infuriated Shortland gave the order to fire, and an 'eye-witness' has stated that the day was saved by the quick thinking of the officer in command of the troopers, who struck up the muskets with his sword, then stepped in front of his men and ordered; 'As you were!'[5] Both sides must have been aware how close they had been to tragedy, for as Shortland and his men left the yard in silence, no cat-calls, taunts or abuse followed them.

Hayes had indeed been in the prison, concealed in a tiny cavity under the stone-flagged floor. He was almost dead from suffocation, when released by a fellow prisoner, saying that his hiding place was even worse than the *cachot*, where he would rather be than have his life ended by a bayonet's thrust. His preference was soon granted. It seemed that the close brush with death had a salutary effect on the prison authorities, in that the hunt had been abandoned. The yard had quietened down and after a few days some of the prisoners arranged a celebratory meal, which fool-hardy Hayes decided to attend. He was recognised by a guard and handed over to his old Irish jailer, Carley. He was returned to the *cachot* to rejoin his cell-mates, and they were all released ten days later, to sit out the long uncomfortable days before they were repatriated.[6] The festive season of 1814 was crowned by tidings of great joy which gladdened the hearts of all the Yankee prisoners. On Christmas Eve, news reached Dartmoor that the Treaty of Ghent had been signed and the war between Britain and America was at an end. The 'War for Free Trade and Sailors' Rights' had been a loss to both sides, in ships and men and money. After only a very few years, it was often referred to as 'The Forgotten War'. One might imagine that the important and the niggardly recriminations which had brought about unnecessary hostilities between the two nations, would have been sorted out at Ghent; but the Royal Navy still retained, and practised, its hated right to 'stop and search' for the next forty years. It was rescinded in another treaty, the Declaration of Paris in 1856, which ended the Crimean War.

To begin with, the combined spirit of Christmas and Peace brought merriment and joy to both sides. Bands played, patriotic songs were sung, and maybe a few rare friendly words, passed between captor and captive. Remembering how speedy had been the repatriation of the French, the Americans felt certain that they would be back in their homeland early in the new year. They were to be sadly disappointed, although they were technically free men, as four more unbearable months would have to be endured before the Treaty was ratified. The prisoners – for prisoners we must still call them for want of a better word – found it difficult to await patiently the tardy dotting of the i's and the crossing of the t's, and were frustrated to see that, instead of jubilant drafts of Yankees passing out of the gates, more prisoners were being checked in. These were the last dregs from the final clearout of the hulks, Millbay and other depots. Included in the very last draft of forty-six American latecomers, was another diarist, who arrived in Dartmoor on the 30th January, 1815, a month after the war had ended. His published work: *'A Green-Hand's First Cruise, roughed out from the Log-Book of Memory, by a Yonker'* (Josiah Cobb), was published in Baltimore in 1841.

Compared with the anti-British flavour which pervades the otherwise excellent work of Charles Andrews, Green-Hand's memoirs contain only comparatively slight traces of bitterness; for he took more pleasure in recording the colourful scenes and characters he saw around him. His sea-going career as a privateer had lasted less than three weeks, when his brig was captured by three British frigates, without a shot being fired. After only five months in the Depot, he was released on the 5th July, 1815. On the 11th October of the previous year, another noteworthy diarist, author of *'A Journal of a Young Man of Massachusetts'* (Benjamin Waterhouse), had arrived. He spent only six months in Dartmoor before repatriation in April 1815. Waterhouse was a Surgeon on a privateer at the time of his capture. He was first imprisoned on Melville Island, Halifax, Nova Scotia, before being sent to England, where he spent some months on the *Crown Prince* hulk at Chatham, before being sent to Dartmoor. He was the first of the prisoner-historians to publish his reminiscences in New York in 1816. He, too, was less bitter than Andrews, but slightly more so than the Green-Hand. In fact, his were feelings more of

disappointment than hatred, for he came from a good Federalist family and, pre-war, had admired Britain and her navy. Those three and a few others, such as Valpey, Browne and Little, have left us a vivid and detailed image of the everyday life of the American prisoner of war.

On the 17th January, Captain Shortland received notice from the Admiralty, that he could release prisoners as and when their Agent, Reuben Beasley, was ready to arrange their repatriation. However, he was not even ready by the 20th March, 1815, when the United States vessel, *Favorite*, arrived from America with the ratified Treaty of Ghent. His defence was, as usual, that he had no funds or positive instructions – he had already stopped the monthly Government allowance of 6s.8d. once peace had been declared, saying that he considered it a wartime grant, and they were no longer at war! He further upset them by insisting that no man would be discharged unless he had been inoculated against smallpox, 'which I hear has been very mortal among you.'

The cruellest of their deprivations was the withdrawal of the daily 'tuppence-ha'pennies'. A large proportion of the prisoners had lived for that monthly payment, which meant extra food and drink – and perhaps even an occasional flutter on the 'Wheel of Fortune' or the 'Keno' booth. Now, however, enraged and resentful, they went hungry and were unable to afford the solace of the fragrant weed, so important to all sailors of the period, tobacco for smoking or chewing, the latter known as 'chaw-plug' or 'pigtail'.

By now, the Depot had became almost unmanageable. Many of the infuriated prisoners decided not to wait, and escape attempts became rife with some of them successful. On the 25th March, the abominable Beasley was called to trial in effigy, in a court convened by the Committee. The verdict was read to the court with great solemnity:

> 'At this trial, held at Dartmoor on the 25th day of March, 1815, you, Reuben G. Beasley in effigy were found guilty by an impartial and judicious jury of your countrymen, upon the testimony of 5,700 witnesses, of depriving many hundreds of your countrymen of their lives by the most wanton and cruel deaths, by nakedness, starvation and exposure to pestilence. It therefore becomes the duty of this court, as ought to be the duty of every court of justice, to pronounce that sentence of the law which your manifold and heinous crimes so richly deserve. And it is with the deepest regret that I am compelled to say our country has been imposed upon by a man whose crimes must cut him off from among the living. You this day must be hanged by the neck on the top of prison No.7 until you are dead; your body is then to be taken down and fastened to a stake and burned to ashes, which are to be distributed to the winds, that your name may be forgotten and your crimes no longer disgrace our nation.'

On that same day, Captain Shortland was threatened by a warning painted on a wall of his house: 'BE YOU ALSO READY'.

At this distance in time, it is not easy to see why it was thought necessary to keep thousands of free men as closely pent as they had been before peace was declared. We know that Shortland had been advised in January that they could be released as soon as Reuben Beasley could arrange their departure. It is very likely that he really was strapped for cash enough to carry out such a large operation. The initial cause of delay was a disagreement between the two governments. The Americans contended that each nation should be responsible for its own prisoners; that it was the duty of Britain to convey all Americans back to the United States, in return for which they would ship all British prisoners held in their prisons – but only as far as Bermuda or Nova Scotia! Lord Castlereagh thought this an unfair deal – and so the Dartmoor Yankees – calculated as 5,430 – continued their long impatient wait. Why though were they still guarded by hundreds of armed soldiers? It is true that if they had been given some sort of parole, which allowed them to enter or leave the Depot as they pleased, a fair number would have 'escaped' and found their own way home, by signing on to work their passage in British or foreign vessels (which is exactly what happened when they were finally released and their drafts reached Plymouth). The British Government still supplied their food and accommodation, so the majority would have returned to eat, drink and await their cartels – and what a great deal of acrimony, time, expense, worry and finally tragedy could have been avoided.

During the last months of the war the general atmosphere had been one of prosperity. Except for the idlers, the work-shy, and unsuccessful gamblers, the prisoners were doing well. Their take-over of the markets had been a huge success, and there had been work of all kinds for any so inclined. Every man had his monthly subsidy from the States – and there were more than 2,000 Americans who had fought for Britain against the French, until their own war was declared. These men had served as Royal Naval tars in British men-of-war and were owed quite large sums in prize-money. The British Government kept faith and paid up every cent of their debt. Therefore, prisoners were coming into Dartmoor well-breeched, some with as much as £1,000 or more in their pockets.

It would appear that the new and much appreciated Chief Surgeon, the tall, thin, one-eyed, George McGrath, secretly thought that perhaps they had more money than was good for their health. Writing in a medical paper after his retirement he said:

> 'During my service there (Dartmoor) malignant measles and smallpox were imported from other contaminated sources. These diseases attained to great virulence among Americans, chiefly arising from habits of indulgence from the ample pecuniary resources they possessed, and the facilities of obtaining spirits and sumptuous articles of diet from the market people, which no vigilance on the part of the authorities could suppress or obviate. The latter disease degenerated into an exasperated species of peri-pneumonia accompanied by low typhoid symptoms, which became very unmanageable and destructive.'

We know from the diarists that the prisoners did not spend their private hours in melancholy waiting, but filled in the time with escape plans, sports and games, gambling, composing more petitions, cursing both governments, or dreaming of the annihilation of Beasley and Shortland. In fact, as we shall see, it was a game in one of the yards which brought about the last great Dartmoor happening.

After the 20th March, 1815, and the reception of the ratification, the markets went into decline. It was not a sudden shut-down, in fact they were, for a short while, better stocked than ever before. The American producers of prisoner of war mementoes stocked their stalls with all their remaining artifacts. At the same time, the local farmers and traders, emptied their stores of every imaginable merchandise to tempt those valuable customers, who would soon be lost forever – and they never needed to reduce their prices.

On the 3rd April, one effort to off-load old stock caused a brouhaha, with serious repercussions. It was usual for depots to keep quite huge stocks of hard tack, or ships-biscuit, against emergencies, such as the shortage in the winter of 1813/14. Now, one of the bread suppliers had arranged with the Agent, to supply the Dartmoor prisoners with biscuit in place of the usual daily issue of one and half pounds of soft white bread per man. Worse still, each twenty-four ounce loaf was to be replaced by only sixteen ounces of hard ships-biscuit.

It was impossible for the indignant prisoners to appeal to Shortland, who was at that time in Plymouth, but they refused to accept it. Trouble and scuffles continued throughout the day, one Yankee tried to get into the market square by climbing the picket fence, but was knocked to the ground by a musket butt, which provoked his comrades into even greater fury. The junior officer left in charge, who had only 300 Militiamen at his disposal, was in a quandary. He could see no alternative but to instruct the contractor to order the usual ration; then send a message to Plymouth; and to promise the unruly mob that, if they returned to their prisons peaceably, the biscuit would be cancelled. Unappeased, they continued to demonstrate until, some hours later, the contractor's bread waggons rumbled into the depot, bearing 9,000 soft white loaves.

It is understandable that when the Captain returned next day, he should have been annoyed that his subordinate should have countermanded his orders. However, that ever-present eye-witness, the anti-Agent, Andrews, is to be doubted when he reported that Shortland swore, that had he not been away, he would have seen that the Yankees would have been brought to order at the point of the bayonet, *and that he was determined to create an opportunity for revenge.*

A couple of days later, on the 6th April, trouble was brewing in the airing yard of prison No. 7. As in all the other yards, men were gathered together in groups, some just talking, joking, arguing, whilst others watched the more energetic of their countrymen indulge in competitive sports and games. A small crowd had gathered to watch a hand-ball match, similar to squash, which was being played against one of the walls of the prison. The Green-Hand (Josiah Cobb), who was in the yard that day, tells us that the four players had been captured whilst on boat duty, from the USS *Superior*, Commodore Chauncey's flag ship, on Lake Ontario. Green-Hand emphasised that these young men prided themselves on having sailed with so renowned an officer; 'they were no ways riotous, but were known throughout the prisons for being, in seamen's phrase, "ready dogs and ripe for fun… fun."' In the course of the game, the ball was often thrown by accident over the wall, into the barrack-yard, and for some time, was as often thrown back by the sentry on the other side, till he through sulkiness refused to toss it again to the players. They tried to persuade him again to give it to them, as it was the only one they had, it affording them amusement and recreation, and lessened the tediousness of their captivity. The only answer they could get from the sulky sentinel, was to 'come and take it.'

The story from then on is simple, with versions which vary only in slight, but important slanted details, according to the nationality of the narrator. The Americans were peeved and, making a show of accepting the sentry's invitation, attacked the wall between No. 7 and the guards' barracks; whilst in another part of the Depot a number of Rough Alleys climbed the picket fence and amused themselves by throwing turfs to annoy the guards. There was no way that a hole in the wall large enough for more than a single body to pass through, could have been achieved without proper tools –

and could never have been mistaken for an escape attempt (into a barracks of armed soldiers!). Their Committee tried, but failed, to stop the attack on the rubble wall, for they were guilty of damaging Government property. Meanwhile, Shortland had been informed of the trouble in No.7 yard and that a group of rowdies, probably Rough Alleys, had somehow managed to break the chain on the main gate to the market square. He was also told, falsely it transpired, that the boundary wall of the Depot had been breached in five places.

Sincerely believing that what all Agents must secretly have feared – a general uprising – the Captain first ordered the recall bell to be sounded, which summoned all off-duty military men back to the Depot. However, it also brought many hundreds of prisoners hurrying from their *casernes* to the market-place, to see what was afoot. Shortly after five o'clock in the afternoon, a company of men of the Somersetshire and Derbyshire Militias, with the Agent at its head, entered the market square. Shortland and McGrath who had accompanied him, tried their best to persuade the noisy assembled crowd to return to their quarters forthwith, the Captain warning that if they refused they would face a bayonet charge. A good number of the muttering mob would have obeyed had they been able, but so many more were surging through the gate behind them that few could retreat. A hundred soldiers of the garrison, under two lieutenants and an ensign, were ranged in double line across the market square. Shortland, realizing that force was unavoidable, 'ordered a file of fifteen who were directly opposite the gate', to charge the crowd with fixed bayonets. The soldiers were too close to the Americans to make a charge, but somehow managed to usher most of them out of the square into the passage under the military walk, 'which was densely packed with people, howling, hooting' and hurling jibes and insults at the Captain and the soldiers. The stubborn Yankees still refused to be moved, in fact, a group of them tauntingly invited the Agent to give the order to fire!

Somebody *did* give that order, but we shall never know for certain who that someone was. The first volley was fired over the heads of the protesting Americans, and it is possible that this humane action did more harm than good. American voices from the rear of the tight-packed mob called out that the soldiers were firing only 'blank cartridges', and the prisoners stood their ground. The second volley, however, was fired into the midst of the unarmed crowd, killing some and wounding many more: such was the beginning of a crazy nightmare – the 'Dartmoor Massacre'.

Most of the soldiers were now completely confused and out of control. Shortland and two of the officers had stepped out in front of the militiamen, which halted the shooting temporarily, and Lieutenant Fortye had managed to keep his section of the guards under orders. Unfortunately, a number of soldiers had dashed off in mad pursuit of fleeing survivors, firing their muskets and bayoneting as they ran. Unbelievably, the sentries and guards on the walls joined in with the senseless slaughter, firing down from their platforms on to the desperate men as they made for the shelter of their prison blocks. All was confusion and madness. When the Americans reached their *casernes* it was difficult for them to enter, for except for one door to each prison, all entrances had been locked, by the turnkeys. Great panic ensued, as the fugitives tried to force their way into the buildings, past men inside who were trying to get out through the same opening, to discover what all the noise was about.

It was not unusual for the turnkey to leave only one door unlocked, as it made for easier head-counts, and it was now about six o'clock and muster time. However, a number of American writers claimed that Captain Shortland had ordered the closure, the easier to carry out his revenge!

There is some evidence to show that several of the soldiers swept up in the chase fired high, and that their shot could be heard rattling on the slated rooftops; but others were guilty of unforgivable homicide.

One unlucky American, a merchant seaman named John Washington, who had earned a reputation among his fellows as a peace-maker, was endeavouring to calm the rowdies in the square, when he was struck by a ball from the first volley. Propping himself against a wall as the pursuing soldiers raced by, he cried out for mercy for himself and fellow Americans, but one of them shot him through the brain.

I have read or heard of only one English 'casualty' in this sorry affair. A young private in the Somersetshire Militia was detailed to act as Lamp-lighter, and was lighting the lantern at the gate to No.5 prison when the first shot was fired. A moment later he was swept off his feet and carried along by the madly rushing Americans, fleeing for shelter. For a while his fate was in the balance; some thought it called for a lynching party, but wiser heads decided against it. Next morning, when the wounded were being carried to the hospital, the militiaman, terrified and not believing his luck, was thrown out of the yard.

This outrage, probably the most disgraceful in British prisoner of war history, took only a few minutes to perpetrate, but in that short time sixty-three American men and boys were laid low. Seven were killed outright by musket shot and bayonet thrust, and two others were mortally wounded and later died in Dartmoor Hospital; twelve were very seriously wounded, some of them becoming amputees, and forty-two suffered lesser injuries.

There was no argument between the nations as to the number of killed and wounded; but some American writers echoed Andrews' dark suspicion: that many more were killed, but Captain Shortland had spirited them away and had them secretly buried, before Dr McGrath visited the prisons next morning.

There followed a whole series of investigations and inquiries by authorities from both sides of the Atlantic. Two days after the dreadful event, on the 8th April, an inquest was held on the seven luckless Yankees. It took place under the jurisdiction of Joseph Whitford, Coroner to the County of Devon, and a jury of twelve Dartmoor farmers, farmers who brought in the unsatisfactory, but not unusual, verdict of 'Justifiable Homicide'.

It is obvious that murder was committed that day, yet no one ever hanged for it. It is puzzling, too, that none of the many enquiries, American or British, fully explained why thousands of free men had been closely impounded, for so long after the two countries were at peace. It was said that they were rioting, but if so, surely it was against false imprisonment.

The conclusions of the two main Courts of Inquiry, gave no solace or satisfaction to the surviving Americans. The first trial was a British review of the available evidence, under Admiral Sir John Duckworth, the Commander-in-Chief at Plymouth, and Major-General S. Brown. They questioned a number of eye-witnesses, under oath, from amongst the turnkeys, guards and sentinels, none of whom had heard Captain Shortland give the order to fire, (it is not surprising to find that, at the international trial which followed later, most American witness swore that he *did* give such an order).

Nevertheless, the Joint British and American Commission, represented by the American Commissioner, Charles King and Commissioner Francis Seymour Larpent, for Britain, came to much the same conclusions as the Duckworth inquiry, and found Shortland 'Not Guilty' of starting the affray. So the Captain was exonerated thrice over, by the inquest and both national investigations; but, to use a modern American expression, surely the buck should have stopped with him to some extent, as the senior man present on that day.

The prisoners, though undeniably rowdy and intimidating, were absolved from any plans to attempt escape or cause an uprising; but no one was found guilty or punished for any part in the inglorious affair. The International Commissioners, King and Larpent, summed up their lengthy investigations by stating that they had endeavoured to 'ascertain if there was the least prospect of identifying any of the soldiers who had been carried to the particular outrageous lengths here alluded to, or of tracing any particular death at that time to the firing of any particular individual, but without success, and any hopes of bringing the offenders to punishment would seem to be at an end. In conclusion, we the undersigned, have only to add that we lament, as we do most deeply, the unfortunate transaction which has been the subject of this inquiry, we find ourselves unable to suggest any steps to be taken as to those parts of it which seem to call for redress and punishment.'

The US Government at first called for Shortland to stand trial, but after some consideration did not pursue the matter. Realising that many of the sworn witnesses were badly wounded ex-prisoners, who would have to be shipped back to England, so they let sleeping dogs lie. The British Government took the positive action of granting pensions to the wounded Americans, and to the families of all who had died. It is recorded that in the 1840s, one of those pensioners was the peg-legged gate-keeper at the Washington Medical College.

The Agent at all times protested that he had never ordered the troops to fire on the helpless prisoners, or that he had ordered a bayonet charge, saying that such actions were beyond his remit and came under military authority – he also strenuously denied that he had been drunk at the time! Dr McGrath testified to the untruth of the latter accusation, that he had been with the Captain that evening, 'and that generally no man could be more abstemious.'

Captain Robert Shortland must have been aware of how close he had come to disgrace, and thanked God and the Commissioners that his so far brilliant career remained unbesmirched. Whilst First Lieutenant of H.M.S *Melpomene* in 1798, he was promoted to the rank of Commander, for gallantry in cutting out the French brig *L'Aventurier*. After his eventful term as Agent at Dartmoor, he was appointed Captain of H.M.S. *Magnificent*. He later became Commissioner of the Port Royal Dockyard at Jamaica, where he died of yellow fever in 1825. All the writers who had been prisoners of war in Dartmoor at that time, ended their diary, journal, memoir or book, with his account of the massacre; telling it as he saw it – or hoped that America and the world would believe he saw it. To show the similarities and differences, a few extracts are included here. It took thirty-eight small-type pages of venom, for Charles Andrews to 'analyse' the story of the 'Dartmoor Massacre', in justification for his accusation that he had heard Captain Shortland swear that he was determined to create an opportunity for revenge:

' …the soldiers now advanced, making a general massacre of men and boys, whom accident or impossibility had left with-out the doors of the prison; they advanced near to the crowded doors, and instantly discharged another volley of musketry on the backs of those furthest out, endeavoring their passage into the prison. This barbarous act was repeated in the presence of this inhuman monster, Shortland – and the prisoners fell, either dead or severely wounded, in all directions before his savage sight.

'But his vengeance was not glutted by the cruel murder of the innocent men and boys that lay weltering and bleeding in the groans and agonies of death along the prison-doors, but turned and traversed the yard, and hunted a poor affrighted wretch, and dared not move lest he should be discovered, and immediate death be his lot.

'But, alas! The unhappy man was discovered by these hell-hounds, with this demon at their head, and with cool and deliberate malice, drew up their muskets to their shoulders and dispatched the unhappy victim, while in the act of imploring mercy from their hands. His only crime was not being able to get into the prison without being shot before.'

Without correcting the spelling mistakes, or introducing punctuation, I submit the following extract from young Joseph Varley's diary:

'On the sixth day of April as the prisoners of No five and seven Prisons made a Small hole in the wall near the Barracks when Capt Shortland gave Orders for the Soldiers to fire in upon the Unarmed Prisoners and a Dreadful Massacree took place in the first place he sent the Turnkeys for to Lock three of the doors out of four so that escape to the prison's was Impossible and after we had got Mostly in at the Remaining door and those that was at the lower ends of the yard and knew nothing of the Disturbance was mostly killed or wounded – in No one and three where there was no offence given and without any provication they fired and then Charged Bayonet Many were killed and wounded in this yard and to Compleat the scene of slaughter and death a Simeler Scein took place in No 4 Yard it appears that the Blacks were near the gates of there Yard Gamboling and not Mistrusting any harm when a dreadful fire from the top of the wall killed several and wounded many the Soldiers kept a Cross fire upon the only Remaining door that we had open – so that it was Impossible for any to Escape i have not yet Received the true list of the killed and wounded.

'On the seventh as soon as it was daylight i went round for to view the yards i found a Consider Blood in our yard and in No four but not so much in No one at 10 in the four noon i Received the list of the Killed and wounded but thanks be to God there was but seven Killed and fifty wounded and the Most of them has lost there Legs or there arms and several Mortally wounded – i Cannot but help Remarking the fait of one Young Man – after he was wounded and Making the Best of his way for the prison five of the British Soldiers came up with him and put there Musquets to his head and Blow'd his brains out a gainst the wall.'

Josiah Cobb – the Green-Hand – did not pretend to witness everything which took place, and reported unsensationally:

'So little did this crowd of prisoners suppose they were in peril, that one, who has since told me the fact, was carelessly looking through the gratings, a little apart from the body, nor dreamed his person was in jeopardy, till the squad of soldiers approached, one pointed his musket downwards, within a foot of his knee, and blew all about to a jelly, splintering and mangling the thigh above in a horrible manner – almost beyond the hope of cure, till the third amputation alone staid mortification. This man is still living and can testify to the above remarks.

'To show the wanton cruelty of the soldiery, I will relate but one instance, which came immediately under my observation, and one that is not mentioned in any report I have seen, although his name is among the list of wounded from the hospital, where he was sent after being brought into the prison. This boy, belonging to No.5, was in the yard when the firing began, gained the door in the rear of the building, found it fastened, ensconced himself closely in its recess, till the firing had entirely ceased, and he could see none in the yards, when he ran out, with the intention of reaching the one at the farther end of the building, and while at his greatest speed, was levelled at by those upon the wall, and shot through the thigh.'

A rumour, current at the time, suggested a reason why soldiers joined the sentries on their platforms and opened up with deadly cross-fire. Ridiculous though it was, it made a change from the pan-American belief that Shortland was the root of all evil. The story goes that, shortly before the catastrophe, the Americans had bribed soldiers to bring forbidden hard liquor into the Depot, and had paid up promptly when the spirits were received. It was only later discovered that their payment had been made in base coinage and forged paper money. They had little chance of redress, and were aware that to make a fuss might call attention to their own transgressions – smuggling could earn an incredible number of stripes, and to be caught in possession of, or uttering false money was a capital charge. So, the rumour said, the soldiers took advantage of the pandemonium to show that the Yankees could not cheat them with impunity!

The Young Man of Massachusetts, Benjamin Waterhouse, was a particularly interesting writer. As indignant and embittered by the harshness of his treatment as any other American prisoner of war, his journal reveals that he had a sense of humour, and was something of a philosopher. Published within a year of the massacre, his journal contains the sworn depositions of sixteen ex-prisoner eye-witnesses; the names of the killed and wounded; international inquiries and letters.

Waterhouse was a young man of strong prejudices, but although he may never have learned to love the French, Spaniards or Scots, his regard for all things English was renewed after he had left Dartmoor – except for Captain Shortland and anyone connected with the British prisoner of war service:

'I did not see the beginning of this affray. I was, with most of the other prisoners, eating my evening's meal in the building, when I heard the alarm bell, and soon after a volley of musketry. There were, I believe, before the alarm bell rung, a few hundred prisoners scattered here and there about the yards, as usual; but I had no idea of any particular collection of them, nor had I any suspicion of any commotion existing, or meditated. But I forbear; and will here insert the report of the (American Prisoner of War) Committee, in the correctness of which I place an entire confidence.'

[*Concluding paragraph*]
'We deem it necessary here to remark, as some editors have manifested a disposition to vindicate Shortland's conduct, that, allowing every circumstance to be placed in the most unfavorable point of view for the prisoners, suppose for a moment, it was their intention to break out, and a number had collected in the market square for that purpose, when, being charged upon by the military, they retreated out of the square into their respective prison yards, and shut the gates after them without making any resistance whatever; under such circumstances no further opposition could have been expected, and consequently, their intention must have been completely defeated. What justification can there then be made to appear for the subsequent brutal, unprecedented butchery and mutilation? NONE! The most shameless and barefaced advocates and apologizers for British injustice cannot produce any.

Signed
Walton Colton
Thos. B. Mote
Wm. Hobart'

The whole story of the 6th April, has such a touch of incompetence and madness about it, that it was almost inevitable that it should end tragically. The Yankees had been unable to accept that they were legitimately taken prisoners of war, and had unwisely made things difficult for their keepers from the start. Furthermore, those keepers were, in the main, a few hundred comparatively inexperienced country militiamen who, between them, had to oversee five or six thousand troublesome and sometimes violent captives, for twenty-four hours a day. They had endured constant abuse, insults and imaginative and savage threats of what would happen to them if ever they fell into American hands. With nerves ajangle, it is no wonder that some of them cracked under the strain when faced with desperate emergency.

The 7th April dawned on to a very different Dartmoor Depot. The prisons were unnaturally quiet, and some prisoners decided not to leave their quarters, lest the one-sided battle of yesterday be resumed. However, when they did venture into the yards, it was to find no sentries had been posted on the walls and scarcely a soldier was to be seen. The Americans were not put under any discipline and were left to act as they wished. Many deeply depressed men wandered the yards, turning over in their minds images of slaughter they could hardly believe they had seen; members of the Prisoners' Committee were interviewing witnesses for the statement they were preparing to send to London; whilst a few talented others kept their minds active, and their pockets lined, by drawing, painting, sculpting or carving mementos of the carnage, for sale in what was left of the market.

The parsimony of both governments in the matter of repatriation, which was largely responsible for the debacle, had to be abandoned. The indolent Reuben Beasley, who had carried out his duties so badly, was now put hard to work, arranging vessels and draft lists, etc. but it was two weeks before the first cartel arrived at Plymouth. Meanwhile security was so lax that seventy-eight Americans escaped in five days, some of them scaling the walls with their baggage in broad daylight, as the sentries watched on with fascinated inaction. Beasley allowed some of these absconders to board the first cartel when it arrived, but some had no such luck. The Hundred Days War, which broke out in the previous month, after Napoleon's escape from Elba, had brought the press-gangs to Plymouth, who must have been delighted to snatch such likely lads to build up the crews of British men-of-war. Protesting their nationality, they were released after confirmation that they were indeed Americans, they were returned to the Depot, their names to be listed in the last draft to leave England.

At last, on the 19th April, forty days after ratification, the first cartel, the Swedish ship *Maria Christiana*, arrived, and on the 20th the first batch of 249 men were at the gate, impatient to begin the march to Plymouth. Their baggage was loaded on to wagons and they had created a large white standard upon which was depicted the Goddess of Liberty, weeping over a murdered sailor at her feet, with a tomb in the background. They left no fond farewells to the monstrous cage they had just vacated, but great cheers for the depot-mates they hoped would soon follow. When they reached Plymouth, eight of them left the cartel to serve under French colours on board a brig bound for France.

The drafts were generally selected according to the length of time served in the prison; men like Andrews, who were among the first to enter Dartmoor more than two years earlier, were the first to leave. Subsequent drafts were made up in a similar fashion, but the very last to depart were chosen as a punishment, the negroes for being negroes, the Rough Alleys for their uncontrollable villainy, and other offenders. The Green-Hand would also be among the last to leave; as a late-comer to the Depot – he arrived after the ratification – he realised he was way down the list of departees. Together with a few other tail-enders, a ruse was tried by which they might jump the queue. The idea was to assume the names of prisoners who were known to have escaped, who otherwise would have been higher up the embarkation list. This involved quite a lot of preparation, as a fairly full description of each captive was entered in the Depot Registers on arrival; name, height, hair colour, complexion, scars, etc. and no doubt this information was available to the clerks who prepared the lists.

Green-Hand almost made it, but another prisoner had chosen the same escaper to impersonate, and when the name was called and he went to the gate, he found that he had been pipped at the post. He returned to his *caserne*, unpacked his baggage, and went back to his journal. We must be pleased that he did, for without it we would have little knowledge of Dartmoor's last three months.

The second draft was delayed for a while. The 350 Yankees had actually moved off when it was noticed that they had, insensitively, been given as escort a unit of the Somersetshire Militia. They immediately came to a halt and returned to the gate, saying that they would not risk their lives in the care of 'such cut-throats'. Only when a detachment from a nearby barracks arrived, would they continue the march to Plymouth. Berths still had to be found for 5,193 Americans. Beasley informed them that he had finally managed to secure eight cartel vessels from various ports, which were on their way to Plymouth. However, it took until mid-July before the last draft embarked for the USA. Meanwhile, many of the Americans were in a desperate condition. It has been mentioned already that a great number of them were suffering from depression and semi-starvation in both food and tobacco, and now many of them were worried that when their turn came, they might have to face the long march to Plymouth barefoot, for they had no shoes. Beasley was quite aware of their sorry state, but true to himself he neglected them to the end.

Letters arrived at the Depot from prisoners who had been taken to London, to give their depositions to the Lord Mayor and members of the Transport Board. On completion of their evidence, these men had been given passports for their release. Andrews tells us that 'any one might obtain a passport who could procure a friend to make application for their release, and informing Mr Beasley that they required no assistance from him to convey them to the United States. In obtaining a passport in this way from Capt. Shortland they needed no other protection in this country' – but the number qualified to grasp this lifeline were few.

The 4,000 Frenchmen captured at Ligny during the Hundred Days, had not had time to re-establish the markets and Frenchify their part of the prison. They were released soon after Waterloo, and were back in France before the last of the Americans left our shores. Although the returning Frenchmen did not know it, their beloved Emperor had been captive in Plymouth, on board the *Bellerophon* (the 'Billy-Ruffian' of the sea-shanty) between the 26th July and the 8th August, before going into exile on St Helena.

The Green-Hand wandered the yards noting the changes which had taken place since his arrival in January. The colour and spirit had faded as the inner markets disappeared, and the traders and farmers found it hardly worth while to continue with the main market in the square. Without the US allowance the prisoners were no longer customers, but had to rely on Government rations. The Green-Hand reported on the character changes which were noticeable in half-starved and tobaccoless men. Some grew quarrelsome and morose; others fell into a sort of lethargy; others again were seized with fits of causeless passion, when they would stride up and down with staring eyes, and turn savagely upon their best friend.

It may be remembered that when the French left Dartmoor in 1814, each man had to return his hammock and bedding, known as the 'Kings Kit', to the quartermaster of the Depot, on the morning of his release. This same procedure applied to the Americans and everyone was aware of it. To be unable to comply meant that the offending prisoner's name would be called only in the very last draft. This was of some concern, particularly to losing gamblers and the Rough Alleys. Unlike the French 'Romans' the leaders of the lawless Americans allowed them to keep their hammocks; but a number lost theirs on the tables. Amongst those losers were the two chiefs, Sodom and Gomorrah, who committed a crime almost as bad as stealing a mess mate's meal – they stole the hammocks of two decent fellows already assigned to an expected cartel. Late on the evening of the 27th June the ship arrived and the listed were ordered to be ready to embark at daybreak. News of the missing hammocks spread throughout the prisons and such a thorough search was made that, within an hour, the crime had been traced to Sodom and Gomorrah.

There was no time to convene a court through the Committee, so the unholy pair suffered summary justice, which could have been fatal. They were stripped of their shirts and hung by their thumbs between two iron posts, with their toes hardly touching the ground. A crier then traversed the prison, calling upon anyone who had a score to settle with 'the greatest thieves in Christendom', to take his turn at the whip.

During the recent short war with France, the Depot had largely been given over to French captives, and the Americans, about 900 almost equally divided into black and white, had again been segregated into No. 4 prison. Flea-bitten and miserable, it was not an ideal waiting room, but the blacks coped with it better than the whites. Big Dick and some of the better behaved negroes, had been included in an earlier release, and without his regal authority the remainder, for the most part, rejoiced in the absence of supervision. Not all, for some of them may have qualified for earlier cartels, but after noticing that the destination was a southern port of America, they decided to wait, for fear of being sold into slavery on their arrival. The rest took an unbelievable step by cancelling the Sabbath, a day which had been held sacrosanct, but was now given over to gambling and pleasure. Perhaps Deacon John felt let down by the Archangel Gabriel, who had given him his personal promise to destroy Dartmoor. On the first Sunday in July, 1815, a reverend gentleman had gained permission to deliver his favourite sermon in No. 4 prison. He set up his pulpit in the yard and found himself surrounded by all sorts of activity. Just a few feet away a Keno table was doing brisk business with three card games in progress and a gang of negroes playing penny pitch-and-toss. As he began to preach, the players matched the rhythm of his speech, with their own loudly delivered calls relating to the games they were playing so that he gave up, saying 'I must give up, I cannot hear my own voice.'

On the 4th July the attempt to celebrate was a dismal failure, but on the next day the Green-Hand's name was called. Joyously, he recalled every detail of his repatriation; of the friendly escort who fraternized so wholeheartedly at a stop-over inn that some prisoners helped by carrying their belts and muskets! And as if to show that the useless war was over, the draft was cheered by kindly countryfolk and townspeople, as they neared the harbour and saw their cartel ship lying a mile offshore.

The remaining Americans were picked up by two more cartels which sailed into Plymouth soon after. The very last healthy prisoners to leave in mid-July, were the Rough Alleys and the negroes, but the Depot was not closed until sick Yankees were discharged from hospital in February 1816. Then the garrison marched off, the fixtures and fittings were carted away, the Admiralty stores closed down, and the prisons and gates securely locked for the next thirty years.

EPILOGUE

THE FRENCH 'ROMANS'

We have read of young men of good family who, for reasons which perhaps even they could not explain, roamed the yards at Dartmoor, as naked and filthy as any other French Roman. However, there were some among them who made spasmodic returns to normality when a remittance arrived from home. It is possible that, during these short lapses into sanity, a few may have been persuaded to re-enter the human race but the vast majority would never give up their membership of the exclusive club of the Capitole.

One might well believe that when the war came to an end, this evil and lawless band would be dumped ashore on the Continent, where it would split up or disappear into the slums and dives of the ports or Paris. This might have been the fate of most, but there were exceptions.

Sir Basil Thomson quotes a French writer, who tells a remarkable story. Fifteen years after he had been released from Dartmoor, a French officer who had been there as a 'broke parole', was touring Picardy when he stopped to hear mass at a small village church. The curé preached an 'eloquent and spiritual' sermon and was obviously venerated by his community, but it was not the service which impressed the officer. Digging deep into his memory, he suddenly realised that the last time he had seen this 'suave and reverend priest' he had been raking over an offal heap 'in the garb of Adam'. After the service the office knocked at the sacristy door and was courteously invited in. Shaken but with no denial, the curé confessed that although his family had funded him regularly, he had become a Roman as violent as the rest when a young prisoner. Evil example and imprisonment had dragged him down, 'but God had worked a miracle on my soul.'

In August 1846, one of the most prestigeous of administrative posts in Louis-Philippe's Government was filled by a man of great ability, lionised by the Press and generally admired. Yet many in the country knew that he too had been a Roman and that the breast that was now plastered with decorations had once been bare to the icy winds of Dartmoor.

In Paris in 1844, there was a particularly successful merchant, who constantly bored his only slightly less wealthy friends with stories of his war experiences, particularly the leading part he had played in managing the internal affairs whilst a prisoner of war in Dartmoor. His chief importance, in real life, was that no one was better at sniffing out fish offal from the garbage heaps!

---

1. Varley also tried his hand at poetry.

2. See *The Arts and Crafts of Napoleonic and American Prisoners of War 1756-1816*, Chapters 2 and 3 – THE DEPOT AND INNER MARKETS.

3. A contemporary note records the complaint that the many flue-pipes which hung from the unglazed windows of the sleeping accommodation spoiled that aspect of the building!

4. Verification of part of Charles Andrews' recollections of the tunnelling was revealed by two more recent excavations. In 1881, the stone-filled shaft of No.5 was exposed when foundations were being laid for a new block at Dartmoor. In 1911, Sir Basil Thomson the ex-Governor wrote to Francis Abell to tell him that another tunnel had been discovered which was probably the interrupted second attempt as the shaft was only 14 feet deep and the passage stopped at 20 feet.

5. Maybe Captain Shortland, in a moment of frustrated anger, *did* give the order to 'Fire' but it is possibly an American effort to back up a similar accusation on a more tragic occasion a few weeks later, the 'Dartmoor Massacre'.

6. Many years later Simeon Hayes became the landlord of The Baltimore House, in Baltimore. It is said that he liked nothing better than to regale his customers with the *full* story of his adventures at sea and in Dartmoor.

PROSPCT af PRESONGEN GREENLAW, som ligger 10 engelske Mile SO. fra EDINBURGH op i Landet, hvor 697. Danske og Franske Priso nere ere indstullede. Signid i Grenlaw Prison, den 20de August 1809.

Chapter Twenty

Part One

Prisoner of War Depots in Scotland
Edinburgh Castle

EDINBURGH CASTLE WAS THE ONLY WAR PRISON in Scotland for the whole of the eighteenth century, in fact until 1803. Overlooking the city from a prominence some 450 feet above sea-level, there has been fortified buildings on Castle Rock certainly since the eleventh century, and perhaps as early as the sixth century AD. It is probable, therefore, that the Castle dungeons had housed foreign captives taken in the many wars earlier than the period of our study.

The most interesting and informative source of details regarding the prisoners of war in Scotland and Edinburgh Castle as their prison, are the Macbeth Forbes Papers in the Scottish Records Office and the article which he published in the March 1899 issue of *The Gentleman's Magazine*[1]. Francis Abell, who knew Forbes personally, depended on the latter's research when writing at the beginning of the twentieth century.

Edinburgh, like Bristol and Liverpool, was an appropriate point for the reception of prisoners of war captured at sea. Privateers infested our coastal waters throughout the Seven Years' War and later wars, and the northern towns of Scotland were particularly vulnerable. In 1746 they had been disarmed for having aided the Stewart cause in Bonnie Prince Charlie's '45 Rebellion. More than a decade later, during the Seven Years' War, the Royal Burghs of

Scotland appealed to the Government on behalf of the deprived towns. As a result, each town was allowed '200 stands of arms' to protect themselves against depredation by French privateers or men-of-war; but more effective, was the setting up of British warship patrols in those dangerous waters.

The first prisoners to enter Edinburgh Castle came from a French vessel appropriately named after one of France's most famous naval – or privateer – heroes of the seventeenth century – the *Chevalier Bart*. Jean Bart was born in Dunkirk in 1650 – and spent his youth at a time when possession of that town was constantly changing hands, which left him in a strange nationality quandary. At various times he was a French, Spanish or English subject – and in 1667, when he was seventeen, he was serving under the Dutch Admiral de Ruyter on the occasion of his historic attack on the English fleet in the Medway. After Bart's death a number of ships, both great and small, naval and letter-of-marque, bore his name with pride.

The small French privateer *Chevalier Bart*, armed with ten carriage and eight swivel guns, was cruising in the entrance to the Firth of the Forth in April, 1757, when she was spotted by HMS

Above. View of Greenlaw. Painted by a Danish Prisoner.

Solebay. The 28-gun frigate gave chase and captured the French vessel off Tynemouth. The prize was taken to Leith and, by the end of the month, its crew of twenty-eight were sent to Edinburgh Castle, thus earning themselves the doubtful distinction of being the first prisoners to enter its dungeons in the Seven Years' War. Many more were soon to follow; the most to arrive in a single delivery of captives being 108 privateersmen, in July of that same year.

The word 'dungeon' brings to mind the image of a small, damp, claustrophobic, underground stone cell, with iron rings set into the walls and something of the torture-chamber about it. Some may have indeed fitted that image, but Macbeth Forbes' description of the Edinburgh prison paints a somewhat different picture:

> 'The dungeons – partly rock and partly masonry – of Edinburgh Castle… are situated to the south and east of the castle, and the date of them goes far back. The corridor leading to the seven dungeons and vaults on the south has a strong outer and inner iron gate, and each of the dungeons must have had, originally, an iron entrance door with heavy chains and padlock, though a few of the doors are now of wood. Some of the vaults are led up to by steps from the ground floor of the corridor; others have steep steps leading down to them, one having as many as nineteen steps. They are thus in two tiers [he said that they were 'strongly arched', and gave the measurements of one dungeon as 54 ft. by 22 ft. 3 ins., and 11 ft. 6 ins. in height].
>
> 'There were peep-holes in each dungeon to which light was admitted by iron-barred loop-holes looking to the Grass Market.
>
> ' …there are other dungeons on the east side, now used as beer and coal cellars for the troops.'

As many as forty prisoners were housed in each of the dungeons. It would seem that there was no facility to sling their hammocks but 'extemporised wooden frameworks' were set up so that they could convert their swinging cots into static bunks.

Forbes says that the floors were of wood and that the walls had been plastered since the dungeons were vacated, and that 'no carvings of names thereon remain'. However, when Abell visited the Rock just before the First World War, he noticed some inscriptions on the wall of the narrow footway near the entrance to what had been the French prisons:

'Charles Jobien, Calais, 1780.'
'Morel de Calais, 1780.'
'1780. Proyol prisonnier nee natif de bourbonnaise.'

Dr J.Cameron, visiting the Castle in the 1950s, also says that the initials of some of the inmates can still be seen carved on the walls.

Edinburgh Castle was unusual in that it had no prisoner of war market place in the sense which just about all other land depots enjoyed. They were, however encouraged to exercise any profitable talent they possessed. There were small sheds and workshops in the airing yard where prisoners could practise their often amazing skills during the day, before being returned to their dungeons at sunset. There was just enough space between the bars of the palisades for the craftsmen to pass their handiwork through to the buying public in return for cash – and, if the records of other depots are a guide, it is probable that some prisoner of war work may have been sold on commission in the city by guards or even depot officers. As in all other depots, the most popular labour for the semi-skilled was the manufacture of straw-plait for bonnet-making – until later when the craft was banned. The 'upper class' of prisoner of war workers were the bone-model makers, and the straw marquetry artists, but there was a market for every type of skill – legal and illegal. The first Castle-produced forgery of a Scottish guinea banknote made its appearance in 1811!

As the Seven Years' War progressed, so did the number of prisoners. Many of them arrived at Edinburgh in a sorry state, as one sympathetic Scot complained in a letter to the *Edinburgh Evening Courant* late in 1759. He said he had 'lately beheld some hundreds of French prisoners, many of them about naked (some of them without any other clothing but shirts and breeches, and even these in rags), conducted along the High Street to the Castle.' The writer added that many of the public who saw this pathetic sight were moved to tears, and he appealed for contributions of clothing to assist them in their distress. He concluded: 'It is not necessary to urge the topics that enforce compassion to prisoners of war. These will readily recur to every generous mind :- *Homo sum, humani nihil a me alienum puto!* Hast thou a human heart! 'Tis written there. No human woe is foreign to thy care.'

Similar reports of destitute and half-naked prisoners are to be found in the histories of all the depots and, sad as they may be, they can usually be traced to the prisoner of war addiction to gambling. However, for prisoners to *arrive* in that condition, calls for a different explanation. It was a common practice, particularly in the case of privateers, for the crews of the capturing vessel to claim the clothes, and many of the possessions, of the defeated enemy, except for the clothes they stood in at the time of capture – not that the prisoner would have got away with it if he wore his best suit into battle!

The publication of the letter brought about a variety of responses mostly showing concern for our unfortunate captives. At that time in 1759, the Castle vaults held 362 prisoners, eight of them officers, and a visit revealed that many of the other-ranks were desperately short of clothing and generally in a 'miserable condition', which was likely to worsen with the approach of winter.

There was an immediate and favourable response from the citizens of Edinburgh. A subscription book was opened, and the requirements listed: of the 362, 'no fewer than 238 had no shirts, and 108 possessed only one.' The shirt shortage was soon taken care of, when the 'City Hospitals for Young Maidens' offered to make the shirts at a cost of twopence a time – and 'sundry tailors to make a certain number of jackets and breeches for nothing'.

The appeal played on the heart- and purse-strings of many generous Scots – so many that, before the year was out, the committee controlling the relief-fund announced that they had all the money they needed, and a few months later the fund was wound up.

This does not mean that no Scot at that time could be accused of canniness when it came to generosity. There were among them 'revilers' of the charity, who thought that the public were being duped and imposed upon; that the ill-clothed were 'idle fellows', who sold or cut up their old clothes, shoes and hammocks, hoping that the charity would replace them with new.

When the Seven Years' War ended with the Treaty of Paris in 1763, there were still five hundred French prisoners confined in the various Castle dungeons; but by the spring they were preparing for their journey home, no doubt polishing up their buttons and selling off the remainders of their stocks of prisoner of war work. Early in May they were escorted in two divisions to Leith, where they embarked onto the transport vessels, and sailed for France.

Prisoner of War Depots in Scotland

We have no record of American prisoners in Edinburgh Castle during the War of Independence, which is perhaps surprising. John Paul Jones, himself a Scotsman by birth – though an American by adoption and loyalty – had cruised Scottish waters with devastating success, and had indeed 'invaded' Whitehaven. There were, however, captives taken from America's ally, the French, when John Howard visited the Castle in 1779. His report tells us that he found sixty-four prisoners in what had once been two barrack rooms, but does not mention dungeons or vaults. In one room the prisoners slept in hammocks with mattresses, whilst the other was, for some reason, fitted out with 'straw-lined boxes', or bunks, each wide enough to sleep two men. Another fourteen prisoners were under treatment in a nearby hospital building, which was reported as clean, and the medical attention superior to that in many other depots. The Agent must have been a conscientious overseer as the regulations regarding prisoners' allowances were prominently posted up in the rooms and Howard said that the provisions were good!

Edinburgh Castle again received its quota of mainly privateer French prisoners after the French Revolutionary War began in 1793. The accommodation was limited compared with many other war prisons. It is probable no more than five hundred captives occupied its vaults at any one time; between 1796 and 1801, the total number confined was 1,104.

Although Edinburgh was a war prison until the end, in 1814, its importance as such was superseded by the opening of the Penicuik prisons at Esk Mills, Valleyfield and Greenlaw and the building of the great depot at Perth.

As more and more prisoners of war flooded in to Scotland, the Castle on the Rock took on a new and important prisoner of war function. It became the headquarters and centre for the distribution of prisoners of war in Scotland. Apart from the logistics involved in directing thousands of ordinary captives, of a wide range of nationalities, to one or other of the Scottish closed depots, after 1810 between one and two thousand officers had been transferred from English parole towns in the south. These parolees had been sent north for fear of a general uprising in England. In most cases they were shipped to Leith, thence passed through the administrative sieve at the Castle and directed to one of the dozen or more border town *cautionnements*, which must have been the most pleasant of open prisons in Britain. (See PAROLE IN THE SCOTTISH BORDER TOWNS Chapter 23.)

The majority of the Edinburgh inmates were French, though Spain and Holland were to a lesser extent represented. In 1797 there were Dutch prisoners in the Castle who complained bitterly of ill-treatment and lack of clothing. There must have been some truth in their allegations, which were stated in a petition to the Transport Office, as they were later transferred to Fountainbridge.

An interesting little story of French influence over a British boy in Edinburgh Castle, echoes to some extent the story of the young George Borrow at Norman Cross. It may be remembered, that George's father was a lieutenant in the West Norfolk Militia at Norman Cross, and that, as a nine-year-old, he had spent much of his time with the prisoners. He witnessed the 'straw-plait-hunts' and their other hardships which left a deep impression on his young mind. Forty years later, when he wrote his famous book *'Lavengro',* he recalled with unpatriotic prejudice and bitterness, the treatment of our captive Frenchmen. The Scottish parallel is another father-and-son story.

When Lord Elphinstone was Governor of Edinburgh Castle, his son, Mountstuart, had virtually a free run of the prison yards. Mountstuart was much drawn to his father's exotic, though reluctant, guests and spent much of his time talking with them in their own language and learning their patriotic songs. The officers of the guard watched with impotent disgust as their Governor's son, his hair worn long in Revolutionary style strutted around the castle singing the *Marseillaise, Les Aristocrates à la Lanterne* and *Çaira*.

The difference between the two tales is, that whilst George Borrow never came to terms with his memories, Mountstuart outgrew his boyhood fascination, later becoming the 11th Lord Elphinstone and Governor General of Bombay.

It would have been almost impossible for inmates to escape from the Castle by either of the two favourite prisoner of war methods – tunnelling or climbing – but some unusual escapades did occur. In 1799, two determined prisoners obtained a sword-blade, either smuggled in by a bribed guard, or surreptitiously passed through the courtyard palisading by visiting friends. This blade they transformed into a toothed saw – iron barrel-hoops had likewise been converted on the hulks – and with this tool they painstakingly sawed through the bars of their dungeon.

Once outside, they were aided by an unlikely accomplice, the Revd FitzSimmons, Minister of the Episcopal Chapel in the Cowgate. FitzSimmons first hid them in his home, then arranged for a Newhaven fishing boat to take them to the Isle of Inchkeith and thence to France. The Minister was brought before the High Court of Judiciary, on a charge of aiding the four fugitives in their escape. He was extremely lucky to receive a sentence of a mere three months in the Tolbooth.

In that same year, an individual attempt took place, which required a different sort of ingenuity, and some fortitude. A French prisoner had carefully noted the time at which the prison dung-cart was due to arrive in the airing yard, to make ready to discharge its contents over the wall. Just before its arrival he had himself concealed in the hand-barrow which conveyed the dung to the top of the wall, and was covered with manure. He was duly wheeled off and tipped over – but the noise of his heavy crash landing alerted the guard. Before he could hide, he was surrounded by sentinels with muskets trained on him. Bruised, terrified and malodorous, he stayed on his knees until the guards arrived to conduct him to the *Cachot.*

Another 'dung-cart' story is told of Valleyfield. The prisoner involved had bribed the carter who visited the depot each morning to collect the horse-droppings. It was arranged that the prisoner should conceal himself in the cart, covered beneath a mound of manure as they passed the sentries. The field where the muck-spreading took place was on the outskirts of the village, and once there the absconder was to depart on the next stage of his adventure. All started well; the cart passed through the gate, passed the first, second and third sentries, and was close to where the Free Church manse now stands, when a friend of the carter hailed him in a loud voice. The cart pulled up, and the poor prisoner, thinking that this was the signal, jumped out, and was shot down before he had gone many yards.

The most spectacular escape attempt in the Castle's history, took place in 1811. Forty-nine prisoners contrived to get out by cutting through the bottom of the parapet wall at the south-west corner, below the Devil's Elbow. This daredevil and dangerous plan involved letting themselves down by a rope made up from short lengths, smuggled in bit by bit over a period of weeks. They restored the rope reliably enough, but one poor fellow lost his grip and crashed to his death on the Castle Rock. 'Five were retaken the next day, and fourteen got away along the Glasgow Road. Some were retaken later near Linlithgow in the Polmouth plantations, exhausted with hunger' [they had lived on raw turnips for three days]. Their plan had been to make for Grangemouth, where there was a good chance that they might pick up a smuggler-escape-agent, who would ferry them to France. Six of the fugitives had stolen a small boat, sailed up the Firth and landed near Hopetown House, with the intention of then travelling overland to Port Glasgow. None profited from their heroic efforts. One man had died, and every one of the remaining forty-eight were eventually recaptured.

It is of interest to note that Robert Louis Stevenson used this thrilling true-life story of escape in his novel, *'St Ives'*, though setting it in 1813, and not 1811. Stevenson did not overstate the degree of courage needed in such an enterprise, when he had St Ives say:

'From the heel of the masonry, the rascally, breakneck precipice descended sheer amongst the wastelands, scattered suburbs of the city, and houses in the building. I had never the heart to look for any length of time – the thought that I must make the descent in person some dark night robbing me of breath; and, indeed, on anybody not a seaman or steeplejack, the mere sight of the Devil's Elbow wrought like an emetic!'

A year later, in July 1812, seven double-offending Frenchmen caused something of a stir in Edinburgh. They had been detected in the forgery of bank-notes, and had been taken from the Castle to the Tolbooth, there to await trial in a civil court. However, they did not 'await' and the story of their escape, again by rope but much shorter than that used in the descent from the Devil's Elbow, made the Scottish news-sheets. It is told in the chapter dealing with the prisoner of war forgers and coiners.

It is said that when the Peace was declared in 1814, the exulting ex-prisoners were escorted through torchlit streets lined by thousands of kindly Scots, who cheered and waved them farewell. For many Edinburgh citizens the last memory of the Castle captives would have been the fading sound of the 'Marseillaise', as they marched to the cartel ships at Leith.

---

1. J.Macbeth Forbes: *'French Prisoners of War in Scotland'*, etc. Printed in *The Gentleman's Magazine*. March, 1899.

Part Two
The Great Valleyfield Depot at Penicuik

'The new prisons added at Valleyfield were about six in number, from about 80 to 120 feet in length, chiefly of wood and of three storeys; they had no glass in the openings for light and air, which were closed at night by very strong wooden shutters, and secured by strong iron stanchions, nor were there any fireplaces or artificial heat, for it was expected that the animal heat would suffice for their comfort, the prisoners having been stowed away as close almost as herrings in a barrel.

'The prisons and level ground on which they were erected were surrounded by a strong wooden stockade or palisade, with a carriage road outside, and guarded by military – generally a regiment of militia.'

C. COWAN: *The Reminiscences of Charles Cowan, Edinburgh, 1878.*

IT IS DIFFICULT TO IMAGINE THE CHAOTIC STATE into which the prisoner of war management at Penicuik would have fallen after the unexpected demise of Esk Mills as a depot, had not the Government obtained possession of the Valleyfield Paper Mills just prior to that calamity. The property was bought on the 6th February, 1811, the purchase and conversion costing some £75,000, and every effort was made to speedily convert the existing buildings into a secure war prison. At the very beginning of the Esk Mills fiasco, the Transport Office had ordered that two additional prisons should be immediately added to the Valleyfield complex, each designed to confine one thousand two hundred captives. A fair amount of conversion work must have been well under way before the actual purchase date, for we know that the first 2,489 prisoners arrived from Esk Mills only four weeks later, on the 11th March, 1811. We also know, from the Valleyfield records, the identity of the first of those prisoners to be entered in the Depot's books. Ian MacDougall's[1] research into those records revealed that the first name on the new depot's Register was that of Thomas Paumier, a twenty year old privateer seaman. He was captured on *Le Vengeur* in October of the previous year and was described as '5 feet six inches tall, slender build, with a sallow complexion, oval face, black hair and eyes…'

The Valleyfield Paper Mills had been the property of Messrs Alexander Cowan & Sons and the home of the Cowan family until 1811.

After its purchase, the Cowans moved to Edinburgh and all the established buildings at Valleyfield, including the family home, the extensive mill buildings, stores and out-houses were quickly denuded of furnishings and machinery and were fitted out for the reception of prisoners of war. The large family house was transformed into the Prison Hospital; the gardens flattened to make room for the quite vast areas which would be required as airing yards for both the converted mill-building prisons and the new wooden prisons which were already under construction. Space had to be found for cookhouses, workshops, stores, accommodation for guards and officials and, not of least importance, the prison market.

All this activity must have brought a boom to the Scottish building industry in the locality, for construction work was not confined to the new Valleyfield Depot alone. Advertisements in the local newspapers also called for tenders for building work at the recently abandoned Esk Mills, where the largest of the buildings were to be fitted out as a Military Barracks. As a prisoner of war depot, Valleyfield was as successful as Esk Mills had been a dismal failure. Building work went on throughout the rest of the war years, and Valleyfield was eventually thought of and remembered as one of Britain's greatest repositories for the captured enemy, capable of housing more than five thousand prisoners at one time.

The total number of prisoners whose names were recorded in the five Valleyfield registers between March 1811 and June 1814, was well over seven and a half thousand. In addition to date, and name, each entry was furnished with personal details, rank or rating, town and country of origin, and how and where captured (or re-captured).

In the autumn of 1811 about 1,800 prisoners were marched or shipped in from a whole variety of places; mainly from Plymouth and Portsmouth, and some from the Border parole towns of Scotland. Among the 2,182 who were added to the Valleyfield prisoner population over the following twenty-one months, were 783 who were brought in from Greenlaw in September 1812. America had declared war on Britain in June of that year and Greenlaw was expected to be the depot designated to house a fair percentage of the large number of Americans who immediately became prisoners of war. Almost all of these would have been seamen, either from captured merchantmen or Americans serving in our Royal Navy when war broke out. The vast majority of the latter refused to fight against their country and became prisoners of war, first sent to the hulks, then later to Dartmoor – where many were still left captive for some time after the French had returned to their homeland. As it turned out, and despite all the preparations, only very few Americans were sent to Greenlaw. Towards the end of the war, quite a number of 'broke-parole' officers from the parole towns – Selkirk, Jedburgh, Kelso, Biggar, Hawick, Lauder, Peebles, etc. – were brought into Penicuik: twenty-two were recaptured escapees, 'including some from Valleyfield itself.'

The Valleyfield captives had been gathered in from the oceans and seas of the world and battles great and small in Europe and the West Indies. Many of them had experienced captivity in other prisoner of war establishments – some better, some worse – before their arrival in Scotland. For those who had been transferred from the dreaded English hulks, or had spent time in prison ships at Jamaica whilst awaiting transport to Britain, Valleyfield would have been a welcome improvement. For 'broke-paroles', who had enjoyed all the privileges of Britain's lightest form of imprisonment, the change must have been hell – although even after breaking their word of honour, most officers would have received a higher standard of accommodation and treatment than the unoffending common masses. They were of many nationalities, principally French, but with a sprinkling of Spanish, Danish, Dutch, Portuguese, etc. Before 1810, the great majority of the Penicuik captives were seamen taken whilst serving as privateers, or in the national navies or merchant marine. The captives taken after the battles of the Peninsular Wars soon began to level out the soldier-sailor equation, and of the roughly two and a half thousand who formed the first Valleyfield intake in 1811, roughly half were military men.

Charles Cowan, an extract from whose *Recollections* heads this chapter, was not the only young boy to recall his memories of Valleyfield in later years. William Chambers, who later was to become the publisher of *Chambers' Journal,* was taken by his father to nearby Penicuik to see the great Depot, which was only a few miles from their home in Peebles. Decades later, he set down his clear recollection of that visit:

> 'Here on a level space in the depth of a valley, was a group of barracks, surrounded by tall palisades, for the accommodation of some hundreds of prisoners, who, night and day, were strictly watched by armed sentries, ready to fire on them in the event of outbreak. The day on which we happened to make our visit was a Sunday, and the scene presented was accordingly the more startling. Standing in the churchyard on the brink of the hollow, all the immediate surroundings betokened the solemnity of a Scottish Sabbath. The shops in the village were shut. From the church was heard the voice of the preacher. Looking down from the height on the hive of living beings, there was not among them a vestige of the ordinary calm of Sunday – only Dimanche! Dressed in coarse woollen clothing of a yellow colour, and most of them wearing red or blue cloth caps, or particoloured cowls, the prisoners were engaged in a variety of amusements and occupations.
>
> 'Prominently, and forming the centre of attraction were a considerable number ranked up in two rows, joyously dancing to the sound of a fiddle, which was briskly played by a man who stood on top of a barrel. Others were superintending cookery in big pots over open fires, which they fanned by the flapping of cocked hats. Others were fencing with sticks amidst a circle of eager onlookers. A few men were seated meditatively on benches, perhaps thinking of far distant homes, or the fortune of war. which had brought them into this painful predicament. In twos or threes, some were walking apart to and fro, and I conjectured they were of a slightly superior class. Near one corner was a booth – a rickety concern of boards – seemingly a kind of restaurant, with the pretentious inscription, *'CAFÉ DE PARIS',* over the door, and a small tricolor flag was fluttering from a slender pole on the roof. To complete the picture fancy several of the prisoners, no doubt the more ingenious among them, stationed at small wickets, openings with hinges in the tall palisades, offering for sale articles, such as snuff boxes of bone, that they had been allowed to manufacture, and the money got by which sales provided them a few luxuries.'

Chambers recalled prisoners selling their artefacts through wicket openings in the palisades. This does not mean that Valleyfield did not have a main and bustling market place on certain days of the week. There the Scottish merchants would do profitable business with the trustee prisoners who bought wholesale to stock the retail stalls in the inner markets. There, too, trustee stall-holders sold the often brilliant offerings of talented prisoner of war work craftsmen. However, it should be remembered that young William Chambers was making his observations on a Scottish Sunday, when it is hardly likely that all the high jinks and liveliness of the open market would have been encouraged on the holy day.

Escapes and attempted getaways were as frequent at Valleyfield as at every other depot in Britain and a number were successful. Some were copy-cat exploits, where news of original techniques had passed through the grapevine from depot to depot. The story of one such attempt – an 'escape by dung-cart' – from Valleyfield, has already been related in the chapter on Edinburgh Castle, where the same ruse had been tried at least once. A similar, but less smelly, attempt was made by three prisoners who had designed and manufactured a false bottom to the prison dust-cart. They got clear of the Depot, but were spotted by a soldier who accosted them; but as the odds were three to one against him and he was unarmed, he decided that discretion was the better part of valour and let them go. Like so many of these stories which cannot but inspire some sympathy for courageous men amongst our enemy captives, this one ended with their recapture a short time afterwards. Valleyfield was probably as labyrinthine as elsewhere, with tunnellers continually digging beneath the prisons and yards, their above-ground accomplices trying all manner of means to get rid of the displaced soil. Some were quite ingenious, but the usual method was for numbers of helpers to carry it about their persons, secretly tipping it out a pocketful at a time, and treading it in as they walked the exercise yards. This was the method used in one large scale tunnelling enterprise, which may have led to a mass exodus had it been successful. Literally tons of earth must have been removed and sent to the surface by shifts of prisoner miners who had completed a tunnel three hundred feet long. It was begun in one of the converted old brick-built Cowan buildings and then went under the airing ground to one of the new wooden *casernes* then under construction – this would have been early in the Depot's history, at the end of 1811 or the beginning of 1812. From the new prison, the tunnel went under the adjoining yard and beyond its surrounding stockade. Such a massive effort deserved some success, or at least a glorious end; certainly not a ludicrous conclusion. The man who was chosen to be the first up and away mistook the time of the day and, instead of emerging under cover of darkness broke surface in broad daylight!

Many of the stories of attempts and getaways are too similar to ones already told to merit repetition; but one escape-related tale is amusing enough to end with. The Depot guard included members of the Ayr and Kirkcudbright Militia, who were encamped at the top of a hill near Kirkhill Village. Answering one particular call to arms on hearing the alarm call which told that prisoners were escaping from Valleyfield, the guards acted with perhaps too much alacrity. Rushing into action, they dashed towards the Depot with their horse-drawn artillery, but the hill was too steep. Unable to slow down their headlong careering, men, horses, big guns and carriages, all ended up in the river!

There is more than enough evidence to lead us to believe the probability that there were at least some women inmates in most of Britain's prisoner of war depots and, improbable as it may seem, even on the prison hulks. A very few may have been captured after following their men into battle, but most would have been officers' womenfolk or passengers on captured merchant ships, who, though quartered in the prisons for a relatively short time, were soon repatriated or granted parole. However there were others who had not been captured but came to Britain voluntarily to share their husband's period of captivity. The great majority of the latter were the wives of officers confined to one or other of the many parole towns in England, Wales and Scotland.

After 1803, there were many British women in Verdun, among the *détenus* unfairly taken hostage by Napoleon at the resumption of hostilities in that year; and some others later crossed the Channel to be with their captive loved ones. (See Chapter 21 – PAROLE D'HONNEUR) Both Britain and France granted some sort of maintenance allowance to these loyal ladies, whether voluntary prisoners or not.

More than one source can be called upon which mentions women prisoners in Britain. In his memoirs the renowned escaper, Tom Souville, says that when a prisoner on the *Crown* prison ship at Portsmouth in 1797, there were French women on the hulk, *'de basse extraction et extrêmement grossières'*. Also, Francis Abell, in his chapter on international recriminations, cites a complaint from France as to our terrible treatment of prisoners of war generally. This was delivered in 1798, at a time when, for good reason, we had temporarily cancelled the privilege of parole. It read, in part: 'There is now no parole for officers, All are pell-mell together, of all ranks *and of both sexes.* A woman was delivered of a child, she was left forty-eight hours without attention, and even a glass of water was denied her.' There was no doubt some exaggeration in that complaint but a Board of Inspection examination of the Plymouth based Hospital Ship *Renown*, in February 1814, revealed an abominable state of affairs on board:

> 'Fever and dysentery have been the prevalent complaints among the prisoners from Pampelune, whose deplorable state the Board of Inspectors are in full possession of. Among these were some forty women "in so wretched a state that they were wholly destitute of the appropriate dress of their sex." Two of the British officers' wives collected money for the poor creatures and clothed them.'[2]

A couple of references to women captives in Portchester, may come as a welcome relief from such tales of hardship and misery. The first tells of a French girl whose sailor boyfriend had been captured by a British warship and was sent to the Portchester Castle Depot. Distraught, she joined the crew of a French privateer dressed as man, thinking that if her vessel too was captured she would at least be in the same country as her lover. It was captured, and somehow, perhaps by coincidence, she too ended up in Portchester Castle. 'For some months she lived there without revealing her sex, until she was taken ill, and sent to the hospital, where, of course, her secret was soon discovered. She was persuaded to return to France on the distinct promise that her lover should be speedily exchanged.'

There are numerous instances of French prisoners of war – and captives of other nationalities – marrying British girls; but the Portchester Church register records a much rarer happening, showing as it does that an English gentleman married a French prisoner of war! A number of French lady passengers were among the prisoners taken by a British cruiser from a vessel on its way to the then French possession of Mauritius. They were all sent to Portchester, the crew to the Castle, the females billeted as parolees with local families, 'and being young and comely, were largely entertained and fêted by the gentry of the neighbourhood'. One of these comely lasses was Josephine Desperoux, whose name entered the register when she married an English squire, Patrick

Bisson, in Portchester Church in 1812.

There is no lack of evidence of women in the Scottish depots and parole towns. George Penny, in his *Traditions of Perth,* says that there were some women among the four hundred prisoners who came up from Plymouth via Dundee, and were the first to enter the new Perth Depot in August 1812. The *Edinburgh Evening Courant* for the 26th August, 1811 reported: 'This morning a number of prisoners of war were brought from Leith and marched to Penicuik. There were four women with them.' And Macbeth Forbes wrote: 'Several women, the wives of prisoners, arrived from time to time at Valleyfield and they used to go to Edinburgh and offer the knick-knacks made by their husbands to likely buyers.'

Ian MacDougall's delving into Admiralty and Transport Board records revealed a number of interesting references to women prisoners in Scotland:

> 'The Transport Board instructed Malcolm Wright, agent for Greenlaw, on 6 June 1808, "You will transmit to us a List of all the women and children in your Custody, stating the allowance of provisions they respectively receive from Government and the dates of our orders for making those allowances, and also their ages and whether any of them be Englishwomen or the children of Englishmen." …In January 1812, Captain Moriarty, R.N., agent at Valleyfield, was told by the Transport Board, "We have received your letter of the 11th Instant and direct you to state who the Woman is, you mention to have accompanied the Prisoners from the *Zealous*; and to which of the Prisoner she belongs." When the Board received Moriarty's reply, they told him: "…the Woman therein mentioned is to be Victualled while she remains; but she may proceed when she pleases to France." Three months later the Board again wrote to Moriarty; " …the Agent for Parole Prisoners at Biggar having stated that Catherine Didon, wife of a Prisoner named Louis Didon at Valleyfield, intends to reside at Biggar, you will state whether this Woman be a Frenchwoman and if so by what Authority she resides in Scotland." And on the 4th May the Board instructed Moriarty "to send the Woman Catherine Diedont [*sic*] to Portsmouth by the return of H.M.S *Regulus* to be delivered into the charge of Captain Woodriff, Agent for the prisoners of war at that port."
>
> 'In August 1813 the Board told Lieutenant Glinn, Admiralty agent at Leith, that when unfit and disabled prisoners were sent from depots and parole towns in Scotland to the Nore for repatriation to France, "Women and boys under 12 years of age are to be allowed to embark with the prisoners." '

A Mr M'Rae, Chaplain to the Canadian forces in France during the First World War, said that whilst visiting some French families after that war had ended, he met an old French lady who was interested by the fact that he came from Scotland and from Edinburgh. She told him that her grandfather had been an officer in Napoleon's army, had been captured and sent to Penicuik. 'He was then a young man and newly married. When his wife got the particulars she sailed to Scotland and joined him there. They lived in lodgings in a house with pillars each side of the door, and there her mother was born.' When she was young the old lady had visited Penicuik and had tea in that house where her mother was born.[3]

When the war ended, the Valleyfield property was put up for sale, but despite advertisements and several failed auctions, years went by without a serious offer. Then, in 1820, Cowan repurchased it for £2,200, and the family moved back into Valleyfield House which, for more than three years had been the Prison Hospital.

Charles Cowan – an extract from whose *'Reminiscences'* heads this chapter – had been a ten year old lad when his father sold the home and paper mills. He lived until his eighty-ninth year; but it must have been another member of the family who showed Francis Abell round what remained of Valleyfield Depot at the turn of the new century. There was however but little to be seen, as the last of the original *casernes*, or prison blocks, had been demolished a few years earlier in 1897. For many years it had been used as a rag store, rag being an important commodity in the paper-making industry; blotting paper and some of the better quality writing papers were made almost exclusively from cotton fibres retrieved from recycled rags.

Abell noted traces of the building which showed it to have been three hundred feet long, with walls 'eleven feet six inches thick [?]'. If that wall measurement was not a printer's error, it cannot be thought of as an escape deterrent, but may be explained by the fact that in the days before its conversion into a depot, the paper-making business had required great quantities of water, and a waterway had originally run through the centre of the Mills. This stream was later diverted so as to encircle the periphery of the establishment, thus providing an additional discouragement to would-be escapers.

Some years after the Cowan family returned to their old home at Valleyfield, Alexander Cowan decided to erect a monument to the memory of those foreign captives who were destined never to return to their homeland, but would remain forever in land which he had sold to the Government in 1811. It was sited in the hillside gardens of Valleyfield House, and was unveiled on the 26th June, 1830. The inscriptions, in English and French, read:

> **'The mortal remains of 309 prisoners of war who died in this neighbourhood between 21st March, 1811, and 26th July, 1814, are interred near this spot.**
>
> *Grata Quies Patria sed et Omnis Terra Sepulcrum.*[4]
>
> **Certain inhabitants of this parish, desiring to remember that all men are brethren, caused this monument to be erected in the year 1830.'**

And on the reverse side:

> **'Près de ce Lieu reposent les cendres de 309 Prisonniers de Guerre morts dans ce voisinage entre le 21 Mars 1811 et le 26 Juillet 1814. Nés pour bémir les vœux de vieillissantes mères par le sort appelés à devenir amants, aimés époux et pères.**
> **Ils sont morts exilés. Plusieurs Habitants de cette Paroisse, aimant à croire que tous les Hommes sont Frères, firentè élever ce monument l'an 1830.'**

MONUMENT AT VALLEYFIELD TO PRISONERS OF WAR.

Postscript.

During the almost three and a half years of the Depot's existence the mortality rate was very low. From all causes – disease, accidents, duels, fights, and those who lost their lives whilst attempting to escape – the total was only 309.

As we began these notes on Valleyfield Depot with the name and a few facts regarding the Depot's first unwilling guest, it is appropriate to end it with similar details of the holder of the last name on the fifth and last Register. Prisoner No. 7,659, Jean Baptiste Destrais, was a seaman captured whilst serving on the frigate *L'Amphitrite*, off Martinique in February, 1809. He had spent some time in Edinburgh Jail, 'where he had been confined for stabbing a soldier' during an attempt the previous year, 1813, to escape from Penicuik. Destrais entered Valleyfield on the 14th June, 1814 and was freed the next day 'as part of the general release of all prisoners, the war having ended two months earlier.'

1. Ian MacDougall. *The Prisoners of Penicuik.*

2. It is to be doubted that their condition came about through neglect in the hospital ship. A great number of prisoners arrived in Britain after long nightmare voyages from their place of capture, in transport vessels or the holds of men-of-war.

3. Told by J.L.Black, early 20th century local historian, and quoted by I. MacDougall.

4. This Latin quotation is from the poet Saumazarius and was suggested by Sir Walter Scott.

Part Three
Perth Depot, Perthshire

THE PRINCIPAL SOURCES OF INFORMATION concerning the great Depot for prisoners of war at Perth, are George Penny's *'Traditions of Perth'*, published in 1835, when memories of its construction and occupants were still fairly fresh, and William Sievwright's detailed study, published in 1894, under the lengthy title of, *'Historical Sketch of the old Dépôt or Prison for French Prisoners of War at Perth.'*

Although the introduction of a war prison usually brought prosperity to the chosen part of the country, not every Perthshireman was enamoured at the prospect of a massive repository for prisoners of war in his locality; and there was considerable opposition to the proposed site if they had to have one.

In the early 1800s, Perth was in need of a replacement for its ancient and crumbling civic Town Jail, which stood at the end of the High Street, and the Council had its eye on a controversial substitute. In 1809, when the need for large prisoner of war depots was becoming desperate, a rather devious deal between the Government and the local council, gave the nation a new prisoner of war Depot and Perth its new Town Jail.

After the '45 Rebellion, Perth Town Council had made a magnificent presentation to William, Duke of Cumberland[1], to celebrate his victory at Culloden. It was in fact the centuries-old Gowrie House, at Perth. Showing little appreciation of this generous gift, the Duke soon sold the historic buildings to the Government; and it was this stately home which the Council visualised as the site for its new civil Jail and a County Hall.

Determined to achieve their end, the Council purchased a number of acres of land from the Moncrieff family, and this they offered to the Government in exchange for Gowrie House and its lands. So the Government now had a site for the great Perth Depot, and the Council for their civil Jail.

After the exchange, sometime in 1810, both parties got quickly down to work. The Depot was started in the following year, and progressed at great speed and at great expense – the total building costs amounting to £130,000. However, at this time of Government construction, the Council was occupied with a work of destruction. They first, by means of 'shameless jobbery', unnecessarily condemned Gowrie House as unsafe, then proceeded to demolish it. George Penny condemned 'the whole transaction', as 'one of the most shameful ever done in Perth', regretting that a paltry jail now replaced the 'venerable pile which formed one of the principal ornaments of Perth.'

Work on the Depot was begun in the autumn of 1811 and carried on through the severe winter which followed. Some 1,500 men were employed on the site, and fires were kept burning throughout the coldest months to thaw the lime and keep the mortar from freezing. Kingoody and several other stone quarries were opened up, roads built and great numbers of horses and wagons employed to deliver the cut stone to the site, where it was covered with layers of straw to protect it from frost. Incredibly, by August 1812, one part of the Depot was so far advanced as to be able to open its gates to its first 400 unwilling guests, and by the end of the year it was virtually completed.

The great Perth Depot, including its yards occupied between nine and ten acres of land; stretching about 600 feet along the Great North Road, then 700 feet eastward, to the banks of the River Tay. A view of the site from the air would have revealed a hexagon with three equal sides to the east, the elongated northern and southern sides stretching westwards towards the 600-feet-long western wall. It was built of flint-like whinstone, a hard basaltic rock, and Sievwright says that the original structures were reckoned architecturally to be the finest of their kind in Scotland.

The establishment comprised five main prison buildings, each three storeys high, 130 feet in length and an internal width of 30 feet, with external open stairways at either end of each building. Each of these prisons had its own airing yard, fenced-in with high iron palisading; and these five yards converged onto a common central square, itself separated from the yards by tall iron railings. This great square was the most important and memorable spot in the life of all prisoners of war – the Depot Market Place. It was the captives' only real contact with the outside world; where they might gain at least some idea of British civilian life, through visual or direct contact with some of the many thousands of men and women of all classes who had visited the daily market.

Perth Depot, with its vast captive population, its spacious yards and large market square, was a fascinating and colourful attraction, not only for the local citizens, but for visitors from all over Scotland. The uniforms of the regular soldiers and militia regiments which guarded the Depot, the cocktail of prisoner of war costume, from Transport Office issued garments and odds and ends of continental regimentals, to the well-cut suits, ruffles and cockaded hats of *'Les Lords'*.

All this would have provided a good-natured entertainment for the visitors and excellent business for both the Scottish market traders and the 'trustee' prisoner of war stall-holders, who displayed their delightful wares on stands around the periphery of the market square. Some of those artefacts are still to be seen in Scottish museums – although some of those pieces once on display would seem to be, at least temporarily, 'lost'.

Dr J. Cameron[2], writing as recently as 1985, mentioned several articles on display at the Scottish Prison Service College Museum at Polmont, including 'a figure of a girl curiously carved out of coal, a handsome pewter box and a long-stemmed pewter pipe with a minute bowl. Naturally keen to view these items I contacted Polmont, only to discover that the museum itself no longer exists. Subsequent enquiries at Inverary, Edinburgh and elsewhere have failed to track down the subterranean store room where they may now lie. However, one of the most interesting of the Depot relics is preserved in Perth Museum. This is a small volume of reminiscences written by a French prisoner of war at Perth. Its descriptive label speaks for itself:

'THE SELECTOR containing a Variety of Interesting Facts, Pleasing Anecdotes and Biographical Sketches. Perth, 1811.(?) Superscription: "Written by a Bombardier in Perth for the support of his family, disposed of by raffle and gained by Alexander Pitcairn who now presents it to his niece, Charlotte Pitcairn 21st February 1811." '

In the centre of the Market Place was a lofty multi-storeyed observation tower complete with flag-staff and guard rooms. In the basement were some grim dark cells, which were the Perth punishment *cachots* or Black Holes.

There were two other smaller prison buildings with individual airing grounds, and sundry official dwellings, also offices, stables, prison kitchens, bake-house, wash-houses, store-rooms, etc. The two first mentioned, were substantial two-storey structures, one on the southern and one on the northern sides of the square. Both were known as hospitals, but Peacock, in *'Annals and Archives of Perth'*, says that a large part of the southern 'hospital' was a petty-officer prison, 'which contained 1,100 inmates'. Another subdivision of one of those buildings housed officers who had broken their *Parole d'honneur*.

Within the two outer walls of the Depot, a moat, ten feet wide and very deep, encircled the prisons and yards as a security measure, but was 'chiefly valuable for sanitary purposes'(!). Beyond the moat was another deterrent against escape, the high iron palisades of the Inner Wall. A spacious courtyard lay between this and the massive stone Outer Wall, a remarkable structure, about twelve and a half feet in height and posted with lamps every few yards. A view from the outside would have revealed thirty great inverted triangular recesses each fitted with stairways, up which the sentinels climbed to military walks just below the very top of the wall, vantage points from which the sentries could observe just about everything which was happening within the Depot.

The Perth Courier. 9th July 1812

'The Depot forms altogether the greatest establishment of the kind in Britain... the ingenious and unusual mode adopted for ventilating, and introducing fresh air into the different prison buildings, and other means for ensuring the health and cleanliness of the prisoners and the secure manner in which every part of it is constructed, it is certainly the most complete Depot or Place of Confinement which has yet been erected...While it is to be deplored that the necessity of such establishments exists, it is at the same time satisfactory, and creditable to the country, also that such accommodation is provided for our prisoners as admits of enjoying every comfort and convenience, consistent with their unfortunate situation.'

'Enjoying every comfort'!... It is difficult to imagine the cramped sleeping accommodation available to six or seven thousand captives, being comfortable or in any way enjoyable. Francis Abell quoted William Sievwright as saying that their night quarters at Perth were so crowded that they had to sleep 'spoon fashion'; this latter statement, however, is questionable.

In all my reading and research, I have only encountered such a method of fitting men into inadequate sleeping space, where reference was being made to the down-and-out lowest ranks of prisoner of war society, *Les Raffelès* on the prison hulks, and *Les Romains,* or 'the Romans', in Dartmoor and their equivalents in other land depots. The Baron de Bonnefoux, on the *Bahama* hulk at Chatham, described how the half-naked *Raffelès* slept, close-packed, spoon-fashion, side by side on deck; how, at midnight, one of their number would give the order, *'Par le flanc droit!'* and all would roll over on to their right sides. Half way through the night came the call *'Pare à virer!'* – 'Prepare to tack!' – and they rolled to the left.

There are a number of memoirs which mention 'spoon-fashion' sleeping in the cocklofts of Dartmoor. L. Catel, an ex-prisoner of the Depot on the Moor, in his *'La Prison de Dartmoor, 1809–1814'*, wrote of as many as five hundred 'Romans' sleeping naked on the cold stone upper floors of the prison, areas which they referred to with pride as their *'Capitole'*. However, in every case, only the dregs of the depots were ever described as existing in such an extreme of nocturnal discomfort – never where men had maintained possession of their hammocks. Therefore, doubting that such conditions were ever the norm at Perth, I went back to the source of Abell's quote – William Sievwright.

Sievwright had, indeed, found it difficult to figure out how some 380 men might have arranged their dormitory accommodation on each of the three floors (measuring 130 x 30 feet) of the five buildings; and despite having made some mathematical conjectures as to the possible positioning of hammocks, he had certainly not reached a categorical conclusion. He said, 'I *fancy*[3] there must have been some resemblance' to the American prisoners at Libby, who were obliged 'to lie spoon fashion', in their 'hard hammocks', and had '*possibly*[3] got the word of command..."Attention! Squad number four! Prepare to spoon! One – two – spoon!!"' Had he chanced upon the memoirs of the French Colonel Lebertre, a 'broke-parole' on the *Brunswick* prison ship at Chatham, he would have learned how an even greater number of prisoners spent their nights in a space similar to, but less convenient than, a single floor at Perth.

The orlop deck of the *Brunswick* was 125 feet in length, and 40 feet at its widest, and narrower fore and aft. The height was only 4 feet 10 inches, so only boys or very short men could pass through it without stooping. Yet within this claustrophobic accommodation, 431 prisoners slung their hammocks each night. At the time of Colonel Leberte's observations, the French prisoners on the hulk numbered 460, so 29 had to sleep on the deck beneath their suspended hulkmates! So the orlop deck of the *Brunswick* – which was generally regarded as one of the 'better' prison hulks – had to find room for eighty more sleepers than one of the storeys at Perth, where the superior height in the latter would have allowed for several additional tiers of hammocks.

Perth Depot may have had its share of deadbeats, who slept as best and wherever they could – and it is possible that some well-planned dormitory arrangements adopted space-saving 'head-to-tail' and other layouts. However, having slept in hammocks for a number of years, I cannot see the advantage of being told when to turn one way or another!

The 'ingenious and unusual mode' of ventilation, mentioned in the *Perth Courier* article, was an important contribution towards Perth's reputation as the healthiest prisoner of war depot in the whole of Britain. The Medical Report for July 1813, when the Depot was nearing its maximum of 7,000 captives, states that only twenty-four prisoners were on the sick-list, and only four of these were in-patients. Over the following months the reported numbers were lower still and in February 1814, not one of the hospital beds was occupied! The figures in these reports must have been confined to cases of illness and disease. It would be quite unbelievable that, with seven thousand men packed into a few acres, there would not have been cuts, bruises, and broken bones, resulting from fights, accidents and escape attempts.

Escorted by a company of the Durham and Fifeshire Militia, the first contingent of French prisoners passed through the gates of the almost-completed Depot, in August 1812. George Penny, who may well have been an eyewitness to the event, wrote in his *'Traditions of Perth'*:

> 'The first division that arrived, consisting of 400 men, were landed from a frigate [the *Matilda*] in the Tay at Dundee, and marched up through the Carse. Never was there such a turnout in Perth, as there was to witness this novel sight. On their way from Dundee, they were lodged for the night in the church at Inchture. During the night they found means to extract the brass nails, and to purloin the green cloth from the pulpit and seats, with every other thing they could lay their hands on. This division were in pretty good condition, and had some women with them.'

One of the sacrilegious Frenchmen who looted the Inchture church went a step too far and stole a couple of 'mort cloths'. This offence disgusted his fellow prisoners who organised an impromptu court marshal, which sentenced him to twenty-four lashes. He suffered seventeen stripes before passing out – but once recovered, received the balance of his punishment.

The inhabitants of Perth experienced more than just excited curiosity at the prospect of thousands of war prisoners being concentrated so near their homes. There was a good deal of alarm at the possibility of breakouts and even uprisings, however well the Depot was guarded. The fact that four regiments were to be quartered in the neighbourhood, and some three hundred men would be mounting guard each day, may have been reassuring security-wise; but there was genuine concern that, with the population being increased by their presence, prices would inevitably rise and provisions become scarce. Their worries proved groundless. Many local businesses, both small and large, profited by supplying in bulk to the daily Depot Market Place, or by dealing with individual prisoners through the palisades.

Many of the bigger operators, the producers of all manner of foodstuffs for contractors to supply the Depot, were in on a get-rich-quick market. Particularly successful were the speculators who planted out many acres of potatoes in the vicinity of the prison. With the departure of seven thousand of their daily customers, in 1814, the potato farmers faced ruin, but almost immediately their output was taken up by the London market. So Scottish potatoes, originally planted for the French consumer, were sent south to the English – and Perth became an important potato producer well into the next century and, indeed, to this day.

The first four hundred French prisoners to enter Perth in August had arrived in a fair state of health, but of the great numbers which were marched in over the following winter, many were in a pitiable condition. Most had been taken after Wellington's victory at the Battle of Salamanca on the 22nd of July, 1812. They were landed in the Firth of Forth, and George Penny, once again writing as a personal observer, said they were marched through Fife, 'the weather was dreadfully wet, and the roads bad. The poor creatures, many of them half-naked, were in a miserable plight; numbers of them gave up on the way and were thrown into carts, one above the other; and when the carts were capable of holding no more, others were tied to the back with ropes and dragged along.'

Perth Depot had been officially opened on the 10th September, 1812, and, according to a local newspaper report, by the 4th December, 4,620 French prisoners of war had already been lodged in the new war prison. With prisoners flooding in from the Peninsular, the Depot was soon nearing its full capacity, the official figure for the 21st January, 1813 was 6,788.

Although it was one of the very few custom-built war prisons, its design based on three-quarters of a century of experience in the inexact art and science of warrior incarceration, it was not escape-proof. Within thirty days of its opening a prisoner, 'genteelly dressed' in a black civilian suit, duped the turnkey and walked out through the gate. He deserved better luck, but had got no farther than Friarton Toll, less than a mile away, when the alarm was raised and he was marched back to short rations and a spell in the *cachot*. There were other small-scale attempted escapes during the last few months of 1812, but few were free for long.

Sievwright recorded a number of these escapades, including a couple of successes. One was achieved by a dedicated absconder named Petite, who made his first breakout at the end of that year. He made for the coast, and was recaptured at Montrose, some fifty miles away. There he was lodged in 'secure' accommodation, before the long march back to Perth, but overnight he managed to unscrew the locks from three doors, and was once again on the run. He then struck inland, but was again captured, this time at Ruthven; from whence he was taken to the punishment cells under the tower at Perth. Not long afterwards, it was decided to transfer him, under strong guard, to Valleyfield Depot at Penicuik, which, until the building of the depot at Perth, had been Scotland's largest war prison. A sergeant and eight men escorted their now notorious prisoner without trouble as far as their first stop-over point, Kirkcaldy, where Petite was locked into a cell in the local gaol. Next morning the inefficient sergeant and escort found what they should have foreseen and guarded against – an empty cell, and that was the last that we hear of the elusive Frenchman.

Sometime early in January 1813, three prisoners celebrated the new year by getting clear of the Depot. Exactly when and by what means they had made their exit, was never discovered. There was strong suspicion that bribery and depot guards were involved; and a Court of Enquiry held on the 21st, subjected sentinels and other possible conspirators to close examination. Later information revealed that the three had made their escape at a time when Perth was enveloped in a thick fog, which enabled them to get undetected to Broughty Ferry, on the Forth. On the way they stopped for a meal at Dundee, and a little further on they entered a shop to stock up with provisions, buying up all the bread on offer, and 'presented a leathern bottle to be filled with spirits'.

At nine o'clock, on the evening of the 21st January – the day when the Official Enquiry was delving into their disappearance back at Perth – the nerveless trio boarded and took possession of a sloop, the *Nancy*, belonging to a local merchant, Mr Grubbs, weighed anchor and were soon homeward bound.

Morning, however, disclosed the secrets of the night, and it was discovered that the good ship *Nancy* had become the unlawful prize of an enemy. The vessel was fifteen tons burthen, and provisioned for ten days. It contained a quantity of oatmeal, salt, etc. It was suspected that the prisoners had been assisted in their escape by persons who had given them information regarding the means they adopted.

The exhaustive Official Enquiry met with some success; two Renfrewshire Militiamen and a women were arrested on suspicion and held for trial and a contemporary newspaper account takes the story one step farther. The report began:

'On Monday morning (9th February, 1813) about 8 o'clock, the jailer [of Perth Jail] having gone into the prison, unaccompanied by any of the town officers, and having released the prisoners from their cells [presumably as part of some routine practice], was suddenly knocked down from behind, and dreadfully bruised on the head with a bottle.'

As he lay unconscious, the jailer's keys were taken from his pocket and he was dragged to a cell and locked in. Later, when his cries drew attention to his plight, it was found that four men had flown the coop: one a soldier confined for desertion, but a fifth man, one of the two Renfrewshire militiamen thought to be involved in the *Nancy* affair, though freed from his cell, was still there. When asked why he had not run with the others, he said with some dignity, that he had declined to do so as he was innocent of the charges brought against him!

That most escapes depended on the co-operation of civilian or military assistance is proved by a number of instances where loyal guards accepted the bribe but reported the proposition to the Depot authorities. In most cases, this led to a rather cruel cat-and-mouse game. In a typical example, the military 'conspirators' were instructed to play along with the freedom-seekers until the last moment. The turnkeys were ordered to be lax in their counting that evening, when all prisoners were locked up for the night. About one and a half hours later, just before the fixed time of departure, a patrol marched to an out-building where they knew they would find seven disillusioned would-be escapers. The poor fellows had been well prepared for what they imagined would be a glorious journey home. A search revealed carefully made scaling-ladders and all manner of escape accessories – and cash aplenty: 'twenty-nine pieces of foreign gold coin and a considerable sum in Bank notes' and 'an excellent gold watch'. The money and watch were taken from them; but, with a not unusual fairness (see Chapters 2 and 3, *The Arts and Crafts of Napoleonic and American Prisoners of War 1756-1816*, THE DEPOT AND INNER MARKETS), their wealth was restored to them in small amounts over a long period.

In some other cases the military cat allowed the prisoner mice to get even farther before it pounced. On the 5th May, 1813, six prisoners, who thought they had bought the aid of a trooper in the Durham Militia with a large bribe, were allowed to get past all barriers as far as the great outer wall and there set up their scaling-ladders. Four climbed the wall and then descended onto the outside road and into the arms of the waiting patrol; the other two were captured in the Depot burial ground just inside the north wall. All were sent to the punishment cells.

Here a touch of poetic justice enters the story of their betrayal. Had the Durham militiaman really been a traitor, his bribe could have proved a dangerous possession. Apart from his disappointment on finding that the promised 'doubloons' were in fact English three-shilling pieces, the main part of the bribe was paid in bank notes – all of them forgeries. Had he been detected of trying to pass even one of those false notes, he would have faced capital punishment.[4]

There were comparatively few escape attempts from Perth which involved digging and tunnelling, but those few were examples of imaginative planning, courageous dedication and hard labour. I have no doubt that they could have made, or obtained, almost any kind of tool or implement required to carry out such work. Their main problem would have been the disposal of the excavated earth and debris; but much of it would have disappeared down the sewers – and the moat was probably shallower than it would otherwise have been!

There is, however, one record of unusual, and dangerous, storage. An observant sentry noticed a suspicious activity among the officers in No. 6 Prison, often involving buckets. He informed the captain of the guard who, on investigating, found 'about thirty cart loads of earth heaped up in the two ends of the cock-loft', immediately under the roof. There was some belief that the sentry had been tipped off by prisoners who were worried that the ceilings might fall in on them at any time.

Three French officers who had broken their *parole d'honneur* and lost the privileges of their parole town, were sent to Perth and lodged in the Officers' Prison, No. 6. When it was found that one had experience in the catering profession, he was given a coveted job in the cookhouse. It was a fatal privilege, however, as a few days later he fell into one of the huge copper boilers and was so dreadfully scalded that he died a few hours later.

In Perth Museum there is an interesting Account Book, which details all manner of financial matters concerning French prisoners of war in the Depot. One sad entry records that the poor fellow who 'had fallen into a boiler and died the same day' had made a death-bed declaration that he would like his pay made over to a named friend.

Some weeks before the 'false note bribery' case, two valiant, but failed, attempts were made to get out, one from No. 2, the other from No. 3 Prisons. There was little doubt that the diggers had been betrayed by an informer among their fellow prisoners. On the 4th April a military search party went straight to a particularly well-designed bolt-hole in No. 2. The excavation was twenty feet deep, and about six feet from the bottom a tunnel had been dug with an upward gradient. The idea was that any water would drain down the tunnel into the pit below. Nine days earlier, a three feet square tunnel which led some forty-two feet from the latrine in No. 3, towards the wall, was discovered with similar ease, only a day before it may have opened up outside the Depot.

The prime suspect was a French prisoner in the Depot hospital, and it was decided that once discharged he would suffer the punishment they had decided upon – he should lose both his ears. On the day he was released, a group of furious prisoners attacked him, beating him severely and cutting off one of his ears, before tying a rope round his neck and dragging him along the edge of the moat, whilst other prisoners jumped on him. His life – and one of his ears! – were saved by the timely intervention of militiamen.

There was one more attempt to get out of No. 2 Prison via a latrine route. During the early hours of the 24th August, 1813, a mass escape got under way through a tunnel which took the fugitives to the bottom of the southern outer wall. Twenty-three prisoners actually got clear of the Depot, and who knows how many would have followed, except for a clumsy mishap. One of them attempting to jump a stream which skirted the north side of the Depot, landed in the water. The mighty splash alerted a nearby sentry who fired his musket into the darkness in the general direction of the noise. The shot raised the general alarm and it was not long before ten had been retaken. Most of them were found in the vicinity of the river: one had tried to swim the Tay and was picked up exhausted and two had climbed aboard a small vessel but were driven off by the skipper. That still left thirteen unaccounted for, but a few days later the *Caledonian Mercury* reported the fate of eight of them:

'Four of the prisoners who lately escaped from the Perth Depot were discovered within a mile of Arbroath on August 28th by a seaman belonging to the Custom House yacht stationed there, who procured the assistance of some labourers and attempted to apprehend them [the recapture of a prisoner of war was rewarded by a guinea and reasonable expenses] upon which they drew their knives and threatened to stab any one who lay hold of them, but on the arrival of a recruiting party and other assistance the Frenchmen submitted.

'They stated that on Thursday night they were on board a vessel at Dundee, but which they were unable to carry off on account of a neap-tide, which prevented her floating. Other three or four have been apprehended and lodged in Forfar jail. It has been ascertained that several others had gone northwards by the Highland road.'

Considering its size and great prisoner population, Perth had a good security record. During the year from September 1812, to September 1813, there were fourteen escape incidents at Perth. Half of these were complete failures, and the other seven were roughly fifty percent successful. Sixty-one absconders got beyond the prison walls, but of those thirty-one were eventually recaptured.

By the middle of April, 1814, news of Bonaparte's abdication reached Perth by a coach which was decorated with ribbons, flags and colourful descriptive placards. The prisoners must have guessed the news before the facts reached the Depot. Over recent months the depot 'grape-vine' would have prepared them for the inevitability of Napoleon's dethronement. Now, from midday on the 14th April, the clamour of bells from all over the city, would have confirmed what must been, at least for some, their worst fears. However, joyous thoughts of release must have predominated; on that same day they sent a petition to Captain Moriarty, the Governor of the Depot – and earlier Agent at Valleyfield – requesting that they be allowed to illuminate and decorate the prisons, to celebrate the prospect of peace and their own liberation. Moriarty readily agreed, and ordered that the great tower in the Market Place should be illuminated.

Talented artists and scenic designers were soon busily creating banners and bunting to bedeck the buildings, and 'transparencies' which would sparkle from the windows when the prisons were lit from within at night – and the prisoner-poets put their emotions into words. A work by one captive poet, M. Canette, who had spent some years as a prisoner of war in Britain before being sent to Perth, was published – in French – in the *Perth Courier*, early in May. It may well have read much better in French than in the following translation!

This happy period, long desired,
　Now cheers my breast, and lulls its woes;
　A change of fate, with joy I learn,
　Will soon my hours of durance close.

Ah, cruel state of bondage here!
　One gleam now gilds the closing day;
　I see succeed the horrid storm,
　A soothing calm, a cheering ray.

O, Liberty! Thou much beloved.
　How sweet thy smiles to me appear:

The Gods, while quaffing Nectar round,
　Enjoy not blessings half so dear.

'Tis this transports my heart with joy,
　The comforts thou insur'st at last;
　For, ah, the golden age returns,
　The iron age will soon be past.

O, France do then, my country dear,
　Receive the fervent vow I take
　To serve thee, while my life endures,
　My hope – my happiness, I stake.

Six years a wretched captive here,
　To thee I've kept a faithful heart;
　And when I reach thy happy shores,
　My sufferings cease – now I depart

To friendship henceforth I devote
　The quiet that remains to me;
　To my fond parents home I fly;
　And, ah, my country! Home to thee.

My faithful foreign sweetheart sends
　A flattering – a last adieu.
　And now I must go! – no more a slave,
　I go to taste of pleasures true!

On the same day, the *Courier* also printed a small epigram which, whether written by a French Royalist or a Britisher, was appropriate to the French addiction to gambling:

' What **shuffling tricks** this gamester **plays**
His **cut** false **honours** brings:
He **deals** with **queens** in various ways,
And makes his **knaves** all **king**.'

The clearance of Perth Depot began on the 1st June, 1814. Six transport vessels had arrived about ten miles down river, at Newburgh where, over a period, the French ex-prisoners would embark for their native land. The first 120 were taken by boat down the Tay to the embarkation point, followed next day by a further 400, who were to march the ten miles to Newburgh, cheered from the walls of the Depot by those who awaited their own release.

At Newburgh they were allowed free range of the town, where they took full advantage of this last opportunity to trade with their captors. Great crowds had gathered to bid adieu to their foreign guests, many with genuine regret, as the departure of the French brought an end to many small local businesses – and it is probable that a number of romances which had blossomed in the Market Place, or through the iron grills of the palisades, would have faded as they mounted the gangplank to freedom. It will have been noticed that in his poem, M. Canette had mentioned his 'faithful foreign sweetheart'.

As soon as each contingent arrived, the talented and industrious amongst them – who had brought with them unsold 'prisoner of war work' articles – set up an exhibition of their handiwork on the quayside: 'and much traffic went on between them and the inhabitants of the vicinity. All, however, was conducted honourably, while the additional grace of French politeness made a deep impression on the natives of Fife, both male and female.'

Not quite so 'honourably conducted', was their disposal of a gift from an Edinburgh Missionary Society. At the beginning of July many hundreds of copies of the French New Testament were distributed to prisoners as they left Perth Depot. It was said that with few exceptions these were sold for trifling sums before they boarded their transports. If true, these French vendors must have been super-salesmen, for one cannot help wondering where they would have found so many Scots desirous of possessing a New Testament in French!

At the beginning of the evacuation there had been well over 6,000 prisoners in the Depot, but as more and more transports arrived, parties varying in number from 200 to 500, left the Depot, but it still took nearly two months before all had left. The transports wasted no time once loaded – except for one which ran aground below Flisk! – and within a day or so, as tides allowed, they sailed first to Dundee, then to France, some to Dunkirk, others to Boulogne or Calais.

The great Depot for French prisoners of war at Perth was officially closed on the 31st July, 1814.

Postscript.

For many years after 1814, the old war prison was used as a military depot for the storage and repair of clothing and other military equipment. Large numbers of women and boys were employed in the cleaning and mending of uniforms and other garments – until it was discovered that the cost of employing so many people far exceeded the cost of replacing the old with the new.

In his *Traditions of Perth*, George Penny was of the opinion that Perth Depot would be an ideal substitute for transportation and Australia. Had the judicial authorities of that time been more inclined towards reformation than harsh punishment, such common sense might have prevailed. Penny had said:

> ' …it [Perth Depot] might be far better occupied as a national bridewell [an old English word for prison or reformatory] where convicted felons, instead of being sent out of the country at so great an expense, could be employed in labour to maintain themselves.'

He went on to theorise that if they were overseen by men of good character it would have 'better effect than a hundred task-masters with the whip over them'. And if they were paid a small sum to support them on their release, they may emerge 'better men than when they went in'.

It was not until the middle of the nineteenth century, when transportation to the Antipodes came to an end, that two great prisoner of war Depots, Perth and Dartmoor, became our principal civil prisons.

---

1. Prince William, Duke of Cumberland, was remembered in Scotland as 'The Butcher', whilst in England a flower of the *Dianthus* family was named 'Sweet William' in his honour. It is said that this old-fashioned flower was more often known north of the Border as 'Stinking Billy'.

2. J. Cameron: *Prisons and Punishment in Scotland from the Middle Ages to the Present.*

3. Author's emphasis on 'fancy' and 'possibly'.

4. He would have been slightly luckier than anyone 'uttering' false currency south of the Border. There he would almost certainly have been hanged. However, in Scotland he was more likely to get away with a few hundred lashes or fourteen years in Australia.

Chapter Twenty-One

Parole D'Honneur

'By a custom which reveals at once the honour and humanity of Europeans, an officer, when taken prisoner, is released on his parole, and enjoys the comfort of spending the time of his captivity in his own country, surrounded by his own family and the side which has released him remains as perfectly sure of him as if it held him confined in chains.'

Emric de Vattel.
Les Droits des Gens. 1758

THE CAPTURED OFFICER WHO GAVE HIS WORD OF honour that he would not attempt to escape, and agreed to accept a few simple and reasonable conditions, was allowed a great deal of freedom. In fact, the word 'prisoner' did not apply to him in the sense that a man confined to hulk or depot would have understood it.

Until the French Revolution, the officer who gave his *parole d'honneur* was released to live where and how he pleased in the country of his captor. Within reasonable bounds he could choose the town or city where he would spend the period of his captivity. He could live in a manner consistent with his social and financial standing and, if he could afford it, lease, buy, or even build a house.

And the advantage of being an officer – and therefore, it was presumed, a gentleman and a man of honour – did not end there. For the greater part of the period covered by this book, an officer who promised that he would not plot, plan or take up arms against his captors, might be allowed the supreme privilege of returning to his own country. There he could live as a free man with his family for the rest of the war, or until he was exchanged for an officer of equal rank from the other side; at which time he would be released from his parole and could return to active service for his country.

The document which he was asked to sign was simple but explicit.

FORM OF PAROLE ENGAGEMENT.
WHEREAS the Commissioners for the Conducting of his Britannic Majesty's Transport Service, and for the Care and Custody of Prisoners of War, have been pleased to grant me, the undersigned .... as described on the back hereof, late of ....………… and now a Prisoner of War, leave to return to France, upon my entering into an Engagement not to serve against Great Britain, or any of the Powers in Alliance with the Kingdom, until I shall be regularly exchanged for a British Prisoner of War, of Equal Rank; and upon my also Engaging that, immediately after my arrival in France, I shall make known the Place of my Residence there, to the British Agent for Prisoners in Paris, and shall not change the same on any account, without first intimating my intention to the said Agent; and moreover, that at the Expiration of every Two Months, until my Exchange shall be effected, I shall regularly and punctually transmit to the said Agent, a Certificate of my Residence, signed by the Magistrates or the Municipal Officers of the Place.

Now, in Consideration of my Engagement, I do hereby declare that I have given my Parole of Honour accordingly, and that I will keep it Inviolable.

Given under my Hand at ....…………… this ...………… day of .... 17……….

On the reverse of this document was entered a full description of the officer paroled, under such headings as: Name, Rank, Age, Stature, Person, Visage Complexion, Hair, Eyes, Marks or Wounds, etc. A similar document was placed before the British officer paroled home from France. It constituted a legal agreement in both civil and military law and breaches were severely dealt with, and in the early days instances of such dishonourable conduct were rare indeed.

Until the later years of the eighteenth century this implicit faith in the *parole d'honneur* was as real in France as it was in Britain, and in both countries it was almost unthinkable that such a promise would not be respected. The paroled officer who might contemplate escape had more than his own personal and family sense of honour to consider. The breaking of his word would be thought shameful and despicable by his captors, but, and perhaps of even greater importance, he would also be disgraced in the eyes of his fellow countrymen.

Of course, officers on both sides did escape. Many had refused to give their parole in the first place, choosing to be sent to a closed prison or even a prison ship, from either of which escape would be considered laudable and in no way dishonourable. Others, who had admittedly given their word, escaped only after convincing themselves that the treatment which they had received at the hands of their captors constituted a breach of agreement on the latter's part – and so felt themselves released from their given word. However, they had more than themselves to convince. In all cases of escape, the onus was on the 'broke-parole' to satisfy an investigatory board, in his own country, that he had not cynically broken his solemn promise. Furthermore, his efforts to convince were not always successful.

In Britain, such investigations were carried out with a court martial-like thoroughness by the Transport Board and the Admiralty. The records clearly show that these inquiries were no mere formality, aimed at white-washing a parole-breaker so that he could return to active service. On the contrary, the 'broke-parole' faced a rigorous court of honour.

In many cases the officer concerned was able to prove that his signed parole had been abnegated by the manner in which he had subsequently been treated; but the entry, 'Decided a Parole Breaker', was not uncommon. The consequences of such a judgement were terrible indeed, not only to the man as an officer, but also to his reputation as a gentleman. If the circumstances of his case were considered particularly bad, he might be dismissed his regiment, gaoled in this country, or even returned to captivity in France.

In 1757, long before the high ideals of *parole d'honneur* had been cheapened by the French during the Napoleonic Wars, René Brison, Second-Captain of the *Prince de Soubise,* broke his parole and fled back to France. He was judged to have no excuse for breaking his word as a gentleman, and the King sent him back to England and captivity.

In any event, his chances of promotion were slight, however long he continued in army or navy. This was bad enough, but perhaps the greatest and longest-lasting punishment for his crime was that society would never allow him to forget that he was a man of blemished honour.

At its best, the parole system was a system of fair exchange, which could only have survived in its original form so long as both belligerents paid it the same degree of respect. If later it began to fall apart, the entire blame can only be placed on the other side of the Channel. The French Revolution and *égalité* made the 'officer-therefore-gentleman-therefore-you-can-rely-on-his-word' syndrome somewhat anachronistic and, by the time of the Napoleonic War, when many French officers of all ranks had no military or naval background and tradition to live up to. Parole-breaking in this country had become so frequent that it is a wonder that the system survived at all. In the three years up to 1812, nearly seven hundred French officers abused their privilege of comparative freedom in the parole towns of Britain.

One might well imagine that, based as it was on mutual trust and respect, survival of the system could only be feasible whilst both sides played the game. However, perhaps with more sense of honour than common sense, the British played strictly to the rules until the very end. As late as March 1814, a Lieutenant Roger Sheeny was returned to France and captivity, after the Board had decided there were no valid circumstances to mitigate against the breaking of his word of honour. An Englishman's word was his bond with a vengeance!

I cannot resist stepping outside the bounds of this book by more than a hundred years, to recount the story of a British officer who honoured his parole with old-fashioned formality and correctness in World War II. In December 1939, three British Hurricanes attacked twelve Messerschmitt fighters over France. One of the three Hurricanes, piloted by Flying Officer Richard Martin, was badly damaged by cannon-shell. With great courage he decided not to bale out, and with a skill to match that courage, he managed to land his crippled plane in what he thought was still some part of France. He was in fact in Luxemburg, and the Duchy had captured its first prisoner of war.

The young officer was treated like visiting royalty. His oil-stained uniform was taken away to be dry-cleaned and he enjoyed a good bath. Whilst awaiting the return of his uniform, the Mayor of Luxemburg requested him to pledge his parole of honour that he would not try to escape. He gave it reluctantly, but at the time it seemed the only thing he could do.

Overnight, Flying Officer Martin, RAF, became a world figure, as the 'Prisoner of Luxemburg' he was front-paged everywhere from London to Melbourne, from Rio to Chicago. The hospitality was quite overwhelming. He was allowed to wander wherever he wished and his autograph was much in demand. He must have had a great time for a while, but after reading of the exploits of his old squadron in the English newspapers which had been sent to him, he felt that he must get back into action as soon as possible. He wrote to his Commanding Officer and, after apologising for having got himself interned, he ended his letter with: 'and now I'm going to see the Mayor to take back my parole... I hope to be seeing you all soon. Merry Christmas.'

He was as good as his word, went to the Mayor – who thought he must be joking – and withdrew his parole.

On Christmas Day, 1939, Luxemburg was blanketed in a fog and, whilst the locals were enjoying the festivities, the 'Prisoner of Luxemburg' wandered off into it and made his way back to France and his squadron. However, to return to the period of our study.

A simple comparison of the number of parole-breakers on each side, between the early years of the 1790s and the end of the wars, would indicate too black and white a picture. On the one hand we would have the shining figure of a British officer-gentleman whose word was sacrosanct and, on the other a Frenchman who, although an officer, was no gentleman, if the criterion was the inviolability of his word of honour.

Yet this would be just a little unfair, for the virtues and failings were inspired from the top. It must be remembered that, whereas the British officer who escaped would have to face a searching enquiry before he could expect any sort of open-armed welcome home, no real equivalent of the Transport Office's Court of Honour existed in Napoleonic France – and Buonaparte would have been only too pleased to have his officers back, even with tarnished honour. Perhaps we should be more surprised that the great majority of French officers *did* keep their word.

If the French Government had been as meticulous as the British in its observation of the Code, it would have been to the great advantage of captive officers of all nations. Unfortunately, it was not, and the chances of a quick release by exchange, and the maintenance of all the privilege of the system, grew less as the war progressed.

For an absolutely trouble-free system of fair exchange to have worked, an impossibly ideal set of circumstances would have had to exist. In the first place, each nation would have to hold exactly the same number of officer captives – although numbers would not have been enough. For man-for-man exchange – general for general, major for major, captain for captain, and so on – the number of officers of each rank would have to match on each side of the Channel.

We always held something like five 'Frenchmen' (including allies) to every Briton held in France, and sometimes the proportion was as great as ten to one, so nothing like that ideal state of affairs could ever have existed.

The matter of exchange, whether of officers or other ranks, was the cause of complaint and counter-complaint which filled the correspondence between the nations throughout the wars. Agreements were reached and broken and we always came out of it as a creditor who was never repaid. The Dutch and the Danes owed us hundreds of officers, and France and her allies were, by 1796, in debt to us to the tune of 5,000 prisoners, if all ranks were included.

For some time after 1780, a ransom system of money for men had been agreed upon, but it was no answer and was abolished in 1793. An Admiral or Field-Marshall was valued at £60; a Captain at four men or £4; a common soldier or sailor was thus valued at one pound.

In 1798, the French Commissary in London, Monsieur Otto, made what was probably a tongue-in-cheek suggestion that all prisoners in Britain should be exchanged for all prisoners in France – fully aware that, at that time, the exchange would be over-balanced by at least five to one in favour of France. His suggestion came about as the result of a rather clumsily worded reply to a French complaint regarding the quality and quantity of rations issued to French prisoners of war. Mr Otto was told that 'the [British] people were not better fed than the prisoners.'

The French Commissary jumped on this indiscretion and replied:

'If the scarcity is so notorious that the Government, not-withstanding its solicitude, cannot relieve the wants of its own people, why should the Government unnecessarily increase the consumption by feeding more than 22,000 [captive] individuals?

'I have already had the honour of laying before you Two Proposals on this subject, namely, that of Ransoming the Prisoners, or that of sending them back to France on Parole. Either of these alternatives would afford an efficient remedy for the evil in question.'

Conscious as the British were that, with so much parole-breaking and such an imbalance of exchange, it was very much a one-sided bargain, they still tried to keep the system working; but changes had to be made. The custom of allowing an officer to return home under parole was virtually dead; and greater restrictions on his general freedom of movement had to be introduced.

The foreign officer no longer had unlimited choice as to where he could spend the period of his captivity and, towards the end of the wars, no choice at all. Strict limits were placed on the distance he could travel from the centre of his appointed town, or *cautionnement*; he had to report regularly to the Prisoner of War Agent of that town, and a curfew was imposed. In such circumstances of distrust which had made these restrictions necessary, it would have been foolish to continue the practice of allowing parolees to return to their homelands before exchange.

Nevertheless, the possibility was never entirely ruled out, although the chance of British officers being given the same privilege was slight indeed. A number of officers were allowed to return to France, without insistence on exchange, even late in the war; but their luck and the degree of our generosity must be somewhat diluted by the fact that they were usually all either very old and or very ill. By the time that Monsieur Otto was writing his letter to the Transport Office, the greatest parole advantages an officer could hope for had gone, never again to be seriously considered. The form of parole, whilst still reasonable, had undergone a number of changes for the worse, and now read as follows:

FORM OF PAROLE ENGAGEMENT

By the Commissioners for conducting H.M.'s Transport Service, and for the care and custody of Prisoners of War.

THESE ARE TO CERTIFY to all H.M.'s officers, civil and military, and to whom it may concern, that the bearer...as described on the back hereof, is a detained French Prisoner of War at................................and that he has liberty to walk on the great turnpike road within the distance of one mile from the extremities of the town, but that he must not go into any field or cross road, nor be absent from his lodging after five o'clock in the afternoon during the six winter months, viz. from October 1st to March 31st, nor after eight o'clock during the summer months. Wherefor you and every one of you are hereby desired to suffer him, the said .... to pass and repass accordingly, without any hindrance or molestation whatever, he keeping within the said limits and behaving according to the law.

All letters home were censored and the form which the paroled officer now signed contained the condition:

' …that he will not directly or indirectly hold any correspondence with France during his continuance in England, but by such letters as shall be shown to the Agent of the said Commissioners under whose care he is or may be, in order to them being read by his Superiors.'

As can well be imagined, this was the most frequently broken of all parole promises. All this was a far cry from the trust and freedom of the good old days, and yet the French officer was in a number of ways better off than his British counterpart across the Channel.

Before moving deeper into the everyday life of the parolee in Britain, it may be well to take a glance at the other side of the story and the other side of the Channel. In earlier wars than the Napoleonic, there was little to choose between the conditions of, and attitude to, parole in the two countries; but by 1803 things were different indeed. Britain had had good reason to tighten its hold on paroled captives, and now Napoleon found reasons, but less valid ones, to go even further.

With the peace of March, 1802, British visitors had flocked to France in great numbers. The ferries were crowded on every crossing with T.G.s, or 'Travelling Gentlemen', as well-to-do tourists were then called. Noblemen and gentry of all types; businessmen picking up the threads of continental trade interrupted by the war; Government officials and just plain travellers, many with families and servants.

The French Revolution had naturally discouraged the British upper classes from visiting the Continent, although in those days war was between kings and emperors and did not make travel to the enemy's country completely impossible or even remarkable. However, with the onset of the Revolution, the ferry service between the two countries had virtually ceased to operate. Now, though, with the Peace of Amiens, for the next fourteen months many hundreds of Britishers set off to enjoy once again the pleasures of continental travel.

J.G. Alger[1] estimated that amongst them were five dukes, three marquises, thirty-seven earls and countesses, eight viscounts, seventeen barons and forty-one elder sons and other heirs – two-thirds of the House of Lords at that time!

The short period of peace ended when war broke out again in

May, 1803 and, to their cost, many of the T.G.s were unprepared for such a happening. Maybe most were not seriously worried; certainly no one could have foreseen that Napoleon would create an almost completely new category of prisoner of war – the *détenus*, or *otages*, as he himself described them – but with its creation, almost all of his civilian visitors were caught in a trap.

On the 23rd May, he issued an edict which decreed that all British persons (within certain classifications) should be detained as prisoners of war. Not only commissioned officers of the army and navy, or enrolled militiamen, but all civilians between the ages of eighteen and sixty, were covered by the new edict – in fact, practically everyone. Napoleon's excuse for including civilians in his atrocious order, was that men between the ages specified were liable to be enrolled in the militia in Britain if called. The excuse was a weak one, but the notice with which the *détenus* were presented makes it clear:

Buonaparte, the First Consul.
B.Marot, the Secretary of State.

Consequently, within the space of 24 hours from the present notification, you will please to constitute yourself a Prisoner of War at the house of the Town Mayor of the City of Amiens. I tell you beforehand that no pretext, no excuse can exclude you, as, according to British laws, none can dispense you from serving in the Militia. After having made this declaration within 24 hours, you will be permitted to remain a prisoner upon Parole. In case you have not made your declaration within 24 hours, you will no longer be allowed to give your Parole, but will be conducted to.......................the control point of the military division that will be fixed upon by the Minister of War.

I Salute you.

With that one infamous decree, Buonaparte netted in some eight hundred British civilians and if he was disappointed with the size of his catch – some French authorities estimated the number as eight thousand – it at least included some very big fish. Very few other than the obviously very young, or those who appeared positively ancient, were exempted. Only a small number of the visitors would have carried written proof of their age – birth certificates were a rarity at that time – so with only twenty-four hours to convince a prejudiced official that you were younger or older than you looked, it was wisest not to argue.

At first the parolees, officers and civilians, had some choice as to their parole town, but in November, 1803, Napoleon ordered that the fortress town of Verdun should henceforth be the one and only *cautionnement* for British officers and *détenus*.

Conditions and treatment in prisons or parole towns anywhere, in either country, were always as good or bad as the Governor or Agent who controlled them, and the prisoners at Verdun could not have been more unlucky in the man who was sent to take charge of them soon after they arrived. Despite the many privileges which went with their position in the hierarchy of prisoner of war society, for the next five years the parolees suffered under the tyranny of General Wirion, General de Gendarmerie, Commandant at Verdun until 1809.

When studying the reminiscences of prisoners of war and their recollections of individual characters, it is well to be aware of the possibility of some exaggeration. However, there is too much evidence, from paroled officer and *détenu* alike – and finally from the judgement of the French authorities – to doubt that Wirion was anything other than a corrupt and loathsome character. One memoirist, writing after the war, described the –

'...multifarious instances of knavery and extortion, fraud, insolence, and despotism, practised by the ever execrable Wirion and his vulgar spouse. During the reign of that contemptible tyrant there was nothing odious in power abused by vulgar hands, nothing base in meanness or rapacity, but what was exercised with impunity against the feelings, property and persons of the *détenus* and prisoners of war.' Wirion never missed a chance to make a dishonest franc. He milked their allowances, condoned false lotteries designed to fleece the prisoners, and used his great powers to make sure that he did not lose at games of chance. His frequent, and uninvited, attendance at private card parties was always greeted with secret dismay; the prisoners knew that they must let him win, 'to avoid being sent to the dreaded dungeons of Bitche or Sedan.'

Among his many unpleasant resources to increase his power over his charges, was his order to all residents who rented lodgings and apartments to the prisoners: that they should act as unpaid spies and report on the personal details and conduct of their tenants.

The stories of General Wiron's bad administration and downright crookedness are too numerous to be recounted here. Anyone interested in further confirmation that the parolees in no way overstated the obnoxiousness of this Commandant, should refer to Edward Boys' *'Narrative'*; Edward Fraser's *'Napoleon the Gaoler'*, and Michael Lewis' *'Napoleon and his British Captives'*. For five years Wiron got away with it, partly as a result of his influence in high places – Marshal Berthier, the Minister of War, being a particularly close acquaintance. The numerous complaints of his conduct went unheeded, either because they never reached the Minister, or were ignored when they did. General Wirion's downfall came only when his friend Berthier was replaced by General Clarke as Minister of War and a Court of Inquiry was set up.

Wirion, no doubt certain of the outcome, did not wait to hear the Court's findings. On the 8th April, 1810, the *'Police Bulletin'* a confidential daily report for Napoleon's inspection, stated:

'General Wirion went yesterday morning at 10 o'clock in a hackney coach to the Bois de Boulogne. Alighting a few yards from the Port Maillot, he blew out his brains... '

With such a man ruling the prisoner community, one might well imagine the Verdun of that day as a dreary, miserable and unhappy town, its inmates condemned to long days of dull monotony and longing for home. Doubtless the longing for home was ever-present, but the rest of the imagined picture would be very wide of the mark.

Before 1803, Verdun was a quiet enough place of no great prosperity, but now, with its elevation to the position of *the* parole town of France, a rapid change took place. The introduction of great numbers of officers, often well-to-do, and *détenus*, many of them men of considerable wealth, brought almost immediate prosperity to the town.

The *détenus* had good reason to think that their detention would be of short duration, as the French decision to intern non-combatant travellers was without precedent. Nevertheless, they soon became bored with this unexciting fortress town and began to create for themselves a society in which they could enjoy at least something of the lifestyle to which they had previously been accustomed. By November, when all paroled British officers arrived in Verdun, they were well on the way to achieving their aim.

One of the first to arrive – in fact he claimed to be the first British Naval officer – was Lieutenant William Henry Dillon. Dillon, who later achieved the rank of Vice-Admiral and was knighted, spoke of the changes which had taken place during the first few months of his arrival:

> 'On our arrival the wives of the bourgeousie were dressed like maid-servants, and not a white stocking was to be seen among them. But in a few months their whole costume was improved by silks and muslins. The shops which were nearly empty, were now crammed with articles for sale. The improvement in the town was daily perceptible. One street in particular in its lower part from its bustle and noise we called Bond Street.'

This street, the Rue Moselle, had had only three or four good shops and a number of smaller ones selling gingerbread, matches and other small merchandise; but now it had its bespoke tailors, a fashion house and shops catering for all manner of luxuries which the wealthier *détenus* and officers might demand.

Some of the new businesses were established by London traders who had been caught in the net, and the French shopkeepers had never had it so good – small wonder that the latter called this new gold-mine *Bon* Street. To be able to walk along a street which displayed such signs as 'Stukey, Tailors and Ladies' Habit makers', 'Anderson, Grocer and Tea-Dealer, from London', must have supplied a little of the atmosphere of home for both *détenu* and the paroled prisoner of war, confined to the bounds of this small walled town. This, and the fact that he was likely to see civilians of his own race; English women, the wives, daughters or mistresses of *détenus*, shopping or passing by in their carriages, probably lessened those feelings of strangeness and loneliness which the French officer must have experienced on his first arriving in an English or Scottish country parole town.

The efforts to create a little London-overseas included the establishment of a number of English-style clubs. The more exclusive of these had strictly limited membership, reserved in the main for detainees, although some paroled officers were admitted as members. Others were welcome meeting places where the not so well-off could spend their idle hours in greater comfort than was possible in their often humble lodgings. It may be true that the best things in life are free, but to the man who was himself not free, money made all the difference. For the wealthy, whether *détenu* or officer, Verdun could now cater for most of his requirements however extravagant; but, for the officer who had to try to exist on his meagre allowance, life became very hard indeed, as inflation set in and the prices of everything, even necessities such as food and lodgings, soared at an alarming rate.

It was inevitable that, with so much unexpected gold flooding into the town, the French traders and shopkeepers and those with accommodation to let, would become greedy. However, they almost killed the goose with its golden egg as by the end of 1804 prices were getting really out of hand. The rent, for example, of a former 30-franc room had now risen to 300 francs a month.

This particular instance of overcharging was mentioned in Napoleon's reply to complaints which had reached his ears. He warned the landlords and traders that if they did not do something about it, the golden egg would be laid elsewhere. This was a stern warning indeed, and must have seriously worried the get-rich-quick townsfolk. For there were plenty of French towns who would have been only too willing to shoulder the prisoner burden in return for its rewards.

Unfair trading was not the only means by which the Briton was relieved of his cash. One of the worst aspects of life at Verdun was gambling, and the scandal of its excesses is dealt with in another chapter (see THE GAMBLERS AND BROKERS, Chapter 9, *The Arts and Crafts of Napoleonic and American Prisoners of War 1756-1816*) but it must be briefly mentioned here as an integral part of the picture of life at Verdun at that time. Chevalier Henry Lawrence, himself a *détenu*, tells us that soon after his arrival at the parole town, 'the game of Hazard having been introduced at the Caron Club, General Wirion sent a gendarme to suppress it; but the act proceeded from the most corrupt of motives. The General was resolved that the English should only lose their money at the bank in the winnings of which he had a share.'

A gambling house was opened, the tables reserved for English players only, designed as a lure for all conditions of prisoner. Large sums were lost by men who could probably afford their loss, but the real evil lay in the fact that others, for whom so many other things had been priced out of the market, were tempted to risk the little they had in the hope of at least temporarily improving their lot. These first flutters often resulted in debt and distress, particularly among the younger officers, which further increased their hardship over the remaining years of captivity. 'Happy it would have been,' says Lawrence, 'if many of our countrymen had never quitted the sober amusements of the clubroom for the tempting delusions of the gaming table, which were carried to dreadful excess at this depot.'

The parolee who could cope with the high cost of living, and avoided the dangers of 'rouge-et-noir', was able to live a reasonably normal life – as normal as was possible under the conditions of his parole. He could select his lodgings and was usually allowed to change them if he first intimated his intention. He could wander at will within the limits of the town, and was even permitted to pass beyond the walls for a few hours at a time and with special permission. These excursions were brief, however, as the *appels*, or roll-calls, were frequent.

At first the prisoners had to muster daily between eight and ten o'clock in the morning and again between two and four in the afternoon. By local rules these hours could be altered at the whim of the Commandant. Later, the frequency of muster was made more reasonable, especially for senior officers who had to report only once a month, and lieutenants every five days.

Once outside the walls, the parolee could walk through quite pleasant countryside and visit the villages round Verdun, but had always to be back to collect his 'passport' at the gate. Failure to attend *appel* was regarded as a serious breach of parole, equivalent, at least in the Commandant's eyes, to attempted escape.

There was no lack of entertainment. All manner of diversions were organised to brighten each day. Apart from the clubs and the gambling, there were dances and theatricals, concerts and banquets, cock-fighting, drag-hunts, fishing and even well-organised race-meetings. However, it must be admitted that most of these things were available only to the lucky ones; high living was not for all.

Although one visitor to Verdun spoke of the British prisoners as 'playing, dancing, drinking and singing all day long,' there were many who could only just make ends meet through the generosity of their fellows, occasional hand-outs from the charitable subscriptions which were sent out from England or by running themselves into debt to the French traders. Some, through pride, necessity and a reluctance to accept charity, hired themselves out as odd-job men to *détenus* or the wealthier among the officers. Others, possessed of various skills, found ways to add to their small income; but the British prisoner, in general, showed none of the profitable ingenuity of his French counterpart, in the manufacture of articles for sale.

Not all of our officers spent their time in search of frivolous amusement, even those who could afford to do so. The more serious-minded studied, painted or pursued other hobbies. One, Lieutenant Tuckey, who had been captured in 1805 whilst serving on the *Calcutta*, concentrated his interest on marine geography, and had something to show for his nine years of captivity at Verdun. When he returned to England in 1814 he published his three-volume work on that subject. Edward Fraser mentions another man who combated boredom in his own way. This was Captain Molyneux, who designed and constructed an 'ice-boat' which he successfully sailed on the Meuse. Another of his inventions, a sail-driven horseless-carriage 'which could run at seven or eight miles an hour' was successful in its object, but 'its evolutions frightened horses on the high road, and one day ran into a cart and upset it, after which the peasants took to stoning the inventor when they met him out on his runs. The experiments were finally stopped by order of the Governor.'

Doubtless there were many other parolees who, with so much time on their hands, spent some of it in a creative manner – and several artists left us specimens of their wartime work – but examples which can be confidently labelled 'British Prisoner of War Work', whilst not unknown, are rare indeed.

It might be reasonable to suppose that once *any* British officer had given his signed promise that he would abide by the rules of parole, his word would be valued at the same rate as that of any other paroled officer, irrespective of rank – if not, why offer him parole in the first place? In fact, rank did mean a great deal to the French when it came to the amount of freedom allowed to an individual. We have seen that senior officers and lieutenants were excused daily muster, but that even here the period between reporting varied greatly according to seniority. For the rest, each day was sliced into by roll-calls. Midshipman Edward Boys calculated that, based on the fact that Field Officers and Naval Captains reported only once a month and he twice daily, his word of honour could only be valued at one-sixtieth part of that of a Field Officer!

The French could never quite understand the rank or rating of a British midshipman, who, whilst not commissioned, was recognised as an officer in his own country. This means that they did not understand or fully respect a high percentage of their naval-officer captives, for more than half were of midshipman rank.

However great their puzzlement, there was certainly no excuse for the harsh and unfair treatment meted out to these young lads, many of them still in their early teens. Not all 'middies' were granted the privilege of parole, and perhaps those that were would have been better off without it. At least they would have felt free to attempt escape without loss of their honour.

From the first days of captivity midshipmen were treated in a very different manner to commissioned officers. Whereas the latter were granted 'the favour of proceeding freely and without escort to the place assigned to them to reside', midshipmen were marched under guard, often for long distances. By the time Edward Boys reached Verdun, he and his companions had walked over 950 miles in five and a half months. After their long march, journey's end must have seemed a blissful prospect; but from their first experiences of their new Commandant they must have wished they could have carried on marching.

We have seen that over the heads of all the captives at Verdun, hung the threatening shadow of Wirion and his 'rapacious understrappers'. He could, and did, send paroled men to closed prisons and dungeons for reasons more personal than patriotic; but the poor midshipmen came in for his special dislike.

He had no respect for them at all, either as officers, as gentlemen or even as men, referring to them as the 'sweepings of the sweepings' of the gutters of England. Any trouble which they gave him was the direct result of his own prejudice, and his failure to understand that their sense of honour was as great as that of any fully commissioned officer.

It could be said, whilst remembering that even the limited degree of freedom which they enjoyed would have been envied by 'other-ranks' in the depots of Bitche or Sedan, that midshipmen were not paroled at all, in the original sense of the chivalrous ideal. In addition to their own promise, most midshipmen at Verdun had to be spoken for and guaranteed by a senior officer or *détenu* of distinction, as a sort of underwriting of their word of honour.

For one reason or another, they were constantly under punishment and in and out of the Citadel of the fortress. Furthermore, this was not always the direct result of an individual's 'crime' – when one offended, all were punished. Midshipman Robert Bastard James, who was only sixteen years old but in command of a small prize vessel when captured, recorded that he and most of his fellow middies had spent two-thirds of their time at Verdun confined to the Citadel.

A system of fines for minor offences and the fact that their small allowance of fifty sous a day – about £1.20p a month at that time – was 'doctored' in the Governor's favour, left many midshipmen in very poor straits. Midshipman Boys' *'Narrative'* tells of a particularly bad instance of harsh treatment and physical violence inflicted on paroled lads who were themselves innocent of offence. It occurred on one of the infrequent and much anticipated occasions when Boys and some friends had, quite legitimately, passed through the gates and set out on what they thought would be a pleasant couple of hours' hunting:

> ' …four of us were rambling about the country with a pointer and a silken net, catching quails, when the gun was fired. [the signal gun which was fired to alert the gendarmes to escape attempts] On our return, in passing through the village of Tourville, we were surprised by two gens-d'armes, one of whom instantly dismounted and seized me. Uttering the most blasphemous epithets, he tied my elbows behind, and then, slipping a noose round my bare neck, triced me up to the holsters of his saddle, remounted, and returned with his prize to the town, exulting in his cowardly triumph and pouring forth volleys of vulgar abuse; every now and then tightening the cord, so as to keep me trotting on the very extemity of the toes to obtain relief, then again loosening it, as occasional gutteral symptoms of strangulation seemed to indicate necessity.
>
> 'Vain would be the attempt to convey an adequate idea of the impotent rage then boiling within me at the insult offered to my juvenile dignity, [he was not yet seventeen at that time] whilst a determined haughtiness distained to betray the slightest indication of

submission or complaint. My companions were secured around the middle, with utmost violence and brutality; and thus we were conveyed to the town.'

It is surprising in these circumstances to find that these 'Young Gentlemen', to give them their official title, knowing that their word of honour was treated with contempt by the enemy, should have paid such high regard to it themselves, and so seldom devalued it. Few attempted to escape without first subjecting themselves to a conscientious soul-searching; but those few put paid to the remnants of parole left to midshipmen in Verdun, and ended their stay in that town.

It began when one midshipman, who, untypically, could not be called a 'young gentleman' in the way in which he acted, broke his parole in a most cavalier fashion, without the vestige of an excuse greater than they all had. Eighteen months later, in August 1808, as the result of a second escape, all one hundred and forty-two midshipmen were first imprisoned in the Verdun Citadel and then sent to depots at Valenciennes, Sarrelibre and Givet.

Once they had been released from their parole by being placed under lock and key, the young gentlemen became a constant source of worry to their gaolers, their one thought and full-time occupation, escape and plans for escape. 'I wish to God,' said a harassed French officer at Bitche, the punishment depot, one evening at dinner, 'I knew what to do to keep those English middies within bounds.' A lady at the table advised him, 'There is only one way, Sir. Put them on their honour.'

Had the French authorities been as wise as this lady, they would have saved themselves a great deal of aggravation – and kept a lot more prisoners in their grasp. Of the one hundred and three commissioned and junior officers who made successful escapes, ninety-three were 'Young Gentlemen'. Those ninety-three were the successful absconders, so the number of attempts must have been many times greater.

A *détenu*, the Reverend Robert Wolfe, followed the middies who had been sent to Givet, in an effort to carry on the good work among them which had occupied him for the past two years at Verdun. He tells us that had his charges received the full trust and privileges of parole, life would have been easier for both prisoner and captor alike. Wolfe also remembered a letter which illustrated the fact that an officer's word was of more than just personal importance. Edward Boys was at Givet and the letter was from his mother. After telling her son that she had heard of some midshipmen breaking their word and escaping home to England, entreated him on no account 'to let any personal suffering, or ill-treatment, or example, induce him to do what would disgrace himself, distress his family beyond measure, and cast a reflection upon his country.'

After General Wirion made his exit in the Bois de Boulogne in 1810, the Commandancy fell into the hands of Colonel Courcelles, who carried on in the General's footsteps, but with greater subtlety. After two years of undetected crime he, too, was exposed and deposed. He managed to shift most of the blame onto the shoulders of his assistant, the Lieutenant of Police, who took the same way out as Wirion.

It is pleasant to be able to end this short account of parole life at Verdun by telling that, for the remaining two years of war, the prisoners were free of tyranny. The last two Governors, Baron de Beauchesne and Major de Meulan, were as generous and considerate as the previous pair had been grasping and vile.

Before 1803 the inhabitants of any number of French towns may well have met, or at least seen, the occasional paroled British officer in their neighbourhood; and he, in turn, may have spent different periods of his captivity in a number of French towns. After that date, however, with the establishment of Verdun as the central point of parole, it is probable that the only news of British officers to spread beyond its walls would have been of extravagant high living and of the English addiction to the gaming tables. There was little opportunity for social intercourse between the Briton and the Frenchman of his class, and the manner in which he spent his captive years must have been a closed book to the average Frenchman outside Verdun; as was the life of the French prisoner inside the depots and prison hulks to the average Englishman.

In Britain, however, there was never any such central parole area, and officers of many nationalities became part of the daily scene. For more than half a century before 1815, the presence of 'war-like strangers' was accepted, and often welcomed, in towns and villages all over the country. Undoubtedly they brought comparative prosperity to some of the smaller and poorer parole towns – and their spending power was sorely missed by the traders and landladies when they left at the end of the wars. However, as the notes on individual parole towns will tell, the townsfolk were generally fascinated by the very foreignness of their unwilling guests and admired their usually cheerful resourcefulness, their education and refined manners.

The news that a small, quiet, country town or village had been selected as a wartime home for paroled prisoners would have caused a great stir among the local residents, and the arrival of the first batch awaited with mixed feelings. Some would have resented the presence of enemy officers in their town, and foreseen only trouble; but for most the feelings would have been of excitement, curiosity and perhaps a little nervousness.

There would have been a great bustle of cleaning up and preparation of unoccupied rooms, shopkeepers dusting off their stock in anticipation of expanded trade – and no doubt a secret flutter in the hearts of the local lassies. It should be remembered that many of the local youths were away at the wars, and that these gentlemen-prisoners would, from then on, represent quite a high percentage of the male population of the place.

When the official returns relating to prisoners of war for the year 1810 are viewed against the Census Returns for that year, it transpires that roughly two percent of all males of military age in Britain must have been Frenchmen. Most were, of course, confined to depots or prison ships, but the number of thousands who were granted the privilege of parole were concentrated in a small number of *cautionnements*, and therefore represented a far higher proportion, in some cases fifteen or twenty per cent or even higher.

Everyone would have read the notice which was prominently displayed in all parole towns:

'**NOTICE IS HEREBY GIVEN**, that all prisoners are permitted to walk or ride on the great turn-pike road within the distance of one mile from the extreme parts of the town (not beyond the bounds of the Parish) and if they shall exceed such limits or go into any field or cross-road they may be taken up and sent to prison, and a reward of Ten Shillings will be paid by the Agent for apprehending them.

'And further, that such prisoners are to be in their lodgings by 5 o'clock in the winter, and 8 in the summer months, and if they stay out later they are liable to be taken up and sent to the Agent for such misconduct. And to prevent the prisoners from behaving in an improper manner to the inhabitants of the town, or creating any riots or disturbances either with them or among themselves, notice is hereby given that the Commissioners will cause, upon information being given to their Agents, any prisoners who shall so misbehave to be committed to prison.

'And such of the inhabitants who shall insult or abuse any of the Prisoners of War on parole, or shall be found in any respect aiding or assisting in the escape of such prisoners shall be punished according to the law.'

This notice, similar to the parole form which each officer had signed, made it plain that if the parolee was to enjoy the privileges, and the townsman was to enjoy the benefits which his presence might bring to the economy of the town, both must behave themselves.

Most of the inhabitants would have taken heed of the warning that the expected additions to the local population were to be treated with respect, but, as we shall see, there were always the unprincipled few who taunted, or grasped the opportunity to cash in on petty infringements of parole rules, which would have been better ignored.

At last the great day would come. Small groups of travel-stained men would straggle in; naval and military officers of all ranks, some with their servants; privateer captains and their lieutenants, merchant master and mates and perhaps even the odd civilian of importance or supercargo, taken on board a merchantman or privateer.

The colourful variety of uniform, cocked hats and dress caps, the babble of strange tongues, Polish, German, Italian, Dutch, Danish, American and, of course, French, would have created an atmosphere of fascinated curiosity and expectancy only experienced on those rare occasions when the fair or circus came to town.

As the weary men arrived they would be directed to the Parole Agent for that town. He would already be in possession of all the relevant details regarding each of his charges. Officials at the port of disembarkation had already gone deeply into each man's qualifications and suitability for the privilege of parole: his rank, description, social (and probably financial) standing, his character generally and, above all, whether he could be regarded as a gentleman – for, remember, only a gentleman's word was worth taking. The senior officer, or the captain of the vessel on which the prisoner had been taken, was expected to attest to the veracity of all such information, and to stand as guarantors for the young boys they were allowed as servants.

Armed with all this knowledge and of the accommodation available in the town, the Agent would then assist in finding lodgings appropriate to their financial resources. He would, no doubt, also acquaint them with some details of their new home town and remind them of the limitations of their freedom. They would soon begin to realise that their Agent was the most important person in their lives as parolees. At intervals they would have to report to him for musters (but nothing like as frequently as at Verdun); he was responsible for distribution of their Government allowances and their 'banker' for handling remittances from home.

All letters addressed abroad had to pass through his hands for onward transmission to the censors at the Transport Office, and he was the recipient of all their worries, problems and complaints. If he carried out his duties as laid down by the Board – and it would seem that most Agents did – the prisoners could be sure that their own complaints would be dealt with as fairly as those directed against them.

All in all, the position of Parole Agent was no sinecure. The monthly reports to the Transport Board, the day-to-day problem of looking after the interests of anything from fifty to four hundred foreign officers, much of it niggling detail, could not have left him much free time; particularly if, like most, he had his own profession or trade to attend to. One might suppose that the rewards would be great, for there was never any lack of applicants for the post; but, officially at least, they were small indeed. He received five per cent of all disbursements for the subsistence of prisoners under his care, a stationery allowance and a few incidental expenses; so if he was Agent of a small *cautionnement* he needed to keep his day job.

There were, in fact, additional, if not exactly legitimate, rewards which could have made the job more worthwhile. The 'perks' which went with such a job were numerous and varied, from appreciative offerings for favours received, to small rake-offs for handling remittances or deals with contractors. However, so long as he did not go too far – and there was certainly no Wirion or Courcelles among them – such small perquisites would be taken for granted in that age.

Inevitably, there were a few who did go too far, but they were a small minority who did not get away with very much for very long. The Transport Office was ever vigilant in this matter and was quick to reprimand the Agent who treated his responsibilities with insufficient thoroughness, and were just as quick to dismiss the few who were proved to have criminally abused their position. Anyway, it would have been a very clever rascal who could have persistently avoided the watchful eyes of both the Transport Office and intelligent foreigners who were well aware of their rights as paroled officers.

The stories of individual Parole Towns will tell of Agents who offended, of some who were offended against, and of others who won the respect, thanks and even friendship of prisoners in their towns. Until quite late in the wars, any man whose education and background would make him a suitable person to deal with and control gentleman-prisoners, might gain the post of Agent; but later only Royal Navy lieutenants of not less than ten years standing were considered. Whilst it would seem appropriate that a commissioned officer of long experience should command more respect from an enemy officer than a civilian might expect, the fact that many of his charges could be of much higher rank than himself, cannot have made his job an easy one.

Some of the parolees were of very high rank indeed. Among our captives were famous admirals and generals, captains and commanders, and even the Emperor's brother, Prince Lucien. Lucien had earned Napoleon's displeasure by not agreeing to an arranged political marriage between himself and the Queen of Etruria. Instead he married the girl of his choice and decided to settle in America. His plans were thwarted when the ship which was taking him to the United States was captured by a British cruiser and he was brought a prisoner to England.

Lucien was paroled to Ludlow in Shropshire and lived for some time at Dinham House. In his case, parole was a mere formality and it is very unlikely that any of the usual restrictions applied. He later bought Thorngrove, near Worcester, and made it his home until the

Peace of 1814.

Most of the more important prisoners enjoyed special privileges, particularly as regards the distance they could travel from their place of parole. Many were allowed to retain their swords but none was allowed to wear them. The French Commander in Chief, Admiral Villeneuve, captured at the Battle of Trafalgar, was permitted to select any town for himself and his staff, so long as it was at least thirty miles north or west of London. He chose Reading and there he stayed until April 1806, when he was returned to France in exchange for four British post-captains.

These special privileges were, no doubt, granted on the assumption that as the serviceman's main qualification for parole was that he must be a gentleman, then the higher his rank and position in society, the more faith one could have in his honour and integrity. If this was so, the British Government must have been often saddened by the way in which some very senior French officers abused their trust. Take, for example, General Lefèbvre-Desnouettes, Officer of the Legion of Honour, General of Division, Colonel Commanding the Chasseurs à Cheval de la Garde. One can sense the pained disgust of the Commissioners of the Transport Office, who would have come down heavily on one of our own officers – even a young midshipman – who had offended against his word, when they wrote:

> 'He was allowed unusually great privileges on parole – to reside in Cheltenham, to go thence to Malvern and back to Cheltenham as often as he liked; his wife was allowed to reside with him, and he was allowed to have two Imperial Guardsmen as his servants. Yet he absconded, May 1st, 1812, with his servants and a naval lieutenant Armand le Duc, who had been allowed as a special favour to live with him at Cheltenham. Lefèbvre-Desnouettes escaped disguised as a German count – some say as a Russian General Officer – with his wife dressed in boy's clothing travelling as his son, and his aide-de-camp in the character of a valet. Lefèbvre's party travelled unhindered to London, where they stayed in an hotel in Leicester Square, and then made its way quite openly to Dover, thence to France.'

It is scarcely believable that when such distinguished prisoners were recaptured after unsuccessful escape attempts, the Government, despite its disgust, seldom dealt out appropriate punishments. Whereas offenders of lesser rank would be considered to have abnegated their officer status and sent to the hulks or closed prison, the more exalted were treated with comparative leniency. Retaliation from the other side had to be considered to a certain extent, but the French held so few of our very senior officers that, though tit-for-tat was unfairly used on occasion, it could not have loomed large as a consideration.

General Simon, who was captured at the Battle of Busaco on the 27th September, 1810, was a constant source of trouble and parole breaking for the next four years. In October he arrived in England and was paroled to Odiham in Hampshire. He arrived wounded but after recovery treated his parole with complete cynicism. While in the parole town he founded the pseudo-Masonic Lodge of The Secret Order of the Lion², formed with the object of arming, and bringing about the general uprising of all prisoners in England.

General Simon escaped from Odiham in 1812, but was free for only a short while. Reward notices were posted: 'One Hundred Pounds is offered for the capture of the French General Simon, styled a Baron and a Chevalier of the Empire, who lately broke his parole and absconded from Odiham.' He was recaptured through the smart work of the Bow Street Runners, who followed leads to several addresses in London, picking up a number of 'broke-paroles' on the way, and finally tracing him to Pratt Street, Camden Town.

This time Simon was sent to Dumbarton Castle, where he was allowed a servant at Government expense and still received a prisoner of war allowance of one shilling and sixpence per day. His accommodation was two rooms, fitted out in the manner of a senior officer's apartment, and he was allowed all reasonable requests, including writing materials and newspapers.

These latter and a few other privileges were withdrawn when it was later discovered that, from Dumbarton Castle, he was acting as an escape-agent for 'broke-paroles', through accomplices in London. News of this treatment reached France and brought about reprisal. The Minister of War arrested General Lord Blayney, and had him confined in the Citadel of Verdun, stating in a letter that this action was in retaliation for Simon's detention and that Blayney would 'answer with his head for whatever the British Government might do to General Simon.'

General Lefèbvre was not the only paroled officer who brought his wife to England. A number of senior officers and other wealthy or distinguished parolees were allowed to send for their spouses to share their captivity. A Government return for June, 1812, showed that out of 3,232 paroled prisoners in Great Britain, 115 were women and children. However, not all the women were wives of prisoners, a few were prisoners themselves.

Among the people arrested by the Bow Street Runners at Camden Town, were two French women escape-agents and a number of French girls were among the captives taken on a vessel bound for Mauritius. The sailors were sent to the depot at Portchester Castle, but the girls were allowed to live with residents in the town. It is not surprising to learn that a great fuss was made of these young ladies and that they were wined and dined by the gentry of the neighbourhood. One of them, Josephine Desperoux, married a local squire named Patrick Bisson in 1812.

All foreign commissioned officers down to gardes-marines – a rank roughly equivalent to our midshipmen – and army sous-lieutenants, were eligible for parole. The masters and mates of merchantmen over fifty tons also qualified, as did passengers of importance. In the case of privateers, captains and lieutenants of vessels with a crew of one hundred or more were normally granted the privilege, but only if their vessel was not under eighty tons – and mounted at least fourteen carriage guns of four pounds or more rating. This last stipulation was designed to discourage the understandable practice of ditching as much armament as possible before striking their colours to the enemy.

There were others who sometimes, but not always, qualified such as pilots, surgeons, chiefs-of-prizes, chaplains, boatswains; also civilians who were judged to be 'respectable persons'. Amongst ordinary soldiers and sailors who enjoyed the comparative freedom of the parole towns, were the lucky ones who had won jobs as officers' servants, and men with special skills, such as carpenters, whose talents could be usefully employed. There was also the mysterious category of 'gentleman volunteer'.

As has already been noted, the parole town officers were usually collectively referred to as 'French' – even in contemporary writings – and in many cases the prisoner-population could be correctly so described; but a great many other nationalities were to be met with in these towns at different periods over the various wars. As well as the French there were Dutch, Italian, Danish, German, Spanish, Portuguese, Breton, Norwegian, Polish, Russian, Belgian, and, during the War of American Independence and again after 1812, American officers.

As lack of respect for parole had necessitated the tightening up of the rules, particularly as to the greatly reduced freedom of choice of place of residence, many of the captives found themselves in surroundings and among people depressingly different from their life-style before capture. Only in a few fashionable centres such as Bath, Cheltenham or London could the sophisticated parolee enjoy anything of the elegant society, with its attendant entertainments and diversions, appropriate to his station. However, these places were reserved to the exceptionally privileged and to the upper class convalescent. The town of Reading was similarly available to only the officer of distinction, his aides and his servants. For the rest, it could be believed that, at least during the last years of the war, the selected parole towns were chosen for their dullness.

For any man confined to prison the prospect is bleak enough. For the prisoner of war there are additional worries and uncertainties. He has no fixed sentence and his gaoler is his enemy. Nevertheless, it might be supposed that the paroled officer had little to grumble about and, when the system was equally respected and working at its honourable best, this was perfectly true. Later, when the best of its advantages had been decayed by abuse, this was less likely to be the case.

The common soldier or sailor of the period was accustomed to a hard life, little pay, poor provisions and tough, even brutal, treatment at the hands of his superiors. Often he was a man pressed into service at sea and thus could hardly be called free, even before his capture. Unless he was unlucky enough to be sent to a prison hulk, or found it impossible to resign himself to captivity, it may well be that his life as a prisoner of war in England was no worse than his life as a free man.

How different for the officer, however, who, only a short time before, may have been in command of a warship or battalion, and now found himself under the command of, perhaps, the local banker of a small town, or a naval lieutenant. The sudden change from an active, demanding life and participation in the progress of a war, to one of idleness and monotony; the drastic drop in his standard of living and income – all this would have taken a far more drastic adjustment. Furthermore, he had bound himself by his word to stay a prisoner and, with the likelihood of exchange growing ever more remote, this could be for a very long time. Something like one in ten of all paroled officers did not honour their pledge, but that still left nine who did. I suppose we should remind ourselves that they did not *have* to give their *parole d' honneur* in the first place, and that some may have given it with the idea of escape – it was easier to escape from a town than from a depot or a prison ship.

Therefore, how then did these men settle into their *cautionnements* in Great Britain? It would seem that after the first trauma of captivity and introduction into a strange environment, most were intelligent and adaptable enough to make the best of their predicament. The impression which they left on the parole towns varied to a degree according to the nationality of the prisoners.

We read of the serious-minded and untroublesome Dutch; of the sober Dane and of the Americans who were, alas, 'a rougher lot,

who broke things up a good deal'. The French, and not only through sheer numbers, left the most lasting and affectionate impression. Memoirs of the period speak of their 'great mannerliness', their 'buoyancy of spirit', and always, wherever they were settled, their quite amazing ingenuity.

A Chesterfield lady remembered 'Their large hooped gold ear-rings, their pink or sky-blue umbrellas, the Legion of Honour ribbons in their button-holes; their profuse exchanges of embraces and even kisses in the public street; their attendant poodles carrying walking sticks in their mouths and their vociferous talking. A great source of amusement was their training of birds and dogs.'

Although she found these colourful characters interesting, she was much less impressed by their womenfolk. The wives who had been permitted to join their husbands she dismissed as 'very dingy, plain-looking women.'

The injection of such colour, fashion and continental manners into an unexciting community, must have quickened the life of many a dull parole town and one might reasonably expect that the effect upon it would be lasting. It is therefore surprising to hear that enquirers at the end of the last century found that the memory of this exotic addition to the wartime population had almost completely faded.

Today it is, as one might guess, rare to find valued remembrances which have been passed down through a family in any of the towns. Even the descendants of prisoners who married their wartime sweethearts are difficult to trace, as many anglicised their surnames when they settled in this country. Nevertheless, the author has managed to talk to members of a few of those families, some of whom have preserved records of forebears who once fought on the other side.

The most frequent reminder to the exile that he was in a foreign land came at meal time. If he ate at his lodgings the French palate must often have been offended by the offerings of his English, Welsh or Scottish landlady. For this reason and also for reasons of economy the officers often preferred to cater for themselves, either individually or communally. Even so, those who had to depend entirely on the Government allowance found it hard to make ends meet, as the cost of eating in Britain was far higher than in France.

That this was a serious matter is proved by the number of complaints received by the Agents and the Transport Board of the inadequacy of the allowance. M. Rivière of the French Admiralty stated that whereas a British Officer could survive in France on 9d. a day, a Frenchman in England would need 2/- a day to do as well. The Transport Office, with much fairness, set about checking this statement in a practical way. They called in an officer, Lieutenant James Wallis, who had recently escaped from France (we hope honourably) to draw up a list of comparative prices in the two countries. As a result of the table he prepared the allowances were increased:

AN ENGLISH GENTLEMAN IN
ENGLAND WILL REQUIRE DAILY:

	s.d.
1lb Bread	0.2
1lb Beef	0.4
¾ of Beer (this measure is not known)	0.1
Beer, very bad, is 3d a	

Bottle, Wine 7d; say they are taken alternately, a bottle a day.	0.5¼
Vegetables and Fruit (Vegetables are very cheap)	0.0½
Milk	0.0½
Expense of cooking	0.1
Wood (at Verdun very dear, 35 livres a corde) 2d per day probably	
1 day's subsistence in France according to M. Rivière.	0.9
1 day's subsistence in France according to Lieut. Wallis' Price List.	1.5½
Average of the Estimates	1.1¼

A FRENCH GENTLEMAN IN FRANCE WILL REQUIRE DAILY:

	s.d.
½ Quartern-Loaf of Bread	0.5
¾ lb Beef, 10d lb at least	0.7½
2 quarts of Beer	0.6
A Pot of Porter	0.5
Vegetables, including Apples	0.2
Milk	0.2
Cooking, at least	0.2
1 day's subsistence in England, according to M. Rivière.	2.0
More probably	2.0½

Wherever the fishing was good – and those paroled to the Border Towns of Scotland would have been particularly lucky – they were able to enjoy the occasional luxury of salmon or trout. However, they were resourceful enough not to depend on rivers alone to supplement their menu – sometimes in ways which shocked the locals.

Much as the inhabitants of the parole towns admired the culture and manners of these likeable men, they could never get used to some of their eating habits. Their taste for snails, frogs and small birds gave many people the shudders. The 'Southern Counties Register' for 1866, says that the older people of Kelso remembered as their most singular peculiarity, 'their gathering for use different kinds of wild weeds by the roadsides, and hedge-roots, and killing small birds to eat – the latter a practice considered not far removed from cannibalism.'

Officers were often to be met with, early in the morning, scanning garden walls and searching under leaves for snails for breakfast. Although it was said, almost certainly maliciously, that 'they found a good plump cat an acceptable substitute for hare,' the most eagerly sought after and obtainable delicacy was frog, and many a landlady complained that her kitchen table was ruined when used as a chopping block for the preparation of frog fricassee.

Francis Able recorded an amusing frog story, told by an old Dumfries man who remembered the prisoners' culinary peculiarities. The occasion was a festivity in the town, in honour of St Crispin, the patron saint of shoemakers. A local man named Renwick was elected 'King of the Cobblers' and he was delighted to accept the hospitality of a group of French officers, who invited him to a dinner which he never forgot:

'The Crispin ploy, ye ken, cam frae France, an' the officers in the big hoose askit the King O' the Cobblers tae dine wi' them. They had a gran' spread wi' a fine pie, that the Maister Renwick thocht was made o' rabbits toshed up in some new fangled way, an' dinna miss tae lay in a guid stock. When it was owre, they askit him how he likit his denner, an' he said "First rate". Syne they lauched and speered him if he kent what the pie was made o', but he wasna sure. When they tell't him it was paddocks [frogs], it was a' ane as if they had gien him a dose of pizzen. He just banged up and breenged oot the hoose. Ooor bit winnock lookit oot on the Frenchmen's backyaid, an' we saw Maister Renwick sair, sair forffochen, but after a dainty bit warlse, he an' the paddocks pairtit company.'

Another old character from the same town remembered that 'the first siller I ever earned was for gatherin' paddocks for the Frenchmen.' Craig-Brown, in his 'History of Selkirk', mentions yet another old Scot whose father was the landlord of an inn at Heathenlie, where the parolees used to call in for their morning tots of rum, who told him: 'they made tea out of dried whun blooms and they skinned the verra paddas'. The French prisoners in Britain have left so much evidence of ingenious craftsmanship and a whole variety of talents, that it is only to be expected that they would employ some of this talent in a matter as important as food, and that some would be possessed of culinary expertise. We know that in more than one *cautionnement*, officers set themselves up as pastry cooks, bakers and confectioners. And William Chambers of Peebles, describes in his 'Memoirs' a sort of communal messing which may have been typical of the arrangements made by the less fortunate in other towns. He recalled that, 'in a friendly way, at least as regards the daily mess, or 'table d'hôte', the richer helped the poorer which was a good trait in their character. The messing together was the great resource, and took place in a house hired for the purpose, in which the cookery was conducted under the auspices of M. Lavoche, one of the prisoners who was skilled in cuisine.'

As youngsters, William Chambers and his brother greatly increased their pocket-money by rearing rabbits in their backyard, and became suppliers to M. Lavoche's 'hotel'.

Not all parolees were entirely dependent on their own resources in the matter of good eating. Apart from the hospitality of the humbler townsfolk and neighbouring farmers, some were entertained in more exalted spheres. Their education and culture – and perhaps their value as curiosities – gained them entry into the society of the local gentry and the county families. As it is recorded that they often dined with their body-servants behind their chairs, it is probable that invitations to the grander functions were more often extended to the higher ranks – who were, presumably, less in need of the treat – than were junior officers.

These social gatherings, almost the only opportunity which the parolee had to mix with British people of his class – unless he was a Freemason – were often the starting points of lasting friendships, sometimes based on mutual political sympathies, for not all who fought for Napoleon were Buonapartists at heart. And speaking of hearts, whilst their tales of adventure and war-like encounters on land and sea no doubt enthralled the hosts, their charm, elegant dress or ornate uniform and prowess on the dance floor, often captivated the daughters. That the girls were smitten by the charms of these captive romeos is evident from the stories of affairs, romances, jiltings and marriages, which span the wars from the Seven Years' to the Napoleonic.

Even earlier, in 1748, the correspondence between two young ladies who met French officers paroled at Deal, indicates that they found them overwhelmingly attractive. One simpering letter, which I cannot bear to quote in full, speaks of their 'universal agreeableness'; that they sang, wrote poetry and panegyrics, and goes on to tell of a French officer she had met at an assembly 'who was very entertaining. Miss Hall and I shared him by way of partner and between us did not suffer him to sit down a single dance, which perhaps you may think somewhat unmerciful; but surely there is no need to scruple about a Frenchman, a species of creature composed entirely of air and fire, with no principle of lassitude in it.'

The outcome of many of the associations between foreign gallants and British girls was marriage. However, far more ended unhappily, with scandal, disgrace and misery for the girl and, unless he could support a child born out of wedlock, civil prison for the prisoner responsible. Under the law he was required to maintain his illegitimate off-spring, the only alternative being the public gaol – an experience which could be extremely unpleasant in those days.

Of course, the better off officer got away with it at what, to many, must have been small cost, and the unfortunate girl suffered most from the liaison. When Abell was making inquiries in the Falmouth area in the early years of this century, a local vicar told him that whilst he had no evidence of marriages to French parolees, 'some St Budock girls appear to have made captivity more blessed for some of them.' George Sweetman, in his pamphlet, 'The French in Wincanton', says:

> 'Here, as in all other parole towns, a large number of children were born out of wedlock, whose fathers were reported to be visitors. Some indeed took French names, and several officers had to pay large sums of money to the Parish authorities before they left. One of the drawbacks to the sojourn of so many strangers amongst us was the increase of immorality. One informant said: "Not the least source of attraction to these gallant sons of France, were the buxom country maidens, who found their way into the town, but lost their way back." '

The amorous nature of many of these young men, made them obvious targets for accusations in paternity cases. The numerous complaints and denials which reached the Transport Office from indignant prisoners, would suggest that, perhaps at least sometimes, their usually better financial standing and prospects made them more desirable candidates for the post of unmarried-father than the local lads.

Even the girl who legally married a Frenchman was not in a very secure position. The French Government did not recognise the validity of such marriages, and if, when the war was over, she accompanied her husband on his return to France, she might well be refused admission into the country. The difference in attitude of the two governments in the matter of marital and extramarital affairs is difficult to understand. In the case of the English wife being allowed to join her British prisoner husband in France, she could expect no financial help from the French; but the French wife granted a similar privilege was supported by our Government, as were her children. Yet the poor English girl, who had literally been left holding the baby, received no such Government aid and was flung on the often uncertain charity of the Parish.

Although the records contain abundant proof that many continental 'gentlemen' took advantage of their country's view of Anglo-French marriages and abandoned their British wives and war-babies, there are many families in this country today who owe their origins to the happy endings to true romance and love-matches which began in parole towns in Britain.

So much for the gastronomic and amatory adventures of the officer prisoner of war; but obviously cooking and courting did not occupy all of the hours of their enforced leisure. In the winter months they passed their time in their clubs and meeting rooms at billiards, or discussed such news of the progress of the war as could be gathered from the news-sheets, or from prisoners newly arrived in the town. The musically talented and the thespians organised entertainments for the rest – concerts and plays which were well attended and enjoyed by the residents of the town.

A surprisingly large number were Freemasons, and in many parole towns they had their own Prisoner of War Lodge, but were often welcomed into the Lodges of their British Brethren, either as visiting Brothers or initiated as members into the local Craft.

The less affluent among them who possessed any talent or tradeable knowledge or ability, showed enterprising industry in adding to their funds. Some created little articles for sale from the most unlikely of odds and ends; others taught dancing, drawing, painting and music. The academics set themselves up as teachers of science and mathematics, and almost every parole town had its language masters, who were available for the instruction of the youth of the area. The youths themselves may have been less delighted at the introduction of so many teachers to the town, but their presence must have been a considerable educational asset to these little communities.

The small industries which occupied their time brought them into close contact with the local peoples, and resulted in a mutual friendliness, inspired on the one hand by their cheerfulness in adversity and, on the other, by the generally sympathetic attitude of the inhabitants. After all, these alien additions to the population were no nine-day-wonders; some of the towns were *cautionnements* for so many years that the presence of a substantial foreign element became part of everyday life. If the old adage is true that it takes twenty-five years to become accepted into an English village or small town, then a few of the parolees were prisoners long enough to qualify for at least half membership.

With so many men, ranking from General to Carpenter or Officer's-Servant, and of so many nationalities, over so long a period, one can only gather a general impression of the effect they had upon the towns; but it says much for the behaviour of the majority that when they were remembered it was more often for their qualities than their faults.

No doubt the Transport Office would have had a different memory. Whilst most parolees gave little trouble, this still left many hundreds who caused them thousands of hours of work, voluminous correspondence and outraged concern. Parole-breaking, in its most serious form – successful or attempted escape – was practised to a degree which would never have been tolerated in France.

The magnitude of this abuse can be judged from the fact that, in 1778, 1779 and the first six months of 1780, no fewer than 295 'broke-paroles' had made successful escapes from parole towns; add to this the number of failed escape attempts and the many hundreds of lesser parole offences and it is surprising that the French method of 'If one offends, punish all' was not more often adopted. The following report of 1812 speaks for itself:

Transport Office 25th June 1812

NUMBER OF ALL FRENCH COMMISSIONED OFFICERS PRISONERS OF WAR, ON PAROLE IN GREAT BRITAIN.

	Total No. of Comm. Officers on Parole	No. that broke their Parole	been Retaken	Effected Escape
Year Ending				
5th June 1810	1,685	104	47	57
5th June 1811	2,087	118	47	71
5th June 1812	2,142	242	63	179
		464	157	307
Besides the above Commissioned Officers, other French Prisoners such as Masters and Mates of Merchant Vessels, Captains and Lieutenants of Privateers, Civilians holding situations connected with the Army and Navy, Passengers and other Persons of Respectability have broken their Parole in the three years above mentioned ………………		218	85	138
		682	242	440

N.B. The numbers stated in this Account include those Persons only who have actually absconded from the Places appointed for their Residence.

A considerable number of Officers have been ordered into confinement, for various other breaches of their Parole Engagements.

(signed) RUP. GEORGE: J. BOWEN: J. DOUGLAS.

There were seven hundred escape attempts in three years by French officers alone, and almost two thirds of them successfully accomplished. How, then, did so many manage to get clear away? Clever as many of them may have been, few could have reached the coast and crossed the Channel without the aid of British accomplices.

In the eighteenth century there had been little love lost between the English country people and the French prisoner of war, and the offending paroled officer could expect little of the tolerance shown to his brothers in later wars. By the time of the Napoleonic Wars, when parole breaking was at its height there was a strange softening of feeling and most of our countryfolk were well disposed towards them – even to the extent of turning a blind eye to the occasional bending of minor rules. Even so, there were few who would have taken an active part in the escape plans of a prisoner.

So much for the majority, but there were others who were interested in the major and minor disobediences of the officers from a different and unprincipled point of view – personal gain. These fell into two groups whose activities would, at first glance, seem to have no point of contact.

The first was the most unpleasant, as he took no risk – the professional parole town snoop. These mean-minded men made their money by spying on the parolee in the hope of catching him out in small technical breaches of his parole engagement. Had they stuck at that, it could be argued that, though without admiration for those who practised the trade, they were at least of assistance to the Agent; and that after being picked up on small points, the offending officer might be discouraged from committing more serious infringements. However, some went despicably further, by encouraging and provoking prisoners to commit offences which they could then 'discover' and claim the guaranteed ten-shilling reward.

The second group was made up of the get-away experts, the escape-agents who were the organisers of most successful home runs. Both of these types had one thing in common. Neither would have been in business if the paroled officer had kept strictly to the letter of his pledge; but their activities touched at another point – the persecution by the first group was often the professed reason why the prisoner patronised the second. It can be understood that an officer, smarting under a fine or punishment brought about by the word of a lout, might well feel unjustly used, to the extent of releasing him from his word of honour.

The lucrative trade of escape-agent became very highly organised, and one particularly businesslike operator, Thomas Feast Moore, who worked out of Folkestone, had sub-agents and contact-men near depots and *cautionnements* throughout the land. Charles Jones, the Solicitor to the Admiralty in 1812, was aware of the methods used by the professional escape merchants, and described them in detail:

1. 'By means of the smugglers and those connected with them on the coast, who proceed with horses and covered carriages to the depots by arrangement, rendezvous about the hour of the evening when the prisoners ought to be indoors, about the mile limit and thus carry them off, travelling through the night and in the daytime hiding in the woods and coverts.

    'The horses they use are excellent, and the carriages constructed for the purpose. The prisoners are conveyed to the coast, where they are delivered over to the smugglers and concealed until the boat is ready. They embark at night, and before morning are in France. These escapes are generally in pursuance of orders from France.'

2. 'By means of persons of profligate lives who, residing in or near Parole towns, act as conductors to such of the prisoners as choose to form their own plan of escape. These prisoners usually travel in post-chaises, and the conductors' business is to pay the expenses and give orders on the road to the innkeepers, drivers &c., to prevent discovery or suspicion as to the quality of the travellers.

    'When once a prisoner reaches a public-house or inn near the coast, he is considered safe. But there are cases when the prisoners, having one among them who can speak good English, travel without conductors. In these cases the innkeepers and postboys alone are to blame, and it is certain that if this description of persons could be compelled to do their duty many escapes would be prevented.'

Until 1812 the detected escape-agent was charged with committing an offence not much more serious than a misdemeanour, and if found guilty was likely to receive a sentence of two or three years in gaol. Added to this there was usually the punishment of being exposed to the ridicule and abuse of the public in the pillory on market-days for a month or two. The landlord of the Red Lion at Rye and his two assistants, who had arranged the escape of General Phillipon and Lt. Garnier, were each gaoled at Horsham, but had to spend the first month pilloried on the coast, 'as near to France as possible'. The sentences were light considering the treacherous nature of the offence, but in 1812 a Bill was passed which made it a felony, which carried the penalty of transportation. The period of their Australasian imprisonment was most often seven, fourteen or twenty-one years, but some escape-merchants were transported for life. The escape-management profession became a hazardous occupation from then on, but with such high rewards, from £25 a head to £400, the usual fee being about £150, (£50 down, the balance on delivery to the coast and the escape vessel) business continued brisk until the end.

Escape was made easy in most cases by the unscrupulous among our own countrymen, but does not excuse the 'broke-parole', unless the latter had convinced himself that he had been absolved by unfair treatment at the hands of his captor. Had a Court of Honour similar to our own existed in France, it is probable that a number could have proved their case, but a far greater number could only have been judged out-and-out breakers of their word, with nothing to be said in their favour.

If analysis had revealed that parole-breaking was mainly confined to privateer or junior officers, a high percentage of disregard for an honourable system might have been expected. The undisciplined and adventurous privateer who, usually, had not been indoctrinated into a jealous regard for the traditions of regimental or naval service, had only his personal sense of honour to consider – and a point might be stretched in the case of the very young junior officer, on the grounds of youth and inexperience. However, as we have seen, the example was set by the most senior officers of army and navy, and when excuses were offered they were usually unconvincing tokens.

The *Moniteur*, the government-controlled French newspaper, published a blanket exoneration for all absconders when, on the 9th August, 1812, it stated that, 'as French officers only surrendered on the understanding that they would be allowed to retain their weapons', we had only ourselves to blame! The fact that they were not *forced* to pledge their word, was not mentioned.

The cynical abuse by the ten percent or so, made things far less comfortable for the remaining majority. Security, which had been almost unnecessary in the great days of mutual trust, now made it essential to keep a closer watch on all our captives; to smarten up our Agents and, on a few occasions, to take measures inspired by despair. It had happened before. In 1797, when an invasion and uprising was expected at any time, all parolees in Britain were taken from their towns and marched to close confinement for a spell, mostly to Norman Cross, in Huntingdonshire.

In November, 1811, escapes had become so alarmingly frequent that Wincanton and some other parole centres were cleared and their prisoners transferred to new *cautionnements* in the Border Towns of Scotland.

Recaptured 'broke-paroles' were usually severely dealt with. It was decreed that they 'shall from that time be considered and treated in all respects as common men', which meant at least transfer to a closed depot or, if judged an incorrigible or the circumstances of the escape particularly bad, to a taste of the dreaded hulks. Surprisingly, some were given a second chance, resurrected from the level of 'common man' and allowed to pledge their word of honour for a second time – not always, sad to relate, with any more sincerity than the first.

The dream of freedom, as ever-present in the minds of those who served out their parole with patience as it was for those who could not wait, at last became reality for them all, with the declaration of Peace. At the end of each war, with the long uncertainty over, whatever the outcome, thoughts of family, home and the world beyond the one-mile limit, would be uppermost in the minds of the now ex-prisoners.

Those inhabitants who could remember their coming, years before, would now witness a scene as opposite as it could be; a joyous clearing out of rooms; an impatient packing of possessions for the homeward journey; the craftsmen hurriedly disposing of remaining stock-in-trade; a clubbing together to pay for transport to the coast – and some fond farewells to British friends and sweethearts with promises of correspondence, often soon forgotten.

This air of jubilation would have been common to prisoners released at the end of each of the wars, but the Peace of 1814 brought about some soul-searching amidst the celebrations. News of the abdication of Napoleon and of the new regime in France was promulgated to the depots and parole towns in the form of a printed circular, and sides of the fence had to be quickly chosen.

Some of the officers could not bring themselves to serve the new Monarchy, and elected not to return to their home land; but many a 'devoted Buonapartist', who had suffered deeply when the British celebrated their victories over his hero, executed a smart about-turn and donned the white cockade.

The following loyal address, sent by officers who had been paroled to Hawick in Scotland, is typical of the many received by the French Commissioners appointed to deal with the repatriation of prisoners of war:

> ' ...The happy events which have taken place in our country, and have placed on the throne of their ancestors the illustrious family of the Bourbons. We lay at the feet of the worthy descendant of Henry IV. The homage of our entire obedience and fidelity.'

The rejoicing of the released prisoners, though great, was eclipsed by the general rejoicing throughout Great Britain at the victorious outcome of so many years of war. For that day at least, even the inhabitants of the parole towns must have joined in the celebrations, in spite of the financial hardship which would hit a large part of the community with the departure of their paying guests.

Every town and every village had its parades and festivals and local records abound with reports of the great occasion. Typical are the diary entries in *'The Norfolk Annals,1801 to 1850'*:

> 'APRIL 6. 1814. – With colours flying and the passengers decorated with the white cockade, the Newmarket Mail brought to Norwich news of the entry of the Allied Army into Paris on March 31st. The church bells were rung, and a bonfire lighted in the Market Place. The rejoicings were renewed on the 9th, 10th and 11th, upon the receipt of the intelligence of the counter Revolution, Bonaparte's

abdication, and the restoration of the Bourbons. On the last mentioned day the horses were removed from the mail coach, and the people dragged it thrice round the Market Place.
> The Chevalier de Bardelin, a French emigrant gentleman, formerly in the service of the King of France, left Norwich, where he had resided 15 years, to accompany Louis XVIII to Paris.'

And later in the same month:

> 'APRIL 19th 1814. – A grand *fête* was held at Yarmouth in honour of the victories. It commenced with a pageant called "The Triumph of Neptune." The "sea god" landed upon the beach and headed a procession round the town. In the procession was an effigy of Bonaparte in fetters. Afterwards 58 tables were laid on the Quay from north to south, each accommodating from 120 to 150 persons, to whom roast beef and plum pudding were served. After dinner there was a naval procession to the Dene, where there were donkey races and other sports took place; a bonfire concluded the day's rejoicings. The public subscription to defray the cost of the celebration exceeded £1,000.'

With true collector's luck, I found pasted to the back cover of an old book, a pamphlet which contained the programme of the Peace celebrations and procession which took place in the old parole town of Moretonhampstead, in June 1814.

The pamphlet was the published record of a lecture read by J. D. Prickman in 1901, entitled 'Fragmentary Notes of the French Prisoners in the West of England and other Places in the Early Part of the Nineteenth Century'. Most of those 'notes' were quotes from Captain Vernon Harris, ex-Governor of Dartmoor Prison and snippets from *The Times* of 1814; but the really interesting contribution is the detailed plan of the Moretonhampstead peace procession, which ended with a banquet well supplied with cider. It must have been an impressive spectacle and, even now, the names of the old trades, professions and occupations represented in the parade make fascinating reading.

The pages which follow tell something of the particular stories of each of the Parole Towns in Britain. It will be seen that the degree of comfort or hardship experienced by the parolee depended on four main factors: which war he had fought in; the town in which he found himself paroled; the extent to which he could adapt and honour his word of honour and, not the least consideration, whether he was strapped for cash or well-to-do.

The French officer, captured during the Seven Years' War and paroled to a Kentish town, would probably return home after the war with bitter memories of an unfriendly and hostile people. Kent was too close to France and retained far too many memories of friction and war to roll out the carpet for a captured enemy officer. At least the captive cousin, at the beginning of the War of American Independence, could expect to be less than welcomed, and regarded as a rebel, renegade or pirate. If those same officers could have fought in the Napoleonic Wars and found themselves paroled in a Scottish Border Town at the Peace of 1814, they may well have been among the signatories to one of the many eulogistic testimonials to the kindness and hospitality of the inhabitants, which were published in the newspapers of that time.

1. J. Godsworth Alger: *Napoleon's British Visitors.* 1904.

2. See Chapter 8, *The Arts and Crafts of Napoleonic and American Prisoners of War 1756-1816*, THE FREEMASON PRISONER OF WAR.

Chapter Twenty-Two

Parole in England

An interesting parole story is told concerning Captain Brenton of H.M.S *Minerve*, which went aground under the batteries of Cherbourg, on 3rd June, only a few days after the resumption of the war in 1803. All four hundred or so of the British prisoners, officers and seamen alike, were marched off well inland to the town of Epinal. Their first halting-place was St Lo, where they stayed overnight.

The French commander at St Lo was General Delgorge, who received them with a degree of friendliness; a friendliness which, on their departure next day, shocked a young and unworldly midshipman who whispered to his mate, 'Look! That French General is kissing our Skipper!'

Once they had left St Lo the gendarme officers in charge of the march were less pleasant, and caused Captain Brenton to remonstrate, stating that officers who had given their parole of honour should thereafter not be placed under restrictions.

'*Je me moque de votre parole d'honneur*' was the impolite reply, '*je ne sais pas ce que c'est moi.*'

'Then I will describe it to you,' said Captain Brenton, 'it is, to a British officer, stronger than any prison you have in France!'

As WE HAVE SEEN, DURING THE PERIOD COVERED by this study, the chivalrous ideals which had inspired the humane system of parole and exchange had been gradually corrupted through lack of respect. Furthermore, by the early nineteenth century, it had deteriorated to a point where implicit faith in a man's word became tainted with mistrust, and imposition of restrictions and precautions became inevitable. Even so, and even at its worst, what remained of the system was still a great improvement on the practices of past centuries.

The fate of the prisoner of war in early times depended entirely on economic considerations of his incarceration and subsistence. If the possibilities of his usefulness as a slave were unlikely to justify his drain on the food supplies, or it seemed unlikely that ransom would be forthcoming for his release, he would be slaughtered on the battlefield or cast overboard at sea. Such atrocities were also calculated to increase the strength of the captor by putting fear into the heart of his adversary.

That this attitude towards the captive was at least recognised even as late as the early seventeen-hundreds, is shown in a passage from Daniel Defoe (1660–1731), where he has Robinson Crusoe worrying whether he was hypocritical in condemning cannibals who slew and ate their captives, concluding:

' …I was certainly wrong in it; that these people were not murderers in the sense that I had before condemned them in my thoughts; any more than those Christians were murderers who often put to death the prisoners taken in battle; or more frequently, on many occasions, put whole troops to the sword, without giving quarter, though they threw down their arms and submitted.'

And a century and a half later old 'Blood and Iron' Prince Bismarck once said – perhaps deliberately outrageously and not entirely seriously – 'Prisoners! You shouldn't have taken any: You should have killed them all!'

Exchange was almost unheard of as a method of disposing of ordinary prisoners; but even then the captured 'gentleman' stood a better chance of living to fight another day. If he belonged to the upper and wealthier stratum of warlike society; lord, leader, chief –

or *senior officer* as we would call him today – he might regain his freedom by the payment of ransom – an exchange for cash.

By the early seventeenth century the treatment of the prisoner of war began to feature in the deliberations of political philosophers in their considerations on the laws of war, almost for the first time. The most significant of these, the Dutch legal scholar Hugo Grotius, said in his masterpiece, *On the Law of War and Peace 1625*, that whilst he did not deny that the captor had the legal right to enslave his enemies, he recommended the alternatives of ransom or exchange. However, as late as the reign of Queen Anne, prisoners of war were, on occasion if not often, put to what would soon after become unacceptable employment. After the Battle of Ramilles in the War of the Spanish Succession, in 1706, the Duke of Marlborough had all his French prisoners drafted as pressed men to serve in British warships.

Officially, at least, the ransoming of officers, or common prisoners of war, came to an end in 1793. As noted in the previous chapter, the ransom rates agreed upon between the two countries up to that time had been fixed at £60 (or sixty common soldiers or sailors) for one Admiral or Field-Marshal, down to £1 (or one soldier, sailor, privateersman or merchantman) for an equivalent ordinary rating on the other side.

By 1810, the earlier excellent system of exchange, too, had begun to stagger towards a halt; but, like all the other aspects of parole and exchange, ransoming never completely died out: A number of the *détenu* members of the British aristocracy were released from Verdun and returned to England without apparent exchange – there was certainly no equivalent group of French civilian *détenus* in Britain who could have been swapped, man-for-man, quality-for-quality, so it may well be that ransom was the most likely alternative employed. The British rules of exchange never allowed for the barter of captive French officers in return for even the most elevated of our civilian detainees in France, until the war was nearly over. A few senior naval or military officers in the forces of France, Denmark, Holland or other continental allies, could be exchanged rank-for-rank, as so few British senior officers were ever captured by the enemy. However, sometimes we accepted a number of lower ranks in exchange for a senior captured officer, but here, too, some sort of ransom might have been involved in the deal.

For the short period from the early eighteenth century until the beginning of the Revolutionary War in 1792, the Parole of Honour System flourished in, if not all, most of its glory. Against the assurance given by no more than a signature, both sides allowed officers to return home, or at least allowed great freedom in the country of their captor, until exchange had been agreed upon – and there was seldom occasion for either side to regret the confidence placed in their word. Of course, no system was ever one hundred per cent perfect, and a very few did break their word, even in those early days; although, as already discussed, the man adjudged a 'broke-parole' suffered greatly and permanently by besmirching his word of honour.

The rot began to set in soon after France signed the treaty of alliance with America in February, 1778, during the War of Independence. Over the following three years, successful escapes from English parole towns, by French officers alone, averaged more than two a week. Compared with later years, this was a very small number; but, when added to the many attempted escapes and lesser parole offences, Agents, militia and the Transport Office had good reason to wake up to the security risks and reconsider the suitability of some parole towns – their proximity to the sea being a prime consideration.

After the French Revolution, parole-breaking became more and more common on the part of French officers, and as the Transport Board would never have condoned such dishonourable conduct by a British officer on a tit-for-tat basis, no matter how many captive foreign officers proved untrustworthy, the whole thing became a very one-sided affair.

It could be said that the greatest parole-breaker of all was the French Government itself. During the Napoleonic period, it made a mockery of the *parole d'honneur* given by great numbers of its officers, through no fault on the part of the latter. The whole system was based on methods of fair exchange, with cartels of officers and men being returned home by one side, in full expectation of a like number being received in exchange from the other. It is something of a mystery why the British Government should have been so trusting – unless it was more interested in reducing the great numbers (and expense) of prisoners in Britain than in receiving the balance due.

In 1808, by which time we had good reason to have lost all faith in promises, France was in debt to us for more than 750 officers and many times that number of other ranks. Even ten years earlier, Holland had returned only sixty-four British officers in exchange for 316 Dutch parolees returned to Holland.

During the Seven Years' War, 1756 to 1763, at least thirty-two towns in England and Wales had been designated parole centres. A few more towns may well have been used for housing officers for short periods, whilst awaiting exchange, or release on the promise of returning a British officer of equal rank after reaching home. Over those seven years, parolees could not be certain of a friendly reception as a matter of course. Although they were generally accepted without initial animosity, there was nothing of the warmth and welcome which would often have greeted them half a century later, particularly if they were paroled to Scotland. The records of the hundreds of complaints received by the Commissioners, from both inhabitants and prisoners, show that they were most prolific

during the Seven Years' War. Townsfolk complained of parole offences, arrogance, unsettled debts, loose morals, competition with local trades, etc. Officers lodged great numbers of complaints – many adjudged well-founded – of ill-treatment at the hands of roughs and troublemakers, and persecution from small-time bounty-hunters, forever on the look-out for the small rewards to be gained from reported petty parole offences.

The rules of parole were then more strictly enforced than in later years, and the 'broke-parole' could find himself condemned to a prison hulk, or, if he made a successful – but inexcusable – escape, might be sentenced to a civil gaol in his own country or returned to his captors. Decisions in these matters were dealt with through the 'Commissioners for Taking Care of Sick and Wounded Seamen and for Exchange of Prisoners of War', commonly known as 'The Sick and Hurt Office'; only after 1799 was the care of prisoners of war placed under the authority of the Transport Office.

Many were the complaints from 'broke-parole' officers who ended up on the hulks or in closed prison depots. However, the substance of their grievances was less often the fact that they were so punished for what, after all, they had brought upon themselves, but that they were confined with common soldiers, sailors or privateersmen. These complaints were taken seriously by the Commissioners and eventually special prison ships and areas in the prisoner of war depots were set aside for 'broke-parole' officers – at least for first-offenders.

Others, who had not broken their parole, were equally indignant that they should have to mix with a lower class of people in the parole town to which they had been sent – whether local inhabitants or their own junior officers and privateer or merchant officers who had been granted parole. The French Revolution was thirty or more years in the future, so England gathered in a goodly number of the French aristocracy and gentry among her captives. Many of these gentlemen had high expectations of privileges due to them, as the following translations of their complaints and requests will show.

The multi-titled officer who wrote (in the 3rd person), this letter in 1756, the first year of the war, was clearly shocked that he should be transferred from Bristol to a parole town in the country:

> 'Having been informed... in your letter of 14th that Monsieur De Bethune, Knight of St Simon, Marquis of Arbest, Baron of St Lucie, Lord of High and Low Justiciaries of the parishes of Chateauvieux, Corvilac, Laneau, Pontmartin, Neung and other areas, was granted parole along with the other officers of his keeping. I would be better able to appraise you that a man of the calibre of Monsieur De Bethune, who is addressing you at this moment, was not put on earth to be in such a deserted place as the country, in view of the fact that on both his parents' sides he is related to the most powerful Kings who ever walked the face of the earth. A place of his choice, such as London or Bristol is more appropriate for yours truly,
>
> De Bristol; le 15 Xbre. 1756'

It would seem that the authorities were less than impressed; but further correspondence reveals that M. De Bethune still remained confident that one of his standing must certainly eventually be allowed to live in London.

There was a constant flow of requests and petitions to be allowed transfer to London, Bath, or any other places of culture and liveliness. Abell gives the example of the Prince de Rohan who could not adapt himself to his parole at Romsey: '...although he had the most rare privilege of a six-mile limit around it, [he] wrote on July 4, 1758, requesting permission for himself and three or four officers to go to Southampton once a week to make purchases, as Romsey Market is so indifferent, and to pass the night there. The six-mile limit, he says, does not enable him to avail himself of the hospitality of the people of quality, and he wants leave to go further with his suite. He adds a panegyric on the high birth and honour of French naval officers, which made parole-breaking an impossibility, and he resents their being placed in the same category with privateer and merchant captains.'

The Commissioners, whilst not doubting the Prince's word, doubted the wisdom of setting a precedent by granting visits to a sea port: 'Petition Not Granted'. The year before, 1757, an officer paroled to Tenterden, Kent, wrote – not for the first time – to the Commissioners complaining of ill-treatment by trouble-making groups in the town:

'If I must stay in England, permit me once more to entreat you to send me to a better place, as I have not yet been able to ingratiate myself with the people of this village. Since I was here many Frenchmen have complained to the Mayor, who has, in turn, put up a notice which forbids any Frenchman to be insulted.

Any such notice has promptly been ripped down the same day. It is really unpleasant to be in a town where the people have to be forbidden to insult prisoners... I have heard that Frenchmen who are held as prisoners in Maidstone are fine and have never been insulted... but what has also spurred me into asking to be sent elsewhere is that, when walking down the street, we run the risk of being thrown into the mud even if we intend stepping off the pavement to let the person pass.

Tenterden, 1757.'

One can feel sympathy for his indignation, even at this distant point in time, and hope that the Sick and Hurt Office had given it their attention. They did, but not as he would have wished. They strongly criticized the Agent, that they should have to hear such complaints from prisoners and not from him; but informed him that the complainant should stay where he was – as he had already spent time in Sissinghurst Castle Prison for having previously broken his parole!

There is little doubt that in most of the towns there were unruly elements who, for profit or from simple-minded aggression, made the life of parolees something of a hell. Even in the later wars such despicable types were sometimes in evidence – and were often punished. Soldier and sailor captives with experience of war and action must have been enraged to the point of violent retaliation, but most were wise enough to take it – though not without complaint – as this petition, signed by eighteen officers at Torrington, points out:

'We are abused at every step, hurled numerous insults and threats, often pursued by the rabble as far as our doors with rocks and sticks. What is more, Sir, the day before yesterday at 5 o'clock in the evening a lead bullet fired from a rifle came within range of the doorway of our lodgings. Fortunately whoever fired it was not a good marksman. There are those of us in all the villages bent on retaliation and eager to see justice done, but will take no action and are forced to silently put up with the situation for fear of making matters worse and inciting people's anger further.

Torrington. 1758'

In that same year one group of officers attempted to retaliate in a different way. They circulated a leaflet which read:

'AS A RESULT of deliberations made by and upheld by the body of Frenchmen detained in this town, it has been ordered that and in accordance with this Agreement, any Merchant, Manufacturer, Shop Keeper etcetera in this town who insults or is aggressive towards a Frenchman of any rank, and if this is substantiated, then a Notice will be pinned up in a public place forbidding any Frenchman for any reason whatsoever to patronise that place. Whoever violates this will be considered a traitor and will be punished accordingly.

'LA FRANCE' 1758.'

The above extracts from 'Sick and Hurt' correspondence could give a false impression of parole life in Britain. Doubtless, even at that time, the average tradesmen and townspeople acted reasonably, even if only from self-interest – and it would have been foolish for the parolee to deliberately antagonize the inhabitants. That much unnecessary trouble in this world, nationally, internationally or locally, is inflicted on the many by a few was as true then as now, is typified in yet another complaint. It was sent by more than thirty French prisoners who had been attacked in their Kentish *cautionnement*, but a more significant document was a testimonial which accompanied it, signed by nine Englishmen:

'We, the inhabitants in the Parish of Goudhurst, Certifie that we never was insulted by the French Gentlemen, nor to their knowledge have they caused any Riot except when they have been drawn in by a Parcel of Drunken, Ignorant, and Scandalous men who make it their Business to ensnare them for the sake of a little money.

Signed. Goudhurst. November 9. 1757.'

The British officers and others who were normally considered eligible for parole during the Seven Years' War and later in the eighteenth century were as listed below. This changed little during the wars up to 1815. It was matched in the case of our enemy captives:

ARMY	All Officers down to Sub-Lieutenant.
NAVAL	Captain, Lieutenant, Ensign, Purser, Master, Chaplain, Surgeon, Surgeon's Mate, Pilot, Midshipman, Boatswain, Gunner, Carpenter, Master Sailmaker, Master Caulker, Coasting Pilot and Gentleman Volunteer.
MERCHANT & PRIVATEER.	Captain, Second Captain, Two Lieutenants for every hundred men, Chief of Prizes, Pilot, Surgeon, Chaplain, Gentleman Passenger.

For the Privateer Officers to qualify, their vessel had to have an armament of at least fourteen guns of not less than four-pound rating, and be of more than 80 tons burden.

Like our midshipmen at Verdun, there was an additional restriction placed on British privateer and merchant officers when captured by the French. They were not so much 'paroled' as 'bailed'. Their *parole d'honneur* alone was not good enough; each had to find a guarantor who would deposit a sum of money with the French Government, as reinforcement to the 'semi-gentleman's' pledge.

Parole, in any of its forms, was the most valuable privilege which any prisoner of war could hope for or desire, and being so desirable it is not surprising that on occasion it proved to have its cash price.

Blank parole forms signed by unscrupulous officials; prisoners assuming the names of dead officers; forged parole documents, and other tricks were discovered sufficiently often to make the following Transport Board directive necessary:

' …namely that no blank form of parole certificates be sent to the Agents at the Depots, but to transmit them to the Agents, properly filled up whenever their ranks have been ascertained at this office, from lists sent by the Agents and from the extracts from the *role d'Equipage* of each vessel captured.'

The number of paroled prisoners in any particular town was constantly changing. Exchange, new arrivals, gaol sentences or confinement in the hulks for serious parole offences, transfer, escape, sickness and death meant that the parolee population grew or diminished almost daily.

The number of prisoners of war of all ranks in Britain during the Seven Years' War averaged about 19,000 – comparatively few in the early years, but building up to a total of some 40,000 to repatriate in 1763. Of that nineteen thousand average, about two thousand would have come within the categories eligible for parole. In 1797, as a result of recriminations between the British and French Governments over exchange in general – the unreasonable refusal to exchange Captain Sir Sydney Smith in particular – and the British apprehension of invasion or an uprising of the prisoners, the parole towns lost all their officer-boarders for a short period.

The French landing at Fishguard on the 22nd February, which was to be remembered as 'The Last Invasion of Britain' – although something of a fiasco as invasions go – did nothing to calm British nerves and did in fact inspire thoughts of rebellion among the prisoners.

Therefore, on the 25th November, 1797, all paroled prisoners in Britain were transferred from the only slightly restrictive freedom of their parole towns, to closed imprisonment at the newly-built Norman Cross Depot, which had first opened its gates in April of that year. Even so, the officers were not lodged with other ranks; a block in the south-east corner of the prison had been made ready, with its own airing yard, for their reception.

The organization of this transfer must have been a logistical nightmare for the Transport Office and the Agents of the many towns affected. Carts and wagons had to be hired or commandeered to carry the mounds of baggage and chattels; suitable transport obtained to convey sick or invalid parolees, and militia to escort the prisoners on the long marches, some over hundreds of miles, to Peterborough and Norman Cross.

The strict day-and-night guarding of the officers on these lengthy treks must have been of particular importance, for whilst they had needed little supervision when they travelled to their parole towns – their *parole d'honneur* acting as good as any overseer – even the most scrupulous must have considered their contract now broken as they marched towards confinement in a closed prison.

However, they were not held for long, and some may have been included in the great number of exchanges which took place a year or so later, in 1799. In that year only 25,646 prisoners remained in this country and the number of parolees was down to about twelve hundred.

For the rest of the war, all of the great depots had special officer-only quarters in their layouts. Although it was seldom that even small numbers of parolees were sent *en masse* into a depot, there are many records of 'broke-paroles' being sentenced to those quarters. It has already been noted that even the parolee multiple-offender whose misbehaviour had earned him a spell on a prison ship, was often sent to a hulk reserved for such tainted 'gentlemen', or to a slightly better accommodation, if available, on a run-of-the-mill floating prison.

PAROLE TOWNS IN BRITAIN AT VARIOUS TIMES DURING THE WARS.

ABERGAVENNY	FAREHAM
PERTH	ALRESFORD*
FOXTON	PETERBOROUGH
ANDOVER*	GOUDHURST*
PETERSFIELD*	ASHBOURNE
GREENLAW	PLYMOUTH
ASHBURTON*	GUERNSEY*
PONTEFRACT	ASHBY-de-la-ZOUCH
HAMBLEDON	PORTCHESTER
ASHFORD*	HAWICK
PORTSMOUTH	BANDON
HELSTON*	READING
BASINGSTOKE*	JEDBURGH
REDRUTH*	BATH
KELSO	REGILLIAK
BECCLES*	KNARESBOROUGH
RICHMOND	BEDALE
LANARK	ROMSEY*
BIDEFORD*	LANDORE
ROSCOR	BIGGAR
LAUDER	SANQUHAR
BISHOPS CASTLE	LAUNCESTON*
SELKIRK	BISHOPS WALTHAM*
LEEK	SEVENOAKS*
BODMIN	LICHFIELD
SODBURY*	BOROUGHBRIDGE
LLANFYLLIN	SOUTH MOLTON
BRECON	LOCKERBIE
STAPLETON	BRIDGNORTH
LOCHMABEN	TAVISTOCK*
BRISTOL*	LONDON
TENTERDEN*	CALLINGTON*
MAIDSTONE*	THAME
CARLISLE	MELROSE
TIVERON	CARNARVON
MILL Prison Hospital	TORRINGTON*
CHATHAM	MONTGOMERY
TONBRIDGE*	CHEPSTOW
MONTROSE	TYNEMOUTH
CHESTERFIELD	MORETONHAMPSTEAD
VALLEYFIELD	CHIPPENHAM*
NEWCASTLE-On-Tyne*	WAKEFIELD
CRANBROOK*	NEWTOWN
WANSFORD	CREDITON*
NORMAN CROSS	WANTAGE
CUPAR	NORTHAMPTON
WELSHPOOL	DARTMOOR
NORTH TAWTON	WHITCHURCH*
DERBY	ODIHAM*
WIGAN	DOVER
OKEHAMPTON*	WINCANTON
DUMFRIES	OLDHAM
WINCHESTER	DUNDEE*
ORMSKIRK	WISBECH
EDINBURGH	OSWESTRY

WYE (KENT)*   EXETER*
PEEBLES   YORK
EYE   PEMBROKE
(BAYFORD/Wincanton)   FALMOUTH*
PENRYN   (WANSFORD/Peterboro')
PENRITH

* During the Seven Years' War.

Some of these towns were used as *cautionnements* during subsequent wars up to 1815. The stories of some of these *cautionnements* is set down in the following pages.

Parole in the Scottish border towns is dealt with in the next chapter (Chapter 23).

ALRESFORD.

Alresford in Hampshire, where Admiral Rodney lies buried near the eighteenth century church, began, like most of the other parole towns at that time, by being a much complained-of place of open imprisonment. However, as inhabitants and prisoners got used to one another and learned the profitability of mutual tolerance, the parolees merged into the townscape – as much as such colourful characters could merge, though the temper of both Briton and officer-prisoner was always a bit uncertain. Certainly Alresford had a high percentage of successful escapes, forty-five in the eighteen months preceding June 1780. At that time, there had been many official complaints from parolees of 'being constantly molested and insulted' by the inhabitants of Arlesford, and pleas to be transferred to another town – and the complaints were not all one-sided. A letter from the Marquess of Buckingham to the Foreign Secretary, Lord Grenville, in 1793, suggests that he would approve of almost any means of returning French officers to France.

He began by informing Lord Grenville of reports he had received of the 'inundation' of French prisoners on the march from Portsmouth to Bristol, and that 'the language of the common men was, with very few exceptions, equally insolent, especially on the subject of the monarchy'. He went on to say:

> ' …I am very anxious that you should come to some decisions about your parole prisoners who are now nearly doubled at Arlesford and Waltham, and are hourly more exceptionable in their language and in their communication with the country people. I am persuaded that some very unpleasant consequences will arise if this practice is not checked, and I do not know how it is to be done.
>
> 'Your own good heart will make you feel for the French priests now at Winchester to whom these people (230 at Arlesford, 160 at Waltham) they openly avowed massacre whenever the troops are removed…
>
> 'Pray think over some arrangement for sending your parole prisoners out of England, for they certainly serve their country here better than they could do at sea or in France (so they say openly).'

It would seem from the above that the 'country people' were if anything too friendly with their unwilling guests – which might account for the high rate of successful getaways from the town. The Marquess may have gone a little far with his scaremongering, but it may well have been wiser than complacency over such a serious matter.

Francis Abell found an interesting item in the Arlesford Parish Records, which tells of happier fraternisation between captors and captives:

> '**1779**. The Captain and officers of the Spanish man-of-war who behaved so gallantly in the engagement with the *Pearl*, and who are [paroled] prisoners of war at Arlesford, lately gave an elegant entertainment and ball in honour of Captain [George] Montagu and his officers, in testimony of the high sense they entertain of the polite and most generous treatment they received after their capture.
>
> 'Capt. Montagu and his officers were present, also Capt. Oates and officers of the 89th Regiment, and many of the most respectable families from the neighbourhood of Arlesford.'

The Spanish vessel must have been the 28-gun frigate *Santa Monica*, and its captain Don M de Nones. The *London Gazette* for the 28th September reported that the Spanish frigate had been taken by the English frigate H.M.S *Pearl* a fortnight earlier off Fayal in the Azores, The *Santa Monica* was a superior vessel to the *Pearl* and was later added to the British Navy[1].

Two senior officer 'broke-paroles', who we have already met on the Chatham prison ships, spent some time in Arlesford before making abortive escape attempts. One was General René Martin Pillet, who was taken captive at the Battle of Vimiera in 1800. He was paroled to Arlesford but, although he must have chosen to sign the parole agreement like any other parolee, he never felt bound by his pledge – to his cost. He was first sent to Norman Cross Depot, where his conduct was so disgraceful that he was committed to harsher imprisonment in the *Brunswick* hulk at Chatham. The other was Colonel Lebertre who experienced prison-ship life in the *Canada*. Both these men wrote bitter memoirs – which, incidentally, included gross exaggerations and not infrequent downright lies – but both forgot to mention that the reason for their sufferings and discomfort was brought about through their loss of honour as officers and gentlemen.

Ensign Bazin, the talented young artist, whose watercolour of Jedburgh is illustrated on page 371, was first paroled to Wincanton in 1805 and then to Jedburgh, in 1812, when a fear of a general uprising cleared many southern *cautionnements* in favour of the Scottish Border Towns. Towards the end of the following year, Bazin was sent to Arlesford, with a strong recommendation for his 'exchange at the first opportunity. [He] has been long imprisoned and is a great favourite'.

The Church Registers record ten burials of French prisoners in the churchyard, between July 1794, and August 1812. Tradition has it that the clock in the church tower, which carries the date 1811, was given to the town by French parolees, as a token of appreciation for their kindly treatment.

ASHBURTON.

Although this small Devonshire town was one of the very earliest English *cautionnements*, it had housed both American and continental internees during the War of American Independence and could still boast a few French officers late in 1815. Little of the history of their stay, however, has been preserved. Even at the beginning of this century, when Abell was searching for material and enquiring from the people whose grandparents may have known the parolees, there was little to unearth. The earliest note is one of complaint. In 1756, the *aumonier*, or chaplain, to the Comte de Gramont bemoaned the fact that the Agents appointed to see to the needs of the paroled prisoners were prejudiced in favour of the inhabitants.

He said that they were tradesmen – 'here a shoemaker, here a tailor, here an apothecary' – who dare not, for business reasons, take sides with the prisoners. His personal complaint was that the inhabitants of Ashburton were *'un peuple sans règle et sans education',* who insulted, hissed and stoned him; and that when he reported this conduct to the authorities, he was pinioned (*garrotté*) and taken to Exeter Prison. He was probably telling only one half of the story. The Agent must have had good reason to have had him carted off to prison.

Between 1795 and 1797, about three hundred paroled prisoners, most of whom had first been held in Millbay Prison, were sent to Ashburton, but in 1797, which as you will recall was a year when fear of a French invasion on the south coast of Britain was at its height, the majority were sent to towns farther inland from the coast.

Later, and until the end of the Napoleonic War, Ashburton was host to many French and other continental privileged captives, and after 1812 the town was selected as a *cautionnement* for American officers: so over a long period the people of this small town would have become familiar with officers of a very wide range of rank and nationality. J.H. Amery, writing ninety or more years ago in *'Devon Notes and Querie',* says that over the years until 1815:

> ' …a number of educated foreigners formed part of the society of our towns. At one time they were lively Frenchmen, at others sober Danes or spendthrift Americans. They lodged and boarded in the houses of our tradesmen; they taught the young people modern languages, music and dancing; they walked our streets and roads and took general interest in passing events; yet today hardly a trace can be discovered beyond a few neglected milestones… and here and there a grave in our parish churchyards. This is particularly the case with Ashburton.'

In the case of a large town or city it might not be so surprising to find that, with all the alarums and excursions of such centres of activity, the temporary residence of a few hundred foreign captives had soon faded from the public memory. Yet it is amazing that they did not leave a deeper impression on small unchanging 'stick-in-the-mud' towns.

One of the early Ashburton Agents was a gentleman whose credentials would have been found acceptable even by the Comte de Gramont *and* his *aumonier*. Joseph Gribble was a solicitor and the County Coroner, who treated his charges with more than fairness. There were seven milestones marking the one-mile limits on the turnpikes in and out of the town, and to venture beyond these markers or wander onto byroads off the turnpike was normally treated a serious offence; but as long as the one-mile distance was respected, it would seem that his parolees had more or less free-range of the countryside.

In general the parolees were liked and were well-behaved but Ashburton had its fair share of broke-paroles – eighteen escaping between 1778–80 – a few during the considerate Gribble's period of office.

We know that the prisoners had their own Freemason's Lodge, called *Des Amis Réunis*, and that in 1814, nine Americans, professing to be members of the Masonic Fraternity, petitioned the Grand Lodge of England for relief (see Chapter 8, *The Arts and Crafts of Napoleonic and American Prisoners of War 1756-1816*, THE FREEMASON PRISONER OF WAR).

One of the last of the French officers to reside in Ashburton – or any other parole town for that matter – must have been General Cambronne, who was wounded at Waterloo whilst leading the Imperial Guard. The General did not leave Ashburton until November 1815. Francis Abell says that, in his own day, a portrait of the General which he had presented to his landlady, Mrs Eddy, was still hanging in the Golden Lion Inn in the town.

For all his valour and service to France, he only just missed the penalty for treason after the war had ended and his Emperor fallen. With Napoleon stowed away on St Helena, General Cambronne, like many other Bonapartists, switched his allegiance to the new Bourbon monarchy. From Ashburton he wrote to Louis XVIII offering his service and his loyalty, then set off for France and home. On arrival in Paris he was arrested and charged with making an armed assault on France; betraying the King and using force on behalf of Bonaparte. It was a horrifying reception but he was eventually exonerated on all three counts.

There is a record of two American officers being buried in Ashburton churchyard whose details cannot now be traced, and the headstone of a French officer's resting-place could be seen until recent years. It was inscribed:

> 'Ici Repose François Guidon
> natif de Cambrai en France
> Sous Lieutenant au 46ème Regt
> de Ligne. Decédé le 18 7bre 1815
> Agé de 22 Ans.   Requiescat en Pace.'

Ashburton Museum has a 'Peace Handbill' which gives some details of the Peace Procession which was 'to assemble at 9am precisely on the 21st of July, 1814':

ASHBURTON FESTIVAL ON THURSDAY
21st JULY, 1814
IN COMMEMORATION OF PEACE
Order of Procession.
Constables; Band; Austrian Standard Bearer;
English Union Bearer; Russian Standard Bearer;
Bearer of Standard of Peace on Horseback
supported; Town Arms Bearer on Horseback
supported; The Portreaves; Clergymen in their
Gowns; Fifty Flower Girls; Haymakers and
Agriculturists; Four Shepperdesses [*sic*];
Woollen Manufacturers;
Two Unions carried by a Soldier and Sailor;
Taylors; Flag Bearers; Tanners;
The Bailiff of the Borough on Horseback supported;
Union Bearer; Bearer of the French Standard;
Union Bearer; Twenty Flower Girls; Sailors;
Britannia in Triumphal Car drawn by Four Horses abreast;
Sailors; Twenty Flower Girls; Band; Shoemakers;
Carpenters; Sawyers; Coopers; Blacksmiths; Butchers;
Painters; Curriers; Clock-makers; Gardeners; Stocking
Weavers; Flags; Boys of Different Schools;
Standard Bearers; Women's Clubs; Forty Flower Girls;
Bearers of the Standard of PEACE;
Band; Flag Bearers; Constables.
GOD SAVE THE KING

ASHBOURNE & DERBY.

Ashbourne in Derbyshire was another of the eighteenth century parole towns which was still active as an open prison in the later wars. It appears that some officers were also paroled to the city of Derby itself. An extract from the *All Saints Parish Book* for the 20th June, 1763 – a few months after the end of the Seven Years' War – gives a truly contemporary report on some aspects of parole town life, and a rare account of officer-prisoners being employed on public works. It also confirms that, at that time, the paroled prisoners were not so easily accepted into these towns as they were to be in later wars:

'…these men (the prisoners during the Seven Years' War) were dispersed into many parts of the nation, 300 being sent to this town [Derby] on parole about July 1759, where they continued until the end of the War in 1763.

'Their behaviour at first was impudent and insolent, at all times vain effeminate, and their whole deportment light and unmanly, and we might venture to say from our observation and knowledge of them, that in any future war this nation has nothing to fear from them as an enemy

'During their abode here, the road from this place to Nottingham was by Act of Parliament repaired, the part from St Mary's Bridge (which by reason of the floods was impassable) being greatly raised. Numbers of these people were daily employed, who worked in their *bag-wigs, pig-tails ruffles*, etc., etc., a matter which afforded us much amusement. But, to their honour let it be remembered, that scarce one act of fraud or theft was committed by any of them during their stay among us. These men were allowed 6d. a day each by the British Government.'[2]

Although there was no lack of evidence that the French fighting man, soldier or sailor, deserved a better opinion of their masculinity than that expressed above, their effervescent spirits and lack of control over their emotions, were a puzzle to the more reserved and sober-minded English, Dutch, Danish and Americans. Half a century later Benjamin Waterhouse, the American 'Young Man of Massachuetts', whilst admitting that the French were a brave people, wrote of the French prisoners on the *Crown Prince* prison ship at Chatham: ' …they would scold, quarrel and fight, by slapping each other's chops with the flat hand, and cry like so many girls… Perhaps such a man as Napoleon Bonaparte could make any nation courageous.'

Whilst the better-off officers were a godsend to the landladies and shops in all the parole towns, there were groups of junior officers who found it difficult to make ends meet. It is probable that the road workers, in their 'bag-wigs and ruffles', were recruited from the comparatively impoverished – or some parolees may have joined in to occupy their boringly idle time – although we know that there, as in most other parole towns, any with ability added to their allowances by teaching, or by creating and selling items of 'prisoner of war work'.

It is said that a building was erected in Ashbourne to accommodate prisoners who could not afford to lodge and eat in private houses, where they could practise economy through bulk-buying of provisions and communal messing. These hard-up fellows were generally of far less bother to the authorities than were some of their very senior officers, men who one might expect to have been shining examples of integrity and honour.

After the resumption of the war in 1803, Ashbourne was the *cautionnement* of a number of generals, most of whom were far more troublesome to the Agent and the Board than the lower ranking officers. Though allowed extraordinary privileges, they were never satisfied, making demands which were often backed up by petitions from influential friends among the local gentry.

There was General Pageot who, in 1804, received a quite amazing indulgence on the part of the Transport Commissioners by being allowed to reside for a week at Wooton Lodge, the country seat of a Colonel Wilson, well beyond the bounds of his parole. The Colonel must have been a gentleman of particular influence, and it would seem that the Commissioners gave their permission with some reluctance, warning him not to repeat such a request: 'as our own paroled officers in France could never expect to receive such favoured treatment'.

Although the Commissioners permitted this bending of the normally strict rules of parole on this occasion, they kept a watchful eye on the General – particularly on his mail. Some time later Colonel Wilson received the following information:

'As it appears by letters between General Pageot and some of his countrymen that he is paying his addresses to a Lady of Respectability in or near Ashbourne [a Miss Bainbridge], the Board think it proper that you should be informed that they have good authority for believing that he is actually a married man, and has a family in France.'

Soon after, the Commissioners wrote to the girl's uncle, giving him the no doubt welcome news that the General had been transferred from Ashbourne to Montgomery in Wales:

'From Motives of Public Duty the Commissioners, when they first heard of the intended connection between General Pageot and Miss Bainbridge, they caused such suspicious circumstances respecting the General as came to their knowledge to be communicated to the young lady's mother, and that it affords them very much satisfaction to find her Friends are disposed to prevent an union which could promise very little comfort to her or Honour to her Family.'

In 1804, at the time when General Pageot's philandering and enjoyment of Ashbourne high-life was being foiled by the Transport Board, there were two other French Generals in the town whose conduct soon made them notorious for their parole offences – senior officers who were a headache for the Transport Office for most of the eight years they were detained in various parts of Britain.

Generals Donatien Rochambeau and Jacques Boyê (or Boyer as his name was often misspelt) enjoyed even more extravagant privileges than were usually granted, even to officers of equal distinguished rank. A house was specially fitted out for their residence; their allowances would have been greater, and they were certain to obtain extension of the milestone bounderies. Although they might ignore the recriminations of the more honourable among their fellow French officers, it is amazing that they should have so disregarded the contempt of the enemy who had fairly captured them.

Many French generals and other high-ranking officers who had given their supposedly sacred word of honour, acted in a manner which would have been thought disgraceful in an offender of the lowest commissioned military officer or a naval middie. General Phillipon, the defender of Badajoz, paroled to Oswestry; Generals Lefèbre, Maurin and Brenier at Wantage; General Simon at Odiham; General Pillet at Alresford and many others – all these were 'broke-paroles', some of whom spent time on the prison hulks or in the closed prison of Norman Cross for their sins.

Something of the histories of Generals Rochambeau and Boyê will be told after the end of these notes on Ashbourne.

Ashbourne has its stories of escape and romance: one English girl, dressed as a lad, eloped with a French colonel when he made his getaway in 1814, and there is the story of another Ashbourne girl who, in March 1812, was charged with aiding parolees to escape from the town. She took strong exception to the suggestion that there had also been an 'improper relationship between her and the Frenchmen', and published a remarkable and plucky denial of the charges. But although the case was later withdrawn, it was decided that her denials could not be accepted:

'To the Christian Impartial Reader.

I the undersigned Susanna Cotton declares that she had nothing to do with the escape of French prisoners, although she has been remanded at Stafford, and there has been no improper relationship as rumoured.

'Judge not that ye be not judged. Parents of female children should not readily believe a slander of their sex, nor should a male parent listen to the vulgar aggravation that too often attends the jocular whispering report of a crime so important. For it is not known what Time, a year or a day, may bring forth.

'Misses Lomas and Cotton take this opportunity (tho' an unpleasant one) of returning their grateful acknowledge of Public and Individual Favours conferred on them in their Business of Millinery, and hope a continuance of them, and that they will not be withheld by reason of any Prejudices which may have arisen from the Slander above alluded to.'

TWO FRENCH GENERALS: Rochambeau and Boyê.

The story of these two officers is remarkable, perhaps less for their exploits than for the amazing degree of tolerance shown by the Transport Board when dealing with their parole offences. Men guilty of lesser infringements, but of less exalted rank, would have been most severely punished, even to the extent of sitting out the rest of the war in the discomfort of a prison ship. Perhaps it was not so much a reverence for their rank and titles that inspired this delicate handling, but rather a suspicion of possible reprisals against the relatively few British senior officers and the many titled *détenus* held by the French at Verdun.

General Donatien – Marie-Joseph-de-Vimeur, Vicount de Rochambeau was the son of the Comte de Rochambeau, who was Commander of the French Forces in America during the War of Independence – the great military leader so influential in the defeat of the British at Yorktown in 1781. The Viscount went to America in 1780 as Adjutant-General to his father and, except for a trip to Paris with dispatches, served there until the end of hostilities.

For short periods during the last years of the eighteenth century he served as Governor-General of the Leeward Islands and the Island of San Domingo and by 1802 was again in the West Indies. In that year Bonaparte had sent ships and troops to subdue the negro Republic of San Domingo. This was achieved by treachery and shameful methods which left the negroes seething with hatred. The French had by no means got off scot-free: apart from war casualties, some twenty-five thousand of their troops had died from yellow fever. Inspired, it is said, by the French Revolution, the black population, mainly negro slaves under Toussaint-L'Ouverture, had revolted and taken over the western, French-held, part of the island.

Such was the situation which had brought Rochambeau back to the island. This time he came as 'General-in-Chief of the Army of Santa Domingo', with Jacques Boyê as his 'General of Brigade and Chief of Staff', his task was the conquest of San Domingo (Haiti). Soon after the short peace, and resumption of the European War in 1803, the arrival of a Royal Naval squadron under Commodore Loring put paid to the French hopes of success in their objective. With the aid of the British, the negoes soon ousted the French from most of those areas of the island where the latter had been in control – except for Cape François, which was under General Rochambeau's command. Blockaded by the British and under siege by the blacks, his forces were soon weakened and depleted and apprehensive of the fate which awaited them if they capitulated to the revolutionaries.

It has been said, with some truth, that the French owed their very lives to their British captors. Had they not surrendered they would have been massacred to a man by the negroes 'in revenge for the barbarities practised upon them by the French Commander-in-Chief, Rochambeau'.

On the 30th November, 1803, the French evacuated Cape François under terms which included the surrender of all French warships in the port to the British, but only after they had cleared the harbour. A fine 40-gun frigate, the *Surveillante*, and a number of smaller vessels left the harbour and struck their colours to Commodore Loring; but another 40-gun frigate; the *Clorinde*, ran aground on the rocks off Fort St Joseph. It seemed that both she and her ship's company of 900 souls were doomed – either by drowning if the ship broke up under the violence of wind and sea, or massacre by the blacks if they managed to reach the shore. In fact, the negro gunners were already preparing to sink the grounded vessel with red-hot shot. However, once again the British – or rather *one Briton* – came to the rescue, and saved both ship and men.

Acting-Lieutenant Nesbit Willoughby, of H.M.S. *Hercule*, who was in charge of his ship's launch, decided on his own initiative and responsibility to return to the aid of the *Clorinde*'s crew. Nearing the stricken vessel, he realised that his launch would be swamped by the desperate Frenchmen crowding the *Clorinde*'s rails if he came alongside. So he procured a small punt and boarded the ship alone.

Once aboard, Willoughby managed to persuade General Lapoype to strike the ship's colours and surrender the ship to him. The general was at first hesitant, as his ship had not cleared the harbour and the strict formalities of honourable surrender had not been observed[3]; but, wisely, he acquiesced – and Lt. Willoughby hoisted the Brish flag.

This was a brilliant move. As the *Clorinde* was now a British prize, Willoughby was able to obtain help from General Dessalines, commander of the black revolutionaries ashore, and together with boats from the British ships outside the harbour, under Willoughby's direction, the *Clorinde* was refloated. Thus, one gallant English junior officer gained another fine 40-gun frigate to add to the Royal Navy, and 900 prisoners who would otherwise have perished[4].

The prisoners, many of them in a poor state of health after suffering hunger and all manner of privation during the siege, were taken to Jamaica before being shipped to England. Rochambeau and Boyê together with about three hundred of their officers were put on board a man-of-war on the 1st December, arriving at Portsmouth on the 3rd February, 1804. Over the following weeks the officers were interviewed and assigned to various parole towns – Generals Rochambeau and Boyê, as we have seen, to Ashbourne.

A large number of the San Domingo officers were sent to Chesterfield. One report of parolees in that town states, probably inaccurately, that 'Commander-in-Chief Rochambeau, who with

Generals d'Henin, Boyer [*sic*] and Lapoype [the general who had surrendered to Lt. Willoughby], Commodore Barrê, and other naval officers with the staffs of the generals, were all at Chesterfield.'

If our two generals were indeed seen in that town, thirty or so miles from their appointed place of parole, it must have been with the knowledge of the Transport Office, and with their permission to pay a short visit.

At Ashbourne the generals would have been housed to a high standard and allowed to bring their servants with them. The chief of these were Pierre Courpon, Rochambeau's negro attendant, and Boyê's Italian servant, Albert Violett.

Neither of these high-ranking captives were forced or persuaded to give their parole of honour, but give it they did, without the slightest intention of honouring it in any way. The flamboyant and arrogant Rochambeau, in particular, almost immediately displayed an air of superiority towards the Ashbourne Agent, and downright contempt for the Commissioners of the Transport Board. The Board was perfectly aware that they amused themselves by writing letters in which they abused *'Les mermidons de transport service'*.

It was one such letter, containing 'expressions which appear to the Board to be of an extraordinary Nature' which constituted the generals' first parole offence: they had been in Ashbourne less that a week when an attempt was made to smuggle it out of the town. There was nothing neurotic about the importance which the Board placed on the suppression of illicit correspondence with France at that critical time.

The great number of prisoners of war of all ranks and ratings pouring into Britain was always a matter of security concern. *The Times* commented:

> '…The prisoners already in our hands and those who may be added, will occasion infinite perplexity. The known licentiousness of their principles, the utter contempt of all laws of Honour which is generally prevalent among the French Republicans, and the audacity of exertions which may arise from a desire of co-operating with an invading force, may render them extremely dangerous… '

One parole town memoir says of General Boyê: 'whilst attentive to the ladies, [he] did not omit to curse, even to *them,* his fate in being deprived of his arms, and without hope of being useful to his countrymen when they arrive in England'. And Rochambeau, throughout his long captivity, was confident that one day Napoleon would turn up on England's doorstep!

Over their next eight months in the little Derbyshire town, the parole offences from this troublesome pair came thick and fast, from the petty to the serious. Some were designed just to annoy and others with more dangerous intent. Every attempt by the Commissioners to bring the generals into line was in vain, and every concession was treated with arrogant disdain. However, at last they stretched the Board's patience too far, and they were informed that they were to be transferred to a Welsh *cautionnement,* Montgomery in Powys – and then only if they renewed their *parole d'honneur* by signing a new agreement. It may be remembered that, in that same year, General Pageot's romantic dreams had been blighted by transfer to Montgomery, and the two troublemakers had no desire to follow him there.

They tried everything from argument and indignant anger to professions of poverty to prevent their transfer; saying they must be given travelling expenses before they signed their parole. More expense was probably the hardest thing for the Board to take, and they turned the demand down flat – telling them to sign or be sent to a closed prisoner of war depot.

Rochambeau and Boyê, probably not believing that the Transport Board would have the audacity to send them to a closed prison, still refused to sign. One can imagine their incredulity, fury and cursing when when they were placed under house arrest, a constable guarding their quarters. On the 9th October, a military guard arrived to escort them on their way to Huntingdonshire – and confinement in the great Norman Cross Depot.

On arrival at Norman Cross these two senior 'broke-paroles' were segregated, even from officers in the established 'Officers' Prison' within its walls. There was no question of their being allowed the freedom of nearby Peterborough, or the little village of Wansford on the Great North Road where a number of French officers were on parole at about that time.

Certain wards of the Military Hospital within the confines of the Depot were adapted – at a cost of £20.15s. 6d. – for use as their special, closely guarded prison; with sentries at the doors and patrolling the small airing-yard where they were permitted to exercise. They were allowed to keep their servants, Courpon and Violett – who had to follow them into prison as they had into the freedom of a parole town – but most other privileges were denied them. Access to newspapers, periodicals and writing materials was forbidden; their special allowances for the purchase of wood, coal or candles were cancelled, and the Agent, Captain Pressland, was given strict instructions by the Board to prevent any communication between the generals and any other prisoners of war.

Despite this great change in their fortunes, the generals, particularly General Rochambeau, felt sure that the war was nearing its end – and had no doubt that England would be the loser. On many occasions during the wars, there were periods of rumour and panic when an invasion of Britain seemed imminent; and Rochambeau, who in some mysterious fashion had access to intelligence from outside in spite of the communication ban, felt sure that he knew the very date of Napoleon's entry into this country.

The inmates of the Depot were in a state of confident unrest and excitement at that time and *The Times* reported:

> 'The French prisoners on the prospect of an invasion of this country begin to assume their Republican fierte [*pride or hauteur*] they tell their guards:- "It's your turn to guard us now, but before the winter is over it will be our turn to guard you." '

Great Bonapartist as he was, and secure in his knowledge, the General appeared in the airing-yard one morning, attired in full dress uniform, resplendent with decorations and orders, booted and spurred, he confidently awaited the arrival of his beloved Emperor. After two days he realised his action was premature – but many years later he did rejoin his great leader – in the 'Hundred Days Campaign' which ended with the Battle of Waterloo.

Captain Pressland had reported favourably on their general conduct; but without effect, and in April 1805, after six months of restrictions, a crack appeared in Rochambeau's rigid determination, and he asked the indulgence that they be sent to Odiham in Hampshire, a town much favoured by paroled officers. However, the Transport Commissioners, no doubt appreciative of a whole half-year free of trouble from the disturbing pair, informed them that they alone were responsible for their own misfortune, and that their imprisonment at Norman Cross was due only to their ungentlemanly contempt for the honourable system of *parole d'honneur* – consequently their request must be turned down.

It was March 1806, almost two and a half years after the surrender of San Domingo, that the Commissioners relented and Rochambeau and Boyê were permitted to sign fresh papers and their parole was given for a second time. Once again they were allowed to reside in the same parole town, this time Wincanton in Somerset.

For the moment we shall leave them in Norman Cross, and discuss parolees at Peterborough, before continuing their story at Wincanton and beyond.

PETERBOROUGH, NORMAN CROSS & WANSFORD

Although we know that French and Dutch officers were sent on parole to Peterborough in 1797, the year which saw the opening of the great Norman Cross Depot, there is little evidence to show that officer captives were sent to the town or its neighbouring hamlets in any great number during the second period of the Napoleonic Wars after 1803. Some were sent to the village of Wansford, about five miles from the Depot, but it would seem that many were housed in an 'officer block' within the prison itself, although allowed the usual milestone limit beyond its walls. Dr Thomas J. Walker's exhaustive research for his book *The Depôt for Prisoners of War at Norman Cross*, unearthed only slight information regarding the officers paroled at Peterborough, only a few miles from the Depot. When he was researching, at the end of the nineteenth century, there were still some persons living who recalled inmates of the Depot among the memories of their early youth and, of course, a large number of Peterborough people whose parents must have observed the day to day life of the paroled officers. Yet few traditions of this period of the city's life were handed down. The Doctor, himself, was surprised that memories should be so short and that the officers had not left a more enduring impression. He said:

> 'This is strange, for the presence of one hundred foreigners of varying social position in and round about a quiet little cathedral city, such as Peterborough was a century ago, must certainly have modified the usual routine of the social life of its citizens, and of the dwellers in the neigh-bouring villages in which some of the prisoners lodged.'

The first French officers to be paroled at Peterborough, were the captain, four lieutenants, purser, first pilot, and surgeon of the 18-gun *La Jalouse*, arriving there in June, 1797. The *Jalouse*, which was later added to the Royal Navy, was captured after a short encounter in the North Sea with the British 28, H.M.S *Vestal*, Captain Charles White. The crew of the French vessel must have been among the earliest to enter Norman Cross Depot, passing through its gates only a few weeks after its opening on the 7th April.

After the Battle of Camperdown in that same year, Dutch prisoners greatly outnumbered the French, both in the closed prisons of the Depot and officers on parole in the neighbourhood. Admiral Duncan defeated the Dutch fleet under Admiral de Winter in the great naval action off Camperdown, which took place on the 11th October, 1797, and the majority of the almost 5,000 prisoners taken were sent to the newly opened Depot.

A parole register (1795–1800), in the Public Records Office, gives the names of about one hundred Dutch prisoners on parole at Peterborough between the 10th November, 1797 and the 3rd July, 1800; but none of these Dutchmen could have spent long in captivity. In February, 1800 they were sent home to Holland under the Alkmaar Cartel Exchange agreement. In almost all the parole towns, we have heard the French officers described as lively, amorous, frivolous, mercurial, lightweight characters; the Danes as sober and plodding; the Americans as troublesome and the Dutch as rather dull and serious-minded. However, the Marriage Register of St John's Church in Peterborough would suggest that, short as was their stay, the latter were certainly serious-minded in their intentions towards the Huntingdonshire maidens. It contains no mention of nuptials between the 'amorous' French prisoner and English girl, but records five marriages in the years 1800 and 1801, where a Dutchman was the bridegroom.

The Registrar, with more regard for sensitivities than for history, recorded the groom's name but did not mention that he was a prisoner of war. Dr Walker, however, matched up those names with the Public Record Office parole register entries, which made it possible to identify both the grooms and the Dutch witnesses to the marriages – and provides the account appended to these notes on Peterborough.

The Agent for the supervision of paroled prisoners, was Mr Thomas Squire, a Peterborough banker and merchant. His residence, the Bridge House, could not have been more ideally situated for the reception of prisoners. Many who were consigned to Norman Cross were brought by barge from Lynn, and disembarked at a point where the canal ran through the Agent's land.

Thomas Squire is mentioned in an interesting little book, *The French Prisoners of Norman Cross. A Tale,* by the Revd Arthur Brown. Set in the second part of the war, *c*.1808, and built round a paroled French captain, he peopled his simple, spiritually-slanted romance with some real-life characters, and despite the fact that the Revd Brown overestimated the saintliness of the prisoners' chaplain, the Bishop of Moulins – of whom more later – he researched his story well.

Brown met an old countryman who remembered, as a boy, seeing groups of French officers strolling out from the barrack-yard of their Norman Cross *cautionnement*, along the Yaxley Road as far as the milestone limit – 'some very well dressed, others in tatters, few in uniform'. If they did not look back at the depressing mass of the prison buildings, their walk would have been pleasant enough, through wooded countryside dotted with small homesteads and farms and just off their road towards Whittlesea, a good sized lake, a joy for the fishermen among them.

Although these men were quartered some six miles from Peterborough and did not have the advantage of individual lodging and all the facilities that urban dwelling has to offer, they were not entirely cut off from association with local inhabitants, or denied access to shop goods and merchandise which they might desire and could afford. The prison market within the walls was open each morning from ten o'clock to noon, a great privilege and one to be envied by the British prisoners in France.

As with all other prison markets, a wide range of foodstuffs would be on display, plus luxuries such as tea, and clothing and odds and ends in great variety. The prison market, with its 7,000 potential customers, was, in fact, bigger and often busier than that in the small cathedral city itself.

The market vendors and the visiting public were given some sort of search at the main gate, to guard against the introduction of weapons or any kind of liquor (although ale and beer could be purchased from the canteens within each of the inner *casernes*). Sentries and market guards were always on the alert, for whilst the facility had a calming effect on the natural restlessness of the captives, it also provided a meeting place for all manner of illegal associations between prisoners and public; from trading in forbidden goods, to outside assistance in escape attempts.

The parolees were required to report to the Agent only twice weekly, although the curfew bell was sounded nightly. On these muster days he would issue to each man his Government money allowance, distribute any incoming correspondence, and keep them informed of new orders or details of possible exchange cartels. The muster days were probably staggered, to allow the Agent to attend the various places where his charges were centred. Obviously, they could not all report to Peterborough, some five to eight miles beyond their respective milestones.

The parole limit of the French officers who were lodged in the village of Wansford was Stibbington, on the Great North Road, and they were lucky in that their milestone coincided with their favourite rendezvous – a coaching inn called 'The Wheat Sheaf'.

Both the Revd Arthur Brown and Dr Walker met the nonagenarian son of the wartime landlord, who showed them what had once been the officers' recreation and smoking room, which he may just have remembered as a child. The main attraction of the inn was not so much its beverages, but the certainty of getting 'a recherché dinner', as his grandmother was 'renowned for her cooking, and could even please the fastidious taste of the French officers'.

There were two other 'Officer Quarters' within Norman Cross Depot, but these were closed ones with no privileged wanderings outside the walls. There was the already-mentioned specially converted quarters for Rochambeau and Boyê, and the south-eastern block for the incarceration of 'broke-paroles'. Not that all were would-be absconders: some had honourably refused to give their pledge in the first place; some had over-stretched their mile beyond excuse; some were punished for fighting, duelling, or troublemaking between themselves or local inhabitants. If apprehended in an escape attempt, the officer was considered to have doubly offended compared with the man who had not given his word – and was punished accordingly. Not only was it unlikely that he would ever regain the comparative freedom of parole (unless he was of very high rank or nobility!); but all rations and allowances would be reduced until all the costs involved in his recapture had been paid off.

As has been mentioned elsewhere, cases were not unheard of where men, sometimes not even officers, had assumed false identities or the names of dead or distant officers. One example of this ruse, which landed the culprit in the 'other ranks' *casernes* of Norman Cross, was a Pierre Dussage who tried to pass himself off as Mathuren Nazarean, first lieutenant of the *Alerte*, who, it was discovered, was at that time ill in Portugal. Such offenders and double-broke-paroles were lucky if they escaped the hulks or civil gaol – and, as we know, forgery and murder were punishable under both civil and military law:

> **' *Stamford Mercury*. 16 September, 1808**
> Early on Friday morning last Charles François Maria Boucher, French officer, a prisoner of war in this country, was conveyed from the County Gaol at Huntingdon to Yaxley Barracks [Norman Cross Depot, also known as Stilton Barracks] where he was hanged, agreeable to his sentence at the last Assizes, for stabbing with a knife, with intent to kill Alexander Halliday, in order to effect his escape from that prison. The whole garrison was under arms and all the prisoners in the different apartments were made witnesses of the impressive scene.'

Some captives who did not qualify for parole by rank or as officers' servants, were also granted the privilege. By a reciprocal agreement between the two countries, fishermen were generally temporarily paroled before being released to return home:

> 'Andreas Anderson, 1st Steerman; Johanna Maria Darata Anderson, Woman, his wife; Margrita Dorothea Anderson, child. Received in Custody 31st May 1800. 3rd June, On parole at Peterborough.'

The mountains of documents in the Records Office which refer to Norman Cross, deal mainly with its establishment and administration, often in great detail, but the registers which record its inmates, are generally less informative. It might be expected that the many thousands of ordinary prisoners who passed through its gates would have proved too much of a clerical task to record in much greater detail than their numbers; but it is surprising to find that so little has been set down regarding the comparatively few paroled and 'broke-parole' officers at Peterborough and Norman Cross. Nevertheless, one would suppose that the Agent would have had up-to-the-minute detail of those under his supervision; but the following extract from a letter dated the 8th August, 1798, indicates otherwise. James Perrot, Agent for the prisoners at Norman Cross Prison (Thomas Squires was Agent for officers and parolees generally), wrote to Captain Daniel Woodriff, R.N., Superintendant for the Transport of Prisoners, who later succeeded Perrot as Agent, telling him of a rumour that a number of prisoners were planning an imminent escape:

> ' ...they were counted both that night, but with little effect from the addition made to their numbers by the men you brought from Lynn, and yesterday morning and afternoon, but in such confusion from the prisoners refusing to answer, from others giving in fictitious names, and others anwering for two or three. In consequence of all these irregularities I made all my clerks, a turnkey, and a file of soldiers, go into the southeast quadrangle this morning at five o'clock, and muster each prison separately, and found that six prisoners from the Officers' Prison have escaped, but can obtain none of their names except Captain Dorfe, who some time ago applied to me for to obtain liberty for him to reside with his family at Ipswich where he had married an English wife. The officers remaining have separately and conjunctively refused to give the names of the other five, for which I have ordered the whole to be put on half allowance tomorrow...'[5]

The majority of the French captives were followers of the Roman Catholic faith, but there were many others from the Protestant areas of France. There is a faint tradition that a Yaxley clergyman was recognised as 'Protestant chaplain to Norman Cross' and that before 1803, at the prisoners' request, Catholic priests were allowed to live within the prison. It is therefore surprising to find that, although at least 1,770 prisoners were buried in the prisoner of war cemetery just outside the Depot, there is no entry in a church register, Catholic or Protestant, which records religious rights having been carried out at their burial. This is not to say that no private service was carried out, for the prison may have been considered 'extra-parochial', but of this we have no evidence or memoir.

It would seem that the 'resident' priests had earned the distrust of the authorities, who had evidence that they comforted their community in ways other than spiritual, mainly by the illicit traffic in uncensored correspondence.

When war broke out again, in 1803, the Transport Board instructed the new Agent, Captain Pressland 'that, profiting from experience gained during the previous period of war, no priests were to be admitted, except in extreme cases, and then under carefully arranged restrictions, as they had abused the privileges allowed them,' and that a 'turnkey or clerk was to be present during the whole time they were in the hospital.'

In the following year, it was decided that, whilst priests could live outside the prison, they were still debarred from residing within. Tarring all French clergy with the stain of the few, they determined that such a privilege could not be granted to foreigners 'of that *equivocal description'*.

However, three years later, the Roman Catholics had a chaplain of very high office to attend to their spiritual needs. This was the Rt. Revd Stephen John Baptist Lewis de Galois de la Tour, the Bishop of Moulins. This prelate left an impression on the county which lasted long after the memory of the prisoners themselves had begun to fade. He built for himself an image and reputation, partly merited partly unjustified, which inspired a number of writers, including the Revd Arthur Brown, to perpetuate his legend. The latter wove the Bishop into his romantic tale as a self-sacrificing saint who gave up his high and financially rewarding office in France, to 'voluntarily come to England out of pure compassion for his imprisoned countrymen, and with true missionary zeal was giving himself up to their spiritual welfare. He was a venerable-looking man, much respected by the prisoners generally. It was a noble act of self-sacrifice.' Both the Revd Brown and another admiring writer, the Revd G.N. Godwin, wrote in almost identical words that they 'hoped 'ere long more will be known of this worthy prelate.' And more *was* heard of him.

Although la Tour did not live amongst his flock – he boarded at the 'Bell Inn' at Stilton – there is no doubt that he did do much good, and his image as a great ecclesiastical figure must have injected hope and strength into some of his fellow Catholics; but there were a number of facts which, if known at the time, would have discouraged his eulogists.

He did not 'voluntarily come to England'. He was not an emigré, but a deportee, having been expelled from France in 1791. He first went to Italy as the Chief Chaplain to the Bourbon Princess, Victoire of France, on whom he was financially dependent. Only when she died did he come to England and soon became seriously involved with money-lenders which, inspired him to write a number of self-justifying and begging letters to the Catholic Lord Fitzwilliam.

The true story of the Bishop came to light exactly one hundred years after those letters were written, when, together with a short autobiography/curriculum vitae and other papers, they were lent by the Fitzwilliam family to Dr Walker. The Bishop was not 'living on his own resources and upon remittances from France'. He received

nothing from France; his main income was a £240 a year allowance from the British Government, twice the sum allowed to emigré Bishops. Although no parish register records the burial of Norman Cross prisoners, there is evidence that the Bishop and other French priests officiated outside the prison, at baptisms and other services. He was also allowed a personal servant, a young prisoner released from Norman Cross to attend on him. The story of the Bishop's abuse of this privilege (which would have earned a British soldier at least a couple of hundred lashes) is told in another chapter (see Chapter 4, *The Arts and Crafts of Napoleonic and American Prisoners of War 1756-1816* – THE STRAW WORKERS).

Despite their stated wish to hear more of the man they so admired, it is to be hoped that the Revd Arthur Brown and the Revd Godwin never saw the manuscripts which tended to 'de-halo' their saint.

Marriages between Dutch Paroled Prisoners and English girls, recorded in the register of St John's Parish Church, Peterborough. 1800–1801.

17 Feb. 1800. Albertus Coeymans married Ann Whitwell. B. Pletz and James Gibbs. Witnesses. [Albertus Coeymans was the 2nd Lieutenant of the *Furie*; B. Pletz was his Captain. Both arrived Norman Cross, 19th Nov. 1798. 'Discharged to Holland', 19th Feb.1800.]

17 Feb. 1800. Adrian Roeland Robberts Roelans married Mary Kingston. Joseph Little and James Gibbs. Witnesses. [A.R.R.Roelans was a midshipman on the *Jupiter*. He arrived at Norman Cross 4th November 1787.

The witness Joseph Little, an Englishman, was married to Mary Roelans, probably Adrian's sister – in the same church nine years later. 'Discharged under the Alkmaar Cartel'.]

18 Feb. 1800. Charles Peter Vanderaa married Lucy Rose. J. Ysbrands and James Gibbs. Witnesses. [Charles Vanderaa was Lieutenant of a Brig of War. Paroled Peterborough 11th June1798. J. Ysbrands, Captain of the *Courier*, was paroled to Peterborough 21st June 1798. Both 'Discharged to Holland' 19th Feb. 1800.]

20 Aug. 1800. Antoni Staring married Nancy Rose. E. B. Knogz and James Gibbs. Witnesses. [A. Staring, Captain of *Duyffe* man-of-war. E. B. Knogz, Surgeon on the *Duyffe*. Both arrived Norman Cross 27th May 1800. Both released 26th Aug. 1800.]

.... Berthold Johannes Justin Wyeth married Sarah Wotton. B. Pletz. Witness. The other witness was probably James Gibbs, the Parish Clerk. [Barthold Wyeth was 2nd Lieutenant of the *Furie*. Received on parole 19th Nov. 1798. Not exchanged under the Alkmaar Cartel. A prisoner until 16th Oct. 1801. This marriage must have been held at about the same date as the others, as the witness, Capt. B. Pletz probably left in 1800.]

Dr T. J. Walker, who devoted many years of study to the history of Norman Cross, saw daily evidence of the one-time presence of French prisoners in the Depot. Miss Habart, his consulting room attendant, was the granddaughter of Jean Marie Philippe Harbart, who was captured on a small fishing boat, the ten-ton *L'Abondance*, off Calais on the 20th June, 1803. Young Jean Habart suffered the frightening experience of a short spell on the prison hulk *Sandwich*, at Chatham, before being transferred to Norman Cross, arriving on 27th August. There, he was treated as a civilian prisoner of war – not fully paroled yet not exactly imprisoned – and was allowed to work as a baker to one of the contractors who supplied the huge amounts of bread required by the Depot each day. Eight long years went by before his release; years made brighter by the frequent visits of the daughter of a Stilton farmer who supplied the prison with milk.

He was released on the 20th June, 1811, and returned to his home town on the North coast of France, where he found that his father, a prosperous gunsmith, had died and left him an inheritance. After a while he returned to England and married Elizabeth Snow, the dairy farmer's daughter, and settled in Stilton as a baker and corn chandler.

Over the years the prison *casernes* which had held so many of his countrymen had disappeared and the forty acres of the barracks had returned to grassland. By 1846, forty-three years after Jean Marie Habart had passed through its gates, Norman Cross was for most a dim and distant memory.

Within sight of those fields, the otherwise happy story of his life ended tragically, On the 24th of January, 1846, after completing his round, he had called in at a Peterborough inn where, it was later supposed, someone had noticed his well-filled money bag. On the Norman Cross Road, about three miles from Peterborough, Jean was found with his head battered, pockets rifled, and his empty purse in a nearby meadow.

ODIHAM.

The delightful village or small town of Odiham in Hampshire was in its day one of the most easy-going of English parole towns. A solicitor, Charles Shebbeare, was the Agent for the prisoners of war, and in him they had a man whose interpretation of rules and regulations was usually in favour of his charges: though leniency did not always equate with wisdom. An over-considerate Agent was seldom rewarded with a reduction in the rate of parole-breaking or escapes in any parole town.

With its ancient stocks and its numerous listed buildings it is not difficult for the modern visitor to imagine it as it was in the days when interned officers, many of senior rank, strolled its High Street. Some would have been accompanied by their young boy servants, and at least one may have strolled with his French wife and children. Even now, at the end of the twentieth century, Odiham retains much of the old world charm which must have greeted its captive guests at the beginning of the nineteenth. An almost unique characteristic of the place, is that most of the townspeople seem to have at least a smidgen of knowledge that during the Napoleonic Wars their town had been a centre for paroled officer prisoners. They are annually reminded of this fact by a simple little ceremony which takes place in the churchyard of All Saints Church. On Founder's Day, which celebrates the life of a philanthropic seventeenth century mercer [dealer in fabrics], posies of flowers are placed on the graves of two French prisoners

of war. These two permanent exiles from their homeland were a naval officer, Pierre Julian Jouneau, who died in 1809, and an army captain, Pierre Feron, who was buried in 1810. Their tombstones stand to the left of the north door of the church.

Neither of these French officers had long to enjoy the pleasures of Odiham. Pierre Jouneau, an administrative officer to the French Navy, was captured with the merchant vessel *Le Rozambo* on the 15th August, 1805. The first four years of his parole he spent in London before being sent to Odiham where, only a few months later, he died on the 4th September, 1809. Captain Feron was captured in the West Indies, when Guadeloupe fell to the British on the 8th February, 1810. He arrived at Odiham on the 7th April, and four short weeks later he was dead[6].

A living reminder of the parolees' one-time presence is the 'Frenchman's Oak', which still thrives on the common, near the milestone which marked the one-mile limit to the prisoners' wanderings: and another parole-limit marker takes the form of a large 'B' on the park wall near the milestone on the Farnham Road. However, the reminders do not end with tombstones and mile-markers. Odiham has its own 'prisoner of war haunted house!'

Most of the commissioned officers were lodged in Bury Square near the the original site of the old stocks, and in private houses on the High Street – as 'Frenchman's Cottage' and a house called 'Frenchmans' still bear witness. There was, however, another building at the end of the High Street called 'Laburnum Cottage', which was used as a meeting house or recreation centre and where, if they were typical Frenchmen, a billiards table would have taken pride of place.

It was there that some sort of rumpus took place, probably a quarrel over a local girl, which ended with a young French officer being killed – and it is said that he still makes an occasional brief return to his old wartime home.

Junior and non-commissioned officers were housed in comfortable, though less opulent, accommodation near the Chalk Pit on the outskirts of the town. These red-brick cottages which were specially built for the prisoners, were remembered as still *in situ* when Francis Abell and J. T. Thorp visited Odiham in the early 1900s; but most have now been demolished. Some of the existing cottages have decoratively plastered ceilings which are said to be the work of the prisoners, and the two plaster plaques on a bedroom wall of the 'Frenchman' bear designs reminiscent of French military badges.

Odiham with its French Clubhouse, a Philharmonic Society and Theatre, their own Masonic Lodge – *'Des Enfans de Mars et de Neptune*– and the 'Old George Inn', where parolee and public could meet, was the popular choice of many who were granted the privilege of parole. Not a few of these officers were very senior indeed, who one might think would have found Bath or Reading more to their liking, but plumped for Odiham – and not all were accepted. Generals Rochambeau and Boyê petitioned the Transport Office but were quite rightly turned down on the grounds of their 'ungentlemanly contempt for the honourable system of *parole d'honneur*'. It may be that these pampered but untrustworthy officers had heard that the Agent was less unbending in his application of parole restrictions. It is difficult to understand how Odiham's genuine French Freemasons were allowed to enjoy their Lodge, after the Anglophobic General Simon had set up his phoney lodge in the town – the 'Secret Order of the Lion' – which preached rebellion and uprising, and brought about a change in the General's status from parolee to State Prisoner.

Although there were a few troublemakers, the majority made the best of their open-imprisonment. Some occupied their captive hours in the usual prisoner of war pursuits – model-making, drawing, teaching languages. Some married local girls and one, at least, settled in Odiham after the war. The officer who may have been seen in the town with his family was Lieutenant Claude Augustin La Croix who had sent for his wife, Pierrette and their three children, François, Josephine and Caroline, to share his captivity. Their fourth child, Augustina, was born in Odiham in 1811. Two years earlier a son, Louis Pierre François, was born in the town to another paroled officer, Jacques Gilliet and his wife Terese Castinazzi. The incidence of women sharing their husband's incarceration was unusual but not extremely rare – there is evidence that some had voluntarily joined their partners on the dreaded hulks! – but this possibility was only enjoyed by the fairly well-off. There was no Government allowance for wives and offspring – and had there been, the number of foreigners in our smaller parole towns might well have exceeded the native population.

The *Mémoires du Baron De Bonnefoux, Capitaine De Vasseau, 1782–1855,* contains many appreciative references to the Baron's all-too-short stay in Odiham; and his description of parole life there as 'by no means approaching the unbearable' can be taken as a genteel understatement. In fact he had an enjoyable and eventful time that many would have envied, which was regretfully ended by the Transport Board's exaggerated reaction to his breaking of a parole restriction.

The Baron de Bonnefoux was captured in the West Indies in 1806, whilst serving on the *Belle-Poule*, at the same time as Louis Garneray who was quartermaster's-mate on that corvette. On reaching England, Garneray was sent to the Portsmouth hulks, whilst Bonnefoux, after signing his *Parole d'Honneur*, was sent to Thame in Oxfordshire. Thame was a pleasant enough town and the gregarious Baron soon fitted in with both the parolee population and the local gentry, who were generous with their hospitality. He particularly enjoyed the company of their charming daughters, but still found time to study languages and drawing. The one blot on the parole town's landscape was a group of troublemakers to whom all Frenchmen were anathema.

Inevitably, he fell foul of their jostlings and taunts, and his strong retaliation resulted in an Anglo-French brawl. Smith, the Thame Agent, whilst realizing that Bonnefoux was not the instigator, feared reprisals from the Thame ruffians if he brought them before the courts. Smith compromised and transferred the Frenchman to Odiham.

He left the town with the sad adieus of both his English friends and his fellow countrymen – and a lock of hair from *'la jeune Miss Harriet Stratford aux yeux bleus, au teint éblouissant, à la physionomie animée, à la taille divine'.*

The news of the Thame experience had reached Odiham before his arrival, and he was greeted there as something of a hero. Possessed of an engaging personality, well-educated, wealthy and generous, he soon had as many friends in Hampshire as he had left behind in Oxfordshire – and like a true sailor, found a girl, or girls, in his new parole port of call.

Proof of his generosity was soon forthcoming. English law dictated that any prisoner who fathered an illegitimate child should pay six hundred francs towards its support, or face imprisonment in a civil gaol. A naval officer named Le Forsiney, who was more amorous than he could afford, was in despair until Bonnefoux came forward and paid for his fellow officer's 'mistake'.

With all its diversions and amusements, pleasant walks through beautiful countryside, music and a good theatre, there was little for a well-heeled prisoner to complain about. Then, in June 1807, an English friend named Danley suggested that they make a surreptitious – and parole-breaking – trip to Windsor, which appealed to Bonnefoux's adventurous spirit.

They left the town undiscovered and after an exhilarating outing, during which they caught a glimpse of King George the Third, they returned safely to Odiham, swearing never to speak of their venture in the presence of any other English person. All went well until a day in September, when he and some friends were chatting, in their own language, beneath the window of a local widow. Unfortunately this lady had been educated in France, and even more unfortunate, some months earlier she had discovered an unsigned letter addressed to Mary, a pretty young nurse in her employ, which read: 'Tomorrow, I shall have the grief of not seeing you, but I shall see your king'.

Putting two and two together, the conversation and the billet-doux, the infuriated eavesdropper decided to denounce the Baron. The easy-going Shebbeare could not avoid placing a full report before the Transport Office and, despite Danley's willingness to shoulder the blame, it was decided that the Baron de Bonnefoux should be sent to the *Bahama* prison ship at Chatham.

Whilst awaiting the transport which was to take him to the Medway and the hulks, Bonnefoux was kept under guard in the 'George Inn' in the High Street. Released from his parole of honour by the sentence, he somehow managed to get past the guards and for the next three days he was kept under cover by friends in one of the Chalk Pit cottages. On the last day he was visited by a particularly smitten local damsel, who convinced him that she could smuggle him as far as Guildford in Surrey. Sarah Cooper, daughter of a local pastry-cook, was as good as her word. One cannot but feel sorry for the courageous though traitorous Sarah, when we read that they arrived in Guildford at dawn the next morning, her Sunday best ruined by torrential rain. There, after fond farewells, they parted, she in a coach back to Odiham, he heading for London. Bonnefoux said:

'Je dis alors à Sara que je pensais qu'il pleuvrait pendant la nuit. Elle répliqua que peu lui importait; enfin j'objectai cette longue course à pied, sa toilette et ses capotes blanches, car c'était un dimanche, et elle leva encore cette difficulté en prétendant qu'elle avait du courage et que dès qu'elle avait appris qu'elle puvait me sauver elle n'avait voulu ni perdre une minute pour venir me cherche... Je n'avais plus un mot à dire, car pendant qu'elle m'entrainait d'une de ses petites mains elle me fermait gracieusement la bouche.'

Baron de Bonnefoux had many further adventures, which are recounted elsewhere.

Another Odiham officer who broke his parole was one Du Baudier who was sent to Stapleton Prison for his offence. He obviously had friends in high places, as the Transport Office received a letter from the Duc de Chartres appealing for his release. Their reply shows that, like William Chambers in Peebles and traders in other towns, the creditors in Odiham had to be careful who they trusted. The request was turned down, the Transport

Office telling the Duke that Du Baudier had run up debts in Odiham and had given his creditors bills on his sister in France. All well and good; but the Duke was also given a copy of a letter written to the sister, instructing her not to honour his debts in the town. It read:

'Les Anglais nous ont agonis de sottises, liés comme des bêtes sauvages, et traités toute la route comme des chiens. Ce sont des Anglais; rien ne m'étonne de ce qu'ils ont fait... ce sont tous des gueux, des scélérats depuis le premier jusqu'au dernier. Aussi je vous prie en grâce de protester ces billets... je suis dans la ferme résolution de ne point payer.'

A sad entry in the Parish Records notes the death in 1806 of B. Blagin, a young French boy aged twelve, who was probably an officer's servant. Another, and we hope happier, entry records the marriage of Jean Marie Pasquire to Sophia Brooker. Abell adds another: Alfred Jauréguiberry, second captain of the privateer, *Austerlitz*, to a Miss Chambers.

Three births are recorded, though there were probably more:

1805 Adelaide.   Daughter of Henrie Barnè de Lau. Commodore and Officer of the Legion of Honour + Anne Webb.

1809   Louis Pierre François. Son of Jacques Gilliet + Terese Castinnazzi.

1811   Augustina. Daughter of Claude Augustine + Pierrette Lalette La Croix.

Odiham has no museum and there is reference to only a few artifacts remaining in the town: one an unusual piece called the 'Odiham Grotto', described as 'an intricate little seascape made out of shells, coral and little figures [a diorama]' with a large magnifying glass in front of it. I could not locate it but have seen a photograph.

WINCANTON.
In 1869 the pamphleteer, George Sweetman, began gathering together all the scraps of information he could discover relating to the history of his Somersetshire home town during its eight years as a parole town. He found there was a paucity of documentary material and that, as with many other one-time parole towns, memories were exceedingly short. However, Sweetman was lucky. There remained two aged locals, Henry Olding and Jonathan James, who had clear recollections of the captured officers and of the town as it was in their day. I, too, was fortunate on my visit to the old parole town. With that mystical touch of serendipity which any devoted collector would recognise, I found a rare copy of the result of Sweetman's research (which he published twenty-eight years later) – his little 'One Shilling' pamphlet, *'The French in Wincanton'*.

By 1869 many changes had taken place in the town, but between them the two octogenerians were able to paint a fairly detailed word-picture of the town as the first prisoners would have found it, on their arrival in 1804. Their reminiscences, backed up by an excellent engraving by a local man, Robert Newman, depict a not unattractive but rather poverty-stricken small town, set in a hilly landscape, and with a population of about 1,800 inhabitants. The streets were narrow and the roads bad, although many coaches and wagons passed through the town each day. In winter the steep hills in and out of the town were difficult to negotiate, coach wheels sometimes sinking to the hub in mud. At that time there were few bridges across the streams and, consequently, the fords could be positively dangerous.

Apart from a number of empty cottages, there were about 380 occupied family houses in the parish, a third of the occupants of working age employed in agriculture; but by far the majority were engaged in one or another aspect of the linen-weaving industry as loom-makers, flax-dressers, spinners or weavers.

'At the lower end of the town was a long row of weaving shops, extending from Church Street to Mill Street, where the clatter of looms, and the merry voices of the workers were continually heard. There were over 200 looms kept going in the parish at this time, inasmuch as those who occupied one room only, managed to keep a loom as a necessary part of the furniture.'

As is intimated by that last sentence, much of the work was carried out as a cottage industry and there was little for the workers to be 'merry' about. Times were hard and wages low, and such small manufactories as theirs were being overwhelmed by the great weaving towns of Lancashire. Women and children did much of the work and almost every cottage housed at least one cumbersome loom, some as many as three, plus spinning wheels. Poor harvests, the steep rise in the price of corn and animal foodstuffs and other wartime hardships, had forced at least sixty of the small community into the town's Workhouse or Poorhouse. Although for the present most just about survived on their poor income, by the middle of the century the 'clatter of looms' was heard no more in Wincanton.

When, in 1804, Wincanton became a parole town, the prisoners could not have come at a better time – at least for the inhabitants. The first to arrive were sea-going officers and captives from the French Colonies. Most were French, but over the years the prisoner community became a cosmopolitan group made up of Spanish, Italian, Dutch, Portuguese, Danes and other nationalities; 'Generals, Captains, Lieutenants, Midshipmen and Officers of every grade'.

Both Sweetman and Abell say that a number of those first parolees were captives from the French ship *Didon*. If that was so, then the memories of the two old Wincantonians were a year adrift, and Wincanton was a *cautionnement* for seven, not eight, years. The 40-gun *Didon*, Captain P. B. Milius, was taken by the British 36-gun H.M.S. *Phoenix*, Captain Thomas Baker, after a three and a half hour battle, on the 10th August, 1805[7], so her officers could not have been in Wincanton in 1804.

On arrival, the prisoners would have been received by the Agent, George Messiter, a popular and highly respected lawyer and, as they would later discover, they could not have been more fortunate in their Commissary. George Messiter was twenty-eight years of age in 1804, and was described by one of Sweetman's old informants as ' ...a gentleman well qualified for the office he held: of noble mien, brave, and held in high respect by all who knew him. Under his direction the captives were supplied with every accommodation he could give them'. Over the years, he was remembered by both locals and his prisoner-charges alike, as a remarkable and admirable character.

In the preparation of his novel, *The Westcotes*, Sir Arthur Quiller-Couch leant heavily on George Sweetman's little pamphlet on wartime Wincanton, which had been published a year or two earlier. This romance of life in Axcester (Wincanton) in its days as a parole town, centres round French officer captives and the Commissary's imaginary sister. The 'Orange Room', 'The Dogs', the 'ting-tang' and a great many other accurate details crop up throughout the tale. In fact, the opening words of the novel are based on the memorial plaque to the one-time Agent to the Prisoners of War in the town. It began: 'A mural tablet in Axcester (Wincanton) Parish Church describes Endymion Westcote (George Messiter) as 'a conspicuous example of that noblest work of God, the English Country Gentleman'. [*The actual inscription on the tablet describes him as* 'A bright example of God's noblest work.']

At first there were about 350 prisoners for the Agent to inspect, direct and instruct as to the restrictions of their parole commitment, and to settle them in. Nineteen of the empty houses were rented and taken over completely by groups of the more affluent officers and servants, but 'the greater number of them were of course in lodgings, and very glad indeed were the inhabitants to have them as lodgers. Many of them paid well, and what country is there, where money does not secure a welcome?' Henry Olding said that the number sometimes decreased through exchange or transfer, but at others rose to as many as five hundred – although some of these were lodged in the adjacent hamlet of Bayford. At all events they represented a significant percentage of the population of Wincanton, and would certainly have outnumbered the young men of that small town. He went on to say that it was:

> ' …quite obvious that some of them were patricians of France, and were frequently guests of the best families in the neighbourhood. The times then were stirring and the blood in the bodies of the sleepy Somerset people flowed more quickly than ordinary. Many a gossip found his or her way into the Market Place daily, and when there was no news, went home disappointed.'

This could not have been often. Although inland, Wincanton was by no means cut off from the latest news and reports of the progress of war. The post-chaises which carried mail and dispatches from Plymouth to London passed through Wincanton, stopping at the 'Greyhound Hotel and Posting House', for change of horses. Jonathan James remembered:

> ' …the post-boys were always booted and spurred; the horses were harnessed day and night ready for any emergency. Directly a coach was seen descending Lawrence Hill the alarm for two or four horses was given, and before the carriage had reached the town, the horses, with post-boys mounted, were in readiness, and as soon as the other horses could be released, they were attached. The change occupied two minutes only. Often the dispatches contained news of a great battle, and if an ensign or eagle appeared, or the word 'Victory' was spoken, the prisoners who were present returned with downcast heads, and the inhabitants sent up a shout of joy.'

Although the internees would no doubt have preferred a larger and more sophisticated town or city for their stay, there were many far less well-equipped to satisfy their needs than Wincanton, with its comfortable and inexpensive lodgings, its public houses, inns and hotels, and regular market in the Shambles. This was the principal market for the district and it became even busier and better-stocked with the introduction of the prisoners; there 'were 20 butchers who attended the market. Game and fish also were brought into the town in abundance, by the 17 coaches and wagons which arrived and departed every day.'

Olding said that the better-off officers lived comfortably in their hired houses or in the best of the lodgings and dined regularly and well, but that those who had only the Government allowance, did not 'fare sumptuously every day... but took their two meals a day at the *Restaurant pour les Aspirants*. The main staple of their diet consisted of onions, leeks, lettuce cucumbers, dandelions, &c.' With such a good market at hand, it is to be doubted that any French officer would have dined quite so simply, however hard up, particularly if they were organised for communal eating, as they were known to do in other parole towns.

Opposite the Market House near the High Street was a group of houses forming what was called 'Polly Carpenter's Corner','which projected so far out as to seriously impede the turning of the stage coaches and other large vehicles; indeed, it was the scene of many an upset.' Farther down there was a shop, a large bakehouse and a wheelwright's shop, all thatched, and a mansion known as 'The Dogs', so called because of the two hounds which decorated the gate pillars. Sweetman was told a sad but heroic little story of 'Polly Carpenter's Corner'. One of the buildings was Mr Carpenter's ironmongery. One day he sent a young girl assistant to the cellar to draw oil. She descended into the darkness with a lighted candle and, unable to draw the oil with one hand, she stuck the candle into a full but open-topped barrel – a gunpowder cask! She returned with the oil, unaware of what she had done, intending to go back for the candle, but Carpenter realised what had happened and told her what a perilous situation they were in. Lacking the courage to retrieve the candle himself, he called a young boy in from the street intending to send him to fetch it. Although trembling and terrified, the girl, preferring to risk her own life rather than sacrifice than that of the boy, rushed down the stairs and saved the day – at great cost to herself. She was ill for the rest of her life, seized with hysterical fits which never left her until her death.

The 'Greyhound Hotel and Posting House', whilst one of the most important, was not the only hostelry in the town – there were nine others. The other principal inns, the 'Bear Hotel', the 'White Horse' and the 'Swan Hotel' were all in the High street, as were 'The Dolphin', and the 'Angel Inn' – whose landlady, being of 'portly dimensions', was known as 'The Fat Angel'. Opposite Angel Lane was a veterinary surgeon whose house bore the marks of a cannon ball fired by the troops of Oliver Cromwell.

Understandably, these hotels and the public houses became busier and more prosperous than ever before; but they were of greater importance to the parolees than merely places to eat, drink or carouse. Nearly all of these establishments had club and assembly rooms and these featured greatly in their efforts to create something of an atmosphere of home-from-home, and also for entertainments to which the locals were invited. They had their operatic and theatrical groups and frequently arranged musical evenings (see Chapter 10, *The Arts and Crafts of Napoleonic and American Prisoners of War 1756-1816*, THE ENTERTAINERS).

The pamphleteer was told that, as in other towns, the prisoners were allowed to walk out of the town about a mile in each direction. On the London road, the boundary was 'Bayford Elm'; on the Ilchester road, 'Anchor Bridge'; on the Castle Carey road, 'Abergavenny Gate'; and on the Bruton road, 'Gooselands'.

> 'They frequently promenaded the streets in great numbers, four abreast. The large rooms in the public houses were often rented for

holding meetings of various kinds. On one occasion the large room at the 'Swan Inn' was used for the lying in state of a mason, who was buried in a very imposing manner.'

Another very senior officer lay in state at the 'Greyhound Hotel'; and it is recorded that when Rear-Admiral de Wailly-Duchemin died in Wincanton, he lay in state in the panelled 'Orange Room' of the afore-mentioned mansion known as 'The Dogs', not far from 'Polly Carpenters Corner'. The room was so called because it was said that William of Orange slept there when his party stopped overnight at Wincanton, on his way to London to lay claim to the English throne.

'Many died from various causes incidental to captivity. They were buried in the churchyard, and a stone there marks the resting place of one who was said to have died of grief. One of them committed suicide, which caused great sorrow both to his fellow captives, and the townsfolk in general. Another poor fellow became demented, and every day might have been heard playing on a flute, a mournful dirge, from which tune, if tune it might be called, he never changed.
'Others bore their estrangement from home less sorrowfully, and employed their time in athletic sports or in carving various articles out of different kinds of wood and bone. Some were allowed to visit friends at a distance, [this must have been a rare concession granted to a few very privileged or senior officers] always returning faithfully to their parole.'

The above statement, that some prisoners were allowed to far exceed their one mile parole limit, is borne out by the fact that one young parolee was known to have visited a hamlet some fifteen miles from Wincanton, on more than one occasion. Charles Aubert, one of a number of young prisoner-artists, had painted mural panels of three of the Muses on the bedroom walls of Jonathan James's house in the High Street, which George Sweetman had been able to inspect more than eighty years after their execution. They had been papered over until, during redecoration, they were rediscovered and restored in 1896.

At that time he met a Miss Impey, of Street, who showed him some drawings, pastels, and watercolours by Aubert, including a picture of Wincanton seen from the Bruton Road. These, she said, had come to her through inheritance from her great grandfather, a Mr Tuttiet, who lived at Somerton, where 'the young artist was allowed to pay visits occasionally'. Rooms in other buildings occupied by prisoners were decorated with wall paintings and stencilling, and the 'Orange Room' in 'The Dogs' at one time housed a 'large number' of their paintings. Sometime in the first decade of this century, Francis Abell was allowed by the then owner 'to inspect the paintings on the panels of this and the adjoining room, which were executed by French officers quartered here, and represent castles and landscapes, and a caricature of Wellington, whose head is garnished with donkey's ears'. There must have been, and possibly still are, examples of the work of another talented artist, Ensign Jean Marie Bazin, who spent seven years in Wincanton before his transfer in 1812[8].

Apart from the rooms in inns and hotels the prisoners had other places of entertainment. They probably had a lot to do with the conversion of a barn on 'Tout Hill', which was fitted out as a theatre, (and there was a Wincanton Theatre, though it would seem there is no record of where it was situated). There was also a building in what was then called 'Oborn's Yard', which was specially built, either by or for them, as a recreation room for the French. It may have also been used as their Masonic Hall[9], but, whatever else, it would certainly have housed a billiards table. After the war this building became Wincanton's first Baptist Chapel.

They had few restrictions on their 'freedom'. However, a check on their continued presence in the town was an understandable necessity. 'Every morning the town bell – the ting-tang – rang to assemble the prisoners.' The roll was then called, each man being expected to answer to his name, and at six in the evening the bell rang again for the same purpose. It rang again as a curfew at a later hour, when every one had to retire to his lodging for the night. The actual timing of the 'ting-tang' would have varied with the seasons; but if any parolee was found on the streets after this third bell without specific permission or excuse, he was liable to be taken before the Commissary, for reprimand or punishment.

The constant addition and subtraction to the prisoner of war population, would have prevented any stagnation in the flow of wartime information and rumour. One can imagine the eager questioning of newcomers as they arrived in the town. Some would have been captured in small skirmishes, taken in merchant, naval or privateer engagements; others in great battles on land or sea, but all would have their stories to tell. Wincanton was allotted its portion of captive officers after the victory at Trafalgar, in 1805.[10] This group numbered about one hundred and fifty officer prisoners, mostly captured in the battle itself, and others from the four French ships of Admiral Dumanoir-Lepelley's division, captured a fortnight later. The public houses and club rooms would have been abuzz with excitement and enquiries as they learned the details of that great action; and if, as was quite possible, any of the French officers had seen *Le Moniteur's* distorted, pro-French, report of the battle before arriving at Wincanton, they may well have thought their internment would be short-lived!

More arrived in 1806, among them generals Rochambeau and Boyê, re-paroled after their confinement in Norman Cross; so we can resume the story of these most notorious and troublesome of parolees. Rochambeau and Boyê soon made their presence felt in Wincanton, as they had elsewhere. They carried on with petty niggling infringements of parole in spite of the fact that in George Messiter, the Agent, they were answerable to a man who commanded the respect of most other parolees. However, it was inevitable that Rochambeau would sooner or later overstep the generous mark of Messiter's forbearance.

Rochambeau's dominant and intolerant personality was no doubt all part of his self-image as a powerful, although at present militarily impotent, general. It made him impossible to control as a paroled prisoner and led him and his fellow transgressor into committing one of the meanest of their many parole offences – an offence which should have placed them back in Norman Cross with even fewer privileges than before.

In July 1807, about fifteen months after their arrival in Wincanton, Rochambeau, Boyê, and other officers from the town, embarked on an escapade which took them four or five miles beyond the milestone limit for normal captive mortals. They had their dogs with them, and were no doubt attended by their servants and aides, and at one point left the turnpike to wander over farmland. The farmer, seeing a group of men and dogs on his land, was understandably annoyed and as it was obvious that they were prisoners of war – Richambeau, in particular, was always attired in resplendent uniform – made his annoyance plain.

The generals were affronted that a mere farmer should address them and set upon him, giving him a thorough thrashing. They eventually returned to Wincanton in a foul mood, causing something of a riot on their way back into town, fighting with the locals and threatening to set fire to the town.

The French officers were overcome after a struggle and secured under lock and key. I do not know what happened to the other parole-breakers, but one might expect to hear that the two persistently offending generals had at last cooked their goose. However, they were merely separated and again sent to parole towns – Boyê to Crediton and Rochambeau to Mortonhampstead, towns which were to be their comfortable prisons for the following three and a half years.

In 1810, after the capture of Mauritius, there was another influx of some fifty officers for Agent Messiter to take under his wing. Among them were some men of considerable means: it was reputed that they brought 'half a million sterling' into the town and, as old Henry Olding would have said, 'Where does money not ensure a welcome?'

For the first few years as Agent, George Messiter had little trouble in the management of his sizeable responsibilities and, unlike many other parole town Agents, there appears to have been no record of personal complaint from his captive charges. In times of real trouble, he was not of course expected to control such a large group of men alone, and troops were at hand when needed. At the top of the town, beyond the two wooden gates known as the Toll Bar, there was the Common, a hundred or more acres where the Militia and Volunteers drilled and exercised and practised with cudgel and singlestick. Henry Olding tells us that 'many pigs and geese were kept [on the Common], for bacon and feather beds', before going on to say: 'in consequence of the disturbed state of the country through the badness of the times and the apprehensions of a French invasion, there were large numbers of citizen soldiers. Wincanton had three companies of Volunteers and a troop of Yeoman Cavalry'.

It would seem that old Henry's memory failed him at this point in his story. There appears to be no record of a Wincanton Yeoman Cavalry until the Coronation of George IV, in 1821, when it was then formed – Henry may have been confused by the fact that its very first commander was the one-time Prisoner of War Agent, Captain George Messiter.

Towards the end of the decade an air of restlessness among the prisoners led to many infringements of their parole commitments. Attempted and successful escapes became frequent and, by 1811 the number who were not there to answer when the 'ting-tang' called them to muster, increased alarmingly.

Sweetman wrote in an understanding manner of the ever-increasing incidence of parole breaking, quoting 'Hope deferred maketh the heart sick'[11], to excuse the fact that as time passed, 'some of the prisoners became more impatient of restraint and longed more for home'. The fact is that the ever-increasing number of desertions from the town was only made possible by the encouragement and assistance of English and French professional escape agents, the former putting personal gain before patriotism at a time when invasion by the enemy was a very real possibility.

These smugglers and their fishermen accomplices were as busy in Wincanton as they were elsewhere in West Country parole towns situated no great distance from the coast.

Salisbury Journal, August, 1811.
'George Culliford, a notorious smuggler, has been committed to Ilchester jail, for conveying from Wincanton, several of the French prisoners of war from that depot. Culliford is said to be one of the gang that for some time past has infested the neighbourhood, and been aiding the escape of the prisoners from Wincanton to the Dorsetshire coast, whence they have been conveyed to Cherbourg, and it was with great difficulty and perseverance he was taken in consequence of a large reward.'

George Messiter, whilst always fair in his dealings with the parolees – and, if the tales are true, sometimes exceeded his authority by allowing some, like Charles Aubert, beyond their strict milestone limits – was still very conscious of his official duties and kept the Transport Office informed of the trouble brewing in the town. At his request, a company of Infantry was stationed in the town and 'were kept lively'. Nevertheless, in the closing months of the year a further twenty-two French officers disappeared from the town and this was just too much. Individual escapes and planned attempts by groups of two or three absconders had been fairly common in most parole towns, but now getaways were organised on a grand scale. At the beginning of 1812, of thirty who made their escape from Andover, Wincanton and Tiverton, four were generals and eighteen colonels!

In November George Messiter reported that, even with his Militia and the additional troops, there was little hope of preventing further escape and requested that Wincanton should be closed down as a parole town. Such reports from Agents and the constant fear of a general uprising in the country inspired rapid action on the part of the Government and orders were issued to the effect that all paroled prisoners were to be removed from the town and distributed through certain Border Towns of Scotland which had recently been appointed as *cautionnements*. Lower ranks were to be marched to London for embarkation and officers of the rank of captain and above were to be sent to Forton Depot at Gosport to await transport by sea to Scotland. During the first week in December the first batch were on their way:

'*Salisbury Journal*, December 9, 1811.
On Saturday last upwards of 150 French prisoners lately on their parole at Wincanton were marched by way of Mere through this city under an escort of Wilts Militia and a party of Light Dragoons, on their way to Gosport, there to be embarked with about 50 superior officers for some place in Scotland. Since Culliford, the leader of the gang of smugglers and fishermen who aided in these escapes, was convicted and only sentenced to six months' imprisonment, they have become more and more daring in their violation of the law.'

Culliford may have got away with six months' gaol on this occasion – although this seems a suspiciously light sentence for a man known to have been an habitual offender – but in the following year, when the law was changed he would have risked transportation to Australia for at least seven years.

The decision that the town was to be completely cleared was kept a close secret for fear of even greater unrest. The departure of the remaining Wincanton internees who left on their journey north, took place early in the New Year: and came as a shock to the prisoners involved:

'About the time of the morning roll-call, one day in the month of February 1812, a company of Infantry and a troop of Cavalry arrived at the 'South Gate'. Before the roll had been completed the Troop entered the town and surrounded the captives. The Infantry followed, and those who had not presented themselves at roll-call, were sent for. So sudden had been the call, that although many had wished for years to leave, they were unprepared when the time came. At 4 o'clock those who were ready departed; some had not even breakfasted, and no one was allowed to have any communication with them. They were marched to Mere [in Wiltshire] where they passed the night in a church. Early next morning, those who were left behind, after having bestowed their goods (for many of them had furnished their own houses), followed their brethren, and, joining them at Mere, were marched to Kelso [I very much doubt that they were 'marched' this great distance. They were almost certainly shipped to Leith for reassignment to a parole town], where they awaited until they were exchanged for British prisoners of war [a forlorn hope for many!].

'Deep was the regret of many of the inhabitants at the losing of so many, to whom they had become much endeared by ties of interest and affection. A great gap was made in the life of the town which took years to fill.'

Although Wincanton was 'cleared', not every officer left the town. A few escaped the exodus of February 1812, through the intercession of the Commissary, backed up by petitions from the inhabitants. The story of one particularly well-regarded officer, Louis Michel Duchemin, who had married Elizabeth Clewett, the daughter of the local printer, is told in another chapter.[12] There were a few other marriages between parolees and local girls.

There was William Bouverie, a popular French military officer, better known in the town by his nickname, 'Billy Booby'. Bouverie married a Wincanton lass and was probably married twice, leaving a 'Sophie Curtis' his widow when he died in 1848. John Peter Pichou, who was described in the Register as 'of Wincanton', was married by licence during the war, at Stoke Trister to Dinah Edwards in 1808, and another, Andrée Joseph Jantrelle, married Mary Hobbs in 1809.

However, one ex-parolee, who settled in Wincanton after the war was over is of special interest, adding another small paragraph to our story of the two dissident generals. This was an Italian, Alberto Biolotti, who was, in fact, none other than Albert Viollet, who had been servant to General Jacques Boyê since 1804! [Some years ago I tracked down descendants of Alberto, who visited my home in Surrey, kindly bringing with them documentary mementoes of the founder of their family in England.]

Alberto Bioletti, who married two English girls, died aged ninety-two in 1869, the year that George Sweetman began his research. Unfortunately, they never met. Alberto set himself up as a hairdresser in Wincanton after the war. His first wife died in 1834, his second in 1858, eleven years before Alberto himself passed away, and was buried in Portsea Cemetery.

As in many other parole towns, some of these romances ended in misery rather than marriage, and Sweetman's comments on these unhappy affairs are noted in the previous chapter. His homily ended with: 'I regret to say that our little town was becoming a veritable hotbed of vice.'

According to the Parish Register, between July 1806 and May 1811, seventeen French parolees who were never to leave Wincanton, were buried in the Parish Churchyard; seven of that number victims of 'the frosty and wet season of 1809'. Only one memorial stone is recorded, which bore the following inscription:

'Hic Jacet Petrus Dionysius Jacquet

Galls. Obiit Anno. Domini 1806.
He was a prisoner of war
But death has made him free.
Etiam, Jes. Bta. Fioupe Gall.
Anno Domini 1807.'

MORETONHAMPSTEAD

The Devonshire town of Moretonhampstead did not become an established parole town until rather late in the war. Except as an overnight stopping place for groups of officers on their way to begin their detention in other towns, or more fortunate ones on their way to exchange and the cartel ships at Plymouth. Moretonhampstead saw little of prisoners of war until it received its first complement of 'permanent' paroled officers in 1807.

A diary entry for November 1803 mentions that sixty-four officers spent a night in Moreton, before continuing their march to Lichfield, and an 1805 entry records that twenty-four Spanish officers made a similar stopover on the journey from Crediton to Plymouth[13]. No doubt a number of such short, in-transit visits occurred over the years and prepared the local inhabitants for foreign lodgers by the time their town itself became a *cautionnement*.

The first to arrive, on the the 23rd January, 1807, was a French officer, followed a month later, on the 22nd February by a Spanish surgeon. Over the next few months of that year the Prisoner of War Agent, Mr Ponsford, had to find lodgings for thirty or more new arrivals, mainly French and Spanish naval officers; and at the beginning of 1808, about twenty Danes were added to the town's colourful mixture of gentlemen captives. Moretonhampstead never received anything like the maximum number of prisoners allowable by the Transport Office regulations; the most for any one year was 250 in 1811.

The diary which tells us of many interesting events relating to the parolees, was kept by a jack-of-all-trades-businessman from 1799 to 1810. Silvester Treleaven, the town's postmaster, shopkeeper, stationer, chemist and barber, was probably as popular with the officers as he was with his local customers. The corner of the Chagford Road, where his shop was located, became known as 'Treleaven's Corner', and itself enjoyed some local fame. Another recorder of local events, Cecil Torr[14], tells us that, 'If the smoke blew downwards at Treleaven's Corner, rain was sure to follow – let the quicksilver be High or Low'.

Within six months of his appointment, Agent Ponsford had his first serious parole-breaking to deal with. On the night of the 27th and 28th September, a French captain and three *aspirants*, or midshipmen, were missing and Treleaven recorded in his diary:

'This morning it was found that four French officers had broken their parole, and supposed they were gone to the sea coast, which proved to be true, for in the evening all four were brought back again by the Officers of the Gang at Teignmouth; they had taken a pleasure yacht and were making out of the harbour when the alarm was given, an armed boat was got off, fired several rounds at them and they surrendered. They were kept under guard of our Volunteers at the Bell Inn all night.'

That same day a local farmer named Potter was arrested as an accomplice in their attempted getaway. Treleaven's entry for the 29th reads:

'This day the aforesaid French officers were conveyed in a post-chaise to Drewsteignton before Justice Roberts, who committed them to the High Gaol.'

Arriving so late on the scene as a parole town, Moretonhampstead had to contend with just about the worst period of parole-breaking of the wars, when the ideals of the parole promise had been forgotten or ignored with contempt by so many of the French and their allies. Of ninety-three officers who arrived in the town during March 1810, thirty-three were soon involved in escape attempts. It is understandable that the juniors should have been influenced by the dishonourable example of their seniors. Cecil Torr stated that they 'ran' in groups of four to six men at a time, and that among those thirty-three there were '8 captains, 8 Commanders and 14 other naval officers'.

Farmer Potter was not alone in giving – or rather selling – aid to would-be absconders. Few successful escapes were ever accomplished without the help of local inhabitants, or the professional escape-agents who carried out their operations all over the country.

In mid-1812, by which time the law had been changed, fines, inappropriate sentences to local gaol, with perhaps a spell in the pillory, had been replaced and more realistically severe punishments were being imposed. The Exeter Assizes came down exceedingly hard on three Devon men: Richard Tapper of Moretonhamstead, who worked as a carrier, and Thomas and William Vinnacombe, two smugglers from nearby Cheriton Bishop, had been involved in the attempted escape of Moretonhampstead parolees, a privateer captain, a midshipman and two merchant captains. All three were found guilty and sentenced to transportation for life.

One might expect that such a punishment would have sent Britain's escape agents scurrying into retirement; but at about the same time that Richard Tapper was on his way to Australia, a notorious member of the traitorous fraternity visited Moretonhampstead with the intention of expanding his business. Waddle, a smuggler and agent, worked out of Dymchurch in Kent, but had contacts countrywide. At the time of his visit he was on £400 bail from Maidstone, in connection with his part in the escape of General Lefèbvre-Desnouettes from Cheltenham.

After thinking that he had been successful in recruiting a local man named Robins, they retired to a local tavern where Waddell, in his cups, boasted that their first job would be to carry out a £300 commission he had arranged in France – the organised escape of a General Reynaud and his aide-de-camp from Mortonhamstead.

The rumour spread and the General soon got wind of the suspicion that he was bribing escape-agent Waddell. Perhaps he was, but wisely he wrote to the Transport Office, emphatically denying the accusation. Whether or not Robins would have become an accomplice had it not been for the tipsy indiscretion, who can say; but he, too, acting wisely, informed Agent Ponsford and Waddell was arrested. The Transport Board Commissioners accepted General Reynaud's refutation, but reminded him that: 'In consequence of the very disgraceful conduct of other French officers of high rank, such reports cannot fail to be believed by many.'

From July 1807 until early in 1811, by far the most senior and best known of Moretonhampstead internees was that tormentor of Agents, General Donatien Rochambeau. One might expect to read of three and a half years of parole-breaking and petty troublemaking, and it is true that Agent Ponsford could never be sure of him from one day to another, but it would seem that with his partner-in-crime, General Jacques Boyê, miles away at Crediton the leopard had changed at least some of his spots

His arrival in Moretonhampstead had caused something of a sensation, as much for his negro servant, Pierre Courpon, as his apparel – bemedalled uniform, cockaded, booted and spurred. The General would certainly have turned out in even greater finery a month later, on the 15th August, Napoleon's birthday, which the prisoners celebrated with a band, cheers and speeches; but 'in such a manner as not to give offence to the inhabitants of the town'.

The appearance of a negro in the town was a rare event, the first black man many had ever seen, and attracted much interest and curiosity among the inhabitants of Moretonhampstead – and particularly so to at least one local girl. Treleaven's diary records:

'**17th October, 1808:** Peter [Pierre Courpon] the black servant of General Rochambeau was married to a Susanna Parker.'

On the 19th February, 1811, Rochambeau's eight-years-long confinement to Britain came to an end. An Order arrived for the release of the prisoners taken at Cape François, San Domingo, when the General surrendered to the British in November 1803. Together with General Boyê from Crediton and fifteen from Tiverton, the parolees were conducted to Plymouth, picking up another hundred prisoners on their way to the coast. At Plymouth a cartel ship was waiting to take them to Morlaix.

Memories of the escapades of the two, lingered longer than most in the parole towns where they had left their infamous impressions. Over the years some of those memories were mis-recalled and turned into legends – one of which will be set down later in this chapter. At least three parolees, two lieutenants and an *aspirante*, ended their days in Moretonhampstead:

Ici repose le corps de
M. ARMAND AUBRY
Lieut. Du 70 me Regt.
D'Infantrie de Ligne
Agé de 42 Ans.
Décédé le 10 juin 1811.
[Crossed Swords]

A la Mémoire de
JEAN FRANÇOIS ROIL
Aspirante de la Marine
Imperiale, âgé de 21 ans.
Décédé le 22 janvier 1811.
[Emblem of Sword & Anchor crossed]

In the case of one of the lieutenants there is an additional sadness to the record of a young man dying a prisoner of war in a foreign land. His tombstone records:

A la Mémoire de
LOUIS AMBROISE QUANTIN
Lieutent. Du 1'44 Regt.
Du Corps Impérial d'Artillerie
de Marine. Agé de 33 Ans.
Décédé le 29 avril 1809.
[Masonic symbol of Compass & Dividers]

The Treleaven diaries tell us that the documents for Lt. Quantin's exchange and return home arrived at Moreton only the day before his death. On the 1st May, 'he was interred with Masonic Honours, with 104 French and Danish officers on parole attending his funeral, as well as most of the respectable inhabitants of this place'.

A Legend of the French Generals and the Dartmoor Ockery.

In common with many folk memories of the famous and infamous, the names of the two generals crop up in places where they may never have been. We have heard of them in Chesterfield when they were in fact in Ashbourne. We also read of a French officer named Boyer in Belfast, writing to 'his brother the General, on parole in Montgomery', telling him that the Emperor would not agree to an exchange of prisoners unless the Hanovarians were recognised as prisoners of war and of Boyê's attention to the Tiverton ladies in 1803, months before he arrived in England! Then there was a letter to him from General d'Henin, supposedly addressed to Montgomery in October 1804, by which time both he and Rochambeau had been ejected from Ashbourne and placed under close confinement in Norman Cross Depot.

Many inconsistencies exist concerning General Rochambeau. All of them are a little puzzling; but the most mystifying is how a story came about that a cottage was specially built to house our blemished heroes, Rochambeau and Boyê, on Dartmoor, at about the time of the founding of that prison.

> 'A great many of the Frenchmen cherished the fond hope that Napoleon would compass their release by the invasion of England and this hope was sustained by reports circulated by the market people.
>
> 'The indulgence of this hope excited two generals who lived in the picturesque little cottage at Ockery Bridge just outside of the prisons; the Commissioner on one occasion reports "Generals Rochambeau and Boyer are at present quiet. When the former thought that the invasion was at the point of being effected, he appeared two days in his garden in full dress with boots and spurs…"'
>
> Capt. Vernon Harris.

It is probable that the above extract from *Dartmoor Prison, Past and Present* by Captain Vernon Harris, a late nineteenth century Governor of Dartmoor, was responsible for this much-repeated myth. It was repeated by some Devon writers and refuted by others: William Crossing, in 1882, described the Ockery and mentions its occupants: '…a cottage built somewhat in the style of a Swiss chalet', having a verandah surrounding its four sides and a thatched roof. It stood on a bank of the Blackabrook stream opposite the Ockery clapper bridge which carried the packhorse track between Plymouth and Moretonhampstead.

William Crossing went on to say, '…during the time the French prisoners of war were confined at Princetown, two generals on parole named Rochambeau and Boyer lived at this house'. So maybe Vernon Harris picked up the story from Crossing.

Basil Thomson, a later Governor of Dartmoor Prison, wrote, in 1907, of the exploits of the famous French escape artist, Louis François Vanhille, which 'created sufficient stir in Devonshire to become the basis of a myth that a French general was confined in the cottage at Ockery Bridge'. Unfortunately, Thompson did not go on to explain what possible connection there could have been between a paroled French General and the escape-expert purser of a French privateer!

We know that special attention had always been given to the housing of distinguished captives, no matter how often they offended, (such as the fitting out of quarters in Norman Cross).

Therefore it is not impossible that the Ockery was built for a very senior officer or officers, but why so dangerously near a war prison?

Some sound research through the Public Records Office by Elizabeth Stanbrook produced some interesting background matter but could not solve the nearly two hundred year old mystery. However, she did offer one interesting and possible solution. When the San Domingo prisoners were released in February 1811, General Rochambeau, with Boyê from Crediton and the officers from Tiverton, would have travelled down the Moretonhampstead packhorse road to their cartel ship at Plymouth. At some point along their route they would have broken their journey, as their military guard were detailed to pick up 102 more San Domingo prisoners from the *petit cautionnement* at Dartmoor Prison, about half way between Moretonhampstead and their embarkation point.

So, as *something* had to spark off the story – and as this was the first time the generals had been together in Devon – it is conceivable that they did stay at the Ockery, if only for the night of the 2nd/3rd March, 1811! And perhaps we can stretch this a little further. If the collection of the prisoners from Dartmoor, and the paperwork involved in the release of more than a hundred men took longer than a one-night halt, then Captain Vernon Harris may well have been right when he said that Rochambeau 'appeared two days in his garden in full dress with boots and spurs'.

However, he was wrong as to date and probable reason for dressing-up. We have seen that he put on a show of sartorial splendour whenever there was cause to celebrate, so one can be sure that he would have presented a long-remembered sight to locals and guards, when the cause was freedom after eight years of captivity – and perhaps the similar story of his 'invasion' wait in the airing-yard at Norman Cross is of equal credibility.

PRINCETOWN, DARTMOOR

Dartmoor Depot, like Norman Cross, had its 'Officer's Prison'. The 'broke-paroles' were housed in a large building, walled off from the other *casernes* and yards, outside the inner iron-grill fencing which surrounded the prison proper. To the prisoners it was known as *'Le Petit Cautionnement'* – and to their captors as the 'Petty Officers' Prison', although commissioned officers of all ranks were represented. Basil Thomson[15] says that the peace-time professions of the inmates included 'lawyers, doctors, merchants, actors, musicians, artists, soldiers and sailors'; and there was also one negro General who was refused parole because of his colour.

They had their own airing-ground and access to the prison market, where just about anything was obtainable if the cash was available. They were able to furnish their messes with tables and chairs from the Depot stores and had servants to wait on them and cooks to prepare their food. Cooks, cleaners and personal attendants were recruited from ordinary captives in the other prisons, and were paid three pence a day for their efforts to provide their officer masters with an easy way of prison life.

All in all, these men who had forfeited what was less a type of closed imprisonment than a type of restricted freedom, were treated with greater consideration than was shown to those in the rest of the Depot, many of whom had not offended – other than getting caught – but could not claim the quality of being 'gentlemen'.

The internal discipline of the *Petit Cautionnement* was to a great extent under the control of prisoner-appointed officials selected from among their own number. As with all six *casernes* which went to make up the main prison, a *Commissaire de Salle* was elected, to act as 'governor, magistrate and chief of police'. These Commissaires held great power and were inferior only to their President – who in turn was responsible to Captain Isaac Cotgrave, the Governor of Dartmoor Prison. Article XVII of the Regulations which were posted up in all the prisons, in English and French, stated that a number of prisoners should be nominated by the Agent to preserve good order and see that all established regulations were attended to and misbehaviour reported to the Agent. From among those nominated the prisoners elected their *Commissaire de Salle.*

Most disturbances and troubles, and the punishments awarded, could be handled efficiently without recourse to Captain Cotgrave or external courts, although serious offenders were brought before the Governor, or tried at the Exeter Assizes. The internal trials in the *Petit Cautionnement* were conducted with all the strictness of a court-martial or civil court-room, as is shown by the 'Case of the Stolen Shirt':

> 'A search of all the chests was made, and the thief was hauled before a tribunal composed of a President, two assessors, an *accusateur* [prosecutor] and a *greffier* [Clerk of the Court]. The accused, who was defended by an able speaker, was found guilty, but instead of the extreme penalty of expulsion [from *Le Petit Cautionnement*], he was made ineligible to vote in any election, to belong to any Mess, or hold any communication with his fellows except such as was indispensable. The humiliation so wrought upon the wretched man that he took to his hammock and refused to eat. He was removed to hospital, where in a few days he died of a broken heart.'

Many duels were fought in Dartmoor and the officers in particular were possessed of a touchy 'susceptibility to wounded honour'[!]. Captain Vernon Harris, who was a predecessor of Basil Thomson in the governorship of Dartmoor Prison, gives us the amazing information that fencing was permitted among the many other distractions and amusements allowed, such as boxing, dancing, acting, etc. He said:

> 'For some time foils were allowed for purpose of recreation; but it was found that among a community trained to arms, the least provocation led to the guard button at the point being removed, and the harmless toy converted into a very good imitation of a "small sword". The evil grew to such an extent that the use of foils was forbidden.'

This ban did not, of course, put a stop to duelling at Dartmoor – or elsewhere where the excitable French spent time in enforced idleness. We read of weapons constructed from knives fitted into sticks, with hilts made from tin, scissor-blades and compass-legs mounted into wooden handles; even razor blades attached to sticks. Duels were fought in most parole towns and prisons, often over the most trivial of grievances – one which took place at Stapleton in 1809 between a military and a naval officer, and resulted in the death of one of the duellists, was fought over a game of marbles!

In June 1812, at Dartmoor, a fierce duel was fought with daggers, which resulted in the death of both contestants. The verdict of the jury – 'homicide by accident'.

Deaths from fights, duels and suicide at Dartmoor led the Plymouth Coroner to complain of the burden thrown on the parish treasury which had to pay 8d. to each of the jurors who attended these inquiries. In February, 1810, Mr Whiteford, the Coroner, spoke of the inquests on French prisoners 'who have laid violent hands on themselves or been otherwise killed' which in a single year in the war prison had outnumbered all inquests he had held in the fourteen preceding years.

Apart from the parole towns in the West Country, which were Ashburton, Tavistock, Okehampton, Moretonhampstead, Callington, Launceston, Bodmin, Roscrow, Crediton and Regilliack, there may well have been a few quartered in Princetown.

For the first few years of the Depot's existence, Princetown itself – described by one writer as 'unquestionably the bleakest place in Devon'[16] would certainly have been too small for it to have been a suitable place as a parole centre: just a few cottages and an inn called 'The Plume of Feathers', on the road which crossed the moor from Tavistock to Moretonhampstead, all the buildings no older than twenty-five years. However, once the prison became occupied with its thousands of inmates, the growth of the nearby town went forward apace – much of it with the aid of French – and later, American – prisoner-labour.

British prisoners of war in France were employed outside their prisons, under the strict surveillance of military overseers – and welcomed the opportunity to earn even a small wage, as they had not the advantage of prison markets where they could buy and sell – but it was less usual for prisoners of war to be employed on public works in this country.

The story of the building by Dartmoor captives, of Princetown Church, the construction of houses for British officer prison staff, and the heightening of their own prison walls, has been told in Chapter 19, DARTMOOR. It is, therefore, reasonable to suppose that some paroled officers may have been lodged in the town, at least whilst such work was in progress.

There were a number of escapes from the Officers' Prison and many more failed attempts. The most famous and well-recorded story was that of Louis François Vanhille, Purser of the French corvette *Pandour*. A man of great personality, Vanhille was elected a representative of the *Petit Cautionnement* dealing with matters between the officers and the prison authorities.

The first officers to escape from Dartmoor made their getaway only five days after the opening of the prison. A naval surgeon, Sevegran, and a naval officer, Auvray, had made careful note of the uniforms and arms of the guard which marched into the prison each evening to see that all prisoners were clear of the yards before nightfall. With great speed and typical French ingenuity, they made overcoats and glengarry bonnets from blankets, and 'armed' themselves with wooden guns and bayonets of tin. When the fifty-strong company of soldiers left through the outer gate, Sevegran and Auvray tagged on at the rear and gradually dropped back in the dusk, and as the detachment turned left into the barracks, they carried on through the village towards Plymouth.

To gain time, an agreement had been made with friends to cover their absence at roll-call on the following morning. As the officers were being counted, a mock quarrel broke out between two prisoners, which soon developed into an equally mock fight and soon attracted a crowd of prisoner spectators. With many threats of the *cachot*, the turnkey called two soldiers to his aid and the trouble quickly subsided – but the turnkey had by this time lost count. That evening three more left the Officers' Prison by almost identical subterfuge and got clear away. Auvray and Sevegran, who spoke fluent English and were not short of money, had reached Plymouth without incident and had no trouble in booking a coach to London.

Other officers absconded disguised as British military, but the majority of successful attempts depended upon corruptible guards and escape agents. The sums involved were surprisingly small considering the drastic risks they ran. Sometimes crooks fell out and there was trouble over the share-out of the ill-gotten gains. The disgruntled soldier might well report the matter to the officer of the guard and his post would be secretly filled by another sentry.

Two French officers would probably have got away, but for one such disagreement. It seems that they had paid well over the odds to four sentries belonging to the Nottinghamshire Militia. Everything was arranged, the officers had been supplied with a pistol 'to intimidate the countryfolk in case of pursuit', and one dark night in February, 1811, they were ready to go. However, one of the soldiers, considering himself unfairly dealt with in the distribution of the generous bribe, alerted the guard. A picket was waiting as the officers descended the wall, and another picket took the three sentries into custody.

On February 28th 1811, privates Keeling, Smith and Marshall, were tried by court martial at Frankfort Barracks in Plymouth, and were each sentenced to 900 lashes. Some time later, Smith and Marshall were pardoned, but Keeling, who had supplied the pistol, actually received 450 lashes – in the presence of pickets from every regiment in the Dartmoor Garrison.

Not all paroled officers who spent at least some of their captivity in Dartmoor's *Petit Cautionnement* were 'broke-paroles', as is shown by the following report:

> ***'Plymouth & Dock Telegraph**. 16 November 1811.*
> On Tuesday last an officer's guard belonging to the Somerset Militia proceeded to Launceston for the purpose of escorting all the French prisoners of the rank of midshipmen [*aspirantes*] on parole at that place to the prison at Dartmoor. The number of prisoners so sent off amounted to 37. Their removal has been occasioned by the order of the French Government to imprison all midshipmen amongst the British prisoners of war in France.'

The 'luxury' of the officer-only accommodation at Dartmoor came to an end in 1812, not as a result of escapes and attempted getaways, but because of the inevitable result of overcrowding in other parts of the Depot. The unhygienic conditions in which thousands of men were confined brought typhus and all manner of illnesses. With an infirmary insufficiently large to accommodate all the prisoner patients even in normal times, the outbreak of the epidemic made the extension of the hospital space an urgent necessity. So the broke-parole officers lost their comfortable *petit cautionnement,* which was made into a hospital, and in the autumn of that year they were housed wherever space could be found within the prison casernes. This was a severe blow to men who had first enjoyed the great privilege of parole, and then, after losing it,

the second-class advantages of the officers' prison, but were now reduced to sharing in the discomfort of their 'other ranks'.

They could hardly have expected a warm reception into the already jam-packed prison accommodation. Conscious of this and unwilling to integrate, it is said that some officers bought second-hand hammocks from which they made partitions and screens to shield them from their 'common' countrymen.

Notes.
In April 1810, the number of captives of all ranks rose to 44,583, the parolees numbering 2,710. Two months later the figures were 49,583 gross, paroled 3,193.

The Parliamentary Papers in the appendices to T. J. Walker's work on Norman Cross Depot include a detailed statement of French and Danish prisoners of war in this country at 26th June, 1812, from which I have abstracted those parts which refer to paroled prisoners. It could have been of only temporary accuracy: America had declared war on Great Britain on the 4th June, 1812, three weeks before the date of its issue, and American prisoners by the thousand were soon filling the hulks, their officers adding to the parole town quotas.

It is also uncertain whether all prisoners were included in this return. A great number of nationalities made up Napoleon's armies and, as was often the case, these allies may well have been grouped together under the heading 'French'.

Transport Office,
26th June 1812

On Parole.	French Prisoners	Danish Prisoners
Officers, Army.	1,615	-
Officers, Navy.	718	-
Masters & Mates of Merchant Vessels.	211	33
Captains, etc., of Privateers.	176	-
Passengers and other Persons of Respectability.	211	3
Servants to Officers.	149	-
Women and Children.	115	-
	3,231	36

Rup. George, J.Bowen, J.Douglas.

The complete return included a breakdown of the number of prisoners confined at that date. The totals were: French Prisoners, 52,649, Danish Prisoners, 1,868 (which, incidentally, shows 37 women and children as being in closed prison).

1. W.L.Clowes: *The Royal Navy. A History.* 1899.

2. This last sentence is ambiguous. The 6d. a day was probably his PoW allowance. If he was given another 6d. per day for his road working efforts he would have been doing very well indeed.

3. The formality of surrender required the captor to fire a symbolic shot across the bows of the enemy, who would reply with one last broadside.

4. Acting-Lieutenant Nisbet Josiah Willoughby eventually became a Rear-Admiral and was knighted.

5. In 1805, Captain Daniel Woodriff was himself to experience life as a paroled prisoner of the French. As commander of the 54-gun *Calcutta* he was convoying a merchant fleet from St Helena to England when he fell in with a squadron of five French ships-of-the-line. After putting up a valiant fight, which allowed his convoy to escape, he was overpowered by the enemy battleships and struck to the 74-gun *Magnamine* on the 26th September. Captain Woodriff was paroled to Verdun where he remained until his exchange and return to England in 1807.

6. Pierre Jouneau had a brother who was paroled to Launceston. When Pierre died, the Transport Office instructed the Agent to forward his belongings to his brother – together with a bill for two guineas – the cost of his funeral!

7. The 40-gun, 1,091 ton, *Didon*, which had lost 27 killed and 44 wounded of its 330 ship's company, was repaired and added to the British fleet.

8. See Chapter 23 – PAROLE IN THE SCOTTISH BORDER TOWNS – Jedburgh.

9. See Chapter 8, *The Arts and Crafts of Napoleonic and American Prisoners of War 1756-1816*, THE FREEMASON PRISONERS.

10. After the battle, the Spanish prisoners were detained at Gibraltar and the officers from the *Achille, Berwick, Duguay, Trouin, Formidable, Fougueux, Intrepid,* and *Scipion,* about two hundred and ten in number, were sent to Wincanton and others to Crediton.

11. PROVERBS. XIII. 12.

12. See Chapter 8, *The Arts and Crafts of Napoleonic and American Prisoners of War 1756-1816*, THE FREEMASON PRISONERS.

13. S.Treleaven: *Chronological Occurrences in Moretonhampstead, 1799–1810.*

14. Cecil Torr: *Small Talk at Wreyland.*

15. Sir Basil Thomson: *The Story of Dartmoor Prison.* 1907.

16. Nicholas Pevsner: *The Buildings of England – South Devon.* Penguin. 1952.

Chapter Twenty-Three

Parole in the Scottish Border Towns

BY 1811 THE EVER-INCREASING NUMBER OF prisoners of war flooding into England had become a matter of considerable concern to the Government. After the capture of the Isle of France, of Guadaloupe and Martinique, not only the depots and hulks, but the English towns assigned as centres for paroled officers, were becoming alarmingly overcrowded. This, and the not unfounded fear of a general uprising of the captives, convinced the authorities that it would be wiser to spread the load.

As early as 1757, Edinburgh Castle had been used for the imprisonment of rank-and-file prisoners of war and had continued to be employed as a closed prison throughout the Seven Years' War, the Revolutionary and Napoleonic Wars. The great mansion house at Greenlaw, some nine miles away, had been put to similar use from 1804 onwards; but compared to the vast numbers crowding the hulks and depots south of the Border, the prisoner of war population of Scotland was very small. For political reasons, Ireland was considered out of the question as a possible recipient of a share of the overflow and so, from 1811 until the end of the war, Scotland was to shoulder a greater part of the prisoner burden.

The great depots at Valleyfield and Perth were set up for the accommodation of ordinary prisoners of war and, for the first time in the North, a number of towns and villages were selected as suitable *cautionnements* for paroled officers. A few officers had been sent to Peebles in 1803, and it is possible that a few others had been paroled to the vicinities of Edinburgh and Greenlaw in the past for short periods; but this would have been only in exceptional circumstances, and none were paroled to Scottish towns as a matter of policy before the end of 1810. The towns selected to receive officers on their parole were:

BIGGAR	KELSO	MELROSE
CUPAR-FIFE	LANARK	PEEBLES
DUMFRIES	LAUDER	SELKIRK
HAWICK	LOCKERBIE	SANQUHAR
JEDBURGH	LOCHMABEN	

The first officers sent to Scotland had already had some experience of parole-town life. They were transferred from certain English towns which were considered danger spots in the event of an uprising; almost every prisoner on parole at Wincanton, for example, being transferred to one or another of the Border towns.

These officers, almost the first to be paroled north of the Tweed, may well have been worried and apprehensive when they learned of their destination. Before leaving Wincanton, some of them had been warned that the Scots 'be a nation of naked sauvages' and, being aware that amongst the reasons for their relocation was the increasing incidence of parole-breaking and escapes in the English towns, they probably thought that they were being sent north as some sort of fiendish punishment. Imagine then, their relief and surprise when they found the 'naked sauvages' were both fully-clothed and kindly, hospitable folk, who generally treated them with generosity and understanding.

After reading everything I could unearth in the Scottish Public Records Office, in books, pamphlets and letters bearing on the subject, I am truly amazed at the warmth of their reception. Anyone who has read the preceding chapters will no doubt agree that the lot of the captive officer, paroled to an English town, was, with few exceptions, no harder than he himself might make it – but those who were sent to the Scottish Borders were lucky indeed.

In researching for other sections of this book, I have often felt a pang of genuine pity, when a letter or record has revealed a glimpse of the soul-destroying misery of a man penned up in a foul hole afloat, or lost in the hopelessness of an over-populated depot. A man whose only crime was that he had fought for his country and suffered the misfortune of captivity. But in writing the story of the enemy officer on parole in Scotland, no such feelings are aroused. Here the sympathy must be reserved for the British serviceman at the seat of war, who would seem to have been almost completely forgotten amidst the excitement which these glamorous men from a different world brought to the Scottish towns.

The above is a general statement, for not all border town *cautionnements* were at first equally welcoming, but, despite the fact that parole-breaking and escapes were not infrequent from the beginning, pro-prisoner feeling was detectable in perhaps the majority of parole-town Scots. The extraordinary degree of compassion exhibited by the public, towards prisoners who had been taken in actions against their own countrymen, can be gauged from the following extract from Wallace's *History of Blyth*:

'One Sunday morning in the year 1811, the inhabitants were thrown into a state of great excitement by the startling news that five Frenchmen had been taken during the night and lodged in the guard-house.

'They were officers who had broken their parole at Jedburgh, and in making their way home had reached the neighbourhood of Blyth; when discovered they were resting by the side of the Plessy wagon-way beside the "Shoulder of Mutton" field. A party of countrymen who had been out drinking, hearing some persons conversing in an unknown tongue, suspected what they were, and determined to effect their capture. The fugitives made some resistance, but in the end were captured, brought into Blyth and given into the charge of the soldiers then quartered in the town.

'This act of the countrymen met with the strongest reprobation of the public. The miscarriage of the poor fellows' plan of escape through the meddling of their captors, excited the sympathy of the inhabitants; rich and poor vying with each other in showing kindness to the strangers. Whatever was likely to alleviate their helpless condition was urged upon their acceptance; victuals they did not refuse, but although money was offered them, they steadily refused to accept it.

'The guard-house was surrounded all day long by crowds anxious to get a glimpse of the captives. The men who took the prisoners were rewarded with £5 each, but doubtless it would be the most unsatisfactory wages they ever earned, for long after, whenever they showed their faces in the town, they had to endure the upbraiding of men, women, and children; indeed it was years before public feeling about this matter passed away.'

After paroled officers, described everywhere as pleasant and agreeable characters, had spent months or years in a town which they had enlivened, it is to be expected that fraternisation would have brought some friendship and cordiality between native and prisoner. However, this attitude towards the escapers is difficult to understand, and yet the reaction of the people of Blyth was not at all unique. This can be gathered from the newspaper-cutting reproduced here; the sympathy was all with the prisoners who had broken their word of honour, and this mystified the judge as much as it does me.

The case referred to, concerned the escape of two other Jedburgh parolees, Benoit Poulet and James Girot, in 1813. At the trial of their British accomplice, James Hunter of Whitton, near Rothbury, the crowd in court cheered and applauded when a verdict of 'Not Guilty' was brought in; the judge said in disgust that he seemed to be in an assembly of Frenchmen rather than a British court of law.

Perhaps this fellow-feeling towards the French officer-prisoners arose from a conscious or subconscious affinity with France from earlier times. Mary Queen of Scots, whose first language was French and had been Queen-Consort of France for a while, met her end at English hands, and their French-exiled Bonnie Prince Charlie had been defeated at Culloden by 'Stinking Billy'[1] – an interesting subject for discussion, but perhaps not here.

These, then, were the sort of people amongst whom the parolees from the southern towns were to settle; and they soon discovered other advantages of their transfer. Food was cheaper than in England, lodgings could be obtained for a very few shillings a week, the conditions of parole engagement were less likely to be so strictly enforced, and almost everywhere they were met with friendly interest. Everyone, from Sir Walter Scott – with reservations – to the local tradesman seems to have gone out of his way to bid them welcome.

As was the case in all parole towns anywhere in Britain, the Scottish shopkeepers, traders, and householders with vacant rooms, were not slow to see financial gain in the form of this addition to the population and their clientele. However, very soon after their arrival, the officers began to be appreciated for their amiable and intellectual qualities, as well as their cash. Where particular acquaintanceships were struck up and friendships formed, the officers would have been known and addressed by their proper names and titles; but, probably owing to the fact that many of those names were difficult to remember and their pronunciation did not come easily to the Scottish tongue, they were generally referred to as 'Mrs McDonald's Frenchman', or 'Nannie Tamson's', according to the family name of the landlady with whom they lodged.

They were, in general, educated, well-mannered men, whose refinement, ingenuity and strange culture fascinated the natives of the normally uneventful little Scottish towns. They were also welcomed into the society of the wealthier county families and were never short of invitations to dances, dinners, parties, in fact to almost every function which took place in the vicinity of their *cautionnements*. Sometimes they were present at celebrations which not all of them could have enjoyed – our victories over their Emperor.

The dangers inherent in too-close fraternisation were appreciated by some thinking men and a worry to the authorities. Sir Walter Scott, at that time Sheriff of Selkirkshire, who was frequently host to French officers at his home in Abbotsford – well outside the one-mile limit – was at the same time conscious of the dangers which lay in forgetting that we were still at war. In a letter dated the 3rd May, 1812, he wrote:

'I am very apprehensive of the consequences of a scarcity [of Militia?] at this moment, especially from the multitude of French prisoners who are scattered through the small towns in this country; as I think very improvidently.

'As the peace of this county is entrusted to me, I thought it necessary to state to the Justice Clerk that the arms of the local Militia were kept without any guard in a warehouse in Kelso; that there was nothing to prevent the prisoners there, at Selkirk, and at Jedburgh, from joining one night, and making themselves masters of this depot; that the sheriffs of Roxburgh and Selkirk, in order to put down such commotion, could only command about three troops of yeomanry to be collected from a great distance, and these were to attack about five-hundred disciplined men, who, in the event supposed, would be fully provided with arms and ammunition, and might, if any alarm should occasion the small number of troops now at Berwick to be withdrawn, make themselves masters of that sea-port, the fortifications of which, although ruinous, would serve to defend them until cannon was brought against them.'

Had an opportunity like this presented itself in any of a number of parole towns south of the border, at this stage of the war, it is unlikely that it would have gone ungrasped. It is inexplicable that the possibilty of such rebellion did not trouble more minds in these northern communities, into which large numbers of war-like, though likeable, foreigners had suddenly been thrust. The majority were young men – the average age at Lauder was twenty-six – high-spirited and resourceful; but perhaps they were too well treated at the start to have taken action as drastic as Sir Walter envisaged – although individual escapes were not rare.

With good cheap lodging, beautiful countryside through which to walk, enviable trout and salmon fishing and friendly folk to help make less bitter the longing for home, it is not to be wondered at that friendships grew which lasted long into the years of peace.

The bare statistics, the numbers, names and dates relating to paroled officer captives, are fairly easily researched in public records offices, whether the prisoners were quartered north or south of the Border. However, more personal details, the happenings which, though of small national importance, may have been sensational locally; the impressions left on townsfolk and local gentry; the minutiae of parole-town life – these things have to be sought after elsewhere, in pamphlets, newspapers, letters, memoirs and family histories. Furthermore, these sources of information are more readily available concerning Scotland than elsewhere. Although the new, post-1811, parole centres were host to captives for no more than four years, a number of English towns had been used as *cautionnements*, on and off, for more than fifty years.

Towards the end of the nineteenth century, J. Macbeth Forbes of Edinburgh, gathered together all that he could find which related to the Border towns and their wartime charges. At that time he was able to record fascinating and still-fresh family memories of those days. In the early 1900s Francis Abell, armed with the historical notes of Forbes, William Chambers and others, visited the Scottish parole towns in search of further material. By that time almost all memories had disappeared, but, by diligent scanning of the newspapers of a hundred years before and filtering through the notes and transactions of the historical and archaeological societies of the little towns, he was able to add to the recorded knowledge.

When, more than three-quarters of a century later, I followed in their footsteps and made my own enquiries in each of the fourteen old parole towns, it was with little hope of finding fresh information, but rather to get closer to my subject than was possible through the notes and findings of others.

Expecting little, I was all the more delighted with what I found. This journey to Edinburgh and the Border Towns, which would have been pleasant enough in its own right, produced some interesting results. There was the rediscovery of two prisoner of war paintings, one of which had been described but never before reproduced; the unearthing for the Bank of Scotland of the 'impliments of forgery', used by the prisoners in the production of false guinea notes; the inspection of all Forbes's original notes and letters; the finding of a number of prisoner of war artifacts, and an interesting little illustrated pamphlet, the reminiscences of a French officer paroled in a border town.

Perhaps the most interesting, however, was a visit to a house on the River Jed, which had welcomed foreign officer prisoners one hundred and eighty years before, and where I was welcomed by descendants of their host and shown fascinating evidence of their visits.

The pamphlet. which I found in Selkirk, was an English translation of *Souvenirs Militaires de Doisy Villargennes*. 'The French Prisoners of War in Selkirk'. Sous-Lieutenant Adelbert Doisy de Villargennes was captured in May 1811 and released in 1814, and the time which elapsed between his captivity and the writing of his memoirs must have further softened even the mildest of hard feelings which he may once have felt for his captors. His own period of captivity was spent with no real hardship, and he was lucky in his English friends from the moment of capture onwards. Even so, his compliments showered on the British treatment of prisoners of war generally are somewhat over-effusive, much as one would like to believe in them. He makes Forton Prison, at Gosport, seem like a holiday camp and dismisses the prisoners on the hulks as 'refractory and incorrigible'. Both these things we know to be nonsense; none of the depots and prisons were comfortable quarters and many men were sent to the hulks as a matter of expediency – and others, because they happened to be serving on the wrong type of vessel, with the wrong number of guns, at the time of capture.

All in all, his lack of sympathy for compatriots who had no more committed crime than he, but were unfortunate in being of lower rank – his own, by the way, was the lowest eligible for parole – does not read well, coming as it does from one who professed to support equality and fraternity. However, his reminiscences of parole life are of great interest, and it is of equal interest to know something of the pre-capture service life and background of men who ended their war in British *cautionnements.*

Doisy, the son of an old army officer, was born in Paris on the 30th January, 1792, so was still a young man when he arrived in Selkirk. He had been impatient to enter the French service and could hardly wait for his schooldays to end, so that he could take part in the stirring events taking place at that time. He chose action at sea rather than on land and when the time came, he obtained a commission as a gardes-marine – a rank somewhere between our midshipman and sub-lieutenant. This was made easy by the fact that Admiral Magendie was a relative of Doisy's mother and so, at the tender age of fifteen, he was serving on a flagship, the *Vasco da Gama*, bound for Portugal. The French occupation of Portugal did not last for long, and after the Battle of Vimeira young Adelbert was back in France and transferred to a frigate, the *Pallas.*

After serving for two years on this vessel, he awoke one morning to find himself a soldier – his sailing days at an end. It appears that his father, in the belief that promotion was quicker on shore than afloat, had obtained for him an army commission and he was now

Sous-lieutenant Doisy of the 26th Regiment of the Line. The Regiment was at Strasbourg, on its way to Germany, and he joined it just in time to see action in the Battle of Essling, where he was wounded by a shell splinter. Although the campaign did not last long, the 26th lost over four hundred men in Germany before marching back through France to Bayonne.

Doisy was in action at Ciudad Rodrigo, Almeida, at Busaco and at Torres Vedras. At Torres Vedras the rains had begun and the French army was in terrible condition; 'food, forage, clothing, even ammunition being very scarce.' The army was reduced to the necessity of marauding and eight hundred and fifty of Doisy's regiment were without boots or shoes.

In writing of the search for foods and the general shortage of provisions, Doisy tells a story which illustrates the surprising fact that, despite the miserable conditions under which both sides were suffering and fighting, there was little real hatred between the English and French armies when not in actual combat:

'One day in February, 1811, my company was on outpost duty; our first lieutenant had been in search of provisions all the previous night, and instead of returning to camp, found it more convenient to stop at our first post, which happened to be in his way. Among other booty secured by him was an old bull. Captain Grignon, our commander, was so transported by joy that, unwilling to allow another the honour of slaughtering the victim, seized a gun and hastily fired at the head of the bull. The poor animal, not being fastened to a post, took one great leap and bolted precisely in the direction of an English outpost invisible from our position, but which we knew to be about half a mile distant. Without any hesitation the following note was written on the flap of an old letter:

"Captain Grignon, 26th of the Line, presents his compliments to the officer in command of the English outpost and begs him to return his bull."

'This was certainly not a clear case for extradition, but our gay captain was no casuist, and did not hesitate a second. This laconic message was given to the care of a corporal and four men (without arms) and sent without delay. This would be about 8 am. Several hours passed without the reappearance of our men and early in the afternoon I accompanied the captain in search of them and to bring them back to the camp, fearing for the result of his chivalrous confidence in the enemy. No news could be had of the men and the vision of court-martial began seriously to haunt the mind of the captain. However, about five o'clock we heard a great racket proceeding from the vicinity of the English outpost. Although by this time it was nearly dark we perceived some fifty red-coats accompanying, with great hilarity, our five men to our lines. Our men were rolling from one side of the road to the other, drunk as Bacchus, yet able to join lustily in the delirious laughter of their enthusiastic escort. The English halted as they came within range of our sentries and returned to their own camp after shaking hands heartily with our men. The latter rejoined us and threw their packages to the ground; these consisted of sundry pieces of beef, several loaves of bread, and two bladders filled with wine.'

Doisy says that it was impossible to get any sense out of the inebriated emissaries, and it was only next day that the corporal remembered that he had a letter for the captain from the English camp, and three English newspapers. The letter, which was written in French, read:

'Major……… of the……… Regiments presents his compliments to Captain Grignon, and regrets sending him only part of the bull, beef being such a rare article in his camp. By way of compensation, however, he begs the Captain to accept a few loaves of bread and a little wine.'

A good story, but it did not end there; word of the incident got to the notice of the Commander-in-Chief. Captain Grignon was called before him and was lucky to get away with no more than a severe reprimand and admonishment against any such future conduct. The following day an order was issued to the whole army, threatening the most dire penalties on anyone guilty of transmission of any communication to the enemy.

Only a few weeks later, Adelbert Doisy was with the retreating army which made its stand at Almeida, the last French stronghold in Portugal. On the 3rd May, 1811, he was taken prisoner in the nearby village of Fuentes D'Onores, and his short but eventful military career was at an end.

He described his last day of active service and the events leading up to his capture. He was on outpost duty with forty of his men that night after a day of sharp-shooting, when General Loyson ordered him to take twenty men and lead him to where he thought the nearest outpost might be. The General left after a while and Doisy and his men walked into trouble:

> ' …the night was exceedingly dark and there fell a fine rain; we marched in silence along a narrow road bordered on either side by hedges. The General had not left us more than ten minutes when, arriving at an open spot, a perfect avalanche of blows assailed my detachment for the space of a minute. Not a shot was fired, only the bayonet and the butt ends of muskets doing the work. And strange to say, among all those who were more or less wounded, an old drummer was the only one who was killed outright. As for myself, 'ere I could guess what kind of wasp's nest I had fallen into, I was laid prostrate by a blow on the head and a bayonet or sword thrust on my left shoulder. When I recovered my senses I found myself surrounded by red-coats. An officer, whom I afterwards knew to be Sir Charles Stewart addressed me in very good French in the most encouraging terms. Soon a surgeon appeared and declared that the most serious wound was that on the head and that I should be alright in a few days.'

Doisy must have had a very likeable personality, for from that time on he was literally nearly killed by British kindness. In hospital he was befriended by a Scottish captain who he was to meet again at Fort Bellin at Lisbon, where all prisoners were held whilst awaiting embarkation to England. At the Fort he was in luck again. Bellin was garrisoned by the 26th English Regiment, and when one day an English officer noticed the coincidence of the regimental number '26' on Adelbert's shako and buttons, he was more or less adopted by the regiment and allowed to live in their quarters during his detention at Lisbon. He was still not fully recovered from his wounds, and the extravagant hospitality, the feasting, drinking and general high living, following so closely upon a period of hard living and illness, brought about a relapse, and a warning from the regimental doctor that if he continued in this way he would 'soon be consigned to the Portuguese soil'.

Back in hospital, he was fortunate enough to meet again his Scottish friend, Captain A. Pattison, who was waiting to be invalided home. By mysterious pulling of strings, Pattison arranged a berth for Doisy on the same warship which was to take him to England, thus avoiding the discomfort of a ten-day trip to Portsmouth on a prisoner of war transport vessel.

Arrived at Gosport, he and other French officers were, somewhat unusually, allowed on their parole to wander about the town and visit their other-rank compatriots in the depot at Forton. Gosport was a distribution centre from which officers were allocated to specific parole towns. Doisy de Villargennes was first sent to Odiham in Hampshire, but was there for only a short time before he was caught up in the new policy of sending parolees to the Scottish borders, and he was included in a group shipped to Leith.

I make no apology for dwelling so long on the experiences of young Doisy, in a chapter devoted to Scottish parole towns. He was probably not untypical of many French officers, old in experience though often young in years, who made their entry into these sleepy little towns, where the majority of the inhabitants lived quiet and uneventful lives; to whom a trip to Edinburgh would have been a great occasion.

After disembarkation at Leith, all officers who had been granted parole were taken to the distribution centre at Edinburgh Castle. From there they were marched to their allocated towns – in Doisy's case Selkirk, about thirty-six miles to the south of the city. About nine miles into their march they would have stopped at Pennicuik where, at nearby Valleyfield, the old Esk Mills had recently been converted into a war prison, the great Valleyfield Depot, designed to accommodate up to 5,000 continental captives.

SELKIRK

On leaving Penicuik, those of the one hundred and ninety officers who were assigned to Selkirk still had a long march ahead of them. However, on arrival at their destination, the county town of Selkirkshire situated on the River Ettrick, they would have found an attractive little place of mainly thatched houses, and a population of about two thousand inhabitants.

> 'The town is encircled by beautiful hills on the sides; in the centre it had a square adorned with a fountain; a very fine bridge crossed the Ettrick. An ordinary looking building belonging to the National Church, and a much larger one owned by the Presbyterians, or rather the sect known by the name of "Anti-Burghers"… were the only buildings in Selkirk worthy of notice.'

Doisy said that when his party arrived they at first found considerable difficulty in procuring lodgings but, 'matters quickly altered in this respect; the Selkirk inhabitants found presently that we were paying cash.' This would make it appear that Doisy's group was the first to be sent to the town and that the Selkirk landladies were inexperienced in the lodging of parolee boarders, but his remark can be discounted on two counts.

About one hundred officers, including a number of army surgeons, had been there since the Spring of 1811 and were well settled in by October, when Doisy arrived. And in each parole town the Agent for the prisoners was always well prepared for their reception and fully acquainted with all the details of the accommodation available. It would have been quite ridiculous for them to have been left to find their own lodging on a door-to-door enquiry basis.

J. J. Vernon found that the Day Book of the Selkirk Subscription Library recorded that, from April 1811, when the first party of officers had arrived until the town was cleared, the prisoners were avid borrowers and were 'omnivorous readers, with a penchant for History and Biography, but devouring all sorts of literature from the poetical to the statistical.'

Most of the officers found their resources sufficient to cope with the cost of accommodation and provisions in the Scottish towns – where prices were cheap compared with England. Their weekly prisoner of war allowance of a half guinea was paid out regularly by the Agent, and the majority received additional cash from

THE
French Prisoners of War
IN SELKIRK:
BEING THE REMINISCENCES OF
Sub. Lieut. ADELBERT J. DOISY
(26th Regiment of the Line).

ILLUSTRATED BY
GEO. HOPE TAIT,
F.S.A. (SCOT).

LIMIT OF PRISONERS OF WAR SELKIRK

G. LEWIS & CO., PUBLISHERS.   PRICE 3D

France. This money reached them through the London banker, Thomas Coutts, who had been selected by each Government to arrange the transfer of cash between countries. Some, like one Selkirk prisoner named Belleville, were wealthy and received as much as £1,000 a year from home, whilst Adelbert Villargennes was remitted an annual £50, doled out in quarterly payments. With lodgings costing only 2/6d. a week, cheap provisions and the fact that they formed themselves into messes of two to six members, even the poorest among them could make ends meet. There was also the advantage of the nearby streams and rivers:

> '…some of us were passionately fond of fishing, and excelled at it, the Ettrick and the Tweed abounded with trout and eels of excellent quality; a lake in the neighbourhood supplied an abundance of very delicate pike. No one ever thought of depriving us of this very agreeable pastime, which proved a valuable asset for us in the culinary sphere.'

Like all the other Scottish parole towns, Selkirk soon had its French club-house, cafe, its twenty-five-piece orchestra – 'superior to all those to which the echoes of our Scottish residence had ever till then resounded.' Later on they hired a building and set up the theatre which is discussed in another chapter and, of course, they had to have a billiard table to cater for their favourite pastime.

Billiards was almost a necessity, and tables could be found not only in the Border towns but in *cautionnements* everywhere else in Britain. 'However, this was not an exclusively upper-class diversion; every prisoner of war depot had its tables – there was certainly a large number spread over the seven *casernes* or prisons which went to make up Dartmoor Depot – and although it may be hard to conjure up the picture, there is undeniable evidence that many of the overcrowded hulks had facilities for play. (Though play must surely have been confined to fair-weather days, as billiards would have been impossible if wind or sea put the hulk into even the slightest pitch or toss; unless the tables were suspended from the deck-head or in gimbals!)

The evidence for the existence of the tables in closed prisons is most often found in the form of orders for the banning of the game and the destruction of the tables for, in the depots and on the prison ships, the billiards table was less often the venue for a friendly game and pleasant pastime, than the equipment for serious, and often vicious, gambling.

Similar things were happening in all the other Border towns, and it cannot be doubted that their comparatively superior culture, their liveliness and the glimpse which they afforded of a largely unknown outside world, made these men the centre of public interest during those last few years of the long drawn-out wars.

The most often broken of all parole engagement rules (except, perhaps, for the smuggling out of uncensored letters), was that which limited excursions beyond one mile in any direction from a specified point, and it is understandable that the distant stretch of road or strip of river should seem more attractive than the selfsame thing within bounds. In most of the parole towns north of the Tweed the rule could be at least slightly bent with a reasonable degree of safety. That is, so long as the technical offender did not go too far and commit the more serious infringement of returning to his lodging after the curfew hour, which varied according to the time of the year. Milestone stories, of officers who found ways, usually humorous, of extending their rambles, are to be found in the memorabilia of many parole towns, and Selkirk was no exception.

> 'On each of the four roads leading into the town, at a distance of one mile, there was placed a post on which was inscribed the words – "Limit of the Prisoners of War". A practical joker pulled up one of these posts and carried it a mile further on, to the amusement of the inhabitants, who, we must say to their credit, never on any occasion took advantage of a regulation, in virtue of which whoever might see anyone of us outside the fixed limits was entitled to one guinea, payable by the delinquent.'

Maberley Phillips tells the story of one officer whose interest was archaeology, and asked the Agent for permission to go a little distance beyond his parole limit at Jedburgh to visit some ruins. The Agent refused to officially give his permission but said he would turn a blind eye nevertheless.

> 'But the Frenchman had given his word of honour and could not break it. He borrowed a wheelbarrow one afternoon, and with it and the necessary implements proceeded out to the obnoxious milestone. Having unshipped the milestone, he raised it on to the barrow and then triumphantly wheeled it to the required distance, where he fixed it [but he had not gone beyond it].'

For generations the stone stood where the Frenchman placed it, no one being any the worse off for the extra extent of the Scotch mile.

One such misplaced milestone could still be seen *in situ* a hundred years later; but this time the offender was an Englishman. Sir Windsor Hunloke, Bart., of Wingerworth Hall, Chesterfield, wished to make it possible for Roman Catholic parolees to visit him, but his home was beyond the limit; so he had the milestone moved to the other side of Wingerworth Hall where it stayed until the early years of this century.

In spite of the milestone limits, officers were frequently invited to the homes of families living beyond the bounds, in the neighbourhoods of all the Scottish towns. There must have been some sort of understanding between the Agents and the hosts, but this would have been quite outside the strict rules laid down by the Transport Board.

Sir Walter Scott – notwithstanding his warning to others of the danger that fraternisation might result in an uprising – seems, himself, to have both fraternised and often abetted infringements of parole He was particularly impressed with one, Tarnier, another of the young French officers who had been captured in Spain: 'a young man of brilliant talent, excellent education, and of a remarkably exuberant spirit.

> 'Soon after they met, Tarnier was invited to Abbotsford [more than two miles beyond the parole boundary marker]. At first Tarnier was the only foreign invitee, but later he was allowed to bring with him three friends and de Villargennes, who would never have missed a social opportunity, was included on a number of these occasions. The mode of procedure seems a little suspect and covert: "…in the twilight, those who were invited repaired to the boundary – [the milestone which had already been placed beyond its legal distance] there a carriage awaited us, which took us at a good pace to Abbotsford, where we were most graciously received by our host."'

Sir Walter was just plain Mr Scott at that time, a respected lawyer and Sheriff of the county, and few people knew that he was the 'Great Unknown', the author of 'Waverley'. Neither could his prisoner guests have known that there was a motive, other than a desire for intellectual stimulation and a philanthropic gesture towards gentlemen in adversity, which inspired the invitations to his home.

On the streets of Selkirk, Scott gave the impression of being a cheerful, good natured person, of rather ordinary appearance, whose lameness made his progress slow. At Abbotsford they found a changed man, welcoming and warm, receiving them 'in a fashion as amiable as it was delicate' and the table, without being lavish, was, on the whole 'recherché'.

Whilst politics as such was not generally the subject of their table conversation, Sir Walter, for his own good reasons, always managed to guide the discussions towards a subject which seemed to fascinate him – Napoleon Bonaparte. Traits and anecdotes, minute details of the French army, he could never hear enough – and his guests, Bonapartists to a man, never tired of speaking of their beloved Emperor.

In a sense, they sang for their supper. One can imagine their sense of bitterness and betrayal when, ten years later, Sir Walter Scott published his work entitled 'A Life of Napoleon Bonaparte', and they could then read, as free men, what they considered a corruption of the information they had appreciatively given to a genial host in the days of their captivity.

However, there were many other gentlemen who, without self-interest, treated the Frenchmen with great kindness. Selkirk was unusual amongst the Border towns, in that the gentry of the town had formally decided, before arrival of the captives, that they should not be admitted into their society. This could not have included any of the gentry who were Freemasons – we know that, by the Spring of 1812, more than a score of French Masons had been admitted as members of the Scottish Selkirk Lodge.

The non-fraternisation determination was not, of course, rigidly adhered to over the years, and was more than made up for by the hospitalty of families outside the town. Particularly treasured, were the memories of a couple of gentlemen farmers: one a keen fisherman who took great pleasure in entertaining the fellow-anglers among the officers, and welcomed them to his strip of river. The other was determined that they should savour the delights of the Scottish culinary art, by serving them offerings of such delicacies as haggis, grilled lamb's head, salmagundi (a salad of odds and ends: meat, onions, anchovies, etc.), hotch potch and a marvellous cheese of his own making. Then there was a wealthy old lawyer who enjoyed his dram, and tried, without success, to teach them to keep pace with him in the 'superabundant libations' which he urged upon them.

Although there is more to be said of Selkirk and its wartime history, we will leave it now to see what was happening elsewhere in the Border towns.

MELROSE

An interesting little burgh on the Ettrick river, Melrose once had an Abbey of importance, where, it was said, the heart of the fourteenth century Scottish king, Robert the Bruce, was buried at the high altar. By the time of the town's use as a *cautionnement*, the paroled officers would have seen only scant ruins of Melrose Abbey, left after its destruction by the English in 1546. Soon after the end of the war Sir Walter Scott, who lived at nearby Abbotsford, supervised the restoration of part of the Abbey and, although a ruin, its south front is still an impressive sight today.

Parole life in Melrose can have been very little different from that experienced by the parolees in Selkirk, only seven miles away. Indeed, there is evidence that Melrose prisoners were regular visitors to Selkirk. Whilst the Agents would sometimes slacken off the reins and allow fishing and hunting trips a mile or so beyond the boundary on occasion, everything in the rules of their parole engagement should have made it impossible for officers to have made these excursions between the towns – yet it is certain that some of them did. Three Melrose-based French officers visited Professor George Lawson's Selkirk Subscription Library after learning that he was particularly fluent in the French tongue. They were made welcome on numerous occasions and were given free run of the library, where they found many books in their own language. Among these were some rare works by old French authors, but they found that the ancient spelling and idiom was too much for them to cope with – but not for the Professor: 'the savant, in an easy and fluent way, entertained them by reading the whole.'

Impressed as they were by this performance, they were less impressed by his efforts to convert them to what he considered to be the only true faith, and on their return to Melrose, one of them, August Bouard, whose English was not as good as Dr Lawson's ancient French, wrote him the following letter:

> 'Dear Sir, I beseech you do leave off of speaking against

The Roman Catholic Church, because as often as you do
speak against her, as often you sin.
You do like St. Paul before his conversion to our Lord
Jesus Christ'.

The proof of such visits, so many miles out of bounds, led J. John Vernon to state in a paper to the Hawick Archaeological Society that the officers paroled to Melrose were not restricted to the usual one mile limit; and James Brown, in his 'History of Sanquhar', says that the parole limits in that town, too, were wider than elsewhere.

In neither case can I believe that this was an instance of official favouritism shown to those two particular towns, a perk which all of the officers paroled to those towns would have been able to enjoy. I think that a possible explanation may be hidden in the coincidence that, in Melrose, Selkirk and in Sanquhar, the French officers operated quite strong Masonic Lodges. These prisoner of war Lodges – in the case of Melrose, the 'Bienfaisance' – were on extremely good terms with the British Lodges in those towns, and it may well be that the favoured few, rather than the general run of parolees, obtained very special privileges through the influence of their British Brethren.

A manuscript exists which shows that the French Lodge was never just another wartime diversion for men at a loose end; but was formed by serious Masons who had hailed from Lodges in many parts of the world – Naples, Martinique, Senegal, Guadaloupe, Cayenne and even Canada. The 'Lodge Bienfaisant' was made up of thirty Brethren, nineteen Founders, two Affiliates and nine Initiates – French army, Navy and mercantile marine officers – but it also had its Honorary Members, eleven prominent Brethren of the British Lodge of St John at Melrose.

KELSO

More than in any other of the old parole towns, there is a something about Kelso which makes it easy to imagine some one hundred and eighty years ago, when it played its wartime part by accommodating its share of the captured officers of Napoleon's army and navy.

It has seen its changes, but an atmosphere of the unchangeable remains. Then, as now, it was a prosperous agricultural town, with its spacious market square, old Town Hall and attractive Georgian frontages. Its people, too, can have changed little – at least as far as amiability goes – possessed as they are of a refreshing calm and friendliness towards the total stranger.

Nearly two hundred years ago their ancestors gave a similar welcome to strangers who they might well have regarded as enemies – prisoners of war from the fighting in Spain and Portugal, and some from the West Indies. The first few officers entered the town on the evening of the 28th November, 1810, and during the following weeks their numbers grew, until, by the end of January, 1811, about two hundred and forty had arrived. Some were naval officers and a few privateersmen, but the greater number were military men. Most were French, but there was a group of twenty Italian officers and a few of other nationalities – including at least one American.

As each party arrived in the town it was met by the Agent, Mr John Smith, a Bailee of Kelso, 'usually garbed in knee-breeches and silk stockings.' He was assisted by Robert Darling, one of the legal staff of the Company of Writers, of which John Smith was the head. Both of these men were held in high regard by the officers over the years that followed. The fact that there was very little trouble in that town, and fewer escapes than the average for the towns, can be attributed to their consideration and fairness. Kelso was more used to visitors and strangers than many of the other Border towns, situated as it was on an important coach road from England into Scotland, and it soon became accustomed to the presence of men of such different backgrounds and cultures.

The officers themselves settled in with ease and were soon found accommodation, for the most part in private dwellings. The first to 'get their feet under the table' were the Freemasons. We know that the first group of officers arrived in Kelso late on the evening of the 28th November. A document which had to be signed by all visitors, is preserved by the British Kelso Lodge, No.58, and the signatures of fifteen French officers appear under the date, the 30th November, 1810, only two days after their arrival!

As was the case in most parole towns, the financial standing of the Kelso detainees ranged from the very well-off to the very hard-up, some at first depending entirely on their half-guinea Government allowance. These latter soon found various and individual ways of making ends meet. Some earned a few shillings by painting miniatures and watercolour landscapes of the surrounding countryside, or made saleable articles in straw plait, such as baskets, trays and suchlike, basing their designs on the plait used in the making of the straw hats[2] so popular with the ladies of that time. Some may have made inlaid boxes of fine-split straw although this type of craftsmanship was more often the product of the depots, where teams made up of various talents worked on masterpieces of straw-marquetry. Others, with special skills or interests employed them usefully, whether for monetary reward or as a round in the fight against boredom and depression. Most often, of course, they became language masters, teaching their native tongue. One of them 'Mrs Matheson's Frenchman', an ex-privateer officer, who had some faith in the power of advertising, was enterprising enough to place the following advertisement in the *Kelso Mail*:

Mr Brement, Professor of Belles-Lettres
and French Prisoner of War
Respectfully informs the
Ladies and Gentlemen of Kelso
that he teaches the French and Latin Languages

Apply for terms at Mrs Matheson's
near the Market Place

It was said that M. Brement's advertisement paid off and he made his stay in Kelso a profitable captivity. With so many opportunities and a pleasant environment for their pursuits, only the most indolent would have been really short of cash or supplies. At any rate, none who was handy with rod and line need have gone hungry. Situated as it was, and is, in beautiful countryside and on the River Tweed, just below the junction with the River Teviot, the Kelso parolees, like those at Selkirk, had the privilege of a first class sport and an additional source of food. Indeed, the Kelso officers are credited with being the first to practise a winter-fishing method of catching salmon through holes in the ice, when the Tweed was frozen over.

Unlike Selkirk, there was never any agreement among the town's big-wigs to avoid over-familiarity with the foreigners. In fact, Macbeth Forbes records that, in a very short time after their arrival, the town took on a new spirit of liveliness and that, 'the time of their stay was said to have been the gayest Kelso had seen since fatal Flodden.' Soon they were being sought after as guests by both town and country families, who appreciated them for their conversation, their stories and their wit – and the hospitality was not all one-sided. The officers quite often hired rooms in the local inns and arranged dinners, parties and private balls, inviting all those who had shown them similar kindness.

Most were usually attired in white trousers or breeches and jackets, which were always immaculate, but on these occasions they were particularly smartly dressed, resplendent in gaily-coloured coats, frills at neck and cuffs, and long white stockings. The *Southern Counties Mail* described them as: 'frivolous we will admit, as many of them wore earrings, and one, a Pole, had a ring to his nose, while all were boyishly fond of amusement, and were merry good natured creatures.' And the *Kelso Mail* tells us that their deportment 'was uniformly conciliatory and respectable'. But the *Imperial Gazeteer of Scotland* was not quite so smitten and described them as men 'who, in a very noticeable degree, inoculated the place with their fashionable follies, and even, in some instances tainted it with their laxity of morals'.

The first part of the *Gazeteer*'s judgement was perhaps unnecessarily sour. The cheerful prisoner who made the best of his misfortune and faced his captivity with constructive resignation after signing his parole, caused less trouble for both his captors and himself; and we have seen how, in the closed prison of depot or hulk, the more adaptable Frenchman fared better than the bitter and rebellious American. However, the last part of the *Gazeteer*'s critical comment was fully justified. The unhappy outcome of illicit amours were common to all parole centres, and Kelso and all the other Border towns had their share of the problem.

James Brown of Sanquhar, commented in similar vein, but perhaps with more understanding:

> 'They were Frenchmen, Italians and Poles – handsome young fellows, who had all the manners of gentlemen, and, living the life of enforced idleness, they became great favourites with the ladies, with whose hearts they played havoc, and, we regret to record, in some cases with their virtue'.

Duels were fought over parole town beauties. One at Selkirk went on for more than half an hour before the combatants retired unhurt; and another which took place at Lauder – where the chosen weapons were razors fastened to the ends of walking-sticks – was, surprisingly, also fought without loss of blood. This duel was probably the result of a similar quarrel. Duelling between prisoners of war was illegal in Britain, and two Selkirk duellists each spent a month in a civil gaol as a result of their encounter.

Napoleon, on the other hand, could see no good reason why British officers should be denied the privilege of killing each other whilst captive in France, and issued no such order. It should, of course be mentioned that, in Kelso, as in most Scottish *cautionnements*, romances between foreign captives and Scottish lasses sometimes ended in marriage.

The old Kelso Theatre, described in another chapter, was taken over and revived to popularity by the prisoners. The lack of changing-rooms meant that the town was often treated to the strange sight of men exotically dressed in costume for their theatrical roles, passing through the town to the theatre. It was on the occasion of one of these prisoner of war productions that the local postmistress earned herself a bad name in the town. Whilst the residents showed warm-hearted friendliness towards the parolees, it was possible to exceed the bounds – even in Scotland. This married lady committed the indiscretion of accompanying one of the actor-officers clad in costume and make-up, from her home to the theatre. The local busy-bodies were scandalised and 'this was accounted a terrible proceeding on her part and the gossips let loose their meddling tongues on her for some time afterwards'.

The author arrived in Kelso just too late to see the last remaining relics of the old 'Horse Market Theatre'. Mr Sandy Blair, the local horologist, told him that it had been demolished only a few years before. Until recent times, some of the decorative work on the ceiling – which Francis Abell had seen in the early 1900s – had still survived, although the gilded woodwork of the proscenium surrounding the stage had been dismantled many years before.

Sandy Blair directed the author to another building in the town, where he thought some prisoner of war wall paintings might still be seen. In spite of going along expectantly to the old house, where at one time paroled officers had lodged, the very old gentleman who greeted him explained that if they did still exist then they were under the layer upon layer of wallpaper, applied over a century and a half of redecoration. He was apologetic and seemed sad that he could not strip his walls to help with the research.

Although the officers were, on the whole, easy-going and adaptable and could have found little to complain of in Kelso, they were still prisoners, with no idea how long that condition might last. It would have been remarkable if, among so many captives, none had put thoughts of home or active service before his 'parole d'honneur'.

Surgeon-Major Jacques Voillard, who had served on the French corvette *Hebe*, was the first to make his getaway. A reward notice was posted up which offered one guinea for his recapture, and *Hue and Cry* described him as about twenty-three years of age, of swarthy complexion, with black hair and eyes, 'a long visage and walking with long strides'. He was traced for some distance, but it would seem that his 'long strides' took him to freedom, as there was no report of his recapture.

His escape took place on the 25th July, 1811, and ten days later Ensign Parnmagen, of the privateer *Hautpol*, was away, followed a couple of weeks later by a Lieutenant C. Rossignal, of the *Angelice Nightingale*. There was one more escape in November of that year and, in June of the following year, Lieutenant Angalade of the French Army – one of the Freemason signatories who visited the Kelso Lodge – broke his parole and headed for France.

A year later, at the end of June 1813, a group of French officers attempted a mass exodus, assisted by an American. They very nearly made it but were recaptured, and the American was arrested for his part in the conspiracy.

A few more got home from Kelso by legitimate means. Although exchange of prisoners was becoming an exception rather than the rule, a small number benefited when agreements between the nations were arrived at. A French merchant who was detained in Kelso was exchanged for the supercargo of the *Clyde*, a British merchantman. A French midshipman and a merchant mate were swapped for their British equivalents; but not all exchanges were arranged on a one-for-one basis – a French midshipman and the master of a sailing vessel were considered fair exchange for a British Engineer Captain.

There was a third group of parole town prisoners which returned to France under less happy circumstance. Badly wounded or infirm captives were invalided home without exchange, but only if they were definitely considered 'unfit in any capacity for future service, either military or naval'.

With the Spring of 1814, Kelso's 'gayest period' came to an end. The officers left Kelso with the good wishes and regret of the good people of the town and with some of their cash. As we shall see, Mr Chambers of Peebles was unlucky in his experience of prisoner of war debtors, so it is pleasant to record that, in the case of Kelso, nearly all debts were honoured.

Many Prisoner of War Agents were remembered long into the years of peace. Some, particularly the worst of the Commissaries of the closed prisons, depots or hulks, such as the American, Reuben Beasley, were immortalised as ogres in prisoner of war memoirs and journals, whilst a few were remembered with appreciation for their consideration and humanity.

The Agents for the parole towns had a less harrowing, and perhaps easier, task – though even so, a few were dismissed as unsatisfactory characters. However, many, such as George Messiter at Wincanton, John Romanes at Lauder and John Smith at Kelso, formed life-long friendships, based upon mutual respect, with their former charges. That the general kindness of the inhabitants and 'parental care' of the Kelso Agent was appreciated can be gathered from the following letter, written a few years after the war:

Paris, on the 6th day of May, 1817

Dear Sir,
I have since I left Kelso wrote many letters to my Scots friends, but I have been unfortunate enough to receive no answer. The wandering life I have led during four years is, without doubt, the cause of that silence, for my friends have been so good to me that I cannot imagine that they have totally forgotten me.

In all my letters my heart has endeavoured to prove how thankful I was, but my gratitude is of that kind that one may feel but cannot express. Pray, my good Sir, if you remember yet your prisoner, be so kind as to let him have a few lignes from you and all news about all his good old friends.

The difficulty I have to express myself in your tongue, and the countryman of yours who is to take my letter, compel me to end sooner than I wish, but if expressions want to my mouth, be assure in revange that my heart shall always be full of all those feelings which you deserve so rightly.

Farewell, I wish you all kind happiness,
Your friend forever,
LE CHEVALIER LEBAS DE STE. CROIX

'My direction [address]': à Monsieur le Chevalier Lebas de Ste. Croix
Capitaine à la Légion l'Isère, Caserne de la Courtille à Paris.

P.S. All my thanks and good wishes first to your family, to the family Waldie, Davis, Doctor Douglas, Rutherford, and my good landlady Mistress Elliot.

To Mister John Smith Esq.
'bridge street'
Kelso, Scotland.

PEEBLES

Peebles was alone among the Border Towns in having had experience as a parole town before the end of 1810. A small number of foreign officers had been housed there as early as 1803 but that was not the town's first experience of accommodating prisoners of war. In September, 1798, a French squadron under Commodore Bomparte had sailed with three thousand troops in an attempt to invade Ireland. This intention was thwarted when a British squadron, under Commodore Sir John Borlase Warren, captured seven of the ten French men-of-war.

Two thirty-six gun frigates struck to the British 36-gun *Melampus*, These were the *Coquille* and the *Résolue* and many of the prisoners taken from those vessels were sent to Peebles. Abell says that they were 'probably confined in the town jail', but I cannot imagine that Peebles would have had such a commodious gaol at that time. I agree with him, however, that in writing of Peebles as a parole town, one cannot do better than quote at some length from 'The Memoirs of William and Robert Chambers'. It is a rare and interesting opportunity to read a first-hand account of captured officers as they entered their parole town and of how they lived when settled there. William Chambers, who was a young lad when he witnessed their arrival, said of that day in 1803:

'Not more than twenty or thirty of these foreign exiles arrived at this early period. They were mostly Dutch and Walloons, with afterwards a few Danes. These men did not repine. They nearly all betook themselves to learn some handicraft to eke out their scanty allowance. At leisure hours they might be seen fishing in long leather boots, as if glad to procure a few trout or eels.

'Two or three years later came a *détenu* of a different class. He was seemingly the captain of a ship from the French West Indies, who brought with him his wife and a negro servant-boy named Jack. Black Jack, as we called him, was sent to school, where he played with the other boys on the town green, and at length spoke and read like a native [of Scotland, presumably].

'He was a good natured creature, and became a great favourite. Jack was the first pure negro whom the boys at that time had ever seen.

'None of these classes of prisoner broke his parole, nor ever gave any trouble to the authorities, They had not, indeed, any appearance of being prisoners, for they were practically free to live and ramble about within reasonable bounds where they liked.'

William Chambers first learned of a fresh influx of officer prisoners in 1810, when, one Sunday, he was sent on an errand to the local chandler:

'Here sat Candle Andrew in his Sunday best, with an under red-silk waistcoat, and his bald head lightly powdered. Before him lay a large open folio of Matthew Henry's Bible, covering nearly the whole table. Above it, and about the same size, lay *'The Star'*. Candle Andrew, who I esteemed to be a great man, as Dean of Guild, was so kind as to speak to me, and what he said was momentous. "Great news, Willie, my man – terrible battles in Spain – thousands of French prisoners – a number of them brought to Leith, and I shouldn't wonder if some were sent here. However, here's *'The Star'*..."

'Little did I know that what Candle Andrew had hinted at, was destined to shape the whole existence of my brother and myself, indeed the whole family, father and mother included. Inspired by the notion that there was something of importance in the intelligence, I hastened home, but before I arrived my father had received a glimmering of the news. A neighbour had called to say there was to be immediately a great accession to the prisoners of war on parole.

As many as a hundred and eleven were already on their way to the town, and might be expected in a day or two.

'There was speedily a vast sensation in the place. The local Militia had been disbanded. Lodgings of all sorts were vacant. The new arrivals would on all hands be welcomed. On Tuesday, the prisoners in an unceremonious way began to drop in. As one of several boys, I went out to meet these new prisoners of war on the road from Edinburgh. They came walking in twos and threes – a few of them lame. Their appearance was startling, for they were in military garb, in which they had been captured in Spain. Some were in light hussar dresses, braided, with marks of sabre wounds. Others were in deep blue uniform. Several wore large cocked-hats, but the greater number had undress caps. All had a gentlemanly air, notwithstanding their general dishevelled attire, their soiled boots, and their visible marks of fatigue.

'Before night they had all arrived; and through the activity of the Agent appointed by the Transport Board, they had been provided with lodgings suitable to their slender allowance. This large batch of prisoners on parole were all, of course, in the rank of naval or military. Some had been pretty high in the service, and seen a good deal of fighting. Several were doctors, or, as they called themselves, *officiers de santé*. Among the whole, I think, were about a dozen midshipmen [probably *aspirants* or *gardes-marines*, approximating our naval rank of sub-lieutenant].

'A strange thing was their varied nationality. Though spoken of as French, there was in the party a mixture of Italians, Swiss and Poles, but this was found out only after some intercourse. Whatever their origin, they were warm adherents of Napoleon, whose glory at this time was at its height. Lively in manner, their minds were full of the recent struggles in the Peninsular.'

William Chambers goes on to speak of a number of things which we have discussed elsewhere: of the officers' addiction to billiards and of their table at Peebles, obtained 'through the considerateness of an enterprising grocer', of their well-attended theatre, of their catering arrangements and of how the richer often helped the poorer: 'the fortunate circumstance of a number of them having brought money – foreign gold pieces, concealed about their person, by which stores were supplemented by remittances from France'.

The prisoners settled into Peebles so well that the enriched economy of the town seemed assured for the rest of the war. It was therefore of concern and puzzlement to many inhabitants when, early in 1811, all *gardes-marines* were deprived of their parole and marched off to the great other-ranks depot at Valleyfield. I cannot find evidence that they had in any way personally offended, but the action was probably related to the treatment of our own midshipmen at Verdun. If so, it had taken the Transport Board a long time to decide on retaliation. General Wirion, the tyrannical Commandant of the French fortress parole town, had an obsessional dislike of our 'Young Gentlemen'; did not understand or accept their rank, or even acknowledge that they were officers, and had marched all our midshipmen off to closed prisons. But that was nearly three years before, in August 1808!

Early in 1812, the real calamity hit the town's landladies and tradesmen. An Order arrived from the Board commanding that the whole of the parolees were to quit Peebles and were to march to other towns, chiefly to Sanquhar in Dumfriesshire. The reason for their transfer was the imminent arrival of a Militia Regiment which would need quartering in the town.

It would seem that William and Robert Chambers' mother was in some ways the wiser of their parents. Whilst she was kind enough to the parolees, she was worried by their mounting debts. William said that she never approved the 'extraordinary intimacy which had

been formed between the French officers and my father. Against him giving them credit, she constantly remonstrated in vain. It was a tempting but a perilous trade'. For a while they had paid well and on time, which encouraged William Senior to give extensive credit to 'these strangers – men who, by their position, were not amenable to civil law, and whose obligations, accordingly, were altogether debts of honour.' The consequence was what should have been anticipated. The officers left with fond farewells and fervent promises that, should they reach their homeland all their debts would be discharged.

'They all got home at the peace in 1814, but not one of them ever paid a farthing. A list of their names, debts, and official position in the army of Napoleon, remains as a curiosity in my possession. It is not unlikely that a number of these returned exiles found a grave on the field of Waterloo. Whatever became of them, there was soon a crisis in my father's affairs.'

Prisoner of war debts were always a worry to the creditors, particularly when parolees were transferred to other towns. Some creditors in the south, even petitioned the Transport Office in an effort to detain prisoner-debtors who were being sent up to Scotland. The Board was never sympathetic, considering such private contacts the concern of the civil courts – well knowing that civil actions would be a complete waste of time.

In most of the parole towns needy officers found local people who were willing to lend them money, or supply them with goods on credit; and most of these debts were honoured. Therefore, Mr Chambers' reckless trust – a contributory factor in the downfall of his company – was particularly unfortunate. To a certain extent he was the victim of circumstance, for the transfer of the Peebles prisoners had occurred two years before the end of the war in 1814.

It may well be that after the transferred officers had settled in Sanquhar, they may have added to their debts by borrowing from the traders in that town. Whilst not excusable, it is at least understandable that they may have better remembered, and appreciated, the most recent debts – which helped them on their joyful journey home – than the debts of yesteryear. Collectively, they left behind in Sanquhar owings amounting to about £160, which were redeemed by the French Commissioners in 1814. This makes one wonder why the unfortunate Mr Chambers could not have been similarly reimbursed. Perhaps this kindly Scottish gentleman placed too much faith on the word of his foreign officer friends and expected them, eventually, to pay up; perhaps he left it too late before making his claim – or perhaps he believed, as his son surmised, that they may have met their end at Waterloo, before they could discharge their debt of honour.

At times, the younger William Chambers could appear as gullible as his father. Writing in *Chambers' Journal*, he remembered a piece of prisoner of war work which his mother had treasured – a work-box, *'made from a bit of fuel-wood and the straw from the poor captive's bed'* [my italics] and he described 'ingenious toys and knick-knacks… fashioned out of larger meat-bones which the prisoners' teeth had previously well polished'. He also once opined that the prisoner forgers (who could be hanged for indulging in their specialised prisoner of war work) made paper money 'to relieve the tedium of their dismal incarceration!' He has left us valuable information regarding the paroled officer prisoner, but it would seem that he knew little of what went on inside the closed depots and hulks!

SANQUHAR

This ancient town on the banks of the Nith, derived its strangely spelled name from two Celtic words – Saen Caer – meaning 'old fort'. Pleasantly situated twenty-five miles north-east of Dumfries, verses found on a window-shutter of an inn and attributed to Robert Burns, paint an idyllic picture:

'As on the banks of wandering Nith
Ae smiling morn I strayed.
And traced its bonnie howes and haughs,
Where linties sang and lambkins played,
I sat me down upon a craig,
And drank my fill o' fancy's dream,
When, from the eddying pool below,
Up rose the genius of the stream.'

However, few of the officers who had been uprooted from Peebles and sent to Sanquhar could have considered their move a change for the better. It was surprising that the Transport Office should have chosen Sanquhar as a suitable parole centre in the first place. War had brought poverty to the weaver inhabitants, and accommodation and fresh meat were in short supply and insufficient for the needs of this addition to that small town's population Some of the officers were lucky enough to find quite comfortable quarters in the homes of local families, but the majority were billeted in outhouses, barns and sheds; a far cry from the lodging they had enjoyed in Peebles. At least one officer wrote to their old friend – and probable creditor – Chambers, acquainting him with their distress and complaining that beef and mutton were just about unobtainable. Nevertheless, their great adaptability allowed them to gradually settle in; busying themselves in sketching, fishing and rambling; indulging in the usual and profitable manufactures in wood and bone (when available). Swimming was a popular diversion, at a spot which was still known as the 'Sodger's Pool' at the beginning of this century.

By June, 1812, they had established their own Masonic Lodge, the name of which – *De La Paix Désirée* – indicates that it was most probably founded by officers who had begun their parole life at Wincanton in the south before being transferred first to Peebles, then to Sanquhar. The Lodge was in existence there for only one year, which suggests that the Brethren were once again on the move to another town. James Brown, in his *'History of Sanquhar'*, says:

'The pride which, in spite of the poverty and misery they had to endure, the people took in the successes of the British arms, bore testimony to their heroic spirit. It was the common topic of every fireside, and the children, catching the spirit of their sires, went about the fields with sticks slashing the heads off the thistles, taking the weeds for Frenchmen.'

For all that, once they had arrived in the town, the officer prisoners of war were treated as well by the people of Sanquhar as they were elsewhere in Scotland. James Brown went on:

'The large number of French prisoners who fell into the hands of the British were distributed over the country. The party sent to Sanquhar was composed of certain officers with their servants. They were stationed here for several years on their *parole d'honneur*, but were not allowed to pass beyond a circuit of three miles [?] from the town. They were of all nations – French, Italians, Poles &c. – for soldiers of fortune of almost all continental nations flocked to Napoleon's standard. One was named Dufaure, another Wysilaski, another

Delizia, and so on. They were handsome young fellows, [and] had all the manners of gentlemen…The banks of the Cranwick would appear to have been a favourite resort of theirs. On a rock in the Holme Walks one Luogo di Delizia has inscribed his name, with the date '1812' underneath. Lower down is cut the date '1814' in similar style.'

True to form, the Sanquhar officers 'played havoc' with the hearts of the local maidens. There were a few marriages, many more romances and one fatal duel. An old resident told the local historian, Tom Wilson, that on the day of the duel, he had followed a trail of blood to Carlton Court, later renamed Baron's Court. J. B. Arnaud, was fatally wounded in a duel which took place on the Washing Green, between rivals for the favours of a local girl. There was a cover-up story that he had died from some illness or other, and his friends set up a stone over Grave No.206 in Sanquhar Kirkyard:

In Memory of
J. B. ARNAUD
Aged 27 years
Lieutenant in the French Navy
Prisoner of War on Parole at Sanquhar
Erected by his Companions in Arms and
fellow prisoners as a testament of their esteem
and attachment. He expired in the arms of friendship
9th November, 1812.

The champion wooer of Sanquhar, and possibly the Border Towns, was the Polish officer, Wysilaski, mentioned in the above quote from James Brown's history of the town. Brown does not mention his romantic activities but does record a beneficial outcome some seventy-five years later.

Wysilaski, reputedly the grandson of the last King of Poland, left the mark of his two years in the town in the form of two illegitimate sons by two different local girls. One of these boys, Louis Wysilaski, lived all his life in Sanquhar. The other, John, was a lad of ambition and adventurous spirit. Whilst still little more than a boy, he set off to seek his fortune in Australia – and found it. John Wysilaski died a very wealthy man, and ensured that the name Wysilaski would be remembered for philanthropy as well as philandering. He bequeathed £4,180 to his mother's favourite place of worship, the South United Presbyterian Church at Sanquhar, the annual interest to be added to the Minister's stipend.

The last prisoner to leave the town departed early in 1815. This still left a few who decided to make Scotland their home. There was one, Auguste Gregoire, who could be said to have grown up in parole towns. He was captured in 1803, whilst serving as a cabin boy on the French privateer *Jeune Corneille*, and was lucky enough to be paroled as a servant to an officer with the first group to enter Peebles, and later Sanquhar. He married a Peebles girl and in 1814, after eleven years as a parolee, Scotticised his French name to Angus MacGregor, and remained in the town as a teacher of dancing and deportment.

James Brown also tells of another, of almost identical name – Angus McGregor – who can only be described as a Scottish-Frenchman. His father had taken refuge in France after playing his part in the '45 Rebellion, more than half a century before. Angus had learned the local craft of hand-loom weaving whilst paroled as a 'French' officer in Sanquhar, and stayed on to practise the trade.

DUMFRIES

Those of the Peebles officers who had not been transferred to Sanquhar, had been sent on the much longer march to Dumfries and were much more fortunate in their new *cautionnement*. There the accommodation was good and plentiful – though expensive.

At first the Dumfries householders were extortionate in their demands, some asking as much as twenty-five shillings a week – ten times the going rate in some of the other parole towns. However, a realistic compromise was reached and they began to settle in to a town at least as friendly, pleasant and hospitable as any they had experienced.

The prisoners numbered about one hundred and Francis Abell made the point that, as Dumfries is quite close to the sea, few of those paroled there had been sailors; the majority being surgeons, military officers and a few servants. Despite the fact that there was hardly any complaint by the parolees of their treatment after the matter of rents had been settled – and a number liked the town and its people sufficiently well to settle there after the war – the number of escapes and attempted escapes over the three years amounted to forty or more. With an average prisoner population of not much more than a hundred this figure is extraordinarily high, and the circumstances of some of the attempts quite remarkable. The notes of Macbeth Forbes and Abell record many interesting facts concerning the Dumfries parolees, including the information that the Dumfries Agent, Mr Francis Short, allowed some of them 'Fishing-licences' which extended the parole limit by a fair distance. Four officers abused his generosity by gradually getting all their possessions away to another parole town, Lochmaben, nearly ten miles away. They were captured when, their transfer of belongings completed, they tried to make their getaway. Nearly all who made their dishonourable bid for freedom were quickly recaptured and ended up in close imprisonment in the Valleyfield Depot. One would-be escaper deserves special mention, for it seems that he really did regret that he was breaking his word. In a gallant, but futile, effort to excuse himself, he wrote to the commanding officer of the Dumfries Garrison, in words which attempted to resurrect that earlier system of parole, so much admired by Emric de Vattel, where an officer, under certain conditions, could return home prior to exchange. He apologised for breaking his *parole d'honneur* and promised that he would get an English officer of equal rank returned from France; that he would not take up arms against Britain until that exchange had come about; and that he would repay all the kindnesses which he had received while on parole in Scotland. It is almost a pity that he had no second opportunity to prove that he could keep his given word. His escape attempt failed and he, too, spent the war in Valleyfield as a broke-parole.

Dumfries has its full share of prisoner of war stories; of officers released as a reward for their courageous fire-fighting in the town; of hospitality given and reciprocated; of foreign officers who became prominent and respected citizens in Dumfries when the war was over; of romances and marriages – all typical of events taking place in the everyday life of all parole towns everywhere. However, one unusual and moving little story was found in 'The Memorials of St Michael's, Dumfries' and lies behind the inscription on a stone in St Michael's Churchyard. It tells that Anna Grieve, 19, died in 1813, followed by the words:

'Ta main, bienfaisante et cherie,

D'un exil vient essuyer les pleurs,
Tu me vis loin de parens, de patrie,
Et le même tombeau lorsque tu m'as
Renfermé nos deux coeurs.'

One of the French prisoners had fallen in love with Anna, and she with him, and when she died he was overcome with grief and wrote the words which were to be engraved on her tombstone. Nearly fifty years later a man of about seventy visited St Michael's and asked in broken English to be directed to the grave. He read the epitaph with deep emotion, 'for it was engraved on the tablets of his memory'.

LAUDER

Lauder has the distinction of being the only Royal Burgh in Berwickshire. So far unspoiled, this out-of-the-way county town, with its ancient castle, its four-aisled church and old Tolbooth, probably presented an even more delightful picture at the beginning of the nineteenth century. Tucked away as it was, it must have been a tranquil and peaceful little town in those days, when news and information travelled so slowly and the war would have seemed a very long way off. That is, until it was brought nearer when fifty or sixty French and German officers were lodged in the then-thatched houses and cottages of Lauder.

The 10th December, 1811, was a day of great excitement and curiosity for the burgesses of the town. On that day the first eleven continental captives were marched in and placed under the care of John Romanes, the Town Clerk, who had been given the additional appointment of Government Agent for prisoners of war paroled to the burgh. They had been marched the long trek from Valleyfield Depot and an eye-witness remembered that they rested, fatigued, on the steps of the Town Hall, awaiting their orders and assistance from Mr Romanes. On the following day, another ten arrived. All twenty-one were midshipmen – *gardes marines* – of the French navy, captured when their vessels, the *Minerva*, *Nieman*, *Junon*, *Pluton*, and others had been taken off the French coast in 1808 and 1809. These were the same youngsters who had been removed from Peebles and elsewhere, in November 1811 and confined in Valleyfield. If their transfer to a closed prison had indeed been intended as a reminder to Napoleon that we were aware of Wirion's abominable treatment of our midshipmen in France, and that we too could play the same game; it was a feeble gesture. The French lads had to endure only a few weeks of discomfort and then were soon redistributed among the Scottish towns, whilst our middies suffered in France until the end of the war.

On the last day of 1811, a further eight officers, including three surgeons, who had been captured earlier in the year, were sent to Lauder from the distribution centre at Edinburgh Castle. In John Romanes, they found they had a kind and understanding overseer and in return they gave him a mostly trouble-free period as Agent. His most regular and important duty was to ascertain that none had escaped and each evening the bell in the Town Hall belfry, like the 'ting-tang' at Wincanton, was tolled at the appropriate hour to call them to muster – five o'clock in winter, eight in summer. I cannot resist including the unimportant scrap of information that a Lauder worthy, named James Thomson, earned an easy ninepence each day by ringing the muster bell dead on time.

Lodgings were cheap and comfortable and the typical Border-Scottish hospitality was as freely given as elsewhere. Here, as elsewhere, the friendliness sometimes went beyond the bounds of discretion and commonsense. In ignoring or condoning parole offences, they were doing more harm than good. The parolees were often welcomed to balls, banquets and parties in the neighbourhood and on one occasion some were invited to a dinner party at Brodie's Farm at Pilmuir. Pilmuir was well out of the parole limit and the prisoners went off without the knowledge of the Agent. Had they asked his permission or returned in time for muster they would have got away with it, or suffered no more than a warning or rebuke. However, they misjudged the weather and were caught in a severe snowstorm, so when James Thomson tolled his bell they were marked absent.

Such a blatant infringement could not be overlooked or covered up by even the most considerate of Agents, and Romanes had to include the escapade in his next report to the Transport Office. That the easygoing acceptance by the inhabitants – and to an extent by Romanes – of small parole infringements was not shared by the central authority in London, was shown when one of the Scottish guests at that dinner, the Parish Minister, the Revd Peter Cosens, wrote to the Transport Board on behalf of the offenders, and received a rap over the knuckles for his pains. The reverend gentleman was informed that they 'were surprised that one in his position should have given countenance to these prisoners breaking their parole, and should then seek to palliate or excuse the offence'.

Yet such upsets were rare in Lauder and John Romanes can have had few bad memories of his charges. Only one escape from Lauder is recorded – a privateer captain who had spent only six weeks in the town, during which time he spoke only French. He made his getaway in civilian clothes and spoke English without a trace of accent. This was a Captain Louis Pequendaire of the privateer *L'Espoir*; and his Second Captain, Jacques Angot, also got back to France at about the same time – but by legitimate means. He was given his freedom as a reward for gallant efforts in rescuing seventy-nine British seamen who were wrecked off the coast of St Valery.

In 1812 the prisoner community was increased by a further twenty officers who had been captured at Badajos in April of that year. They were shipped direct from Spain to Scotland and eventually arrived at Lauder. Twelve were German officers from the Hess-Darmstadt Infantry Regiment which was at that time siding with Napoleon.

One of them, Lieutenant-Adjutant George Maurer, is described in the Admiralty records as being a fresh complexioned youth of twenty years; five feet nine and three quarter inches in height; hazel eyes and a small sword scar on his left cheek. This young officer is to be remembered by a small watercolour of Lauder and its surroundings.

Writing at the beginning of this century, Macbeth Forbes mentioned Maurer's painting as once hanging in one of the rooms of Thirlestane Castle, the ancient residence of the Earls of Lauderdale. Although it was described it had never been reproduced, and I wondered whether it still existed.

Some weeks later, whilst searching through prisoner of war-related material in the Scottish Records Office, I had come across three glass photographic plates, one of which I felt sure was the negative of the Maurer watercolour. I wrote to the Earl of Lauderdale, care of the House of Lords, enclosing a print from the glass negative kindly supplied by the Record Office, with my enquiry. His Lordship replied, informing me that he had inherited

the title but not the Castle, and helpfully put me in touch with the present owner, Captain, the Honourable Gerald Maitland-Carew.[3]

A search was made of the many-roomed Castle – some of which had been unused and unentered for years – but without success, and it seemed that George Maurer's little painting had disappeared. However, nine months later it was rediscovered, in a drawer of an old bureau, and the Captain invited me to view it at Thirlestane Castle. He seemed as delighted as I was that my enquiry had brought it once again to light. The painting bears the inscription: 'Painted by G. Maurer, prisoner of war on parole at this place. August, year 1813.' and Maurer has included himself as the artist painting the scene. If other parolees dressed as he did on his painting trip – white knee-breeches, swallow-tailed uniform coat and tartan tam-o'-shanter – the inhabitants must have appeared dull by comparison.

Maurer and the other Germans found it just as easy to settle in as had their French brothers-in-arms and were as well-received by the townsfolk. They were included in the usual round of invitations to the homes of the local gentry and, in January 1813, George and seven of his compatriots were admitted as Freemasons into the St Luke's Lodge of Lauder. Their names are listed as Carl Seenkenberg, Louis Roeder, Frederick Damin, Louis Foigt, Emil Scriba, Christian Fresenius, Frederick Roeder and, of course, George Maurer. Some of the French prisoners were tranferred to Kelso, Jedburgh and Dumfries during 1813. and another three had been invalided back to France, so when the Germans at Lauder together with their countrymen in other parole towns, were released very early in 1814 the Agent was left with only about twenty prisoners to oversee.

At the beginning of 1814 Germany had changed sides and in February the twelve were freed to return to the Continent, this time to fight against Napoleon. From that day they were, of course, our allies, and the night before their departure for Harwich the town's magistrates gave them a great send-off at the Black Bull Inn – plus a Transport Board handout of five pounds a man to help them on their way. George Maurer survived those last few months of war and often returned to Lauder, to dine and talk over old times with his one-time Agent, John Romanes.

On the 3rd June, 1814, the last twenty-two Frenchmen left, and the town returned to memories and its old unruffled calm. The last entry in the Agent's account book read 'To: Paid for carrying: prisoners' baggage to Leith ... £1.0.3d.'

HAWICK

The first thirty-seven officers to arrive in Hawick were old hands as parolees. They had been sent up from Wincanton, where some had already spent a number of years on parole. However, the forty-one who followed two days later, on the 15th January, 1812, were inexperienced as prisoners of war. They had been taken in the Peninsular, shipped to Leith, then marched into Hawick.

By November, Hawick's quota of officers had risen to 120, the newcomers transferred mainly from Launceston in Cornwall, and two French surgeons from the depot at Greenlaw. These last two men had probably not been close confined at Greenlaw, but served as part of the depot's medical team. Their transfer to Hawick was no doubt to appoint them doctors to the officers paroled there.

The number was made up almost equally of military and naval men, the latter being mainly French, whilst the army was represented by a mixture of French and South German officers. They ranged in rank from captains, ships' masters and mates, to *enseignes* and *aspirants* – ensigns and naval cadets – and a few officers' servants. As usual, their financial standing covered as wide a range as their ranking. Forbes saw an old receipt, dated the 6th July, 1813, which showed that a Captain Grupe received a monthly allowance of £13.4s.6d, from Paris, a Mr Thomas Turnbull of Hawick disbursing the remittance on behalf of M. Faber, the Paris banker. Whatever the source of their income – remittances from home, earnings from their private enterprises as teachers or souvenir-makers – the spending power of the parolees was as significant in Hawick as in any other parole town. It has been estimated that each prisoner spent on average one pound a week in the town and that, during its 122 weeks as a *cautionnement*, with a fluctuating prisoner population which averaged about 140, this would have amounted to the grand total of £17,000. This sum was probably greater than the income from local manufactures during that period.

It is known that the artistic among them found a ready market for their efforts and, even if the prisoners kept within their one mile limit in any direction from Tower Knowe, there was an abundance of beautiful landscapes to inspire the gifted wielder of the brush. These paintings and sketches were purchased and preserved as much as mementoes of the artists themselves and a unique period in the history of the town, as for their intrinsic artistic quality or topographical interest. As a profitable hobby, painting and drawing was a pleasant way of avoiding boredom in their restricted freedom, and some of the more professional taught painting in watercolours to the young ladies of the neighbourhood. I have tracked down a few examples of the graphic work of the Hawick parolees, but there are probably many more tucked away, unrecognised, and waiting to be discovered in the old houses of the district.

Two prisoner of war landscapes are preserved in the museum at Wilton Lodge, the old mansion house at Hawick. One, a watercolour by an unknown officer, is a well-executed view of the town as it was in 1813, and the uplands to the north of it. The other is a very fine monochrome of Hawick as seen from Mary's Manse, and in this case the artist is known. He was Louis Joseph Fereday Prefort, an ensign aboard a French man-of-war until his capture off Catalonia in October 1810. After a year and a half as a prisoner of war in Spain, he must have appreciated the comparative comfort of his parole to Hawick in April 1812.

Another midshipman, who arrived in Hawick on the same day as Prefort, also left a pictorial memento of his stay. He was Pierre Louis Thirat, a native of Oranienbaum, who had also been captured at Catalonia on the *Atalane*, a month before Prefort's vessel was taken. His little monochrome shows the Slitrig Water crossed over by a small bridge and, between the churchyard and the river, there is a building of particular interest, as it was the place rented by the French officers for use as their club-house. It was there they created their little bit of France, introduced their essential billiards table, the first seen in the town; and where they met to discuss the progress of the war – their spirits no doubt rising or falling according to the newspaper reports of victories or defeats abroad. There, too, they arranged musical and theatrical evenings, the proceeds from the small admission charges pooled towards more ambitious future efforts.

I have tried, unsuccessfully, to discover the present whereabouts of Thirat's little watercolour and reproduce it here from one of the three glass plates, which I found in the Records Office in Edinburgh. Pierre Thirat got home a few months ahead of most of

his fellows. He was exchanged for four British seamen and released in December 1813.

The parolees soon found billets in the town, some as individuals boarded with local families, whilst others, for reasons of economy, found communal accommodation. A number of them lodged in the rooms and attics of a three-storeyed house at No.44 the High Street. One of its occupants left a sketch – reproduced here – of his now long-since-demolished war-time home.

Parole life at Hawick was pleasant enough to inspire some officers to make application to the Transport Board, requesting that captive friends and relatives be allowed to join them there. In May, 1812, a Captain Baumbauch requested that a M. Preen, of the 6th Regiment of the Confederation of the Rhune, might be transferred to Hawick, 'as he is only 18 and left under my care by his parents'. In August of the same year, Lieutenant Lafont, of the corvette *Tapageuse*, made a similar request, pleading that his cousin, the Lieutenant of a privateer, was ill and in need of assistance. The records show that neither request was granted, but not all such applications were automatically turned down. An elderly captain, Louis Paillard, had two sons who were captives at Edinburgh Castle. Both were *aspirants*, or naval cadets, one from the French vessel *L'Alexandre*, the other from the *Scipion*. The old man asked that they should be allowed to join him at Hawick, as he was himself aged and infirm and his sons very young. The Board was not heartless but at the same time economical. They decided in his favour and agreed to the transfer, but added that 'they may go [to Hawick] at their own expense'. The Captain himself was later invalided home to France.

Not all of the officers remained in Hawick until the end of the war. Some were exchanged, some, like Captain Paillard, were repatriated for medical reasons and one, at least, was given his freedom as a reward for his services to this nation. It appears that, in some unguessable way, a *garde-marine*, Joseph Lapeyrere, was instrumental in saving the British frigate H.M.S. *Solbey*. Her commander, Captain Dundas, brought this mysterious fact – which was said to have occurred in 1802 – to the attention of the Transport Office, who ordered his release in February, 1813.

Even when considered in the context of the friendliness of the Border Towns in general, Hawick stands out as a particularly pleasant place of parole; which may explain why there is no record of escapes from the town. Macbeth Forbes said that Hawick had a reputation of being an I'm-as-good-as-you-are sort of place, but with no personal claims to superiority, and that this was in accord with the doctrine of 'Liberty, Equality and Fraternity'. Robert Wilson, who published his *History of Hawick* in 1825, and gained his information at first hand, tells us that the officers were appreciative and conscious of the qualities of their hosts. He says, 'there is a familiarity of manners and an equality of intercourse among the inhabitants of this Border burgh, antipodal to such distinctions in society,' and that 'the levelness of rank and the promiscuous association of the people forcibly struck these paroled foreigners'. Wilson goes on to report a conversation which he overheard, between a local tradesman and a French infantry captain. In his book he has attempted to reproduce the Frenchman's enunciation by writing 'de' for 'the', and 'dat' for 'that' and so on, and I have taken the liberty of his effort for the sake of easier reading:

"'The weather," said the Scotsman, "must be very uncomfortable to you who have been accustomed to a more genial climate".

"It is the Devil's weather," said the Frenchman, "but you have the heaven country for all that; you have the cold, the snow, the frozen water and the sober dress; but you have the grand constitution, and the manners and the equality that we did fight for so long. I see in your street the priest and the shoemaker, the banker and the baker, the merchant and the hosier, all meet together, be companions and be happy. This is the equality we fight for and never got, not the damned thing the English newspapers say we want. Ah, Scotland be the fine country and the people be wise good men."

'The tradesman asked him what he thought of England: "England is the Devil," exclaimed the fiery Gaul, "the English tell me at Wincanton that Scots be naked savages. It was a lie – the English be the savages and the Scots be the civilized people. The high Englishman be rich and good; the low Englishman be the brute. In Scotland [The Captain could have seen no more of Scotland than a mile or two from the centre of Hawick!] the people be all the same. The commonman be wise and good, like the Magistrate and the Commissaire. O, Scotland be a fine country!"'

There simply has to have been a French equivalent to the Blarney Stone in those days – and the Captain must have kissed it often.

BIGGAR

So far I have been unsuccessful in locating much information regarding prisoners of war in Biggar; but the Biggar Museum Trust has the unpublished typescript of a family history which I hope to inspect on my next journey north. The Trust also possesses a few relics of the parolees' stay, including a cocked hat left by one of the officers to the Tyler of the local Masonic Lodge and it is still worn occasionally. This latter artefact is of particular interest as it ties in with a reference to Freemasonry in 'Biggar and the House of Fleming'. The works of Francis Abell and the masonic researches of J. T. Thorpe do not mention a prisoner of war Lodge in the town, but the reference suggests that one may well have existed:

'A number of French prisoners stationed at Biggar on their parole of honour, towards the close of the war with France, were Freemasons. In the beginning of 1813, they applied to the members of the Biggar Lodge [The Lodge of Free Operatives] for the use of their hall, the master's chair, the warden's tools, etc., in order that they might constitute a lodge of their own. This application was acceded to, and Brothers Elias Berger and Francis Renaudy became security for any damage that might be done. The French masons were here wont to practise their rites, which were somewhat different from those of Scottish brethren. One of their number, resident in Westraw, having died, was interred with masonic honours, and a funeral lodge was held out of respect to his memory. The Biggar Lodge had the honour of enrolling in its ranks one of these prisoners, a distinguished Polish nobleman and freemason, married François Mayskie, and received from him a fee of one guinea.'

LOCHMABEN

A tiny town in the Dumfries and Galloway area, Lochmaben was made a royal burgh in 1298. Situated near several small lochs in the Annandale Valley, it afforded excellent fishing for both inhabitant and paroled alike, and beautiful, though restricted, walks for the latter. Like many other Scottish parole towns it had its ancient history of battles with the English, and tradition has it that King Robert the Bruce was born in Lochmaben Castle. There were seldom more than twenty officers paroled to the town, although their number was increased for a day or two when four officers made it a stop-over point in their attempted escape from Dumfries. eight miles away.

LOCKERBIE

An even smaller town to the east of Lochmaben in the Gallway/Dumfries district, Lockerbie was never host to more than a couple of dozen prisoners of war, and there is scant record of even those few. (Maybe I shall unearth some detail when I visit nearby Biggar.)

CUPAR

The story of Cupar as a *cautionnement* is very similar to that of its neighbouring parole towns. It was a royal burgh and market town in north-east Fife, and the centre for the administration of justice for Fifeshire. It still retains something of its old importance today.

By now we have become used to reading of the warmth of welcome which greeted captive enemy officers introduced into these northern towns; a warmth which could not have been exceeded had it been our own servicemen returning from the Peninsular or war at sea. The reception was also no less enthusiastic and friendly in the case of Cupar, as Keddie tells us in 'The Story of a Middle-Class Scottish Family':

'The residents treated the jetsam and flotsam of war with more than forbearance, with genuine liberality and kindness, receiving them into their houses on cordial terms. Soon there was not a festivity in the town at which the French prisoners were not permitted – nay heartily pressed to attend. How the complacent guests viewed those rejoicings in which the natives, as they frequently did, commemorated British victories over the enemy is not on record. However, there was no thought of war and its fierce passions among the youth of the company in the simple dinners, suppers and carpet dances in private houses. There were congratulations on the abundance of pleasant partners, and the assurance that no girl need sit out a dance or lack an escort if her home was within a certain limited distance beyond which the prisoners were not at liberty to stray.'[4]

As can be expected, romances and affairs were many, resulting in at least three marriages, one between a French colonel and the daughter of a local vicar. However, as the too-welcoming inhabitants of other parole towns had discovered, hospitality and fraternizing could go too far. The Transport Office got to hear of the possibly dangerous degree of intimacy between captor and captive; and when the prisoners completed the building of their own theatre to which the local people were to be welcomed, only one performance was enjoyed before all the officers were suddenly transferred to other towns.[5]

LANARK

Much of the following information regarding prisoners is gleaned from the papers of Hugh Davidson FSA Scot.[6] In the late 1850s, Davidson formed a close friendship with one of the parolees, Captain Augustus Francis Marie Brard, who settled in Scotland after the wars. Fifteen years of conversation, correspondence and reminiscences resulted in the papers, which recorded many interesting events during the two or three years when Lanark had been a parole town.

The Lanark allocation was typical of the mixed bag of nationalities which were added to the populations of the small Scottish parole towns; French, of course, German, Italian, Swiss, Spanish and men of other nations who fought under the banner of France. The parolees in the town never numbered more than twenty-eight or thirty. A list exists which names twenty-three of them:

1. PETER AUGUSTUS AYMER. French Captain and Adjutant Major Aymer died on 23rd September 1813, and was buried in

Lanark Churchyard, where a tombstone marked his grave.

2. PETER FORTINI CLEMENT BERARGI.
3. SAINT CYR BERTRAND.
4. AUGUSTUS FRANCIS BRARD.
5. MONSIEUR BUSNEL. Captain French Army.
7. JOHN BONANI.
8. DOMINIQUE CRAMPS. From Venice.
9. MONSIEUR D'BLUE.
10. CHARLES ETIEN. A German Lieutenant.
    17th Dragoons.
11. CHARLES FOUCALD. Lieutenant.
    26th Regiment of Foot.
12. BENOIT PAUL GRANDJEAN. Lieutenant de Granades.
    65th Regiment of the Line.
13. ANTOINE GORGIES. Sub-Lieutenant.
    70th Regiment of the Line.
14. M LEVASSEUR.
15. VICTOR MARISTIN. La Concord No.88 in the
    City of Cuba.
16. PIERRE MARTYS. Captain. 4th Swiss Regiment.
17. MONSIEUR MEUDELL.
18. JOSEPH OLIVER.
19. WILLIAM LOUIS QUESTEL.
20. JEAN PURE THEVEANON.
21. JEAN BAPTISTE TOURY. Midshipman. French Navy.
22. LOUIS ZILL DE SILLS.
23. JACOB WEIN.

We can now add a few more names to that list: The Library of the Grand Lodge of Scotland holds a Masonic Certificate issued by the Lanark prisoner of war Lodge, *Des Amis Réunis dans l'Adversité* – 'Friends United in Adversity' – to a German parolee, MAURICE SCHAUENBURG, Adjutant of the 11th Regiment of Dragoons, in 1812, and bearing the signatures of other Mason internees. Yet another of the twenty-eight, DENIS ELIE LEFROTTER DE LEZEVERNE, features in a small book, *'Les Voyageurs Français en Ecosse, 1773–1818'* by M. I. Bain. It is said that Lezeverne spent the first part of his captivity on the hulks before being sent to Lanark, where he settled in to appreciate Scotland and the Scots.

We know something of the lives of a number of these educated and sophisticated officers who integrated so well into the comparatively unworldly society of this Clydeside town. Lefrotter de Lezeverne, who Bain referred to as 'the first French romanticist in Scotland', spent his enforced stay studying the works of Robert Burns and Ossian, and in writing his own prose and poetry. Thus inspired, much of his work comprised descriptions of his surroundings, so idealised as to be surprising as the work of a prisoner. The small volume of poems which he published in France in 1818, tells of his Lanark years in his poem, 'Plaisirs d'un Prisonnier en Ecosse'.

Most of them would have been recipients of local hospitality and three, at least, received more than normal hospitality. With the assistance of two inhabitants – obtained either through friendship or bribery – Charles Etien, Charles Foucald and Pierre Martys made an unsuccessful attempt to escape a year or so after arrival. These 'broke-paroles' would have been severely punished, but their Scottish accomplices suffered a worse fate:

'On 22nd August 1813, Janet Hislop and James Hislop were brought before the High Court of Justiciary, accused of aiding them to make their escape, and pleading guilty to the charge, were sentenced to seven years transportation beyond seas.'

A variation on the 'one mile on the turnpike' limitation to a parolee's wandering is mentioned more than once in Davidson's notes, and referred to as a 'five mile circuit'. This occurs in a story of the only daily newspaper which reached that part of the country at that time. The tenant of Draffan Farm in the Parish of Lesmahagow had a relative who worked in the office of the *London Courier*, who regularly sent him a copy of that paper by the London to Glasgow mail coach.

Draffan Farm was about eight miles from Lanark, but the news-hungry prisoners learned of this fountain of information, so temptingly near, though yet so far beyond their parole point. On most days a number risked their privileged freedom by going to Draffan Farm. Obviously, they must have been confident that none of the countryfolk would betray them; although reward notices would have been posted up in Lanark, as in every other parole town; but...

'One spring evening [in 1814] an inmate of the farm-house went down to Burnfoot on his customary errand to get the newspaper from the guard of the passing mail coach... The coach approached with a white flag on top, and the guard as he threw from him the newspaper shouted high above the rattle of the wheels, "Boney's beat."'

Thus the parole-breaking officers were the first to hear news of the surrender of Paris, the downfall of their great hero and the return of the Bourbons.

Not all French officers could foresee a future under the new regime and opted for exile. A number of them found ready employment as teachers of their native tongue, some of them to the offspring of distinguished families. M. Lavasseur became French master to the children of the great social reformer, Robert Owen, whose cotton mills were in Lanark; and Captain Augustus Brard, who settled in Lanark after the war, could count among his one-time pupils, Sir Henry Campbell-Bannerman, Prime Minister of Great Britain.

Hugh Davidson left a potted biography of his old friend, Brard, which tells something of his adventures and long post-war life in Scotland. Augustus Francis Brard was born in Normandy in the year 1789. As a young lad he decided on a military career and was sent to the Military College of St Cyr, which he left at the age of eighteen, in 1807, to join Napoleon at Fontainbleau, as a lieutenant in the French Army. After seeing action in Spain under Murat, which ended with defeat, his legion was sent to the Balearic Isles, where his military service was interrupted by captivity until 1814. Lieutenant Brard and a number of his fellow officers were taken prisoner and shipped to Scotland, where those who chose to give their *parole d'honneur* were first sent to Cupar-Fife. From what we know of parole life in Cupar, Brard and his compatriots could have found little to complain of in the year they spent there:

'Certainly the foreign officers were made curiously welcome in the country town [Cupar], which their presence seemed to enliven rather than offend. The strangers' courageous endurance, their perennial cheerfulness, their ingenious devices to occupy their time and improve the situation, aroused much friendly interest and amusement. The position must have been rendered more bearable to the sufferer, and perhaps more respectable in the eyes of the spectators, from the fact, for which I am not able to account, that, undoubtedly, the prisoners had among themselves, individually and collectively, considerable funds.'

At the end of that year, the officers were transferred to Lanark,

369

where, with short interruptions, Brard was to spend the rest of his life. With the peace of 1814, he returned to France and rejoined his old regiment. Like many of his fellow officers, he felt sure that Napoleon would not stay long a prisoner on Elba, but until then he was reluctant to serve under the Bourbon flag. He obtained leave to return to Scotland to marry his Scottish sweetheart, Jean Currie, daughter of James Currie, Procurator to the Sheriff Court at Lanark. Ten days after they married, the news reached England that Napoleon was once again on the warpath – and that same day, Brard was packed and on his way to Leith, thence by boat to Gravesend and Dover, where he paid a fisherman to ferry him to France.

Reaching Paris, once again with his regiment and now a captain, he had the unforgettable experience of witnessing his own and all the other regiments receive new eagles from the hands of Napoleon himself in the *Champ de Mars*, where a quarter of a million onlookers cheered the ceremony. At Waterloo Captain Brard was in command of a force of 120 men, but in the battle he was wounded by a Prussian shell and became a prisoner of war for a second time. He was taken to the rear of the English lines where it was discovered that he spoke English, which earned him an appointment as interpreter to two British generals. He was brought to England on a man-of-war and again granted parole, this time to Ashburton in Devon. His wife, Jean, joined him at Ashburton and at the conclusion of the war, they visited France, but were ordered out of the country as Brard was considered too dedicated a Bonapartist. Back in Scotland, he was involved in a business venture in Glasgow which failed, then established himself with more success, as a master of the French language, instructing members of some of the leading families in the city. About 1850, Brard moved once more to Lanark, with his now enlarged family[7], where he comfortably spent the rest of his long life.

Davidson ended his reminiscences of Augustus Brard by remembering him as:

> ' …a quiet and unobtrusive citizen and much esteemed by all who had the privilege of his acquaintance. Though his ashes rest in Lanark churchyard far from his friends and the place of his birth, they rest among a people who can appreciate and admire his patriotism, even knowing that he fought valiantly against them on the plains of Waterloo'.

A curious footnote to a page in 'The Lanark Manse Family'[8], mentions that it was said that Brard had his tombstone constructed during his lifetime and inscribed – except of course, for the date and his age. Eventually it read:

AUGUSTUS FRANCIS BRARD,
a Native of Paris,
who died 26th August 1873, aged 84

JEDBURGH

Jedburgh was the last, and most rewarding, stop on my tour of the old Scottish Border parole centres. This very ancient town, with its memories of Mary Queen of Scots and Bonnie Prince Charlie, its eleventh century Abbey and twelfth century, three-arched, Cannongate Brig, had already seen its share of war-like strangers long before the arrival of the French prisoners of war in 1811.

Situated as it is, only ten miles from the Border, it was, in days gone by, the scene of frequent invasions from the south – but this new 'invasion' was welcomed rather than resisted by most of the inhabitants of Jedburgh. At the end of March, one hundred and seven officers, transferred from southern towns, were marched in from Leith. Only twenty-five were military men, soldiers who had been captured at Baylen, the remainder were mostly naval officers. A year and a half later the number was made up to one hundred and thirty by the arrival of another twenty-three – Jedburgh's share of the officers taken at Badajos – and this number was not exceeded during its time as a parole town. Their Agent, Mr George Bell, housed most of them amongst the townsfolk and billeted the rest in quarters under the Clock Tower. They were well enough received by the people of Jedburgh, although perhaps not with that same almost unnatural welcome which officers paroled to such towns as Kelso and Lauder seem to have enjoyed. A Jedburgh pamphlet, the 'False Alarm', says that 'the officers were very polite, and not infrequently put us roughspun Scotsmen to the blush with their polished manners.' They came in the course of time to be liked but it seemed that some of the older members of the community could never be brought to fraternise with them. One old man actually pointed his gun at them and threatened to fire because they had exceeded their walking limit. This attitude was, as we have seen, unusual in a Scottish town (though not unique; Doisy de Villargennes told us that, in Selkirk, the town's gentry had not been over-friendly) and not shared by the majority of the townspeople. However, perhaps this less than complete acceptance may account for the higher than usual incidence of parole-breaking and escape attempts – or it could be that the Agent was not as vigilant as he might have been. An historical note referring to prisoners at Hawick says that they occasionally met up with a party coming from Jedburgh at Denholm Village, five miles from each of the parole towns.

Those who settled in to make the best of their situation, and respected their *parole d'honneur*, found Jedburgh a pleasant enough place to spend their captive years. There were ways in plenty to occupy their minds and hands. Mrs Grant, in her *Memoirs of a Highland Lady*, says: 'the ingenuity of the French Prisoners of all ranks was amazing, only to be equalled by their industry' and those unskilled in the higher arts made things for sale from anything that came to hand and that their productions were 'eagerly bought up by all who met with them'. Whilst in the town I sampled 'Jedburgh Snails', a humbug-like confection said to have been originally made and sold by enterprising French sweetmaker parolees – and still on sale in Jedburgh.

The work of the artists: silhouettes, miniatures, sketches and watercolours, were just as eagerly sought after, and they were never at a loss for subject matter. The countryside surrounding Jedburgh – which Robert Burns described as 'Eden scenes on crystal Jed' – was, and is, truly beautiful. I was lucky enough to view *in situ*, a number of these artistic efforts, and other rare prisoner of war works in a private house where they had been presented as tokens of appreciation by officers who had been welcomed there during those last three years before Napoleon's downfall. The more serious-minded or intellectual among the officers must have been particularly downhearted when they heard that they were being paroled to towns north of the Border. The voluble French captain who we left at the end of the notes on Hawick, has told us that, before leaving England, they had been warned that they would find themselves among a primitive and uncouth people; and they could have had little hope of intellectual stimulus from their Scottish hosts.

Those whose interest was in the fields of science and mathematics must then have been truly amazed when they found that, in this

VUE DE L'ABBAYE DE JEDBURGH
Dédiée à Mr. James Veitch à Inch-Bonny
le 1er. Aout 1812. Hommage amicale de Bazin.

Details of Ensign Bazin's Watercolour which hangs at Inchbonny, Jedburgh.

'Vue de l' Abbaye de Jedburgh'
d'après Nature. pt. Jn Mrie Bazin de St Malo.
Dediée à Mr James Veitch à Inch-Bonny.
le 1er Aout 1812. Hommage amicale de J.M.Bazin.

This view of Jedburgh was painted from the house at the corner of Abbey Place, where Bazin shared a room with Charles Jehenne. The focal point of the painting is the Abbey itself, but of the greatest interest there are the tiny figures which were said to have been recognisable portraits of prisoners and local characters. The bottom right-hand corner depicts a hearse and a funeral party which has come in from the country. The mourners with their plaids and 'mauds' (shawls or blankets) wound round them, are preceded by the bellman ringing the Dead Bell (now in the Jedburgh Museum), while a crowd of local townswomen are looking on. On the High Rampart: The lady in the white costume on the extreme left is Miss Jenny Somerville, who married General Sir Henry Elliot. Next are two Prisoners of War and a Soldier. The figure moving out from the railings is 'Jumping Joseph', the soubriquet of the Revd Joseph Thomson, Minister of Morebattle. The next five figures are Parolees with a newspaper between them. The two officers on the extreme right of the Rampart, are Lieut. M. Scott, in his 'long grey coat', and Ensign Jean Marie Bazin himself. Foreground:The two-horse coach is the Stewartfield Carriage (Stewartfield was the seat of Lord Stratheden and Campbell) and this is followed by a groom on horseback. The man walking with the wheeled barrel is a local worthy known as 'Will the Maltman'. The man carrying a handful of letters next to 'Will the Maltman' is another local character, 'Johnnie Wark'. To the right again is Mr Shortbreed, the Sheriff-Substitute, who was a friend of Sir Walter Scott, and Agent for the British Linen Company Bank. He is in conversation with James Veitch himself, to whom this painting is dedicated. They are on that part known as the 'Lower Rampart'. The figure to the left of the two horsemen following the flock of sheep is a French officer, wearing a cocked hat and the usual white breeches.

particular Border town, there were men – and women – of great accomplishments: Mary Somerville, the famous mathematician; Robert Easton, astronomer and botanist; George Forrest, gunsmith and inventor; Gibson, the horologist, telescope and barometer maker; Alexander Scott, who experimented with balloons and bombs; George Noble, poet, and the young, and later famous, David Brewster. All these and many others were frequent visitors to Inchbonny House, less than a mile outside the town and well within the parole limit. After their short walk out of town, which for some invited parolees was a daily trip, they headed for the workshop of the most remarkable man of them all – James Veitch of Inchbonny.

James Veitch, a ploughwright by trade, was a man of great natural genius. Philosopher, mathematician, astronomer; well-versed in optics and a number of other sciences, he was entirely self-taught; having received only a very ordinary education. He was also a craftsman of great skill. When Jedburgh became a parole town in 1811, James Veitch would have been about forty years of age, and already thought of as one of the finest of scientific instrument makers. It was with a telescope of his own construction that he was the first in this country to observe the comet which appeared in the northern hemisphere in the August of Jedburgh's first parole town year. The comet, which still shone on in 1812, was thought by the more superstitious of the town's unwilling visitors to be a forewarning of disaster for Napoleon, and of his retreat from Moscow:

> 'Now shines it like a comet of revenge,
> A prophet to the fall of all our foes,'[9]

Sir Walter Scott was a friend and sincere admirer of this very talented man and described him as 'one of the most extraordinary persons I ever knew'. In a letter to a friend, Sir Walter recommended: 'If you cross the Border, you must see him as one of our curiosities; and the quiet, simple, unpretending manners of such a man who has, by dint of private study, made himself intimate with the abstruse sciences of astronomy and mathematics, are as edifying as the observation of his genius is interesting.'

People did come from far and wide to seek advice and instruction. His most successful student was David (later Sir David) Brewster, the son of a Jedburgh schoolmaster. Under the direction of James Veitch young David was making telescopes at the age of ten, and was thus set on the road to fame and a knighthood. However, James Veitch himself never sought fame. He was one of those rarest of happy men, content with his lot and with no wish for the limelight; but who delighted in intelligent conversation and the company of kindred spirits. His scientific interests did not interrupt his making of ploughs, which were recognised as the finest in the kingdom, nor prevent him from serving with the local militia volunteers, among whom he was respected as a fine marksman. Furthermore, as though he was not already fully occupied, he was also Inspector for Weights and Measures for the County of Roxburgh!

The Veitch workshop was the haunt of all manner of interested folk, from the local college student to such famous men as the geologist, Professor Sedgwick, Lord Jeffrey and Sir Humphrey Davy, all of whom, delighted not only in his craftsmanship but also in his conversation, which was not limited to scientific matters but covered a great range of subjects, from philosophy to theology. Into this brilliant circle the paroled officers were welcomed, and a

number took full advantage of that welcome.

A regular, almost daily, visitor to Inchbonny was Charles Jehenne, who had been captured at the Battle of Trafalgar. On that great day he was at the masthead of his vessel, the *Didon*, when he saw Nelson's fleet bearing down upon them. 'They saw us before we saw them', he would ironically remark when telling of the days before his capture. Ensign Jehenne was an amateur astronomer and could not have been more fortunate in his chance selection for parole to Jedburgh. He soon became a great favourite of Veitch, who gave him the use of his tools, and no doubt the benefit of his guidance, to enable him to build a telescope for his own use. He spent many hours scanning the heavens through the splendid equipment at Inchbonny – sometimes more hours than he was entitled to by the strict conditions of his parole, as he was often still concentrating on the stars when the muster bell was tolled at Jedburgh.

These minor fractures of his parole engagement were either never discovered or ignored; or perhaps his friends covered for him. On those occasions James Veitch would lend him an enveloping plaid cloak and Jehenne managed to get back to his lodging undetected. Sir David Brewster's daughter recalled another prisoner-scientist who regularly visited the workshop, an old naval officer, Lieutenant M. Scott, who dressed in his 'long grey coat, was to be seen with every gleam of sunshine at the meridian line, resolved to determine the problem of finding the longitude'. However, all was not serious work and study at Inchbonny. It is said that some of the officers constructed an 'electrical gadget' which was capable of producing a mild electric shock, which they wired up to a plate on one of the windowsills, and had great fun by luring the local girls up to the windows.

The Inchbonny welcome was not restricted to scientifically-minded parolees. One of the most frequent and appreciative of the French visitors was a talented young artist, Ensign Jean Marie Bazin, who had made many friends in Jedburgh – and patrons for his works. This was the fifth time I had encountered Ensign Bazin in the course of my research: First, in Sweetman's little pamphlet, *The French in Wincanton*; and I was even familiar with his signature, as it appears on the Louis Duchemin Masonic Certificate which had been added to my personal collection a few years earlier – and again, on the print taken from the third of the glass negatives which I had found in the Scottish Record Office. Therefore, to read of his visits to Inchbonny was like hearing news of an old friend.

Ensign Jean Marie Bazin, of St Malo, was captured on the French corvette *La Torche,* on the 16th August, 1805, and spent the next six years on parole at Wincanton, where he was a member of the French Masonic Lodge, *'De la Paix Desirée'.* In Jedburgh he was one of a small group of artists who accepted commissions, and was almost certainly the painter mentioned in *Memoirs of a Highland Lady*. Mrs Grant wrote: 'Lord Buchanan, whom we met there [Jedburgh], took us to see a painting in progress by one of them; some battlefield, all the figures portraits from memory. The Picture was already sold and part paid for, and another ordered which we were very glad of, the handsome young painter having interested us much.' The painting of very small figures was certainly a Bazin specialty. As a token of his appreciation of the hospitality which he had enjoyed at the Veitch's home, he had painted just such a picture, with tiny portraits of Jedburgh acquaintances and characters, and dedicated it to his friend James Veitch.

He had entitled his watercolour, *'Vue de l'Abbaye de Jedburgh'* and inscribed it:

'd'après Nature. pt. Jn Mrie Bazin de St Malo.
Dediée à Mr James Veitch à Inch-Bonny.
le 1er Aout 1812.
Hommage amicale de J.M.Bazin.'

This inscription was executed with the same meticulous care as the rest of the painting and is a fine example of penmanship. Dividing the dedication is a drawing of Veitch's famous improved plough. All these details I knew from my print from the glass plate and a black and a white reproduction in a 1912 issue of *'Hawick Archaeological Society Transactions'*, so, wondering if the painting might still be preserved in a library or museum, I wrote to the town Clerk of Jedburgh to ask if he knew of its whereabouts. He regretted that he did not, but asked whether it might not still be in Inchbonny House.

Somehow, probably as the result of past disappointments, I had taken it for granted that Inchbonny was no more, that it would have been converted or torn down after so many years. As soon as I could make the journey, I was back in Jedburgh, asking the way to Inchbonny. My knock on the door of the lovely old stone house, beautifully situated about half a mile up the Jedwater, on the Jedburgh to Newcastle Road, was answered by a friendly lady, who was not at all surprised by my enquiry: 'I am researching details of a Mr Veitch, Inspector of Weights and Measures for the county'. 'Really,' she replied, 'you must mean my husband.' Incredibly, more than one and half centuries after James Veitch had held that post, I was invited in to meet Mr William Veitch, Chief Inspector for Weights and Measures for Selkirkshire! My visit led me to believe that hospitality might well run in families, and I was left with a vivid impression of the earlier Veitch, as friendly as his descendants, receiving his foreign visitors in those very rooms, so many years ago.

Inchbonny House, itself, which has been in the family since 1732, stands on a bank about a hundred yards from where the Howden Burn joins the River Jed. The old workshop, the meeting place of talents both native and foreign, was demolished at the end of the last century, but many examples of Veitch's excellent workmanship are still preserved in the house. Dismissing my apologies for intrusion, Mr and Mrs Veitch could not have been more interested and cooperative. Together we examined some fifty telescopes, hoping to find the one made by Charles Jeheene; although it and other prisoner-made examples may well have been there, without a great deal of additional study, positive attribution would have been difficult. Neither could we locate the 'electrical gadget' which amused or annoyed the border-town lasses, but maybe these and other relics will turn up later. Meanwhile there was plenty to make up for their absence. For me, the *pièce de résistance* was Jean Marie Bazin's *'Vue de l'Abbaye'*, which still takes pride of place on the wall where it was originally hung in 1812; but there were also sketches, miniatures, silhouettes and other interesting mementoes to handle and discuss.

I have to thank the present-day Mr and Mrs Veitch for their kind help with my research by supplying me with so much information concerning their hospitable forebear; for the pamphlets which they allowed me to take away to study, and their permission to reproduce some of their treasures here.

Paroled officers were well received by a number of other local families, to dinners, card-clubs and parties, but it cannot be expected that more than a small percentage of individuals among the hundred and more captives would have enjoyed anything like regular invitations. Some of the less well-dressed, less talented or less socially presentable, must have envied their more fortunate fellows. It is said – possibly with some exaggeration – that some of the hardest-up youngsters, who Mr Bell, the Agent, had billeted under the Clock Tower, eked out their stock of bread by hoisting the loaves to the ceiling-beams on ropes, to avoid the temptation of eating between meals. Others, it is alleged, with insufficient talent to convert bones into saleable souvenirs, found a novel use for these 'osseous remains'. They ground and pounded them into a fine powder and added it to their food, and it seems that they 'flourished on this dissolved phosphate of lime and gelatine'. It was common, in all towns, north or south of the Border, for British victories to be celebrated with open-air parties and festivities, from which the prisoners were not debarred. While almost all forms of excitement were welcome breaks from monotony, what they witnessed was sometimes hurtful. An old Jedburgh woman remembered when:

> 'A great bonfire was kindled at the Cross, and an effigy of Napoleon was set on a donkey and paraded round the town by torchlight, and then round and round the bonfire and then cast into the flames. I have often heard an old gentleman, who had given the boots and part of the clothing, say he never regretted doing anything so much in his life, as helping in that great show, when he saw the pain it gave to those poor gentlemen-prisoners, who felt so much at seeing the affront put upon their great commander.'

As the war progressed, these celebrations became more frequent, and the prisoners more despondent. At Selkirk, the parolees were depressed when news of yet another great Wellington victory in Spain was announced by the joyful ringing of all the bells in the town; but they rejoiced at the opportunity to retaliate when, a short time later, they got news of a French victory in Russia. The next day, a Sunday, two officers attended a religious service and hid inside the church when it closed that night. At midnight they let half a dozen of their comrades in through a window, and fastened a very long rope from outside the building to the church bell, and in the early hours, 'six vigorous arms made the instrument vibrate to the breaking point and in a few minutes astonishment and consternation spread throughout the town'. By the time the townsfolk had tumbled from their beds and reached the church the prisoners were back in their lodgings with honour satisfied.

There was one date which was celebrated in Jedburgh and everywhere else that prisoners were housed, in every *cautionnement*, depot and prison ship – Napoleon's birthday. This was a great day of speeches, feasting, rejoicing and patriotic songs. Our old friend, Doisy de Villargennes recorded the banquet which was held in their club-house at Selkirk. The officers there had subscribed towards a sumptuous feast which was shared by about a hundred continental celebrants, but when everyone had eaten and drunk their fill, the table was still laden and some bottles unopened. The merry captives decided that this excess should be shared among the crowd which had been attracted by their roistering – but with one stipulation. Any of the townsfolk who wished to partake of their generosity and their drink, must first remove his cap and cry 'Vive l'Empereur Napoleon'. Although some of the officers stood outside and proffered portions of ham, fowl and roast beef, and tempted the townsfolk with glasses of wine, whisky and brandy, none came forward – until they spotted a local man who they collectively employed as a sort of general dogsbody. This individual they knew as 'Bang Bang' and, being either simple or thinking he might lose his profitable employment with them, he was persuaded to conform to their wishes. The crowd were incensed and at times menacing, but when they saw that 'Bang Bang' was rewarded with almost a whole turkey and liquor, enough of them followed suit for the table to be cleared. The price of patriotism was a full belly! Doisy tells us how 'Bang Bang' got his nickname:

> 'He was always at the beck and call of his many masters and constantly tormented by simultaneous appeals for his services. His reply was always, "By and by". This expression, incomprehensible to most of us, was changed into "Bang Bang", which was as near the pronunciation as we could get; and he was referred to by us always by that euphonious appellation.'

Many of the foreign prisoners had difficulty with our language and knew little or no English – and even less Scottish – when they first arrived in their place of parole. One would imagine that, with so many language masters among them, it would not have been long before they were all fluent. However, some never were, and this resulted in any number of parole-town stories of allegedly humorous misunderstandings. One is reputed to have gone into a shop to buy eggs, and successfully mimed his requirement by sitting down with his cloak around him, flapping his arms and clucking. Furthermore, when they had mastered the rudiments of the tongue they often had trouble with the pronunciation, even after years in an English or Scottish Town. Some of the Jedburgh officers who had used their time in making little articles for sale, decided to dispose of surplus stock by auction – or roup (a Scottish and northern English dialect word for auction). One of them visited the Provost, who had a shop in the Canongate in order to obtain permission to hold the sale. He presented himself at the counter and, using the right word but strange enunciation, informed the Provost, 'Ve vant a Roup'. The helpful Provost offered the bewildered officer the choice from a selection of second-hand ropes, cords and twines.

A number of the parolees married local girls, some the daughters of the gentry, before they left for France, and one, at least, returned to Jedburgh and made Scotland his home. He was another of the talented who would have undoubtably been an Inchbonny visitor. Lieutenant François Espinasse, Chevalier de la Légion d'Honneur and naval officer. The Chevalier had served for six years on the frigate *Le Junon*, before he was taken in February, 1806. From Halifax, Nova Scotia, he was sent to England and first paroled to Crediton, where he stayed until the introduction of the Scottish Border *cautionnements* in 1811. His first few weeks in Scotland were spent in Lauder, before being transferred to Jedburgh where he stayed until the end of the war. Although he had spent such a short length of time in Lauder, he, like the German artist Maurer, became a lifelong friend of the Agent there, John Romanes. In

Jedburgh, Espinasse set himself up as a teacher of French conversation and literature, and thus laid the foundations of a new career which, after the war, was to make his name respected throughout Scotland, many distinguished inhabitants of his parole town becoming his students.

Espinasse was a devoted Bonapartist and his loyalty to Napoleon never faltered throughout his life. At the end of the war, he returned to France, but, like so many like-minded Frenchmen, could not bring himself to serve under the new monarchy. He came back to Scotland and settled in Edinburgh, where he opened classes which became famous.

W. H. Langhorne, in his *Reminiscences of Inveresk*, says that 'in the opinion of Lord Jeffrey, it was also a school of philosophy and moral training, the Chevalier imparting to his pupils a tone of an exceptionally valuable kind, and illustrating his lectures by reference to maxims from the best French authors'.

Many years later, about the year 1860, the old Lauder Agent, John Romanes, sent his son to study under Espinasse in Edinburgh. The poor young lad must have been startled on his first day, when he was greeted with the words, 'Ah! Once your father had me – now I have you!'

The epitaph which Chevalier François Espinasse desired should be engraved on his tomb was a compliment to the kindly people of the Scottish Border parole towns – and a fitting ending to these notes on the old *cautionnements*:

**MON COEUR A MA PATRIE,
ET MA
RECONNAISSANCE A L'ECOSSE.**

**MY HEART TO MY COUNTRY
AND MY
GRATITUDE TO SCOTLAND**

CAPTAIN AUGUSTUS FRANCIS BRARD
Receipted Invoice for his services as a Language Master. 1819
Augustus Brard was paroled first to Cupar-Fife and later to Lanark where he settled after the war.

THE OFFICERS' CLUB HOUSE. HAWICK
Monochrome Watercolour. Signed and dated 'P. THIRAT fecit, 1813'
In the foreground is the Slitrig, crossed by the little bridge known as the 'Wire Brig'; between the churchyard and the stream and to the left, is a house by the parolees as a club house. It was quite spacious, with two main floors, attics and an area basement.

COMMUNAL RESIDENCE OF PAROLED OFFICERS 1812–1814
44 High Street, HAWICK. Prisoner of War artist unknown.

---

1. After Culloden, or the Battle of Drummossie, the victorious Duke of Cumberland, Prince Willliam Augustus, was honoured with Handel's 'See the Conquering Hero Comes', and an English flower, the 'Bunch Pink', was renamed the 'Sweet William'. However, to this day it is known in Scotland as 'Stinking Billy'.

2. They would have had to be extremely careful not to come up against the strict laws against the making of straw hats, or producing plait in quantity for the crooked dealers. See Chapter 4, *The Arts and Crafts of Napoleonic and American Prisoners of War 1756-1816*, THE STRAW WORKERS.

3. Captain Maitland-Carew is a descendant of Sir Richard de Matulant, one of the great Scottish barons of the thirteenth

century, and numbers among his ancestors statesmen, soldiers, and sailors prominent in the service of Scotland and England. One, of particular interest to us here, was Captain Maitland of HMS *Bellerophon*, who took Napoleon prisoner at Rochefort in August 1815. The *Bellerophon* ended her great career soon after, and was put to meaner work from 1816 to 1825 – as a civil convict prison hulk at Sheerness.

4. S. Keddie: *Three Generations – The Story of a Middle-Class Scottish Family'*.

5. See Chapter 10, *The Arts and Crafts of Napoleonic and American Prisoners of War 1756-1816*, THE ENTERTAINERS.

6. H. Davidson: *The French Prisoners of War in Lanark*. Printed for private circulation.

7. *The Parish Register of Lanark 1800–1819*, records the birth of Francis Elizabeth Brard, born 26th June, 1816. *The Glasgow Registers* record the births of two more daughters and a son: Janet, born 25th June, 1818. Augustus Henry, born 16th July, 1822. Cornelia Elizabeth, born 14th December,1824.

8. *The Lanark Manse Family*. Printed for private circulation, 1901.

9. There was one warlike – though not prisoner of war – relic preserved at Inchbonny which fascinated Sir Walter Scott. It was the sword which Ringan Oliver had wielded to such deadly effect at the battles of Killiecrankie and Bothwell Bridge. It had been handed down to Veitch through his grandmother, who was Ringan Oliver's sister.

Bibliography

ABELL, Francis, *Prisoners of War in Britain 1756-1815*. Oxford University Press, 1914.

ALGER, John Goldworth, *Napoleon's British Visitors and Captives*. Constable, London, 1904.

ALLEN, Col. Ethan, *Narrative of Col. Ethan Allen's Captivity*. Burlington, Chancey Goodrich, 1846.

ANDREWS, Charles, *Dartmoor Prison: a Prisoner's Memoirs*. New York, 1852.

ANDROS, Thomas, *The Jersey Captive: Narrative of the captivity*. Boston, William Peirce, 1833.

BECK, Herbert, *Journal of Ensign Thomas Hughes 1779-1780*. Lancaster County Historical Society, 1954.

BERCKMAN, Evelyn, *The Hidden Navy*. Hamish Hamilton, London, 1973.

BOWIE, Lucy Leigh, *German prisoners in the American Revolution*. Maryland Historical Magazine.

BOYS, Edward, *Narrative of a Captivity and Adventures*. Dove, London, 1831.

BRANCH-JOHNSON, W., *The English Prison Hulks*. C. Johnson, 1952.

BROWN, Revd Arthur, *The French Prisoners of Norman Cross*. Hodder Brothers, London, 19??.

BUSHNELL, Charles, *The Adventures of Christopher Hawkins New York*. Privately printed, 1864.

BUSSELL, Peter, *The diary of Peter Bussell 1806-1814*. Peter Davies, London, 1931.

CALLENDER, Geoffrey, *The Naval side of British History*. Christophers, London, 1924.

CAMERON, Joy, *Prisons and Punishment in Scotland*. Canongate, Edinburgh, 1983.

CAREY, George, *A Sailor's Songbag – an American Rebel in an English Prison 1777-1779*. Amherst, University of Massachusetts Press, 1976.

CHOYCE, James, *The life of a Jack Tar; or Master Mariner James Choyce*. Fisher Unwin, London, 1891.

CLUBB, Stephen, *A Journal*. Boston, 1809.

COBB, Josiah, *Green Hand's First Cruise – The log book of memory*. Volumes 1 & 2, Cushing & Brother, Baltimore, 1841.

COFFIN, Capt. Alexander, *The Destructive Operation*. Privately Printed, New York, 1865.

COGGESHALL, George, *American Privateers and Letters-of-Marque*. George Putman, New York, 1861.

COGLIANO, Francis, *American Maritime Prisoners in the Revolutionary War*. Annapolis Naval Institute Press, 2001.

CONWAY, Stephen, *The American War of Independence 1775-1783*. Edward Arnold, London, 1995.

CORBETT, Julian, *England in the Seven Years' War*. Greenhill Books, London, 19??.

DE CURZON, Alfred, *Dr James Currie and the French Prisoners of War in Liverpool 1800-1801*. Howell, Liverpool, 1926.

DEACON, Audrey, *The Prisoner from Perrecy*. Hertfordshire Record Society, 1987.

DOISY, Adelbert, *French Prisoners of War in Selkirk*. Hawick Archaeological Society, *c*.1830.

DRING, Capt. Thomas, *Recollections of the* Jersey *Prison Ship*. H. H. Brown, Providence, 1829; *A Young Man of Massachusetts: a journal written by himself*. Rowe and Hooper, Boston.

ELTON, Oliver, *Locks, Bolts and Bars – French Prisoners 1759-1814*. Frederick Muller, London, 1945.

FITCH, Jabez, *The diary of Jabez Fitch: a Prison ship martyr of 1776*. William Abbatt, New York, 1903.

FORBES, J. Macbeth, *French Prisoners of War in the Border Towns*. (Publisher unknown.)

FOX, Ebenezer, *The Revolutionary War*. Charles Fox, Boston, 1838.

FRASER, Edward, *Napoleon the Gaoler*. Methuen, London, 1914.

FRENEAU, Philip, *Some account of the capture of the Ship Aurora*. Mansfield & Wessels, New York, 19??.

FURNEAUX, Rupert, *The Seven Years' War*. Hart-Davis, London, 19??.

GARNERAY, Louis, *The French Prisoner*. Merlin Press, London, 1957; *Voyages, Aventures et combats*. Vols 1& 2 Editions De La Roue Solaire Brussels 1944; *Mes Pontons-Neuf années de captivité*. Editions Excelsior, Paris, 1933.

GEYL, Pieter, *Napoleon:For and Against*. Peregrine Books, London, 19??.

GILLE, Philippe, *Louis François Gille: The Prisoners of Cabrera, a memoir of a conscript of 1808*. Victor Havard, Paris.

HAIN, Sir Edward, *Prisoners of War in France 1808-1814*. Duckworth, London, 1992.

HALL, George, *Two escapes from French Prisons during the war with Napoleon*. Reprint by Truslove & Hanson, London, 1860.

HERBERT, Charles, *A Relic of the Revolution of 1776*. Charles Peirce, Boston, 1847.

HIBBERT, Christopher, *Redcoats and Rebels–The War for America 1770-1781*. Grafton, London, 1993.

HICKEY, Donald, *The War of 1812: a forgotten conflict*. University of Illinois Press, Chicago, 1989.

HOPKINS, R. Thurston, *Famous Bank Forgeries*. Stanley Paul, London, 1936.

JACKSON, John, *The Defense of The Delaware 1775-1781*. Rutgers University Press, New Jersey, 1974.

JAMES, William, *Naval Occurrences of the late war*. Egerton, London, 1817.

JOHNSTON, T. A., *Extracts from the history of the Royal Burgh of Sanquhar*. Grieve & Sons, Dumfries, 19??.

JONES, Stuart, *The Last Invasion of Britain*. University of Wales, 1950.

KEMP, Peter, *The British Sailor*. Dent & Sons, London, 1970.

KROG, Jens, *A Danish Prisoner in England 1807-1814*. Carl Roos, Denmark, 1953.

LAVERY, Brian, *Nelson's Navy*. Conway, London, 1989.

LEARY, Lewis, *That Rascal Freneau*. Rutgers University, Columbia, 19??.

LECKIE, Robert, *George Washington's War*. Harper Collins, New York, 1992.

LEECH, Samuel, *A Voice from the Main Deck–six years in a Man-of-War*. John Neale, London, 1844.

Bibliography

LEPPER, John Heron, *Freemasonry and the Sea.* Pollard, Oldham, 1946.

LEWIS, Michael, *Napoleon and His British Captives*; *Napoleon and His Captives.* London Allen & Unwin, 1962.

LITTLE, George, *Life on the Ocean:or Twenty years at sea.* Waite Peirce, Boston, 1845.

LYNCH, Malcolm, *The Dartmoor Yankee.* Tabb House, 1992.

MACDONALD, James, *Danish Prisoner.* Phillips, London, 1810.

MACKENZIE, A. D., *The Bank of England Note.* Cambridge University Press, 1953.

MAITLAND, Capt. F. L., *Narrative of the Surrender of Buonaparte.* Henry Colburn, London, 1826.

MASSON, Philippe, *Les Sépulcres Flottants.* France Quest 1987.

MILLER, John, *Origins of The American Revolution.* Faber, London.

NAPIER, William. *The War in the Peninsular.* Folio Society Reprint, 1973.

NATIONAL LIBRARY OF WALES, *Fishguard. An Authentic account of the Invasion by The French Troops 1797.* Perkins, Haverfordwest, 1853.

O'BRIEN, Donat Henchy, *My Adventures during the late War 1804-1814 of England.* Bodley Head, London. 1908.

ONDERDONK, Henry, *The Revolutionary Incidents of Queens County.* Leavitt Trow, New York, 1846; *The Revolutionary Incidents of Suffolk and Kings Counties– and the British Prisons and Prison ships at New York.* Kennikat Press, New York, 18??

PARKINSON, Roger, *The Peninsular War.* Hart Davis, London, 1973.

PEEL, Albert, *The Life of Alexander Stewart–Prisoner of Napoleon and Preacher of the Gospel 1815.* Oxford University Press, 1947.

PHILLIPS, Maberly, *Straw-plaiting & French Prisoners.* *Connoisseur* Magazine, London, 1908.

PITOU, Louis-Ange, *Voyage à Cayenne.* Paris 1805.

POCOCK, Tom, *Battle for Empire.* Michael O'Mara, London, 1998.

PRICKMAN, J. D., *Notes of the French Prisoners in the West of England.* Privately printed, 1864.

READ, Jan, *War in the Peninsular.* Faber & Faber, London, 1977.

RHODES, A. J., *Dartmoor Prison.* Bodley Head, London, 1933.

RIBTON-TURNER, C. J., *A History of Vagrants and Vagrancy.* Chapman and Hall, London, 1887.

RICHARDSON, Hubert, *A Dictionary of Napoleon and His Times.* Cassell, London, 1920.

ROBINSON, Charles Napier, *The British Tar.* Harper Brothers, London, 1911.

RUDE, George, *Revolutionary Europe 1783-1815.* Fontana-Collins, London 1964.

RUSSELL, J., *The History of the War between the United States and Great Britain 1812-1815.* B.& J. Russell, Hartford, 1815.

SCHWARTZ, Seymour, *The French & Indian War 1754-1763.* Greenhill Books, London.

SEITZ, Don C., *Paul Jones–His exploits in English Seas 1778-1780.* Dutton & Co., New York, 1917.

SENER, Samuel, *The Lancaster Barracks: British and Hessian Prisoners.* Harrisburg Publishing Co., 1895.

SHERBURNE, Andrew, *Memoirs of Andrew Sherburne.* William Williams, Utica, 1828.

SHERBURNE, John Henry, *The Life of Paul Jones.* Murray, London, 1825.

SMITH, Denis, *The Prisoners of Cabrera.* Fair Walls, New York, 2001.

STEVENSON, Robert Louis, *St. Ives.* William Heinemann, London, 1898.

SWEETMAN, George, *The French in Wincanton.* Sweetman, 1897.

TAYLOR, George, *Martyrs to The Revolution in the British Prison Ships.* W. H. Arthur, New York, *c.*1876.

THOMSON, Basil, *The story of Dartmoor Prison.* Heinemann, London, 1907.

THORP, Jennifer, *Lady Harriet Acland and The American War.* Hampshire County Council, 1994.

THORP, John, *French Prisoners Lodgers.* Leicester Lodge of Research Freemasons, 1935.

TUCHMAN, Barbara, *The First Salute.* Michael Joseph, London, 1989.

U.S. STATE PAPERS, *A Message from The President.* Washington 1814; *A Report from The President: Impressed American seamen in Dartmoor Prison.* Washington, 29 April 1816.

VALPEY, Joseph, *Journal of Joseph Valpey of Salem 1813-1815.* Detroit Burton Historical Collection, 1922.

VERNON, Fred, *History of Freemasonry: Roxburgh, Peebles and Selkirkshire.* Kenning, London, 1893.

VIBERT, Lionel, *Masonry among Prisoners of War.* Evans, Liverpool, 1925.

WALKER, Thomas James, *The Depot for Prisoners of War At Norman Cross, Huntingdonshire, 1796-1816.* Constable, London, 1913.

WATSON, George, *James Veitch of Jedburgh.* Smail, 1899.

WHEELER, H. F. B. and **BROADLEY,** A. M., *Napoleon and the Invasion of England.* Bodley Head, London, 1908.

YOUNG, Brigadier Peter, *Edward Costello–The Peninsular and Waterloo Campaigns.* Longman Green, London, 1967.

YOUNG MAN OF MASSACHUSETTS, A., *A Young Man of Massachusetts: a journal written by himself.* Charles Fox, Boston, 1838.

Index

(Page numbers in **bold** refer to illustrations.)

Index

Index